Mastering
Autodesk® Revit® 2017 for Architecture

Mastering
Autodesk® Revit® 2017 for Architecture

Marcus Kim

Lance Kirby

Eddy Krygiel

Senior Acquisitions Editor: Stephanie McComb
Development Editor: Kelly Talbot
Technical Editor: Eric Bogenschutz
Production Editor: Rebecca Anderson
Copy Editor: Kim Wimpsett
Editorial Manager: Mary Beth Wakefield
Production Manager: Kathleen Wisor
Executive Editor: Jim Minatel
Book Designers: Maureen Forys, Happenstance Type-O-Rama; Judy Fung
Proofreader: Nicole Hirschman
Indexer: Robert Swanson
Project Coordinator, Cover: Brent Savage
Cover Designer: Wiley
Cover Image: John Miler, Hendrich Blessing

Published simultaneously in Canada

ISBN: 978-1-119-24000-6

ISBN: 978-1-119-24001-3 (ebk.)

ISBN: 978-1-119-24003-7 (ebk.)

Manufactured in the United States of America

Library of Congress Control Number: 2016938155

10 9 8 7 6 5 4 3 2 1

Acknowledgments

Ah, acknowledgments. Although all the glory of writing a book is mostly consumed by the authors, it takes so many more people than just us to actually make this happen. Just like building design, the process of writing and publishing a book is truly a team sport—and without the hard work, dedication, and willingness to put up with the authoring team, this book would have never have happened.

Of all the people to thank, first of all, we'd like to thank the staff at the Revit Factory. Without their fine work, this would be a very empty book. A special thanks to the three Product Managers, Harlan Brumm, Sasha Crotty, and Steven Campbell. And a huge thank you to the rest of the Factory - thank you guys and gals, for your hard work, innovative ideas, and desire to stay in touch with current design and construction issues.

Finally, a big thanks to our technical team. They dot our i's, cross our t's, and chide us every time we turn in something late. Their work and effort ensure that we as authors can produce something that you the reader can actually follow. So a thank-you to our amazing and patient developmental editor, Kelly Talbot, for putting up with our excuses and typos; to copyeditor Kim Wimpsett and proofreader Nicole Hirschman for taking our slang and making it readable; and to production editor Becca Anderson for putting all the pieces together and getting it ready for print. Thanks also to Mary Beth Wakefield for watching the schedule and allowing us to use you as an excuse not to visit family on weekends or holidays during "Book Season." A thank-you to Eric Bogenschutz, technical editor, who has given a careful and detailed eye to all of our Revit workflows, and to our excellent support team at Sybex, who helped us develop all this foxy content.

The building photograph on the cover was designed by SOM and is the Chicago Public Library, Chinatown branch. The Chinatown Branch Library is a new civic, educational, and social hub for Chicago's Chinatown neighborhood, providing a much-needed public gathering place geared toward inclusive community activities and driven by technology-based learning. An array of vertical shading fins juxtapose an ultra-transparent, high-performance glass curtain wall that maximizes visibility for both library patrons and passersby during the day, while presenting the image of a glowing lantern at night. The building's south-facing entrance, softened triangular shape, and gentle interior circulation reference Feng Shui design principles and resonate with the values held by the community. Like a traditional Chinese courtyard plan, all spaces connect to the central atrium room, providing clear orientation and spatial cohesion.

`http://www.som.com/projects/chicago_public_library_chinatown_branch`

About the Authors

Marcus Kim is a senior business consultant with Autodesk. Marcus focuses on enterprise adoption of Revit and BIM workflows for AEC customers and has traveled all over the globe providing BIM services to domestic and multinational customers. Marcus received his bachelor's degree in architecture studies from the University of Illinois in Chicago and an associates of arts and sciences degree from the American Academy of Art in digital media. During the early part of his career, Marcus pursued design and technical architecture, but he was given the opportunity to participate in a Revit pilot program where he excelled. Throughout his career, until his transition over to Autodesk, Marcus managed the BIM on complex and high-profile projects such as the NATO World Headquarters for SOM Chicago, developing and implementing workflows during a time when producing BIM projects and BIM management was in its infancy. Marcus has used Revit since version 7.0 and has lectured at Autodesk University on topics such as BIM management, BIM architecture workflows on large-scale projects, and design visualization.

At Autodesk, Marcus provides both technical and business process thought leadership to his customers, helping them adopt and improve new and existing BIM workflows, training, content, and standards. He has taken BIM concepts common to AEC and applied them to other industries ranging from manufacturing to energy to mining.

Marcus is based out of the Chicagoland area and spends much of his spare time chasing after his toddler and sneaking in moments of relaxation by pursuing his other two passions, digital art and painting little toy soldiers.

Lance Kirby is a senior AEC business consultant with Autodesk. Lance's primary focus is accelerating the adoption of BIM and VDC practices among owners and their supply chain of designers and contractors. He received his bachelor's degree in architecture from Mississippi State University's College of Architecture, Art, and Design and also studied at the Budapest University of Technology and Economics, coincidentally alongside the creators of Graphisoft's ArchiCAD. He spent six years in various architecture offices helping to produce everything from 400-square-foot fast-food kiosks in shopping malls to 7,000,000-square-foot federal prisons.

In 2000, he left a prominent architecture firm to join a new tech start-up outside Boston to help produce a new design tool called Revit. Helping to develop Revit since version 1 and create its early tutorials, Lance has supported hundreds of BIM projects and trained thousands of its users over the past 15 years. Coincidentally, he has also supported all the previous and current authors of this book at some point in his career. Although this is his first published book as an author, he routinely pens 1,000+ pages in customer reports a year.

Although Lance has been based in Atlanta since 1995, he is often out of town. When he is not traveling globally in support of Autodesk customers, he may be traveling globally with his flight attendant wife, Scarlett. He enjoys fiction, analog/digital gaming, gastronomy of the smoked meat variety, and heavy down-tuned music.

Eddy Krygiel is a principal business consultant with the AEC team with Autodesk Consulting. Eddy focuses on BIM and technology workflows for AEC clients. He received his bachelor's degree in architecture from the University of Kansas School of Architecture and Urban Design. He has almost 20 years of experience in architectural offices and on a range of projects from single-family residential to office, federal, civic, and aviation clients. Eddy has helped firms around the United States at both the firm level and the project level.

His most recent project was the Mexico City International Airport, where he had the role of BIM manager for the Centro de Integración, Capacitación y Operación BIM. The BIM role involved supporting and steering stakeholder workflows from design through construction while not affecting the overall project fee or schedule. The final deliverable to the airport was a facility management–ready BIM model for both vertical and horizontal assets. Eddy has also led or been involved in other large-scale projects that have taken BIM beyond documentation.

Eddy is the author of more than 16 books on BIM and sustainability including the Mastering Revit series and *Green BIM*. He has also taught BIM, construction documents, and architectural communication at the University of Kansas School of Architecture.

About the Contributor

Seth Edwards authored Chapter 21. Seth is a technologist and educator for the AECOO industry specializing in design methodologies, implementation, and change management procedures. He currently works as a technical consultant for Autodesk engaging in BIM and computational design strategies. Prior to his current role, he led internal knowledge management initiatives as an associate director of building intelligence at WeWork, a shared workspace service provider. As a design professional, Seth worked on a number of high-profile projects at both SHoP and Grimshaw Architects. As an implementation and business consultant at CASE, he worked with a number of prominent clients including HDR, AECOM, and Woods Bagot. Seth has taught computational design at IE Business School in Segovia and is a volunteer for SmartGeometry, a nonprofit organization promoting digital design. He has been a speaker at the AIA Convention and the Venice Biennale, among others.

Contents at a Glance

Contents

Introduction

"A world which sees art and engineering as divided is not seeing the world as a whole."
—Sir Edmund Happold

What you hold in your hands is regarded as the definitive source of Autodesk Revit expertise available in written form. It has been a leading book in educating novice and experienced users alike for the better part of a decade. Those of you who have read previous editions know there is a wealth of information regarding the practical usage and application of the program in producing many different architectural designs. If you have used these preceding editions to help you gain a better understanding of this complex application, then you know that new information is provided in each edition to update you on the newest features and how they might improve your workflow every day. What you may not know is that this specific edition seeks to go further. Its purpose is to provide you with not only the best understanding of the available tools but also many of the skills sorely needed by professionals to manage these tools in an architectural BIM workflow.

Often when working with architects around the world, we find that the terms *Revit* and *BIM* are used interchangeably in describing what is new about the profession and the way we execute work. From the typical user all the way to the principal members of a firm, there is a misconception that if you're using Revit, you are doing BIM. The challenge, of course, is separating the tool from the technique. Although Autodesk Revit is a wonderful apparatus for joining three-dimensional geometry with incredibly powerful and accurate data, it's not a process or a road map for producing architectural work. Although Revit is an important foundational asset to a BIM-based workflow, it is still a resource that needs associated procedures and the intent for reaching planned deliverables. Where is technology without technique?

BIM is a methodology used to produce a complete design, construction, and operations solution. It has become a catalyst for transforming design and production processes in the architecture, engineering, and construction industry. A decade ago in 2005, BIM was represented solely as architectural design and documentation authoring tools. By 2016, BIM has grown to form the basis of the process from design discipline authorship to construction and operation management of built assets. It is also being adopted for infrastructure as well as buildings. As the use of BIM tools and processes has become more mature, nations have changed legislation to accommodate the immediacy of centralized collaborative working practices in contrast with traditional sequential paper workflows. Global organizations within specific industries have defined exchange classifications such as Industry Foundation Classes (IFC) and COBie, and owners and their customers now expect to see full 3D media to describe a building at any stage of the design and build process. They even expect to see it as part of the construction process on-site, controlling and validating the build environment.

The challenge for any company in the AEC industry is to recognize the BIM areas that match its business niche and to ensure that the information that it attributes to a model can be generated efficiently and maximized by all other information-model users. With this comes much more responsibility to users of the tools and managers of the information, beyond lines and arcs generated by zeros and ones. It entails that you work with intent beyond what you see displayed on monitors. It is not enough to know every button and setting contained in the program; the BIM practitioner must know why to use a feature and when it is appropriate. It is not enough to know how to customize the templates for your specific workflow; it involves user understanding, knowing when customization is needed to create a specific output and when settings are best left unchanged. It is not enough to know how to create iterative forms through the manipulation of Python coding; it also requires an understanding of design criteria and how BIM uses align with them. And most important, it is not enough to just have the knowledge of how to model a thing; it is necessary to have the wisdom to know when and why to do so.

Rest assured, this book's purpose is to educate you on the best techniques and practices of Autodesk Revit, regardless of your responsibilities as an architectural project team member. New users will find a plethora of information regarding everything from simple concepts to complex techniques in executing modeling, documentation, and data input/output. All the while, we have included some lesser-known tips and tricks for seasoned veterans. All readers, regardless of their experience, will benefit from the authors' knowledge in planning, collaborating, governing, and supporting BIM projects with Revit at the center. The goal is not to turn all readers into BIM managers but to extend the amazing information provided in previous volumes with additional recommendations for supporting your work for more efficiency and better quality.

Anyone involved in any aspect of BIM, even tangentially, can benefit from knowledge of the bigger picture. This edition's coverage of the collaboration process, the management of practices, and the governance of data standards has been expanded so that even novices can increase their value to the team. By understanding principles that show that every action should have a method and every method should have a purpose, readers will continue to progress their expertise in providing precise modeling and valid data to their teams at the right time and in the right format.

If you seek a greater understanding of the BIM process and strive to transcend your traditional responsibilities, this edition will help you toward the goal of BIM management. Pursuing knowledge of planning, organizing, leading, and controlling your projects through new techniques and tools will help you take those next steps. By planning, you will establish strategies for achieving BIM use objectives. By organizing, you will be structuring the workflow to maximize the collaborative integration of your team. By leading, you will optimize your project team's potential for providing quality deliverables efficiently. By controlling, you will be able to measure the team's performance and provide continual self-improvement with the goal of raising the level of excellence. Regardless of your role, you will contribute more.

As you begin delving into this book, keep an active mind about how each of the provided recommendations might fit your company's culture, your experience, and your customer's needs. Not all of these ideas may be of interest or value to every project, but the goal of this book is that you will grow beyond any of the tools or techniques you deploy on your BIM projects, that the tools become second nature and an extension of your creativity, and that through this you will realize great architecture.

Architecture is the process of turning a thought into a space. Although it's so simple to convey that in the written word, the actual act of doing so is much more than it is possible to write. It's glory, it's torment, it's frustration, it's freedom, it's the realization that one miscalculation means a complete redesign, like blowing on a house of cards, and it's the 3 a.m. epiphany when you realize that the new design was what you were meant to get to in the first place. With all of that, it's also the burning desire to work relentlessly to make something better one step at a time.

Autodesk® Revit® Architecture software is one of the many tools we employ to help us through this organic process. It's one tool in the toolbox, but it can be much more than that. It can be the workflow that helps to empower a team. That team is the designers, the contractors, and ultimately the owners who are all looking to speak the same language.

We hope that in the process of using this book, you'll experience a bit of the struggle to realize a bit of the satisfaction of finding the solution. We hope what you learn in this book helps inspire you to your own bit of greatness, because what's most important is that architecture isn't about buildings. It's about what we are able to accomplish with what little time we have. This is the elegant essence of Revit. Before we go much further, we have a few semantics to discuss.

First, all the tutorial files necessary to complete the book's exercises plus sample families are hosted online at `www.sybex.com/go/masteringrevit2017`.

Don't have a copy of Revit 2017? Download the trial version of Revit Architecture at `http://usa.autodesk.com/revit-architecture`, where you'll also find complete system requirements for running Revit. Are you a student or educator? Someone with an .edu e-mail address? You can get a copy of Revit for free at `http://students.autodesk.com`.

For the clearest direction when following the exercises in this book, please make sure to install all the Revit support files that come with the default installation. We reference them heavily, and you'll need them to best leverage the software.

Beginning with Revit 2017, there is only a single version of Revit which offers Architecture, Structures, and MEP packages in one application. We have focused this book on the Architectural features and have set the user interface to remove some of the Structural and MEP tools for better visual clarity. The variations will be slight and hopefully manageable, which really means you have some extra tools for Structure and MEP design. For the ease of reading, we removed those from the book's images.

Finally, Revit comes with some additional options that you can download and install separately, including access to cloud rendering, storage, and analysis, which we demonstrate in Chapter 9, "Conceptual Design and Design Analysis." You can go to `http://accounts.autodesk.com` to create an Autodesk® A360 account to access those additional tools.

Who Should Read This Book

This book is written for architects and designers who have had some exposure to Revit and are eager to learn more. It's for architects of any generation—you don't need to be a computer wizard to understand or appreciate the content within. We designed the book to follow real project workflows and processes to help make the tools easier to use. The chapters are full of handy tips to make Revit easier to leverage in your day-to-day world.

This book is also for the entire range of architects, from those who are fresh out of school to seasoned project managers. We have endeavored to include content for all walks of the profession so that regardless of your role on a project, you can learn how BIM changes both workflow and culture within a project team. With that, a basic understanding of Revit will make it easier to work through the book. Revit is a very robust tool requiring more than one project iteration to master.

For BIM managers, the book offers insights into the best practices for creating good project or office templates; these managers should also take a sneak peek into the powerful world of building content and Revit families. We've added many time-saving and inspiring concepts to the book, supported by examples from our own projects and the rest of the real world, to help motivate and inspire you on your journey through building information modeling.

What You Will Learn

This book will help you take the basics of Revit and BIM that you already know and expand on them using real-world examples. We will show you how to take a preliminary model and add layers of intelligence to help analyze and augment your designs. We'll show you how to create robust and accurate documentation, and then we'll help you through the construction process.

We go beyond introductory topics. To that end, we won't be starting a project from scratch or teaching you how to build a simple BIM model. If you are interested in learning at that level, we strongly recommend you pick up *Autodesk® Revit® Architecture 2016 Essentials* (Wiley, 2015) before plunging headlong into this book. Instead, this book begins with a brief overview of the BIM approach. As you are already aware, BIM is more than just a change in software; it's a change in architectural workflow and culture. To leverage the full advantages of both BIM and Revit in your office structure, you will need to make some changes to your practice. We've designed the book around an ideal, integrated workflow to help you make this transition.

Starting with the project team, standards, and culture, we'll discuss how BIM changes your project approach and how to best build your team around a newer workflow. From there, we'll delve into conceptual design and sustainability studies, continuing through best practices for design iteration and refinement. You'll learn how to use powerful modeling techniques, how to design documentation best practices, how to make compelling presentation graphics, and how to take advantage of parametric design with the Family Editor. We'll explore workflow topics such as tracking changes and worksharing as well as some strategies that move beyond traditional concepts of BIM. The book concludes with an appendix on troubleshooting and best practices so you can avoid common pitfalls. Throughout the book we've shared our practical experience with you, particularly in the form of real-world scenario.

Whether you're studying Revit on your own or in a class or training program, you can use the "Master It" questions in the section called "The Bottom Line" at the end of each chapter to test your mastery of the skills you've learned.

Free Autodesk Software for Students and Educators

The Autodesk Education Community is an online resource with more than 5 million members that enables educators and students to download—for free (see the website for terms and conditions)—the same software used by professionals worldwide. You can also access additional tools and materials to help you design, visualize, and simulate ideas. Connect with other learners to stay current with the latest industry trends and get the most out of your designs. Get started today at `www.autodesk.com/education/free-software/featured`.

The Mastering Series

The Mastering series from Sybex provides outstanding instruction for readers with intermediate and advanced skills, in the form of top-notch training and development for those already working in their field and clear, serious education for those aspiring to become pros. Every Mastering book includes the following:

- Real-world scenarios, ranging from case studies to interviews, that show how the tool, technique, or knowledge presented is applied in actual practice
- Skill-based instruction, with chapters organized around real tasks rather than abstract concepts or subjects
- Self-review test questions, so you can be certain you're equipped to do the job right

What's New?

The Autodesk Revit team works continuously to improve the software, add new features, and eliminate bugs. It's a constant evolution. Here's a list of the items that have been added or enhanced in the 2017 release:

Links Managing links has become easier based on the ability to see the Manage Links status note when an RVT link is unloaded for the current user. A new Auto – Project Base Point To Project Base Point positioning option for RVT links, which aligns the link to the host model's project base point (using the link's project base point as the origin), has also been added.

Imports A command was added to import a 3D file (SAT or Rhino) and to use the imported geometry to produce a generic model in the current document or a shape in the current family. Revit's Import Shape tool also now allows the importing of shapes that include conical surfaces.

Multiple Wall Joins Several enhancements have been made to wall joins.

- You now have the ability to specify Allow or Disallow for automatic wall joining as a default option in wall creation.
- Display options (Clean Join/Don't Clean Join/Use View Setting) when selecting multiple wall joining have been enabled.
- The existing wall joining type switch function of Miter, Butt, and Square-off have been expanded to multiple wall joining.

Views A read-only parameter was added to the new Underlay group in the view properties: Range: Top Level reports the top level of the underlay range, as well as improves filtering by adding support for Filter By: Contains.

Schedules With this release, several improvements to schedules were made.

- The ability to save additional fields for view templates, including all the available parameters from the Fields, Filter, Sorting/Grouping, and Formatting tabs, was added.
- Schedules can now be filtered using a global parameter.

- The material take-off schedule now includes the material unit weight parameter so that the table can calculate the total weight of a model.
- The Align tool now works with schedules on sheet views.

Annotation The ability to maintain text note orientation when using the Rotate Project North tool was also included in this release.

What to Expect

Mastering Autodesk Revit 2017 for Architecture is divided into five parts, each representing a milestone in your progress toward becoming an expert Revit user. Here is a description of those parts and what they will show you.

Part 1: Fundamentals

This book is not intended for novices, but we recognize that not everyone will know how to find every tool or have a complete understanding of the workflow. The chapters in Part 1 help you build a foundation of essential tools and knowledge.

Chapter 1, "Introduction: The Principles of BIM," covers principles in building information modeling within your office or project environment.

Chapter 2, "Applying the Principles of the User Interface and Project Organization," details the Revit interface and general organization.

Chapter 3, "The Basics of the Toolbox," explores the commands and tools within Revit. It gives you an overview of where to find them and leaves the deep dive into their use for the chapters ahead.

Chapter 4, "Configuring Templates and Standards," discusses the tools you'll need to develop and manage graphic standards in a project template.

Part 2: Collaboration and Teamwork

Part 2 sets you on the path toward using Revit on a team or throughout your firm and takes a deep dive into a successful BIM workflow.

Chapter 5, "Working in a Team," discusses the critical tools to working with Revit on any project team.

Chapter 6, "Working with Consultants," covers the basics of working with team members outside your office.

Chapter 7, "Interoperability: Working Multiplatform," details the tools you'll need to share your Revit files with other team members who don't use Revit as a design tool.

Part 3: Modeling and Massing for Design

In this part, you'll delve into the use of Revit starting from the early stages of design through analysis, iteration, and visualization.

Chapter 8, "Advanced Modeling and Massing," details the creating of forms and shapes with the conceptual Revit toolkit.

Chapter 9, "Conceptual Design and Design Analysis," gives you an overview of conceptual Revit tools and using those in energy analysis.

Chapter 10, "Working with Phasing, Groups, and Design Options," takes the next step after the initial design and analysis: iteration.

Chapter 11, "Visualization," takes the design work you've created and shows you how to create stunning renderings and imagery of your design.

Part 4: Extended Modeling Techniques

Part 4 takes the conceptual forms you create in Part 3 and expands them to the real world using walls, floors, roofs, and other building components to create the elements behind a building.

Chapter 12, "Creating Walls and Curtain Walls," delves into the use of the Wall and Curtain Wall tools.

Chapter 13, "Modeling Floors, Ceilings, and Roofs," demonstrates a variety of ways to work with the horizontal components of a building: floors, ceilings, and roofs.

Chapter 14, "Designing with the Family Editor," shows you how to work with parametric families to create a host of content for the building design.

Chapter 15, "Creating Stairs and Railings," demonstrates a variety of ways and techniques to use the Stair and Railing tools—for their intended purpose and for others.

Part 5: Documentation

Once the building is designed, it becomes necessary to create the views and documents needed to build the project. This section shows you how to detail, document, and annotate the design.

Chapter 16, "Detailing Your Design," works with the building design you created in previous chapters to add 2D components for documentation.

Chapter 17, "Documenting Your Design," works with the newly created views and helps you organize them on sheets.

Chapter 18, "Annotating Your Design," takes the next step in the documentation process and works with keynoting and dimensioning.

Part 6: Construction and Beyond

This section focuses on what to do once the design is resolved, taking it into the construction process and working with presentation tools.

Chapter 19, "Working in the Construction Phase," focuses on the tools Revit has to keep track of changes during construction.

Chapter 20, "Presenting Your Design," shows you how to take the completed design and display the results in a variety of 2D and 3D methods.

Chapter 21, "Computational Design with Dynamo," teaches you how to use new tools that provide parametric design environments to enable users to create unique geometry as well as develop automated processes and sophisticated data manipulation techniques.

Part 7: Appendixes

Finally, three appendixes supplement the chapters' coverage of Revit software features.

Appendix A, "The Bottom Line," offers solutions to the "Master It" questions in each chapter's "Bottom Line" section.

Appendix B, "Tips, Tricks, and Troubleshooting," is just what the title describes—a collection of tips and tricks for troubleshooting and working effectively with Revit.

Appendix C, "Autodesk Revit Architecture Certification," describes Autodesk's certification exam for Revit Architecture and how this book can be used as a supplementary tool for test preparation. Throughout the book, the symbol shown on the left marks significant coverage of exam objectives.

Contacting the Authors

We welcome your feedback and comments. You can find the authors on Facebook at Mastering Revit and on `Twitter @MasteringRevit`, or you can contact them via e-mail at `masteringrevit@gmail.com`.

We hope you enjoy the book.

Part 1

Fundamentals

Although this book is focused on helping you master Autodesk® Revit® Architecture software, we recognize that not everyone will know how to find every tool or have a complete understanding of the workflow. The chapters in Part 1 will help you build a foundation of essential knowledge and may even give the veteran Revit user some additional insight into the basic tools and concepts of building information modeling (BIM).

Chapter 1

Introduction: The Principles of BIM

In this chapter, we cover the principles of a BIM approach within your office environment and summarize some of the many practices used in today's architectural workflows. We explain how you and your organization can achieve some of the many possible benefits from BIM by sharing the processes that these new technologies support. As you will see, these practices are oriented to industry BIM uses that provide advantages such as more thoroughly explored design concepts, better coordinated documentation, and better executed construction methods.

In this chapter, you'll learn to:

- Focus your investment in BIM
- Understand a BIM workflow
- Leverage BIM processes

The Fundamentals of a BIM Approach

Building information modeling (BIM) is an integrated model-centric methodology that delivers validated and coordinated knowledge about a building project throughout planning, design, construction, and operation. When this collaborative, interdisciplinary approach is optimized, it can improve an organization's operations. BIM provides designers, contractors, and owners with a process to improve decision making, quality, and timeliness. At the core of this BIM approach are model-centric workflows (geometric and data models) that support project execution and asset lifecycle management. These workflows determine the methodology for creating data-rich geometries, integrated deliverables, and a model-based process to develop projects from planning through the operation and management lifecycle phases. BIM can be defined through technology, processes (its governance through standardization), and people. The technology system is central to the processes of creating, storing, and using models. With processes, the success of BIM requires all stakeholders in the project ecosystem to follow a series of steps, both as individuals and as a team. Ultimately, the users of these new techniques and technologies are committed to improving their design process, successfully integrating both geometry and data.

To succeed with these practices in this new environment, a business needs to make fundamental changes in the way it operates, whether by moving into a new market or by changing its methods of operation. It requires an alignment of the organization's activities relating to its people, processes, and technology with its business strategy and vision. Through collaboration and data management during an asset's lifecycle, sharing information efficiently and effectively can support better integration and interoperability among all project stakeholders. Along with this data comes the possibility of integrated analysis. By making these analyses easily accessible, derivatives of this model-centric workflow can provide a better understanding of design opportunities and decisions' consequences. With the availability of valid geometry-based data, 2D, 3D (visualization, clash detection), 4D (time), 5D (cost), and beyond are possible. Taking advantage of these capabilities is a must in keeping architecture firms competitive in today's market. Transforming your organization's business quickly and efficiently will be the difference between maintaining your market share and taking that next evolutionary step forward.

The Management People Inside a BIM Project Team

The architectural marketplace is changing and is influencing staffing decisions to some degree as skills needed for BIM projects can be different than traditional CAD skillsets. Some of your organization's leadership may be aware of this change and are organizing BIM teams and resources to better anticipate new processes. Others are unsure of how BIM may change how they plan projects, from staffing to hiring. When looking to acquire BIM-skilled staff, savvy firms look for process experience in their new hires beyond those with tool expertise only. The primary factor is always professional experience, but knowledge of a BIM workflow supports these professional skills very well.

When planning project staffing, architecture firms generally focus on deliverables produced by a project hierarchy of managers, designers, engineers, interns, and draftspersons. BIM roles and responsibilities are based on the availability within the project team, rather than composing the best fit based on model-based workflows. This does not constitute a project problem, as much as it decreases efficiency in two ways: roles/responsibilities are not clearly defined and team members must adjust to BIM project needs during the project. Managers, who are making staffing decisions, may not have the resources to judge BIM experience level or tool/process skillsets, other than hearsay or previous project experience with similar circumstances. BIM managers have a better understanding of these capabilities, but do not generally make staffing decisions for projects. There may be project managers who know to confer with BIM managers over this need at project start-up; however, this is uncommon.

Typically, professionals are hired based on project experience, education, and certifications. For architecture firms in general, BIM experience is nice to have, but not typically required. In today's market, more and more professionals have BIM experience on their résumés in the form of project experience and trained tools, as they anticipate skillsets being required more frequently. Not having these skillsets does not preclude new staff from being successful BIM project team members, but it does impede the ability of managers to access the probability of their successful contribution to these projects.

Regardless, whether you are making staffing decisions or are a hardworking BIM project team member, understanding how these new workflows are changing the planning and execution of projects is important. Being prepared by understanding the people, processes, and technology of BIM is a must.

Staffing for BIM

As the building industry's process of design and documentation is transforming, one of the fundamental changes teams need to address is staff planning in a BIM process. A common misconception of project management is that staffing the BIM project will be the same as it has been in CAD workflows. Unfortunately, many times this is not the experience of many architecture teams. Because a BIM-based project can significantly alter the project workflow, many of the standard timetables for task completion are no longer valid. Although fundamental deliverables remain the same (drawings, schedules, etc.), the processes to reach these outputs are different. For example, in a CAD workflow a user can create a plan as a single one-off entity. In a BIM workflow, the same user would need to generate a model before a floor plan could be produced. The investment in the nD model requires more time upfront, and therefore the floor plan to be produced necessitates a longer schedule. However, once this model has been produced, many other derivatives can be produced with less effort. As a model is developed, the ability to pull accurate and precise drawings, schedules, and analysis improves geometrically. To leverage this workflow, the staff and processes need to take into account the gathering of momentum early in the cadence of execution in later phases.

Years ago, Patrick MacLeamy, CEO of Hellmuth, Obata, + Kassabaum, explained this workflow movement with a diagrammatical description of the shift of workload and the ease of affecting change in the construction process forward. The graph, which has come to be known as the MacLeamy Curve (Figure 1.1), is not simply intended to imply a shift in labor earlier in the design process; rather, it stresses the importance of being able to make higher-value decisions earlier before changes become too difficult or costly to implement. The x-axis of the chart represents project phases from conceptual design through occupancy, whereas the y-axis represents the amount of effort in each phase.

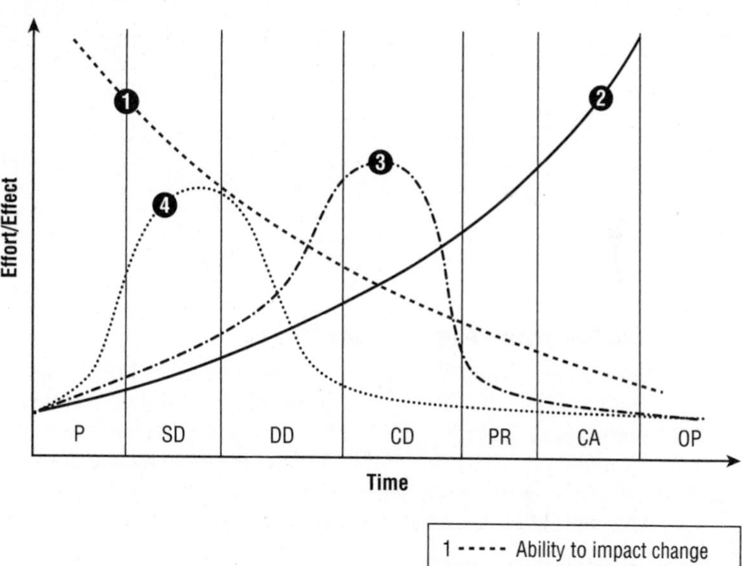

FIGURE 1.1
The effort curves in the design and construction industry

Another important aspect of a BIM workflow is its ability to leverage decisions earlier in the process. As shown in Figure 1.2, implementing BIM in earlier project phases allows teams to make and share better information earlier, so that the entire project team can benefit earlier.

On the basis of the BIM uses, a common industry term we will refer to later in this chapter, project teams may need to adjust labor in the planning and design stages in order to prepare an environment for geometric and data to develop together. In a CAD workflow, different project roles may be tasked with separate tasks in order to move the design forward. A planner may be developing a program, just as a designer may be producing massing studies. In a BIM workflow, these roles may be continuing the same task but in the context of a single model allowing them to interact through geometry and information. Because of this interaction and its ability to allow better decision making, project teams may be deploying additional staff to help support this collaboration in BIM. Depending on the uses, teams might increase staff to build a model or to perform energy analysis; however, deploying a BIM workflow will not necessarily provide more proficiency or quality than a CAD-based project without proper planning and governance.

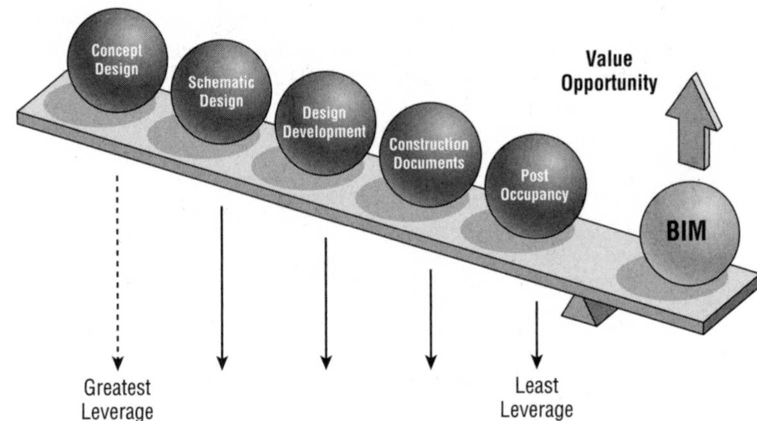

FIGURE 1.2 BIM provides more leverage when it is implemented earlier in the design.

Understanding Project Roles

It's also important to understand how the significant changes to tools and processes provided by BIM affect the roles and responsibilities of the project team. Project managers need to plan staffing and labor required to complete tasks in every project phase. BIM projects are supported by a few primary roles that will allow the team a level of predictability, although the specific effort and staffing will vary between offices (and even projects). Here are three primary roles that should be considered on every BIM project:

Design Architect Generates design intent from the planning stage through early design

Technical Architect Produces the deliverables, ensuring the design intent is building

Coordinator Directs the BIM workflow between design and production

These roles represent efforts and general tasks that you need to take into account on any BIM project. For larger projects, these roles could represent multiple people, whereas smaller projects might constitute the same person filling multiple roles. For many architecture firms, designers and production staff may be tightly integrated and have very little differences in the responsibilities. For other firms, there may be a clear demarcation between the first two roles. Regardless of the interaction between designers and production roles, every BIM project has some coordination responsibilities. We will now explore each of these in more detail and discuss how these roles affect the project workflow.

The Role of the Design Architect

The role of the architect is to generate the design intent, typically focused on the project from pursuit through planning to design development. These staff may include licensed architects and interns. Designers typically interact with the BIM process by first transferring their conceptual ideas into digital form. For many planners this is going from two 2D layouts to a 3D model. For more sophisticated designers it might be to create a conceptual massing model based on sketched geometry or is something as sophisticated as iterative design calculations. Whatever the case, designers may be the origin for models of the project.

For some workflows, designers may stay in a more traditional process, and technical architects begin the BIM process based on their designs. As creative processes and digital capabilities align, designers moving forward are more likely to use digital authoring tools for their work, rather than traditional ones, such as hand sketching and physical modeling. With this, the BIM process will start earlier in the project timeline. Following this workflow, designers have the capability of making better decisions for the project team earlier based on the intelligence they provide to their geometric-based designs. What becomes most important at this stage is having a workflow specific to design work in BIM projects that allows creativity but properly sets the stage for production staff to develop the designs into buildable instructions. With this in mind, the typical responsibilities for design architect include:

- Create initial design intent models through the creation of 3D geometry through conceptual massing or iterative design processes
- Lead the creation of architectural elements and building from within the model
- Design around code requirements and other building logistics

The Role of the Technical Architect

The role of the technical architect is to ensure that the project is buildable. These staff can be a wide-ranging group from experienced licensed architects and architectural technologist, to interns that are learning how buildings go together. As with design architects, technical architects are a role in the BIM process not because of their professional skill sets but because of their responsibilities to the project workflow. As models are developed, technical architects solve issues such as constructability, wall types, and managing the program of spatial and equipment requirements, as well as other issues involving code compliance and client relationships.

Primarily concerned with deliverables, production staff are manipulating models to create the needed outputs, such as drawings and schedules. The role of these staff is to create sheets and embellish associated views with annotations or other details. This role applies standards to the project (as in wall types, keynotes, and so on) and organizes the document set. Technical architects are responsible for the bulk of the work needed to document the project. In earlier stages of the project, this role is typically assumed by either the architect or the modeler, but as documentation progresses into later phases of design, this can quickly become the role of multiple people on a larger project. This role includes the following tasks:

- Validate the constructability and detailing aspects of the design
- Produce smart deliverables from well-coordinated models
- Follow the established Level of Development (LOD) or Model Development Specification (MDS) to ensure models comply with requirements of the stated BIM uses
- Ensure the models and valid data are passed to construction and operation phases of the project lifecycle

The Role of the Coordinator

BIM coordinators supervise the overall project modeling techniques and discipline-specific BIM output through all project phases. They are responsible for checking that all models produced by design and production staff comply with the standards set out by the BIM project execution plan (PxP). They check that models are correctly named and are the current version and that all relevant asset metadata has been completed with appropriate values. They coordinate requests for supplier information from the design teams and determine whether model details already exist in the library of design objects. Where model components do not already exist, they create or delegate their creation in the context of standards and set responsibilities. Their BIM duties are to:

- Author and maintain the technical sections of the PxP
- Determine project file organization and model splitting strategy
- Define file sharing protocols for the project
- Determine team training needs and organize training if needed
- Assemble and maintain any multidiscipline models
- Manage publication of files
- Create project delivery output from assembled files matching all the firm's BIM standards
- Review models for adherence to project standards
- Maintain the team's access to the correct tools for BIM authoring, aggregation, and analysis
- Oversee the application of BIM technologies and ensure that the model adheres to all internal and client-specific goals and standards
- Oversee the development of the content of a specific model element to the LOD/MDS listed for a particular phase of the project
- Assist all team members in BIM processes at all stages of the project
- Lead 3D coordination meetings

These BIM roles for architectural project teams generally work for most firms and building types; however, it is ultimately up to each organization and its management to decide how team members share in the responsibilities of managing geometry and connected data specifically for its needs. As long as there is an expectation set at the beginning of the project and a workflow defined during its phases, any number of roles and responsibilities should help ensure that the project is completed successfully. In support of that, project managers have a responsibility to help maintain the integrity of this new workflow. Although they may not be directly developing models, they are making important staffing decisions based on this new workflow and have the responsibility to ensure that the deliverables from this process meet contractual obligations. With that, we suggest that project managers have enough knowledge of BIM people, processes, and tools to do the following things:

- Understand the impact BIM has on a project delivery schedule
- Allocate time as planned for BIM management activities for the BIM coordinator and any BIM administration and support requirements
- Be familiar with BIM concepts and uses on a project so that they are able to effectively manage the project team and communicate progress and requirements to the client
- Oversee the administrative and contract sections of the BIM project execution plan (PxP)

Establishing a BIM Execution Plan

To optimize your results with BIM, you need to start with the end in mind. Although a lot of tasks are possible with BIM, before you draw your first wall, you will want to create a BIM project execution plan. We go into more detail about creating these plans and some resources for them in Chapter 6, "Working with Consultants," but essentially a BIM plan helps to drive the direction of the modeling effort and modeling outcomes. How will your consulting team share models? Will your project need to provide BIM deliverables such as a reference model or databases in the Construction Operations Building Information Exchange (COBie) format? Does the owner have expectations for a model deliverable for operations and management? All of those possibilities and more are explored and documented in a PxP. It gives the project team a definitive outcome to develop and enrich the models toward.

Creating a standard BIM project execution planning process will help project teams to plan and execute the required processes to achieve the anticipated goals. Using a PxP template and a planned methodology, the project team members should actively pursue these concepts:

- All parties should clearly understand and communicate the strategic goals for implementing BIM on the project.
- Teams should understand and communicate their roles and responsibilities in the project execution.
- The plan should outline resources, training, or other competencies necessary to successfully implement BIM for the intended uses.
- The baseline plan should provide a goal for measuring progress throughout the project.
- The plan should provide a benchmark for describing the process to future participants who join the project.

Teams carry additional process risk when implemented by teams that are not experienced with the BIM process, as many team members, managers and users alike, are not familiar with the strategies and processes of this new workflow. If the process is well planned and communicated, the project team will set expectations of what is to be done and how, thereby reducing the overall risk to the project. To ensure a successful project execution planning process, the team should do the following things with the PxP:

- Modify the plan to meet the project's needs.
- Build the plan with the entire consulting team.
- Create an LOD or an MDS with the entire consulting team to facilitate model and staff planning, unless it is already required by the owner.
- Review the plan early and often, making needed changes as project experience grows.

For those who are responsible for developing the PxP for your team, begin your plan by referencing industry-based templates, such as the Penn State Project Execution Plan or the Autodesk BIM Deployment Plan, that can provide you shortcuts to a well-organized and consistent PxP process. Determine what is needed by your project teams and then modify the plan to match your requirements. Additional language specific to the type of facility and construction should be added to the plan to make it more appropriate. A comprehensive PxP should include these sections:

- Restatement of project goals and objectives
- Intended BIM uses
- Team structure and deliverables
- Roles and responsibilities
- Data transfers
- Phase-based data requirements
- Intended authoring, analysis, and aggregation tools
- Governance information

By doing these things, project teams should have no problem developing a comprehensive project execution plan that will benefit them on a daily basis.

The Optimization of BIM Processes

According to the National Institute of Building Sciences (`www.nibs.org`), BIM is defined as "a digital representation of physical and functional characteristics of a facility" that serves as a "shared knowledge resource for information about a facility forming a reliable basis for decisions during its lifecycle from inception onward." Although this is the definition of the noun used to represent the electronic data, the verb form of building information *modeling* is equally important. BIM is both a tool and a process, and one cannot realistically exist without the other.

Building information modeling implies an increased attention to more informed design and enhanced collaboration. Simply relying on tools to replace your current processes without an updated corresponding methodology will yield limited success. In fact, it may even be more cumbersome than using traditional CAD tools to execute project work.

Regardless of the design and production workflow you have established in the past, moving to BIM is going to be a change. Moving to BIM is a shift in how designers and contractors approach the design and documentation process throughout the entire lifecycle of the project, from concept to occupancy. In a traditional CAD-based workflow, represented in Figure 1.3, each view is drawn separately with no inherent relationship between drawings. In this type of production environment, the team creates plans, sections, elevations, schedules, and perspectives as stand-alone entities and must coordinate any changes between these views manually.

FIGURE 1.3
A CAD-based workflow

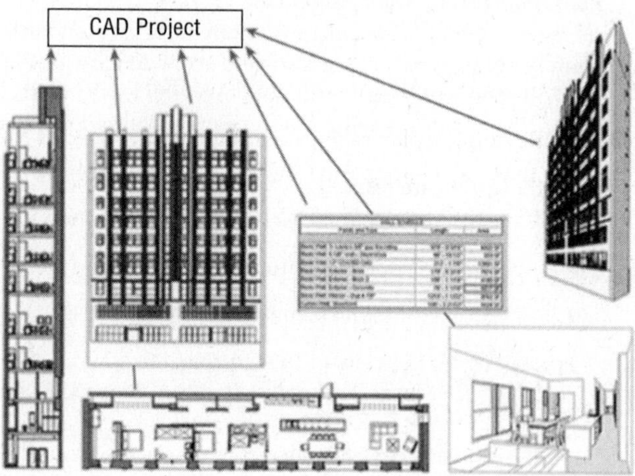

In a BIM-based workflow, the team creates 3D parametric models to generate the drawings necessary for documentation and analysis. Plans, sections, elevations, schedules, and perspectives are all by-products of creating a building information model, as shown in Figure 1.4. This enhanced representation methodology not only allows for highly coordinated documentation but also provides the basic model geometry necessary for analysis, such as daylighting studies, energy usage simulation, material takeoffs, and so on.

FIGURE 1.4
A BIM-based workflow

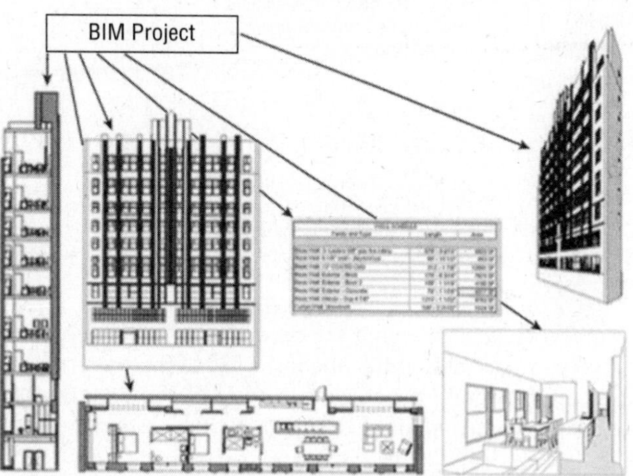

Identifying and Planning BIM Uses

We encourage you to explore ongoing research from organizations such as Penn State University, buildingSMART International, and the UK BIM Task Group. Penn State (`http://bim.psu.edu`) has developed a catalog of BIM uses and project implementation guidelines that have been adopted into the National BIM Standard-United States, version 2 (`http://nationalbimstandard.org`). Another important aspect of supporting numerous BIM uses is the development of open standards. The organization known as buildingSMART International (`www.buildingsmart.org`) provides a global platform for the development of such standards. The UK-based BIM Task Group is helping the region adopt BIM practices through building standards and educational support. Groups from a number of regional chapters around the world are generating information exchange standards that will soon have a profound impact on the ways in which we share model data with our clients and partners. The following are some of the latest developments:

- Industry Foundation Classes (IFC) version 4
- Construction Operations Building Information Exchange (COBie)
- Specifiers' Properties Information Exchange (SPie)
- BIM Collaboration Format (BCF)

For a general overview of the approach to standardizing exchanges with information delivery manuals (IDMs) and model view definitions (MVDs), visit `www.buildingsmart-tech.org/specifications`.

As the industry continues to build processes around the technology behind BIM, its potential continues to grow. Many new applications are now possible using building information modeling. As more and more benefits are achievable through BIM, teams find new uses to explore and develop. Figure 1.5 shows some of the potential opportunities that have been identified by the AEC industry and clearly organized by Penn State.

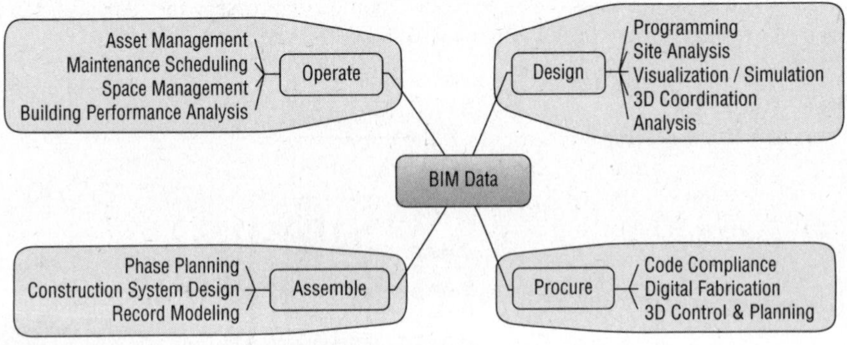

FIGURE 1.5 Service opportunities that BIM supports

When you are trying to plan and manage your organization's BIM and methodology, it's very important to think about the use of these processes and technology to achieve your project goals. One of the primary ways of understanding this is through BIM uses. These many uses can be organized into five basic activities: gather, generate, analyze, communicate, and realize.

Gather To collect and manage building information

Generate To create information about the building

Analyze To examine aspects or components of the building to make better decisions about how to plan, design, construct, or operate it

Communicate To shared information about a building collaboratively

Realize To build or manage a physical element using building data

Understanding how benefits are derived from these uses will help focus your teams' efforts in planning, managing, and governing new BIM processes.

Gather

As architects pursue work and plan awarded projects, they gather information about budgets, required functionality, site context, and anything else that is significant knowledge required to make the best decisions for the project. In an analog process, this information may be gathered in the building program, a contract, or even a cartoon set of drawings required. The advent of BIM processes and technology is changing this. BIM not only allows the acquisition of smartly acquired contextual data about the project but also becomes an improved repository for information gathered in traditional ways.

One example of these traditional processes is the creation of the space program. These are usually done by interviewing user groups that are to occupy the building and gathering information about the things that they do and the equipment they need in the adjacencies of the spaces they occupy. These processes are collected in a spreadsheet or in graphical layouts that explain their qualities. This type of data is typically used in parallel with the design process, with many planners manually pulling information into CAD layouts. With BIM, this process takes on a more evolved approach to connecting design data to programmatic requirements. Using a BIM process, a designer can input spatial information directly into the model database even before conceptual massing or area plans are generated. This allows the designer to take directly from the program information to lay out his or her design and get instant feedback whether it meets the required tolerances for these requirements.

Another example of gathering intelligent data could be in the form of laser scanning. There is sophisticated technologies that allow the generation of point clouds in pre-existing spaces. The generation of these spatially located points can be used as an accurate underlay in the building of existing conditions. With millions of points available, designers have at their fingertips a massive amount of data in which to begin to understand the context of their designs. This has incredible applications for complex renovations or spatially challenged sites or even historical preservation efforts.

Through this kind of information gathering, the qualification and quantification of data can empower the design team to understand both the implicit and explicit attributes of its projects. These processes can also help support estimating and cost forecasting efforts. During the early design phases of a building, quantities may be generally estimated but become more certain as the contract documents are created and construction processes proceed. All along the stored information becomes more and more accurate with respect to design intent.

Toward the later part of the construction process and into operations and maintenance, processes can help establish real-time performance measurements within facilities to help owners understand energy usage, operation costs, and many other metrics. As an example, an integrated O&M system may be tracking electrical costs on an hourly, daily, weekly, monthly, and yearly basis to help owners understand where they're maximizing their energy investments and where there is waste that they may reduce. Information gathering can be important throughout the entire lifecycle of a BIM project.

Generate

One of the most common aspects of building information modeling, and the one most accessible to new users, is the creation of intelligent geometry. As users draw a wall, a mass, or a new level, they are generating not only form but also data that helps them make informed design decisions. For example, when a wall is drawn in an authoring tool, that object can immediately have attributes such as length, width, and height. It may also have multiple materials, structural and finish, as well as cost and a fire rating. In a CAD process, the users must maintain the intelligence that they attribute to the objects they are drawing. They may be able to quickly generate four lines to represent a wall that could understand length and width, but that's where the distinction stops. These CAD drawings, although they can contain additional information, are inherently based on the output, whereas building information models inform the outputs rather than vice versa. A wall in a model database is the design. In CAD, the outputs represent what the users conceptually maintain in their mind. As smart as we are as architects, we can't maintain all the information needed to be communicated to the contractor in building our designs. That's where BIM can begin to support us by maintaining the information for us.

When users generate information about the project through both geometry and integrated data, they are prescribing attributes, arranging elements, and determining real-world dimensions. Within the context of the lifecycle of the building, the designers during the planning and design phases are the primary generators of geometry and data. During the construction phase of the project, the subcontractors will manage most of the data in the models. For sophisticated BIM projects, the construction phase management of as-built data can be created to build a foundation for the operations phase where that information could be used to operate and maintain the building. This database that they might maintain could be updated with new information throughout its entire lifecycle. This might include new equipment installed or renovations made to existing structures.

As experts generate both geometry and data for the project, they are specifying qualities and generating design data. The planner of a building may define particular spaces in the building, just as a structural engineer may define structural grid. Later in the project, a contractor might define a specific construction sequence as attributes of materials, just as the owner's construction manager may define the need for a specific piece of equipment. Because all these ideas are generated inside the building information model or linked systems that influence this database, generation of building data can happen in every phase.

As designers make decisions about the spatial configurations of the building, they are in a range elements in three dimensions. This is the beginning of 3D coordination processes, which is a major asset to BIM practices in terms of collaboration and problem solving. This can begin with the arrangement of spaces; move to an arrangement of structural systems, through mechanical, electrical, and plumbing systems; and end with coordination of trades that are constructing the build. Because of all these aspects that occupy space and therefore have some relationship with one another, the model becomes a spatial organizer for this arrangement.

Before the opportunities that BIM affords us were available, subcontractors may only have determined that services in the building they were installing may have issues as they were designed. This might include a piece of ductwork that does not quite have enough room to move around a beam or a doorway that does not have enough clearance from the edge of the stair riser. With the ability to simulate these relationships as designers, engineers, and other consultants coordinate spatially, we now find many of the problems we found in the past in the field during the 3D coordination process. This ability to solve problems earlier in the arrangement of these three-dimensional objects affords designers and builders a great opportunity of designing better outcomes with much more cost-effective and timely solutions. In the end, it's much cheaper to fix it in the computer than in the field.

The sizing geometry also is an important aspect to the generation of information in these models. Just as spatial organization is important, the ability to estimate the correct dimensional aspects of building systems in the specification of specific equipment is important. Generating sizing information in a 3D model might take the form of creating types based on standard industry specifications. Being able to specifically model objects that have real sizes and tolerances help designers be able to make the right decisions about specifying common building elements and complex building systems. Typical offering programs have tolerances built in for the level of detail that's required to have buildings constructed accurately. Users have the capability of modeling much more accurately than they ever could in the field. Of course, the caution here is that teams need to realize that though they can be more accurate in the model, the ultimate purpose of the model is to get the building built and into operation efficiently and effectively. This means sizes should be based on the requirements of the construction trades; any more information or accuracy beyond that is not needed. However, where BIM shines above typical CAD processes is its ability to share truth. It is much more work to hide the true sizes than it is to display them accurately. This may frustrate some users who are used to applying their own dimensions, until they realize that the models represent what they designed, whether it is to a standard dimension or not.

Analyze

The primary purpose for the authoring environment is creation and not analysis. Because geometry and data are combined together in a single database, confidence in that interaction allows us to begin to understand what it is it will create. This first step into analysis begins at the planning stages. However, it's common to pull information from the authoring environment into one specifically built for analysis. You'll find that many processes and tools specifically built for analysis work in parallel, and sometimes perpendicular, to model authoring. The real value in BIM beyond design documentation is the interoperability of model geometry and metadata between applications. Consider energy modeling as an example. In Figure 1.6, we're comparing three energy-modeling applications: A, B, and C. In the figure, the darkest blue bar reflects the time it takes to either import model geometry into the analysis package or redraw the design with the analysis package. The lighter blue bar reflects the amount of time needed to add data not within the authoring environment, such as loads, zoning, and so on. The lightest bar represents the time it takes to perform the analysis once all the information is in place.

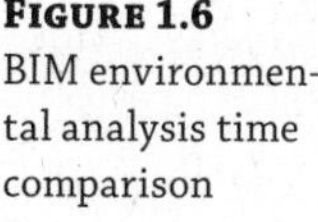

FIGURE 1.6
BIM environmental analysis time comparison

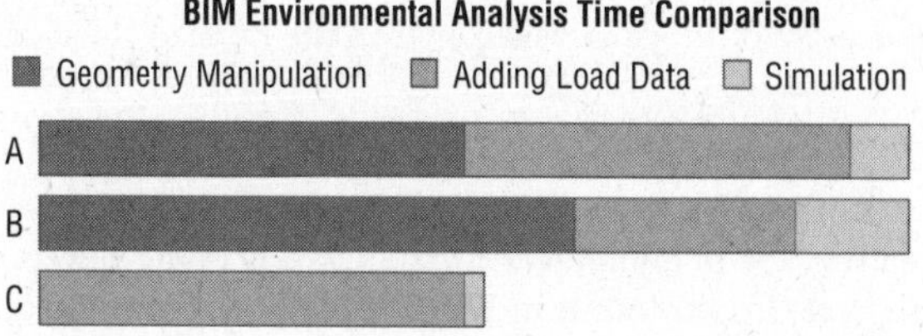

In some instances, models authored in one platform may not work directly with analysis platforms, such as the example in A and B. This caused the re-creation of the geometry directly in the analysis tool and also required time to coordinate and maintain the design and its iterations between the two models. The trend of these tools is moving toward better integration or additional analysis tools embedded inside the authoring applications. In application C, you can see we were able to import the model geometry directly into the analysis package, saving nearly 50 percent of the time needed to create and run the full analysis. Using this workflow, you can bring analysis to more projects, perform more iterations, or do the analysis in half the time.

The same workflow is true for daylighting (Figure 1.7) and other types of building performance analysis. By designing directly in the authoring tool, designers are able to move away from anecdotal or prescriptive design solutions and begin to rely on calculated results.

FIGURE 1.7
Daylighting overlay from Autodesk® 3ds Max® Design software

Building analysis can reach beyond just the design phase and into the whole building lifecycle. Once the building has been occupied, the use of BIM does not need to end. More advanced facilities management systems support tracking—and thereby trending—building use over time. By trending building use, you can begin to predict usage patterns and help anticipate future uses such as energy consumption or expansion. This strategy can help you become more proactive with maintenance and equipment replacement because you will be able to perceive how equipment performance begins to degrade over time. Trending will also aid you in providing a more comfortable environment for building occupants by understanding historic use patterns and allowing you to keep the building tuned for optimized energy performance. The application of this analysis comes in the Realize stage of BIM uses covered later in this chapter.

Communicate

Using BIM to better visualize a building is very powerful way to communicate design intent. Creating documentation and visualization using BIM gives teams the added advantage of being able to communicate the design of the project in 3D, where it is more accessible to project participants. It is especially persuasive for those who are typically involved directly with the construction process but are still important decision makers. Owners can benefit greatly from this type of communication. In this, visualization is an important tool for making design or construction decisions.

Although this was initially conceived as one of the "low-hanging fruits" of a BIM workflow, this benefit has led to an explosion of additional perceptions of the design, including isometric details, renderings, animations, class detection reports, and so on. This provides a much better way to communicate design opportunities and decisions between project stakeholders.

In the 1990s, if you wanted to create a rendering, a physical model, a daylighting model, an energy model, and an animation, you would have had to create five separate models and use five different pieces of software. There was no ability to reuse model geometry and data between model uses. One of the key uses of BIM is the opportunity to repurpose the model for a variety of visualizations. This not only allows you to not have to re-create geometry between uses but also ensures you're using the most current information in each visualization because it all comes from the same source. As the capacity of cloud rendering and analysis grows, the feedback will no longer need to process locally and you'll be able to receive feedback faster.

This digital creation of the project has given us a variety of tools to communicate its aspects. Because the model is a single source of truth, it can be used in many different applications for communicating. Models may be imported into a gaming engine for an interactive virtual experience, allowing clients to virtually tour the building at their own pace, to help understand how this building will accommodate their functional and aesthetic needs. These same virtual models can also be physically printed through rapid prototyping methods, creating small models (Figure 1.8) in a fraction of the time it would take to build one by hand. Many other forms of communicating through BIM are emerging as you read this book.

FIGURE 1.8
An example of rapid prototyping using BIM data
Source: HOK

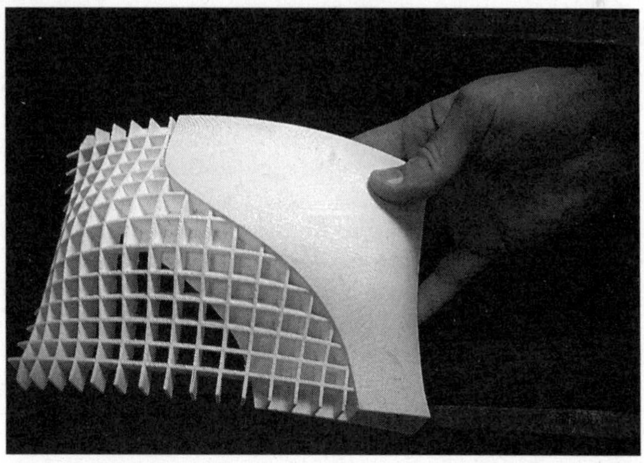

If we consider a broad spectrum of representations, from tabular data to intelligently generated 2D documentation and 3D visualization, our traditional design deliverables become transformed. Schedules give you instantaneous reports on component quantities and space usage, whereas plans, sections, and elevations afford you the flexibility to customize their display using the information embedded in the modeled elements. For example, the plan in Figure 1.9 shows how color fills can be automatically applied to illustrate space usage by department. Because this is live in the model, changes can be made easily, providing confidence to the communicators and the receivers of this information that what they are seeing is accurate and can be the basis of valid decision making.

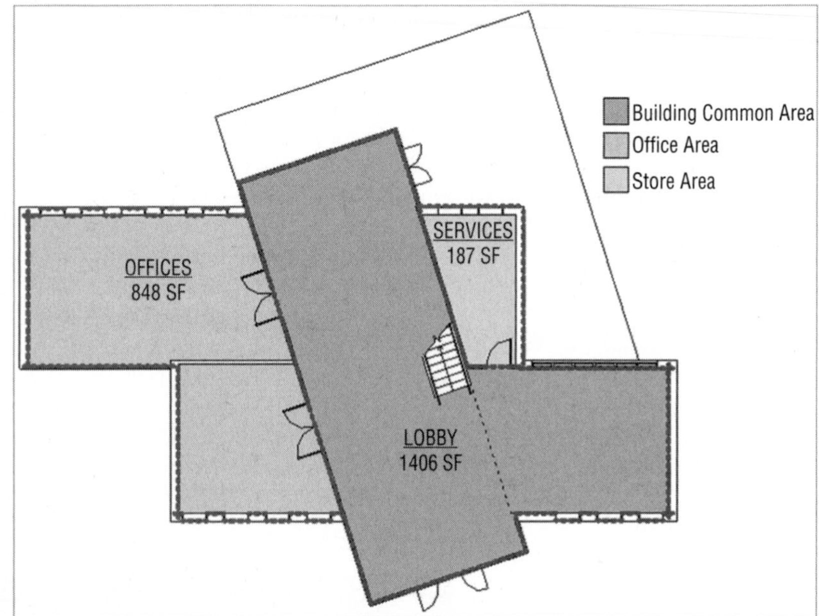

FIGURE 1.9
Even 2D views can evolve to illustrate and analyze spatial properties.

Expanding 2D documentation to include 3D imagery also gives project teams the ability to clearly share the intent of more complex designs. It also has a positive effect on construction by reducing translation errors with illustrative documentation, rather than cryptic details and notations. Figure 1.10 shows a basic example of a drawing sheet composed of both 2D and 3D views generated directly from the project model.

Another obvious benefit to creating a complete model of the building is the ability to generate a wide variety of 3D images for presentation. These images are used not only to describe design intent but also to illustrate ideas about proportion, form, space, and functional relationships. The ease at which these kinds of views can be produced makes the rendered perspective more of a commodity. As shown in the left side of Figure 1.11, materiality may be removed to focus on the building form and element adjacencies. The same model is used again for a final photorealistic rendering, as shown in the right side of Figure 1.11. As the model contains information of both form and function, it's up to the communicator to decide what information is shared. A plan, perspective, and schedule can share common information. Because they come in different forms, the intent of the communication can be different. That is the great boon of having an intelligent model; you decide where and when information is communicated in any of the outputs with the confidence that it is the single source of truth.

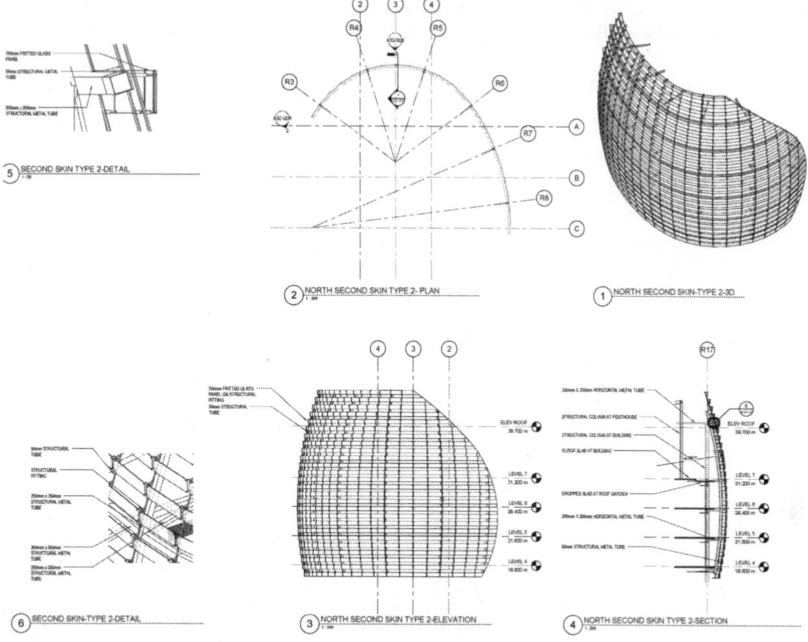

FIGURE 1.10 Construction documentation can begin to transform from 2D to 3D.
Source: HOK

FIGURE 1.11 Two different methods of using 3D presentation views
Source: HOK

By adding materials to the BIM elements, you can begin to explore the space in color and light, creating photorealistic renderings of the building. These images can convey information about both the intent and content of the design. Iterations at this level are limited only by processing power and user intent. The photorealism allows for an almost lifelike exploration of color and light qualities within a built space even to the extent of allowing analytic brightness calculations to reveal the exact levels of light within a space, but with the added benefit of being derived directly from the working models. In this case, renderings can be an embedded process or a perpendicular instantaneous output. The first option would be rendering within the authoring tool. This would produce timely renderings based on the current models, but they are not of the typically required quality for presentation purposes. More high-end renderings used for marketing would normally require exports from models brought into specific rendering tools. These renderings can be more stylized or photorealistic; however, they are a snapshot in time of the working model and take additional preparation in order to be useful. This in effect ends their BIM connectivity.

The next logical step is taking these elements and adding the element of time. In Figure 1.12, you can see a still image taken from a phasing animation (commonly referred to as a 4D simulation) of a project. Not only do these simulations convey time and movement through space, but they also have the ability to demonstrate how the building will react or perform under real lighting and atmospheric conditions. All of this fosters a more complete understanding of the constructability and performance of a project before it is realized. This is also a common method when trying to understand construction sequencing by contractors as they are planning the building of the facility.

FIGURE 1.12 A still from an animation showing accurate physical conditions for the project
Source: HOK

Realize

The use of BIM can potentially remove the direct human input to develop specific elements of the facility. Using the data generated through BIM-based planning and design processes to fabricate or manage building elements of the facility allows facility owners to realize some of the most beneficial aspects of the entire endeavor. Using BIM for facility management can enable owners to take advantage of the facility data throughout the building's lifecycle to support safe, effective, and efficient environments. The maintenance of this data can improve efficiencies through having accurate as-builts. It can promote the optimization of operation and maintenance of the facility's systems to reduce energy usage. Let us explore two main concepts of BIM realization: assemblage and control.

By developing building information modeling, you can re-plan building elements way before they are actually fabricated and assembled. This can include the specific specification of existing systems or the design of custom systems to be installed in the facility. Examples include picking a water pump that fits both the functional requirements and the spatial requirements of a mechanical space or the opportunity to free fabricate a custom receptionist desk for a highly designed lobby space. During the projects' early phases, these processes can be used to generate multiple design schemes. For construction, these processes can help the contractors to understand the process of bringing materials on-site and how and when they should go together. It might also inform them how to pre-assemble custom systems for delivery to the project site, preventing cumbersome storage or barriers to successful assemblage such as poor weather or misinterpreted documents. Being able to assemble systems with the aid of machines, such as CNC systems, can reduce not only costs but also the time needed to install components in the facility. Examples of prefabrication might include wall systems, ductwork, and curtainwall.

Building information modeling also allows operators of the facilities to help manage and maintain the equipment and systems once they are installed on-site. If a database was created during the planning, design, and construction phases of the project to ensure that all as-built systems are well documented with specific properties associated with each system, operations and maintenance stakeholders not only will have a better knowledge of what systems they have but also may have some automated processes that could schedule maintenance requests or connect in with building system analysis tools. When you do an analysis of the lifespan of a building, you will see most of the time is in the occupancy stage. This really means that most of the money spent on the facility is running it. If BIM can help reduce the costs of operating and maintaining a facility, this becomes a huge benefit to owners that can be realized through a building information modeling process. As architects we are the primary origin of this information that can help owners achieve these benefits. A good model-based database can help an owner solve maintenance issues more quickly, may be able to find potential issues more readily, and can be able to plan future construction much more easily. The use of this data to regulate facility systems potentially allows facility operators to optimize their operations. It is even possible that in the future, building systems could be automated because of information generated by BIM. Be able to plan the system integrations ahead of time allows for more intelligence built into the facility. An example of this is when a thermostat is programmed to modify the settings of the HVAC system in response to pre-programmed rules by its connection to an intelligent monitoring system, enabled by the BIM. Benefits such as these can really help owners optimize the operations and maintenance of the facilities and demand more services from its designers, such as yourself.

The Integration of Tools Inside a BIM Workflow

As you have read with the explanations of people and processes involved with BIM, the last aspect to discuss is the technology. Without the technology you would not be here. It in effect, it supports all the other things that make building information modeling possible. The thing you may not realize is that even though it is the foundation of all these other great opportunities and benefits, it is still a lesser aspect of the entire BIM ecosystem. This may confuse some readers, but in our experience we find that the most meaningful changes happen with the people deploying these processes and the methodology they take in transforming their work. The tools that people use in their workflows to generate geometry and data change only slightly from year to year. Technology is constantly being improved, made more efficient, and better integrated with other tools in the market. You as an individual user have little influence over this. Understanding the existing capabilities of tools is important; however, change in the technology sense is much more limited than improvements to your process and skillsets.

The purpose of this book is to connect your knowledge as a person with the best understanding of authoring tool's capabilities. That specific authoring tool, of course, is Autodesk Revit. Coming to this realization, the user must understand that an expert of the software is not an expert in BIM. Many people know the functions of the tool based on learning or experience but still do not have a grasp on why they should do something and when they should do it. That comes with having a better understanding of not only why BIM is beneficial but also how all these things come together to create an architectural zeitgeist. Throughout this volume we hope to make contributions to your understanding of all three and to help you make the connection between opportunities in the application and a methodology to deploy them, with the overall sense of what it means to your project and to your organization.

What Is Revit?

Autodesk Revit software is a BIM application for authoring parametric 3D models that generate geometry with embedded information for the design and construction of buildings and infrastructure. From these intelligent models, plans, sections, elevations, perspectives, details, and schedules—all of the necessary instruments to document the design of a building—can be derived. Drawings created using Revit are not a collection of 2D lines and shapes that are interpreted to represent a building but live views extracted from virtual building models. These models are a compilation of intelligent components that contain not only geometric attributes but also data informing decisions about the building at every stage of the process, including occupancy.

Elements in Revit are managed and manipulated through a series of parameters that we will discuss in greater detail throughout this book. These elements have bidirectional associativity, allowing the user to change the 2D views to change the 3D model, or the model to change the views. If you move a door in a plan, that door is moved in all of the elevations, sections, perspectives, etc. in which that object appears. In addition, all of the element's properties contain information internally, which means that intelligent annotations are directly linked to the objects. These tags display the object's data directly, rather than a manual entry interpreted by the user. When contrasted with traditional CAD tools that store element information only in the annotation, Revit gives you the opportunity to more easily input, manage, and export your project data for project coordination and execution.

The Bottom Line

Focus your investment in BIM. Since using Revit software is a change in workflow, it is also important to understand the change in staffing and who is needed to perform what roles on a project.

Master It What are the three primary roles in a Revit project, and what are the responsibilities of those roles?

Understand a BIM workflow. Understand how projects are completed in BIM and how the use of Revit software on a project can change how information within a project is created.

Master It Explain one of the primary differences between a more traditional 2D CAD-based workflow and producing documents using Revit.

Leverage BIM processes. Understanding the level of risk your firm is willing to take in new technologies will help you establish goals for your future use of BIM.

Master It Using the three areas of firm integration (visualization, analysis, and strategy), define how those areas overlap for your firm or project.

Chapter 2

Applying the Principles of the User Interface and Project Organization

After more than a decade in the architecture, engineering, and construction (AEC) industry, Autodesk® Revit® software continues to be unique in its combination of powerful features and ease of use. Revit may not be the absolute best tool to design and document every imaginable building type, but its features and functions make the vast majority of production tasks much more efficient and accurate.

Revit is a completely bidirectional, multiuser working environment, unlike other 2D computer-aided drafting (CAD) or 3D building information modeling (BIM) tools. Instead of layers and vectors, you will be using terms such as *projects, components,* and *parameters* along with tools like Wall, Door, and Floor. The concepts and terminology should seem familiar if you have experience in the building industry; however, transitioning to them can be a daunting task if you are more familiar with drafting terms than construction. This chapter provides an overview of the Revit user interface (UI) as well as the key aspects of data organization within a project.

In this chapter, you'll learn to:

- Understand the user interface
- Understand project organization

Understanding the User Interface

The UI is based on the Windows ribbon framework that is also found in software applications such as Microsoft Office. Within Revit, you will find many commands and tools that use similar dialog boxes and workflows. For example, you will not find disparate dialog boxes for door properties versus window properties. Persistence of tool location is another key to increased usability. Even though tools remain contextually exposed or hidden, the majority of them can be found in the same place relative to the overall UI.

As you're learning the interface, keep in mind that the interface presents a tooltip for every element. This tooltip has two stages. The first stage, which appears when you first mouse over the tool, provides the name as well as an option to find out more information from the Help menu by pressing the F1 key. Most tools provide a second stage that gives you an additional description about what the tool is typically used for. A new user can learn a lot just by mousing over various parts of the interface.

You have the ability to access all three disciplines of the Revit software suite—Architecture, Structure, and MEP. This functionality is addressed in the "Getting to Know the Ribbon" section of this chapter.

Figure 2.1 shows the Autodesk® Revit® Architecture 2017 UI. To illustrate some different project views, we've tiled four view types: plan, elevation, 3D, and sheet. In the following sections of this chapter, we will review the major components of the UI.

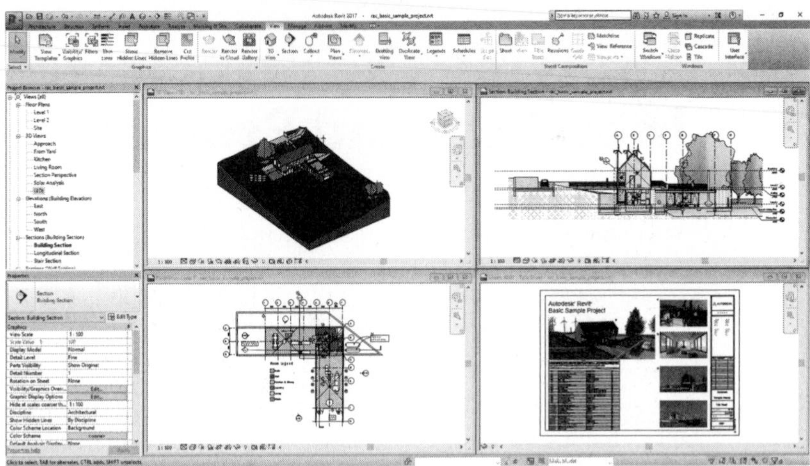

FIGURE 2.1 The Revit Architecture 2017 UI

Accessing and Using the Application Menu

Click the big R in the upper-left corner of the UI to open the Application menu and access commonly used commands such as New, Open, Save, Print, and so on. You can also export your project to a number of 2D and 3D formats from this menu. In the upper-left corner of the dialog there are two icons for both recent documents and open documents. Recent Documents lists the last several files that you've opened, no matter the location. Open Documents shows you all the files you currently have open, as Revit allows you to load multiple files at once. This is a great tool in case you have many views open and you want to quickly go to a specific file you're working on. Many of the tools that allow you to open or save multiple formats include extensions that help you specify different options. For example, when you have a project open and you choose Save As, you can save your project as a typical Revit file or as a template to be used as a basis for future projects. Dialogs like this will also limit you to the operations that you can do currently. If you have a project file open, you cannot save it as a family file; Revit will gray that option out, visually informing you that this is not a valid operation. These dialogs are also nice in that you can customize locations for opening and saving certain file types. When you open the Open dialog, you'll see a list of shortcuts to the left that give you quick access to your desktop, favorites, and even the history of your most recent navigation. What's nice about this dialog is that you can also create additional locations based on your current workflow. Creating a shortcut to a library of components or to your project folder will help save you time when you're navigating between files. The Publish option lets you upload exported formats (DWF, DWG, DXF, DGN, and SAT) to Autodesk® Buzzsaw® to share project documents with your team. Use the Close command to quickly close a project or family without closing every open view.

When accessing some of the flyout commands in the Application menu, be aware that there may be additional commands or options on the flyout that are hidden. This is most evident on the Export command flyout, in which you must scroll to the bottom of the flyout to access exporting options for IFC (Industry Foundation Classes) and others. If you click the button without choosing the flyout, you are choosing the default option.

Using the Quick Access Toolbar

The Quick Access toolbar (QAT) allows you to keep frequently used tools at your fingertips. Some commonly used commands are included by default in the QAT, but you can customize it to meet your own needs.

Right-click any button in one of the ribbon tabs, and you will find the command Add To Quick Access Toolbar. By clicking the small, down-facing arrow to the far right of the QAT, you'll find that tools may be further customized, grouped, or removed from the toolbar (Figure 2.2). By default, the QAT bar is above the ribbon, but you also have the option to show the QAT below the ribbon.

With the QAT you also have the option of temporarily hiding quick access tools based on the flyout arrow on the far-right side. With this, you could quickly provision or unprovision tools based on your current workflow, without having to re-create the shortcut.

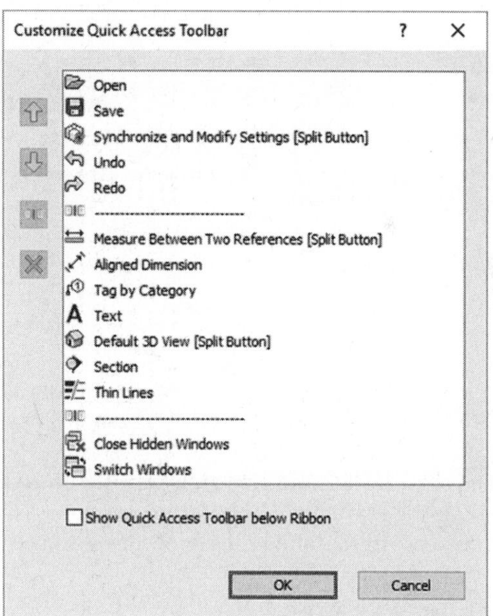

FIGURE 2.2
Customizing the QAT

Using the InfoCenter

To the far right of the QAT is the InfoCenter (Figure 2.3).

FIGURE 2.3
The InfoCenter

From left to right, you have the ability to search for help solutions, access the Subscription Center, open the Communication Center, show Favorites (saved articles and solutions from the Communication Center), sign in to other Autodesk services (such as cloud rendering or Collaboration for Revit), launch the Autodesk Exchange for Revit (Exchange Apps), and open the help content.

Because Autodesk continues to move toward more cloud services, we recommend making sure you have a login for your system. This helps with other things such as collaboration, but it is going to make it easier for you to take advantage of all the capabilities that the software has to offer.

Getting to Know the Ribbon

The ribbon is the primary location for accessing the commands and tools you will use in the application (Figure 2.4). Every program using Microsoft's ribbon interface is different, and some software developers and companies develop their own unique interfaces and ways of working. Revit is a great example of this. You can launch commands and tools by selecting icons in the ribbon, or you can create customized keyboard shortcuts as an alternative. Refer to Chapter 3, "The Basics of the Toolbox," for more information on keyboard shortcuts. Throughout this book, we will refer to the ribbon frequently, so you should be familiar with its basic parts: tabs and panels. Tabs are the categories of tools, and panels are the subcategories organized into icons.

FIGURE 2.4
The ribbon

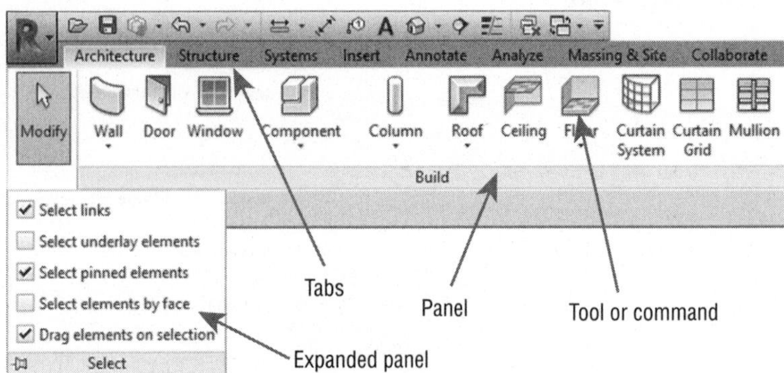

The organization and size of the icons within each panel on the ribbon will change slightly as you scale the size of your application window. As the application window gets smaller, the icons will decrease in size and will sometimes stack, or the descriptions will be hidden.

Touring the Tabs

Tabs are the highest level of organization and are used to select from among the various groups of functionality. There are up to 11 tabs along the top of the ribbon. We'll take a moment to briefly describe them:

Architecture, Structure, or Systems When you install Revit, you will have access to the tools for all three design disciplines, and you can control the visibility of these tabs (Architecture, Structure, and Systems) from the Options dialog box (accessed from the Application menu), as shown in Figure 2.5. It has become common for architects to have all three disciplines visible to improve collaboration. These tabs contain tools you will use to create or place content specific to each design discipline. At the end of the tabs bar, there is a tool that allows you to cycle through variations of displaying tabs and panels. This is really useful only if you are trying to increase the real estate that is available to your working views.

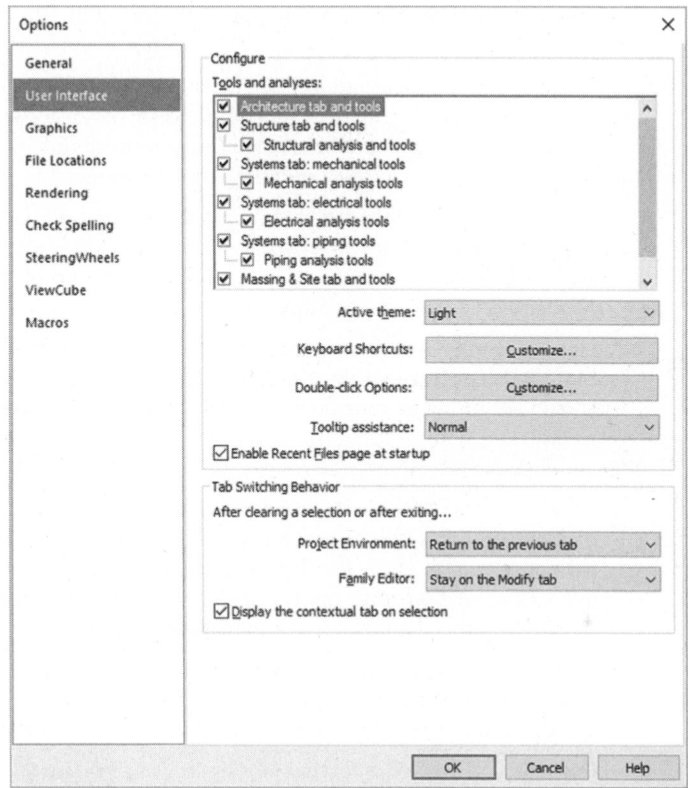

FIGURE 2.5
Setting the UI options

Insert The Insert tab is used to link external files (2D, 3D, image, and other RVT files) as well as search for external content via Autodesk® Seek. To insert content from family files, you can use the Load Family command from this tab; however, this same command is available with most modeling commands in the contextual tab of the ribbon. Learn more about linking Revit files in Chapter 6, "Working with Consultants," and using other file formats in Chapter 7, "Interoperability: Working Multiplatform."

Annotate The Annotate tab contains many of the tools necessary to annotate, tag, dimension, or otherwise graphically document your project. Learn more about these tools in Chapter 16, "Detailing Your Design," and Chapter 18, "Annotating Your Design."

Analyze The Analyze tab contains the tools necessary to modify energy analysis settings and to run an energy simulation via Green Building Studio®. This feature requires an Autodesk Subscription account to access the online analysis engine. Learn more about conceptual energy analysis in Chapter 9, "Conceptual Design and Design Analysis."

Massing & Site The Massing & Site tab contains the tools necessary to add massing- and site-related elements such as toposurfaces and property lines. Learn more about modeling site context in Chapter 3, "The Basics of the Toolbox," and conceptual design massing in Chapter 9.

Collaborate The Collaborate tab contains the tools that you'll use to coordinate and manage the project within your own team as well as across other teams and their linked files. Learn more about worksharing in Chapter 5, "Working in a Team," and interdisciplinary coordination in Chapter 6.

View The View tab contains the tools that you'll use to create all your project views, 2D and 3D, as well as schedules, legends, and sheets. You can also modify your UI from this tab, including your keyboard shortcuts. Learn more about creating multiple project views and sheets in Chapter 17, "Documenting Your Design."

Manage The Manage tab contains tools to access all your project standards and other settings. You will also find the Design Options and Phasing tools on this tab. Additional tools such as Review Warnings and Select By ID are found in the Manage tab and will help keep your project running smoothly.

One of the most important settings that you'll use during your project is Object Styles on the Manage tab. Selecting this option will allow you to manage the global visibility settings for just about everything in your project: how it projects, how it cuts, and its associated color and pen weight. Learn more about this and other project settings in Chapter 4, "Configuring Templates and Standards."

Add-Ins The Add-Ins tab appears when additional extensions have been installed. It contains the tools that can do a variety of things based on additional applications created through the API. Many third-party companies, such as Ideate, BIMObject, and even Autodesk itself, have written additional applications that supplement the functions of Revit. These may include enhanced analysis or management processes.

Modify The Modify tab contains the tools used to manipulate the content that you're creating in your project. You'll find tools like Cut, Join, Move, Copy, and Rotate, among many others. Learn more about common editing tools in Chapter 3.

Contextual Tabs Contextual tabs are revealed when specific elements are selected or element creation commands are launched. For example, the Modify | Walls contextual tab (Figure 2.6) is displayed when a wall is selected. These unique tabs are usually colored green to help you distinguish them from other static tabs in the ribbon.

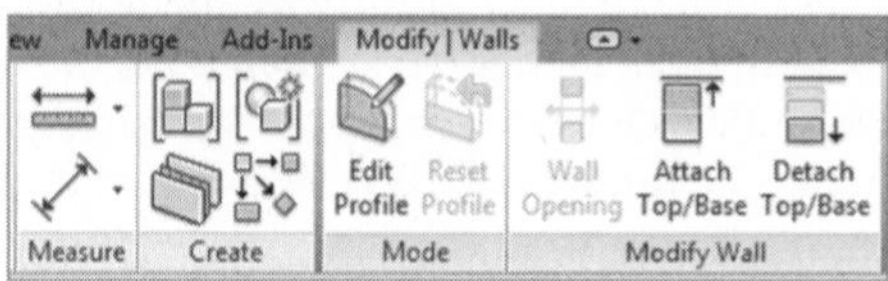

FIGURE 2.6
Example of a contextual tab

A simple, yet important, setting that may be exposed on the contextual tab when placing model content is Tag On Placement. Modeling commands like Door, Window, and Component allow you to enable automatic tagging to reduce overall documentation time. If you are working in an early design phase, you may wish to disable the Tag On Placement setting, unless you have separate presentation views created.

Placing Panels

Within each tab in the ribbon are groups of tools and commands referred to as *panels*. If you want to make any panel consistently available for easy access, you can pull it out of its tab and arrange it anywhere on your computer screen. To relocate a panel, drag the panel out of the ribbon using your mouse pointer on the panel title bar (Figure 2.7). The panel will snap to alignment with other panels you have previously dragged from the ribbon if you hover over other floating panels while dragging. These changes are persistent beyond your use of the software and will retain their new position every time you restart Revit until you choose to change them again.

Figure 2.7
Panels can be relocated anywhere in the UI.

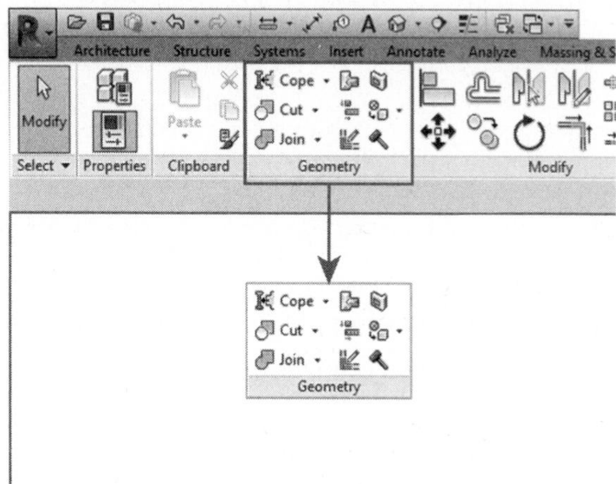

To return a panel to the ribbon, hover the mouse pointer over a floating panel and the panel's border will appear. Click the arrow in the upper portion of the gray bar at the right of the floating panel.

On some panels, you will find that settings can be accessed from the panel's title bar. An example of these features can be seen in the Annotate tab of the ribbon. In Figure 2.8, the small arrow on the Text panel is known as a *dialog launcher* and will open the Type Properties dialog box for Text (not shown in Figure 2.8). Clicking the down arrow on the Tag panel exposes an *expanded panel* that displays the Loaded Tags and Symbols command.

Figure 2.8
Special panel features

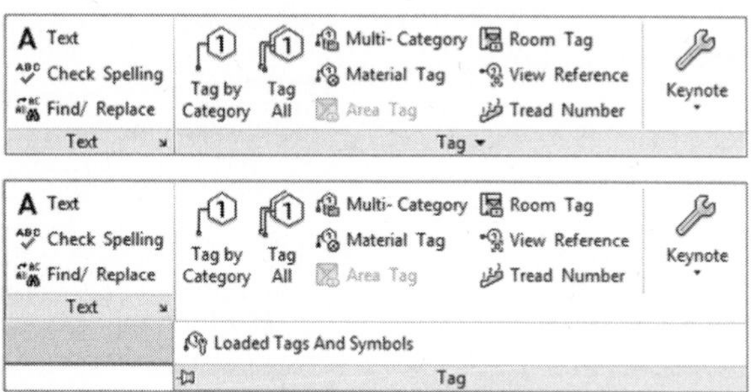

Using Other Aspects of the UI

Now that we've covered the fundamental elements contained in the ribbon, let's look at other important aspects of the UI.

Options Bar

The Options bar is located directly below the ribbon and is a contextually sensitive area that gives you feedback as you select tools and objects. In Figure 2.9, you see the options available below the ribbon when the Wall tool is active. You can also use the Options bar when an object already placed in a project or family is selected.

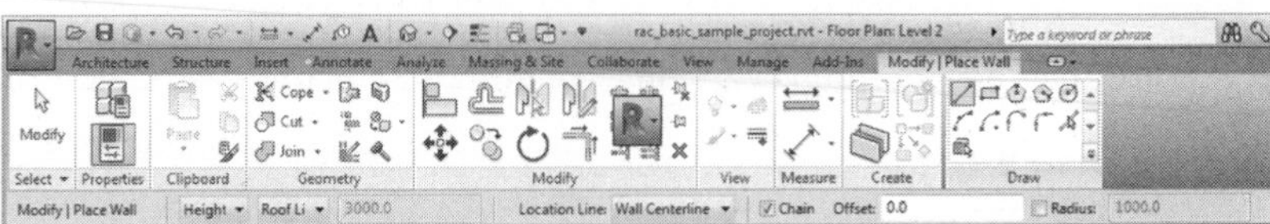

Figure 2.9
Options appear in a bar below the ribbon.

An especially important and frequently used option is included with any annotation symbol—the ability to include or exclude a leader. This will help you place tags in the clearest location within your documentation while maintaining a parametric relationship to the associated model element. Look for this option when you use the Tag By Category command from the Annotate tab in the ribbon.

Properties Palette, Project Browser

The Properties palette contains the parameters of whatever you're currently working on and shows the instance parameters by default. In this palette, you will find the Type Selector, a selection filter, and the Edit Type button (Figure 2.10). You'll learn more about filtering selected objects in Chapter 3, as well as much more about parameters in Chapter 14, "Designing with the Family Editor."

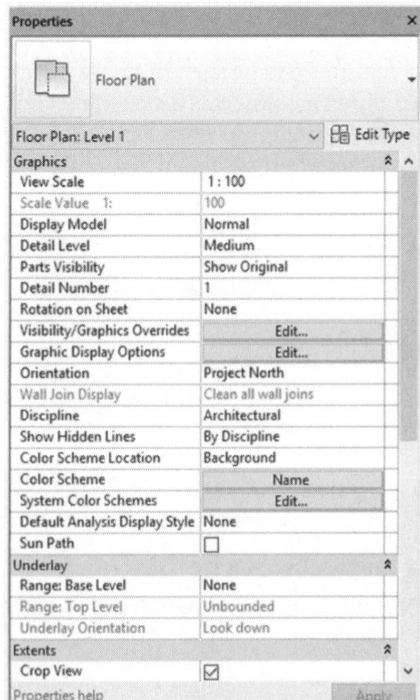

Figure 2.10
Properties palette

The Project Browser (Figure 2.11) is a hierarchical listing of all the views, legends, schedules, sheets, families, groups, and links in your project. You can expand and collapse the project tree by selecting the + and – icons.

FIGURE 2.11
Project Browser

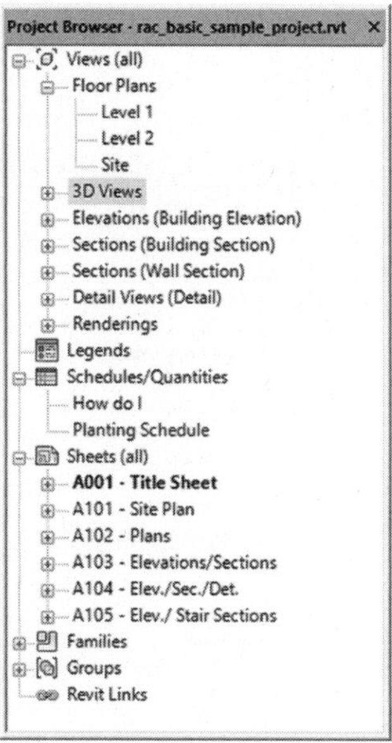

You can search for elements by right-clicking on any item in the Project Browser and selecting Search from the context menu. The simple search function will highlight any view, sheet, family, or type with the matching text in its name.

The Project Browser can also be filtered and grouped into folders based on a number of user-defined parameters (see Figure 2.12). To access the Browser Organization Properties dialog box, right-click the Views portion at the top of the palette. You can also access this tool in the View tab under the User Interface flyout button. Learn more about Project Browser customization in Chapter 4.

FIGURE 2.12
Browser Organization Properties dialog box

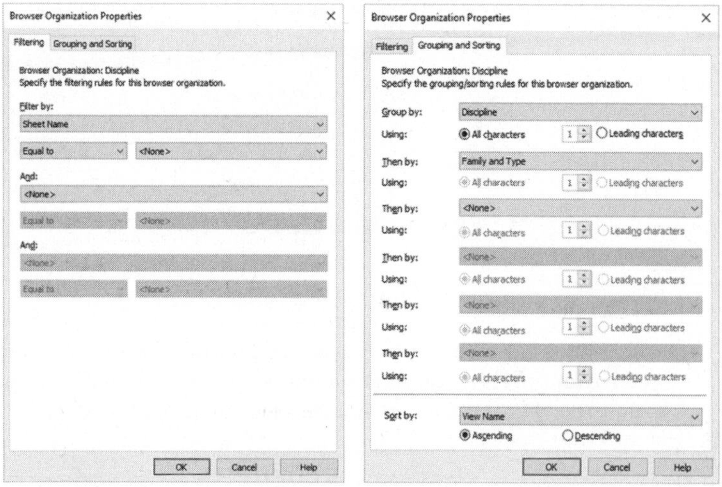

The Properties palette and Project Browser can be undocked from the main UI and can also be placed on a secondary monitor simply by dragging or double-clicking the top border of either palette. You can also drag these UI elements onto each other to use them in a unified tabbed or stacked palette, as shown in Figure 2.13. Dragging one palette onto the top border of the other will create a tabbed palette, whereas dragging it just below the top border will result in a stacked palette.

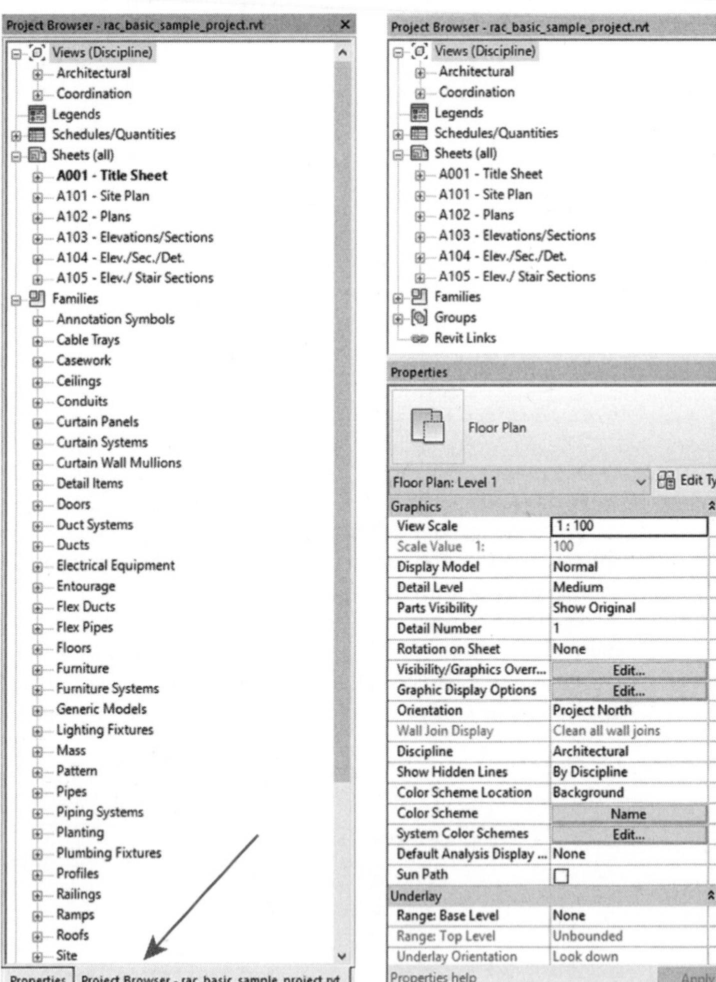

FIGURE 2.13 Properties palette and Project Browser combined in a tabbed or stacked palette

STATUS BAR

The status bar at the bottom of the UI provides useful information about selected objects and active tools. When you start a tool, the status bar will display prompts about the next step required of the tool. For example, select an object and start the Rotate command; the status bar will read "Click to enter rotate start ray or drag or click the rotation center control." It is also useful when you are using the Tab key to toggle between object snap points or when selecting chains of elements.

Toward the middle of the status bar, you will find toolbars for worksets and design options. Showing the current worksets during a collaborative project will help ensure you are placing elements on the correct workset. Worksharing will be covered in Chapter 5. If you're using design options (covered more in Chapter 10), the status bar can also show you which option you're currently exploring.

At the far right end, you will see a filter icon next to a number. When you select objects in a view window, the number of selected objects will be displayed here. Click the Filter icon to open the Filter dialog box and refine the selection set. The five icons next to the Filter icon determine which objects in your model are eligible for selection. We will discuss selecting elements in greater detail in Chapter 3.

Drawing Area

The drawing area is the window into your design space. As shown previously in Figure 2.1, you can tile several views from any number of open files or you can maximize the view windows. When the view windows in the drawing area are maximized, press Ctrl+Tab on the keyboard to cycle through the open views. To reverse the cycling, press Ctrl+Shift+Tab. To go directly to the view you want to see, choose the view from your Project Browser.

If you decide to use tiled views when you work in Revit, you should be aware of a subtle limitation. You'll be able to zoom into only the extents that are defined by the drawing area. If you want to get around this limitation, here's a helpful tip: Create a new sheet, but then delete the sheet border. This is now a workspace for any view of the project. Just be sure to label it as a working sheet apart from your documentation set. Now you can create duplicate views of any of your project views and assemble them in this working space (Figure 2.14). Zooming in and out is much more fluid, and you're not limited to the extents of one drawing area. You can create a keyboard shortcut to activate and deactivate views, which is helpful as well.

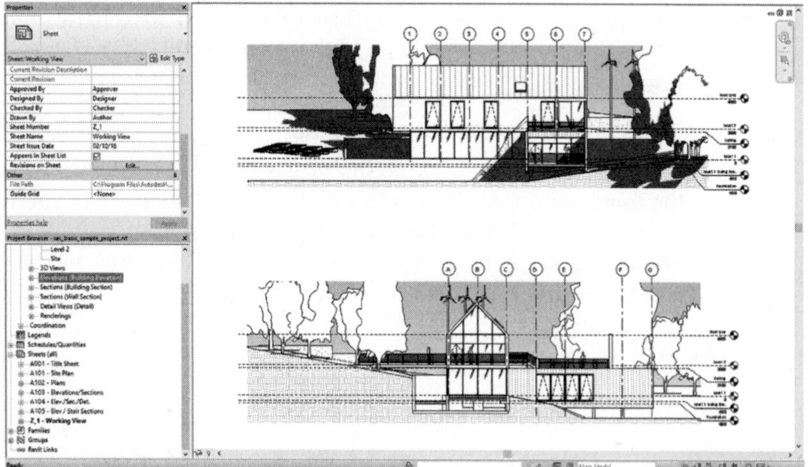

Figure 2.14
Working sheet view

VIEW CONTROL BAR

The view control bar is at the bottom of every view and changes slightly depending on the type of view (Figure 2.15). For example, sheet views have only four buttons, and perspective views do not have a scale option. In Figure 2.15, we have tiled three view windows to illustrate some of the differences in the view control bar. From top to bottom, you can see a drafting view, a plan view, and a 3D view.

FIGURE 2.15
View control bar examples

Some of the buttons in the view control bar are just shortcuts to view parameters that are also available from the Properties palette. Scale, Detail Level, Crop View, and Show/Hide Crop Region are found in both the view control bar and the Properties palette. The Visual Style button allows you to select from a short list of graphic display modes that can be customized in detail with the Graphic Display Options in the Properties palette.

Other buttons in the view control bar are unique commands. One example is the Temporary Hide/Isolate command, which helps users more readily see specific elements while working in a view. When you select an object in a view window, use this button to select from various tools to hide or isolate either the selected objects or the entire category of objects. Temporary visibility states do not affect printing, and the view window will display with a turquoise border until the temporary visibility is reset. Next to the Hide/Isolate button is the Reveal Hidden Elements button. Use this tool to highlight any elements that are hidden in the current view, either temporarily or through other methods.

The Worksharing Display button is available only on projects where worksharing is enabled. Worksharing Display can be enabled and configured in any view to illustrate Owners, Checkout Status, Model Updates, and Worksets. Refer to Chapter 5 for a detailed explanation of these visibility features.

The Show/Hide Analytical Model button allows you to quickly display analytical graphics that are commonly used by the Structural or MEP tools in Revit. Finally, the Reveal Constraints button temporarily displays all of the model-based constraints visible in the current view. This is useful for troubleshooting model elements that might not be behaving as expected.

TEMPORARY VIEW PROPERTIES

You may also temporarily modify view properties or apply a view template. When you click the Temporary View Properties icon in the view control bar, you will have a choice of Enable Temporary View Properties or Temporarily Apply Template Properties, as shown in Figure 2.16. Because these applied properties are only temporary, they will not affect printing and they will not be saved with the project.

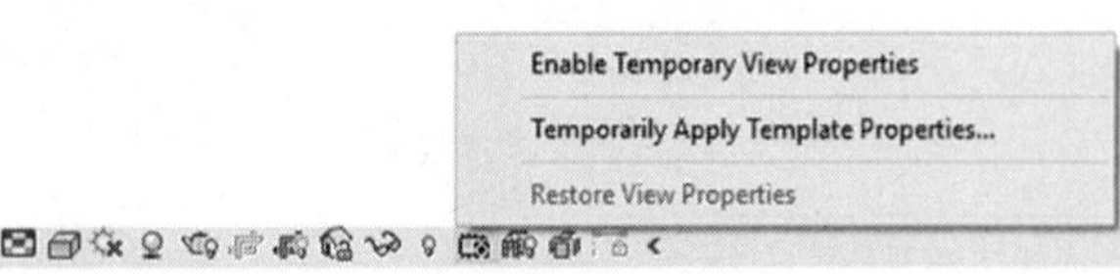

FIGURE 2.16
Temporary View Properties command

If you select Temporarily Apply Template Properties, you can select from any view template established in your project. Once a view template is applied to the view with this tool, the view will be highlighted with a purple boundary, as shown in Figure 2.17. Refer to Chapter 4 for a detailed review of view templates.

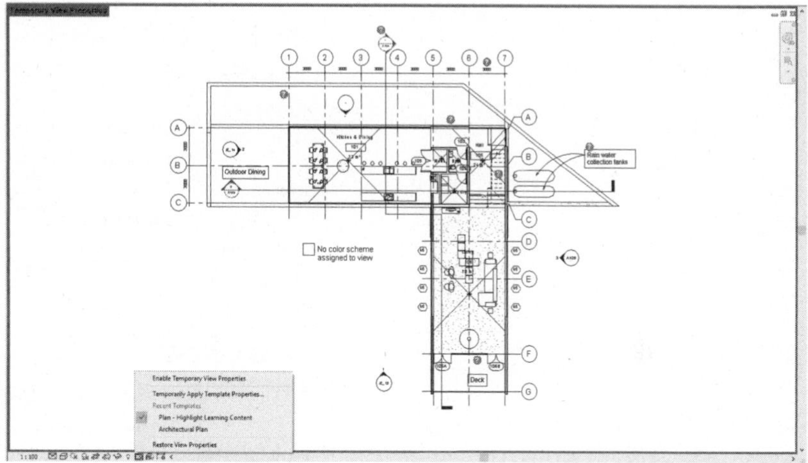

FIGURE 2.17 Active view with Temporary View Properties applied

Referring to Figure 2.16, you will notice that any recently applied view templates will appear in the Temporary View Properties menu. This allows for rapid application of templates to increase your productivity when manipulating views for various working scenarios.

The other command selection is to Enable Temporary View Properties. This mode allows you to change any view properties manually. The result is the same as temporarily applying a view template, but you can tweak any setting to your needs. For example, you might want to temporarily hide all the furniture in a view.

To remove the temporary settings, you can simply wait until you close the project file because the temporary settings are not saved. Otherwise, click the Temporary View Properties icon again and select Restore View Properties.

Graphic Display Options

The Graphic Display Options dialog box gives you access to some of the same settings you can select in the view control bar; however, more refinement options are available. From the Properties palette, click Edit in the Graphic Display Options property field, and explore the graphic settings you can customize for the current view (Figure 2.18). As an alternative, you can click the Visual Style icon (the small box) in the view control bar and choose Graphic Display Options from the pop-up menu.

Many graphic options are available, including customized backgrounds, photographic exposure, and a transparency slider. Experiment with a variety of the settings to see which ones meet your presentation and documentation needs. By saving them as view templates, you can group various settings for better comparison and contrast. You will learn much more about graphic styles in Chapter 11, "Visualization."

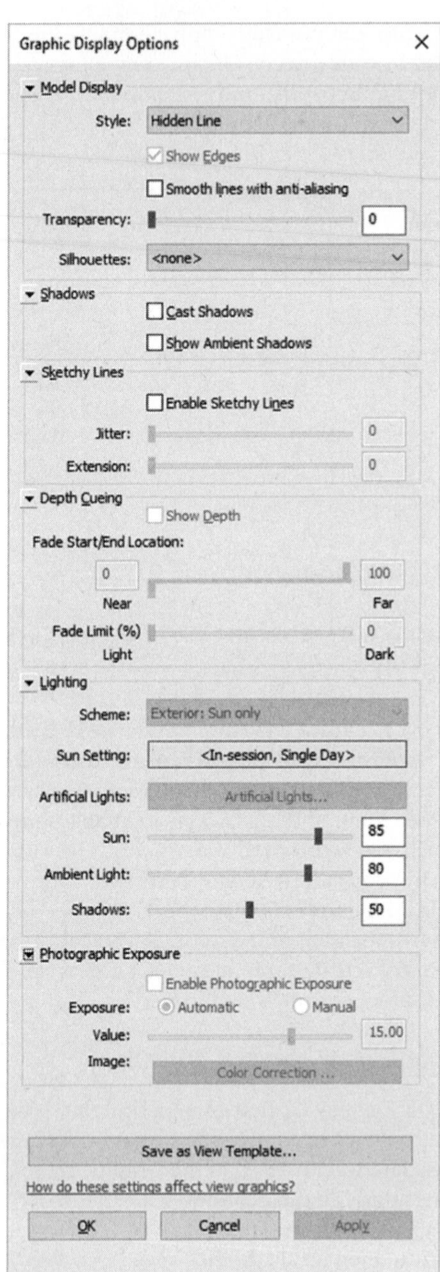

FIGURE 2.18
Graphic Display Options dialog box

WORK PLANE VIEWER

Most modeling tools and commands require an active work plane on which to place geometry. When you are working in a plan view, the work plane is usually set to the current level associated with the view. In a 3D, section, or elevation view, the definition of an active work plane may be a bit more confusing. In addition to levels, work planes can be defined as reference planes, a structural grid, or a surface of another object. To help you visualize an active work plane, a work plane viewer is available in Revit. Be aware that an active work plane could be perpendicular to your orientation if the view is adjusted three dimensionally.

The Viewer option is located on the Work Plane panel of the Architecture tab. This viewer is available from all model views when you're in the project environment. By default, the work plane is based on the active work plane of the last active view. But when you enter Sketch mode (for example, when you are creating a floor or a roof), the active work plane is that of the sketch (Figure 2.19). So even if the project window shows a 3D view, the viewer shows the plane of the sketch—and you can sketch directly in the work plane viewer! This is useful for working on sloped surfaces such as roofs.

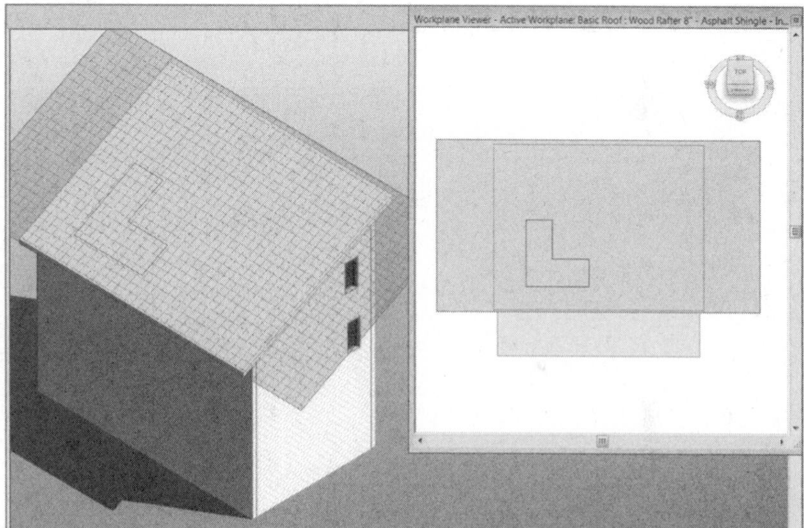

FIGURE 2.19 Sketch mode with active work plane

Navigation Methods

One of the challenges of any 3D modeling software is creating methods of navigation that are intuitive. If you have used more than one modeling application, such as Rhino, SketchUp, or Digital Project, you will know that there is no standard 3D navigation functionality. As is the case with Revit, Autodesk has consistent navigation tools across most of its industry-based applications such as AutoCAD® and Navisworks®. These include the ViewCube® tool, the SteeringWheels® tool, and basic mouse controls.

VIEWCUBE

A 3D navigation tool known as the ViewCube is available in most Autodesk design software. This tool will appear by default in the upper-right corner of any 3D view. Click any face of the cube to orient the view to that face, or click a corner of the cube to orient to an axonometric angle. Press and hold the left mouse button while moving the mouse pointer over the ViewCube to orbit the view freely. Press and hold the left mouse button while hovering over the compass, and the view will rotate as if it were on a turntable. The selected tool, the cube or compass, will highlight with a shade of blue when active.

Hovering over the ViewCube with your mouse pointer reveals the Home option (the little house above and left of the ViewCube) that you click to return to your home view. Right-clicking the ViewCube opens a menu that allows you to set, save, and orient your view (see Figure 2.20). Selecting Options from the context menu takes you directly to the ViewCube options in the Options dialog box, which you can also access from the Application menu. The ViewCube options allow you to customize the placement, transparency, and functional behavior of the tool.

FIGURE 2.20
ViewCube context menu

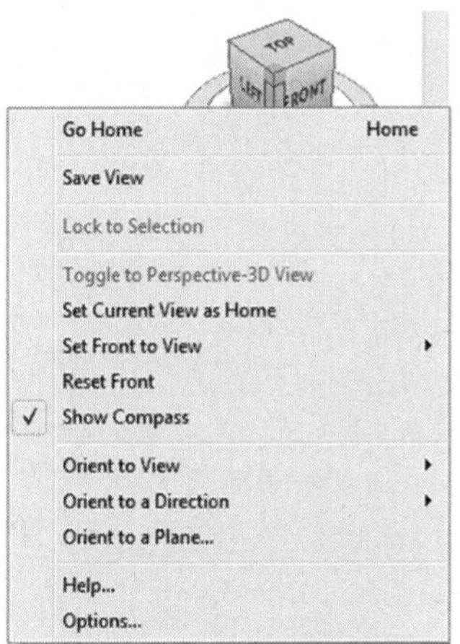

STEERINGWHEELS

Another method of navigation that is unique to Autodesk software is the SteeringWheels tool. This tool can be activated by pressing the F8 key, by pressing Shift+W, or from the Navigation bar. The SteeringWheels will follow your mouse pointer as you move about a view and will stop when the mouse movement slows, allowing you to hover the mouse pointer over one of the command areas on the wheel. As you hover the mouse pointer over a navigation command, press and hold the left mouse button while moving the mouse to activate the corresponding navigation method. There are many ways to customize the SteeringWheels, all accessible through the Wheel menu in the lower-left side of the tool. This is easier to demonstrate than explain in text, so feel free to try the various modes of the SteeringWheels tool as you continue through this book.

If you use a laptop or mobile workstation without the benefit of a mouse, the SteeringWheels tool can be a welcome substitute for traditional pointer-based navigation. The touchpads or pointing sticks on most laptops do a poor job of emulating the press-and-drag motions of a mouse along with simultaneous keyboard button combinations that drive native navigation in Revit. If you're struggling without a mouse connected to your laptop, try the SteeringWheels tool and you might thank us!

Navigation Bar

Access to the most common navigating tools is also provided in the Navigation bar located at the right side of the drawing area. From here you can launch any of the SteeringWheels and all of the zoom/pan commands from the flyout buttons.

Navigating with the Mouse

As with most modern design applications, the mouse can also be used to navigate in any view. You are not constrained to using the ViewCube, SteeringWheels, or Navigation bar. You might have already figured out that pressing the left mouse button selects objects and the right mouse button is used to access context menus. We discuss selection methods with greater detail in Chapter 3. For now, let's review how you can use the mouse to navigate the views in Revit.

To pan in any view, press and hold the wheel button on your mouse while moving it around your mouse pad. Hold the Shift key and use the wheel button on the mouse to orbit a 3D view.

The mouse wheel can be used to zoom in and zoom out of any view, but the zooming may be somewhat choppy. Hold the Ctrl key and press the wheel button while moving the mouse forward to zoom out (pushing the model away) or backward to zoom in (pulling the model toward you). You will also notice that the views will zoom in and out with a focal point based on the location of the mouse pointer.

In camera views, zooming works a bit differently. Scrolling the mouse wheel zooms in and out but includes the view's crop region. To adjust the view within the crop region, only the SteeringWheels and the ViewCube can be used.

Defining Project Organization

If you have experience with 2D CAD software, you are likely familiar with many of the terms and concepts related to designing and documenting a project, but not all of them have exact equivalents in Revit. You may be comfortable with thinking in terms of what needs to be drawn and coordinated: plans, sections, elevations, details, schedules, and so on. Such information is likely stored in a plethora of separate files that have to be linked together in order to reference other parts of a building design. For teams collaborating in the design process, you are also likely accustomed to allowing only one person in one file at a time. With this, maintaining all your project settings and standards is a struggle across so many disconnected files.

Working in the Revit environment affords you much more control and efficiency in managing these issues. From within a single, bidirectional database, Revit organizes these project organization aspects: datum, objects, content, views, and project management. Figure 2.21 shows what we like to think of as a Revit organizational chart, which gives you a visual description of these four categories and what these categories contain. In the following sections, we'll discuss each of these categories and describe its particular role in your Revit project environment.

Introducing Datum Objects

Data (plural) are sometimes referred to in Revit as *datum objects* and consist of references, grids, and levels (Figure 2.22). Datum objects establish geometric behavior by controlling the location and extents of your content (the building, the stuff that goes in a building, and the stuff you need to document your building).

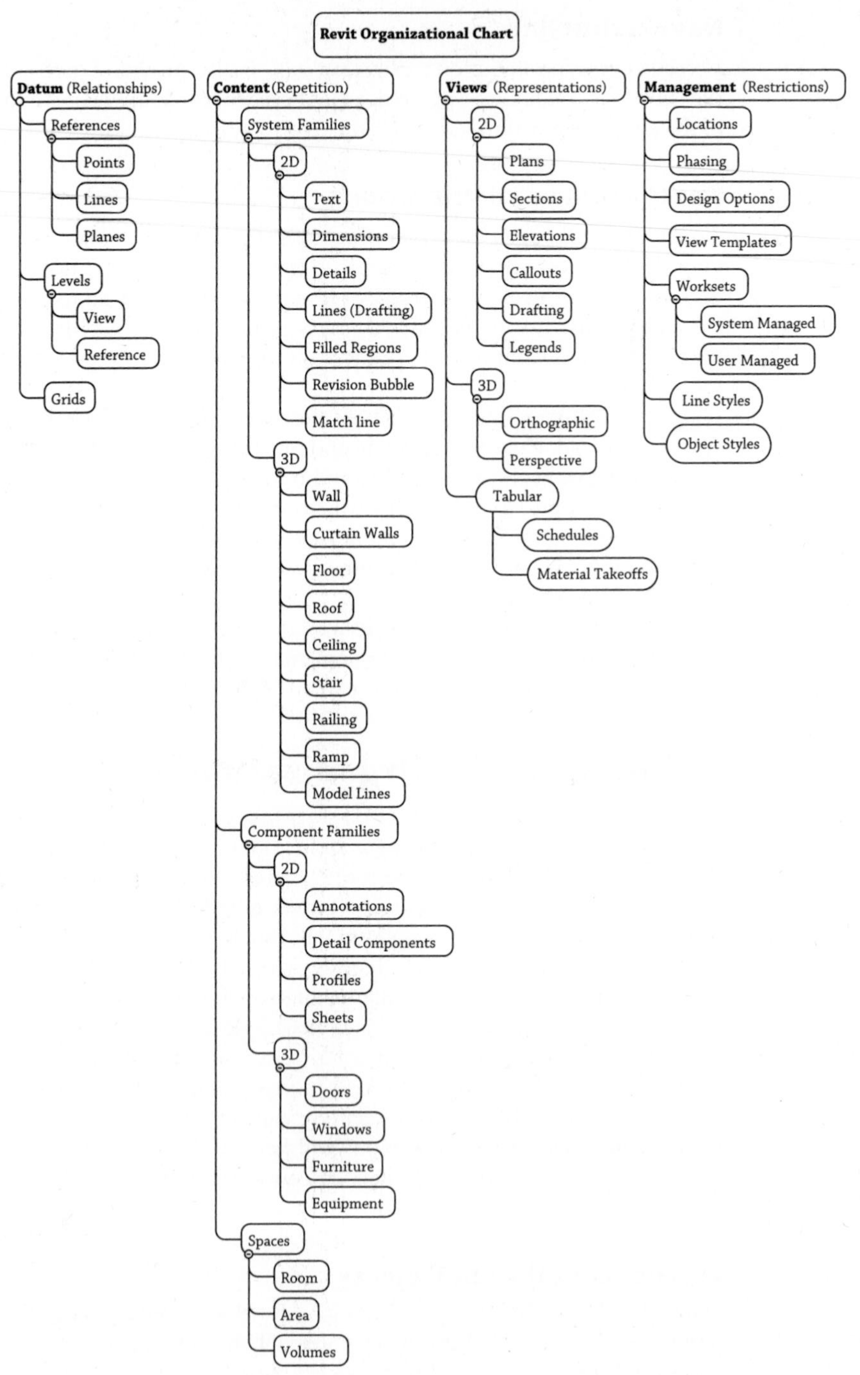

FIGURE 2.21 Revit organizational chart

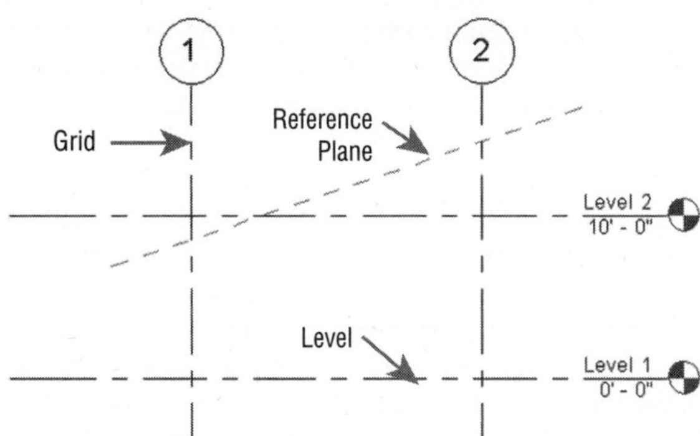

FIGURE 2.22
Datum objects

Reference planes can be created in any 2D view from the main ribbon tabs (Architecture, Structure, or Systems), but once created, they may not be visible in 3D. After you add reference planes to your project, they can be set and seen from the Work Plane panel. This will allow you to work with respect to the desired work plane.

Grids are used to locate structural elements in your project. You are not required to include grids in your project, but they are quite useful in managing structural walls and columns. Like reference planes, grid lines can be added to any 2D view. Keep in mind that grids can only be perpendicular to levels. Furthermore, grids are only visible in views that are perpendicular to the grid. So if the grid is in a north–south orientation, you'll be able to see it only in plan and from the east–west orientation.

Levels are datum objects that are parallel to the ground plane. They serve several purposes. First, they are the main method for placing and managing the elevation (or Z-location) of content. Virtually all content placed in a Revit model has a Level parameter. You can even move objects from one level to another simply by changing this property in the Properties palette. Levels also function as constraints for objects such as walls and columns. These objects have top and bottom constraints that can be set to levels so that they will automatically update if the levels are adjusted. Levels may be seen and created only in elevation and section views; therefore, you can't create levels in plan, and they can't be diagonal to the ground plane.

Creating any datum is easy. Simply select the desired tool from the Architecture tab, and then pick two points to define the start and end locations. Despite their two-dimensional appearance, all datum objects have three-dimensional extents that help you manage their appearance throughout a project. You will explore this further in the section "Explaining 3D and 2D Datum Extents" later in this chapter.

CREATING AND DUPLICATING LEVELS

In the previous section, we discussed the overall purpose of datum objects; however, there are special conditions related to the creation of levels. First, you should understand that a level does not always require an associated plan view. Levels that have plan views will have a blue graphic symbol at the end (double-click it to go to that view), whereas those that don't will have a black graphic symbol. The blue represents hyperlinked data, which you can find on levels, section heads, and other annotations. When you create a new level, you have the option to create a corresponding plan view by using the Make Plan View option from the Options bar.

Copying an existing level will not create the corresponding plan views. This is useful if you are working on a larger project, such as a high-rise, and you want to quickly configure multiple levels without creating them one at a time. You might also want to use levels just as a reference for content but not for a specific plan, such as for an intermediate landing or mezzanine.

Although it is easy to create many levels by copying or arraying, only create the levels that are necessary to manage major parts of your project and that need to be shown in your documentation. You do not need to create a level for every slab, stair, or floor offset, as objects can be shifted in the Z direction offset for any level. Too many levels can have a negative impact on your project's and your performance, as they take resources to manage.

Let's explore the creation and duplication of levels with an exercise. First, download and open the file `c02-Levels-Start.rvt` or `c02-Levels-Start-Metric.rvt` from this book's web page at `www.sybex.com/go/masteringrevit2017`. Then follow these steps:

1. Open the exercise file and make sure the Project Browser is open—remember that it may be in a tabbed palette with Properties. Expand the Views tree and then expand Elevations. Double-click on South to activate that view in the drawing area.

   You will see two levels that are usually present when you create a new project using the default template.

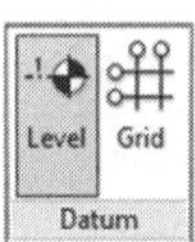

2. From the Architecture tab in the ribbon, find the Datum panel and click the Level tool. In the Options bar, ensure that the Make Plan View option is selected.
3. From left to right, draw a new level exactly 10′-0″ (3000 mm) above Level 2.

   When you hover the mouse pointer anywhere near either endpoint of the existing levels, you will see alignment guides (dashed lines) that help keep the extents of the datum objects consistent.

4. Click the Modify button or press the Esc key, and you will notice that the new level has a blue target. Double-click the target for Level 3, and the Level 3 floor plan will open.
5. Return to the South elevation view and select Level 3. From the Modify tab in the ribbon, click the Copy tool. In the Options bar, select the Multiple option.
6. Create two copies of Level 3: one that is 2′-0″ (600 mm) above Level 3 and one that is 9′-0″ (2700 mm) above that one, as shown in Figure 2.23.
7. You can change the names and elevations of levels by selecting a level and then clicking the name or the elevation value. Rename Level 3 to **Level 2B**, Level 4 to **Level 3**, and Level 5 to **Roof**. If you are prompted to rename the corresponding views, click Yes.

As we stated previously, plan views are not created for levels that are copied or arrayed. This gives you the flexibility to quickly generate levels for taller buildings without all the associated views that may increase your project file size unnecessarily. Although this workflow may be beneficial for you in early design phases, what do you do when you need all those floor plans and ceiling plans for that high-rise design?

If you want to convert a level that doesn't have a view to one that does, find the Create panel on the View tab and then select the Plan Views flyout and then the Floor Plan command. This opens the dialog box shown in Figure 2.24. You can select among all the levels without corresponding views in your project. Only the levels you copied in the previous exercise are listed in the dialog box.

FIGURE 2.23 Create multiple copies of levels.

FIGURE 2.24 Adding views to levels

You can also use this command to create duplicate views of existing levels. Clear the Do Not Duplicate Existing Views option at the bottom of the dialog box to see all the levels in your project.

Select the Roof level and click OK. A floor plan will be created for the Roof level, and that floor plan will be opened. It is important to note that every plan you create with this method will be opened as you complete the command. Remember to use the Close Hidden Windows tool (available in the Quick Access toolbar) to avoid slower performance in your work session.

Explaining 3D and 2D Datum Extents

Datum objects—specifically grids and levels—have two types of extents: 3D (analytic) and 2D (graphic). These extents are expressed as grips that are shown at the endpoints of the grids and levels in plans, sections, and elevations. The analytic grips control the extents of the datum across the entire project and all views. The analytic grip is shown as an open circle and the indicator displays as 3D, as shown in Figure 2.25.

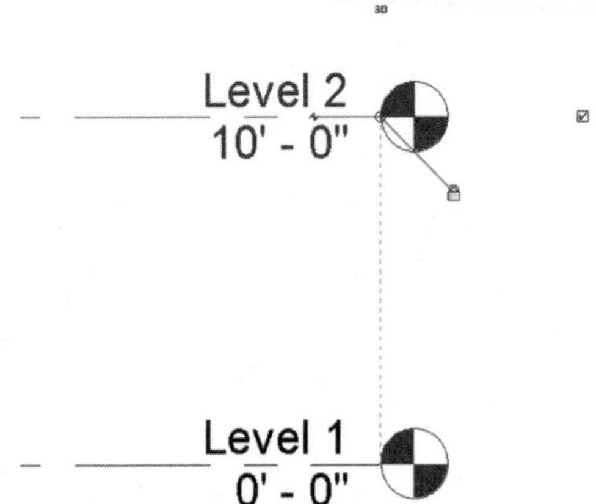

Figure 2.25
Controlling the 3D (analytic) extents of the datum

If you want to adjust the 2D extents of your datum in only the current view, click the 3D icon and it will change to 2D. You can then modify the 2D extents of the datum object without affecting the 3D extents. We will explore this further in an exercise later in this section.

Datum objects are visible only in views that intersect their 3D extents. The elevation in Figure 2.26 shows four grids and four levels. Grid lines 3 and 4 are not visible on Levels 3 and 4 because their 3D extents are not intersecting those levels.

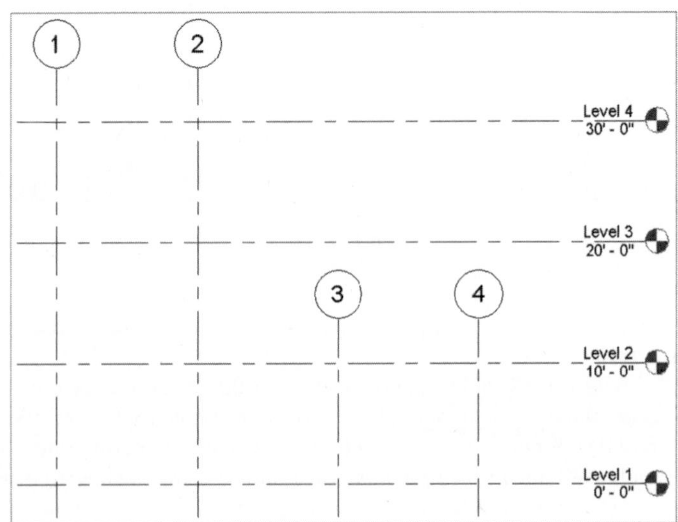

Figure 2.26
3D (analytic) extents affect visibility of datum objects.

You can use the 3D and 2D extents to your liking in any view. In Figure 2.27, for example, the 3D extents of the grid lines extend through Level 1 and Level 2, but the 2D extents are set above Level 2. This means that the grid datum would still be visible in both levels, even though it looks like they do not intersect the levels.

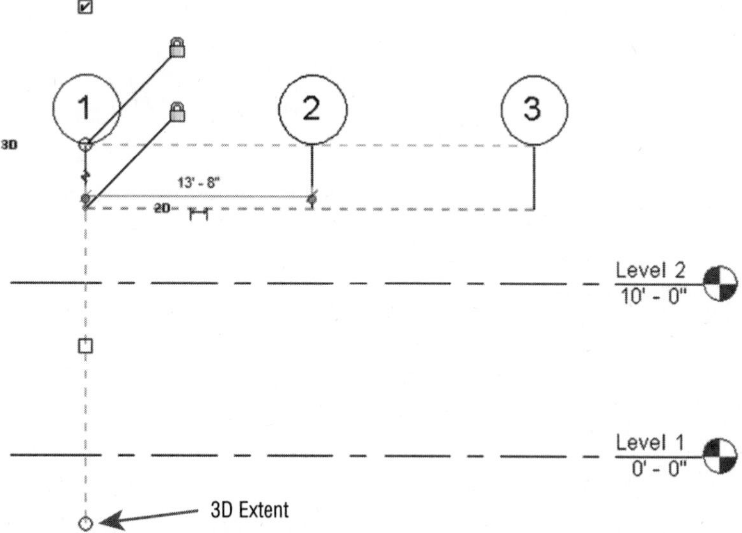

FIGURE 2.27
Customizing 3D and 2D extents of datum objects

When you move a datum object, one way or another, content is going to respond. If you move a level, walls and furniture are going to move accordingly. If you move a grid, structural elements associated to the grid are going to relocate. And if you move references, the elements associated with them will update. As a matter of fact, you will often constrain or pin datum objects in order to restrict their movement as your project is starting to develop.

Let's continue with the exercise from the section "Creating and Duplicating Levels" and edit the 2D extents for one of the levels you copied. Remember that although this exercise uses levels, these methods can be applied to grids as well. Here are the steps:

1. Open the South elevation view again, and you'll notice that the label for Level 3 is slightly overlapping the label for Level 2B because they are relatively close. You'll need to adjust the 2D extent of Level 3.
2. Select Level 3, and you'll see two items at the right endpoint with which you'll need to interact: the 3D indicator and the lock symbol. First, click the lock symbol to unlock the right endpoint. This will allow you to move the endpoint for the selected level without affecting all the other levels.
3. Click the 3D indicator so that it changes to 2D. Now you are ready to modify the 2D extents of the level.
4. Drag the 2D extents grip (the solid circle) to the right. The result should look like the image shown in Figure 2.28.

5. As a final option, you can choose to break the end of a level or grid line so that the tag or label will clearly display. Click the Add Elbow symbol near the label at the right endpoint of Level 3. We have indicated the location of this symbol in Figure 2.28.

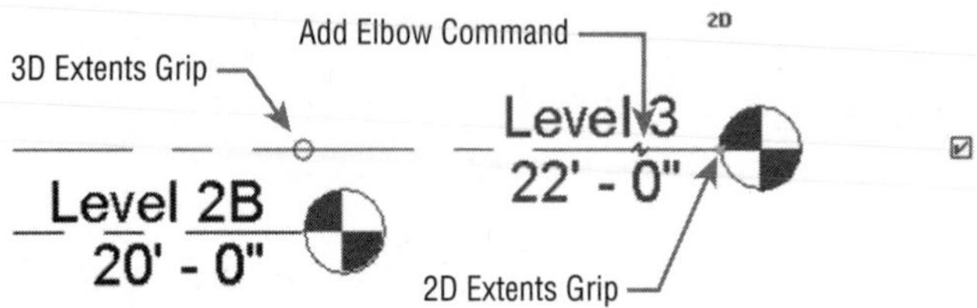

FIGURE 2.28
Adjusting the graphic extents of a level

6. Use the additional line grips to adjust the level endpoint so that it resembles the image shown in Figure 2.29.

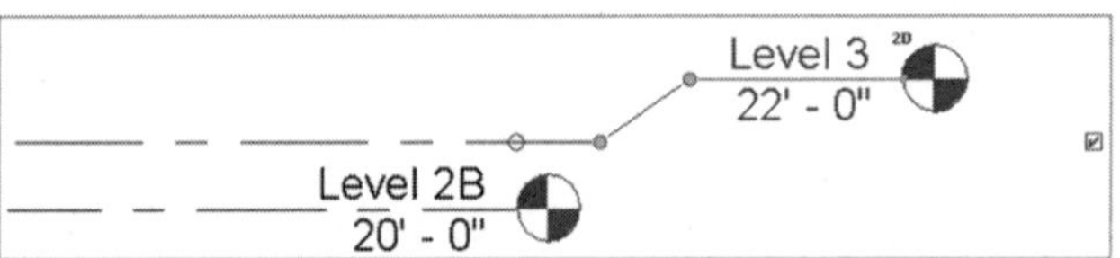

FIGURE 2.29
Adding an elbow to a level

PROPAGATING EXTENTS

Quite often you will adjust the extents of datum objects that need to be replicated in several other views. Fortunately, there is a tool to help you accomplish this—Propagate Extents. The premise of this tool is simple, but you must be aware of the subtleties in applying it to a three-dimensional model.

The Propagate Extents tool pushes any modifications you apply to a datum object from one view to other parallel views of your choosing. This tool does not work well on levels because the parallel views are essentially mirrored views of each other. For example, the orientation of the South elevation is the opposite of the North elevation; therefore, if you make a change to the extents at the right end of a level in the South elevation, those changes would be propagated to the left end in the North elevation.

The best way to apply the Propagate Extents tool is with the 2D extents of grids. Why only the 2D extents? Because changing the 3D extents affects the datum object throughout the project, independent of any specific view. Let us examine this behavior with a quick exercise:

1. Download and open the `c02-Grids-Start.rvt` file from this book's web page, and then activate the South elevation.

   You will see three levels and four grids.

2. Select grid 3 and click the 3D indicator at the bottom endpoint. Notice that the lock symbol turns off automatically, allowing you to immediately adjust the graphic extents of the grid.

3. Drag the 2D extent of grid 3 up toward the top. Repeat this process for grid 4 so that the result looks like the image shown in Figure 2.30.

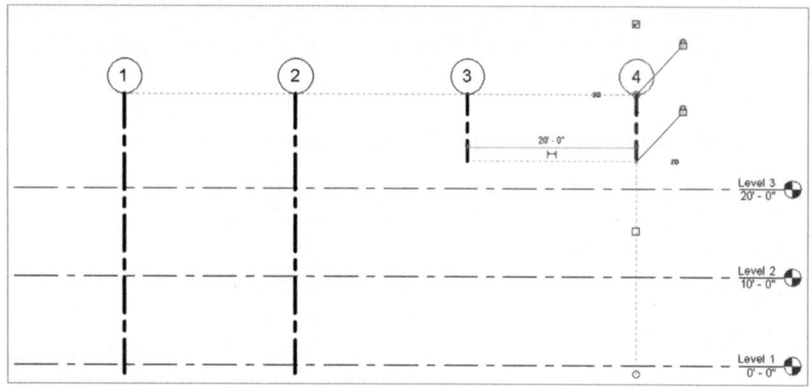

FIGURE 2.30
Adjusting the 2D extents of grids

The line weight of the grid lines has been increased for clarity.

Before you continue, open the Level 1 and Level 2 floor plans and observe that grids 3 and 4 are still visible. If you had adjusted the 3D extents of the grids in the South elevation view, those changes would already be reflected in the other views. We're using this method because we want to maintain the 3D extents but modify the 2D extents only in the South elevation view.

4. Return to the South elevation view and select grids 3 and 4 while pressing the Ctrl key. From the contextual tab in the ribbon, click the Propagate Extents button, and the dialog box will appear as shown in Figure 2.31.

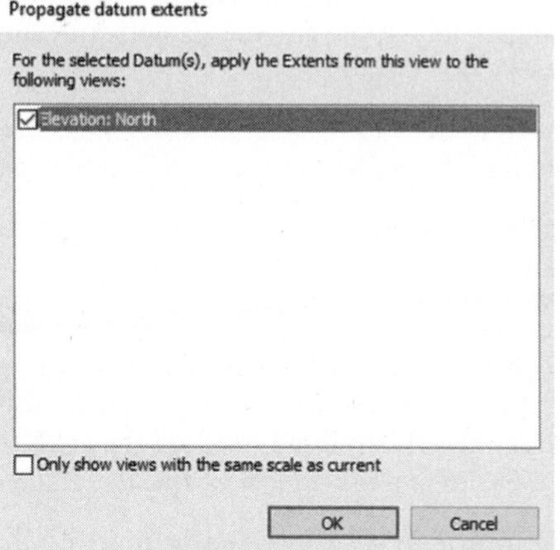

FIGURE 2.31
Propagating extents to other views

5. In the Propagate Datum Extents dialog box, select the North elevation view.
6. Click OK to complete the command and then activate the North elevation view. Observe that the 2D extents of grids 3 and 4 now match the modifications you applied in the South elevation view.

You can use the Propagate Extents command to easily copy datum settings to any parallel views in your project. This is especially effective for propagating grid extents to many plan views in high-rise buildings.

Resetting or Maximizing 3D Extents

Two commands you might need when adjusting datum object extents are ones that give you the ability to reset or maximize the 3D extents. These commands are available in the context menu when you have a datum object selected (Figure 2.32).

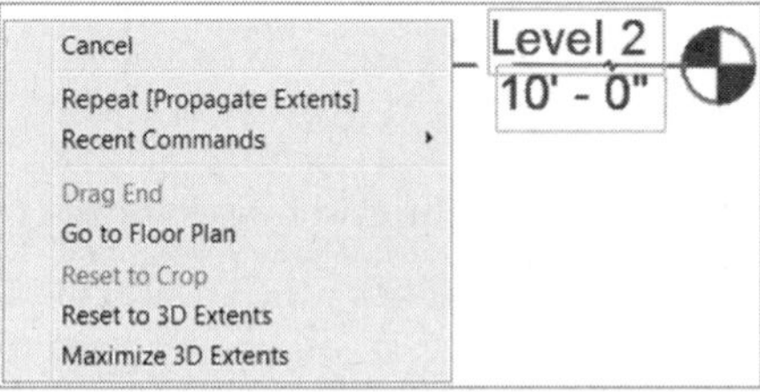

Figure 2.32
Extent commands in the context menu

The Reset To 3D Extents command allows you to reset any graphic extent modifications back to the analytic extents. Let's apply this command in the continued exercise file:

1. In the `c02-Grids-Start` file, return to the South elevation view. Right-click grid 3, and select Reset To 3D Extents from the context menu. Repeat this step for grid 4.
2. You will see the grid lines return to their original condition; however, this has been changed only in the current view (South elevation). Activate the North elevation view to observe this behavior.
3. Return to the South elevation view and select grids 3 and 4. Click the Propagate Extents button in the contextual tab in the ribbon, and select the North elevation view.
4. Click OK to close the dialog box, and the reset 2D extents will be applied to the grids in the other views.

   The other command in this pair serves a similar purpose in dealing with datum objects. Maximize 3D Extents is most often used if your levels or grids are exhibiting strange behavior. There are various reasons why this happens, but you'll realize it when it does. You can use this command to set the analytic extents of a datum object to the outer boundaries of your project geometry.

   Continuing in the exercise file, activate the Level 1 floor plan and notice that grid line C seems to be displayed like all the other grids. Now activate Section 1 from the Project Browser or by double-clicking the section head shown in the floor plan. You'll notice that grid line C is not visible in the section view. This is because someone mistakenly pulled the analytic (3D) extents far to the left in plan while the graphic (2D) extents remained consistent with the other grids. Let's continue the exercise and repair this problem.

5. Activate the Level 1 floor plan and select grid line C. Right-click and from the context menu, choose the Maximize 3D Extents command.

6. It may not seem like anything happened, but activate the Section 1 view and you'll now see that grid line C is visible.

7. Return to the Level 1 floor plan, select grid line C again, and then click the 2D indicator at the right endpoint so that it indicates 3D.

USING REFERENCE PLANES

Objects in the Revit model are able to maintain relationships with other objects; however, you may not always have other model elements (like walls, floors, and roofs) to relate to other geometry. This is why datum objects are so important.

If you have been using Revit for a reasonable amount of time, it seems obvious that levels and grids would control content, but reference planes aren't often appreciated. Here's a simple exercise to demonstrate this special kind of relationship between reference planes and walls:

1. Download and open the file `c02-Walls-Start.rvt` from this book's web page. Activate the Level 1 floor plan, select the wall segment, right-click, and then choose Create Similar from the context menu. Use the Tangent End Arc option from the Draw panel in the contextual tab of the ribbon to create a series of concentric walls starting from the left endpoint of the provided wall, as shown in Figure 2.33.

FIGURE 2.33
Concentric walls

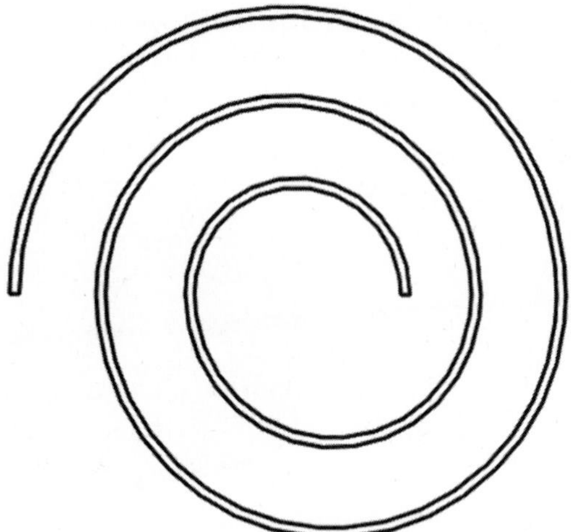

2. Go to the South elevation view. From the Architecture tab in the ribbon, click the Reference Plane tool and add two angled planes (dashed lines) as shown in Figure 2.34.

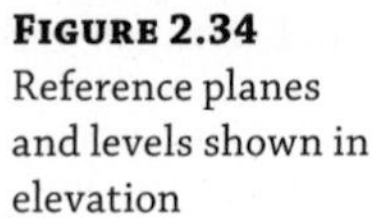

FIGURE 2.34
Reference planes and levels shown in elevation

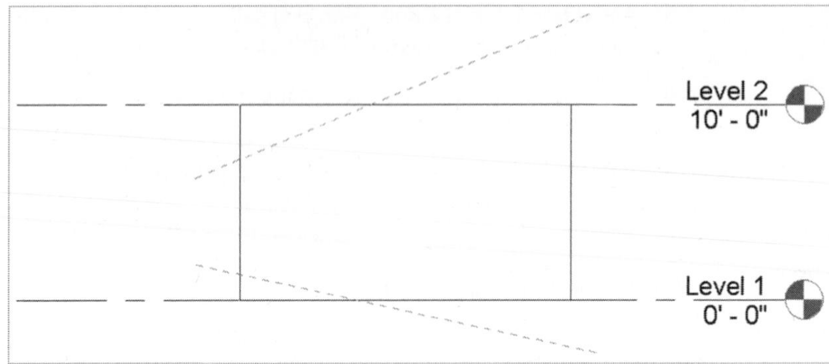

If you move Level 1, you'll notice that the walls all move with it. You don't have to select the walls; it's in the properties of the walls to maintain a relationship to the Level 1 datum. You could make the top of the walls maintain this same kind of relationship to Level 2.

3. You can also create a relationship to the reference planes. To do so, simply select all the walls (just hover your mouse over one wall, press and release the Tab key, and then left-click to select the chain of walls), and then click the Attach Top/Base button in the ribbon. Note that Attach Wall ➢ Top is the default selection in the Options bar, so first pick the upper reference plane. Click the Attach Top/Base button again, make sure Attach Wall ➢ Base is selected in the Options bar, and then pick the lower reference plane.

Figure 2.35 shows the results in a 3D view, once you've attached the top and bottom of the walls to the upper and lower reference planes.

FIGURE 2.35
Finished walls

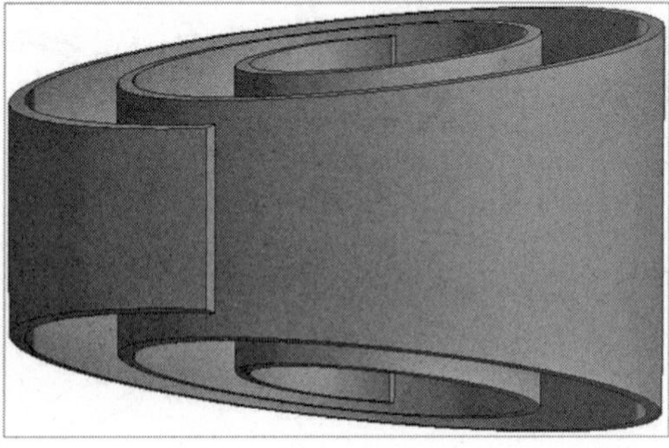

Try moving and rotating the reference planes, and notice that the walls will maintain their relationships to the planes. This is shown in a section view of the walls in Figure 2.36.

Although you can use levels, grids, and reference planes to customize model elements, there may be situations where you need to establish relationships with non-planar geometry.

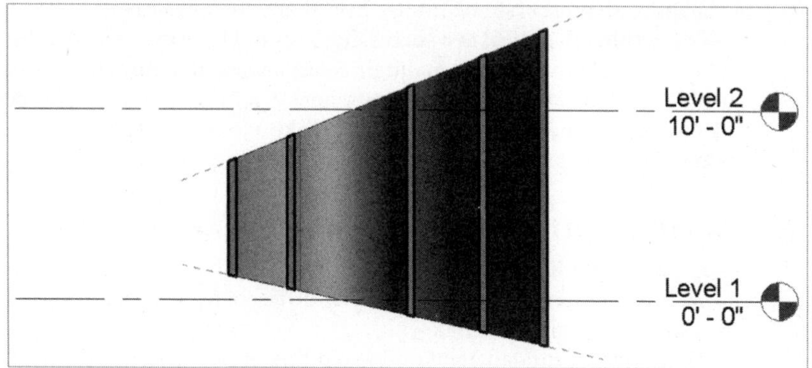

FIGURE 2.36
Section view

Using Content

Effective use of content is all about repeated elements in a hierarchy (project, family, type, instance) that you put in your Revit project to develop and document your design. Content can often maintain relationships with other content, but more important, they maintain relationships to datum objects. As you can see from the Revit organizational chart shown previously in Figure 2.21, content includes system families, component families, and spaces.

System families (also called *host families*) are content that is part of the Revit project environment and are more akin to rule sets rather than physically constructed components. These families are not created and stored in external files (RFAs)—they're found only in the RVT project file. If you need another type of a system family, you will duplicate an existing type from within the project. System families can be 3D elements such as walls, floors, roofs, ceilings, stairs, and railings or 2D elements such as text, dimensions, revision bubbles, and insulation.

Component families are created in the Family Editor and are either 2D or 3D content. This means that you will have to create and load these kinds of families outside the Revit project environment as RFA files. When you start to create a component family, you'll need to select an appropriate family template (Figure 2.37). By selecting the right family template, you will be certain that the component that you're creating is going to behave, view, schedule, and (if necessary) export properly.

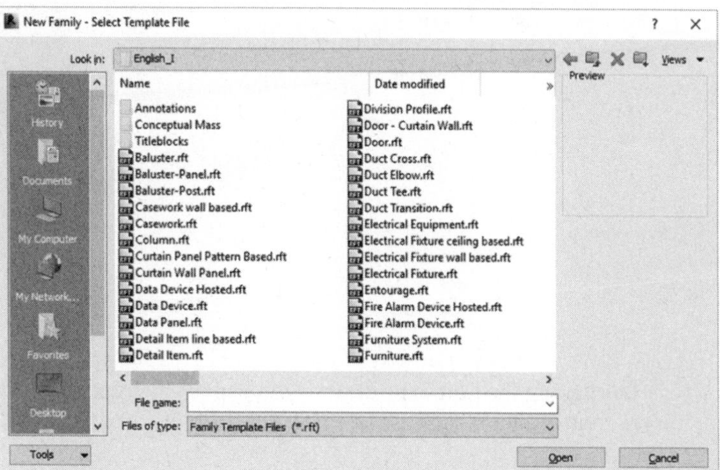

FIGURE 2.37
Selecting a family template

Although most system families help shape the physical aspects of a building, the occupied voids within are critical to a successful design. These elements are *spaces*, which take the form of rooms and areas. Spaces maintain relationships to datum objects but also to model elements including floors, walls, ceilings, and roofs. In addition to spatial properties, rooms are used to document finishes within your project. Take a look at the properties of a room, and you will find Floor Finish, Base Finish, Wall Finish, and Ceiling Finish.

Working with Type and Instance Parameters

All content in a Revit project has *parameters*, which are simply the information or data about something. Parameters can affect many different aspects of an object, such as visibility, behavior, size, shape, and material.

To develop a fundamental understanding of parameters, you must note that there are two kinds of parameters: *type* and *instance*. Type parameters control information about every element of the same type. For example, if the material of a piece of furniture is designated as a type parameter and you change it, the material for all the furniture of that type will change. Instance parameters control only the instances that you have selected. So if the material of the piece of furniture that you have selected is an *instance* parameter, you will be editing only the selected elements.

Instance parameters can be constantly exposed in the Properties palette. Selecting something initially displays the instance parameters. Figure 2.38 shows the instance parameters of a wall that control the relative height, constraints, and structural usage.

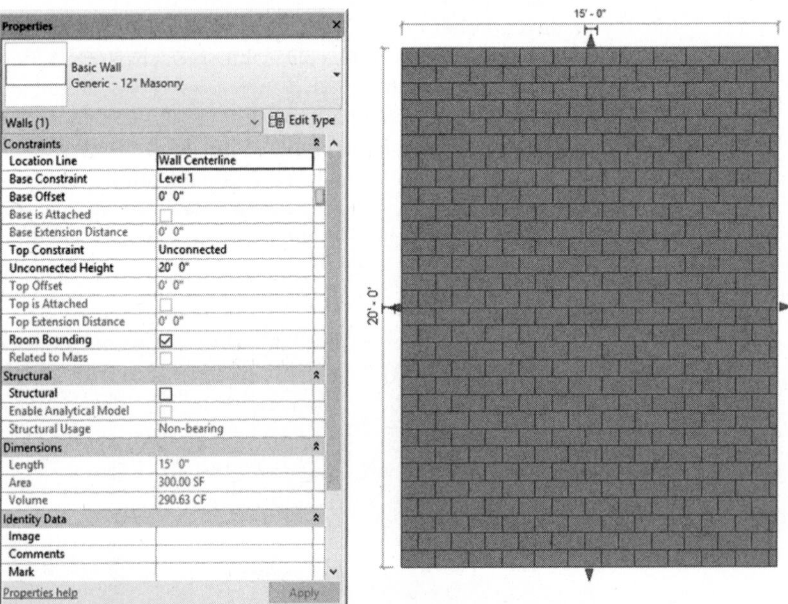

Figure 2.38
Instance parameters of a wall

By clicking the Edit Type button, you expose the type parameters (Figure 2.39). These parameters control values such as the structure, graphics, and assembly code.

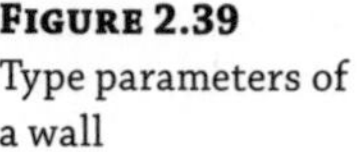

FIGURE 2.39
Type parameters of a wall

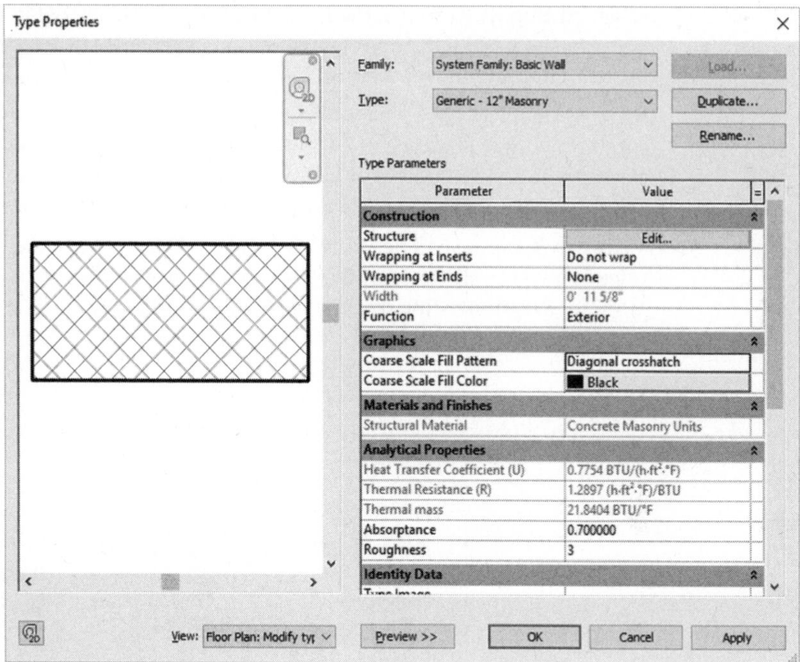

This section provided you with a basic overview of families and parameters; you will learn much more about these concepts in Chapter 14.

Working with Views

Views are the means by which you will interact with, perceive, and document the project. As you can see in the Revit organizational chart shown previously in Figure 2.21, there are both 2D and 3D views. Two-dimensional views are oriented to specific coordinates such as plan, elevation, and section. Schedules and material takeoffs are yet another way of viewing information in a project that is neither 2D nor 3D. Three-dimensional views are either orthographic or perspective (camera view) in nature. Views also have type and instance parameters that control properties such as name, scale, detail level, phase filter, and graphic display options. We will review each type of view again in more detail in Part 5, "Documentation."

Reviewing the Common Properties of Views

Let us first review, in detail, some of the properties that apply to most views. All of these are found in the Properties palette when no objects are selected; however, some properties may also be accessed in the view control bar. The most common view properties are as follows:

Crop Region With the exception of schedules and drafting views, the extents of all views can be limited using crop regions. The visibility of the crop region itself can be turned off, but you can choose to hide all crop regions in the Print Setup dialog box when using the Print command. Although you might feel the need to keep crop regions visible to allow easier editing, you can use the Reveal Hidden Elements tool in the view control bar to temporarily show hidden crop regions. Buttons to enable/disable and show/hide the crop region are available on the view control bar.

View Scale The view scale is the proportional system used to represent components of measured drawings. The scale of a view not only controls its printed size but also automatically controls the relative weight of line work as well as the size of annotations such as text, dimensions, and tags. The view scale is displayed on and can be modified from the view control bar.

Visibility/Graphics The Visibility/Graphic Overrides dialog box (Figure 2.40) allows overrides of a view's elements in two essential ways: visibility (turn object categories on/off) and graphics (customize line thickness, color, and fill pattern).

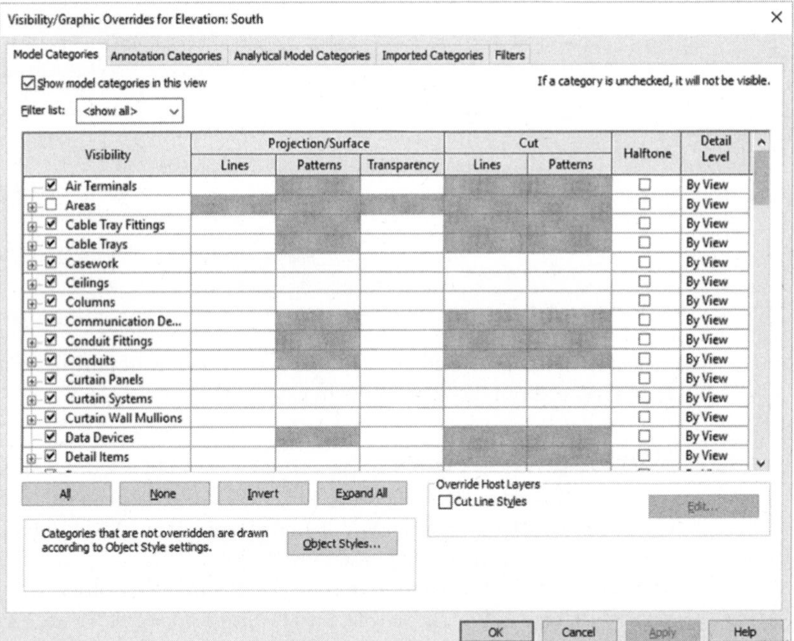

FIGURE 2.40 Visibility and graphic overrides for an elevation

Detail Level The Detail Level parameter can be set to one of three predefined choices: Coarse, Medium, or Fine. A representation for each setting is defined during the component's construction and sets the level of detail in each view level. It can help improve model performance and avoid cluttered views by limiting the visibility of smaller model elements. Detail Level can be set with a button on the view control bar.

View Template View templates are a selection of view properties, which can include properties that change the scale, detail level, and visibility of objects in the view. As an aid to standardization, view templates can help you organize common view settings and apply them to groups of views throughout your project and other projects within your office or firm. View templates are covered in detail in Chapter 4.

Creating and Duplicating Views

You can create views in various ways in order to work with your project in a manner that meets your needs. Although creating views is quick and easy, you should avoid populating your project file with too many unnecessary views. An overabundance of unused views will increase the amount of management your team will need for the project's organization. Views that do not have a specific purpose are just another object to maintain, search through, and store. Keep it simple, and routinely purge valueless views. Let's review the procedures to create different view types and see how to control their extents after they're created.

New views can be generated from the Create panel on the View tab of the ribbon (Figure 2.41), and the process is quite simple. Click one of the buttons and a new view is activated and stored in the Project Browser.

Figure 2.41
Creating new views from the ribbon

Another quick way to create new views is to right-click a view name in the Project Browser and select one of the Duplicate View commands (Figure 2.42). You can also duplicate the current view by using the Duplicate View button in the Create panel of the ribbon.

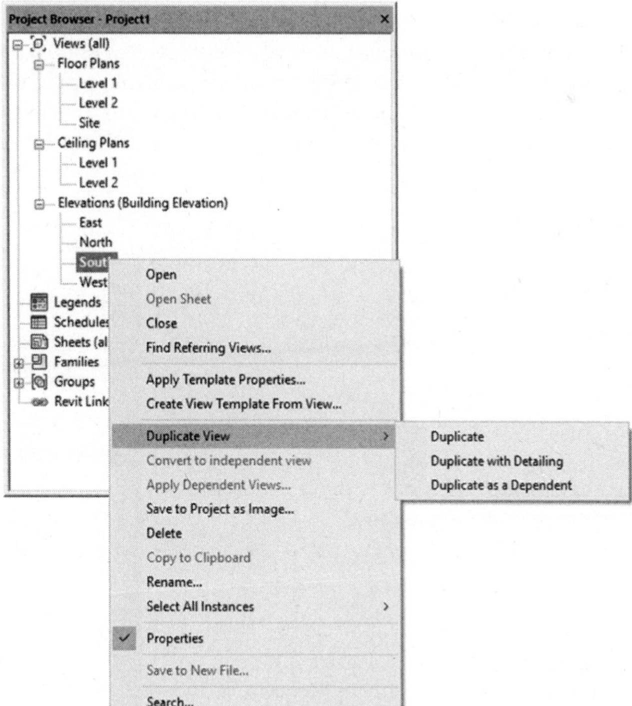

Figure 2.42
Duplicating views from the Project Browser

As you can see in Figure 2.42, there are three choices in the Duplicate View flyout command: Duplicate, Duplicate With Detailing, and Duplicate As A Dependent. Let's take a quick look at what each of these options means:

- **Duplicate:** This command will create a copy of the selected view but will not replicate any of the annotations in the view. Use this command when you need a fresh copy of a view in which you will create a new annotation for a different documentation purpose or even a working view without clutter.
- **Duplicate With Detailing:** As its name suggests, this command will create a copy of the selected view with all of the annotation in the view. We don't recommend using this command too often because replicated annotation is often a sign of an inefficient production process.
- **Duplicate As A Dependent:** This command allows you to create a series of partial views that assume the properties of one parent view. Using dependent views does not mean that you can have a parent view with a larger scale like 1:100 and then create dependent views at larger scales such as 1:50. The parent view has all the same properties as the dependents, but you can manage the crop regions and settings from the parent view. This is used most commonly with large plans and elevations that cannot fit on the project's standard sheet size.

Creating Floor Plans and Ceiling Plans

As you learned in the section "Creating and Duplicating Levels" earlier in this chapter, when you create a level in an elevation or section view you have the option to create a plan view for that level in the Options bar. If you have levels without corresponding plan views, you can also use the Plan Views tool from the ribbon to create a plan view.

The vertical extents of plans and ceiling plans are controlled by the View Range settings. The View Range settings, as shown in Figure 2.43, define the vertical range of the view.

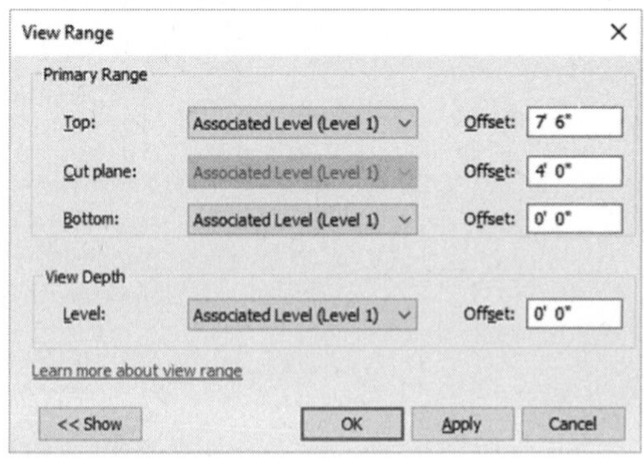

Figure 2.43
View Range dialog box

The view range properties can be difficult to understand, so we created a diagram to illustrate the principles. In Figure 2.44, you will see that the primary range is the zone you usually see in a default floor or ceiling plan. If an object crosses the cut plane, the object's Cut values are used. If the object is below the cut plane but above the bottom, the object's Projection values are used. Cut and Projection values can be found in Visibility/Graphics.

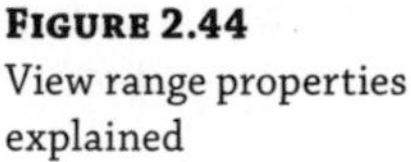

FIGURE 2.44
View range properties explained

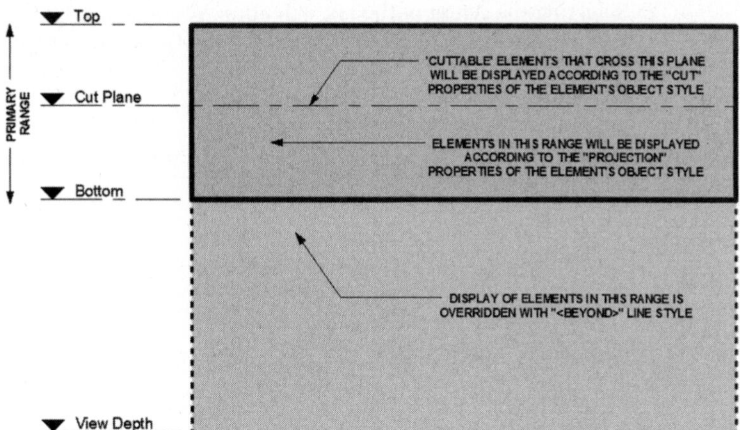

For most views, the Bottom and View Depth parameters are set to the same plane. Therefore, objects below the bottom of the view range simply won't appear. So, what happens if you need to show objects on a lower terrace for reference in the current view? When you set View Depth to Level Below or Unlimited, objects that are below the bottom of the view range but within the view depth will be overridden with the <Beyond> line style.

Perhaps you only need to apply a different view range setting to isolated areas of a view. This can be accomplished with the use of the Plan Region tool. You can find this tool in the Create panel of the View tab along with the other Plan View tools. The Plan Region tool allows you to sketch a boundary within which the View Range dialog box will be available to make specific changes. You can use this method for areas such as windows that might be placed in a wall above the cut plane but need to be shown on the plan for documentation.

Another useful property of plans is known as an *underlay*. Although this property may function more like a tool, it is found in the Properties palette along with the other view properties. An underlay allows you to use any other level as a reference in the current view. You can use the underlay to display ceiling soffits in a floor plan, to display furniture layouts in a ceiling plan, or to use another level as a reference for replicating partition layouts.

Creating Elevations

Selecting the Elevation tool on the View tab creates elevations of various types. You'll also notice that as you place an elevation tag, the elevations automatically orient to walls (Figure 2.45). If there's no host element nearby to reference, they'll automatically orient to the left.

FIGURE 2.45
Elevation tag orientation

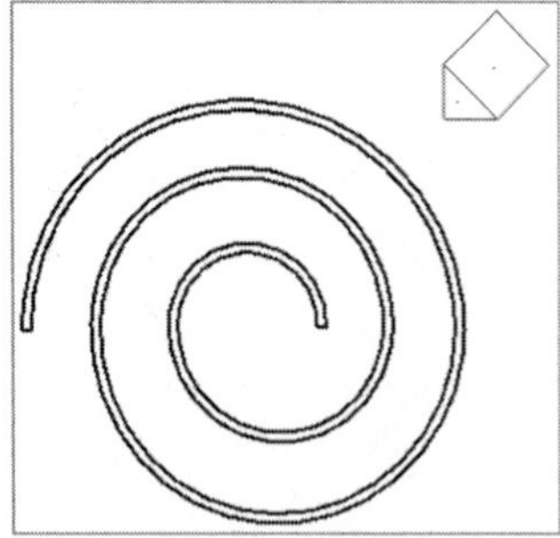

Selecting the center of the tag will allow you to create additional elevation views (more typically done for interior elevations) by selecting the unchecked boxes that surround the elevation tag (Figure 2.46).

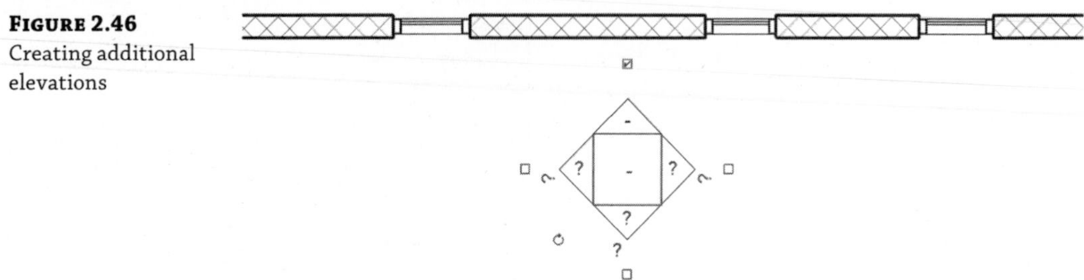

FIGURE 2.46
Creating additional elevations

If you select the directional point of the elevation tag, you will see a blue line that defines the beginning of the cut plane for the elevation as well as a dashed line that defines the side and rear extents (Figure 2.47). This allows you to control the analytic extents of the elevation without moving the graphic tag, which is useful if you want the tag in a particular location but you want the cutting plane to start somewhere else.

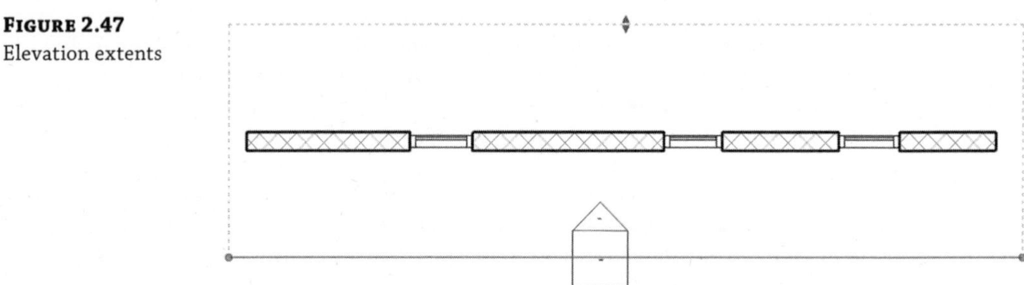

FIGURE 2.47
Elevation extents

Finally, there are three types of elevations in a Revit project: exterior, interior, and framing. Their differences are more than graphic. *Exterior elevations,* by default, do not have an active crop boundary, only a starting cut plane. *Interior elevations* have their crop boundary on by default and attempt to find boundaries of host elements, like walls, floors, and ceilings. *Framing elevations* can be placed only along a grid line, and their cut plane corresponds to the respective grid.

CREATING SECTIONS

Selecting the Section tool on the View tab creates sections. By default, three types of sections are available from the Type Selector: Building, Wall, and Detail. This allows them to be grouped with better clarity in the Project Browser, but there are also other important properties.

Unlike with elevations, the cutting plane of a section must correspond with its graphic line. Figure 2.48 shows the instance properties of a Building section. The far and side cut planes of a section can also be controlled. This goes for both Building and Wall sections.

FIGURE 2.48
Section properties and extents

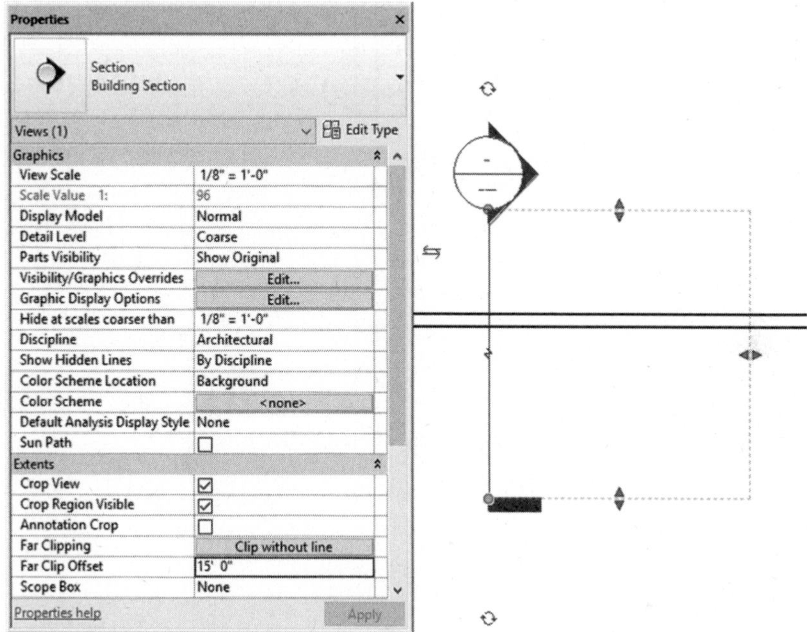

Building and Wall sections must be created in a perpendicular orientation with respect to levels. But after you create them, they can be rotated in elevation. However, doing so would lead to confusion in your project because, once rotated, the section wouldn't be displayed in plan view because the section cutting plane would no longer be perpendicular to the plan view.

A Detail section will have a different graphic symbol by default, although you can customize this to your liking. We discuss this form of customization in Chapter 4. Beyond the differing graphic symbol, Detail sections will have a smaller clipping region than a Building or Wall section. In Figure 2.49, a Building section is shown at the left of the image and a Detail section is shown to the right.

It's important to know that a Detail section created in plan will automatically display as a callout in any Building section or Wall section if the Detail section overlaps a larger section. Of course, this is not an ideal workflow for architectural documentation. We discuss the process of using callouts from larger sections in Chapter 16.

Also note the color of callout and section heads in Figure 2.49. These blue icons act as hyperlinks to the other views in your project. Double-click on any of these blue heads to activate that view.

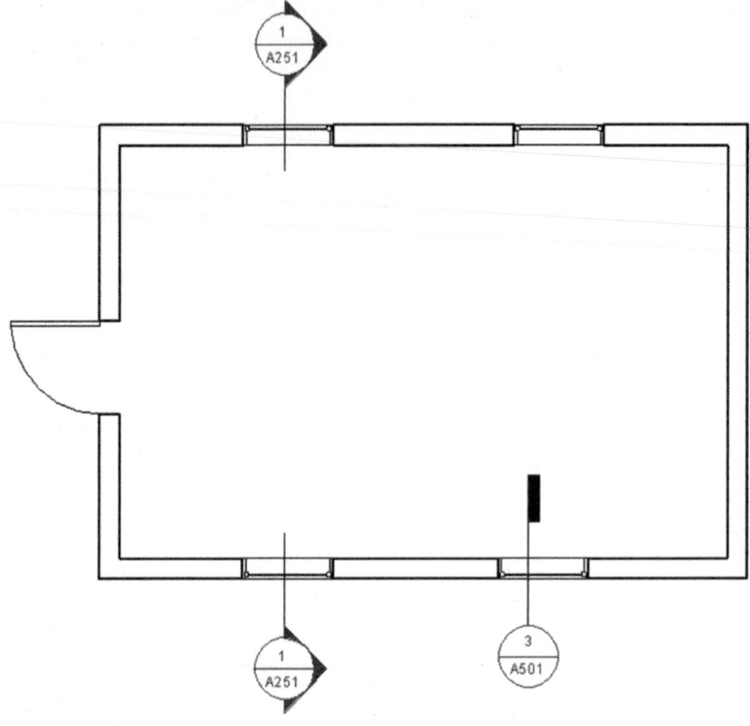

FIGURE 2.49
Building and Detail sections shown in plan view

CREATING CALLOUTS

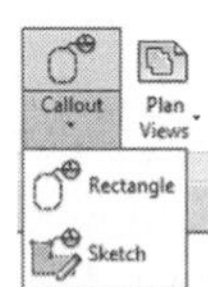

The Callout tool allows you to create views that are intended to be enlarged from the scale of the parent view in which you create the callout. When you are in a parent view—a floor plan, section view, or elevation view—you can create a callout from the View tab in the ribbon within the Create panel.

The most important aspect of the Callout tool you need to understand is the difference between the types of callout views you can create. When you activate the Callout tool, click on the Type Selector in the Properties palette. You will see several choices that depend on what kind of view you currently have activated. For example, if you are using the Callout tool in a floor plan view, you will see Detail and Floor Plan listed in the Type Selector, as shown in Figure 2.50. Two types of callouts are available in the Type Selector: Detail and Floor Plan. Although Detail callouts may look like Detail sections graphically, they are not visible inside other perpendicular views. So a callout created in plan view will not be visible in elevations or sections like a Detail section.

In the example shown in Figure 2.50, if you select Detail, the callout view you create will be listed in the Project Browser under Detail Views. If you select Floor Plan, the callout view will be listed under Floor Plans. You cannot change a callout view from one type to another after it is created, so plan the configuration of your views carefully.

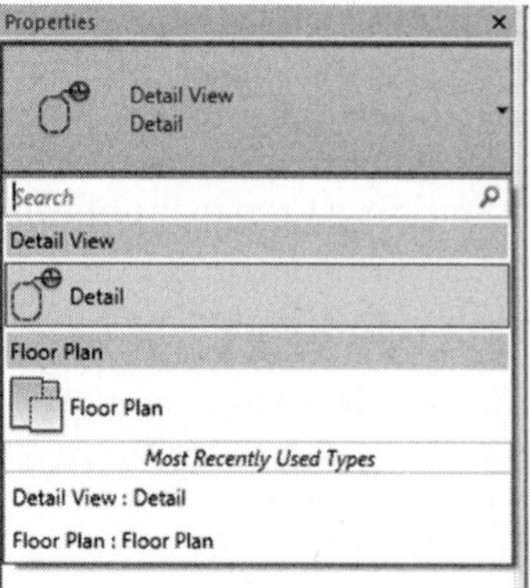

FIGURE 2.50
Be aware of the different types of callouts you can create from the Type Selector.

Beyond the organization of callout views in the Project Browser, choosing the right type for your callouts affects other functionality as well. The Detail callout has a unique property called Show In. This property can be set to either Parent View Only or Intersecting Views. If the callout is set to show in Intersecting Views, this type of callout in plan would display as a section detail mark in an intersecting view such as a Building section. In Figure 2.51, you can see the callout added to the floor plan (left). When the Show In property of that callout is set to Intersecting Views, it displays as a detail section mark in the building section (right).

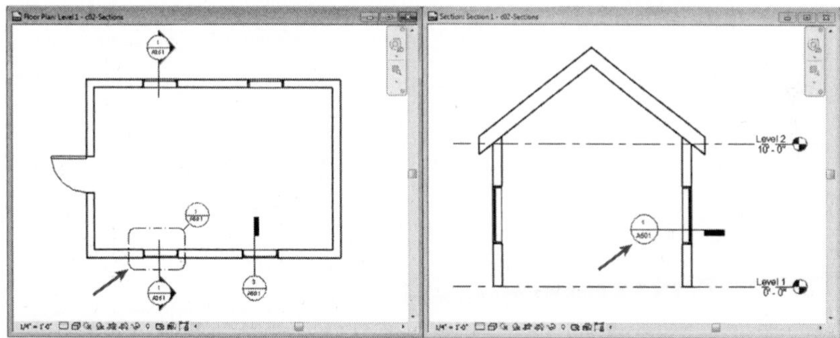

FIGURE 2.51
Detail callouts can be set to show in intersecting views.

If you create a callout using the same type as the parent view, the callout view will also have all the same view controls as the parent view. In the floor plan example, you will still have view properties such as Depth Clipping and View Range. In a Detail callout, the property called Far Clip Settings can be set to either Independent or Same As Parent View.

Take a moment to note the grips on the boundary of a callout when one is selected. You can use these grips to change the size of the callout boundary, but this also modifies the crop region within the callout view. As you might assume, if you modify the crop region in the callout view, the callout boundary also changes.

Callouts can be created in either a simple rectangular shape or in any custom sketched shape. You will see these two tool options in the Callout flyout button in the ribbon, but you can always edit a rectangular callout by first selecting a callout and then selecting Edit Crop from the contextual tab in the ribbon. You can also return a custom shape callout to a simple rectangular shape by clicking Reset Crop in the ribbon.

Using Drafting Views

Not every view needs to be connected directly to the model. Drafting views give you the ability to draw without first creating a reference to something in your project. They may contain Detail and Repeating Detail components and any other annotation content. Drafting views are great for quickly documenting typical conditions that don't require an actual model geometry.

Once you create a drafting view, you can refer to this view when creating an elevation, section, detail, and so on that would normally rely on an actual view of the model. As you start to create a standard project view (Figure 2.52), simply select the Reference Other View option from the contextual tab of the ribbon, and then you'll be allowed to select a reference view from all the other like views in your project as well as any drafting views. You can even use the search bar to easily locate specific view names instead of scrolling through a long list of all project views. Drafting views can also be saved out of the project as common reusable details. This will be covered in more depth in Chapter 16.

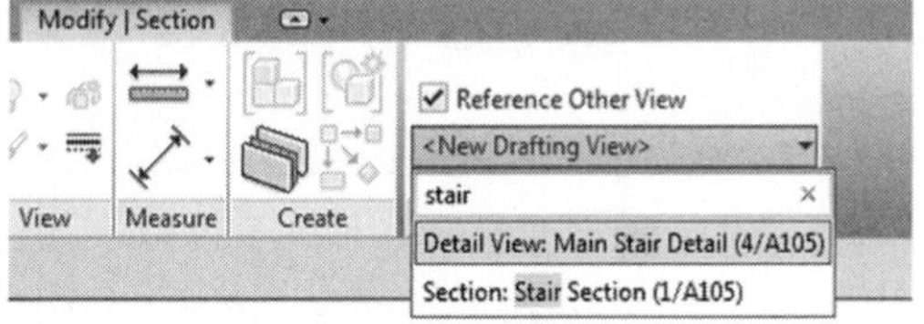

Figure 2.52
Use the search bar with the Reference Other View option.

Using Legends

Legends are views in which you can display samples of model elements that will not affect schedules and quantity takeoffs. There are two types of legends: legends and keynote legends. Regular legends are used to assemble analytic views of content in your project, graphics, geometry, tags, and so on—anything that lives in your project. Legends may contain Detail, Repeating Detail, and Legend components—which are live representations of 3D model elements. Legends are unique in that they are the only view that can be placed on more than one sheet.

A Legend component (Figure 2.53) is a special live representation of a system or component family that may appear only in legend views (not drafting views). If you make a change to an element in your project, the representation of that element in the legend will change as well. When you are creating a legend view, the Legend Component tool is located in the Component flyout button on the Detail panel of the Annotate tab in the ribbon.

FIGURE 2.53
Legend components

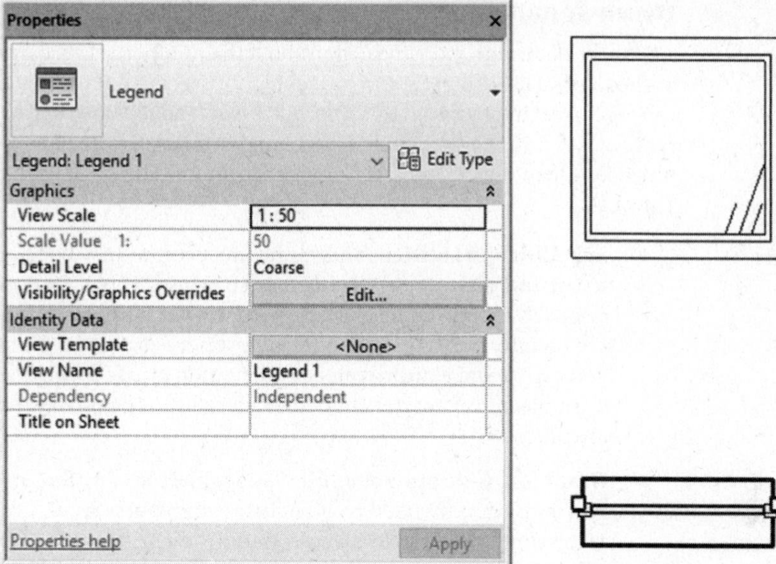

Keynote legends are special schedules. When creating a keynote legend, you will be prompted much the same way as you are when creating a schedule (Figure 2.54). These types of legends are meant to be placed on either one sheet or multiple sheets. If the legend is placed on every sheet in which keynotes are used, the Filter By Sheet option should be selected on the Filter tab of the Keynote Legend Properties dialog box. With this option selected, only those keynotes that appear in views placed on a sheet will appear in the sheet's keynote legend.

FIGURE 2.54
An example of a keynote legend placed on a sheet

KEYNOTE LEGEND	
061000.01	FRAME EXISTING OPENING TO MATCH.
061000.02	DOOR LANDING - TREATED WOOD STRUCTURE, TREX RAILS AND STEPPING SURFACES
061000.04	COMPOSITE RAILING SYSTEM, TIMBERTECH RADIANCERAIL OR SIM.
074600.01	VINYL SIDING OVER 1/2" RIGID INSULATION
077200.02	BREAK-FORMED ALUMINUM FASCIA OR COMPOSITE TRIM (WHITE)
092100.01	1/2" GYPSUM BOARD, PAINT BY OWNER (TYP.)
096800.01	LAMINATED WOOD FLOORING (FURNISHED AND INSTALLED BY OWNER) OVER 3/4" PLYWOOD SUBFLOOR ALIGNED WITH EXIST. SUBFLOOR
096800.02	MARMOLEUM OR VINYL FLOORING (FURNISHED AND INSTALLED BY OWNER)
238100.01	DUCTLESS HEATING AND COOLING UNIT

Using Schedules

All model elements have information about their properties such as size, material, and cost. In Revit, a schedule is a list of any type of element in a project or linked models and their characteristics. You can report and interact with this information in tabular views known as schedules. There are six types of schedule views that can be accessed from the Create panel in the View tab of the ribbon: Schedule/Quantities, Graphical Column Schedule, Material Takeoff, Sheet List, Note Block, and View List.

- **Schedule/Quantities:** This is the most commonly used schedule type, allowing you to list and quantify all the element category types. You would use this type to make door schedules, wall schedules, window schedules, and so on. These schedule types are usually limited to scheduling properties within the same category; however, you can create a multi-category schedule or use some fields from other elements. For example, many model elements can refer to the properties of the room in which they are placed.
- **Graphical Column Schedule:** This schedule is different from the other schedule types and is commonly used by structural engineers. Structural columns are displayed according to their grid intersections, indicating top and bottom constraints as well as offsets.
- **Material Takeoff:** This type of schedule lists all the materials and subcomponents of any family category. You can use a material takeoff to measure any material that is used in a component or assembly. For example, you might want to know the volume of concrete within the model. Regardless of whether the concrete is in a wall or floor or column, you can tell the schedule to report the total amount of that material in the project. Material takeoffs will report material properties across multiple categories.
- **Sheet List:** This schedule allows you to create a list of all the sheets in the project.
- **Note Block:** This tool creates a unique schedule that lists the properties of a generic annotation symbol used in a project.
- **View List:** This schedule shows a list of all the views in the Project Browser and their properties. A view list can be a valuable tool to help you manage your project's views efficiently.

One important aspect that we want to reiterate is that schedules are derivatives of the model. Often, if the schedule is not accurate, the model is not accurate. A schedule can also deal with the tolerances the team has set in the units of the file and may be based on the template.

Using Sheets

Printed contract documents are still a common way that architects are paid. You will use sheets to organize views and other annotation for the purpose of issuing printable (physical or digital) documents. Sheet borders can be customized, but the important fact to realize is that sheets are always scaled at 1:1. The important thing to remember is that you are not going to select a scale when you print a sheet; it's really more like printing than plotting. If you need your she smaller or fit on the desired page, these options are available, and using them is little di than printing from a word processing application.

You will learn more about creating sheets in Chapter 17.

Using 3D Views

Two kinds of 3D views are supported: orthographic and perspective. The Default 3D view is orthographic, whereas the Camera and Walkthrough views are in perspective (Figure 2.55). You can right-click on the View Cube and select the Toggle To command in the context menu. To enable the ability to toggle between isometric and perspective, you must have a crop region activated in the view. We'll also cover 3D views in detail in Chapter 11.

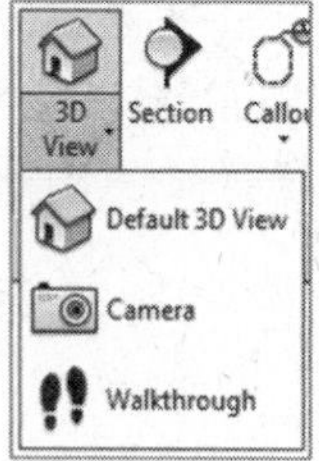

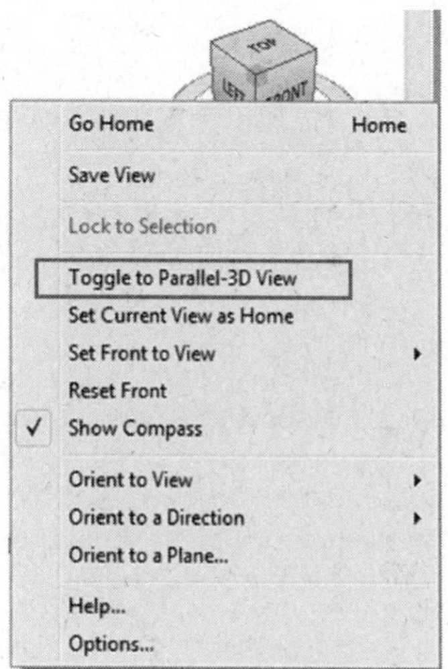

Figure 2.55
Creating 3D view types and toggling between them

Orthographic views will always show parallel edges along Cartesian x-, y-, and z-axes. Orthographic views are best if you need to show model information to scale. Many people do not realize that it is possible to dimension and detail in Revit inside a 3D orthographic view. For a more thorough explanation of annotating a 3D view, refer to Chapter 20, "Presenting Your Design."

Create camera views by placing the start and end points of a camera (typically from a plan view). The first point you select in plan is the point from which the view will be taken, but the second point is also the rotation origin for the view (Figure 2.56). This is important because if you select a second point that is far beyond your view, when you open the view and attempt to modify it, it will rotate around a target that doesn't seem to make sense. That's because the target location of the view is off in the distance.

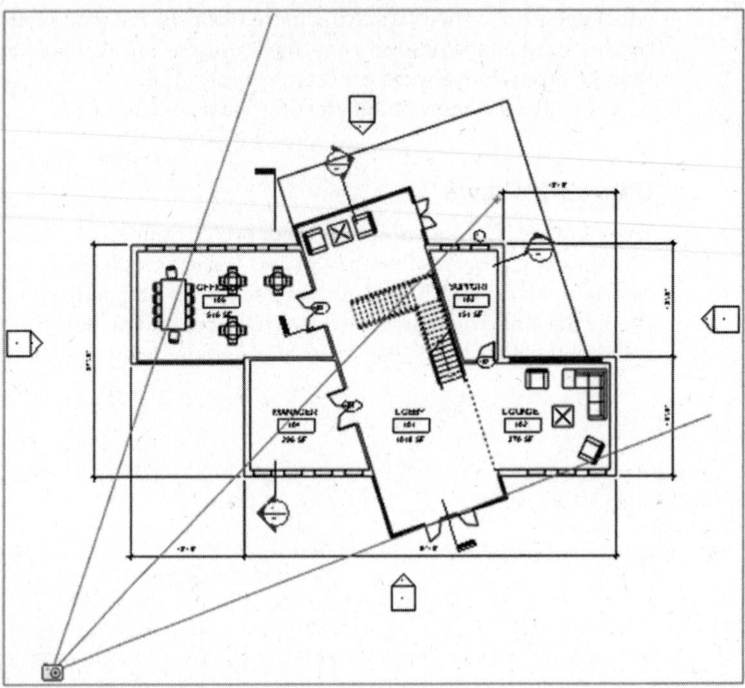

FIGURE 2.56
Setting camera and target origins

A perspective view will not be to scale, but it can be made relatively larger or smaller by selecting the view's crop region and then selecting the Size Crop button from the Modify | Camera tab. Once you do this, you will have the option to change the view size and field of view, proportionally or not proportionally (Figure 2.57). You can also simply drag the nodes of the bounding box.

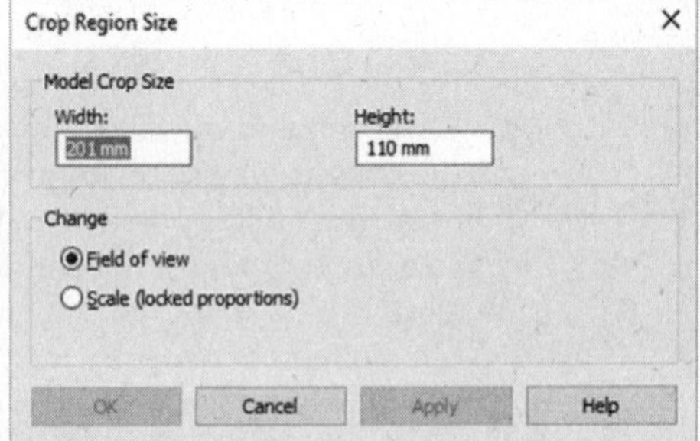

FIGURE 2.57
Modifying the view size and field of view

Camera extents are defined by the Far Clip Offset option, accessed in the Properties palette for the view. If the Far Clip Offset is too low, the view may resemble the image shown in Figure 2.58. Geometry that you'd expect to see will be "clipped" in the view.

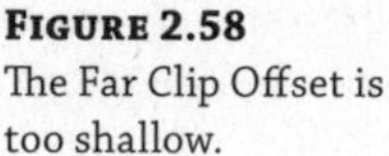

FIGURE 2.58
The Far Clip Offset is too shallow.

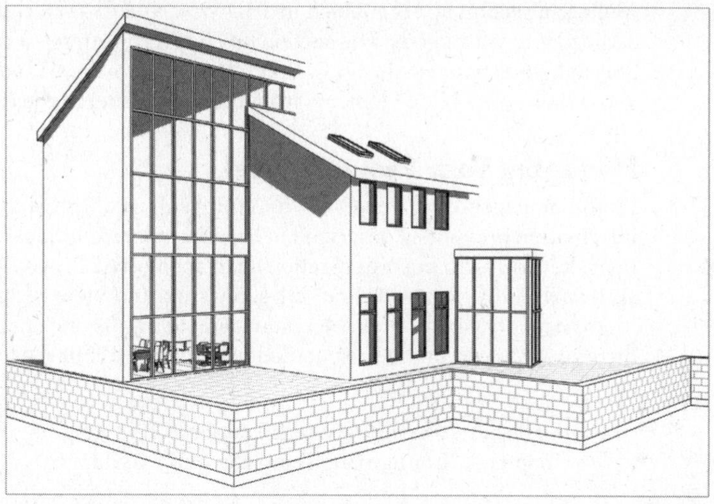

Simply increase the Far Clip Offset value to show more of the model. You may also do this graphically by returning to a plan view, right-clicking the camera view in the Project Browser, and then selecting Show Camera. Once the camera is shown in your plan view, you can select the node at the far end of your clipping plane and manually drag the node to extend the far clip offset of your view in a similar manner to that shown in Figure 2.57.

Finally, the extents of 3D views (even walkthroughs) can be customized with the use of section boxes. You'll find the Section Box option in the Properties palette for a 3D view. This will allow you to control how much of the project is shown (Figure 2.59) and is helpful for creating cutaway visualizations in real time or in renderings.

FIGURE 2.59
Section box applied to a 3D view

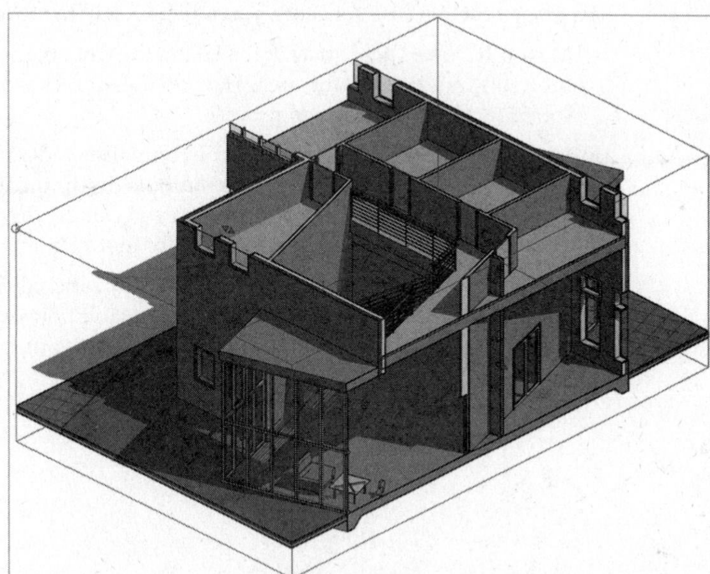

Once a section box is enabled in a 3D view, you can select it in order to stretch or rotate it according to your needs. The section box is not considered a crop region, and therefore it is not affected when you use the Show Crop Region command. If you want to hide a section box, select it and then select Hide Elements from the View panel in the ribbon.

Managing Your Project Model

Project management involves all the settings that control (and therefore restrict) the graphic information previously described in this chapter as relationships, repetition, and representations. Returning to the organization chart in Figure 2.21, you'll see that a Revit project is managed with settings such as line styles, phasing, and view templates.

To cover all aspects of project management in this one chapter would be overwhelming; therefore, you can find more detailed information about the following topics throughout this book:

- For object styles, line styles, fill patterns, line weights, and view templates, refer to Chapter 4, "Configuring Templates and Standards."
- For worksets and worksharing, refer to Chapter 5, "Working in a Team."
- For phasing and design options, refer to Chapter 10, "Working with Phasing, Groups, and Design Options."
- To learn about locations and shared positioning, refer to Chapter 3, "The Basics of the Toolbox."

The Bottom Line

Understand the user interface. In addition to understanding how your project is organized, to use the Revit software well you must understand how the UI is organized. Once you grasp both of these concepts, you will be ready to move ahead.

Master It The "big" areas of the UI are the ribbon, the Properties palette, the Project Browser, and the drawing area. How do these areas work together, and what tabs correspond to an iterative design process?

Understand project organization. The compelling advantage of being able to design, document, and manage your project across multiple disciplines—the architectural, structural, and mechanical disciplines—is something that you can do only in Revit, and understanding project workflow is key to getting off on the right foot.

Master It Thinking back to the Revit organizational chart shown in Figure 2.21, what are the main components of a Revit project, and how can you apply them to your design process? How do these categories directly affect your design workflow?

Chapter 3

The Basics of the Toolbox

The road to mastering Autodesk® Revit® Architecture software will always include reinforcement of fundamental skills. Just as an accomplished musician will practice her scales, here you will "practice" by reviewing the fundamental selection and editing tools throughout the Revit Architecture program. There are many tools that can assist you in refining your models and project designs. Some are simple geometry-editing functions, whereas others possess more powerful capabilities.

In this chapter, you'll learn to

- Select, modify, and replace elements
- Edit elements interactively
- Use other editing tools
- Create site context for your project

Selecting, Modifying, and Replacing Elements

Knowing how to select, modify, and replace elements efficiently is fundamental to working productively in Revit software. These interface operations are the foundation on which you will build skills to create and edit your project models. In the following sections, we will review methods for selecting, filtering, and modifying properties.

Selecting Elements

Revit was one of the first programs that had the ability to pre-highlight elements as you hovered the mouse pointer over them, before actually clicking to select. Not only does this give you a clear idea of what you are about to select, but it also displays information about that object in the status bar and in a banner near the mouse pointer. When you hover over an element, it pre-highlights; click the highlighted element and it turns blue, indicating that it is selected.

Once an element is selected, the ribbon changes to Modify mode, where consistent editing tools are located on the left side and context-sensitive tools appear to the right. Notice the subtle differences in the ribbon, as shown in Figure 3.1, when a roof, wall, and floor are selected.

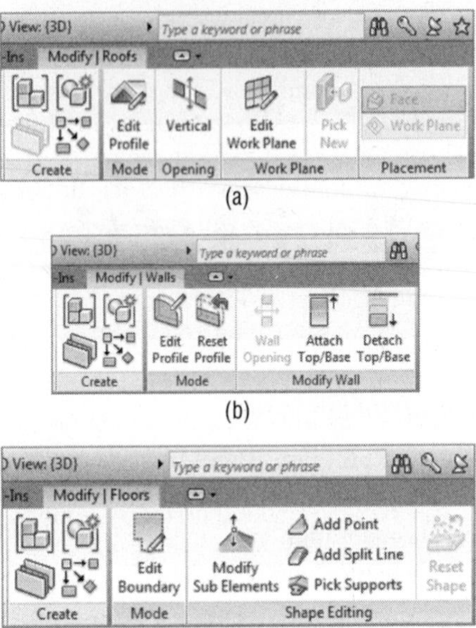

FIGURE 3.1
The right end of the Modify tab changes based on the element that is selected: (a) the Modify | Roofs tab; (b) the Modify | Walls tab; (c) the Modify | Floors tab.

> **CHANGING SELECTION COLORS**
>
> You can customize the default colors for selection, highlighting, and alerts to your own color palette. To do this, click the Application menu and select Options. In the Options dialog box, select the Graphics option on the left to edit the settings for colors.

You can select elements in many ways:

Add or Subtract You can build a selection of individual elements by using the Ctrl and Shift keys on your keyboard. Hold down the Ctrl key while picking to *add* elements, and hold down the Shift key while picking to *remove* elements. Notice that the mouse pointer will indicate a plus (+) when you hold the Ctrl key and a minus (–) when you hold the Shift key.

Window To select a large number of elements in a view window, you can click and drag the mouse to form two different types of selection windows. Click and drag from left to right, and only the elements completely within the window will be selected—this implied window is displayed as a solid line. Click and drag from right to left, and any element within or crossing the window will be selected—this implied window is displayed as a dashed line. To activate either window-selection tool, you must begin by clicking in a blank area (not on an element) within the view window.

Chain Chain-select is an intelligent method for selecting connected elements such as walls, lines, sketch segments, and line-based components. To activate this mode, hover your mouse over (but don't click) one linear element that is connected to several other linear elements. While the element is pre-highlighted, press the Tab key once and the connected elements will be pre-highlighted. You can then click to select the chain of elements. When selecting objects, use the Tab key to cycle through all available objects near your mouse pointer. If a floor edge happens to be near the edge of a wall that you are trying to chain-select, you can skip the chain of walls and select the floor. Be sure to look at the status bar; it will indicate "Chain of walls or lines" when you have selected correctly.

Select Previous Command A little-known feature allows you to select elements you had previously selected. Either right-click and choose Select Previous from the context menu or press Ctrl and the left-arrow key on your keyboard.

Selection Options

You have the ability to choose elements that will be included or excluded when you click on elements in a model. There are two ways to adjust these settings, as shown in Figure 3.2: Click the drop-down menu under the Modify button in the ribbon, or use the icons at the right end of the status bar. Note that the icons in the status bar will change slightly to indicate the status of each option. When a mode is disabled, a small red X will be displayed on the icon. One of these selection options is Select Elements By Face, which allows you to select elements simply by picking any face of the element.

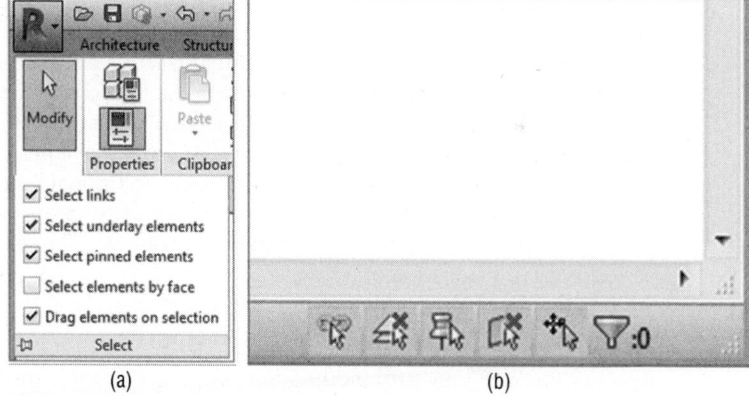

FIGURE 3.2
Use selection options to avoid picking elements, such as links or pinned elements. These options are found in the Select expanded panel (a) and the status bar (b).

Filtering Your Selection

Once you have elements selected, a count of selected objects is displayed at the right end of the status bar. You can also filter the selection into object categories by clicking the Filter icon in the status bar or ribbon. Just as when selecting folders in Windows Explorer, you can select multiple categories while holding the Shift key or add a single category by holding the Ctrl key. This tool allows you to select large numbers of elements and then focus your selection by removing categories you don't need, as shown in Figure 3.3. For example, if you window-select an entire floor plan, you will have a selection set of many different categories. Using the Filter tool, you can limit the selection to just the Doors category—or perhaps Doors and Door Tags.

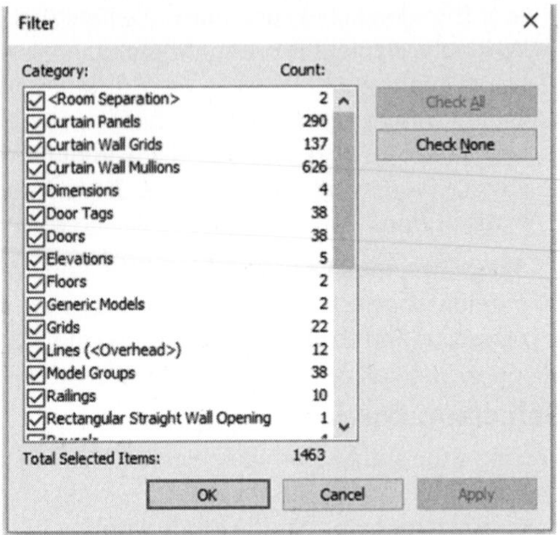

FIGURE 3.3 Use the Filter dialog box to fine-tune your selections.

You can also use the Properties palette as a filter; see the section "Using the Properties Palette" later in this chapter for more information.

Using Selection-Based Filters

If you need to save a selection of elements for future editing, you can save a selection-based filter. When you have a number of elements selected, click Save in the contextual tab of the ribbon and a named selection set will be created in the active project model. To load or edit any saved selection-based filter, go to the Manage tab in the ribbon and locate the Selection panel. Click the Load button to activate any of the saved selection sets, and then you can use other tools such as Temporary Hide/Isolate to continue your task work. These selection sets remember the items selected within the categories and will not select additional items made after the selection set was created. You may update the selection set with new items by loading the existing set and using your Ctrl key to add and the Shift key to subtract. The selection set can be saved over the previous set or made as another set.

Selecting All Instances

Another fast and powerful method for selecting objects is the Select All Instances function. When you right-click a single object in the drawing area or a family in the Project Browser, the Select All Instances tool gives you two options: Visible In View or In Entire Project. Selecting the Visible In View option will select only those items you can see in the current view. This will *not* select elements that have been either temporarily or permanently hidden in the view.

Use the In Entire Project option carefully because you could modify elements in many places that you did not intend to change. Always remember to look at the selection count in the status bar when you use Select All Instances. Here are some common situations where you might use this tool:

- View titles—when updating graphics
- Walls—when switching from generic to specific types

- Title blocks—moving from design to detail documents
- Viewports—useful when trying to purge unused viewports

Note that Select All Instances does not work on model lines or symbolic lines. This limitation exists because lines not only are drawn in project views but also are integral parts of other objects such as filled regions and shaft openings.

Using the Properties Palette

The Properties palette is a floating palette that can remain open while you work within the model. The palette can be docked on either side of your screen, or it can be moved to a second monitor. You can open the Properties palette by using one of the following methods:

- Click the Properties icon in the Properties panel of the Modify tab in the ribbon.
- Select Properties from the context menu.
- Press Ctrl+1 or PP on your keyboard.

As shown in Figure 3.4, the Type Selector is located at the top of the Properties palette. When you are placing elements or swapping types of elements you've already placed in the model, the palette must be open to access the Type Selector.

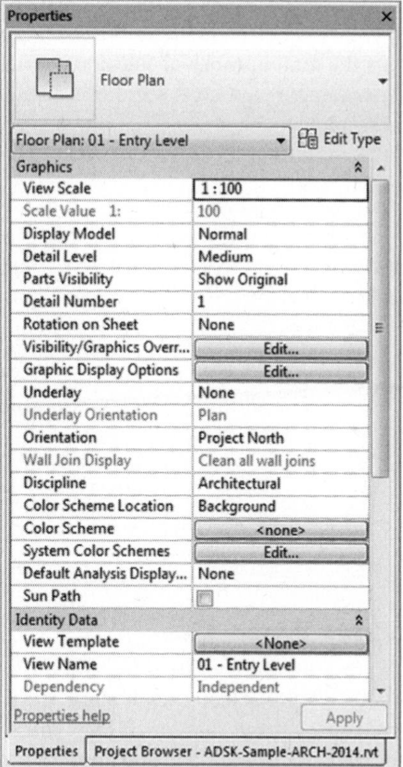

FIGURE 3.4
The Properties palette contains the Type Selector and is used to set view properties when no objects are selected.

When no elements are selected, the Properties palette displays the properties of the active view. If you need to change settings for the current view, make the changes in the Properties palette and the view will be updated. For views, you do not even need to use the Apply button to submit the changes—simply move the mouse out of the Properties palette, and the changes will automatically be accepted.

Customizing the Apply Button Behavior

The behavior of the Apply button in the Properties palette can be modified by editing the `Revit.ini` file. If you want to disable the automatic application of settings when you move the mouse pointer from the palette into the drawing area, add the following code to the `Revit.ini` file:

```
[UserInterface]
DisableMppAutoApply=1
```

If the bracketed text `[UserInterface]` already exists in the `Revit.ini` file, simply add `DisableMppAutoApply=1` below it. You should restart the application after making any changes to the `Revit.ini` file.

Finally, you can also use the Properties palette as a filtering method for selected elements. When you select elements from different categories, the drop-down list below the Type Selector displays the total number of selected elements. Open the list and you will see the elements listed per category, as shown in Figure 3.5. Select one of the categories to modify the parameters for the respective elements. This process is different from the Filter tool in that the entire selection set is maintained, allowing you to perform multiple modifying actions without reselecting elements.

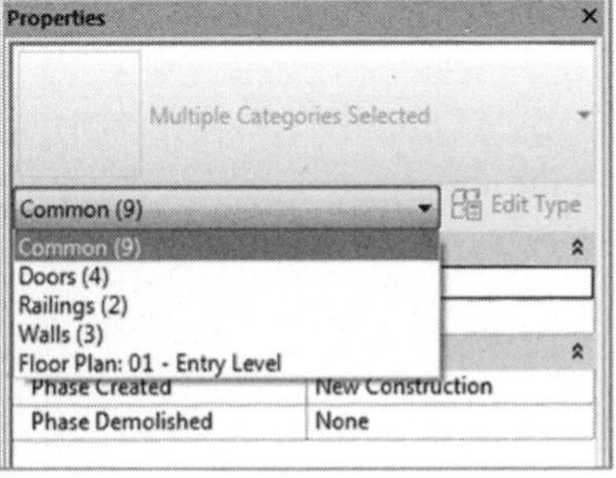

Figure 3.5
Use the Properties palette to filter selection sets.

Matching Properties

Located on the Modify tab of the ribbon in the Clipboard panel, the Match Type Properties tool allows you to select one element and apply its type and instance properties to other elements of the same category. Once you select one element, the brush icon near the mouse pointer appears filled. Each subsequent pick on elements of the same category will replace the selected element with the properties of the first element picked. Clicking in an open space will clear the brush icon and allow you to pick a new source object without restarting the command.

If you want to use the Match Type Properties tool for multiple objects in a more controlled manner, click the Select Multiple button in the contextual tab of the ribbon after the source object is selected. Proceed to use any of the usual selection methods described earlier in this chapter. When your selection is complete, click the Finish button on the ribbon.

Be careful when using this tool with walls, because not only does it change the wall type, it also changes the top and bottom constraints of the walls being matched. One best practice for changing wall types without affecting height constraints is to pick a wall and use the Type Selector to modify its type.

Using the Context Menu

The context menu that appears when you right-click in the view window contains several options. You can activate the last command or select from a list of recent commands, as shown in Figure 3.6.

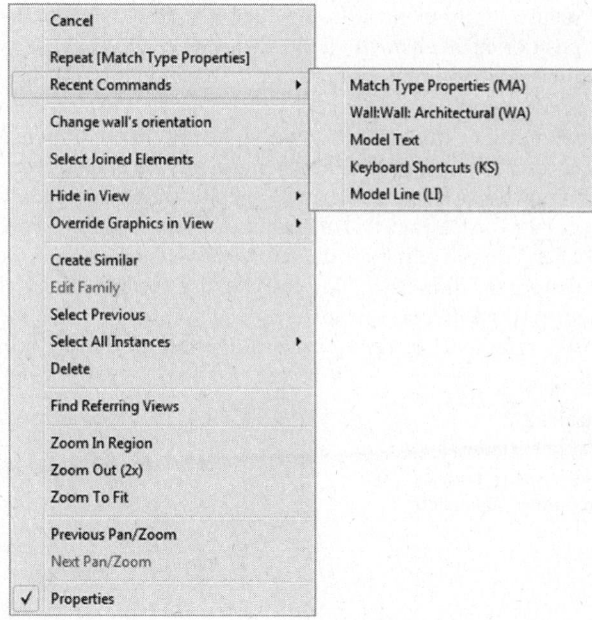

FIGURE 3.6
Run recent commands from the context menu.

In addition to the other right-click commands listed throughout this chapter (such as Create Similar), zoom commands, including Previous Pan/Zoom, are on the context menu. There are also useful commands when you right-click views in the Project Browser. For example, activate a plan view and then try right-clicking a 3D view in the browser. Select Show Section Box, and you can edit the extent of the 3D view's section box while in a floor plan.

Editing Elements Interactively

The Revit software provides a range of options to edit elements in the model interactively. The most obvious are selecting elements and then dragging them on screen, or using the blue control grips to extend walls, lines, shape faces, and region boundaries; however, you often need more precise ways of moving and copying objects. Let us look at some ways to do that.

Moving Elements

You can move elements in several ways, ranging from choosing traditional tools to using interactive dimensions that appear on the fly when you select elements. Become familiar with each method and determine what is best for your workflow.

Using Temporary Dimensions

You have likely noticed by now that dimensions appear when elements are selected or newly placed. These dimensions are called temporary dimensions and are there to inform you of the location of the elements relative to other elements in the model, as well as to help you reposition them. Clicking the blue dimension value (the text representing the distance measurement) makes it an active and editable value. Type in a new value, and the selected element will move relative to the element from which it is dimensioned. Remember that when you are editing the position of an element via the dimensions, it will always be the selected element that moves. You can't modify a dimension value if an element is not selected.

If a temporary dimension is not referencing a meaningful element, you can choose a different reference by dragging the small blue dot on the dimension's witness line to a new, parallel reference, which will highlight when the mouse moves over it (Figure 3.7). For example, if you want to position a door opening at a specific dimension from a nearby wall, you will need to drag the grip of the temporary dimension that references the center of the door to the side of the opening. Then you can edit the value of the dimension as required. When you are dragging the grip of a temporary dimension, you can also use the Tab key on the keyboard to cycle through available snapping references near the mouse pointer. To learn more about how to add references to families, refer to Chapter 14, "Designing with the Family Editor."

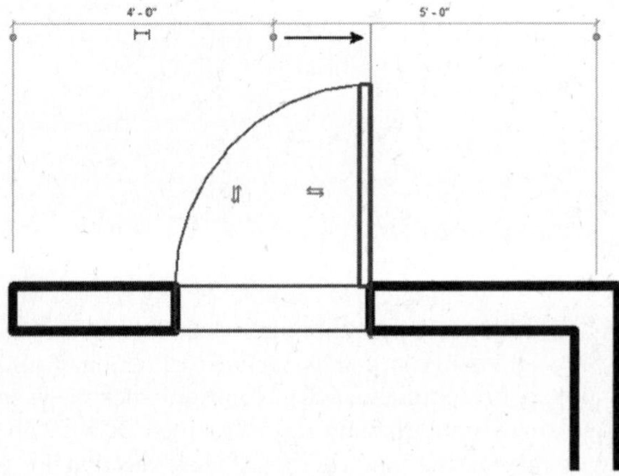

Figure 3.7
Drag or click the blue grip to change the reference of the temporary dimension.

If you click a blue grip, it cycles to the next possible reference in the element. For example, clicking the grip of a dimension to a door or window cycles between the left and right openings and the center reference. The same applies to walls: Try clicking the grip on the temporary dimension extending from a wall and see how the dimension cycles through the various references in the wall (interior face, centerline, exterior face). Note that when you drag a temporary dimension reference to a different position, the new reference is remembered when you return to the element for future editing.

You can also change the default behavior of temporary dimensions using the Temporary Dimension Properties dialog box, shown in Figure 3.8 (on the Manage tab, click Additional Settings and then select Temporary Dimensions). Here you can specify how temporary dimensions will independently reference walls, doors, and windows.

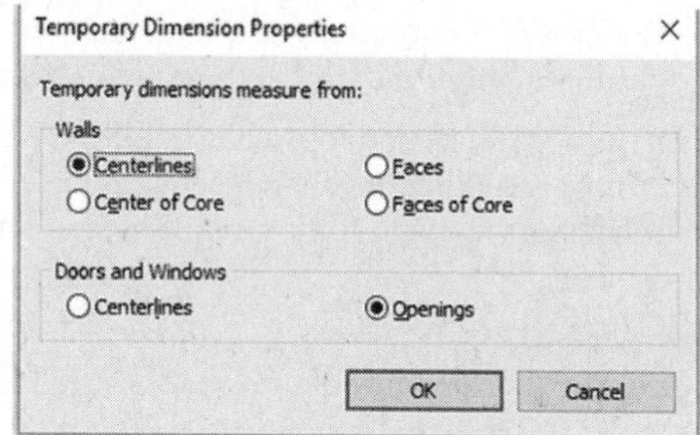

FIGURE 3.8 The Temporary Dimension Properties dialog box lets you define default behaviors based on your modeling needs.

You can modify the font size and transparency of temporary dimensions in the program options. To customize these values, click the Application menu and select Options. In the Options dialog box that opens, switch to the Graphics category and locate the Temporary Dimension Text Appearance settings. Adjust the text size and transparency according to your needs.

If you have several elements selected at the same time or select an element within the proximity of a large number of other elements, temporary dimensions sometimes don't appear. Check the Options bar for the Activate Dimensions button; clicking it will make the temporary dimensions appear in the view.

BEHAVIORS FOR MODIFY TOOLS

As in Autodesk AutoCAD software, you have the option to activate the Modify tools without any elements selected. If you choose this method, you must press the Enter key after selecting the objects you intend to modify.

You can also switch between any of the Modify panel tools while you have elements selected. For example, if you initially chose Mirror – Pick Axis and selected an element during the command, you can simply activate the Mirror – Draw Axis command without reselecting the elements.

Using the Move Tool

To relocate elements with more precision, use the Move tool rather than simply drag them. The tool allows you to type in values or use temporary dimensions as helpers.

Moving elements is a two-click process: First, you define a start point, and then you click to define a destination. If you know you need to move something a specific distance, it does not matter where your two picks take place. All that matters is that the distance between the two clicks is the specified distance and in the specified direction. Alternatively, you can guide the mouse pointer in the desired direction of the move and key in the desired dimension value.

There are a few options on the Options bar to be aware of when the Move command is active:

Constrain When this option is selected, it constrains movement to horizontal and vertical directions relative to the view. Deselecting it allows you to move the element freely as long as the element is not hosted. Hosted elements, such as windows or doors, always move in a constrained manner parallel to their host's axis.

Disjoin The Disjoin option is helpful when you need to move elements and eliminate any joining relationships the moved elements might have with other objects. This is particularly useful with walls in some circumstances where you may be rapidly iterating through design scenarios.

You might also attempt to use the Disjoin option to move a hosted element, such as a door, to a new host. Don't use the Move tool to perform this action; instead you must select the hosted element, and from the contextual tab in the ribbon, click Pick New Host. The object will be relocated to the new host you select. This method is also preferred over deleting and re-creating because it maintains the data associated with the original element instance.

Multiple The Multiple option is not active for the Move tool. This option is available only when you switch to the Copy tool.

Nudging Elements

Nudging is a simple way to push things around quickly, as you would in software programs such as Adobe Photoshop. When elements are selected, you can use the arrow keys on the keyboard to move the elements horizontally or vertically in small increments. Each press of an arrow key nudges the element a specific distance based on your current zoom factor. The closer you zoom, the finer the nudge. Note that your snap settings do not affect the nudging distances set by the zoom level. However, holding the Shift key while using the nudge tool increases the distance of the nudge.

Moving with Nearby Elements

A simple way to constrain freestanding elements is to use the Moves With Nearby Elements option. This setting is designed to capture logical relationships between elements without establishing an explicit constraint. When furnishing a space, for example, you probably want to align the bed or dresser with an adjacent wall. If you change the design of the space, you want the furniture to follow the wall to the new location. For this purpose, select the furniture and then select Moves With Nearby Elements in the Options bar, as shown in Figure 3.9.

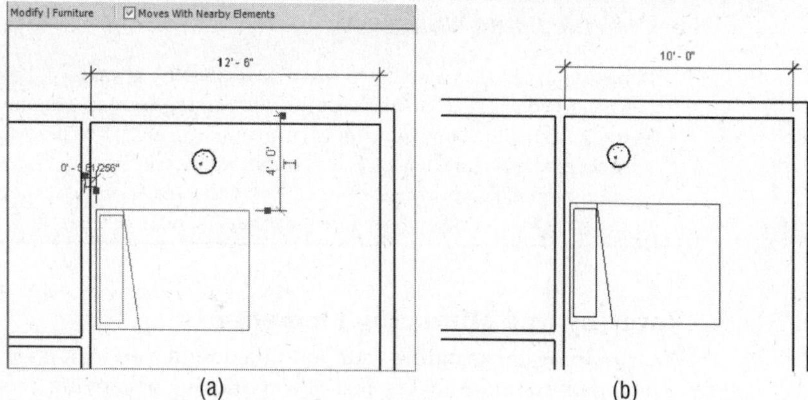

FIGURE 3.9 Once an object is selected, it can be set to move with nearby elements: (a) Select the furniture, and then select the Move With Nearby Elements tool; (b) note that the elements keep their relationships.

By setting this option, you create an invisible relationship between the bed and the wall so that each time you move the wall, the bed moves with it. To clarify the difference between this approach and other constraint relationships, you could create a wall-hosted family, but that would limit your placement options and would subject instances to deletion if the host is deleted. You could align and constrain the family to its host, but too many explicit constraints will adversely affect model performance.

The Moves With Nearby Elements option is also a simpler alternative to using a hosted family. When a component family does not need to cut or carve the host geometry, consider using a freestanding family or just a face-based family in conjunction with the Nearby Elements option. Refer to Chapter 14, "Designing with the Family Editor," for more information about hosted versus non-hosted values.

Copying Elements

The Copy tool is another modifying tool that is nearly identical to the Move tool, but it makes a copy of the selected element at the location of the second pick. This tool doesn't copy anything to the Clipboard; it copies an instance of an element or selection of elements in the same view. If you change views while using this tool, your selection is lost.

To activate this tool, either choose elements you want to copy and then select the Copy tool in the Modify tab in the ribbon or activate the Copy tool first, select elements you want to copy, and then press the Enter key to start the copy process. Using the Options bar, you can choose to make multiple copies in one transaction by selecting the Multiple option.

An alternative to using the Copy tool is to use standard Windows accelerator keys to copy elements. To quickly copy a single element without the precision of the Copy tool, click and drag an element while pressing the Ctrl key on your keyboard. This technique is useful for quickly populating a quantity of elements in a design without the required precision of the multiple picks of the Copy tool.

COPYING USING WORKSETS

If you are working in a model in which worksharing is enabled, be careful when performing any method of copying. These methods include pasting from the Clipboard, mirroring, and arraying, as well as using the Copy tool. Copied elements will always be placed on the active workset, not the workset of the original object. For example, if you are copying chairs that have been placed on the workset named Furniture but your active workset is Structure, the copied chairs will be assigned to the Structure workset. For more information, refer to Chapter 5, "Working in a Team."

Rotating and Mirroring Elements

When refining or expanding your building design, you will likely find a frequent need to rotate or mirror one or more objects. Just as with moving or copying, there are a few methods for these types of interactive operations. We will review these methods in the following sections.

USING THE SPACEBAR

You can use the spacebar to rotate an element, both at the time of initial placement and after it has been placed. In addition to rotating an object in 90-degree increments, pressing the spacebar will locate any nearby non-orthogonal references (walls, grids, or reference planes) as rotation candidates. This is a great time-saving command to become familiar with because you can forgo the necessity of using an additional tool, such as Rotate or Mirror, after placing an object. Here are a few examples:

Doors and Windows If you have a door with its swing in the wrong direction, select it and press the spacebar. You can cycle through all four possible orientations of the door using the spacebar. The same holds true for windows; however, many window families only let you flip the window from inside to outside because many windows are symmetrical in elevation. If you are creating an asymmetrical window family, be sure to add flip controls to the window family during its creation. These controls allow the spacebar to work on hosted elements.

Walls If you select a wall, pressing the spacebar flips the element as if it were being mirrored about its length. Walls flip based on their location line, which often isn't the centerline of the assembly. If you aren't sure which direction your wall is facing, select it and look for the flip-control arrows. These are always located on the exterior side of walls (Figure 3.10). You can also use the spacebar to flip the direction of an object. Simply select the object and hit the spacebar, or use it to toggle through placement options while you're locating a component.

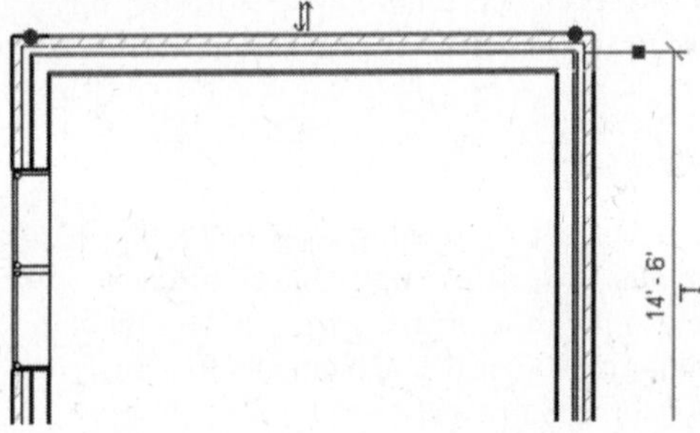

FIGURE 3.10
The flip arrow is another way to reorient an element. For walls, it is always found on the exterior side.

Freestanding Elements If you select a freestanding element, the spacebar rotates the element around the center reference planes defined in the family. Depending on how the family was built, the rotation origin may not make the most sense. If you decide to edit a family in order to change the location of the geometry relative to the center reference planes, be careful: When the family is loaded back into a project, all instances of the family will jump to a new location based on the change you made relative to the reference planes.

USING THE ROTATE TOOL

To rotate an element, select it and click the Rotate tool in the Modify panel. Remember, you can also activate the Rotate tool first, select one or more elements, and then press Enter to begin the operation. This is a two-click operation similar to the Move and Copy tools. The default rotation point is based on the center of the selected elements; however, you will most likely want to designate a more meaningful center.

To choose a new center of rotation, you have a couple of options. You can drag the center icon to a new location before clicking to set the starting reference angle. Note that you might have to zoom out in order to find the center icon. The second option is to select elements you want to rotate and then use the Place button in the Options bar to simply place the rotation point in the desired location without dragging. Once the center is established, begin rotating the element using the temporary dimensions as a reference or by typing in the angle of rotation explicitly.

Note that you can also use keyboard snap shortcuts to refine the location of the center of rotation while dragging it. For example, type **SE** to snap to an explicit endpoint while dragging.

USING THE MIRROR TOOL

The Mirror tool allows you to mirror elements across an axis in order to create a mirror image of an element or multiple elements. You can either pick an existing reference in the model with the Mirror – Pick Axis tool or draw the axis interactively using the Mirror – Draw Axis tool. In Figure 3.11, the centerline of the plumbing chase wall was picked as the axis for mirroring the plumbing fixtures.

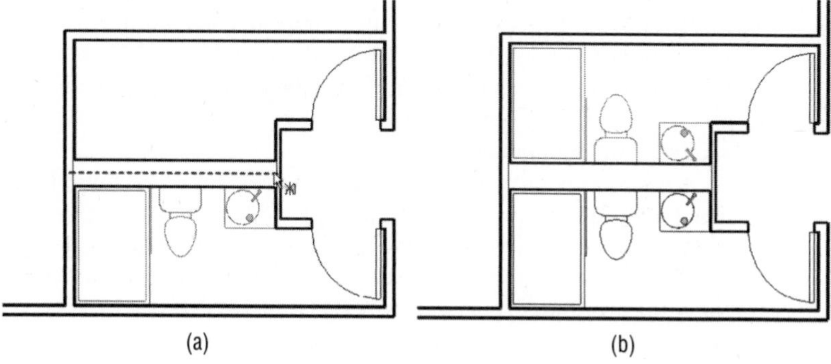

FIGURE 3.11 The sink, toilet, and bath fixtures are mirrored around the centerline of the chase wall: (a) selecting the axis; (b) the mirrored elements.

Like the other Modify tools you have seen so far, the Mirror tools have the option to create a copy of the selected elements or to simply mirror the selected elements to a new position. You can find the Copy option in the Options bar after you activate either of the Mirror tools.

BEING CAREFUL WHEN MIRRORING

The Mirror tools should be used carefully on any type of freestanding elements that may be asymmetrical in design. You can use the Mirror tools on any object, but keep in mind that performing this operation to suit a design may distort a product component. For example, if an asymmetrical chair family was loaded into your model and you decide to mirror it to fit a space layout, the mirrored version of that chair may not be a viable product offered by the manufacturer. Remember that although an object can be scheduled, the schedule cannot determine if the object has been mirrored.

Arraying Elements

The Array tool allows you to copy instances of an element with equal spacing between the instances. You have the option to create intelligent arrays that can be grouped and associated for further refinement, as well as one-off, unassociated arrays. Like the other tools we have reviewed in the Modify tab of the ribbon, the array options are presented on the Options bar.

You can create two types of arrays: linear and radial. *Linear* arrays are set as the default because they're the most common. As you would expect, a linear array creates a series of elements in a line. Each element in the array can be given a defined distance from the previous element (Move To 2nd option) or can be spaced equally based on a defined overall array length (Move To Last option). Figure 3.12 shows a linear array where the Move To 2nd option was selected to define a fixed distance between each instance in the array. Think of this type of array as additive and subtractive: If you change the number, the length of the array increases or decreases.

If you want to arrange elements in a fixed space and the exact spacing between elements is less important, use the Move To Last option. Figure 3.13 shows an array where the location of its last element was picked and the elements were placed equally between the first and last elements. With this option, the length is fixed and the array squeezes elements within that constraint as the number changes.

A *radial* array uses the same options as a linear array, but it revolves around a center point. The Move To 2nd and Move To Last options function as angles instead of distances in a radial array. You can specify the instance angle or overall array angle with two picks, or you can enter a specific value. With this type of array, elements auto-rotate so that each element faces the center of the array, as shown in Figure 3.14.

FIGURE 3.12
The Move To 2nd option is used in the Array tool to set a fixed distance between instances: (a) setting the array distance; (b) changing the number of elements in the array.

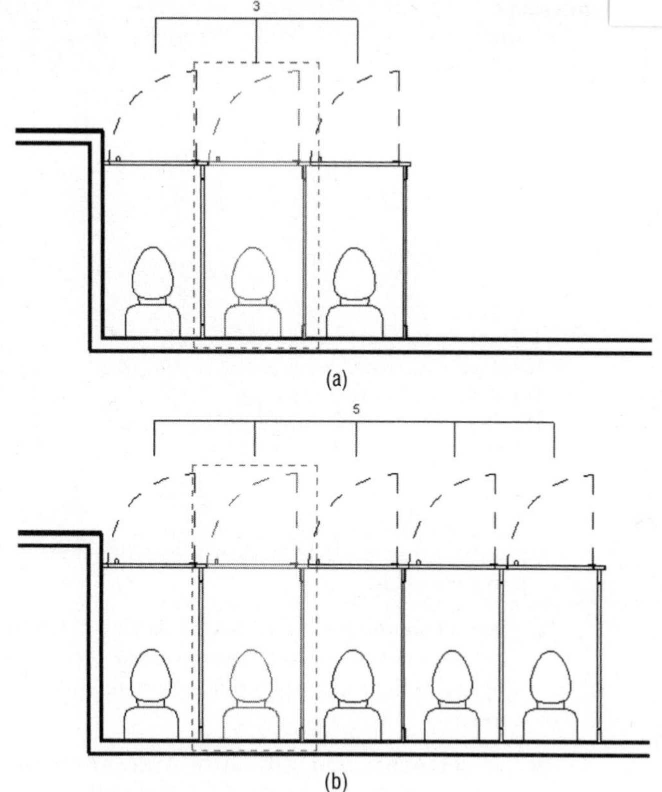

FIGURE 3.13
This array uses the Move To Last option and fills instances between the first and last instances: (a) creating an array first to last; (b) adding more elements to this array to keep the end element in the same location but add more in between.

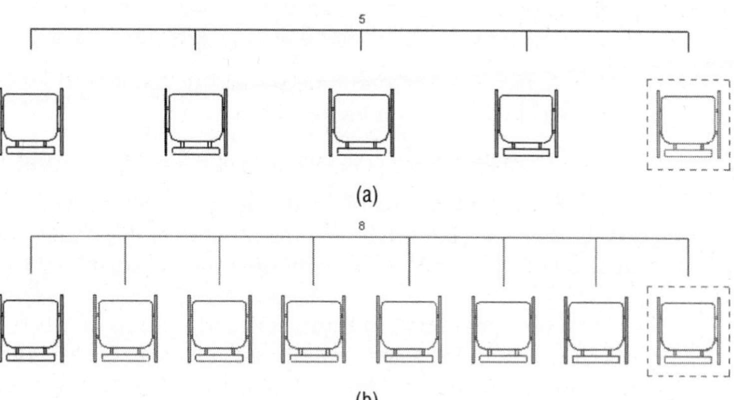

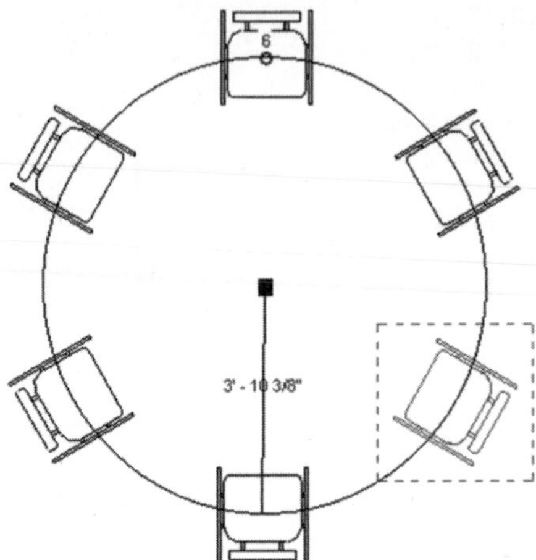

FIGURE 3.14
Elements will auto-rotate in a radial array.

The radial array is a little trickier than a linear array. Here is how to achieve the example shown in Figure 3.14:

1. Download and open the file `c03-Array.rvt` from this book's companion website at `www.sybex.com/go/masteringrevit2017`. Activate the Level 1 floor plan. To assist in starting the radial array, we provided a detail line to help locate the intended center of the array.
2. Select the chair and activate the Array tool from the Modify tab in the ribbon. In the Options bar, select the Radial option button, change Number to **6**, and choose the Move To Last option.
3. In the drawing area, click and drag the grip indicating the center of rotation off the element and to the endpoint of the detail line provided.
4. Click the mouse to define any starting point. An exact starting point is not important, because you will be defining a complete circle in the next step.
5. Do not click a second time; instead, go to the Options bar, type **360** in the Angle option, and press Enter on the keyboard.
6. Press Enter or click on any open space in the drawing area to complete the command.

Enabling the Group and Associate option allows you to treat an array as a group that can be modified later to adjust the number and spacing of the array. If this option is unchecked, the array is a one-off operation and you have no means of adjusting it after it is created.

As shown previously in Figure 3.12 and Figure 3.13, when an element in a grouped array is selected, a control appears, indicating the number of elements in the array. Editing that number changes the number of elements in the array. This tool comes in handy when you are creating certain families because the array number can be associated with a parameter or driven by a mathematical formula. See Chapter 14 for a detailed exercise.

Grouping Arrays of Datum Elements

When developing a project for a multistory building, you may find that using the Array tool is a quick and easy way to generate many levels and grid lines. We recommend not using the Group and Associate option when arraying datum elements. Maintaining grids and levels inside groups can cause problems with elements that refer to those data.

Scaling Elements

The Scale tool lets you scale certain lines and graphic elements in 2D that are appropriate for scaling, such as imported raster images and 2D line shapes. Although it's not an obvious option, the Scale tool can be used in Sketch mode for any type of sketch-based element in a project or for solid and void geometry sketches in the Family Editor.

Keep in mind that you are working with a model made out of real-world objects, not abstract primitive forms. You cannot scale most elements because it's not practical or meaningful and may cause dangerous errors in scheduling and dimensions. For example, you can't scale the size of a door, wall, or sink because they represent real assemblies and scaling them would mean resizing all their components. This would lead to impractical results, such as a sink being displayed as a fraction of its actual manufactured size.

Aligning Elements

If you've been using Revit software for any amount of time, you have likely discovered the power of the Align tool. It can supplant the need to use many of the tools we have already discussed, such as Move and Rotate. The Align tool lets you line up elements in an efficient way that works on almost all types of objects.

With this tool, you explicitly align references from one element to another, regardless of the type of either object. For example, you can align windows in a facade so that their centers or openings are all in alignment. To use the Align tool, activate it from the Modify tab in the ribbon and first select the target reference—a reference to which you want to align another element. Next, select what you want to align to that reference—the part or side of the element whose position needs to be modified. The second element picked is the one that always moves into alignment. This selection sequence is the opposite of the other editing tools we've discussed so far, so remember: *destination first*, then the element to align.

As soon as you make your second pick and the aligned element is moved, a lock icon appears, allowing you to constrain the alignment. If you click the icon, thereby constraining the alignment, the alignment is preserved if either element moves. Figure 3.15 illustrates the use of the Align tool to align multiple windows in an elevation view using the Multiple Alignment option on the Options bar.

The Align tool also works within Filled Region model patterns, such as brick or stone on surfaces of model objects. Select a line on an object such as the edge of a wall, and then select a line in the surface pattern. Use the Tab key if you cannot get surface patterns selected with the first mouse click. Note that the Align tool will also rotate elements in the process of aligning them to objects that are not parallel. This is a real time-saver compared to moving and rotating.

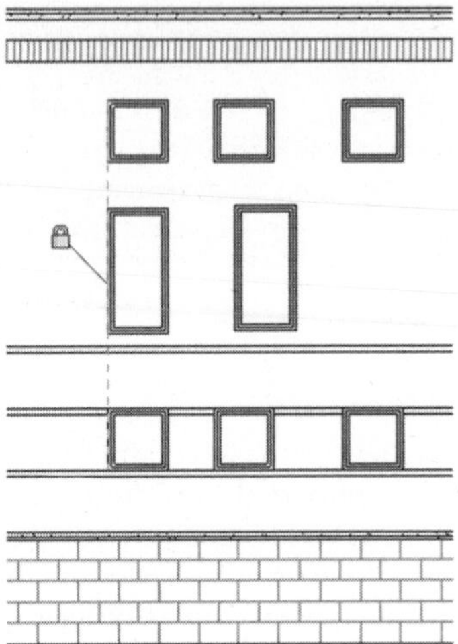

FIGURE 3.15
You can use the Align tool to line up edges of windows in a facade.

Trimming or Extending Lines and Walls

You can trim and extend lines and walls to one another using the Trim/Extend tools on the Modify tab of the ribbon. In older versions of Revit Architecture, this function was assigned to a single button with three options in the Options bar. There are three separate tools in the ribbon: Trim/Extend To Corner, Trim/Extend Single Element, and Trim/Extend Multiple Elements. With the Trim/Extend tools, you first activate the tool and then operate on elements in the model, selecting two lines or walls that need to meet in a corner or as a T-intersection.

The Trim/Extend tools are used frequently for editing sketches of floors and roofs because it's easy to end up with overlapping lines that need to be trimmed to form a closed loop. Keep in mind that with the Trim/Extend tools, you are selecting pairs of elements to *remain*, not to remove. Although the Single Element and Multiple Elements tools are similar to the Extend command in AutoCAD, the behavior of the Trim/Extend To Corner tool in Revit Architecture is more like that of the Chamfer or Fillet command rather than its Trim command.

The Trim/Extend tools for extending a single element or multiple elements function in a slightly different way than Trim/Extend To Corner. To extend a wall or line, first select a target reference; then select the element you want to extend to that target (Figure 3.16). Using the Trim/Extend Multiple Elements tool, you first select the target reference; then each subsequent pick extends the selected element to the target reference. You also have the ability to use a selection box to trim multiple elements.

USING TRIM/EXTEND ON LINE-BASED COMPONENTS

You can use the Trim/Extend tools on line-based families that are either model or detail components. Try this using a line-based detail component for batt insulation or gypsum wallboard. The Trim/Extend tools will help make your detailing process much more efficient and fun!

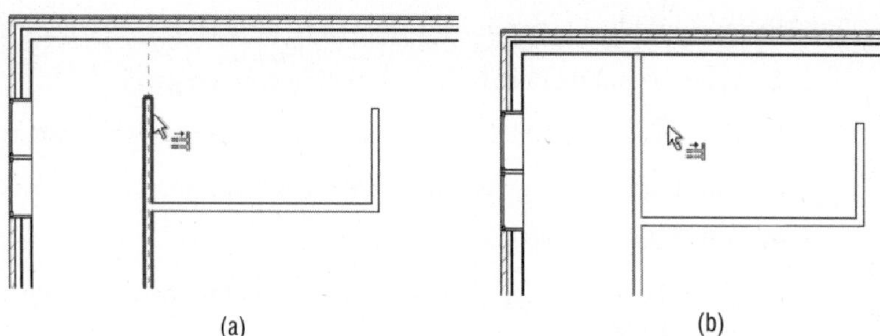

FIGURE 3.16
Extend walls to references by picking the target (a) and then the wall to extend (b).

Splitting Lines and Walls

The Split Element tool operates on walls and lines and lets you divide an element into two pieces. To cut an element, activate the Split Element tool from the Modify tab in the ribbon and place the mouse pointer over the edge of a wall or line. Before you click, you will see a preview of the split line. The split line will automatically snap to any adjoining geometry.

The Options bar displays a nice feature called Delete Inner Segment that removes the need to use any of the Trim tools after a splitting operation. In the example in Figure 3.17, the middle section of a wall needs to be removed so that you end up with a clean set of wall joins. Using the Split Element tool with the Delete Inner Segment option checked, you can accomplish this with two clicks and get a clean condition without having to return with any of the Trim commands.

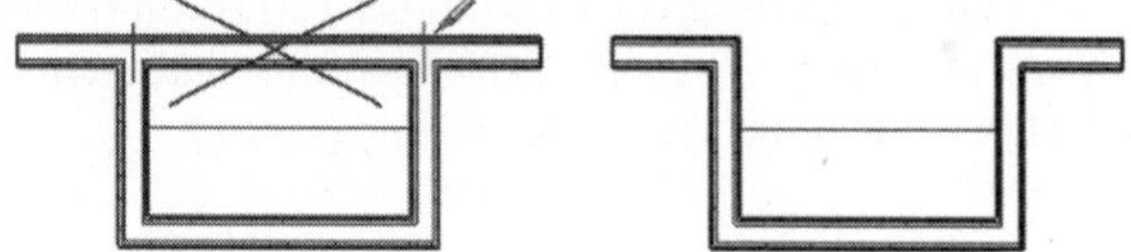

FIGURE 3.17
Using the Split Element tool with the Delete Inner Segment option checked

SPLIT WITH GAP

The Split with Gap tool allows you to specify a gap distance and pick a single point on a wall. Although the wall is divided into two separate segments, the gap distance is maintained with an automatic constraint. To use Split with Gap, follow these steps:

1. Go to the Modify tab, and from the Modify panel, select Split with Gap.
2. Specify the Joint Gap distance in the Options bar. Note that this distance can be set only between 1/16″ (1.6 mm) and 1′-0″ (300 mm).
3. Move the mouse pointer over a wall and click to place the gap.

Once you have successfully split a wall with a gap, select the wall and notice the constraints (locks) on the gap and between the two parallel wall segments. Try to drag either of the wall ends separated by the gap, and you will see that the gap distance is maintained. Try to move the wall in a direction perpendicular to the wall segments, and you will notice that the two wall segments remain aligned.

If you would like to rejoin walls that have been split with a gap, follow these steps:

1. Select a wall that has been split with a defined gap.
2. Click the constraint icon in the gap to unlock the dimension constraint.
3. Select each wall segment and click the Allow Join icon near the end of the wall that was split.
4. Select the other wall and repeat step 3.
5. Drag the wall end grip of one wall segment to the end of the other segment. The walls should join.

Note that on walls with smaller gaps, the segments may automatically join as soon as you select Allow Join; however, rejoined segments may not form a single segment. If you have trouble joining two parallel wall segments into one, try to drag one of the wall ends away from the other and release the mouse button; then drag the segment back to the other end.

Offsetting Lines and Walls

Offset is similar to the Move and Copy tools in that it moves and makes a copy of an element by offsetting it parallel to an edge you select. You can find the Offset tool in the Modify tab of the ribbon. You can also specify an offset distance as an option in the Options bar when you are sketching lines or walls.

This tool is especially useful in the Family Editor when you are making shapes that have a consistent thickness in profile, such as extruded steel shapes. The Offset tool has a Copy option available in the Options bar that determines whether the offsetting operation generates a copy of the selected elements or simply moves them.

Remember that you can Tab-select a chain of elements and offset them in one click, as shown in Figure 3.18. When the Offset command is active, the dashed line appears on the side of the element to which the offset will be created.

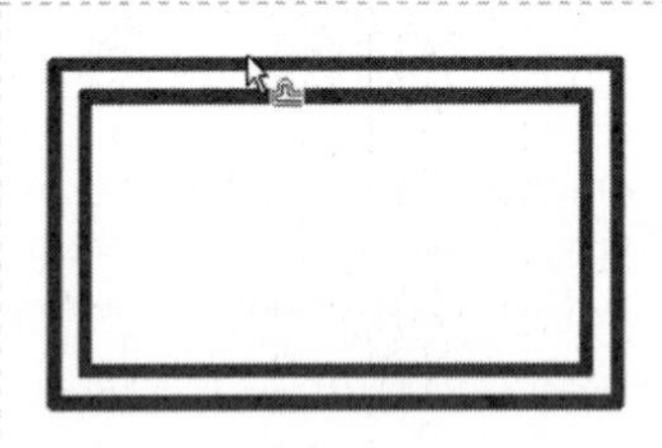

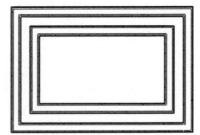

FIGURE 3.18
Use Offset with Tab-select to copy a chain of elements.

Preventing Elements from Moving

In some cases, you may want to make sure some elements in the model never move. An example of this is when you work on a renovation to an existing building. For obvious reasons, you would not want to move existing walls. Other examples include imported drawings, grids, levels, and exterior walls. There are two ways to deal with this and lock certain elements, thus preventing them from moving.

PINNING ELEMENTS

You can restrict an element's ability to move by pinning it with the Pin tool. Use this tool to lock down critical elements that need to remain fixed for long periods of time. As one example, this is an important tool to use on imported CAD files because it is easy to accidentally select an import and drag it or move it. This kind of accidental modification can lead to coordination problems, even in a BIM environment. Use pins to lock down grid lines because you certainly do not want to accidentally relocate those either.

This tool is located in the Modify panel of the Modify tab in the ribbon. Select one or more elements for which you want to prevent movement, and click the Pin tool. If you try to move the element, nothing will happen—you will not even get a preview of a potential move. To unpin an element, select it and click the Unpin tool, which is also located in the Modify panel. You can also unpin an element by clicking the pin icon that appears near a pinned element when it is selected.

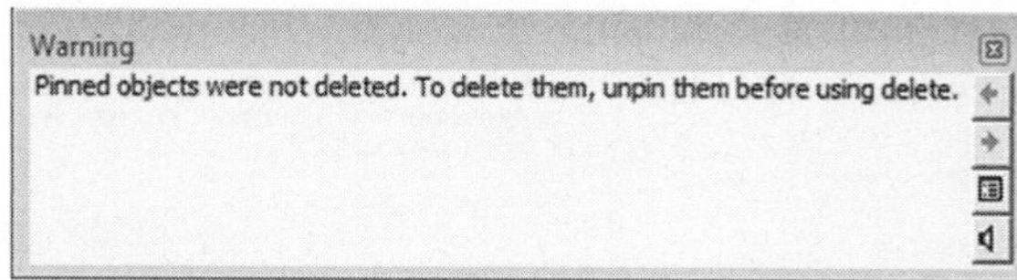

Revit helps you avoid accidentally deleting elements. Instead of permitting the deletion and providing a warning, Revit will warn you that the element is pinned and instruct you to unpin the element before using Delete. If you select multiple elements (some pinned and some not pinned) for deletion, Revit deletes the elements that are not pinned and warns that you must unpin the pinned elements before deleting them.

Combining the Pin tool and the selection filters will allow a BIM coordinator to create a selection set for pinned items. By loading the selection set, the coordinator can double-check that the items are indeed pinned.

CONSTRAINTS

Constraints aren't as rigid as the Pin tool, but they do allow you to create dimensional rules in the model so that elements remain fixed relative to other elements. You can create a constraint using dimensions or alignments and then click the lock icon that appears upon creation of a dimension or completion of an alignment operation.

A simple example of using constraints is maintaining a fixed distance between a door and a side wall. If the wall moves, the door will also move. If you try to move the door, the software will not let you move it. Look at Figure 3.19; the door has been constrained to remain 4″ (100 mm) from the wall face.

This type of constraint is accomplished by placing a dimension string between the doorjamb and the face of the wall and then clicking the lock icon on the dimension. Note that the dimension can be deleted while preserving the constraint. If you delete a constrained dimension, an alert will appear, giving you the option to unconstrain the elements or simply delete the dimension while maintaining the constraint (Figure 3.20). Note that you can determine where constraints were by creating new dimensions; constrained relationships will still display with the lock icon. You can also view these relationships when a constrained element is selected. Simply hover the mouse pointer near the constraint icon, and you will see the dimension constraint represented as a dashed dimension string.

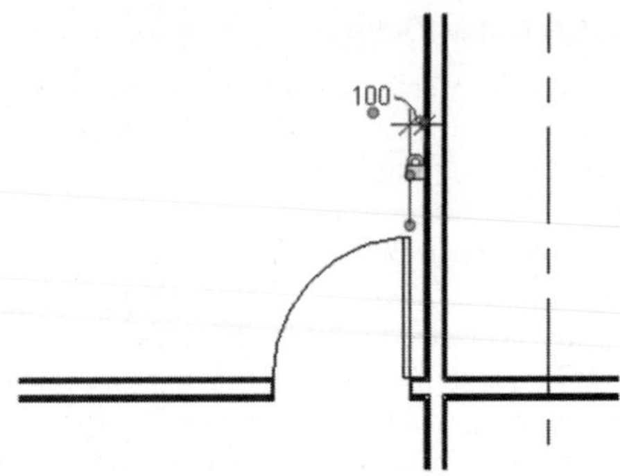

FIGURE 3.19
A door constrained to a wall can't be moved independently of the wall.

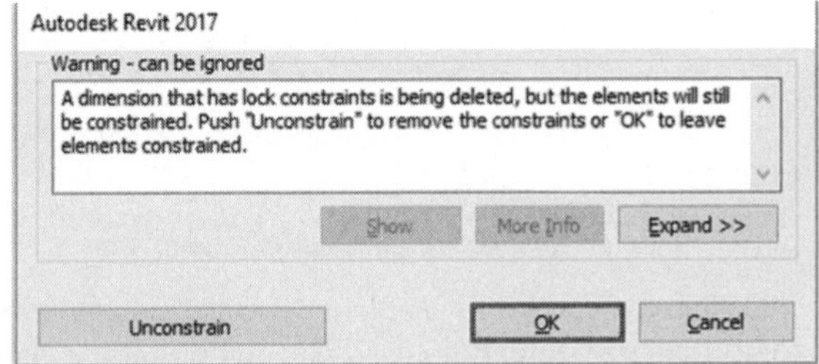

FIGURE 3.20
Deleting a constrained dimension generates an alert.

REVEALING CONSTRAINTS IN A VIEW

You may find that your modeled elements behave in an unexpected way if too many constraints have been applied. To assist in troubleshooting constraints, you can use the Reveal Constraints view mode available on the view control bar. When this temporary view mode is activated, all constraints on visible model elements—even constrained dimensions that have been deleted—will be displayed in red (Figure 3.21).

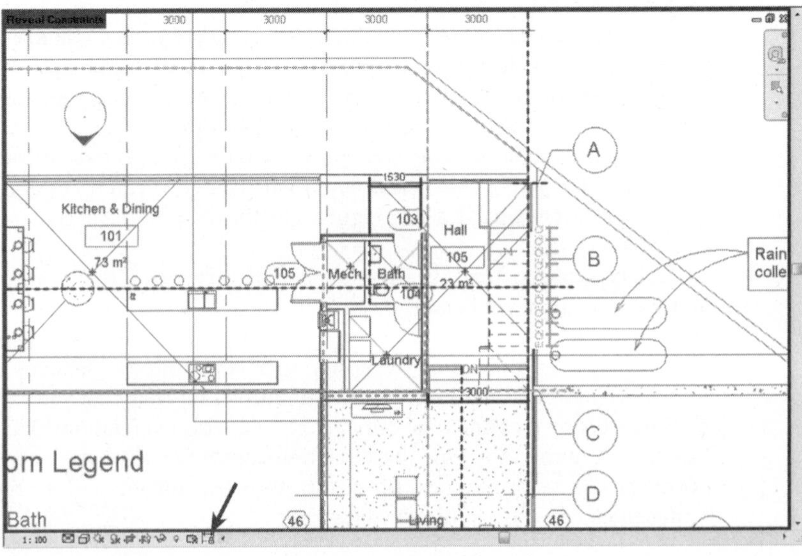

FIGURE 3.21
Using Reveal Constraints view mode

Exploring Other Editing Tools

Many other editing tools are available, and we will cover them in subsequent chapters when they're used in specific operations. However, there are a few you should know about now because they are generic tools you can put to immediate use on any project.

Using the Join Geometry Tool

Joining walls to floors and roofs creates clean-looking drawings, and Revit will attempt to create these joins automatically; however, in some cases, elements don't look right until they are explicitly joined. This is where the Join Geometry tool comes into play. This tool creates joins between floors, walls, ceilings, roofs, and slabs. A common use for this tool is in building sections, where floors and walls may appear overlapped and not joined. Figure 3.22 shows a floor intersecting with some walls that aren't joined. Using the Join Geometry tool, you can clean up these conditions nicely.

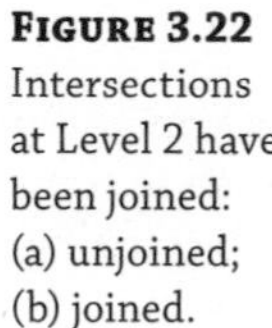

FIGURE 3.22 Intersections at Level 2 have been joined: (a) unjoined; (b) joined.

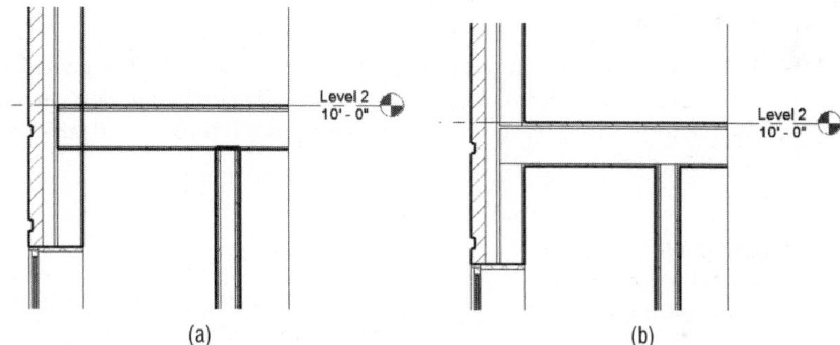

You might notice that some joins—especially in a view set to the Coarse detail level—contain a thin dividing line between two elements. This is usually because the two elements you joined consist of differing materials. Ensuring consistent material application will give you increased graphic quality in your project views.

You should also be aware that joining large host elements to many other elements may degrade model performance. One way to avoid this is to apply a black solid fill to elements in the cut plane of your coarse view sections and avoid overall manual joining; then selectively join for medium and fine views. You can do so easily by selecting the element in question (wall, floor, and so forth) and choosing Edit Type from the Properties palette. By default, the Coarse Scale Fill Pattern is set to No Pattern. Set this to Solid Fill; in all your coarse views, your elements will show as solid black.

Using the Split Face and Paint Tools

Occasionally, you may need to apply a thin material to the face of an object without making a new type of element. You may also need to divide an overall surface into smaller regions to receive different materials. You can use the Paint tool to apply materials and the Split Face tool to divide object surfaces. With the Paint tool, you can apply alternative materials to the exterior faces of walls, floors, roofs, and ceilings. This material has no thickness, but you can schedule it with a material takeoff schedule and annotate it with a material tag. A typical use case for these two tools is the application of a carpet or thin tile to a floor. See Chapter 13, "Modeling Floors, Ceilings, and Roofs," for a detailed exercise on this topic.

Copying and Pasting from the Clipboard

Copying and pasting is a familiar technique used in almost all software applications, and Revit software provides the basic features you would expect (Ctrl+C and Ctrl+V). It also has some additional time-saving options that are specific to working on a 3D model.

To copy any element or group of elements to the Clipboard, select them and press Ctrl+C. To paste, press Ctrl+V. In the majority of cases, the software pastes the elements with a dashed bounding box around them. You then determine where to place the elements by clicking a point to define its final position. In the Options bar, you will find a Constrain option that when clicked will only let you define the location of the pasted content orthogonally to the original elements. With the elements copied to the Clipboard, you'll also find some additional tools on the Clipboard panel of the Modify tab.

Edit Pasted

Immediately after you select a point for the location of the pasted content, you will find a new panel in the ribbon called Edit Pasted (Figure 3.23). You can click Finish to complete the pasting action or start another command. If you are unsatisfied with the pasting action, select Cancel.

Figure 3.23
Additional actions are available when pasting elements.

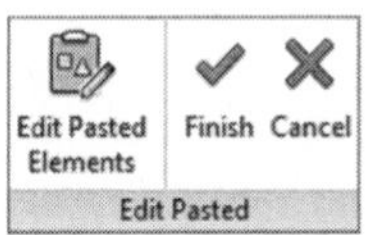

If you select Edit Pasted Elements, a special mode will be started with the Edit Pasted tools appearing at the top left of the drawing area (Figure 3.24). In this mode, only the pasted elements are editable. You can use the Select All or Filter button to refine those elements within the pasted selection. When your edits are completed, click the Finish button.

Figure 3.24
Edit Pasted mode allows additional modification of pasted elements.

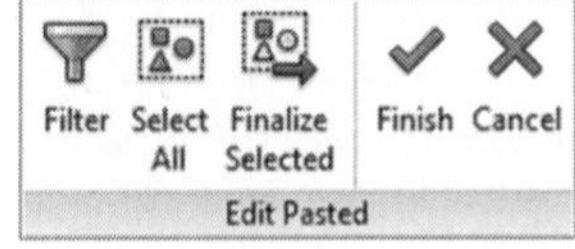

Paste Aligned

If you need to paste elements with greater location control, Paste Aligned offers options to make the process simple and efficient. These options allow you to quickly duplicate elements from one view or one level to another while maintaining a consistent location in the x-coordinate and y-coordinate planes. After selecting elements and copying them to the Clipboard, find the Paste button in the Clipboard panel, as shown in Figure 3.25.

FIGURE 3.25
Paste Aligned options

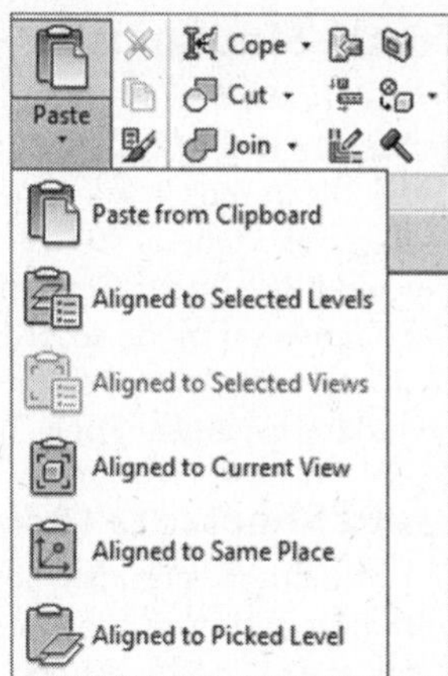

Five options, in addition to the Paste From Clipboard option, are available when you click the Paste drop-down button. Depending on the view from which you copy and what kinds of elements you copy, the availability of these options will change. For example, if you select a model element in a plan view, you will not have the Aligned To Selected Views option. These options are as follows:

Aligned To Selected Levels This is a mode you can use to quickly paste copied elements to many different levels simultaneously. When you select this option, you choose levels from a list in a dialog box. This is useful when you have a multistory building design, and you want to copy a furniture layout that repeats on many floors, and selecting level graphics in a section or elevation would be too tedious.

Aligned To Selected Views If you want to copy view-specific elements, such as drafting lines, text, or dimensions, this option allows you to paste them by selecting views from a list of views in a dialog box. In the list available for selection, you do not see levels listed but rather see a list of parallel views. For example, if elements are copied from a plan view, all other plan views are listed. Likewise, if you copy from an elevation view, only elevation views are listed.

Aligned To Current View This option pastes the elements from the Clipboard into the active view in the same spatial location. For example, if you copy a series of walls in one view, switch to another view in the Project Browser, and paste with the Aligned To Current View option, the software pastes the walls to the same x-coordinate and y-coordinate locations in the view you switched to.

Aligned To Same Place This option places elements from the Clipboard in the exact place from which they were copied or cut. One use for this tool is copying elements into a design option; see Chapter 10, "Working with Phasing, Groups, and Design Options," for an explanation of design options.

Aligned To Picked Level This is a mode you can use to copy and paste elements between different floors by picking a level in a section or elevation. Although you can cut or copy elements from a plan view, you must be in an elevation or section to paste using this option. You might use this paste option to copy balconies on a facade from one floor to another.

Using the Create Similar Tool

Rather than hunting through a list of families or making copies you'd have to edit later, try using the Create Similar tool to add new instances of a selected element to your model.

This tool is available in the Create panel of the Modify tab of the ribbon when an object is selected or from the context menu. To use this method, select an existing instance of the same type of element you'd like to create and click the Create Similar tool, and you will immediately be in a placement or creation mode according to the type of element. For example, if you use Create Similar with a floor selected, you're taken directly into Sketch mode, where you can start sketching the boundary for a new floor.

Using Keyboard Shortcuts (Accelerators)

To increase your productivity even further, you may like to use keyboard shortcuts to speed up common commands and minimize interruptions to your workflow. When you hover your mouse pointer over any tool in the ribbon, the keyboard shortcut is indicated to the right of the tool name, as shown here.

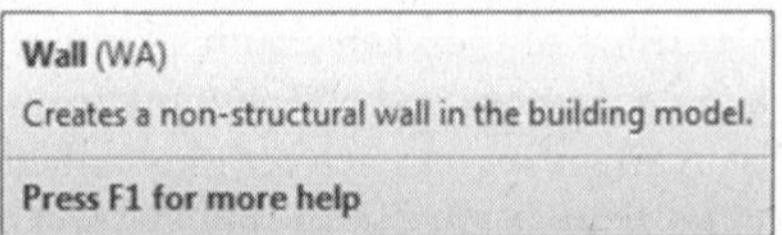

You can customize the keyboard shortcuts assigned to all commands. To access this tool, go to the View tab in the ribbon, find the Windows panel, and select User Interface ➤ Keyboard Shortcuts. When the Keyboard Shortcuts dialog box appears (Figure 3.26), you can search for commands in the Search box.

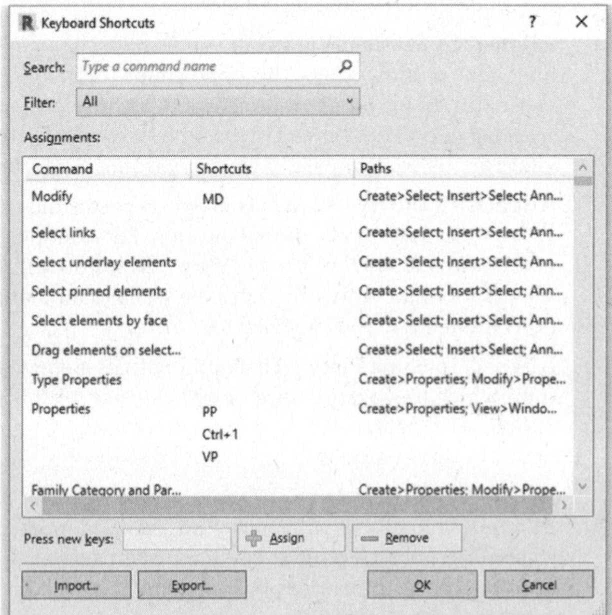

FIGURE 3.26
Customize keyboard shortcuts for commonly used Revit commands.

Once you find a command to which you'd like to assign a shortcut, select it and type the shortcut in the Press New Keys box. Click the Assign button, and you will see the new shortcut added to the selected command. Click OK to close the dialog box, and the keyboard shortcuts will be ready for immediate use. If you choose to modify the shortcut, understand that no two commands can have an identical shortcut. As an example, if you use the shortcut AA for Align, you can't use AA again for the shortcut to another command. Revit will take the one that appears first in the list and ignore any other entries.

Double-click to Edit

Revit allows you to double-click families and components to launch the respective editing mode. Although this may be the epitome of editing efficiency, you also have the ability to customize this behavior—even to completely disable it. From the Application menu, click the Options button. In the Options dialog box, select the User Interface settings, and then click the Customize button next to Double-Click Options. In the Customize Double-Click Settings dialog box, you will see the limits to which you can customize the behavior to your liking. Note that any of the actions can be set to Do Nothing and some can be set to Edit Type or Edit Element.

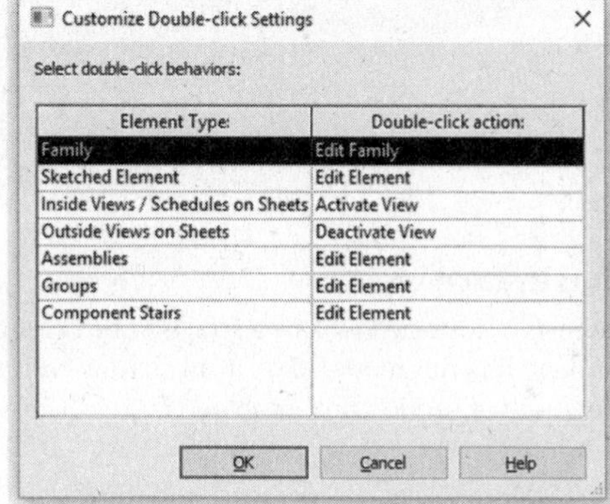

Modeling Site Context

In the previous sections of this chapter, you learned about the fundamental tools for editing and modifying model elements. Other tools you should become familiar with are the site tools. They allow you to create a context within which your building models can be situated. For example, a toposurface will create a hatched area when you view your building in a section, and it will function as a hosting surface for site components such as trees, shrubs, parking spaces, accessories, and vehicles (Figure 3.27).

The site tools are intended for use only in the creation of basic elements, including topography, property lines, and building pads. Although editing utilities are available to manipulate the site elements, these tools are not meant to be used for civil engineering like the functionality found in AutoCAD® Civil 3D® software is.

In the following sections, you'll learn about the different ways to create and modify a toposurface, how to generate property lines with tags, and how to model a building pad within a toposurface.

FIGURE 3.27
A toposurface can host components, such as trees, people, vehicles, and other entourage.

Using a Toposurface

As its name suggests, a toposurface is a surface-based representation of the topography context supporting a project. It is not modeled as a solid; however, a toposurface will appear as if it were solid in a 3D view with a section box enabled (Figure 3.28).

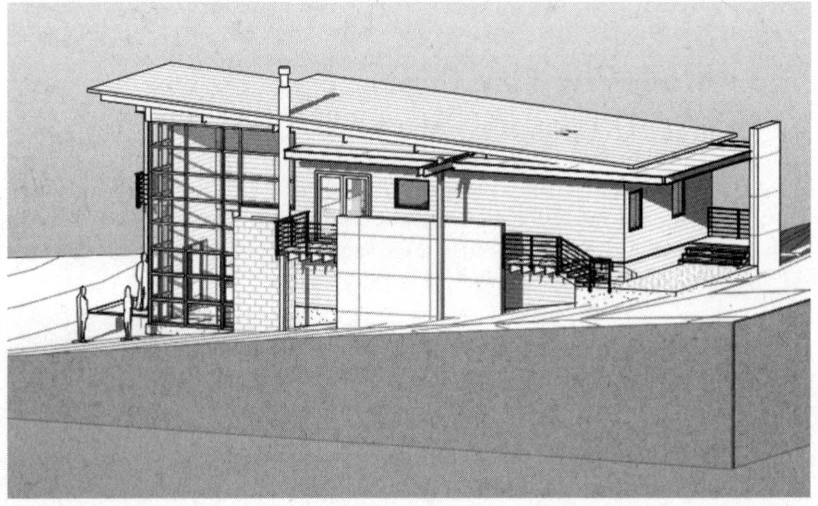

FIGURE 3.28
A toposurface will appear as a solid in a 3D view only if a section box is used.

You can create a toposurface in one of three ways: by placing points at specific elevations, by using a linked CAD file with lines or points at varying elevations, or by using a points file generated by a civil engineering application. We'll examine these techniques in the following exercises.

TURNING ON AND OFF TABS

If you don't see the Massing & Site tab, just navigate to the Application menu and choose Options. From there, select the User Interface category. Here you can turn on and off any of the tabs from the ribbon.

CREATING A TOPOSURFACE BY PLACING POINTS

The simplest way to create a toposurface is by placing points in your Revit project at specific elevations. To create a clean outer edge for your toposurface, draw a large rectangle using detail lines in your site plan. When you are creating a toposurface by placing points, there are no line-based geometry tools; however, points can be snapped to the detail lines. The following exercise will show you how to create a toposurface by placing points:

1. Begin by opening the file `c03-Site-Tools.rvt` or `c03-Site-Tools-Metric.rvt`, which can be downloaded from this book's companion web page.
2. Activate the floor plan named Site, and you will see a rectangle created from detail lines.
3. Go to the Massing & Site tab, and from the Model Site panel, click Toposurface.

   Notice in the contextual tab in the ribbon that the default tool is Place Point.
4. Notice the Elevation value in the Options bar. Set the value of the points you are about to place.

   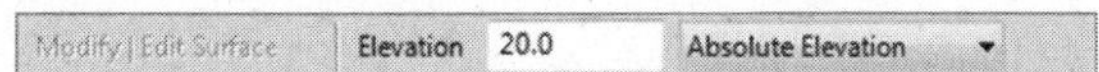

   Also note that the elevation values are always related to the Revit Project Base Point. They do not relate to the elevation of any shared coordinates.
5. With the Elevation value set to 0′-0″ (0 mm), place a point at each of the left corners of the rectangle.
6. Change the Elevation value to 20′-0″ (6000 mm), and then place a point at each of the right corners of the rectangle. You will notice the contour lines of the surface begin to appear after the third point of the surface is placed.
7. In the contextual tab of the ribbon, click Finish Surface (green check mark) to complete the toposurface. Activate the Default 3D view, and you will see the sloping surface, as shown in Figure 3.29. And keep in mind that this will be a thin surface, not a solid. Notice that the 3D view in this project already has the section box property enabled. To adjust the section box, activate the Reveal Hidden Elements tool in the view control bar.
8. Save the file for use in a subsequent exercise in this chapter.

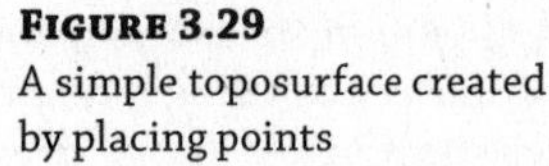

FIGURE 3.29
A simple toposurface created by placing points

CREATING A TOPOSURFACE FROM IMPORTED CAD DATA

A common workflow you may encounter involves the use of CAD data generated by a civil engineer. In this case, the engineer must create a file with 3D data. Blocks, circles, or contour polylines must exist in the CAD file at the appropriate elevation to be used in the process of generating a toposurface in Revit.

In the following exercise, you will download a sample DWG file with contour polylines. You must link the file into your Revit project before creating the toposurface:

1. Download and open `c03-Site-Link.rvt` or `c03-Site-Link-Metric.rvt` from this book's website.
2. Download the file `c03-Site-Link.dwg` from this book's web page.
3. Activate the Site plan in the Project Browser.
4. Go to the Insert tab in the ribbon and click the Link CAD button. Select the `c03-Site-Link.dwg` file and set the following options:
    - Current View Only: Unchecked
    - Import Units: Auto-Detect
    - Positioning: Auto-Center To Center
    - Place At: Level 1
    - Correct Lines That Are Slightly Off Axis: Unchecked
5. Click Open to complete the insertion of the CAD link. Open a Default 3D view to examine the results (Figure 3.30).
6. From the Massing & Site tab in the ribbon, click the Toposurface button. In the Tools panel of the Modify | Edit Surface tab on the ribbon, select Create From Import and then Select Import Instance.
7. Pick the linked CAD file, and the Add Points From Selected Layers dialog box will appear (Figure 3.31). Click the Check None button and then select the layers C-TOPO-MAJR and C-TOPO-MINR.

8. Click OK to close the dialog box. It may take a few seconds to generate the points based on the contour polylines in the linked file, but they will appear as black squares when they have all been placed.

9. If you would like to use fewer points to define the toposurface, click the Simplify Surface button in the contextual ribbon and enter a larger value, such as **1′-0″** (**300** mm).

10. Click the Finish Surface button in the contextual ribbon tab to complete the toposurface. Change the visual style of the view to Consistent Colors to examine your results.

FIGURE 3.30
Linked CAD file as seen in a 3D view

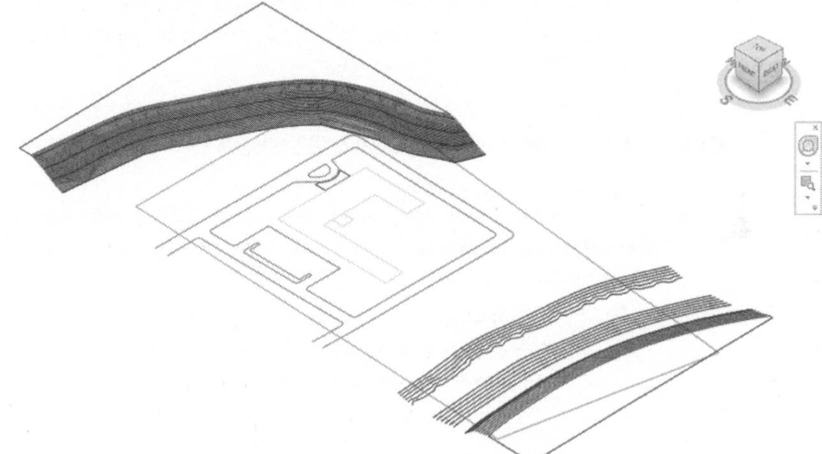

FIGURE 3.31
Select only the layers containing 3D contour information.

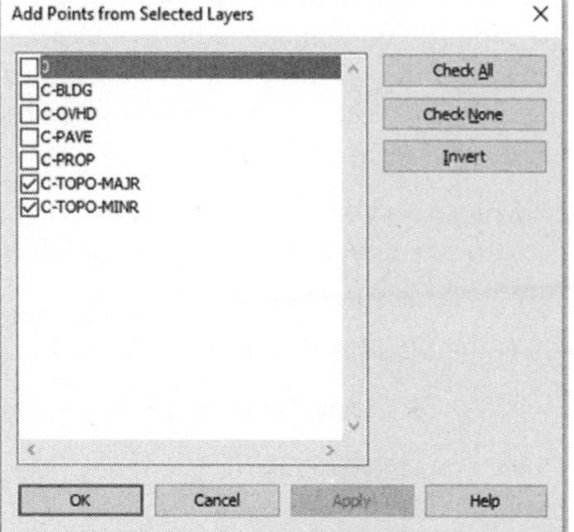

Creating a Toposurface from a Points File

A less-common method for creating a toposurface, although equally effective when using linked CAD data, is using a points file. A *points file* is a text file that is usually generated from a civil engineering program. It must be a comma-delimited file (TXT or CSV format) in which the x-, y-, and z-coordinates of the points are the first numeric values in the file. In the following exercise, we have provided a sample points file that was exported from AutoCAD Civil 3D using the XYZ_LIDAR Classification (comma-delimited) format setting:

1. Open the file `c03-Site-Points-Start.rvt`, which can be downloaded from this book's web page.
2. Download the file `c03-Points.csv` from this book's web page to your local computer.
3. Activate the Site plan in the Project Browser.
4. From the Massing & Site tab on the ribbon, click the Toposurface button. In the Tools panel of the Modify | Edit Surface tab, select Create From Import and then choose Specify Points File.
5. Navigate to the `c03-Points.csv` file and click Open. Note that if you were using a TXT format file, you would change the Files of Type option to Comma Delimited Text.
6. In the Format dialog box, select Decimal Feet. It is important to understand the units of the values in the points file to ensure that the toposurface will be created at the correct scale. Click OK to close the dialog box.
7. Click the Finish Surface button in the contextual ribbon to complete the toposurface. Open the Default 3D view to examine your results. You may have to use the Zoom To Fit command to see the extent of the new toposurface.

Modifying the Surface with Subregion

The points file example in the previous exercise represents a section of terrain across Lake Mead, Nevada. If you wanted to define an area of the toposurface with a different material but not change the geometry of the overall surface, you would use the Subregion tool. In the following exercise, you will use this tool to create a region that will represent the water of the lake:

1. Download and open the file `c03-Site-Lake.rvt` from this book's website, and then activate the Site plan from the Project Browser. In this view, there are dashed detail lines that represent the edge of the water.
2. Go to the Massing & Site tab in the ribbon and click the Subregion tool.
3. Switch to Pick Lines mode in the Draw panel of the contextual ribbon.
4. Hover your mouse pointer over one of the dashed detail lines on the left side of the surface, Tab-select the chain of lines, and then click to select them. You will see a purple sketch line appear.
5. Repeat step 4 for the dashed detail lines at the right side of the surface.
6. Switch to Line mode in the Draw panel of the contextual ribbon, and draw a line connecting each open end of the water edge lines, as shown in Figure 3.32.

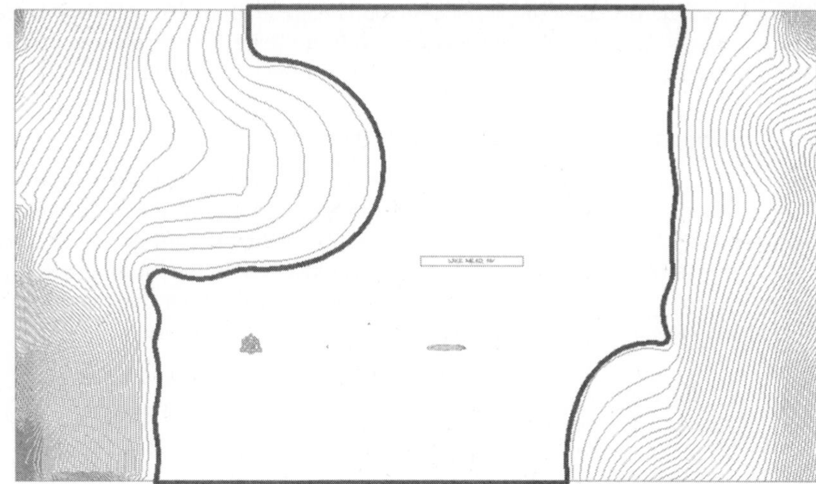

FIGURE 3.32 The sketch boundary for a subregion must be a closed loop but can overlap the edge of the toposurface.

7. Click Finish Edit Mode in the contextual ribbon to complete the subregion.
8. Activate the Default 3D view and select the subregion you created in the previous steps.
9. In the Properties palette, select the Material parameter, and click the ellipsis button to open the Material Browser dialog box. Locate and select the material named Site - Water. Note that you can easily find this material by typing **Water** in the search field at the top of the dialog box.
10. Click OK to close the Material Browser dialog box; you will see the results in the 3D view, as shown in Figure 3.33.

FIGURE 3.33 The subregion is assigned a different material for visualization purposes.

When you use the Subregion tool, the geometry of the original surface remains unchanged. If you no longer need the subregion, you can select it and delete it. Be aware that topographic surfaces cannot display surface patterns assigned to materials.

Using the Split Surface Tool

If you need to divide a topographic surface into separate parts for the purpose of editing the geometry, you can use the Split Surface tool. With this tool, you can sketch a single line along which the surface will be divided into two editable entities. These separate entities can be recombined later using the Merge Surfaces tool. In the following exercise, you will split a topographic surface and edit some of the points. Remember that you can also use Split Surface to delete a portion of a topographic surface. Here are the steps:

1. Open the file `c03-Site-Tools.rvt` or `c03-Site-Tools-Metric.rvt` you saved in the "Creating a Toposurface by Placing Points" exercise.
2. Activate the Site plan in the Project Browser.
3. Go to the Massing & Site tab in the ribbon and click the Split Surface tool. Remember that you should use the Subregion tool if you plan to assign a different material only to the split region of the original surface.
4. Select the topographic surface and you will enter Sketch mode. Using the Line mode in the Draw panel of the contextual ribbon, draw two lines that overlap the edges of the surface, as shown in Figure 3.34.

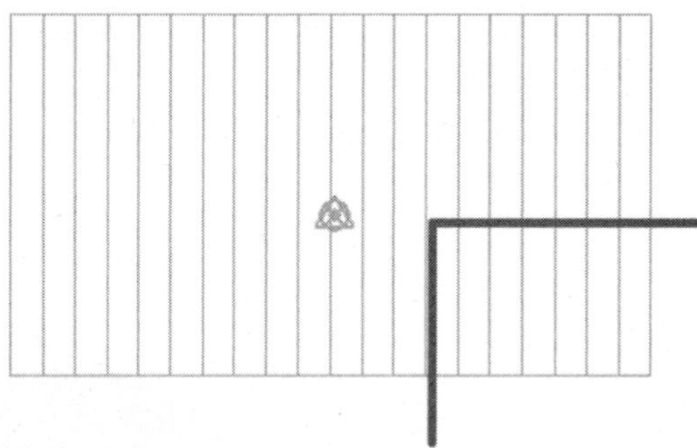

Figure 3.34 Sketch lines that overlap the edge of the topographic surface.

5. Click Finish Edit Mode in the ribbon, and you will see the split surface highlighted in blue.
6. Activate the Default 3D view from the Quick Access Toolbar or from the View tab.
7. Turn off the Section Box option in the Properties palette.
8. Select the split surface, and click the Edit Surface tool in the Modify | Topography tab of the ribbon.
9. Select the point at the outer corner of the topographic surface, and change the Elevation value in the Options bar from 20′-0″ (6000 mm) to **10′-0″** (**3000** mm).

10. Click the green check (Finish Edit Mode) in the contextual ribbon, and you will see the result shown in Figure 3.35.

FIGURE 3.35
A split region after editing the elevation of a corner point

11. To illustrate the difference between a split surface and other topographic surface edits, select the main surface and click Edit Surface in the contextual ribbon. Select the point at the upper corner opposite from the split region and change the Elevation value to **10′-0″** (**3000** mm). Notice the difference in how the surface slope is interpolated between the other points on the surface (Figure 3.36).

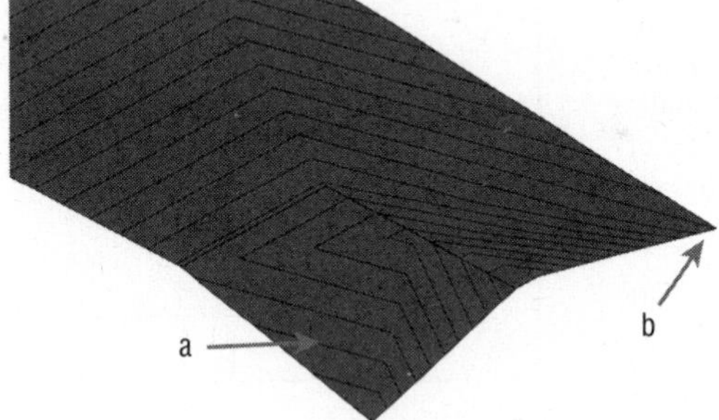

FIGURE 3.36
Compare the difference between an edited split region (a) and an edited point directly on the surface (b).

Creating a Building Pad

A *building pad* in Revit terminology is a unique model element that resembles a floor. It can have a thickness and compound structure, it is associated with a level, and it can be sloped using slope arrows while you're sketching its boundary. The building pad is different from a floor because it will automatically cut through a toposurface, defining the outline for your building's cellar or basement.

The process of creating a building pad is virtually identical to that of creating a floor. Let's run through a quick exercise to create a building pad in a sample project:

1. Open the file `c03-Site-Pad.rvt`, which can be downloaded from this book's web page.

2. Activate the floor plan named Site in the Project Browser. You will see an existing topographic surface and property line. Notice that reference planes were created to demarcate the required zoning setbacks from the property line. Foundation walls have been created within these reference planes.

Note that you don't have to create a property line and walls before creating a building pad. You might create a building pad before any other building elements. Just realize that you can use the Pick Walls mode to associate the boundary of the building pad with the foundation walls.

3. Activate the Cellar floor plan from the Project Browser.
4. Go to the Massing & Site tab in the ribbon, and click the Building Pad button. In the Properties palette, change the Height Offset From Level value to **0**.
5. Switch to Pick Walls mode in the Draw panel of the contextual ribbon, and then pick the inside edges of the four foundation walls. You can use the Tab-select method to place all four lines at once.
6. Click the Finish Edit Mode button in the contextual ribbon to complete the sketch, and then double-click the section head in the plan view to examine your results. Notice that the top of the building pad is at the Cellar level, and the poché of the topographic surface has been removed in the space of the cellar (Figure 3.37).

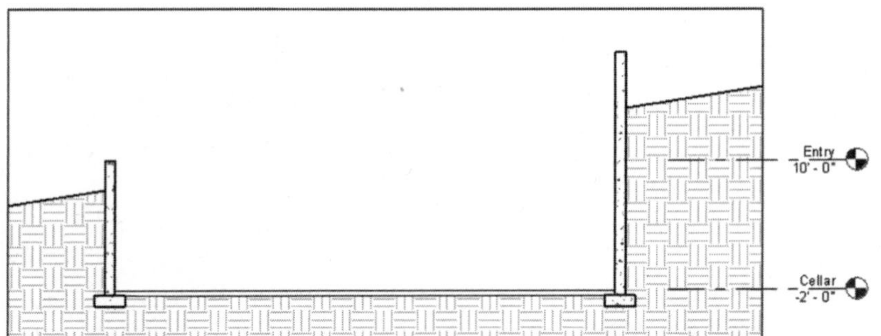

FIGURE 3.37 This section view illustrates how the building pad adjusts the extents of the topographic surface.

If you are working on a project that has a complex site condition that might require several building pads at different elevations, you should be aware that the pads cannot overlap; however, they can share common boundary edges. To help avoid this situation before you get too involved in modeling any of the pads in your project, try using detail lines in your site plan to lay out the pad design first.

ADJUSTING THE SECTION POCHÉ FOR TOPOGRAPHIC SURFACES

If you would like to customize the settings for the fill pattern and depth of poché, click the dialog launcher at the bottom of the Model Site panel in the Massing & Site tab of the ribbon. This will open the Site Settings dialog box, shown here.

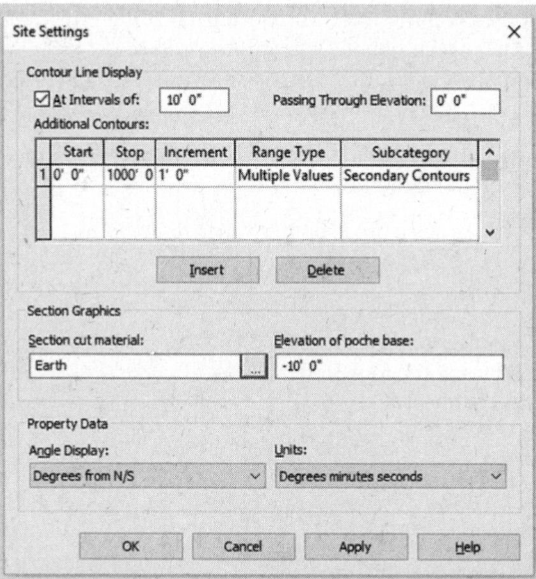

Site Settings

Contour Line Display

At Intervals of: 10' 0" Passing Through Elevation: 0' 0"

Additional Contours:

	Start	Stop	Increment	Range Type	Subcategory
1	0' 0"	1000' 0	1' 0"	Multiple Values	Secondary Contours

Insert Delete

Section Graphics

Section cut material: Earth

Elevation of poche base: -10' 0"

Property Data

Angle Display: Degrees from N/S

Units: Degrees minutes seconds

OK Cancel Apply Help

As you can see in this dialog box, you can change the Section Cut Material and the Elevation Of Poche Base settings. Note that the elevation value is in relation to the Project Base Point. You can also adjust the display format of contour lines shown on topographic surfaces, as well as the units displayed by property lines.

Generating Property Lines

Property lines are used to delineate the boundary of the lot within which your building will be constructed. These special types of lines are different from simple model lines or detail lines because they can be tagged with standard property line labels that will display segment lengths along with bearings. The property line object can also report its area in a special tag.

You can create a property line in one of two ways: by sketching lines or by entering distances and bearings in a table. In the following exercise, you will create a simple property line by sketching and converting the sketched property line into a table of distances and bearings for comparison:

1. Open `c03-Site-Prop-Lines.rvt` or `c03-Site-Prop-Lines-Metric.rvt`, which you can download from this book's companion web page. Activate the Site plan view in the Project Browser.
2. Go to the Massing & Site tab and click the Property Line button. When prompted by the Create Property Line dialog box, choose Create By Sketching.
3. Switch to the Rectangle tool in the Draw panel of the contextual ribbon and draw a rectangle measuring 120′ × 70′ (36 m × 21 m).
4. Click the Finish Edit Mode button in the contextual ribbon to complete the sketch.

5. With the property line still selected, click the Edit Table button in the Modify | Property Lines tab of the ribbon. You will be prompted with a warning that you cannot return to Sketch mode once the property line has been converted to a table of distances and bearings. Click Yes to continue.

   You will now see each vertex of the property line expressed as a distance and a bearing, as shown in Figure 3.38.

6. Click OK to close the Property Lines dialog box.

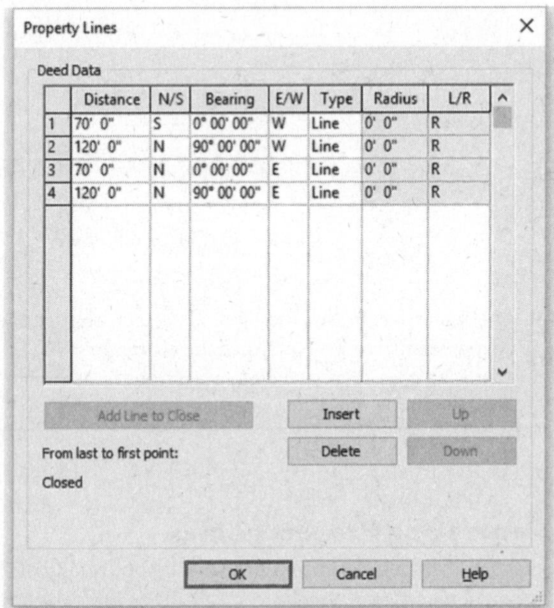

FIGURE 3.38 A property line can be defined in a table of distances and bearings.

TAGGING PROPERTY LINES WITH AREA

In standard construction documentation, it is customary to annotate each vertex of a property line with its distance and bearing. There are two different types of tags you can use to annotate property lines. In the following exercise, you will load these two types from the Revit default library and tag each segment of the property line, as well as display the area contained within it.

1. Go to the Insert tab of the ribbon and click the Load Family button. Navigate to the Revit default library; double-click the Annotations folder and then the Civil folder.

2. Locate the following files and select them both by pressing the Ctrl key (the equivalent metric library families are shown in parentheses):

   - `Property Line Tag.rfa` (`M_Property Line Tag.rfa`)
   - `Property Tag - SF.rfa` (`M_Property Tag.rfa`)

3. Click Open to load both families.
4. Go to the Annotate tab of the ribbon and click Tag By Category, and then deselect the Leader option in the Options bar.
5. Click each segment of the property line to place the tags indicating the distance and bearing, as shown in Figure 3.39.

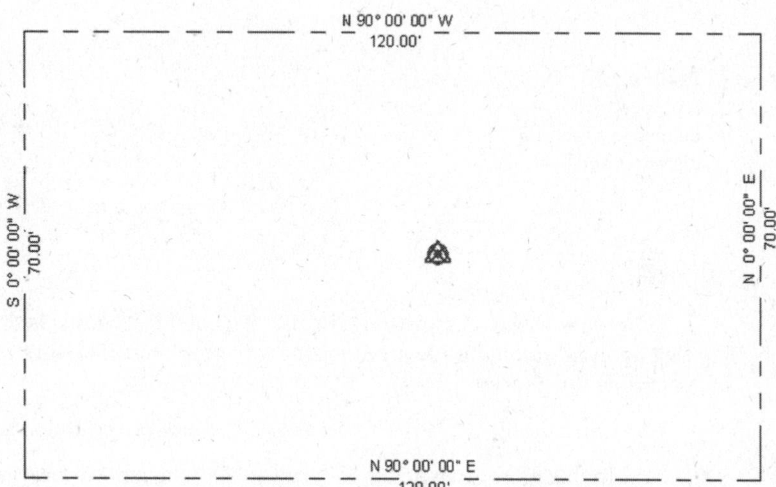

FIGURE 3.39 Tags are applied to display the distance and bearing of each segment of the property line.

Now that you have tagged the individual vertices of the property line, it is time to display the area within the property line. This process is not the same as applying an area tag because an area object doesn't exist for the property line. Instead, the annotation family `Property Tag - SF.rfa` (`M_Property Tag.rfa`) is designed to apply to the property lines when all its segments are selected.

You can try this with the property line you created earlier. Go back to the Annotate tab in the ribbon and click Tag By Category. Instead of picking a single vertex of the property line, hover your mouse pointer over one segment and use Tab-select to highlight the entire chain of property line segments. Click to place the property area tag. Click the question mark above the area to change the name of the property line, as shown in Figure 3.40.

Cut/Fill Schedules

As we mentioned earlier, Revit site tools are not meant to replace civil engineering software programs. We have shown you how to create a topographical surface in a variety of ways as well as some methods of modifying these objects. There is also a way to quickly quantify how much earth is displaced by proposed changes to existing topography. This is commonly referred to as a cut/fill schedule.

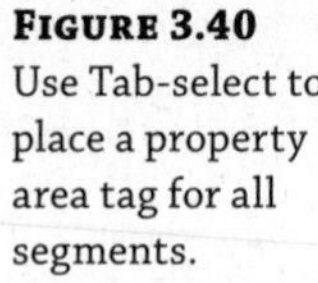

FIGURE 3.40
Use Tab-select to place a property area tag for all segments.

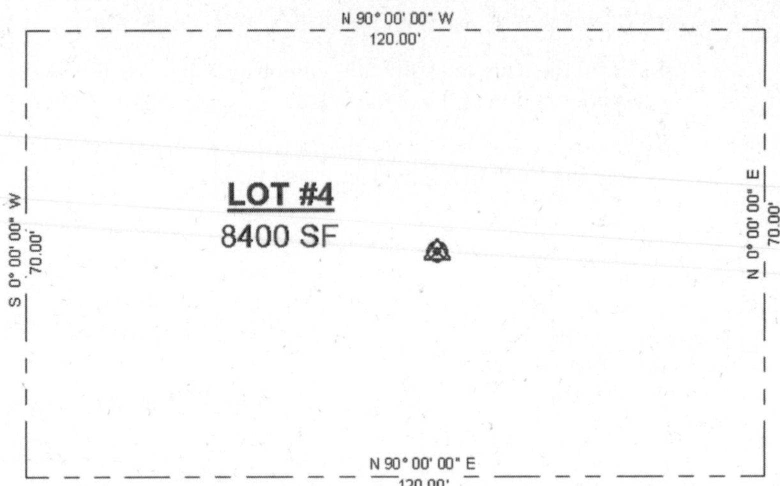

One easy way to demonstrate the use of a cut/fill schedule is through the creation of a building pad that automatically modifies the topographic surface. Let's go through a quick exercise to examine this process:

1. Open the file `c03-Site-Cut-Fill.rvt`, which can be downloaded from this book's web page.

   In this file, open a default 3D view, select the toposurface, and you will notice that the topographic surface has been assigned to the Existing phase in the Properties palette.

2. From the View tab in the ribbon, click Schedules and then select Schedule/Quantities to open the New Schedule dialog box.

3. From the Category list, choose Topography, set Phase to New Construction, and then click OK.

4. In the Fields tab of the Schedule Properties dialog box, choose Name, Projected Area, Net Cut/Fill, Phase Created, and Phase Demolished, clicking Add after each one. Click OK to close the dialog box.

5. While you are still in the working view of the schedule, go to the Properties palette and set the Phase Filter of the schedule to Show Previous + New. This will allow only the modified toposurfaces affected by the Graded Region command to appear in the schedule. The complete existing topography will not be listed in the schedule.

6. Activate the Cellar plan from the Project Browser, and create a building pad in the same way you created one earlier in this section.

   After you complete the creation of the building pad and the topographic surface is modified, notice that the Net Cut/Fill values in the topography schedule still have a value of 0. This is because the Graded Region tool must be used on a surface to generate the differences required to calculate what volume must be cut versus filled in the proposed design.

7. Tile the open Revit windows so you can see both the Default 3D view and the topography schedule.
8. On the Massing & Site tab, click the Graded Region tool, and you will see a dialog box appear with two options to continue the command. Choose the option Create A New Toposurface Exactly Like The Existing One. This option creates overlapping existing and proposed surfaces, which will allow the software to schedule the differences between the two as cut or fill volumes.
9. Select the existing toposurface, and you will see the volume values in the topography schedule update to reflect how the excavation for the building pad affected the overall soil. Note that this type of calculation does not account for various construction methods, such as backfilling.
10. Click the Finish Surface icon in the contextual tab of the ribbon to complete the Graded Region command.

Activate the Section 1 view to see the building pad more clearly. Try selecting the building pad and changing the Height Offset From Level value in the Properties palette. Observe how the Net Cut/Fill values change as the pad defines the scope of excavation for the foundation.

You can also make the topography schedule easier to read by assigning descriptive information to each topographic surface. Select the surface and enter a value in the Name field in the Properties palette. Change the name of the main surface to **Existing Grade** and then locate the surface where the building pad is. Change its name to **Pad Area** and observe the topography schedule once again.

SELECTING TOPOSURFACES WITH THE FILTER COMMAND

If you have trouble selecting the toposurfaces, you can select the objects in the drawing window with a crossing window and use the Filter command to select each toposurface.

If you would like to explore the completed project file for this exercise, you can download `c03-Site-Cut-Fill-FINISHED.rvt` from this book's companion web page.

The Bottom Line

Select, modify, and replace elements. Many fundamental interactions are supported by Revit software to select just what you need and to modify elements efficiently.

Master It How can you quickly select only the door tags in a plan view and switch them to another type?

Edit elements interactively. The editing tools in Revit are similar to those found in other CAD and BIM software programs. Tools such as Move, Copy, and Trim are available on the Modify tab of the ribbon.

Master It How do you create a parametric repetition of an element?

Use other editing tools. Beyond the basic editing tools are more advanced commands to help you consistently and intelligently populate a building model with content.

Master It How do you copy model elements in the same location for a multistory building?

Create site context for your project. The site tools allow you to create context for your building models, including topographic surfaces, graded regions, and property lines.

Master It Describe the different methods used to create a topographic surface.

Chapter 4

Configuring Templates and Standards

In this chapter we discuss how to configure and manage standards through the development and use of a project template. Such templates can be rich with information that goes beyond the out-of-the-box content that Autodesk provides. We will present proven methods for establishing template settings and content, as well as explain how the reuse of work will increase productivity with each successive project.

In this chapter, you'll learn to:

- Define settings for graphic quality and consistency
- Organize views for maximum efficiency
- Create custom annotation families
- Start a project with a custom template
- Develop a template management strategy

Introducing Project Templates

Like many other applications, the Autodesk® Revit® Architecture application allows you to start with a basic template and then evolve your own custom templates to suit specific needs. As your knowledge of the software progresses, you will begin to create new and reusable content such as wall types, roof types, ceilings, stairs, tags, and other families in order to meet your design and documentation needs. This is also the case with regard to the graphical language that you or your firm has established and needs to implement within Revit. How you graphically present elements such as text, dimensions, annotations, keynotes, and hatch patterns defines your graphic style of design documentation. In reality, the architectural profession tends to develop stylized graphics to convey design intent, and Revit respects this by enabling the customization of almost all aspects of the project template.

You can configure project templates by one or more of the following methods:

- Predefining all project graphic requirements
- Preloading the model with annotation families and styles
- Defining standard system families

We will explain these methods in greater detail throughout this chapter. For now, know that you can save the completed settings as a new project template (with the filename extension `.rte`) and use these templates whenever you start a new project. You can create templates by using a completely blank project, by saving an existing project as a template, or by using one of the default templates provided with the Revit installation.

To start from scratch, click the Application menu and choose New ➢ Project. In the New Project dialog box, shown in Figure 4.1, choose None for the Template File option, and choose Project Template for the Create New option. Once you click OK, you will be asked to choose a default unit of measurement—imperial or metric. This dialog box also appears when you press Ctrl+N or click New in the Recent Files window.

FIGURE 4.1
Starting a new project template from scratch

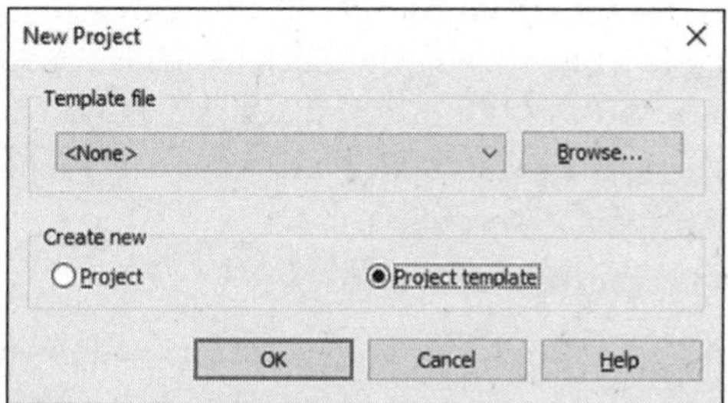

Starting a new project template without a base template requires you to develop *all* common content such as levels, grids, sections, callouts, tags, and model elements. Before you start loading all new graphic content, do a review comparing your requirements to the default symbology. Determine whether you can use or modify existing families before you begin creating new ones to load into your new template. If you have only custom graphics and system families, this approach would be appropriate; however, if much of your graphic style is similar to the defaults, we suggest you start with one of the default templates and edit it as necessary. This is also a much faster approach to get you up and running. You can find these templates by clicking Browse in the Template File area of the New Project dialog box. By default, the template files are installed in the root folder of the templates directory: `C:\ProgramData\Autodesk\RVT 2017\Templates`.

Customizing Project Settings for Graphic Quality

One of the most common complaints from teams implementing Revit software on their first projects is poor graphic quality of printed documents. When you first install the software, only some default settings are defined to approximate a standard graphic appearance of architectural drawings. For example, walls cut in sections are thicker than those shown in projected views and callout boundaries are dashed; however, almost all annotation categories are set to a line weight of 1. Fortunately, you can easily overcome these problems with some basic configuration.

Discovering Object Styles

The primary means of controlling graphic consistency throughout a project is through *object styles*. To access these settings, select the Manage tab and choose Object Styles from the Settings panel. As shown in Figure 4.2, the dialog box is divided into four tabs: Model Objects, Annotation Objects, Analytical Model Objects, and Imported Objects. Settings for Line Weight, Line Color, Line Pattern, and Material are established for each category.

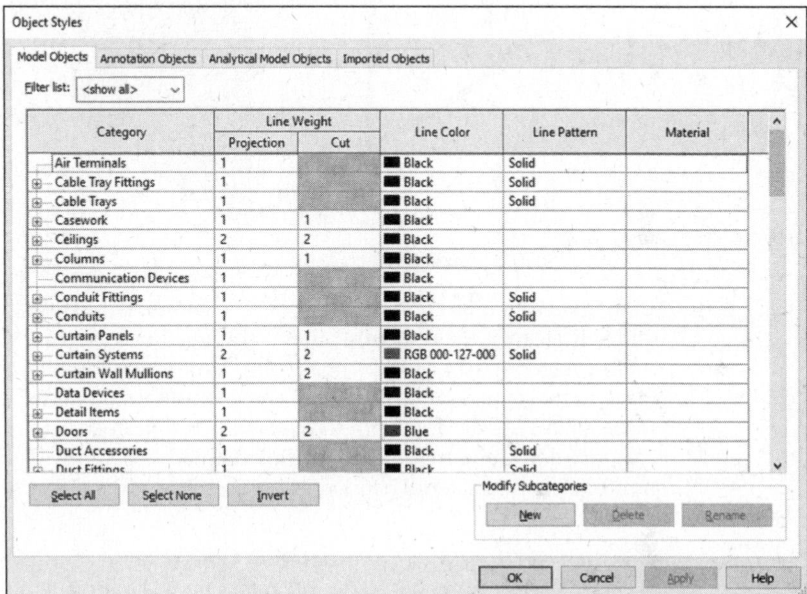

FIGURE 4.2
The Object Styles dialog box gives you graphic control of all Revit categories and their subcategories.

Model Objects The Category column on the Model Objects tab lists all available categories and subcategories of model elements. It is important to note that the subcategories for model and annotation objects are created in families, which are loaded into the project or template. This will be discussed in greater detail in Chapter 14, "Designing with the Family Editor."

The next two columns, under Line Weight, define the line weight used when the elements are displayed in projection or cut view. You use a projection view when you are looking at the object from a distance; you use a cut view when your view plane is intersecting the element as in a section. In some categories, the Cut setting is unavailable; these element categories will never be cut in plan or section views, regardless of the location of the view's cut plane. For categories that enable cut display, you can set element geometry in the Family Editor to follow that rule or not, as shown in Figure 4.3.

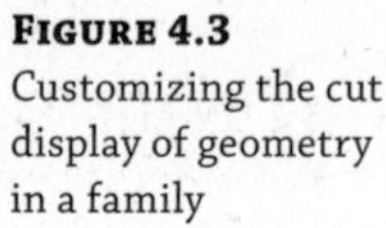

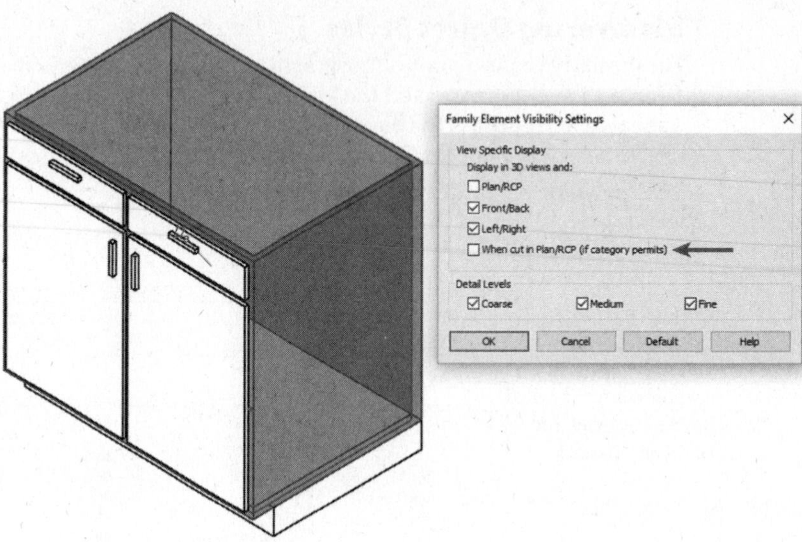

FIGURE 4.3
Customizing the cut display of geometry in a family

Line Color and Line Pattern allow you to customize the display properties of each category and subcategory, but remember that printing a Revit view is WYSIWYG (what you see is what you get)—colors will print as colors unless you override them to print as grayscale or black in the Print Setup dialog box. The last column, Material, allows you to define a default material to be associated with the category or subcategory in case family components in that category don't have materials explicitly defined. If a family has materials set to By Category, it references the material defined in the corresponding object style within the project environment.

Annotation Objects The Annotation Objects tab is similar to the Model Objects tab except there are no material definitions. There is also only one column for line weight (Projection) because lines do not have three-dimensional properties like model objects and cannot be "cut."

Analytical Model Objects This tab allows you to color the various physical conditions in the building that correspond to the building's structural components. Analytical settings only apply to structural and MEP analysis tools within Revit and are beyond the scope of this book.

Imported Objects You can control the graphic appearance of layers (DWG) and levels (DGN) within linked or imported CAD files throughout the project on the Imported Objects tab of the Object Styles dialog box; however, we will cover this in greater detail in Chapter 7, "Interoperability: Working Multiplatform."

ASSIGNING LINE WEIGHT 1

You may want to avoid assigning line weight 1 to objects because this is the weight used by most fill patterns. Reserving its use will help object profiles stand out compared to their patterns.

Using Line Settings

You can use lines in a variety of ways. Some lines relate to obvious tools, such as detail lines and model lines, whereas you can place others with filled regions and by using the Linework tool. Lines also relate to the graphic representation of model and annotation elements, as previously discussed. Achieving the desired graphic quality requires a review of line weights, patterns, and styles.

SETTING LINE WEIGHTS

To open the line weight settings, click the Manage tab and choose Additional Settings ➤ Line Weights. The dialog box shown in Figure 4.4 manages the printed line weights relative to a numbered assignment from 1 to 16. For model objects, heavier line weights vary between view scales. If you require more granular control between scales, click the Add button to insert another scale value column and edit the line weights as required. In the Perspective Line Weights and Annotation Line Weights tabs there is only one column to specify line weights. This is because annotation is always displayed at 1:1 scale and perspective views are not defined at any measurable scale.

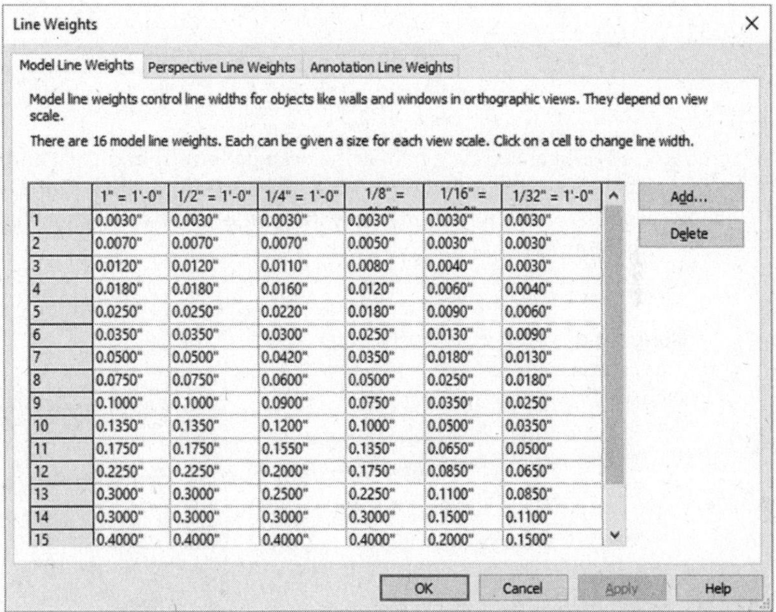

FIGURE 4.4 Model line weights vary depending on the view scale.

We recommend that you first customize the graphic appearance of model and annotation elements with object styles before trying to manipulate any of the information in the Line Weights dialog box. You should attempt to refine the line weight settings only with a rigorous investigation of printed views in multiple scales, because changes in one area can have an impact on several others.

SETTING LINE PATTERNS

Line patterns are created from a repetitive series of dashes, spaces, and dots. To edit or create line patterns, switch to the Manage tab and choose Additional Settings ➢ Line Patterns. The Line Patterns dialog box, shown in Figure 4.5, displays a list of existing line patterns in the project.

FIGURE 4.5
This dialog box displays all line patterns in the project.

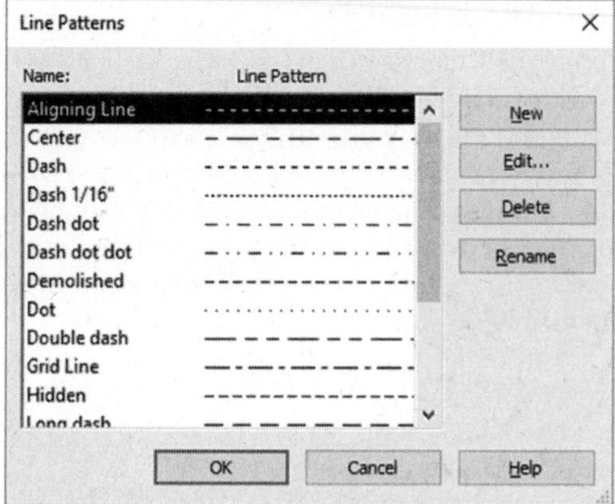

To edit an existing pattern, select a pattern from the list and then click the Edit button. Click New to create your own patterns. You create and edit patterns by specifying dash and space lengths, which will form a repeating sequence, as shown in Figure 4.6. For dots, a length value is not required.

FIGURE 4.6
Line patterns consist of dashes, spaces, and dots.

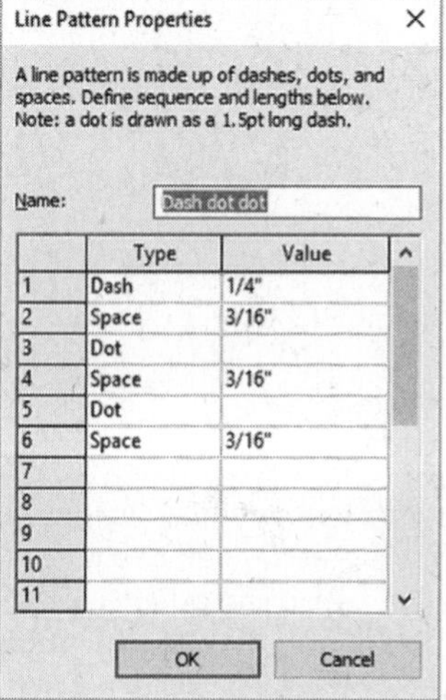

Using Caution When Deleting Line Patterns

Before deleting a line pattern, you must verify that it hasn't been used anywhere in your project because Revit does not have any method for purging unused line patterns. You can do so only by manually checking Object Styles, Line Styles, and Visibility/Graphic Overrides. If you fail to do so, all line styles using the deleted pattern will be assigned as Solid.

Frequently, a line pattern is required to include a symbol or text for elements such as fence lines, piping, or underground utilities. In Autodesk® AutoCAD® software, shape definitions can be used within linetype definitions to achieve the desired results. In Revit, these special lines can be created as line-based detail components. Samples of this type of custom line can be found by downloading the file `c04-Lines.rvt` or `c04-Lines-Metric.rvt` from this book's companion web page at `www.sybex.com/go/masteringrevit2017`.

Creating a New Line Pattern

Follow these steps to create a new simple line pattern:

1. Switch to the Manage tab and choose Additional Settings ➢ Line Patterns.
2. In the Line Pattern dialog box, click New.
3. In the Name field, type **MARA Pattern**.
4. Define the sequence, as shown in the following image.

   Any dash or dot must be followed by a space, and all dashes and spaces must have a defined length.

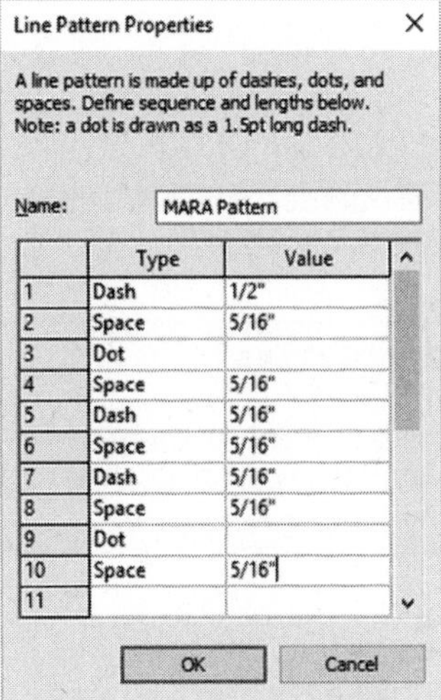

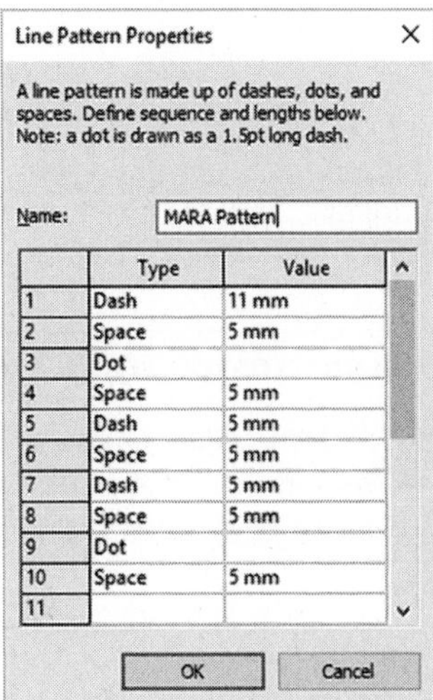

5. Confirm by clicking OK.

   The resulting line pattern looks like this:

Setting Line Styles

Now that we have discussed the basic components of lines—weight and pattern—the two are combined with a color to create *line styles* for use in detail lines, model lines, filled regions, and masking regions. They are also available when the Linework tool is used to override a part of a model element. To open the Line Styles dialog box (shown in Figure 4.7), switch to the Manage tab and choose Additional Settings ➢ Line Styles. Note that you may need to expand the list of line styles by clicking the plus sign next to Lines.

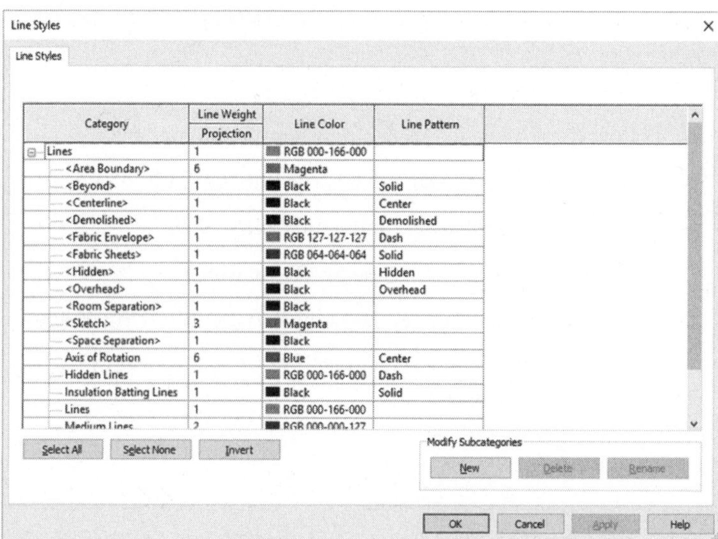

Figure 4.7
Line styles consist of weight, color, and pattern.

In the Line Styles dialog box, notice that some of the style names are bracketed—for example, <Hidden>. These are internal, "system" types of lines that cannot be renamed or deleted; however, their weight, color, and pattern can be modified.

Using Caution When Deleting Line Styles

If you delete a line style used in a project, any elements using the deleted style will be unable to reference that style anymore. The lines assigned to the deleted style will be reassigned to a common style such as Thin Lines—possibly producing undesirable results.

Establishing the best styles for your templates will be completely up to you, but we will offer some proven examples for inspiration. First, realize that the application already uses common line styles such as Thin Lines, Medium Lines, and Wide Lines. If you are creating a complete array of customized line styles for your colleagues to use, rename the out-of-the-box styles to fit into your graphic standard.

One common approach is to create line styles organized by their weight number along with any variable to their appearance, such as (3) Gray Dashed or +Line 01. The parentheses (or the use of any special characters at the beginning of the line's name) keep your custom line styles sorted to the top of the list in the Line Styles dialog box as well as in the Type Selector when you're using a line-based tool. This approach has proven to be effective and efficient when creating details in drafting views or generating fill or masking regions.

Another approach reserves certain line styles for special circumstances where lines represent aspects of a building in a plan, elevation, or section and must be assigned to a specific layer when views are exported in CAD format. For example, the crossing lines typically used to indicate an area-in plan that is "Open to Below" may need to be assigned to the CAD layer A-FLOR-BELW. This is difficult if you used a line style based solely on weight and pattern such as (2) Dashed. You cannot separately assign that line style to A-FLOR-BELW for the floor plan export and A-DETL-THIN for all other exports. Here are some examples of line styles you could create:

- Open to Below
- ADA Circles
- Curbs
- Fire Rating

In summary, take care to understand the different settings when you are beginning to customize graphic settings for lines in the Revit template. To change the displayed weight of an element in a project, you should make changes not in Line Weights but rather through the Object Styles dialog box. For example, if you want to increase the cut line weight of a wall already set to (5), do not increase the value of (5) in the Line Weights dialog box. You would change this value by selecting (6) or (7) as the cut weight of a wall in the Object Styles dialog box.

Defining Materials

Defining materials in your project template is another important task that can help maintain graphic consistency in many other areas. Materials drive the graphic representation of elements, not just in a rendered view but also in hidden line views that are 2D or 3D. They are also responsible for cleanups between model elements because materials can merge with one another when elements of the same material are joined. In Figure 4.8, the surface patterns and colors are all derived from the material assigned to each element.

FIGURE 4.8
Materials define the surface and cut patterns, color, and render material of the elements.

Materials in Revit are organized into groups of properties called *assets*, consisting of the following: Identity, Graphics, Appearance, Physical, and Thermal. Let us explore these by opening the Material Browser. Switch to the Manage tab and choose Materials on the Settings panel to open the Material Browser (Figure 4.9). The left side of the dialog box shows the materials that exist in the active project, including a search bar to help you quickly find materials for editing. Click the icon just below the search bar to show or hide the Library Panel. On the right, the selected material's assets are displayed as tabs.

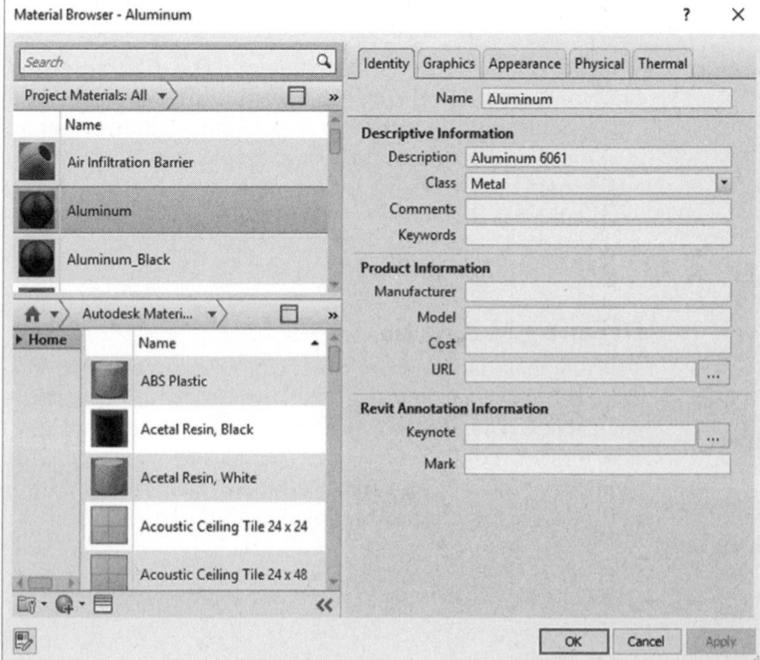

FIGURE 4.9
Manage material properties using the Material Browser.

Material Properties

Select any material in the Project Materials list and we'll step through each of the asset tabs.

Identity Defines schedule values and keynotes for materials. Specifying correct identity data for your standard or typical materials will increase efficiency when you're using annotation such as material tags as well as facilitate quality management by aligning model data such as manufacturer, model, and mark with your project specifications. In Figure 4.10, we've entered some sample identity data. The use of material identity data in project annotation is also discussed in Chapter 18, "Annotating Your Design."

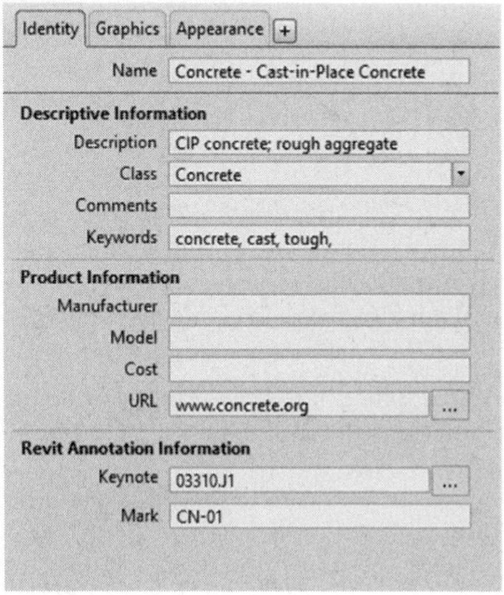

Figure 4.10
Use identity data to classify, find, tag, and schedule materials.

Graphics Defines shading color, surface patterns, and cut patterns. These properties will determine how a model element displays in non-rendered views (Hidden Line, Shaded, or Consistent Colors):

Shading Defines the color and transparency of a material. Note that the color can be dependent on the material's render appearance. If the Use Render Appearance option is selected, the color and transparency are adopted from the Appearance asset settings and the shading controls will be disabled.

Surface Pattern Allows the selection of a *model pattern* to be displayed on the faces of elements in elevation, plan, and 3D views. Note that a material's surface pattern does not appear in rendered views; a pattern can be defined in the Appearance asset tab.

Cut Pattern Allows the selection of a *drafting pattern* to be displayed when an element is cut in a model view. Some elements can't be cut, as discussed previously in this chapter; in these cases, this setting has no effect on the graphic display and the pattern will not display.

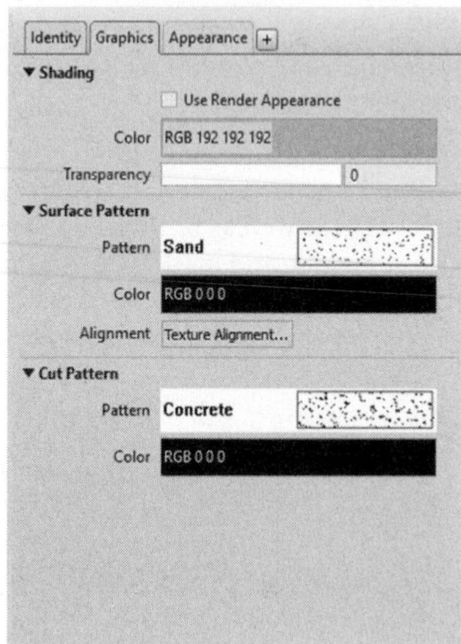

Appearance Defines rendering attributes for use in Realistic and Ray Trace display modes as well as renderings. These properties will become visible only when you render a view and will not affect other graphic display styles, unless the Use Render Appearance option is selected in the Graphics asset under Shading.

Identity, Graphics, and Appearance are the three assets that are required for every material in Revit. You can add Physical and Thermal assets for analysis, if necessary.

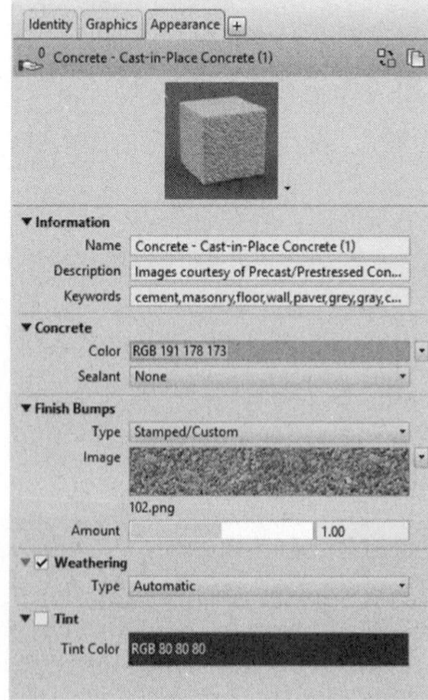

Physical Defines physical properties of a material for analysis.

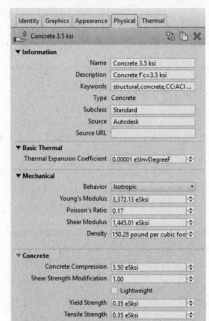

Identity | Graphics | Appearance | Physical | Thermal

Concrete 3.5 ksi

▼ Information

Name	Concrete 3.5 ksi
Description	Concrete f'c=3.5 ksi
Keywords	structural,concrete,CC:ACI ...
Type	Concrete
Subclass	Standard
Source	Autodesk
Source URL	

▼ Basic Thermal

Thermal Expansion Coefficient	0.00001 eSInvDegreeF

▼ Mechanical

Behavior	Isotropic
Young's Modulus	3,372.13 eSksi
Poisson's Ratio	0.17
Shear Modulus	1,445.01 eSksi
Density	150.28 pound per cubic foo

▼ Concrete

Concrete Compression	3.50 eSksi
Shear Strength Modification	1.00
	☐ Lightweight
Yield Strength	0.35 eSksi
Tensile Strength	0.35 eSksi

Thermal Defines thermal properties of a material for analysis.

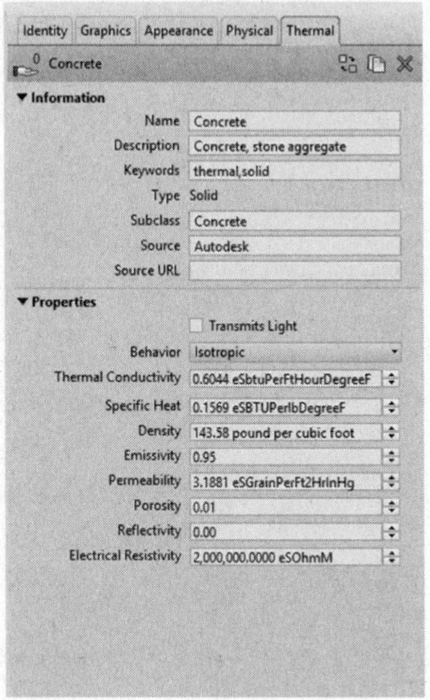

Adding and Replacing Material Assets

You can also replace an asset for Appearance, Physical, or Thermal properties with one from any asset library. Let's review the process to add a new asset to a material. To complete the following exercises, download and open `c04-Materials.rvt` from this book's web page.

1. Select the material Concrete - Cast-In-Place Concrete from the Project Materials list.
2. Click the plus button in the tabbed list of assets and then select Physical.

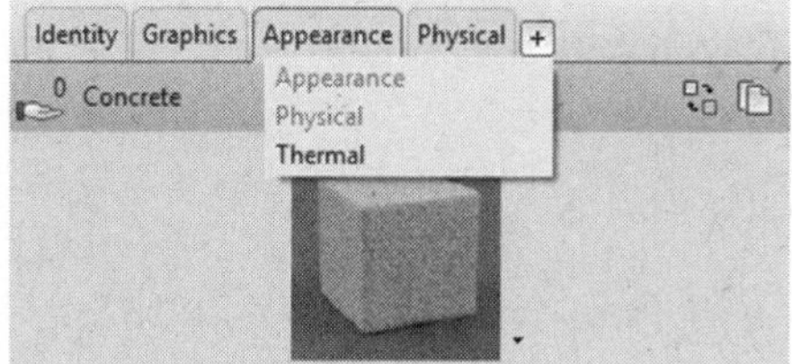

3. The Asset Browser dialog box will open (Figure 4.11). In the asset selection tree at the left, expand the Autodesk Physical Assets tree and navigate to Concrete and then Standard. Find the asset named Concrete 3.5 ksi, and with the mouse pointer hovered over the asset, click the arrow located at the right end of the asset listing.
4. Click the X to close the Asset Browser and return to the Material Browser.

   You will see a new Physical Asset tab next to the Appearance tab.

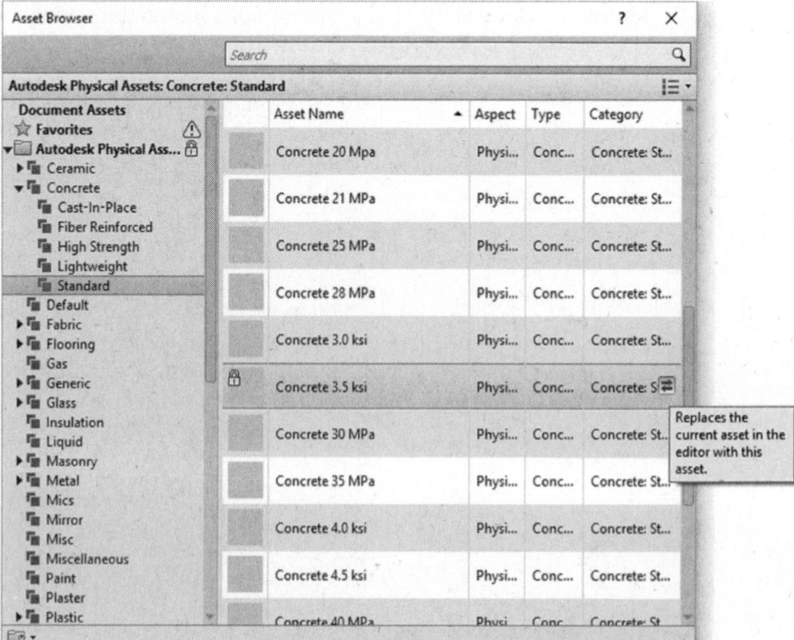

Figure 4.11
Use the Asset Browser to access material assets in the document or a material library.

You cannot change any of the asset properties in the Autodesk Physical Assets library; however, after an asset has been assigned to a project (document), you can change the values. Let's experiment with this process in a quick exercise. Remember that altering any physical or thermal assets may produce undesirable results in analysis or simulation.

1. Continuing from the previous exercise, make sure the Material Browser is open and the Concrete - Cast-In-Place Concrete material is selected. Select the Physical Asset tab.
2. Click the Duplicate This Asset icon at the top of the tab.

   It should change the name of the asset to Concrete 3.5 ksi(1). To change the name of an asset, expand the Information drop-down menu and click in the Name field. Change the name to **Concrete 3.5 ksi (Custom)**.

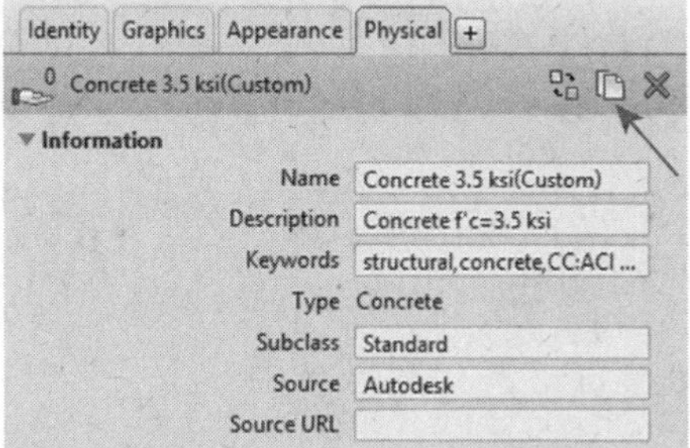

3. Change the Source field to your name and then expand the Concrete drop-down menu. Change the Shear Strength Modification to **1.75**.
4. Return to the Project Materials list and select Cast-In-Place.

   We will now add the customized physical asset to this project material.
5. Click the plus button in the tabbed list of assets and select Physical.
6. In the Asset Browser, scroll to the top of the list of assets and select Document Assets. From this list, you will find Concrete 3.5 ksi (Custom). Hover the mouse pointer over this asset and click the arrow at the end of the row to add it to the selected material.

Another way you can quickly change assets is by using the Replace Asset command. Instead of manually changing each asset property, simply select a material in the Material Browser and in one of the asset tabs, click the Replace Asset icon. Let us explore this functionality with another quick exercise:

1. With the Material Browser still open, select the material named Concrete - Precast Concrete and then select the Appearance tab.
2. Click the Replace This Asset icon in the Appearance tab.
3. In the Asset Browser, navigate to the Appearance Library folder and then click on Concrete.

   Notice that the list of assets is automatically filtered to show only those assets with the Aspect field specified as Appearance.

4. Select the Smooth Precast Structural asset and double-click it, or click the replace arrow at the end of the row, as shown in Figure 4.12.
5. Click the X to close the Asset Browser, and then click OK to close the Material Browser.

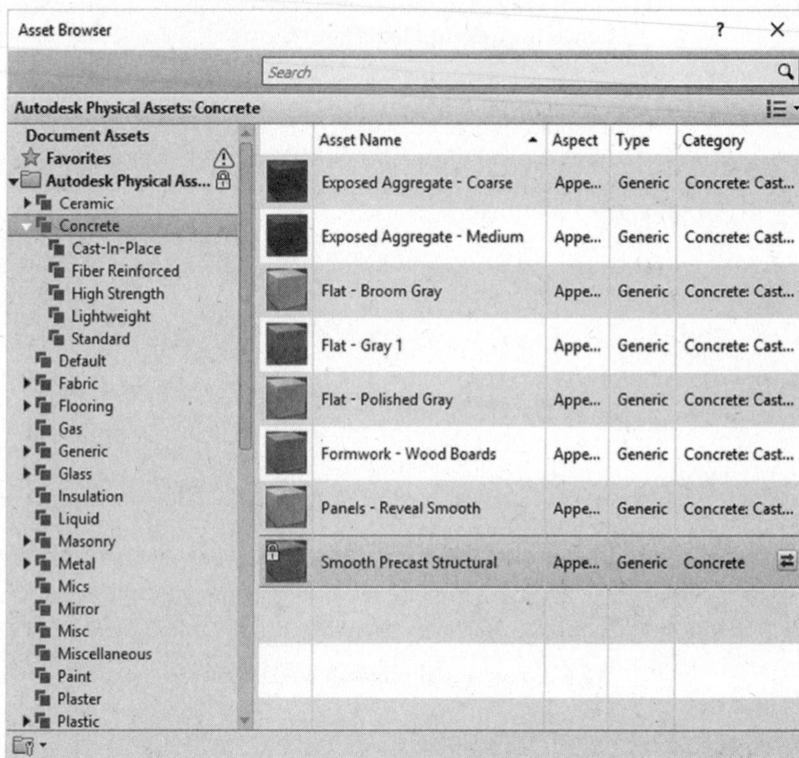

FIGURE 4.12
The Asset Browser can also be used to replace an asset assigned to a material.

PLANNING MATERIAL STRATEGIES

It may seem impossible to imagine all the materials you will need in a project, which may make the process of building a template seem daunting. Think of the basic materials you're likely to use—wood, brick, concrete, glass, and so on—and build from those. Remember, a template is just a starting point, and you can always expand it. If you create a number of high-quality materials over the course of a project, use the Transfer Project Standards function to copy those materials back into your templates. You can also create custom material libraries for your own reuse or for larger project teams.

Your organization's existing graphic standards taxonomy is likely the starting place when you are looking to manage materials. If there is not an existing system, you can create one based on the workflows of your teams. When you start to organize materials by name, there are many prevailing theories too numerous to list here, but here are a few suggestions:

- **By Type:** Each material is prefixed with a descriptor such as *Metal, Paint, Carpet, Wood,* and so on.
- **By Use:** Each material is prefixed with a description of its application, such as *Cladding, Interior, Exterior, Site,* and so on.
- **Alphabetical:** Materials have no prefixes.

- **By CSI Division:** Each material is prefixed with a MasterFormat numerical descriptor corresponding to its specification section.
- **By Mark:** Each material is prefixed with the designation of its Mark annotation parameter (for example, WD01-Wood-Cherry).

Whatever naming convention you choose for materials, the Material Browser can help you organize and manage them efficiently. First, note that you can change the display of the material list, including sorting options, by clicking the icon at the upper right, as shown in Figure 4.13. You can also filter the list of materials according to the Class property by clicking the arrow at the upper right.

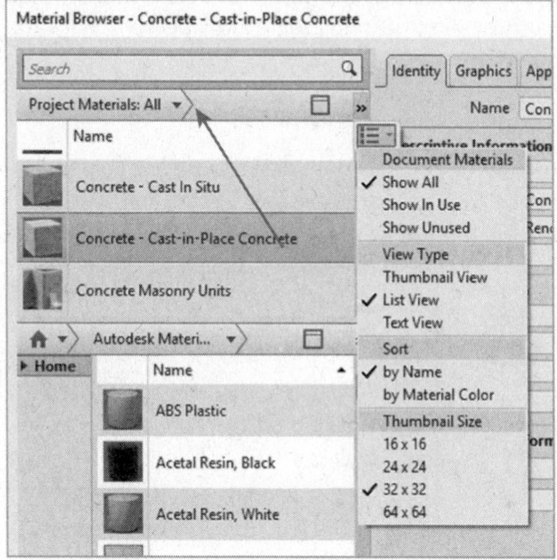

FIGURE 4.13 Accessing different sorting options in the Material Browser

You can also use the Search bar to quickly find matching text in any material property field. For example, try typing **sample** in the Search bar and the list will reflect those materials that include that term in the Keywords property.

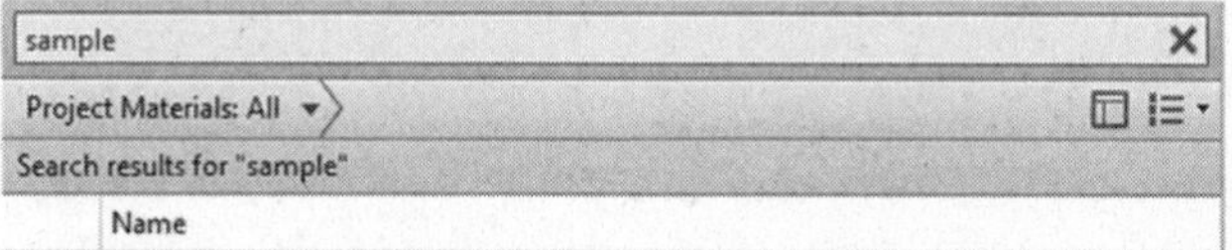

CREATING A SIMPLE EXTERIOR GLAZING MATERIAL

In the early phases of design, you may want to keep the level of detail to a minimum. In fact, guidelines for modeling levels of development may be established as part of a BIM execution plan. (See AIA G202-2013 Project Building Information Modeling Protocol Form at `www.aia.org/contractdocs` or the BIM execution planning guide from Penn State at `bim.psu.edu`. You can also reference a Model Progression Specification at `www.vicosoftware.com/model-progression-specification`.) To simplify the creation of exterior enclosures such as a curtain wall, try creating a glass material with a surface pattern approximating the layout dimensions of a curtain wall system (such as 5′ × 12′ or 1.5 m × 3.5 m). Then create a generic wall type using this material, and you will have a much lighter wall type to explore design options with great ease.

Defining Fill Patterns

Materials are often represented with simple hatch patterns. For any material used, you can define a *surface pattern* and a *cut pattern*. For simple parallel hatches and crosshatches, you can use the patterns already supplied or you can make your own patterns.

For more complex patterns, you need to import an external pattern file (with the filename extension `.pat`). Such pattern definitions can be imported from pattern files used by AutoCAD—a process we explain later in this chapter. To create, modify, or view an available fill pattern, switch to the Manage tab and choose Additional Settings ➢ Fill Patterns (see Figure 4.14). On the left side of the Fill Patterns dialog box, you can view the names and small graphic previews of the patterns. Below those are the Pattern Type options, where you choose what type of pattern to create and specify what type of pattern you want to edit (Model or Drafting).

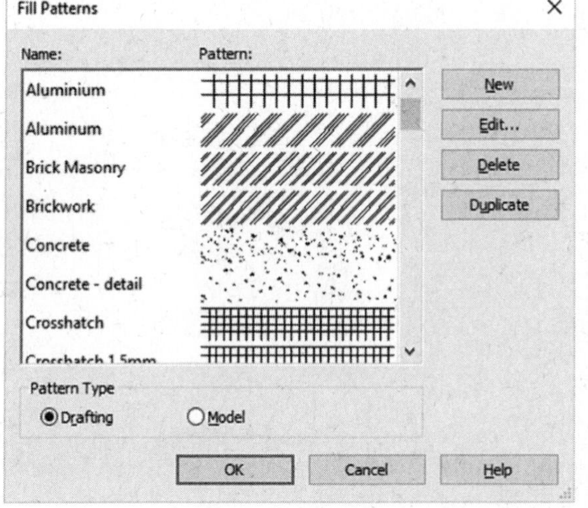

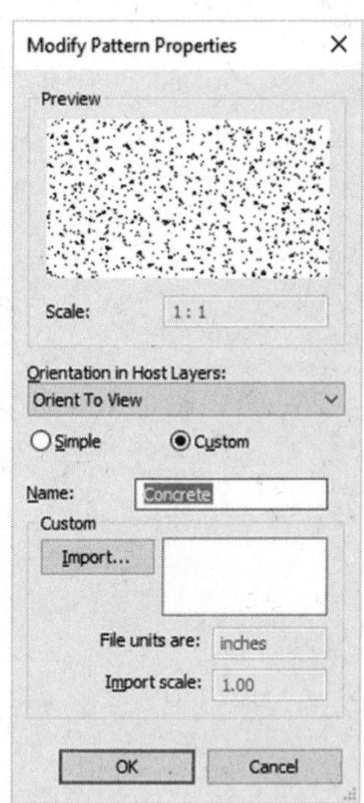

FIGURE 4.14 Fill patterns are defined separately for drafting and model representations.

Model patterns are used to convey real-world dimensional patterns to represent a material, whereas *drafting patterns* are intended for symbolic representations. For example, a model pattern is used to show a brick pattern in 3D and elevation views, whereas a brick drafting pattern is used to represent the material in plan and section. Figure 4.15 shows how concrete masonry units (CMUs) are represented with a running bond pattern (model) as well as a crosshatch (drafting). To display cut patterns in a 3D view, you must enable and adjust a section box to intersect a model element.

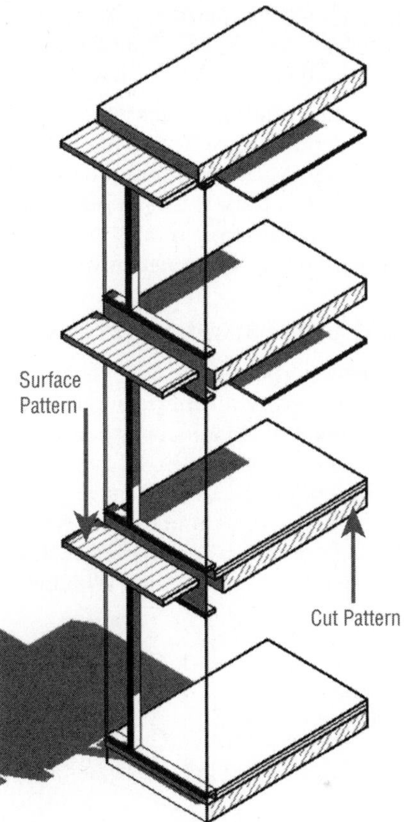

FIGURE 4.15
The CMU wall has both a drafting pattern (cut) and a model pattern (surface) defined.

Model patterns have specific behaviors that are not dependent on any view. The scale you establish in a model pattern will always be that size, regardless of the view scale. In the example shown in Figure 4.15, the surface of the CMU wall displays a block pattern that measures 16″ × 8″ (400 mm × 200 mm). If you were to change the view scale, the pattern would appear larger or smaller but it would always measure the same. With a drafting pattern, the opposite is true: The pattern adjusts with the view scale, so the pattern looks identical in all scales.

Fill patterns are also created as one of two types: simple or custom. Figure 4.16 illustrates some examples of each option.

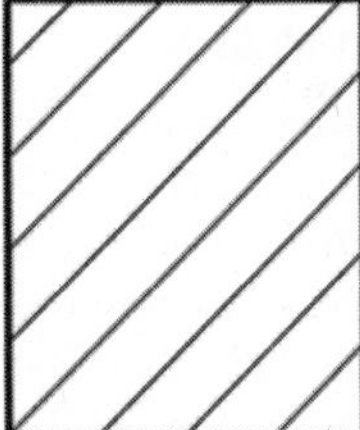

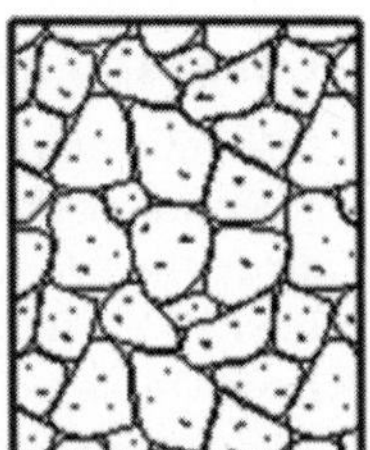

FIGURE 4.16
From left to right: a simple fill pattern, a simple fill pattern with the Crosshatch option selected, and a custom fill pattern

Simple These patterns are generated with parallel or crosshatch lines that can have different angles and spacing. With both the Crosshatch and Parallel Lines options, you can specify only one angle for the entire pattern. Using crosshatch, you can set two spacing values.

Custom To create a more complex custom pattern, you have to import a pattern (PAT) file from an external source. This is often necessary because of the current limitation in creating natively complex patterns. Your office may have a set of established patterns that have been used for years, and the Custom option allows you to import and reuse them without having to make them again from scratch. Custom patterns let you import a PAT file from anywhere on your hard drive or on a network and use it as a base pattern for a new fill pattern.

Creating a New Simple Pattern

To create a new simple pattern, first choose either Model or Drafting, and then click the New button. A generic pattern appears in the New Pattern dialog box. You can then design your pattern and assign orientation behavior.

The option Orientation In Host Layers is particularly useful when you're making drafting patterns. This option allows you to specify how a pattern orients itself relative to host elements such as walls, floors, roofs, and ceilings when they are represented as cut. Note that the option is not available for model pattern types. As shown in Figure 4.17, the orientation options are Orient To View, Keep Readable, and Align With Element.

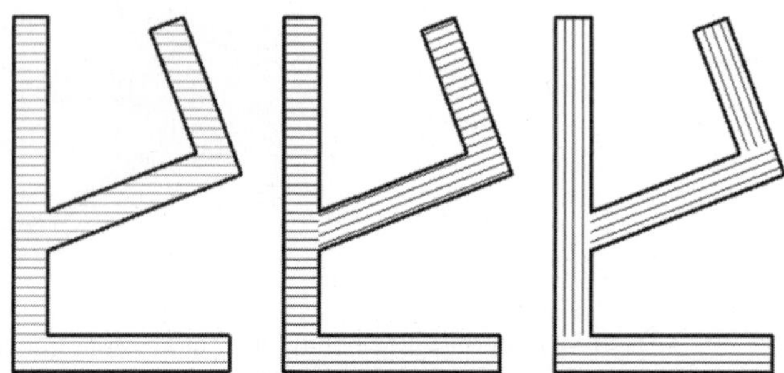

Figure 4.17 From left to right: Orient To View, Keep Readable, and Align With Element

Orient To View When this orientation is applied, the patterns used in the project all have the same orientation and the same origin. They're always perfectly aligned with the origin of the view.

Keep Readable This orientation will maintain alignment with the view (that is, horizontal lines will remain horizontal) but will be adjusted relative to angled host elements.

Align With Element This orientation ensures that the pattern orientation depends on the orientation of the host element. Patterns essentially run parallel with the element.

Creating a Custom Complex Pattern

Custom patterns require an external file that contains the definition of the pattern. The filename extension of that pattern should be `.pat`, which is what you'll make in this exercise by editing an existing AutoCAD PAT file. An advantage of specifying patterns in the template file is that the PAT file won't need to be installed on each computer where the application is installed; patterns are stored internally in the Revit template or project file.

Before modifying PAT files, always make a copy of the original PAT file you intend to use as a base; you don't want to risk messing up other files that might already be using that original PAT file. PAT files can be edited with Notepad or any other text-editing application. For this exercise, you'll choose the AutoCAD pattern called Grass, which you can find in `acadiso.pat` (in metric units) or `acad.pat` (imperial units) located on this book's web page.

Importing a Custom Pattern

Follow these steps to make a custom fill pattern by importing an existing pattern definition:

1. Using Notepad or a similar text editor application, open the file `acadiso.pat` (Metric patterns) or `acad.pat` (Imperial patterns).
2. Highlight the lines that define the pattern, and select them:

    ```
    *GRASS,Grass area
    90, 0, 0, 17.9605, 17.9605, 4.7625, -31.1585
    45, 0, 0, 0, 25.4, 4.7625, -20.6375
    135, 0, 0, 0, 25.4, 4.7625, -20.6375
    ```

    The actual numbers in the pattern may differ slightly, depending on whether you are using `acadiso.pat` or `acad.pat`.
3. Choose Edit ➤ Copy.
4. Open a new text file and paste the selection. (You can also open the Revit `metric.pat` or `revit.pat` file located in `C:\Program Files\Autodesk\Revit 2017\Data`, in which all Revit patterns are already saved. In that case, you can paste the selected text in that file.)
5. This is the important part: In the new text file where you pasted the selected text, add the two lines shown boldfaced here:

    ```
    ;%UNITS=MM
    *GRASS,Grass area
    ;%TYPE=DRAFTING
    90, 0, 0, 17.9605, 17.9605, 4.7625, -31.1585
    45, 0, 0, 0, 25.4, 4.7625, -20.6375
    135, 0, 0, 0, 25.4, 4.7625, -20.6375
    ```

    The first line that you write before the pattern text, ;%UNITS=MM, can appear only once in the text file. It defines the value for the units used in the pattern. In the example, the units are millimeters (MM); if you wanted to work in imperial units, it would be ;%UNITS=INCH. (If you use the option in step 4 to collect all patterns in the master PAT file, then this line already exists and you don't need to add it.)

    The second statement, ;%TYPE=DRAFTING, helps define whether you're creating a drafting or model pattern. In this example, the pattern is the Drafting type.
6. Save your text file with a `.pat` filename extension.
7. On the Manage tab, choose Additional Settings ➤ Fill Patterns.
8. In the Fill Patterns dialog box, verify that the Drafting option is selected, and click New.
9. In the New Pattern dialog box, select the Custom option.

    The lower part of the dialog box offers new options.
10. Click Import, navigate to the place on your hard drive or network where you saved the PAT file, select it, and then click Open.

IMPORTING PAT FILES

It's important to know that when you import a new pattern, the type of pattern needs to be the same as the new type of pattern you're making. In other words, if you're making a new model pattern, you can't import a drafting pattern. If you try to do so, you'll see a warning message like the one shown here:

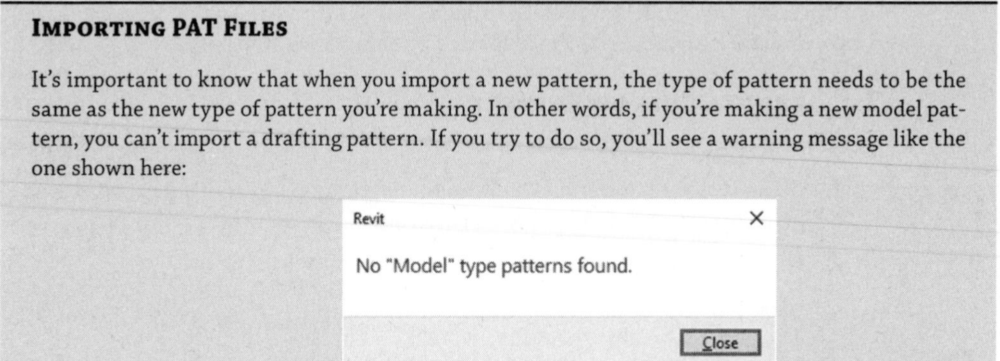

In the list that appears to the right of this button, you can see the name of the pattern you created: GRASS, as shown in Figure 4.18. (If you have a PAT file with many patterns defined, you'll see all the other drafting patterns available in that list.) The name of the pattern automatically becomes the name of your fill pattern, but you can change that if you like.

If necessary, you can adjust the scales of the imported pattern. The Preview window displays the graphic of the pattern, always in 1:1 scale. This informs you if you need to scale the pattern up or down. You'll know that you need to scale the pattern if the preview appears as a solid black box—that means the pattern is too dense. As an alternative, if the preview box shows only white, your scale might need to be reduced.

11. If you're happy with the result, confirm by clicking OK.

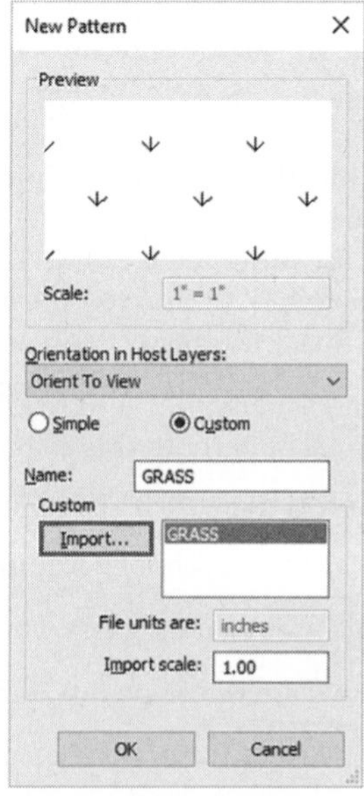

FIGURE 4.18
The New Pattern dialog box displays the imported PAT file in the Custom group.

Now that you have created a fill pattern, you can use the pattern in a number of ways. One of the simplest ways is to assign the pattern directly to a material. We purposely instructed you to create a grass pattern in the previous exercise to illustrate a limitation in Revit—you cannot assign a surface pattern to a material that is associated with a toposurface.

In the following exercise, you will assign the grass pattern to a material in the sample project that has already been assigned to a toposurface. We will then show you how to create a new filled region type in order to create a symbolic representation of grass in the site plan.

1. Continuing with the `c04-Materials.rvt` file, switch to the Manage tab and click Materials.
2. In the Material Browser, find the material named Site - Grass and choose the Graphics tab. Under the Surface Pattern properties, click the Pattern field and then choose the GRASS pattern you created in the previous exercise. Click OK.

   The pattern will be assigned to the material, but you will be prompted with a warning that toposurfaces do not support surface patterns. Next, we will create a filled region type and use it as a graphic indicator on a site plan.
3. In the Project Browser, activate the floor plan named Site. Switch to the Annotate tab and in the Detail panel select Region ➢ Filled Region.
4. In the Properties palette, click Edit Type and duplicate the current filled region type to a new type named **Grass**. Set the Fill Pattern property to GRASS (Figure 4.19).
5. Click OK to close the Type Properties dialog box, and draw a shape on the Site plan using any configuration of lines, making sure your lines form a closed loop.

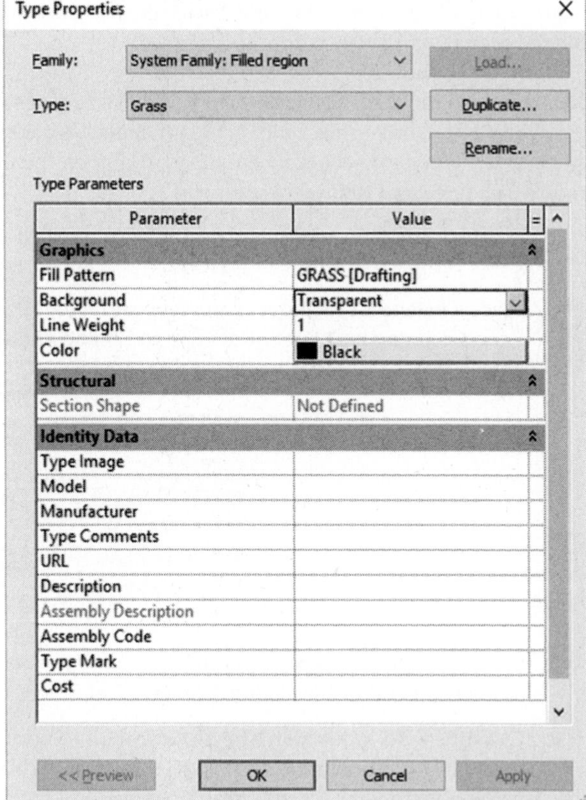

FIGURE 4.19 Create a new filled region type with your new custom fill pattern.

Remember to click the green check mark in the contextual ribbon to complete the sketch of the filled region. You can even experiment with the <Invisible Lines> type to achieve results similar to those shown here.

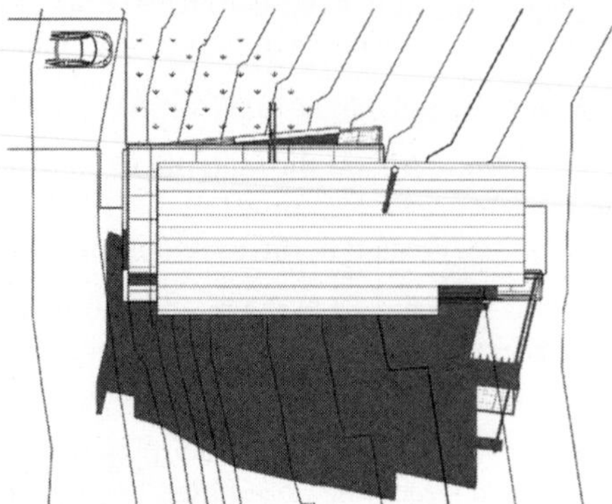

Preconfiguring Color Schemes

The use of color schemes in project documentation will be covered in greater detail in Chapter 20, "Presenting Your Design"; however, for now, just know that you can preconfigure them in project templates for a variety of scenarios. For example, an architect may perform many projects for a single client that uses the same department names in all of its program design requirements. The architect would like to ensure that an identical color scheme is used in the colored plans in all projects for this client.

In the following steps, you will create a new color fill legend with some predefined department values and associated colors. These settings can be saved in either a custom project template (`*.rte`) or a project file (`*.rvt`) that acts as a container for settings to be transferred into another active project file. Download and open the file `c04-Color-Schemes.rvt` from this book's web page and follow these steps:

1. Activate any floor plan view from the Project Browser. On the Annotate tab, choose the Color Fill panel and select the Color Fill Legend tool.
2. Place a legend in the floor plan view, and you will see the Choose Space Type And Color Scheme dialog box. Set Space Type to Rooms and Color Scheme to Department (these choices can be modified later) and then click OK.

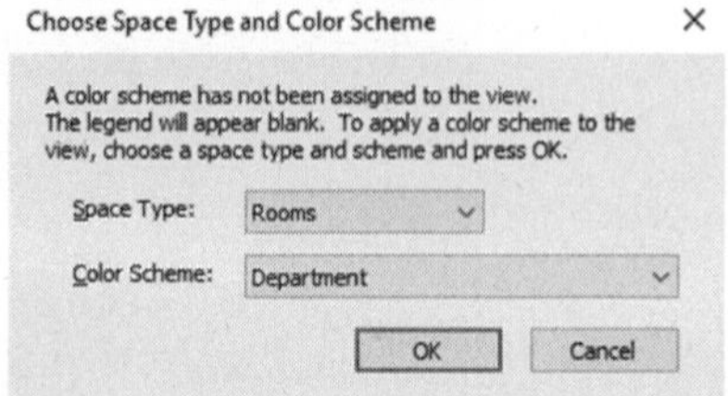

3. Select the color fill legend you placed in the previous step, and click the Edit Scheme icon at the right end of the ribbon. The Edit Color Scheme dialog box will appear.
4. Click the Add Value icon (the plus symbol) to populate the list of departments in the Scheme Definition area. Add the values as shown in Figure 4.20. Choose colors and fill patterns according to your graphic requirements.

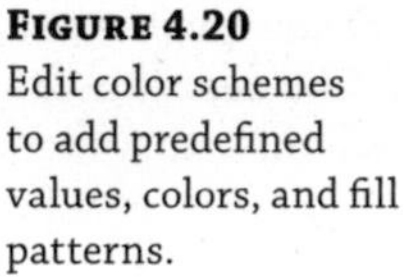

FIGURE 4.20
Edit color schemes to add predefined values, colors, and fill patterns.

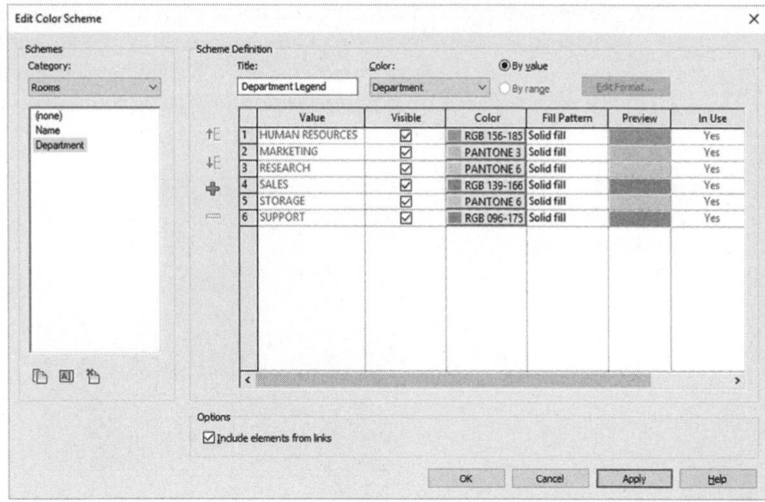

5. Click OK to close the dialog box.
6. Activate the Level 1 floor plan and, from the Architecture tab, choose the Room button and add rooms to the enclosed spaces shown in the plan view. For clarity, we have turned on the Interior Fill and Reference properties for rooms in this plan view. This will make it easier for you to select the rooms in the next step.

   You will not want to let these rooms remain if you save the file as a project template, but it will help to better visualize the color schemes if you can see them placed in a sample model view.

   When rooms are placed, you can either type the values for departments that match the predefined values in the color scheme or select the values in the Properties palette when each room is selected, as shown in Figure 4.21.

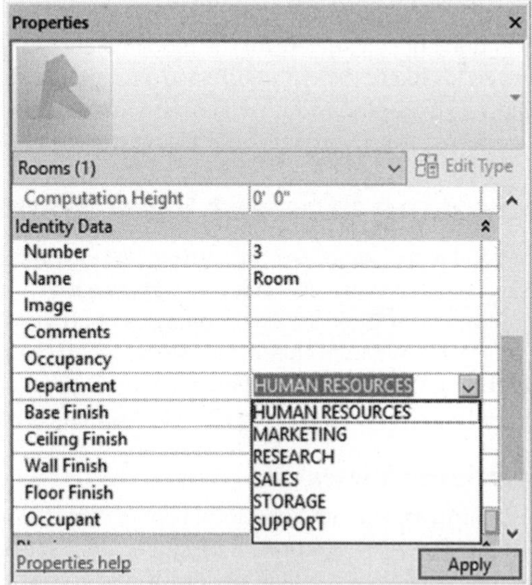

FIGURE 4.21
Select from predefined values in the Properties palette of a room.

7. Select each room that you placed in the plan view, and select a Department value in the Properties palette according to the layout shown in Figure 4.22. The department values used in every project started with your project template will have the same colors and fill patterns according to those specified in the original color scheme. You also have a predefined list of your client's department names.

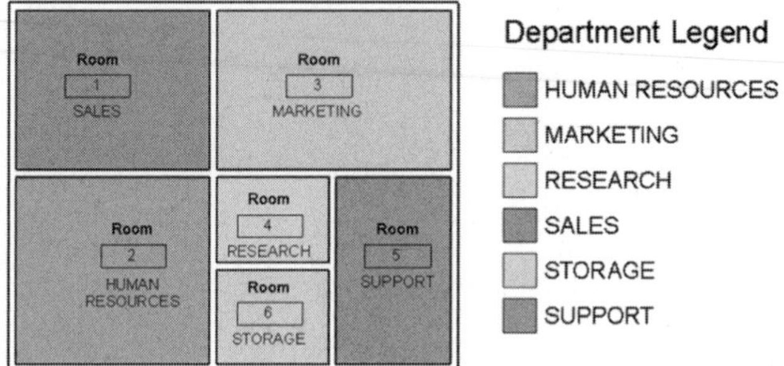

FIGURE 4.22
Color-filled plans can use predefined values in templates.

At this point, you have two options for storing these types of settings. We will discuss strategies for managing templates later in this chapter, but for now you can either save this file as a project template or maintain it as a container file, which is simply a RVT file that holds settings you will transfer into other project files. For a container file, simply leave the file as is, and we will discuss the use of the Transfer Project Standards command later in this chapter. If you want to use this file as a project template, follow these steps:

1. In the plan view, select all the walls, rooms, and room tags, and then delete them.
2. Activate the Room Schedule view under Schedules/Quantities in the Project Browser.
3. Click in the first row of the schedule and then click the Delete button in the ribbon. Repeat this step until all rooms have been removed from the schedule.
4. Go to the Application menu and then select Save As ➤ Template. Name the file **c04-Color-Scheme-Template.rte**.

You don't have to delete all the modeled content and rooms from your project templates; however, it's likely that you will have a unique layout for each project you design. By deleting the sample walls and rooms, you maintained the color scheme settings with the predefined colors, patterns, and department names.

Increasing Efficient View Management

Once you have customized the settings for graphic quality, you can use several other tools and techniques to increase efficiency and ensure that your visual standards are applied consistently throughout your projects. The properties of all views can be used to your advantage in creating a browser organization that meets the needs of your teams. You can apply filters to views for generating graphic overrides based on model element parameters. You can manage and deploy these settings and more in view templates that can be applied to many views simultaneously.

Organizing Views

Maintaining a clear and consistent organization of views within a Revit project can generate measurable increases in project productivity. Especially in larger projects, a Revit file can have more than 1000 views, which can easily cause confusion and wasted time if the right view cannot be found in the Project Browser when needed.

Download and open the file `c04-Browser-Org.rvt` from this book's web page. Most default project templates contain a few simple Browser Organization types that can be copied and/or customized—except for the type named All. To access these settings, switch to the View ribbon, find the Windows panel, click the User Interface drop-down button, and select Browser Organization, as shown in Figure 4.23.

FIGURE 4.23
Accessing browser organization settings in the ribbon

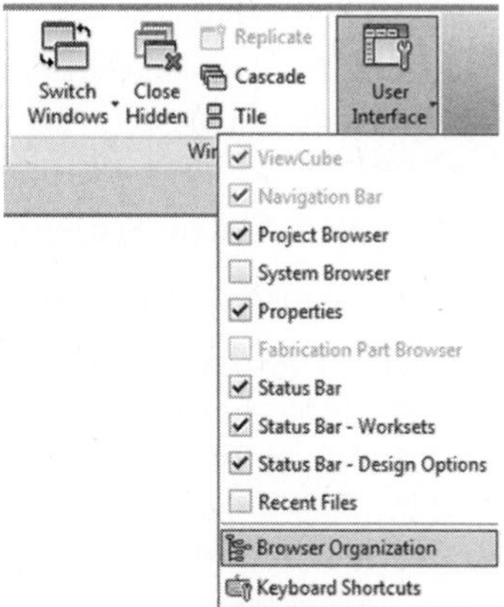

Select any one of the listed types in the Browser Organization dialog box and click the Edit button. Remember, you can't edit or delete the type named All.

In the Browser Organization Properties dialog box (Figure 4.24) are a Grouping And Sorting tab and a Filtering tab. Grouping And Sorting allows you to group views together based on selected view parameters, whereas the Filtering tab gives you the opportunity to display only views that pass selected criteria.

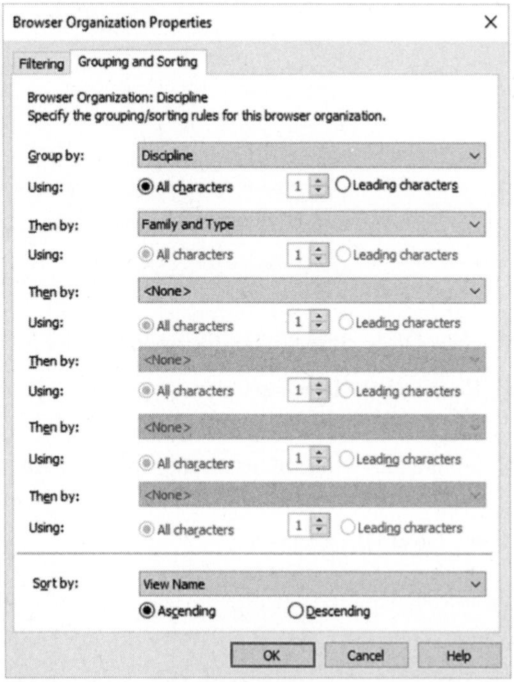

FIGURE 4.24
Use view properties and parameters to create folders for the Project Browser.

Browser Organization Properties
Filtering | Grouping and Sorting
Browser Organization: Discipline
Specify the grouping/sorting rules for this browser organization.
Group by: Discipline
Using: All characters | 1 | Leading characters
Then by: Family and Type
Using: All characters | 1 | Leading characters
Then by: <None>
Using: All characters | 1 | Leading characters
Then by: <None>
Using: All characters | 1 | Leading characters
Then by: <None>
Using: All characters | 1 | Leading characters
Then by: <None>
Using: All characters | 1 | Leading characters
Sort by: View Name
Ascending | Descending
OK | Cancel | Help

Choose the Grouping And Sorting tab to specify three levels of hierarchy to be shown in the Project Browser. Here are some examples:

- Family And Type, Discipline, View Scale
- Phase, Discipline, Family And Type
- Detail Level, Family, Type

To further organize the views in your project, you can create additional project parameters and assign them to views and sheets. The following is one example of adding custom text parameters to views for more refined organization:

1. On the Manage tab, find the Settings panel, and click Project Parameters.
2. In the Project Parameters dialog box, click Add.
3. In the Parameter Properties dialog box, create a parameter named **Zone**; for Type Of Parameter, specify Text. Select the Instance option; then find and check the Views category, as shown in Figure 4.25. You may also set the Group Parameter Under value to Identity Data.

FIGURE 4.25
Create custom project parameters for additional view organization options.

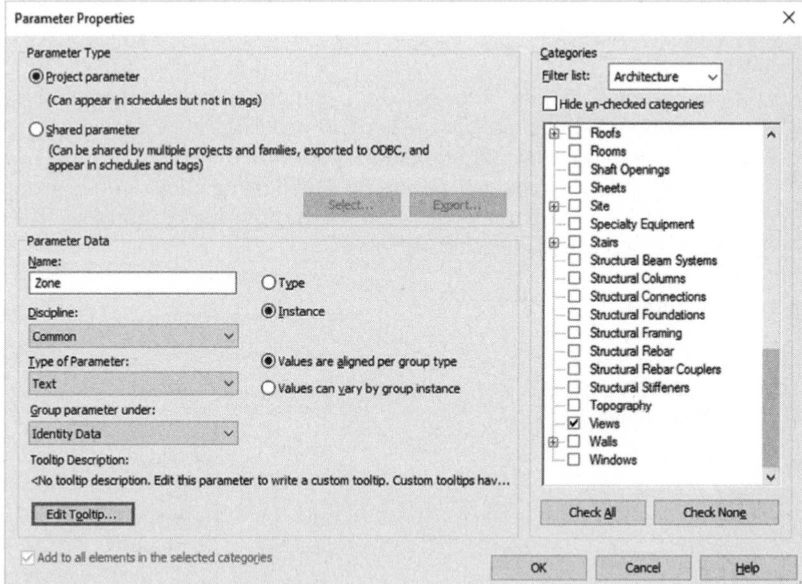

4. Click OK to close both of the open dialog boxes.
5. Return to the Browser Organization dialog box and click New. Name the new type **Zone/ Phase** and click OK.
6. Set the following values on the Grouping And Sorting tab in the Browser Organization Properties dialog box:
   - Group By: Zone
   - Then By: Phase

7. Click OK to close the dialog box and return to the Browser Organization dialog box.
8. Check the box next to Zone/Phase to make this browser setting current and click OK to close the dialog box.

The Project Browser is now ready to support the use of the custom view parameters you created earlier.

It is now up to you to assign values to the custom view parameters created in the previous exercise. These values can be assigned directly to the view properties in the Properties palette or by adding them to view templates. Views that do not have values for these parameters will be found in the browser hierarchy listed as ??? (three question marks). Figure 4.26 illustrates this scenario in which floor plans and ceiling plans have values assigned to the Zone parameters but the elevation views do not.

FIGURE 4.26
Customized Browser Organizations can make larger projects easier to navigate.

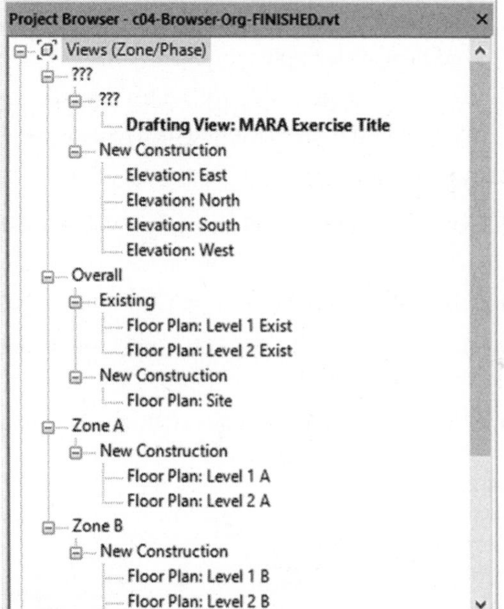

Creating and Assigning Filters

Filters are another view configuration and customization tool that can be developed and deployed in Revit project templates. They are similar to the filters available in schedules in that they can either display or hide elements matching user-specified criteria. However, filters can also override the graphic appearance of elements within a view. The possible combination and application of view filters is virtually limitless, so let us take a look at a few real-world examples.

First, we will review the steps to create and assign a view filter. The fundamental steps are as follows:

1. Create a named filter.
2. Assign it to object categories.
3. Assign data criteria.

4. Add to the Visibility/Graphic settings of a view.
5. Define graphic overrides.

In the following example, you will create view rule-based filters to identify fire-rated walls with different colors. You can download the sample file `c04-Sample-Building.rvt` from this book's web page. Here are the steps:

1. Open the file `c04-Sample-Building.rvt`. Switch to the View tab, find the Graphics panel, and click Filters.
2. Add a new named filter by clicking the New button on the right side of the dialog box. Name the first new filter **Walls-Fire 1**, use the Define Rules option, and then click OK.
3. When the expanded Filters dialog box appears, make sure the Walls-Fire 1 filter is selected, and in the Categories list, find Walls and check the category.
4. In the Filter Rules at the right side, define the criterion to filter by Fire Rating Equals 1 HR and then click Apply.
5. With the Walls-Fire 1 filter still selected, click the Duplicate icon twice (the second icon below the Filters list) and then rename the duplicated filters **Walls-Fire 2** and **Walls-Fire 3**.
6. Select Walls-Fire 2 and change the value in Filter Rules to 2 HR and click Apply.
7. Select Walls-Fire 3 and change the value in Filter Rules to 3 HR, as shown in Figure 4.27, and then click Apply again.
8. Click OK to close both of the Filters dialog boxes.
9. Activate the Level 1 floor plan, open the Visibility/Graphic Overrides dialog box, and select the Filters tab.
10. Click the Add button, select all three filters you created in the previous steps, and click OK.

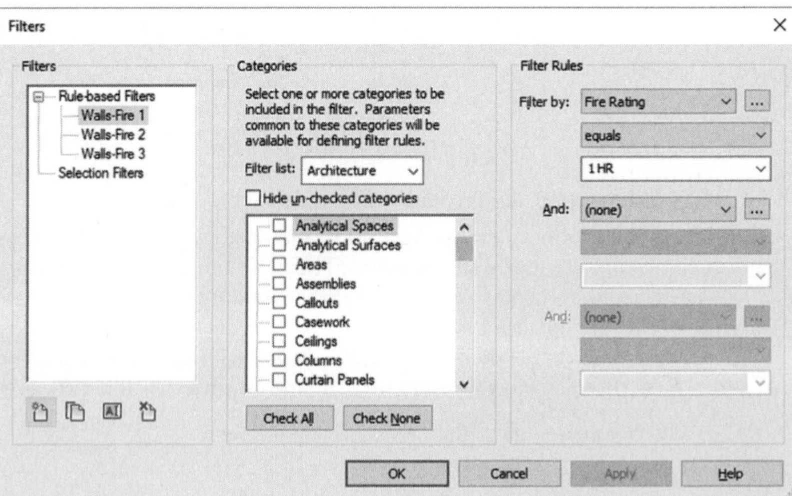

FIGURE 4.27 Filter rules applied to walls for fire ratings

11. Click the Override button in each filter row under Cut-Lines and change the line color as follows:

- Walls-Fire 1 = Green
- Walls-Fire 2 = Yellow
- Walls-Fire 3 = Red

12. Click OK to close the Visibility/Graphic Overrides dialog box.

With the filters now applied to the floor plan, walls that have been assigned a fire rating value will appear with the color overrides you assigned to the respective filters. You can create more filters to define graphic styles for specific model elements such as furniture by owner, interior walls, secure doors, or equipment not in contract.

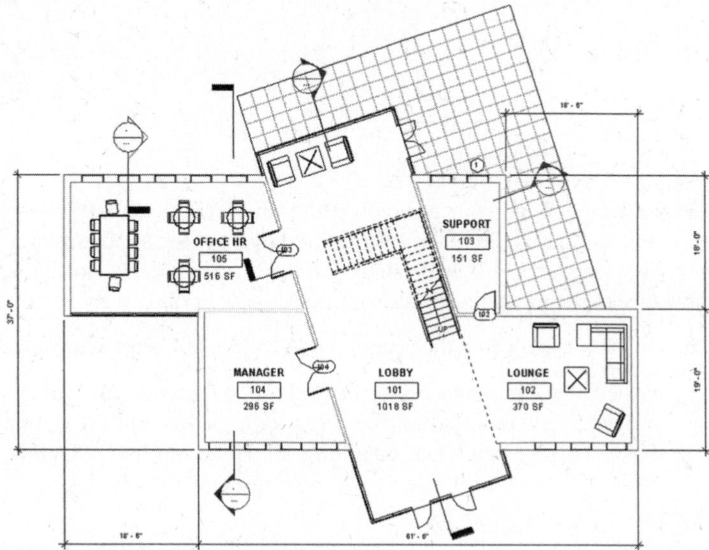

You can also create filters based on selection. This allows you to define the objects to be filtered without a ruleset. This is a useful option when there is no clear rule that will allow the visibility you need. The selection can happen before or after the filter creation, allowing you to add or subtract as needed. To create a selection filter, follow these steps with same file used for rule-based filters:

1. Activate the view Level 1 Design. In the Manage tab, locate the Selection panel.

2. Select Edit. The Edit Filters dialog will appear with a list of rule-based filters and selection filters.

3. Select New.

4. When the Filter Name dialog appears, provide the name **MARA Test** and choose Select. The dialog will close with the ribbon providing the Edit Selection tools. By default, the Add To Selection tool is active.

5. Select several objects in the plan view to add to the set. To remove objects from the set, select Remove From Selection. You will notice the mouse trades its plus symbol for a minus symbol. You will also see that previously unselected objects are now suppressed, allowing you easy access to change your selection set.

6. Once you are satisfied, choose Finish Selection. As shown in Figure 4.28, you now have a filter based on selection, rather than a rule.

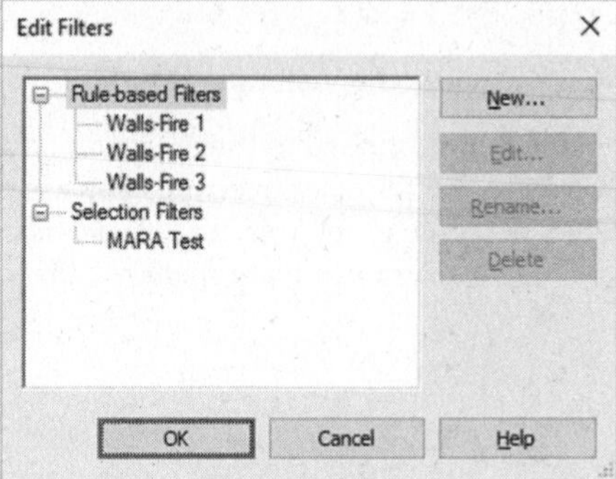

FIGURE 4.28 Filter based on selection, rather than rules

Using View Templates

After you have defined your desired settings in as many view types as possible, you can use view templates to manage these settings and apply them to other views of the same type. The use of view templates will be discussed in various chapters of this book, but we will discuss their importance to the project template in this section. Let's begin by opening the View Templates tool:

1. On the View tab, find the Graphics panel and select View Templates ➤ Manage View Templates.

   In the View Templates dialog box (Figure 4.29), you will find icons to duplicate, rename, or delete view templates below the list on the left. On the right are the view properties that can be applied when the view template is applied to a view.

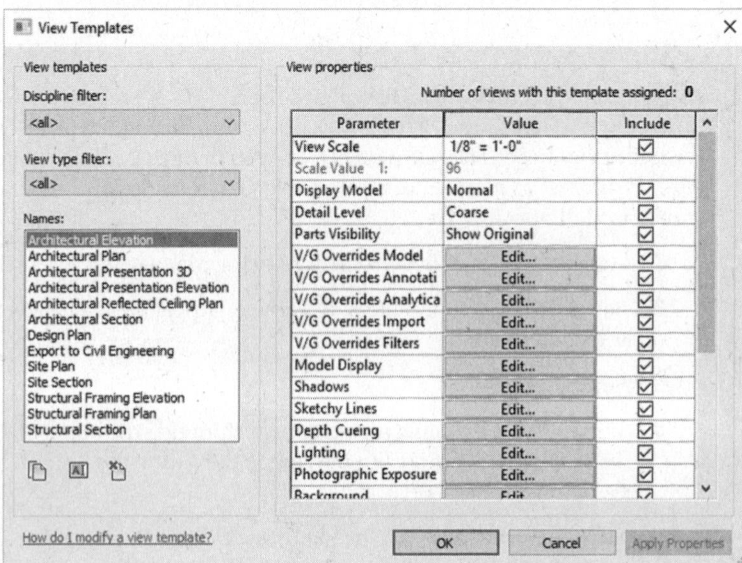

FIGURE 4.29 View Templates dialog box

Notice the column named Include on the right of this dialog box. This column allows you to include or exclude various view properties when you are applying the view template. If you uncheck View Scale and Detail Level settings, you can apply this template to plans of multiple scales and detail levels, while applying settings such as visibility of Object Styles, Phase Filter, and View Range without affecting the View Scale or Detail Level settings.

Also notice in Figure 4.29 the custom view parameter we created earlier: Zone. This value can be applied with the view template, which will have the effect of cataloging the views in a customized hierarchy within the Project Browser. Changes to view templates are automatically reflected in the views to which they have been assigned.

2. Click OK to close the window.

The only way to *assign* a view template to a view is in the Properties palette. Select any view in the Project Browser and then examine the Properties palette to locate the View Template parameter. If the View Template parameter button displays as <None>, then no view template has been assigned. Click the button to launch the Apply View Template dialog box, and choose an appropriate view template. In contrast to this *assigning* workflow, view template properties can be *applied* to individual views. Applying a view template is a onetime application. Future changes to the view template will not change a view where a template was applied. You can apply a template in various ways, including the following:

- Select multiple views in the Project Browser, right-click, and then select Apply View Template from the context menu.
- From the View tab, click View Templates ➢ Apply Template Properties To Current View.
- Select multiple sheets in the Project Browser, right-click, and then select Apply View Template To All Views from the context menu.

Any of these methods will apply the properties of a view template, but it will not assign the view template to the view. If you use these methods and a view happens to have a view template already assigned, a message will prompt you to partially apply the properties that are not being managed by the view template assigned to the view.

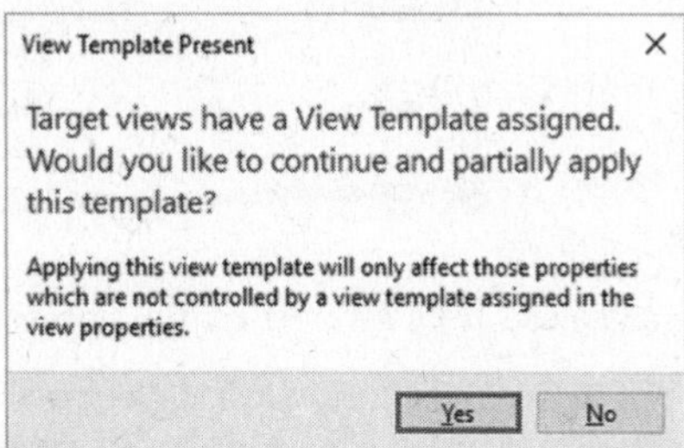

Any properties listed in the View Templates dialog box, shown previously in Figure 4.29, that are selected in the Include field will not be changed if you choose to partially apply view template properties to a view with an assigned template. For example, if model object styles are included in the assigned view template and you are attempting to apply template properties that also have model object style modifications, the model object settings from the assigned view template will not be overridden from the applied properties.

Despite these relatively intuitive methods for applying view templates, you can increase efficiency on larger projects by assigning a default view template for each view type. In the following exercise, continue to use this chapter's exercise file `c04-Sample-Building.rvt` from the filters exercise, and follow these steps:

1. Activate the Level 1 floor plan in the Project Browser, right-click on the Level 1 floor plan, and choose Duplicate View ➤ Duplicate from the context menu. Rename the duplicate view as **Level 1 Design**.
2. With the properties of the Level 1 Design floor plan active in the Properties palette, click Edit Type. In the Type Properties dialog box, click Duplicate to create a new type named **Design Plans**.
3. Click the button in the View Template Applied To New Views field and select the Design Plan view template (Figure 4.30). Click OK.

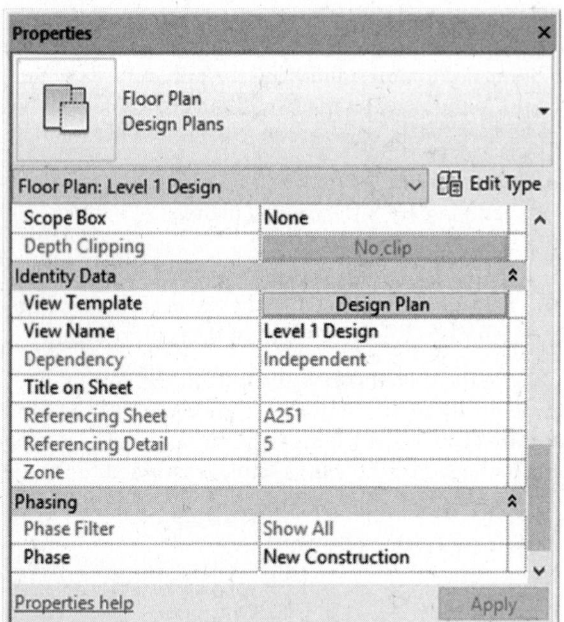

FIGURE 4.30 Specify a view template for new views within a view type.

4. Click OK to close the Type Properties dialog box.

   You should notice that the Level 1 Design floor plan in the Project Browser is now listed under Floor Plans (Design Plans); however, the view template has not been applied to this view yet.

5. In the Properties palette, click the View Template field button, select the Design Plan template, and then click OK.

   The floor plan view should appear changed, no longer displaying any annotation.

6. From the View tab, click Plan Views ➤ Floor Plan. In the New Floor Plan dialog box, select Design Plans in the Type drop-down list and then select Level 2 from the list.
7. Click OK, and a new floor plan for Level 2 will be created that has the Design Plan view template already assigned. Rename this view as **Level 2 Design**.

The workflow described in the previous exercise will help you spend less time configuring view settings and more time focused on your designs. Including view templates in your project template will give your teams the ability to quickly apply your standard view settings. It will also support continued consistency as each building project grows in scope and size. Remember that view templates are easily shared between projects using the Transfer Project Standards tool, which we will discuss later in this chapter in the section "Strategies for Managing Templates."

Creating Custom Annotations

We are avid supporters of global graphic standards for architecture and engineering, such as the United States National CAD Standard (`www.nationalcadstandard.org`), but in reality many architects and designers will likely have their own set of graphic conventions that will need to be implemented in their Revit projects. Placing customized annotation families in your project template will save time when you are starting new projects and ensure maximum compliance with your firm's conventions. You can load tag families into the template using several methods:

- Switch to the Insert tab, and in the Load Library panel, select Load Family.
- Using Windows Explorer, select RFA tag families and drag them into the Revit project environment with the template open. If you try to drag more than one family at once, you are prompted to either open each of those files in an independent window (so you can modify them) or load them all in the current project. Choose the second option.
- Use the Loaded Tags And Symbols tool available in the Annotate tab when you expand the Tag panel (Figure 4.31). This tool allows you to preview all loaded and preset tags and symbols that will be used for respective element categories.

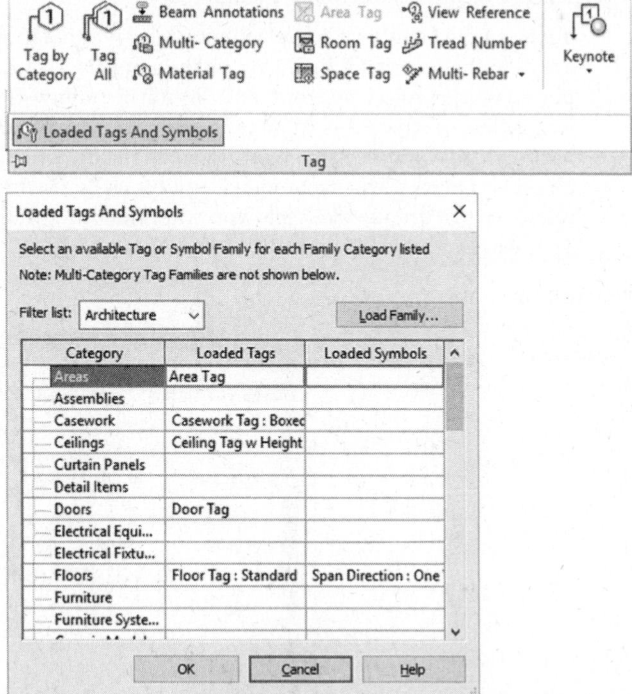

FIGURE 4.31 The Loaded Tags dialog box shows loaded annotation families assigned to selected categories.

In the following sections, we will walk you through creating some common element tags and customizing system annotation.

ARCHIVING AND MANAGING CUSTOM CONTENT

Many new users are unsure where to store custom-created families. It is not advisable to save them in the system folders created during the installation of Revit because you may lose track of them or inadvertently delete them when you reinstall the software. Reinstalling the application erases just about any folder and its entire contents. It is thus wise to keep your personally created content elsewhere, under a separate, independent folder; if you are not a single user, store that folder on a shared network drive. Remember that you can always include additional library shortcuts in the application options. Just select File Locations and click the Places button from the Options menu.

You should also keep your templates up-to-date as you add more content; that way, you need to maintain only a few template files rather than dozens of separate family files. It's even better if you can establish a template manager as a role within the office so everyone isn't making graphical changes to your templates.

Introducing Tag Family Fundamentals

Tags in Revit have various similarities and differences to annotation symbols you might find in a CAD application. They are similar in that they are created at 1:1 scale and contain lines and other graphic elements. The main difference is that Revit tags merely *report* information from model elements, whereas a CAD-based symbol usually holds an attribute value that does not directly relate to the annotated building element. These dynamic annotation elements are referred to as *labels* within a Revit family, whereas static annotation is simply known as *text*.

Before you begin to customize annotation families or create your own, let's take a detailed look at the difference between text and labels.

Text In the Family Editor, placing text in an annotation family or title block means you are defining text that will always be the same and is unchangeable when that family is placed in the project environment. Figure 4.32 shows the words *AREA* and *VOLUME* as text. Regardless of where this room tag is placed, the text will always say AREA and VOLUME. Section tags work the same way: If you add static text, that text appears exactly the same for all section marks. This technique is not typically used for sections because each section is a reference to a unique view, and you want that information to be dynamic and parametric. That is where label functionality comes into play.

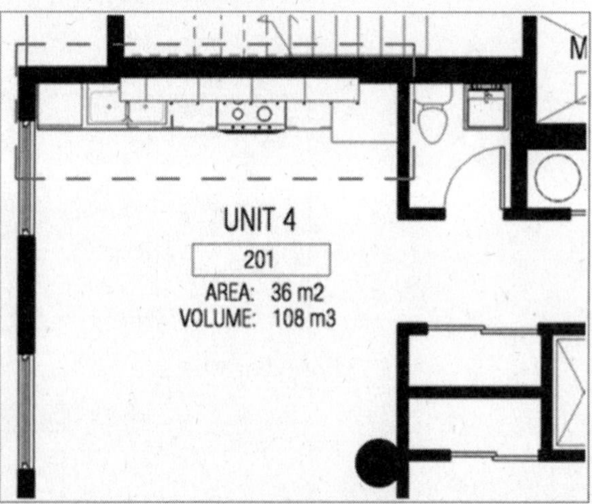

FIGURE 4.32
Floor plan showing the room tag

Labels Like static text, a label offers textual information; however, it is a live reference to a parameter value of an element in the project. For example, if you add an Area label, it will pull the value of the area of the room; if you add a Sheet Number label in a Section Head family in the Family Editor environment and then use that section head in a project, the label will automatically display the actual sheet number on which the section view is placed in the project. If you move the section view from one sheet to another, the label will automatically report the new sheet number. In Figure 4.32, UNIT 4 is a label reporting the room name; the number 201 is a label reporting the room number. The label behaves as dynamic text and is always fully coordinated with the value of the model element parameter it represents.

Creating a Custom Door Tag

Imagine you could use the actual width and height of a door element to drive the tag value. You can! As an example of creating custom tags for a basic model element, use the following steps to create the custom door tag shown in Figure 4.33. You can download the template files from this book's web page if you can't find them in the default location.

FIGURE 4.33

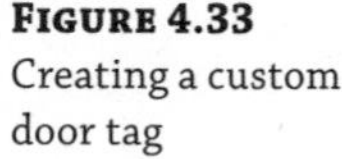

Creating a custom door tag

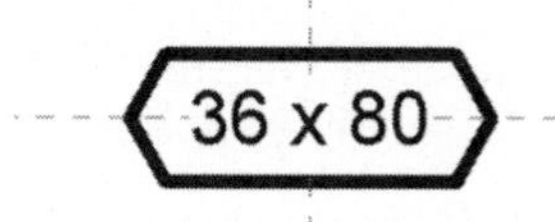

1. Click the Application menu and select New ➤ Annotation Symbol.
2. In the New Annotation Symbol dialog box, select the family template called `Door Tag.rft` or `Metric Door Tag.rft`, and click Open.

   The Family Editor opens in a view with two crossing reference planes, the intersection of which represents the origin of the tag. To avoid problems later, don't move these planes.
3. On the Create tab, find the Text panel and select Label. Click the intersection of the two planes to position the label.

   Note that text and labels do not snap to geometric references; therefore, you will have to manually adjust the placement of labels to achieve the desired alignment.
4. In the Edit Label dialog box that opens, select Width from the column on the left, and click the Add Parameter(s) To Label icon between the Category Parameters and Label Parameters fields. Then do the same for Height, as shown in Figure 4.34.

FIGURE 4.34

Adding more than one parameter to a single label

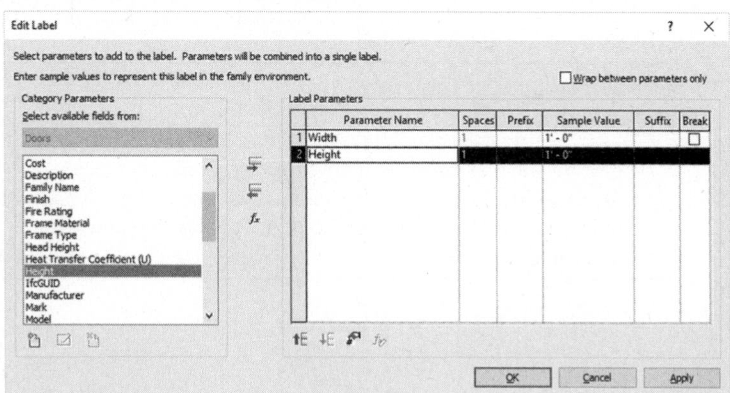

The Width and Height parameters will be concatenated in a single label, which will display the actual size of the door in the tag. In the subsequent steps, you will customize the display of the label.

5. Add a space and the letter **x** in the Suffix column of the Width parameter, and change the number in the Sample Value column to **36** (in) or **1000** (mm). Change the sample value of the Height parameter to **80** (in) or **2000** (mm).
6. With the Width row selected (click on row 1), click the Edit Parameter's Units Format icon. In the Format dialog box, uncheck the Use Project Settings option and set the following:
   - Units: Decimal Inches (or Millimeters)
   - Rounding: 0 decimal places
   - Unit Symbol: None
7. Repeat the previous step for the Height parameter.
8. Click OK in all open dialog boxes.
9. On the Create tab, activate the Masking Region tool and sketch a six-sided polygon, as shown previously in Figure 4.33.

   Remember to finish the sketch by clicking the green check mark in the Mode panel. A masking region is used instead of just lines because it will allow the door tag to obscure any geometry if it is placed over a model object. If you do not need this graphic convention, simply create the tag outline with lines.
10. Save your tag and load it into your project template.

    Make sure that it is specified as the default tag for doors in the Loaded Tags And Symbols dialog box, and use the Tag By Category or Tag All Not Tagged tool or place new doors with the Tag On Placement option. Using concatenated parameters in tag labels allows a great deal of flexibility while utilizing actual parametric values. In this example (Figure 4.35), the actual Width and Height parameters driving the door size become the text displayed in the tag.

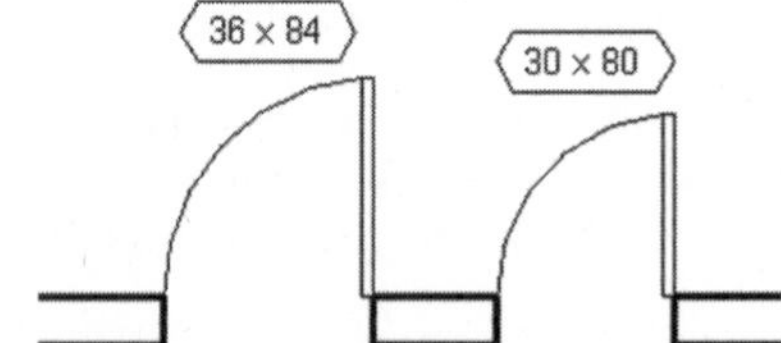

FIGURE 4.35
The custom tags applied to doors comprise actual door sizes.

SETTING SOME DEFAULTS

To aid the users of your custom templates, take some time to establish default values for common elements, such as doors, windows, rooms, grids, sheets, and levels. Create one of each element and change the Mark value to a number just below the value at which you would like your users to begin. As an example, enter a value of **0** if you want your users to begin with 1. Unfortunately, this approach does not work for letters because nothing comes before *A*.

Customizing View Tags

Section, callout, and elevation tags are graphic indicators that reference (link to) other views in your project. The graphics for these elements can be customized to meet most scenarios. To create a custom section tag, for example, you have to first create a custom section tag family and a section tail family and then load them into a template or project. You must then associate them with a section tag system family type, which is then assigned to a section type. Switch to the Manage tab, and choose Additional Settings ➤ Section Tags; you will see the application of separate section head and tail families in a section tag system family type, as shown in Figure 4.36.

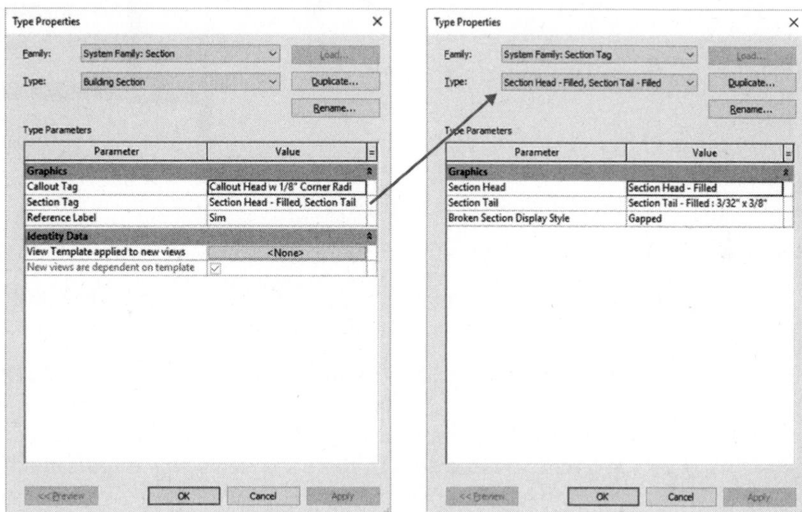

FIGURE 4.36 Creating a SIM type section tag

In simple terms, view tags are organized in the following hierarchy: The view type refers to a Callout Tag type (and a Section Tag type for section views); the Section Tag type then refers to a section head family and a section tail family.

By default, there is a predefined view tag for each view type. The graphics can vary depending on the language version of Revit you have installed on your machine. The view tags shown in Figure 4.37 are displayed and available by default in the U.S. English version.

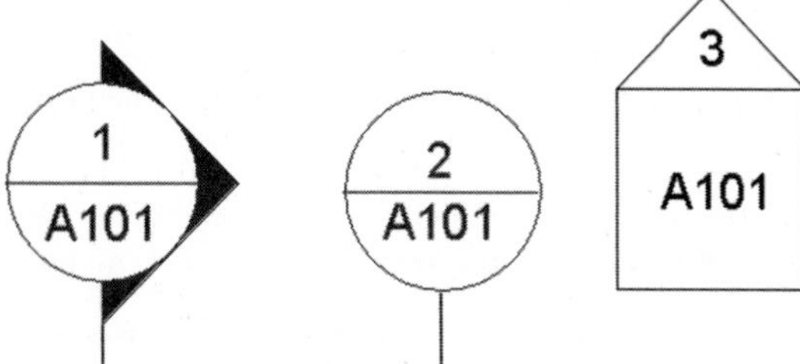

FIGURE 4.37 The default tags

CREATING A CUSTOM SECTION TAG

In the next exercise, you will create a section tag that looks like the one shown in Figure 4.38. You will first need to create a section tag family using the Family Editor before loading the section tag family into the template. You can download the template files from this book's web page if you cannot find them in the default location.

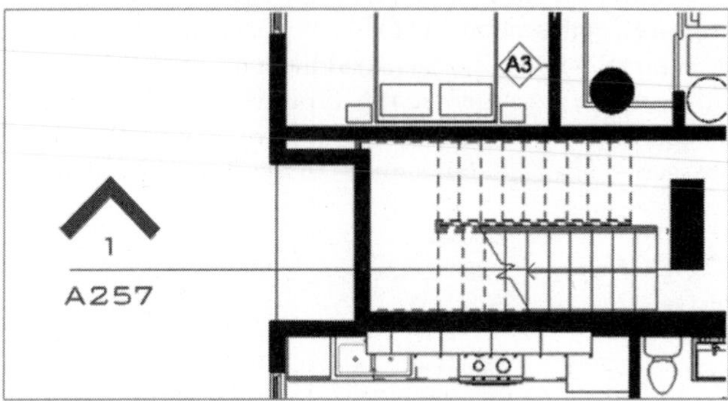

FIGURE 4.38
Customizing the section tag

To begin, follow these steps:

1. Click the Application menu, and select New ➤ Annotation Symbol.
2. In the New Annotation Symbol dialog box, select the family template called `Section Head.rft` or `Metric Section Head.rft`, and click Open.

   The Family Editor environment automatically opens, and the drawing area shows a view in which three green reference planes (two vertical and one horizontal) have already been drawn. Do not change the position of either the horizontal reference plane or the vertical reference on the right. In some templates, this is indicated with help text in red (which you can later remove).

   The intersection of the horizontal and the right reference planes defines the connection location with the section line. This means your annotation will be located in between the two intersections points.

   A proposed geometric shape is drawn for the annotation: a circle (two arcs) and a horizontal line. The default shape is there to help you visually understand where to begin drawing your new tag geometry.

3. Select the arcs that create the circle and delete them.
4. On the Create tab's Text panel, click the Label button. Position your cursor between the two vertical reference planes and below the horizontal plane, and click to position the start of the label.
5. In the Edit Label dialog box, select Sheet Number. Click the Add Parameter(s) To Label button. In the Sample Value column, you can enter a value; the default is A101. Click OK.

   The label is placed and displays blue grips when selected. These let you change the length of the label text field. The length is important because any value that is added (in a project) that is longer than the length of this box will begin to wrap and could cause undesirable results.

6. Following the same principle, place the label Detail Number above the horizontal reference plane but still between the vertical reference planes, as shown in Figure 4.39.

You can reposition a label by selecting it and using the Move button to move it around. For more precise positioning, use the arrow keys on your keyboard to nudge elements in small increments. You can also help yourself by zooming in for a better view. (Zooming in refines the increment for the nudge tools.)

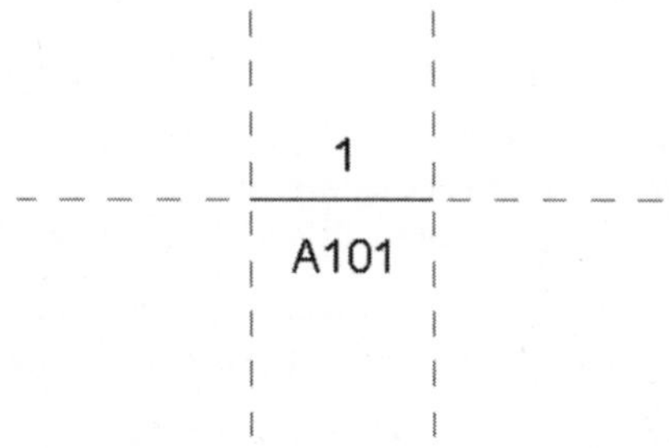

FIGURE 4.39
Place labels for Detail Number and Sheet Number.

7. On the Detail panel of the Create tab, click the Filled Region button. You'll be put into Sketch mode. Using the Line tool, draw the shape shown in Figure 4.40. In the Properties palette, click Edit Type. In the Type Properties dialog box, check that Color is set to Black and Cut Fill Pattern is set to Solid Fill. Click OK to close the Type Properties dialog box and then make sure the lines you sketched form a closed loop (no gaps or overlapping lines).

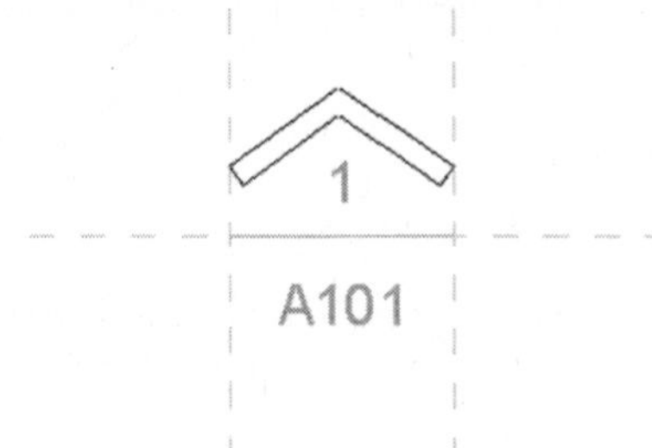

FIGURE 4.40
Draw the outline of the filled region to form the section arrow.

8. Click Finish Edit Mode on the Mode panel of the Modify | Create Filled Region Boundary tab.
9. Save the tag you just created as **`Custom Arrow.rfa`** on your hard drive or network, and you're ready to use it in the template or a project. To load it into your project, click the Load Into Project button located in the Family Editor panel. Choose the project where you want to use the symbol and click OK.

Next, you will assign this tag to a section mark system family type in the context of a project or template.

Creating a Section Type with a Custom Head/Tail Graphic

To create a section type that uses the section head family you created earlier, you need to load the new section head into the template file (if you've already loaded the custom arrow family in the previous exercise, skip to step 3):

1. If the family is not already loaded, switch to the Insert tab, and on the Load From Library panel, choose Load Family.

2. In the Load Family dialog box, find the `Custom Arrow.rfa` section head you created previously, select it, and click Open.
3. Switch to the Manage tab and select Additional Settings ➤ Section Tags.
4. In the Type Properties dialog box, click Duplicate.
5. In the Name dialog box, name the new type **Custom Filled Arrow**, and click OK.
6. In the section head's Type Properties dialog box, click the drop-down menu for Section Head and select Custom Arrow. For Section Tail, click <none>. This means the other end of the section line will not use a symbol. Click OK.

   The final step is to create a customized section view type, which will use the new section tag type you created in the previous step.
7. Switch to the View tab, and on the Create panel, select Section.
8. On the Properties palette, select the Edit Type button.
9. In the Type Properties dialog box, select Duplicate.
10. Name the new type **Design Sections**, and click OK.

You can now place a section in your drawing area and see the results shown in Figure 4.41. Note that in our sample the section is referencing a view that has already been placed on a sheet.

FIGURE 4.41
The completed custom section tag

You can repeat the previous exercises using a callout tag family template instead of a section tag template to achieve results similar to those shown in Figure 4.42.

FIGURE 4.42
Customizing the callout tag

CREATING A CUSTOM ELEVATION TAG

Elevation tags are a bit different from section or callout tags because one tag can simultaneously reference up to four views. You must, therefore, create and nest various parts of a custom elevation tag into one family in order to create custom graphics. Here is how it works:

1. Click the Application button, and select New ➤ Annotation Symbol.
2. In the New Annotation Symbol dialog box, select the family template called `Elevation Mark Body.rft` or `Metric Elevation Mark Body.rft`, and click Open.
3. Using steps similar to those in the section tag exercise, place the Sheet Number label and draw lines as shown in Figure 4.43.

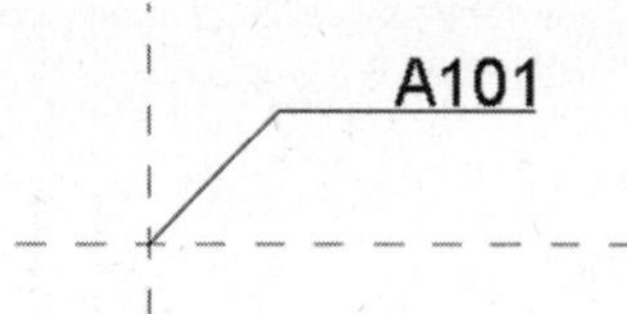

FIGURE 4.43
Define the custom linework and sheet number for the elevation mark body.

4. Make sure the properties Keep Readable and Fixed Rotation are checked for the label.
5. Save the family as **`Custom Elev Head.rfa`**.
6. Click the Application menu and select New ➤ Annotation Symbol.
7. In the New Annotation Symbol dialog box, select the family template called `Elevation Mark Pointer.rft` or `Metric Elevation Mark Pointer.rft` and click Open.
8. Using methods similar to those in previous steps, place labels for the Detail Number and Reference Label parameters. Draw a diamond with lines and a small, triangular, filled region, as shown in Figure 4.44.

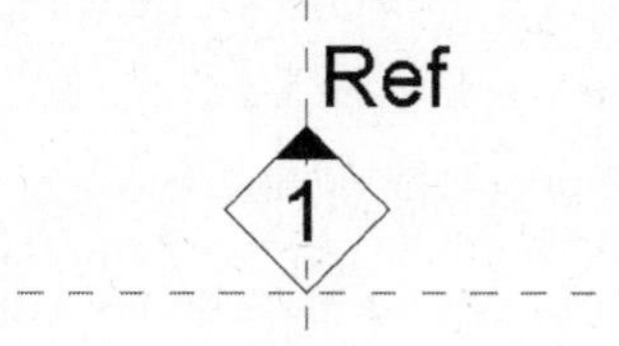

FIGURE 4.44
Custom elevation pointer composed of lines, filled region, and labels

9. Again, remember to make sure the properties Keep Readable and Fixed Rotation are checked for the labels.
10. Save the family as **`Custom Elev Pointer.rfa`** and load it into the `Custom Elev Head .rfa` family.
11. Place four instances of the Custom Elev Pointer family around the intersection of the visible reference planes, as shown in Figure 4.45.

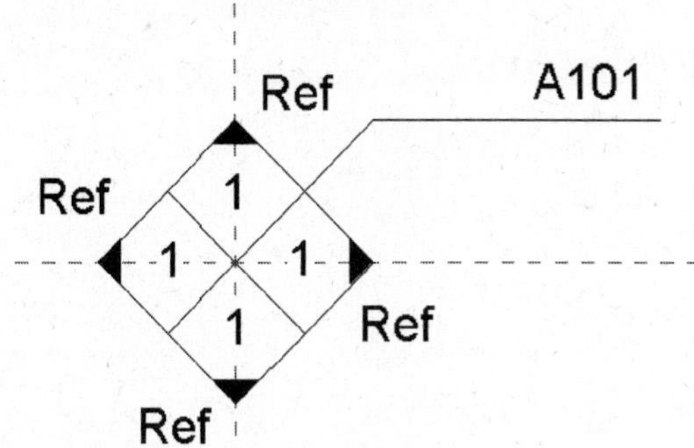

FIGURE 4.45
The nested pointer family is placed four times in the head family.

When this custom elevation tag family is loaded into a project and associated with an elevation type, it will function much like standard elevation symbols.

After the views are placed on a sheet, you get a preview of the completed elevation symbol, as shown in Figure 4.46.

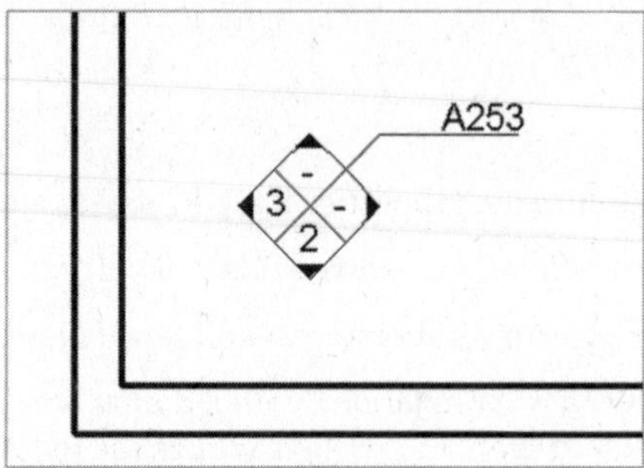

FIGURE 4.46
A customized elevation tag for interior elevations

Starting a Project with a Custom Template

Now that we have covered many areas of customization within project templates, you can configure Revit to use any of your custom project templates. To do so, follow these steps:

1. Click the Application menu and at the bottom of the menu click Options.
2. In the Options dialog box, select the File Locations category. The list of Project Template Files allows you to select several RTE files that will be displayed on the Recent Files screen. You can see these files in a drop-down list when you launch the New Project command either from the Application menu or by pressing Ctrl+N on the keyboard.
3. Click the green plus to add RTE files, and use the up and down arrow icons to modify the order of the templates in the list (Figure 4.47).

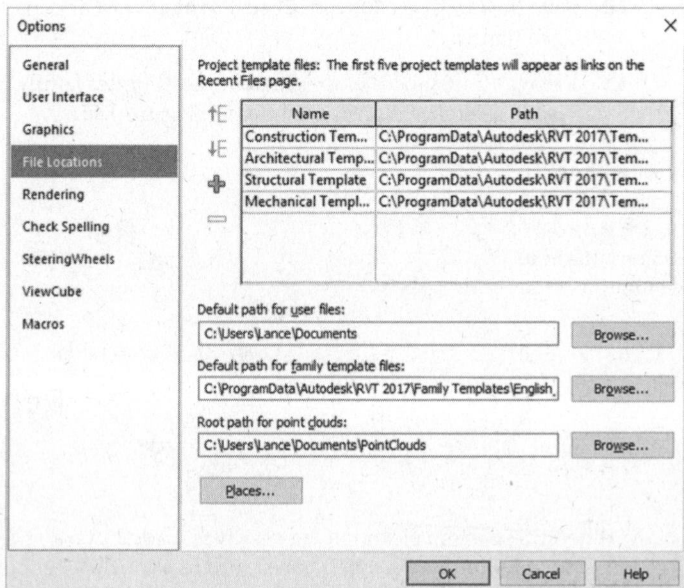

FIGURE 4.47
Add your custom project templates to File Locations in the Options dialog box.

Strategies for Managing Templates

During implementation, you can take one of two approaches when managing project templates: additive or subtractive. An *additive* approach, as shown in Figure 4.48, assumes that more than one project template will be developed to manage standards and content for a single project. Typically, a "base" template is used to start a project with a minimum amount of settings, whereas content and settings from "supplemental" templates are appended based on region, project type, or project style. In this scenario, each template file is lighter, but managing the templates becomes more difficult because changes in common settings or families must be applied to all templates.

FIGURE 4.48
Additive template approach

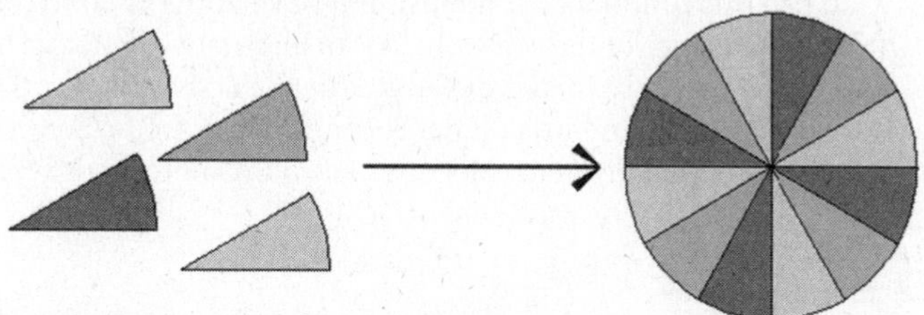

In contrast, the *subtractive* approach, shown in Figure 4.49, uses a single master template that contains all standard settings and content and relies on the project teams to remove and purge unused content. Although the file size of these templates tends to be larger, graphic settings are easier to manage within a single file.

FIGURE 4.49
Subtractive template approach

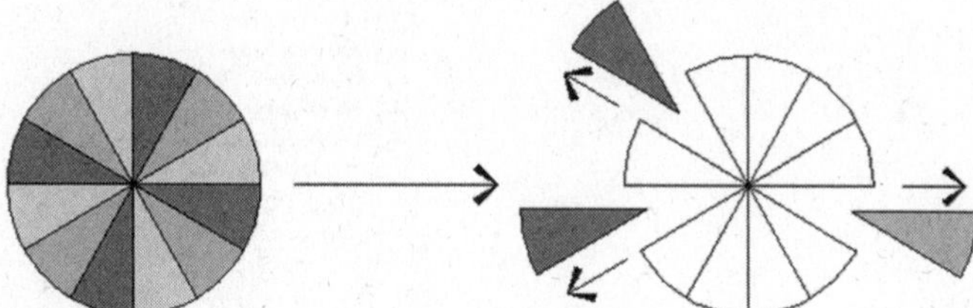

Aggregating Template Data

Whether you are managing the settings between templates or developing a project with multiple templates in an additive approach, you have useful tools within Revit to help share data between projects, such as Transfer Project Standards, Insert Views From File, and Insert 2D Elements From File.

TRANSFERRING PROJECT STANDARDS

You can easily share Revit families between project files by loading their RFA files; however, most other types of content must be transferred with the Transfer Project Standards command. Types of elements commonly transferred with this command include, but are not limited to, the following:

- Materials
- System family types (Walls, Floors, Roofs, Stairs, and so on)
- Text and dimension styles

- Filled regions
- Grid and level types
- Schedules
- Line styles and patterns
- Object style settings
- Viewport types

To use this command, you must first have both the source and target Revit files open within the same instance of the software. As an alternative, you can have the source file linked into your target file. Next, make the target file the active project. Switch to the Manage tab, and select Transfer Project Standards on the Settings panel. In the Select Items To Copy dialog box (Figure 4.50), choose as many item categories as you want to transfer, and then click OK.

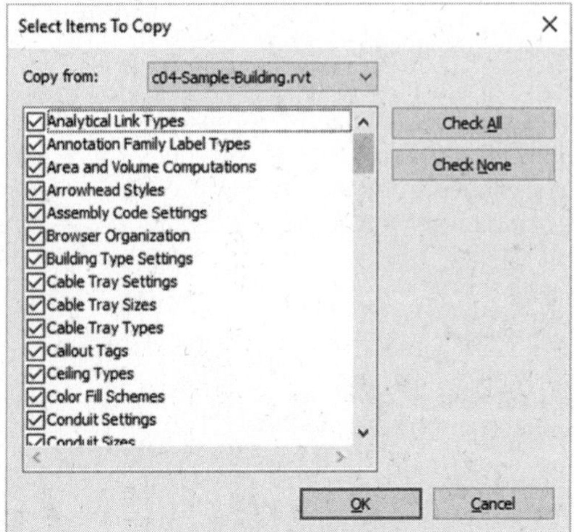

FIGURE 4.50
Select categories to be transferred between projects.

If you choose an element category containing some of the same types that already exist in your current project, you will be prompted with the option to overwrite the existing types or import the new types only (New Only), as shown in Figure 4.51.

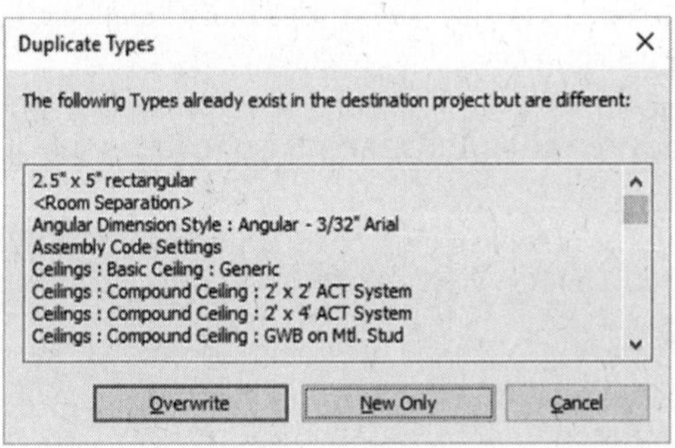

FIGURE 4.51
Transferring project standards with duplicate types

Real World Scenario

USING PROJECT TEMPLATES TO REDUCE REDUNDANT WORK

In a survey conducted by Robert Manna for an Autodesk University class, the majority of responders indicated that they develop two to five project templates primarily to differentiate between project types and/or market sectors. For example, if you work for an architectural firm that is usually contracted to perform work on large transportation sector projects, you might need to create a Revit file just to manage the site data for every project.

In that case, you would use a specific template as a site project template. Within such a template, you could use the following settings to reduce the amount of redundant work every time different teams attempt to establish a site model to which other building models are linked:

- Name levels Sea Level and First Floor Reference.
- Set default view scales to larger sizes.
- Change default project units to reflect civil engineering.
- Add a Cut/Fill schedule.
- Create dimension types useful for large drawings.
- Pad types, including "gravel."

INSERTING VIEWS FROM A FILE

The Insert Views From File command is useful for sharing views between project files—especially if you use the additive method of template management we mentioned earlier. This command allows you to copy drafting views, renderings, or schedules from one project to another. It can also insert entire sheets with all attached drafting views and associated properties. This procedure is quite useful if you use Revit project files as containers for your standard or typical details. An entire sheet of details can be inserted with one command!

Switch to the Insert tab, and choose Insert From File ➤ Insert Views From File in the Import panel.

Browse to a Revit project file (with the filename extension `.rvt`), and you will then see the Insert Views dialog box (Figure 4.52). In the left pane, all eligible drafting views, sheets, and schedules will be listed. If necessary, use the Views drop-down list to filter the choices.

If one or more sheets are selected in the Insert Views dialog box, all eligible drafting views placed on those sheets will be inserted into the current project as well. Note that repeating this process will not update the drafting views in the project but instead create new renamed drafting views and sheets. Also note that any custom view parameters are maintained during the transfer and can fit right into your customized Project Browser organizations, as we discussed earlier in this chapter.

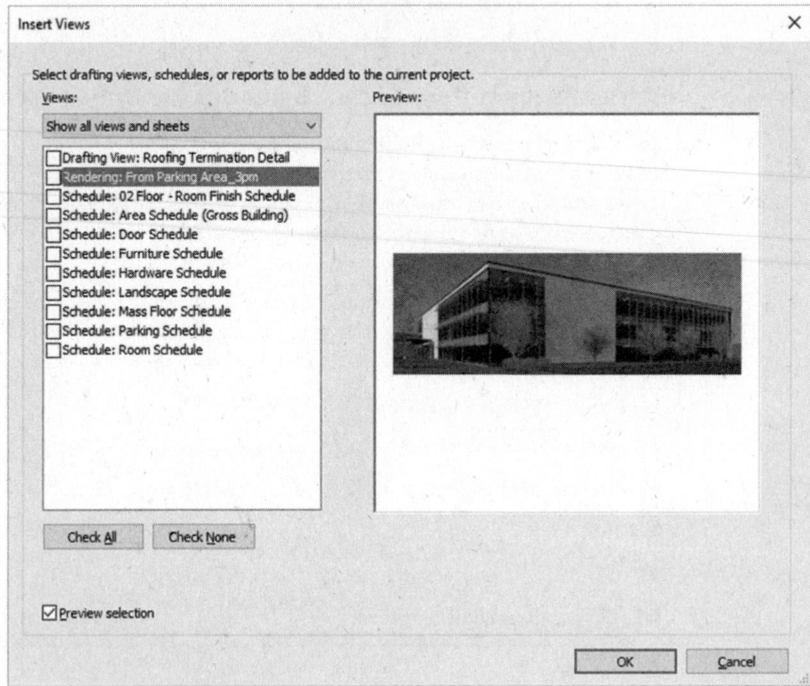

FIGURE 4.52 Insert Views can be used to transfer an entire sheet of drafting views into your project.

INSERTING 2D ELEMENTS FROM A FILE

The Insert 2D Elements From File command is similar to the Insert Views From File command, but instead of inserting an entire view, it will transfer only the view-specific elements from the selected view to the active view in the current project. You can select only one view from the selected file. This command allows you the flexibility to insert various view-specific elements such as detail lines, filled regions, text, and color fill legends. These elements can be imported from any view—not just drafting views.

On the Insert tab, find the Import panel, choose Insert From File ➤ Insert 2D Elements From File, and then navigate to a project file. Choose one of the available drafting views in the Insert 2D Elements dialog box (Figure 4.53).

For consistency, be sure to select the Transfer View Scale option to convert the scale of the active drafting view to that of the view you are inserting. You can move the elements into position using the Move command, and after placing the 2D elements, be sure to click Finish in the Edit Pasted panel or double-click anywhere outside the elements to complete the command.

DUPLICATE TYPES WHEN INSERTING

When using Insert Views From File or Insert 2D Elements From File, be sure to watch for warnings about existing types not being overwritten, as shown here, because new element types from the inserted source may contain more desirable properties.

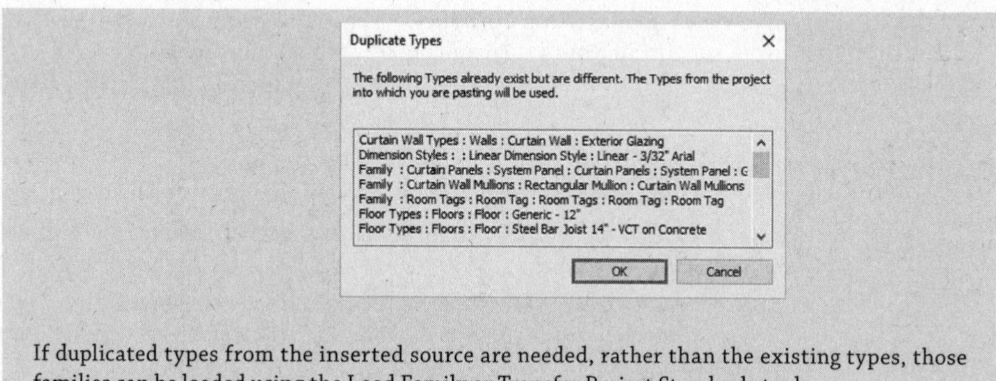

If duplicated types from the inserted source are needed, rather than the existing types, those families can be loaded using the Load Family or Transfer Project Standards tools.

FIGURE 4.53
Insert 2D Elements dialog box

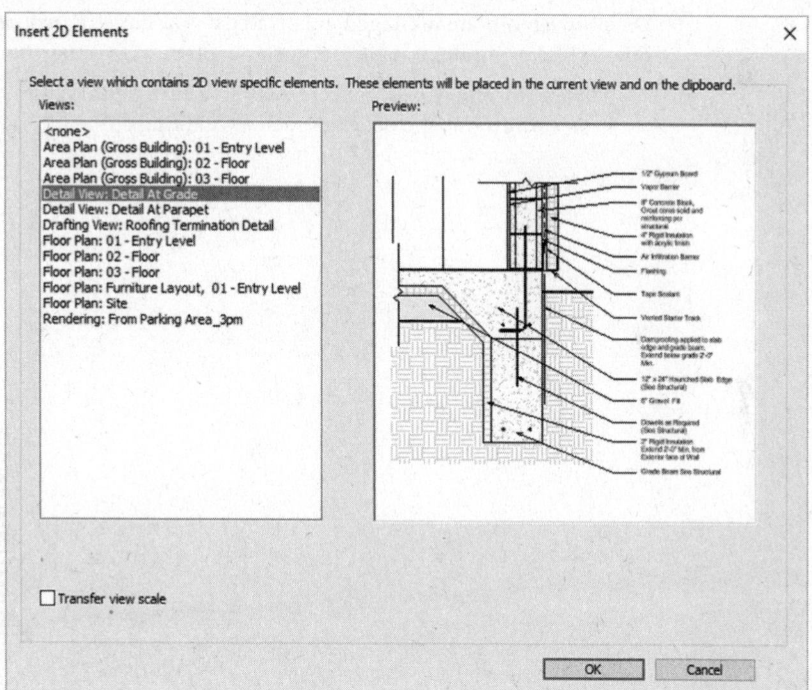

The Bottom Line

Define settings for graphic quality and consistency. The fundamental building blocks for any template are the customized settings for object styles, line styles, fill patterns, materials, and more.

Master It How can a complex custom-fill pattern be imported?

Organize views for maximum efficiency. The project template can be used to capture a framework supporting your visual and organizational standards.

Master It How can you customize the Project Browser to support your business needs?

Create custom annotation families. Developing a graphic style to match your standards will usually require you to edit some annotation families or create them from scratch.

Master It Can a single label display more than one parameter? How are custom view tags loaded into a project?

Start a project with a custom template. Making your custom template available for new projects ensures that all future projects will maintain the same level of graphic quality and efficiency you expect.

Master It How do you set your own custom project template to be the default for new projects?

Develop a template management strategy. Organizing your standards, content, and settings while using Revit tools to transfer content will make your effort more efficient.

Master It How do you insert your standard details from one Revit project to another? How do you transfer settings such as materials?

Part 2

Collaboration and Teamwork

In Part 1, you became familiar with the Autodesk® Revit® Architecture user interface and editing tools. Now we will take a look at what makes a Revit project tick. Part 2 sets you on the path toward using Revit software as part of a local team or as part of a larger project organization.

Chapter 5

Working in a Team

Most projects involve more than one person working together at any given time. It is common in design for many people to work collaboratively to meet deadlines and create a set of construction documents. Autodesk® Revit® Architecture software has tools that allow for a collaborative design and documentation process while giving multiple people simultaneous access to its single-file building model. This unique functionality is known as *worksharing*.

In this chapter, you'll learn to:

- Understand key worksharing concepts
- Enable worksharing on your project
- Organize worksets in your model
- Manage workflow with worksharing
- Understand element ownership in worksets
- Collaborate in the cloud

Understanding Worksharing Basics

Worksharing refers to the use of *worksets* to divide a model for the purpose of sharing project work among multiple people. A workset is a customizable collection of building elements that can be used to manage project responsibilities. By associating various building elements with worksets, the design team has the ability to subdivide the model to retain additional control over element ownership. Using worksets, several people can collaborate and work within the same file without fear that their decisions will conflict directly with their teammates. By default, worksharing is not enabled when you start a project because it is assumed you are in a single-user environment.

Worksharing is commenced when worksets are enabled and a project file is saved as a *central file* located on a network drive. This central file becomes the repository where all the design team's work is saved. Team members then create a local copy of the central file on their own workstation in which they will work as usual. The local copies of the model are individual versions of the file connected to the central file (Figure 5.1).

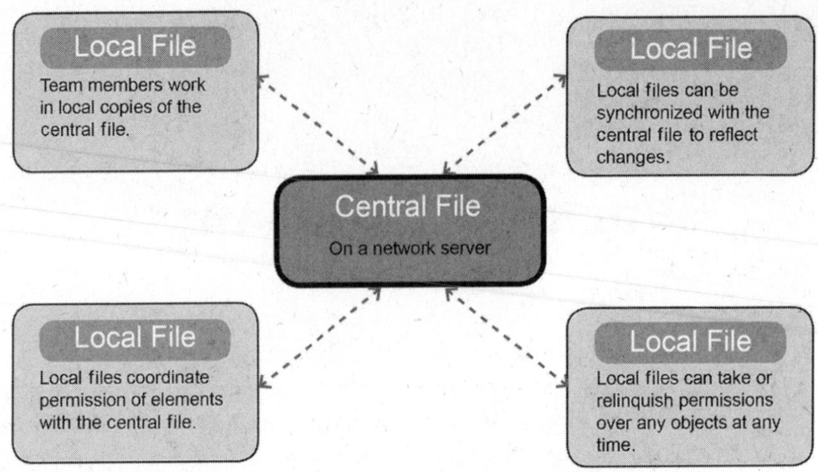

FIGURE 5.1 The worksharing concept

The only information that flows instantly between the local copies and the central file is permissions. Edits to model elements or settings are not transferred among the project team members because this would significantly decrease performance and would be distracting to your workflow to see the model constantly changing on the screen. In other words, the only way another team member knows you are editing something is by seeing that you own the element. Even though worksets are established to break a model into manageable chunks, permissions for a worksharing-enabled project are managed at the object level. This means that you could have a worksharing-enabled project with only one workset. Remember, a project file is essentially a database. As you are working on elements within the model, you are automatically obtaining permission to edit elements from the central database. Once permission to modify an element is granted, no one else can make changes to that element until the changes are reconciled with the central file. This occurs when you use the Synchronize With Central (SWC) command on the Collaborate tab to save changes you have made back to the central file and simultaneously update your local file with any other changes that have been published to the central file by other team members.

THE LIBRARY WORKSHARING ANALOGY

Another way to understand worksets and how they relate to object permissions is to think of a workset as a shelf of books in a library and the model objects as individual books on the shelf. If you are working on a paper about beavers, you can go to the library and do one of two things: check out the entire shelf of books about animals or check out the book about beavers. Checking out an entire shelf of books within a certain category is the same as making an entire workset editable—no one else can do their animal research paper because you have all the animal books. You have become the owner of that workset, and there can be only one owner per workset.

As an alternative, you would likely borrow only the book on beavers so that your fellow students can access other animal books to complete their papers. You have become an element borrower, and there can be many borrowers within each workset. Of course, the teacher probably made a mistake if she assigned two students to complete a report on the same animal. This mistake may also hold true when your team is working in Revit. The same model object cannot be edited simultaneously by more than one person. After all, you probably should not be working on the same model area as your teammate anyway, right?

The actual use of worksets can vary greatly from project to project. Quite frankly, creating more worksets beyond the defaults is technically not necessary; however, you can use worksets to take advantage of other benefits:

- Use worksets to control the visibility of groupings of building components, such as building skin, core, interior walls, and so on, without the need to use temporary view settings or control visibility manually.
- Close worksets as needed to remove those parts of your project from active memory, thus improving performance.
- Use workset ownership to prevent others from editing a part of the project you are currently designing.

Enabling Worksharing on Your Project

The worksharing feature can be enabled in any Revit project file. You can begin worksharing, create and remove worksets, or move elements between worksets during any stage of the project.

> **WORKSHARING IN THE PROJECT PROCESS**
>
> When the team has chosen to enable the worksharing feature, make sure everyone is aware of the change to the file and that it is planned within the project process.

To follow along with the text in this chapter, you can download the sample building project file from this book's companion website at `www.sybex.com/go/masteringrevit2017`. One version of the project does not have worksets, whereas the other has retained worksets but is not configured for worksharing. Open the file `c05-Sample-Building_Start.rvt` and switch to the Collaborate tab in the ribbon. The worksharing tools are shown in Figure 5.2.

FIGURE 5.2
The Collaborate tab

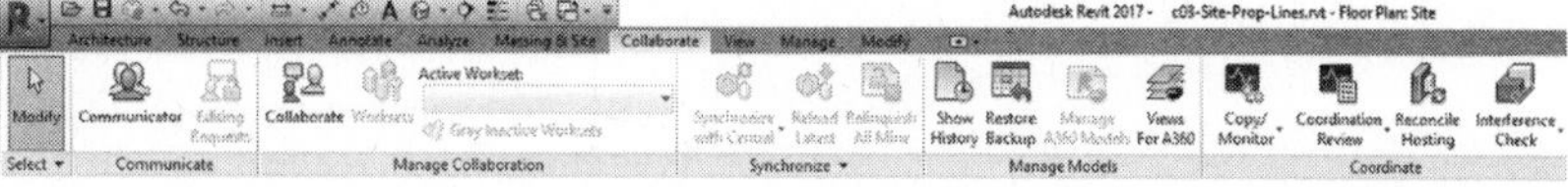

You can initiate worksharing by clicking the Collaborate button. It will initially be the only active button on the Manage Collaboration panel. Selecting this tool opens the Collaborate dialog box, alerting you that you are about to enable collaboration for your project (Figure 5.3). You can choose to Collaborate within your Network or with Autodesk 360. You can only choose A360 if you have that application installed. Both options allow you to enable Worksets. To start worksets, select the Worksets button in the Manage Collaboration Panel. Two worksets are automatically created within your project: Shared Levels and Grids, to which any existing levels and grids in your project will be assigned, and Workset1, to which all other building elements will be assigned. You can rename these worksets; however, we recommend not renaming Workset1 because you can never delete that workset—even if it has been renamed. You will read about an alternative way to use Workset1 in the section "Organizing Worksets" later in this chapter.

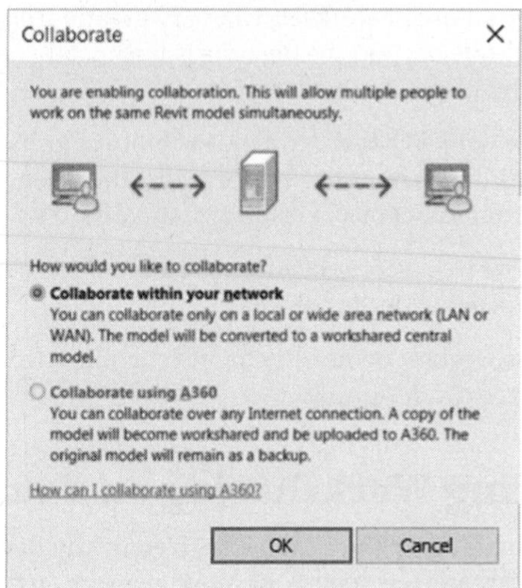

FIGURE 5.3
Activating worksharing

Click OK to confirm that you want to enable worksharing. Depending on the size of your model and your processor speed, this process can take a few minutes to complete. Once it is done, the Worksets dialog box opens (Figure 5.4).

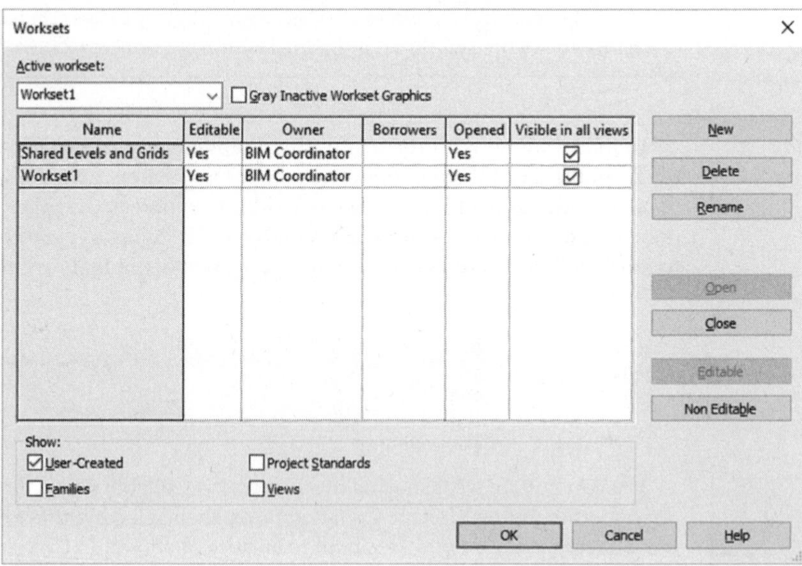

FIGURE 5.4
The Worksets dialog box

In the Worksets dialog box, you can create as many user-defined worksets as necessary; we offer some tips in the section "Organizing Worksets" later in this chapter. By default, when a new workset is created, it does not contain any model elements or components. You can add model elements to worksets as you build them or reassign existing elements to worksets. The Worksets dialog box also lets you take and relinquish permissions over existing worksets. First, you should understand the different types of worksets illustrated by the options in the Show area at the bottom of the Worksets dialog box, shown in Figure 5.4.

Types of Worksets

There are four types of worksets in any project: user-created, families, project standards, and views. User-created worksets such as Shared Levels and Grids and Workset1 are shown by default, and you have the option to list the others by selecting the check boxes at the bottom of the Worksets dialog box:

User-Created Worksets In addition to the two worksets automatically generated when you first enable worksharing, all of the worksets you add in the Worksets dialog box will fall under this category. All building elements, spaces, and datum objects you place in the project are assigned to user-created worksets. Only elements in user-created worksets can be moved to other user-created worksets.

Families Worksets For each family loaded in the project, a workset is automatically created. When editing the properties of a family, you will automatically take ownership over that family.

Project Standards Worksets The project standards workset type is dedicated to all the project settings, such as materials, dimension styles, annotations, tags, line styles, and so on. Any time you need to edit a project standard, such as modifying the type properties of dimensions, you will be taking ownership of the element's workset.

Views Worksets Every view created in a project has its own workset. The views workset type controls ownership of the view properties and any view-specific elements, such as annotations, dimensions, tags, detail lines, and so on. You can take ownership of a particular view workset by selecting it from the workset list and clicking the Editable button, but this is not necessary to start working in a view. You can also take ownership of a view by right-clicking the view in the Project Browser and choosing Make Workset Editable from the context menu. This can be a helpful shortcut in construction documents when much of the effort on the project is more view specific. Regardless of ownership, any team member always has the ability to *add* annotation elements to any view—you just cannot *change* any existing view-specific elements when another user owns a view workset.

We will get back to worksets in the "Organizing Worksets" section of this chapter. For now, you should establish the workset-enabled project model as a central file.

Creating a Central File

After you enable worksets in a project model, you must save the project as a central file to enable others to collaborate on the model. This is the file that will collect all the work done by your team members and allow them to receive regular updates of changes being made to the model and documentation.

You can use one of two commands to establish a workset-enabled model as a central file: Save or Save As. If you click Save from the Application menu, you will be presented with a warning telling you that this is the first time the file will be saved since worksharing was enabled (Figure 5.5). If you select Yes, the file will become a central file with only the default settings in its current location.

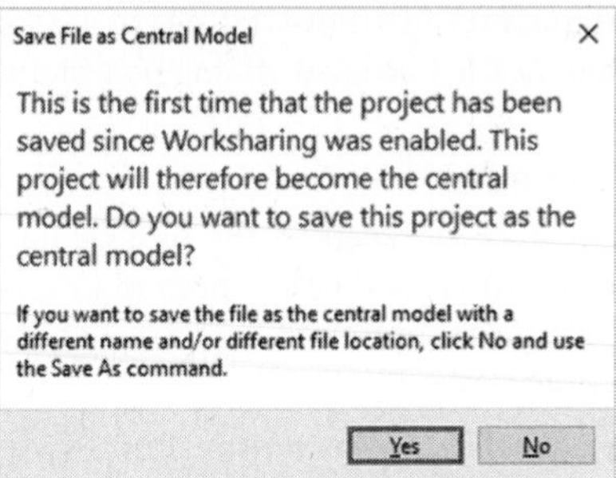
Save File as Central Model

This is the first time that the project has been saved since Worksharing was enabled. This project will therefore become the central model. Do you want to save this project as the central model?

If you want to save the file as the central model with a different name and/or different file location, click No and use the Save As command.

Yes No

FIGURE 5.5
The Save command will create a central file with only the default settings.

As an alternative, we recommend using the Save As ➤ Project command from the Application menu. When you click this button instead of Save, the Save As dialog box will appear. In the Save As dialog box, click the Options button to access the options shown in Figure 5.6.

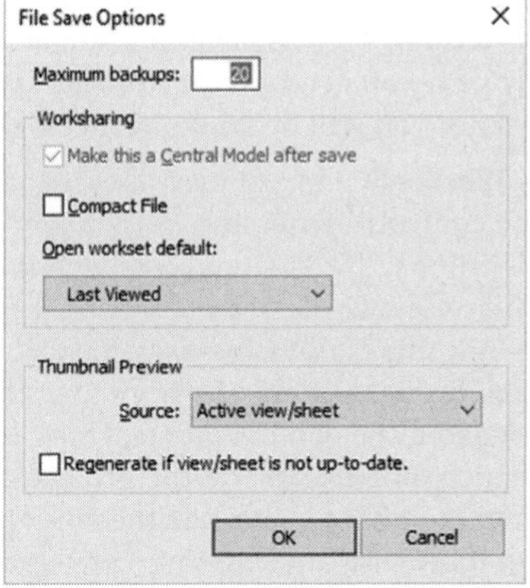

FIGURE 5.6
Options for saving a project file

This dialog box contains some important settings. At the top, you can set the number of backups the file will keep in the folder history after saves. The default value is 20. Depending on the storage availability on your network, how often your network is backed up, and the number of people working in the model (remember, local files are also backups), you might want to increase this number. For example, if three users are using Synchronizing With Central every 30 minutes; that might be 48 saves before the next backup. Better safe than sorry. Also, the Make This A Central Model After Save check box is selected and grayed out. This is because we have activated worksharing in this file and it is assumed that we will be making a central file on the next save.

You can also specify default settings for opening the project file (shown as Open Workset Default). We will discuss opening a file in the section "Creating a Local File" later in this chapter, but we recommend setting this option to Specify for most project scenarios. This will always prompt your team members with the Worksets dialog box when a local file is opened. Click OK to exit the File Save Options dialog box.

Back in the Save As dialog box, choose a network location that everyone on the team has access to for your central file. Be sure that when you are naming your new central file, you choose a new name. Do not save over the existing Revit project file. There are two reasons for this: First, it automatically gives you a backup of your file as it existed before worksharing was enabled. Second, saving over an open Revit file can sometimes cause corruption, even if it is the same model. It is also a good idea to name the file with some clarity that helps identify it as a central file, such as `MyProject-Central.rvt`.

FILE NAMING IN REVIT

When you are working with a project team in Revit, it is important to give your various team members some guidance when you name your files. We just touched on the idea of making sure you include "Central" in your filename so team members know they will need to make a local copy when opening the file, but there are some other guidelines you might want to consider.

When working with other disciplines, consider naming your file with a denominator to let the larger team know which file is architectural, which is structural, and so on. Also, because your office might be working on several Revit projects at one time, you might be working in more than one version of Revit if you're working on more than one project. So it's a good idea to include the Revit version in your filename so team members don't accidentally open the file with a newer version. An example filename might be `c05-Sample-Building-A16-Central.rvt`. c05-Sample-Building is the project name, A designates the discipline as architectural, 16 is the version of Revit (2016), and Central notes it is a central file.

Once you have entered a new name for the file, click the Save button to save the file. Now that your file is saved to the network, close all the open view windows. As one final step, you need to make sure you don't accidentally retain any rights over the objects and elements within the central file, thereby prohibiting anyone from editing those elements.

To do this, go to the Collaborate tab, find the Synchronize panel, and click the Synchronize With Central button. This button is a flyout button that contains two commands: Synchronize And Modify Settings and Synchronize Now. You will want to use Synchronize And Modify Settings in this case. In the Synchronize With Central dialog box, shown in Figure 5.7, make sure you select any available check boxes in the middle portion to relinquish ownership of all worksets. You can also add a comment to identify the action taken during this synchronization.

FIGURE 5.7
Synchronizing with central to relinquish permissions

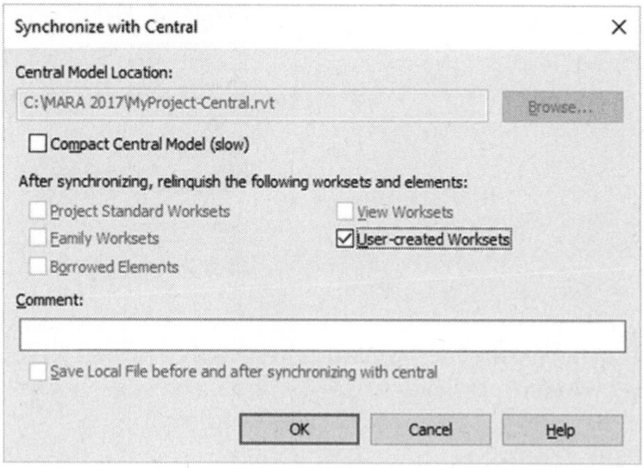

Yes, it might seem odd to use the Synchronize With Central command when you are actually in the central file, but this method is the fastest way to relinquish all worksets and complete the setup of the central file. Click OK to complete the synchronization.

Using a Revit Server Accelerator

If your project team is distributed in various geographic locations, an alternative to synchronizing with the central model directly over the wide area network (WAN) is to use a Revit Server Accelerator. This technology was developed by Autodesk to support extended collaboration through the use of server technology that creates a layer of virtual central models. The Revit Server then manages changes into a single central model without burdening the WAN with full synchronization traffic.

You may learn more about A360 Collaboration for Revit, which we discuss more in the "Collaborating in the Cloud" section later in this chapter.

Selecting a Starting View

On the Manage tab of the ribbon, locate the Manage Project panel and click the Starting View command. With this command, you can select any project view to be the first view displayed when the model is opened (Figure 5.8). Because 3D views take longer to regenerate when your project opens, we recommend you select a 2D view to speed this process; you can even create a drafting view that contains the project name and image as the starting view.

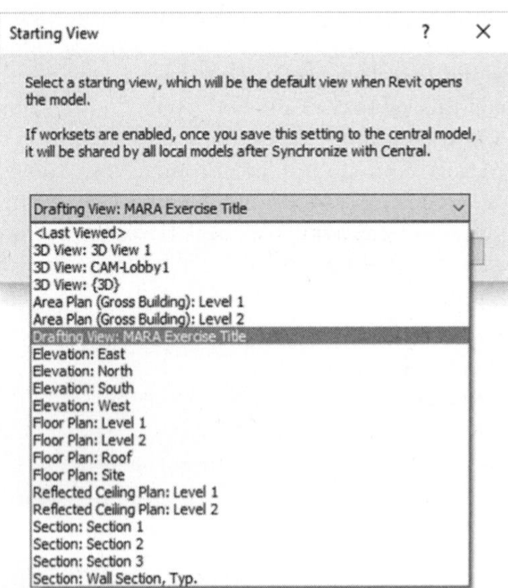

Figure 5.8
Selecting the starting view

Another use for the starting view is as a project bulletin board. Simply create a drafting view for the starting view and keep it populated with project standards, modeling action items, and other notes your team might need to know.

Synchronize the central file once again, and remember to relinquish any worksets you might have obtained during the configuration of the central file. From the Application menu click Close to close the central file.

Using Caution When Using a Central File

Once you have created a central file, there are a couple of things you cannot do. Do not open it directly again and do not change the filename. Opening the file will change its attributes, and none of your team members will be able to synchronize with central. If they were actively working in the local file, their work would be lost. The same problem occurs if you change the filename—those with a local copy will lose their association to the central file and they will not be able to save their work.

Creating a Local File

Now that you have made a central file, you will need to create a local copy of it in which you will organize worksets for team collaboration and continue your design and documentation. There are several ways to perform this action. One option is to simply open the network location of the central file and copy the file from the network to your desktop or anywhere on your local hard drive. Be careful not to *move* the file—only copy it. It is also a good idea to rename the file to something that identifies it as a local file, such as `c05-Sample-Building-Local.rvt`.

Another method of creating a local file is to use a script or macro. There are many variations of this method, so we will not discuss them in detail here. We believe the simplest example of a script is to use common Windows commands in a BAT file. You can create a BAT file in any simple text editor such as Windows Notepad, and you will find a command-line reference in Windows Help and Support on your computer (search for *commands*). You can also find a free tool on David Baldacchino's blog:

`http://do-u-revit.blogspot.com/2008/03/streamlining-local-file-creation.html`

The last and most predictable method for creating a local file is to use the functionality integrated with the Open command. Using any common method to open a file, you will get to the Open dialog box (Figure 5.9). Navigate to the central file, and when it is selected, you will have the option to create a new local file at the bottom of the dialog box. Whenever you select a central file through the Open dialog box, this box is checked for you as a safety precaution against you opening the central file directly.

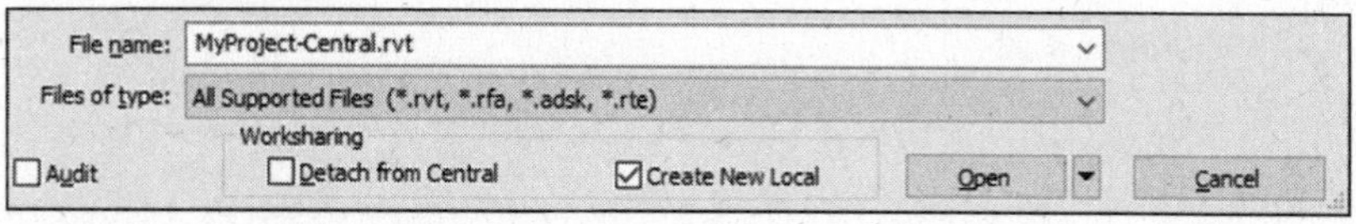

Figure 5.9
Create a new local file from the Open dialog box.

File name: MyProject-Central.rvt
Files of type: All Supported Files (*.rvt, *.rfa, *.adsk, *.rte)
Worksharing
☐ Audit ☐ Detach from Central ☑ Create New Local Open Cancel

The local file is created in the location specified as the default path for user files. This setting can be found in the application options, under the File Locations settings. The default location for this setting is the My Documents folder. If you choose this method, the local file will be appended with your workset username. If you have already created a local file with this method, you will be prompted with a warning the next time you attempt to create a new local copy from the central file (Figure 5.10). You have the option to either overwrite the existing local copy or append a time stamp to the existing file.

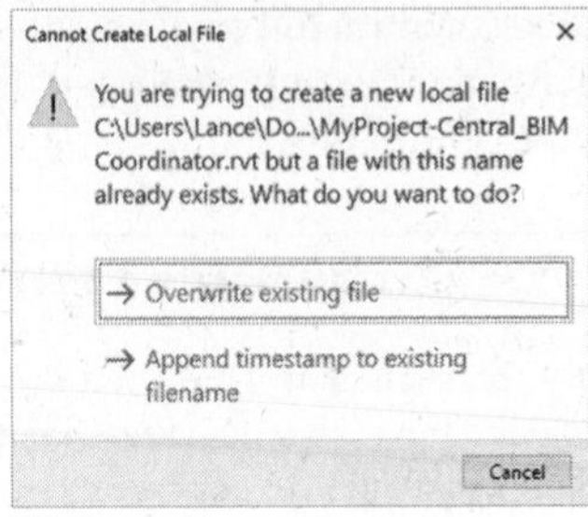

FIGURE 5.10 Overwriting existing local files

Before you proceed to open the file, you can change the way you interact with worksets. If you click the small arrow to the right of the Open button, you will see a list of options, as shown in Figure 5.11.

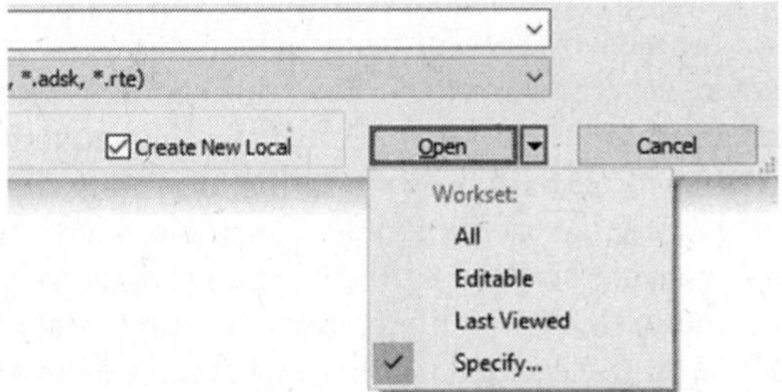

FIGURE 5.11 Workset options when opening a file

The default setting for opening worksharing files is Last Viewed, but each of the available settings is helpful to your workflow. Let's review these settings in detail:

All This setting opens all available user-created worksets.

Editable This setting opens only those worksets that you have previously made editable. If you did not retain ownership of any worksets the last time you worked on a local file, none of the user-created worksets will be opened. To retain ownership of worksets when you close a file, you will be prompted with the alert shown in Figure 5.12. Choose the option to keep ownership of elements and worksets. We do not recommend this workflow because it restricts others on your team from working on elements for which you retain ownership.

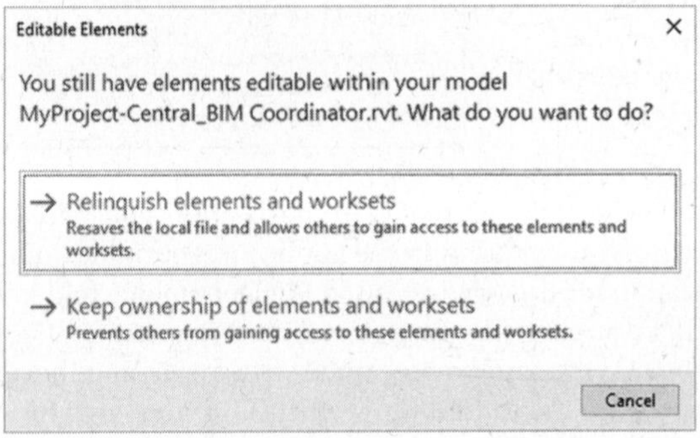

FIGURE 5.12 Closing a file while relinquishing ownership of worksets

Editable Elements

You still have elements editable within your model MyProject-Central_BIM Coordinator.rvt. What do you want to do?

→ Relinquish elements and worksets
Resaves the local file and allows others to gain access to these elements and worksets.

→ Keep ownership of elements and worksets
Prevents others from gaining access to these elements and worksets.

Cancel

Last Viewed The file will be opened with the Last Viewed worksets configuration. If you use this option when opening a new local file for the first time, all worksets will be opened.

Specify We highly recommend this option because it will give you the most flexibility when opening a local file. When Specify is selected, you will be presented with the Worksets dialog box immediately after you click the Open button. You can then choose the worksets you would like to open or close before the file is loaded into memory.

To continue your exercise, choose the Specify option and then click the Open button. The first time any local file is opened using a method other than the Create New Local option, you will see a warning message alerting you that you are opening a local file. This is simply a notification that you have made a local copy of a central file and you will be the owner of the local file. If this warning appears, click Close to dismiss the warning and continue the file-opening process.

The Worksets dialog box will be displayed if you used the Specify option to open the file. At this point in the exercise, you will still have only Shared Levels and Grids and Workset1, but in the future, you will have the ability to close any workset you may not need for editing in your work session. Click OK to close the Worksets dialog box.

USING CAUTION WHEN USING A CENTRAL FILE

Using a worksharing environment allows you to do something your IT department typically asks you *not* to do: work directly on your workstation's hard drive. Although working off a network file is typically a good idea, there are several reasons why a local copy offers additional benefits:

- It allows more than one user to make changes to the central file by editing local files and synchronizing those changes with the central file.
- Your local copy will be more responsive than a networked local file because your access speed to your hard drive is much faster than it is across most networks.
- If anything bad happens to your network or your central file, such as file corruption, each local file is basically a backup that can be used to create a new local file by performing a Save As operation and selecting the option to make this a new central file.

Using Worksharing Usernames

Each local file is automatically associated with your worksharing username once it is opened; after it is opened, it cannot be edited by any other user. By default, your Windows login name is used as your worksharing username. When you use the Create New Local option to open a worksharing-enabled project, the username is appended to the end of the local filename—for example, `c05-Sample-Building-A16-Central_YourName.rvt`.

It can be a good idea to adjust the naming convention for usernames to help team communication. In a smaller office, it might not be as necessary, but in a larger office or multi-office team, clarification of element ownership is vital. One option is to change your workset username to first name, last name, and phone extension. This way, team members can quickly identify and contact you if they need you to relinquish permission of an element.

To make this modification, follow these steps:

1. Close all your open projects files. You can change the username only when no workshared projects are open (you cannot change your username while it is active in open projects). After you change your workset username, you will need to create a new local file because the old local file is associated with a different username.
2. From the Application menu, choose Options at the bottom.
3. In the Options dialog box, select the General category.
4. In the Username field, enter a new value (Figure 5.13). Click OK to exit.

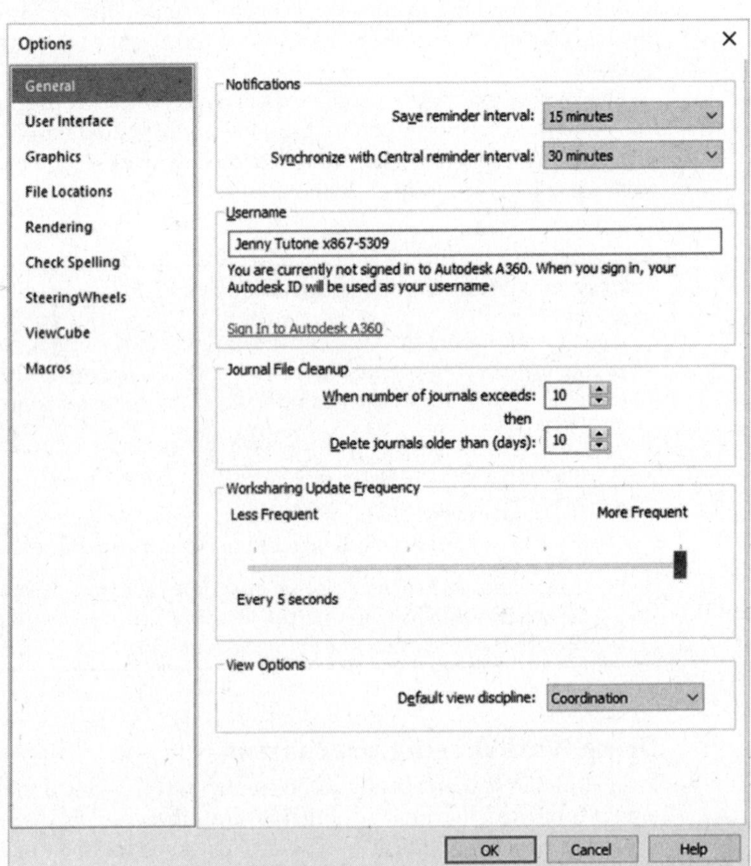

FIGURE 5.13 Changing the default username

If you have signed in to an Autodesk® 360 (A360) services account, your username will automatically switch to your A360 username, which may not include your telephone number but will give you access to other ways of communication such as instant messaging through applications such as C4R. A360 is an online service with Autodesk accessible from the upper-right portion of your application window. If you are not signed in, you should see the button as a small figure with Sign In next to it. More information on the A360 account is provided later in this chapter.

Organizing Worksets

Now that you have enabled worksets and configured your project file for worksharing, you have the opportunity to further organize your model into more worksets. When dividing your project into worksets, it is important to think about the larger building system rather than try to isolate its individual components. In other words, worksets should not be used like layers in a CAD application. A good way to think about dividing up worksets is to consider the building elements and the number of people working on each of these elements. A basic breakdown of a project's components might include the following:

- Exterior skin
- Core
- Interior partitions (in a larger building, by floor)
- Site
- Furniture, fixtures, and equipment (FF&E)

This breakdown mirrors some of the roles and responsibilities on the project as well. There might be a small group working on exterior skin design and detailing, another group working on interior partitions, and a third working on FF&E. And for larger projects where you have linked files (possibly from other disciplines like mechanical, electrical, and plumbing [MEP] or structure), it is helpful to associate those linked files with their own worksets.

How Many Worksets Do You Need?

A good rule of thumb is that you should have one or two worksets for every person working on the project (besides Shared Levels and Grids). On a small project with two or three people, you might only have three or four worksets. On larger projects, you could have a dozen or so.

Also keep in mind that once you have six to eight people working in a project, the performance of Revit slows somewhat, not to mention that you spend a bit more time saving local files because each person actually saves twice (once to save changes to central and another to download everyone else's changes). If your project is large enough to warrant more than six to eight people working concurrently in the model, consider dividing the model into multiple files, as we discuss in Appendix B.

Continuing with the Sample Building exercise file, open a local copy of the central file and click the Worksets button from the Collaborate tab or from the status bar. Click the New button and create each of the following new worksets (keep the Visible In All Views option selected each time):

- Exterior and Structure
- Furniture
- Interiors

When you have done this, you should see a total of five user-created worksets, as shown in Figure 5.14. The worksets we have set up demonstrate how a typical breakdown might occur in a project of this size, but creating, defining, and assigning worksets is by no means limited to this scheme. Depending on how you structure work in your office, the worksets might be quite different.

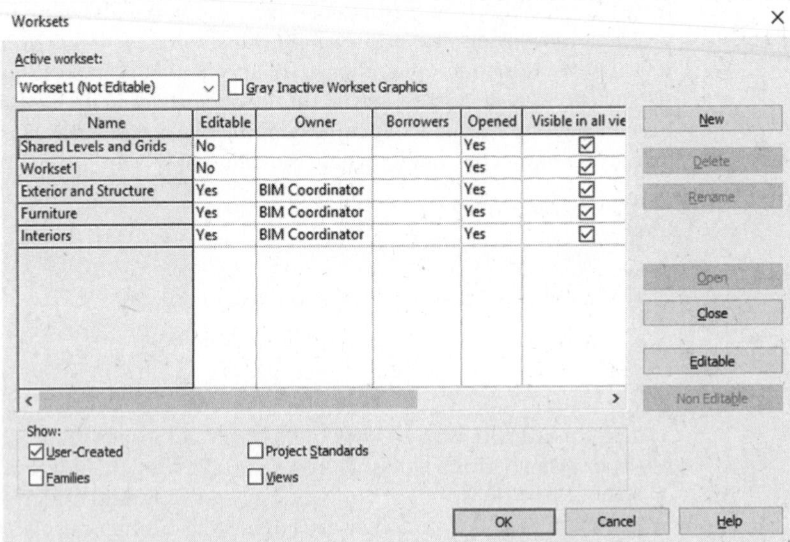

FIGURE 5.14 Creating new worksets in the project

SHOULD YOU KEEP WORKSET1?

Why keep Workset1? Well, it is a great holding place when new users need to work on the project but they are not certain to which workset they should assign the new elements they create. Tell them not to worry! Simply ask them to make Workset1 their active workset. After they have finished their work, they can isolate all the elements they have created and then assign them to the right workset later (maybe with some oversight). You can even have a 3D view with only Workset1 visible.

As we stated previously, one of the biggest challenges facing teams new to Revit is understanding the difference between layers in a CAD application as compared to worksets. These teams typically want to try to manage worksets as they managed layers in CAD, which can result in worksets named Doors, Windows, Walls, and so on. Although this is effective management in a CAD environment, you do not want to create all of this structure for worksets. Not only is it time-consuming, but it does not provide any benefit.

Much like layers, the workset is a tool that the team will need to understand in order to use it successfully. Worksets should be structured by a team's BIM coordinator or a project manager familiar with a BIM workflow. Ultimately, though, it is up to the team members to place elements in the proper worksets and ensure that project standards are being followed.

Moving Elements between Worksets

With this chapter's exercises, you are applying worksharing to an existing model; therefore, you will need to assign the existing model elements to the worksets you have created. The easiest way to move elements between user-defined worksets is by using a customized 3D view. The following exercise will walk you through moving elements from Workset1 to the new worksets you have established, using a subtractive method to reassign the model geometry. This should be done by a single person who owns all the elements to ensure that no permissions issues occur when elements are being moved between worksets. This is also best done with only one person actively working on the file. If you have other users with local copies, ask them to not use the model while you're moving elements.

To move the elements between worksets, follow these steps:

1. Open the default 3D view so you can see the entire model. By selecting a 3D view, you cannot accidentally select view-specific elements (like elevation or sections) or datum—you'll be selecting only model elements that can be assigned to user-defined worksets. Now open the Visibility/Graphic Overrides dialog box and choose the Worksets tab. Choose to hide all the worksets except for Workset1 (Figure 5.15), and click OK. This will turn off any elements that are visible on those worksets and allow you to "subtract" elements from this view as you move them to the nonvisible worksets.

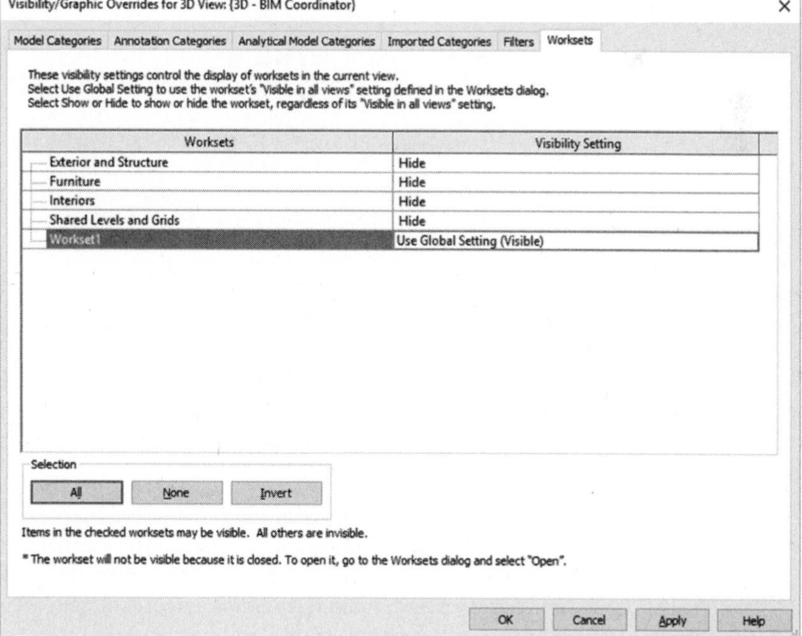

FIGURE 5.15
Isolating Workset1 in Visibility/Graphic Overrides

In a worksharing-enabled file, the default 3D view is unique to each user participating in the model. The name of the view will be appended with the team member's username; for example, {3D – BIM Coordinator}.

2. To select model elements and assign them to different worksets, you have a few options:

   - For a smaller model, select a comfortable number of elements using the Filter tool and then modify the Workset parameter in the Properties palette. What constitutes a "comfortable" number of elements depends on your computer's capabilities. As an example, if you window-select all the elements in our Sample Building model, you can click the Filter button in the ribbon and choose to keep the Furniture category active and uncheck the remaining items (Figure 5.16). Click OK. In the Properties palette, assign these elements to the Furniture workset.

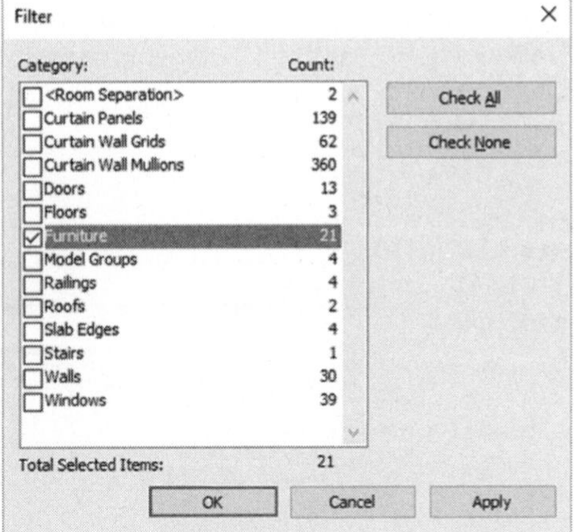

FIGURE 5.16
Use the Filter tool to select specific object categories.

   - For a larger model, it might first be necessary to select some individual components and move them separately. Although the process remains the same (select elements, change the workset in the Properties palette), the selection system can vary. Another example of moving elements by selection would be to highlight an exterior wall and use the Tab key to select a chain of exterior walls. Those exterior walls can be moved to the Exterior and Structure workset.
   - You can also select one or more types of elements in the model and use the Temporary Hide/Isolate tools in the view control bar. In the exercise file, try to locate a single window and select it. From the view control bar, click the Temporary Hide/Isolate icon and select Isolate Category. The boundary of the 3D view will be highlighted, indicating a temporary view setting, and you will see only windows. Window-select all the windows and then go to the Properties

palette to assign them to the Exterior and Structure workset (Figure 5.17). Return to the Temporary Hide/Isolate icon in the view control bar and select Reset Temporary Hide/Isolate.

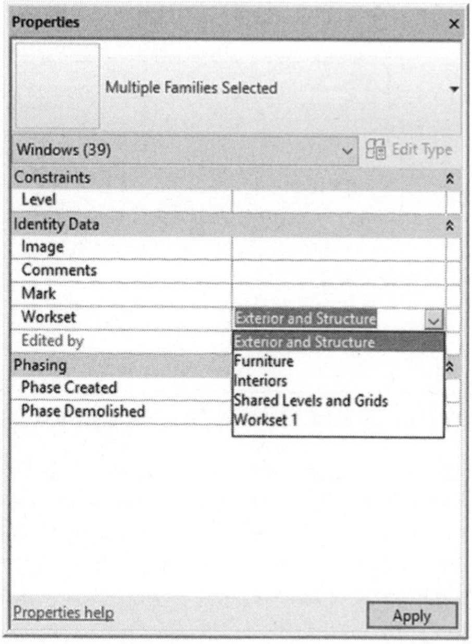

FIGURE 5.17
Assign the Workset property to multiple elements.

3. Using the same technique, you can move the remainder of the model elements to their respective worksets. When the default 3D view is empty, you will know that all the elements have been reassigned to new worksets.

For even easier workset management and quality control, you can create a 3D view named according to each workset. In each of these views, isolate the respective workset in the Worksets tab of the Visibility/Graphic Overrides dialog box. After these views are established in the project, you can periodically examine them to fix any workset assignment mistakes. For example, someone might have placed plumbing fixtures on the Site workset.

As you continue to assign model elements to worksets, you should be aware of some special conditions that might exist in your project. Some elements that can be selected and/or filtered are actually subcomponents of other systems, and as such their Workset property cannot be changed independently of the parent system. For example, you can select and filter curtain wall panels and mullions, but you can change only the Workset property of the curtain wall object, which is simply categorized as a wall.

Another special condition to look for is the presence of groups. Grouped objects will show up in the filter list as Groups and not in their respective categories. As an example, in Figure 5.18, the filter list shows Model Groups. Select only Model Groups in the Filter dialog box and use the Isolate Elements command in the view control bar, and you will see that the groups contain elements in the Casework and Furniture categories.

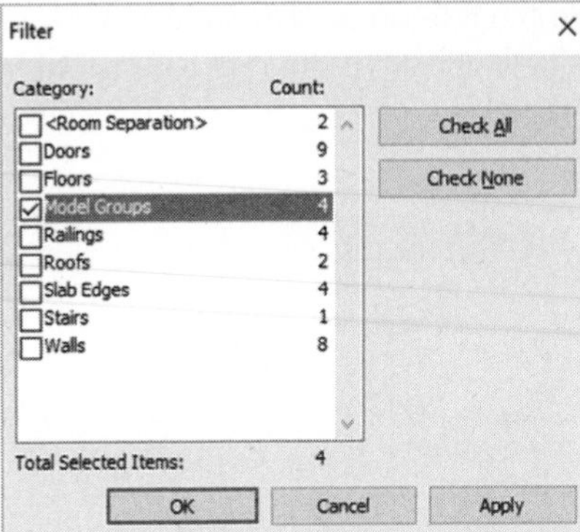

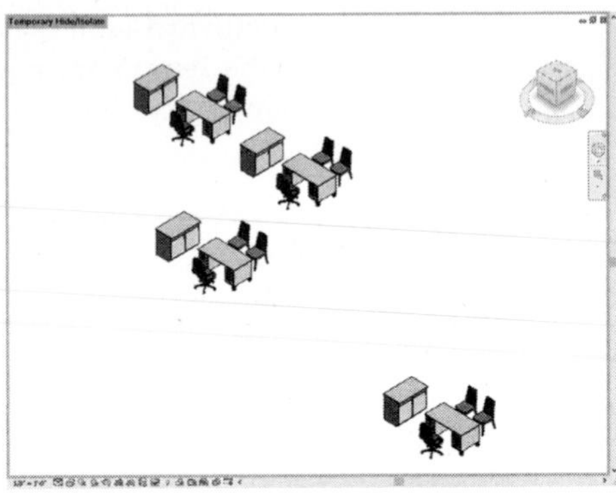

FIGURE 5.18 Select only Model Groups in the Filter dialog box.

> **MOVING EVERY INSTANCE OF AN ELEMENT**
>
> A quick way to move every instance of an element type to a new workset is to use the Select All Instances option from the context menu. For example, select a chair in the model and right-click it. From the context menu, choose Select All Instances ➤ In Entire Project. This selects all the family elements in the entire model, allowing you to quickly move them all to the same workset in the Properties palette.
>
> Another way to select all instances of an element is to right-click the family name in the Project Browser under the Families node. Simply navigate to your family in its proper category.

At any point in this process, you can check your work by opening the Workset tab in the Visibility/Graphic Overrides dialog box and setting all but one workset to Hide. Use this method to inspect the contents of each workset.

The workflow described in the preceding exercise is necessary only if you have developed a model *before* enabling worksharing for collaboration. You can always start a new project enabled with worksets, and your team can develop the model simultaneously. The only important thing to remember is to ensure your team uses the appropriate active workset when working in a worksharing-enabled project. We will cover that in greater detail in the following section.

Managing Workflow with Worksets

Now that you or your BIM coordinator has established a central file and organized your project into worksets, you can get ready to work by creating a local copy of the central file. Do you need to do anything special to begin working in a project that is enabled with worksets? No. You can simply start adding or editing content in your project because permissions are being automatically managed as you work. Just remember that you cannot edit any elements (2D or 3D) that someone else is already editing.

You do not have to make any worksets editable unless you want to prevent other team members from editing certain parts of your project until you have completed some work. Remember the library analogy earlier in this chapter.

Do Not Work in the Central File

Make sure that you *never* work directly within the central file. Doing so will change the file attributes on the server and prohibit anyone with a local file from being able to synchronize with the central file. The possibility of losing a lot of work and effort from team members exists, so it is safer to err on the side of caution by simply never opening the file.

The most important thing to remember when you use worksharing is that every element in the file and added to the file belongs to a workset. To make sure you are placing elements in the proper workset while working, know there are a few tools to ensure that you select the right workset.

One such location is on the Collaborate tab, where you originated worksharing. As shown in Figure 5.19, the active workset is Exterior and Structure. This also tells you that the Exterior and Structure workset is not editable. What this means is that as a user, you have not taken ownership of this workset. However, as we mentioned previously, you do not need to own a workset to add elements to it. It just needs to be active in this window.

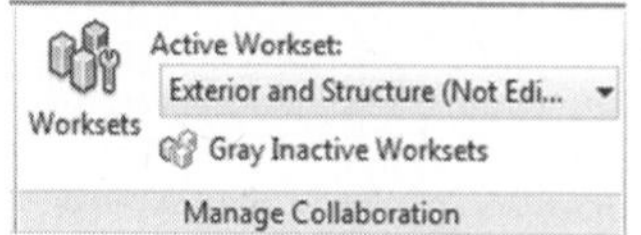

Figure 5.19
Setting the active workset in the ribbon

The second location is in the status bar at the bottom of the application (Figure 5.20). The drop-down menu on the left serves the same function as the Active Workset drop-down in the Collaborate tab, but it allows you to verify that the proper workset is active without the need to bounce between tabs in the ribbon and interrupt your workflow. From this location you can also change the active workset and even open the Worksets dialog box using the small button to the left of the drop-down menu.

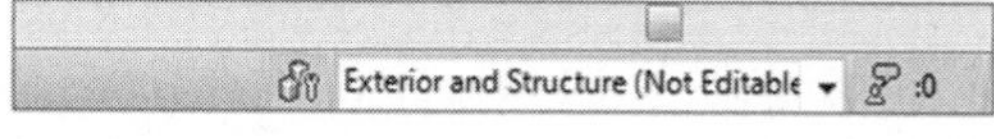

Figure 5.20
Setting the active workset in the status bar

Another helpful tool located on the Collaborate tab is the Gray Inactive Worksets button. This dims all the elements that are not on the active workset, helping you identify what elements are in your current, active workset. This is a temporary view state and will not affect any printing or other output.

In addition, you can always view an object's workset assignment by hovering your mouse pointer over the object and viewing its workset in the status bar (Figure 5.21). This location will also display an object's family and category. In the example shown here, the wall is in the Exterior and Structure workset, in the Walls category, and its type is Exterior - EIFS on Mtl. Stud. There are three locations in this figure where you can see the workset: one in the Properties palette, one in the status bar, and one in the tooltip shown when you hover over an element.

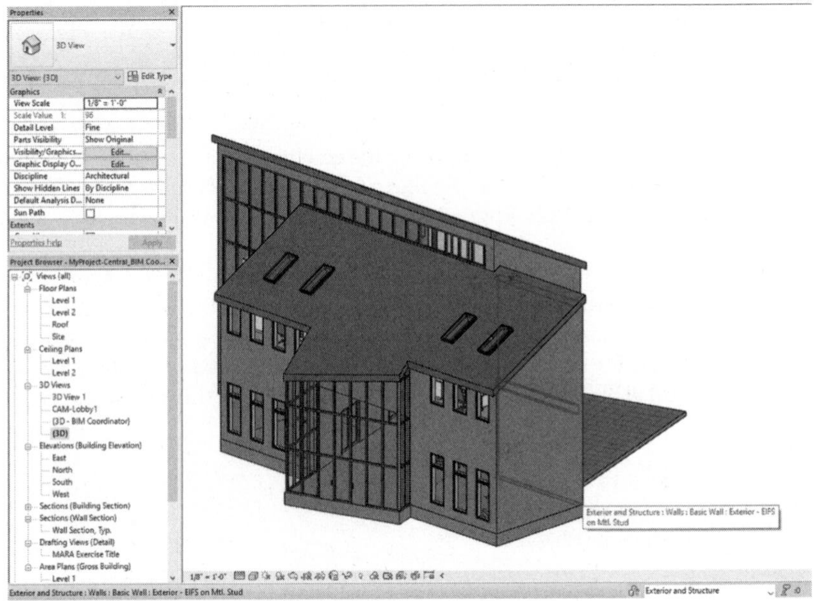

FIGURE 5.21 Workset assignment displayed in status bar, Properties, palette, and pop-up information.

Saving Work

It will eventually become necessary to save your work and share your progress with others in the model. You have three ways to both save your work and view the work of others: Save, Synchronize And Modify Settings, and Synchronize Now.

Save The Save button saves the work you have done to your local file only; the work is not shared or published back to the central file. This can be a useful step if you are in the middle of a process and want to make sure your work is saved but are not ready to share the changes with the rest of the team. You can find the Save tool either by choosing Application ➤ Save or by clicking the Save icon on the Quick Access toolbar (QAT).

Synchronize With Central ➤ Synchronize And Modify Settings When you are ready to publish your work for the rest of your team to see, you have two command choices to synchronize with the central file. The first of two synchronizing commands is known as Synchronize And Modify Settings. You can access this command in a couple of ways. The first is on the Collaborate tab in the Synchronize panel, as shown in Figure 5.22. The Synchronize With Central flyout button is located on the left of this panel.

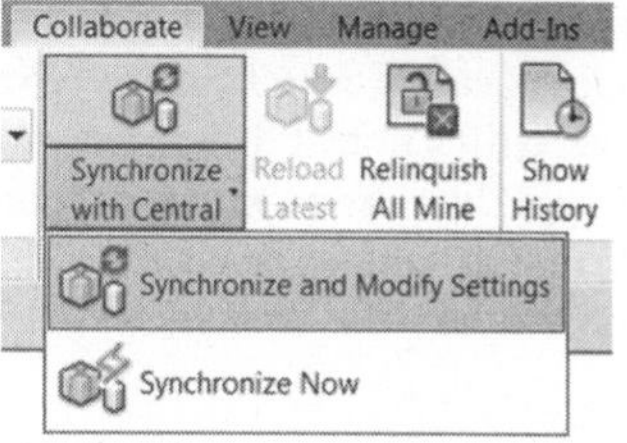

FIGURE 5.22
Synchronize With Central command on the ribbon

As an alternative, you can use the Synchronize With Central button located on the QAT. Both buttons perform the same action and will open the Synchronize With Central dialog box (Figure 5.23). This dialog box gives you some additional tools to assist your workflow:

- The Compact Central Model check box allows you to compact the model to save on disk space. It will take some additional save time, but it can temporarily decrease your file size significantly. This should not be seen as a permanent solution to managing a large file, however. Compaction will decrease the file size, but use of the file will expand the compacted elements. Tips and techniques for reducing file size are discussed in Appendix B.
- Five additional check boxes will be available (depending on what work you have done to the file) to allow you to relinquish or keep permission over the elements you have previously edited. Unchecking these boxes means that you will retain ownership over all the elements you currently own with the model. This can be useful if you are planning to continue working on the same elements and want to publish only recent changes of the model.
- You can add comments to the synchronization that can be useful for tracing potential model conflicts later in the production process.
- A final check box, Save Local File Before And After Synchronizing With Central, allows you to save your changes locally, get any new changes from the central file, and then save locally again, ensuring that your local copy is up to date. This is the save option that takes the longest, and you might choose to uncheck this periodically if you have pressed for time or have a large file that typically takes longer to save.

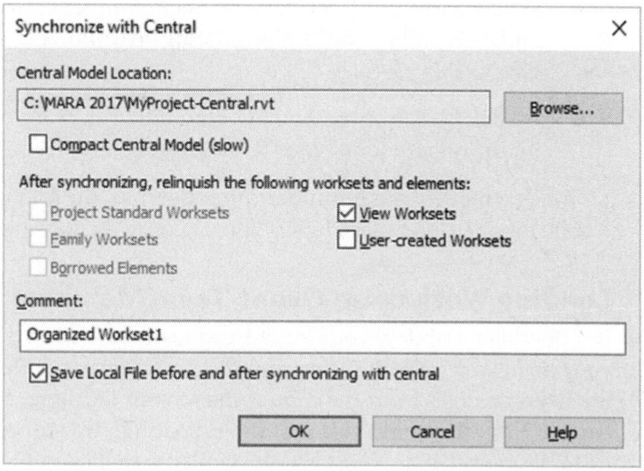

Synchronize with Central
Central Model Location:
C:\MARA 2017\MyProject-Central.rvt
Browse...
☐ Compact Central Model (slow)
After synchronizing, relinquish the following worksets and elements:
☐ Project Standard Worksets
☐ Family Worksets
☐ Borrowed Elements
☑ View Worksets
☐ User-created Worksets
Comment:
Organized Workset1
☑ Save Local File before and after synchronizing with central
OK | Cancel | Help

FIGURE 5.23
Synchronize With Central dialog box

Synchronize With Central ➤ Synchronize Now The second command choice to publish your changes is called Synchronize Now. Choosing this option allows you to bypass the Synchronize With Central dialog box and simply sync your file immediately. With this option, you will be relinquishing all your permissions over any elements you have borrowed; however, you will remain the owner of any worksets you have made editable in the Worksets dialog box.

Saving at Intervals

You will be prompted to save your work at regular intervals. Once worksharing is enabled, you will receive an additional reminder to synchronize with the central file as well as to save your work (Figure 5.24). You can dismiss these dialog boxes by clicking Cancel at the lower right, but remember, it is a good idea to save regularly so you do not lose any work.

Figure 5.24
Changes Not Synchronized With Central dialog box

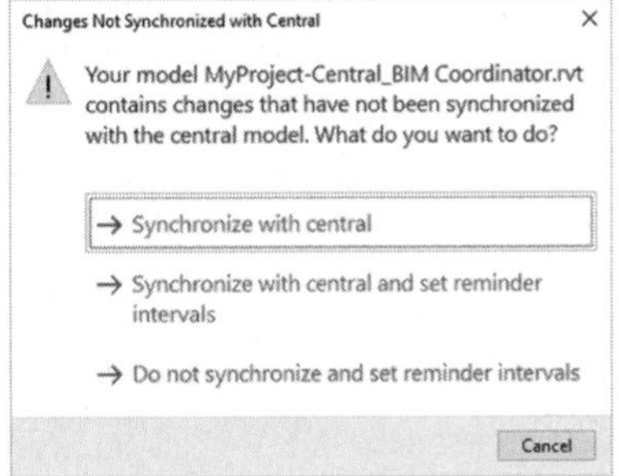

If the Changes Not Synchronized With Central dialog box appears, you will have three options to choose from:

- Synchronize With Central, which will perform a save operation identical to that of the Synchronize Now command
- Synchronize With Central And Set Reminder Intervals, which will synchronize your file and then pull up the Options dialog box, allowing you to set the intervals in which you receive this message
- Do Not Synchronize And Set Reminder Intervals, which will cancel all future reminders for the remainder of your Revit session

You can modify the reminder time shown in the dialog box at any time by clicking the Application button, selecting Options, and then choosing the General tab.

Loading Work from Other Team Members

It is possible to update your model and load work from other team members without publishing your own work back to the central file. This process, called Reload Latest, basically downloads the latest changes from the central file to your local file. Because you are only downloading content from the central file and not uploading, this process takes only a portion of the time a full SWC does. To do this, click the Collaborate tab on the ribbon, and choose Reload Latest from the Synchronize panel. The default keyboard shortcut for this command is RL.

Using Worksharing Visualization

Sometimes it helps to have the ability to graphically display worksets and their status in the project. With worksharing visualization, you can visualize four different values: ownership status, individual ownership, updated elements, and workset assignment. You can open the settings from the view control bar.

To display any of the values, select the desired setting. When any value is selected, the temporary view condition is indicated by colored highlighting around the edges of the view window.

Select the Worksharing Display Settings menu item to customize the graphic appearance of the visualization overrides. The Checkout Status tab of the Worksharing Display Settings dialog box shows three values: what is owned by you, owned by others, or not owned at all (Figure 5.25).

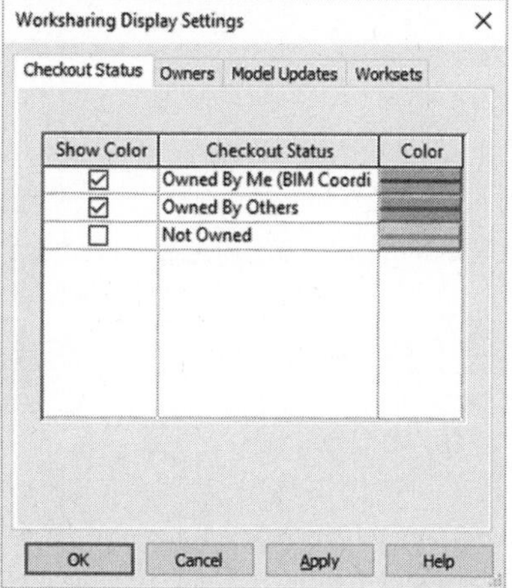

FIGURE 5.25
Checkout Status tab

The Owners tab of the Worksharing Display Settings dialog box illustrates which elements are owned by the users in your project. If you see users listed who do not have any enabled elements or worksets, you can remove them from the list by selecting their username and clicking the Remove User icon at the lower left (Figure 5.26).

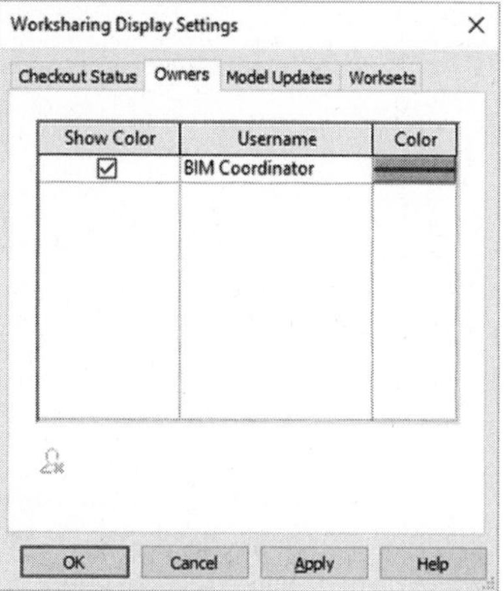

FIGURE 5.26
Owners tab

The Model Updates tab of the Worksharing Display Settings dialog box indicates changes to the central file that may not be apparent until you have synchronized with the central file (Figure 5.27).

FIGURE 5.27
Model Updates tab

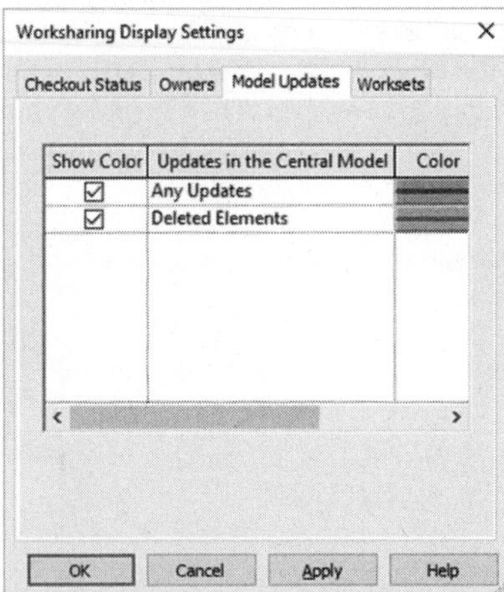

The Worksets tab allows you to color-code the model based on the workset assignment of all the building elements. Color-coding is also helpful for keeping track of your active workset (Figure 5.28).

FIGURE 5.28
Worksets tab

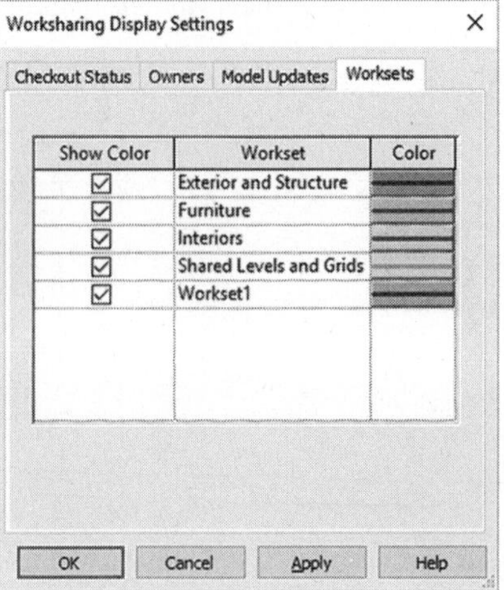

Finally, how often the display settings update in your project is up to you. To modify these settings, choose Application ➤ Options to modify the Worksharing Update Frequency option (Figure 5.29). Moving the slider to the far left will set the description below the Updates slider to Manual Updates Only, and the update will occur when you use Reload Latest or Synchronize With Central. Slide just a bit to the right and you will see that the display will update every 60 seconds. Slide it all the way to the right and your display will update every 5 seconds.

FIGURE 5.29
Modifying the settings for Worksharing Update Frequency

Managing Workset Visibility in View Templates

As we described in the section "Moving Elements between Worksets," worksets can be used as a different way to visualize your project using the Visibility/Graphic Overrides dialog box. Workset visibility can also be managed as part of a view template. To modify these settings, go to the View tab, locate the Graphics panel, and select View Templates ➤ Manage View Templates. In the View Templates dialog box (Figure 5.30), select V/G Overrides Worksets to modify the visibility settings in any view template. Refer to Chapter 4, "Configuring Templates and Standards," for more information on view templates.

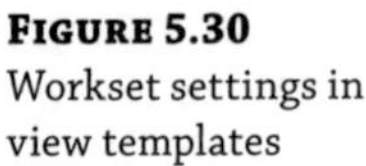

FIGURE 5.30 Workset settings in view templates

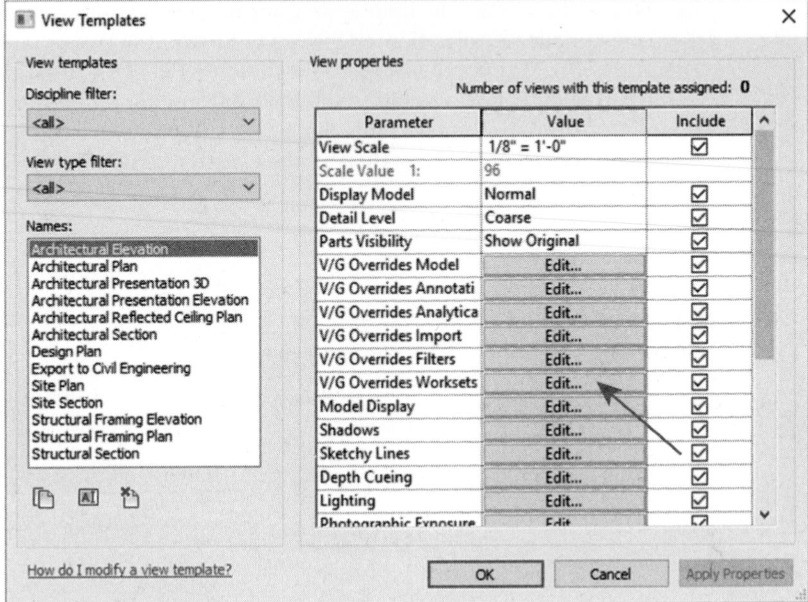

Closing Revit

Eventually, you will need to close your project and leave for lunch, attend a meeting, or go home for the day. Do not worry—the project will still be there tomorrow. But in the meantime, it is important to understand how to close the project correctly so you do not accidentally retain permission over any elements. This situation—where a team member has accidentally left the office and not closed the project file or relinquished permissions—leaves the other team members without a way to edit elements for which the team member had permission or even request permission. So that you are not the unfortunate victim of their wrath upon your return, make sure you close the application properly.

The most thorough way to close the file is to simply quit the application completely. You can do this by clicking the X at the upper right or choosing Exit Revit from the Application menu. You will be presented with a dialog box in which you can choose to Synchronize With Central, save your changes locally, or discard the changes (Figure 5.31). Obviously, the best choice is to use Synchronize With Central, allowing your changes to be published and any objects you own to be relinquished; however, you might be in the middle of a design study and not ready to share your changes. In that case, you may choose to save locally and retain ownership of certain elements. Just be aware that no one else on your team can edit elements you own until you relinquish them. Our recommendation is to always relinquish all elements at the end of your work session.

What if you were only reviewing the model and making some minor changes, and you do not want to save the changes? Close the file or application with any of the methods previously mentioned and select Do Not Save The Project from the Changes Not Saved dialog box. You will then be presented with another dialog box with two choices concerning borrowed elements (Figure 5.32). In the Close Project Without Saving dialog box, you can either relinquish any borrowed elements and worksets or retain ownership of them. Clearly, the best choice is to relinquish all elements and worksets.

FIGURE 5.31
Saving options when closing a local file

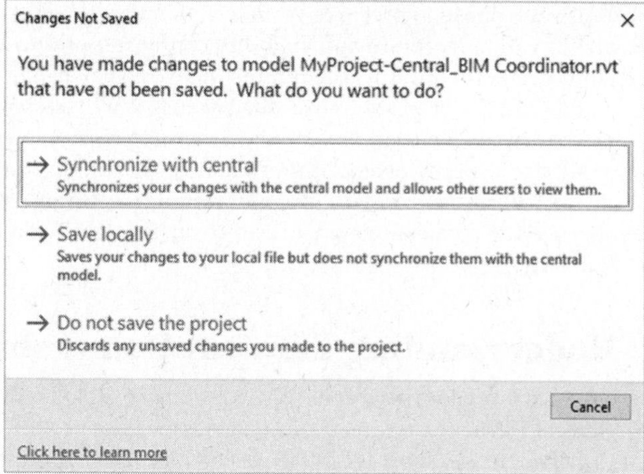

FIGURE 5.32
The Close Project Without Saving dialog box

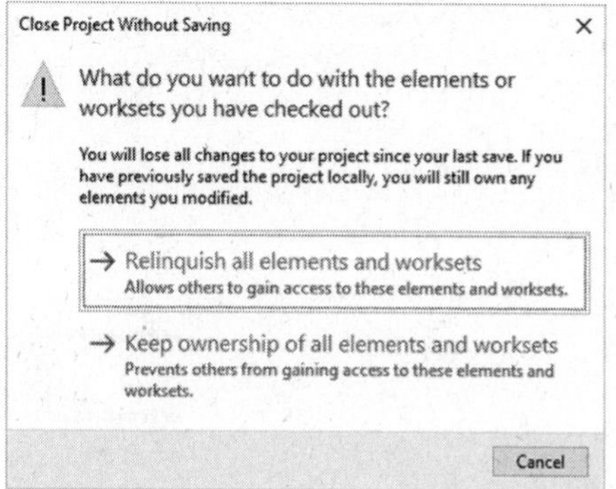

Disabling Worksharing

In a few cases, you might decide that you have enabled worksharing too soon, or after enabling worksharing you would rather go back. Worksharing may be disabled as part of the Detach From Central functionality. This option can be found at the bottom of the Open dialog box. When you elect to detach a copy of the central file, you have the option to discard worksets, as shown in Figure 5.33.

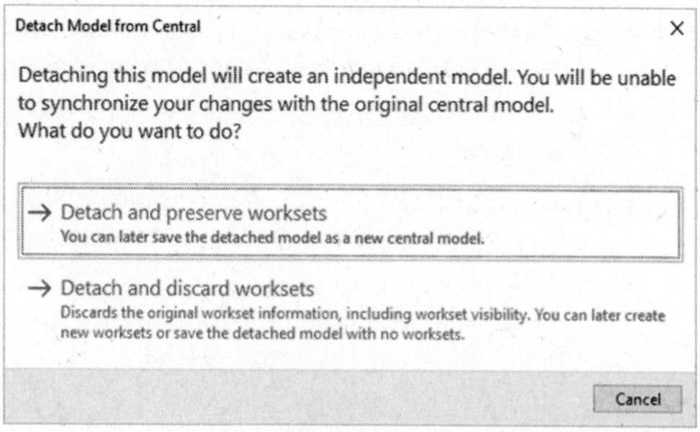

FIGURE 5.33
Disabling worksharing

Detach Model from Central

Detaching this model will create an independent model. You will be unable to synchronize your changes with the original central model.
What do you want to do?

→ Detach and preserve worksets
You can later save the detached model as a new central model.

→ Detach and discard worksets
Discards the original workset information, including workset visibility. You can later create new worksets or save the detached model with no worksets.

Cancel

If you choose to preserve worksets, the worksharing functionality remains in the file. This allows you to maintain any visibility configurations you have established that depend on worksets. Although this file retains the worksharing capability, it can no longer be synchronized with the original central file because it will become a new central file as soon as you save it after detaching. This method can also create a file for review by a project manager or quality control reviewer without the fear of changing the model accidentally. If you elect to discard worksets, you will lose any visibility settings established from worksets. You will also need to create all new worksets from scratch if you decide to enable worksharing again in the future.

Understanding Element Ownership in Worksets

One of the fundamental concepts in a model enabled with worksharing is the ownership of elements. When you directly edit an element in a project, you automatically take ownership of that element—as long as no one else owns it. Determining whether you own an element is fairly easy. Simply select it. If you do not own it, you will see a worksharing icon, as shown on the selected element in Figure 5.34.

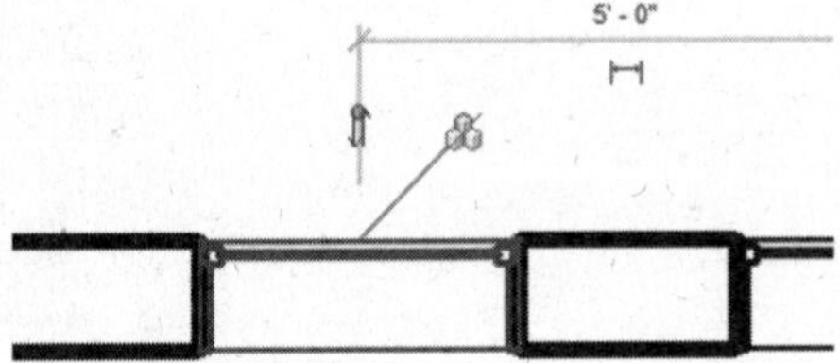

FIGURE 5.34
The worksharing icon on a selected element

By borrowing elements, team members can take ownership of only portions of a workset, leaving the remainder of the workset to be edited by someone else. Taking ownership of elements in this style creates a more "take what you need" approach to editing and usually results in less overlap between team members.

Besides automatically borrowing elements when they are edited, you can obtain ownership of an element or group of elements in a few other ways:

- In the Worksets dialog box, you can make any workset editable. You then become the owner of the workset instead of borrowing elements within one.
- Select any element or series of elements, and take ownership of them by clicking the worksharing icon.
- You can right-click any element in the Project Browser under the Families node. In the context menu that appears, you can take ownership of families, groups, or views.
- You can right-click any element in a view and choose Make Elements Editable from the context menu (see Figure 5.35). You also have the ability to make editable the entire workset to which the selected object is assigned.

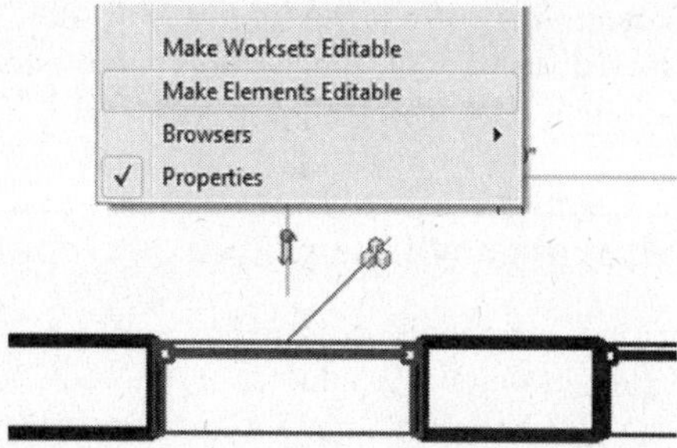

FIGURE 5.35
Making an element editable using the context menu

If you use any of these options, if the selected element is already owned by another team member, Revit will alert you and you will not be able to modify the element or make it editable.

ACCIDENTS HAPPEN

As proficient as any team is, accidents may occur on a project, and elements will get modified or deleted unexpectedly. It is important to know how to recover your work when these accidents occur.

On one project a team developed, someone new to Revit software and new to the team was working on window details in a three-sided building. In the detailing process, the new team member accidentally deleted one of the walls in the project. By deleting the wall, this person also deleted the elevation, as well as all the wall sections associated with that wall, along with the details in plan and section. When the new team member deleted the element, he was not aware of the mistake and performed a Synchronize With Central, publishing all the deletions to the central file. Fortunately, the error was caught before everyone else performed a Synchronize With Central, and the team did not have to resort to restoring the model from the previous night's backup. The team was able to use another member's local file to create a new central file, thereby minimizing the loss of work. Once everyone on the team made a new local copy, he was able to get back to work.

Had the deleted elements been more isolated (like a conference room layout), recovery would have been much less invasive. In such a case, you simply create a group from all the elements you would like to save and then right-click the group in the Project Browser. You will have the option to save the group out of the file, which can then be inserted into a different project file and ungrouped again.

Understanding Editing Requests

When working in a worksharing project, you do not always have to take ownership of an entire workset in order to begin editing elements. As we discussed earlier in this chapter, it is possible to take ownership of individual model elements. This process is referred to as *borrowing*. Remember, there can be only one *owner* of a workset but multiple *borrowers* of elements within a workset.

If you need to work on elements that already belong to someone else, you will receive an alert that you cannot edit the elements until the other person relinquishes them, and you will be given the option to place an editing request.

Understanding the editing request workflow is critical for multiuser teams; it allows users to transfer permission of objects without having to constantly save all their work to the central file and relinquish all worksets. Let us look at this interchange of permissions in more detail.

SIMULATING A WORKSHARING ENVIRONMENT

Practicing with a multiuser environment is not easy to describe in text, although it is possible to configure on your own computer. If you would like to work through the exercises in this section, you can launch the Revit application twice. Remember to change the worksharing username in the application options before you create a new local file each time. And of course, remember to restore your original username once you have completed the training exercises.

Placing an Editing Request

Imagine you are happily working away on your model in a worksharing environment and you try to edit an element that someone else owns. What do you do? When that situation occurs, you will be presented with a dialog box that allows you to request permission to edit the element from the other user (Figure 5.36).

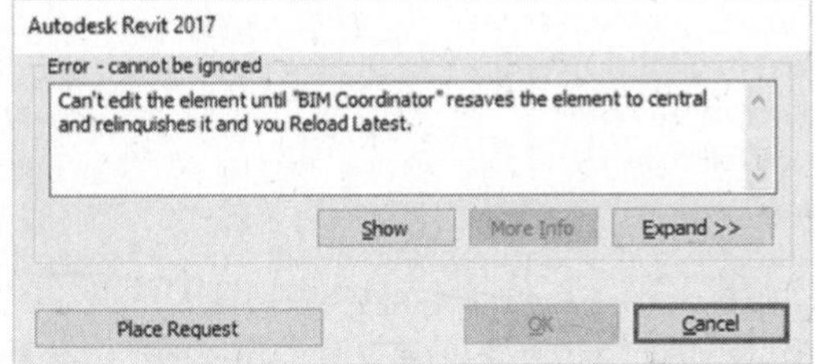

FIGURE 5.36
Placing a request for permission

Looking at the dialog box, you have two options:

- You can click Cancel and not take possession of the element, and then focus your efforts on another part of the design.
- You can click Place Request to ask your team member to relinquish possession over the element in question. When you click Place Request, the dialog box shown in Figure 5.37 opens.

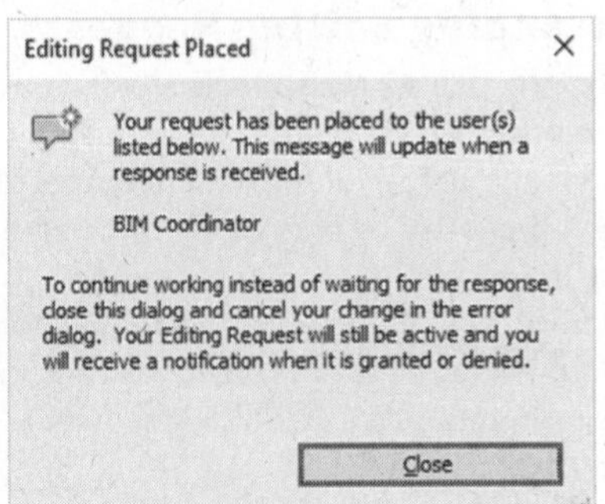

FIGURE 5.37
Editing Request Placed dialog box

Once you have placed your request, you are in a bit of a holding pattern. You cannot continue to edit this element until the other user has granted you permission to edit it, and you cannot continue working on other portions of the project. This situation applies only if you are editing an element and you need to make an editing request related to that element. If you simply want to request permission to edit an element and not edit it right away, you could close the request confirmation box and continue working on other elements in your project.

The recipient of an editing request will see a pop-up notification appear at the bottom of the application, as shown in Figure 5.38. The notification gives the recipient instant information about the element in question and who made the request and provides buttons to grant or deny the request. It also provides a Show button that finds the element in a view so the recipient can determine the most appropriate response to the request.

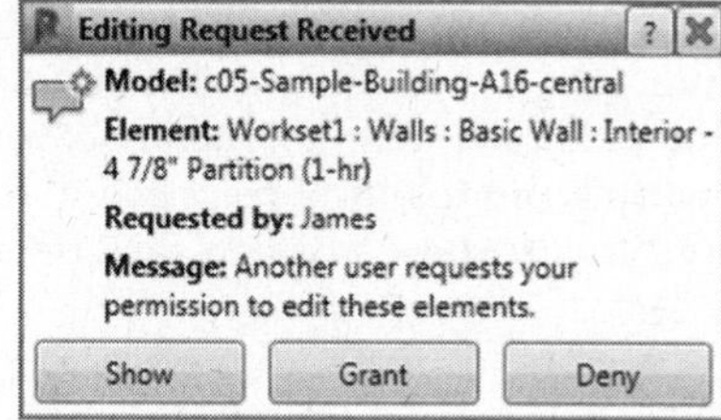

FIGURE 5.38
Editing request notification

If you happen to miss or accidentally close the request notification, there is also a small visual indicator on the status bar at the bottom of your screen.

It indicates whether there are any outstanding requests (both to and from you). Clicking this icon opens the Editing Requests dialog box (Figure 5.39). Any requests indicated by an asterisk require you to Synchronize With Central before granting the editing request.

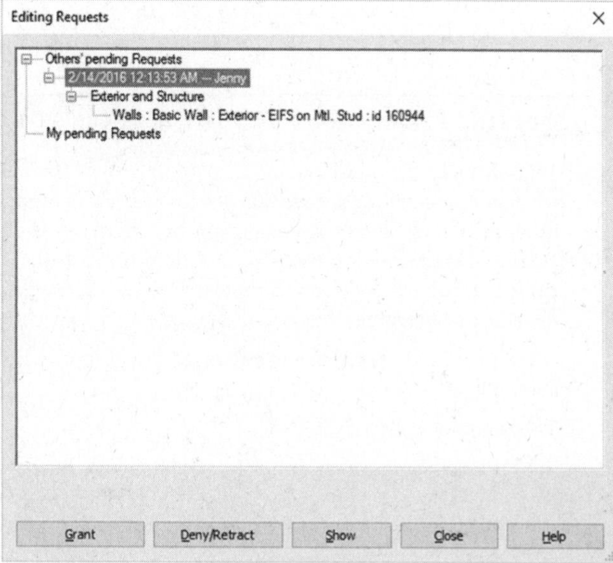

FIGURE 5.39
The Editing Requests dialog box

Granting an Editing Request

Let's now observe the other side of this scenario. If you are the recipient of an editing request and you are ready to grant it, one of two things will happen. If you have not changed the element, you can simply click Grant and the permission for the element will be transferred to the requesting team member.

If you have modified the element or one that is dependent on or hosted by the element in question, you will be alerted that you will need to SWC before the request can be granted. The team member who placed the editing request will subsequently need to use the Reload Latest command or SWC to receive the recent changes, and then he or she can edit the most recent version of that element. Permission requests that require an SWC are flagged in the Editing Requests dialog box by an asterisk next to the request.

After your editing request has been granted, you will receive a notification similar to those shown in Figure 5.40. If the request did not require an SWC from the other team member (as indicated in the left image in Figure 5.40), you can continue the editing command that prompted the request. Otherwise, you will need to Reload Latest before you can continue the editing command. If you need to return to a view of the element or elements related to the editing request, you can click the Show button. Click the X to close the notification box.

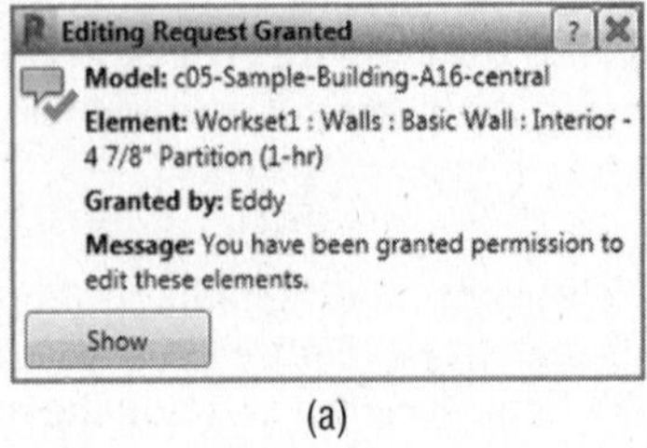

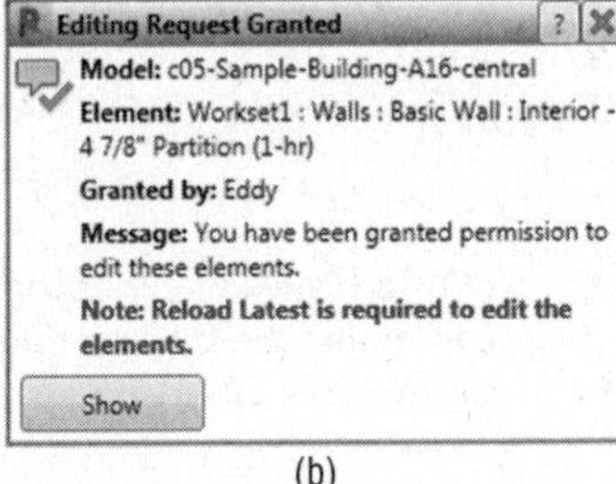

FIGURE 5.40
(a) Notification of a granted editing request (b) Alternate notification of a granted request alerting you to Reload Latest

GETTING PERMISSION FOR SOMEONE ELSE'S OBJECTS

This situation may happen on one of your projects; someone leaves for a meeting or goes home without relinquishing permission of borrowed elements and worksets. This scenario would prevent other team members from editing any of the borrowed elements until that person returns to the office and synchronizes the changes with the central file. If that person cannot return to the office, there is a workaround for this problem. The workaround will result in the loss of the work by the missing team member, but it will clear up all the permissions issues.

If the immediate team needs outweigh the potential loss of the missing person's work, follow these steps:

1. Open a new session of Revit.
2. Click the Application menu, select Options, and choose the General tab in the resulting dialog box.

3. Change the name listed in the Username field from your username to the person's whose permissions you are looking to release.
4. Create a new local file of the project and open it. Now simply SWC, and all the person's elements will be available to the team to edit. Then close the file.
5. Before closing Revit, be sure to go back to the Application menu, click Options, and select the General tab so you can change the username back to your own.

Relinquishing Permission

It is not always necessary to wait for a request from another team member to relinquish permission over your elements. Fortunately, there is a tool to do just that. On the Synchronize panel of the Collaborate tab is a button called Relinquish All Mine (Figure 5.41). This feature returns the permissions for any elements you have not edited back to the central file so they are available to the rest of your team.

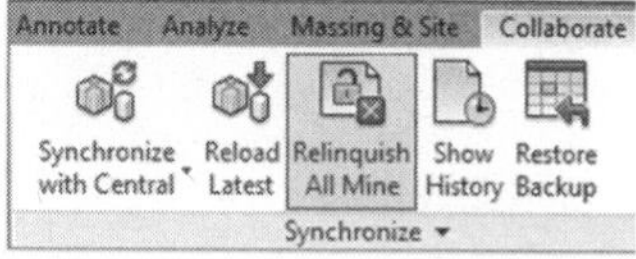

FIGURE 5.41
Relinquish All Mine

Using the Worksharing Monitor

If you are an Autodesk® Subscription customer, you will have access to a useful extension application called Worksharing Monitor, shown in Figure 5.42. When you are working on a team project that is enabled for worksharing, this utility gives you real-time information about the users participating in the project file. It also has a convenient resources monitor to keep you informed of your computer's available RAM, virtual memory, and disk space.

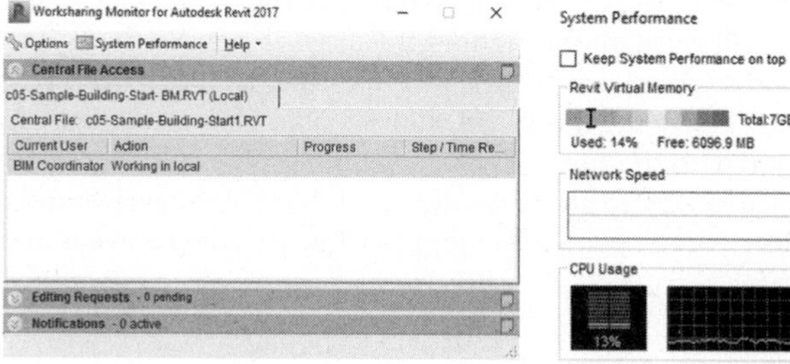

FIGURE 5.42
The Worksharing Monitor is available for Autodesk Subscription customers.

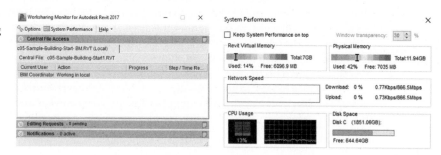

Collaborating in the Cloud

Eventually you will need to collaborate with other designers. Maybe this partnership—if it is with your structural engineer or MEP designer—will require the both of you to share models. Maybe you simply need to share your modeling work with people within your own office who are not Revit savvy enough to be able to negotiate their way through the software, and you are looking for an easy way for them to view and comment on what you have created. Fortunately, there is a way for you to not only share your model but also comment on models created by your team.

Autodesk has created a web-based resource to share and mark up Revit files. The site is A360 Drive (`360.autodesk.com`). The site requires an A360 account, which you can register for on the website. Once signed up, you can sign in through Revit to take advantage of online applications like daylighting or cloud rendering (see Chapter 9, "Conceptual Design and Design Analysis") or use the site as an online collaboration portal.

The site (Figure 5.43) allows you to upload and share models with collaborators. You can make models public or you can share them with only certain individuals.

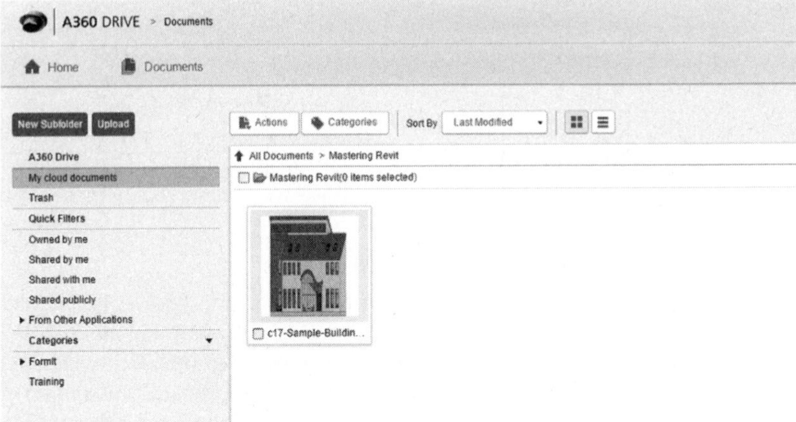

FIGURE 5.43 Viewing models online with A360 Drive

One of the great benefits of the site beyond just document management and sharing is the ability for non-Revit users to be able to navigate the model in a read-only format. Using the sample model we will work on throughout this book, a non-Revit user can navigate any of the views within the model (plans, elevations, 3D views, and so forth) as well as spin the model around in an interactive 3D format. Figure 5.44 shows a plan view and some of the additional model metadata that is stored on the site.

This is an easy way to share models and allow nonusers to make comments on preset views. The site works best with Google's Chrome web browser and works on either a Mac or a PC.

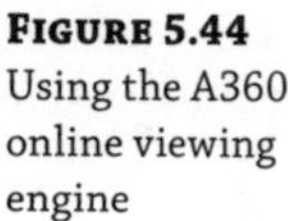

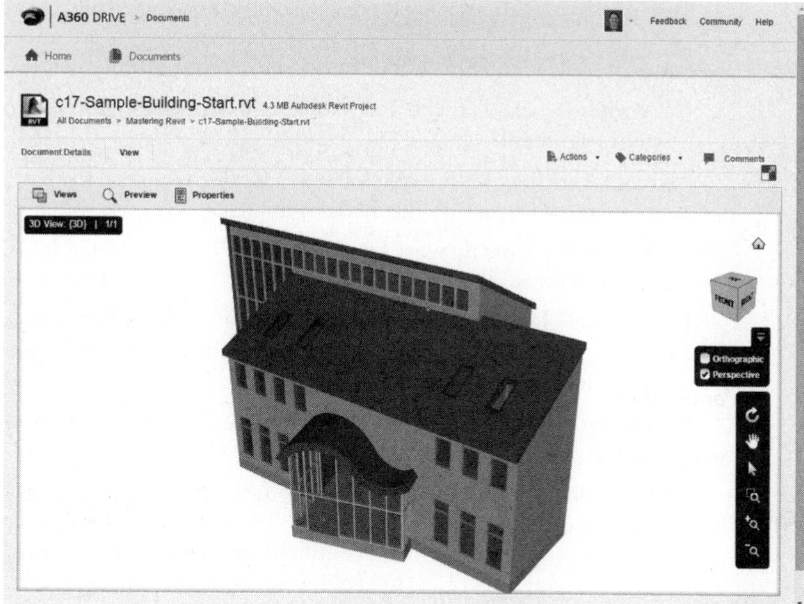

FIGURE 5.44 Using the A360 online viewing engine

A360 Collaboration for Revit

Although the A360 Drive website allows you to upload and download files as well as view Revit models, it does not provide an alternative to true collaboration with Revit worksharing. A new service called A360 Collaboration for Revit (C4R) allows teams to synchronize changes using Autodesk's cloud services instead of a Revit Server Accelerator on your WAN.

A360 Collaboration for Revit is a paid service that can be purchased per registered user. You can learn more about the service at `www.autodesk.com/products/collaboration-for-revit`.

The Bottom Line

Understand key worksharing concepts. Once the team has created local files, it is necessary to understand how to keep both the local files and the central file up to date as changes occur on the project. Doing so ensures that everyone is working from an updated and recent copy of the model at all times.

Master It Once you have begun working in your local file, how do you publish your changes to the central file? How do you download changes from the central file to your local file?

Enable worksharing on your project. Knowing how to activate and use worksharing is indispensable to working in a team environment using Revit.

Master It How do you transition a single-user Revit file to a multiuser environment using worksharing?

Organize worksets in your model. There is no single rule for organizing worksets in your project models; however, they can be used to your team's advantage. You can use worksets to better organize larger projects and for additional visibility control.

Master It How do you assign objects to worksets? How do you change an object's workset assignment?

Manage workflow with worksharing. Once the central file has been created, you will need to organize and structure the model into logical worksets to maintain workflow with Revit.

Master It How do worksets differ from layers in 2D CAD? What are some logical ways to create worksets within a model?

Understand element ownership in worksets. Editing elements in a central file means you have sole ownership over further changes to those elements. Understanding the permissions is critical to working in a team.

Master It How do you edit an element in the model if someone has already taken ownership of it in a worksharing environment?

Collaborate in the cloud. Not all of your team members will be Revit-savvy and know how to use the tools. In addition, not everyone on the team will have a copy of Revit, but you might still need their input and comments on the design. Learning to leverage complementary tools to Revit is critical to keeping a project moving smoothly.

Master It How do you use the cloud to get feedback from non-Revit users on a project team?

Chapter 6

Working with Consultants

Whether you work on large or small projects—residential, commercial, or industrial building types—collaboration is an almost certain aspect of the workflow you will encounter when implementing BIM. This chapter discusses important considerations for interdisciplinary coordination as well as the tools within Autodesk® Revit® software to help you manage the process. This chapter covers aspects of collaboration solely utilizing the Revit platform, and Chapter 7, "Interoperability: Working Multiplatform," focuses on collaborating with other software programs.

In this chapter, you'll learn to:

- Prepare for interdisciplinary collaboration
- Collaborate using linked Revit models
- Use Copy/Monitor between linked models
- Run interference checks

Preparing for Collaboration

Working alone in the Revit environment will deliver measurable increases in productivity, quality, and consistency; however, the true benefit of building information modeling (BIM) is the ability to effectively collaborate between design disciplines, share model data with contractors, and deliver useful information to facility operators.

The difference between these working paradigms has been described as *lonely BIM* versus *social BIM*. Lonely BIM can be thought of as the use of isolated BIM techniques for targeted tasks such as architectural design or structural analysis. Social BIM is the act of sharing model data between project stakeholders in order to enhance collaboration while developing a building design. The importance of increased efficiency in collaboration is the underpinning for the goals set forth by organizations such as buildingSMART International (`www.buildingsmart.org`) or the UK's BIM Task Group (`www.bimtaskgroup.org`).

The ability to support high-quality information exchanges necessitates the proper use of 3D models and nongraphic data in a highly collaborative environment. Although we will be discussing collaboration solely within the Revit platform in this chapter, the buildingSMART Alliance and the National BIM Standard (NBIMS-US) stress the need for open interoperability between BIM applications.

Once a project team decides to participate in social BIM—either through desire or the requirements of a client—they must decide how to collaborate with BIM in a manner that is useful to all constituents throughout the project life cycle. Whether or not your client requires it, you should develop a BIM execution plan in order to set clear expectations related to the use of BIM.

The buildingSMART Alliance (www.buildingsmartalliance.org), in an effort sponsored by the Charles Pankow Foundation, the Construction Industry Institute, the Penn State Office of Physical Plant, and the Partnership for Achieving Construction Excellence (PACE), has created a "BIM Project Execution Planning Guide" and template for a BIM execution plan. You can find this information at the Penn State Computer Integrated Construction (CIC) website: http://bim.psu.edu.

One of the most critical parts of a BIM execution plan is the definition of the project goals and uses of BIM to achieve the stated goals. If you are just beginning your implementation of Revit software, you may be using it to create 3D visualizations, or perhaps you are attempting to increase your drafting productivity. Defining clear and concise reasons for implementing BIM on each project will help you define where to concentrate your modeling efforts. According to the buildingSMART Alliance, "[A] current challenge and opportunity faced by the early project planning team is to identify the most appropriate uses for Building Information Modeling on a project given the project characteristics, participants' goals and capabilities, and the desired risk allocations." A listing of the common uses of BIM along with potential value opportunities and required resources is also available on the Penn State CIC website. For our European counterparts, you can find another list here: aecuk.wordpress.com/documents.

According to the American Institute of Architects' "Integrated Project Delivery: A Guide," a BIM execution plan "should define the scope of BIM implementation on the project, identify the process flow for BIM tasks, define the information exchanges between parties, and describe the required project and company infrastructure needed to support the implementation." To be clear, the development of such a plan does not imply the application of integrated project delivery (IPD). IPD is "a project delivery approach that integrates people, systems, business structures and practices into a process that collaboratively harnesses the talents and insights of all participants to optimize project results, increase value to the owner, reduce waste, and maximize efficiency through all phases of design, fabrication, and construction." For the purposes of this chapter, we will consider only the collaboration and coordination between members of a project design team, not the interactions with a client or contractor.

For additional reading on IPD, refer to these sources:

- Integrated Practice/Integrated Project Delivery: www.aia.org/ipd
- Whole Building Design Guide: www.wbdg.org

Managing the Coordination Process

The coordination process in a Revit environment begins with linking multiple files together to form a composite view of your building project. Even though smaller projects might be coordinated within a single Revit project file, most moderate to large projects will be designed by multiple disciplines or trades working in different offices. A project can be divided in many different ways to meet a variety of workflow requirements. Most often, each discipline will develop at least one separate Revit project file, and many of these project files will be linked into each other for reference. Because there are several workflow possibilities, this chapter will focus on the coordination among a traditional design team consisting of the following:

- Architect
- Structural engineer
- Mechanical, electrical, and plumbing (MEP) engineers

The workflow within a traditional design team is more complex than you might assume. If you were to graph the dependencies and coordination between these parties (Figure 6.1), you would see a web of primary relationships (architect to/from structure, architect to MEP) and secondary relationships (structure to/from mechanical and piping).

FIGURE 6.1
The relationships of interdisciplinary coordination

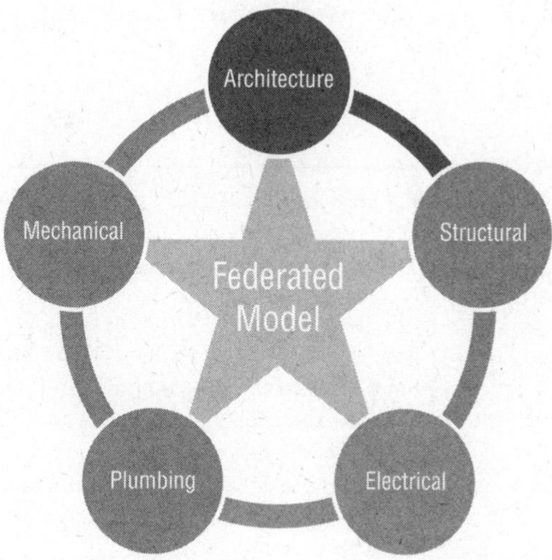

These relationships can be further parsed into physical and logical relationships. If we use mechanical and electrical as an example, you can see that a physical relationship means making sure a light fixture is not hitting the bottom of a duct, whereas a logical relationship means making sure the electrical design properly accounts for the load of the heating coil in a variable air volume (VAV) box (being designed by the mechanical engineer).

It is the complexity of these possible workflow scenarios that makes this process prone to errors and illustrates the importance of proper coordination between the different disciplines of a design team. So, what are the tools that can be used for collaboration between Revit products? Three distinct tools are typically used in a collaboration scenario:

Linked Models Linking models together using the Link Revit tool provides full visual fidelity of the referenced content, showing the complete context of the other disciplines' data, fostering a complete understanding of their geometry. The data can also be controlled and shown in any manner appropriate to the use. You can turn it on or off, half-tone the data, or enhance it with color or line pattern overrides. Linking also provides support for the Interference Check, Copy/Monitor, and Coordination Review tools.

Copy/Monitor Copy/Monitor is a powerful tool available in all products built on the Revit platform and is considered the most intelligent of the coordination tools. It offers several benefits. It lets you link Revit files from other team members (structural engineers or MEP engineers) and copy key elements from their model into yours. Once that link is created, you can monitor that relationship and know if the element has moved or changed when you receive updated models from your team members. A basic example of using this tool would be copying the structural grid into your architectural file. If the grid moves or changes with subsequent updated models, you will be instantly alerted to the change.

Interference Check In many cases, the only workflow requirement is to verify that items from another discipline are not interfering with your items. The Interference Check tool can be used to check between categories within a single model or between linked models.

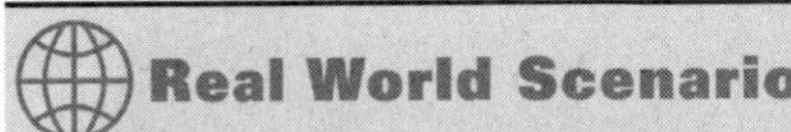

INDIANA UNIVERSITY BIM REQUIREMENTS

In 2009, the University Architect's Office at Indiana University (`www.iu.edu`) announced that it would require the use of BIM on all projects with a capital value of over $5 million. Accompanying the announcement was the release of the IU BIM Standards and Project Delivery Requirements, which included a BIM execution plan template and IPD template—developed under the guidance of Autodesk and SHP Leading Design (`www.shp.com`). Although the university's BIM requirements may seem new, the desire to ensure the maximum reuse of information has been evolving at IU for several years, beginning with its implementation of integrated GIS tools for campus and facility management in 1996.

One important excerpt from these requirements focuses on the organization of the interference checking (aka clash detection) process. Within the IU BIM Standards & Guidelines for Architects, Engineers, & Contractors, rules have been established for classifying clashes between modeled elements. Level One clashes are considered critical and include ductwork and piping clashing with ceilings, rated walls, or structure; equipment clearances interfering with structure are included in Level One as well. Level Two clashes are less critical but include casework clashing with electrical fixtures and structure vs. specialty equipment. Finally, Level Three clashes are still important but are a lower priority. These include casework clashing with walls and plumbing interfering with mechanical equipment.

These requirements may be defined differently by other clients, but it is critical to understand the importance of using interference-checking tools for logical groups of model elements. Checking for clashes throughout an entire model will yield a plethora of unusable data and will limit the effectiveness of model-based coordination.

For more information, visit the IU BIM site at `www.indiana.edu/~uao/iubim.html`.

Given the range of available Revit tools for collaboration, they are not necessarily applicable to all interdisciplinary relationships. As shown in Figure 6.2, only the most appropriate tools should be applied to each collaborative situation. These situations are merely suggestions based on the experience of the authors. The needs for your collaborative workflows may vary.

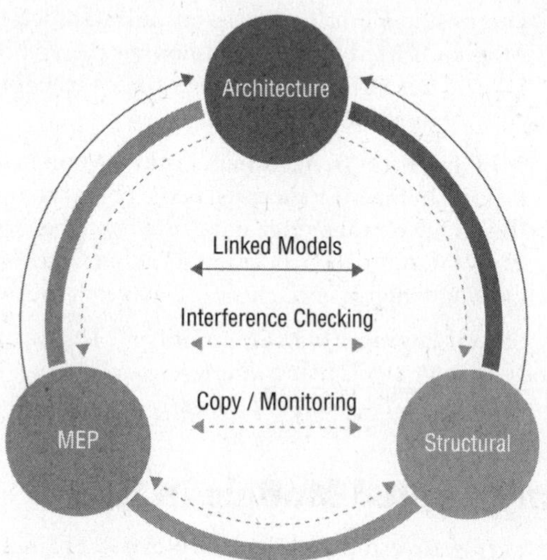

FIGURE 6.2 Suggestions for collaboration tools to be used between disciplines

Architect to Structural Engineer The relationship between the architect and the structural engineer is becoming closer as we strive for lighter structures and more innovative design. In many respects, structural engineers may be affecting the building aesthetic as much as the architects. Thus, this workflow may be considered the most crucial and should be bidirectional.

Architect to Structural Engineer: Copy/Monitor and Coordination Review By using Copy/Monitor, structural engineers are able to create a strong, intelligent link between the structural and architectural models. In doing so, they can easily track the changes in the architect's model that will affect the structural design. They are also able to create geometry in their model using these tools, which can be directly or indirectly related to architectural elements such as walls and floors.

Remember that coordination of relationships for datum (grids and/or levels) should be established at the beginning of a project. For example, does the architect "own" the levels and the grids—or will the structural engineer? Conflicts due to a lack of proper planning will negatively impact the effective use of the Copy/Monitor tools on your projects.

Structural Engineer to Architect: Interference Check The architect's primary requirement for the structural model is to include the structure in context and to know if the structure is interfering with any architectural elements. For this workflow, it is recommended that the architect link in the structural model and use interference checking. The rules governing what clashes are considered critical may be established by a client's BIM standards and protocols.

Architect to MEP Engineer The relationship between architecture and MEP is not quite as dynamic as that between architecture and structure but represents specific opportunities to benefit from collaboration.

Architect to MEP Engineer: Copy/Monitor and Coordination Review The MEP engineer needs to link in the architect's model to have the architectural model for context and positional relationships for ceiling-based items and the avoidance of clashes. Copy/Monitor is used to copy and monitor the architect's levels and rooms. These room objects take on the additional properties, such as light levels and airflow. Levels are required to copy or monitor the rooms.

MEP Engineer to Architect: Linked Models The architect's primary benefit from linking in the MEP model(s) is the ability to reference this geometry within the context of the architectural model and drawings. There is usually no compelling reason to use the Copy/Monitor and Coordination Review tools from the MEP on the architectural project, although interference checking may be required under certain circumstances.

Structural Engineer to MEP Engineer This relationship is almost always best served by cross-linked models using interference checking. The most important aspect of collaboration between these disciplines is the early detection and correction of clashes.

Using Linked Models in Revit

The first rule governing all Revit-to-Revit coordination situations is that all linked project files must be generated with the same Revit platform version, such as Autodesk Revit 2017. In a worksharing environment with other disciplines, it is important to ensure that the computers of all team members working on a project have the same Revit build installed. As discussed previously in this chapter, a BIM execution plan should include an agreement on all modeling and coordination software to be used on a project, including the version of each listed program.

You can find the build information for your Revit product by clicking the Help drop-down button in the InfoCenter and selecting About Autodesk Revit 2017 (Figure 6.3). The build appears at the upper right of the About Autodesk Revit 2017 dialog box.

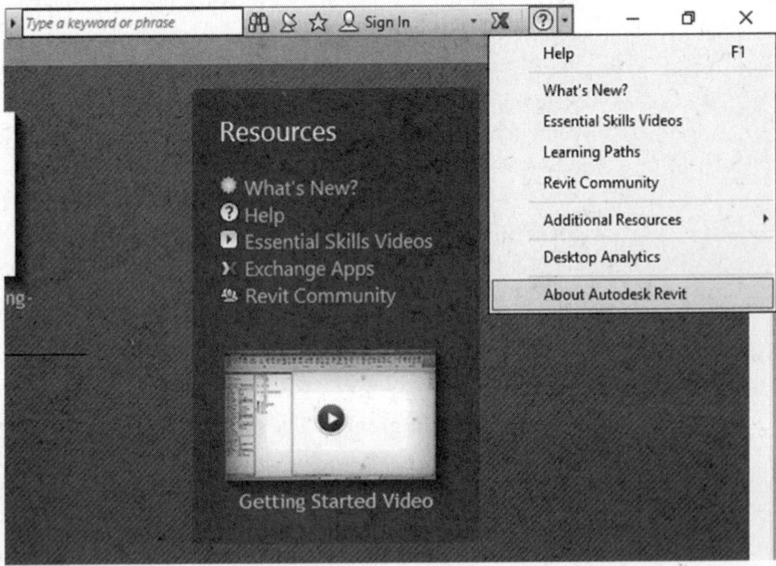

FIGURE 6.3
Linked files must use the same platform version, and all worksharing team members should use the same build. The build number can be found in About Autodesk Revit.

Shared Positioning

In the collaborative process of sharing information via linked models, the coordinated positioning of each model is of paramount importance. To ensure accuracy, every project's BIM execution plan must include agreement on a common coordinate system and origin. This section will help you develop a fundamental understanding of the coordinate systems within Revit so you can configure and manage them in your projects.

We will begin our description with a simple statement: There are two coordinate systems in a Revit project, *project internal* and *shared*. Each system has essential features and limitations.

Project Internal Every Revit project has an internal coordinate system referred to in several places as project internal. The origin of this coordinate system is at first marked by a project base point; however, this reference point can be moved away from the internal origin. We discuss the project base point in greater detail later in this chapter.

The project internal coordinate system cannot be changed, and your model should be constructed within a *one-mile radius* of the internal origin. The true origin in Revit is referred to as the Project Start Up Point, and the project base point can be reset to this point by setting it to Unclipped, right-clicking the icon, and selecting Move To Startup Location.

A complementary component of the project internal coordinate system is the view orientation of Project North. This setting is the default and can be found in the View Properties of any plan. We strongly recommend that your model be created in an orthogonal relationship to the project or as you expect the plans to be oriented on a typical sheet. Your project's actual relation to true north will be established via shared coordinates.

Shared Coordinates In simple terms, shared coordinates are just a way for the project team to use the same work point. In other words, the shared coordinate system consists of a single origin and true north orientation that can be synchronized between models and even Autodesk® AutoCAD® drawings. In the diagram shown in Figure 6.4, you can see an architectural model and structural model linked together. Each model was created using a different project internal origin (not the recommended method), but their shared coordinates were synchronized.

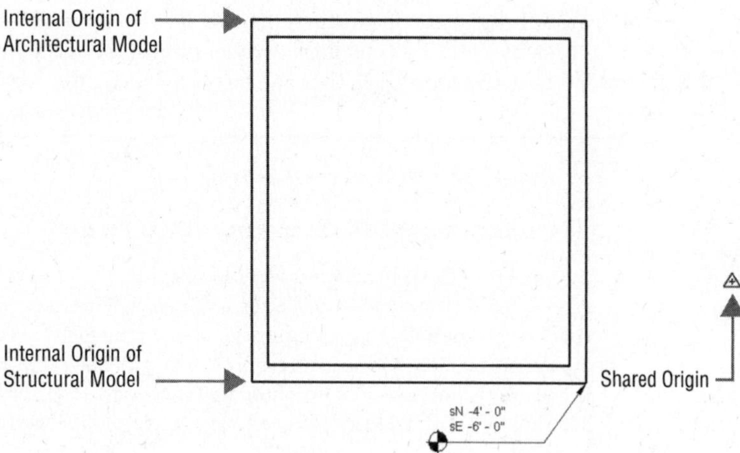

FIGURE 6.4 Diagram of the relationship between project internal origins and shared coordinates in linked models

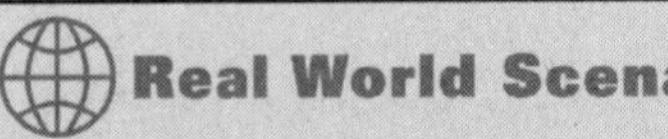

Limitations on Using Shared Coordinates for Exporting

Although you can use either Project Internal or Shared as the setting for Coordinate System Basis when exporting CAD formats, there are some limitations. If you are exporting sheet views, the plan data will always use the project internal coordinate system. Using the Export Views On Sheets And Links As External References option during export does not change this limitation. We recommend using plan views—not sheets—for issuing 2D CAD backgrounds to project participants who are not using Revit. Refer to Chapter 7 for more detailed information on exporting.

Acquiring or Publishing Coordinates

When you attempt to synchronize shared coordinates between linked projects, there are two tools to achieve this: Acquire Coordinates and Publish Coordinates. A simple way to understand the difference between these tools is to think of them in terms of pulling versus pushing:

- Acquire = pull
- Publish = push

It is important to understand the situations in which you would pull or push coordinates between linked files. A typical workflow for establishing a synchronized, shared coordinate system on a single building project is as follows:

1. A site model is generated in which the survey point (SP) in the Revit project is coordinated with geodetic survey markers or station lines. The site model is linked into the architectural Revit model. This file can be placed manually and then moved and rotated into a position relative to the building. ***Do not move or rotate your building to the linked site model!***
2. From the Manage tab, select Coordinates ➤ Acquire Coordinates. Pick the linked file and the origin of the shared coordinate system, and the angle of true north in your Revit model will be synchronized with those in the linked file.
3. All engineers or consultants using Revit should obtain a copy of the site model and repeat steps 1 and 2. When linking other project models that have already been synchronized with the site model, they can be placed using the Auto–By Shared Coordinates option.

Real World Scenario

Acquiring Coordinates from a CAD File

A common scenario in a project workflow begins with the architect beginning a design model and receiving a 2D survey file in DWG format from a civil engineer. The survey is drawn in coordinates that are geospatially correct but may not be orthogonal to true north. The architect should create the model close to the internal project origin; however, the architect will need to ensure that the building and survey coordinates are synchronized for properly oriented CAD exports and for coordination with additional linked Revit models from engineers in later phases of the project.

The architect will link the 2D CAD file into the Revit model but will first manually place it—moving and rotating the CAD file to be in proper alignment with the building model. Once the link is in place and constrained (or locked), the architect will acquire the coordinates from the DWG survey by switching to the Manage tab, selecting Coordinates ➤ Acquire Coordinates from the Project Location panel, and then clicking the DWG link. This will not affect any views that are oriented to project north—only those set to true north will display the orientation established by the coordinates acquired from the survey file.

For a campus-style project in which you might be creating multiple instances of a linked building model, you would most likely use Publish Coordinates to push information from a site model into the linked building model. Here is how that would work in a hypothetical scenario:

1. Assuming a site model and building model were created in Revit, you would begin by opening the site model and linking the building model into the site.
2. Adjust the position of the first instance of the linked building model to location A.
3. From the Manage tab, select Coordinates from the Project Location panel, and then click Publish Coordinates. Pick the linked building model.
4. The Location Weather And Site dialog box will open, and you will create a duplicate location named Location A.
5. Copy the linked building model as required for each subsequent location. Repeat steps 2 through 4 for each copy. As shown in Figure 6.5, there are three locations (Location A, Location B, and Location C) that represent each instance of the linked project model.
6. When you close the site model and open the building model, you can link the site model to the building using any of the named location references you *pushed* into the building model.

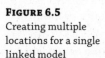

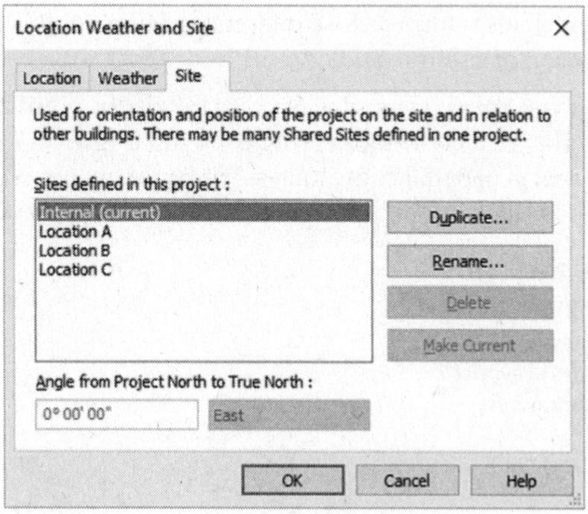

FIGURE 6.5
Creating multiple locations for a single linked model

Using Project Base Point and Survey Point

Revit provides two graphic objects to identify the *project base point* and the *survey point*. In the default templates, these points are visible in the floor plan named Site; however, they can also be displayed in any other plan view by opening the Visibility/Graphic Overrides dialog box, selecting the Model Categories tab, and expanding the Site category, as shown in Figure 6.6. You can also use the Reveal Hidden Elements command in the view control bar to temporarily display these points.

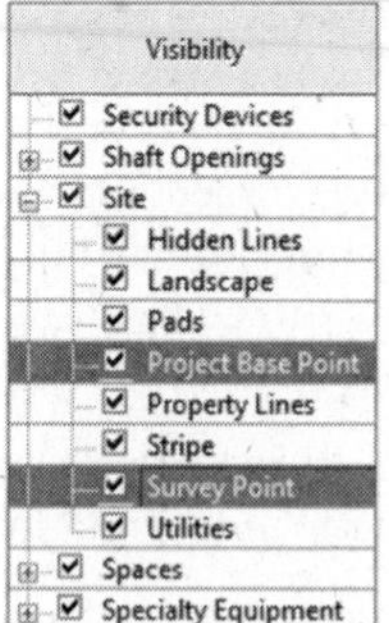

FIGURE 6.6
The Project Base Point and Survey Point settings are found under Site in Visibility/Graphic Overrides.

Project Base Point The project base point (PBP) is a reference point that is usually located at the origin of the internal project origin. The PBP is used to define a common reference for project-specific annotation such as spot coordinates. The PBP cannot be used for exporting your project to CAD or Navisworks® formats. The only choices you have for exporting are Internal or Shared. Remember, the internal project coordinates cannot be modified, but you can move the PBP. Let us review what the paper clip icon means when you need to relocate the base point.

The unclipped PBP *can* be moved in relation to the internal origin, thus creating a secondary reference point for spot coordinates, spot elevations, and levels—as long as the measuring parameter (either Coordinate Origin or Elevation Base) is set to Project Base Point in the respective type properties of such annotation elements. Moving the clipped PBP icon is the equivalent of using the Relocate Project tool, moving the project relative to the shared coordinates system.

Unless your project requires the use of a secondary point of reference other than the survey point, we recommend that you do not adjust the PBP and that you make sure your building model lies within a close reference of this point, such as the corner of a property line or intersection of column grids A and 1.

Survey Point The survey point (SP) is the equivalent of a station pin or geodetic survey marker in a civil engineering drawing (Figure 6.7). This is the point that will be coordinated to real geospatial coordinates. For coordination with Autodesk® Civil 3D® software, the SP is used when a Revit project is exported to the ADSK file format.

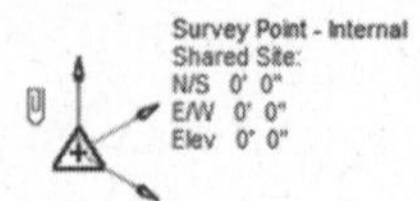

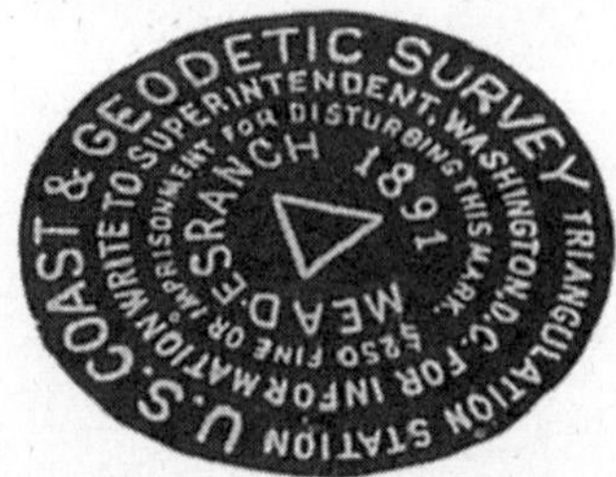

FIGURE 6.7
The survey point can be considered similar to a real-world geodetic survey marker.

Specifying a particular location for the SP based on civil engineering data is not a requirement. For smaller projects, the SP and shared coordinates may never be used at all; however, they are critical in the use of analytical tools for daylighting and solar analysis.

To further expand your understanding of these points and what happens when they are modified, we created a sample file for your reference. Open the file `c06-Shared-Points.rvt` from this book's web page (`www.sybex.com/go/masteringrevit2017`). In this file you will find three copies of the Level 1 floor plan. One view is configured to display the project coordinates, another view displays the shared coordinates, and the third view displays a combination of the two. There are also two types of spot coordinates: one indicating project coordinates in which the values are prefixed with the letter *p* and the other indicating shared coordinates with the prefix of *s*. You can open these three floor plans and tile the windows (click the View tab, select the Window panel, and choose Tile, or type the keyboard shortcut **WT**) to get a better sense of how these points affect one another (Figure 6.8).

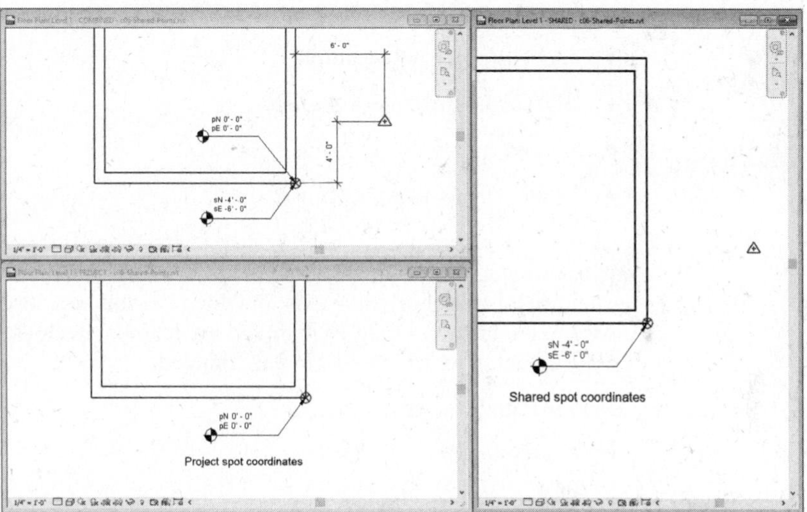

FIGURE 6.8
Using tiled windows helps you examine the effect of project and shared coordinates.

In this sample file, you can explore the effects on your model's coordinates of moving the project base point and survey point. When selected, the project base point and survey point have paperclip icons that determine the behavior of the points when you move them. Clicking the paperclip icon changes the state from clipped to unclipped and back to clipped.

The following list shows the possible point modifications and how they affect the project. In most cases you should not have to move the project base point or survey point if you are using a linked Civil 2D or 3D file and acquiring the coordinates from the linked file.

- Project Base Point: Clipped
    - Move the PBP.
    - PBP coordinates change relative to the survey point.
    - Project-based spot coordinates do not change.
    - Model elements "move" relative to shared coordinates.

Moving a clipped PBP is the same as using Relocate Project—that is, the model elements maintain their relationship to the PBP, but the relationship of the PBP to the survey point is changed.

- Project Base Point: Unclipped
  - Move the PBP.
  - PBP coordinates change relative to the survey point.
  - Project-based spot coordinates change.
  - Model elements do not move.

Unclipping the PBP essentially detaches it from the internal project origin. Moving the unclipped PBP is only used to affect the values reported in spot coordinates set to the project origin base. It does not have any effect on exported files.

- Survey Point: Clipped
  - Move the SP (survey point).
  - SP coordinates do not change.
  - Shared spot coordinates change.
  - Model elements do not move.

The clipped SP represents the origin of the shared coordinate system. Moving it is the equivalent of setting a new origin point. Use caution if you must move the shared coordinates origin if linked models already exist in which the shared coordinates have already been synchronized. In such a case, each linked model must be opened and manually reconciled with the model in which the origin has changed.

- Survey Point: Unclipped
  - Move the SP.
  - SP coordinates change.
  - Shared spot coordinates do not change.
  - Model elements do not move.

Moving an unclipped SP essentially does not do anything. It does not affect spot coordinates, and it does not affect the origin of exported files.

 **Real World Scenario**

USE PINNING TO PROTECT COORDINATE ORIGINS

An excellent way to prevent accidental modification of your project's coordinate systems is to pin them. To do so, you must first make sure the survey point and project base point are visible in a view (as we discussed previously in this section). Next, select each point and click the Pin button on the Modify panel when the Modify | Project Base Point or Modify | Survey Point ribbon appears.

Comparing Attachment to Overlay

Linked Revit models use what we will call a *portability setting* that is similar to the way Xrefs are handled in AutoCAD. Although this setting is not exposed when you initially link a Revit model, you can modify the setting by switching to the Insert tab and selecting Manage Links. Change the setting in the Reference Type column as desired (Figure 6.9).

Figure 6.9
Determining the reference type of linked Revit models

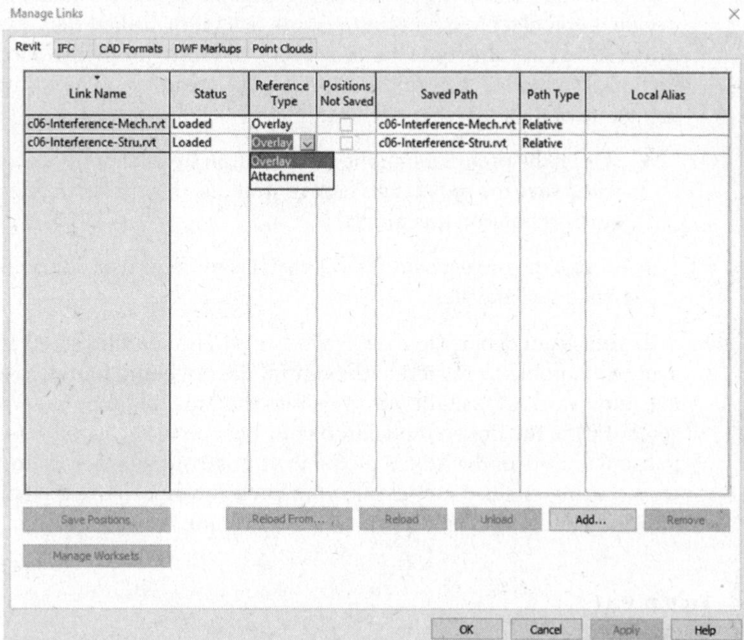

- **Attachment:** The Attachment option ensures that the linked model will be included if the host model is subsequently linked into other hosts. For example, if Project A is linked into Project B as an *attachment*, when Project B is linked into Project C, Project A will automatically be included as well.
- **Overlay:** The Overlay option prevents linked models from being included if the host model is subsequently linked into other hosts. For example, if Project A is linked into Project B as an *overlay*, when Project B is linked into Project C, Project A will not be included. When you initially link a model that contains other linked models with the Overlay option, you will be notified that those links will be invisible (Figure 6.10).

Figure 6.10
Notification of nested models using the Overlay setting

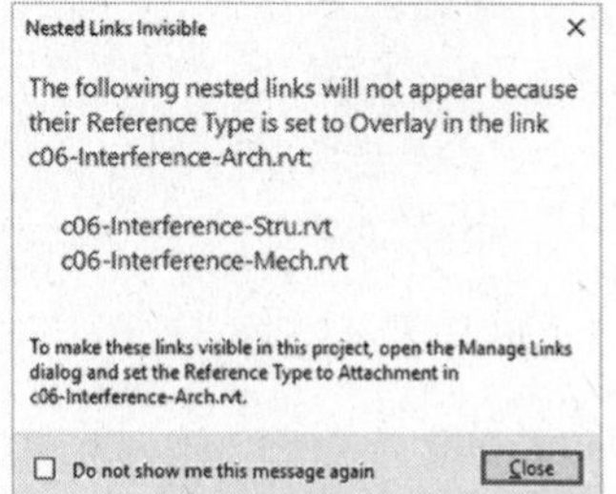

Linking with Worksharing Files

If you are using linked Revit models where one or more of the project files have worksharing enabled, there are a few guidelines to follow as well as some tangible benefits, such as linked visibility control between worksets. Be sure to read more about worksharing in Chapter 5, "Working in a Team," before continuing with this section.

When you are linking worksharing-enabled files from consultants, you will first need to decide if you need to maintain the worksets in the linked files. Even though you may not have direct access to your consultants' servers, the software will attempt to reconcile the location of each project model's central file location. We recommend handling each received project file using one of the following options:

- Open the project using the Detach From Central option, choose Preserve Worksets, and then save the project as a new central file on your server. Refer to Chapter 5 for specific instructions on this process.
- Open the project using the Detach From Central option, choose Discard Worksets, and then save the file.

If your team decides to disable worksets in linked files received from consultants, you will avoid any problems related to the central file not being found; however, you will not be able to extend workset visibility settings into the linked files or use worksets to selectively load content from the linked model into your host project. If you preserve worksets, you can continue to use worksets in the linked model to your advantage. For example, when you first link a worksharing-enabled model into your project, you can use the Specify option associated with the Open button in the Import/Link RVT dialog box, as shown in Figure 6.11.

Figure 6.11
Use the Specify option to close worksets when linking.

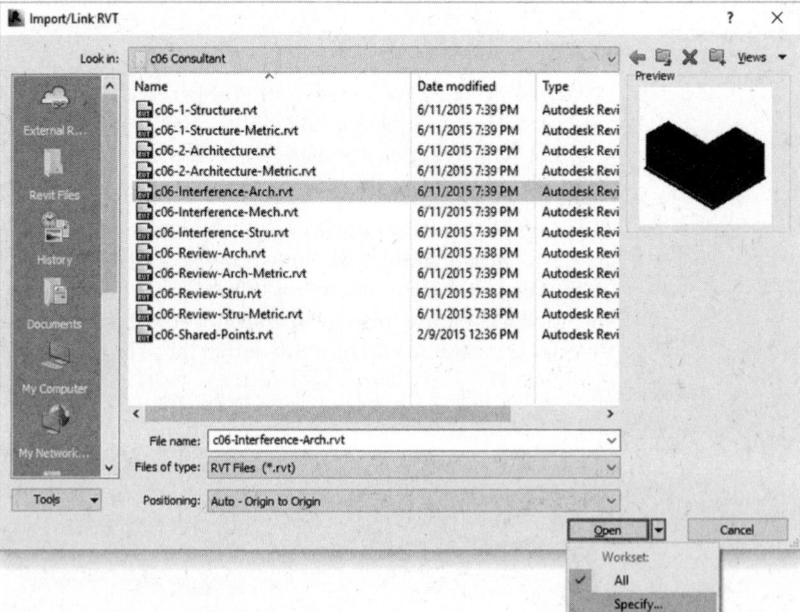

At any time throughout the development of the project, you can adjust the loaded worksets from linked files very easily. From the Manage tab or the Insert tab in the ribbon, click the Manage Links button. In the Manage Links dialog box (Figure 6.12), select one of the linked RVT files, and if it is a worksharing-enabled file, click the Manage Worksets button to open the Worksets dialog box. We describe this process in greater detail in the next section of this chapter.

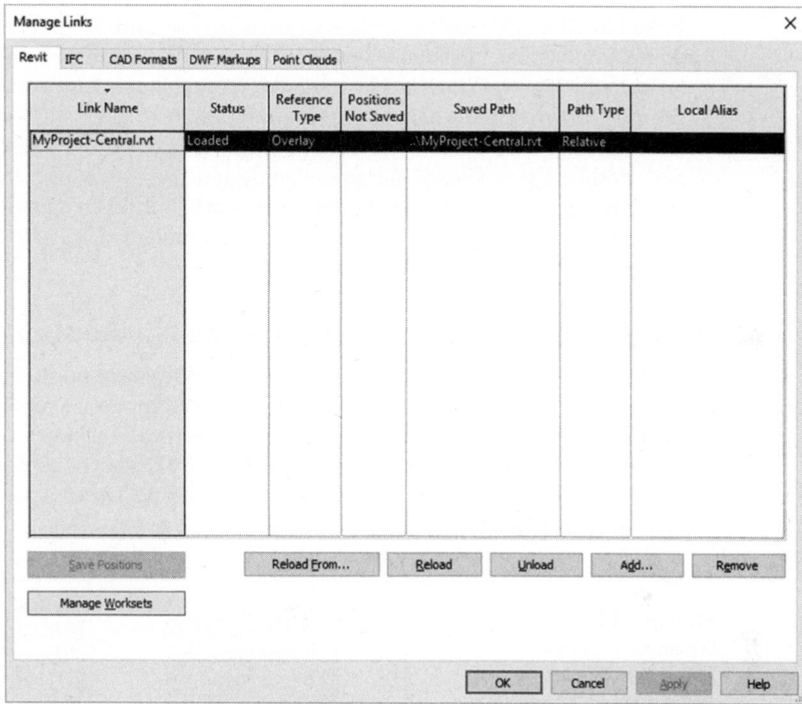

FIGURE 6.12 Access worksets of linked files from Manage Links.

In addition to the workset-loading control, you can apply visibility settings automatically to linked models—as long as the worksets in any linked files are named exactly as they are in the host file. For example, if you linked a model that had the default workset named Shared Levels and Grids, and your host model also had that same workset, you can hide the workset in both the host and linked model in one step. Open the Visibility/Graphic Overrides dialog box, select the Worksets tab, and then set Shared Levels and Grids to Hide. You will see that any datum objects assigned to that workset—in either the host or linked model—are hidden. You do not need to perform a separate visibility override on the linked file.

Although the automated visibility linking of worksets can be beneficial, it can also be problematic when you need to coordinate content between the host and linked models. In the same scenario described previously, what if you wanted the Shared Levels and Grids workset to be visible in the host model but hidden in the linked model? This is common when you are coordinating datum objects between architectural and engineering models. The grids and levels from a linked model should be visible for use with the Coordination Monitor tools described in this chapter, but then the linked references might need to be hidden. In this case, you might choose to access the Manage Worksets button discussed earlier and close the Shared Levels and Grids workset in the linked file. You could also adjust the linked view; however, this would require you to adjust every view in which the linked model appears. We discuss linked views in greater detail in Chapter 17, "Documenting Your Design."

Using Worksets to Organize Linked Models

As we discussed in Chapter 5, we recommend that you create and reserve a workset for each linked Revit model, such as Link-RVT-Structure or Link-RVT-HVAC. This simple step will allow your team members to choose whether they would like any, all, or none of the linked models to be loaded when working on a host model. To enable this functionality, use the Specify setting in the drop-down options next to the Open button.

When the Worksets dialog box appears, select the worksets reserved for the linked models and set their Open/Closed status as you desire. The benefit of using worksets to manage linked Revit models is the flexibility it offers a project team. When a team member closes a workset containing a linked model, the linked model is unloaded only for that person—it does not unload for the entire team.

Expanding Workset Properties for Linked Models

Additional flexibility can be leveraged with the Workset parameter in both the instance and type properties of a linked model. In a large and complex project that consists of multiple building elements where some of the elements are identical, each may consist of multiple linked models: architecture, structure, and MEP. Figure 6.13 shows a simplified representation of such a design where the Podium has one set of models and Tower A and Annex are identical to one another, as are Tower B and the Penthouse.

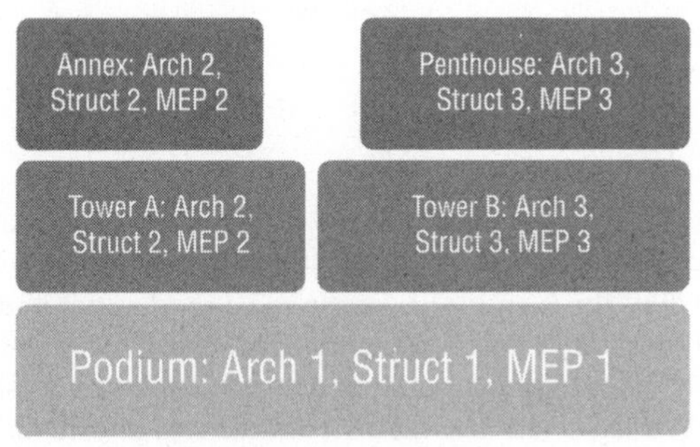

Figure 6.13
Schematic representation of a complex project assembled with multiple linked models

In Figure 6.13, there are three Revit models that represent the podium and the two towers (A and B) for each discipline (Arch1, Arch2, and so on). There are multiple instances of several of the linked models. For each instance of a linked model, you can specify the Workset parameter so that the workset instance property represents the building element, and the type property reflects either the entire discipline or one of the discipline models, as in this example:

- Instance workset: Tower A
- Type workset: Link-Architecture1 or simply Link-Architecture

Using this example, you can choose to open the Tower A workset, which would load all the discipline models but only for Tower A, or you could choose to open the Link-Architecture workset, which would load only the architectural models but for all the building elements. You can modify the workset-type properties only after placing a linked model in your project. Access this setting by selecting an instance of a linked model and opening the Properties palette, and then click Edit Type. Although this functionality can offer a variety of benefits to your project team, it should be used with care and proper planning because it can adversely affect model visibility if you are using worksets for visibility manipulation.

Worksharing-enabled linked models also afford you the flexibility to adjust the visibility of project elements for the entire project, without relying on individual settings per view or maintenance of view templates. For example, grids and levels are not usually displayed from linked models because their extents are not editable in the host model and the graphics may not match those in the host model. Without worksets, the owner of the host model would have to establish visibility settings for the linked model within all views and hopefully manage those settings in view templates. Assuming the owner of the linked model maintains the levels and grids on an agreed-upon workset such as Shared Levels and Grids, you will be able to close that workset in one place, thus affecting the entire host project. To modify the workset options for linked Revit models, follow these steps:

1. Open the Manage Links dialog box and switch to the Revit tab.
2. Select one of the linked files and click the Manage Worksets button.
3. In the Manage Worksets for Link dialog box, select the worksets you would like to close, click the Close button, and then click Reload.
4. Click OK to close the Manage Links dialog box.

Real World Scenario

RELATIVE PATHS OF LINKED MODELS

If your team is working in a situation where your project file(s) is regularly transferred between multiple locations throughout the design process, you may find it difficult to maintain linked files (they are unloaded when the file is returned), even if you are using relative paths. To alleviate this problem, try keeping the linked models and CAD files within subdirectories of the central file. For example, if your central file is saved in W:\Architecture\BIM, try keeping linked CAD files in W:\Architecture\BIM\Links-CAD and linked Revit models from consultants in W:\Architecture\BIM\Links-RVT.

Summarizing the Benefits and Limitations of Linked Models

Let us review some of the benefits and limitations of using linked Revit models. You should carefully consider these aspects not only when preparing for interdisciplinary coordination but also when managing large, complex projects with linked files.

The following list highlights some of the benefits and limitations:

- **Tagging Elements in Linked Files:** Most model elements from a linked model can be tagged in a host model. Linked views can also be used if the annotation exists in the linked model and needs to be displayed in the host.
- **Scheduling Elements in Linked Files:** In the Fields tab of the Schedule Properties dialog box, check the option Include Elements In Links.
- **Copying/Pasting Elements from Linked Files:** In a host model, use the Tab key to select any individual element within a linked file, and you can use standard copy-and-paste techniques to create a copy of the element in the host model.
- **Hiding Elements in Linked Files:** In addition to having full control of a linked model's visual fidelity through object styles, you can use the Tab key to select an individual element in a linked file and use the Hide In View commands as you would on any element within the host model.

The following list highlights some of the limitations:

- **Joining Walls:** Walls cannot be joined between linked Revit models. Consider alternative graphic techniques such as using coarse-scale black solid fill to mask unjoined walls.
- **Opening Linked Models:** You cannot have a host model with loaded linked models open in the same Revit session as the linked model files. Either separate Revit sessions must be launched or the host file must be closed before opening a linked model. If you choose not to follow either of these options and open the link in your current session, the linked model will be unloaded and need to be reloaded after the edits are made.

Using Linked Models—Exercises

Before you begin the exercises in this chapter, download the related files from this book's web page. The project files in each section's exercise should be saved because the lessons will build on the data. In this first exercise, you will do the following:

- Link the architectural model to a structural project.
- Establish shared coordinates.

The structural model is essentially a blank project with a few element types specifically built for this chapter's lessons. Let us get started working with shared coordinates:

1. Open the sample project file `c06-1-Structure.rvt` or `c06-1-Structure-Metric.rvt` and activate the Level 1 floor plan.
2. Switch to the Insert tab and select Link Revit.

   On the Revit tab of the Manage Links dialog box, click the Add button to add a new linked model. To make the steps easier to follow, the rest of this chapter will use the Link Revit button on the Insert tab, but both buttons will give you the same result.

3. Navigate to the file `c06-2-Architecture.rvt` or `c06-2-Architecture-Metric.rvt`.
4. Set the Positioning option to Auto – Center To Center and click Open.
5. Activate the South elevation view and use the Align tool to bring the linked model's Level 1 down to align with Level 1 in the host model if necessary.

   Remember, linked models should be aligned to the geometry in the host model. The modeled elements in the host model should be as close to the internal project origin as possible.
6. Switch to the Manage tab, and from the Project Location panel, select Coordinates ➤ Acquire Coordinates. Pick the linked model.

   The elevation value displayed in the level within the host file has changed to match the shared elevation in the linked file. This is because the Elevation Base parameter of the level's type properties has been set to Survey Point.
7. Save the project file for subsequent exercises in this chapter.

Modifying Element Visibility in Linked Files

Once you have linked one or more Revit files into your source project file, you may want to adjust the visibility of elements within the linked files. By default, the display settings in the Visibility/Graphic Overrides dialog box are set to By Host View for linked files, which means model objects in the linked files will adopt the same appearance as the host file. In the following exercise, we will show you how to customize these settings to turn the furniture off in the linked file and then display the room tags:

1. Continue this exercise with the structural model that you saved with the linked architectural model.
2. Activate the Level 1 floor plan from the Project Browser.
3. Go to the View tab in the ribbon, locate the Graphics panel, and select Visibility/Graphics. In the Visibility/Graphic Overrides dialog box, select the Revit Links tab.

   You will see the linked architectural model listed as an expandable tree. Click the plus sign next to the name of the linked file, and you will see a numbered instance of the link. This allows you to customize the visibility for each instance of a linked file if you have multiple copies of the link in the host file.
4. In the row displaying the name of the linked file, click the button in the Display Settings column that is labeled By Host View.

   Doing so opens the RVT Link Display Settings dialog box.
5. To begin customizing the display of elements in the linked file, you must first choose the Custom option in the Basics tab, as shown in Figure 6.14. This enables all the options in each tab of the RVT Link Display Settings dialog box.

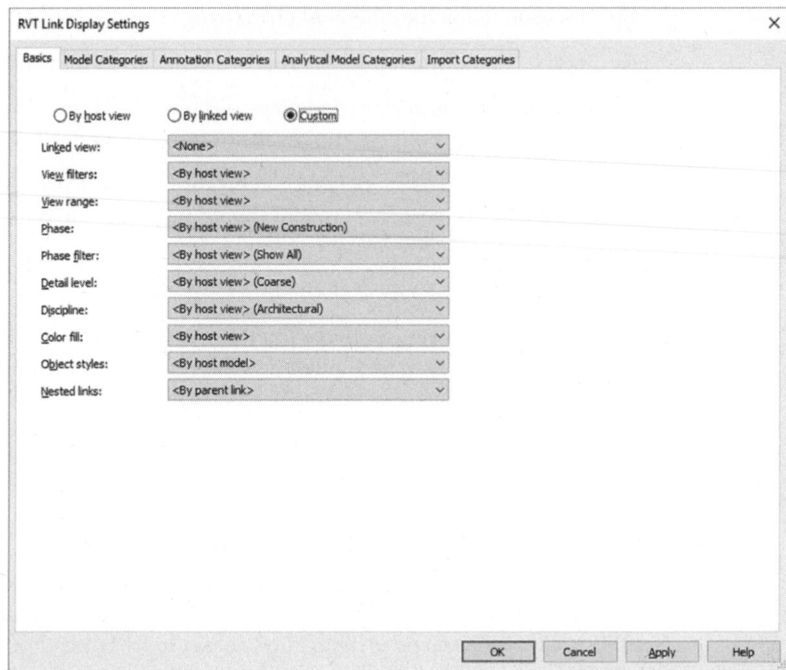

FIGURE 6.14 Enable all custom display settings for a linked RVT file

6. Select the Model Categories tab and choose <Custom> in the drop-down list at the top of the dialog box, as shown in Figure 6.15.

FIGURE 6.15 Enable custom display settings for model categories of a linked RVT file.

RVT Link Display Settings

Basics | Model Categories | Annotation Categories | Analytical Model Categories | Import Categories

Model categories: <Custom>

Show model categories in this view

If a category is unchecked, it will not be visible.

Filter list: Architecture

Visibility	Projection/Surface			Cut		Halftone	Detail Level
	Lines	Patterns	Transparency	Lines	Patterns		
☑ Areas						☐	By View
☐ Casework	Override...	Override...	Override...	Override...	Override...	☐	By View
☑ Ceilings						☐	By View
☑ Columns						☐	By View
☑ Curtain Panels						☐	By View
☑ Curtain Systems						☐	By View
☑ Curtain Wall Mullions						☐	By View
☑ Detail Items						☐	By View
☑ Doors						☐	By View
☑ Electrical Equipment						☐	By View
☑ Electrical Fixtures						☐	By View
☑ Entourage						☐	By View
☑ Floors						☐	By View
☐ Furniture						☐	By View
☐ Furniture Systems						☐	By View

All | None | Invert | Expand All

Override Host Layers

Cut Line Styles | Edit...

OK | Cancel | Apply | Help

7. Clear the check marks from the following categories: Casework, Furniture, and Furniture Systems.
8. Click OK to close all open dialog boxes.

You should observe that all the furniture and casework from the linked architecture file are no longer visible in the Level 1 floor plan. In a standard architecture-to-structure collaboration scenario, the structural engineer is likely to have a view template in which typical architectural elements are already hidden. In such a case, the default By Host View settings would be sufficient. The previous exercise illustrates a scenario where additional visual control is required.

USING LINKED VIEWS

Whereas the previous exercise focused on the display of model elements, a slightly different approach is required to use annotation elements from a linked file. In the following exercise, we will show you how to display the room tags from the linked architectural model. Many other tags can be applied to linked model elements. Here are the steps:

1. Continue with the structural model saved from the previous exercise and make sure you have activated the Level 1 floor plan.
2. Open the Visibility/Graphic Overrides dialog box and select the Revit Links tab.
3. The button in the Display Settings column should be labeled as Custom based on the previous exercise. Click the Custom button to open the RVT Link Display Settings dialog box.
4. Select the Basics tab and click the Linked View drop-down box. You will see the floor plans available for reference in the linked file. Only view types similar to the current view in the host file will be available for use as a linked view.
5. Select the linked view named Level 1-A-Anno.
6. Click OK to close all open dialog boxes.

After completing these steps, you should see the room tags from the linked architectural file in the host file. Remember that you can tag other model elements in linked files. Try using the Tag By Category tool to place some door tags on the linked architectural model.

Using the Coordination Tools

Once you have established the configuration of linked Revit models for your project, the next step is to create intelligently bound references between specific elements within the models. In the past, CAD users might have referenced files containing grid lines or level lines to establish a level of coordination between one user's data and another's. These elements in CAD are merely *lines*—not datum objects as they are in a Revit model. If these referenced elements were modified in a CAD setting, the graphic appearance of the referenced lines would update, but there would be no additional automated response to the geometry. It would be the responsibility of the recipient to update any referring geometry in their host files.

The coordination tools in Revit—Copy/Monitor and Coordination Review—allow a project team to ensure a high degree of quality control while achieving it at an increased level of productivity. These tools can function on datum (levels and grids) as well as model elements such as columns, walls, floors, and fixtures. The Copy/Monitor command is used first to establish the intelligent bonds between linked elements and host elements, whereas the Coordination Review command automatically monitors differences between host and linked elements that were previously bound with the Copy/Monitor command.

Although these tools are indeed powerful and have no similarities to CAD workflows of the past, it is important to employ proper planning and coordination with your design team. The familiar adage of "quality over quantity" holds true for the implementation of coordination tools. It may not be necessary to create monitored copies of all structural elements within the architectural model. How would these affect project-wide quantity takeoffs for the sake of minor improvements in graphic quality?

We reiterate the necessity of developing a BIM execution plan to determine important aspects of the collaboration process. When using specific coordination tools such as those in Revit, teams might plan on issues such as these:

- Who is the "owner" of grids and levels?
- Who is the "owner" of floor slabs?
- Are structural walls copied, monitored, or just linked?
- How often are models exchanged?
- How are coordination conflicts resolved?

A seemingly powerful BIM tool will not replace the need for professional supervision and the standard of care implicit to respective disciplines in the building industry. Thus, there is no substitution for the most important part of effective collaboration: *communication*. Without open and honest communication, the coordination tools will discover conflicts, but the results may be ignored, dismissed, or overwritten, to the detriment of the team's progress.

Using the Copy/Monitor Command

The Copy/Monitor command allows you to create copies of linked elements for better graphic control of the elements while maintaining an intelligent bond to the linked elements. If the linked element changes in a subsequent iteration of the project file, the changes are detected in the Coordination Review tool, which we will discuss next.

With the structural model saved from the "Using Linked Models" exercises, switch to the Collaborate tab and select Copy/Monitor ➤ Select Link. Pick the linked architectural model, and the ribbon will change to Copy/Monitor mode. Click the Options icon to open the dialog box shown in Figure 6.16.

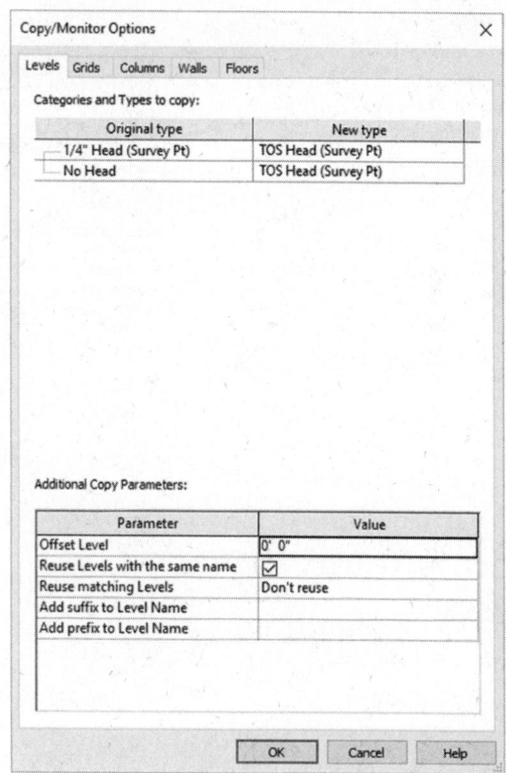

FIGURE 6.16
Element tabs available for Copy/Monitor in Revit Architecture

As shown in Figure 6.16, the Copy/Monitor Options dialog box in Revit is divided into five tabs representing the elements available to be copied and/or monitored. For each element tab, there is a list called Categories And Types To Copy. As shown in Figure 6.17, the Floors tab lists the available floor types in the linked model in the left column and host model floor types in the right column. Notice that any of the linked types can be specified with the option Don't Copy This Type. This feature can be used for quality control if your project's BIM execution plan states that certain elements are not to be copied. For example, if walls are not to be copied, switch to the Walls tab and set all linked wall types to Don't Copy This Type. You can also use the option Copy Original Type if the element type exists in the linked file but not in the host file. After one or more of these elements are selected using Copy/Monitor, the type mapping will be synchronized.

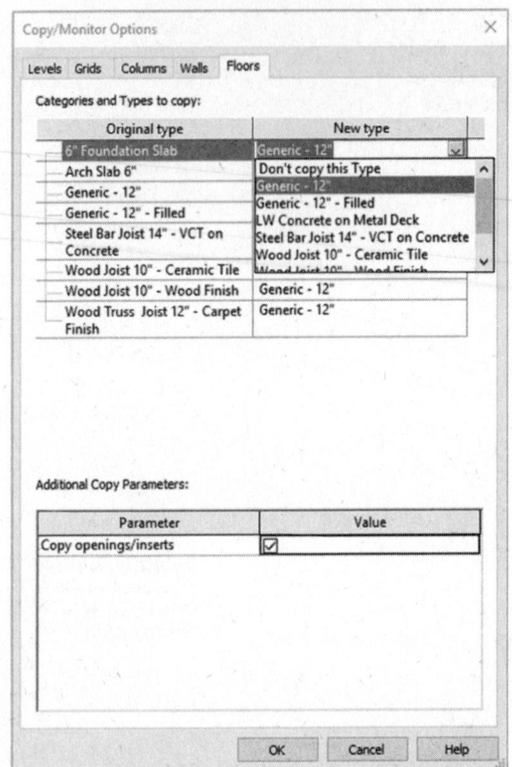

FIGURE 6.17
The Copy/Monitor Options dialog box allows customization for intelligent collaboration.

At the bottom of the Copy/Monitor Options dialog box, you will find a section called Additional Copy Parameters for each element tab (refer to Figures 6.16 and 6.17). The additional parameters are different for each element category. For example, when levels are copied and monitored, an offset and naming prefix can be applied to accommodate the difference between the finish floor level in a linked architectural model and the top-of-steel level in the host structural model.

Let's take a closer look at each of the element category options available for the Copy/Monitor tool:

Levels In most cases, the difference between the location of a structural level and an architectural level may lead to the presumption that you would not want to copy levels between files. However, maintaining an offset between linked and host levels can be quite desirable. Keep in mind that the offset will apply to all copy/monitor selections. Thus, if a structural level needs to be offset by a different value, create the level in the host model and use the Monitor command to create the intelligent bond to the linked model's level. The difference will be maintained through any modifications in the linked model.

Grids Copying the grids is usually a strong workflow. You can use the options on these tabs to convert the grid bubbles used by the architect into those used by the structural engineer. It is also possible to add a prefix to the grid names. For instance, you could add the value S- in the prefix field, and then grid A from the architectural model will come into the structural model as S-A.

Columns The structural engineer can choose to replace any column—architectural or structural—in the architectural model with an appropriate structural column; however, this implies that the architect will maintain an understanding of where differentiating column types would exist. Realistically, the structural elements should exist only in the structural engineer's model and then link into the architectural model. The architect may then choose to either copy/monitor the linked structural columns with architectural columns (which act as finish wrappers) or place architectural columns along the monitored grid lines. In the latter option, architectural columns will move along with changes in grid line locations but will not update if structural columns are removed in the linked model.

Walls and Floors Similar to columns, structural walls that are important to the coordination process may be better managed in the structural model and linked into the architectural model. If you decide to use a copy/monitor relationship for these types of elements, it is best to create uniquely named wall types for structural coordination. Name such wall types in a manner that makes them display at the top of the list in the Copy/Monitor Options dialog box. You can do so by adding a hyphen (-) or underscore (_) at the beginning of the wall type name.

Finally, make sure you select the check box Copy Windows/Doors/Openings for walls or Copy Openings/Inserts for floors so that you also get the appropriate openings for those components in the monitored elements.

Using the Copy/Monitor Command—An Exercise

Continue with the structural model saved in the previous exercise in this chapter. In this exercise, you will do the following:

- Use Copy/Monitor to establish new levels and grids.
- Use Copy/Monitor to create floors.
- Link the new structural model back to the architectural model.
- Use the Monitor option for grids in the architectural model.

These steps will establish the intelligent bonds between elements in the host file with the related elements in the linked model. With the structural model open, activate the South elevation view. Then follow these steps:

1. Switch to the Collaborate tab and select Copy/Monitor ➢ Select Link. Choose the linked model.
2. On the Copy/Monitor tab, click the Options button.
3. Select the Levels tab, and under Categories And Types To Copy, make sure the rows under New Type are set to TOS Head (Survey Pt). In the Additional Copy Parameters section, set the following options:
    - Offset Level: –0′ –6″ (-150 mm)
    - Add the prefix (note the order in the dialog box) to Level Name: **T.O.S.**
4. Select the Grids tab, and under Categories And Types To Copy, make sure the rows under New Type are set to 1/4″ Square (6.5 mm Square).

5. Select the Floors tab and set the following options under Categories And Types To Copy:
   - Arch Slab 6" (150 mm): LW Concrete on Metal Deck
   - Set all other entries under Original Type to Don't Copy This Type.

   Remember that you can select multiple rows in the Categories And Types To Copy list by pressing the Shift key while selecting a range of rows. You may then make a selection in the New Type column for any row, and all the selected rows will be modified.

   In the Additional Copy Parameters section, set the following option:
   - Copy Openings/Inserts: Yes (checked)
6. Click OK to close the Copy/Monitor Options dialog box.
7. From the Copy/Monitor tab of the ribbon, choose the Copy button.
8. Select the Level 2 and Roof levels in the linked model. Levels in the host model should be created 6" (150 mm) below the linked levels with the prefix T.O.S. (Top Of Structure).

   There is already a Level 1 in the host model. You will need to use the Monitor tool to establish a relationship to the Level 1 in the linked model.
9. From the Copy/Monitor tab of the ribbon, choose the Monitor button and select Level 1 in the host model.

   You can only select levels in the host model for the first pick.
10. Select Level 1 in the linked model to complete the monitored relationship.

    You will see an icon appear near the midpoint of the level indicating that it is now monitoring the level in the linked model.
11. Activate Section 1 and return to Copy mode by clicking the Copy button in the Copy/Monitor tab of the ribbon.
12. Select the floor in the linked model at Level 2.
13. Activate the Level 1 floor plan and make sure the Copy tool is still active. Check the Multiple option in the Options bar.
14. Select all the visible grids using any selection method you prefer.
15. Click the Finish button in the Options bar to complete the multiple copy process for the grids. Do not click the Finish icon in the Copy/Monitor tab of the ribbon without finishing the Multiple selection mode first.
16. Click the Finish icon in the Copy/Monitor tab of the ribbon to exit Copy/Monitor mode.

If you now select any of the grids or levels in the host file, you will see a monitor icon near the center of the element. This icon indicates that the intelligent bond has been created between the host and the linked element and will evaluate any modifications in the linked file whenever the file is reloaded.

Save and close the structural model and then open the architectural model, `c06-2-Architecture.rvt` or `c06-2-Architecture-Metric.rvt`. Using the procedures you have learned in this chapter, link the structural file into the architectural model. Placement should be done in the Level 1 floor plan using Auto – By Shared Coordinates positioning.

Use the Copy/Monitor tools in Monitor mode to establish the relationships of the grids between host and linked models. Doing so will ensure that changes to grids in either model will be coordinated.

Using the Coordination Review Tool

After intelligent bonds have been established between elements in linked models, it is the purpose of the Coordination Review tool to support the workflow when datum or model elements are modified. This tool was designed to allow the recipient of linked data to control how and when elements in host models are modified based on changes in the linked models.

When a linked model is reloaded—which will happen automatically when the host model is opened or when you manually reload the linked model in the Manage Links dialog box—monitored elements will check for any inconsistencies. If any are found, you will see a warning message that a linked instance needs a coordination review.

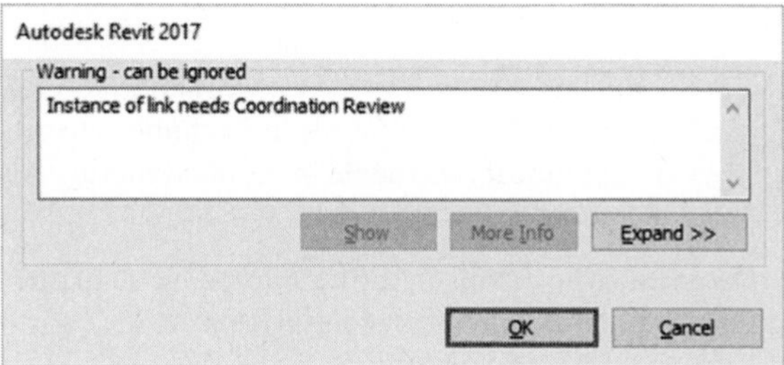

The Coordination Review warning is triggered when any of the following scenarios occur:

- A monitored element in the linked model is changed, moved, or deleted.
- A monitored element in the host model is changed, moved, or deleted.
- Both the original monitored element and the copied element are changed, moved, or deleted.
- A hosted element (door, window, opening) is added, moved, changed, or deleted in a monitored wall or floor.
- The copied element in the host file is deleted.

To perform a coordination review, switch to the Collaborate tab and click Coordination Review ➤ Select Link. After picking one of the linked models, you will see the Coordination Review dialog box, which lists any inconsistencies in monitored elements (Figure 6.18).

FIGURE 6.18
The Coordination Review dialog box lists inconsistencies in monitored elements.

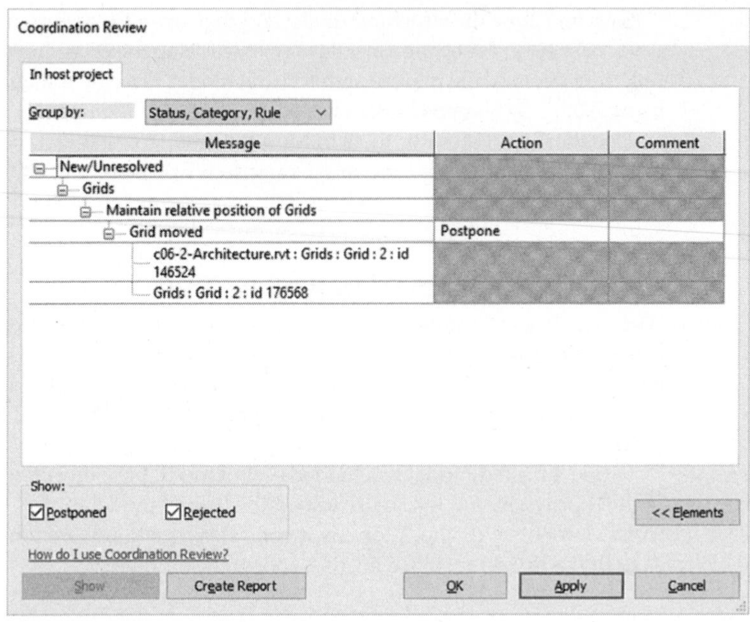

For each of the changes detected in the Coordination Review dialog box, one of the following actions can be applied. Actions that result in changes to elements will be applied only to the host model; they do not modify elements in a linked model. Also, not all options are available for all monitored elements.

- **Postpone:** Takes no action on the monitored element and changes the message status so that it can be filtered out or considered later.
- **Reject:** Select this action if you believe the change made to the element in the linked file is incorrect. A change must then be made to the element in the linked file.
- **Accept Difference:** Accepts the change made to the element and updates the relationship. For example, if a pair of grids was 8″ (200 mm) apart and one was moved to 12″ (300 mm) away, the change would be accepted and the relationship would now consist of a dimensional offset.
- **Modify, Rename, Move:** The command name changes based on the action. If the name of the monitored element has changed, the command reads Rename. If a column or level is moved, the command is Move. If a grid is changed or moved, the command is Modify.
- **Ignore New Elements:** A new hosted element has been added to a monitored wall or floor. Select this action to ignore the new element in the host. It will not be monitored for changes.
- **Copy New Elements:** A new hosted element has been added to a monitored wall or floor. Select this action to add the new element to the host and monitor it for changes.
- **Delete Element:** A monitored element has been deleted. Select this action to delete the corresponding element in the current project.

- **Copy Sketch:** The sketch or boundary of a monitored opening has changed. Select this action to change the corresponding opening in the current project.
- **Update Extents:** The extents of a monitored element have changed. Select this action to change the corresponding element in the current project.

As you can see, Coordination Review can be a powerful tool to support the collaboration process. Remember that such a tool may not be appropriate for all elements at all times. For example, instead of copying and monitoring columns and grids, it may be sufficient to copy and monitor only grids because the columns placed in your host model will move with the grids anyway.

Using the Coordination Review Tool—An Exercise

In this exercise, you will use two files that have already been linked together with monitored elements between both files. You can download the files `c06-Review-Arch.rvt` or `c06-Review-Arch-Metric.rvt` (architectural model) and `c06-Review-Stru.rvt` or `c06-Review-Stru-Metric.rvt` (structural model) from this book's web page. In this exercise, you will do the following:

- Modify elements in the architectural model.
- Use Coordination Review to address these changes in the structural model.

Remember that you cannot have a host model and a linked model open in the same Revit session. To make this lesson easier, you can launch a second Revit session. Open `c06-Review-Arch.rvt` or `c06-Review-Arch-Metric.rvt` in one session and `c06-Review-Stru.rvt` or `c06-Review-Stru-Metric.rvt` in the other. Then follow these steps:

1. In the architectural model, activate the Level 1 floor plan and make the following modifications:
   - Move grid line F to the north by 2′-0″ (600 mm).
   - Rename grid 6 to **8**.
2. Save the architectural model and switch to the structural model. Open the Manage Links window, select the linked architectural model, and click Reload. Once the file is done reloading, you are presented with the Coordination Review warning. Click OK to close the dialog box and then click OK to close the Manage Links dialog box.
3. In the structural project, activate the Level 1 floor plan, and then switch to the Collaborate tab and choose Coordination Review ➢ Select Link. Select the linked architectural model.
4. When the Coordination Review dialog box opens, you will see changes to monitored elements detected in the reloaded architectural model. You may need to expand some of the statuses and categories to reveal the detected change and the drop-down list under the Action column.
5. Apply the appropriate modifying action to each of the detected changes. (Modify the moved grid, and rename the numbered grid.)
6. Click Apply and OK to close the dialog box.

In the previous exercise, you might have noticed the appearance of a monitored floor sketch. Why did a floor sketch change if you only moved a grid and renamed another? The answer lies in constraints and relationships. The exterior wall in the architectural model was constrained to be 2′-0″ (600 mm) offset from grid line F. When it was moved, the exterior wall was moved to maintain the offset. The sketches of the model's floor slabs were created using the Pick Walls tools, creating an intelligent relationship to the wall. The modified grid affected the wall, which modified the floor, and the Coordination Monitor tools ensured that all changes were detected and presented to you for action.

Using Interference Checking in 3D Coordination

In addition to asset management, digital fabrication, and cost estimation, 3D coordination is one of the most important uses of building information modeling. It has enormous potential to reduce the costs of construction through the computerized resolution of clashing building elements as well as exposing opportunities for alternate trade scheduling or prefabrication. The key component to achieving 3D coordination is interference checking, also known as *clash detection*.

Real World Scenario

Indiana University Defines Clashes

As we mentioned previously in this chapter, not only are some building and facility owners requiring BIM processes and deliverables for new projects, but they are also defining how these processes are to be used. When you focus on interference checking, myriad potential clashes can be distilled into a prioritized grouping of building elements. Borrowing from Indiana University's BIM Standards & Guidelines for Architects, Engineers, & Contractors, the following is an intelligent approach to the organization of potential interferences. (Always remember that the priorities listed here are based on the requirements of one organization. The needs of your firm and those of your clients may vary.)

Level One Clashes

Clashes in these categories are considered the most critical to the coordination process. They usually relate to systems or construction techniques that are more costly to delay or reschedule.

- Mechanical Ductwork and Piping vs. Ceilings
- Mechanical Ductwork and Piping vs. Rated Walls (for coordination of dampers and other mechanical equipment needs)
- Mechanical Ductwork and Piping vs. Structure (columns, beams, framing, etc.)
- All Equipment and Their Applicable Clearances vs. Walls
- All Equipment and Their Applicable Clearances vs. Structure

- Mechanical Equipment and Fixtures vs. Electrical Equipment and Fixtures
- Mechanical Ductwork and Piping vs. Plumbing Piping

LEVEL TWO CLASHES

These categories of clashes are considered important to the design and construction process but are less critical than those designated as Level One.

- Casework vs. Electrical Fixtures and Devices
- Furnishings vs. Electrical Fixtures and Devices
- Structure vs. Specialty Equipment
- Structure vs. Electrical Equipment, Fixtures, and Devices
- Ductwork and Piping vs. Electrical Equipment, Fixtures, and Devices
- Ductwork vs. Floors

LEVEL THREE CLASHES

These clashes are considered important to the correctness of the model; however, they will usually change on a regular basis throughout the design and construction process.

- Casework vs. Walls
- Plumbing Piping vs. Electrical Equipment, Fixtures, and Devices
- Plumbing Piping vs. Mechanical Equipment, Fixtures, and Devices
- ADA Clear Space Requirements vs. Doors, Fixtures, Walls, Structure

USING THE INTERFERENCE CHECK TOOL

The Interference Check tool is a basic tool supporting 3D coordination. You can use it within a single project model or between linked models. You can also select elements prior to running the tool in order to detect clashes within a limited set of geometry instead of the entire project.

For more powerful clash-detection capabilities, Autodesk offers Navisworks® Manage (`www.autodesk.com/navisworks`), which is a multiformat model-reviewing tool with various modules supporting phasing simulation, visualization, and clash detection. Figure 6.19 shows an example of a model in Navisworks Manage comprising Revit, Tekla Structures, and AutoCAD MEP components. Some of the benefits of using Navisworks for interference-checking over Revit include automated views of each clash, grouping of related clashes, enhanced reporting, clash-resolution tracking, and markup capabilities. Revit models can be opened directly in Navisworks or exported directly to the Navisworks format from the Application menu.

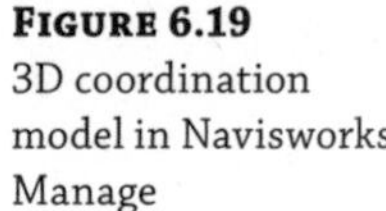

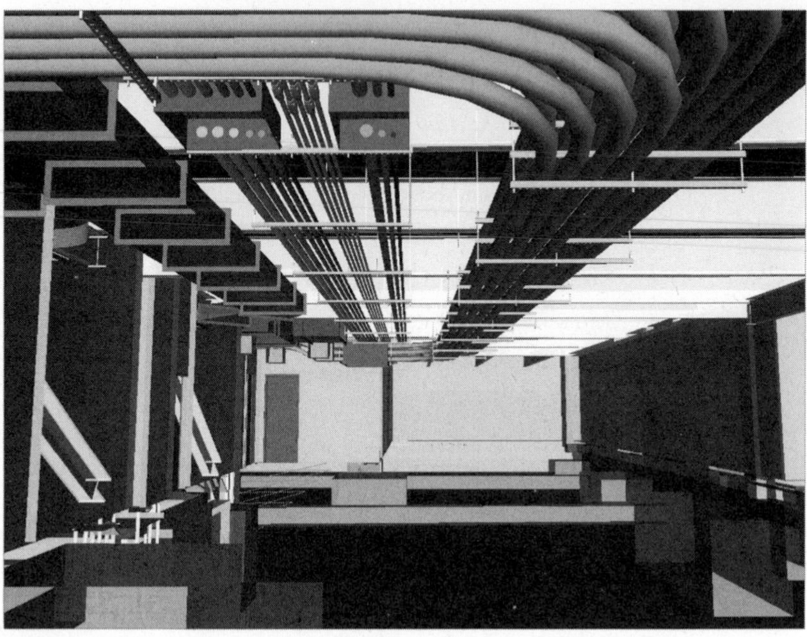

FIGURE 6.19
3D coordination model in Navisworks Manage

RUNNING AN INTERFERENCE CHECK—AN EXERCISE

Let's take a look at the Revit interference-checking process. For this exercise, you will need to download three sample files to your computer or network: `c06-Interference-Arch.rvt`, `c06-Interference-Mech.rvt`, and `c06-Interference-Stru.rvt`. You can download these files from this book's web page. The sample files are already linked to each other using relative paths, so be sure to place all three files in the same folder. Then follow these steps:

1. Open the file `c06-Interference-Mech.rvt` and activate the default 3D view.
2. Switch to the Collaborate tab, find the Coordinate panel, and choose Interference Check ➢ Run Interference Check.
3. When the Interference Check dialog box appears, choose `c06-Interference-Stru.rvt` from the Categories From drop-down list in the left column. Select Structural Framing in the left column and Ducts in the right column (Figure 6.20).
4. Click OK to close the dialog box.
5. The Interference Report window will appear, listing all clashes detected between the categories you selected. The list can be sorted by either Category 1 or Category 2, representing the left and right columns in the Interference Check dialog box, respectively. In Figure 6.21, one interference condition has been selected, and the corresponding element is highlighted in the 3D view.

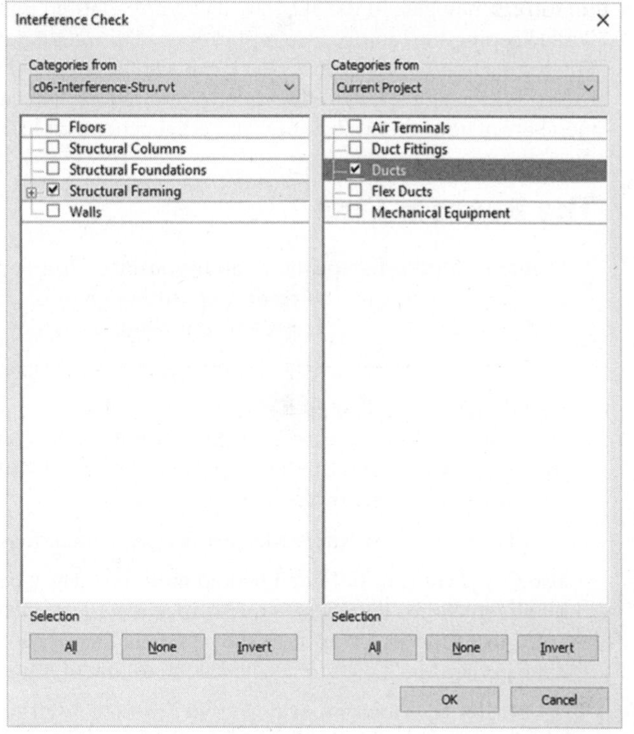

FIGURE 6.20 Select categories to be included in an interference check.

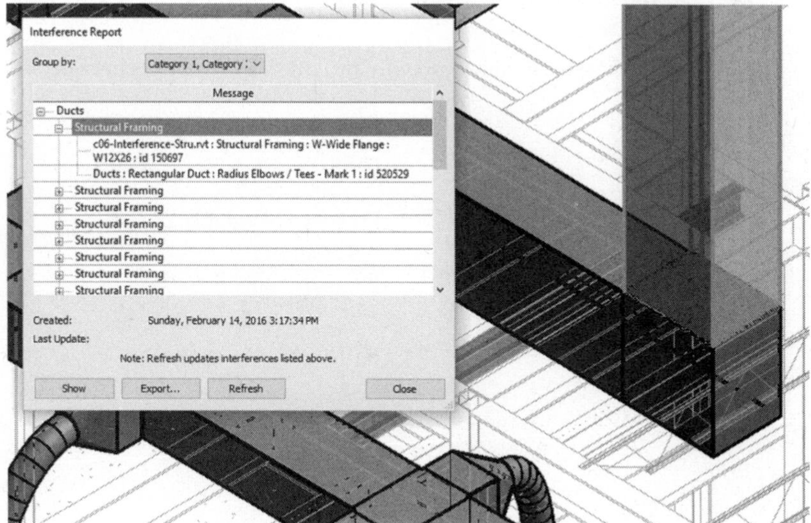

FIGURE 6.21 The results of an interference check are displayed in the Interference Report window.

You can navigate in the 3D view using any method (mouse, ViewCube®, or SteeringWheels®) while keeping the interference report open. This facilitates resolution of the clashing items. The results of the interference check can also be exported to an HTML format report. Click the Export button and specify a location for the report. You can then share this report with other members of your design team for remedial actions on linked models.

The Bottom Line

Prepare for interdisciplinary collaboration. Proper planning and communication are the foundation of effective collaboration. Although only some client organizations may require a BIM planning document, it is a recommended strategy for all design teams.

Master It What are the key elements of a BIM execution plan?

Collaborate using linked Revit models. The most basic tool for collaboration is the ability to view consultants' data directly within the context of your own model. Project files from other disciplines can be linked and displayed with predictable visual fidelity without complex conversion processes.

Master It How can worksharing complement the use of linked Revit models?

Use Copy/Monitor between linked models. The Coordination Monitor tools establish intelligent bonds between elements in a host file and correlating elements in a linked model. They also support a workflow that respects the needs of discrete teams developing their own data, perhaps on a different schedule than that of other team members.

Master It How can grids in two different Revit projects be related?

Run interference checks. Interference checking—also known as *clash detection*—is one of the most important components of building information modeling. It is the essence of virtual construction and has the greatest potential for cost savings during the physical construction process.

Master It How do you find interfering objects between two linked Revit models?

Chapter 7

Interoperability: Working Multiplatform

In the previous chapter, we discussed working with others in an environment in which all parties use Autodesk® Revit® Architecture software; however, often you'll need to work with data from other software platforms. For example, you may need to coordinate data from other disciplines, reuse legacy data, or integrate disparate design platforms. There are several ways to use external data within your Revit Architecture model in both 2D and 3D. We will discuss not only the methods of importing and exporting data but also when to use each method and the reasons for using specific settings.

In this chapter, you'll learn to:

- Use imported 2D CAD data
- Export 2D CAD data
- Use imported 3D model data
- Export 3D model data
- Work with IFC imports and exports

Examining Interoperability on a BIM Curve

On the basis of a 2007 study on interoperability in the design and construction industry, McGraw-Hill Construction reported annual losses of $9.1 billion in the building industry due to insufficient interoperability. You can find the full report online (`http://www.aia.org/aiaucmp/groups/aia/documents/pdf/aias077485.pdf`). Although the study is now a bit dated, it underscores a problem that building information modeling (BIM) as a whole is designed to address. Adequate interoperability will help rectify the problem illustrated in Figure 7.1, sometimes known as the BIM curve. In Figure 7.1, the downward spikes in the lower line at the end of each project phase represent a loss of knowledge and acquired data. This loss usually occurs when a project is exported from BIM to a 2D CAD format or is printed to paper. Project data is then gradually reconstructed in another software platform. The upper line represents a more ideal paradigm where data and knowledge are gradually increased throughout the life of the project—a paradigm supported by BIM and full interoperability.

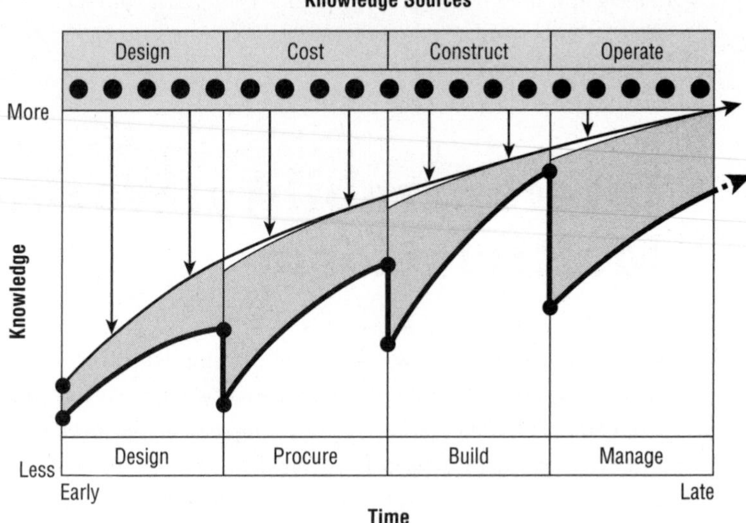

FIGURE 7.1 The BIM curve shows loss of data without interoperability at project milestones.
Source: P. Bernstein, Autodesk AEC Solutions

Although full interoperability between BIM platforms is the ideal scenario, we realize that you are likely to be working with constituents who are using 2D CAD or non-BIM 3D software.

Inserting CAD Data

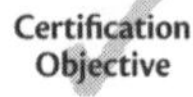

Although Revit software provides ample means to generate 2D documentation based on a rich multidimensional (3D, 4D, 5D, and so on) model, there are a few real-world scenarios in which CAD data must be integrated with the building information model. Such scenarios might include the following:

- Using CAD details developed within your firm
- Coordinating with other firms using CAD software
- Converting projects from CAD to a Revit model
- Using external modeling tools for conceptual massing
- Using complex component models from other software

Using Predefined Settings for Inserted CAD Data

When you are inserting data from a DWG or DXF file, you can establish some predefined settings to control its appearance within the Revit environment. Some settings are controlled at the time you insert a CAD file, but other settings can be configured more deliberately in saved configuration files. The two ways you can configure this data are by mapping layer colors to Revit line weights and converting font types.

Mapping Layer Colors

For inserted CAD files, layers within the file are assigned a Revit line weight based on the weight assigned to each layer by the CAD software application that created the files. If the layer line weights are set to Default in the CAD file, they will follow a translation template you can configure that maps the layer colors to Revit line weights. To access these settings, select the Insert tab and click the dialog launcher at the bottom right of the Import panel. Doing so opens the Import Line Weights dialog box, shown in Figure 7.2.

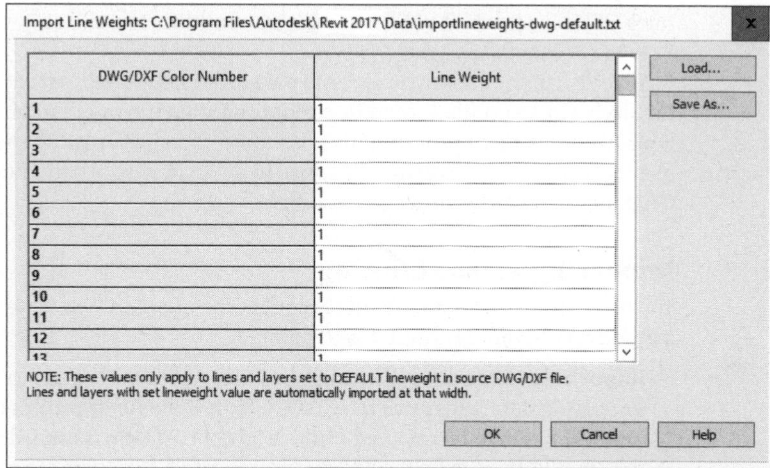

FIGURE 7.2 Defining settings for imported DWG/DXF line weights

As you can see in the title bar of this dialog box, these settings are stored in a text file (TXT) in the Data folder where Revit is installed. There are several predefined text files based on international CAD standards for layer color:

- AIA (American Institute of Architects)
- BS1192 (British Standard)
- CP83 (Singapore Standard)
- ISO13567 (International Standards Organization)

Click the Load button to select one of these predefined line weight templates or your own. On the basis of the unique needs of some projects, you might also consider creating customized import setting files and storing them along with the rest of your project data.

DEFINING THE IMPORTED LINE WEIGHTS TEMPLATE IN *REVIT.INI* FILES

The file location for the imported line weights template is stored in the `Revit.ini` file under the following category:

```
[Directories]
ImportLineweightsNameDWG=&#x003C; Full path to TXT file >
```

If you are using any kind of automation scripts to set up standards, your imported line weights template file location can be written into the `Revit.ini` file for all your users. Doing so ensures consistency for all team members inserting CAD data into your Revit project.

Mapping Font Types

Another important aspect for inserted CAD data is the ability to map shape-based fonts to TrueType fonts. Usually a remnant of older CAD standards based on graphic performance, CAD files may contain fonts such as Simplex, RomanS, or Monotxt that do not have matches in standard Windows fonts. The shxfontmap.txt file defines the mapping of TrueType fonts as substitutes for each specified SHX font. You can find this text file at `C:\ProgramData\Autodesk\RVT 2017\UserDataCache`.

If your firm frequently uses CAD data as an integrated part of your final documentation, the shxfontmap.txt file should be configured to map your standard CAD fonts to your standard fonts used in a Revit project. This file should then be copied to the workstations of all team members using Revit software. Failure to do so may result in undesirable results when using CAD files in a worksharing environment.

Importing versus Linking

You can insert CAD data into the Revit environment in two ways: importing and linking. Each method has advantages and disadvantages.

Importing Similar to the using the Insert command in Autodesk® AutoCAD® software, importing data integrates the CAD data into the Revit project but does not allow the imported data to be updated if the original CAD file is modified. In such a case, the imported data would have to be deleted and reimported. It also does not give you an easy way to purge the layers, linetypes, and hatch patterns of an imported file if it has been exploded and then deleted.

Linking A linked CAD file in a Revit project is analogous to an external reference (xref) in an AutoCAD project. When the original CAD file is modified, its reference is automatically updated in the Revit environment. Linking also allows you to easily unload or remove a file when it is no longer needed, which will leave no trace of the file's contents after removal.

Linked data cannot be modified directly in a Revit project unless it is converted to an import in the Manage Links dialog box (Insert ➤ Manage Links) and then exploded. We discuss this process in the "Manipulating Inserted CAD Data" section later in this chapter. As an alternative, it can be modified in its original authoring application and then updated within Revit.

Linking is the preferred method for external data integration; however, too many linked files will make it slower to open a Revit project. For example, ceiling plan fixture layouts may change with every design iteration (where linking is preferred); however, standard details that all share a minimal amount of standardized layers, linetypes, hatch patterns, text, and dimension styles might be better suited as imports.

Collect CAD Links in a Linked Revit File

Another option to manage many CAD references in larger projects is to create a separate Revit project that contains only the inserted CAD data. If the CAD data is placed with the Current View Only option, you must use linked views between Revit models. If the linked data does not use this option, it will be visible like any other modeled element in a linked Revit model. Refer to Chapter 6, "Working with Consultants," for more information about linked Revit models.

Using Options during Importing/Linking

After you have configured the necessary settings for inserted CAD data and decided whether to import or link, you need to understand certain options during the import/link process. We'll discuss the preferred settings for each of the options based on real-world situations in the sections "Using Inserted 2D Data" and "Using Inserted 3D Data." To place your first CAD file into a Revit project, switch to the Insert tab and select either the Link CAD or the Import CAD button. No matter which tool you use, there will be several important options at the bottom of the respective dialog box, as shown in Figure 7.3.

FIGURE 7.3
Options available for import/link

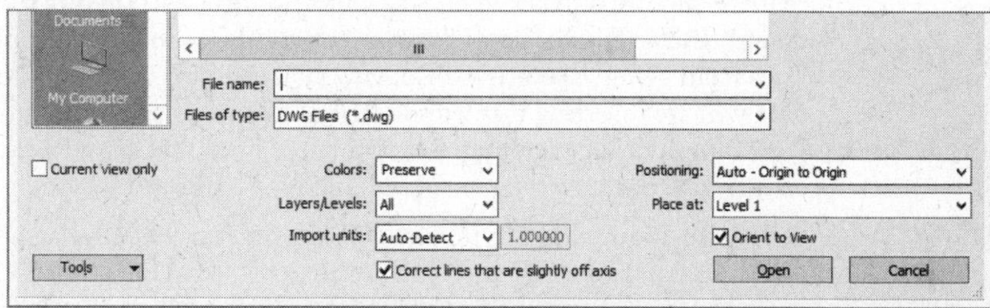

Let's examine the meaning of the settings in this situation:

Current View Only When this option is selected, the linked or imported file can be seen only in the view in which it was inserted and is thus considered a view-specific element. In a worksharing-enabled project, this data will be assigned to the view's workset. More often than not, you will want to choose this option to limit the number of views in which the referenced data will appear. If you need this data in other views, you can copy and paste it from one view to another.

If the option is not selected, the linked file can be seen in all views, including 3D, elevations, and sections. In a worksharing-enabled project, this data will be assigned to the active workset. A benefit to using links in a worksharing environment is the ability to create a workset specifically for linked data and uncheck its Visible In All Views option. The CAD files placed in this manner will not appear in every view but are available when you need them by adjusting the workset visibility in the Visibility/Graphic Overrides dialog box.

Colors Colors don't matter for CAD files being used as a basis to create a Revit model; however, using Invert or Preserve may help distinguish the CAD data from the modeled elements during the conversion process. If you are going to integrate the inserted data with other elements in your project for final design or construction documentation, you'll want to select the Black And White option, because printing from Revit is mostly WYSIWYG (what you see is what you get). Read the section "Using CAD Data for Coordination" for more detailed recommendations on this process.

Layers/Levels These options allow you to import or link all the layers, only the layers visible when the CAD file was last saved, or a selected group of layers you choose from the linked file in a separate dialog box. (*Layers* is a DWG-based term. Revit software supports the same functionality with *levels* from DGN files.)

Import Units For CAD files generated in an original program (that is, DWG from AutoCAD or DGN from MicroStation), the Auto-Detect option works well. If you are linking CAD data that has been exported from a different program, such as DWG exported from Rhino, you should specify the units relative to the respective CAD file.

Positioning To maintain consistency in a multilevel project during a CAD-to-Revit coordination or conversion process, you should use Auto – Origin To Origin or Auto – By Shared Coordinates. Origin To Origin will align the world coordinates origin of the CAD file with the project internal origin. Although Autodesk claims Auto – By Shared Coordinates is only for use with linked Revit files, it can be used with CAD files if the rotation of true north becomes inconsistent using the Origin To Origin option.

Place At This option is available only if Current View Only is not selected; it specifies the level at which the inserted data will be placed.

Correct Lines That Are Slightly Off Axis Selecting this option automatically corrects lines that are slightly off axis when you import or link CAD geometry. This option is selected by default and will help keep your Revit elements (such as walls or linework) that tie to CAD lines from being askew; however, you may need to consider this option carefully. If the CAD data you are inserting is intentionally off axis, the corrections may lead to inaccurate results. For example, a site plan may have property lines that are a fraction of a degree from being orthogonal, but they must be maintained for accurate building placement in your Revit project.

Orient To View This option may be used if True North has been rotated away from Project North. If that is the case and you are linking a CAD file into a view that is set to True North, deselect this option to align the CAD file's World Coordinate System with True North as defined in your Revit project.

If you do check the Orient To View option, the CAD file will align with Project North regardless of the view orientation.

Manipulating Inserted CAD Data

Once you have CAD data imported or linked into a Revit project, you have several ways of manipulating the data to suit your needs:

Foreground/Background This setting applies only to linked or imported CAD files placed with the Current View Only option. With the inserted file selected, a drop-down menu will appear in the Options bar so you can adjust whether the data appears above or below your modeled Revit content. You can also access this setting in the Properties palette when the inserted file is selected.

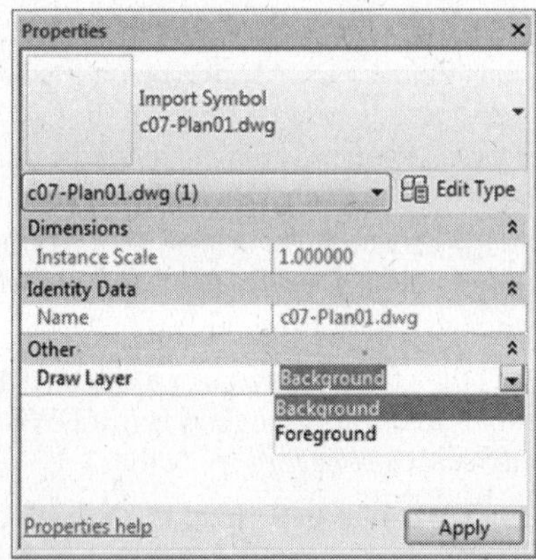

Pay close attention to this option when integrating 2D CAD data with an existing Revit model—sometimes linked or imported CAD data may not appear at all until you set the option to Foreground because of floors or ceilings obscuring the 2D data.

Visibility of Layers/Levels The layers or levels within a linked or imported CAD file can be accessed in two ways, the easiest of which is the Query tool. First, select a linked or imported CAD file; then, from the contextual tab in the ribbon select the Query tool and pick an object in the CAD file.

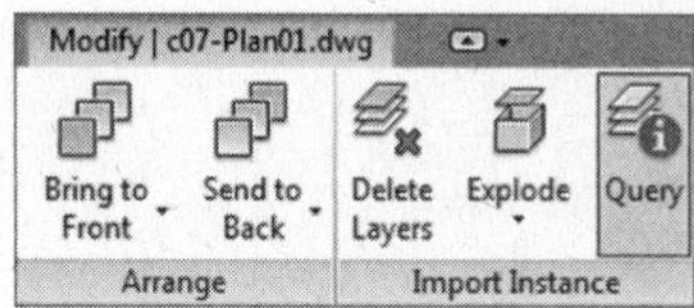

You will see the Import Instance Query dialog box (Figure 7.4). Using this tool, you can hide the layer or level by clicking the Hide In View button. The Query tool will remain active even after you click any of the command buttons in the Import Instance Query dialog box, and you must press the Esc key or click the Modify button to end the command.

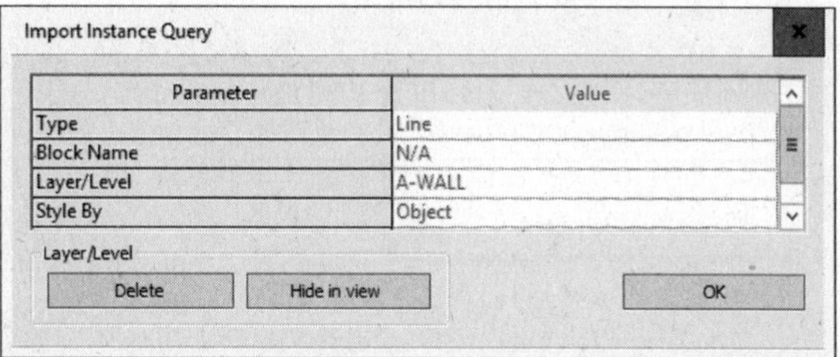

FIGURE 7.4 Querying objects within a linked CAD file

The second way to make layers or levels in imported or linked CAD files invisible is to use the Visibility/Graphic Overrides dialog box by switching to the View tab and selecting Visibility/Graphics from the Graphics panel. Once the dialog box opens, select the Imported Categories tab, as shown in Figure 7.5. Only the inserted CAD files that are visible in the active view will be listed in this tab. Expand any listed file to expose the layers/levels within that file, and use the check boxes to customize visibility of the link within the current view. This method is the only way to restore visibility of layers/levels that were hidden with the Query tool.

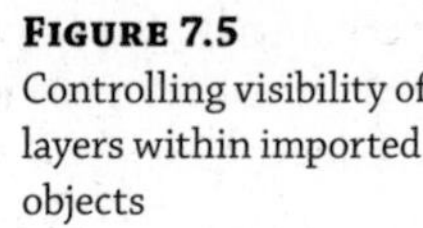

FIGURE 7.5
Controlling visibility of layers within imported objects

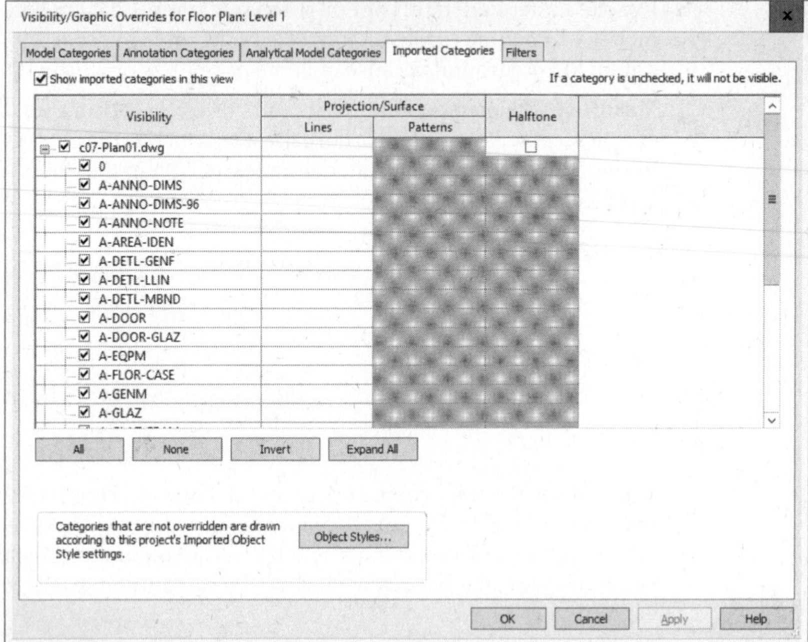

CAD DATA IN FAMILIES

Remember that 2D and 3D data imported into Revit families will be listed under the Imports In Families category in both the Visibility/Graphic Overrides and Object Styles dialog boxes. They will not appear as separately listed files.

Graphic Overrides If you need to change the appearance of the content within a linked or imported CAD file, you can accomplish that at the project level or within an individual view. To change a CAD file's appearance throughout the project, select the Manage tab on the ribbon, and click Object Styles in the Settings panel. Select the Imported Objects tab (Figure 7.6), and expand any of the imported or linked CAD files to change the color, line weight, line pattern, or material of the layers/levels within the referenced file. Changing these properties in the row of the filename does not affect the contents of that file. You can also apply these settings in a specific view using the Visibility/Graphic Overrides dialog box.

Exploding Although we do not recommend exploding CAD data within a Revit project, you can do it to facilitate the modification of such data. Linked content must first be converted to an import in order to be exploded. You do this by selecting the Insert tab on the ribbon, choosing Manage Links from the Link panel, choosing a listed link, and clicking the Import button. To explode the imported file, select it, and choose Explode ➤ Full Explode or Partial Explode from the contextual tab in the ribbon. The lines, text, and hatch patterns will become new line styles, text types, and fill regions in your project. Remember that these types of objects cannot be removed from your project via the Purge Unused command; you must remove them manually.

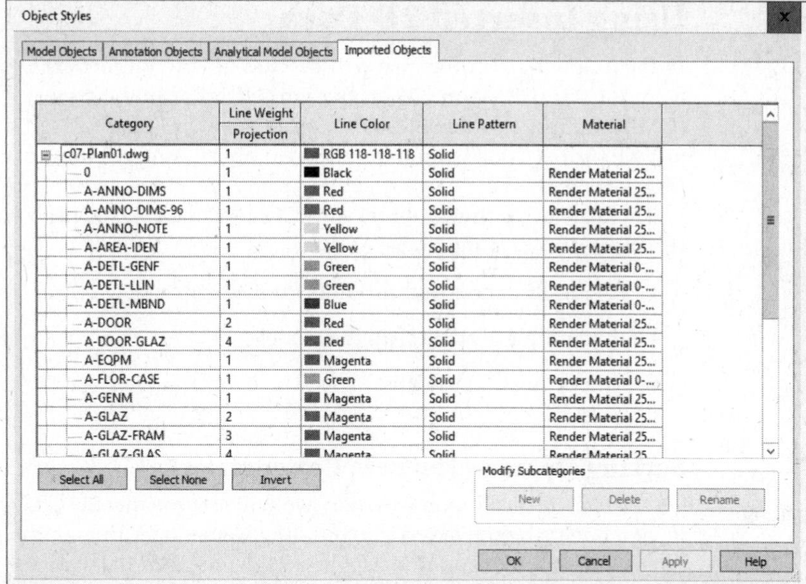

FIGURE 7.6 Changing the graphic appearance of imported layers via object styles

TIPS ON IMPORTING CAD FILES

To minimize the adverse impact of unnecessary styles and types carried into the Revit environment with exploding imported CAD data, we recommend removing extraneous data in the CAD file *before* importing it. Here are some general tips for this workflow:

- If your import contains elements such as hatches or annotations not intended for use in the Revit project, delete them before importing.
- Consider consolidating data within the CAD file to a minimum number of layers or levels. Doing so will ease the process of converting to Revit line styles if the file is exploded. This process will also facilitate graphic overrides.
- If it is allowable within your workflow for the imported CAD file, import it into a family, and then insert that family into your project. This will not reduce the overall file size, but it will make it a lot easier to find and manipulate should your imported CAD file need additional changes. It will also give you some extra control over the graphic display of the imported file.

Revit software doesn't allow line segments shorter than 1/32″ (0.8 mm). Although it might seem like you wouldn't have a lot of lines that length, many manufacturers' details contain small fillets in sections and plans and will fall into this range. Take care when exploding CAD details with very small line segments because they will be removed upon exploding. A good example of this is the manufacturers' details. Many of those CAD files have the level of detail needed to create the part (for example, a window mullion) but are not necessary for architectural detailing. Revit will automatically remove those shorter segments, and in some cases it might be quicker to simply trace over the detail rather than insert and explode it.

Using Inserted 2D Data

In the following sections, we will discuss how to import 2D CAD data from platforms such as AutoCAD (DWG) and MicroStation (DGN) or in the generic Drawing Exchange Format (DXF). You can also use files from other software platforms, but only if they are DWG, DGN, or DXF format. Most commercially available CAD programs are able to export in DWG or DXF format.

There are three fundamental ways 2D CAD data can be used with respect to a building project's floor plans, ceiling plans, or site plans:

- Using 2D data as backgrounds for BIM conversion
- Integrating 2D data with the model
- Importing CAD details

Setting Options for BIM Conversion

On the basis of a common situation, we will assume that 2D CAD data will be linked into the Revit model to be converted into building elements. Although the positioning of the files is important, the color and line weights of the imported data are not.

To begin the next exercise, you will need the files `c07-Plan01.dwg` and `c07-Conversion-Start.rvt`. You can download these files from this book's web page, `www.sybex.com/go/masteringrevit2017`. After downloading, open the `c07-Conversion-Start.rvt` file, and activate the **Level 1** floor plan. Then follow these steps:

1. Switch to the Insert tab and select Link CAD from the Link panel. Browse to the file `c07-Plan01.dwg`.
2. In the Link CAD Formats dialog box, set the following options:
   - Current View Only: Selected
   - Colors: Invert
   - Layers/Levels: All
   - Import Units: Auto-Detect
   - Positioning: Auto – Origin To Origin
   - Correct Lines That Are Slightly Off Axis: Selected
3. With those settings in place, choose Open to link in the CAD file.

Linking Large CAD Data

Use caution when attempting to link or import CAD files with vector data very far from the origin. Revit software has distance limitations on imported vector data that—if exceeded—may result in a warning, as shown here:

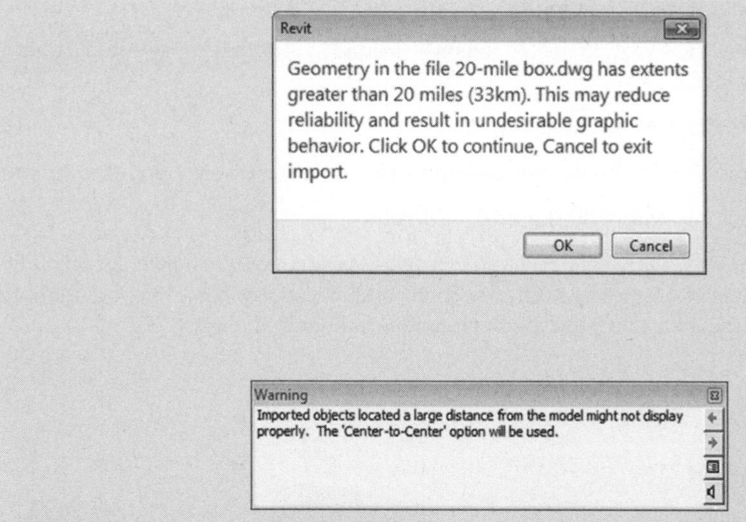

The warning message indicates that the software will automatically use Center To Center positioning if the distance limitations are exceeded. This will preclude you from using the origin of the linked file for Origin To Origin placement. If you must link data that is physically larger than a 20-mile cube—which may occur in projects such as airports or master plans—you should separate the data into smaller portions before linking. If the data is smaller than the 20-mile cube but is located farther than 20 miles from its origin, an alternate origin should be coordinated with your project team, and the data should be moved closer to the origin.

Using CAD Data for Coordination

If you need to use 2D CAD data as an integrated component of your team coordination, different settings become important. Here are a few examples of these types of scenarios:

- Showing light fixture layouts from a lighting designer
- Integrating landscape design into a site plan
- Reusing existing CAD data for a renovation project

Most of the settings and procedures for conversion apply to the coordination process; however, color and the placement visibility will be different. Because this data will be included in the Revit output, you will usually want the color option to be set to Black And White in the options during linking. It is also likely that some sort of background plans will be exported from the Revit model for use in coordination by one or more consultants using a CAD-based program. The data returned in this process may still contain the background information originally exported from Revit; thus, we recommend agreement on a standard that establishes unique layers for the consultants' content. This will help you select layers to be loaded when linking your consultants' files into the Revit project.

Use these options when linking CAD files into a Revit project for plan-based coordination:

- Current View Only: Selected if data is needed in one view; unselected if data is needed in many views
- Colors: Black And White
- Layers: Specify (choose only designated layers to isolate consultants' content)
- Positioning: Auto – By Shared Coordinates

If Current View Only is not selected, the 2D CAD data will be visible in all other views. This could be a nuisance in views such as sections and elevations; however, you might find it useful to visualize the data alongside the Revit model, as shown in Figure 7.7.

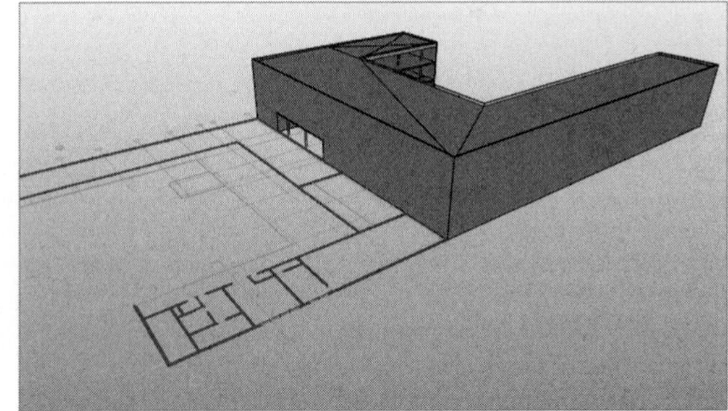

FIGURE 7.7 Existing 2D CAD data integrated with the Revit model

Linking Details

Your company's CAD detail library does not need to go to waste when you start working in a Revit environment. CAD data can be linked or imported into drafting views, allowing you to leverage the powerful view coordination tools within Revit. Entire sheets of CAD details can be inserted to reduce the number of linked files you have to reconcile; however, we recommend linking one detail into each drafting view and using the software's ability to automatically manage the view references with callouts, sections, and detail views. You may also want to name these drafting views with a unique prefix to help keep track of where any linked CAD data might reside. For example, a drafting view might be named `CAD-Roof Detail 04`. Also refer to Chapter 4, "Configuring Templates and Standards," for additional information on view organization.

In this exercise, you will create a drafting view into which a single CAD detail will be linked. This view can be referenced throughout your Revit model using a section, callout, or elevation view with the Reference Other View option selected in the contextual tab of the ribbon, as shown in Figure 7.8.

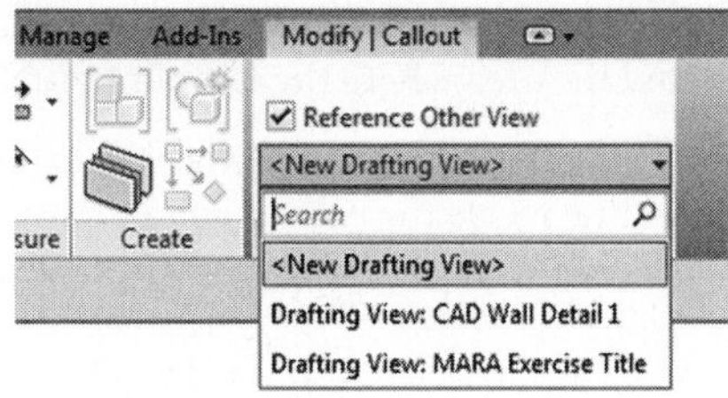

FIGURE 7.8
Creating a view as a reference to a drafting view

To begin this exercise, open the `c07-Sample-Building-Start.rvt` file. You can download this file and the associated CAD file (`c07-Detail.dwg`) from the book's web page.

1. Switch to the View tab and select Drafting View from the Create panel.
2. Name the new drafting view **CAD Wall Detail 1**, and set the scale to 1 1/2″ = 1′-0″. Click OK to close the dialog box.

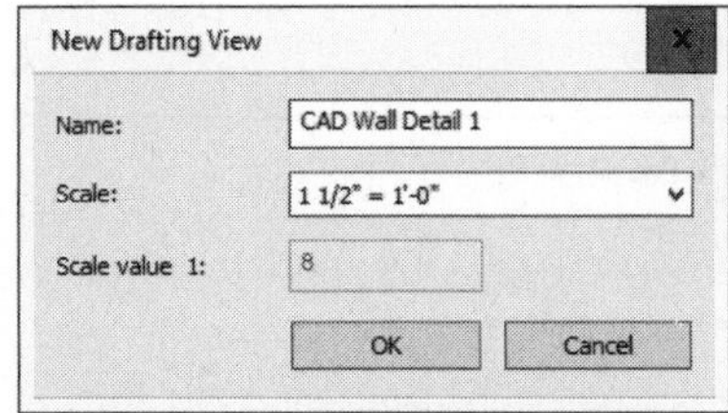

3. Switch to the Insert tab and select Link CAD.
4. In the Link CAD Formats dialog box, navigate to the `c07-Detail.dwg` file and set the following options:
   - Colors: Black And White
   - Layers/Levels: All
   - Units: Auto-Detect
   - Positioning: Auto – Center To Center
   - Correct Lines That Are Slightly Off Axis: Unchecked
5. Click Open to complete the command. If you don't see the linked detail in the drafting view, use Zoom To Fit (ZF on the keyboard) in order to reset the extents of the view.
6. Open the **Wall Section, Typ** view from the Project Browser located under the Sections (Wall Section) node, and zoom to a portion of the view where a floor meets an exterior wall.
7. On the View tab, select Callout from the Create panel, and select Reference Other View in the contextual tab of the ribbon (similar to Figure 7.8). Choose **Drafting View: CAD Wall**

Detail 1 from the drop-down list. In the drawing window, drag the callout rectangle around the area where the floor at Level 2 intersects the exterior wall.

8. After the callout is placed, select the callout you just created and use the grip where the leader line meets the callout head to drag the callout head to the left. The result should look like the image shown in Figure 7.9.

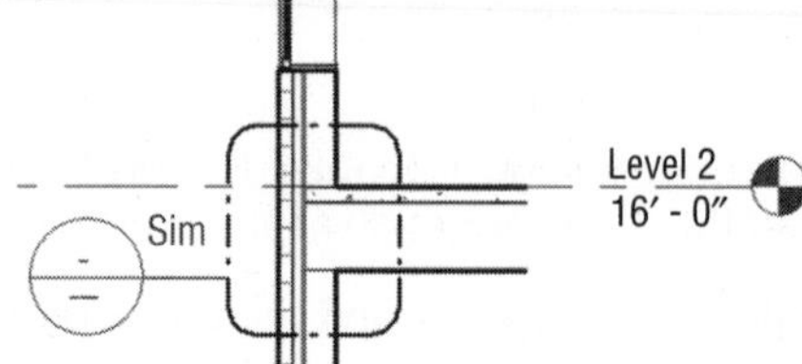

FIGURE 7.9
Callout created to reference a drafting view containing a linked CAD detail

9. Double-click the callout head, and you will be taken to the drafting view with the CAD detail linked in the previous steps.

CUSTOMIZING CALLOUTS

You also have the option to create your callouts with nonrectangular shapes. Additionally, for any view you reference using the previous steps, you can change the target view after you've created the callout or sectional reference. Simply highlight it and choose a new detail to reference from the Options bar.

Using Inserted 3D Data

Now that we have discussed using 2D reference data, we will show you how to use 3D model data from other design software within your Revit project. There are many valid reasons for modeling outside of the Revit environment, including software expertise, the availability of content, and optimization of complex geometry. The following sections will explore some situations in which model data can be shared between programs:

- Inserted data as a mass
- Inserted data as a face
- Inserted data as an object

Using CAD Data as a Mass

In Chapter 8, "Advanced Modeling and Massing," you will learn more about harnessing the impressive modeling toolset in the Revit conceptual massing environment; however, the fast and flexible process of design may lead architects to a tool in which they have more expertise or comfort. This type of massing design workflow is supported in the Revit environment under the following conditions:

- Inserted model data requires solid geometry to calculate volume, surface area, and floor area faces.
- Finely detailed complex geometry should be avoided because the Host By Face tools may not be able to generate meaningful objects.

The following exercise creates an in-place mass by linking an external model—in this case, a SketchUp model. Download the files `c07-SKP-Mass.rvt`, `c07-Mass.skp`, and `c07-Mass-2.skp` from the book's web page and follow these steps:

1. Open the project file `c07-SKP-Mass.rvt`. Activate the Level 1 floor plan, and from the Massing & Site tab (if that tab isn't available, you can turn it on under the Application menu ➢ Options ➢ User Interface), select In-Place Mass from the Conceptual Mass panel.
2. Name the new mass family SKP Mass and click OK.
3. Switch to the Insert tab and select Link CAD from the Link panel; be sure to switch your Files Of Type filter to *.skp files.
4. Navigate to the `c07-Mass.skp` file downloaded from the book's web page and set the following options:
   - Current View Only: Unchecked
   - Colors: Invert
   - Layers/Levels: All
   - Import Units: Auto-Detect
   - Positioning: Auto – Center To Center
   - Place At: Level 1
5. Click Open to complete the link process.
6. Click Finish Mass in the In-Place Editor panel of the ribbon.
7. Activate the Mass Schedule view from the Project Browser and observe the values for Gross Surface Area and Gross Volume.

Now that a new mass has been created, you can assign mass floors and begin to see calculated results in schedules of masses and mass floors. (Refer to Chapter 8 for more information on these processes.) Calculation of volumes, perimeters, and mass floor areas will work well in this workflow, but be careful when using imported model geometry with the By Face tools because face updates will likely be more difficult for the software to maintain than native Revit massing.

Using linking instead of importing enables continued iteration of the form in the original software. In the case of this example, you may edit the original file in SketchUp, which is available as a free download from `www.sketchup.com`, or you can download the file `c07-Mass-2.skp` from this book's web page.

If you modify and save the original SKP file yourself, save, close, and reopen the Revit project. As an alternative, open the Manage Links dialog box, select the SKP file, and click Reload.

If you want to use the alternative file downloaded from the book's web page, use the following steps:

1. From the Insert tab of the ribbon, click Manage Links.
2. In the Manage Links dialog box, switch to the CAD Formats tab, select the SKP file, and click the Reload From button.
3. Navigate to the file `c07-Mass-2.skp` and click Open.
4. Click OK to close the Manage Links dialog box.

With the modified mass loaded, activate the Mass Schedule view and notice the changes of Gross Volume and Gross Surface Area.

Using CAD Data as a Face

Similar to the data as mass workflow, externally modeled data can be used as a planar host for more complex forms. An example might be the need to generate a complex curved roof surface. We will demonstrate this workflow using Rhino by McNeel (`www.rhino3d.com`) to generate a shape, link the shape into the project, and create a roof by face on the shape.

As shown in Figure 7.10, a complex surface is generated in Rhino by drawing two curves and using the Extrude Curve Along Curve tool. Note that some reference geometry was exported from a Revit model to DWG and linked into this study in Rhino.

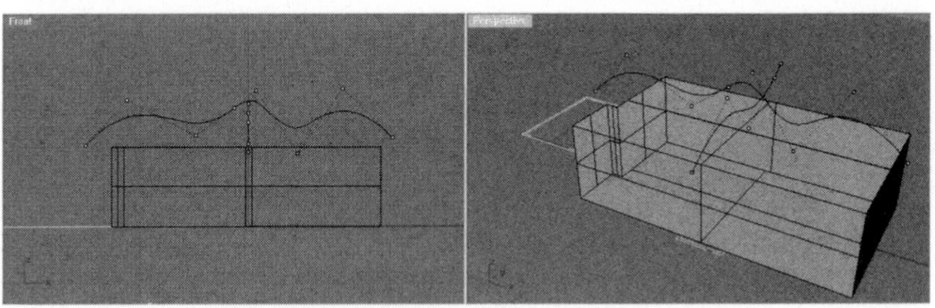

FIGURE 7.10 Curves for a complex surface in Rhino

A flat surface model is enough to generate a roof by face; however, it may be difficult to see the imported surface, so use the Extrude Surface tool to give it a thickness. Once the surface is complete (Figure 7.11), select only the double-curved geometry, choose File ➤ Export Selected Objects, and choose the .sat filename extension. SAT will generate the cleanest geometry for curved solids and surfaces.

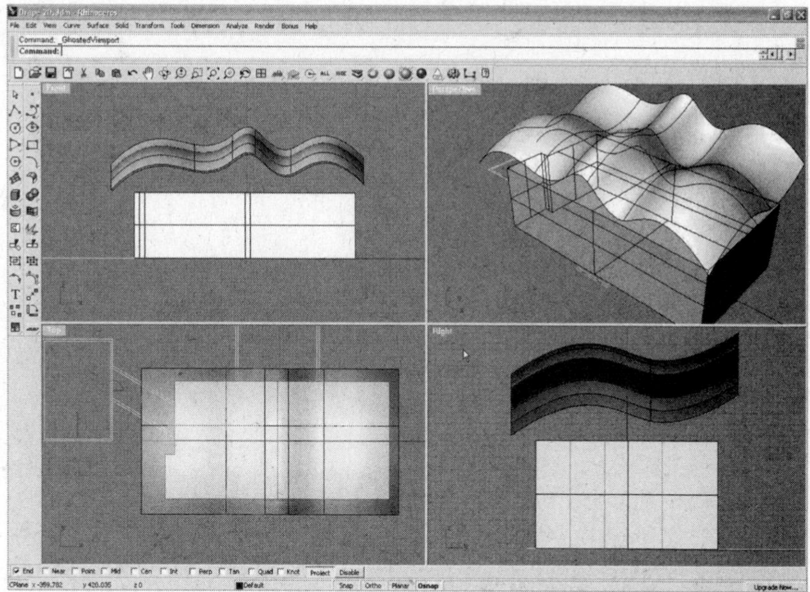

FIGURE 7.11 Completed complex surface in Rhino

You can download the Rhino file (`c07-Roof-Face.3dm`) and SAT export (`c07-Roof-Face.sat`) from this book's web page. You can also download the sample Revit project and continue the process as follows:

1. Open the file `c07-Roof-by-Face.rvt` and open the 3D view named **00-Start**.
2. On the Massing & Site tab, choose In-Place Mass and name it Rhino Roof. You will see an alert that the Show Mass mode has been enabled. You may choose to not show this message again, but you can always use the Show Mass combination button in the Massing & Site tab of the ribbon to toggle between different visibility modes.
3. Switch to the Insert tab and select Link CAD. In the Files Of Type drop-down, select *.sat and navigate to the `c07-Roof-Face.sat` file downloaded from the book's web page.
4. Set the placement options as follows:
   - Positioning: Auto – Origin To Origin
   - Place At: Level 1
   - Import Units: Inch
5. Click Open to complete the link and close the dialog box, and then click the Finish Mass button in the ribbon.

The mass should be seen above the tops of the walls in the Revit model, as shown in Figure 7.12.

FIGURE 7.12
Complex surface linked as an in-place mass

6. Return to the Massing & Site tab and select the Roof tool from the Model By Face panel. Choose **Basic Roof: Generic - 12″** from the Type Selector, and click the top face of the mass created in the previous steps. Click the Create Roof button in the ribbon to complete the command, and the roof will be generated along the mass surface, as shown in Figure 7.13.

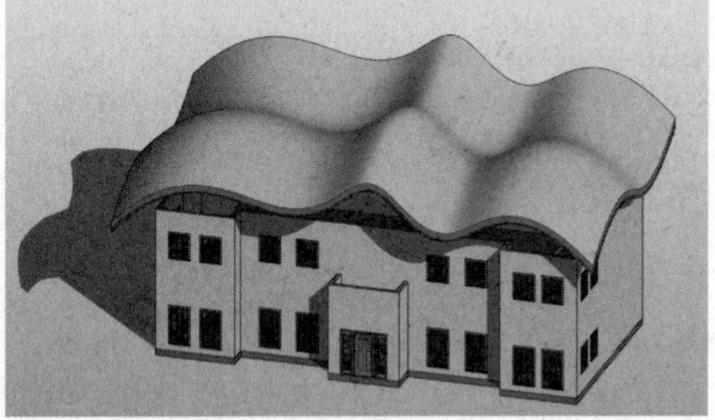

FIGURE 7.13
Roof By Face applied to the mass with linked SAT geometry

7. Select all the perimeter walls, using the Tab key or Ctrl to add them individually to the selection.
8. Select the Attach Top/Base tool from the Modify | Walls tab, set the Top option in the Options bar, and pick the roof by face created in step 6.

   The walls will connect to the underside of the complex roof shape. Activate the 3D view named Camera-Front and you will see the result of the exercise, as shown in Figure 7.14.

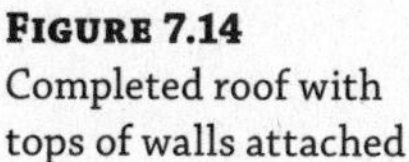

FIGURE 7.14
Completed roof with tops of walls attached

The imported shape can be edited in the original modeling software and will update via the link if the original exported SAT file is overwritten. To update the roof based on the newly modified massing geometry, select the roof and click the Update To Face button in the contextual tab of the ribbon.

Using CAD Data as an Object

Yet another derivation of the reference data workflow supports the use of CAD model geometry for specific instances of building components. Examples of this scenario might include a complex canopy structure being designed in SolidWorks or a building's structural framing being modeled in Tekla Structures. The workflow is again similar to that of using CAD data as a mass or face; however, the file format will help you control the component's visualization. In the previous exercise, we used an SAT format to transfer complex curved geometry from Rhino to Revit; however, a limitation of an SAT file is that the geometry contains only one layer, making it impossible to vary material assignments for different components of the design. We recommend using a solids-based DWG, DGN, or DXF file format, which will maintain a layer structure in most cases.

In the following exercise, you will create an in-place structural framing component that will act as a placeholder for a consultant's structural model, which is in DWG format. You will be using the file `c07-3D-Structure.dwg`, which you can download from this book's web page.

1. Download and open the file `c07-Framing-Start.rvt` from the book's web page. Activate the Level 1 floor plan.
2. Switch to the Architecture tab and choose Component ➢ Model In-Place. Set the Family Category to Structural Framing and click OK.
3. Name the new in-place model DWG Structure.
4. From the Insert tab, select Link CAD.
5. Change the Files Of Type option to DWG Files (*.dwg) and navigate to the file `c07-3D-Structure.dwg`.

6. Set the following options and then click Open:
   - ◆ Current View Only: Unselected
   - ◆ Colors: Black And White
   - ◆ Layers/Levels: All
   - ◆ Import Units: Auto-Detect
   - ◆ Positioning: Auto – Origin To Origin
   - ◆ Place At: Level 1

   The DWG file provided is actually a sample Revit file that was exported to DWG format (Figure 7.15). Models may be provided in this format from any number of other design applications such as Autodesk® AutoCAD® MEP software or Tekla Structures.

7. Click Finish Model in the In-Place Editor panel to complete the process.

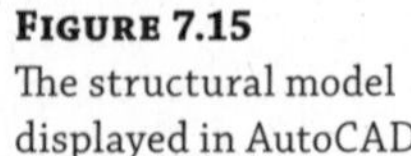

FIGURE 7.15
The structural model displayed in AutoCAD

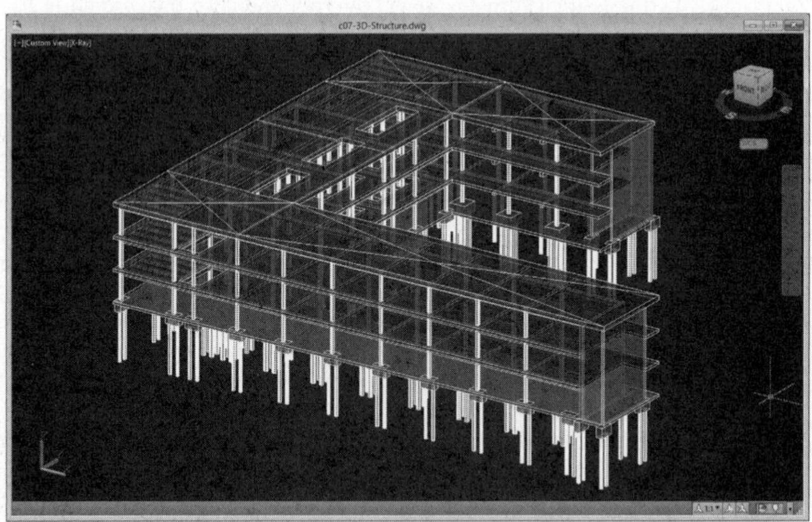

Activate the default 3D view, and you should see the entire contents of the linked CAD model (Figure 7.16). Because the linked content was created as a structural framing model, the linked data will be displayed similarly to any other structural framing element. Examine the linked model in different plans and sections to observe this behavior.

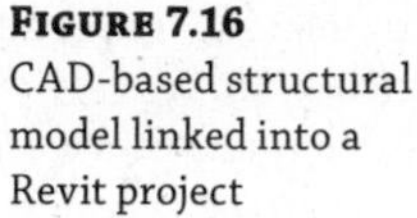

FIGURE 7.16
CAD-based structural model linked into a Revit project

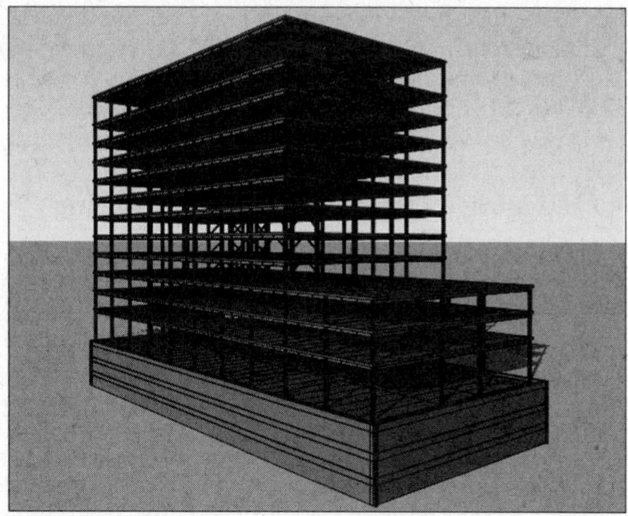

If you're not seeing the model as part of your 3D view, you forgot to uncheck the box for Current View Only in step 6. If that is the case, you'll need to either undo your way back or unlink and relink the CAD file.

Using linked models in DWG, DGN, or DXF format also allows you to modify the graphic representation of the elements within the Revit environment. To adjust these settings, follow these steps:

1. Select the Manage tab, click Object Styles, and switch to the Imported Objects tab.
2. Find your linked file, expand it to expose the layers or levels included in it, and modify the graphic settings as desired.

When you are using linked model data for custom components, the consistency of the data you bring into Revit software from other programs depends on the ability of that software to generate organized information. Some programs use layers, and some don't. Recognizing this difference will give you the best opportunity for success in coordination through interoperability.

Exporting CAD Data

Just as significant as importing data is the ability to export Revit data for use by others. We will now examine various processes for exporting data from your Revit project to other formats. To achieve your desired results when exporting, remember that exporting from Revit is essentially a WYSIWYG process. For example, exporting a 3D view will result in a 3D model, exporting a floor plan will result in a 2D CAD file, and exporting a schedule will result in a delimited file that can be used in a program such as Microsoft Excel.

We will first review the settings to be configured for the exporting process. These methods are similar for almost all exports and will be referred to in subsequent sections.

The process for exporting CAD files from Revit has been streamlined in recent releases of the software. There are basically two steps to export CAD data from a Revit project: create a list of views to be exported, and define the settings in an export configuration.

Preparing a List of Views for Exporting

The first step to any CAD export is to establish the set of views to be exported. You can use the file `c07-Sample-Building-Start.rvt` for this section's exercises. The following steps will walk you through the process of creating a saved list of views for export:

1. You can find all exporting commands in the Application menu when you click the Export flyout. You may need to scroll down this flyout menu to access all the export commands available for use. From the Export menu, select CAD Formats ➢ DWG.

2. You will first see the DWG Export dialog box, as shown in Figure 7.17. The Export drop-down list is set to <Current View/Sheet Only> by default. This is where you would select predefined lists of views to be exported from your project.

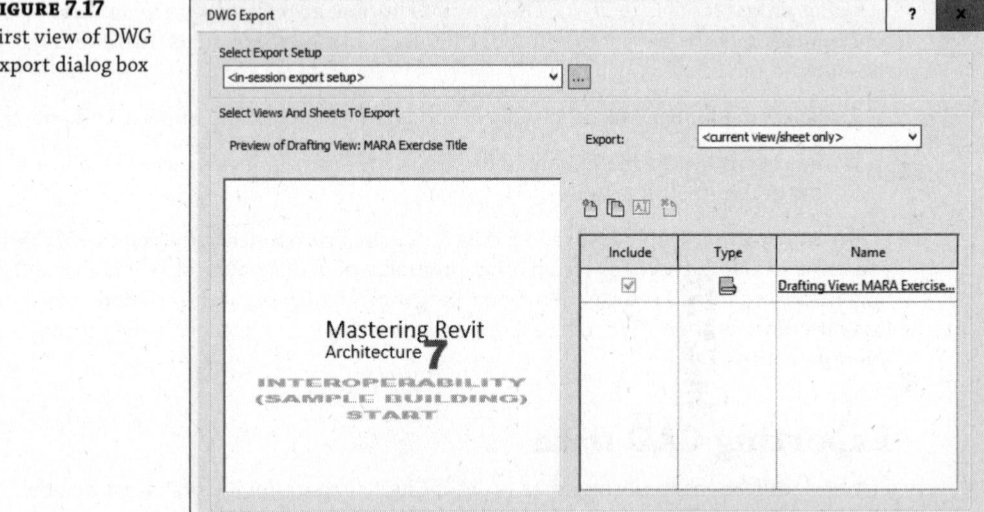

FIGURE 7.17 First view of DWG Export dialog box

3. Begin to create your own list of views and/or sheets to export by choosing <In-Session View/Sheet Set> from the Export drop-down list, as shown in Figure 7.18.

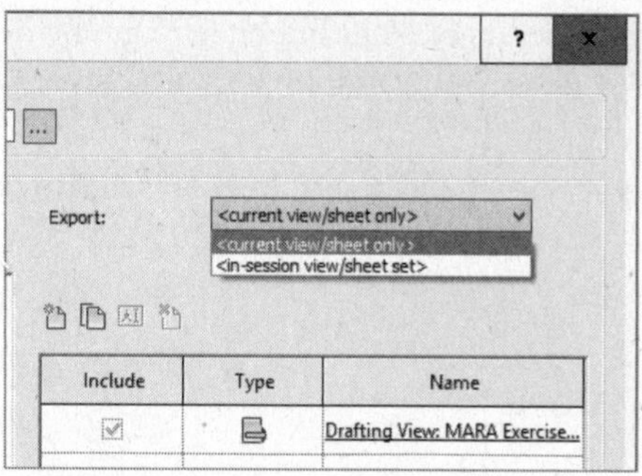

FIGURE 7.18 Viewing available export sets in the model

4. From this point, you can either use a temporary in-session set or create your own named set. We will continue these steps by creating a new named set. Click the New Set icon above the view list, shown in Figure 7.19, and name the set **PLANS**. Click OK to close the dialog box.

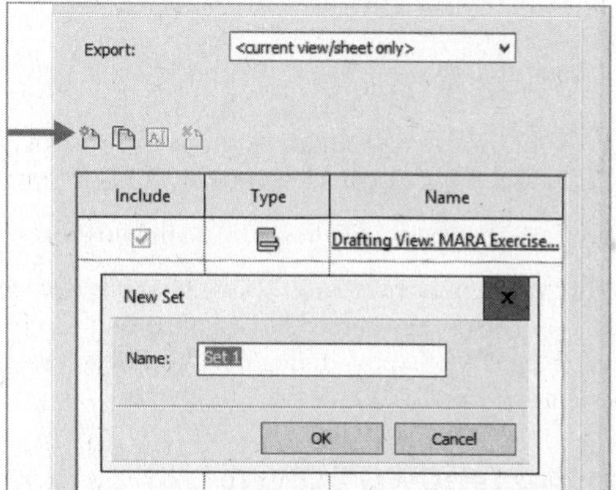

FIGURE 7.19 Create a new export list.

> **USING IN-SESSION LISTS WITH WORKSHARING**
>
> Be careful when using an in-session list for printing or exporting on a worksharing-enabled project. If two or more team members working on the same Revit project attempt to use the in-session set, you may receive errors about the workset not being editable. Instead, always try to use predefined lists for exporting and printing on worksharing projects.

5. To begin adding views and/or sheets to your new export set, from the Show In List drop-down menu, choose Views In The Model.

6. Click the Check None button to clear any extraneously selected views and then find the floor plans with the *A*- prefix. Select these views by checking the boxes next to the views in the Include column.

   Remember, you can sort the list by clicking any of the list headers (Figure 7.20).

FIGURE 7.20
Adding views/sheets to the export list

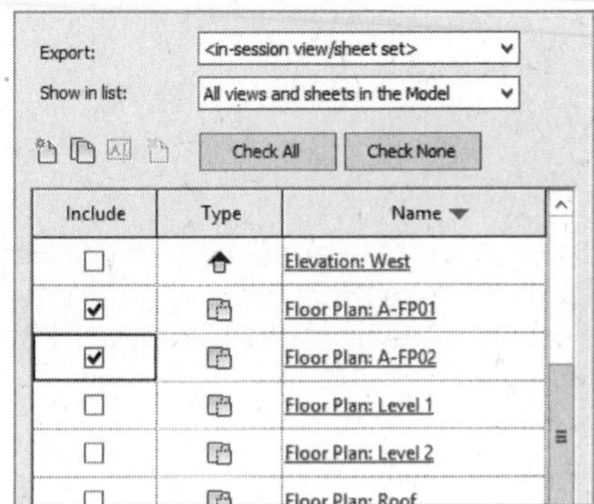

7. For now, we will simply end this exercise by saving the list of views for later. Click the Save Set & Close button and the DWG Export dialog box will close.
8. Save the project file to continue the next exercise.

Now that you have created a saved list of views for export, they will be available for any CAD export processes. You can create as many lists as you need as well as duplicate, delete, or rename them in the DWG Export dialog box. In the next section, we will show you how to adjust the settings for exported DWG files.

Settings for DWG Exports

In addition to saving lists of views for exporting, you have the ability to save predefined exporting configurations. To complete an export, you will select a list of files and an export setup before defining an export location and launching the process. Let's examine the various settings that can be customized for DWG export.

Continuing with the `c07-Sample-Building.rvt` file, go to the Application menu and then choose Export ➢ CAD Formats ➢ DWG. You will return to the DWG Export dialog box. In the previous exercise, you created a named list of views to export. Before we begin an exercise to create a customized configuration for export settings, we will briefly explore the various settings that can be saved and applied to any list of views to complete the export process. Click the ellipsis button at the top of the dialog box. A tooltip will appear showing the associated command as Modify Export Setup. The Modify DWG/DXF Export Setup dialog box will appear (Figure 7.21).

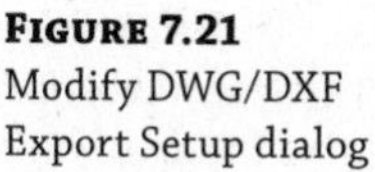

FIGURE 7.21
Modify DWG/DXF Export Setup dialog

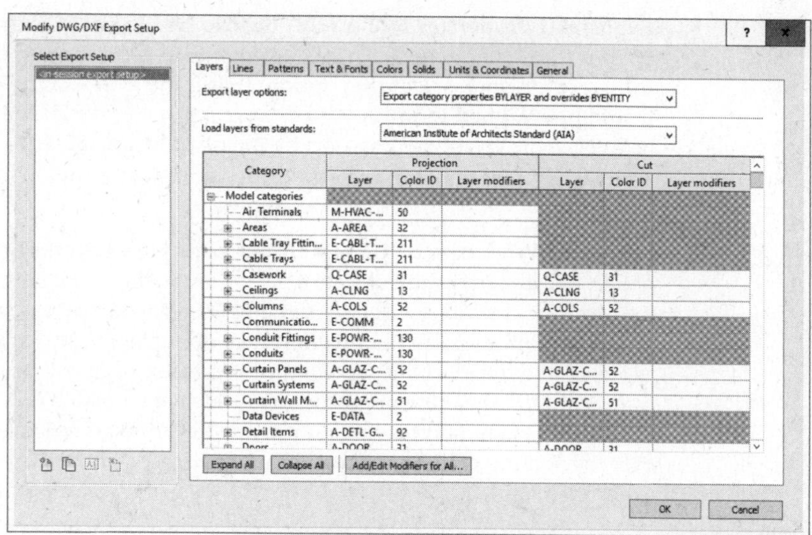

As you can see, a number of opportunities for customization are offered in this dialog box. First, you'll notice at the left side of the dialog box a list of export setups and icons similar to those found in the main DWG Export dialog box. Use these icons to create, duplicate, rename, or delete export setups in your project. Let's take a look at some of the other export settings in greater detail.

LAYERS

The Layers tab was shown previously in Figure 7.21. It contains many options to completely customize the export of object styles to layers. Let's examine each of these settings more closely.

Export Layer Options

At the top of the Layers tab is a drop-down that allows you to specify the overall behavior of exported elements. This setting accounts for any graphic overrides that might be applied in a Revit view. For example, the Linework tool might have been used to modify the edge of a wall to a dashed line. These options determine how that override will be exported to a CAD format.

Export Category Properties BYLAYER And Overrides BYENTITY This option will export unmodified elements to their respective layer assignments, and their properties will remain assigned to the layer. If an object or part of an object has been overridden, the overridden element will still be assigned to the respective layer, but the graphic override will be applied directly to the entity. In the wall example noted previously, the wall edge would still be assigned to the A-WALL layer but would have a DASHED linetype instead of a BYLAYER assignment.

Export All Properties BYLAYER, But Do Not Export Overrides If the recipients of your CAD file will use scripts or macros to enforce their own graphic standards to the exported data, select this option. Using the wall example again, the wall elements would be assigned to the A-WALL layer; however, the dashed line overrides would not be exported. This style of export is usually appropriate for engineers who need to use architectural plans as background information and thus will override all elements to halftone.

Export All Properties BYLAYER, And Create New Layers For Overrides This final option will assign default objects to layers based on their categories; however, any elements with graphic overrides will be assigned to new layers that are subsets of the original layer. When we continue with the previous wall example, the unmodified wall elements will be assigned to the A-WALL layer, but the overridden edge will be assigned to a new layer such as A-WALL-3, where the properties of the element are all BYLAYER and the new layer contains the dashed linetype. In our opinion, this option is less useful because there is no control over the naming of the new layers, thus creating potential confusion for the recipients of the exported files.

Load Layers From Standards

Several exporting templates based on the industry-standard layering guidelines are included (Figure 7.22) with the Revit application and can be applied in the Load Layers From Standards drop-down. Similarly to import settings, you may want to create customized layer export templates and save them with your project data for future reference. Export templates may inherit the layer names of linked CAD files in your active project. Because of this, we recommend saving a copy of your export templates in a ZIP archive in case you need to return to the original template.

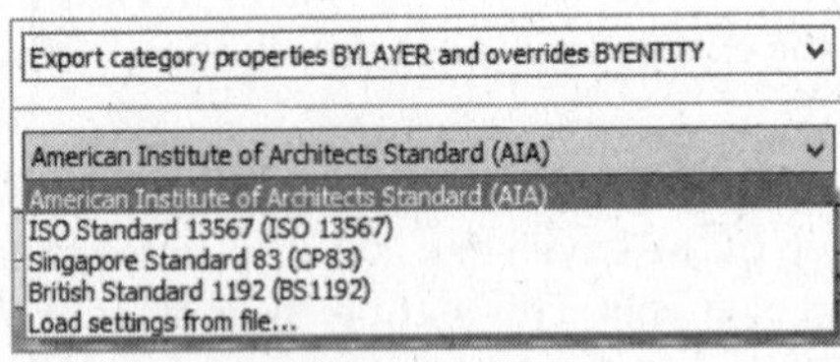

FIGURE 7.22 Industry-standard layering conventions can be applied to export settings.

Layer names and colors can also be customized by directly editing the values in the Layers tab in the Modify DWG/DXF Export Setup dialog box. Each category and subcategory is capable of independent color and layer names.

Layer modifiers can be applied to any or all of the model categories for export. To do this, either click in the Layer Modifiers column for any of the listed model categories and then click the Add/Edit button that appears, or click the Add/Edit Modifiers For All button. Either method will open the Add/Edit Layer Modifiers dialog box (Figure 7.23). Here you can assign modifiers such as phase status, workset, view type, or user-customized fields.

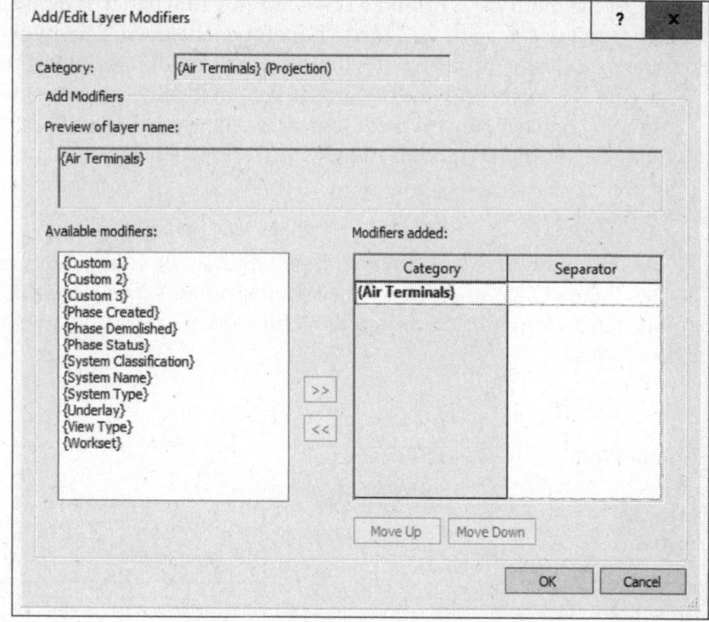

FIGURE 7.23 Modifiers such as Phase Status may be applied to individual or all categories.

LINES

Switch to the Lines tab in the Modify DWG/DXF Export Setup dialog box, and you will find additional settings for assigning Revit line patterns to CAD-based linetypes (Figure 7.24). The first setting at the top of the tab is to assign the linetype scale in the exported CAD files. This option can be configured to Modelspace, Paperspace, or Scaled Linetype Definitions. This setting can be changed by the recipient of the exported files, so it is common to use the Modelspace setting for any model view exports, such as plans or elevations, and the Paperspace setting for sheet views.

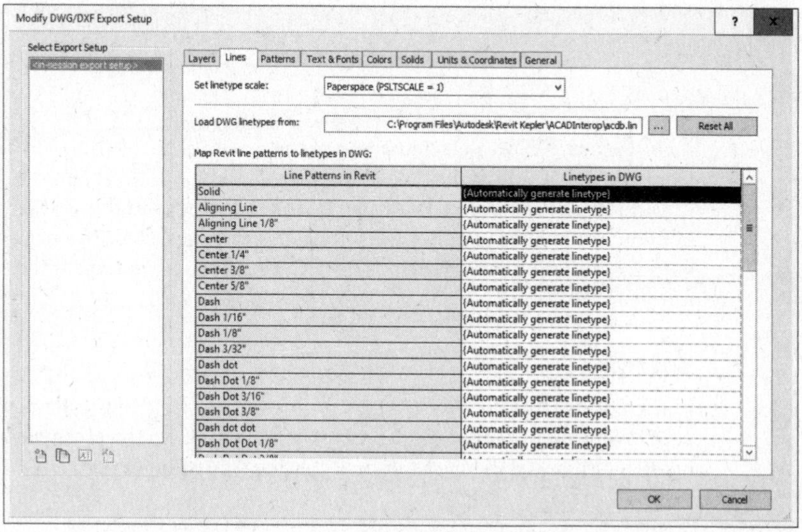

Modify DWG/DXF Export Setup

Select Export Setup: <in-session export setup>

Layers | Lines | Patterns | Text & Fonts | Colors | Solids | Units & Coordinates | General

Set linetype scale: Paperspace (PSLTSCALE = 1)

Load DWG linetypes from: C:\Program Files\Autodesk\Revit Kepler\ACADInterop\acdb.lin | ... | Reset All

Map Revit line patterns to linetypes in DWG:

Line Patterns in Revit	Linetypes in DWG
Solid	{Automatically generate linetype}
Aligning Line	{Automatically generate linetype}
Aligning Line 1/8"	{Automatically generate linetype}
Center	{Automatically generate linetype}
Center 1/4"	{Automatically generate linetype}
Center 3/8"	{Automatically generate linetype}
Center 5/8"	{Automatically generate linetype}
Dash	{Automatically generate linetype}
Dash 1/16"	{Automatically generate linetype}
Dash 1/8"	{Automatically generate linetype}
Dash 3/32"	{Automatically generate linetype}
Dash dot	{Automatically generate linetype}
Dash Dot 1/8"	{Automatically generate linetype}
Dash Dot 3/16"	{Automatically generate linetype}
Dash Dot 3/8"	{Automatically generate linetype}
Dash dot dot	{Automatically generate linetype}
Dash Dot Dot 1/8"	{Automatically generate linetype}

OK | Cancel

FIGURE 7.24 Line styles can be assigned to specific CAD linetypes.

In the main list within the Lines tab, any line patterns defined in your Revit project can be assigned to a specific CAD-based linetype. The default linetype definitions file is included with Revit, but it can be changed with the command buttons above the line patterns list. The default setting for exporting line patterns is Automatically Generate Linetype, which will replicate the graphic pattern but will not integrate well with any other CAD software if the exported files require additional modification by the recipient.

PATTERNS

As with lines, the exporting of fill patterns can be completely customized. Switch to the Patterns tab (Figure 7.25), and you will see similar options to specify a default CAD-based pattern file as well as the ability to assign Revit fill patterns to hatch patterns that are native to AutoCAD software.

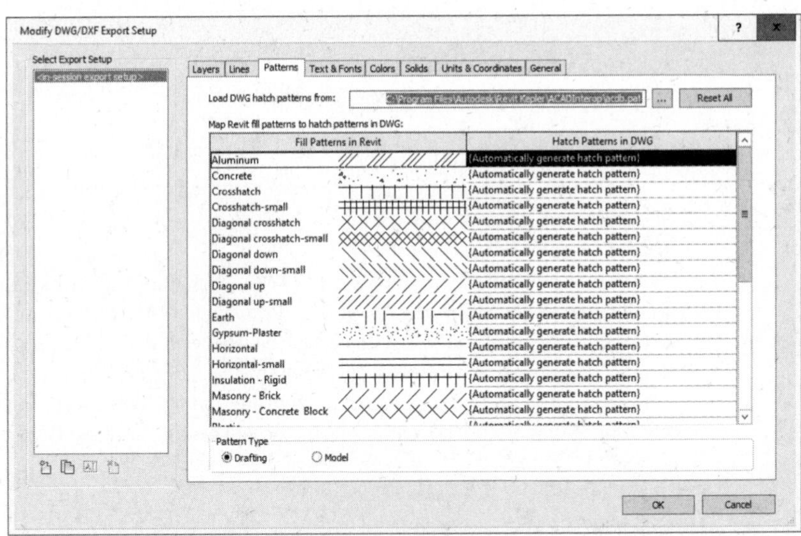

FIGURE 7.25 Fill patterns can be assigned to CAD hatch patterns.

In Figure 7.25, we selected a few of the Revit fill patterns to be mapped to a respective pattern from the AutoCAD pattern definition.

Similar customizations can also be made for fonts in the Text & Fonts tab, and in the Colors tab you can choose to either use specific layer-based color IDs or use the true color RGB values assigned in your Revit project. Let's take a quick look at the remaining tabs and their importance.

SOLIDS

In the Solids tab, you have the option to select either Polymesh or ACIS Solids for exporting of 3D views. For cleaner solid geometry exporting, we recommend the ACIS Solids option; however, this will likely result in larger file size upon export.

Units & Coordinates

One of the most important settings is Coordinate System Basis, which can be found in the Units & Coordinates tab. This option will affect the ability of your exported files to be properly aligned with other project files. Refer back to Chapter 6 for more information on using shared coordinates.

General

Finally, the General tab (Figure 7.26) contains some additional options such as assignment of non-plottable layers, exporting space boundaries, and default export file options.

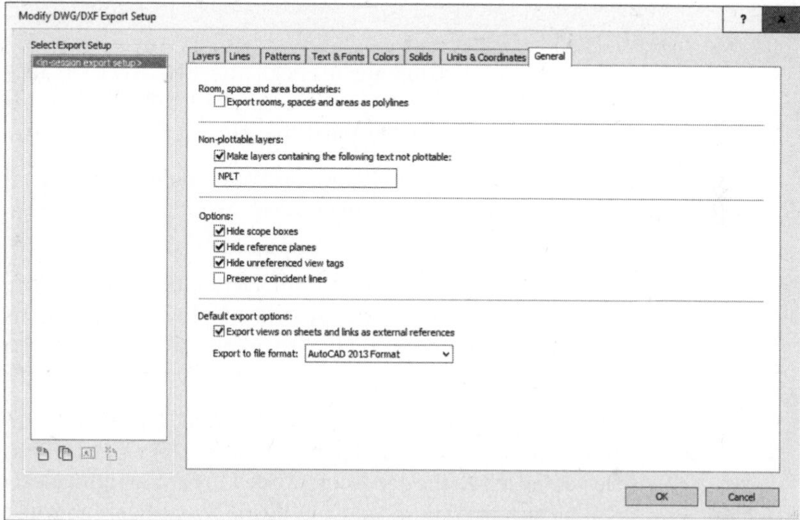

Figure 7.26 General options allow further customization of CAD exports.

At this time, you can click the Cancel button to close both active dialog boxes. In the next section, you will return to these settings and save a configuration to be applied to the export process.

Exporting 2D CAD Data

When you are collaborating with others who require 2D CAD, developing a planned strategy will allow you to share your Revit data more efficiently and consistently. We highly recommend that you determine and document the scope of data to be shared, the schedule by which the files will be shared (when and how often), and the software platforms to be used on a project. These aspects should be compiled in a BIM execution plan, as explained in Chapter 6.

To facilitate the setup and ultimate export of plan data, you can create copies of floor plans and ceiling plans with a standardized naming convention in your Revit project. These should be easy to recognize, and they help in building the export list. Figure 7.27 shows a series of duplicated plans that have been created and assigned to the floor plan type named Export. The view name conforms to the naming convention specified by the United States National CAD Standard (`www.nationalcadstandard.org`).

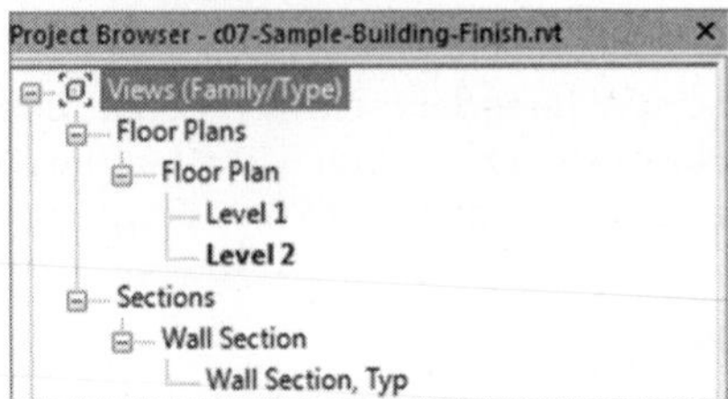

FIGURE 7.27 View organization for plans to be exported

In the following exercise, you will continue to use the `c07-Sample-Building-Start.rvt` project file while using the saved list of views you created in the "Preparing a List of Views for Exporting" exercise:

1. From the Application menu, click Export ➤ CAD Formats ➤ DWG. In the DWG Export dialog box, make sure PLANS is selected in the Export drop-down. Click the Modify Export Setup ellipsis button (three dots) at the top of the dialog box.
2. In the Modify DWG/DXF Export Setup dialog box, select the New Export Setup button from the bottom left to create a new export setup. Name the new export setup British Plans with Phase.
3. In the Layers tab, set the Export Layer Options drop-down list to Export Category Properties BYLAYER And Overrides BYENTITY. Locate the Load Layers From Standards drop-down list and select British Standard 1192. You will receive an error message stating that loading these settings will replace your previous settings. Click **Yes** to accept.
4. While still in the Layers tab, click the Add/Edit Modifiers For All button. In the Add/Edit Layer Modifiers dialog box (Figure 7.28), add the **{Phase Status}** modifier from the list at the left to the Modifiers Added list at the right. Next to {Multiple Categories} in the Separator column, add a hyphen. The preview above should now read **{Multiple Categories}-{Phase Status}**. Click OK to close this dialog box.

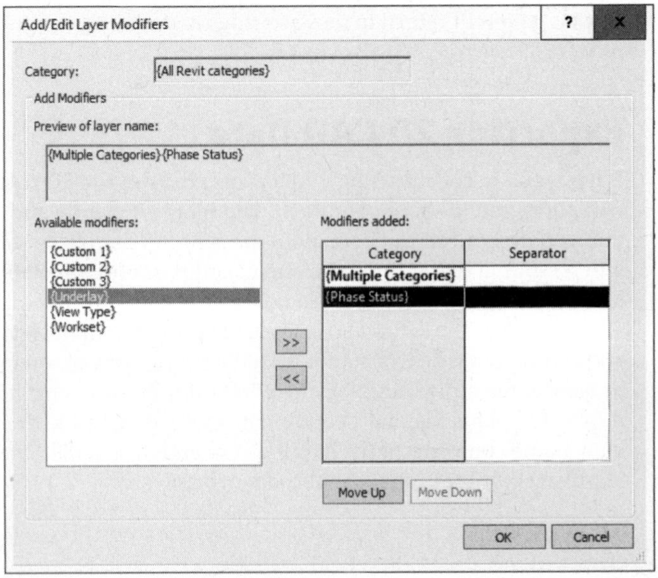

FIGURE 7.28 Add a Phase Status modifier to all categories.

5. Switch to the Units & Coordinates tab and set the Coordinate System Basis to Shared by clicking the radio button. Click OK to close the Modify DWG/DXF Export Setup dialog box.

6. Click the Next button to continue the exporting process. In the Export CAD Formats–Save To Target Folder dialog box, set the Naming drop-down list to Automatic–Short. This will create files named similarly to `FloorPlan-A-FP01.dwg`.

7. Uncheck the Export Views On Sheets And Links As External References setting. Although this setting does not affect this exercise, we discuss its importance after the exercise.

8. Select an appropriate location on your computer or your network for the exported files and then click OK to complete the export process.

Unfortunately, you cannot customize the naming of the exported files when you export more than one view in a batch process. That said, any kind of file-renaming tool can be used to remove the prefix FloorPlan- from exported files using the Automatic–Short option.

There is one more option that you should understand in the exporting process. In the final Export CAD Formats dialog box, you will see the option to Export Views On Sheets And Links As External References. When this option is checked and you are exporting sheet views, any views that are placed on those sheets will be exported as separate files. Those files will then be configured as external references (Xrefs) in the exported sheets. If you also have other RVT files linked into your current model, they too will be exported as separate CAD files and configured as Xrefs in the exported files.

We recommend that you deselect the External Reference option during exporting unless it is absolutely necessary. The exporting process will result in fewer files and more portable and predictable results for the recipients of your exported data.

Exporting 3D Model Data

In the previous section, we showed you how to export 2D views to CAD formats, which will support more traditional collaboration work flows. You can also export your Revit project as a 3D model in several formats for use in other modeling software. A frequent destination for such data is Autodesk® Navisworks® software for its enhanced coordination with contractors during construction. This workflow is supported by a free Navisworks plug-in to Revit that will allow you to export your models as NWC files, which Navisworks uses. More generic exports in DWG, DGN, DXF, or SAT formats can provide numerous opportunities for you to become more creative with the presentation of your designs.

Exporting to SketchUp

Previously in this chapter we discussed using SketchUp for conceptual building massing studies. These studies were imported directly into the Revit environment for further development of a true building information model. Revit model data can also be exported via 3D DWG to SketchUp, where visualization studies can be conducted on an entire project or even a simple wall section.

In the following exercise, we will export a wall section study from the Revit environment to SketchUp using files you can download from this book's web page. To complete this exercise, you will need to download SketchUp from `www.sketchup.com` and install it.

To begin the exercise, follow these steps:

1. Open the file `c07-Sketchup-Wall-Study.rvt`.
2. Activate the Default 3D view and enable the Section Box option in the Properties palette for the view.
3. Set the detail level of the view to Medium or Fine.
4. Select the section box in the 3D view, and shape handles will appear on each face. Grab the shape handle of one side of the section box parallel to the vertical edge of the wall sample, and drag toward the wall until the section box intersects the wall, as shown in Figure 7.29.

   You should see the layers of the wall structure exposed.

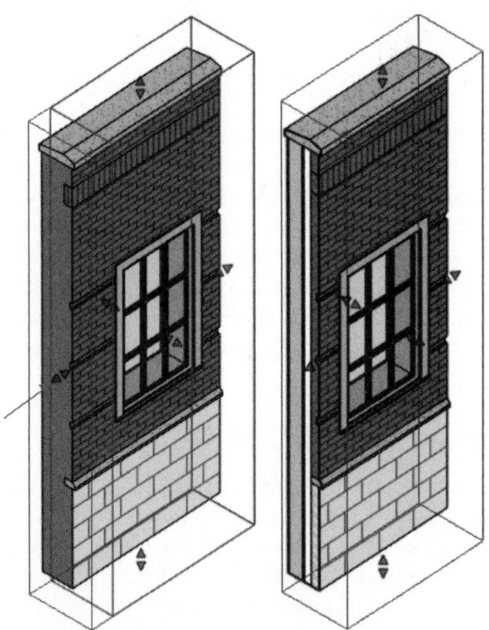

FIGURE 7.29 Using the section box to expose the layers of the wall

5. With the section box still selected, right-click and choose Hide In View ➤ Elements.

   This will prevent the section box from being exported.
6. Click the Application menu and select Export ➤ CAD Formats ➤ DWG Files. Set the Export drop-down list to <Current View/Sheet Only>.
7. Click the Modify Export Setup ellipsis button to open the Modify DWG/DXF Export Setup dialog box. In the Modify DWG/DXF Export Setup dialog box, switch to the Solids

tab and set the option to Polymesh. Click OK to close the Modify DWG/DXF Export Setup dialog box.

8. Click Next and set the Files Of Type drop-down to AutoCAD 2013 DWG Files. Select a location on your computer or network, and then click OK to save the file.
9. Launch SketchUp, and choose File ➤ Import.
10. Switch the Files Of Type option to AutoCAD Files, navigate to the file saved in step 8, and click Open.
11. Switch to the Select tool, select the entire DWG import, right-click, and choose Explode.

This will allow you to directly edit the elements in the SketchUp environment. Other components within the exploded model may need to be exploded again.

Once the DWG model is loaded in SketchUp, you can use the Paint Bucket tool to apply materials to individual components, use the Push/Pull tool to hide or expose layers of the wall construction, and use the line tools to customize the profile of the revealed layers, as shown in Figure 7.30.

FIGURE 7.30
Completed wall study in SketchUp

3D EXPORTS BY LEVEL

Effective coordination between Revit and AutoCAD® MEP software frequently relies on the exchange of 3D DWG files of limited scope with respect to the overall project. MEP engineers

Continues

Continued

using AutoCAD MEP will usually manage their BIM with one model file per level. Even though the entire architectural model can be exported to a single DWG model, they may not be able to reference such a large model efficiently. The good news? Your Revit project can be set up to achieve this by creating 3D views with section boxes for each level.

Begin by creating a series of floor plans designed for exporting (discussed previously in this chapter). In the View Range settings for these plans, set the Top value to Level Above, Offset: 0 and the Bottom value to Associated Level, Offset: 0. Create a 3D view for each level required in the project and rename the views according to your standards. In each duplicated 3D view, right-click the ViewCube®, select Orient To View ➤ Floor Plans, and choose the corresponding floor plan with the adjusted view range. This series of 3D views can be saved in an export list and batch-exported to 3D DWG when needed for collaboration, as shown here:

Using IFC Interoperability

Industry Foundation Classes (IFC) are the data model standard developed by buildingSMART International to support interoperability in the building industry. The IFC model specification is registered by the International Standards Organization (ISO) as ISO/PAS 16739 and is currently in the process of becoming the official International Standard ISO/IS 16739. Because of its focus on ease of interoperability between BIM software platforms, some government agencies are requiring IFC format deliverables for publicly funded building projects.

Some scenarios where IFC exchange may apply and facilitate data exchange include, but are not limited to, the following:

- Linking AutoCAD MEP software into a Revit project
- Using Solibri Model Checker or Viewer for model quality audits
- Coordination between Revit projects and Nemetschek Allplan, Vectorworks, or ArchiCAD
- AutoCodes Project by Fiatech
- COBie (Construction-Operations Building Information Exchange) deliverables
- GSA spatial validation

You can export the Revit model quite effectively to the IFC 2×2, 2×3, BCA ePlan Check, or IFC GSA 2010 formats by clicking the Application menu and selecting Export ➤ IFC. The resulting IFC file (Figure 7.31) can be viewed in a number of programs that can be downloaded at no cost from any of the following websites:

- DDS-CAD Open BIM Viewer from Data Design System (`www.dds-cad.net`)
- Solibri Model Viewer (`www.solibri.com`)
- IFC Viewer (`www.ifcbrowser.com`)
- Tekla BIMsight (`www.tekla.com`)

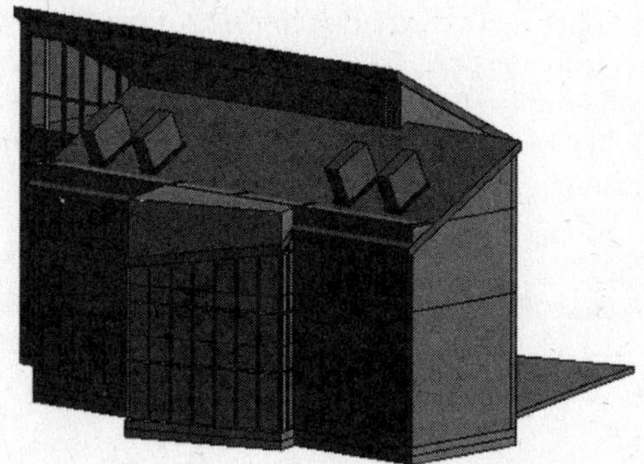

Figure 7.31
Revit model exported to IFC format

Importing IFC data into the Revit environment is similar to the process for importing 3D CAD geometry; however, the data generated is intended to be more intelligent and editable. Although this method has great potential, the accuracy of the Revit IFC import is highly dependent on the software used to generate the IFC output. We recommend the use of one of the free IFC viewers listed previously to inspect IFC data prior to importing into a Revit project.

> **VIEWING THE CONTENTS OF AN IFC FORMAT FILE**
>
> Did you know that an IFC file can be viewed in a text editor such as Notepad? Download a sample file from the book's companion web page and check it out! Right-click an IFC file, select Open With, and choose Notepad.

After you've reviewed the contents of the IFC file, you can link it into a Revit project and integrate it into your coordination process as follows:

1. Start a new project with any default template. From the Insert tab in the ribbon, click on Link IFC.
2. Navigate to the `c07-Structure.ifc` file and click Open.
3. Save the project file.
4. Open the default 3D view and inspect the linked geometry.

If an updated IFC file is received, overwrite the linked file you used in the previous steps. When the host project file is reopened, the linked IFC content will be updated.

DOWNLOADING AND CUSTOMIZING THE OPEN SOURCE IFC EXPORTER

In addition to offering a basic IFC export command in the default installation of Revit, Autodesk has been developing an improved IFC exporter on the website SourceForge.net (`http://sourceforge.net/projects/ifcexporter`). Anyone can download the source code for this exporter and contribute to its development. This allows a larger international community to provide input on the improvement of this important feature.

The open source exporter consists of two separate downloads and installations: the exporter and a custom export UI. After they are installed, you can still launch the IFC export command from the Application menu; however, you will see a new Export IFC dialog box (Figure 7.32). Much like the CAD export process we described earlier in this chapter, this interface allows you to create, customize, and save export setups.

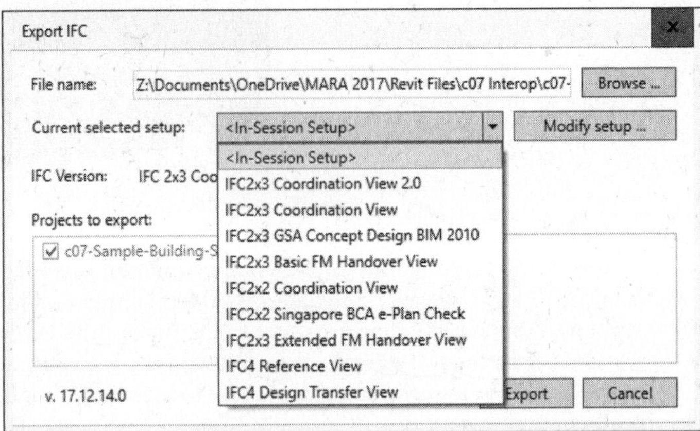

FIGURE 7.32
The open source IFC exporter user interface

For advanced IFC exporting options, choose the Modify Setup dialog box in Figure 7.32. There are several tabs across the top of this dialog box that allow you to customize the IFC export setup (Figure 7.33). In addition to the predefined export configurations, you can create and save your own setups that will be maintained in the Revit project file.

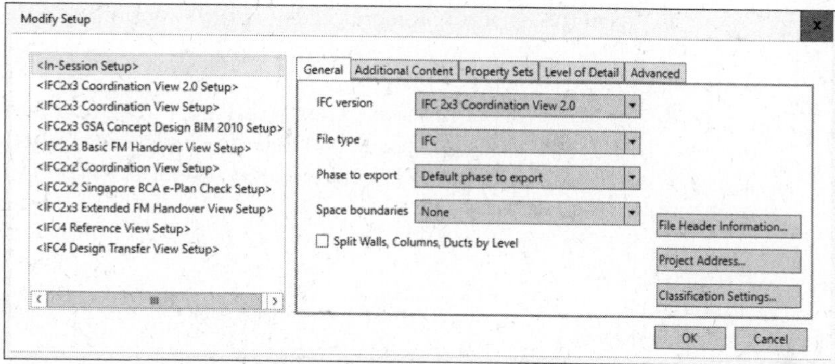

FIGURE 7.33
Customize and save IFC export setups

An excellent resource for IFC interoperability in Revit is the buildingSMART alliance web page for Common Building Information Model Files (`www.nibs.org/?page=bsa_commonbimfiles`). You can download sample files as well as a configuration guide with additional instructions related to customizing IFC exports from Revit.

Classifying IFC Export Settings

Because exporting to IFC format is about converting one model format to another, settings are not related to layer conversions, linetypes, or text, as they are in a CAD export. Rather, it is critical to correctly map the logic of the Revit model organization to the open data standard. In other words, model object categories must be mapped to IFC entities; for example, walls in Revit will be exported as IfcWall entities. This translation seems quite logical for walls and other objects, but consider an electric receptacle. Such a device would be categorized in Revit as an Electrical Fixture; however, it is classified as IfcFlowTerminal in the open standard. Entities are further refined with types—in this case, IfcFlowTerminalType—that would help distinguish an electric receptacle from other IfcFlowTerminal entities such as a faucet or an air diffuser.

The schema of the currently released standard (IFC4) can be viewed at `www.buildingsmart-tech.org`, the portal for the Model Support Group and Implementation Support Group. Although IFC4 is the currently released standard, many workflows still use IFC2x3, including native export from Revit software. If you work with IFC export and import regularly in the Revit environment, you should become familiar with some of the common classifications in the IFC schema. You'll find the IFC2x3 IFC4 schema indexes here:

`www.buildingsmart-tech.org/ifc/IFC2x3/TC1/html/index.htm`
`www.buildingsmart-tech.org/ifc/IFC4/final/html/index.htm`

Click Alphabetical Listing and then Entities, and you will be able to browse through some of the most common IFC classifications related to building elements. For example, find and click IfcCovering, and you will see that this classification is used for wall claddings, flooring, and suspended ceilings.

One aspect of the Revit project model that can be exported to IFC is a structural grid. These datum objects are beneficial to the coordination process if you are using Solibri Model Checker or Viewer or Tekla BIMsight; however, they are not exported if you use the default IFC export settings in Revit. Let's solve that problem with a quick exercise. You can continue to use the `c07-Sample-Building-Start.rvt` file.

1. From the Application menu, click Export ➤ Options ➤ IFC Options.

   You might need to scroll down the Export menu to see the Options flyout.

2. In the IFC Export Classes dialog box (Figure 7.34), find the entry for Grids and set the IFC Class Name to IfcGrid. You must manually enter any IFC entities and types into this dialog box; therefore, you should always refer to the buildingSMART website for accurate classifications.

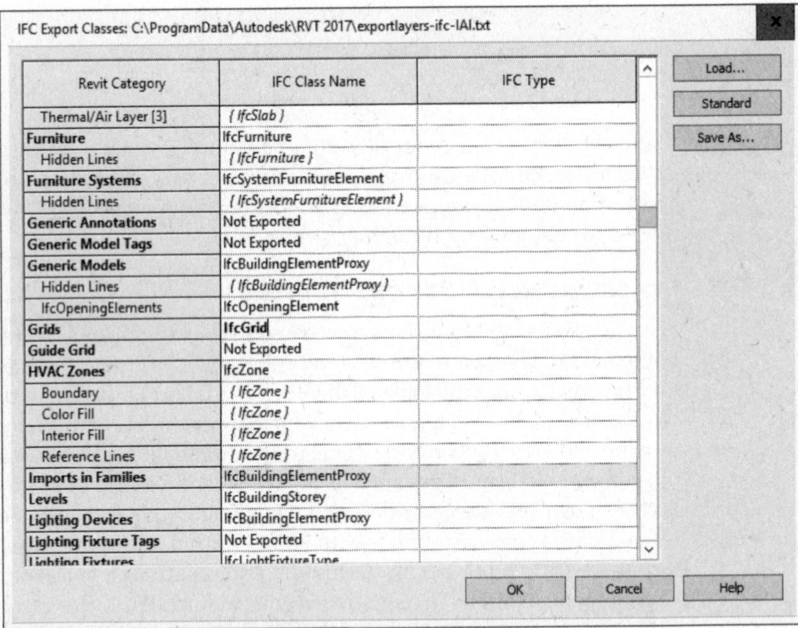

FIGURE 7.34 Customize the mapping of Revit categories to IFC entities.

3. Click OK to close the IFC Export Classes dialog box.

   You can save the IFC mappings to a text file for use in other projects.

4. From the Application menu, click Export ➤ IFC. If you are not using the custom IFC exporter that we discussed earlier in this chapter, simply set the export file type to IFC2×3 and save the file to your computer or network.

5. Open the IFC file in an application such as Solibri Model Checker or Viewer, and you will be able to see the Revit grid lines in the model-only exported format.

There are two other methods to customize the classification mappings for IFC. One is to use subcategories in families. As an example, a Revit family created for an elevator has been assigned to the Generic Models category; however, a subcategory named Elevators was created in the family (Figure 7.35).

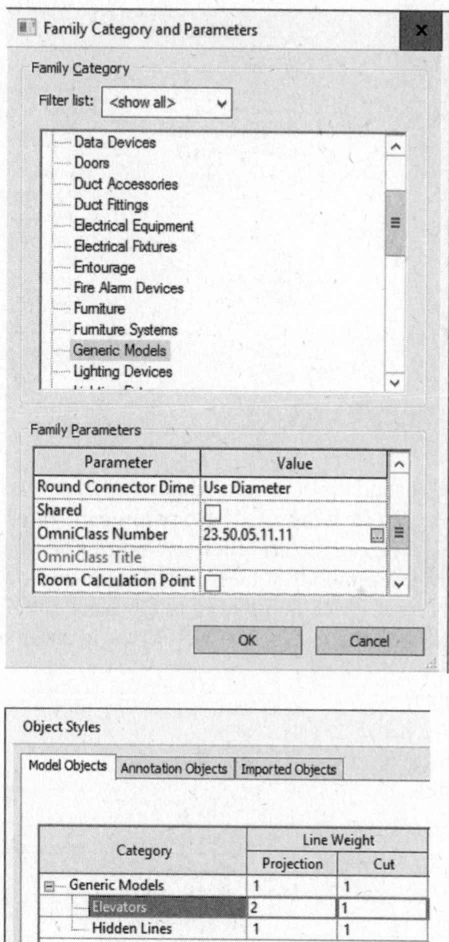

FIGURE 7.35 Create subcategories in a family for customized classification.

After the elevator family is loaded into a project, the new subcategories can be assigned to an appropriate IFC classification. Click the Application menu, and then click Export ➤ Options ➤ IFC Options to open the IFC Export Classes dialog box. Locate the Revit category for Generic Models and you will also see the Elevators subcategory, as shown in Figure 7.36. For IFC Class Name, enter IfcTransportElement and for Type, enter IfcTransportElementType, and you will be ready to export your project with the additional object classifications.

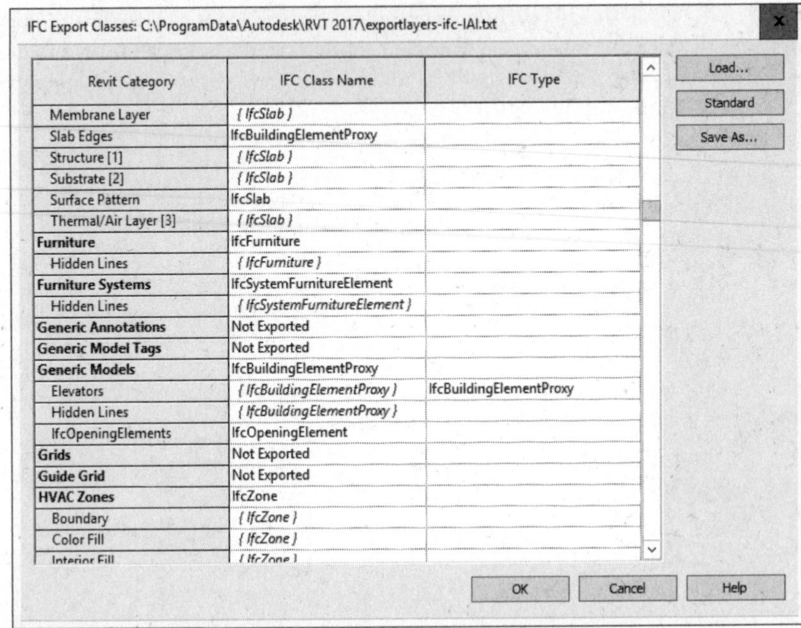

FIGURE 7.36
Subcategories can be mapped directly to IFC classifications.

The second method of classification customization is to use two specific shared parameters associated with a family. These parameters must be named IfcExportType and IfcExportAs, as shown in Figure 7.37, but they can simply be selected from a shared parameters file downloaded from the Common BIM Files web page mentioned previously in this chapter. When these families are loaded into and placed in a project, the IFC classifications will be automatically mapped according to the values specified in these parameters.

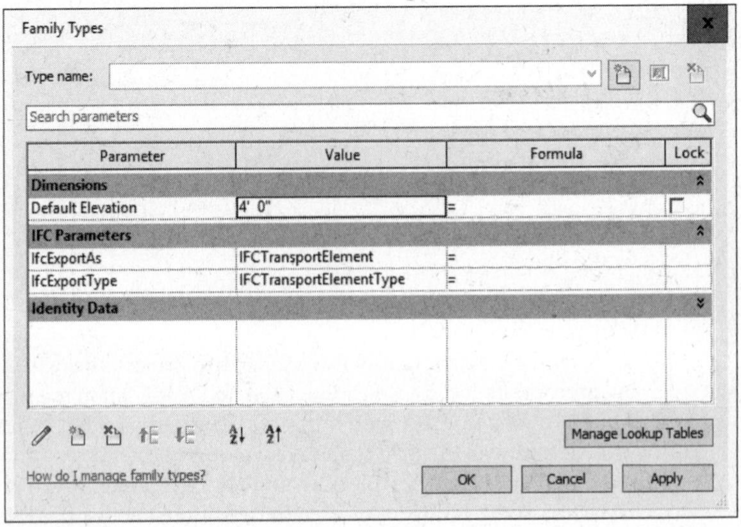

FIGURE 7.37
Use specific shared parameters to customize IFC mapping.

The Bottom Line

Use imported 2D CAD data. CAD data can be integrated into your Revit project in a number of ways: as plans of existing conditions, as fixture layouts from consultants, or as standard details from your company's library.

Master It How can CAD details be used in a Revit project?

Export 2D CAD data. The ability to deliver quality 2D information to other constituents involved in your project is as important as importing it into the Revit environment. Appropriately formatted views, standardized layer templates, and proper coordinate settings will result in happy team members and a smooth coordination process.

Master It Does Revit software comply with the National CAD Standard?

Use imported 3D model data. Model data generated outside of the Revit environment can be integrated into your projects as whole-building systems, massing studies, or unique components.

Master It How can a building's structural model created with the Bentley Structure be integrated into a Revit project?

Export 3D model data. Your modeled elements don't have to remain in the Revit environment forever. Data can be exported to 3ds Max, SketchUp, AutoCAD MEP, and more.

Master It How can you coordinate your architectural Revit model with an engineer using AutoCAD MEP?

Work with IFC imports and exports. Industry Foundation Classes (IFC) is a vendor-neutral model format designed to support interoperability in the AEC industry. It is widely used by some major BIM platforms available around the world.

Master It How is an IFC model integrated into a Revit project for coordination?

Part 3

Modeling and Massing for Design

In Part 2, we covered the topics that help you define important project standards when using Autodesk® Revit® software—within your team as well as across external teams with other consultants. In this part, we'll delve into the use of Revit from the earliest design stages to analysis, iteration, and finally visualization.

Chapter 8

Advanced Modeling and Massing

Every design starts with an idea. That can be shapes drawn out on trace paper, or a chipboard model, or a conceptual form in a 3D model. This idea becomes the basis for your design and ultimately your building. Although you might sketch out several variations to give your ideas shape, there comes a point in the design process where you need to begin testing your assumptions. Does the floor plan fit within the building's massing? Does it meet the client's functional requirements? Is the design energy efficient?

Massing is a set of unique tools within Autodesk® Revit® software specifically created for this kind of early design analysis. By creating the "big" design idea at a macro level, you're able to quickly and easily quantify and analyze the results. This allows you to confidently work from general to specific as your design progresses, without concern about actual building elements.

In addition, the massing tools allow you to create forms and containers to control other building system components. Complex walls, curtain walls, curtain panels, and other elements would be incredibly difficult to make and update without some underlying form to establish and drive their design.

Even though your overall design might not be represented by a complex massing form, it's likely that somewhere in a more conventional design, massing is essential to the success of your project.

In this chapter, you'll learn to:

- Create and schedule massing studies
- Know when to use solid and surface masses
- Use mathematical formulas for massing

The Massing User Interface and Functionality

A *mass* is simply a form with geometric substance (solids and voids) that is not related to any specific building element category. It is intended to allow designers to create a lightweight component that can either represent an entire building or serve as a guide for a single component, such as a complex roof form. When you create a mass in the context of a whole building, you can quantify the surface area, assign functional "floors" to the mass, and perform energy analysis—all without creating a single wall, floor, window, or roof.

After you create a whole-building mass, you can use By Face versions of commands to place system families such as walls, floors, and roofs. When these elements are placed by face, they retain a relationship to the mass elements. The associated building elements are not updated automatically, which means you can freely explore design alternatives to the massing. Once you are confident of your final design decision, the building elements can be updated to match the changes in the underlying mass.

Another important thing to know about massing is that masses can be created in either the project environment or the Family Editor. Much of the functionality overlaps in each case, so what's the difference between the two?

The main difference as to whether you create massing in place or in the Family Editor doesn't depend on the kind of shape or surface you want to create. Solid and surface forms can be created in both the project and Family Editor environments. Rather, it depends on how you want to create the massing and how you want to change the mass once it's been created.

Using in-place masses gives you the ability to model in the context of other surroundings (Figure 8.1). For example, you may be proposing an addition to an existing building or a new building on an existing campus. You may need to create a complex shape for a feature wall or a roof form, and you therefore need the context of the rest of your building design.

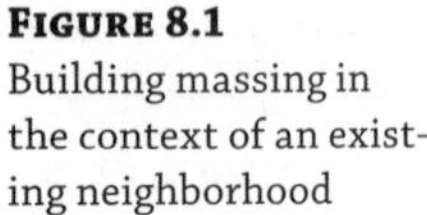

FIGURE 8.1
Building massing in the context of an existing neighborhood

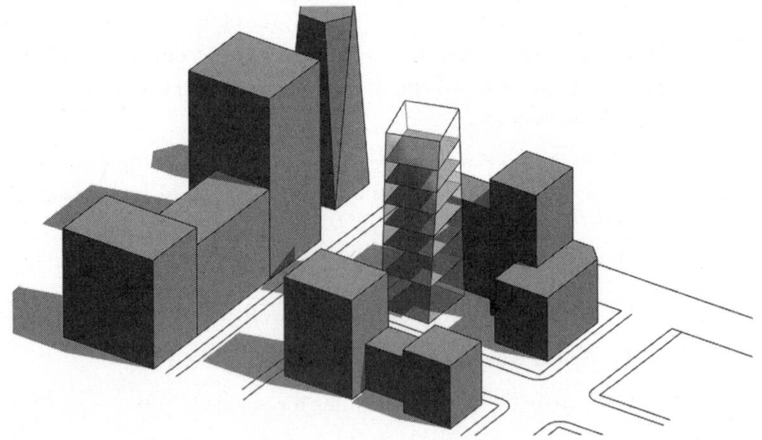

Creating a mass in the Family Editor gives you a slightly different user interface (UI) (Figure 8.2). When you create a Conceptual Mass family, you have the ability to see work planes and levels in 3D views; however, these references are not in the context of your project environment. In addition to the lack of context in the Family Editor, to make changes to massing, you must reload the mass families into your project for face-based elements and schedules to update.

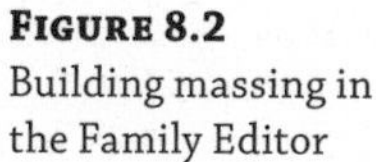

FIGURE 8.2
Building massing in the Family Editor

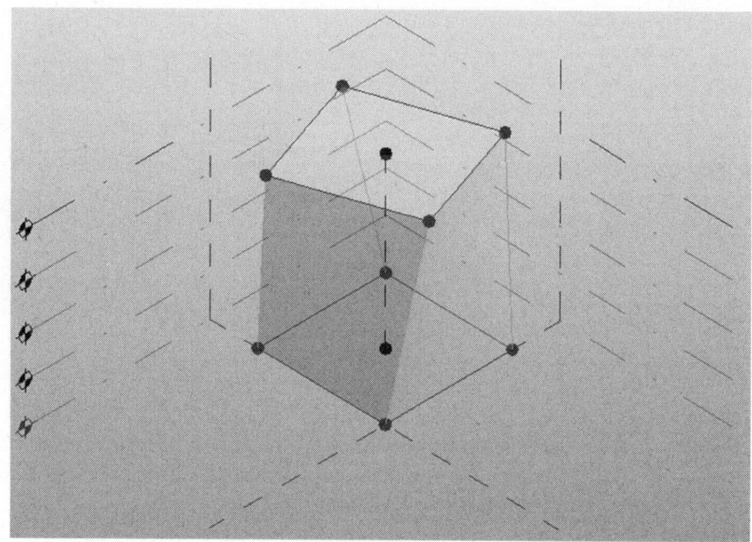

Let's take a moment to clarify the difference between in-place component modeling and massing. If you need to create a custom-shaped building element, such as the wall shown in Figure 8.3, you would use the Model In-Place command. You would set the category to Walls and then use either a blend or a sweep to generate the form of the wall. You'll notice in the figure that the sectional dimensions of the wall are not consistent.

FIGURE 8.3
Custom-shaped wall as an in-place element

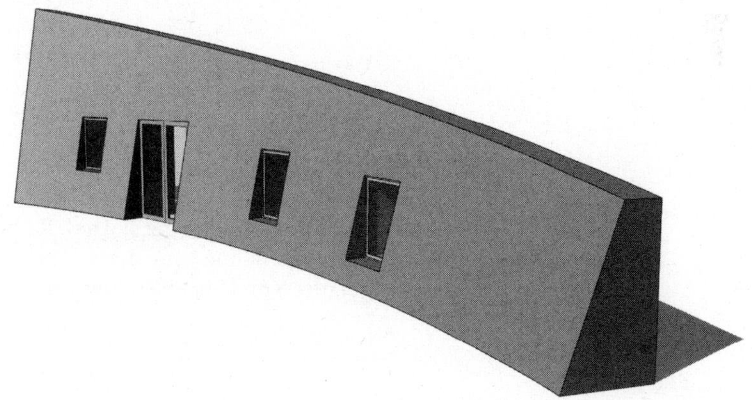

If you wanted to use a wall assembly with consistent sectional dimensions but configure the wall in a complex vertical layout, you would create a mass and then use the Wall By Face command. In the example shown in Figure 8.4, a generic wall is applied to the face of a mass that was created by generating a surface between two splines.

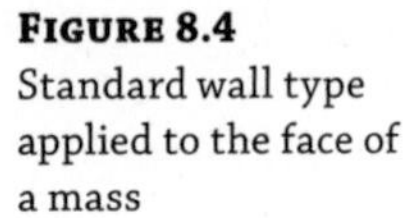

FIGURE 8.4
Standard wall type applied to the face of a mass

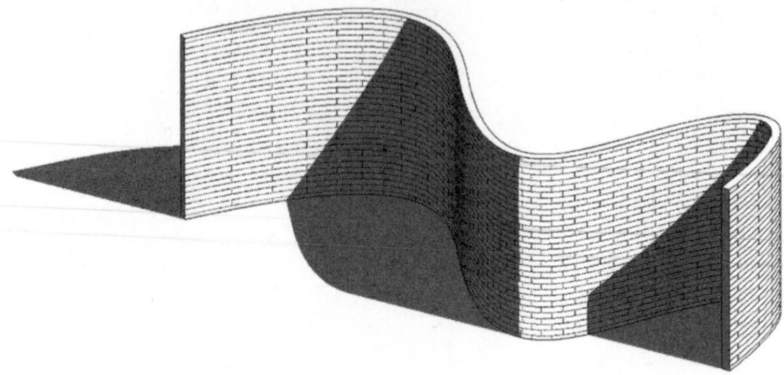

The rest of this chapter will focus solely on the creation of masses for the purpose of whole-building design. You can learn more about component modeling tools in Chapter 14, "Designing with the Family Editor."

Creating Mass Geometry

How you create masses (surface or solid) differs significantly from the UI used to create other standard family content. When you're creating standard project content, you have specific geometry tools such as Extrusion and Sweep (Figure 8.5). In some ways, this is a noun-verb approach: You select a tool for the form that you want to create and then you take action to create it.

FIGURE 8.5
Non-massing form-creation tools

Creating a mass still requires that you know the form that you intend to create, but you're not required to select a particular form type to get started. Rather, you start by simply creating the sketch-based elements that would define your shape. Then you select them as a group and choose the Create Form tool (Figure 8.6). This will allow you to create both solids and voids.

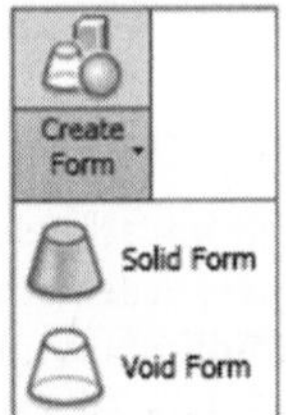

FIGURE 8.6
The Create Form tool

Both solid and surface may be created from model lines or reference lines; however, the differences are important. Keep in mind that your ability to further iterate the form that you create depends on whether you use model or reference lines to generate the form, even though the forms created may look exactly the same at first.

If your intent is to simply create a form that is not likely to require rule-based parameterization, using model lines is fine. Model lines are *consumed* by the form after you use the Create Form tool. In other words, the only way to get back to your original sketch form is to dissolve the shape. But if you intend to control the form with formulas and other parameters, it's best to start with reference lines. Figure 8.7 shows the subtle graphic difference between the two line types. The model line shape is on the left, and the green reference lines are on the right. You will also notice that when reference lines are selected, they have much more capability to serve as multidimensional references for hosting other geometry.

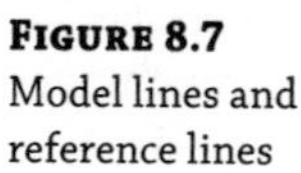

FIGURE 8.7
Model lines and reference lines

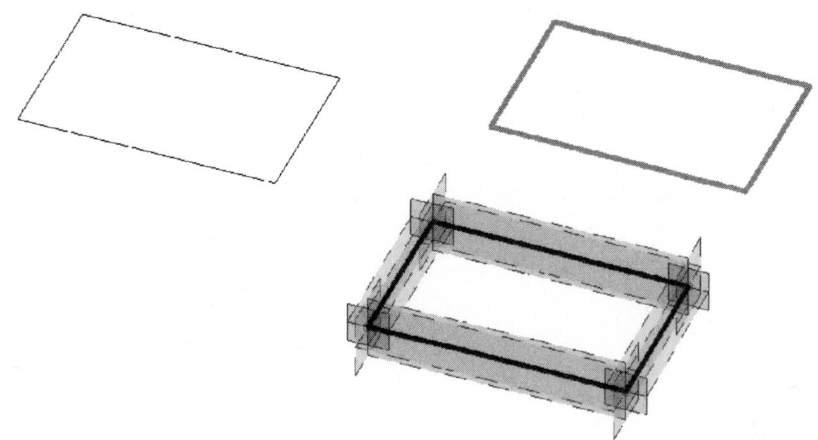

Because the difference is so subtle on the screen, we recommend that you give your reference lines more thickness and lighten the default green color so that they stand out better, and make that a part of your project template.

Creating an In-Place Mass

Now that you are familiar with the difference between massing for components and whole-building massing, let's look closer at the important capabilities that will help you develop building designs. Download and open the file `c08-Massing-1-Start.rvt` or `c08-Massing-1-Start-Metric.rvt` from this book's website at `www.sybex.com/go/masteringrevit2017`. In this section, we will create some simple mass forms, generate mass floors, and then build schedule views to quantify the results. After you open either file, activate the Level 1 floor plan before starting the exercise.

Whether you create masses in place or in the Family Editor, you're able to generate floor faces (not the actual floors) and schedule important metadata before you've even begun to assign actual geometry to the masses. This is important to do early in the design process because the masses will be "light" in your project—they won't have a drastically negative impact on performance. Use them to establish your overall design idea and get a general idea for building size and area.

In-place mass forms can be both solid- and surface-based forms; however, masses that contain only surfaces cannot be analyzed for any sort of volumetric quantities. You can start an in-place mass in one of two ways: The first way is to select the Architecture tab in the ribbon, and on the Build panel, choose the Component ➤ Model In-Place command.

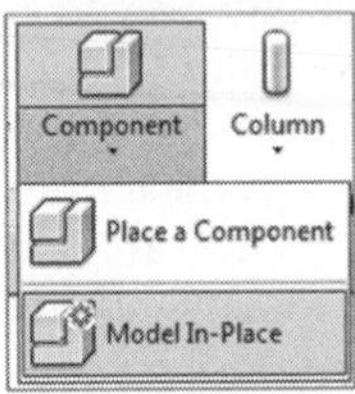

When you select this option, the Family Category And Parameters dialog box appears (Figure 8.8). You will be able to use the other massing tools only if the in-place component is assigned to the proper category. Be sure to select the Mass category and click OK.

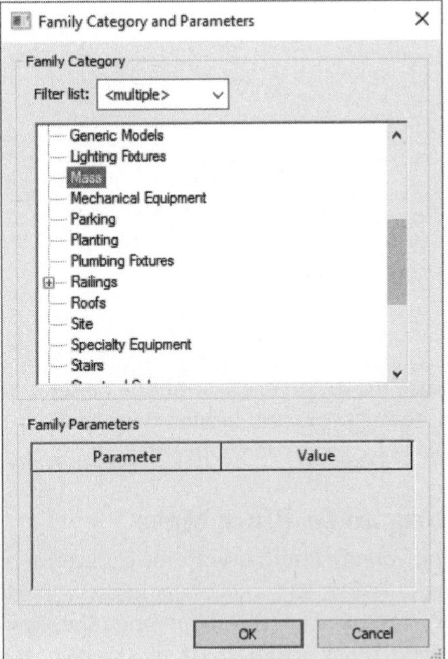

FIGURE 8.8
Selecting the Mass category

WHERE ARE MY MASSING TOOLS?

If you don't see the Massing & Site tab in the ribbon, you might need to activate it. In some installations, these tools are deactivated by default. In the Application menu, click Options and then select User Interface. Make sure that the Massing & Site Tab And Tools option is checked.

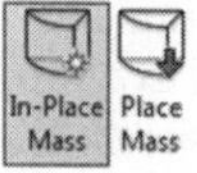

The other way to create an in-place mass is to select the Massing & Site tab in the ribbon and from the Conceptual mass panel, choose the In-Place Mass command. In either case, when you start to create the mass, you'll want to have the Mass category visible (it's turned off by default in all views). Rather than confuse you by allowing you to create objects that wouldn't be visible, the software prompts you to turn the category on (Figure 8.9).

FIGURE 8.9
Enabling the Show Mass mode

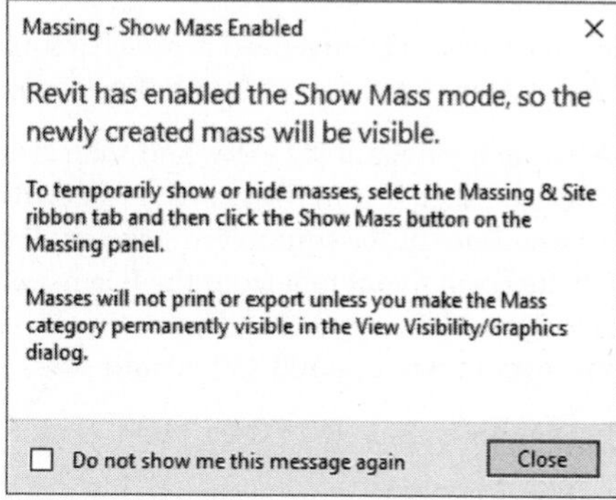

Once you close this dialog box, you'll be given the opportunity to name your in-place mass. In this case, you're going to name the mass Cube (Figure 8.10).

FIGURE 8.10
Naming the mass

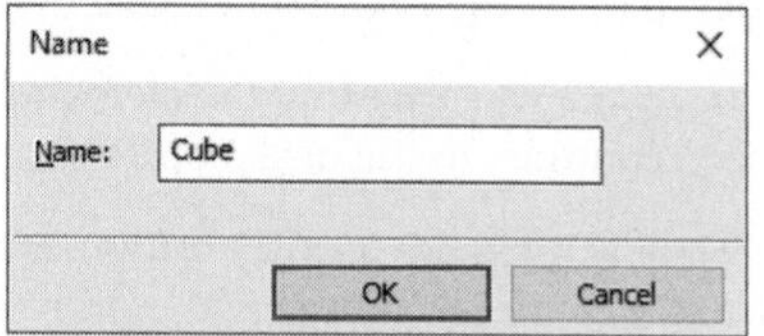

After you've named the mass from the previous steps and clicked OK, you'll be shown the Massing toolset for in-place families. The Create tab contains the tools that you'll use to create solid and void geometry as well as surface-generated masses.

In the following exercise, we will create a cube, pyramid, and sphere (Figure 8.11) to demonstrate some uses for masses. Starting with the cube, its dimensions are 100′ × 100′ × 100′ (about 30 m × 30 m × 30 m). The base of the pyramid is the same size as the cube, with equal sides tapering to the same height. The sphere is the same width as the cube.

FIGURE 8.11
Cube, pyramid, and sphere masses

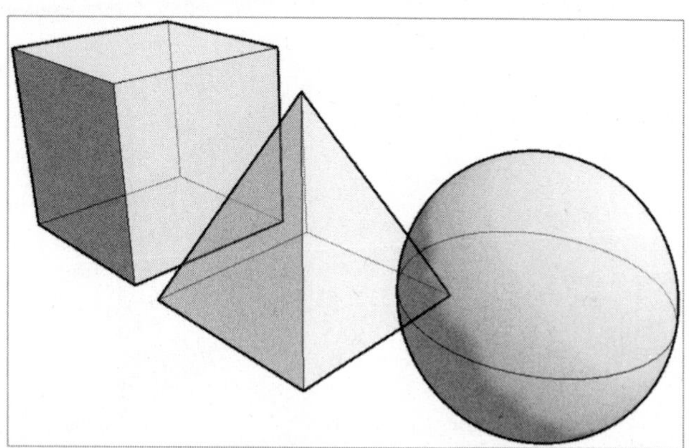

You've already started the command with either the Model In-Place or In-Place Mass command. The next step will be to create the 3D geometry inside the family. Mass geometry is created in a two-step process: First, create the 2D shape of the object; then use the Create Form tool to generate the 3D geometry. This process is different from typical modeling software applications because it does not require you to choose a specific modeling command before you begin to explore your design.

Now, let's get into the details with the following steps:

1. For the cube, you'll first need to sketch a square in a plan view. From the Create tab in the ribbon, in the Draw panel, use the Line or Rectangle tool to sketch a 100′ × 100′ (30 m × 30 m) square.
2. Activate the default 3D view, and then click the Modify button in the ribbon. Select the lines you sketched in the previous step. You may need to press the Tab key to ensure that all four lines of the square are selected. From the contextual tab in the ribbon, choose the Create Form flyout tool from the Form panel, and choose Solid Form. You will see a dimension in the 3D view that indicates the default height of the extrusion. Click the dimension value and then type 100′ (30 m) and press Enter on the keyboard to set the desired height.
3. In the contextual tab of the ribbon, click Finish Mass.
4. Return to the Massing & Site tab in the ribbon, and then click In-Place Mass. Name the next mass Sphere.
5. From the Create panel in the ribbon, select the Circle tool from the Draw panel. In the Options bar, set the Placement Plane to Level : Midpoint. Set the Radius to 50′ (15 m).

   You may get a warning that the elements are not visible in the current view. That's fine for now; continue to the next step.
6. In a 3D view, click the Modify button in the ribbon, and then select the circle. From the contextual tab in the ribbon, choose Create Form ➤ Solid Form. This will pop up two visual options for you (Figure 8.12). One will allow you to simply extrude the circle and create a cylinder; the other will allow you to create a sphere. Choose the Sphere option.

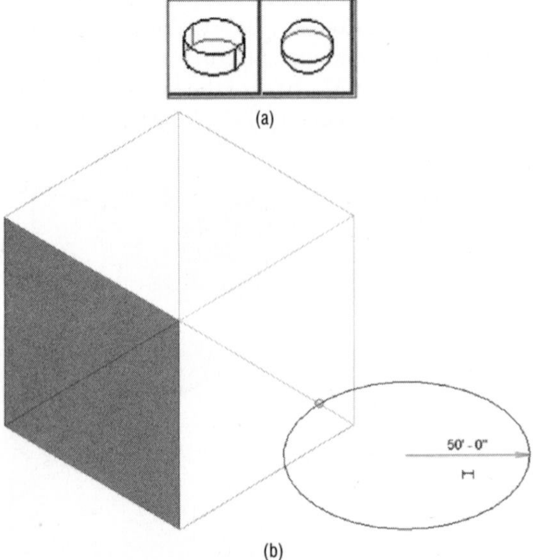

FIGURE 8.12
Create Form options for a circle

7. In the contextual tab of the ribbon, click Finish Mass.
8. Once again, return to the Massing & Site tab in the ribbon, and then click In-Place Mass. Name the next mass Pyramid. For this shape, you will need to sketch a square in plan and a triangle in elevation before you use the Create Form tool.
9. Activate the Level 1 floor plan and sketch a square that measures 100′ × 100′ (30 m × 30 m). From the Draw panel in the ribbon, click the Plane tool. Draw two reference planes—one for each centerline of the square you just sketched (Figure 8.13). Select the horizontal reference plane, and in the Properties palette set the Name value to Pyramid Ctr.

FIGURE 8.13
Draw two reference planes in the pyramid sketch

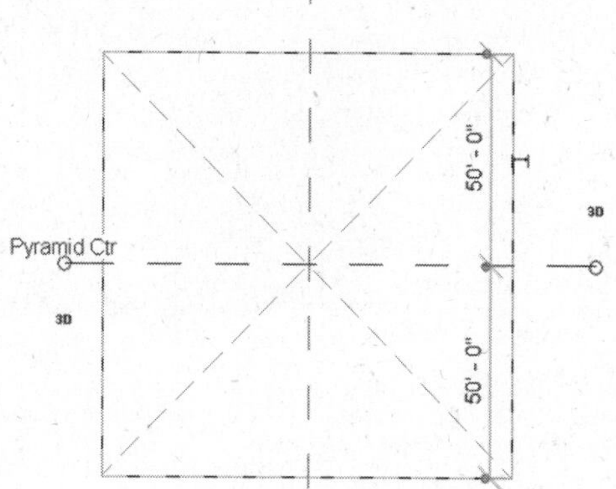

10. Activate the South elevation view. From the Draw panel in the ribbon, click the Line tool. You will be prompted to select a work plane. Choose the Name option, and from the drop-down list select Reference Plane : Pyramid Ctr. Sketch a triangle as shown in Figure 8.14. Make sure to use intersection and endpoint snapping to make the base of the triangle in line with Level 1 and at the intersection of the Top level and the vertical reference plane.

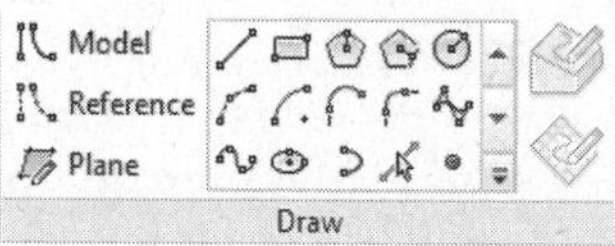

FIGURE 8.14
Sketch a triangle in elevation.

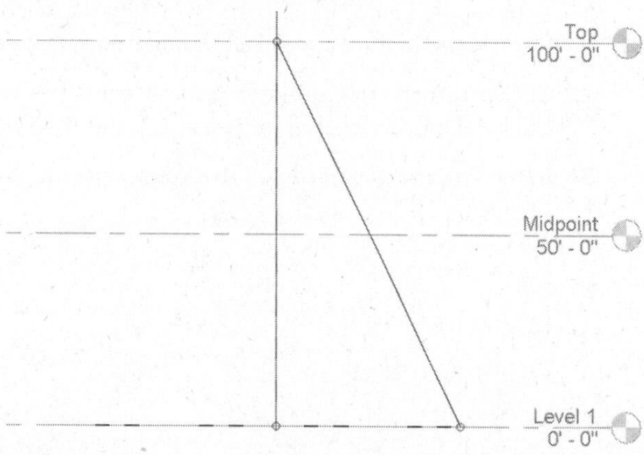

11. In a 3D view, click the Modify button in the ribbon. Select both the square and the triangle, and then select Create From ➤ Solid Form from the contextual tab in the ribbon. The Create Form command will detect that the most likely configuration of these two 2D shapes is to sweep the triangle along the square path, thus forming a pyramid. Click Finish Mass in the contextual tab of the ribbon, and you will see the three masses that you've created: cube, pyramid, and sphere (Figure 8.15).

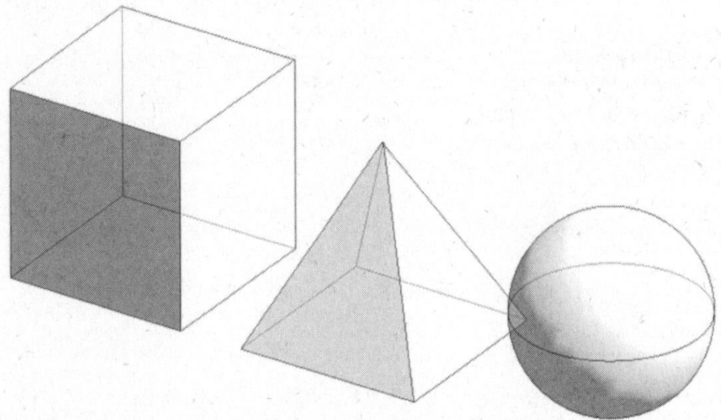

FIGURE 8.15 Cube, pyramid, and sphere.

As each form was finished, the in-place mass was completed, and the process was repeated for each new mass. In the Project Browser, locate the Families branch and the Mass category. Expand the branch and you will see each mass as a separate item.

Placing a Mass

Continuing with the previous exercise, you will now load and place a mass family. There are many premade families in the default libraries for Revit software. We have already loaded a mass family in the project files for this exercise. Continue with the `c08-Massing-1-Start.rvt` or `c08-Massing-1-Start-Metric.rvt` file by following these steps:

1. Activate the Level 1 floor plan. Switch to the Massing & Site tab in the ribbon and click Place Mass. In the Type Selector, make sure that either Gable or M_Gable is selected.
2. Click an area to the right of the mass forms you created in the previous exercise steps. Click the Modify button in the ribbon and then select the Gable mass you just placed.
3. In the Properties palette, set the following values:

   Width: 100′ (30 m)

   Depth: 100′ (30 m)

   Height: 100′ (30 m)

   Eave Height: 50′ (15 m)

When you switch back to a 3D view, you will see the Gable mass family in the same context as the in-place masses you created previously (Figure 8.16). All of the mass forms will function similarly as you assign mass floors, place building elements by face, and create schedules. The main difference is that to edit the geometry of the placed mass, you must do so by changing the values in the Properties palette. Keep in mind that you may also load a different mass family and swap one shape for another. You cannot swap an in-place family for a loaded family.

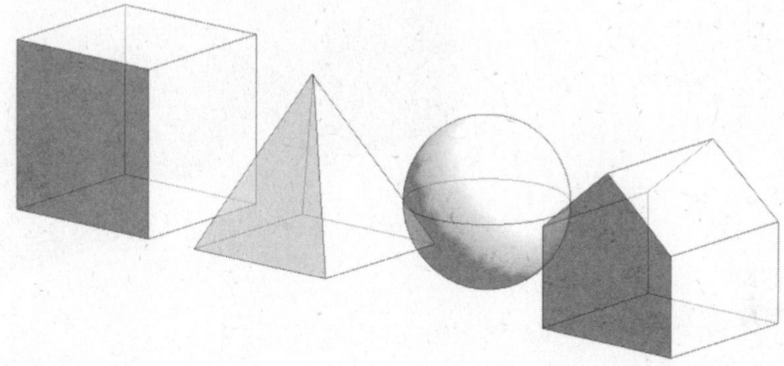

FIGURE 8.16
The Gable mass family is placed and modified.

Creating Mass Floors

Once you have created some solid mass forms, it's important to understand how to create mass floors. The Mass Floors dialog box allows you to generate some quick floor plates and get a rough idea of the floor areas available in your masses. This technique will work equally well with in-place masses or loaded mass families.

To create mass floors, follow these steps:

1. Activate the South elevation view. Use the Copy tool from the Modify tab in the ribbon to create more levels in addition to the three provided in the exercise file. Place the copied levels at intervals of 10′ (1500 mm), so you have a total of 10 levels (Figure 8.17).

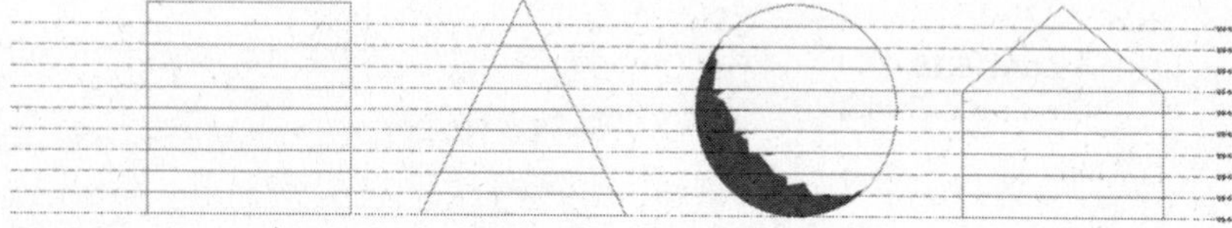

FIGURE 8.17
Create multiple intersecting levels

2. In a 3D view, select all the masses and click the Mass Floors button in the contextual tab of the ribbon.

3. In the Mass Floors dialog box, check the boxes for all the available levels. This allows you to assign a conceptual floor plate wherever each selected level intersects a mass form. Click OK to close the dialog box.

Wherever the selected levels intersect the mass forms, floor faces will be generated, as shown in Figure 8.18. Now the masses and floor faces can be calculated and scheduled. If you select any one of the masses and observe the parameters in the Properties palette, you will see that Gross Floor Area now reports an area that will change depending on how many mass floors are assigned to that mass.

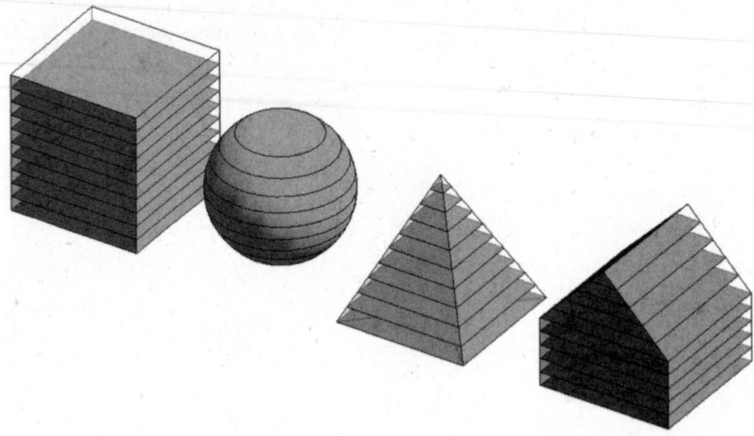

FIGURE 8.18
Floor area faces assigned to mass forms

Scheduling Masses

With the mass floors created, you can now schedule them and begin to understand what kinds of areas you have for floor plates in these shapes. Remember, you can do this exercise with any type of mass shape, and it can be a great way to validate your building's program against a variety of building forms.

Let's continue with the exercise by following these steps:

1. From the View tab in the ribbon, click Schedules ➤ Schedule/Quantities, and you'll be given the option to schedule the Mass category itself or various subcategories, including Mass Floor (Figure 8.19). Select Mass, and we'll schedule the masses so we can do a comparative analysis between the different mass types.

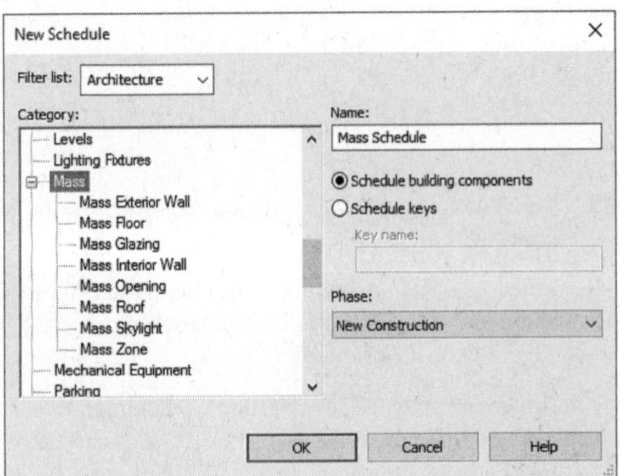

FIGURE 8.19
Creating a schedule

2. Select the fields Family, Gross Floor Area, Gross Surface Area, and Gross Volume, as shown in Figure 8.20. Add them to the Scheduled Fields table by clicking the Add Parameter(s) button.

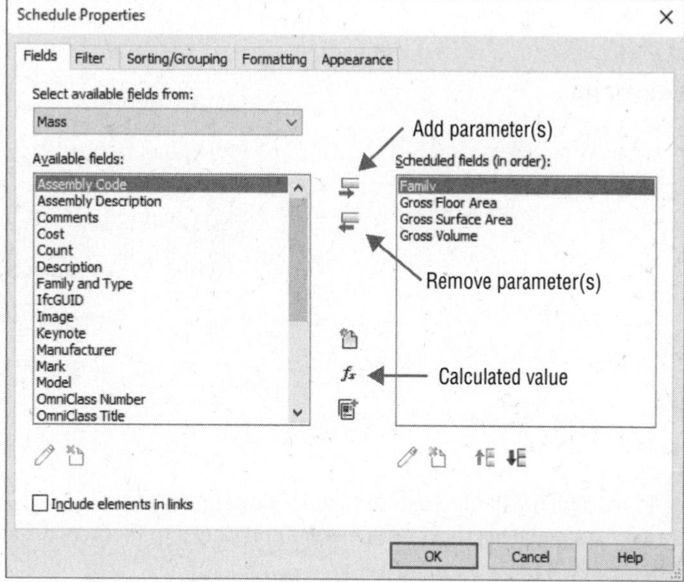

FIGURE 8.20
Scheduled fields

For this example, we'll also show you how to create two calculated values. This will allow you to calculate the overall volume of each mass compared to the floor area, as well as the overall surface area compared to the floor area. Schedules like this will be helpful during the early design process to help you understand how efficient the space of your design is compared to the volume and surface area required to contain that space. Follow these steps:

a. Click the Calculated Value button in the Fields tab of the Schedule Properties dialog box, and name the new calculated value **Volume to Floor Ratio**, as shown in Figure 8.21. In the Formula area, enter the following formula, and be sure to use the correct case: **(Gross Volume / 1) / Gross Floor Area**. In metric units, the formula is **(Gross Volume / 1m) / Gross Floor Area**. To keep the units consistent, you divide the gross volume by 1′ (1 m) before dividing by the gross floor area. Click OK to accept the formula.

FIGURE 8.21
Create a calculated value for volume-to-floor ratio.

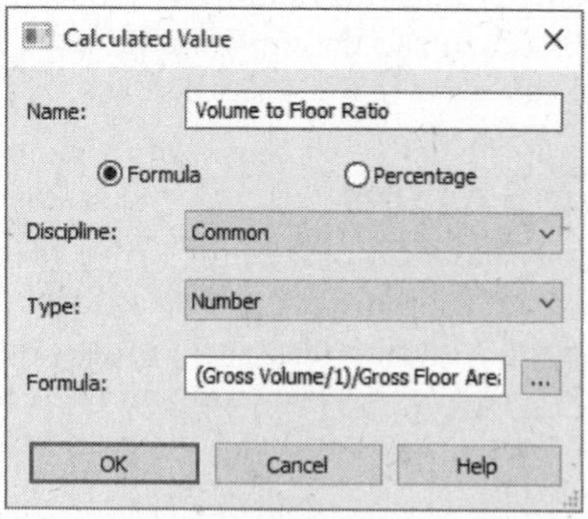

b. To create your next calculated value, click the Calculated Value button again and name this formula Surface to Floor Ratio. In the Formula box, enter the following formula and again be sure to maintain the correct case: **Gross Surface Area / Gross Floor Area**. Once you've entered the formula, click OK (Figure 8.22).

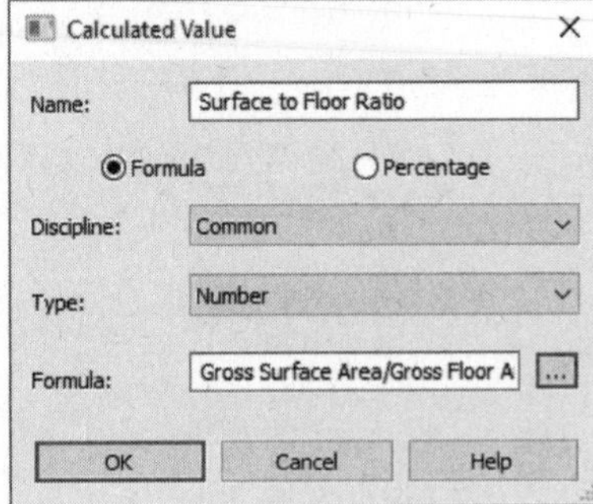

FIGURE 8.22
Create a calculated value for the surface-to-floor ratio.

The finished schedule is shown in Figure 8.23. Notice that, proportionally, a sphere and a cube have efficient floor areas compared to their corresponding surface area and volume.

FIGURE 8.23
Completed schedule

<Mass Schedule>

A	B	C	D	E	F
Family	Gross Floor Area	Gross Surface Area	Gross Volume	Volume to Floor Ratio	Surface to Floor Ratio
Cube	100000 SF	60000 SF	1000000.00 CF	10	0.6
Sphere	51837 SF	31416 SF	523598.68 CF	10.100858	0.606052
Pyramid	39007 SF	32639 SF	338471.06 CF	8.677127	0.836742
Cube1	85000 SF	50806 SF	800000.00 CF	9.411765	0.597721

On the other hand, the pyramid mass will require significantly more surface and volume to create the same relative surface area as a cube or a sphere; thus, a pyramid takes far more surface area than a cube to contain the same amount of space.

You can download the finished file from the book's web page. It's in the Chapter 8 folder and is named `c08-Massing-1-Finished.rvt`.

Massing Surfaces

Now that we have discussed how to create or place solid mass forms, let's review some of the ways in which you can generate massing surfaces. Similar to the process of creating a solid massing form, you can select one or more lines and then use the Create Form tool to generate a surface. Figure 8.24 shows a number of reference line types you can create with the Draw tools: Spline Through Points, Spline, Curve, and Line.

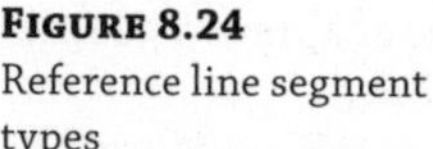

FIGURE 8.24
Reference line segment types

As you can see in Figure 8.25, each of these reference lines has different control points that allow for further control.

FIGURE 8.25
Reference line control points

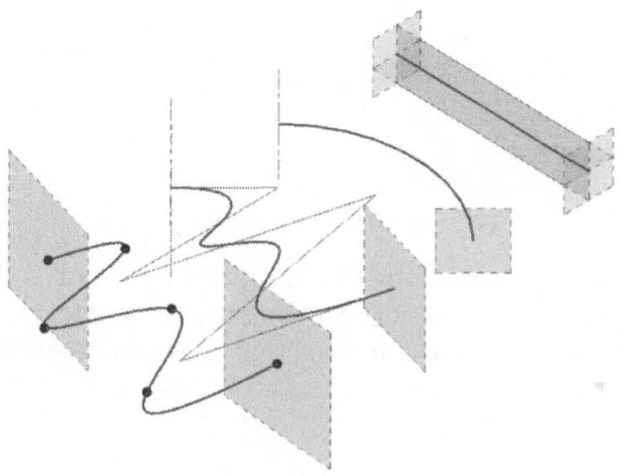

Because these are not closed loops, the form that will generate from each of these segments will only be a surface (Figure 8.26). You generate the form by selecting each of the lines (one at a time, not together) and then selecting Create Form ➢ Solid Form.

FIGURE 8.26
Surface forms

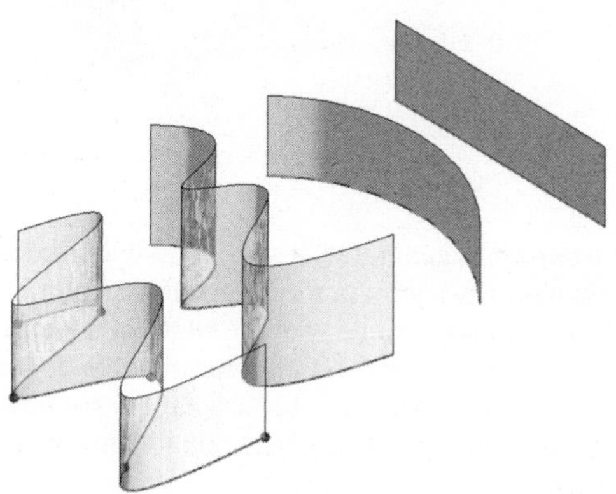

You can also create surface-based forms from more than one line at a time. The result is a surface that can be controlled in more complex ways than a single line.

Take the Spline Through Points line, for example. The form on the left in Figure 8.27 creates a face that is controlled by a single reference line, whereas the form on the right is a face controlled by two (and it could be more) reference lines.

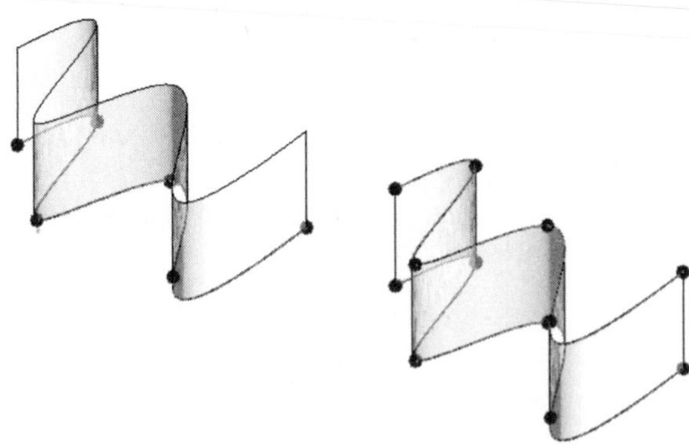

FIGURE 8.27
Surfaces based on multiple splines

Moving the location of the control points on the form on the left maintains a consistent height to the top of the surface previously generated, whereas moving the control points of the surface on the right creates a surface that varies in height (Figure 8.28).

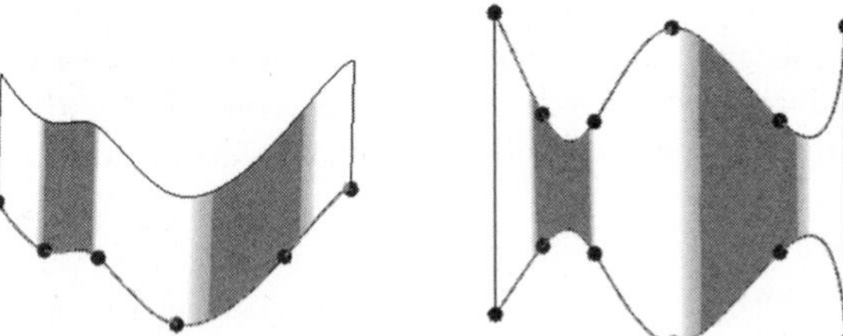

FIGURE 8.28
Single and multi-spline surfaces

After a surface is generated, it's also possible to add more profiles, as illustrated by Figure 8.29. A profile is basically a joint in the form, allowing for another control location. Any profile you add will respond in the same way the edges of the mass respond, by allowing you to modify and manipulate both them and their location. We'll demonstrate how to use this tool and the rest of the Form Element panel later in the chapter. For now, we'll step through some of the tools so you can get an understanding of the relationship of tool to form and see how quickly you can create forms.

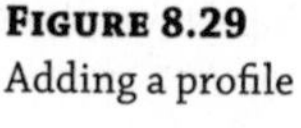

Figure 8.29
Adding a profile

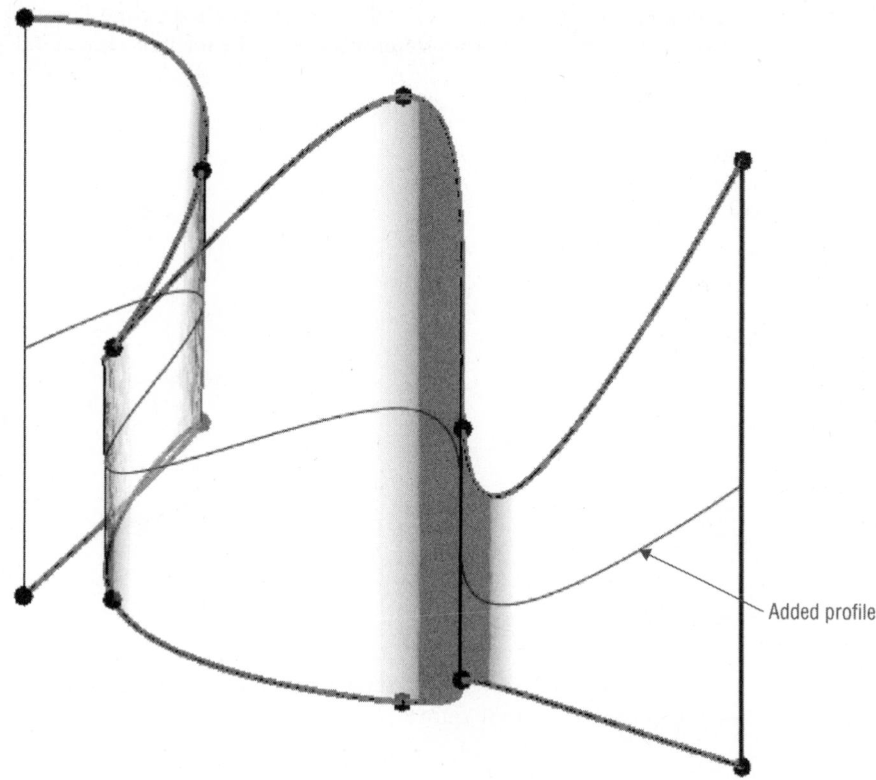

After the profile was added, it was moved to create a bulge in the surface (far right shown in Figure 8.30).

Figure 8.30
Moved profile

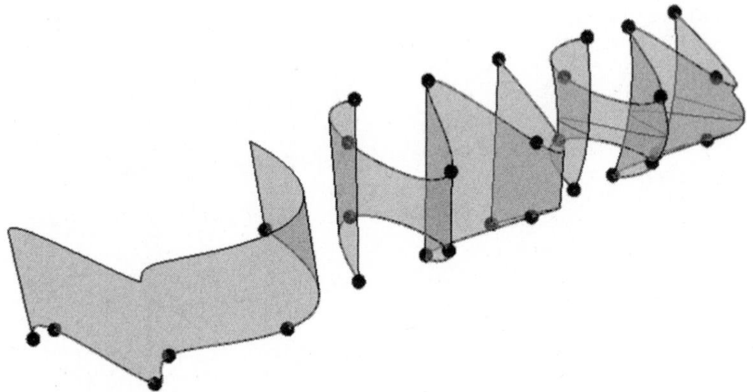

The fourth iteration of the form was created by selecting the surface and then choosing the Dissolve tool in the contextual tab of the ribbon. This removed the surface but left us with all the references used to create the form.

Once the face was dissolved, another reference called Spline Through Points was added between the upper and lower reference splines. The result is shown in Figure 8.31.

FIGURE 8.31
Additional spline added

Selecting all three references and then choosing the Create Form tool stitched them all into a new single-surface form (Figure 8.32).

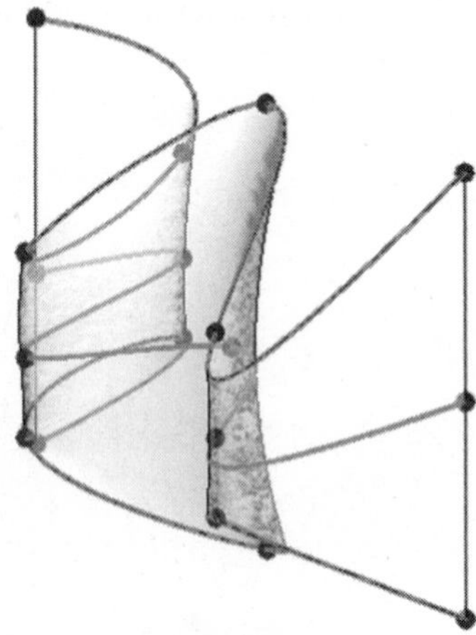

FIGURE 8.32
New surface form

Selecting the points within the middle reference allowed for even more complex surface control (Figure 8.33).

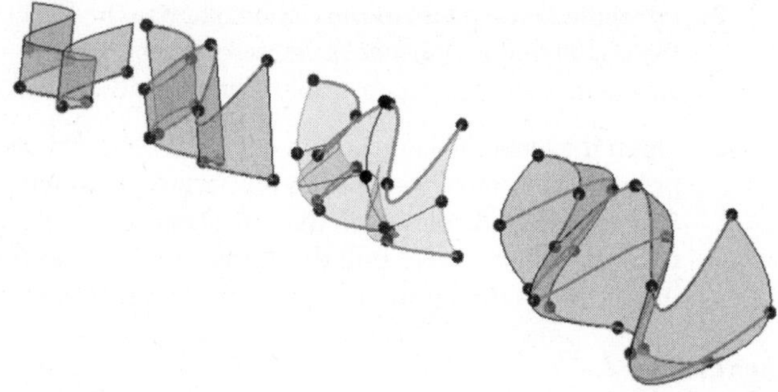

FIGURE 8.33
Edited center spline

Keep in mind that selecting lines or shapes to create forms is a sequential operation (when it's not in a closed loop). Window-selecting all the splines and then creating the surface will result in very different forms than if you were to sequentially select adjacent splines (Figure 8.34). The result is that the surface form isn't interpolated as smooth between the upper and lower splines. Instead, a distinct edge is created between the two splines.

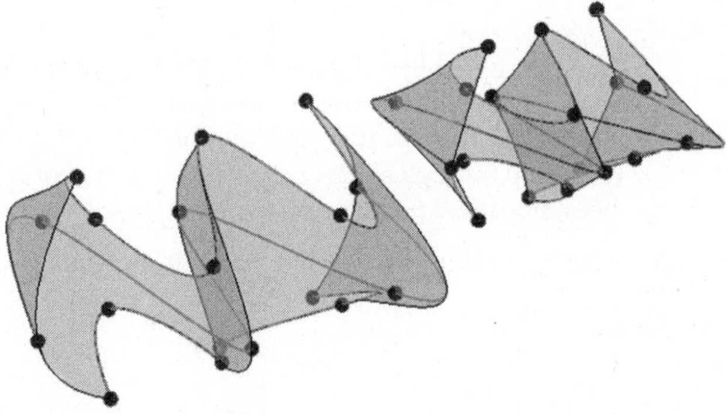

FIGURE 8.34
Spline-based surfaces

As you can see, it's easy to create complex surface forms using reference lines. Now let's begin to create complex forms using reference planes.

Using Free-form Building Massing

Now that you are familiar with the basic functionality of the massing tools, let's learn how to generate and explore building forms in an informal way. The exercise in this section will build on the skills you learned in the previous section, and you will learn how to directly manipulate solid geometry using grips, gizmos, and dimensions.

Start by downloading and opening either `c08-Massing-2-Start.rvt` or `c08-Massing-2-Start-Metric.rvt` from the book's web page. Begin the exercise by following these steps:

1. Activate the Level 1 floor plan. From the Massing & Site tab in the ribbon, click In-Place Mass and name the new family Mass 1.

2. From the Draw panel in the ribbon, choose the Rectangle tool. In the Options bar, check the box to make a surface from closed loops. Sketch a rectangle that is approximately 40′ × 90′ (12 m × 28 m). Specific dimensions are not important; it's more about the proportions.
3. Open the Default 3D view, and click the Modify button in the ribbon. Hover the mouse pointer over one of the lines in the rectangle sketch. Press the Tab key until you see Form: Form Element displayed in the status bar. Select the form element and you will see controls that allow you to pull the surface into a solid (Figure 8.35). Using the control pointing in the up direction, press and drag it until the form is about 140′ (43 m) tall.

FIGURE 8.35
Creating a solid form

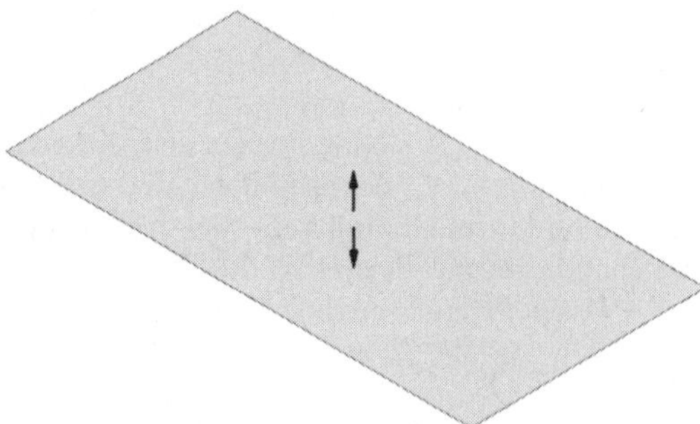

There are a number of shape handles that allow you to modify each face, edge, and intersection. Simply hovering over each face, edge, and vertex will highlight the appropriate control. You can also press the Tab key on the keyboard to select the desired control. We'll step through some of the selections to give you an idea of what the controls for the faces, sides, and points look like.

4. Starting with any vertical face, select it and you'll be given the control shown in Figure 8.36.

FIGURE 8.36
Face control

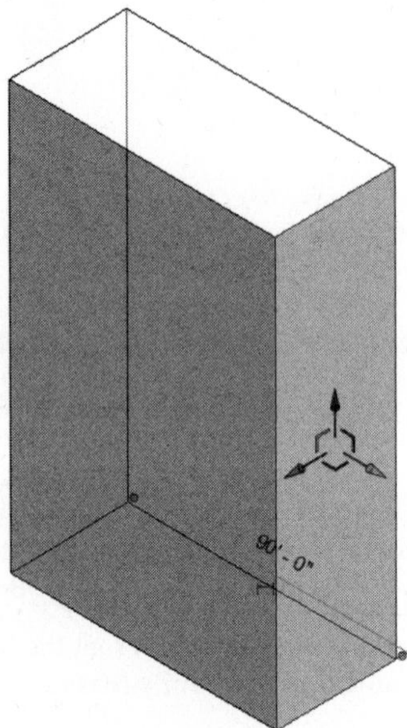

5. Select an edge and you will have the ability to move the edge of a form in multiple directions (Figure 8.37).

FIGURE 8.37
Edge control

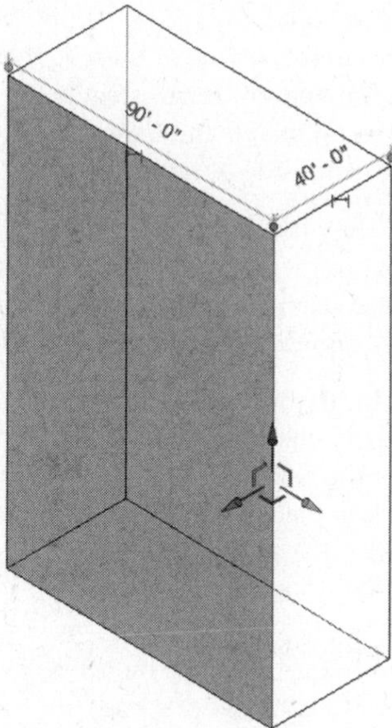

6. Select the point at the intersection of several edges. You will likely need to press the Tab key to select a corner point. This control allows you to modify the location of a vertex (Figure 8.38).

FIGURE 8.38
Vertex control

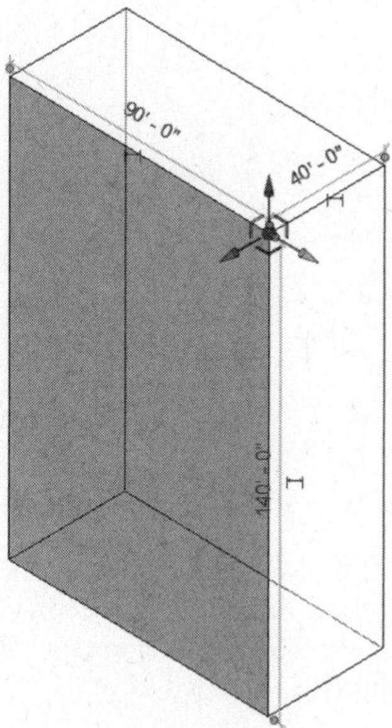

The control arrow allows you to modify the selected element parallel to the direction of the arrow, whereas the angled indicators of the same colors as their corresponding arrows allow you to modify the location of the selected element perpendicular to the arrow.

There are also some tools to help you with the visualizations of the mass, especially as it gets more complex. One of these is the X-Ray tool, which will take a solid and turn it into a semitransparent form. Turn on X-Ray mode by selecting the form and clicking the X-Ray button on the Form Element panel. This will let you see any of the profiles and controls on the other side of the object.

Now that X-Ray mode has been enabled, look at the options that are provided for turning a rather simple, extruded form into something complex. An edge may be added to an existing form from vertex to vertex or parallel with the trajectory of the form (shown as a dotted line from the upper to the lower face).

7. Click the Modify button in the ribbon, and then select the front face of the extruded mass you previously created. From the contextual tab in the ribbon, select Add Edge. As you mouse over the face you've selected, you'll be given a ghosted line to locate the edge. Simply click to place it, as shown in Figure 8.39.

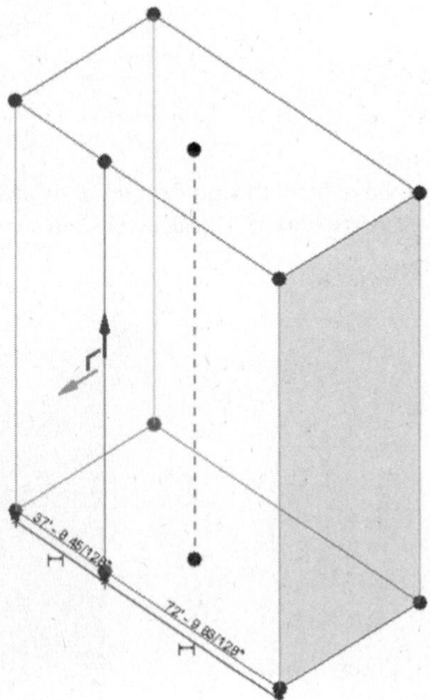

FIGURE 8.39
Adding an edge to a form

8. Once the edge has been added, you can push or pull the face adjacent to the new edge, as shown in Figure 8.40. Click the Modify button, and then select the face to the left of the edge you created in the previous step. Press and drag the green control arrow to move the face back into the extruded form.

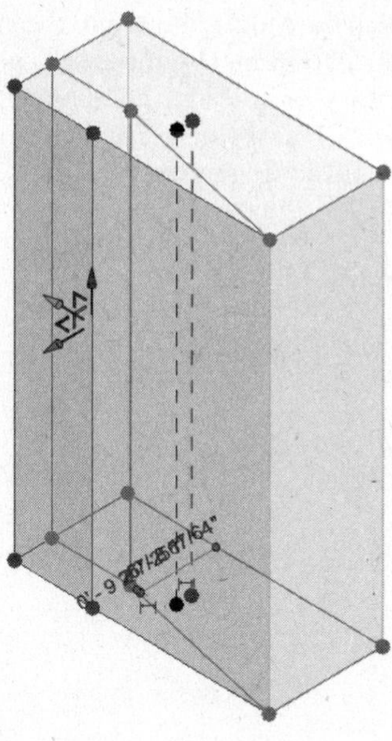

FIGURE 8.40
Pushing the face

9. Select the overall mass form again, and then click the Add Profile tool on the Form Element panel in the ribbon. You'll get the same ghosted line as you did to create the edge, but this time it will be the circumference of your element—essentially representing the profile at that point. Click to place it as shown in Figure 8.41.

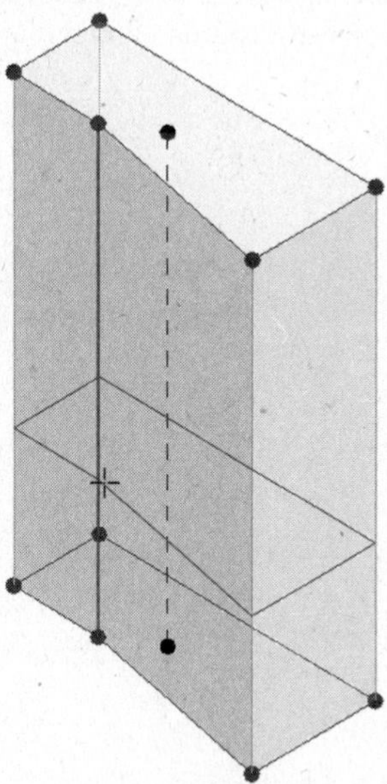

FIGURE 8.41
Adding a profile to the form

10. Again, click the Modify button in the ribbon, and then select the edge at the upper left of the extruded form. Use the green control arrow to pull the edge away from the mass form. Pushing or pulling a point or single edge will create curved and warped surfaces (Figure 8.42). This is fine because the form that you're creating can be rationalized later when you are adding a pattern to the surface.

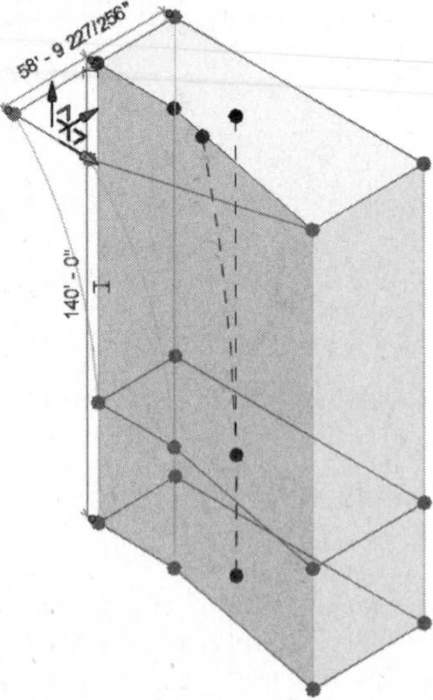

FIGURE 8.42
Pulling the edge to create a warped surface

11. Click the Add Edge button in the contextual tab of the ribbon, and then click the vertices indicated in Figure 8.43 in the order they are numbered. Doing so will force the warped faces to become triangulated and planar, because three points define a plane.

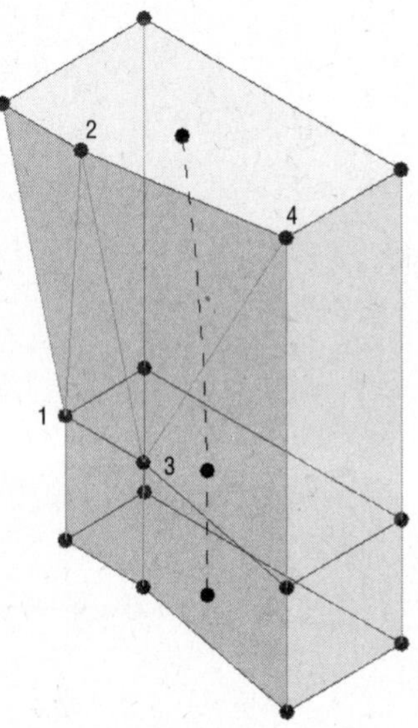

FIGURE 8.43
Adding more edges to eliminate warped surfaces

12. Select the edge at the upper right of the mass form and use the red control arrow to pull it away from the form, as shown in Figure 8.44. Again, it's not necessary to maintain the exact dimensions of what you see here; it's about trying to keep the proportions appropriate. This is what free-form massing is all about!

FIGURE 8.44
Pulling the upper edge

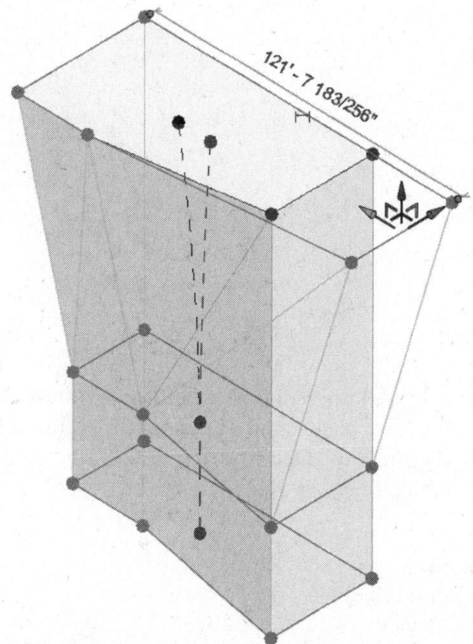

> **ESCAPE THE MADNESS**
>
> By now, you're probably tired of constantly clicking the Modify button in the ribbon when you need to jump between commands to explore the free-form modeling processes. An easier solution is to simply press the Esc key to return to the Modify state.

Dissolving and Rebuilding

Now, let's say you have come to a point in your design exploration when you would like to simplify the mass form you've created and start exploring some other alternatives. The tool to perform this function is called Dissolve. Using the Dissolve function will remove the mass solid and leave behind the profiles that define the solid. The dot in the center of each plane is a control that will allow you to edit the elevation, rotation, and location of each profile.

Continue with the `c08-Massing-2-Start.rvt` or `c08-Massing-2-Start-Metric.rvt` file you used for the previous exercise, and follow these steps:

1. In a 3D view, select the entire form and then click Dissolve on the Form Element panel in the ribbon. Only the profiles will remain, as shown in Figure 8.45.

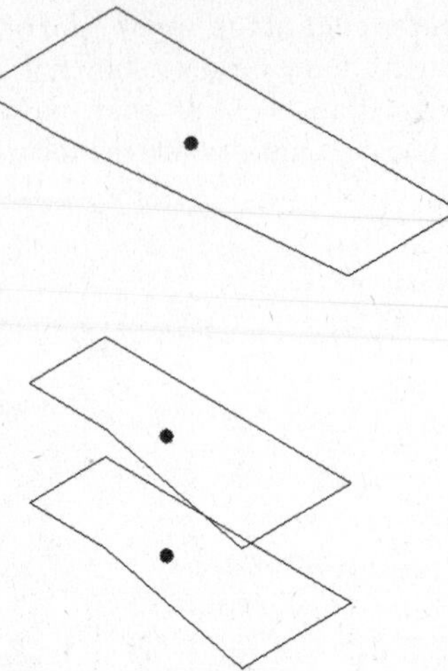

FIGURE 8.45
Using Dissolve to remove the mass solid

2. Select all the remaining profiles and then click Create Form ➤ Solid Form. This will stitch the form back together in a way that interpolates the shape as more of a lofted blend (Figure 8.46). Once the new shape is created, you can add more profiles or edit the shape using the tools we just reviewed.

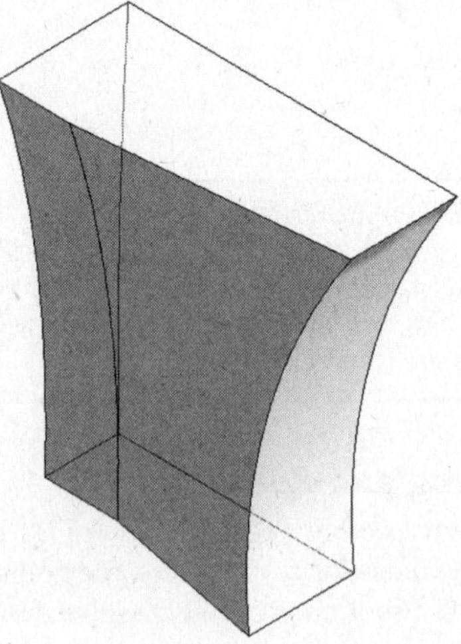

FIGURE 8.46
Making a lofted blend from three profiles

There are a few other ways to generate shapes using the profiles you just created. For instance, if you select only two profiles at a time, then you'll get a form like the one in Figure 8.47. This form was created by first selecting the bottom and middle profiles and then creating the form. Then the middle and upper profiles were selected and another form was created. The result is straight—rather than curved—interpolation between the profiles.

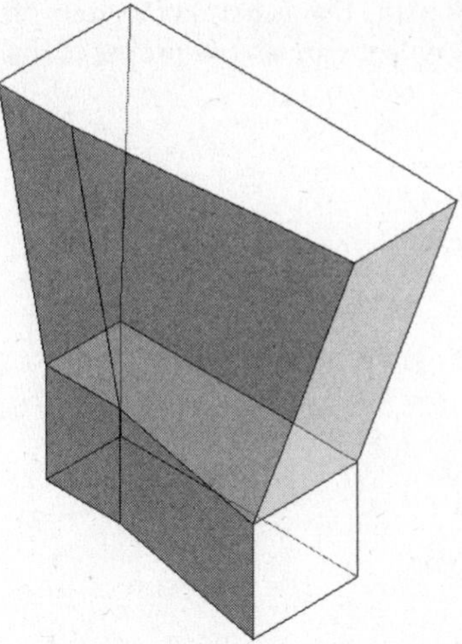

FIGURE 8.47
Making a blend from two profiles at a time

As another way to generate form using these profiles, you can alter the shape of the profiles before you create the form again. In the next steps, you will delete the straight edges along one side of the profiles and then define a curved edge.

3. Start by deleting the existing edges along the right side (you'll have to tab to select just the edges), as shown in Figure 8.48.

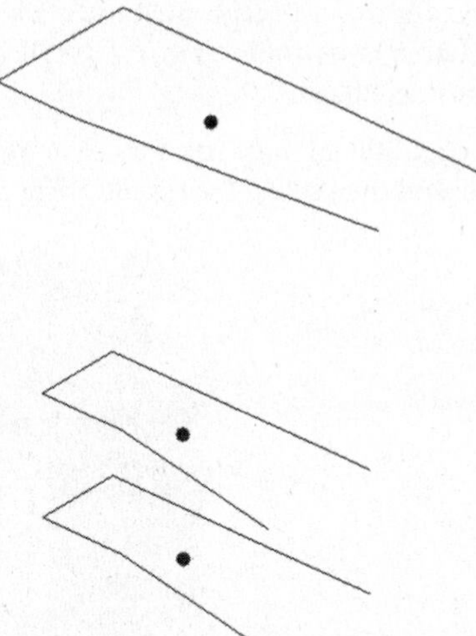

FIGURE 8.48
Deleting the right edge to modify the profile

Now you'll want to draw a fillet arc to rejoin the two remaining edges. Before you can draw the arc, you first have to define the right work plane.

4. Click the Set command from the Work Plane panel. Highlight the control point in the center of the profile, and press the Tab key to cycle through your options until you get a

work plane that is parallel to your profile (Figure 8.49). Click to select. Now you'll be able to draw your arc on the proper plane.

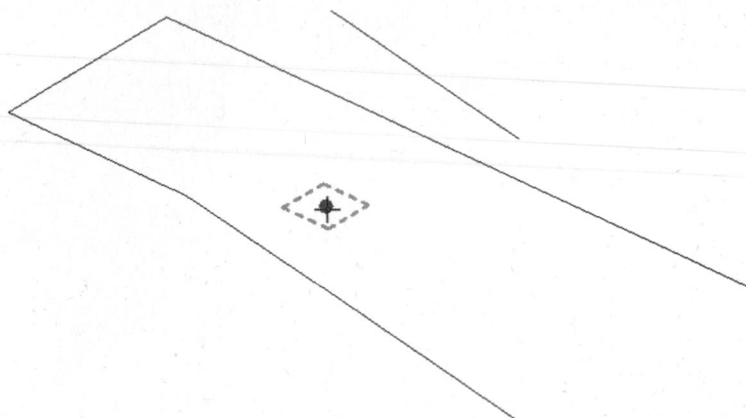

FIGURE 8.49
Selecting the work plane

5. From the Draw panel in the ribbon, choose the Fillet Arc tool. Click each edge on either side of the open end, and then click again to set the arc in place. Once the work plane is selected, you'll be able to draw additional model lines. In this example, you're using a fillet arc to connect the lines. You'll do the same thing for the other two shapes.
6. Repeat steps 4 and 5 for the other two profiles.
7. Select the lower two profiles and click Create Form ➤ Solid Form. Then do the same with the upper two profiles. Finally, you'll want to remove any blends by adding an edge to the opposing edges.

Creating additional mass solids is easy. You can select an existing face, as shown in Figure 8.50, and then select the Create Form command.

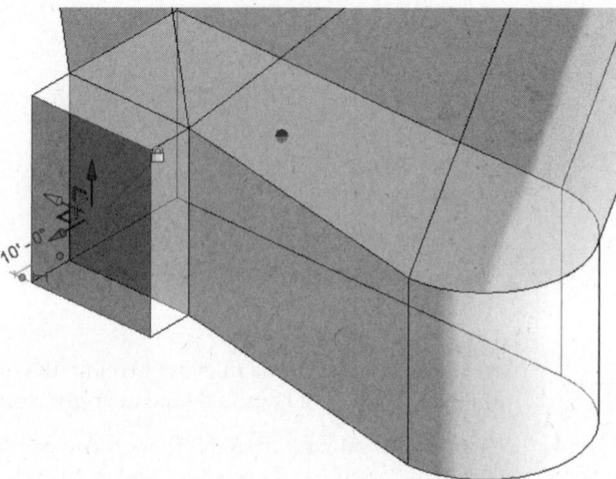

FIGURE 8.50
Creating additional mass forms

The same tools were used to create the form shown in Figure 8.51. Click the Finish Mass command in the contextual tab of the ribbon and return to the regular project environment.

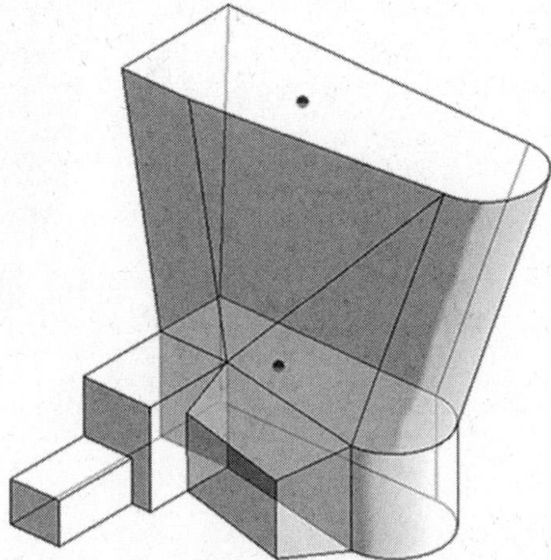

FIGURE 8.51
Creating another form

Once you're out of In-Place Massing mode, you'll notice that if you select the model, many shape handles simultaneously appear in the form of solid blue arrowheads (Figure 8.52). You can use shape handles to push and pull your solid mass, but you won't be able to modify edges or vertices without reentering In-Place Massing mode.

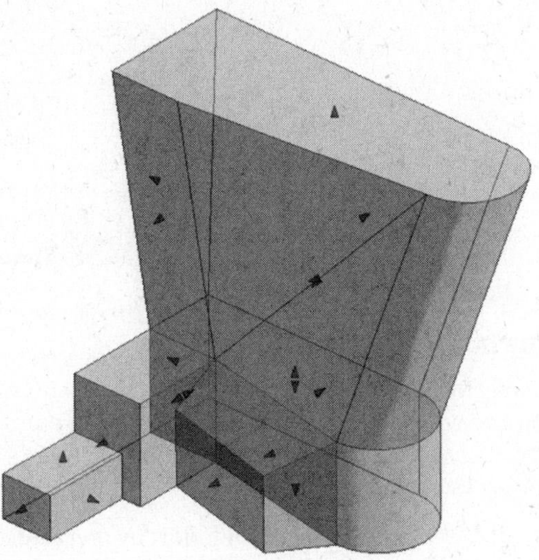

FIGURE 8.52
Using shape handles

Figure 8.53 shows the finished mass in a perspective view. Both solids and voids can be used to complete a mass form. Whereas solids will add more geometry, voids will remove geometry from your mass.

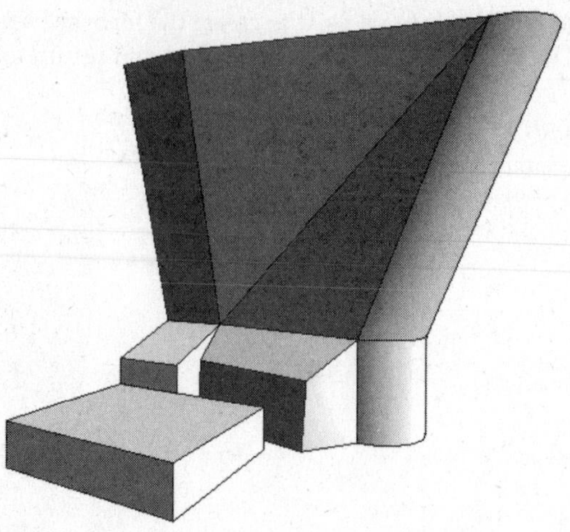

FIGURE 8.53
The finished form

To demonstrate this, we'll return to In-Place Massing mode and create another face on the top of the existing form (Figure 8.54).

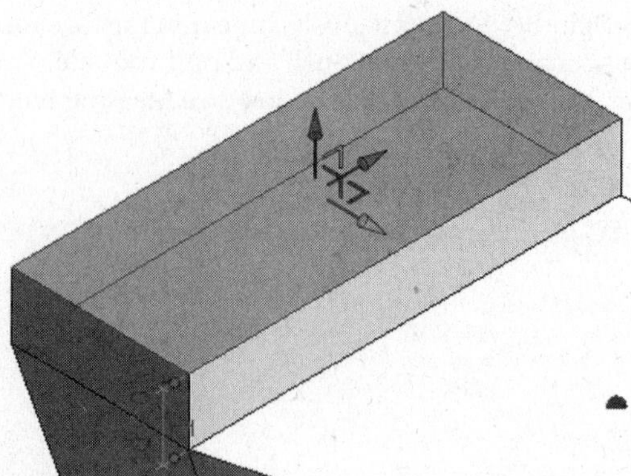

FIGURE 8.54
Creating another form

STARTING VOIDS AS SOLIDS

If you create the void as a void, it will immediately cut the solid mass and become invisible. This can be annoying when you're trying to resolve your design and want to selectively cut after you've intuitively resolved a design idea. Fortunately, there's another way to create the form as a void.

Follow these steps:

1. Rather than creating a void, start by creating a solid of a different color, to keep things clear during your design iteration. You can simply give the new solid a different material type to change the color.
2. Select the solid mass and convert it to a void by changing the Solid/Void property in the Properties palette, as shown in Figure 8.55.

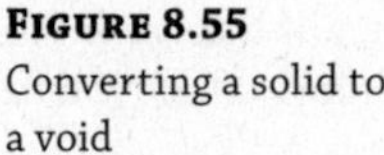

FIGURE 8.55
Converting a solid to a void

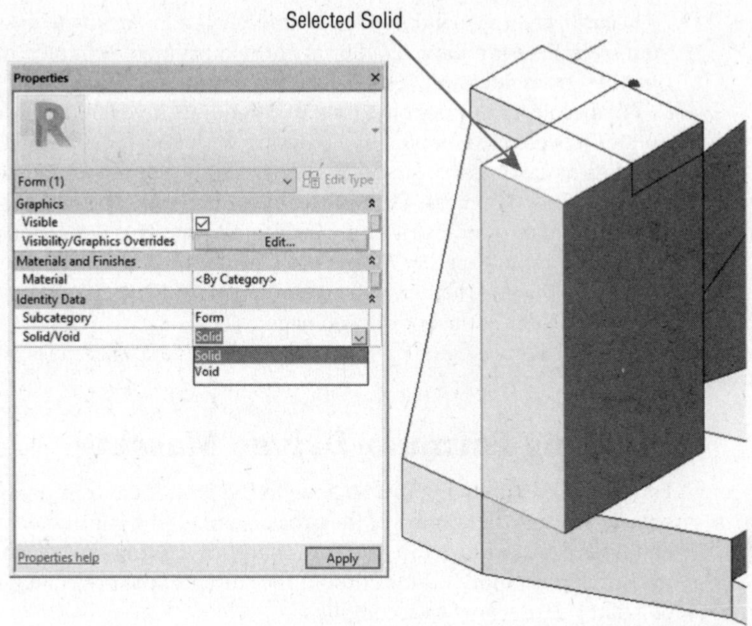

Figure 8.56 shows the result of the void cutting the solid. Note how the form on the left side of the image has changed from Figure 8.53. Keep in mind that if you want to convert the void back to a solid, you'll have to uncut any geometry that was being cut by the void. But the nice thing about this technique (converting solids to voids and then cutting) is that you've selectively cut only the solids that you wanted to cut. Had you originally modeled the void as a void, you would have found that the void was cutting many solids and you'd have had to uncut solids that weren't even overlapping with the void!

FIGURE 8.56
Cutting the void

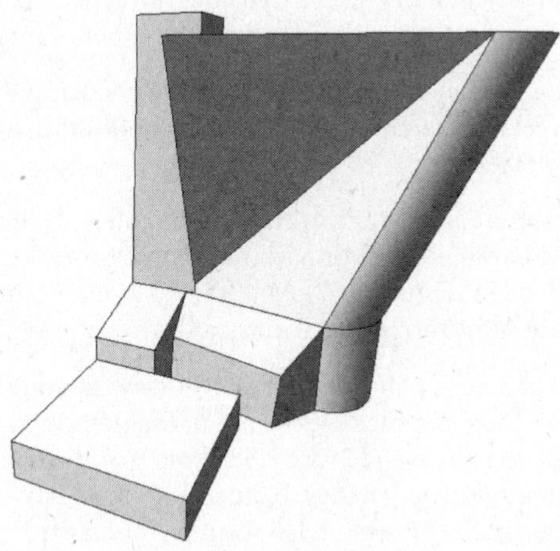

Overall, creating solid masses intuitively is a great way to establish, analyze, and visualize your overall design idea. As you saw previously in the chapter, mass floors allow you to even quantify gross floor areas before you've committed to geometry.

Furthermore, it's possible to put different intuitive massing ideas inside different design options (covered in Chapter 10, "Working with Phasing, Groups, and Design Options") so that many ideas can live in a single Revit project file. Simply initiate worksharing and create worksets for each study mass. Multiple team members will be able to see one another's work at the same time and in context with their design ideas. This is the holistic kind of team approach to design information that makes massing a unique and valuable design tool. If you'd like to investigate this file further, you can download the file `c08-Massing-2-Finished.rvt` from the Chapter 8 folder of the book's web page.

Next, we'll investigate parametric and formulaic solid mass creation in the Family Editor.

Creating Formula-Driven Massing

Formula-driven massing can be done in the project environment, but the challenge is that you have to work in the context of the project, and all the parameters, formulas, reference planes, and lines can start to get in the way. Therefore, having the option of creating form-driven masses in the Family Editor without the clutter of the project environment can help you focus on what you're trying to accomplish.

In this section of the chapter, we will show you two different methods for creating formula-driven massing. First, you will create a generic model family and then load it into the project environment as part of an in-place mass. Second, you will create a conceptual mass family to observe the differences in modeling tools and how they will affect your design explorations.

Creating a Generic Model Mass Family

Although it's possible to create complex forms as a generic model in the Family Editor, they do not behave as masses when you place them in the project. You can assign standard walls, curtain walls, and roofs to the faces, but you can't add patterns, create mass floors, or even schedule the results as a mass. The tools you will use in this exercise are the tools available for building most other 3D content using extrusions, sweeps, and blends. It's good to understand how to use these tools so you're familiar with all the types of modeling in Revit software.

1. Open a Generic Model template by choosing the Application button ➢ New ➢ Family. Select either `Generic Model.rft` or `Metric Generic Model.rft` from the list of default templates.

   In some cases, you can change the category of a family by clicking the Family Category and Parameters button in the ribbon; however, you can't convert a generic model family to a mass (Figure 8.57). You'll need to maintain the family as a Generic Model and then place it into an in-place mass within a project.

2. Go to a floor plan reference-level view in your family. From the Create tab in the ribbon, click the Reference Line tool (not Reference Plane). Draw a reference line along the y-axis (up), as shown in Figure 8.58. Note that the reference line is drawn from the intersection of the reference planes. Note also that we have increased the line weight of Reference Lines in the Object Styles settings for clarity.

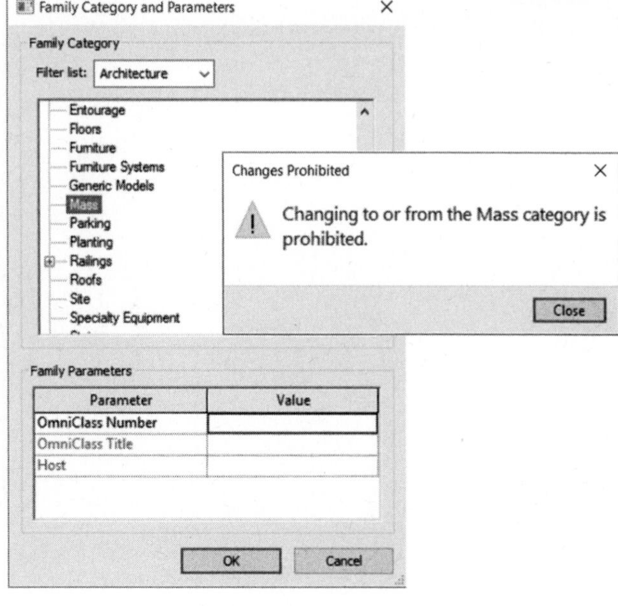

FIGURE 8.57
Message box explaining you can't change the category to Mass

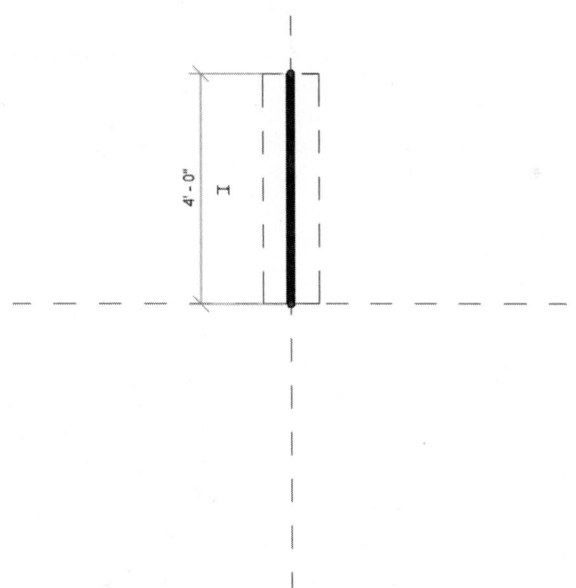

FIGURE 8.58
First reference line

3. Draw another reference line in a downward direction along the y-axis (Figure 8.59). These reference lines will control the angular "twist" in your finished family.

   Now you're going to create a blend that will be associated with the reference lines you just created. The bottom of the blend will be associated with the first reference line, and the top of the blend will be associated with the second reference line.

FIGURE 8.59
Second reference line

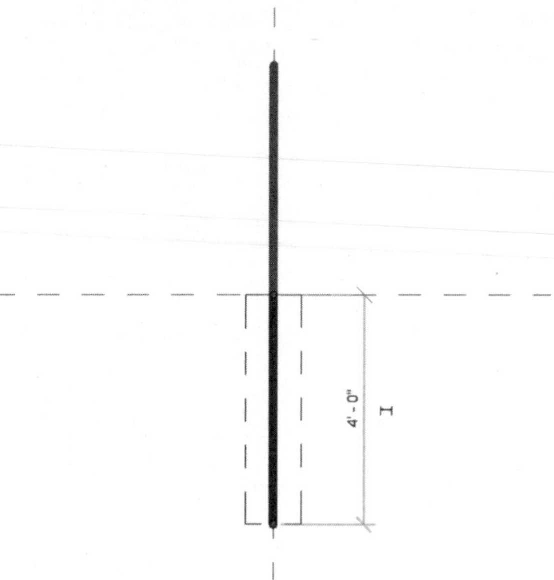

4. From the Create tab in the ribbon, click the Blend tool. By default, you will start by defining the bottom profile of the blend. Click the Set command in the Work Plane panel of the contextual tab in the ribbon. Choose the Pick A Plane option (Figure 8.60), click OK, and then click the first reference line you drew.

FIGURE 8.60
Setting the work plane

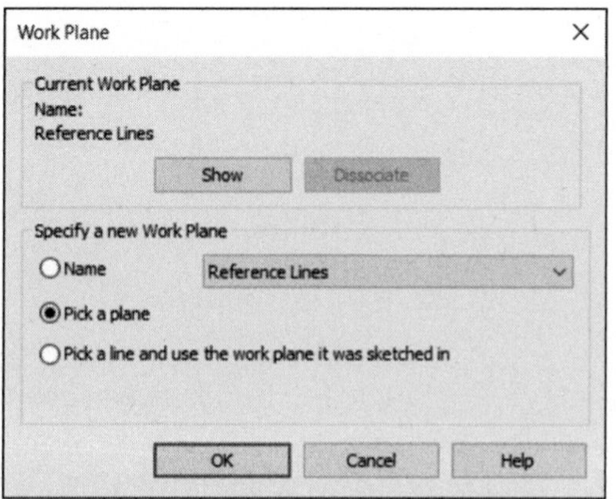

5. From the Draw panel in the contextual tab of the ribbon, choose the Rectangle command and sketch a 20′ (6 m) square in the plan view.

6. Switch to the Annotate tab in the ribbon and click the Aligned dimension tool. Place a dimension on both vertical lines in the square sketch and the vertical reference line—not the reference plane. Click an empty area of the plan view to finish the dimension command. Highlight the finished dimension and click the EQ icon on the dimension string. The plan view should look like the image in Figure 8.61.

FIGURE 8.61
Establish equality dimensions.

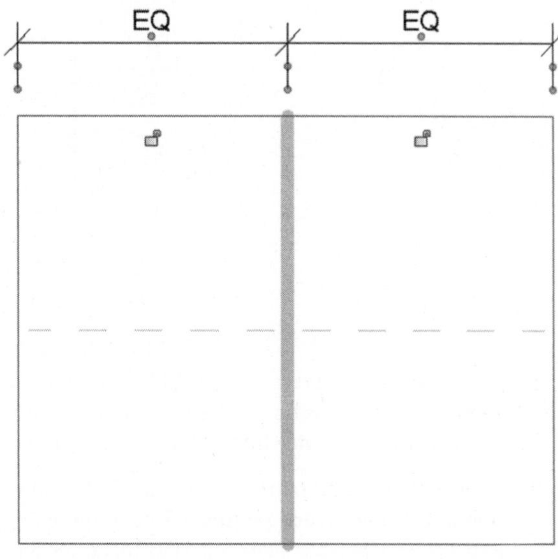

7. Use the Aligned dimension tool again to create dimensions for the vertical and horizontal sketch lines. This time, you'll want to select the Reference Plane as your center dimension. The goal is to make the box equal on all sides and equidistant from the reference planes (Figure 8.62). After you place the two dimensions, select them, and from the Options bar go to the Label drop-down list, and then choose <Add Parameter>. In the Parameter Properties dialog box, set the following values:

   - Name: **BW**
   - Type or Instance: **Instance**
   - Edit Tooltip: **Bottom width of blend**

   The plan view should now look similar to the image in Figure 8.62. You can adjust the value of the BW parameter by clicking the Family Types icon from the Properties panel in the ribbon.

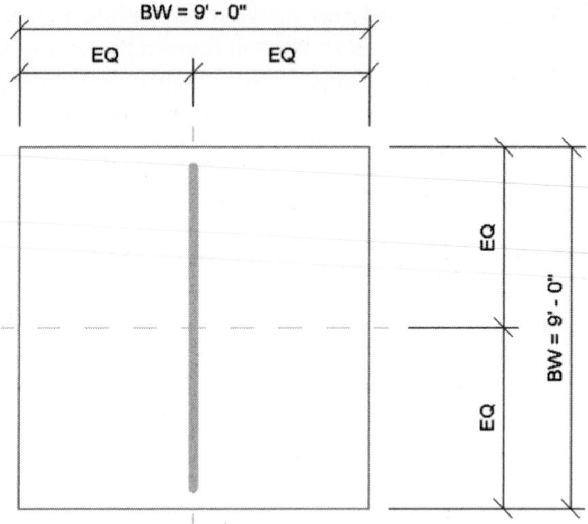

FIGURE 8.62 Parameter dimensions added to the bottom sketch

8. From the contextual tab in the ribbon, choose Edit Top. Click the Set command in the Work Plane panel, choose the Pick A Plane option, click OK, and then click the second (downward) reference line you drew in step 3.

9. Repeat steps 5 and 6 for the top sketch. Equally distribute the overall dimensions in relation to the downward reference line and create the parameters as you did previously, but name the parameter TW (Top Width), as shown in Figure 8.63.

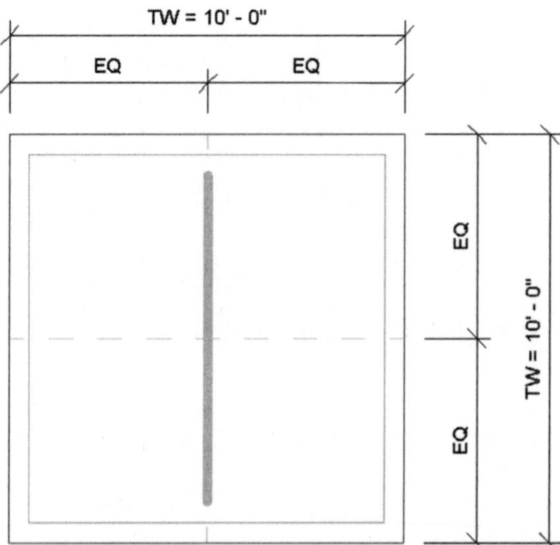

FIGURE 8.63 Top width parameters and sketch

10. In the Properties palette, locate the property named Second End. Click the small button at the right end of the row—this is the Associate Family Parameter button. Click the Add Parameter button. In the Parameter Properties dialog box, set the following values:
    - Name: **H**
    - Type or Instance: **Instance**
    - Edit Tooltip: **Height of blend**
11. Click OK to create the parameter and close the open dialog boxes. Now select Finish Family (the green check mark) from the contextual tab in the ribbon to complete the blended form.
12. You should take a moment to test that the reference lines control the top and bottom sketches of the blend. Activate the default 3D view, select the reference line to highlight it, and then move the end of the reference line. Be careful when moving the reference line. The goal is to test the parameters, so when you move the line, do so by dragging the line slightly. You'll see the resulting forms change. Don't use the Move command—it will break the parameters. The other end remains associated with the intersection of the default reference planes, and the top and bottom sketches rotate, as shown in Figure 8.64.

FIGURE 8.64
Twisting the blend with reference lines

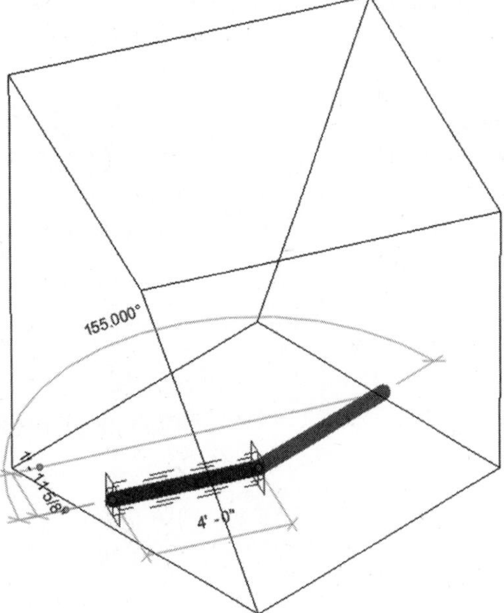

13. From a plan view, move the reference lines so that they're no longer on top of the reference planes. From the Annotate tab, click the Angular dimension tool and place dimensions between each reference line and the vertical reference plane.

14. Select the upper angular dimension, and from the Label drop-down list in the Options bar choose <Add Parameter>. Create a new family parameter with the following values:

   - Name: **BA**
   - Type or Instance: **Instance**
   - Edit Tooltip: **Bottom angle, counterclockwise from 90**

   Furthermore, you can add parameters to control the top and bottom angles of the blend. We've called these instance parameters BA and TA (for bottom angle and top angle, respectively).

15. Select the lower angular dimension and again choose <Add Parameter> from the Label drop-down list. Create another new parameter with the following values:

   - Name: **TA**
   - Type or Instance: **Instance**
   - Edit Tooltip: **Top angle, clockwise from 270**

   Figure 8.65 also shows all the parameters that control this blend. From the Create tab in the ribbon, click the Family Types icon. Go ahead and test the parameter values by changing angles in the Properties palette and clicking the Apply button (or moving your mouse out of the palette). The form should rotate and twist. This is how you will interact with the form after you load it into a project environment.

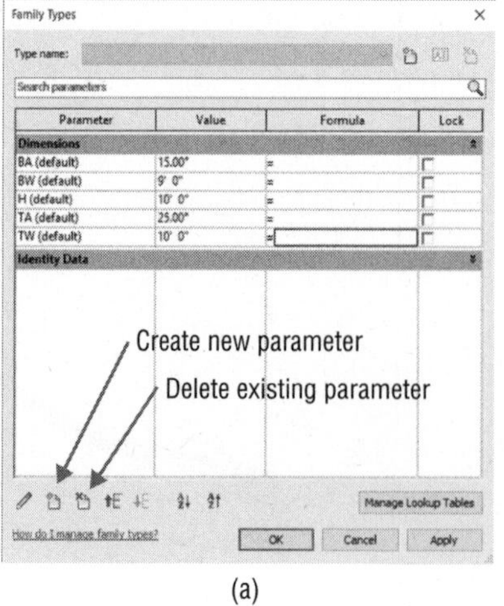

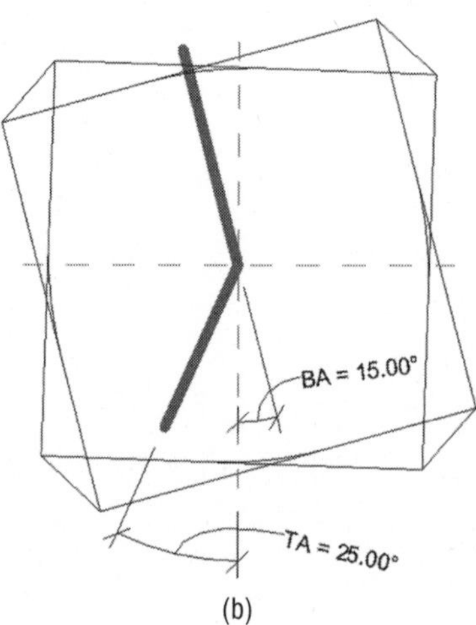

FIGURE 8.65
Test the dimensional parameters before continuing.

16. You're going to use the edges of this blend to drive the geometry that you're going to create, but since you don't want to see this blend, turn it into a void. With the blend selected, use the Solid/Void drop-down list in the Properties palette (Figure 8.66). The blend form will change color to a yellow-orange if you set your visual style of the view to Shaded.

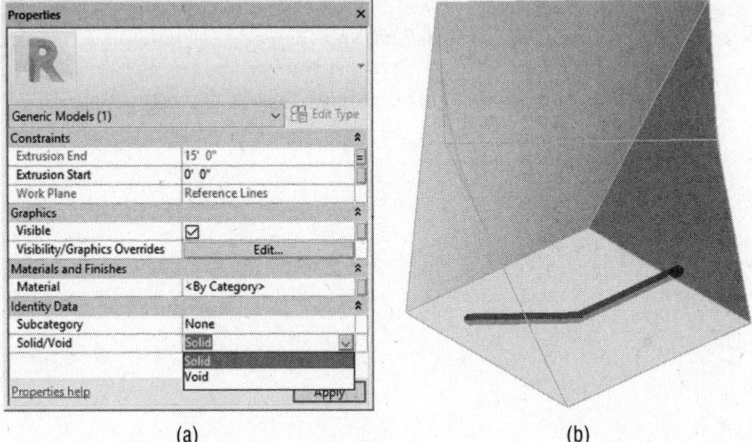

FIGURE 8.66
Turning a solid into a void

17. From the Create tab in the ribbon, click the Sweep tool. Select Pick Path (not Sketch Path) in the contextual tab of the ribbon to select the edges of the blend previously created. Pick the edges of the blend, as shown in Figure 8.67. Note the location of the sketch plane along the lower rear edge. This is because it is the first edge selected.

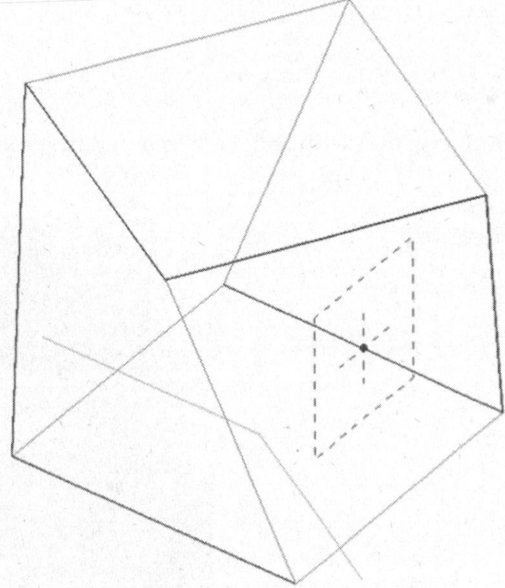

FIGURE 8.67
Selecting the edges of the blend

18. Once you select the edges of the blend, click the green check mark to finish the path. Click the Select Profile icon and select Edit Profile from the contextual tab in the ribbon. Doing so allows you to sketch the profile in direct context of the selected edges.

19. Sketch a profile 5′-6″ (1.7 m) wide × 4′-6″ (1.4 m) high. After you sketch the profile, add aligned dimensions, and then add parameters to the profile width and height as you've done previously in this exercise. We've called the instance parameters PW (profile width) and PH (profile height), respectively (Figure 8.68).

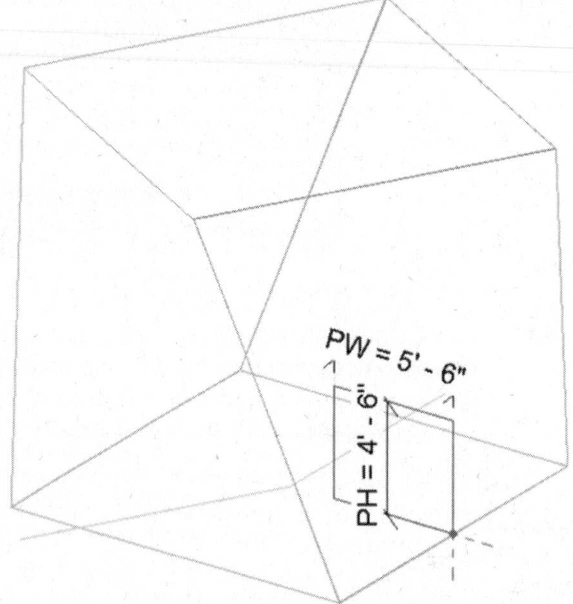

FIGURE 8.68
Adding parameters to the profile width and height

20. Finish the sketch and the sweep, and the profile will generate as shown in Figure 8.69.

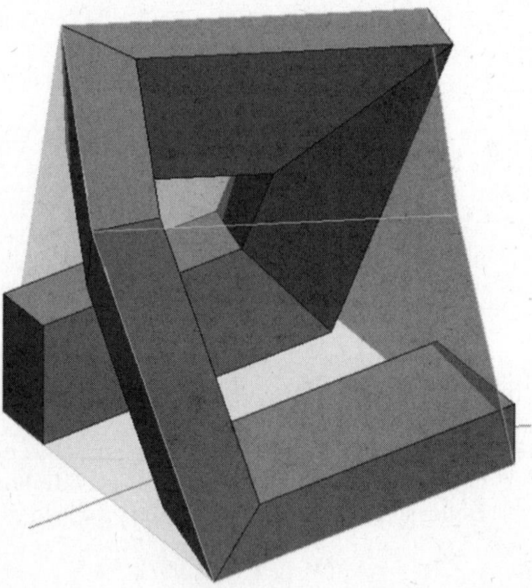

FIGURE 8.69
The finished sweep

Save the family on your computer as `Generic Model Mass.rfa`. With the form created, it's now possible to load this family into your project environment and place it within an in-place mass. To do this, follow these steps:

1. Open a new project using the default Architecture template, and begin by creating an in-place mass from the Conceptual Mass panel of the Massing & Site tab. Name the mass Generic Mass.
2. While still in the In-Place Mass Sketch mode, toggle back to the mass family you just created and click Load Into Project from the ribbon. You should immediately be ready to place an instance of the loaded family, but if not, switch to the Create tab in the ribbon and click Component. Place the generic family as a component into your in-place mass.
3. Select the component you just inserted, and notice in the Properties palette that all the attributes you gave to the mass are available for you to edit. Using these parameters, set the values as follows:
   - BW: 160′ (49 m)
   - TW: 140′ (43 m)
   - H: 160′ (49 m)
   - PW: 40′ (12 m)
   - PH: 65′ (20 m)
   - BA: 22°
   - TA: 22°
4. Now finish the in-place mass by clicking the green check mark, which is the Finish Mass button. Even though this is a generic model family, because you've placed it during In-Place Mass mode, the software treats it as a mass.
5. Activate the South elevation view and add 15 additional levels. Space the levels every 10′ (3 m) apart, as shown in Figure 8.70, so that there are levels that extend across the entire elevation of your massing.

FIGURE 8.70
Adding levels that extend across the elevation of your massing

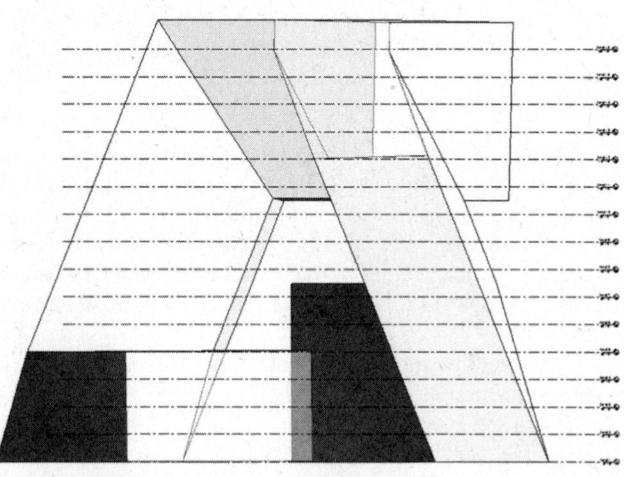

6. Select the mass and click the Mass Floors button on the contextual tab in the ribbon. Select and check the boxes for all the levels, and then click OK to apply the changes and close the dialog box.
7. Select the mass, and on the contextual tab in the ribbon click Edit In-Place. Hover over one of the surfaces on the generic model, press the Tab key until the status bar indicates a face, and then click to select it. In the contextual tab of the ribbon, click Divide Surface. With the face still selected, go to the Type Selector and choose Triangle (Flat). You'll also be able to associate patterns and pattern-based components with your generic massing family (Figure 8.71). Continue to do this for each vertical surface on the generic model, and then click Finish Mass.

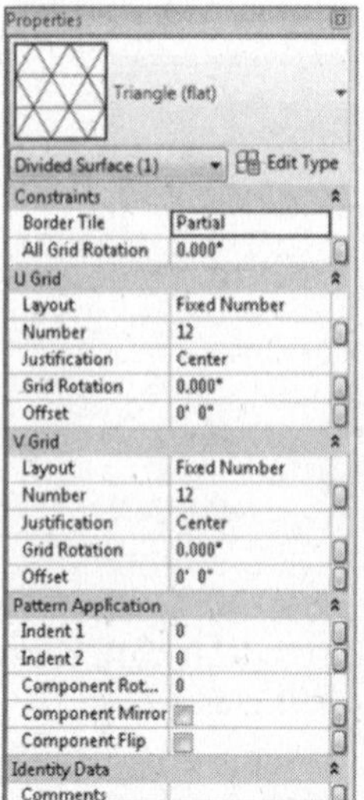

FIGURE 8.71
Adding pattern-based components

8. Finally, switch to the Architecture tab in the ribbon and click Roof ➢ Roof By Face. Click the horizontal surfaces of the mass and then click Create Roof in the contextual tab of the ribbon. Click the Modify button to complete the command. Figure 8.72 shows four perspective views of the completed massing study, all created with the familiar geometry toolset.

We've also rendered the model, as shown in Figure 8.73. The results are quite interesting, and you'll still have the ability to modify the underlying parametric family and then rehost the faces. You'll also be able to schedule the volume, surface, and floor area of the mass.

You can download and further investigate the files that were used to create this exercise in the Chapter 8 folder of the book's web page. Download the project file `c08_Parametric_Generic_Massing_Finish.rvt`, which contains the in-place massing and the loaded generic element.

Now let's begin to investigate how to create parametric massing in the Family Editor using the conventional massing tools.

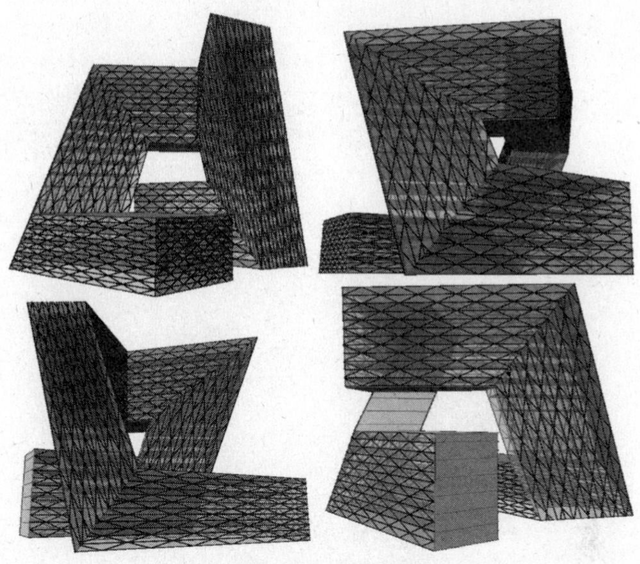

FIGURE 8.72
Perspective views

FIGURE 8.73
Rendering of the generic massing project

Real World Scenario

DESIGN BY VISUAL PROGRAMMING

A new trend in design methodology is becoming more popular—the use of visual programming tools to generate complex forms. We are not talking about parametric design as an aesthetic philosophy, but rather the tools employed to achieve the results. The term "visual programming" refers to the use of a graphic UI to drive code-based scripting that will generate complex geometrical forms. One new tool that is now available and bundled with Revit 2017 is called Dynamo. The website dynamobim.org has learning material, free downloads, and a discussion forum. *Mastering Autodesk Revit 2017 for Architecture* has a brand new section dedicated to Dynamo; check out Chapter 21!

Continues

Continued

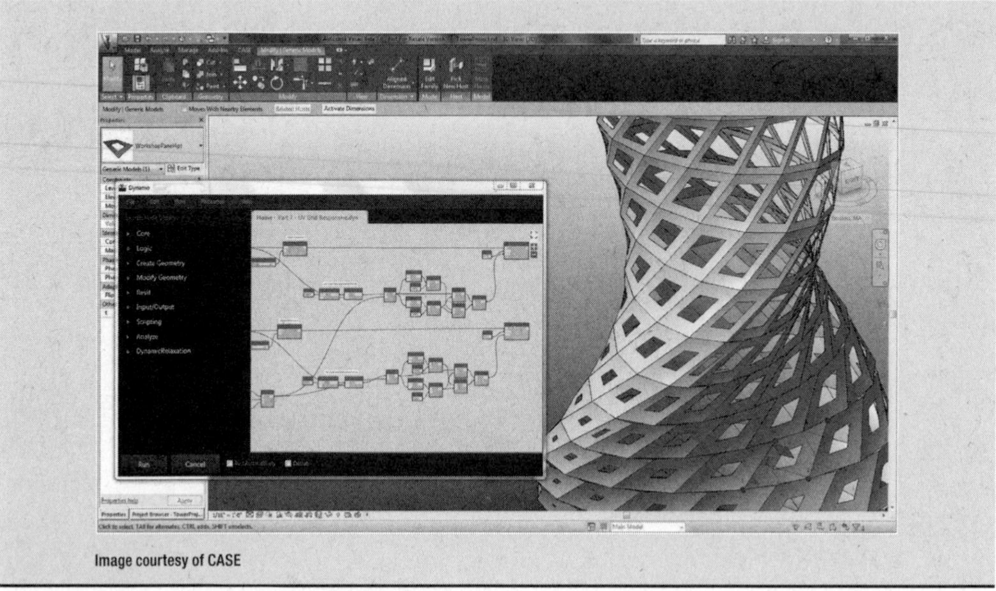

Image courtesy of CASE

Creating a Complex Mass Family

In the previous exercise, we used the basic modeling tools that are available for most family categories. The tools available in the conceptual massing environment are somewhat different. In the next exercise, you will open a conceptual mass family that we have started with a number of datum objects and embedded formulas.

Overall, the UI is not too dissimilar from the project environment. It's as if you're creating masses in-place—except that you're not in the project environment; you're in the Family Editor. One significant difference that you can see is that there is a single level and two reference planes, which also define the origin for a massing family (Figure 8.74). Keep in mind that when you reload this family into your project, it will update relative to the origin in the family.

FIGURE 8.74
The Massing user interface

In the past, the ability to parametrically control objects in the massing editor was done using reference planes and reference lines. The Revit development team introduced reference point elements in 2010, which add another level of control to model elements. Point elements allow for Cartesian X, Y, Z, as well as rotational control.

With all complex and parametrically controlled families, we think it's best to understand complex families to get the basic rules down first. In this case, the rules are the parameters and formulas that will control a twisting, tapering tower.

To begin this exercise, download and open the file `c08-Formula-Massing-Start.rfa` or `c08-Formula-Massing-Start-Metric.rfa` from the book's web page. Open the Family Types dialog box and observe the parameters and formulas that are included with the exercise file, as shown in Figure 8.75.

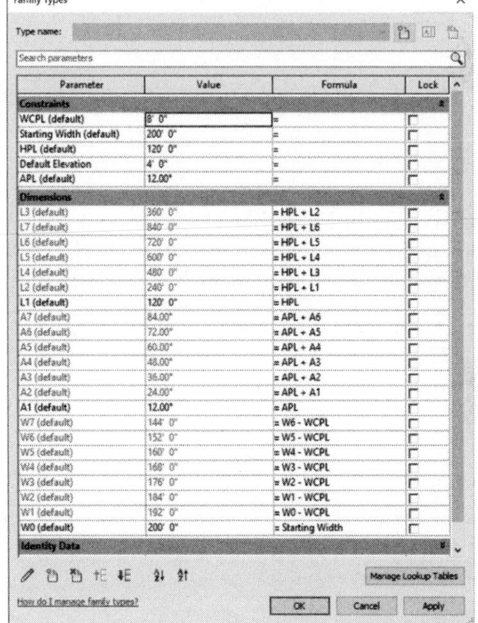

FIGURE 8.75
The Family Types dialog box

We will briefly describe how this conceptual mass family was created so you can get an overview of the process and employ similar techniques on your own designs. Similar to the steps you performed in the previous exercise, reference lines were used to generate a square sketch at the first reference level.

The reference lines were dimensioned with equality constraints based on the reference planes defining the origin. Overall dimensions were placed and associated with the W0 parameter (Figure 8.76). W0 is shorthand for the width dimension on the 0-level.

FIGURE 8.76
Dimensioned reference lines

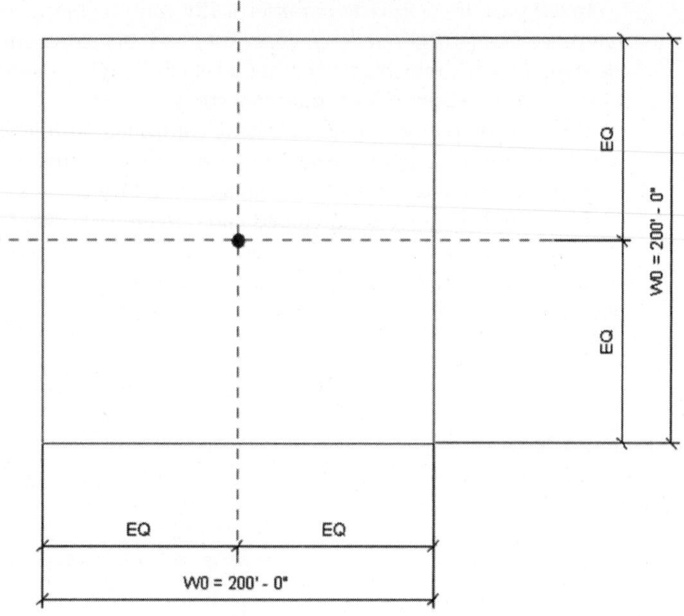

Activating the South Elevation, you can see seven reference points were placed at the intersection of the default reference planes. Each reference point was then elevated manually by dragging the up arrow to move it away from the other overlapping point elements (Figure 8.77).

FIGURE 8.77
Moving the point element

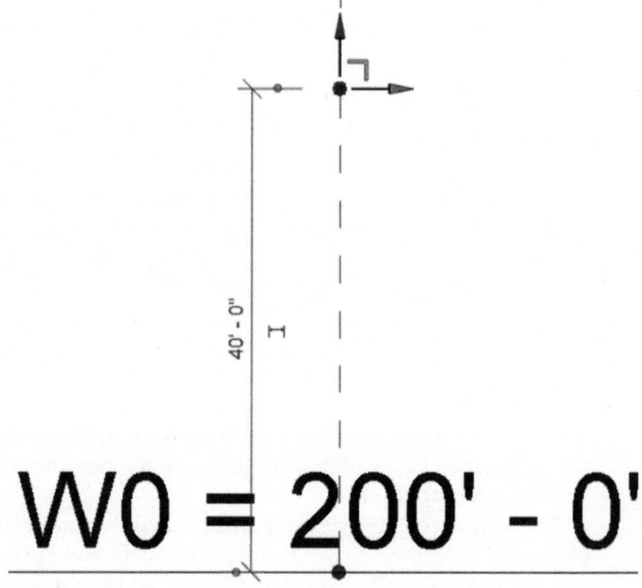

When you select a reference point, you have the option to associate any of the point's properties with any of the family parameters developed for this conceptual mass. This is done by clicking the small button in the Properties palette next to each property value. For each reference point in this exercise file, the Offset property was associated with a corresponding L-parameter (Figure 8.78). The L-parameters refer to the level number of each of your point elements. The first point element is associated with the parameter named L1 because it is reference Level 1. The second point is associated with L2, and so on. When you associate a property with a family parameter, you'll notice that the button fills with a small equal sign.

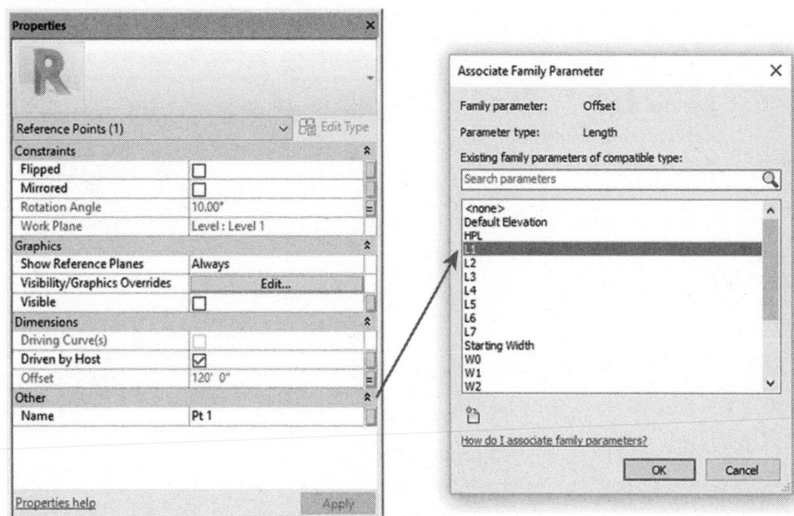

FIGURE 8.78
Adding a parameter to the point element

By default, the reference point elements are just spherical nodes. Their reference planes are not visible. To make them a little more usable for your modeling purposes, you can set them to display their internal reference planes. With a reference point selected, in the Properties palette you will find a property called Show Reference Planes; set it to Always, and the reference planes of the point elements will be visible (Figure 8.79).

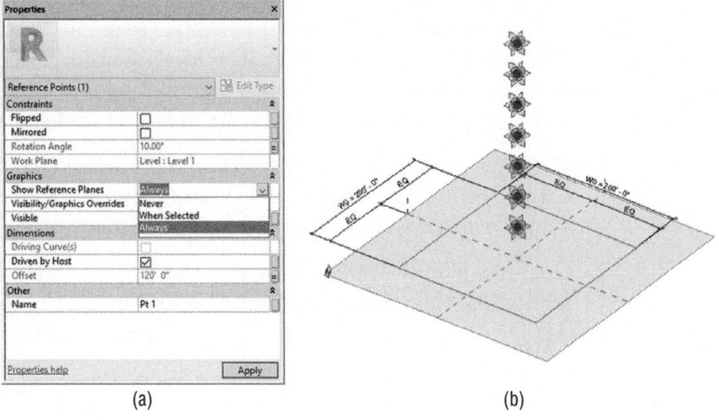

FIGURE 8.79
Selecting Always next to Show Reference Planes

Next, the Rotation Angle property of each reference point was associated with the corresponding family parameter. Point 1 was associated with A1 (angle 1), Point 2 with A2, and so on.

We then used the Set command in the Work Plane panel to use each point's horizontal plane as the working reference to draw a square sketch of reference lines associated with each point. Each sketch was dimensioned in a similar way to the first sketch. The dimensions for the sketch associated with Point 1 are W1, the Point 2 sketch dimensions are W2, and so on. Switching to the 3D with Dimensions view, you can see this (Figure 8.80).

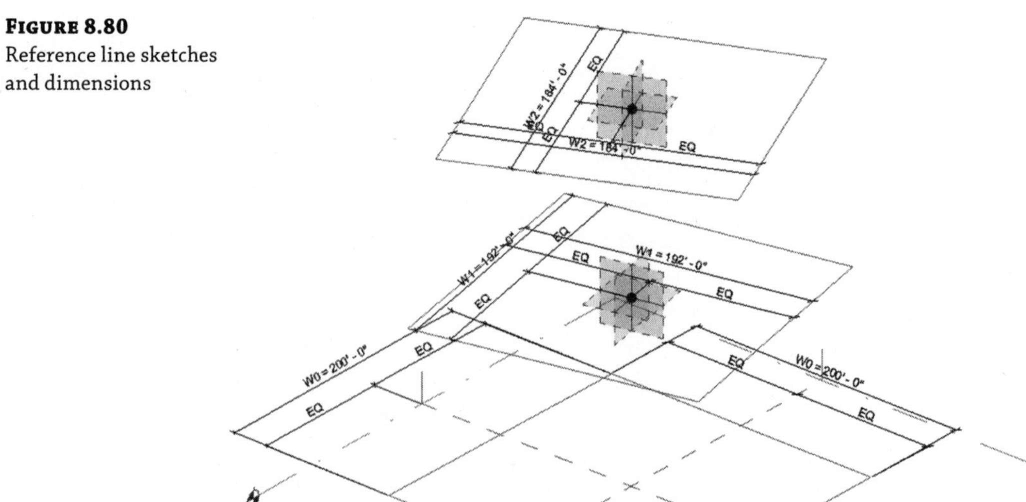

FIGURE 8.80
Reference line sketches and dimensions

For clarity, we've hidden the dimensions in the default 3D view so that you can see all the reference lines and point elements. If you'd like to see all the dimensions configured in this exercise file, activate the 3D view named 3D with Dimensions.

Now let's begin to create some mass forms using the parametrically driven framework of reference lines in this exercise file. Follow these steps to get started:

1. While pressing the Ctrl key, select all the square reference line sketches, and then click Create Form ➤ Solid Form on the Form panel in the ribbon. Although this will look like a simple extrusion, it's actually a blend with many profiles.

2. Open the Family Types dialog box and begin to test the results before loading the family into the project (Figure 8.81). Set the WCPL and APL parameters to 0 and click Apply.

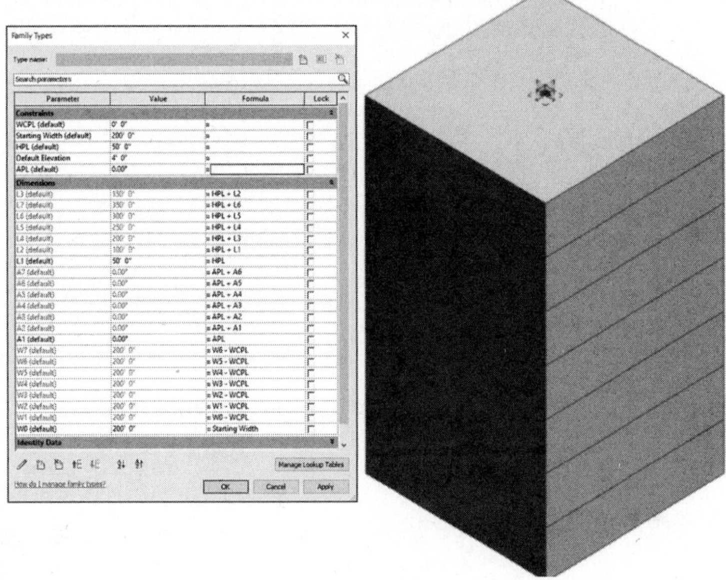

FIGURE 8.81
Testing the parameters driving the form

3. Test the parameter that controls the distance between levels by increasing the HPL instance parameter (which stands for height per level). If you hover the mouse pointer over these parameters, a tooltip will appear telling you what they mean.
4. Now test the ability of the shape to taper (Figure 8.82). Do so by increasing the WCPL instance parameter (which stands for width control per level).

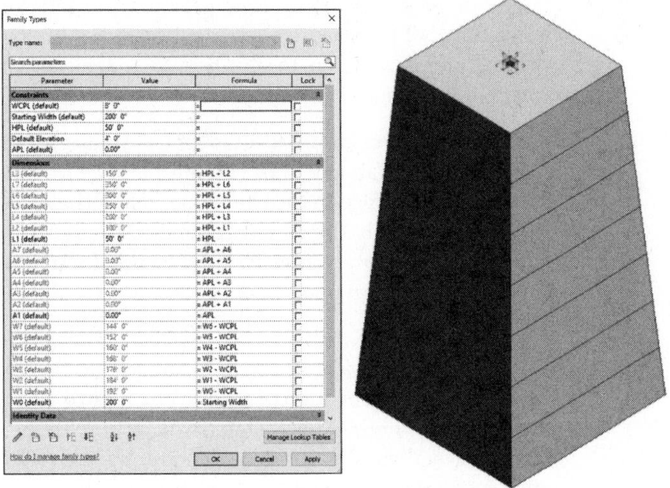

FIGURE 8.82
Increasing the WCPL instance parameter

5. Next, test the parameters that control the amount of angular twist per level (Figure 8.83). Do so by increasing the APL parameter (which stands for angle per level).

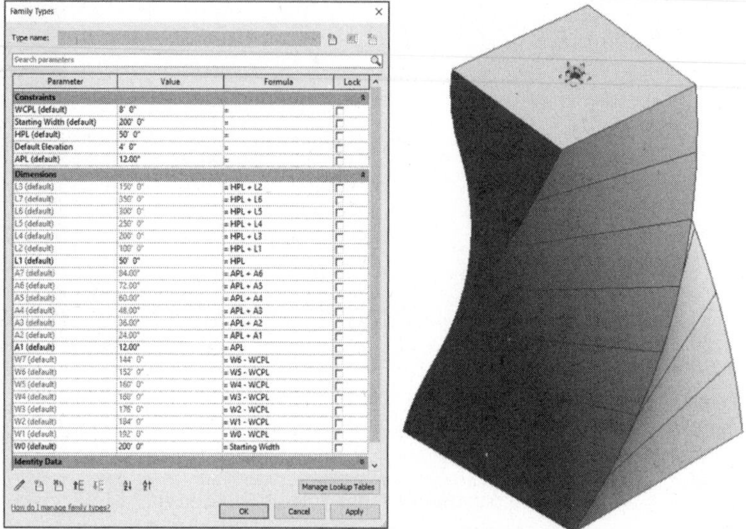

FIGURE 8.83
Increasing the APL parameter

6. Start a new project using the default Architectural template. Switch back to the mass family, and click Load Into Project from the ribbon. Place an instance of the conceptual mass family in the project environment. When you select the massing family, you'll be given access to all of its parameters in the Properties dialog box. You can quickly and easily test the massing parameters to significantly increase the height, width, taper, and incremental rotation of the massing family.

7. Switch back to the family file. Hover the mouse pointer near the edge of any face on the mass, press the Tab key until you highlight a surface, and then click to select a surface. Click Divide Surface in the contextual tab of the ribbon. From the Type Selector, choose Rhomboid to apply the pattern, as shown in Figure 8.84. You will notice in the Properties palette that you can change the properties of the Rhomboid pattern to adjust the pattern to meet your design needs. Repeat this process for the remaining vertical surfaces of the mass.

8. Click Load Into Project to reload the mass into the project. Activate the South elevation view and set the elevation of the Level 2 datum object to 30′ (9 m). Select Level 2 and click the Array tool in the Modify tab of the ribbon. In the Options bar, uncheck Group and Associate, set Number to 60, and choose the Move To 2nd option. In the elevation, click once, move the mouse pointer upward, and then type 15′ (4.5 m). This will create a quick configuration of levels for your tower design. Note that no plans will be created when you copy or array levels.

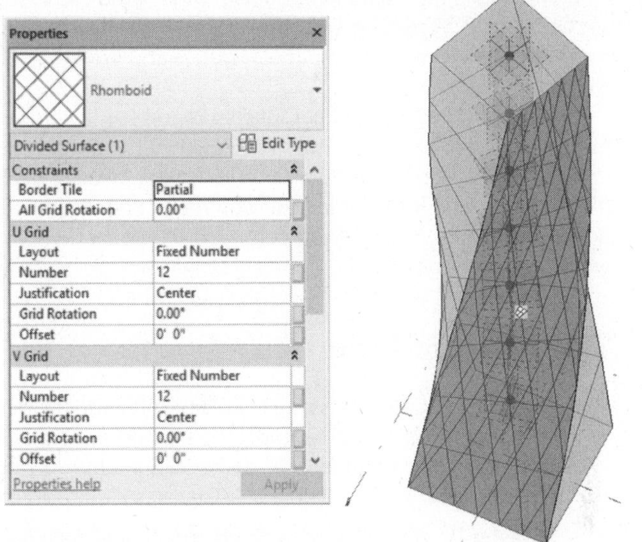

FIGURE 8.84
Adding patterns to the face of your mass

9. Select the mass form and click Mass Floors in the contextual tab of the ribbon. Select and check all the levels in the project, and then click OK to apply the changes and close the dialog box. In Figure 8.85, we applied a section box to the 3D view to illustrate the mass floors.

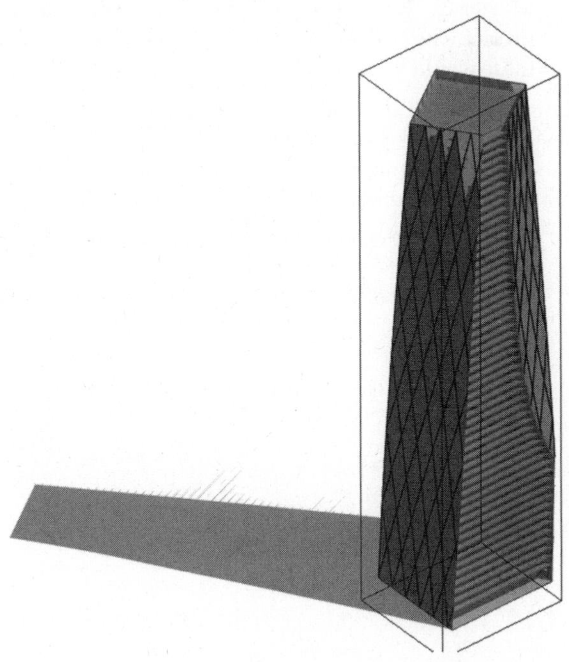

FIGURE 8.85
Floor area faces

If you want to learn more about expanding the use of the divided surfaces on massing forms, see Chapter 12, "Creating Walls and Curtain Walls." In that chapter, we discuss the modeling techniques to create custom panel families and how to apply them to pattern-based curtain walls.

Creating interesting and complex massing studies that can be parametrically controlled isn't just a skill developed over time. The rules that you develop to make and reiterate your designs are also carefully considered aesthetic choices to make decisions rather than blobs! To see this file, go to the Chapter 8 folder and download `c08-Formula-Massing-Project_Finished.rvt`. Be sure to turn on Show Mass Form And Floors on the Massing & Site tab if it's not turned on when you open the file.

The Bottom Line

Create and schedule massing studies. Starting the design process with actual building elements can lead to a lot of unexpected frustration. Walls lead to rooms, which get room tags and eventually scheduled. But if you've failed to fulfill the client's program, you'll wonder where to start over!

Master It You're faced with creating some design studies of a large hospital complex. How would you go about creating a Revit project that would allow you to create a massing study and schedule it against the design client's program?

Know when to use solid and surface masses. Solid masses and surface masses can both be used to maintain relationships to host geometry like walls and roofs, but surface masses can't be volumetrically scheduled or contain floor area faces.

Master It You've been asked to create a complex canopy system for the entry to a hotel project. The system will consist of a complex wave of triangular panels. What kind of mass would you create?

Use mathematical formulas for massing. Not all massing is going to involve intuitive, in-the-moment decision making. By discovering the underlying rules that express a form, you can create the formulas that can iterate and manipulate your massing study. So rather than manually manipulating the mass, you manipulate the formulas related to your mass.

Master It What's the best way to discover and create these formulas?

Chapter 9

Conceptual Design and Design Analysis

In this chapter, we will take a further look at the Autodesk® Revit® Architecture Conceptual Design tools and how you can leverage them for sustainable design analysis. We'll also explore a few other tools, some of which use BIM geometry to support design analysis.

Most building design starts with some simple concepts and forms. Will the building be tall or long? Curved or rectilinear? How will those shapes affect sustainable design concepts like solar gain, daylighting, and energy consumption? To perform these kinds of analyses and explore the initial ideas for building form in Revit, we use masses. In the previous chapter, we discussed how to create several kinds of massing. In this chapter, we'll explore a different type of mass called a Conceptual Mass and use that to generate sustainable design analysis.

In this chapter, you'll learn to:

- Embrace energy analysis concepts
- Create a conceptual mass
- Analyze your model for energy performance

Analysis for Sustainability

Environmentally thoughtful design strategies have been around for millennia, but the practice of sustainable design with quantifiable metrics has seen substantial growth in the past decade. Sustainable design practices can help address many issues, among them energy use, access to natural daylight, human health and productivity, and resource conservation. One of the principal goals of sustainable design is to reduce a building's overall resource use. This can be measured in the building's carbon footprint (`www.architecture2030.org`) or the net amount of carbon dioxide emitted by a building through its energy use.

Before we delve into discussing any specific workflows involving BIM and sustainable design analysis, it's important to recognize that many concepts are both interdependent and cumulative. The more sustainable methods you can incorporate into a project, the "greener" the project becomes.

Take the example of building orientation, glazing, and daylighting. Designing your building in the optimal orientation, using the right glass in the correct amount and location, and integrating sunshading into the project to optimize the use of natural light all build on each other. Using these three strategies together makes a building operate more efficiently while allowing occupants access to plenty of natural light. The amount of usable daylight you might capture will be greatly reduced with the application of highly reflective glass or if the building's orientation is inappropriate for the geography. The appropriateness of any of these individual strategies and the benefits depend on building type and climate.

Revit software has similar characteristics. Because it is a parametric modeler, all the parts are interrelated. Understanding and capitalizing on these relationships typically takes numerous iterations that span multiple projects. Optimizing the integrated strategies and technologies for a high-performance design requires an understanding of how they work together to deliver the best potential. That is where Revit comes in—allowing the ability to iterate and analyze faster than in a more traditional process. The process is built on the following methodology for reducing the energy consumption of buildings:

- Understand climate
- Reduce loads
- Use free energy
- Use efficient systems

Bad Modeling Has Bad Downstream Effects

Like poor ecology, poor modeling can have a negative impact downstream on team members and project stakeholders. If you are choosing to use your model for sustainable design analysis, remember that the more accurate you are in your modeling, the more accurate your results will be.

Conversely, a poorly assembled model will deliver inaccurate results. If you do not establish the proper materials in a daylighting model, for instance, you will not get the right reflectivity and therefore your daylighting study results will be inaccurate. If rooms and volumes are not established properly within the model, your energy performance calculations will be inaccurate. These faulty results may prompt you to make changes in your design that are incorrect or unnecessary.

It is a good idea to establish early on in your modeling process which sustainable design analyses you will be performing based on your model geometry. It is much easier to set the model up for successful analysis when you begin than it is to go back and have to make significant changes to the model to perform analysis.

Creating a Conceptual Mass

To begin performing any kind of analysis, you first need a building design. In the previous chapter, we discussed how to make and schedule building massing using different methods. In this chapter, we're going to step through one more method of conceptual massing in order to generate building geometry and use that to understand the sustainable design tools.

Since we are using the conceptual massing tools in Revit, you're first going to create an *adaptive component*. This type of family can be inserted into a mass to modify its shape, either by application of parameters or by being pushed and pulled in the view window. It will serve as a sort of skeleton, or *rig*, to drive the geometry in a more fluid way. In the twisting tower form exercise from the previous chapter, you used a simple square form that was tapered and twisted. In this chapter's massing exercise, you will create a slightly more complex plan profile, but—more important—that profile will be dynamically controlled by four vertical splines instead of simply twisting the plan shape.

Modeling an Adaptive Component

The first thing you're going to create is an adaptive component family that will act as a diaphragm for designing the building shape. You'll then import this family into a mass and use the solid form tool to wrap a stack of these shapes. This example is a bit advanced and an error in the steps can cause incorrect results, so please follow the steps closely.

To get started:

1. From the Application menu, choose New ➢ Family. Use the family template named `Generic Model Adaptive.rft` or `Metric Generic Model Adaptive.rft`. Switch to the Create tab and click Set in the Work Plane panel. In the view window, click the 3D level line to set the level as the active reference plane. The 3D Level line is the black line represented by a dash-dot pattern and forms the horizontal plane in the view (Figure 9.1). It will look like a normal 2D level line but shown in the 3D view.

   If you prefer to see the active plane in which you will begin modeling, click the Show button in the Work Plane panel.

FIGURE 9.1
Adaptive model default view

2. On the Draw panel, select the Reference type and then the Point Element tool (Figure 9.2). In the view window, create four points. These points aren't location-specific; just lay them out in a way similar to what is shown in the figure. Exact layout isn't critical, but the order you place them in is. Place the points starting at the upper left and moving clockwise. These will later coincide with the object number of vertical elements that you'll create in the mass.

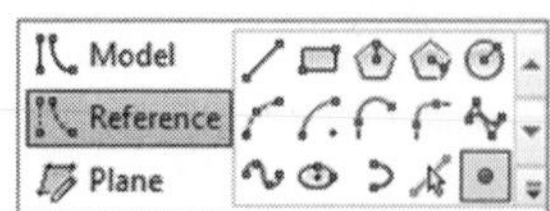

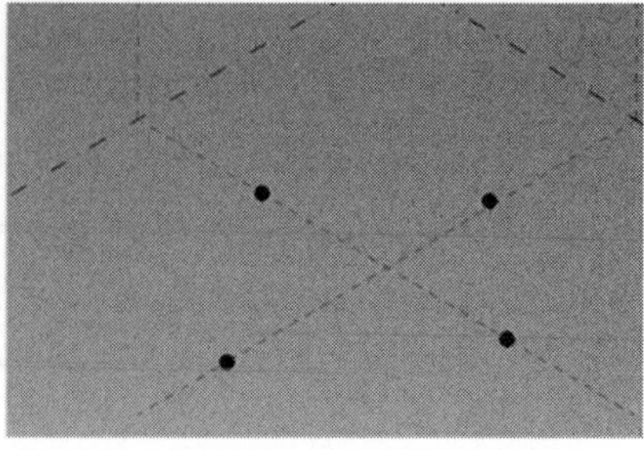

FIGURE 9.2
Placing reference points

3. Once all four points are placed, select all the points, and from the contextual tab in the ribbon, click the Make Adaptive tool.

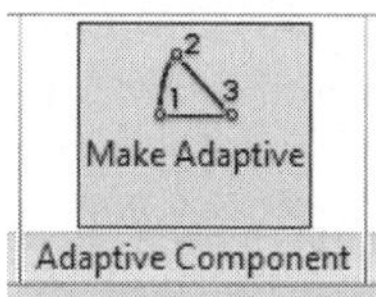

The points will become numbered in the order in which they were inserted, and each point will have its own reference planes (Figure 9.3).

FIGURE 9.3
Making points adaptive

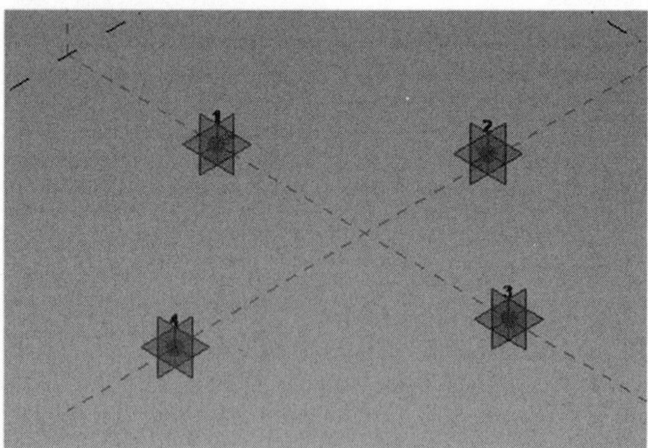

4. Now, from the Create tab click the Reference type; then choose the Line command. Make sure that 3D Snapping is enabled from the Options bar. The order in which you place the reference lines is critical to later steps, so connect the points in this order:

   1. Point 1 to Point 2
   2. Point 2 to Point 3

3. Point 4 to Point 3
4. Point 4 to Point 1

This sets the start and end point of each segment, which has an impact on how the Normalized Curve Parameter will act in the following steps.

Once you're finished, the four reference points form an enclosed shape (Figure 9.4). Once everything is connected, click the Modify button in the ribbon or press the Esc key twice to quit the Line command.

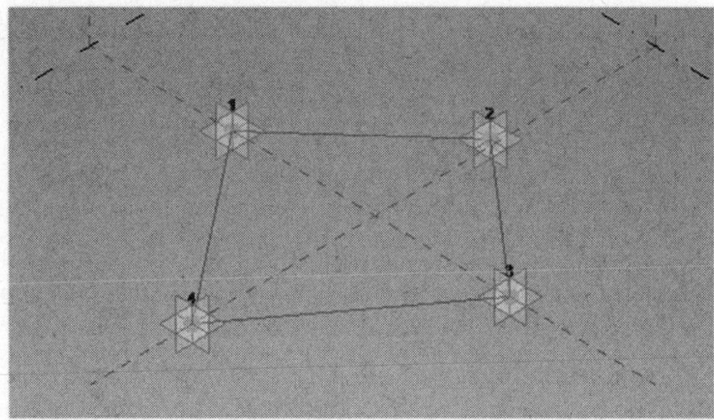

FIGURE 9.4
Connecting the four adaptive points

Now that you have all four points connected forming a rhomboid, you will create a set of points that will round one of the corners of the form. This rounded corner will be associated with a formula-based parameter so you can modify its radius within the mass to change the shape.

5. On the Create tab in the ribbon, click Reference again, and choose the Point Element command. Make sure you choose the **Draw On Face** option to the right of the Draw tools.

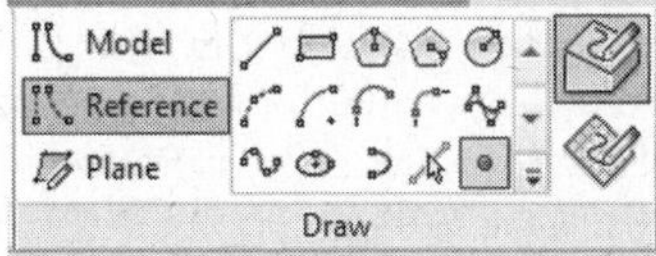

Add two points on the reference lines to each side of one of the corners. We've added points near the corner of Point 4, as illustrated in Figure 9.5. The order in which you add these points is not important to the exercise.

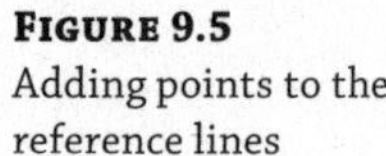

FIGURE 9.5
Adding points to the reference lines

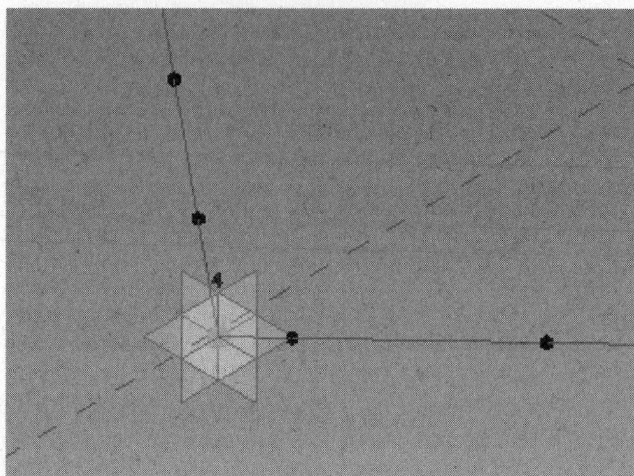

USING POINTS IN REVIT

There are several types of points in Revit, and it's a good idea to know the differences. In this exercise, we lead you through the creation of a few point types. Here's a list of the types and some of their uses:

- **Reference Points**: These are points that identify a specific X, Y, Z location in the conceptual design environment (adaptive components, conceptual masses, and the like). All reference points can be tied to parameters.
- **Driving Points**: These are reference points that control the geometry of a dependent spline. When you select these points, they will allow you to manipulate them with 3D controls. In Revit, these points will appear larger on the screen to distinguish them from the other points.
- **Hosted Points**: These are reference points that exist on a spline, line, surface, or some other element. Visually, they appear as smaller than driving points. Hosted points can be used to drive the manipulation of geometry.
- **Free Points**: These are reference points that are simply placed on a reference plane. Free points will show 3D controls when selected and are movable on their reference plane.

For the next step, you need to add a parameter to control the location of the points along the reference line. This will help form the radius of the curve. One of the default properties of a point in Revit is called **Normalized Curve Parameter**. This property is a ratio of the length of the host line expressed from 0.0 to 1.0. As an example of how to use this parameter, if you want to keep a point at the midpoint of a reference line, this property must always be 0.5.

NOTE If you select one of the placed points and you don't see the Normalized Curve Parameter property, you will need to delete the point and place it again; this time ensure that you select the Draw On Face option in the Draw panel of the ribbon.

To modify the Normalize Curve Parameter, continue with the steps.

6. Start with the point closest to the corner between points 4 and 1 (look ahead to Figure 9.7), and in the Properties palette locate the property named **Normalized Curve Parameter**. Click the small button to the right of the value field to pull up the Associate Family Parameter dialog box (Figure 9.6).

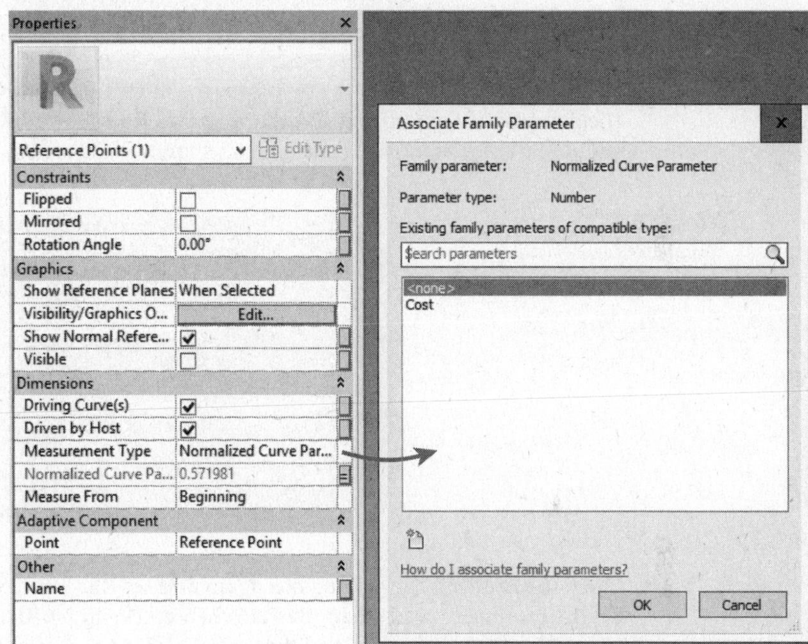

FIGURE 9.6
Adding a family parameter to the point

7. Click the Add Parameter button. This will open the Parameter Properties dialog box. Name the new parameter **Rad_A1**, and click OK to exit each of the dialog boxes. Giving the parameter this name is sufficient; don't worry about the other settings in the Parameter Properties dialog box. Once this is complete, move to the next point. Select the next point on that same line and repeat this process, naming the point **Rad_A2**.

8. On the Create tab, click the Family Types tool from the Properties panel. In the Family Types dialog box, you'll see the two parameters you've created so far. You want to add a formula that will set point A1 at half the distance between Point 4 and A2. In the Formula box for Rad_A1 add the formula **=Rad_A2 / 2** (Figure 9.7). Click OK to exit the dialog box.

FIGURE 9.7
Adding a family parameter to the point

Family Types

Type name:

Search parameters

Parameter	Value	Formula	Lock
Other			
Rad_A1	0.219921	=Rad_A2 / 2	
Rad_A2	0.439841	=	
Identity Data			

9. Repeat steps 6 and 7 with the points on the other line. For the other two points, select them as you did before and add the variables **Rad_B1** and **Rad_B2**. The parameters should be associated with the points as shown in Figure 9.8.

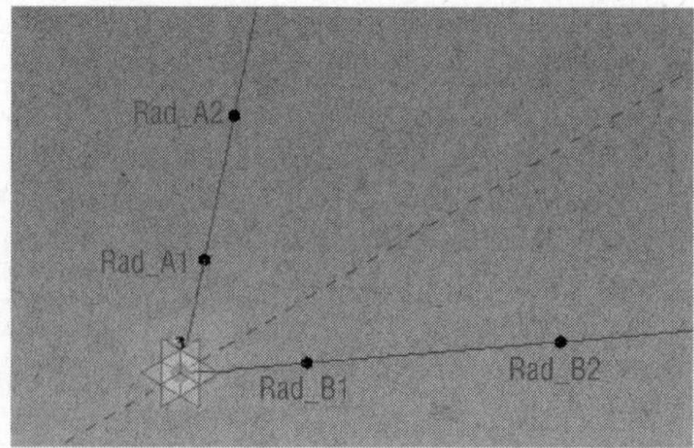

FIGURE 9.8
Parameters associated with points

10. Open the Family Types dialog box again and set **Rad_B2** equal to **Rad_A2**. For Rad_B1 set the formula to read **=Rad_B2 / 2**. When you've finished, the Family Types dialog box should have four variables and three formulas, as shown in Figure 9.9. You can test the formulas by changing the numbers in the Value column and clicking Apply each time. You should see the points move up and down the host reference line.

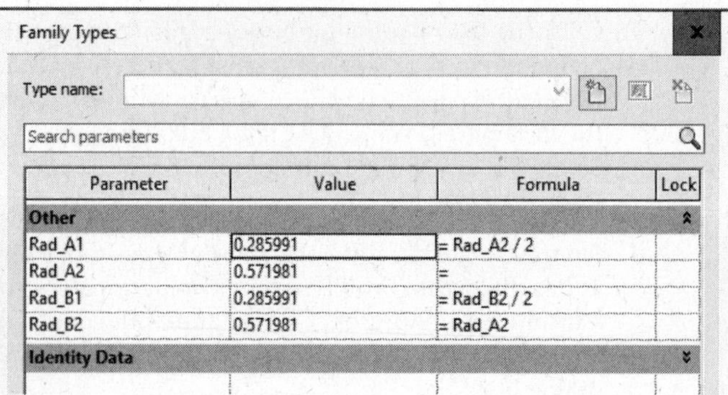

Family Types

Type name:

Search parameters

Parameter	Value	Formula	Lock
Other			
Rad_A1	0.285991	= Rad_A2 / 2	
Rad_A2	0.571981	=	
Rad_B1	0.285991	= Rad_B2 / 2	
Rad_B2	0.571981	= Rad_A2	
Identity Data			

FIGURE 9.9
Add formulas to control the point locations.

11. With the points and formulas in place, you're going to add a few additional elements to create the curve. Add another reference line between the two middle points (Rad_A1 and Rad_B1); be sure to select the 3D Snapping check box in the Options bar (Figure 9.10).

FIGURE 9.10
Add a reference line between the two middle points.

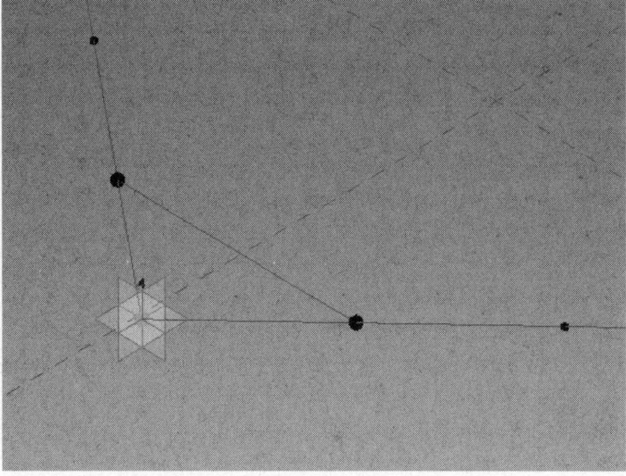

12. Switch to the Point Element command in the Draw panel, and then add a point to the middle of the reference line you added in the previous step.
13. In the Create tab, click the Model style and then select the Spline Through Points tool.

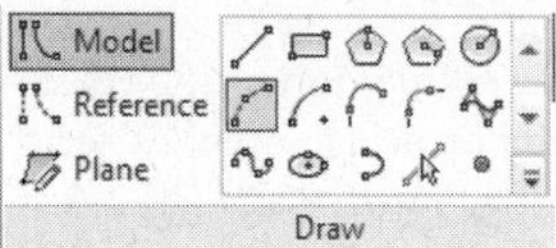

Connect the farther point, Rad_A2, to the midpoint of the line (the point you placed in step 12), to the point Rad_B2. The connected points should create an arc like the one shown in Figure 9.11.

FIGURE 9.11
Add the spline to connect the points.

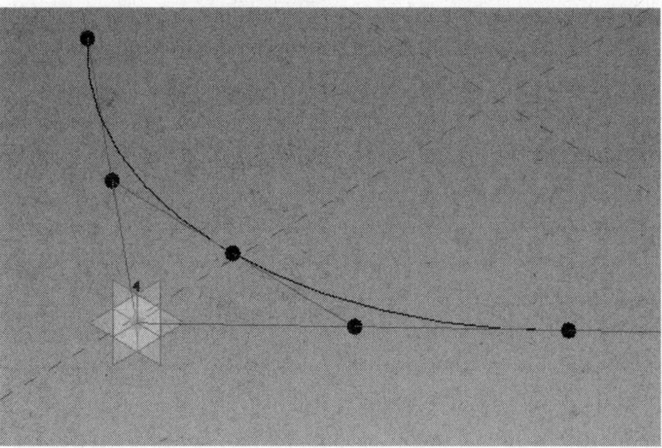

14. Make sure Model is still selected in the Create tab and choose the Line tool. Connect the arc you just created to the other three points, completing the shape now with model lines. The final form will look like Figure 9.12. The order of line placement is not important.

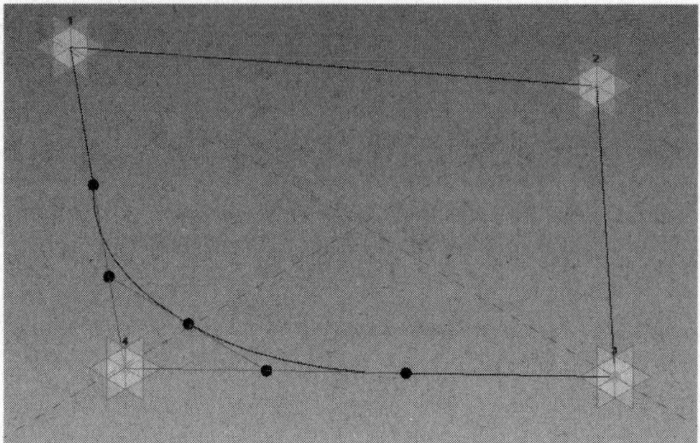

FIGURE 9.12
Adding model lines to connect the other points

15. As the final step to this sequence, you need to apply a surface to the points and lines. Select the model lines you just created. You can select them individually (select one and use the Tab+Select method) or select everything and then use the Filter tool to isolate Lines (Generic Model).

    Next, from the contextual tab in the ribbon, choose Create Form ➢ Solid Form. You'll be prompted with the option to create a solid or a plane. Choose the plane, which will be the option on the right (Figure 9.13). The result should look like the image to the right in the figure.

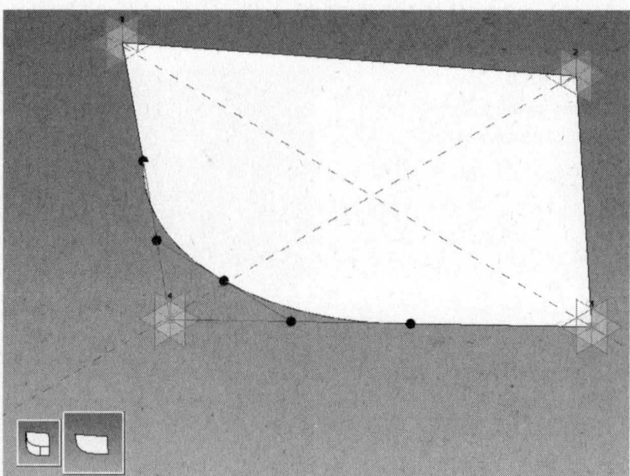

FIGURE 9.13
Creating a form out of the model lines

At this point, you need to save the family for use in your mass. Save the family with the name `c09-Adaptive-Rig.rfa`. You can download the finished file from the Chapter 9 folder on this book's web page, `www.sybex.com/go/masteringrevit2017`.

Building the Massing Framework

Now, you need to create a mass family into which you will load and place the adaptive component family. From the Application menu, choose New ➤ Conceptual Mass. This will open the template-selection dialog box. Choose the `Mass.rft` or `Metric Mass.rft` file. The conceptual mass environment will mirror the adaptive component look and feel. You're going to use this to study forms for an office tower.

The first steps in this exercise will show you how to add some 3D splines, to which each of the four reference points in the adaptive component family will attach. With the new mass family started, follow these steps:

1. On the ViewCube® in the 3D view, click Front. In the Create tab of the ribbon, on the Draw panel, select Reference and choose the Spline tool. Before you place the point, set the Placement Plane drop-down on the Options bar to Reference Plane : Center (Front/Back), as shown in Figure 9.14.

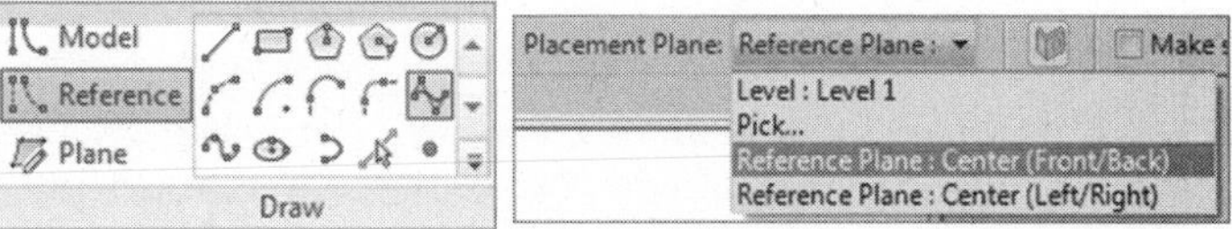

FIGURE 9.14
Select the correct work plane for the spline.

2. Draw one spline to the left and one to the right of the centerline (Figure 9.15). The shape of the spline isn't important—keep it organic but avoid very tight radii. To create a spline, you can click in the view as many times as you like, and then press the Esc key to stop sketching.

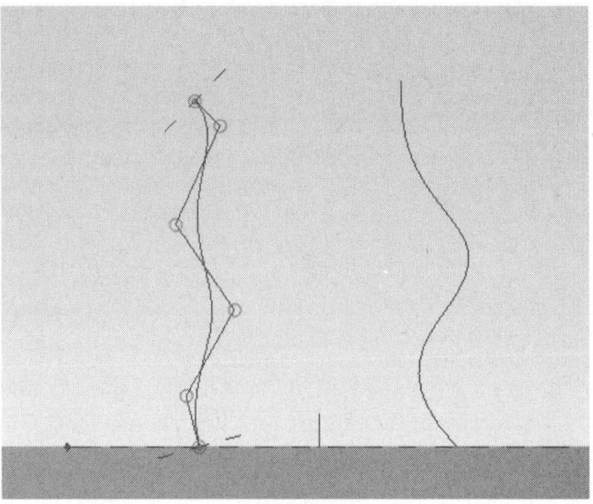

FIGURE 9.15
Draw splines on each side of the work plane.

3. Orbit the 3D view slightly, and then click Left or Right from the ViewCube. Start the Reference and Spline tools again and choose Reference Plane : Center (Left/Right) from the Options bar. Draw two more reference splines, one on either side of the centerline.

4. Your next step is to join the splines with horizontal reference lines. This will allow you to establish some benchmarks for inserting the platform family you just created. For each of the sets of horizontal reference lines you create, you're going to insert another instance of the adaptive component family.

   You'll draw the reference lines in the Left/Right plane to start using the same view you used to draw the last two splines. You want the reference lines to intersect both sets of points but to extend past them on both ends. The length of the reference line will determine how far the adaptive component can stretch. Start by drawing one at the base and extending it past both ends of the spline (Figure 9.16). Do the same for the Front/Back plane, making sure to remember to switch your placement plane. We will create more reference lines in a later step.

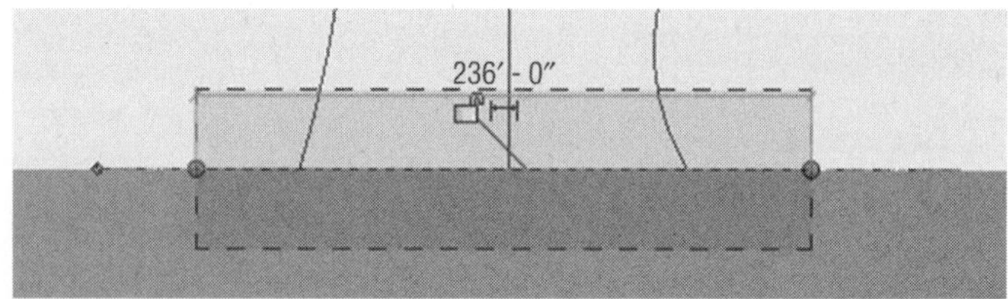

FIGURE 9.16
Adding reference lines

5. Select one of the upper corners of the ViewCube so the view rotates back into an axonometric view. You're going to add points to the splines. Choose the Model style and the Point Element tool and add a point to each of the splines near the intersections of the reference lines you just drew; see Figure 9.17. It doesn't have to be exact—once you get all the points in place you'll perform another step to connect the points to the intersection of the spline and reference line. Add four hosted points, one for each spline.

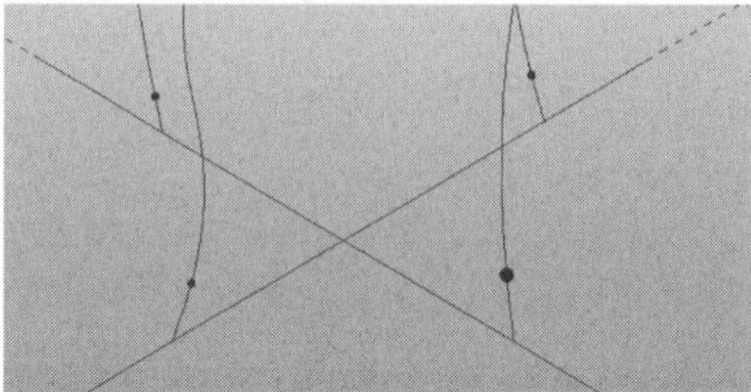

FIGURE 9.17
Adding points to the reference lines

6. As we just mentioned, the next step is to attach the points to the reference lines. Select any one of the points, and then choose Host Point By Intersection from the Options bar. Then select the intersection of the spline and reference line, as shown in Figure 9.18. Do this for all four points.

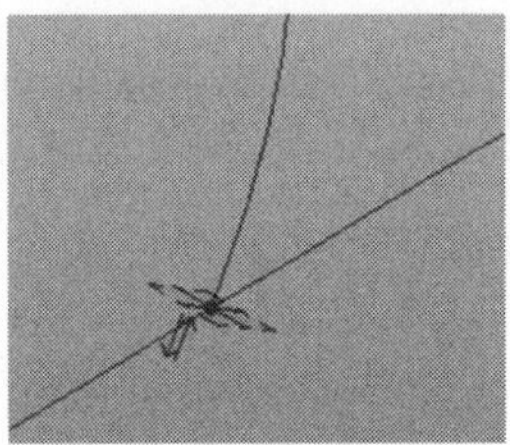

FIGURE 9.18
Aligning the points and reference lines

7. Now, you need to make several versions of these elements—points with intersecting lines—one set for each of your adaptive components. The more sets you create, the more granular control you have over the form. Open one of your elevations (it doesn't matter which one) by selecting one of the elevation sides of the ViewCube. Draw a selection box starting on the left and going right over the ground plane so you encompass the levels, points, and lines you've been drawing. You'll have selected too much, but that's okay. With everything selected, click the Filter tool in the contextual tab of the ribbon. In the Filter dialog box, uncheck Levels, Reference Points, and Reference Planes so that only Reference Lines is selected (Figure 9.19). Click OK to close the dialog box.

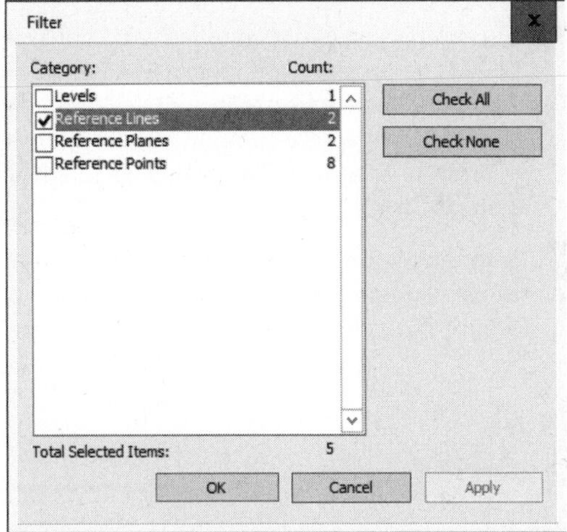

FIGURE 9.19
Filtering the selection

8. With these items selected, you're going to make a few copies. In our example image (Figure 9.20) we've made three copies for a total of four elements. Still in the elevation view, choose the Copy tool from the Modify panel and copy the selected elements, spacing them relatively evenly. You'll need to add points to each of these intersections. It's a bit tedious, but it goes pretty quickly, and it will be good practice to remember the steps. Add the points on the splines and close the reference lines. Then select the points, choose Host By Intersection, and choose the reference line, as you did in step 6. When you've finished, you'll have an array of points and lines, as shown in Figure 9.20.

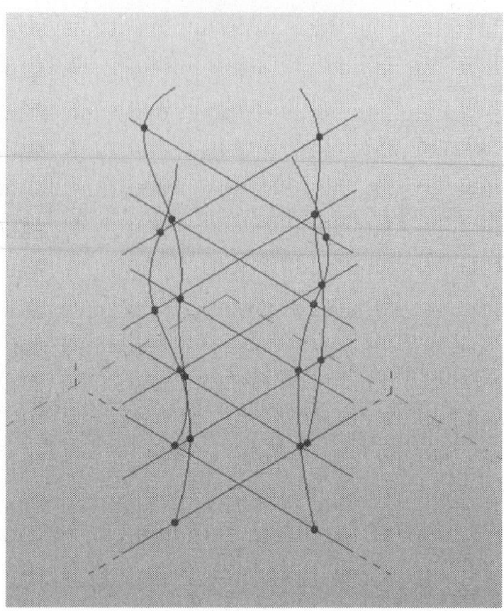

FIGURE 9.20
Creating several instances of the selection and adding points

9. The mass is just about complete, and you're ready to load the `c09-Adaptive-Rig` family into the project. Open the `c09-Adaptive-Rig` family file, or if the family is still open, choose the family from the Switch Windows button on the Quick Access toolbar. When you load an adaptive component into a family or project, it doesn't respond quite like a normal component. The points you created need to be anchored to the points on the spline elements.

   Load the platform family into the conceptual mass. Once it is loaded, one of the first things you'll notice is a small, gray version of your family floating around by your cursor (Figure 9.21).

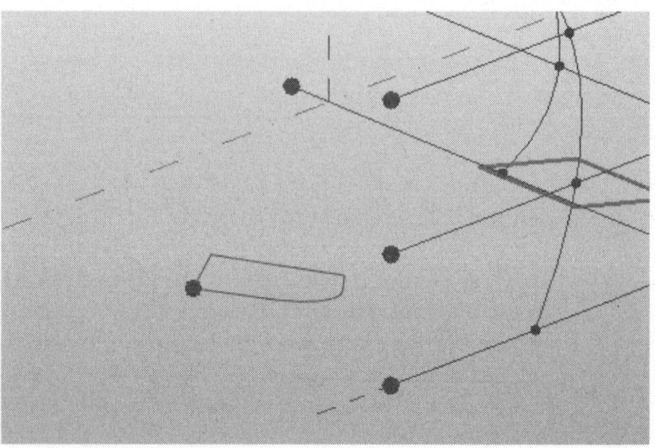

FIGURE 9.21
Inserting the adaptive component into the mass

10. To anchor the family, select one of the points you inserted earlier in this chapter at the base of the splines. Work your way around all the points in the same plane in a clockwise fashion until you've selected all four points at the base of the spline (Figure 9.22). Notice how the curved section you added at Point 4 isn't touching the point on the vertical spline.

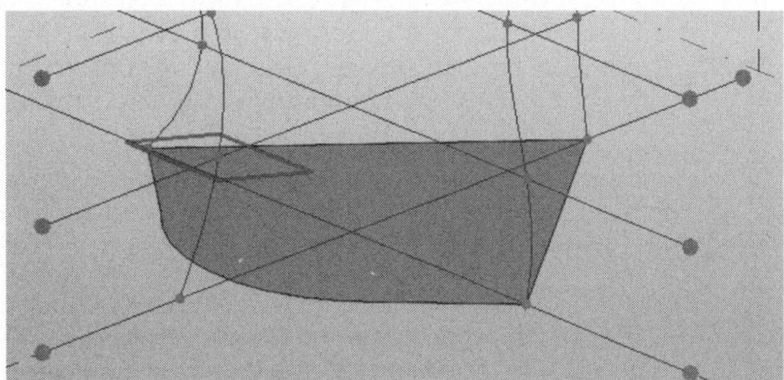

FIGURE 9.22 Anchoring the adaptive component to the mass

It is critical to anchor the family properly. If the family gets placed and appears to have lines between any two points, rather than just along the boundary, your points are not coplanar.

11. Do the same for each of the vertical levels you added. Your mass should look like Figure 9.23. Make sure your first point on each level is on the same spline. This will ensure that all the curved sections at Point 4 stack properly. When your platforms are fully inserted, you can grab any of the splines and push and pull it to see the platforms change shape.

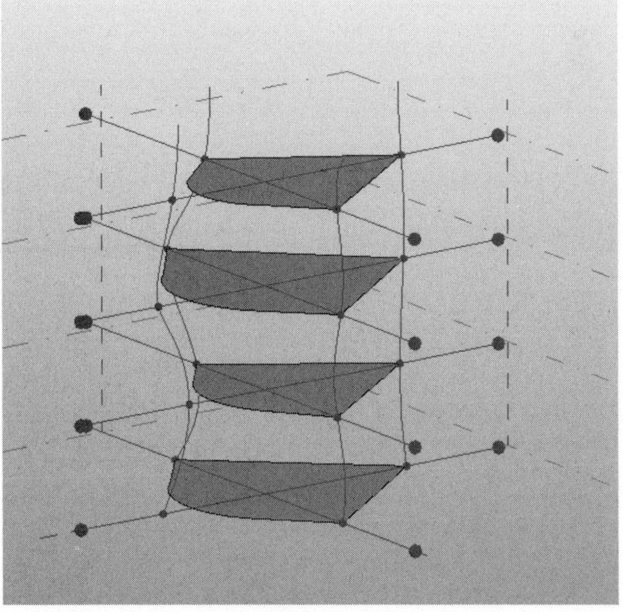

FIGURE 9.23 Creating several instances of the selection and adding points

Before we create the solid form from these adaptive components, you will create a visibility toggle for the generic surfaces. This will allow you to turn them off in the project environment when you don't want to see them.

12. Select each of the adaptive components you have placed in the 3D view. Click the Filter tool in the contextual tab of the ribbon and make sure that only Generic Models is selected. Click OK to close the Filter dialog box. In the Properties palette, click the Associate Family Parameter button for the property named **Visible**. This is the small button on the right of the Visible parameter row. Click Add Parameter in the dialog box.

13. In the Parameter Properties dialog box, set the Name of the new parameter as Show Rig and set the Group Parameter Under drop-down to Visibility (Figure 9.24). Click OK to close all open dialog boxes.

FIGURE 9.24
Setting the visibility parameter

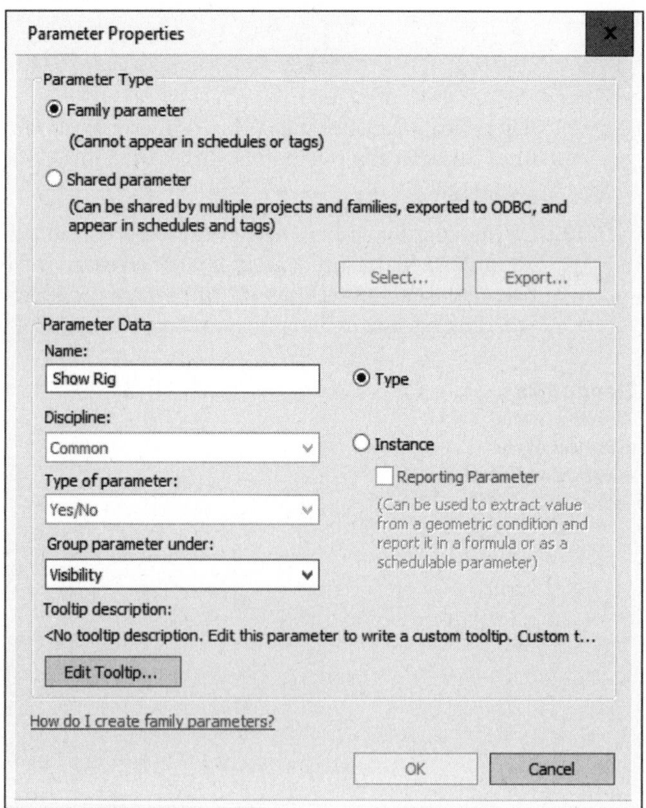

14. Finally, to create the mass, select the surface for each of the rigs. This is a somewhat tricky operation. You'll need to hover the mouse pointer over the edge of a surface, and press the Tab key until you see `Generic Models : c09-Adaptive-Rig : Face` appear in the status bar at the bottom of the application window. Click to select the face. Then hover the

mouse pointer over the next surface, press the Tab key, and repeat the step. When you see the Face element in the status bar, press and hold the Ctrl key while clicking to select the next face. Repeat this process until all the faces are selected.

15. With these faces selected, select Create Form ➤ Solid Form from the contextual tab in the ribbon. Your completed mass will look like Figure 9.25. Remember to save the mass family for use in the next section of this chapter.

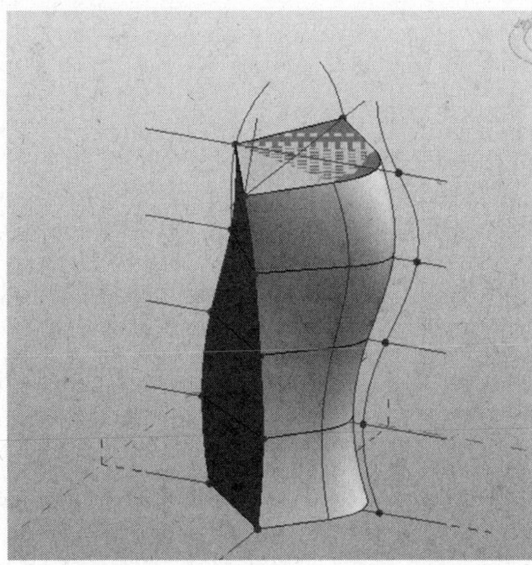

FIGURE 9.25 Creating several instances of the selection and adding points

You can modify this mass by moving any of the nodes on the four vertical splines. You can also select any of the Adaptive Rig elements and click Edit Type in the Properties palette. Change the values for any of the Rad parameters you created in the adaptive component, and the severity of the curved edge will be affected. This exercise was just one example of the almost limitless number of ways you can use parameters and components to drive conceptual geometry. We're going to use this mass family to explore conceptual energy analysis in the next section.

Energy Modeling

Understanding a building's energy needs is paramount to helping the project become more sustainable. According to the U.S. Energy Information Administration (`www.eia.doe.gov`), as of March 2015 buildings in the United States account for 30 percent of the world's energy consumption and 60 percent of the world's electricity use, making the United States the primary consumer of energy in the world (Figure 9.26). This reality should inspire you to build responsibly and to think about your design choices before you implement them.

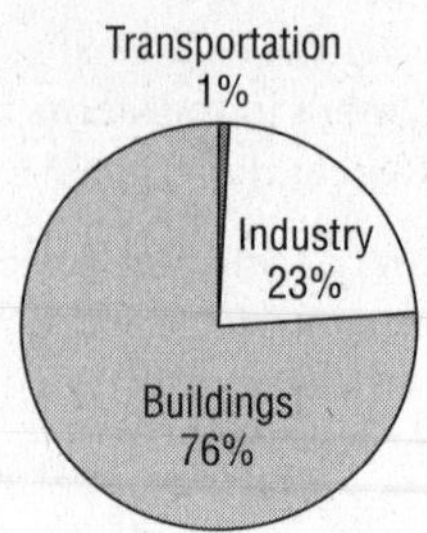

FIGURE 9.26
Energy use in the United States

The energy needs of a building depend on a number of issues that are not simply related to leaving the lights on in a room that you are no longer using, turning down the heat, or increasing the air-conditioning. Many of the components and systems within a building affect its energy use. For instance, if you increase the size of the windows on the south façade, you allow in more natural light and lower your need for electric lighting. However, without proper sunshading, you are also letting in additional solar heat gain, so those larger windows are increasing your need for air-conditioning and potentially negating the energy savings from reduced lighting.

In exploring the use of energy in a building, you must consider all energy-related issues, which is a good reason to use energy-simulation tools. These computer-based models use climate data coupled with building loads, such as the following:

- The heating, ventilation, and air-conditioning (HVAC) system
- Solar heat gain
- The number of occupants and their activity levels
- Sunshading devices
- Daylight dimming
- Lighting levels

The energy model combines these factors to predict the building's energy demands to help size the building's HVAC system. It also combines the parameters of other components properly so you are not using a system larger than what you need, and you can understand the impact of your design on the environment. By keeping the energy model updated with the current design, you can begin to grasp how building massing, building envelopes, window locations, building orientation, and other parameters affect energy demands.

There are two ways you can use Revit Architecture software for energy analysis—by analyzing mass forms directly in the model or by exporting a more detailed model to another application using the gbXML format. The gbXML file type is a standardized XML schema that is used for sustainable design analysis. For either choice, you must first have accurate location and true north settings. Once you have those established, you can approach either analysis with confidence. Let's first take a look at the process for generating a conceptual energy analysis.

Conceptual Energy Analysis

A conceptual energy analysis (CEA) tool was added to Revit software as a Subscription Advantage Pack in 2009. This tool creates a link to the online analysis service known as the Autodesk® Green Building Studio® service. The analysis results will indicate such information as the life cycle and annual energy costs. In our opinion, it is wise to use the CEA tool only to determine relative costs. So, if you run an analysis against a design and then make changes and rerun the analysis, the difference should give you a general idea of performance improvement or performance loss.

In the following exercise, you will load a conceptual mass into a template project to run a series of energy analyses. There are three basic tools for configuration, analysis, and comparison of results on the Analyze tab of the ribbon for both building elements and masses (Figure 9.27).

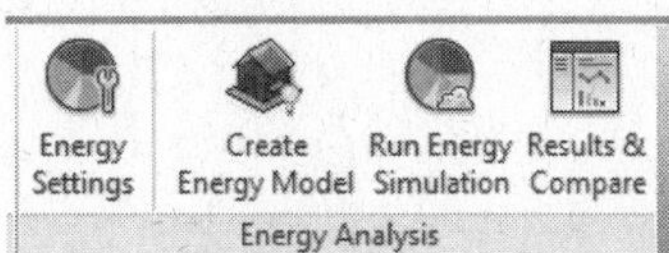

FIGURE 9.27
The Energy Analysis panel in the ribbon

> **NOTE ON GBS AND REVIT CEA TOOLS**
>
> You will need an Autodesk Subscription account to access the Green Building Studio service and use the CEA tools. Not sure if you have a subscription account? Check with your BIM manager or local reseller; however, if you've purchased Revit on subscription, you'll have access to the tools. Another way to gain more limited access is to simply sign up for an Autodesk® 360 account. You can do that from the top-right portion of the Revit software using the Sign In button or by visiting `360.autodesk.com`.

Energy Analysis Setup

Before you can run an analysis for either building elements or massing, you need to do a bit of configuration to give your analysis engine some parameters to run. You're going to use the mass you created, but you're going to insert that mass into an existing building model so you can run the analysis side by side. Let's get started by comparing the two buildings (existing and mass) side by side.

Open the `c09-Analysis-Start.rvt` or `c09-Analysis-Start-Metric.rvt` file. You can download the file from this book's web page. Once the file is open, activate the **Level 1** floor plan, and then load and insert the mass you made earlier in this chapter or the one from the website. You can also download the completed massing family from the web page (`c09-Conceptual-Mass-Finished.rfa`). Position the mass in the center of the plan view.

To begin the configuration of the energy analysis settings, follow these steps:

1. To begin, from the Massing & Site tab, choose Show Mass Form and Floors from the conceptual mass panel. Next, activate the default 3D view, and in the view control bar, set Visual Style to Shaded and turn Shadows on. Select the massing form, and from the Properties palette click Edit Type. Deselect the Show Rig property and then click Apply. This will turn off the generic model faces from the adaptive component you used to build the massing form. Click OK to close the dialog box.

2. Activate the South elevation view. Use the Copy or Array tool to create several new levels that span the height of your massing family (Figure 9.28). Make the levels above Level 2 evenly spaced at **15′-0″** (**4 m**) each. Select the massing family again and from the contextual tab in the ribbon, click Mass Floors. Select all the levels in the dialog box and then click OK.

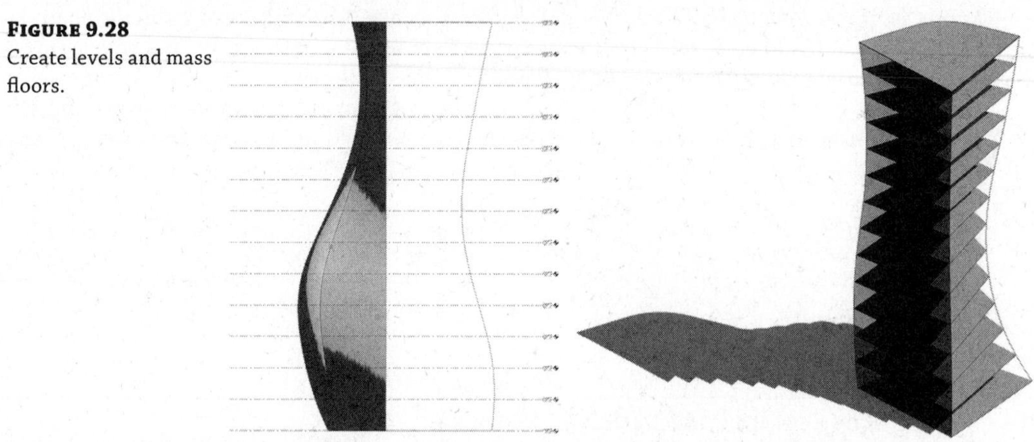

FIGURE 9.28
Create levels and mass floors.

3. On the Analyze tab, click Energy Settings. The Energy Settings dialog box is shown in Figure 9.29. We're going to work our way down this dialog box, making sure you have the settings correct.

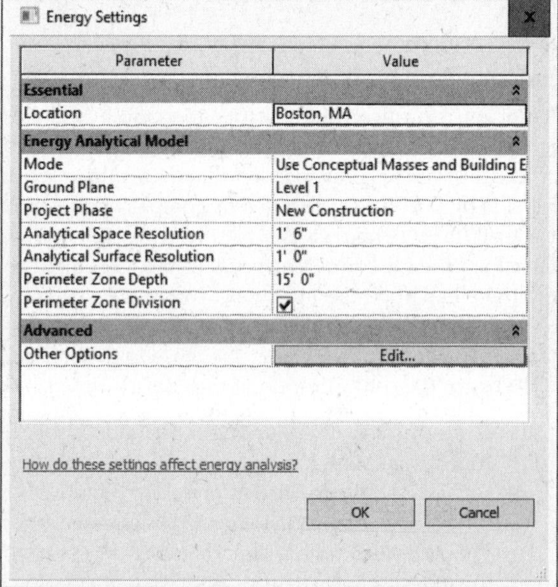

FIGURE 9.29
The Energy Settings dialog box

4. The next step is to establish the correct location of your project. Click the selection button to the right of the Location parameter to open the Location Weather And Site dialog box (Figure 9.30). Insert Boulder, CO, USA (or your hometown) in the Project Address field and click Search. Click one of the closest weather stations (shown by the pin icons) in the list or directly on the map. Finally, choose Use Daylight Savings Time if that is appropriate for your location and time of year. When you've made a selection, click OK to close the dialog box.

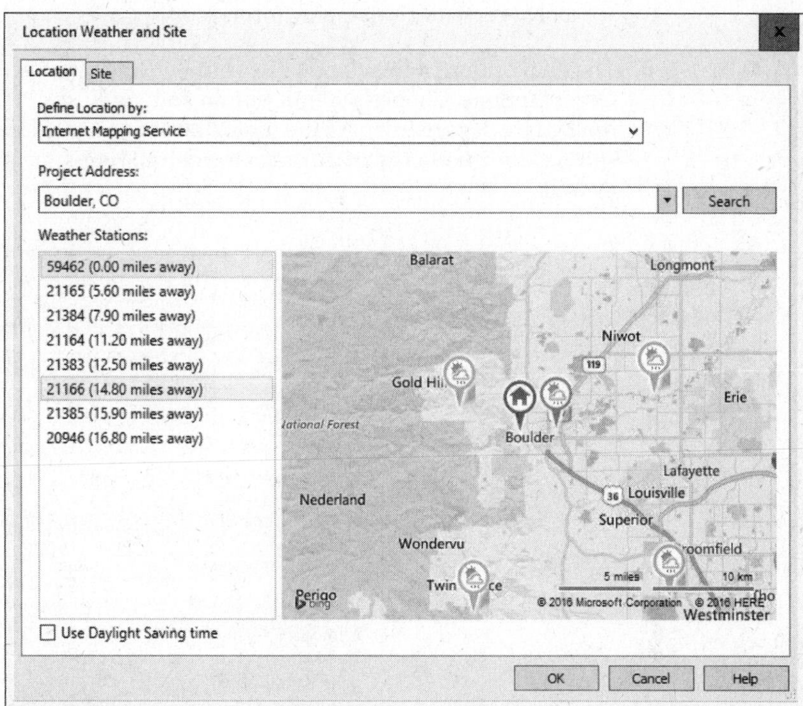

FIGURE 9.30 In Location Weather And Site, first specify the location and weather station.

You'll notice a lot of options in the Energy Settings dialog box—some of them quite complex. To complete the rest of the dialog box, we're going to step through each of the sections. So far, we've completed the Location.

5. In the Energy Analytical Model settings, change the following values:

   - **Mode**: Change this to Use Conceptual Masses.
   - **Ground Plane**: This should be set to Level 1.

   We are going to leave the rest of the settings as they are, but let's review a few of them so you understand their impact to the conceptual model.

   - **Project Phase**: This is the phase the analysis will be run against. Keep the default setting of New Construction, but if you had multiple phases to your project, you could change how the analysis is run here.

- **Analytical Space Resolution and Analytical Surface Resolution**: These numbers dictate the tolerances for Revit to resolve the spaces and surfaces within the model. For our uses, keep the default values.
- **Perimeter Zone Depth and Perimeter Zone Division**: When this setting is enabled (the default), zones are automatically defined around the perimeter of the massing form. If you prefer to create your own zones, disable this setting and set the Core Offset value to 0. Then create more detailed mass forms and use the Cut Geometry tool to combine overlapping forms.

6. The final option in this dialog box is in the Advanced group and is an option for Other Options. Choose the Edit button and you'll see the Advanced Energy Settings dialog box (Figure 9.31). As the dialog box suggests, these are more advanced settings for the energy performance and building systems. Let's walk through these as well.

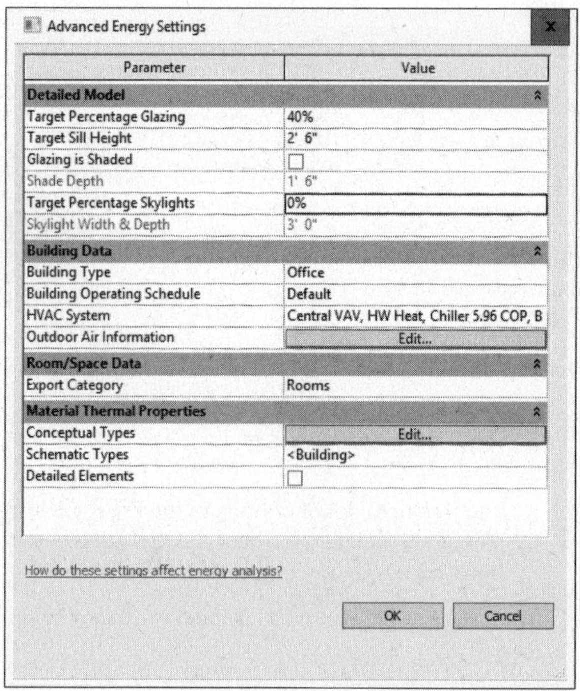

FIGURE 9.31
Advanced Energy Settings dialog box

- **Target Percentage Glazing**: When you click the Show Energy Model button, you will see the Target Percentage Glazing value illustrated as solid and semi-transparent regions on the vertical exterior surfaces of the massing form (Figure 9.32). This value sets the assumed amount of glazing as a percentage of the overall wall area.

FIGURE 9.32
Assumptions for glazing are illustrated on exterior surfaces of the massing form at the default of 40 percent.

- **Target Sill Height**: This is the height of the sill for glazing to begin on each floor.
- **Glazing Is Shaded**: Select this check box if you intend to design sunshading for the glazing. This does not differentiate by building orientation, so if you check the box, conceptual shading elements will be added to the glazing assumptions on all sides (Figure 9.33).

FIGURE 9.33
Conceptual shading elements are added to all sides of the massing form.

- **Shade Depth**: When the Glazing Is Shaded option is checked, you can assign a depth to any assumed sunshading.
- **Target Percentage Skylights**: Like Target Percentage Glazing, this value assumes an amount of skylighting for your model.
- **Skylight Width & Depth**: This value sets the size for skylights if you are using that value.

- **Building Type**: This value sets the type of building use. By default, it is set to Office building, but there are many different building uses. The building use will help dictate the type of load on the building, assumed number of occupants, and so on.
- **Building Operation Schedule**: How often will your building be occupied? Will it have people in it 24/7, or will it be operational only during office hours? This can have a large impact on your heating and cooling cycles.
- **HVAC System**: Here you can set a conceptual HVAC system. That could be a four-pipe system, underfloor air distribution, or a variety of other HVAC system types.
- **Outdoor Air Information**: If you know how many air exchanges you'll be required to produce per hour, you can set that value here.
- **Export Category**: Your option here is either Rooms or Spaces. If you're working from an architectural model, chances are you're using Rooms. If this were an MEP model or you were linking in information from an MEP consultant, you'd want to use Spaces. For this exercise, leave it set to Rooms.
- **Conceptual Types**: The Conceptual Types dialog box allows you to edit the assumed values of building elements for the mass form, as shown in Figure 9.34.

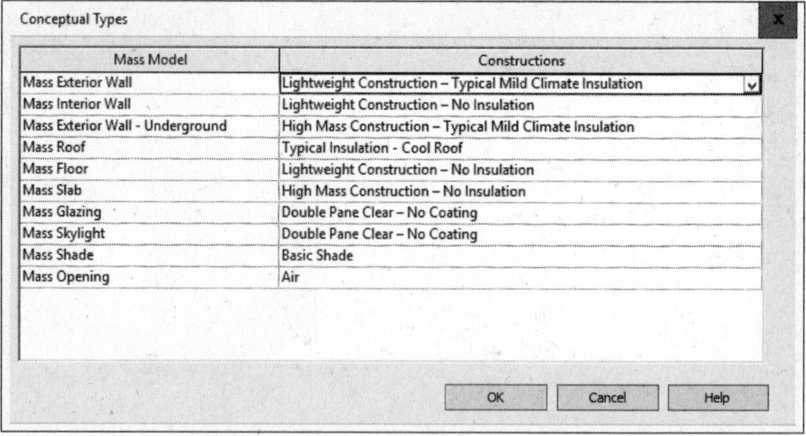

Conceptual Types
Mass Model
Constructions
Mass Exterior Wall
Lightweight Construction – Typical Mild Climate Insulation
Mass Interior Wall
Lightweight Construction – No Insulation
Mass Exterior Wall - Underground
High Mass Construction – Typical Mild Climate Insulation
Mass Roof
Typical Insulation - Cool Roof
Mass Floor
Lightweight Construction – No Insulation
Mass Slab
High Mass Construction – No Insulation
Mass Glazing
Double Pane Clear – No Coating
Mass Skylight
Double Pane Clear – No Coating
Mass Shade
Basic Shade
Mass Opening
Air
OK
Cancel
Help

FIGURE 9.34
Conceptual Types allow you to test assumptions about massing forms.

- **Schematic Types**: The Schematic Types dialog box allows you to edit the assumed values of the U values for each building system. Here is where you can customize the assumptions for the building type for insulation values, as shown in Figure 9.35.

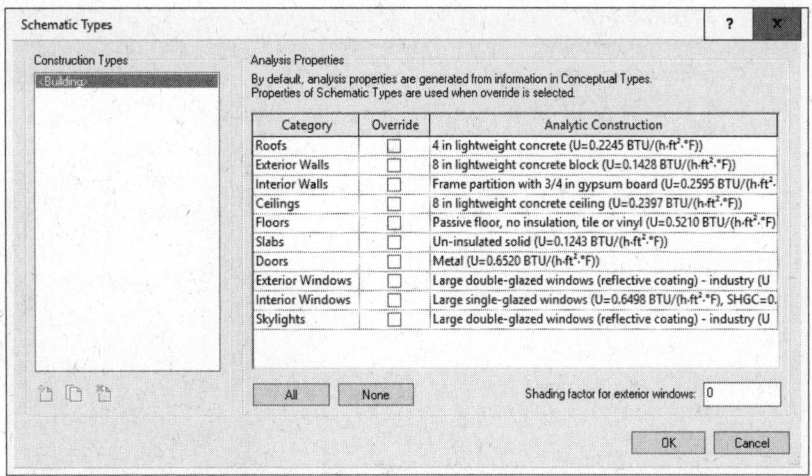

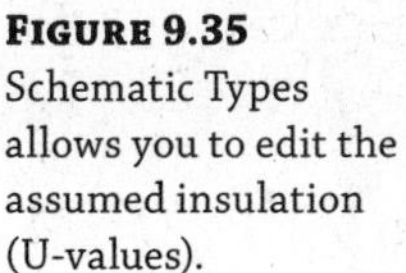
FIGURE 9.35 Schematic Types allows you to edit the assumed insulation (U-values).

- **Detailed Elements**: The final setting in the dialog box is the Detailed Elements check box. This box is unchecked by default, but checking it will tell Revit to use the thermal properties associated with the materials you have in your model. For our analysis, we have no materials assigned, so we will leave this unchecked, but if you are performing an analysis on a more developed model, this option could give more exact results. Be aware that you will need to make sure to have thermal properties assigned to each of your materials in order to get accurate results.

Once those values are set, click OK to exit the dialog box.

Remember that this type of analysis is based on assumptions only and uses the overall size, location, and orientation of your proposed design. After you start analyzing the results, you can examine different massing configurations with the same construction and systems assumptions or varied assumptions on the same massing configuration.

Running Energy Analysis Simulations

After you have established some baseline settings and assumptions for an energy analysis, it's time to create the energy model. This is the final step before running a simulation. Selecting the Create Energy Model button from the Analysis tab will apply the settings we just reviewed to your model. You can see the changes and assumptions it made in Figure 9.36.

Finally, it's time to run the simulation. To do so, follow these steps:

1. Click the Run Energy Simulation button on the ribbon to start the analysis. If you haven't logged into A360, you'll be asked to sign in. Next, you'll get a dialog box asking you to name your new simulation. We've filled this in with some project-specific values, but you can name this whatever you'd like (Figure 9.37). You will need an Internet connection and an Autodesk Subscription account to run energy simulations. Once you click Continue, Revit will begin uploading your energy data.

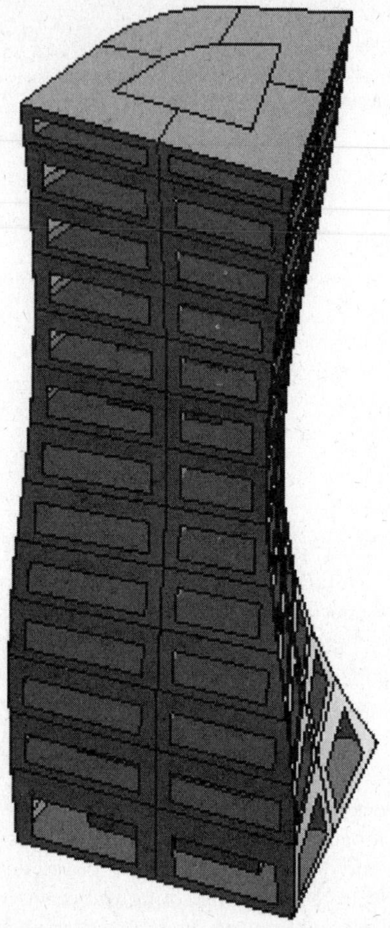

FIGURE 9.36
Creating the energy model assigns the energy values to the form

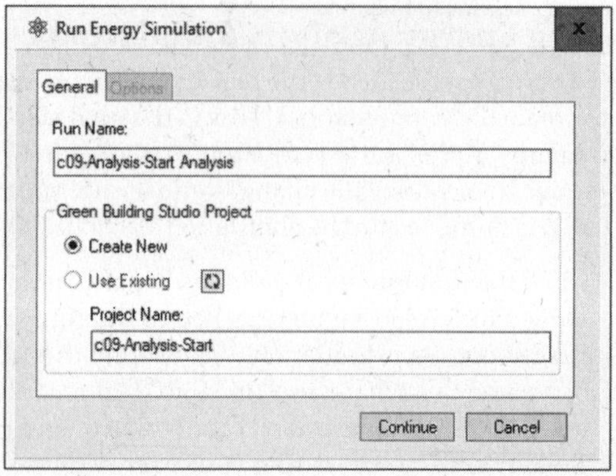

Run Energy Simulation

General | Options

Run Name:

c09-Analysis-Start Analysis

Green Building Studio Project

Create New

Use Existing

Project Name:

c09-Analysis-Start

Continue | Cancel

FIGURE 9.37
Generate the analytical energy model to begin the simulation.

2. In the Run Energy Simulation dialog box, name this analysis Baseline_SouthCurve and click to run your initial analysis. The project name will be the file name by default. The software will start to communicate with the Green Building Studio service online and load your model into the analysis engine. Click Continue to start the analysis. This will take a few minutes to run. Your model data will be sent off to Autodesk's cloud for processing and allow you to continue working while the analysis is being performed.

3. Click the Results & Compare button on the ribbon to view the progress of the upload. If you don't have the Results And Compare dialog box open, an alert will appear in the lower-right portion of the application window, informing you that the analysis is complete. Once the analysis is complete, you will see the run (Baseline_SouthCurve) listed under the name of the model you are analyzing, as shown in Figure 9.38. You can scroll through the list of analyses that are provided.

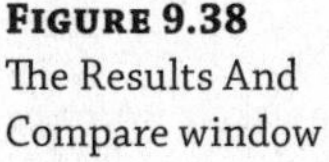

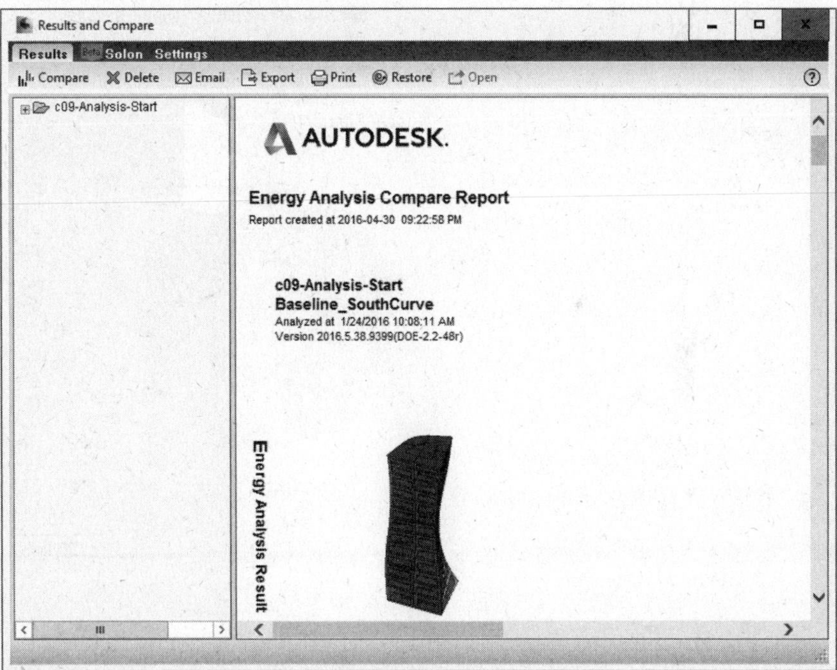

FIGURE 9.38 The Results And Compare window

You can scroll through the results and get a basic understanding of the building loads (Figure 9.39). One of the great uses for this tool isn't looking at the actual reported data but using it as a comparative analysis. If you make changes to the building form, size, or orientation, how does that change your performance?

FIGURE 9.39
Sample results

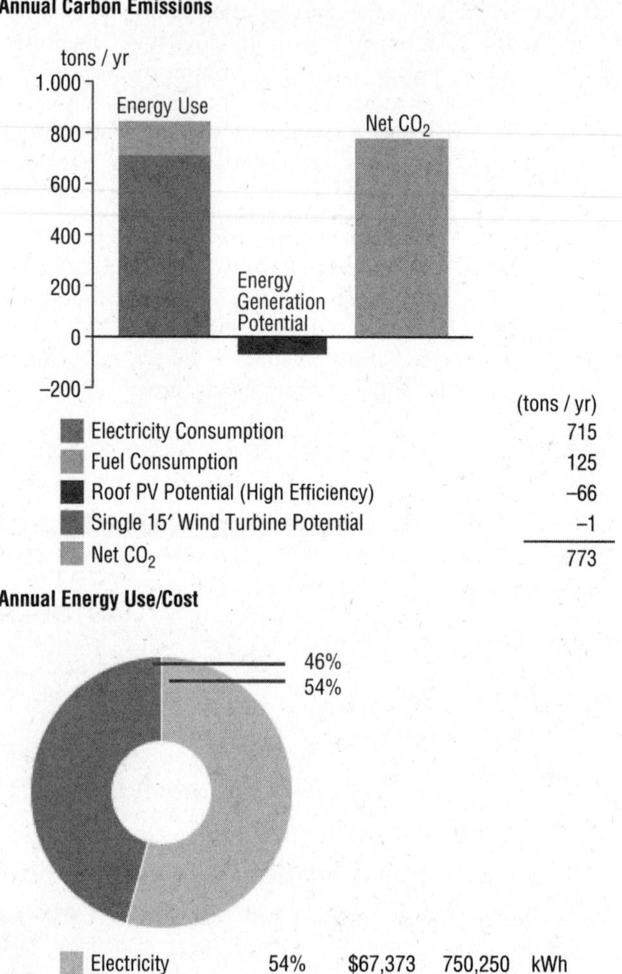

4. Activate the plan view, Site, from the Project Browser. Select the massing family and select the Rotate tool from the contextual tab in the ribbon. Rotate the mass so that the curved face is oriented South (90 degrees counterclockwise).

 Return to the Analysis tab, and let's make some adjustments to the model so we can compare results.

5. Go back to the main application window and click the Energy Settings button on the ribbon. Click the Other Options tool to pull up the Advanced dialog box. Change the following settings:

- Select the Glazing Is Shaded check box and set the Shade Depth value to **2′-0″ (600 mm)**.
- Click the Conceptual Types Edit button and change the Mass Glazing setting to Double Pane Clear - High Performance, LowE, High Tvis, Low SHGC. Click OK to close all three dialog boxes.

6. Click the Run Energy Simulation button again, name this run **Shading + HighPerfGlass**, and choose to use the existing model.
7. After the run has completed, return to the Results And Compare window, press and hold the Ctrl key, and select both the Baseline_SouthCurve and Shading + HighPerfGlass runs. Click the Compare button.

You will see the results of the two analyses runs side by side. Notice that the second run has a lower monthly electricity consumption and lower fuel consumption. Be careful when reading the graphs, because the values in each graph may be different. Take a look at the Monthly Cooling Load graphs. Notice that the values for Window Solar are lower for the second run; however, the values for Light Fixtures are slightly higher. This is due to the addition of the shading, which requires more electric lighting power.

 **Real World Scenario**

Making More Informed Decisions

We have seen so many projects in which design forms were arbitrarily created and presented to clients—only to have them choose the option that looked the most compelling. Cost of construction may come into play for a more complex design against a simpler solution. But what about how each of the design solutions will perform after construction?

Using the conceptual energy analysis tools has allowed our teams not only to present various design ideas to clients but to accompany the forms with performance characteristics as well. One design may cost more to construct but is projected to perform better in terms of heating loads in the winter. We frequently use selected graphs and comparisons from the Results And Compare reports in our early design phase presentations to clients. This enhanced information increases stakeholder confidence in making key decisions when they are most appropriate to drive value in the design and construction process.

Detailed Energy Modeling

Later in the design process, you may want to use your building elements to perform more detailed energy modeling. For this process to be successful, you first need a solid, well-built model. This does not mean you need to have all the materials and details figured out, but you do have to establish some basic conditions. To ensure that your model is correctly constructed to work with an energy-modeling application, there are a few things you need to do within the model to get the proper results. Some of this might sound like common sense, but it is important to ensure that you have the following elements properly modeled or you may have incorrect results:

- The model must have roofs and floors.
- Walls inside and outside need to touch the roofs and floors.
- All areas within the analysis should be bound by building geometry (no unbound building geometry allowed).

To perform an energy analysis, you need to take portions of the model and export them using gbXML to an energy-analysis application. The following are the energy-modeling applications commonly used within the design industry. They vary in price, ease of use, and interoperability with a gbXML model. Choosing the correct application for your office or workflow will depend on a balance of those variables.

- **IES VE**: IES VE (`www.iesve.com`) is a robust energy-analysis tool that offers a high degree of accuracy and interoperability with a design model. The application can run the whole gamut of building environmental analysis, from energy and daylighting to computational fluid dynamics (CFDs) used to study airflow for mechanical systems. Cons to this application are its current complexity for the user and the relatively expensive cost of the tool suite.
- **eQuest**: The name stands for the Quick Energy Simulation Tool (`www.doe2.com/equest`). This application is a free tool created by the Lawrence Berkeley National Laboratory (LBNL). It's robust and contains a series of wizards to help you define your energy parameters for a building. As with Ecotect, it can be a challenge to import a design model smoothly depending on the complexity of the design, although it will directly import SketchUp models by using a free plug-in.

Exporting to gbXML

Before you can export the model to gbXML and run your energy analysis, you need to create several settings so you can export the proper information. The order in which these options are set isn't important, but it is important to check that they are set before exporting to gbXML. If the information within the model is not properly created, the results of the energy analysis will be incorrect.

Project Location

As we mentioned earlier in this chapter, the physical location of the project on the globe is an important factor in energy use analysis. You can give your building a location in a couple of ways. One is to choose the Manage tab and click the Location button. Another way to get to this same dialog box is through the Graphic Display Options dialog box you used for sunshading earlier in this chapter.

Building Envelope

Although this might seem obvious in concept, you cannot run an accurate energy analysis on a building without walls. Although the specific wall or roof composition won't be taken into account, each room needs to be bound by a wall, floor, or roof. These elements are critical in creating the gbXML file and defining the spaces or rooms within the building. These spaces can in turn be defined as different activity zones in the energy-analysis application. Before you export, verify that you have a building envelope free of unwanted openings. This means all your walls meet floors and roofs and there are no "holes" in the building (Figure 9.40).

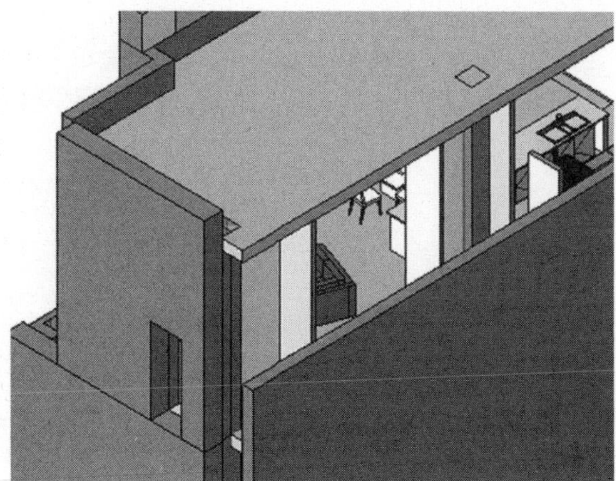

FIGURE 9.40
Make sure your building envelope is fully enclosed.

ROOMS AND VOLUMES

When you export to a gbXML file, you are actually exporting the room volumes because they are constrained by the building geometry. This is what will define the zones within the energy-analysis application. You will need to verify several things to make sure your rooms and room volumes are properly configured:

Ensure that all spaces have a room element. Each area within the model that will be affected by the mechanical system will need to have a room element added to it. To add rooms, select the Room tool from the Architecture tab.

Set room heights. Once all the rooms are placed, each room's properties should be redefined to reflect its height. The height of the room should extend to the bottom of the room above (in a multistory building), or if it is the top floor or only floor of a building, the room must fully extend through the roof plane. When you extend the room through the roof plane, the software will use the Roof geometry to limit the height of the room element and conform it to the bottom of the roof. Rooms should never overlap either in plan (horizontally) or between floors (vertically) because this will give you inaccurate results.

An easy way to set the room heights is to open each level and select everything. Using the Filter tool (Figure 9.41), you can deselect all the elements and choose to keep only the rooms selected. In this way, you can edit all the rooms on a given floor at one time.

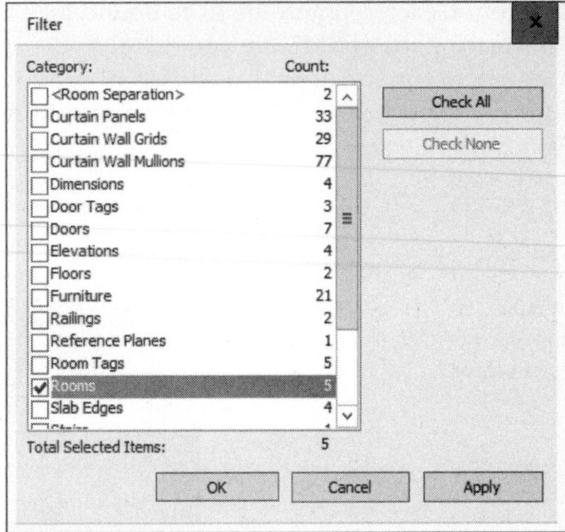

FIGURE 9.41 Use the Filter tool to select only the rooms.

Once the rooms are selected, go to the Properties palette and modify the room heights. By default, rooms are inserted at 8′-0″ high, and the default for metric projects is 4m. You have the option to set a room height directly, or you can modify the room height settings to go to the bottom of the floor above. This second option is shown in Figure 9.42. Note that you'll need to set Upper Limit to the floor above and set the Limit Offset value to 0 (zero). Repeat this same workflow for every floor of the building.

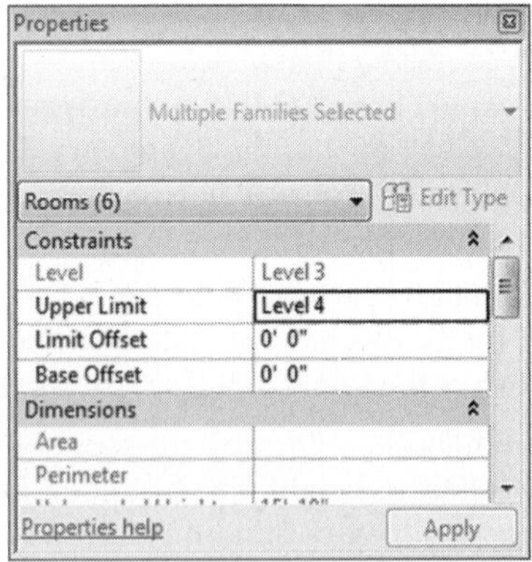

FIGURE 9.42 Modifying the room height

Turn on room volumes. Now that all the heights are defined, you have to tell the application to calculate the volumes of the spaces. By default, Revit does not perform this calculation. Depending on the size of your file, leaving this setting on can hinder performance. Make sure that after you export to gbXML, you return to the Area And Volume Computations dialog box from the Room & Area panel on the Architecture tab and change the setting back to Areas Only.

To turn on room volumes, select the flyout menu from the Room & Area panel on the Architecture tab (Figure 9.43) and click Area And Volume Computations.

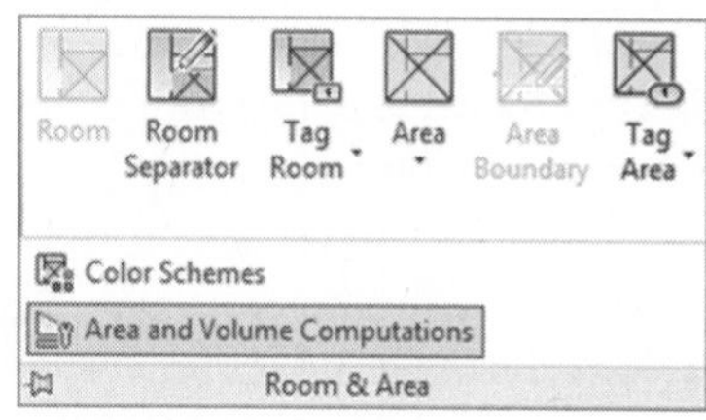

FIGURE 9.43
Opening Area And Volume Computations

Doing so opens the Area And Volume Computations dialog box. There are a couple of simple settings here that will allow you to activate the volume calculations (Figure 9.44). You'll want to select the Areas And Volumes radio button on the Computations tab so that the software will calculate in the vertical dimension as well as the horizontal for your room elements.

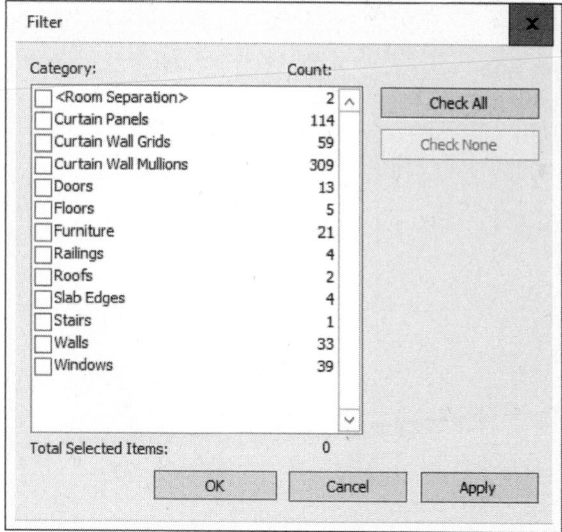

FIGURE 9.44
Enabling volume calculations for rooms

The Room Area Computation setting tells Revit from where in the wall to calculate rooms. If you choose At Wall Finish, the software will not calculate any of the space a wall actually takes up with the model. Arguably, this is also conditioned space. Technically, what you would want is to calculate from the wall centers on interior partitions and the interior face of walls on exterior walls. However, you do not have that option, so choose to calculate from At Wall Center. Once you've modified those settings, click OK.

Exporting to gbXML

Now that you have all the room settings in place, you're ready to export to gbXML. To start this process, click the Application menu and select Export ➢ gbXML. If this step opens the Space Volumes Not Computed warning, be sure to select Yes. This will enable Revit to calculate volumes instead of just areas. Next, you'll need to decide whether you want to calculate the analysis based on your rooms and areas or the energy settings (Figure 9.45). Choose the Use Room/Area Space Volumes option.

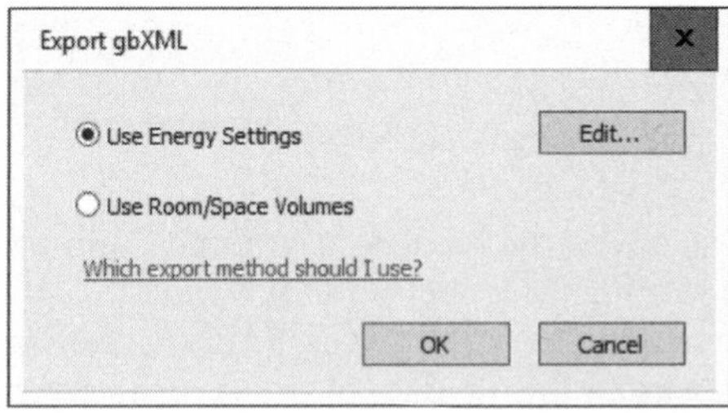

Figure 9.45 Choosing the analysis type

Once you do that, a dialog box like the one in Figure 9.46 will open, allowing you to refine your settings for a gbXML export.

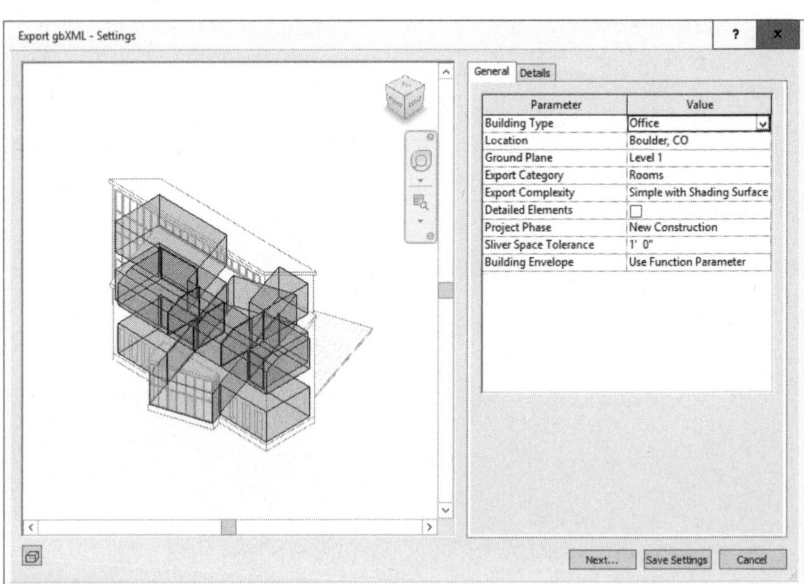

Figure 9.46 Exporting gbXML settings

There are a few things to take note of in this dialog box. First, you'll see a 3D image of the building showing all the room volumes that are bound by the exterior building geometry. You can see in our building visualization that the boundary for the building is not completely full of room elements and that some of the room elements do not visually extend to the floor above.

This would be your first clue that all your rooms do not have room elements placed or set properly, and you'll want to dismiss this dialog box to change those settings.

Second, you'll notice the ViewCube feature at the upper right of the 3D view window. This window will respond to all the same commands that a default 3D view will, directly in the Revit interface, allowing you to turn, pan, and zoom the visualization.

There are also two tabs on the right of this dialog box. The General tab contains general information about your building (building type, location, ground plane, and project phase), and you'll want to verify that it is filled out properly. These settings will help determine the building use type (for conceptual-level energy modeling) and the location of your building in the world. There are two other settings that you'll need to be aware of: Sliver Space Tolerance and Export Complexity. Sliver Space Tolerance will help take into account that you might not have fully buttoned up your Revit building geometry. This will allow you a gap of up to a foot, and the software will assume that those gaps (12″/300 mm or less) are not meant to be there. The Export Complexity setting allows you to modify the complexity of the gbXML export. You have several choices (Figure 9.47) based on the complexity of your model and the export. These are identical to the ones found in the Energy Settings dialog box.

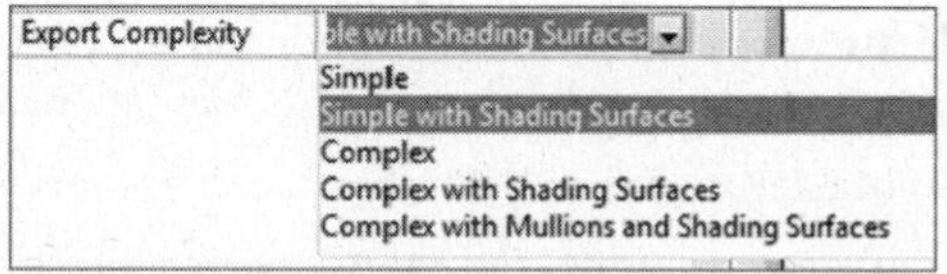

FIGURE 9.47
Exporting complexity settings

The Details tab will give you a room-by-room breakdown of all the room elements that will be exported in the gbXML model. Figure 9.48 shows the expanded Details tab. This is an important place to check because, as you'll also notice, this dialog box will report errors or warnings with those room elements.

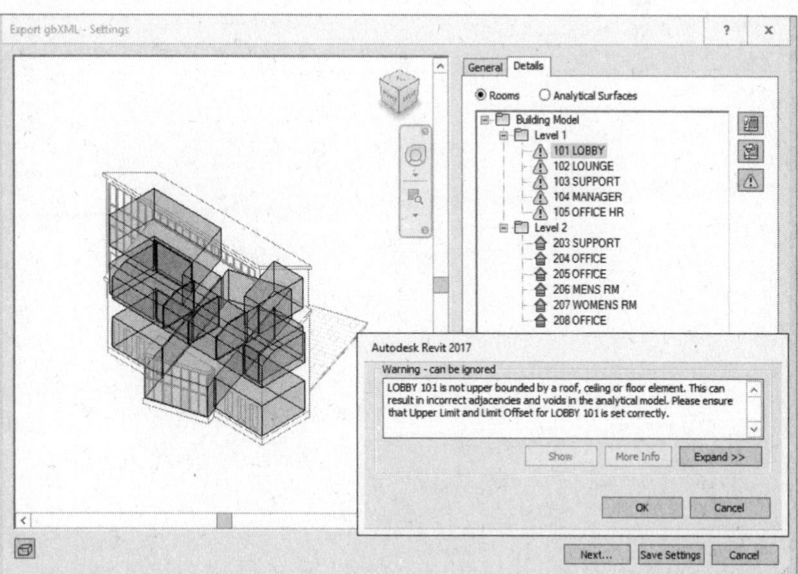

FIGURE 9.48
The Details tab allows you to examine any errors or warnings.

If you expand any of the levels and select a room, clicking the warning triangle will give you a list of the errors and warnings associated with that room. You'll want to make sure your gbXML export is free of any errors or warnings before completing the export.

Once you're ready to finish the export, click Next. This will give you the standard Save As dialog box, allowing you to locate and name your gbXML file. Depending on the size and complexity of your building, a gbXML export can take several minutes and the resulting file size can be tens of megabytes.

You're now ready to import the gbXML file into your energy analysis application to begin computing your energy loads.

The Bottom Line

Embrace energy analysis concepts. Understanding the concepts behind sustainable design is an important part of being able to perform analysis within the Revit model and a critical factor in today's design environment.

Master It What are four key methods for a holistic sustainable design?

Create a conceptual mass. Understand ways to generate building forms quickly and easily to explore a variety of shapes and orientations.

Master It Describe how you can use families to quickly generate form.

Analyze your model for energy performance. Being able to predict a building's energy performance is a necessary part of designing sustainably. Although Revit doesn't have an energy-modeling application built into it, it does have interoperability with many applications that have that functionality.

Master It Explain the steps you need to take to get a Revit model ready for energy analysis.

Chapter 10

Working with Phasing, Groups, and Design Options

Projects will progress through various stages during design and construction. As a result, it's sometimes necessary to distinguish the element of time within your project: when something is created, if it is demolished, and what it will look like when the project is complete. Beyond just phasing, design is also about maintaining relationships between repetitive elements. Sometimes this repetitive element can be a single component in your project, such as a light or a piece of furniture. But it can also be an entire collection of elements, such as a typical room in a hotel or hospital.

Another fundamental aspect of design is the iteration of options. You have to be able to see many ideas simultaneously and in context with other ideas. The client and contractor need to see options and alternates. It's important that these options not be fully independent, separate files so that the results can be analyzed and compared.

This chapter focuses on these three concepts: time, repetition, and iteration of options. In Autodesk® Revit® Architecture software, they're addressed with phasing, groups, and design options, respectively.

In this chapter, you'll learn to:

- Use the Phasing tools to create, demolish, and propose a new design
- Understand and utilize groups
- Create and use design options

Using Phasing

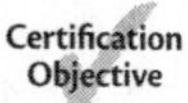

Phasing is the software's method of allowing you to add the element of time to objects in your project. It's easy to think of an architectural design in terms of what something is, where something is, and how it will be assembled. Phasing adds the dimension of *when* something is, which is incredibly useful and powerful.

Phases are most useful for doing the kinds of tasks that require you to show when elements are being introduced into your design: showing demolition and new construction in an existing building, or showing different drawing packages as examples. But a few words of caution and clarification: We don't recommend using extensive phasing to simulate construction sequencing, which is sometimes referred to as 4D. It might seem like a great idea at first, but ultimately it will degrade the performance of your model and lead to confusion across your project team.

There's a far more efficient method of simulating construction sequences that allows model elements to be scheduled, viewed, and even color-coded based on the sequence value that you define: project parameters.

By using project parameters, you're able to create and assign an instance parameter value to everything in your project that you'd want to assign a construction sequence, as shown in Figure 10.1.

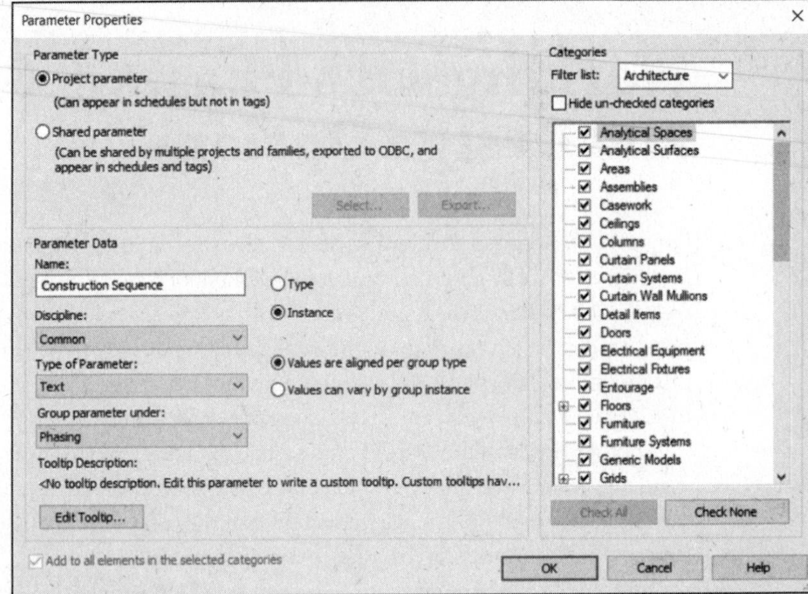

FIGURE 10.1
Creating a construction sequence instance parameter for project geometry

Once you've created this instance parameter, you'll be able to create view filters that override the default display style of an object based on the parameter value, as shown in Figure 10.2. Each construction week value is assigned to a filter rule.

FIGURE 10.2
Developing filters by parameter

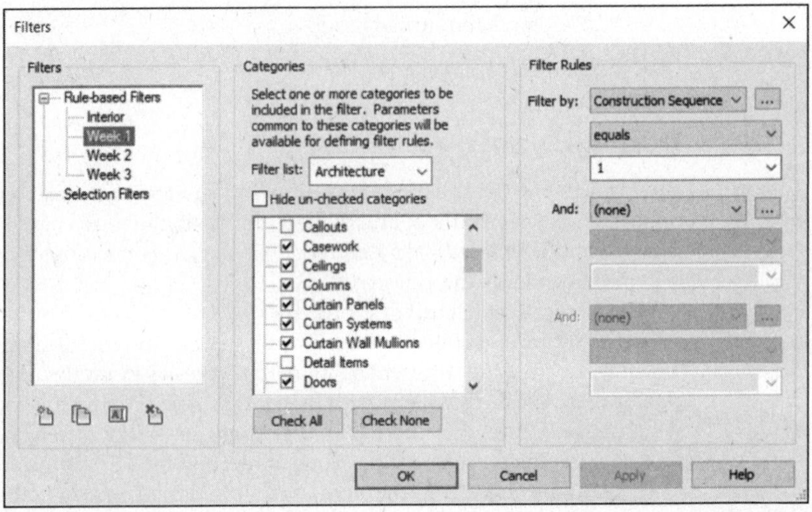

Combined with visibility and graphic overrides, you're able to create a filter that modifies the graphics based on a parameter, as shown in Figure 10.3.

FIGURE 10.3
Applying filters to graphic override settings

Visibility/Graphic Overrides for Floor Plan: Level 1

Model Categories | Annotation Categories | Analytical Model Categories | Imported Categories | Filters

Name	Visibility	Projection/Surface			Cut		Halftone
		Lines	Patterns	Transparen...	Lines	Patterns	
Week 1	☑	Override...	Override...	Override...	Override...	Override...	☐
Week 3	☑						☐
Week 2	☑						☐

As a result of applying parameter-based filters, you will be able to modify the graphics of a view to illustrate some metadata about the objects in a far more flexible and predictable way than the phasing functionality, as shown in Figure 10.4. Another benefit is that this technique is not limited to views of geometry. View filters can be applied to any view, including schedules, which will allow you to group and filter schedules based on your unique project parameter.

FIGURE 10.4
Using parameters and view filters to override graphics

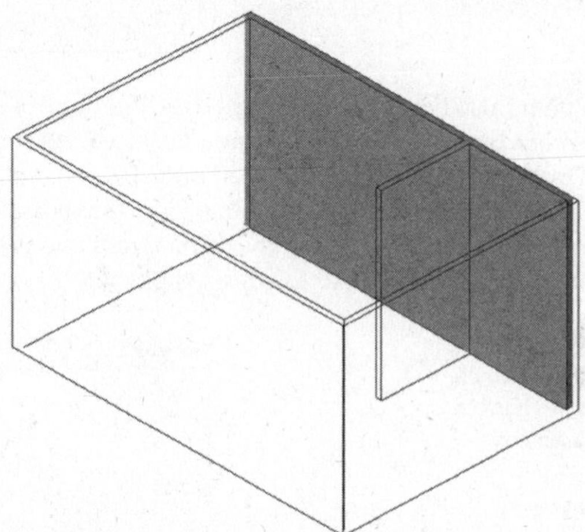

Now that you understand a better way to create sequencing in Revit using parameters and filters, we'll discuss how phasing is best used. To work along with the steps in the following section, download and open the file `c10-Phases-Start.rvt` from this book's web page at `www.sybex.com/go/masteringrevit2017`.

What Can You Phase?

All modeled elements in Revit have two parameters associated with phasing: Phase Created and Phase Demolished. When you place geometry in a view, the Phase Created property by default is the phase assigned to that view. For example, if your view is set to Phase Existing, all elements you place in that view will automatically be assigned to the Existing phase. After an element is placed in the project, the phase can always be changed in the Properties palette, as shown in Figure 10.5.

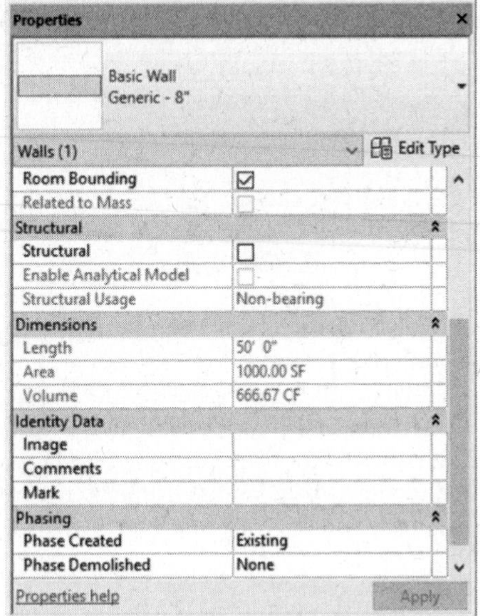

FIGURE 10.5
Changing the phase of geometry (near the bottom of the dialog box)

Rooms also have phasing properties, but there is an important difference: The Phase property of a room cannot be changed after it is placed. As shown in Figure 10.6, the phase is shown in the Properties palette, but it is read only. If you want to change the phase of a room, you'll need to delete and re-create the room in a view that is assigned the desired phase. You also might find it faster to press Ctrl+X to cut the rooms from one view and then press Ctrl+V to paste them into a view that has been set to the desired phase.

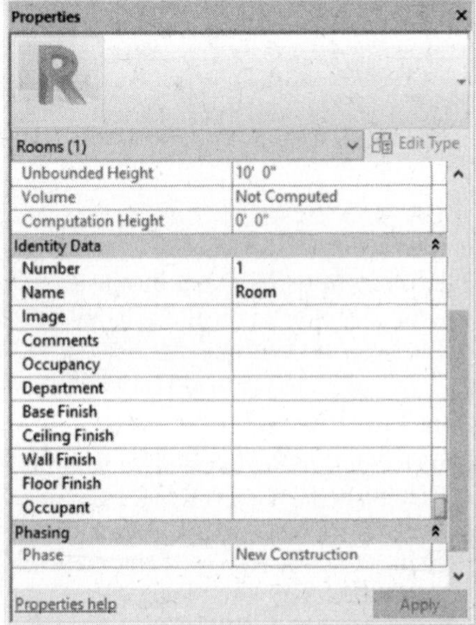

FIGURE 10.6
The phase of a room may not be changed after placement.

The phase of an element when initially placed is often confusing to a new user, but it is quite simple: The phase of the view that you're placing the element into determines the element's phase, as shown in Figure 10.7. This is more critical for rooms than for building elements because the phase of a building element can be changed after placement. But there may be occasions when you're placing many elements that you intend to be in a particular phase, and you'll want to create a view with that phase active. This will allow you to place elements in that view and not worry about changing their phase later.

FIGURE 10.7
Changing the phase of a view

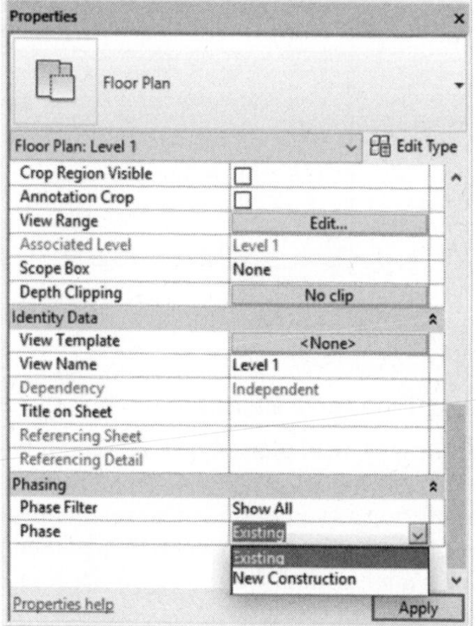

Implementing Phase Settings

Applying the notion of time to your project may seem complicated, but it is quite simple to implement. You need to understand three basic aspects about the settings related to phasing:

- What are the major phases of your project?
- How will you use the phasing properties to filter views within your project documentation?
- What is the graphic convention to convey an object's phase?

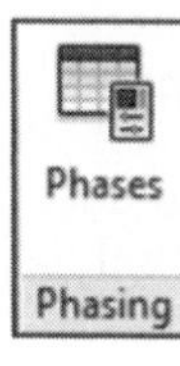

These aspects are expressed in the three tabs of the Phasing dialog box. On the Manage tab of the ribbon, click the Phasing button to open the Phasing dialog box, shown in Figure 10.8.

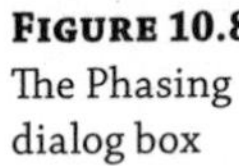

FIGURE 10.8 The Phasing dialog box

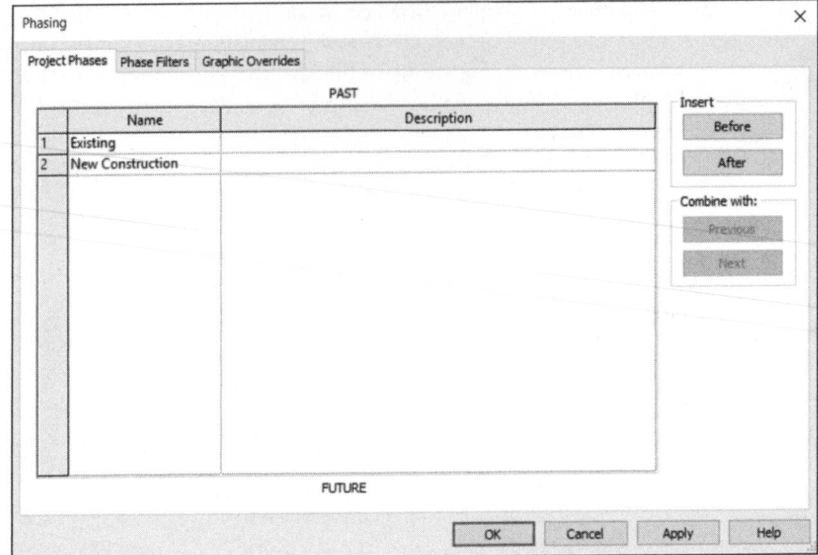

Applying Project Phases

In the most common of phased projects, you'll have views to illustrate Existing, Demolition, and New Construction conditions. On more complex projects, you might have several stages of new construction as you build out larger facilities. Because this dialog box shows only Existing and New Construction, new users will mistakenly create a new phase for Demolition. As we'll demonstrate later, demolished elements are represented with phase filters, not as a dedicated project phase.

So, when do you need to create more than the phases shown by default? As one example, think of a staged construction project that will happen in two new phases. In this scenario, you are designing with a start time for the building shell followed by another phase for interiors, allowing the owner to split funding for the project into two budgets. In phase one, the building core and shell are built. In the second phase, interior construction occurs. Your first phase is labeled Shell and Core. Your other phase is labeled Interiors. This phasing also gives a contractor who is familiar with Revit the ability to use the model to see what needs to be built and when. Depending on how your model is created, the contractor can even do cost estimates by phase.

In the Project Phases tab of the Phasing dialog box, create the two phases as we just described (Figure 10.9). You can simply rename the New Construction phase **Shell and Core**. Click the Insert After button to create an additional project phase and then rename it **Interiors**. We'll use these in a sample exercise in a moment. When you're creating phases, you might notice there's no Delete button. You can't delete a phase once you've added it because you don't want to delete any geometry placed on a phase. Should your planning process change and you want to eliminate a phase, you can merge two phases using either of the Combine With buttons on the right.

FIGURE 10.9
Creating additional project phases

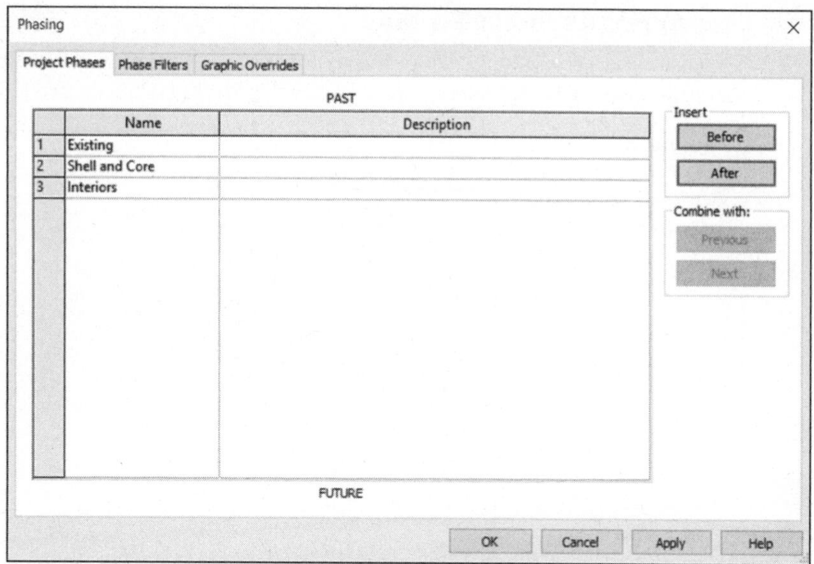

Click OK to accept the changes and close the Phasing dialog box, and then activate the Level 1 floor plan. Once you've created these additional project phases, pick any project geometry and look at its instance parameters. You'll notice in the Properties palette that it can be assigned to any one of these three phases, as shown in Figure 10.10.

FIGURE 10.10
Assigning available phases

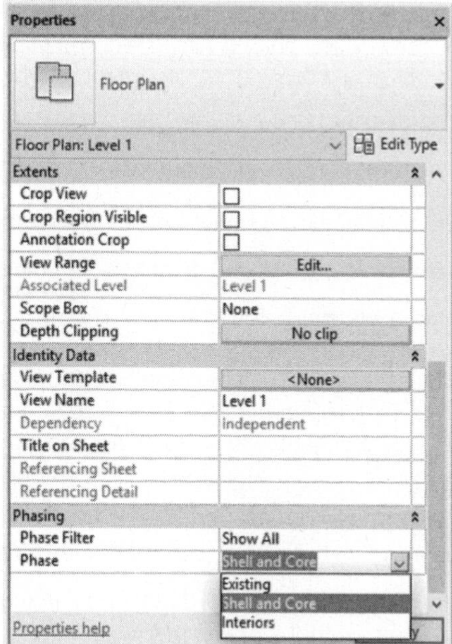

APPLYING PHASE FILTERS

Return to the Manage tab in the ribbon and once again click the Phasing tool. The middle tab in the Phasing dialog box is Phase Filters (Figure 10.11). Seven predefined phase filters are listed.

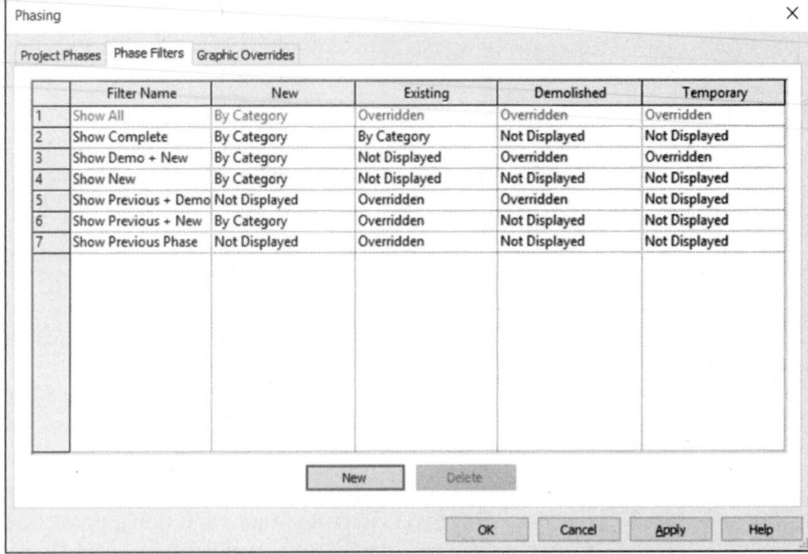

	Filter Name	New	Existing	Demolished	Temporary
1	Show All	By Category	Overridden	Overridden	Overridden
2	Show Complete	By Category	By Category	Not Displayed	Not Displayed
3	Show Demo + New	By Category	Not Displayed	Overridden	Overridden
4	Show New	By Category	Not Displayed	Not Displayed	Not Displayed
5	Show Previous + Demo	Not Displayed	Overridden	Overridden	Not Displayed
6	Show Previous + New	By Category	Overridden	Not Displayed	Not Displayed
7	Show Previous Phase	Not Displayed	Overridden	Not Displayed	Not Displayed

FIGURE 10.11
The Phase Filters tab with seven predefined phase filters

Don't be concerned if the filter names seem a bit cryptic at first. What's really important is the four graphic conditions that can be overridden: New, Existing, Demolished, and Temporary. Let's take a moment to explore how these graphic conditions are applied to a virtually unlimited number of user-defined project phases. Any object you place into a project has certain states relative to any particular phase. In other words, you might ask the following questions about a model element:

- Was it created in the *current* phase? That's *new*.
- Was it created in a previous phase? That's *existing*.
- Was it created in a previous phase and demolished in the current phase? That's *demolished*.
- Is the object created and demolished in the same phase? That's *temporary*.

As you can see, phase filters are relative settings. That is, the filters are relative to the phasing properties of the object and the phase of the view in which the object is displayed. Also realize that although phases are applied to elements, phase filters are applied only to views.

Now let's explore the predefined ways a phase filter can be applied. Select any of the drop-down menus, as shown in Figure 10.12. You'll notice that the phase filter can override the graphics in one of three ways:

- **By Category:** The object can be shown by its category settings or *not* overridden. It will be displayed in the project just as it does by default.
- **Overridden:** This means that you can define a graphic override for that object. We'll get into the graphic overrides in a moment.
- **Not Displayed:** The object is hidden in the view.

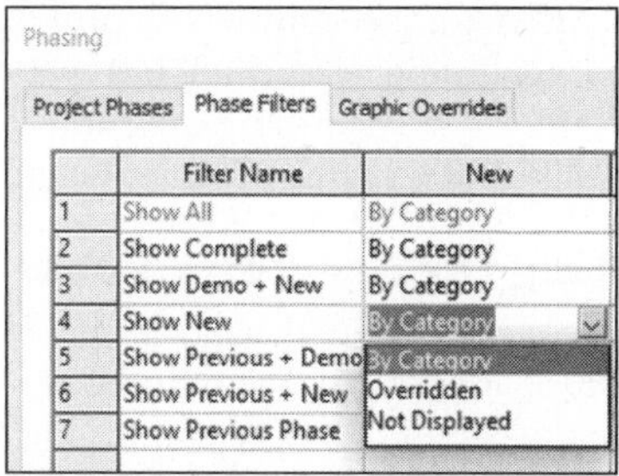

	Filter Name	New
1	Show All	By Category
2	Show Complete	By Category
3	Show Demo + New	By Category
4	Show New	By Category
5	Show Previous + Demo	By Category
6	Show Previous + New	Overridden
7	Show Previous Phase	Not Displayed

FIGURE 10.12
Setting a filter override

Once you understand how each of the phase filters displays objects, phases can begin to make sense. For example, the Show Complete phase filter shows New and Existing elements *By Category*. But Demolished and Temporary elements are not displayed at all. Use this setting when you want to show the model in a finished condition. Another example is to use the Show New phase filter in a schedule such as in a door schedule. The Show New filter will include only those doors that are assigned to the phase that is also assigned to the schedule. The schedule will not list any existing doors or doors that were demolished.

If there's any remaining confusion, it probably involves the naming convention of Show Previous + Demo. A better name might be Show Existing + Demolition, but *Existing* is a bit misleading because this setting is showing the previous phase, which is not necessarily existing elements. They might be temporary elements that need to be demolished. Therefore, Show Previous makes more sense.

USING GRAPHIC OVERRIDES

The Graphic Overrides tab is the final tab in the Phasing dialog box (Figure 10.13). This dialog box relates back to the Overridden assignment of the previous tab.

Phase Status	Projection/Surface Lines	Projection/Surface Patterns	Cut Lines	Cut Patterns	Halftone	Material
Existing				Hidden	☐	Phase - Exist
Demolished				Hidden	☐	Phase - Demo
New					☐	Phase - New
Temporary					☐	Phase - Temporary

FIGURE 10.13
The Graphic Overrides tab

This tab allows you to override geometry in a few areas: the Lines and Patterns characteristics of Projection/Surface and Cut (which refers to the cut profile of objects). You also have the option to just halftone the element. Finally, you can assign a unique Material setting when rendering. Although this ability is helpful for rendering with phase information, it can also be useful for rendering everything to a matte material, something we discuss in Chapter 11, "Visualization." As it is, phasing can show you where you are (new construction) and where you're coming from (existing), but not where you're going (future).

Illustrating the Geometry Phase

Here's a simple exercise to illustrate each of the phases in a single view. Download and open the `c10-Phases-Start.rvt` file from the book's companion web page if you have not already done so. Activate the default 3D view (Figure 10.14).

FIGURE 10.14
Four generic walls

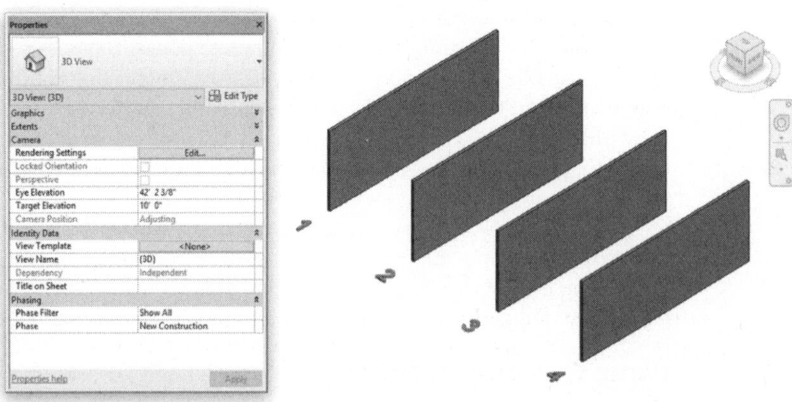

By default, all of these walls have been created in the New Construction phase because the phase of the view is New Construction. Now, selecting each of the walls from left to right, associate them with each of the following phase settings:

- Wall 1: Phase Created: Existing/Phase Demolished: None
- Wall 2: Phase Created: Existing/Phase Demolished: New Construction
- Wall 3: Phase Created: New Construction/Phase Demolished: None
- Wall 4: Phase Created: New Construction/Phase Demolished: New Construction

IT'S HAMMER TIME

Throughout most of this chapter we show you how to set the Phase Demolished property in the Properties palette, but there's a more fun way to change this parameter. In the Modify tab of the ribbon, within the Geometry panel you will find the Demolish hammer. Activate this tool and you can simply click model elements in the active view to set their Phase Demolished property to the phase of the view. It's even been suggested to Autodesk to include a hammering sound effect to this tool!

In Figure 10.15, you'll notice that Wall 1 (Existing/Phase Demolished: None) and Wall 3 (New Construction/Phase Demolished: None) look similar. Graphically, this might not be enough to demonstrate the different phases, so let's change the graphic properties of the Existing wall so it's visually more distinct.

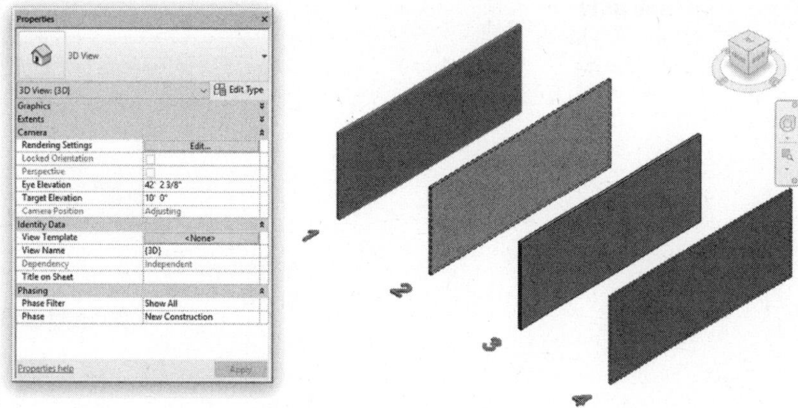

FIGURE 10.15
Default shaded overrides for phasing

From the Manage tab in the ribbon, click Phases; then click the Graphic Overrides tab. Next, select the option to open the Material setting for the Phase - Exist material. You'll click the far right of the Phase-Existing box in the Material column. This opens the Material Browser dialog box highlighting the Phase - Exist material (Figure 10.16).

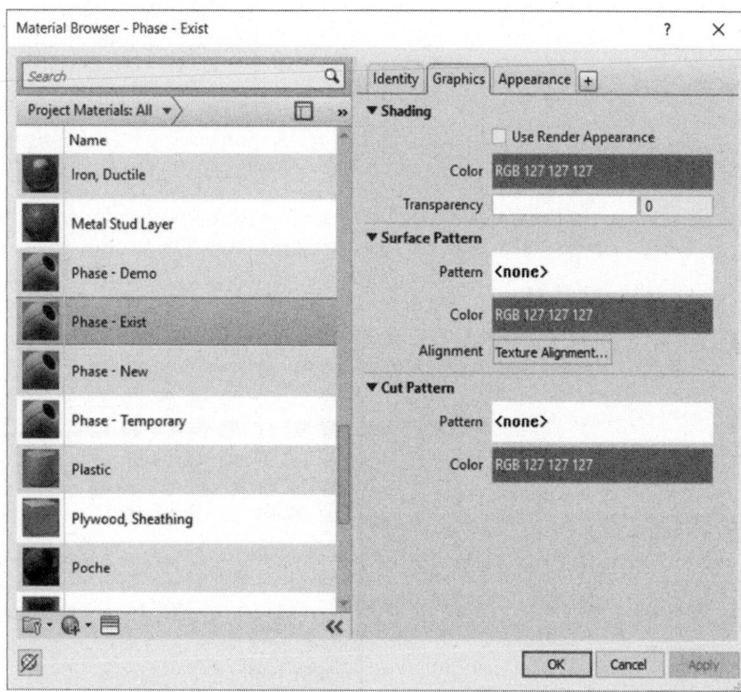

FIGURE 10.16
The Material Browser dialog box

Select the Appearance tab to modify the rendered appearance of the material (Figure 10.17). Click the gray bar that reads RGB 80 80 80 to open the Color dialog box.

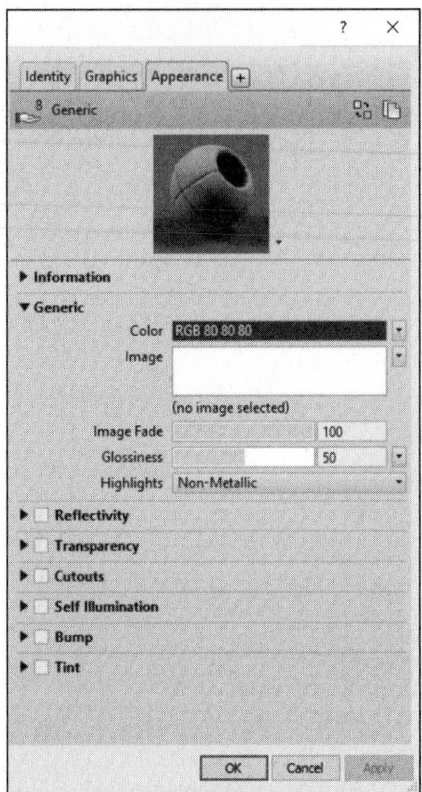

FIGURE 10.17 Editing the Phase - Exist material

In the Color dialog box, assign a lime-green color with the following RGB values: Red = **0**, Green = **255**, Blue = **0** (Figure 10.18). Click OK to close the Color dialog box.

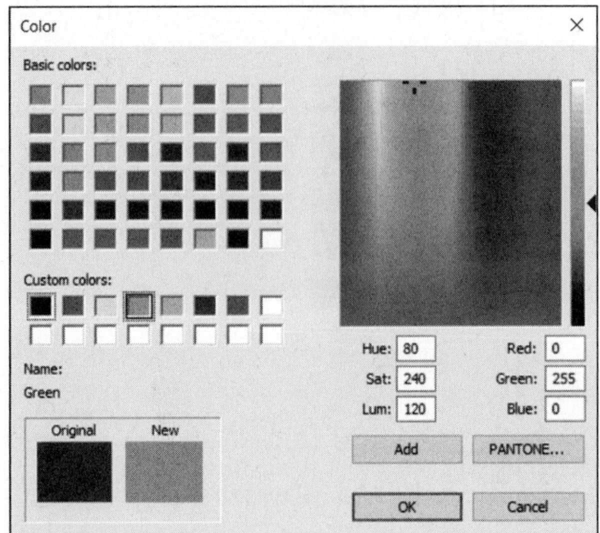

FIGURE 10.18 Overriding the color value

Switch to the Graphics tab and under the Shading properties, check the Use Render Appearance box. This setting will use the coloring of the render material for shaded views as well. Click OK to close the Material Browser. When you finish changing these settings, you'll have the result shown in Figure 10.19, with each phase shown distinctively within the view.

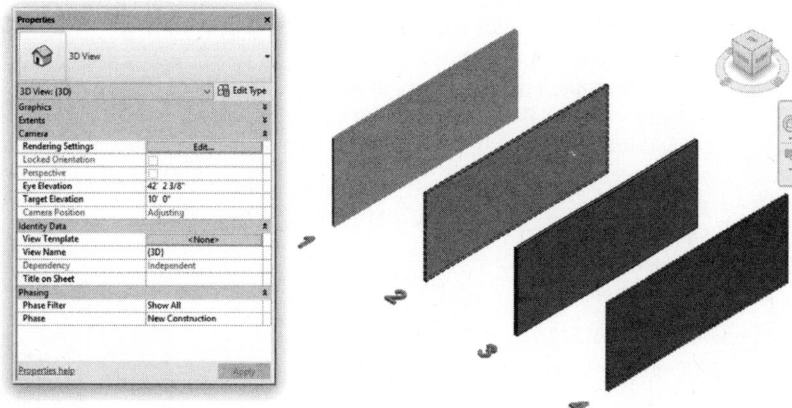

FIGURE 10.19 Finished shading values

Once you settle on a color and graphic scheme, we recommend making this particular setting part of your default project template or your office's standards. That way, new users will be able to distinguish the phase of an object far more clearly, and the standard will be consistent throughout your office.

Using the View Phase

Now that we've discussed the phasing properties of geometry, we'll cover the phase properties of the views. Starting with the 3D view from the previous example, examine the view properties in the Properties palette, provided there are no model elements selected (Figure 10.20). We have collapsed some of the property groups at the top to show the Phasing properties at the bottom of the list.

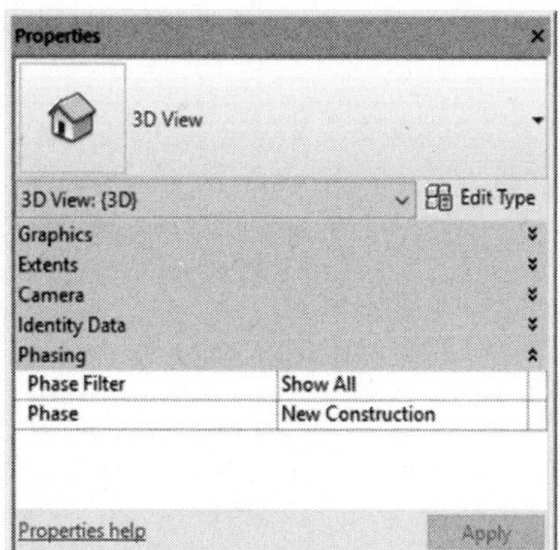

FIGURE 10.20 Phasing options for a view

Remember that all the graphic overrides and filters for phasing are *relative* to the phase that is assigned to geometry or a view. By default, the New Construction phase is assigned to new views created in your project. This phase assignment can be changed at any time from the Properties palette. The phase property can also be assigned to a view template for easier management of this parameter.

The next important step is to apply the most appropriate phase filter. To illustrate how a phase filter changes the way objects are displayed in a view, you will step through several filters in the following exercises.

The default phase filter is Show All (Figure 10.21). This filter will show all the model elements relative to the phase assigned to the view and will override their graphics based on their Phase Created and Phase Demolished parameters. It also gives you a sense of all the elements as they exist in time.

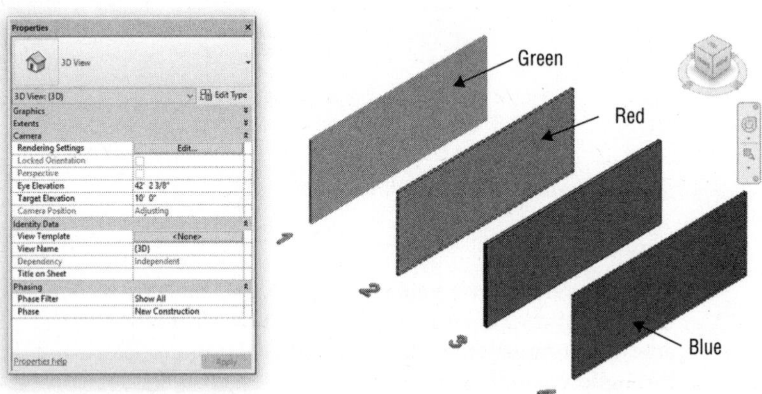

FIGURE 10.21 Show All phase filter for the New Construction phase

Although this is great for 3D views, where every phase has a distinct color, it's also useful for working in a plan, elevation, or section. To turn this graphic visibility on, activate the Level 1 floor plan from the Project Browser and change the Graphic Display setting to Shaded or Consistent Colors. You'll be able to clearly distinguish between objects in different phases, as shown in Figure 10.22.

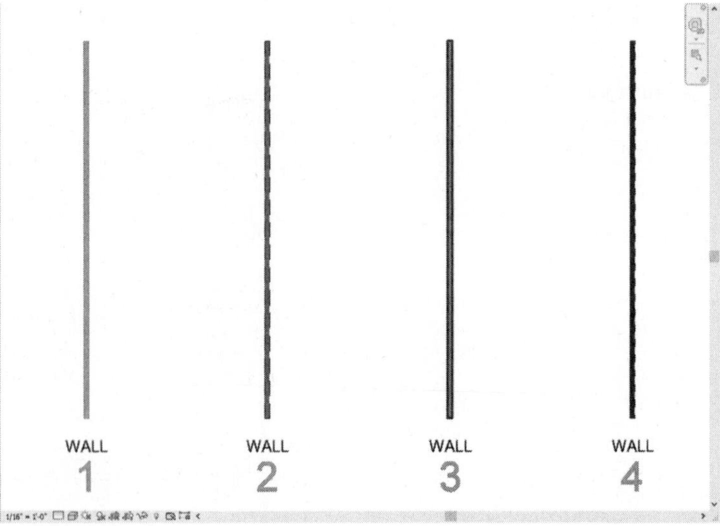

FIGURE 10.22 Shaded plan view of phased elements

Now let's start moving through each of the phase filters. But here's an important note: Rather than moving through the various phase filters from top to bottom, let's move through time by changing the Phase parameter.

Return to the 3D view and keep the Phase Filter set to Show All, but change the Phase to Existing (Figure 10.23). This will show only the objects created in the Existing phase—and their graphics are not overridden. The two walls that were assigned to the New Construction phase are not shown in the view because Revit does not provide a way to see future construction beyond the phase assigned to the view.

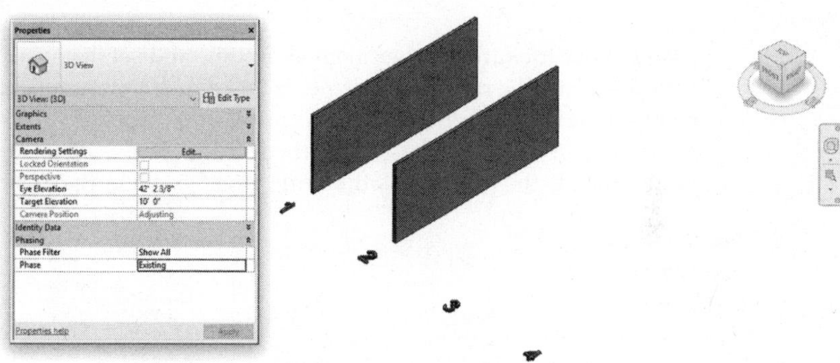

FIGURE 10.23
Show All phase filter for the Existing phase

Set the phase of the view back to New Construction and set the phase filter to Show Previous + Demo (Figure 10.24). This filter still shows only the existing walls (the walls from the previous phase). One of the walls is clearly being demolished. Keep in mind that the graphic overrides that are being applied are relative to what you'd be seeing through the lens of the New Construction phase.

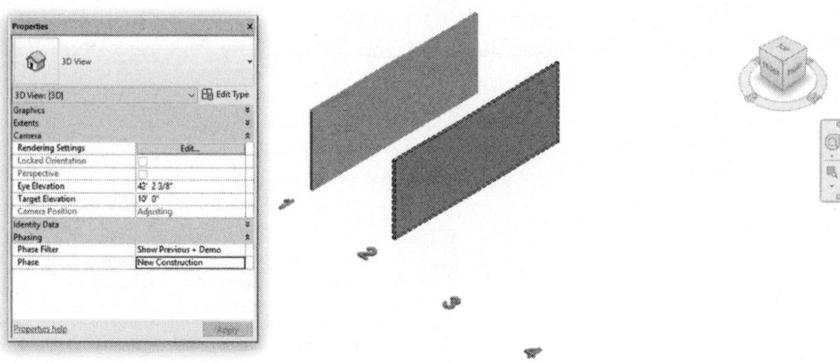

FIGURE 10.24
Show Previous + Demo phase filter

Now select Show Previous Phase as the phase filter, as shown in Figure 10.25. The demolished element is no longer shown.

FIGURE 10.25 Show Previous Phase phase filter

We'll move forward another moment in time and set the phase filter to Show Previous + New. This shows only the remaining elements (not any of the demolished content) from the present and previous views (Figure 10.26). It is not always necessary to click Apply in the Properties palette each time you want to apply the settings you've just changed. Moving your mouse pointer outside the palette has the same effect as clicking Apply.

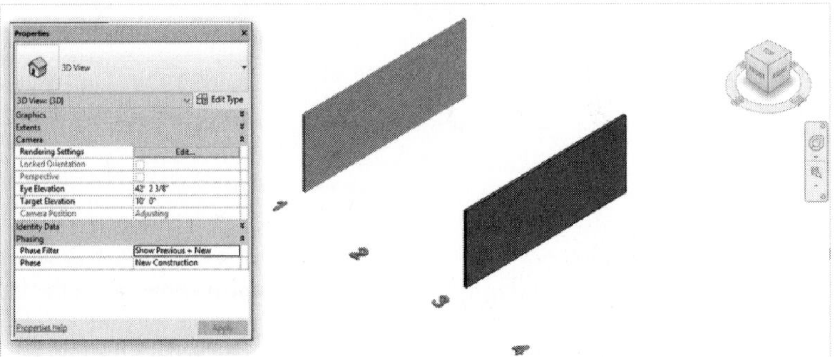

FIGURE 10.26 Show Previous + New phase filter

This visualization brings up another interesting point: Why not show the remaining existing elements as well as the proposed and temporary elements? Although you could also create a new phase filter, for this example we'll change the settings of the Show Previous + New graphic phase filter (Figure 10.27). From the Manage tab on the ribbon, click the Phases tool again. Choose the Phase Filters tab, and in the Show Previous + New row, go to the Temporary column and change the setting to Overridden.

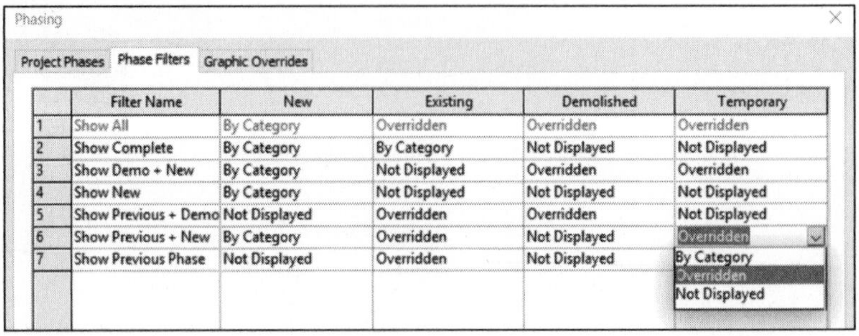

FIGURE 10.27 Changing the phase filter settings

Phasing

Project Phases | Phase Filters | Graphic Overrides

	Filter Name	New	Existing	Demolished	Temporary
1	Show All	By Category	Overridden	Overridden	Overridden
2	Show Complete	By Category	By Category	Not Displayed	Not Displayed
3	Show Demo + New	By Category	Not Displayed	Overridden	Overridden
4	Show New	By Category	Not Displayed	Not Displayed	Not Displayed
5	Show Previous + Demo	Not Displayed	Overridden	Overridden	Not Displayed
6	Show Previous + New	By Category	Overridden	Not Displayed	Overridden
7	Show Previous Phase	Not Displayed	Overridden	Not Displayed	By Category Overridden Not Displayed

Click OK to exit the dialog box. Figure 10.28 shows the result.

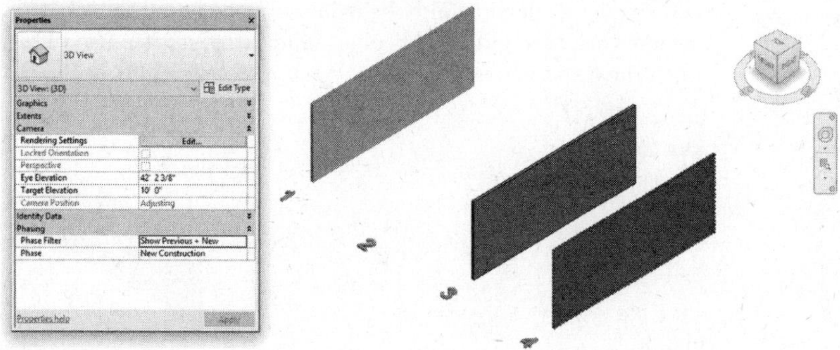

FIGURE 10.28
Show Previous + New phase filter with temporary elements added

The next step in the sequence is to set the view to Show Demo + New, which will show demolished elements from the present phase as well as any new elements from the present phase (see Figure 10.29). The numbers disappeared because they are Model Text elements that were placed on the Existing phase.

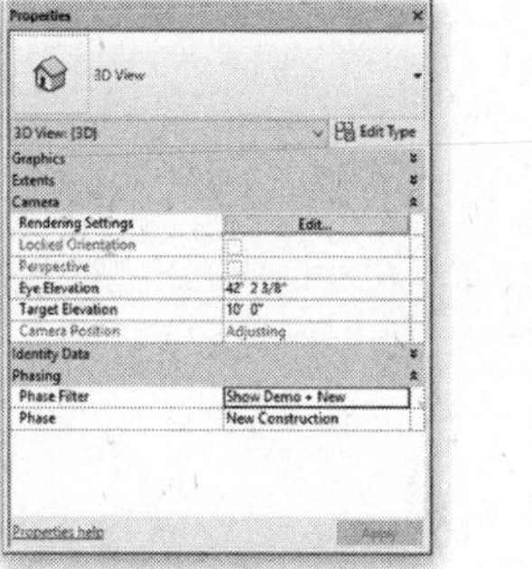

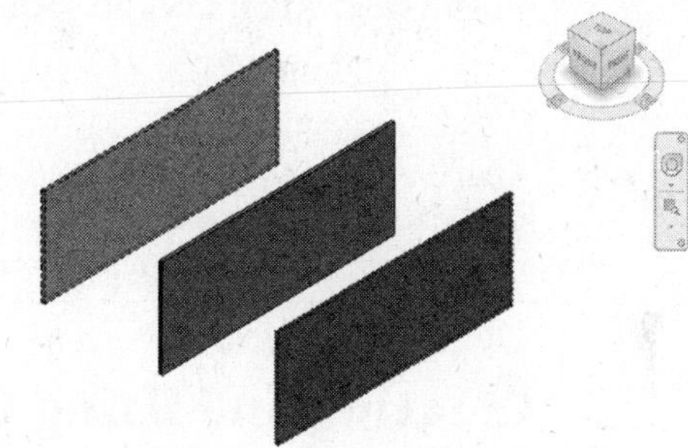

FIGURE 10.29
Show Demo + New phase filter

Moving forward in time, let's now show only the elements in the New Construction phase. Set the phase filter to Show New and only one wall will be displayed, as shown in Figure 10.30.

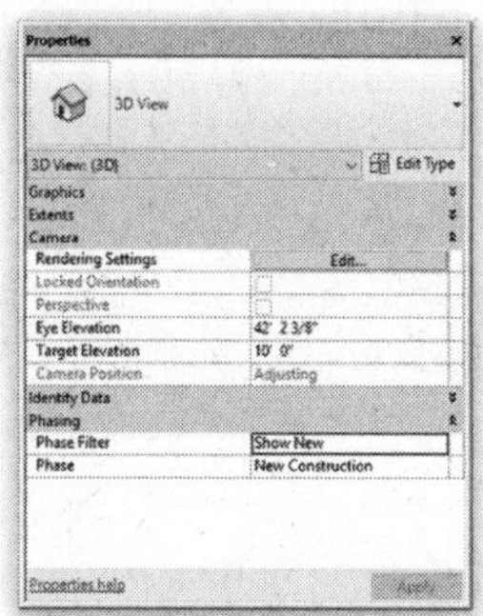

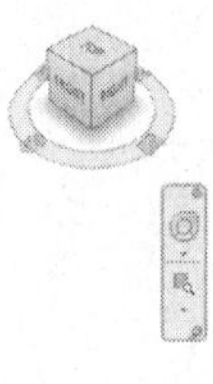

FIGURE 10.30
Show New phase filter

Now comes the final phase filter setting, Show Complete (Figure 10.31). This shows only the existing elements that were not demolished in previous phases up to the phase assigned to the view. Elements that are demolished in any phase are not displayed, and neither existing nor new elements are overridden. This phase filter is most often used for camera views where a rendering of the finished conditions may need to be generated without any sort of graphic overrides.

FIGURE 10.31
Show Complete phase filter

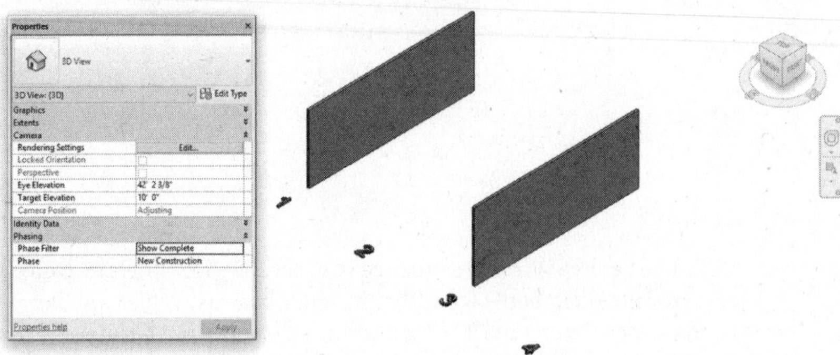

PHASING WITH LINKED MODELS

If you are working on larger-scale projects, you'll want to keep some additional factors in mind when using phasing. To control your phasing between linked models (which could be linked architectural models or consultant models), make sure your phase names are *identical*. If one model has "Existing + Demo" and the other team has "existing+demo," the linked models will see those as different phases. Remember: Consistency is the key.

Creating and Using Groups

It's easy to think of groups as functionally similar to blocks in Autodesk® AutoCAD® software or cells in Bentley MicroStation, but groups can be much more. They are great at maintaining repetition within your project, but there are some major differences:

- Creating groups is quite easy. And whether it's a 2D or 3D group, the insertion point for the group is easily defined and modified. The same can't be said of simple 2D blocks in other applications.
- Updating groups is a breeze. It's easy and intuitive to modify a group after it's been created. Practically anyone on your team can do it, which means that design workflow will not bottleneck in your project team.
- Copying groups throughout your project is also a breeze. Groups can be copied across different levels, rotated, and even mirrored. We cover groups in more detail later in this chapter.

There are a few good practices that you'll want to keep in mind when using groups. But they're so straightforward that you'll wonder how you've ever worked without them.

Creating Groups

You can create two kinds of groups in Revit. One kind is just for geometry, and these groups are called *model groups*. The other is just for view-specific content like text, tags, dimensions, and so on, and these groups are called *detail groups*. You can create one kind of group or the other explicitly. But if you try to create a group with both model and detail elements, Revit is smart enough to create a separate detail group that's associated with the model group.

To demonstrate this, download and open the file `c10-Groups-Start.rvt` or `c10-Groups-Start-Metric.rvt` from this book's web page. Activate the Level 1 floor plan and you will see four walls with dimensions, as shown in Figure 10.32.

FIGURE 10.32
Four walls and dimensions

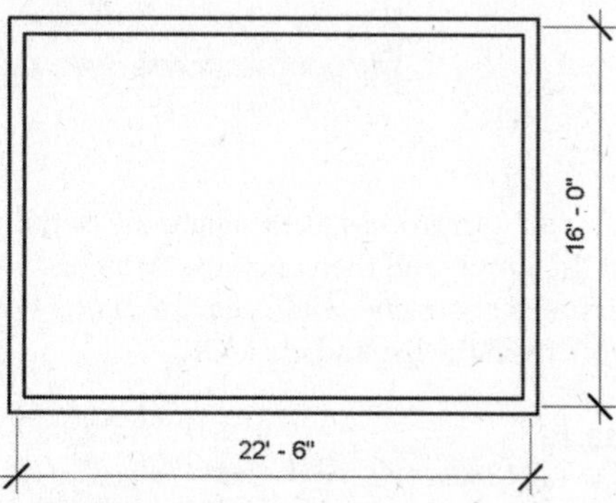

Select the walls and dimensions in the view, and click the Create Group button on the contextual ribbon in the Create panel. Keep the default name, Group 1, for both Model Group and Attached Detail Group (Figure 10.33).

FIGURE 10.33
Creating the model and attached detail group

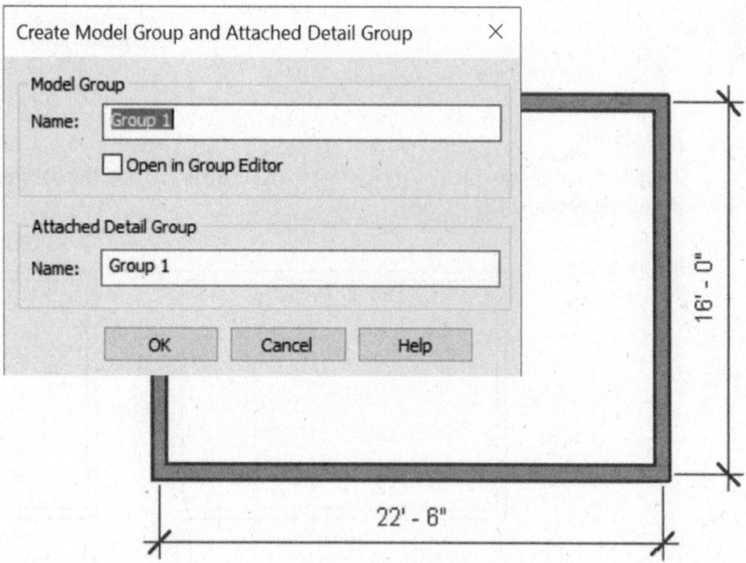

Now select the group of walls and copy it to the side of your original group. You'll notice that only the model-based group is copied, which is fine for now (Figure 10.34).

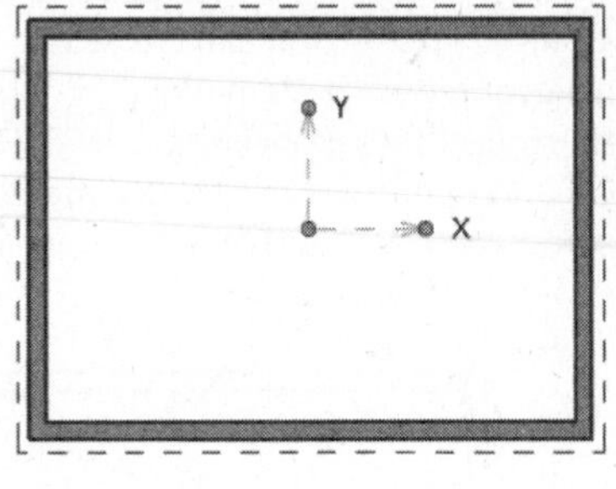

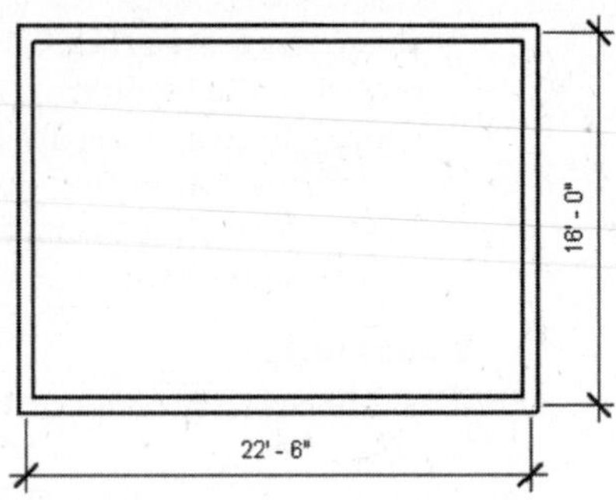

FIGURE 10.34
Copied model group

It is a simple process to associate the detail group to another instance of the model group. Select the group and then click the Attached Detail Groups button on the Group panel in the contextual ribbon, and you'll see the dialog box shown in Figure 10.35. Select the check box for Group 1 from the list and click OK.

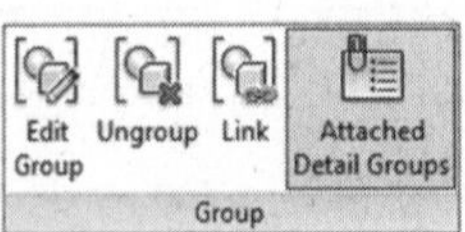

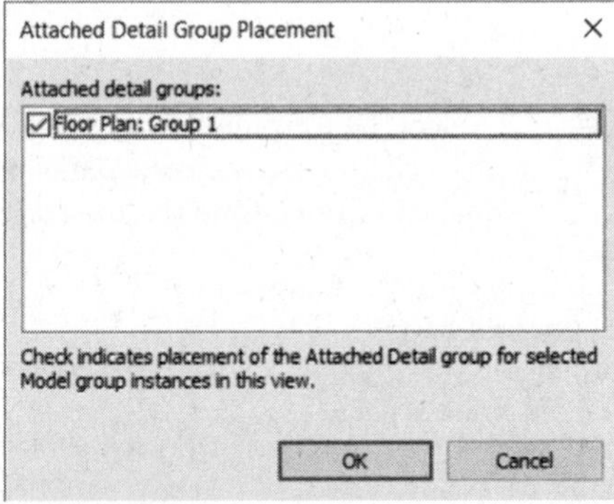

FIGURE 10.35
Attached Detail Group Placement dialog box

The results are fairly straightforward (Figure 10.36). Both groups are now identical with geometry and dimensions.

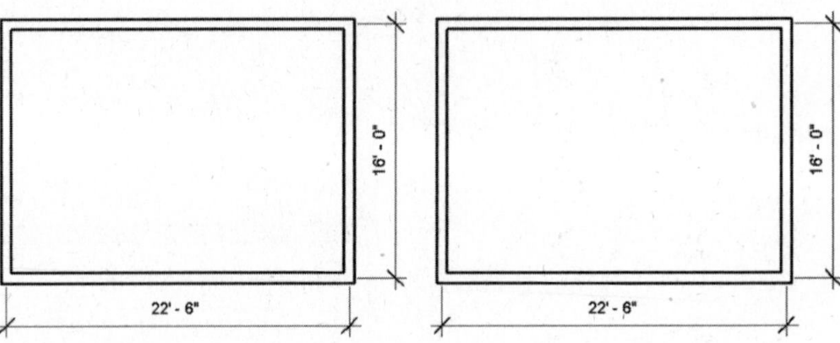

FIGURE 10.36
Identical groups

Modifying Groups

Now that you've created two identical groups, let's add a door to one of the walls that belong to the group, as shown in Figure 10.37. But don't add the door to the group—just place it in one of the walls as you would with any nongrouped wall.

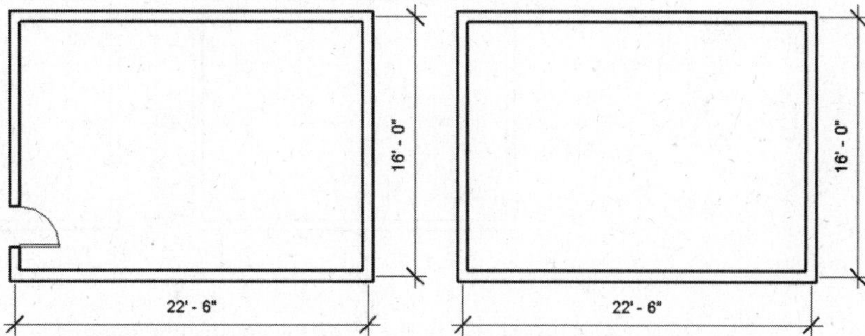

FIGURE 10.37 Adding a door outside of Edit Group mode

Now select the group to the left (the one with the new door) and select Edit Group from the Group panel in the contextual tab of the ribbon. You'll enter a special editing environment, shown in Figure 10.38, and the nongrouped elements will be grayed out. The screen overlay color alerts you that you are in Edit Group mode. The screen will appear with a yellow background in this mode. Here you'll be able to add, remove, and attach other elements to your group.

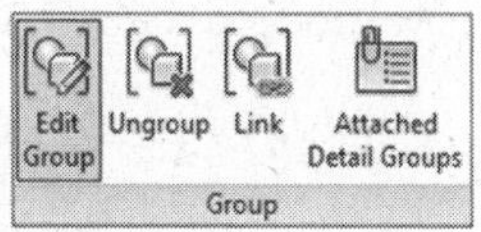

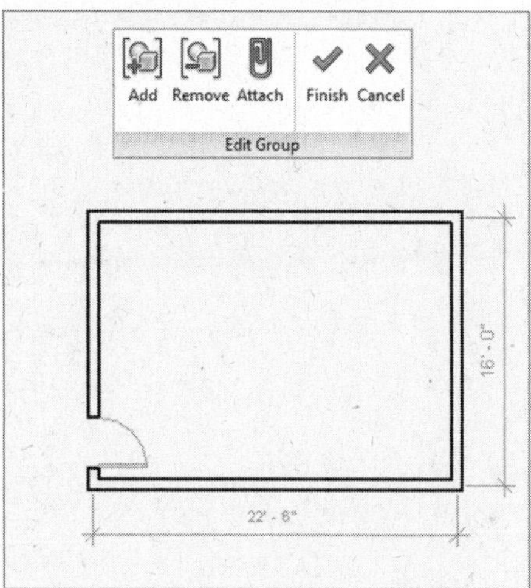

FIGURE 10.38 Edit Group mode

Now add the door to the group by selecting the Add function from the Edit Group panel. When you add an element to the group, it will appear black in the Edit Group mode, letting you know you were able to successfully add it to your group. You'll notice that you can't add the door numbers because this is a model group and tags are 2D components. Now finish the group by clicking the Finish button (the green check), and you'll notice that both groups now have a door in the same location (Figure 10.39).

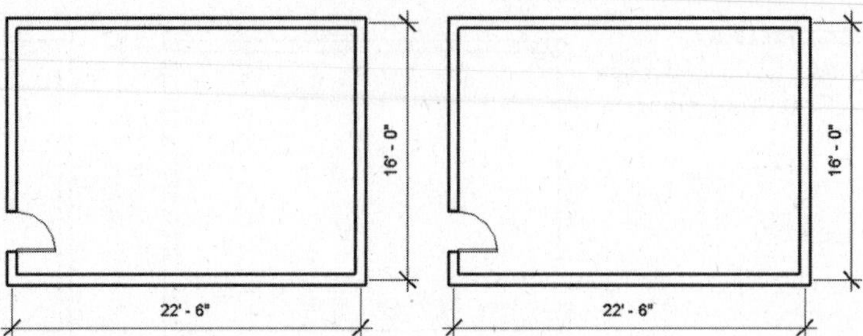

FIGURE 10.39
Finished group

The process is essentially the same for modifying any group: Start the Edit Group mode, make the changes and/or additions, and then finish the group.

Creating New Groups

Sometimes the easiest way to make a new group is to copy and modify an old one. A quick way to do this is to right-click the name of the group you want to duplicate in the Project Browser and choose Duplicate from the context menu, as shown in Figure 10.40. Complete this command and make sure the new group is named **Group 2** in the Project Browser.

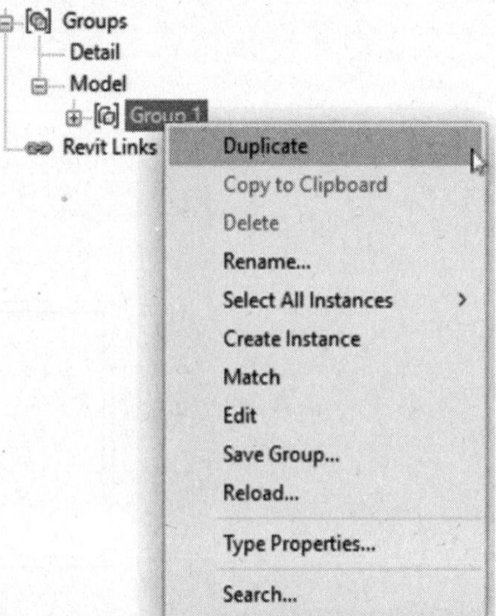

FIGURE 10.40
Duplicating a group

Return to the plan view and select your group. Notice in the Type Selector that you can swap between groups in the same way you can swap between types within a family. Choose Group 2 in the Type Selector so you have one of each group type on the screen.

With Group 2 still selected, click Edit Group from the contextual tab in the ribbon. Edit it by making it 13′-6″ square (4 m), as shown in Figure 10.41; then finish the group.

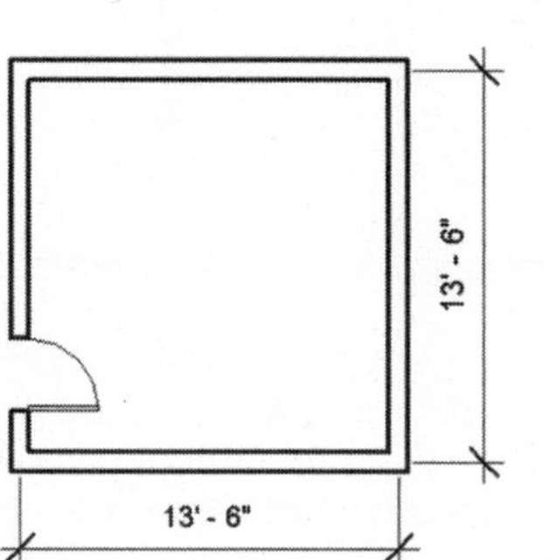

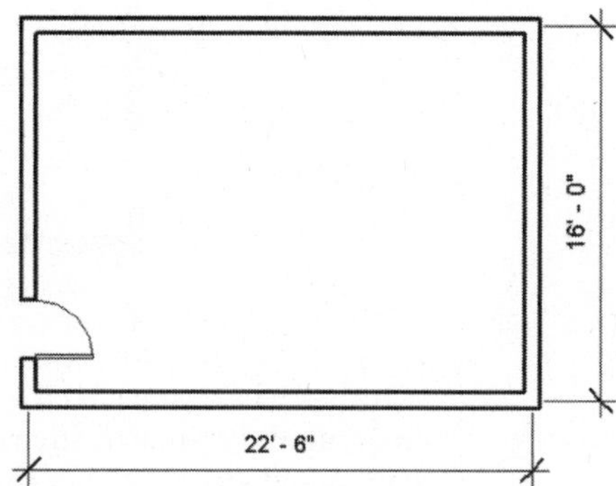

FIGURE 10.41
Modifying the second group type

Groups have insertion points that you need to consider before you exchange one group for another. When you create a group, the insertion point is initially at the geometric center of all the elements in the group. The group's origin is also identified by x- and y-coordinates.

But keep in mind that as you edit the group, the insertion point doesn't move until you deliberately relocate it. This can be seen in Figure 10.42; editing the geometry for Group 2 retains the same insertion point that was active when the group was initially created. Even though we've modified the group, the insertion point remains where it was originally when the group was created. (When editing this group, the left wall was moved to the right and the top wall was moved down to achieve the dimensions.)

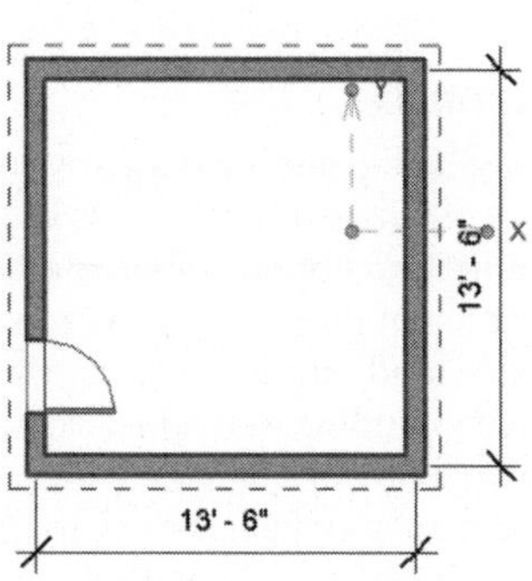

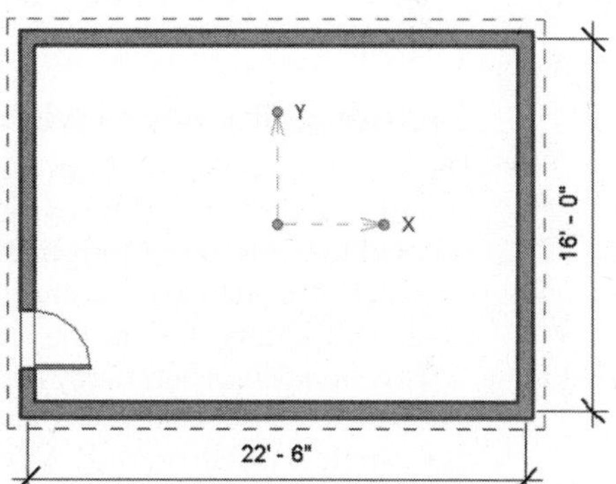

FIGURE 10.42
Insertion points in different groups

Moving the insertion point is an easy matter of dragging (and, if necessary, rotating) the Insertion Point icon to a common location before swapping one group for another (Figure 10.43). Drag the insertion points for both Group 1 and Group 2 to the inside face of the walls at the lower-left corner.

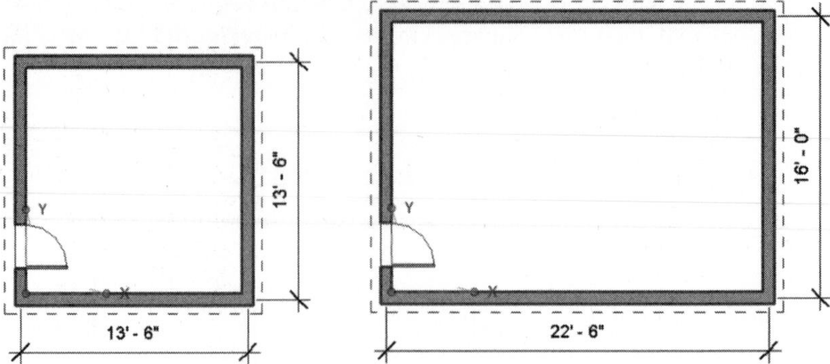

FIGURE 10.43
Relocating insertion points

Once you have adjusted the insertion points of multiple similar groups, swapping groups will occur at the same relative location. Figure 10.44 illustrates Group 1 being swapped for Group 2, and vice versa, but common insertion points are maintained. Select the instance of Group 1 in the floor plan and choose Group 2 from the Type Selector.

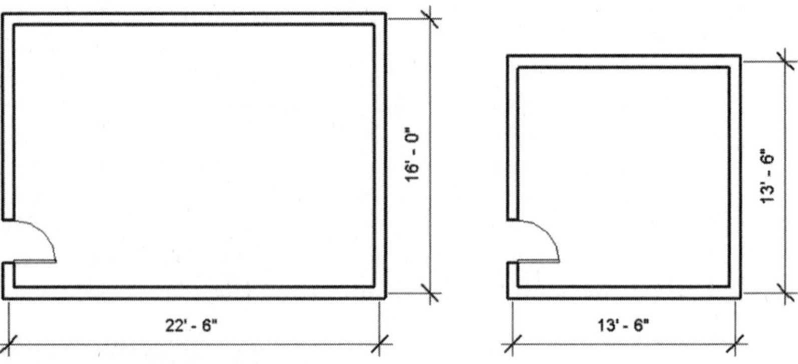

FIGURE 10.44
Exchanged groups

Excluding Elements within Groups

There will be occasions where everything in a group works great and it works throughout the project—except for that one particular case where a condition is slightly different. In the past, you had to create new groups for each slight exception, which might have been conceptually consistent but often led to a much longer list of group variants. You were left with little ability to cohesively modify them as the project size (and number of groups) continued to grow.

This workflow is now deftly handled by excluding individual elements from groups. The original group definitions remain intact, and schedules are aware of excluded elements. Figure 10.45 shows an example of this in practice. We've created another instance of Group 1; however, there's a column right in the middle of the door.

We don't want to destroy the integrity of the group and give up being able to quickly modify similar elements, but we also cannot advance the design with the column located where it is shown. To resolve this, hover the mouse pointer over the door within the group and then press the Tab key until the door is highlighted, right-click it, and select Create Similar from the context menu. This will allow you to place a new door in a better location. This door will not be part of the group. In Figure 10.46, the new door has been placed above the grouped door, and its swing direction has been flipped.

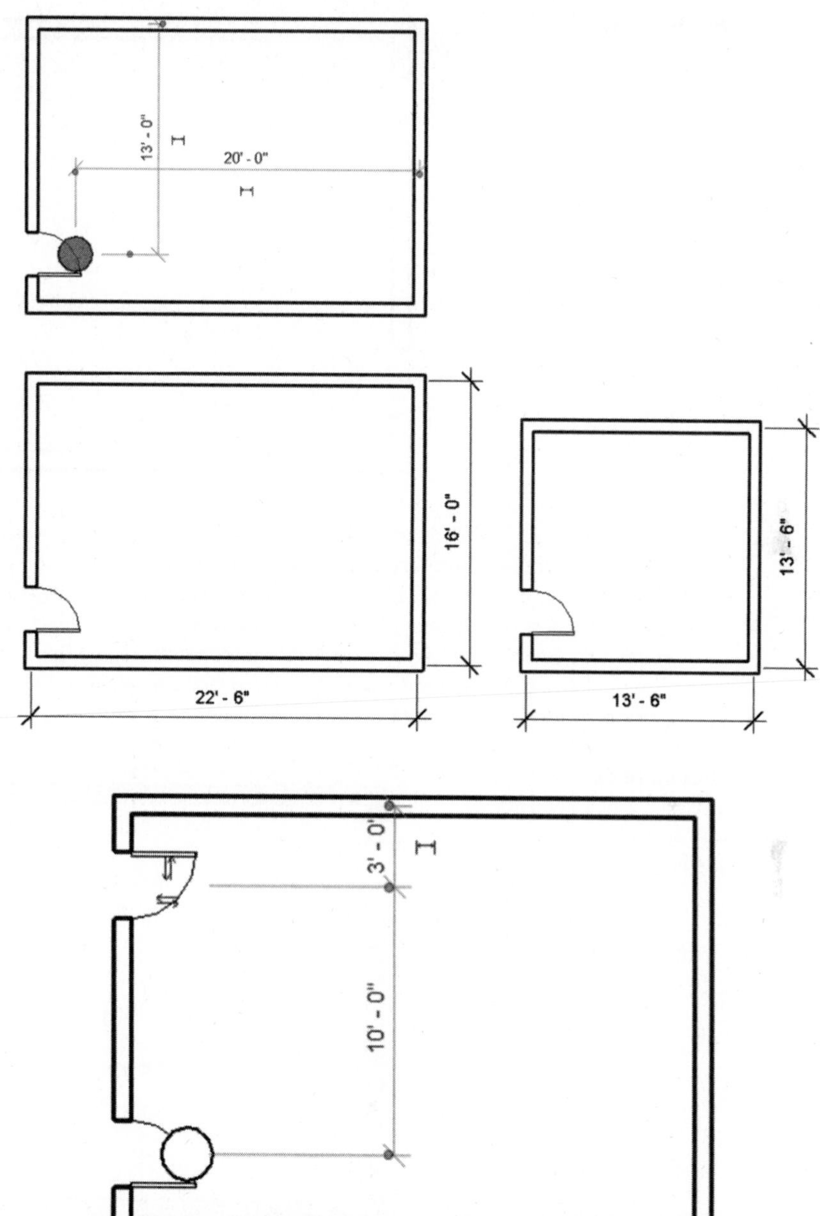

FIGURE 10.45
A column location conflicts with the door in our sample group.

FIGURE 10.46
Adding a new door using Create Similar

Now you can exclude the door that conflicts with the column as an exception to the original group definition. This process can be a bit confusing at first because you don't need to enter Group Edit mode to exclude members from groups. Simply hover the mouse pointer over the door and press the Tab key until the door is highlighted. Select the door, as shown in Figure 10.47.

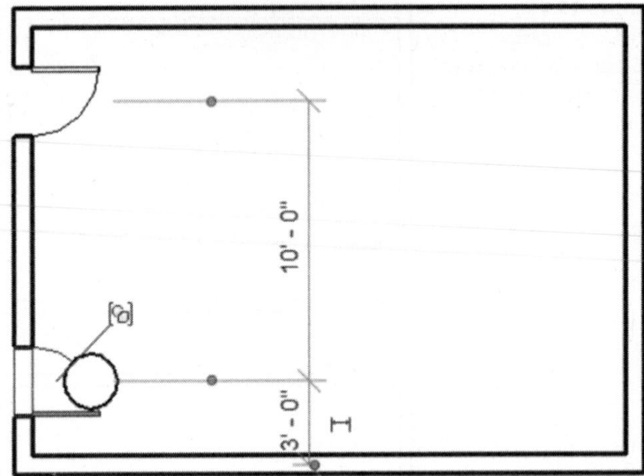

FIGURE 10.47
Selecting elements in groups

Once the door in the group is selected, you'll notice an icon pointing to the door. Clicking this icon will allow you to exclude the door as an exception to the group. The icon will change and show a red hash through it. This means the element is now excluded and will automatically be deleted when you deselect the group. The wall will heal itself as if the door were never there.

How can you tell if a given group has elements that have been excluded? Selecting the group will reveal any hidden elements in the group that are excluded (Figure 10.48). Just tab through to select the hidden door to include the component back into the group.

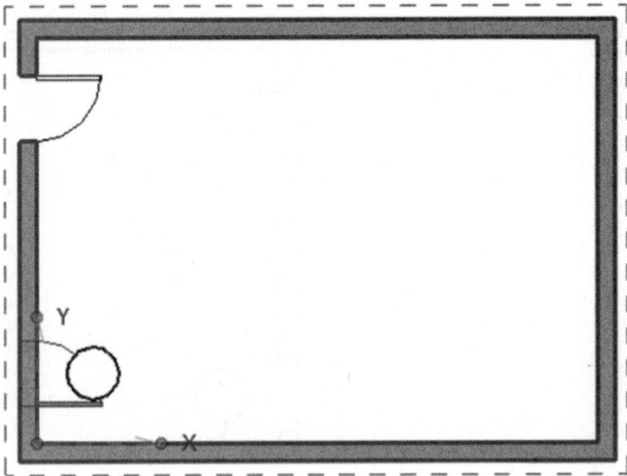

FIGURE 10.48
Excluded group elements will display when the group is selected.

Saving and Loading Groups

Even though we stress the fact that Revit is a whole-process BIM application (by integrating the modeling, documentation, and multiuser workflow into one database), there are times when you'll want to share the data across many files.

Just as you wouldn't want your family components locked up inside a project file, there are good reasons to keep commonly used groups outside your project. You might even want to keep them in a folder just as you do your custom content so you can use them again on similar projects or as part of your office's library. You can do so by saving groups outside your projects.

Saving groups is a simple matter of right-clicking the group name in your Project Browser and selecting Save Group (Figure 10.49).

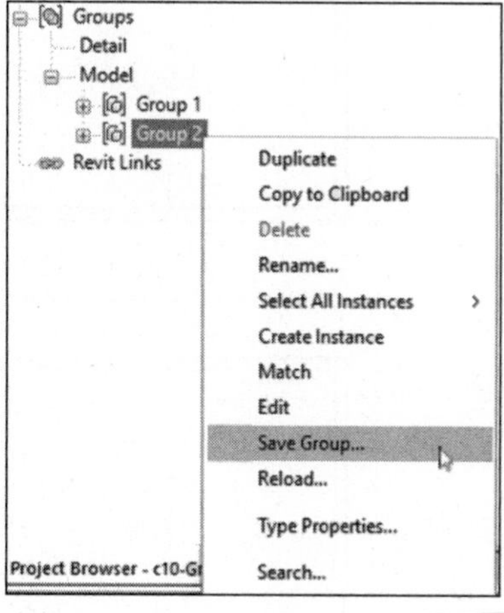

FIGURE 10.49
Saving groups from the Project Browser

You'll then be prompted to save the group as an RVT file. You can open this file as you would any other RVT file if you'd like to modify it later and then reload the group into the project in order to update all the instances. To load an external group into a project, go to the Insert tab in the ribbon. On the Load From Library panel, choose Load As Group.

Be aware that when you load the group in a project, if the group name already exists, you'll be given a warning. You can overwrite the existing group (by selecting Yes) or load with the option to rename the group that's being loaded (by selecting No). Or you can cancel the operation altogether (Figure 10.50).

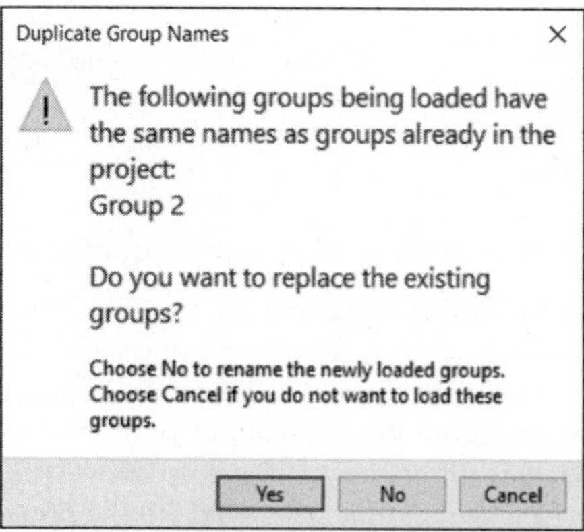

FIGURE 10.50
Loading groups with the same name

What's really great is that when you reload the group, Revit even remembers to exclude previously excluded elements from the group that's been modified in another session. Figure 10.51 shows that a desk and chair have been added to Group 1 in the RVT file saved from the original group. The group has been reloaded, overwriting the original group, but the exclusion remains intact.

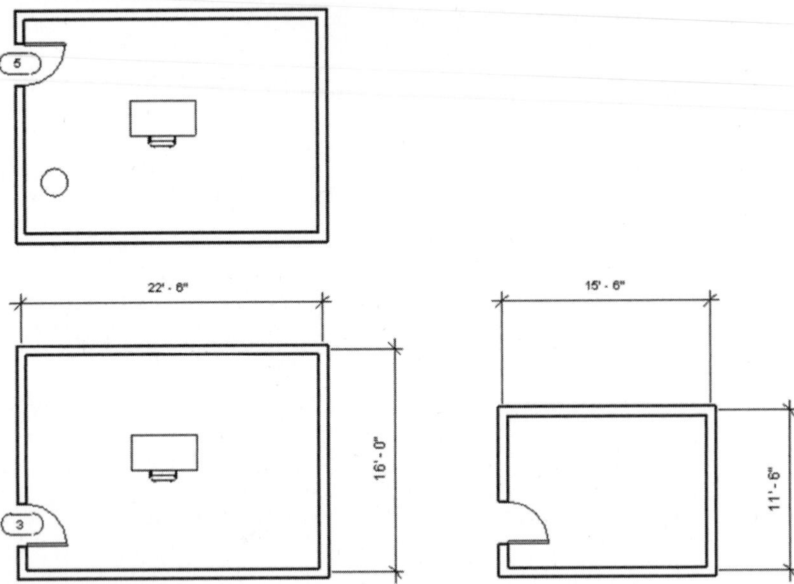

FIGURE 10.51 Retaining excluded group elements

Creating Groups from Links

Because groups are also RVT files, they can be linked into the project environment as well. Although you can't edit a link in place (as with a group), there are some excellent reasons why you might want to start a group as a link and then bind the link at a later time. Binding a linked project will convert it to a group. Groups and links can also exist within design options (more on design options later in this chapter). To follow this workflow, use these steps:

1. From the Insert tab in the ribbon, choose Link Revit from the Link panel (Figure 10.52).

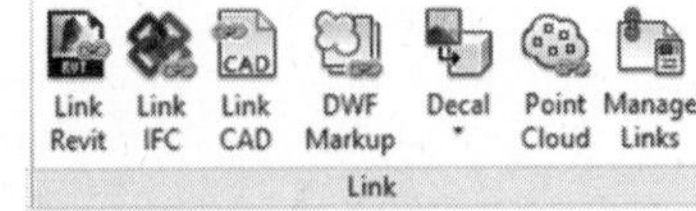

FIGURE 10.52 Use the Link Revit command to add groups as links.

2. Browse to the group you just exported and click Open.

After the link has been placed, you can copy it throughout your project as you would any other element in Revit. Keep in mind that all the functionality between groups and non-grouped elements will not behave the same in links as it does throughout the rest of your project. For example, in Figure 10.53, the upper-right collection of walls and furniture is a link, not a group. As a result, walls are not cleaning up between linked models and groups in the same way they are between groups and other walls in the project.

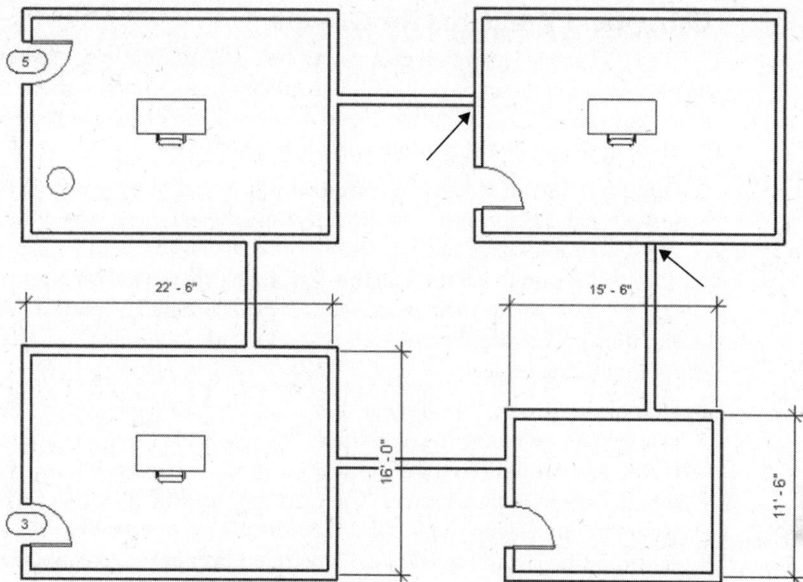

FIGURE 10.53 Walls don't join to linked models.

This graphic restriction may not be a concern during early stages of design, when links allow for a lot of rapid flexibility. After you've resolved your design using linked models, you can bind them into the project environment by selecting each link in a view and clicking Bind Link from the contextual tab in the ribbon.

Rather than explode the linked model into separate and unrelated elements, Revit converts the link to a group. Once this happens, walls easily join across groups, as shown in Figure 10.54.

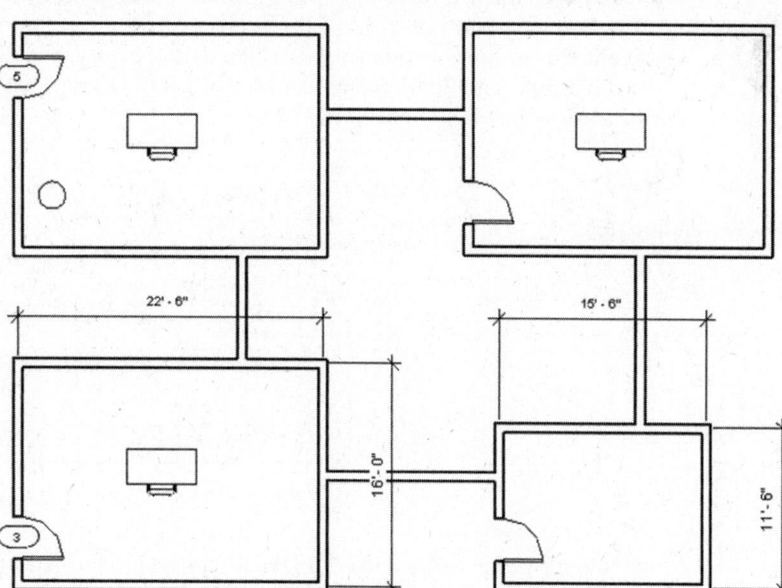

FIGURE 10.54 Wall joins are resolved when linked models are bound in the current project.

Using Best Practices for Groups

So far, you have learned that groups can help you maintain consistency among repeated elements and will facilitate additional design iteration; however, there are some important exceptions that you will want to note. Nearly every time a problem crops up with groups, it's the result of ignoring one of the following best practices:

Don't put datum objects in your group. Avoid putting datum objects (levels and grids) inside your group. First, you can't manage the extents of the datum objects unless you're in Edit Group mode, which can create conflicts elsewhere in your project. Of course, you will have the option to *not* include the datum objects when you bind your link. Again, doing so doesn't necessarily create a technical hurdle, but it can create a lot of confusion. We've seen situations where duplicate levels were deleted only to find out that those levels were hosting content in the project.

Don't nest groups. In other words, avoid creating groups within other groups. Although nesting can save time in some situations when the design is preliminary and your team is trying to distribute content and design ideas quickly, you'll likely find a point of diminishing returns as the design evolves. You can't get to all the features and functionality of Revit when you're in Edit Group mode. And if you're nested deep into groups and trying to modify project properties, you'll quickly get frustrated digging in, out, and across nested groups to go back and forth between your group and the project.

Group hosted elements and their hosts together. Always keep your hosted elements and hosts together. For example, do not group doors and windows without the walls that are hosting them. If any of the windows in a group become unhosted from walls and then deleted, this will delete the respective windows in all other group instances—even if they are properly hosted.

Don't use attached relationships in groups. The top constraints of walls are commonly attached to levels or other hosts like floors and roofs, but these relationships should be avoided in groups. If you manipulate the datum or attached host and the relationship creates inconsistent conditions among the instances of the group, you'll see a warning asking you to fix the groups (Figure 10.55).

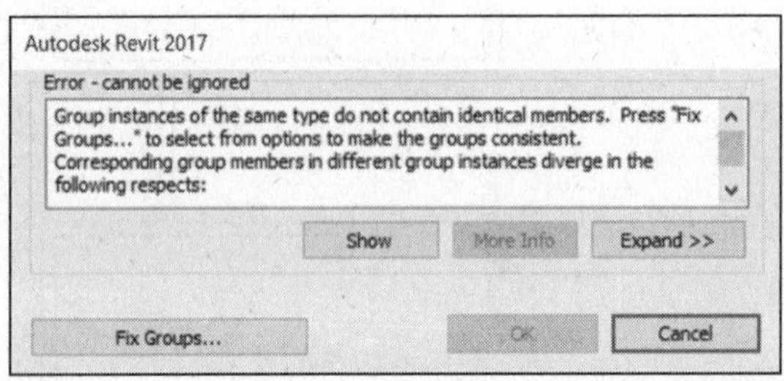

FIGURE 10.55
Avoid attaching with groups.

Fixing the group really doesn't fix the group. It actually explodes it or creates a new group that is no longer referenced to the first group (Figure 10.56).

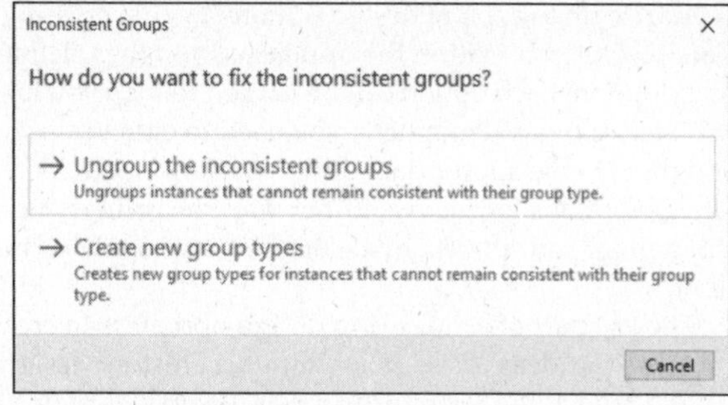

FIGURE 10.56
Resolving attachments warning

Don't mirror groups. Finally, and maybe most important, don't mirror groups. Instead, it's better to create left and right versions. Does mirroring work in concept? Yes. Does it work in the real world? Not really.

Think about it. You'd love to be able to mirror that prototype coffee shop, right? Mirror the coffee shop—and all the equipment in the group—and now the baristas are foaming milk on the right rather than the left. This might look great in a rendering, but it doesn't make sense for the company that manufactures the espresso machines.

And now the display cases have power supplies on the wrong side. The cash register has keys on the wrong side. The desk in the manager's office now has drawers on the left and filing cabinets on the right. And to make matters worse, the sink in the bathroom now has hot water coming from the wrong faucet. Again, it makes all the conceptual sense in the world to be able to mirror a building—and a group. But trying to make it work can cost a lot of time and money. And that's just a coffee shop. If you think it's a good idea to mirror a hospital room or a surgical theater or some other mission-critical building or civil construct, well, it could end badly. Or you will have to work very, very late to resolve the issues.

If you'd like to download the file that has been created during the examples, you can find it in the Chapter 10 folder on the book's web page; the file is called `c10-Groups-Finished.rvt`.

Making Design Options for Design Iteration

Revit software provides a unique set of tools for developing multiple design iterations in the confines of a single-model environment. You can use these tools to explore alternative designs without the need to save multiple independent versions of your model as you move in different directions. You're free to investigate multiple roof configurations or different entry canopies or to explore various furniture, office layouts, and stairs—quite literally anything that can be modeled. This functionality also allows you to create views that show each option so multiple designs can be compared.

Let's begin by establishing a fundamental understanding of the workflow for design options. First, you have a *main model*, which includes all the elements you've learned how to model so far in this book. The main model can be thought of as a backdrop or stage on which different options are displayed. Elements in the main model are always visible by default, whereas design options come and go, appearing and disappearing depending on which design option you're editing or viewing. Put another way, the main model includes everything else that's *not* in the design options.

You begin to explore design options by first creating a named option set—for example, Canopy Options. Within the option set, you then define options, the first of which is the primary option. Each option can be named to help you identify the intent, such as Glass Canopy and Steel Canopy. From here, you need to either select elements you've already modeled and add them to the appropriate design options or edit each option and create the elements with the Design Options tool active. Either way, the primary option in each option set will be displayed throughout your project by default. You can make as many options as you need—there is no limit.

The last part of configuring design options is to create some additional views in which to compare the ideas. As soon as you start creating design options in a project, the Design Options tab is added to the Visibility/Graphic Overrides dialog box. In this interface, you can select a specific option to be displayed for any of the option sets in the project. You can then present them to a client, to the project architect, or to other stakeholders in the design process. At any time, you may set any other option as the primary option. This will affect any views that are displaying the default option.

When an option within a set is finalized, you can *accept* the primary design solution and add it back to the main model. Doing so deletes all elements in the other options within the option set and merges your accepted option back into the main model.

Creating Design Options

Let's now explore the use of design options with a simple exercise. Download and open the file `c10-DesignOptions-Start.rvt` or `c10-DesignOptions-Start-Metric.rvt` from this book's web page. The sample files have a simple layout of walls, as shown in Figure 10.57.

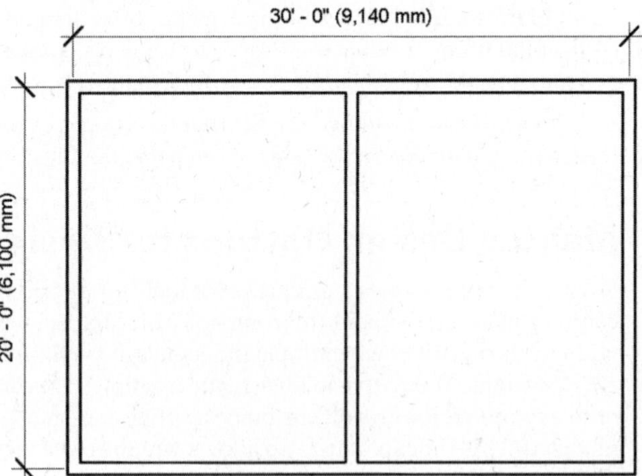

FIGURE 10.57 Create a simple layout of walls to begin studying design options.

Starting in the Level 1 view, you're going to configure this simple space into a design option that divides the space vertically in one option and horizontally in the other:

1. From the Manage tab in the ribbon, locate the Design Options panel (Figure 10.58) and then click the Design Options button.

You can also access the Design Options tool from the status bar at the bottom of the application window.

FIGURE 10.58
Launching the Design Options tool

2. In the Design Options dialog box, click New in the Option Set area to create a new option set. This will automatically create one design option within the set.
3. Click New in the Option area of the dialog box to create an Option 2 option, as shown in Figure 10.59. Click Close to dismiss the dialog box.

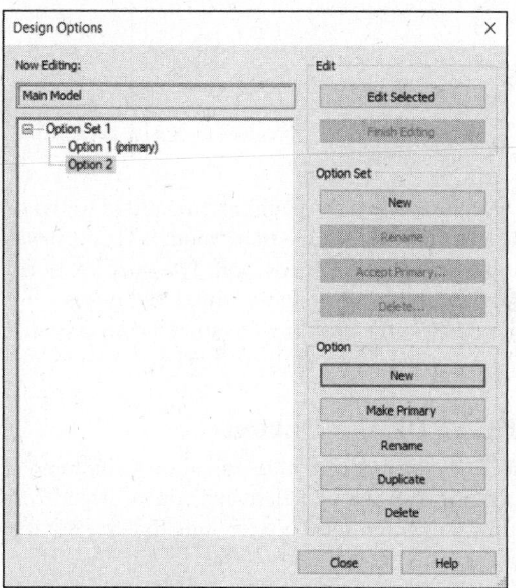

FIGURE 10.59
Creating an option set and two options

Now that you've started creating design options, everything in the project is considered the main model. You can start adding elements to one of the two options.

4. Select the center wall, which will immediately initiate the Modify | Walls contextual tab in the ribbon.

   With the wall segment selected, you can find the Add To Set button in either the Manage tab in the ribbon or the Design Options toolbar in the status bar (Figure 10.60).

FIGURE 10.60
Using the Add To Set tool on the Design Options panel

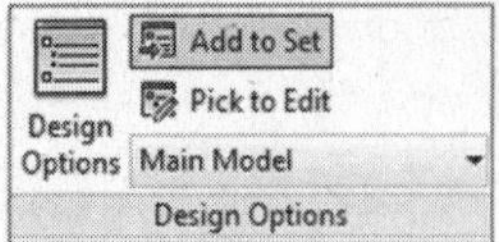

5. In the Add To Design Option Set dialog box, add the wall to Option 1 but not Option 2, as shown in Figure 10.61.

FIGURE 10.61
Adding elements to option sets

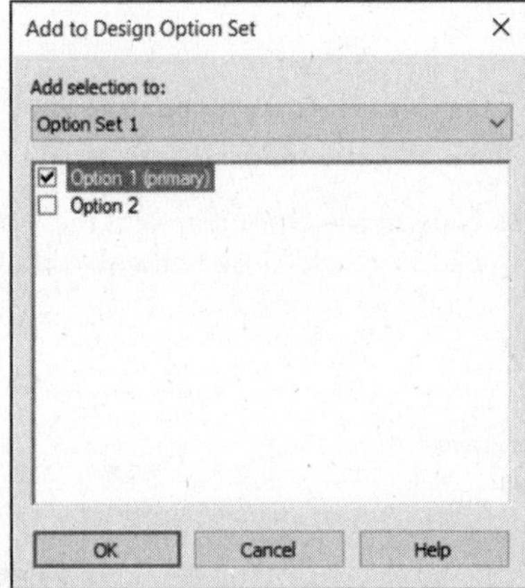

Note that when the elements are added to the option set, you immediately lose the ability to select them within the main model. This is because an option called Exclude Options in the status bar is checked by default. The purpose of this option is to support a workflow in which design options are explicitly edited. Otherwise, it is assumed you are working exclusively on other parts of the building design. Of course, you can disable this option at any time by deselecting the check box in the status bar.

Editing Design Options

Selecting a design option to edit allows you to enter a special mode called Edit Option mode. In this mode, you can add elements you've already created in the main model or create them from within the option set. The elements that are not inside this option set turn light gray, indicating that they are not editable.

Entering Edit Option mode is quite easy. From the drop-down list in the Design Options toolbar or from the Design Options panel in the Manage tab, select the option you want to begin editing (Figure 10.62). In our example, we chose Option 2.

FIGURE 10.62
Accessing Edit Option mode

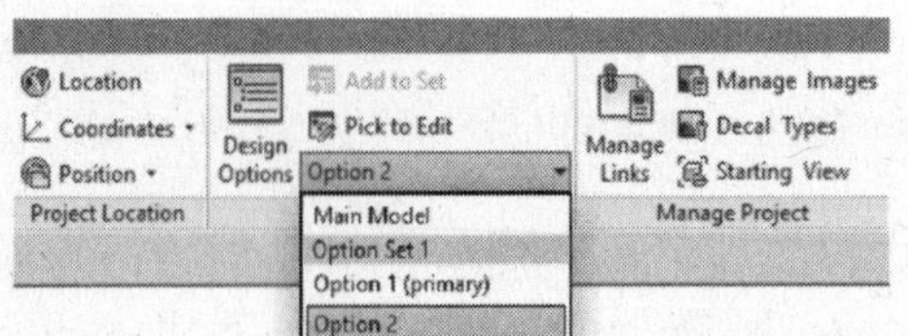

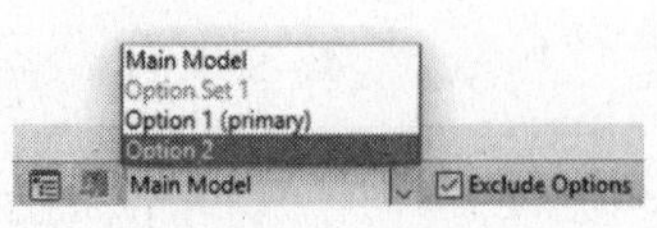

Once you have entered Edit Option mode, you will notice that the wall you added to Option 1 is not visible. Add one horizontal wall dividing the space, as shown in Figure 10.63. Note that anything else you add to the project while in Edit Option mode will be assigned to that design option. You can also modify or delete any elements in the selected option in this mode.

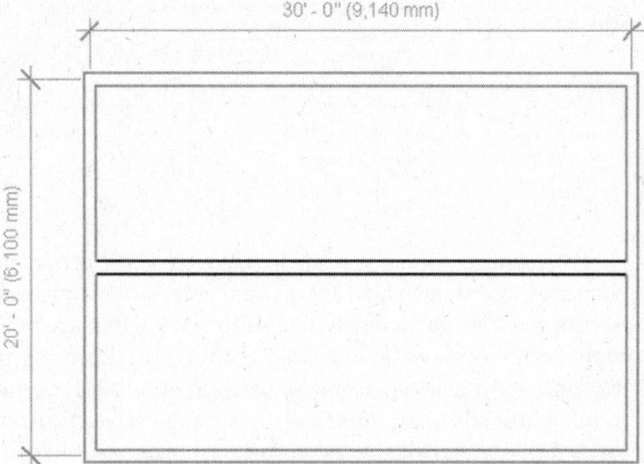

FIGURE 10.63
Adding a wall in Edit Option mode

To exit Edit Option mode, return to the Design Options drop-down list and select Main Model. Remember that only the primary option will appear by default; therefore, when you finish adding the horizontal wall to Option 2 and you return to the main model, the horizontal wall will disappear and the vertical wall will reappear. In the next section, you'll learn how to control the visibility of design options.

Viewing and Scheduling Design Options

You'll notice that whenever you switch between Option 1 and Option 2, the view automatically changes to show the option that you've selected. Initiating design options automatically creates a new tab in the Visibility/Graphic Overrides dialog box. By default, a design option's display shows as <Automatic> (Figure 10.64). This means that the Primary design option (in this case, Option 1) will be shown in the view.

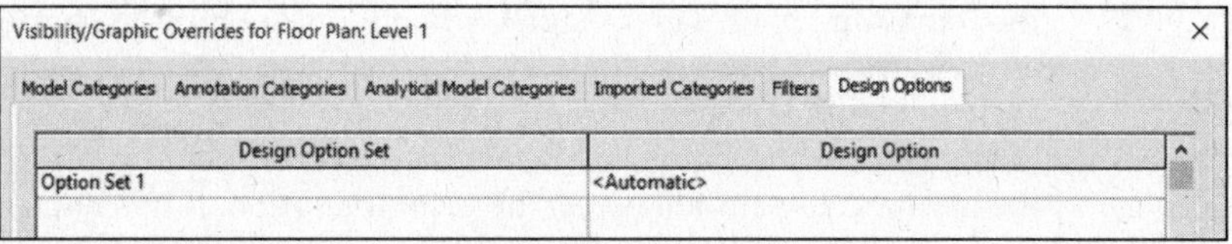

FIGURE 10.64
The Design Options tab displays <Automatic>.

The Design Options tab is available for any view, even for schedules. Selecting the Visibility/Graphic settings in the view properties of a schedule filters the schedule according to the desired design option.

If you want to specify or lock a view to a particular design option, open the Visibility/Graphic Overrides dialog box and select the Design Options tab. From the drop-down list, change the setting from <Automatic> to one of the design options (Figure 10.65).

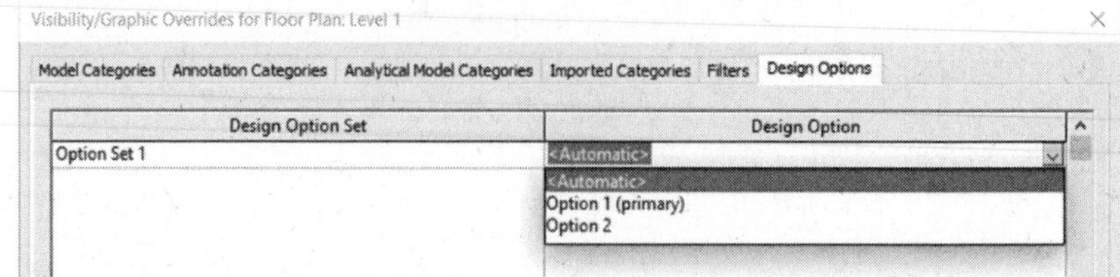

FIGURE 10.65
Locking the view to a design option

For working views, it's fine to leave the view properties set to <Automatic> so that the view switches to actively show the primary design option; however, using the Visibility/Graphic settings can be particularly useful for views that are being placed on sheets. To show multiple design options on one sheet, simply duplicate any relevant views and use the Visibility/Graphic settings to set a specific design option for each view. One of the compelling visualization techniques using this feature is perspective. You can quickly and easily show a variety of design options all from the same vantage point within the model by simply creating a perspective view, duplicating it, and setting the relevant design option in the Visibility/Graphic settings.

Removing Design Options and Option Sets

As your project progresses, it may become necessary to delete an option set, accept the primary design option, or delete a single design option. Although some of these methods might yield similar outcomes, there are important differences. Remember that you can create an unlimited number of option sets and any number of individual options within each set. Maintaining too many design options may have adverse performance effects on your project file, so you should be conscious of the status of all design options. As always, each option set should be named appropriately so that your project team can understand the intended use of each study.

ACCEPTING THE PRIMARY DESIGN OPTION

The most common outcome of a design option study is to accept one option and delete the remaining ones. The Design Option tools are built to support this workflow quite effectively.

To accept the primary design option, open the Design Options dialog box from the Manage tab or the status bar. Select the associated option set from the list. Make sure that the option you want to keep is the primary option. If it is not, select that option; then click the Make Primary button. Once that is complete, click the Accept Primary button, as shown in Figure 10.66.

When you accept the primary option in an option set, the geometry associated with the primary option is integrated into the main model. Any geometry on other options within the selected option set is deleted.

FIGURE 10.66
Accepting the primary design option

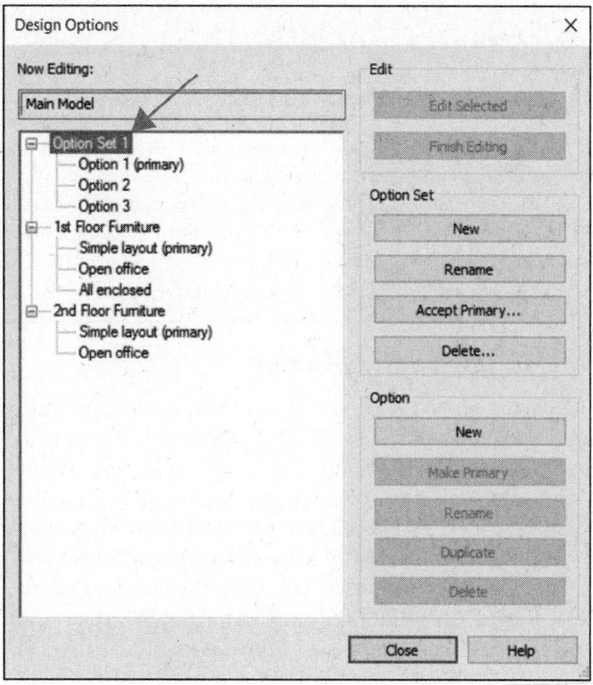

You will proceed through a series of warnings and confirmations before completing the process. If any views are specifically assigned to display the options being deleted, you will have the option to delete or retain such views (Figure 10.67). This is a good way to keep your project file clean and free from extraneous views related to the rapid iteration process of design options.

FIGURE 10.67
Delete or preserve views related to deleted design options.

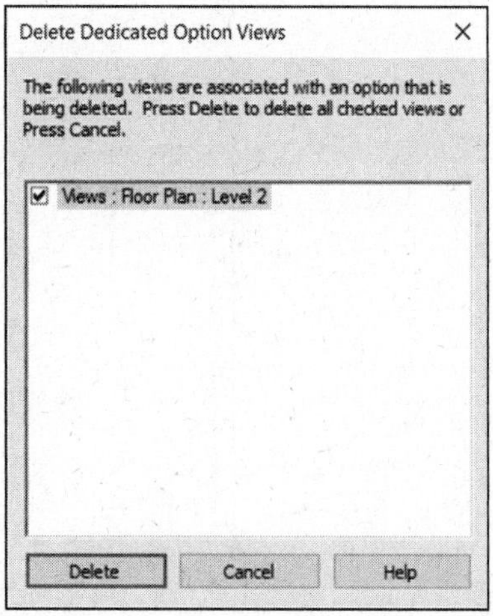

Preserving Your Design Iterations

In our experience, we have heard many stories about vast amounts of effort that have been wiped out when various actions are taken in a Revit model, usually for the sake of improving performance. One classic scenario is when several design options are created and only one is moved forward after certain project milestones. If you use the Design Options tool, be sure to create an archive copy of your project model before you activate potentially destructive commands such as accepting the primary design option or deleting an option set.

Deleting an Option Set

Do not confuse the ability to completely delete an option set with the ability to accept the primary option and delete all other options within the set. If you delete an option set, *all* options within the set are deleted. This workflow is less common because you usually study options for some element of your design that will need to be included in one form or another. Sometimes you may just need to study a potential addition to the scope of your project and it doesn't get accepted. This is where it is useful to completely delete an option set.

To delete an option set, return to the Design Options dialog box and select an option set. Click the Delete button in the Option Set area, as shown in Figure 10.68. As in the previous exercise, you will be prompted with a series of warnings and confirmations because of the content you are about to permanently delete from your project.

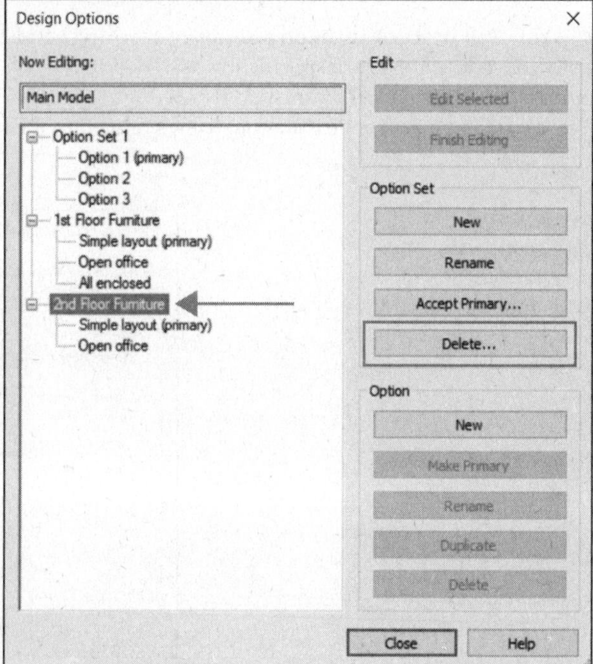

Figure 10.68
Deleting an option set

Deleting an Individual Option

Another common workflow in the iteration of design is to delete just one of the options within an option set. This may occur for various reasons, but let's say you didn't want to continue exploring the option for all enclosed offices in the furniture layout for the first floor of your project. In Figure 10.69, we have the Design Options dialog box open and the All Enclosed option selected within the 1st Floor Furniture option set. From here, you would click the Delete button in the Option area, as shown in the figure.

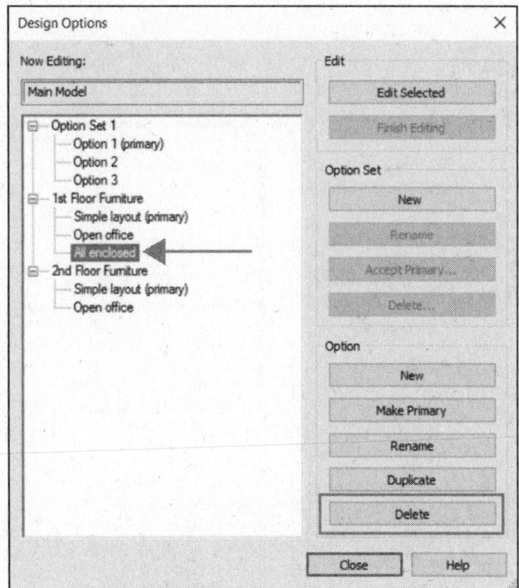

Figure 10.69
Deleting an option within an option set

You cannot delete the primary option in an option set. Some other option must be assigned as the primary option before you can delete the original primary option. To make an option the primary option, open the Design Options dialog box, select an option, and click the Make Primary button.

Combining Phasing, Groups, and Design Options

Now it's time to bring it all together—phasing, groups, and design options. In this exercise, we're going to create a tenant-finish package in two phases. The first phase will start construction on one side of the space, and then we'll turn to the other side of the space to complete the renovation. We'll also rely on groups for collections of components. Finally, we'll create a design option for the second space. Ultimately, you need to visualize the exercise in plan, perspective, and schedule.

Download the `c10-Exercise-Start.rvt` file from this book's web page to get started. Before you start this exercise, remember that this model will be the existing condition. So rather than create the existing walls and then change their phase, let's start by duplicating a view and changing the phase of that view so that the walls and other content are displayed as existing.

1. In the Project Browser, duplicate the Level 1 floor plan and name the duplicated view **LEVEL 1 - EXISTING.**
2. Activate the LEVEL 1 - EXISTING view, and in the Properties palette make sure the phase is set to Existing. Leave the phase filter set to Show All for now.

Don't be concerned that the elevation tags have disappeared in the view. View tags are also phase aware, and they're in the New Construction phase. The finished existing plan is shown in Figure 10.70.

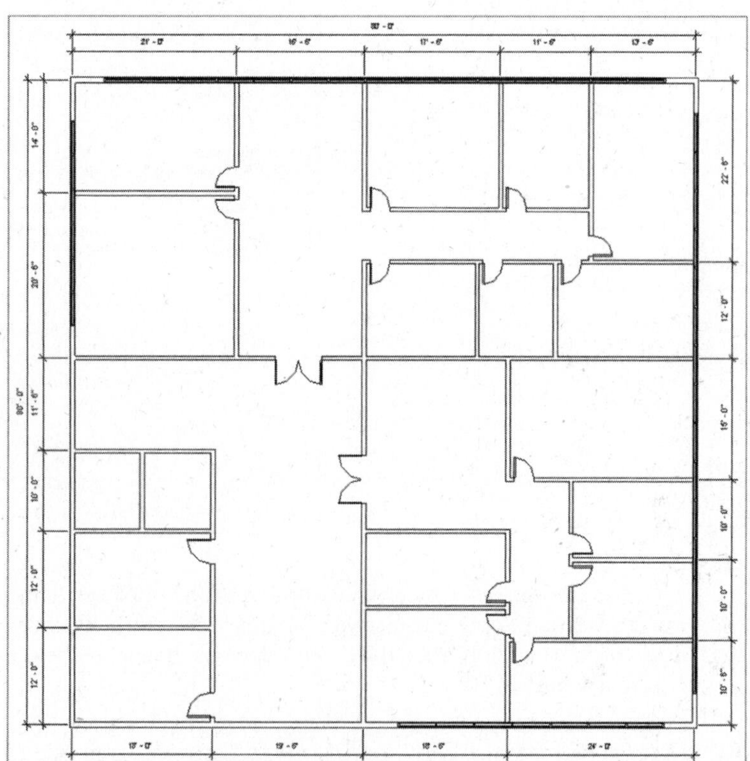

FIGURE 10.70
The existing floor plan

As you can see, the finished existing space is really two areas. In this scenario, the tenant in the lower-left space is expanding and will be taking over the upper space. The idea is that we're going to demolish the space in stages. We don't want to upset the existing tenants to complete the phased work.

Phase 1: Demolition

In the first phase of our exercise project, we will indicate some of the existing walls to be demolished. You don't want to demolish them in the existing Level 1 floor plan view because the demolition should take place at the start of the New Construction phase. That said, there will be two construction phases (so there will also be two demolition phases). Create the new phases and associated plans by following these steps:

1. From the Manage tab in the ribbon, click Phases. In the Phasing dialog box, rename the New Construction phase to **New Construction - Phase 1**. Click the After button and create a new phase named **New Construction - Phase 2** (Figure 10.71). Click OK to close the dialog box.

FIGURE 10.71
Create two new construction phases.

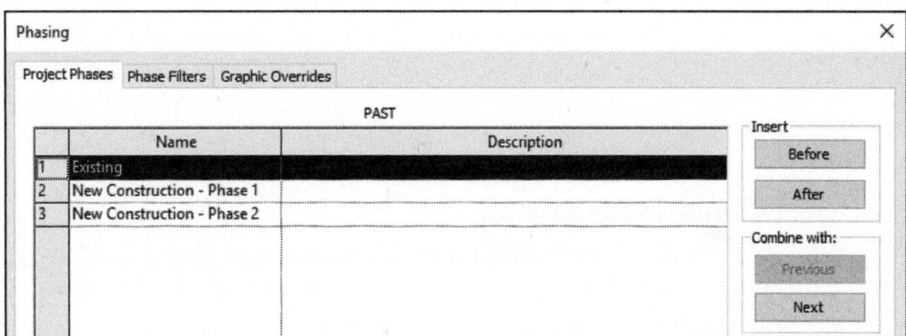

2. In the Project Browser, duplicate the Level 1 floor plan. Activate the duplicated view, and in the Properties palette set the following values:
   - View Name: **LEVEL 1 - PHASE 1 - DEMOLITION**
   - Phase: **New Construction - Phase 1**
   - Phase Filter: Show Previous + Demo
3. Duplicate the default 3D view, listed in the Project Browser as {3D}. Activate the duplicated view, and in the Properties palette set the following values:
   - View Name: **PHASE 1 - DEMOLITION**
   - Phase: **New Construction - Phase 1**
   - Phase Filter: Show Previous + Demo

   You'll notice in the demolition plan that the graphic override for existing walls has been set to include a gray solid fill. This will help to distinguish the existing, new, and demolished walls. In the 3D view, existing elements are shown as transparent green to also aid in the visualization of the phases.
4. Demolish the walls as shown in Figure 10.72 using the Demolish tool (the small hammer) on the Geometry panel of the Modify tab.

   You don't have to demolish the doors if you first demolish the walls that host them.

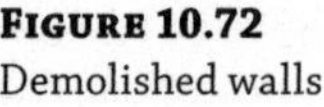

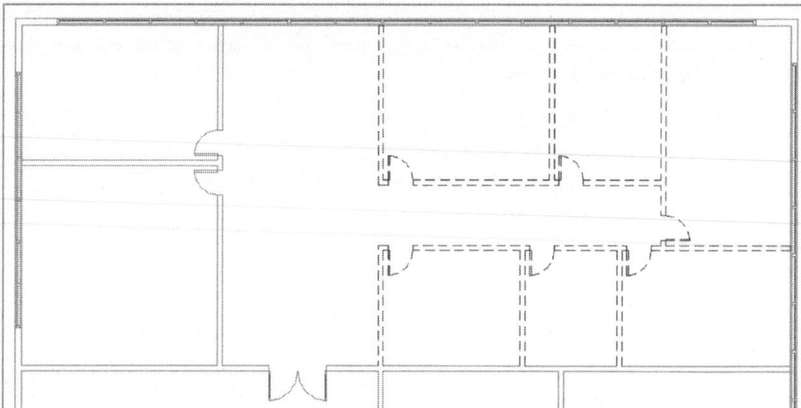

FIGURE 10.72
Demolished walls

Phase 1: Proposed

Now that you've created a demolition plan for Phase 1 and have demolished the interior partitions for that area, we'll need to create another plan view in which you will create a new layout. Follow these steps to continue the exercise:

1. Duplicate the Level 1 floor plan, and in the Properties palette set the following values:
   - View Name: **LEVEL 1 – PHASE 1 PROPOSED**
   - Phase: **New Construction – Phase 1**
   - Phase Filter: Show Previous + New
2. Duplicate the default 3D view, listed in the Project Browser as {3D}, and in the Properties palette set the following values:
   - View Name: **PHASE 1 – PROPOSED**
   - Phase: **New Construction – Phase 1**
   - Phase Filter: Show Previous + New
3. In the LEVEL 1 – PHASE 1 – PROPOSED plan view, you will add the new elements, as shown in Figure 10.73. First, add segments of Curtain Wall: Storefront to the existing walls in the room shown at the lower left of Figure 10.73.

   Because the new storefront is proposed and the interior walls exist, this action will automatically demolish the openings necessary to accommodate the new wall type.
4. Using the furniture families already loaded in the project, add furniture to the proposed space as shown in Figure 10.73.

   You'll add a reception area and other office furniture. Add desks, tables, shelving, and chairs.
5. Add workstation and chair components to the open office area to the right of the Phase 1 area, but group the assembly before you start copying through the office space.

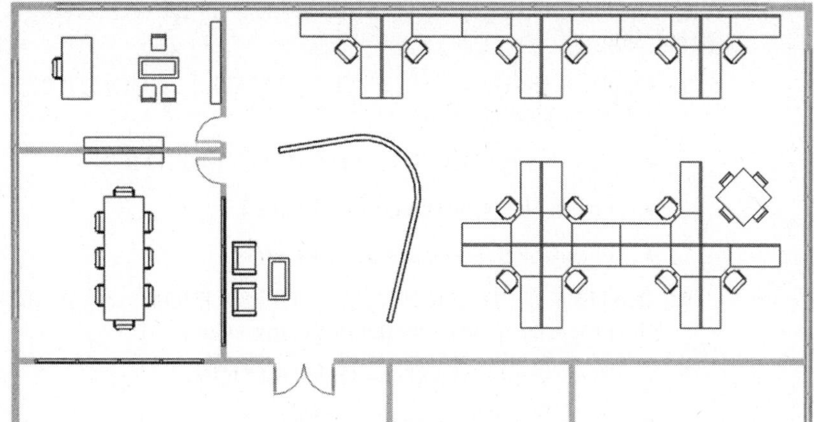

FIGURE 10.73
Phase 1 proposed layout

Use your own judgment and creativity in laying out the new elements in the space. The aim of this exercise is to become familiar with phasing and grouping. Figure 10.74 illustrates the space in a perspective view. Note that the demolished walls are not being shown.

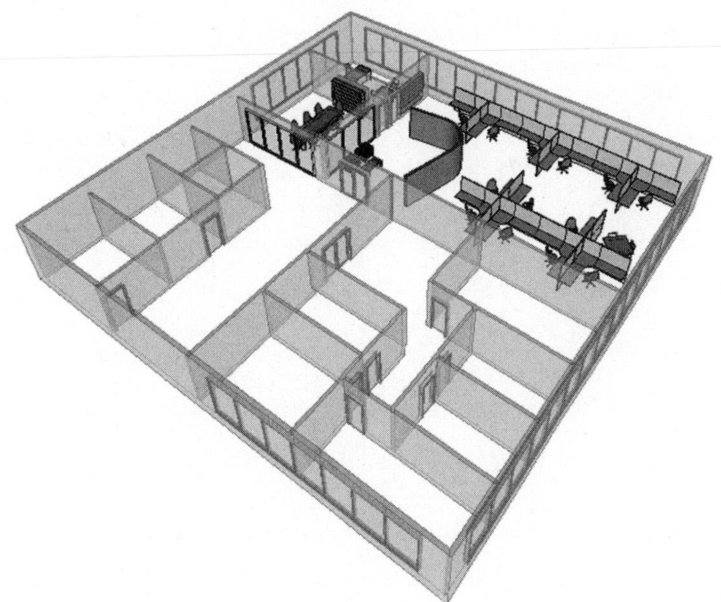

FIGURE 10.74
Phase 1 proposed layout in perspective view

Phase 2: Demolition

Now that we have created a new layout for the first phase of our renovations, we will create similar views for the second phase. In addition to some selective demolition, we will add a design option set to explore two different ideas for the second phase. Follow these steps to get started:

1. Duplicate the plan view LEVEL 1 – PHASE 1 DEMOLITION, and in the Properties palette set the following values:
   - View Name: **LEVEL 1 – PHASE 2 DEMOLITION**
   - Phase: **New Construction – Phase 2**
   - Phase Filter: Show Previous + Demo
2. Duplicate the 3D view PHASE 1 – DEMOLITION. Activate the duplicated view, and in the Properties palette set the following values:
   - View Name: **PHASE 2 – DEMOLITION**
   - Phase: **New Construction – Phase 2**
   - Phase Filter: Show Previous + Demo
3. Demolish the existing walls shown as dashed lines in Figure 10.75 using the demolition tool (the small hammer) from the Modify tab in the ribbon. Note that you'll have to split the long wall between Phase 1 Proposed and Phase 2 Proposed in order to allow only a portion of the wall to be demolished.

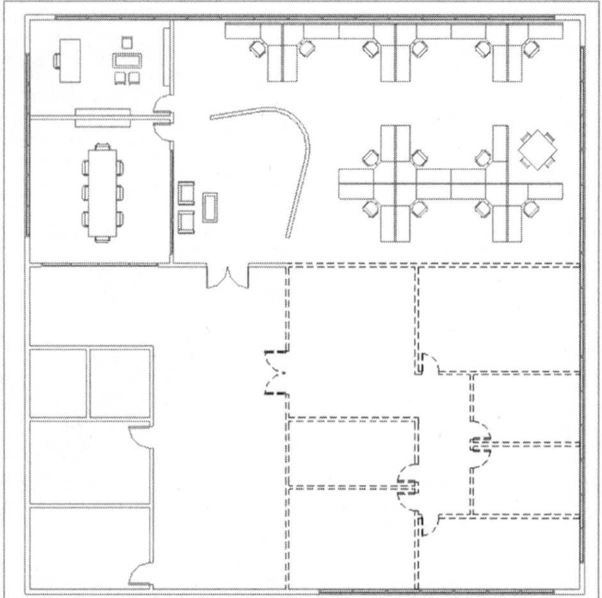

FIGURE 10.75 Demolished walls for Phase 2

4. Return to the 3D view named PHASE 2–DEMOLITION and your view should be similar to the image shown in Figure 10.76. Don't be confused by the proposed content from New Construction – Phase 1 showing as existing. This is correct because that content is now considered existing when seen through the lens of New Construction – Phase 2.

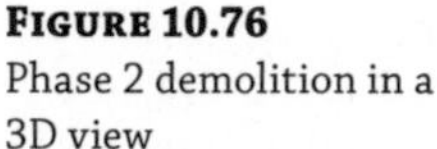

FIGURE 10.76
Phase 2 demolition in a 3D view

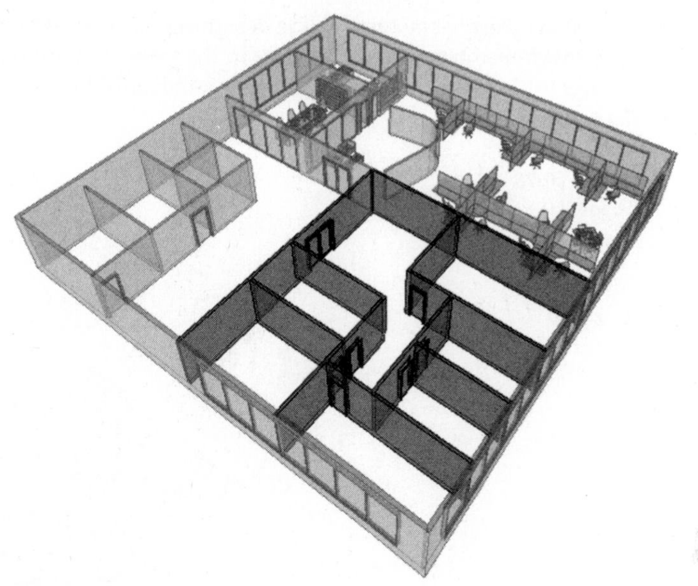

Phase 2: Proposed

In the final steps of our exercise project, we will create two different layouts for the client to review. We will generate a design option set and views that will specifically show the alternate option.

1. Duplicate the plan view LEVEL 1 – PHASE 1 PROPOSED and rename it **LEVEL 1 – PHASE 2 PROPOSED**. Set the Phase to **New Construction – Phase 2**.
2. Start working in your new plan view, adding proposed elements for the primary design layout as shown in Figure 10.77.

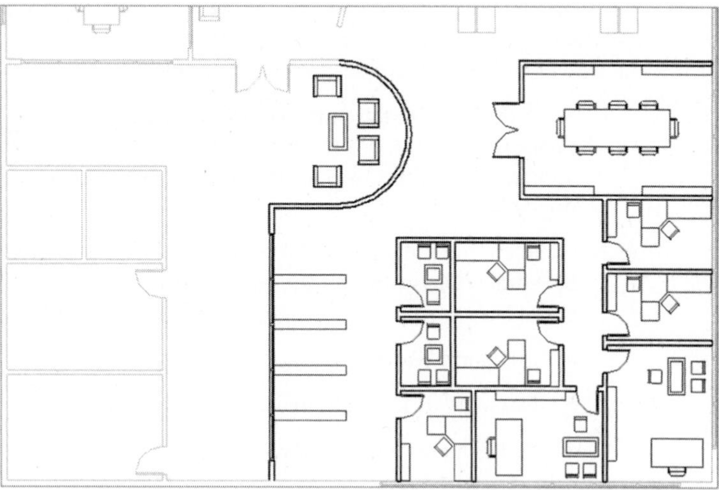

FIGURE 10.77
Proposed layout for the primary option in Phase 2

Don't worry about getting the design right—just get the idea right.

Just remember, adding elements in the view with the appropriate Phase and Phase Filter settings is the easiest way to avoid confusion. Figure 10.78 shows a perspective of the first proposed layout.

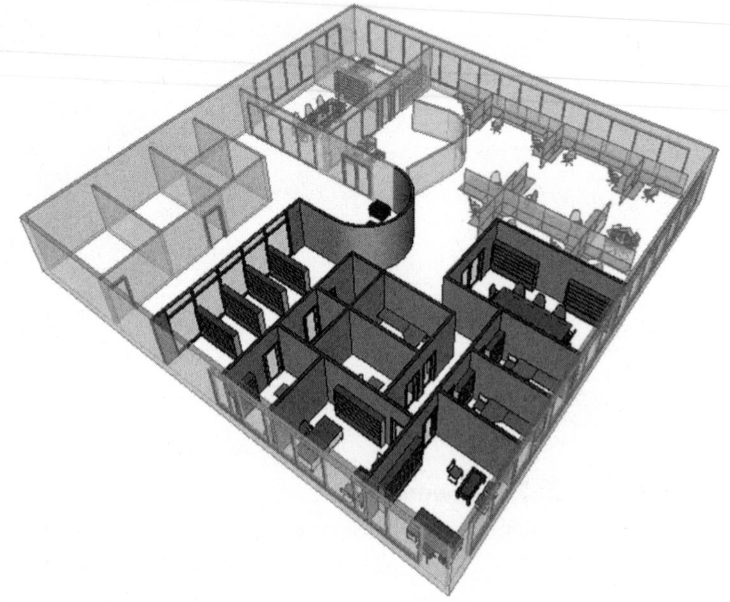

FIGURE 10.78
Proposed layout in perspective

Scheduling

Now let's create a schedule for walls that we will use to provide a volume-based cost for demolition in each phase of the proposed work.

First, you will need to create a phase filter to show only demolished elements. After you create the new phase filter, you can apply it to any floor plan or 3D view to verify what the filter will display. The same elements will be displayed in a schedule. To create the phase filter and the wall demolition schedules, follow these steps:

1. From the Manage tab in the ribbon, click Phases. In the Phasing dialog box, switch to the Phase Filters tab. Click the New button and name the new filter **Demo Only**. Set the New and Existing column values in the table to Not Displayed, and then click OK to close the dialog box.
2. Switch to the View tab in the ribbon, and from the Create panel choose Schedules ➢ Schedules/Quantities. In the New Schedule dialog box, set the following values and then click OK:
   - Category: Walls
   - Name: **Wall Demo Schedule – Phase 1**
   - Phase: New Construction – Phase 1

3. In the Schedule Properties dialog box, make sure you are in the Fields tab. Add the parameters Type and Volume to the Scheduled Fields list, as shown in Figure 10.79.

FIGURE 10.79
Add Type and Volume to the list of scheduled fields.

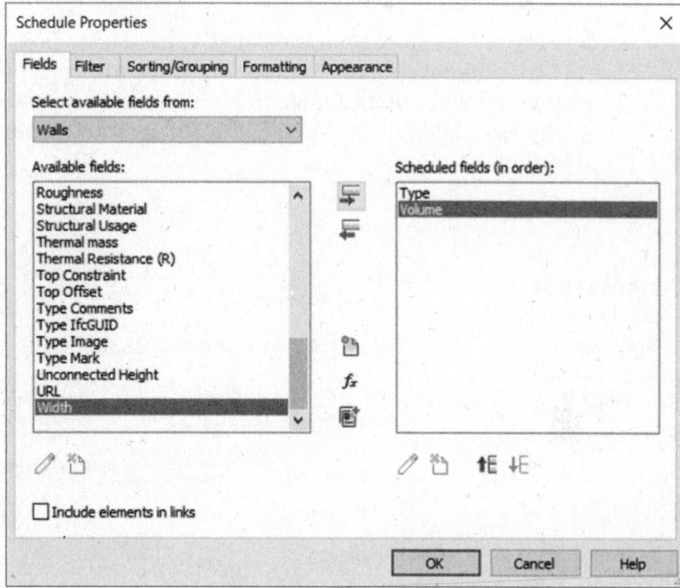

4. Click the Add Parameter button, and in the Parameter Properties dialog box set the following values:

- Parameter Type: Project Parameter
- Name: **Demo Cost Per Unit**
- Type Or Instance: Type
- Type Of Parameter: Currency
- Group Parameter Under: Construction

5. Click OK to close the Parameter Properties dialog box, and then click the Calculated Value button in the Schedule Properties dialog box. Create a new calculated value with the following values. You'll need to add a calculated value in order to multiply the demolished walls' volume by the cost per unit and get the total. Click the Calculated Value button in the Schedule Properties dialog box. We've divided the Volume value by 1 CF to keep the units consistent.

- Name: **Disposal Cost**
- Formula or Percentage: Formula
- Type: Currency
- Formula: **Volume / 1 CF × Demo Cost Per Unit**

In this formula, it is important that the spelling of each parameter be exact because it is case sensitive. We divided by 1 unit (cubic feet in this example) to eliminate the volumetric units in the equation. The result will be a number that is multiplied by the value assigned to the Demo Cost Per Unit parameter.

6. Click OK to close the Calculated Value dialog box, and then switch to the Sorting/Grouping tab. Establish the settings to sort by Type (with the Header option) and then by Volume, as shown in Figure 10.80. Check the box for Grand Totals, and set the associated drop-down list to Totals Only. Deselect the Itemize Every Instance option.

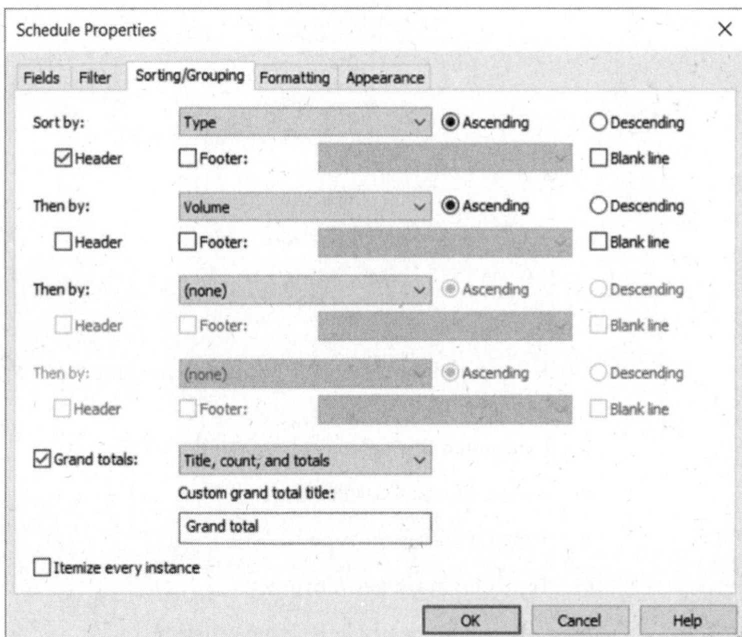

FIGURE 10.80 Set the Sorting/Grouping options for the demolition schedule.

7. Switch to the Formatting tab and select Disposal Cost. Check the Calculate Totals box, and then click OK to create the schedule.

8. In the Properties palette, set Phase to New Construction–Phase 1 and Phase Filter to Demo Only. After you type a value in any of the Demo Cost Per Unit fields, the schedule will look similar to the image in Figure 10.81.

9. For the Phase 2 demolition schedule, don't start over. In the Project Browser, duplicate the previously created schedule and just change the phase in the Properties palette to New Construction – Phase 2.

Figure 10.81
The completed wall demolition schedule

<Wall Demo Schedule - Phase 1>			
A	B	C	D
Type	Volume	Cost Per CF	Disposal Cost
Generic - Type 1			
Generic - Type 1	57.50 CF	$12.00	$1,380.00
Generic - Type 1	58.00 CF	$12.00	$696.00
Generic - Type 1	60.00 CF	$12.00	$720.00
Generic - Type 1	68.00 CF	$12.00	$816.00
Generic - Type 1	77.08 CF	$12.00	$925.00
Generic - Type 1	79.58 CF	$12.00	$955.00
Generic - Type 1	101.25 CF	$12.00	$1,215.00
Generic - Type 1	125.83 CF	$12.00	$1,510.00
Generic - Type 1	184.58 CF	$12.00	$2,215.00
			$10,432.00

At this point in the exercise, you can drag the floor plan views, 3D views, and schedules from the Project Browser onto sheets for publishing, as shown in Figure 10.82. We'll cover sheets in greater detail in Chapter 17, "Documenting Your Design," but for now you can begin to become familiar with the process. Add the plans, 3D views, and schedule for Phase 1 to sheet A101, and then add the views for Phase 2 to sheet A102.

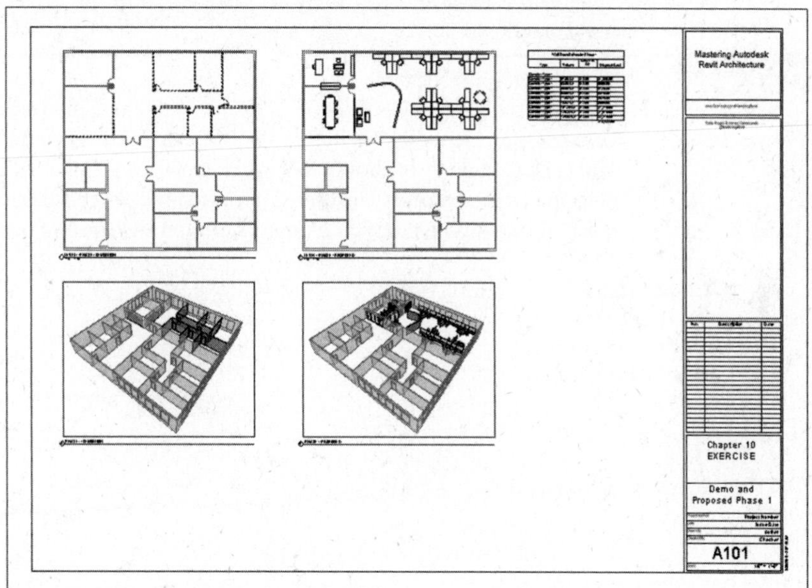

Figure 10.82
Multiple design views assembled on a sheet

Using the Design Option Tool

Everything looks great so far, but our client has asked us to prepare an alternative design for the second phase of construction. We'll accomplish this within the same exercise file using the Design Option tool. Let's get started with the following steps:

1. From the status bar at the bottom of the application window, click the Design Options icon. In the Design Options dialog box, click the New button to create a new option set.

Click the Rename button and name the new set **Phase 2 – Proposed**. Click the other New button to add two options, as shown in Figure 10.83.

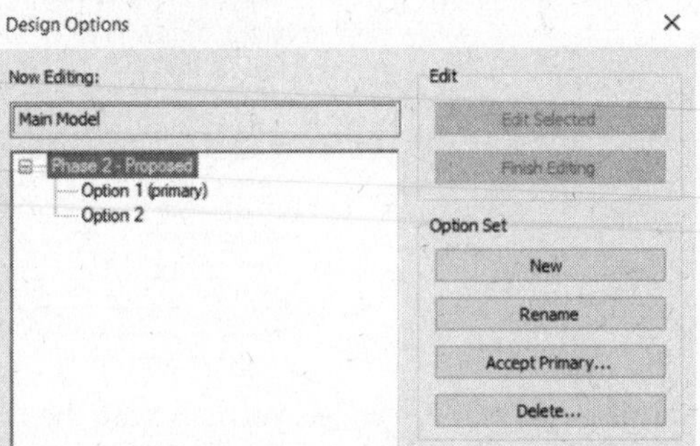

FIGURE 10.83 Create a new design option set with two options.

USING A PHASE FILTER TO START DESIGN OPTIONS

Here's a great tip: To isolate what you need to assign to Option 1, activate the Phase 2 floor plan, and then set the Phase Filter property to Show New. This will turn off any existing conditions from the previous phases.

2. Activate the LEVEL 1 – PHASE 2 PROPOSED floor plan and then select all the new construction elements. Switch to the Manage tab in the ribbon, and click Add To Set. Uncheck Option 2, as shown in Figure 10.84, and click OK. This will add everything selected to the primary design option. If you changed the Phase Filter property to help select the new construction elements, remember to set it back to Show Previous + New.

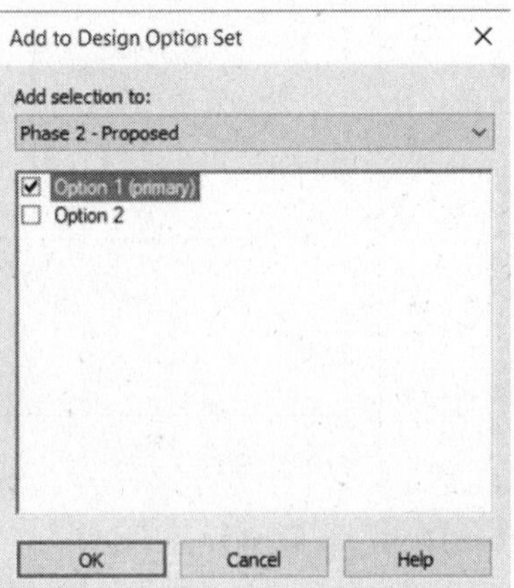

FIGURE 10.84 Add the primary design elements to only the first design option.

3. In the Project Browser, duplicate LEVEL 1 – PHASE 2 PROPOSED and rename it **LEVEL 1–PHASE 2 PROPOSED – OPTION 2**.

   This will be your working view for the second design option.

4. Open the Visibility/Graphic Overrides dialog box and switch to the Design Options tab. Change the Design Option value for the design option set shown from <Automatic> to Option 2. Click OK to close the dialog box.
5. From the Design Options toolbar, select Option 2 in the drop-down list to make Option 2 active for editing and create another design iteration, as shown in Figure 10.85. When you are finished with the alternate layout, set the Design Options drop-down list to Main Model.

FIGURE 10.85
Create an alternate design layout.

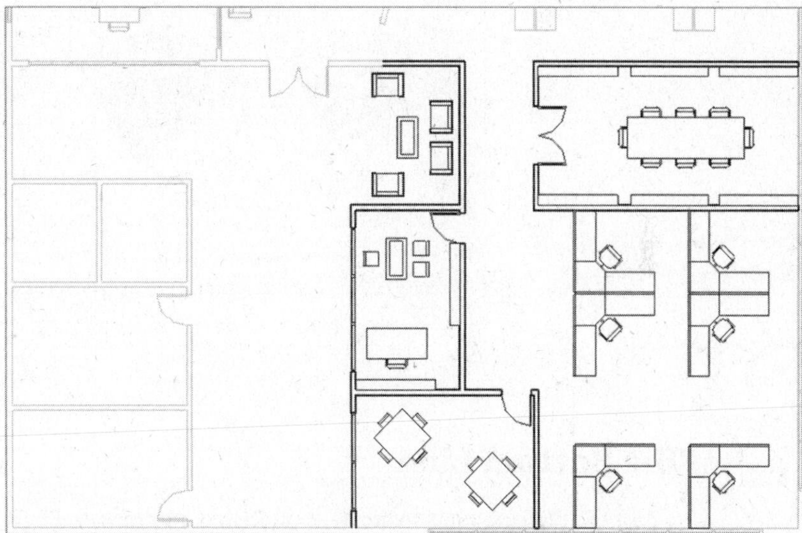

6. In the Project Browser, duplicate the 3D view named PHASE 2 – PROPOSED and name the duplicated view **PHASE 2 – PROPOSED – OPTION 2**. In the Visibility/Graphic Overrides dialog box for the view, set Design Option to Option 2.
7. Activate sheet A102 and then drag and drop the views for Option 2 onto the sheet, as shown in Figure 10.86.

SELECTING ELEMENTS IN DESIGN OPTIONS

You might notice that you can't select model elements that have been added to design option sets. There is a setting in the status bar at the bottom of the application window called Exclude Options, which is checked by default. When you uncheck this setting, you can select elements that are assigned to design options.

If you'd like to download the completed file used for this exercise, you can find it in the Chapter 10 folder at this book's web page; the file is called `c10-Exercise-Finished.rvt`.

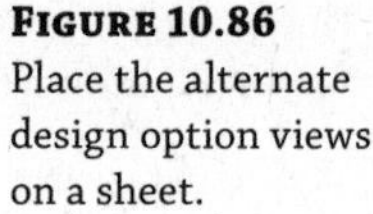

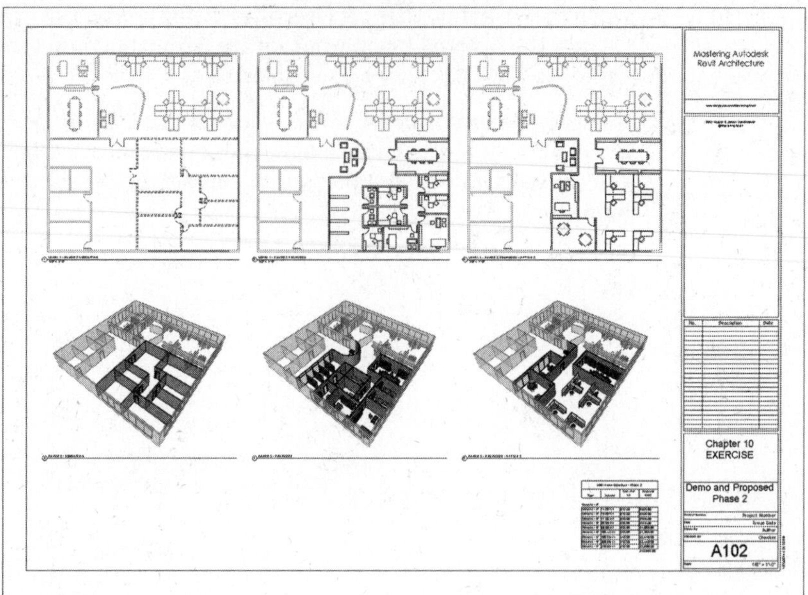

Figure 10.86
Place the alternate design option views on a sheet.

The Bottom Line

Use the Phasing tools to create, demolish, and propose a new design. Time is such an important element to the design process and nearly impossible to capture with traditional CAD tools. Don't use phasing for construction sequencing (there's a better way). Embrace phasing for *communication*, not just *illustration*.

> **Master It** How can you use phasing to communicate your design across a series of key stages? What kind of project is best suited to phasing?

Understand and utilize groups. Groups are great for creating collections of both host and family component geometry. Just remember to apply best practices, and you'll avoid a lot of common roadblocks. Individual model elements within groups will always appear properly in schedules, as you'd expect. And creating exceptions in groups allows you to make subtle changes without creating a new group.

> **Master It** Why shouldn't you mirror groups?

Create and use design options. Like groups, design options work great when you follow the rules. Design options are intended for design iteration that is bounded and well-defined—not for putting multiple buildings in one project file. Remember that links, groups, and phasing can exist within design options. Always keep hosted elements with their host when using design options.

> **Master It** Suppose you have a multistory tower. How could you show multiple design options for the entire vertical exterior enclosure?

Chapter 11

Visualization

Visualization in Autodesk® Revit® software—as with any tool (even a pencil)—isn't an exact science. It still requires a patient, aesthetic eye. The most important thing you can do to successfully visualize your work starts with one thing: the ability to listen. That's right—it's your ears that make you a great artist! You need to be able to understand what your client is trying to accomplish because you're not really trying to visualize something—you're trying to communicate something *for someone else.*

In this chapter, you'll learn to:

- Create real-time and rendered analytic visualizations
- Render emotive photorealistic visualizations
- Understand the importance of sequencing your visualization workflow

Explaining the Role of Visualization

We believe that anyone can use Revit to create compelling, emotive visualizations. What's really great is that your visualizations are based on the same coordinated design information you're using to document your project. But there are a few challenges:

- Creating emotive visualization is usually such a small part of your project's overall workflow that it's hard to spend the time necessary to hone your rendering skills. This is the reason that photorealistic renderings, both still and moving images, are often the realm of a specialist who deeply understands the techniques and workflow needed to create compelling imagery.
- The reality is that visualization is both art and science, but especially art. You'll never be able to just push a button and get a beautiful image. There's a world of difference between something that's photorealistic and something that's emotive and compelling. In other words, the button says Render, not Make Beautiful.
- Most important, visualization is about communication, something that many people forget to take into account. Don't ever create a rendering until you know what you're trying to accomplish. You must know your audience and understand what needs to be communicated (keeping in mind that the person requesting the rendering isn't always the intended audience). Otherwise, you'll spend hours doing something that is beautiful but entirely irrelevant.

You'll likely struggle with two important points about rendering in Revit, and unfortunately there's little that you can do about it, because the two are in tension with each other:

- Although engineers often analyze in order to design, architects often visualize in order to design. But if your intent is to put all of this visual iteration into Revit just to render it, you'll probably get frustrated over all the entourage you're putting into a database that you want to keep light and flexible (particularly during early design). The reality is that Revit is most useful during early design to communicate analytic rather than visually representative information.

- You'll never be able to render out of Revit more than you put into it. The level of detail required to create deeply emotive and detailed visualizations is usually far greater than the level of detail necessary to produce accurate construction documentation.

Even though Revit has the ability to help you create great renderings, the level of detail required at the beginning of a project (when analytical relationships are still being resolved) is too high for schematic design. Even when the project is well resolved and established, the level of detail required for a highly finished and photorealistic visualization is far beyond what's required to complete your project documentation. So what is the point of this chapter?

Our focus is to get you somewhere in the middle. You need to understand how Revit works, but you also need to understand that although something is technically feasible, it may not be practical from a workflow standpoint. Our goal is to help you focus on communication, not just visualization for its own sake. So if you're happy with visualizing your project at its current level of development (not too far ahead and not overly detailed), you're going to have a lot of success rendering with Revit software.

Analytic versus Photorealistic Visualization

Throughout this chapter we will refer to basic modes of visualization as *analytic* as compared to the more advanced modes we will refer to as *photorealistic*. Although photorealistic visualization is self-explanatory, analytic visualization is the most common form of communicating with 3D views in Revit. You will not achieve the true realism of a photorealistic rendering, but analytic views are active views of the model within which you can create or analyze the design. You can even create a camera view with analytic graphic settings to use as a cover sheet for your document set—and you'll never need to remember to regenerate a rendering to update the cover image!

Before we begin to address the two types of visualization techniques in greater detail, let's review the basic controls that are available to help you configure views for further visualization.

Understanding View Controls

In this section, we'll describe the various visual styles that are available in the view control bar with regard to analytic visualization. Figure 11.1 shows the view control bar of an orthographic view and that of a perspective view.

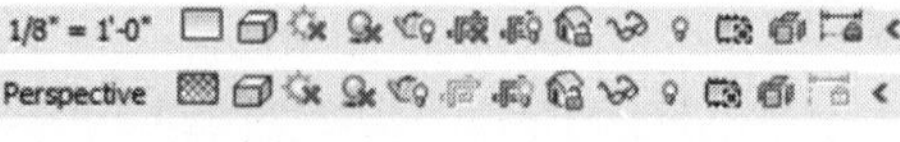

Figure 11.1
2D and orthographic view control bar and perspective view control bar

All of the icons in the view control bar refer to view properties that can also be set in the Properties palette. The view control bar simply gives you quicker access to the most commonly used settings. The first control at the left of the view control bar is the view scale. Because camera views are not scale specific, it simply lists the status as Perspective.

Setting the Detail Level

After the Scale setting, the next icon in the view control bar sets the detail level in the view (Figure 11.2). The Detail Level property can be set to Coarse, Medium, or Fine.

FIGURE 11.2
Level of detail

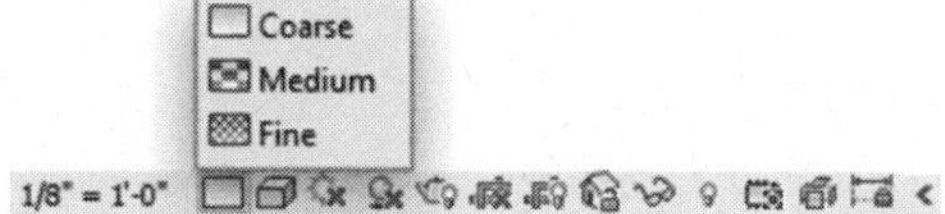

When you create a new view, the default value for Detail Level is initially determined by the scale of the view, as shown by switching to the Manage tab in the ribbon and clicking Additional Settings ➤ Detail Level. Figure 11.3 shows the default settings.

FIGURE 11.3
View Scale-To-Detail Level Correspondence window

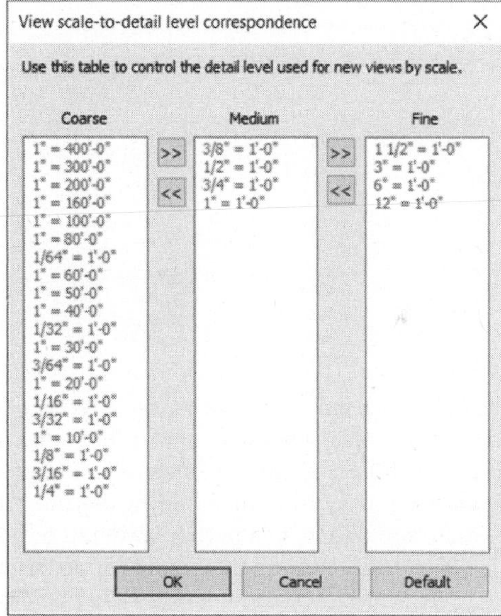

Even though a default value is specified for a new view, the Detail Level setting can be overridden after the view is created. This fact is important for two reasons. First, changing the scale after the view is created will not automatically reset the level of detail. Second, rendering a view with a finer detail level will (generally speaking) take more time. Even though the results may not be visible to the naked eye, the calculations required to render what you won't be able to discern (because the objects are so small) will still be computed.

When you consider this information, you will find it's very important to render at the appropriate level of detail. To understand this, look at the two perspectives in Figure 11.4. Although these two views look identical, one will rotate, refresh, and render faster than the other because they're set to different levels of detail.

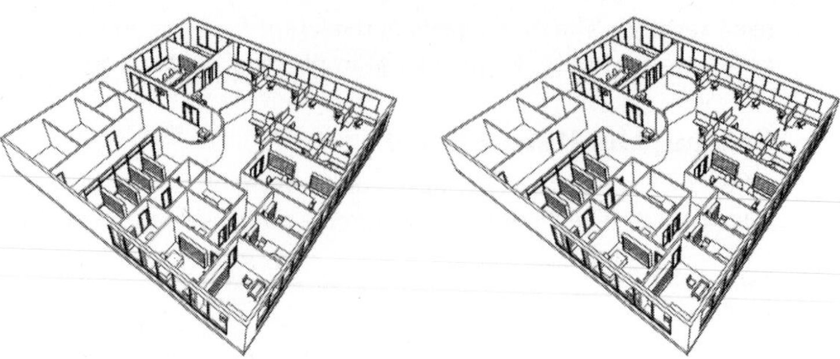

FIGURE 11.4
Nonidentical views

The view on the left is set to a Coarse level of detail, but the view on the right is set to a Fine level of detail. Although this different detail level doesn't have much of an effect on the content in either view, the detail level affects performance.

The Executive Chair family has been modified so that the casters at the base of the chair display only at a Fine level of detail. The results are shown in Figure 11.5.

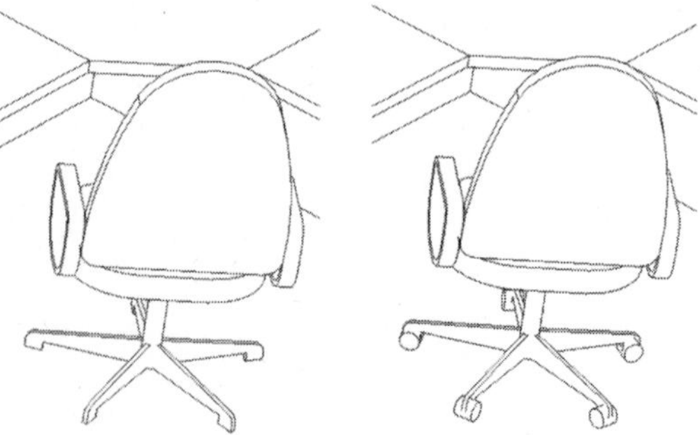

FIGURE 11.5
Detail level of chair

This difference may not have a large effect on a small project, yet it can have a significant effect on your project when you render (not to mention the additional time it will take when you export and print). So be sure that before you render a view, the level of detail is appropriately set. If you're far away from the building or your view is broad, a Coarse detail level is sufficient. But if you're zoomed in on a particular detail or part of the building (or just a single office or room), a Fine detail level might be more appropriate.

We discuss the use of detail level in Chapter 14, "Designing with the Family Editor," where you will learn how to apply this property to your own content families.

Working with Graphic Display Options

The Graphic Display Options dialog box allows you to control all of your views' graphic options (Figure 11.6). These are the Model Display (which we've just reviewed) and the Shadows, Sketchy Lines, Lighting, Photographic Exposure, Background settings, and Depth Cueing (new in 2017). This dialog box also allows you to save views as templates to quickly transfer the settings to other views. It's important to understand how these settings impact the visualization in your view. Since we just stepped through the Model Display options, let's go through the options in this dialog box to round out your understanding of how you can modify the view to get the desired effect in your renderings and visualizations.

FIGURE 11.6
Graphic Display Options dialog box

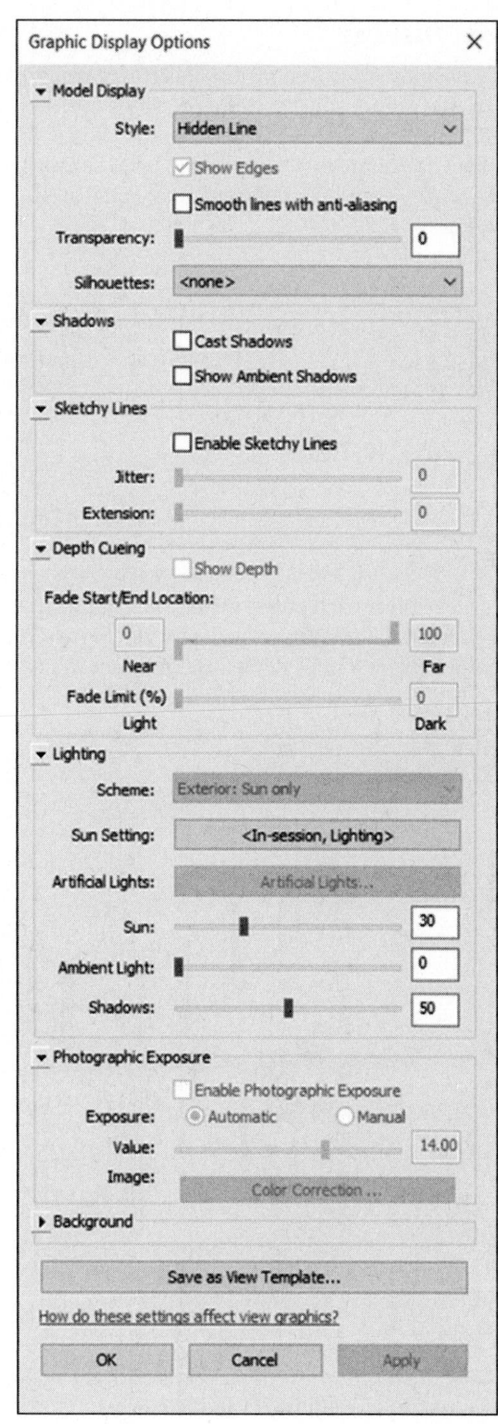

Model Display

Model Display is the first group of settings you will find in the Graphic Display Options dialog box. In this group, you can define settings for the visual style, transparency of model elements, and silhouettes.

Likely one of the most commonly used settings, the visual style of your view can be defined from one of six options. The available visual styles are shown in the context of the view control bar in Figure 11.7.

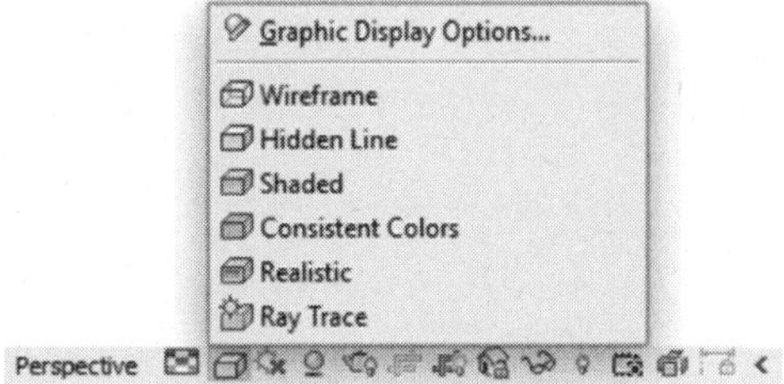

Figure 11.7
Visual style settings in the view control bar

As we explore each of the visual styles, note that the Show Ambient Shadows setting has been enabled. The Wireframe view style (Figure 11.8) maintains only the edges of objects. Faces are hidden. Note that in Revit 2017, ambient shadows are not available in Wireframe view.

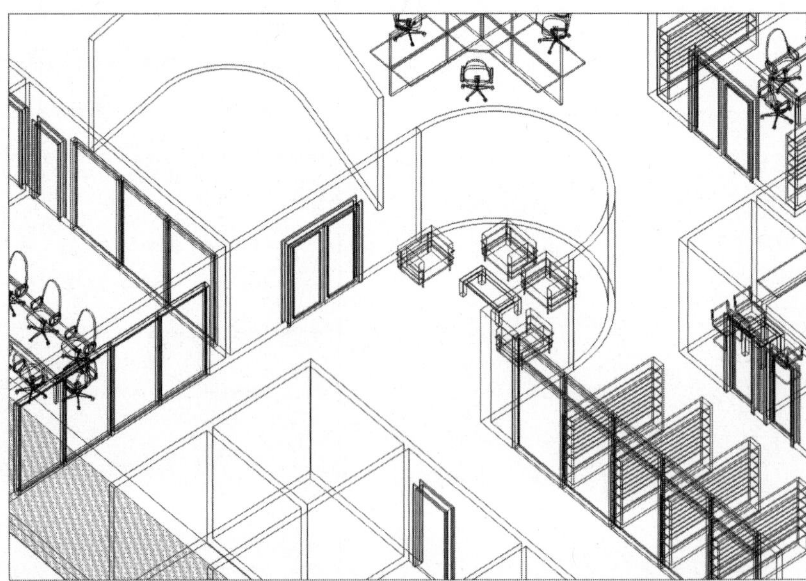

Figure 11.8
Wireframe view style

The Hidden Line view style keeps both the edges and faces visible (Figure 11.9). This view style is used by default in 2D and 3D views.

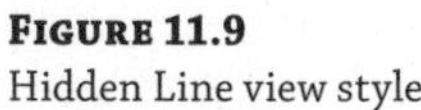

Figure 11.9
Hidden Line view style

The Shaded view style shows faces in their shaded value with accentuated edges (Figure 11.10). Note the change in color depending on an object's orientation. This effect is particularly pronounced on curved surfaces. In addition, if you have a material applied to an element and that material has a color associated with it, you'll see those colors and patterns represented. Glazing appears clear and the shelving and desks have a wood tone to them. Materials with a model pattern (like the brick at the bottom of the image) will show their patterns as well.

Figure 11.10
Shaded view style

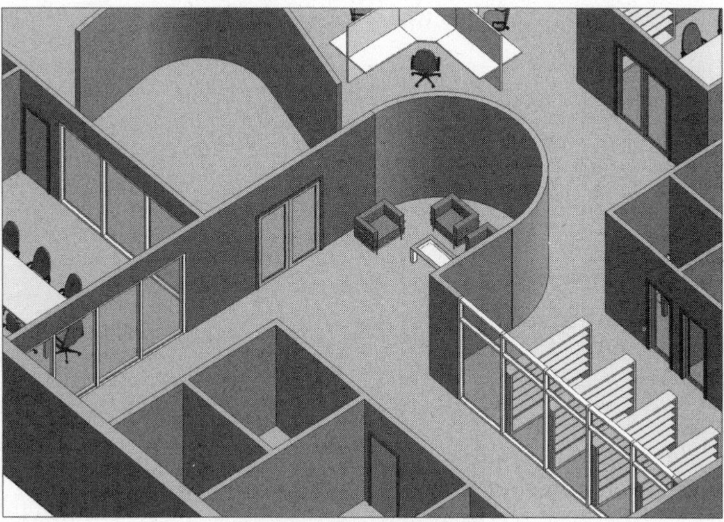

The Consistent Colors view style removes the color variation based on an object's orientation to the viewer. Colors are strict interpolations of the shaded color setting (the RGB value of the material assignment) and therefore have a flatter yet more consistent appearance (Figure 11.11).

The curved wall in the center of the image is stone, so it begins showing as a color that is different from those of the other wall types.

FIGURE 11.11
Consistent Colors view style

The Realistic view style provides real-time overlays of geometry with the material that will be used during a photorealistic rendering, as shown in Figure 11.12. In both Shaded and Realistic view styles, you can turn off Show Edges in the Graphic Display Options dialog box, whereas this mode is always on for all other styles.

FIGURE 11.12
Realistic view style

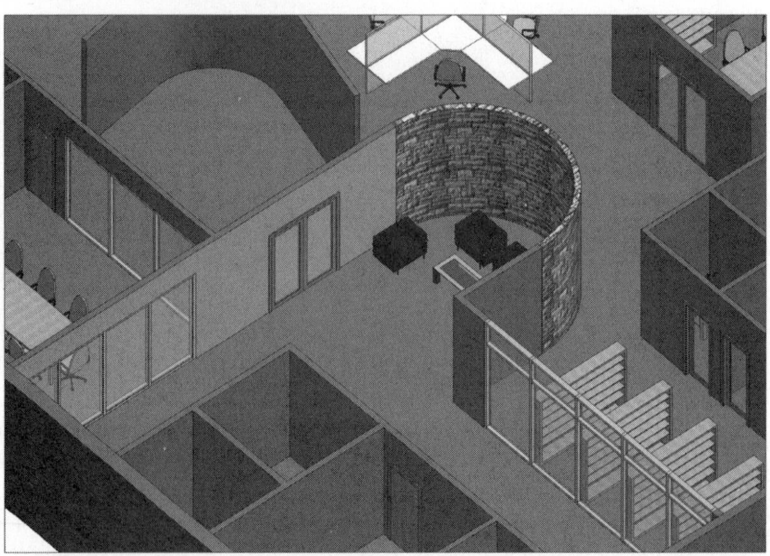

The Interactive Ray Trace mode is available only in the view control bar; it is not available in the Graphic Display Options dialog box. When you select this mode from the view control bar, the application will perform a quick render of the view window based on your current view settings (Figure 11.13). Based on your computer's processor, it may take a bit of time to render the view, but once rendered, the view remains interactive—meaning you can continue to navigate within the view. As you do, the rendering will dynamically update. This is a fairly computationally intensive view type; if you're working in this view, make sure you close other applications that might consume RAM or processor resources so the view you use is quick and fluid.

FIGURE 11.13
Interactive Ray Trace mode

One graphic setting in the Model Display options that's not accessible in the view control bar is Transparency. This slider at the top of the Graphic Display Options dialog box allows you to make all the elements within the view transparent to an equal degree. In earlier versions of Revit, this was the Ghost Surfaces setting, but the percent of opacity/translucency was not modifiable. In Figure 11.14, the view has been set to 40 percent transparency with the Consistent Colors view style.

FIGURE 11.14
Perspective view with Transparency override applied

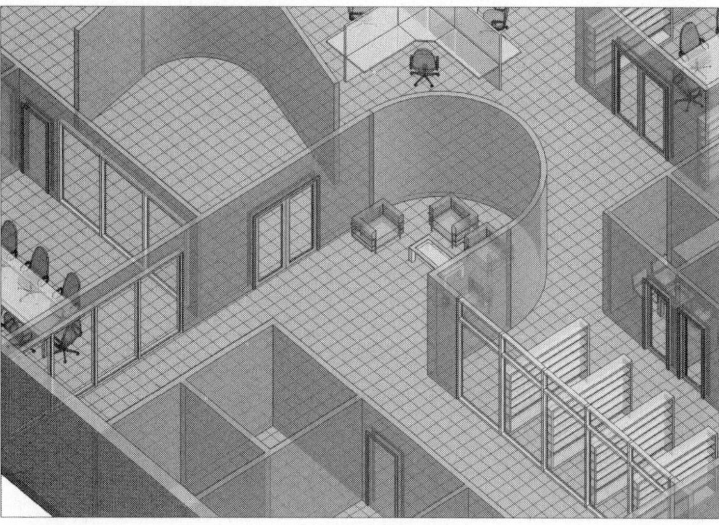

The Silhouettes option allows you to override the edges of objects in the view using your defined line styles (Figure 11.15).

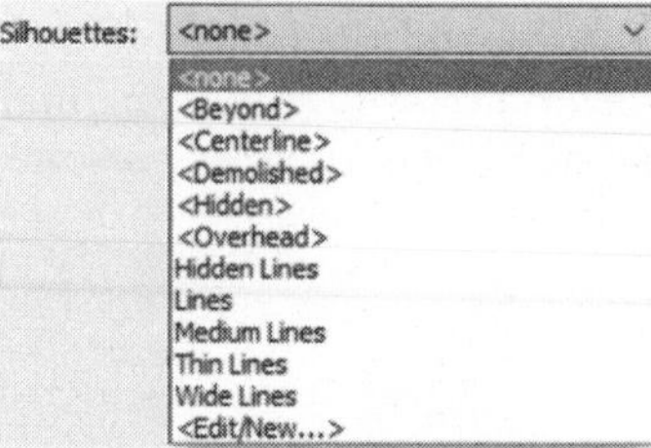

FIGURE 11.15
Silhouettes style

In Figure 11.16, the image on the left illustrates the view without silhouettes, and the image on the right shows the view with Wide Lines enabled.

FIGURE 11.16
No silhouettes versus Wide Lines silhouettes

SHADOWS

The Shadows toggle is available in the Graphic Display Options dialog box, but there's also a toggle in the view control bar. With this button, there is no flyout—simply select it to toggle shadows on and off based on sun settings which we will discuss later in this chapter. The ability to turn shadows on in real time is a terrific feature that helps you add an improved sense of depth to your view (Figure 11.17). Note that the Shadows toggle is not available if a Transparency override is applied.

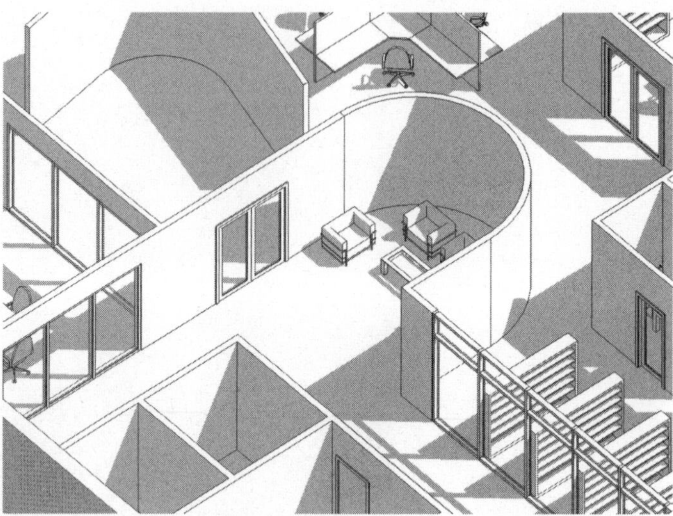

FIGURE 11.17
Default shadows on

Keep a couple of things in mind when turning on shadows. First, it takes a bit longer for the screen to refresh when shadows are turned on. Depending on the complexity of your view and the size of your model, you might want to keep shadows off in your working views as you zoom in, zoom out, and rotate.

Second, the default settings could use adjusting depending on how you like to have the view rendered. Sometimes it's more valuable to show the space well lit than to show an exact time of day for the sun position. To set the sun to an angle that is not dependent on a location and time, choose the Sun Setting button in the Lighting group of options. This button will report the current preset (sunlight from top right). Clicking this button will open the Sun Settings dialog box (Figure 11.18). Notice that the Lighting radio button is selected and an azimuth and altitude are specified as being relative to the view. This will show a sun angle regardless of the building's orientation or location on the globe.

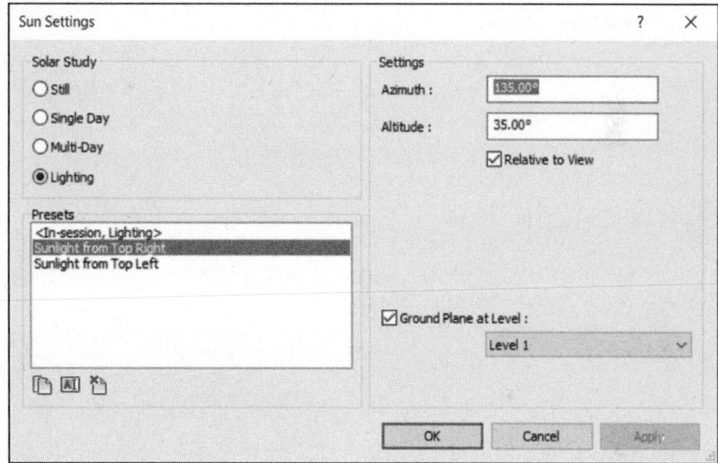

FIGURE 11.18
The Sun Settings dialog box

Back in the Graphic Display Options dialog box, you also have the ability to modify the intensity of the sun, ambient light, and shadows with the sliders (Figure 11.19). Changing these can dramatically change the amount of shade or shadow that appears in your view.

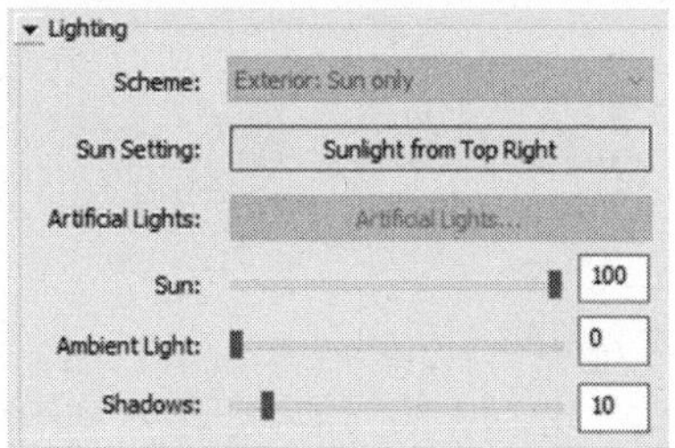

FIGURE 11.19
Increased sun intensity setting

Another important visualization tool in the Shadows settings is the Show Ambient Shadows option. Combined with other graphic options such as edge enhancements and real-time materials, this setting allows you to create emotive, real-time views of your project that do not require renderings.

To activate ambient light and shadows, open the Graphic Display Options dialog box, expand the Shadows settings, and then select Show Ambient Shadows.

The results are noticeable, particularly around the intersections of objects. Shaded elements are embellished by highlights in the center of objects and deeper shading at the edges. The result is almost a watercolor effect that considerably softens the shaded view. The effect can be accentuated when combined with the option to enhance the silhouette of edges for even more real-time effects. Figure 11.20 demonstrates the differences in effect between shadows with and without ambient shadows turned on.

FIGURE 11.20
Activating ambient light and shadows: (top) without ambient shadows; (bottom) with ambient shadows

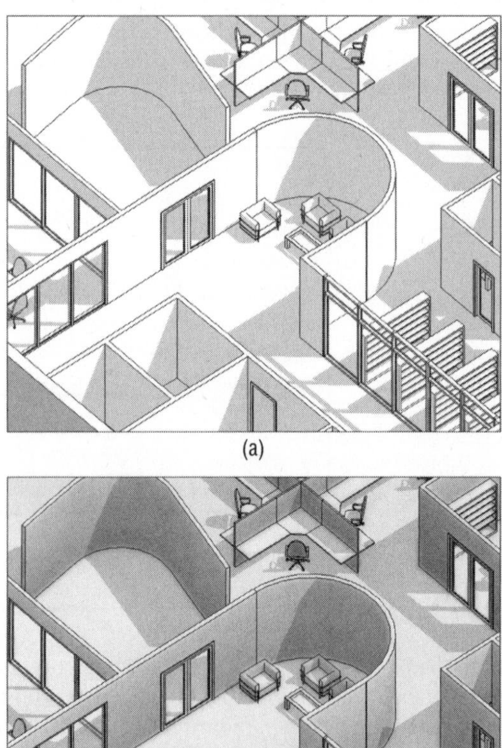

(a)

(b)

SKETCHY LINES

You can apply the Sketchy Lines feature as a graphic display style (Figure 11.21).

FIGURE 11.21
Sketchy Lines options for more informal presentations

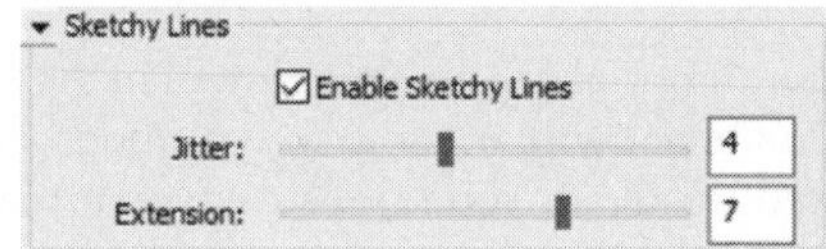

You can adjust settings for Jitter and Extension to create unique interpretations of any visual style, as shown in Figure 11.22.

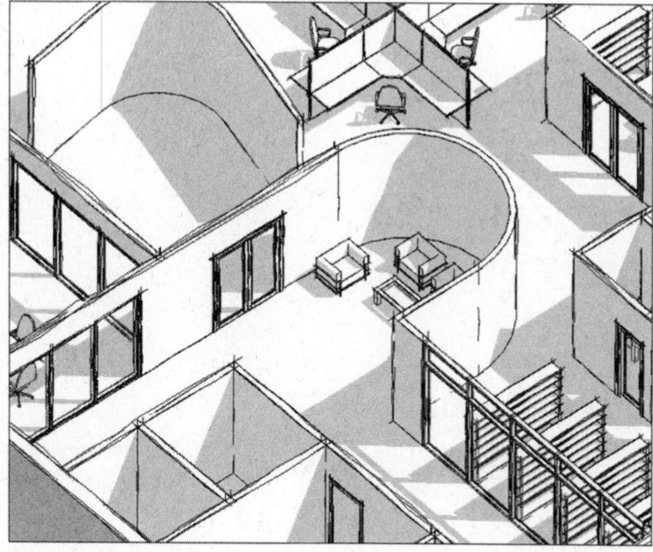

FIGURE 11.22
Sketchy Line options applied to a 3D view

LIGHTING

For most analytic view styles, only sunlight settings are available to cast shadows throughout your model. Lighting controls are fully enabled in the Graphic Display Options when Realistic mode is selected. We discuss the use of artificial lighting settings for photorealistic visualization later in this chapter. If you are using Hidden Line, Shaded, or Consistent Colors, you will have access only to the Sun Settings dialog box we discussed earlier.

Sunlight can be customized to reflect the location of your project at a specific date and time or a position relative to the view. We will discuss solar and shadow studies later in this section.

PHOTOGRAPHIC EXPOSURE

Photographic Exposure allows you to control the color range within the view (Figure 11.23). This option is available only when your model display is set to Realistic.

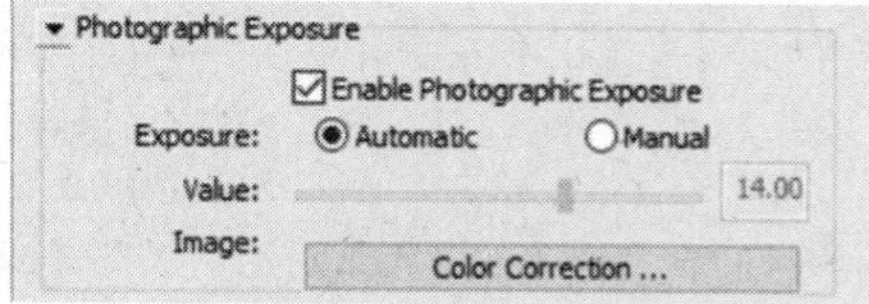

FIGURE 11.23
Photographic Exposure settings

Without this setting enabled, the Realistic view types tend to be rather dark. This setting allows you to lighten the views and correct the highlights, shadow intensity, color saturation, and white point to get the best possible image (Figure 11.24). Photographic Exposure also has an Automatic setting that allows you to let the software pick the best possible combination between those settings.

FIGURE 11.24
Manually modifying the Photographic Exposure settings

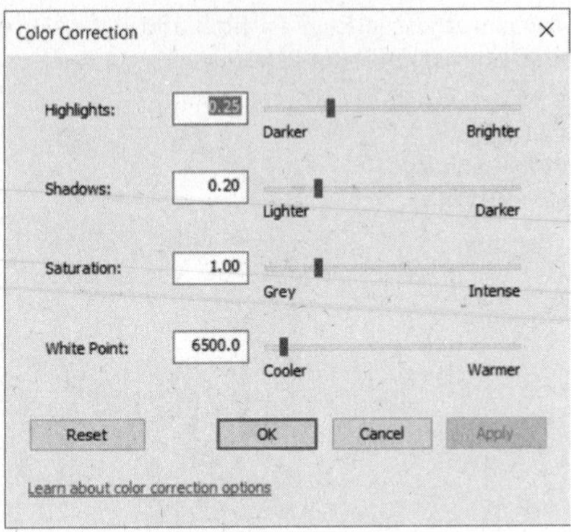

BACKGROUND

The final settings in the Graphic Display Options dialog box are the Background options (Figure 11.25).

FIGURE 11.25
Background settings

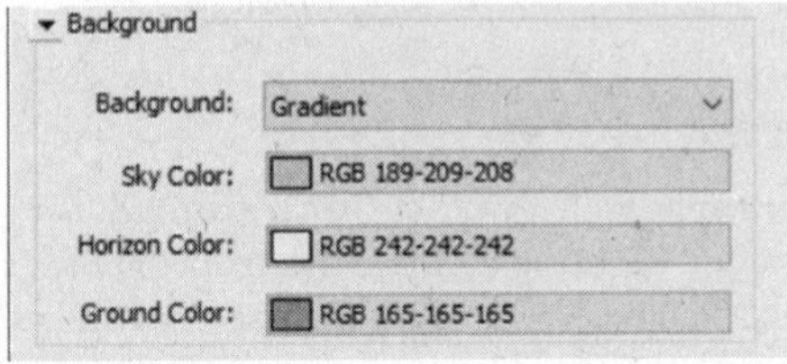

From the Background drop-down, you can choose Sky, Gradient, or Image. With the Gradient or Sky option, you can simulate a ground plane and horizon without rendering. This is a great feature if you're presenting anything live within the model environment because it gives a visual plane for the building to sit on. Figure 11.26 shows the effect of the default Gradient settings on the building section. This setting can also be used in elevation and 3D views.

FIGURE 11.26
Default background settings applied to a section view

DEPTH CUEING

Depth Cueing is a new feature added to Graphic Display Options in Revit 2017. Depth Cueing provides easy controls that can graphically adjust the 3D effect of an image viewed in section or elevation by illustrating objects in the front more vividly than objects in the back. In past versions of Revit, this illustration effect could be achieved only by selecting an object and applying a manual graphic override.

Though this option is listed in Graphic Display Options for any view, it can be activated only within an elevation or section. With an elevation or section open, from the Depth Cueing menu, with Show Depth selected, control sliders can be manipulated to adjust the effect of Depth Cueing (Figure 11.27).

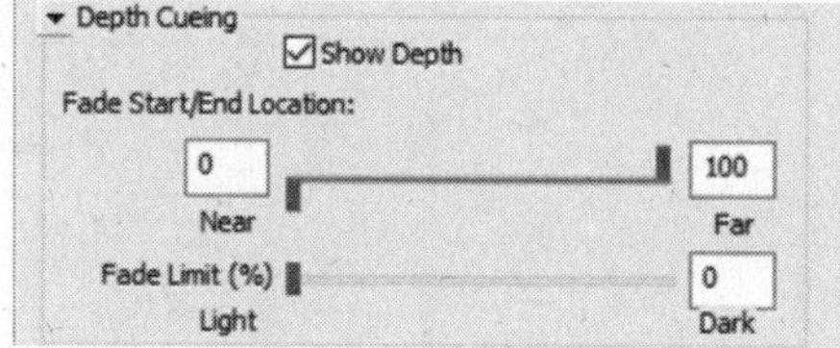

FIGURE 11.27 Default Depth Cueing settings applied to a section or elevation view

The Fade Start/End Location slider represents the overall clipping depth of a section or elevation. The default value of 0 in the Near setting represents the point in which the section or elevation cuts the model. The default value of 100 in the Far setting represents the maximum extent of the clipping plane for the section (Figure 11.28). Adjusting the values for Near and Far is the equivalent of inputting a percentage of the total distance for the clipping plane.

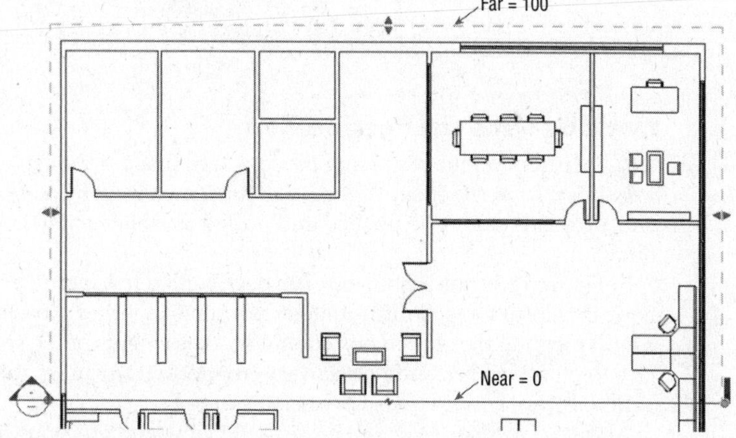

FIGURE 11.28 Representation of default Near and Far settings applied to a section

The Fade Limit (%) slider applies the amount of fading from the Near, where objects are clearly displayed, which then fades to the specified percentage as it approaches the Far distance. The slider ranges from 0 to 100 where 0 denotes objects in the distance that are significantly grayed to 100 where the objects in the distance maintain the same graphic characteristics as set by the object styles. In Figure 11.29, section (a) represents a section with Depth Cueing off, and section (b) represents the same section with Depth Cueing set to Near = 10, Far = 100, and Fade Limit (%) = 5. Note the differences between the two sections and how section (b) denotes objects in various shades of gray, with the furthest wall illustrated in the lightest shade of gray.

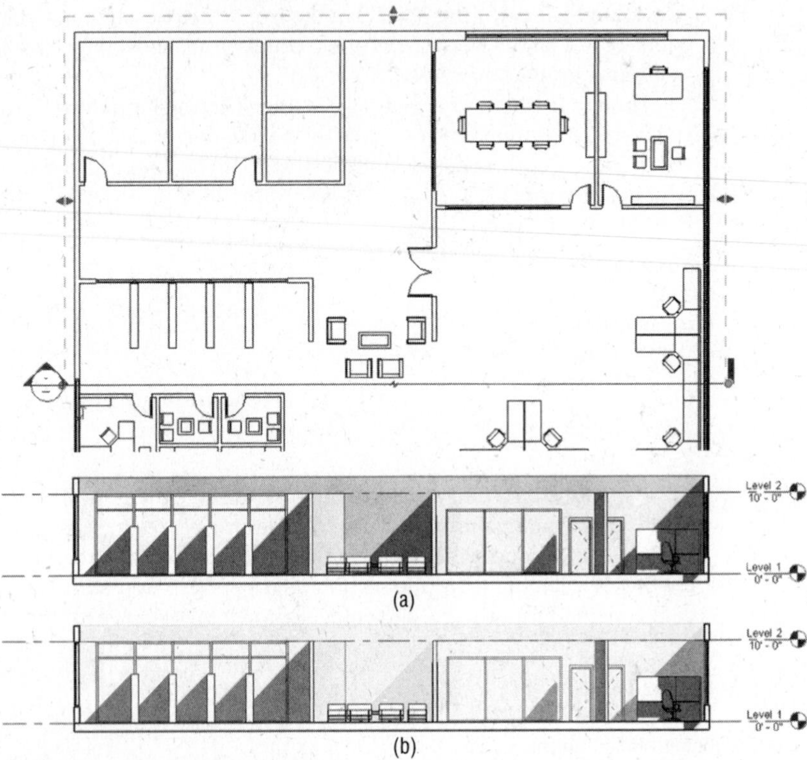

FIGURE 11.29
Fade Limit used with Near and Far settings

Working with the Section Box

Before we get into the rendering process, let's discuss the section box. By selecting the Section Box option from the Properties palette for the view, you create a rectilinear matrix around your project that may be pushed and pulled to isolate a portion of your project within the view.

In Figure 11.30, the section box has been pulled to isolate a portion of the project. This technique is helpful for isolating a smaller portion of a larger project. But a word of warning: Be careful toggling the section box off and on. The extents of the section box will reset and you'll have to pull them back into place. Very frustrating! If you want to see the whole project and the sectional view, it's best to use two separate views.

After you activate a section box in a 3D view and you configure the box to intersect some model elements, you have another graphic tool to aid in your visualization. If the Detail Level option of the view is set to Coarse, model elements that are intersected by the section box will display a color and fill override that can be customized as you see fit. From the Properties palette for the view, select Edit Type. When you open the type properties, you'll notice that there's a Coarse Poche Material setting, which determines the color and fill pattern of the poché.

The poché can be seen in all display types (Wireframe through Realistic), but it is displayed only in a view that is set to the Coarse level of detail. We recommend that you set the default color to black.

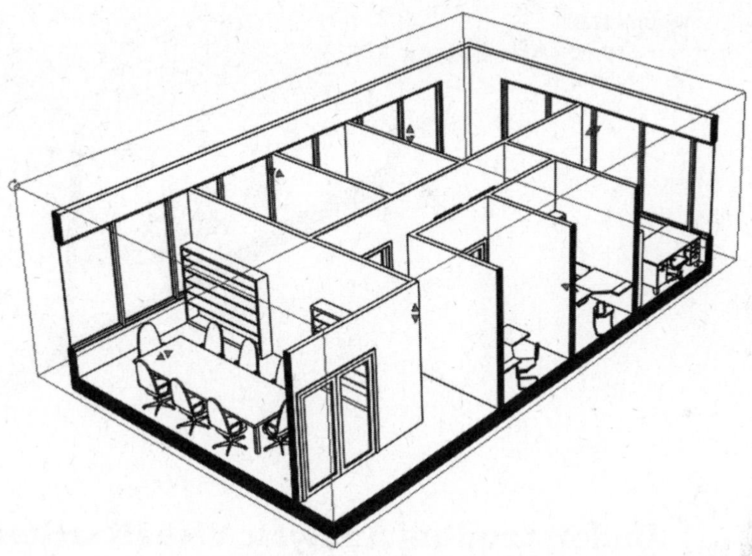

FIGURE 11.30
Pulling the section box to isolate a portion of the project

Here's why you would want the poché color to be black. As shown in Figure 11.31, the regions between host elements (like the walls and floors) are shown as discrete geometries. Notice that you can see black lines dividing the geometry where walls meet floors and so on.

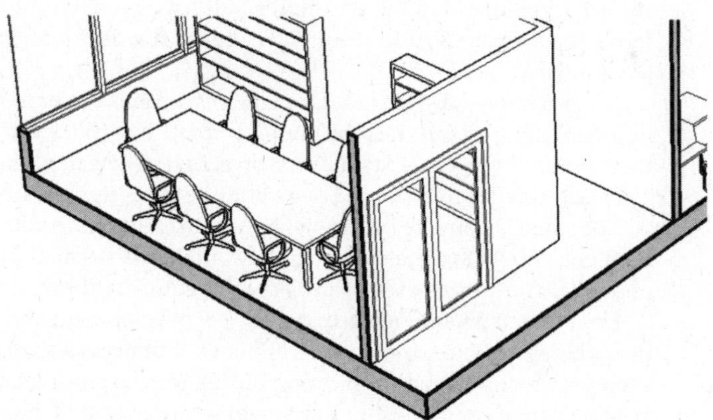

FIGURE 11.31
Regions between host elements are shown as discrete geometries.

You can use the Join Geometry option to clean up the lines between elements. But this approach is time-consuming and often leads to other problems in your file when a lot of things get "joined" just to create a graphic impression.

One simple way to clean this up graphically is to select a poché color that is the same as the color of the lines between elements: black. Again, it's not the most desirable result, but it's fast, doesn't require manual joining of geometry, and reads well (Figure 11.32).

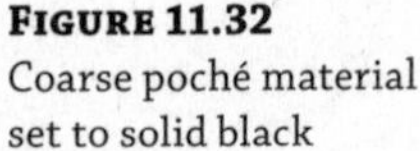

FIGURE 11.32
Coarse poché material set to solid black

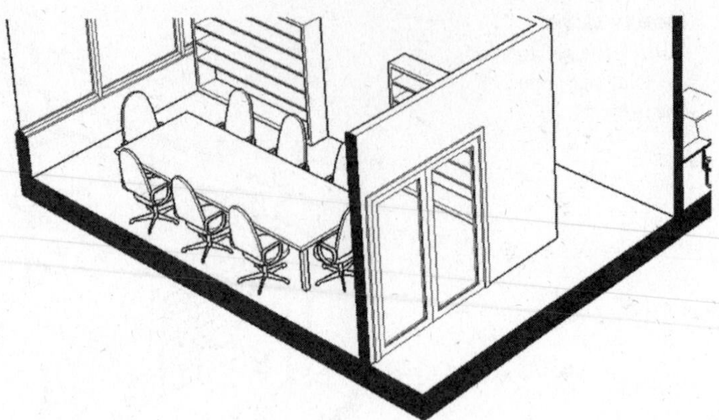

Understanding Analytic Visualization

Now that we have covered the basic view control tools, let's get back to the two types of visualization: analytic and photorealistic. To better understand the analytic concept, think for a moment about Google Maps and how it uses two types of visualization—there's an option to view both Map and Satellite modes. Think of the Map mode as your analytic view and the Satellite mode as your photorealistic view. Both views are important, depending on what you're trying to communicate. If you're simply trying to understand directional information, the Map view is better. But if you're trying to show someone what something looks like with regard to trees and other real-world features, the Satellite view has obvious advantages.

It's also interesting that real-time information is easier to maintain in analytic views. For example, Google Maps has the option to show live traffic data. But this doesn't mean that they're showing actual cars moving on actual streets in photorealistic mode. Rather, they're color-coding the streets based on overall traffic patterns and movement.

The same is going to be true when you're visualizing your project in Revit. More often than not, you'll have the ability to show analytic information in real time; however, producing photorealistic images of your project will require additional time to render.

Even as you get into more of the project development and detail, materials may be a distraction whereas textures may not. Keeping your materials abstract and analytic allows you to help keep your focus on communicating the big ideas of your project. For example, does the spatial arrangement elegantly fulfill the design requirements? How is the vertical/horizontal stacking? We'll show you how to communicate these ideas in the following sections.

Project Parameters

Viewing information about your project in a variety of ways is easy, and one way to do this is with view filters. In this section, first you'll create a view filter based on a project parameter, and then you'll create one to illustrate a user-defined project parameter. A filter can be used to alter the default display properties of elements on a per-view basis. As you can see from the Filters dialog box in Figure 11.33, you can apply up to three filters to a single filter type to override the graphic values of 2D and 3D content as well as spaces.

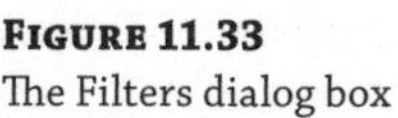

FIGURE 11.33
The Filters dialog box

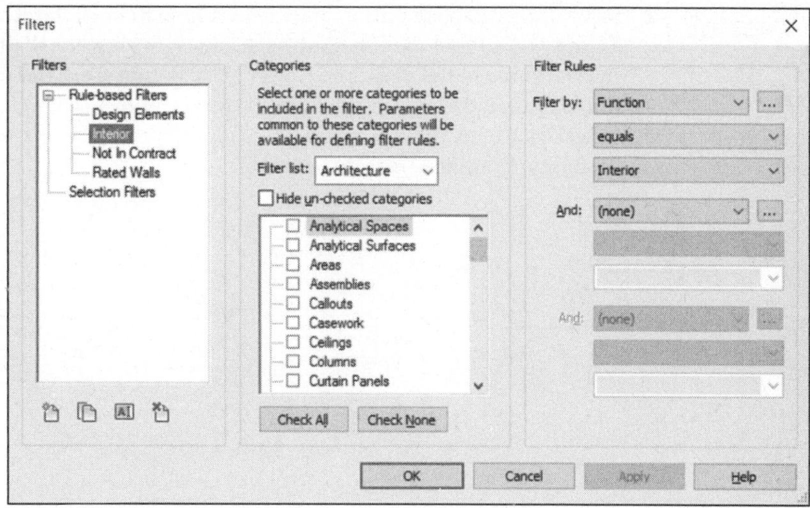

Figure 11.34 shows a simple example of how this works. In the view, there are walls that are two-hour rated. You'd be able to see this in a schedule, but how would you see it in a project view (2D or 3D)? You can easily show that with filters.

FIGURE 11.34
The default view—unfiltered

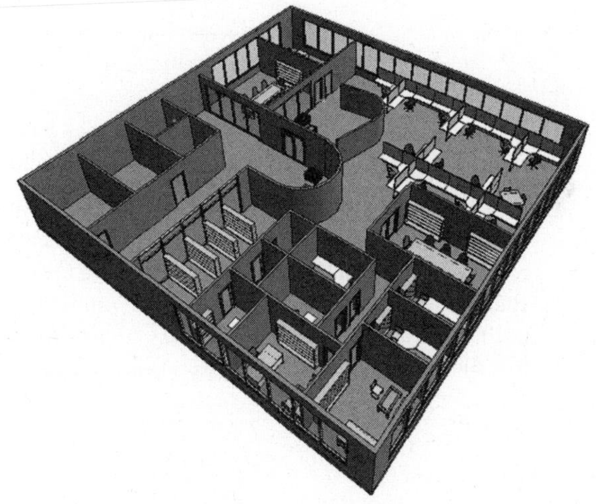

Certification Objective

Let's now explore the use of filters with a simple exercise. Download and open the file `c11-Visualization-Start.rvt` from this book's web page. From the Project Browser, open the ORTHOGRAPHIC VIEW. To apply a filter to your view and visualize the rated walls, follow these steps:

1. First, open the Visibility/Graphic Overrides dialog box (type **VG** on the keyboard or select it in the Properties palette) and choose the Filters tab. Click the Add button to begin the process of creating and applying a new filter.

2. Select the Edit/New button and create a new filter called **Rated Walls**, as shown in Figure 11.35. From the Categories list, check the box for Walls. In the Filter Rules group on the right side of the dialog box, select Fire Rating from the Filter By drop-down menu. Set the filter to Equals in the next drop-down, and from the third drop-down menu, select 2. Make sure the filter is selected in the column on the left, and click OK to add it to your Visibility/Graphic Overrides settings.

FIGURE 11.35
Creating the filter, category, and filter rule

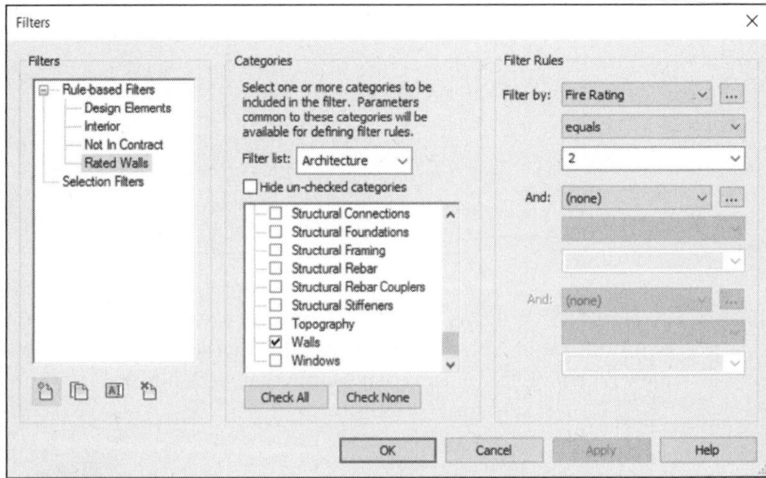

3. When you return to the Visibility/Graphic Overrides dialog box, you'll need to add the filter to your view. Simply click Add, and select Rated Walls.

4. The next step is to customize the Rated Walls filter so that items that fall into the filter category will have a specific graphic effect. Set the Projection/Surface override for Patterns to Red and Solid Fill. To do this, select the Override button in that category to bring up the dialog box shown in Figure 11.36. You'll also want to choose the Override button for both Lines and Patterns under the Cut heading and set each of their colors to Red, as you just did for line graphics.

FIGURE 11.36
Graphic overrides

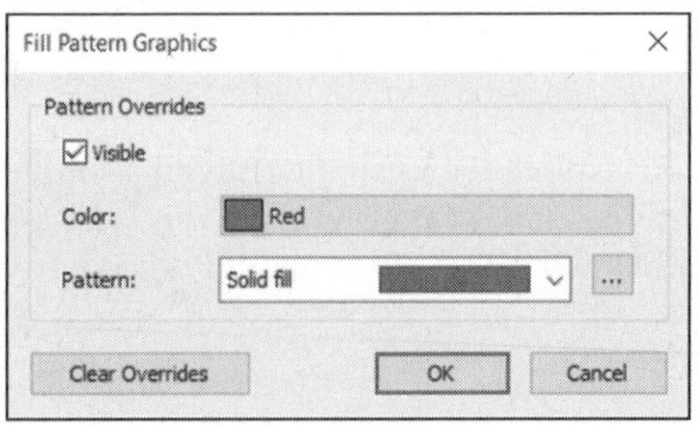

5. When you've finished, click OK to return to the view of the project. You'll see that the filter is overriding the project-defined graphics of the two-hour rated walls (Figure 11.37).

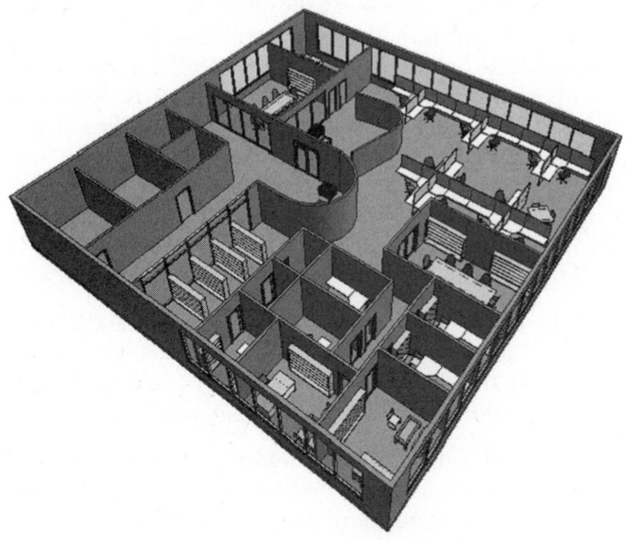

FIGURE 11.37
Applied filter in Shaded view

What's wonderful about this is that you're able to visually coordinate and verify your project schedules with project views that confirm what is being described in the schedules. This even works in Hidden Line view, as shown in Figure 11.38. Changing elements in the schedule or from the project environment will immediately update in all views of your project.

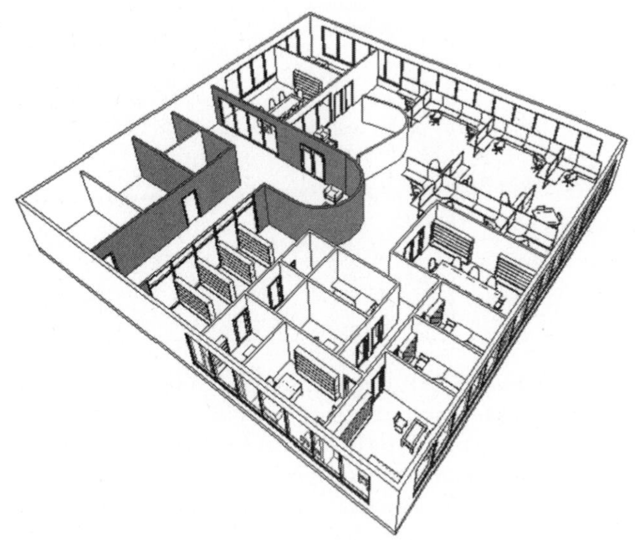

FIGURE 11.38
The applied filter in Hidden Line view

Setting User-Defined Parameters

Now let's look at another example where a particular parameter you might need for a project is not part of the default project environment. In this example, you want to show the space as functionally complete—all the office furniture in place—but a lot of the content that is shown in the image isn't actually in the scope of work for your contract. To demonstrate this, you want to show those furnishings as a separate color. To do this, you'll make two changes to the image.

First, this kind of parameter will have to be applied across many categories of elements—furniture, equipment, appliances, and so on. Second, it may apply to one element but not apply to another element in the very same category, name, and type. For example, under the Furniture category, the designer can specify the desks and cubicles but not the chairs. To make this possible, you'll want to make sure you're using an instance parameter (not a type parameter).

For this exercise, continue with the file from the previous section or download and open the file `c11-Visualization-Start.rvt` from this book's web page.

1. From the Project Browser, right-click the ORTHOGRAPHIC VIEW and duplicate the view. Rename the duplicate view that is created to **PHASE 2 – 2 HOUR RATED WALLS**. In the view, return to your Filters dialog box by opening the Visibility/Graphic Overrides dialog box (**VG**) and create a new filter named **Not In Contract**.

2. Make sure you select numerous categories of elements that you want to be able to distinguish as Not In Contract. For this example, we chose Electrical Equipment, Electrical Fixtures, Furniture, and Furniture Systems, as shown in Figure 11.39. When you finish, select <More Parameters…> from the Filter Rules drop-down list.

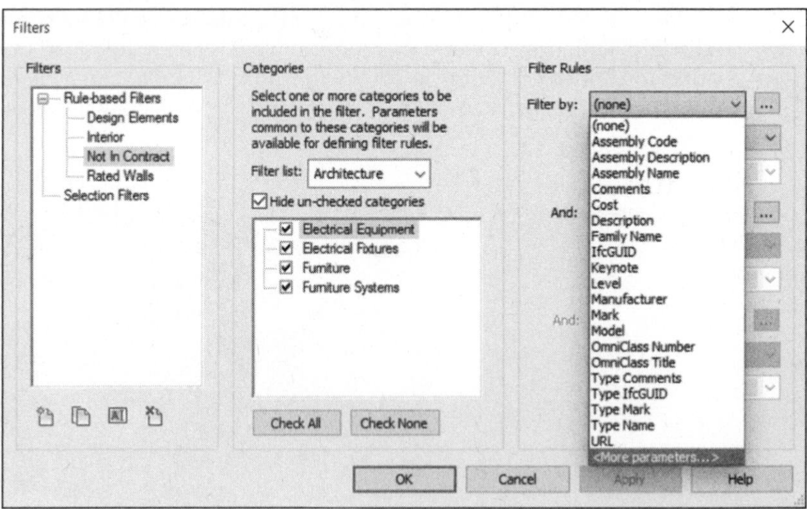

FIGURE 11.39 Multicategory selection

3. The Project Parameters dialog box opens. You need to make a new parameter called **Not In Contract**. Select the Add button. This will take you to the Parameter Properties dialog box. Type in the name of the new parameter, **Not In Contract**. From the Type of Parameter drop-down menu, choose Yes/No. Finally, check the boxes for the following categories: Electrical Equipment, Electrical Fixtures, Furniture, and Furniture Systems, as shown in Figure 11.40.

   This user-defined project parameter will allow you to distinguish elements across a number of categories.

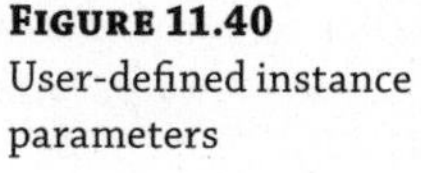

FIGURE 11.40
User-defined instance parameters

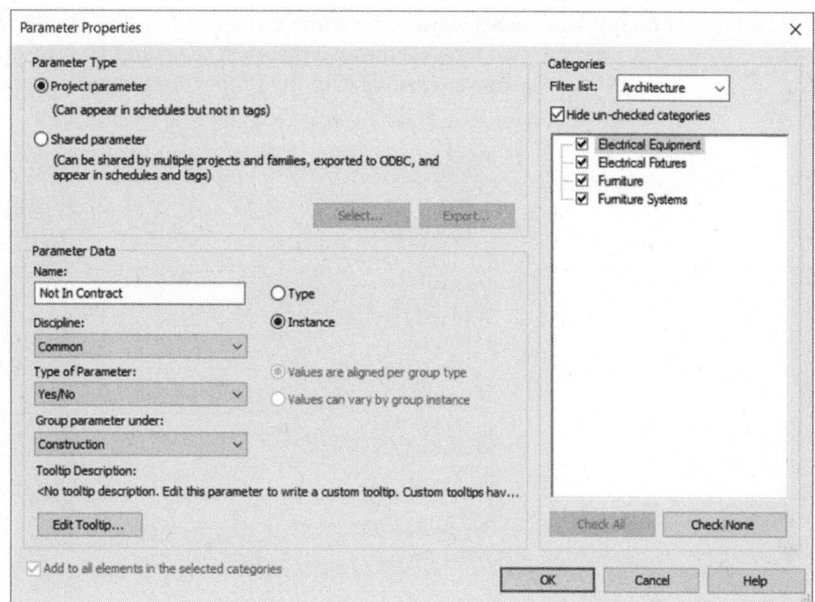

4. Click OK to apply your parameter to the filter.

   In this case, you're instructing Revit to override the graphics when the value of **Not In Contract** equals Yes in the Filter Rules settings (Figure 11.41).

FIGURE 11.41
Filter parameters

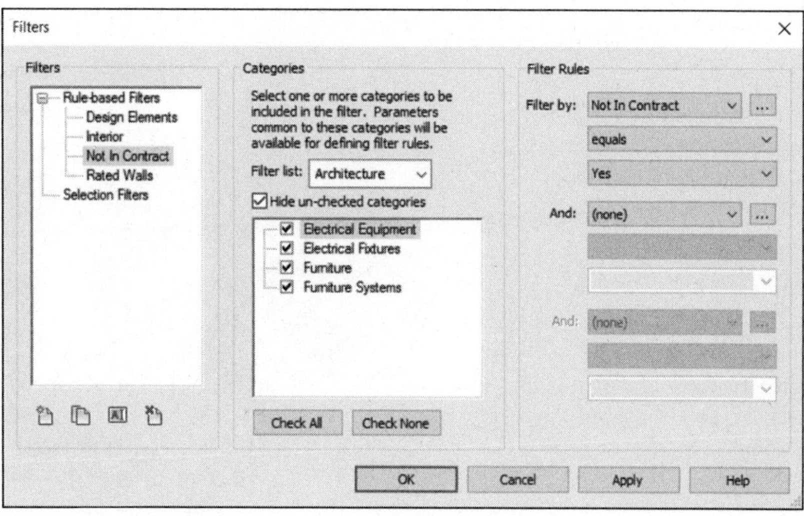

5. You'll return to the Filters tab in the Visibility/Graphic Overrides dialog box, where you'll define how the graphics will be overridden. Once again, add the filter and override the surface pattern with a solid yellow color.

6. Back in the 3D view, select some elements from the categories that you've just created a filter for. You'll notice that as you select the object in your file, the instance parameter for **Not In Contract** is available in the Properties palette (Figure 11.42).

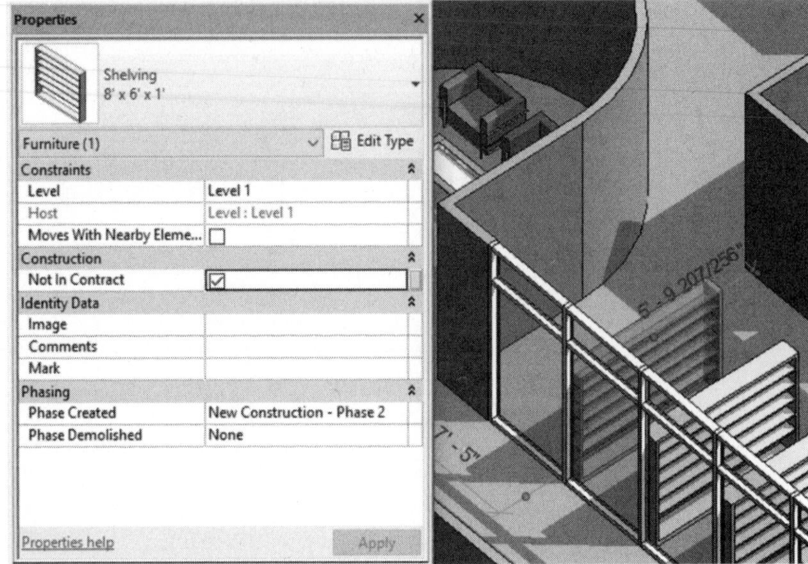

FIGURE 11.42 Instance parameters

7. Select the check box.

   As you do, the solid color will be applied to the components, as shown in Figure 11.43, because the filter that you created now applies to the elements that you've selected, even in Hidden Line views!

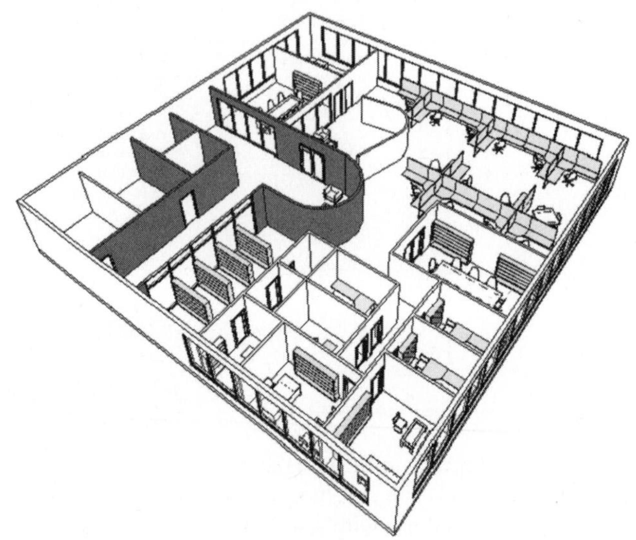

FIGURE 11.43 The Not In Contract graphic override in action

Identifying Design Elements

Another use for this process of using filters is identifying "generic" host design elements as you move between design iteration and design resolution. Figure 11.44 shows a filter that has been applied to a view to highlight any walls, floors, ceilings, or roofs that have the term *Generic* used in their family name.

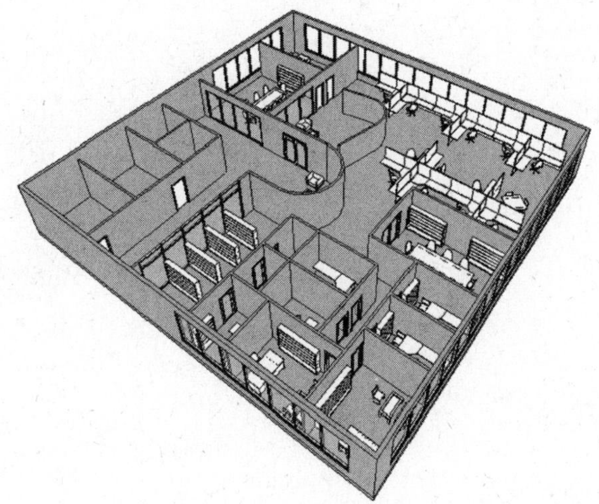

FIGURE 11.44 Identifying generic elements

Typically in a design project, you might create a series of generic elements to replace the ones that have a more detailed label. Using a filter to identify those, you can quickly locate what needs more detail from within your project. The default template already uses the term *generic* to describe basic design host elements, which makes them easy to filter, as shown in Figure 11.45.

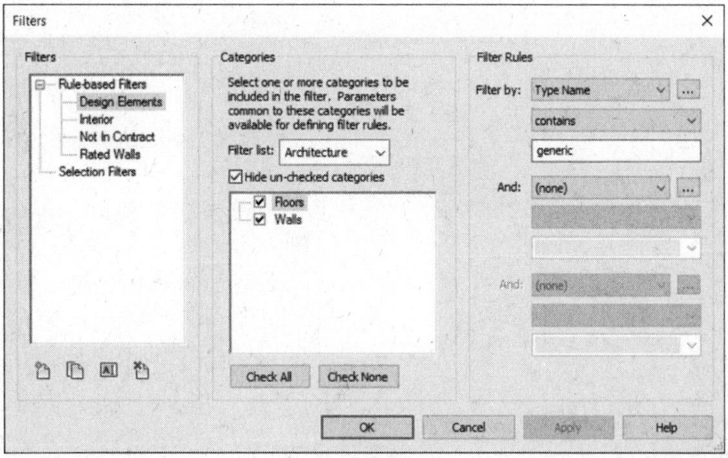

FIGURE 11.45 Generic host element filter

Setting Solar and Shadow Studies

By using solar and shadow studies, you can use another analytic visual style that allows you to communicate natural lighting based on your project's location, orientation, and time of year. The sun's path can also be displayed (Figure 11.46), and you can edit the path of the sun both directly by dragging the sun or sun path within the view and indirectly through time-of-day settings.

FIGURE 11.46
Visual sun path

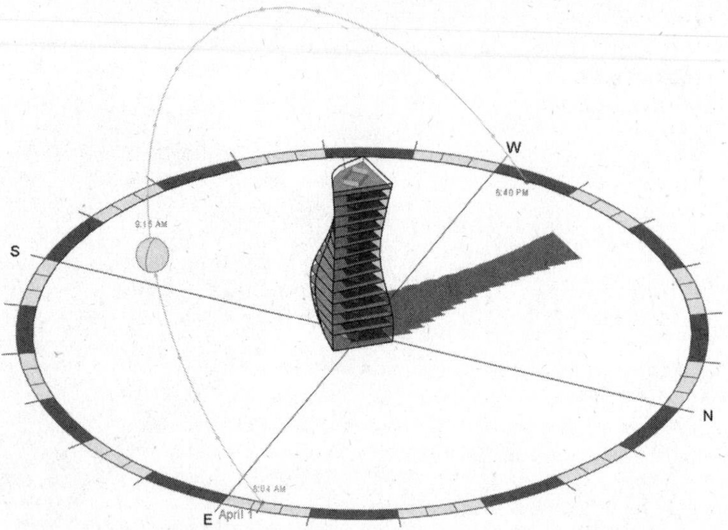

The sun path can be activated from the view control bar. You'll also notice the Sun Settings option in the Sun Settings pop-up menu. This setting will allow you to give an exact location, time, and date for the sun. Selecting Sun Settings (Figure 11.47) allows you to select the settings for your particular view and solar study type. This tool can be used in various view types, including plans, elevations, 3D, and perspectives.

FIGURE 11.47
Sun Settings

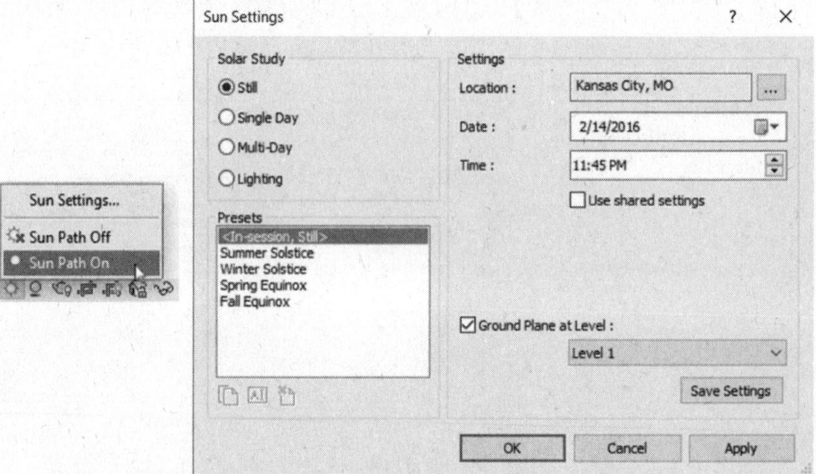

There are four types of solar studies that you can create in Revit:

- The Still setting allows you to create a study of a particular time, date, and location.
- Single Day allows you to create a study over an entire day at intervals of 15, 30, 45, and 60 minutes.
- Multi-Day allows you to create a sun study over a range of dates at intervals of an hour, a day, a week, and a month.
- A Lighting study is not related to a particular time, date, or place. It's more useful for adding graphic depth and texture with "sunlight" from an analytic top right or top left.

Single images are created using the Rendering dialog box. However, animations of single- and multiday solar studies are created by clicking the Application menu and selecting Export ➤ Images And Animations ➤ Solar Study.

For either single- or multiday sun studies, you can set your project location through the Sun Settings dialog box. In the upper-right corner is the Location button. Selecting this button will pull up the Location Weather and Site dialog box (Figure 11.48). Here you can select your project location from the map or via the Project Address drop-down menu. Select your city and click OK to close the dialog box. This will set the location of your project universally for this model, so if you are using the energy modeling tools or sun settings, or exporting the project for use in another application like Autodesk® 3ds Max® software, this setting will locate the project on the globe for all those uses.

FIGURE 11.48
Locating the project

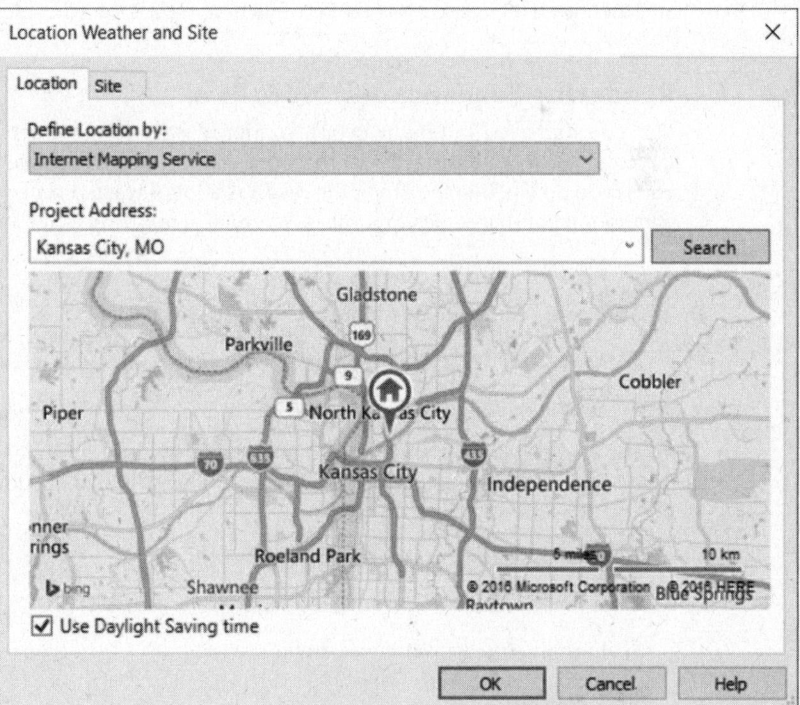

Regardless of whether you choose to use Still, Single Day, or Multi-Day, analytic visualization is incredibly useful for quickly communicating information about your project in a way that isn't literally associated with the actual real-world material assignments of your project elements. Although photorealistic visualization would render wood as "wood," an analytic visualization could be used to identify which wood materials were sustainably harvested, recycled, or LEED (Leadership in Energy & Environmental Design) certified. Analytic visualization is concerned with the actual properties of a material, not just what it looks like. Because analytic visualizations can often be viewed in real time, your project information remains visually concurrent and up to date.

Understanding Photorealistic Visualization

When compared to analytic visualization, *photorealistic visualization* is the expression of the emotive, experiential qualities of your space and content. Materials are carefully selected for accuracy and real-world simulation. Put another way, if analytic visualization is about what something *means*, photorealistic visualization is about how something *feels* or is experienced.

In many cases you'll find yourself tweaking materials and lighting in order to "theatrically" increase the visual interest of the space. Embellishing your model with nonproject entourage is probably essential, and we'll cover important techniques to keep that content from cluttering up the views that are necessary for construction documentation.

In the following sections, we'll review the process for creating camera views and walkthroughs, and then we'll look at some of the settings that impact the outcome of the renderings in Revit.

Rendering Sequence and Workflow

You'd be surprised, but many people render in the wrong sequence. The workflow for creating compelling renderings is not the same one you use to resolve your design process. If you try to do one like the other, the result is a lot of wasted time and frustration. Consider a documentation-based design process to create a building that moves from intent to content:

1. Host components (walls, floors, and roofs)
2. Hosted components (doors and windows)
3. Furniture, fixtures, and equipment
4. Assembly details and documentation

The challenge is that this process does not provide an optimal workflow for creating great renderings. If you're focused on the process of *visualization*, the ideal workflow is more along the lines of the following:

1. Geometry (host and family components)
2. Cameras (setting up your views)
3. Lighting (using matte materials)
4. Materials

Yes, this is as simple as it gets: cameras, and then lights, and then materials. In a documentation-based process, lights don't usually show up until the building is well resolved because you're placing lights meant to be the actual fixtures to be installed in the building, not just for rendering. So the documentation process is simply out of sequence with the visualization process.

In addition, you need to evaluate the lighting neutrally, without materials to distract you. As you're placing your content, a lot of elements already have material assignments. You need to find a way to neutralize the material settings while you figure out lighting. Now you just need to put it all together!

Creating Perspective Views

The tasks of creating and modifying your camera views are almost as important as the model content you're creating. If you're not careful, you can easily fail to impress the viewer by selecting the wrong view and aspect ratio of the camera and controls.

Perspective views communicate far more depth than orthographic views (Figure 11.49). Unless the view needs to be at dimensioned scales, we prefer to use perspective views of the project for renderings.

FIGURE 11.49
Orthographic view versus perspective view

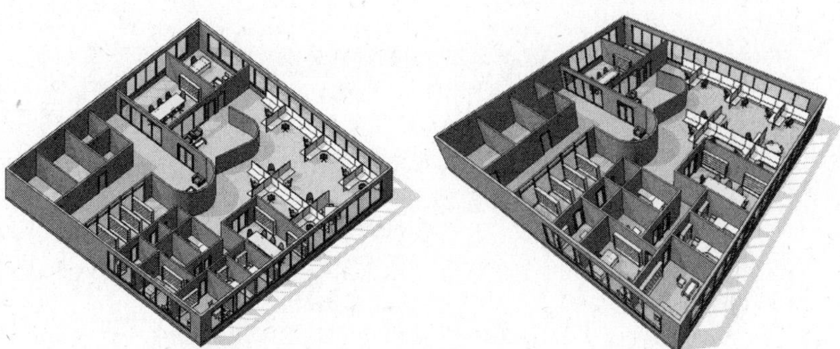

To create a perspective view, switch to the View tab, locate the Create panel, and click 3D View ➢ Camera. This command will not work if you are working in a drafting view, a schedule, or another camera view. When the Camera command is activated, you will need to pick two points. The first point to select is the camera location, and the second point is the target location. Keep in mind that when you rotate your view, the rotation is centered on the target elevation. If you use the Camera command in a plan view, as shown in Figure 11.50, you have the opportunity to specify the elevation of the camera as an exact distance from the associated level in the Options bar.

After creating a camera view, you should understand that there is a boundary box that defines the extents of the view defined by the camera and target locations. If you need to adjust these two locations (other than navigating within the camera view), you can activate the controls by going to another view, like a plan, and then locate the camera view in the Project Browser. Right-click the camera view and choose Show Camera from the context menu, as shown in Figure 11.51.

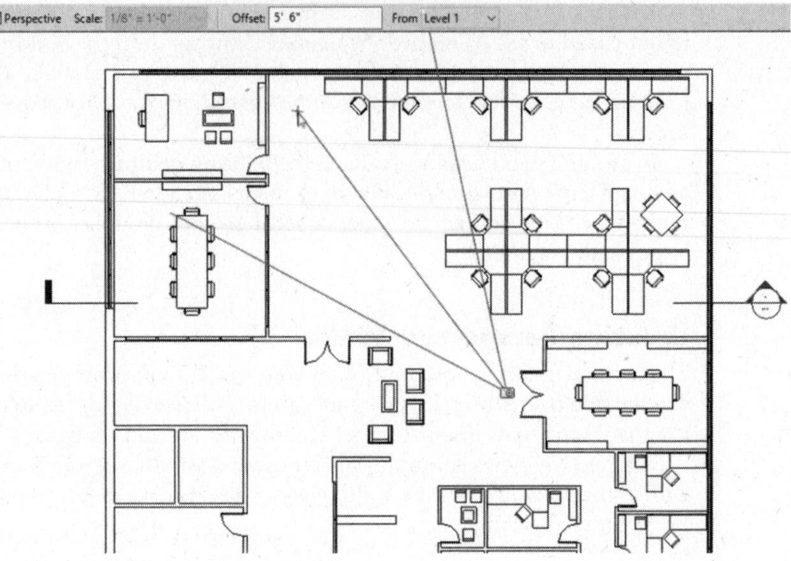

FIGURE 11.50 Placing the camera in a plan view

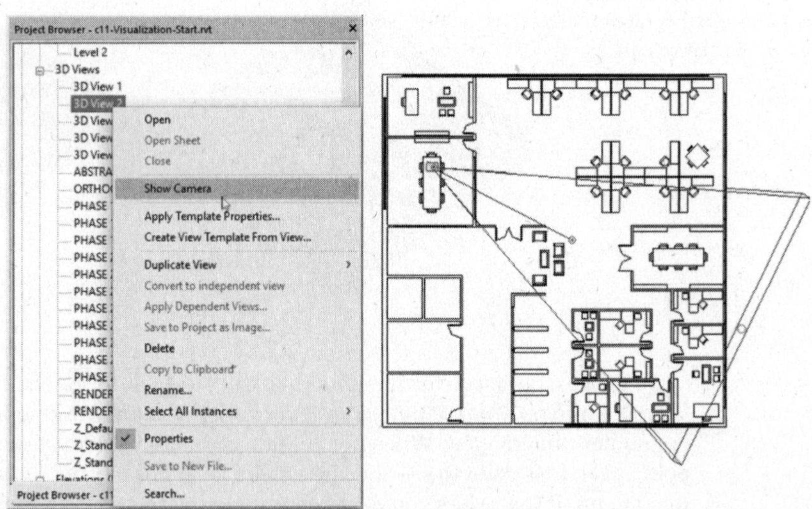

FIGURE 11.51 Reactivate the camera controls with Show Camera.

Once you see the camera, you can select and move it around your project. Doing so allows you to move your camera closer or farther away. You can also select the clipping planes of your camera and edit the front and back planes of your camera's view.

The aspect ratio of your camera view is also important. For example, a television ratio of 4:3 seems far less expansive and dramatic than a 16:9 wide-screen ratio. Figure 11.52 illustrates this; image (a) is 4:3 and image (b) is 16:9. The result is that image (a) seems too tight and constrained, whereas image (b) is far more natural.

FIGURE 11.52
Aspect ratio comparison

(a)

(b)

To change the aspect ratio, select the crop region in the camera view and then click the Size Crop command in the contextual tab of the ribbon. In the resulting dialog box, you can change the aspect proportionally or non-proportionally (Figure 11.53). Keep in mind that this setting doesn't zoom your camera forward and backward; it simply changes the relative height and width of the aperture.

FIGURE 11.53
The Crop Region Size dialog box

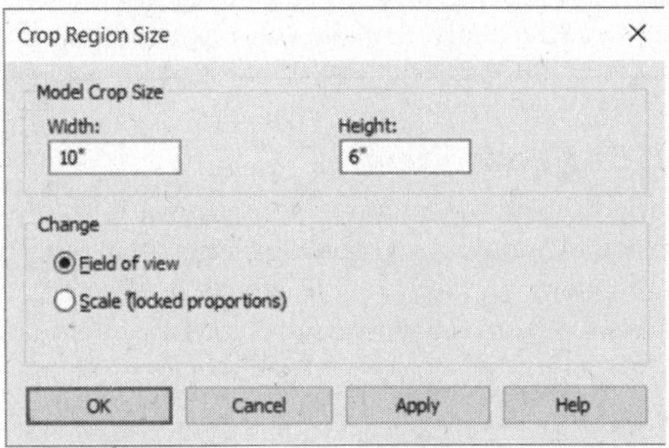

You can also modify the camera position and angle on the fly using the SteeringWheels® (similar to other Autodesk products). Simply activate the Navigation Wheel (Figure 11.54) located on the right side of the view window or press Shift+W on the keyboard. You'll be able to zoom, pan, and orbit as well as control other view features using the Navigation Wheel. This tool can take some getting used to because it will "follow" your mouse pointer across the screen—it's not anchored at the bottom corner as the image might suggest. This is helpful because it will give you a dynamic menu to change and modify your view, but don't forget to turn it off before you start modifying geometry. Selecting the same button again will hide the tool until you need it again.

FIGURE 11.54
The Navigation Wheel

Real World Scenario

COLLABORATING ON YOUR DESIGNS

One of the great features of Revit software is the almost immediate visualizations you can perform within a model for quick yet meaningful collaboration. In many firms, the lead designers tend to work and think with pen and paper. Traditionally, they find it difficult to design in modeling software. Using the visualization tools, it's easy for modelers and non-modelers to speak the same language. Being able to identify some key camera points within the model will allow you to create quick hidden line or shadowed perspectives that a designer can then trace over and collaborate with the team to drive changes in the model. Save those perspectives and they can be printed again and again as the design changes, allowing the designer to see the progress.

Locking Your View

After you create your view, you might want to consider locking it so it can't be accidentally adjusted. Although you can't tag elements in a perspective view, it is a good practice to lock camera views to preserve consistency between rendering iterations. The view-locking tools can be accessed from the view control bar, as shown in Figure 11.55.

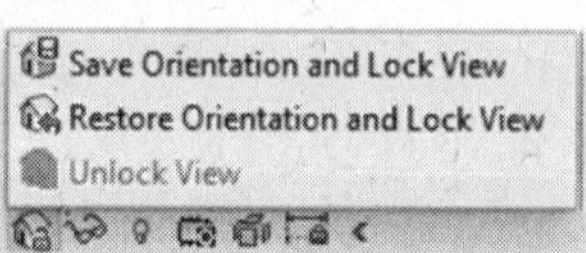

FIGURE 11.55
Lock view settings

Three options are available from the Lock 3D View option. Save Orientation And Lock View keeps the current orientation and prohibits anyone from rotating the view. As its name implies, the Unlock View command unlocks the view and allows you to navigate freely. After you have unlocked a previously locked view and changed the view, click Restore Orientation And Lock

View to return the view to its previously saved orientation. If you unlock a locked view and then choose Save Orientation And Lock View, the previously saved orientation is lost while the new orientation is saved and locked.

Creating a Walkthrough

In addition to still perspective views, you have the ability to create animation paths called walkthroughs. Creating a walkthrough is much like creating a series of connected camera views. Like any other 3D view, a walkthrough can be generated using any of the visual styles and settings we described previously in this chapter. In the following exercise, use the `c11-Visualization-Start.rvt` file.

1. From your Level 1 plan view, start placing a series of cameras by setting the camera location and then the camera direction.

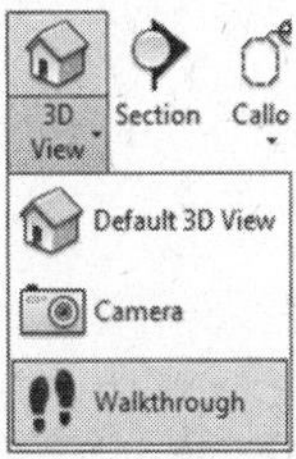

Note that each time you pick a location, these cameras will become the key frames in your animation. When you have placed the last camera, press the Esc key and your finished path will appear (Figure 11.56).

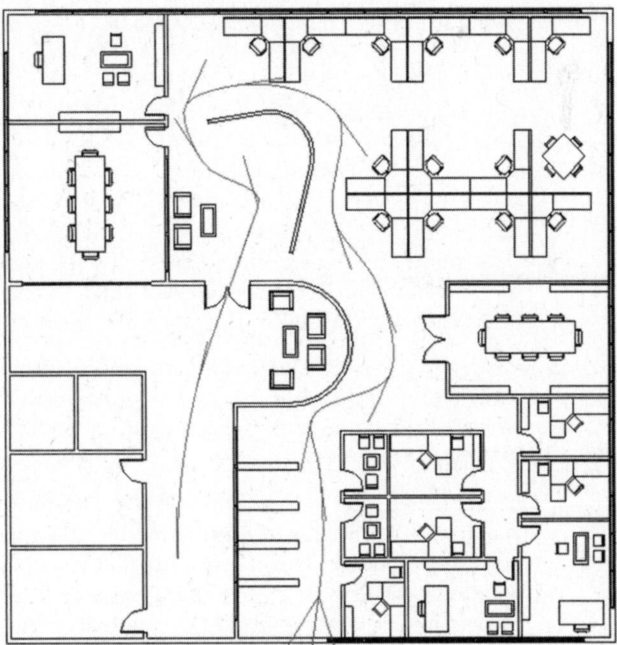

Figure 11.56
The finished camera path

2. Right-clicking the path and choosing Edit Walkthrough will allow you to manipulate each of the series of views that you just created. Right-click the nodes on the path and choose Go To View.

   If your walkthrough path is not displayed, look in the Project Browser for the Walkthroughs category and locate the walkthrough view you just created. Right-click it and select Show Camera from the context menu.

3. Double-click the walkthrough view in the Project Browser to open the view as you would any of the other views.

   Figure 11.57 shows the first view in the path that we've just created along with the Walkthrough view properties from the Properties palette.

   The view you might see when you activate a walkthrough is the last frame in the camera path. You'll need to use the Show Camera method to select the walkthrough and then click Edit Walkthrough to access the frame controls. You can then use the control icons in the ribbon or set the Frame value to 1 in the Options bar to get to the first camera point in your walkthrough.

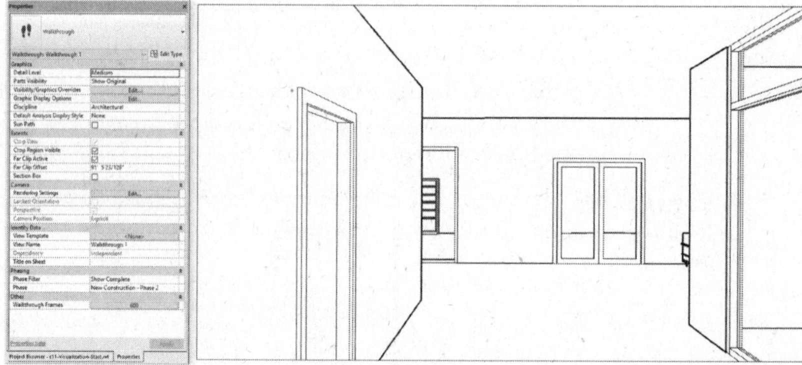

FIGURE 11.57
A walkthrough camera view with associated properties

4. Let's modify the aspect ratio to 16:9. Select the view boundary and select Size Crop from the contextual tab in the ribbon. By default, the view is 6″ × 4 -1/2″ (150 mm × 113 mm). Select the Field Of View radio button and then set the Width value to **8″** (**200** mm).

5. We're going to export a Hidden Line view for testing (especially before rendering), but we want to give the walkthrough more depth. So, in the Graphic Display Options dialog box we reviewed earlier in this chapter, under Model Display change the Silhouettes option to Wide Lines.

   It's not usually desirable to simply walk with the camera facing the same direction that you're walking. So you're going to modify the camera directions to make the visualization more dynamic. This will require that you open a couple of views and tile the view windows, as shown in Figure 11.58. This way, you'll be able to see the results of your work in one view while working in another.

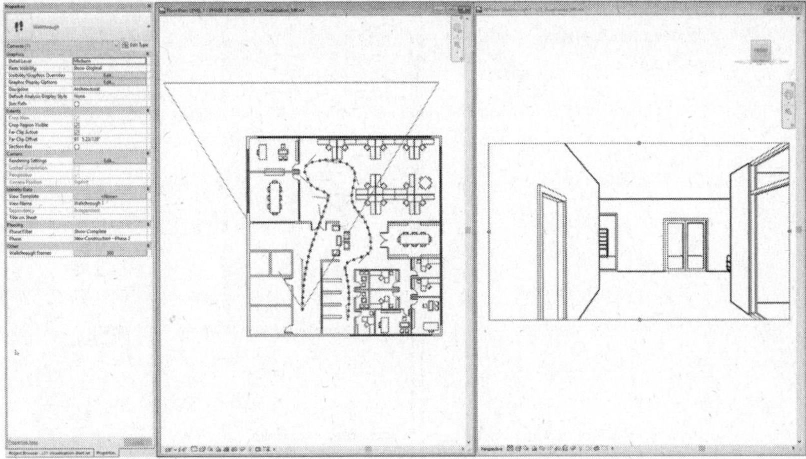

FIGURE 11.58
Tiled camera and plan views

6. Activate the plan view of Level 1, and then click the Close Hidden Windows button from the Quick Access toolbar. Activate the walkthrough, and then tile those views by pressing **WT** on the keyboard. Press **ZA** to activate the Zoom All To Fit command.

   A couple of important points should be noted. First, you're showing the plan and the camera view at the same time. This allows you to see both the graphic and the analytic camera, which is important for modifying views. As you can see, when you select the boundary of the view on the right, the camera path highlights in the view on the left. Since the view is selected, you have the option of editing the crop size just as with any other camera. But you also have the option of editing the walkthrough.

7. Click the Edit Walkthrough option, and you'll see the contextual toolbar, shown in Figure 11.59.

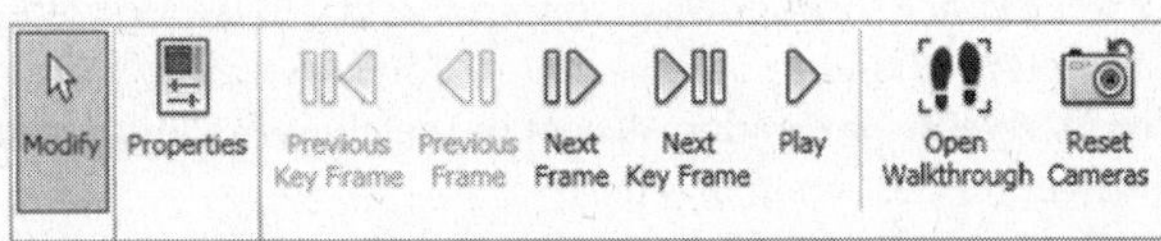

FIGURE 11.59
Edit Walkthrough contextual toolbar

   When you open the Walkthrough Editor, the camera path now shows important controls (Figure 11.60).

   The red dots along the path represent key frame locations (when you placed your camera), and the red dot directly in front of the camera allows you to control the rotational direction. By default, all the cameras face ahead relative to their location on the path. But you can edit the default so that the camera can follow one direction but face another direction.

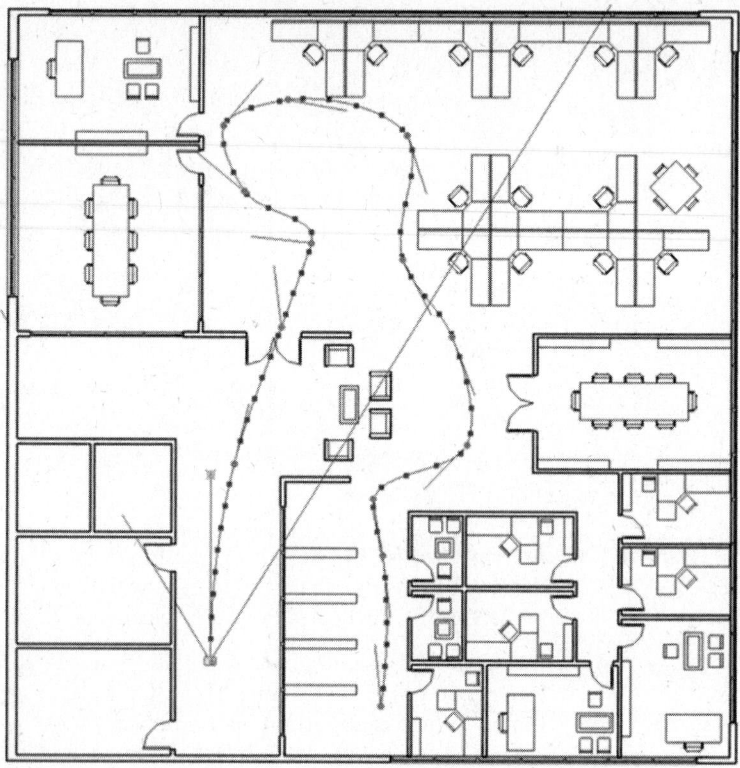

FIGURE 11.60
Camera path and controls

Because the default path is 300 frames in length, it would take a long time to go to each frame and edit what you see. It's better to jump ahead from key frame to key frame, editing fewer locations. When you do this, Revit will interpolate the frames between the key frames for you. As you advance through each key frame, try to experiment rotating the camera to the left and right as well as glancing up and down. You can do so by dragging the target point in the plan view or using the Navigation Wheel in the camera view. Use the Look command from the Navigation Wheel for best results.

Exporting a Walkthrough

After you edit the key frames in the walkthrough, you can export the animation by clicking the Application button and choosing Export ➤ Images And Animations ➤ Walkthrough. The options to export an AVI are the same as all of the options for rendering still images (Figure 11.61).

A 15 frames-per-second (fps) frame rate is minimal to keep the animation smooth. But if you increased the frame rate, the animation length would shorten and it would seem like you were running (rather than walking) through the scene. What can you do to have a longer animation without adding speed? Simply add more frames to your animation.

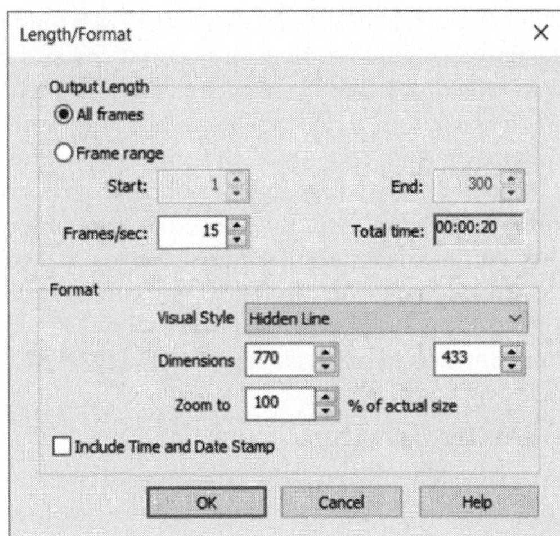

FIGURE 11.61
Graphic format controls

From the Properties palette, open the Walkthrough Frames dialog box (Figure 11.62). By increasing the Total Frames value, you can also adjust the relative frames per second (fps) to maintain the desired speed.

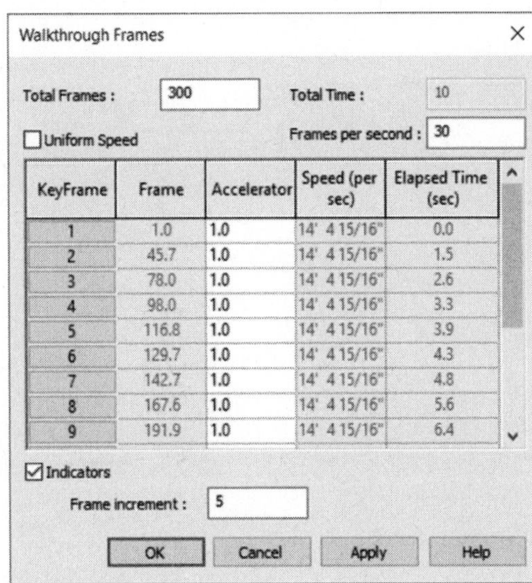

FIGURE 11.62
Default frame count

So, for example, if you wanted to increase the fps to 30 but maintain the same travel speed, you would also increase the Total Frames setting to 600.

Finally, where a lot of people struggle is with the speed of their animation. Unless you're breaking up your animation into separate paths (which will be combined later into a single sequence), it's necessary to be able to speed up or slow down your camera's movement. In Revit, you can uncheck the Uniform Speed option to speed up or slow down the camera during a single animation study.

The same visual effect plays a part in your renderings. The farther you are from something, the faster your camera can move as you fly by and still seem smooth and fluid. But you will need to slow down considerably if you're walking through the building, where a comfortable pace is 6 to 8 feet (2 to 2.5 meters) per second.

We've exported the animation from this portion of the chapter. It's important to understand that when Revit exports video, it exports in an uncompressed format. The file sizes will be large compared to what you might be used to. Any of the videos can be brought into other video-editing tools (iMovie, HandBrake, Movie Maker, and so on) to compress the raw footage. If you want to investigate the file or animation, you can download the `c11-Visualization-Finished.rvt` file or the `c11_Visualization_Animation.avi` file from the Chapter 11 folder on this book's web page at `www.sybex.com/go/masteringrevit2017`.

Rendering Settings

Now that we have covered the processes to create still camera views and walkthroughs, let's discuss some of the settings that are important to understand before you begin to generate photorealistic renderings. You can access the Rendering dialog box by clicking the teapot icon on the View tab in the ribbon or in the view control bar of a 3D view.

Some of these settings are also available from the Rendering Settings dialog box, which is accessed from the Properties palette when you are working with a 3D view. Figure 11.63 shows the Rendering dialog box to the left and the Rendering Settings dialog box to the right.

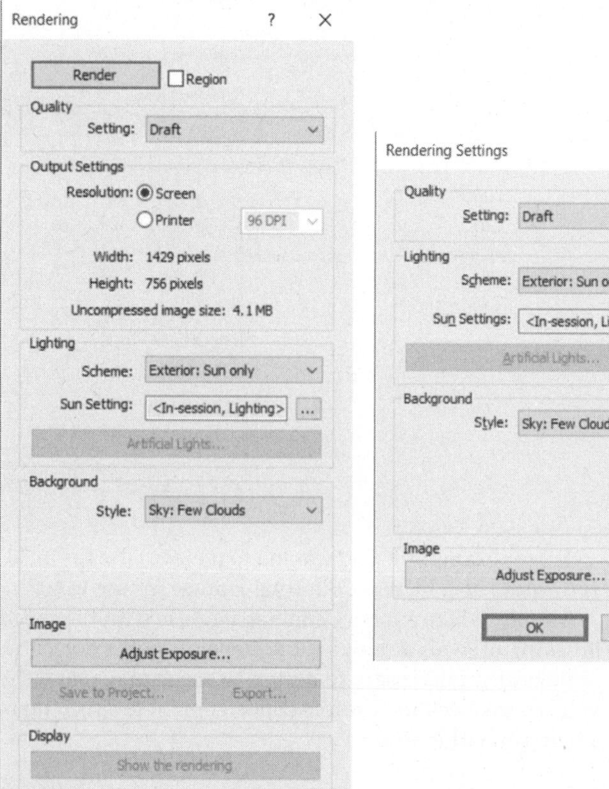

FIGURE 11.63
Rendering dialog box

If you are a veteran to Revit, you will notice that there is a subtle difference with the new Rendering dialog. When Revit 2016 was released, it allowed a user to select a render engine called NVIDIA mental ray® or a new render engine called Autodesk Raytracer®, which had very similar rendering characteristics to the interactive Ray Trace view setting that can be selected in the view control bar. With the release of Revit 2017, NVIDIA mental ray has been removed; instead, Raytracer is the main rendering engine and has undergone incremental improvement from what was released in Revit 2016.

So, what is Raytracer? Raytracer is an iterative rendering engine that renders in a series of passes, with each pass adding to the accuracy of how materials and lighting are represented in the rendered scene. Unlike traditional rendering engines, if you were to stop Raytracer mid-render, the fidelity of the rendered image would be consistent and complete. It would not have missing rendered areas or areas that are partially rendered. This capability brings enormous flexibility in a rendering workflow. With Raytracer, you no longer have to worry if the available time for rendering is sufficient to complete a rendered image. As long as you initiate the rendering process, even if you have only 30 minutes, the end result will be a complete rendering, consistent in its quality. Granted, the previous example represents the direst of circumstances, but in the high-speed architecture industry, this capability is the difference between having something to show at a design meeting and being left empty-handed after working really late hours.

Using Output Settings

An important setting in this dialog box is Resolution. It's easy to spend far too much time creating a rendered view because rendering times increase exponentially when the resolution doubles. Think of it this way: If you're rendering a view at 150 dots per inch (dpi) and then you render the same view at 300 dpi, the image is now four times larger, not twice as large (1 × 1 = 1 and 2 × 2 = 4). If you were to render the view at 600 dpi, it would be 16 times larger (4 × 4 = 16), and you could reasonably expect the 150 dpi image that rendered in a few minutes to take considerably longer at 600 dpi.

How large you need to render something depends on what you're going to use it for: screen or print. Don't expect a rendering the size of a 3″ × 5″ (75 mm × 150 mm) postcard to work for a 3′ × 5′ (900 mm × 1500 mm) banner.

The Output Settings options help you determine the level of resolution at which your image can be saved when rendered. The screen resolution is simply the resolution of the view on your monitor.

You should be much more interested in the Printer settings because of the likelihood that you'll need to print your views. Again, the resolution is important, because you're printing for something that will be viewed at some distance (arm's length or a few feet away) with the naked eye. Rendering beyond what can reasonably be seen is time that can be spent on further refining your design. While the default printer resolutions are shown in Figure 11.64, you can input other values by typing them in the dialog box.

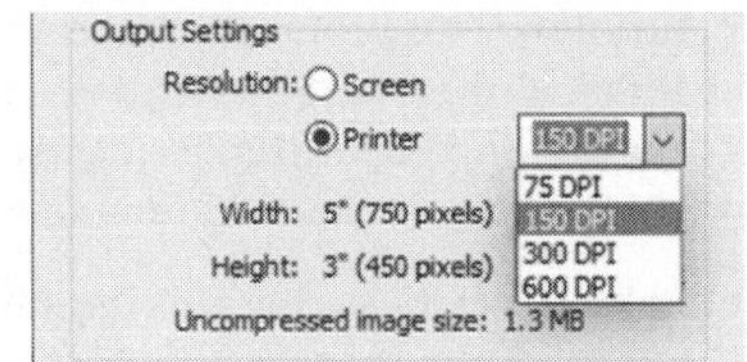

Figure 11.64
Printer settings

Using Quality

Revit's new Raytracer render engine maintains the look of previous quality setting options but provides only four presets: Draft, Medium, High, and Best. The Low setting has been removed because with the speed of Raytracer and how it calculates renderings, there was no difference in the quality of the output between a rendering set to Draft and a rendering set to Low. Figure 11.65 illustrates the new render range for settings between Draft and Best.

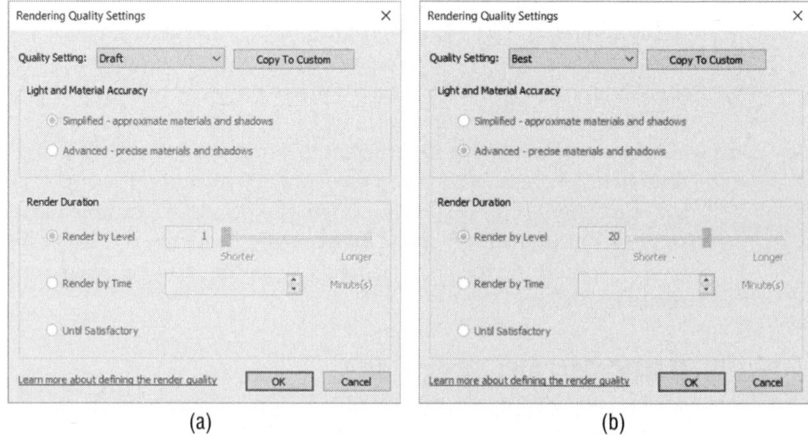

Figure 11.65
(a) Draft setting;
(b) Best setting

There is a drastic difference in the currently available options and what had been present throughout many versions of Revit. Gone are the slider controls that controlled reflection, transparency, and indirect illumination; instead, the Render Quality settings provide five radio buttons grouped under two major categories:

- **Light and Material Accuracy:** This grouping allows you to select one of two rendering accuracy settings.
  - **Simplified – approximate materials and shadows:** Speeds up the rendering passes at the cost of accuracy to materials and shadows in areas such as indirect illumination, soft shadows, reflection, and refraction.
  - **Advanced – precise materials and shadows:** Increases the accuracy of materials and shadow and with each rendering pass tightens the accuracy of real-world effects such as indirect illumination, soft shadows, reflection, and refraction. Using this setting increases the render time for each pass.
- **Render Duration:** This grouping allows you to select one of three duration settings. Remember that with an iterative renderer, it is no longer a matter of whether you have enough time to complete the rendering; it becomes a question of what quality of rendering you can achieve with the available amount of time.
  - **Render by Level:** Selecting this option allows you to specify the number of render passes. The minimum setting is 1, and the maximum setting is 40.

- **Render by Time:** Selecting this option allows you to specify the number of minutes to be dedicated to the rendering process.
- **Until Satisfactory:** Selecting this option will instruct the rendering process to continuously render pass after pass until it is instructed to stop rendering.

These settings will control the quality of the output, but remember, with Raytracer, time is now a correlation to the quality of the rendering achieved (you will always get a complete rendering) instead of a risky proposition of whether the available amount of time allows you to complete a rendering at the desired output (which may or may not be finished). Raytracer's iterative rendering capability and the ability to specify render duration takes away the stress of trying to produce a rendering. We still recommend you perform a quick draft render to get a feel for your scene setup before committing to a rendering of longer duration.

Using Output Settings and Quality

We've discussed both Output Settings and Quality, but for a successful rendering, both must work together. As you start experimenting with your rendering exercises, pay attention to Output Settings and Quality. If you commit to a rendering with a high output resolution such as 600 dpi but have your Quality set to Draft, you will unnecessarily increase the render time for each iterative pass. The end result is a high-resolution image of a low-quality render. The reverse is also true. If you set a low output resolution such as 75 dpi but have your Quality set to Best, you will once again increase the render time for each iterative pass. The end result is a low-resolution pixelated image trying to convey characteristics of a high-quality render. In both cases the results are subpar.

So, what is the right balance? Well, it's probably better to render the output resolution a bit larger than the format in which it will be presented, which will give you some flexibility if you need to increase the size of your image later. Of course, you would want the best quality possible, but you should always consider the audience that is viewing your rendering. If it is an internal design meeting, the Medium setting is probably good enough. If it is a final presentation or a rendering that will be published, you might want to use Best (which defaults to 20 passes) or even set it to Until Satisfactory and let it render overnight. There are many potential combinations, but now with Raytracer, you have been provided with a rendering process that is forgiving. So experiment!

Some Tips for the Resolution You Should Use

Estimating your image resolution is easy. If the image is going to be viewed on a screen, 150 dpi is likely sufficient and even gives you some flexibility if the image has to be slightly larger. If you need to print the image, 300 dpi will work the majority of the time. Now take the longest dimension of your image (height or width) and multiply the dimension by the needed resolution. That's all you need to figure out your image pixel size. If you don't know the size of the final image, guess big: Perform your necessary draft renderings and make the final 2000–4000 pixels. That will work for any large-scale presentation or high-res monitors.

Using Monochromatic Views to Examine Context and Lighting

Now that we have our geometry in a sample model and we have shown you how to create and manipulate camera views, we will move on to lighting before discussing materials. That said, it is difficult to review your design geometry with realistic lighting in Revit without also rendering component materials. If you want to examine spatial context and lighting quality in a monochromatic model, we'll show you how to accomplish that technique in Revit.

Take a look at the rendering shown in Figure 11.66, which has been created by rendering a camera view with all the default materials active.

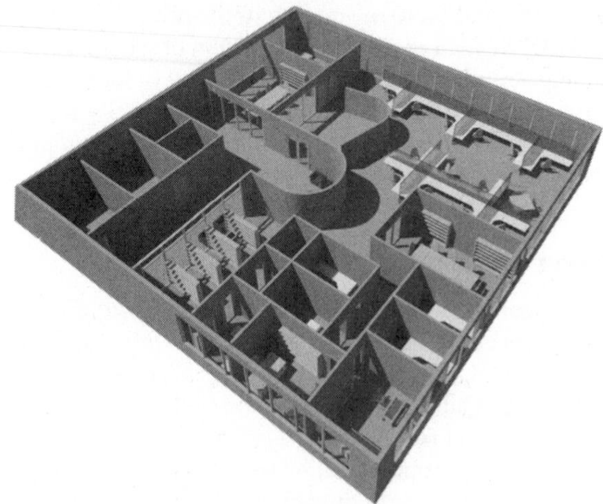

FIGURE 11.66
Camera view rendered with default materials

The challenge is that to get the materials correct, you'll have to commit a significant amount of time to selecting, testing, editing, and refining many material selections for an otherwise simple view that's quite early in the design stage. You don't have time for resolving your design to this level of specificity early in the iterative process.

Figure 11.67 shows the same view rendered abstractly, with all the model objects set to a matte white material.

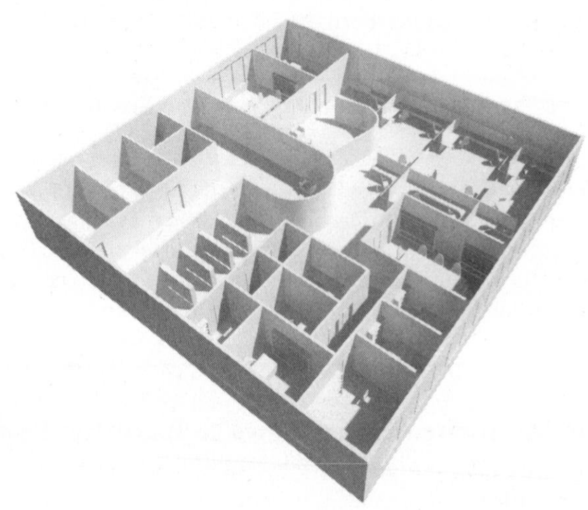

FIGURE 11.67
Abstract rendering

By selecting a matte material for everything in the view, you're able to focus on form-space and light-shadow relationships. Using phase filters, you can create a rendering like this quickly and easily. This technique is much faster than trying to select neutral materials for each element type in your view. To begin the series of exercises in this chapter, download and open the file `c11-Visualization-Start.rvt` from this book's web page. Here are the steps to create a matte rendering using the material overrides in Phasing:

1. From the Project Browser, activate the 3D view named OVERHEAD CAMERA. Press **VG** on the keyboard to activate the Visibility/Graphic Overrides dialog box. In the Model Categories tab, uncheck the Ceilings category and then click OK.

2. In the Properties palette, you should see the properties for this 3D view. Click the Edit button for Graphic Display Options to bring up the dialog box shown in Figure 11.68. Set Style to Shaded, and under Shadows check Show Ambient Shadows. Click OK to close the dialog box.

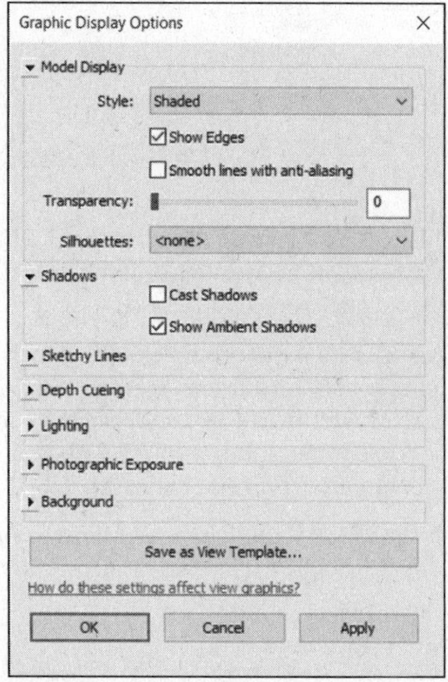

FIGURE 11.68 Graphic Display Options settings

3. On the Manage tab in the ribbon, click the Phases button to open the Phasing dialog box. Select the Phase Filters tab. Click the New button to create a new row in the list of filters. Rename the new filter to **Abstract**. Change the New and Existing column values to Overridden, and then change the Demolished and Temporary column values to Not Displayed.

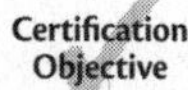

4. Switch to the Graphic Overrides tab, and then create a new material. You'll do this by clicking inside any of the Material boxes and then clicking the Selector button on the right. (For this exercise use the Material box for Existing.) This will open the Material Browser. In this new dialog box, select the Create New Material icon at the lower-left corner. Switch to the Identity tab, change the Name to **Abstract**, and then click Apply (Figure 11.69).

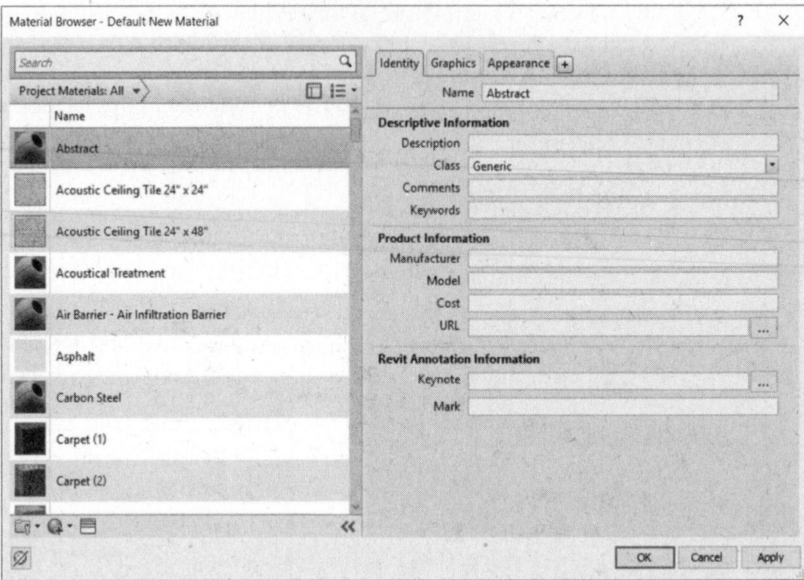

FIGURE 11.69
Create a new default material.

5. This will give you a generic material with some predefined settings. We're going to customize this slightly to make it the universal material we want. Switch to the Appearance tab and click the Open/Closes Asset Browser icon.

   This will open the Asset Browser, which will allow you to select the attributes of a material to match to your new material type. In the Asset Browser, type **Porcelain** in the search bar at the top. In the Asset Browser folder tree, click on Ceramic/Porcelain under the Appearance Library folder and double-click on Neutral Gray to replace the asset in the material definition (Figure 11.70).

   This material will give the rendering a nice overall gray finish without too much reflectivity. Click OK to close the Material Browser.

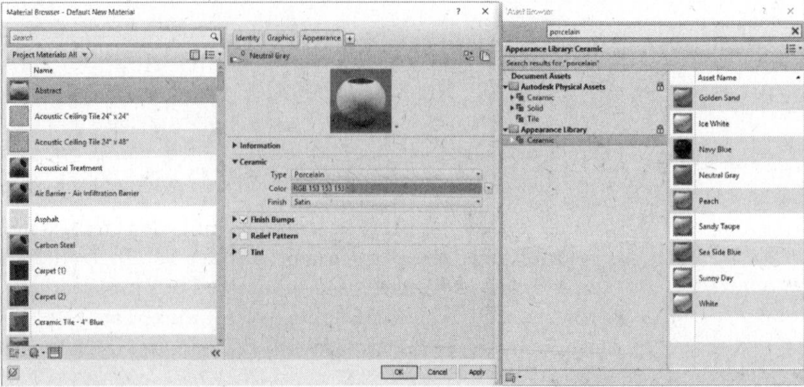

FIGURE 11.70
Assign material appearance from the Asset Browser.

6. Now assign this material to your Existing and New phase objects by selecting this same material for those phases (Figure 11.71). Click OK to exit the Phasing dialog box.

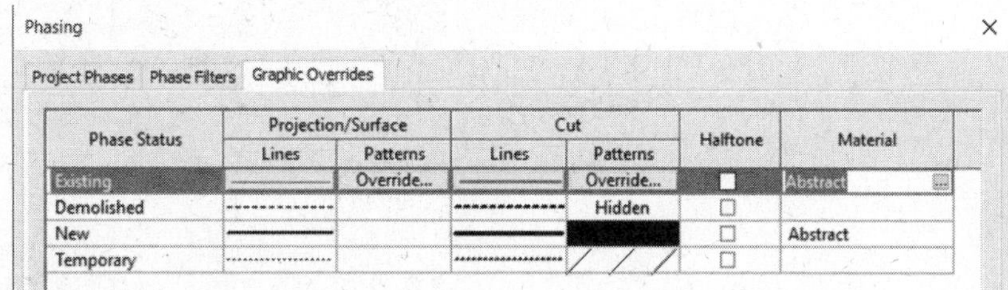

FIGURE 11.71 Assigning the Abstract material

7. This step is important. Because the material you created is associated as an override for the Abstract phase that was created in step 4, for the new material to take effect when you render, change the view properties' Phase Filter setting to Abstract.
8. From the View tab in the ribbon, click the Render tool. In the Rendering dialog box, use the following settings:
   - Quality: Medium
   - Output Settings: Screen
   - Lighting: Exterior: Sun Only
   - Background Style: Color, with color set to White
9. Click the Render button and observe the results in the view window. To toggle back and forth between the rendered view and the shaded display, click Show The Model at the bottom of the Rendering dialog box.

That's it! When you want to render a project view with this abstract material assignment, simply assign the Abstract material to the graphic overrides in the Phasing dialog box and apply the Abstract phase filter to the properties of the camera view.

PHASING AFFECTS THE ENTIRE PROJECT

In the previous exercise, you created a unique phase material override to generate a specific style of visualization. Be aware that phasing settings will affect the entire project; therefore, if you are working on a project with others, your team should be made aware of these changes so other documentation isn't adversely affected.

Adjusting Lighting and Interior Renderings

Let's take a closer look at an interior camera view and how to adjust natural and artificial lighting. You will continue with the `c11-Visualization-Start.rvt` file from the book's web page. From the Project Browser, activate the 3D view named RENDER - CONFERENCE ROOM. As you can see in Figure 11.72, we've already adjusted the shadows and sunlight as well as applied silhouette edge overrides to the live view.

Figure 11.72
Viewing an interior camera view in Hidden Line mode

Now let's render the view. Keep in mind that the rendered material applied to the Abstract phase override is solid white (which we set up earlier in this chapter), so you'll want to turn off the visibility of your curtain panels if you want to see through the glazing. Open the Rendering dialog box by clicking the teapot icon in the view control bar and choose the following settings:

- Quality: Medium
- Output Settings: Printer, set to 300 dpi
- Lighting: Exterior: Sun Only
- Background Style: Color, with color set to White

The reason we're using Printer as the Output Setting is that 300 dpi is sufficient for printing this page. And an 8″ (200 mm) wide image will suffice for the anticipated width of this book.

Figure 11.73 shows the results of the rendering. The scene can be viewed beyond the immediate space of the conference room. Take particular note of the shadows and how the lighting drops off from the edge of a shadow. If the rendering appears too dark or too bright, click the Adjust Exposure button to change the Exposure Value setting.

Figure 11.73
Sun Only rendering

Of course, this image is being rendered with the sun, which doesn't count for interior renderings; it's just a benchmark. But you can begin to see the level of detail and materiality and the "look and feel" of the space. Now that you know what it looks like, you can turn off the sun and start placing some artificial lights.

Because you're rendering abstractly using a phase override, everything is going to be solid white. But if your light source is behind a solid lens, it's not going to render very well. The best way we've found to handle this is to create a unique object subcategory for the lens that surrounds the light source. Doing so allows you to control the visibility of the lens of the lighting fixture, thus preventing obstruction of the light source. Unfortunately, this approach will not give the most realistic effect because many lighting effects result from light passing through translucent objects (like lenses or shades). But it's the best you'll be able to do for now to resolve lighting *before* you resolve materials.

Before you can add lighting, you need to add a ceiling to the spaces. To keep things generic, we've added the default compound ceiling to all the spaces. It's just a placeholder for your ceiling that will change later. But the important thing is that you don't get hung up centering ceiling tiles during your design process. Rooms will change dimensions, and all that time spent centering will go to waste.

Placing Artificial Lighting

Activate the Level 1 ceiling plan and locate the room we have identified with a revision cloud. This is the room in which you will begin placing light fixtures to continue the exercise.

1. On the Architecture tab in the ribbon, click the Component tool, and from the Type Selector, choose the Downlight - Recessed Can family that has been preloaded from the default Revit library. You can use the 6" Incandescent - 120V type.
2. Place fixtures in the ceiling plan along the lower and right walls as shown in Figure 11.74. The exact dimensions aren't important—just get the idea right.

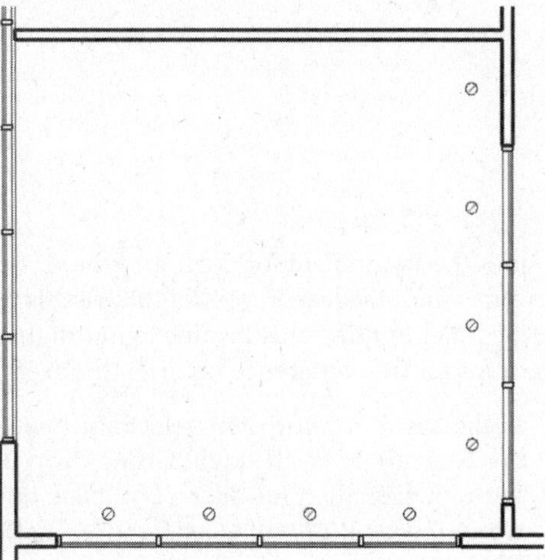

FIGURE 11.74 Placing light fixtures in the ceiling

This light family doesn't have a lens, so you don't have to worry about the light source being obscured. Before you start to render these artificial lights, we need to explain the process and technique of using light groups.

Manipulating Light Groups

There are times when you'll want to isolate the lights that are being calculated and rendered in a particular view. You might want to test the lighting that will result from having certain lights on and others off, just as in a real space. Revit software allows you to create light groups for this purpose. Doing so saves you a lot of time compared to turning individual lights off and on manually.

By default, whenever you place lights in your project, they're not placed in any group. They're "unassigned," just like the lights shown in Figure 11.75. You access this dialog box by clicking the Show Rendering Dialog tool on the view control bar and then clicking the Artificial Lights button in the Rendering dialog box. Here you can assign and create all kinds of light groups.

FIGURE 11.75
Light groups

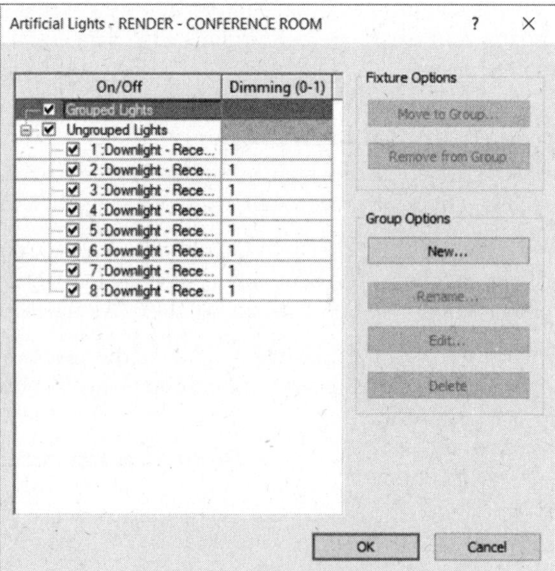

Besides the assignment for the light group, you also have the option of adjusting the Dimming value. One reason you might use this feature would be to dim some of the lighting and leave other lighting at full value to highlight a feature in the rendering. Let's create two light groups for the conference room in this exercise. Follow these steps:

1. In the Level 1 ceiling plan, select any one of the lights you placed during the previous exercise. From the Light Group drop-down in the Options bar, choose Edit/New. In the Artificial Lights dialog box, click the New button to create two groups named **Conference - Right** and **Conference - Left** (Figure 11.76).
2. Now assign the lights to the groups. Just select the lights in either the ceiling plan or any 3D orthographic view, and then assign them to the light group from the Light Group drop-down menu in the Options bar, as shown in Figure 11.77. Place the lights in each group as indicated in the Level 1 ceiling plan.

FIGURE 11.76
Creating light groups

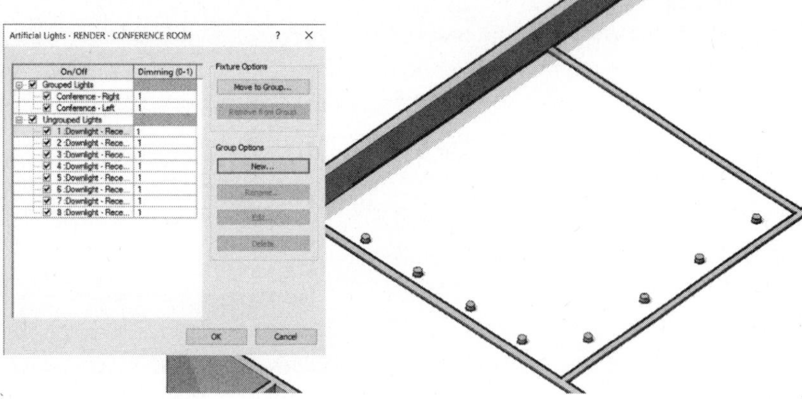

FIGURE 11.77
Assigning light groups

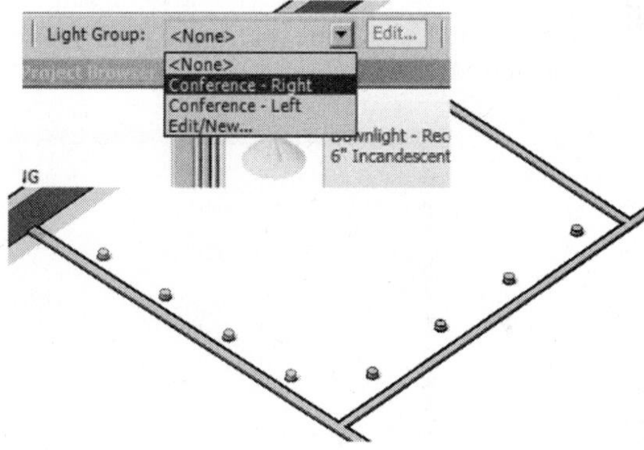

3. Return to the camera view named RENDER - CONFERENCE ROOM. Before you start to render the view, let's test the light groups by rendering only the lights in the Conference - Right group. To do this, from the Properties palette, open the Rendering Settings dialog box, and then click the Artificial Lights button. Turn off the lights in the left group by simply clicking the check box for that group in the Artificial Lights dialog box. Figure 11.78 shows the results after you render with the following settings:

   - Quality: Draft
   - Output Settings: Printer, set to 96 dpi
   - Lighting: Exterior: Artificial only
   - Background Style: Color, with color set to White

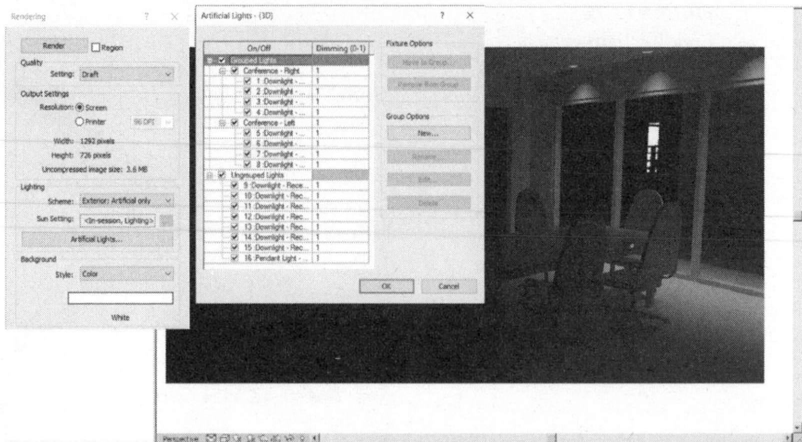

FIGURE 11.78 Rendering with light groups

4. Let's complete the rendering of the space with the other light group turned on. Keep in mind that the more lights you have turned on in your view, the longer the calculations will take and, therefore, the longer it will take to render your view. Figure 11.79 shows the results of this second rendering.

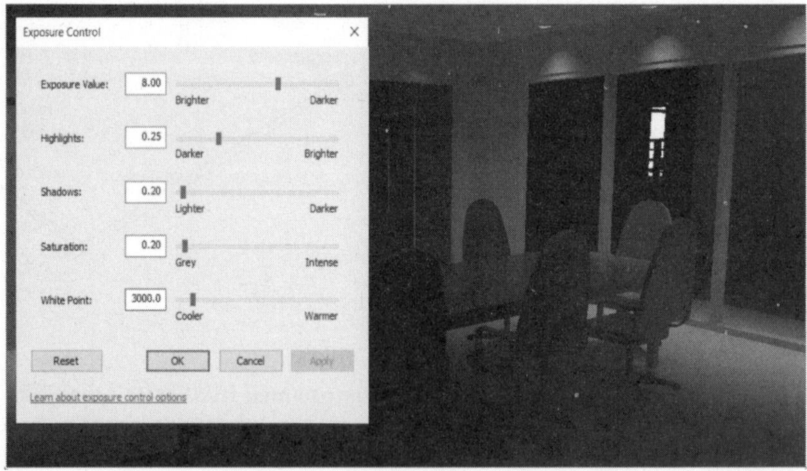

FIGURE 11.79 Rendering both light groups

5. By default, the image will have a sepia tone. You can remove the sepia tone by adjusting the White Point value in the Exposure Control dialog box. In the Rendering Settings or Rendering dialog box, click the Adjust Exposure button.

   Keep in mind that what you're looking for is how the lighting affects the space. Are the lights too close or too far apart? We've added lights to brighten the room by adding the same lighting to the remaining two sides of the ceiling.

6. After you render the space with all the lights, what becomes apparent is that the lights aren't illuminating the conference table (Figure 11.80). You need to add a nice linear

lighting source above the table in order to understand the effect that light will have on the space. Again, it's important that you do this without the distraction of materials.

FIGURE 11.80
Rendering without center lights

7. Return to the Level 1 ceiling plan. We'd like to see the conference table as a reference for placing a new light fixture in the context of a floor plan. In the Properties palette, set the Underlay value to Level 1, and then set the Underlay Orientation to Plan.
8. Start the Component tool again and from the Type Selector, choose the family named Pendant Light - Linear - 1 Lamp and use the type named 96" - 120V. Place one fixture over the conference table, as shown in Figure 11.81. You may need to rotate the fixture for proper alignment.

   The pendant light fixture family has a lens, but it is not assigned to a subcategory that can be turned off when necessary. In the next series of exercise steps, you'll assign the lens to a new subcategory in order to test a rendering with the lens turned off. First, open the Visibility/Graphic Overrides dialog box, and expand the Lighting Fixtures category. You will notice that the only subcategories are Hidden Lines and Light Source. This will change in a moment when you add Lens to the list.

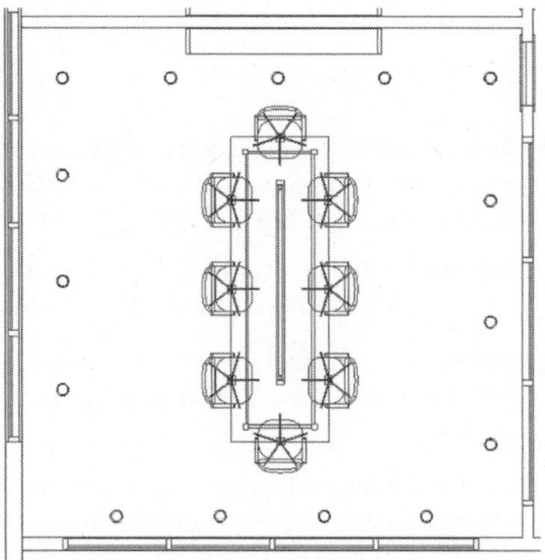

FIGURE 11.81
Placing the light fixture over furniture

9. Select the linear light you placed over the conference table and click Edit Family in the contextual tab of the ribbon to open the family in the Family Editor. Activate the 3D view named View 1.

10. In the 3D view, orbit the model so that you can see the bottom of the light fixture. Select the main cylindrical extrusion and from the view control bar, click the sunglasses icon and choose Hide Element. You will then see a rectangular extrusion that runs the length of the fixture. Select that extrusion and in the Properties palette you'll see that the Subcategory value is None, but the material is set to Glass - White, High Luminance. Actually, it is assigned to a type parameter named Diffuser Material; however, this doesn't help because we are overriding the material of all model objects using the abstract phasing filter we discussed previously in this chapter.

11. From the Manage tab in the ribbon, click Object Styles. In the Object Styles dialog box, click the New button and create a new subcategory named **Lens**. Make sure that it is a subcategory of Lighting Fixtures. Click OK twice to close both dialog boxes.

12. Select the rectangular extrusion again, and from the Properties palette set the Subcategory value to Lens, as shown in Figure 11.82.

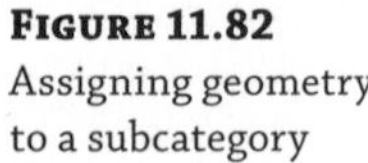

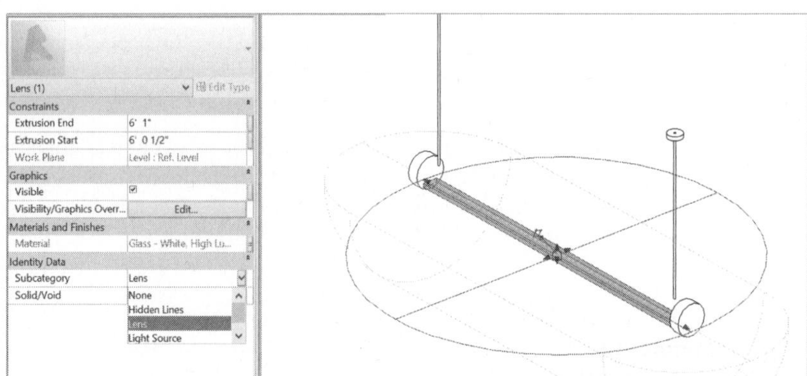

FIGURE 11.82
Assigning geometry to a subcategory

13. From the ribbon, click Load Into Project to reload the light family into your project. At this point, if you were to render the view, you'd notice that light is still obscured by the lens, as shown in Figure 11.83.

    Eventually, the lens will use its assigned translucent material that will allow the light to shine through, but for rendering matte images, you don't want the light blocked.

14. Open the Visibility/Graphic Overrides dialog box for the RENDER - CONFERENCE ROOM camera view. Expand the Lighting Fixtures category and uncheck the Lens subcategory.

15. When you render the view again, the results will look like Figure 11.84. The lens for the linear light isn't showing, but this is fine. You're after the lighting effect of the lighting fixture. The lens will come back on when you render with all the materials showing.

FIGURE 11.83
Rendering with an obscured lens

FIGURE 11.84
Rendered view with light lens turned off

If you want your rendering to seem more complete than just a rendering of the building elements, you'll have to add entourage. But you don't want to clutter all your views with the kinds of things that you want to add that will not be part of your document set.

> **WORKING WITH ENTOURAGE**
>
> Worksets are great for controlling this part of your project. By creating a workset called Entourage, you'll be able to place your project content on a workset where all of its visibility can be quickly and easily controlled. But before creating and assigning elements to a workset, make sure the workset is turned off by default in other views.
>
> This means that entourage will not show up in existing or new views until you turn it on; otherwise, you'll have to turn this workset off in all present and future views. This will save you a lot of time as you add entourage to your project.

Assigning Materials

Now that you have determined the right lighting effects using matte materials, you can set the phase filter of the interior camera view back to Show Complete. You'll also want to turn on the visibility for the curtain panels as well as the Lens subcategory of Lighting Fixtures. Keep in mind that with all the new materials, transparency, and reflectivity, it will take quite a bit longer to re-render the view (Figure 11.85).

FIGURE 11.85 Rendering with materials

Once you render the view and you can start to see the transparency and reflectivity in the curtain panels, the rendering takes on a much more realistic effect. You can also see the materials in the table and chairs as well as the lens for the linear light above the conference table.

At the moment, all of the materials that are assigned to the walls in this view are based on the properties of the wall. And creating surface materials for every different wall would result in a very long list of wall types! A better method of assigning materials on a case-by-case basis is to use the Paint tool. Just be aware that your modeled walls might continue beyond the confines of the space in which you are designing, and painting a material on a surface may affect other spaces.

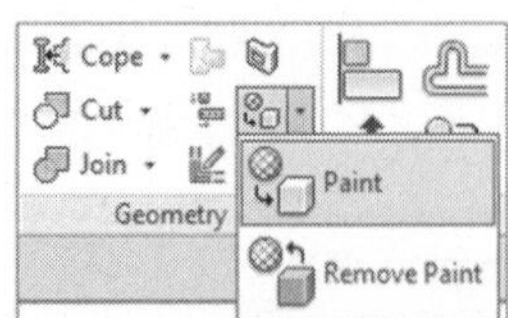

To assign materials to host elements, select the Paint tool on the Modify tab in the ribbon. Select a material from the Material Browser, and then click on a surface in the model. If you need to remove a painted-on material, use the Remove Paint tool from the same flyout button you used for the Paint tool.

Rendering in the Cloud

In addition to rendering on your own computer, Autodesk offers the ability to render "in the cloud." This term simply means that you will be sending data from your computer to remote computers operated by Autodesk for increased processing power and more flexibility. As we mentioned previously in this chapter, the rendering process can be time-consuming—especially when you can't do any other work while renderings are being produced. The cloud option becomes quite compelling when you consider the benefit of gained productivity.

As of this writing, you can create a user account for free at `360.autodesk.com`. With a free account, you will receive some amount of complimentary cloud credits; however, some cloud-rendering processes are free. For example, you can process a still rendering at standard resolution without using any credits. This allows you to send many draft renderings until you are happy with the results and then use your credits to produce the final rendering.

After you create a user account, you will need to connect to the Autodesk® 360 service in the Info Center at the top of the application window, as shown in Figure 11.86.

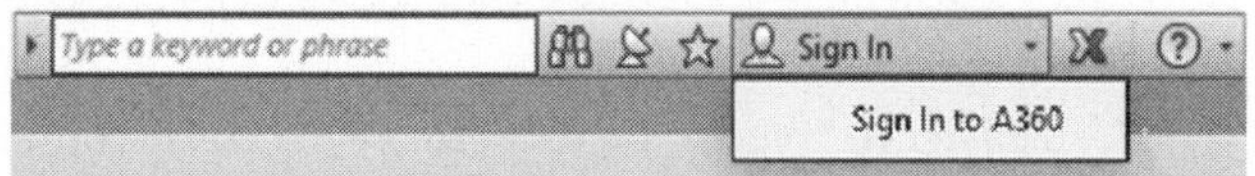

FIGURE 11.86
Sign in to the Autodesk 360 service.

Once you are connected, you can use the Render In Cloud command from the View tab in the ribbon. In the Render In Cloud dialog box, you can select multiple 3D views for rendering, the output type (still image, interactive panorama, or illuminance), image size, exposure (advanced or native), and file format. At the bottom of the dialog box, you can also choose to be notified via e-mail when the cloud rendering is complete. Once you click the Start Rendering button, a small amount of data will be uploaded, and then you can get back to work while the cloud works on your renderings!

After you have been notified that your renderings have completed, you can access and share the renderings from your Autodesk 360 web space (Figure 11.87). Each image has contextual commands that include the ability to download the file and adjust the exposure levels.

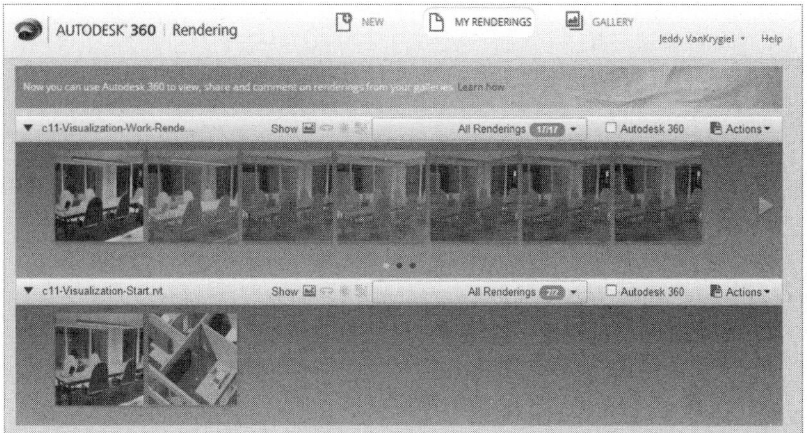

FIGURE 11.87
Viewing renderings on the cloud rendering website

The Bottom Line

Create real-time and rendered analytic visualizations. Analytic visualization is the concept of communicating information about your project in a nonliteral way, and it's very important! It's not about showing real materials in the project but about using filters to visualize important metadata.

Master It During the renovation of a space, you want to reuse the doors rather than throw them away. How would you illustrate this?

Render emotive photorealistic visualizations. Photorealistic visualization is about communicating design ideas but in emotive ways that are much closer to how the space will be experienced, including real lighting, materials, and entourage. Just remember that the time it takes to calculate and render your views will change dramatically based on the quality and resolution of your views.

Master It Would the rendering for a PowerPoint presentation differ from a rendering being printed for a marketing brochure?

Understand the importance of sequencing your visualization workflow. The sequence of design—building, content, materials, and cameras—is not the same as the sequence for visualization (geometry/cameras, lighting, materials). Lighting is far more important than materials of actual objects. Get the lighting right and the materials will look great, but not the other way around.

Master It How do you create a rendering environment that replaces the actual materials with matte materials in order to study the effects of lighting on your design?

Part 4

Extended Modeling Techniques

In Part 3 we covered a variety of topics that are primarily useful in—although not exclusive to—the earlier design phases of a project. As you continue to develop your designs, there will be an increased specificity to the elements required in the building information model. You will need to expand your knowledge of the fundamental components of a building model, including walls, floors, roofs, stairs, and railings. In addition, you will likely be required to understand and create your own families. This part will dig deep into the rich, component-building skills necessary for mastering Autodesk® Revit® Architecture software.

Chapter 12

Creating Walls and Curtain Walls

According to the American Institute of Architects (AIA) document *G202-2013 Project BIM Protocol Form*, there are five levels of model development, ranging from 100 to 500. If you examine excerpts from the model content requirements describing each level of development (LOD) for the design professions—LOD 100, LOD 200, and LOD 300—the evolution of modeling granularity becomes apparent. Although LOD 100 represents a conceptual level of information defined as "overall building massing," LOD 200 and LOD 300 are represented by "generalized systems or assemblies" and "specific assemblies," respectively. This chapter will help you create walls that comply with both LOD 200 and LOD 300.

Four different kinds of walls can be created: basic walls, stacked walls, curtain walls, and in-place walls. In this chapter, you'll explore the skills needed to create and customize walls to meet your design requirements. You will also dive into the new and exciting realm of complex curtain wall and panel generation made possible with the conceptual massing tools in Autodesk® Revit® Architecture software.

In this chapter, you'll learn to:

- Use extended modeling techniques for basic walls
- Create stacked walls
- Create simple curtain walls
- Create complex curtain walls

Using Extended Modeling Techniques for Basic Walls

As you might already know, walls in the Revit environment are made from layers of materials that act as generic placeholders for design layouts to complete assemblies representative of actual construction. These layers are assigned functions that allow them to react to similar layers in other walls as well as in floors and roofs. The function assignments within object assemblies give you a predictable graphic representation when you join these types of overlapping elements.

After you become familiar with the basic modeling functions for walls, you'll probably need to create your own wall types to achieve more complex designs. As you add more information into the source of your building model, you will be able to extract more useful results through intelligent tagging and schedules. In the following sections, we'll show you how to get the most out of your basic wall types.

Creating Basic Wall Types

Walls and curtain walls are *system families*, which means they exist in a project or template but cannot be saved as individual families outside of the project file (as RFA files). Other system families include floors, ceilings, roofs, stairs, railings, and mullions. There are only three ways to create or add new system families to your project:

- Duplicate a type from one that already exists and modify its properties.
- Copy and paste them in as objects from one project to another or group them from one project to another.
- Use the Transfer Project Standards tool.

In Chapter 4, "Configuring Templates and Standards," we discussed different strategies for managing standard content through the use of templates. If you have a series of standard wall types you use on every project, you have the option of either storing them in your main project template using the *subtractive method* or storing them in separate container project folders in an *additive method*. If you need to make new, custom types that are not part of your template, you can create new wall types on the fly at any stage of a project by duplicating existing types, adding or removing wall layers, and adjusting the parameters to meet your requirements. Regardless of which method you employ to manage templates and standard system families, we will show you how to create and customize your own wall types in the following sections.

Within a project file, you can access and edit a wall type in one of two ways:

- In the Project Browser, scroll down to the Families category, locate any wall type, right-click it, and select Type Properties, or simply double-click the wall type name.
- Select a wall in the model or start the Wall command, open the Properties palette, and click Edit Type.

The Type Properties dialog box will appear (Figure 12.1). If you don't see the graphic preview to the left, click the Preview button at the bottom of the dialog box.

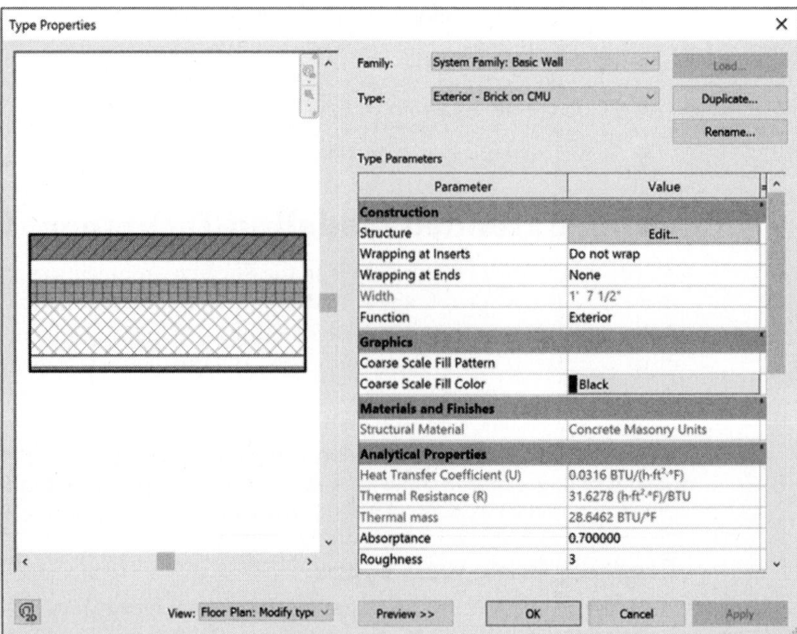

FIGURE 12.1 The Type Properties dialog box for a wall

Using Function and Graphics Type Properties

You can assign basic parameters to the type properties of a wall such as Type Mark, Assembly Code, Type Comments, Fire Rating, Cost, and so on. In addition to these parameters, there are two other type properties that are important to understand: Function and Coarse Scale Fill Pattern. The Function type property of walls is a simple list of values, but it can be used in very powerful ways. A wall's function can be used to filter schedules or views—for example, if you wanted to hide interior walls for a series of drawings showing only core and shell (exterior) elements. The Function property also affects the default placement behavior when you create new walls. The behaviors associated with each function are as follows:

- Interior—Default height for new walls is set to the level above the active level.
- Exterior—Default height is Unconnected: 20′-0″ (8 m).
- Foundation—Default height is determined as Depth, specified down from the active level.
- Retaining—Default height is Unconnected: 6′-0″ (2 m).
- Soffit—Default height is Unconnected: 1′-0″ (250 mm).
- Core-shaft—Default height is Unconnected: 20′-0″ (8 m).

You can also use the Function type property when you export to CAD formats. You can export walls of different functions to specific layers assigned in the Modify DWG/DXF Export Setup dialog box, shown in Figure 12.2. Refer to Chapter 7, "Interoperability: Working Multiplatform," for more information on exporting.

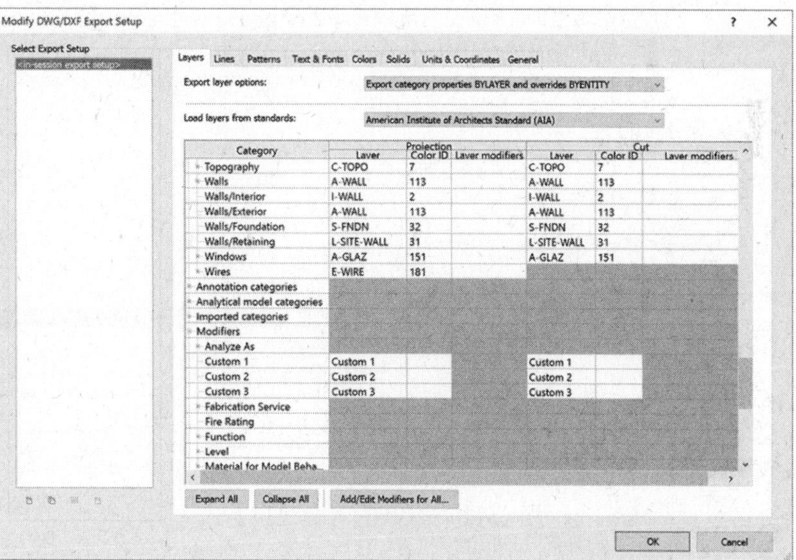

Figure 12.2 Wall functions can be assigned to different layers for exported CAD files.

The Coarse Scale Fill Pattern type property (along with Coarse Scale Fill Color) defines a fill pattern to be applied to the wall type when a view's Detail Level is set to Coarse. These settings are an important tool to help you communicate your designs more effectively. For example, you might want to set all the fire-rated wall types to display with a red solid fill for coarse views. Using these type properties for walls is a slightly different approach than you might use for design plans in which you want all wall types to display with a black solid fill. For the design plan approach, you can override the fill pattern for the Walls category in the Visibility/Graphic Overrides dialog box for a view or a view template.

When the Detail Level property of a view is set to Medium or Fine, the individual layers of a wall type's structure are visible—including any fill patterns that are assigned to the materials in the wall structure (you'll learn more about wall structure in the next section of this chapter). When Detail Level is set to Coarse, the wall type is displayed only with the pattern defined in the Coarse Scale Fill Pattern parameter—if one is defined. This property is best explored with the generic masonry wall types in the default project templates.

Create a new project with any Autodesk default project template, and then place a wall segment using the type Generic - 8″ Masonry (Generic - 225 mm Masonry) in a plan view that is set to Coarse. You will see that a fill pattern is displayed. What you are seeing is the fill pattern that is assigned to the Coarse Scale Fill Pattern type property of the wall—not the pattern that is assigned to the material within the wall structure. Select the generic wall segment you just created, and in the Properties palette click Edit Type. Change the Coarse Scale Fill Pattern to No Pattern, and then click OK to close all open dialog boxes. No fill pattern will appear for this wall type in a coarse view. From the view control bar, set the Detail Level to Medium, and you will then see the fill pattern as it is defined in the material within the wall structure.

EDITING WALL STRUCTURES

We will first discuss editing a wall type's structure. To access these settings, click the Edit button in the Structure parameter field. This will open the Edit Assembly dialog box, shown in Figure 12.3. From here you can add or delete wall layers, define their materials, move layers in and out of the core boundaries, and assign functions to each layer. You can also add sweeps and reveals or modify the vertical constraints of the layers.

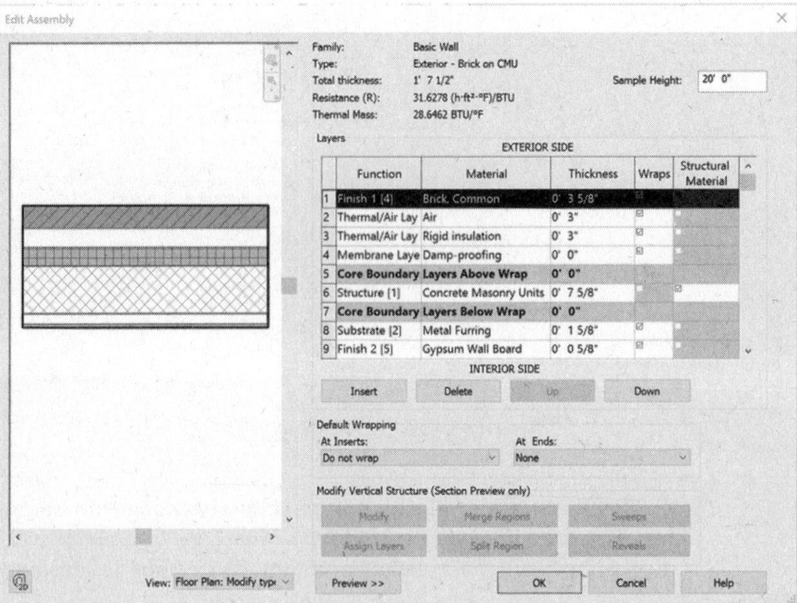

FIGURE 12.3
The Edit Assembly dialog box lets you define the construction layers of a wall type.

This dialog box is divided into four zones: the Preview window, the Layers table, the Default Wrapping option, and the Modify Vertical Structure options (which are active only when the preview is set to section display). The area above the Layers zone holds basic reporting about the wall type: its family name, sample height in the Preview window, and thickness and thermal properties.

Preview Window On the left side of the dialog box, you will see a graphic preview of the wall structure in plan or section. If you didn't activate it in the Type Properties dialog box, click the Preview button at the bottom of the dialog box. To switch from the default plan view to the section view or vice versa, click the drop-down list next to View to choose an alternate viewing option. In the preview, the core boundaries of the wall are shown with green lines. Note that in the section preview, each wall layer is highlighted in blue when you select a row in the Layers table. Also note that you can change the height of the wall shown in the section preview by modifying the Sample Height value in the upper-right part of the dialog box. You can use any mouse-based navigation method to adjust the preview as well as activate the SteeringWheels® feature by clicking the button at the bottom left of the dialog box.

Layers Table The Layers Table is where you add, delete, move, and define layers of the wall structure. The makeup of the wall is organized in a table, and the Exterior and Interior orientation of the wall is identified at the top and bottom. Each wall layer is represented as a separate row of information. Two of the rows are gray, representing the core boundaries of the wall, which will be discussed in greater detail later in this chapter in the section "Creating a Wall Core." The table is divided into five columns (Function, Material, Thickness, Wraps, and Structural Material):

Function This column provides six choices for wall layer functions that relate to the purpose of the material in the assembly. Each of these functions defines a priority that determines how it joins with other walls, floors, and roofs. Note that the numeric priority is more important to understand than the name of the function itself.

- Structure [1] defines the structural components of the wall that should support the rest of the wall layers. This function gives the highest priority to a wall layer and allows it to join with other structural layers by cutting through lower-priority layers.
- Substrate [2] defines continuous board materials such as plywood or particle board.
- Thermal/Air [3] defines the wall's thermal insulation layer and/or an air gap.
- The Membrane Layer is a zero-thickness material that usually represents vapor prevention.
- Finish 1 [4] specifies a finish layer to use if you have only one layer of finish.
- Finish 2 [5] specifies a secondary, weaker finish layer.

With the exception of the Membrane Layer, which has no priority assigned, all the other layers have a priority value from 1 to 5. These priorities determine how to clean up the intersections between various layers when two or more walls are joined. The principle is simply explained: Priority 1 is the highest and 5 is the lowest. A layer that has a priority of 1 will cut through any other layer with a lower priority (2, 3, 4, or 5). A layer with priority 2 will cut through layers with priority 3, 4, or 5, and so on. In Figure 12.4, layers with the same priority clean up when the two intersecting walls are joined. Notice the way the finish layers don't join on the right side of the vertical wall, because one has a priority 4 and the other is priority 5.

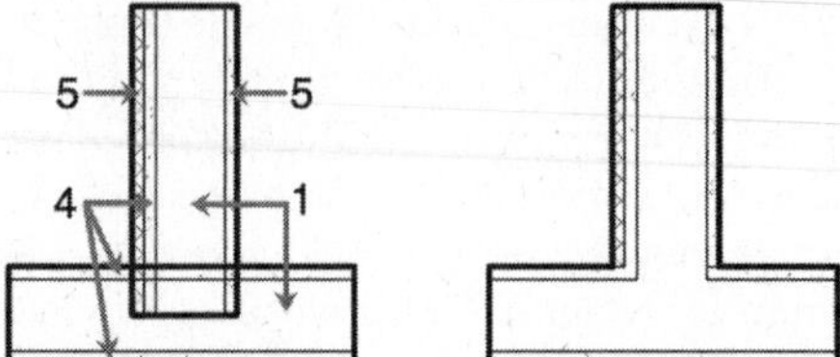

FIGURE 12.4
Layers with the same priority clean up when joined.

Material Associating a material to a wall layer provides graphic (color, cut/surface patterns, and render appearance), identifiable (mark, keynote, description, and so on), and physical characteristics (for analysis purposes) of each wall layer. Using material takeoffs, you can calculate quantities of individual materials used in wall assemblies throughout your project. Keynoting and material tagging functionality are also supported through wall layers and are discussed in greater detail in Chapter 18, "Annotating Your Design."

A material definition also affects clean up between layers of joined walls. If the priority of the layers is the same and the material is the same, the software cleans up the join between these two layers. If the priority of the layers is the same, but the materials are different, the two layers are separated graphically with a thin line. In Figure 12.5 the structure layer of one of the joined walls was simply changed from Metal - Stud Layer to Metal - Stud Layer 2.

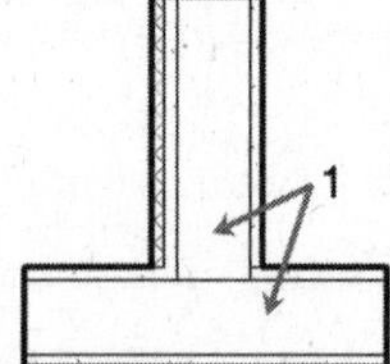

FIGURE 12.5
Two layers with the same priority but different materials. The separation between the two layers is indicated with a thin line.

Thickness This value represents the actual thickness of the material. Note that the membrane layer is the only layer that can have a thickness of zero.

Wraps Wall layers rarely end with exposed edges at wall ends or wall openings, windows, or doors. This option allows a layer to wrap around other layers when an opening or wall end is encountered. Figure 12.6 illustrates the layer wrapping of the outer wall layer based on the closure plane defined in the window family. Layer wrapping will be covered in greater detail later in this chapter.

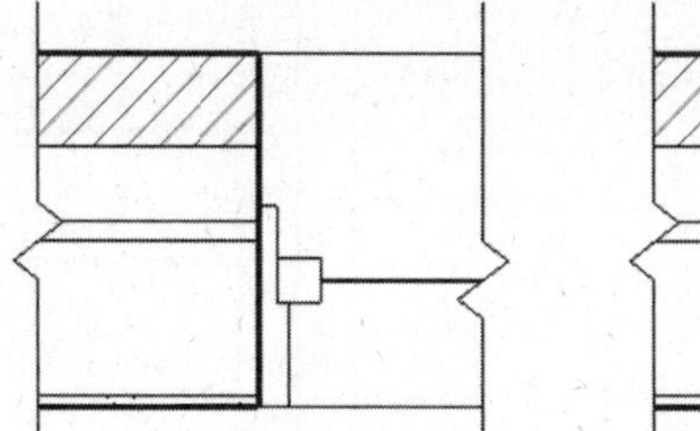
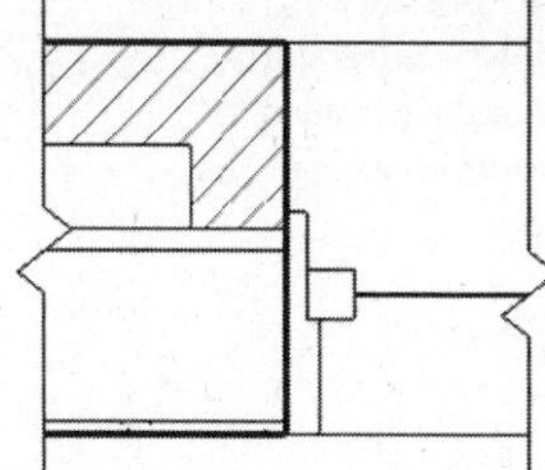

FIGURE 12.6
Layer wrapping is a result of a coordinated approach between wall layers and hosted families such as windows.

Structural Material This value represents whether the material within the wall assembly is load bearing or structurally significant in any way. In the example shown earlier in Figure 12.3, you can see that the Structure [1] functional material, Concrete Masonry Units, was given a check mark by default.

Default Wrapping Although you can specify whether each wall layer will wrap in the Layers table, you must also specify whether these options are activated at all in the wall type. To use this option, you must decide whether the wrapping should occur at openings, wall ends, or both. For inserts, you can choose Do Not Wrap, Exterior, Interior, or Both. Similarly, for wall ends the options are None, Exterior, and Interior. The default wrapping parameters appear in both the Edit Assembly dialog box and the wall's Type Properties dialog box. Refer to the "Creating Layer Wrapping" section in this chapter for more detailed information about wrapping.

Modify Vertical Structure These settings are available only when you enable the **section** view in the Preview window. In this area of the Edit Assembly dialog box, you can add articulation to the wall type using any combination of cornices, reveals, trims, and panels. We will discuss these in the section "Adding Wall Articulation" later in this chapter.

In summary, editing a wall type's structure begins with adding or deleting wall layers. Each layer is assigned a priority, material, thickness, and wrapping option. To move layers up and down in the table or to add and remove layers, use the buttons at the bottom of the Layers table. Next, we will cover some more complex aspects of wall structure in greater detail: *wall cores* and *layer wrapping*.

Creating a Wall Core

One of the unique functions of a basic wall is its ability to identify a core. The wall core is more than a layer of material; in fact, it can comprise several material layers. It defines the structural part of the wall and influences the behavior of the wall and how it interacts with other elements in the model. The core boundaries are references to which you can dimension or constrain sketch lines when you use the Pick Walls selection option for floors, ceilings, or roofs.

The example shown in Figure 12.7 illustrates a sample floor in Sketch mode where the outer core boundary of the wall was selected using the Pick Walls method. The core boundaries of the wall are shown as dashed lines for clarity.

FIGURE 12.7
A wall's outer core boundary is used to define an edge of the floor.

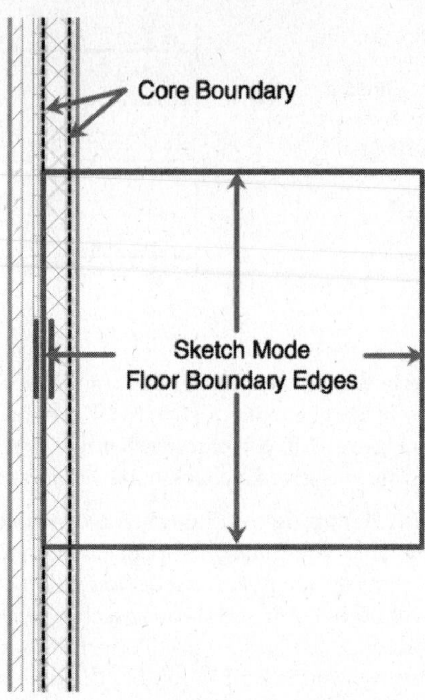

When floors generated with the Pick Walls method intersect the walls that were picked during Sketch mode, you will receive a prompt to automatically join the geometry and cut the overlapping volume out of the wall.

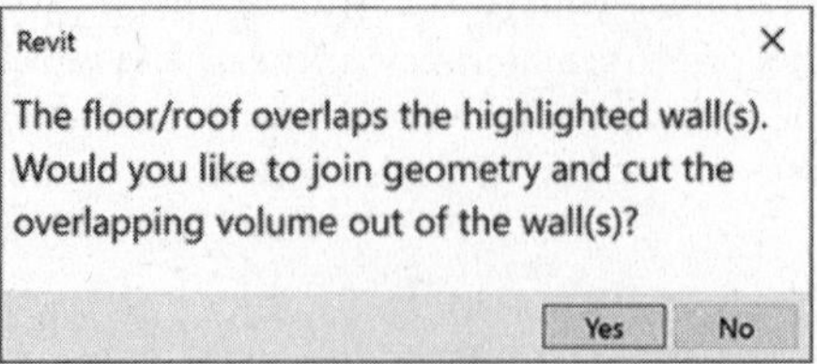

If you click Yes to this message and examine the intersection of the wall and floor in a section view, you will see the result of the joined elements (Figure 12.8). Note that you can get the joining prompt to appear again simply by selecting the floor, clicking the Edit Boundary button in the ribbon, and then clicking Finish Edit Mode (green check mark icon). If any portion of the selected floor and related walls still overlap, but are not joined, the prompt will be displayed.

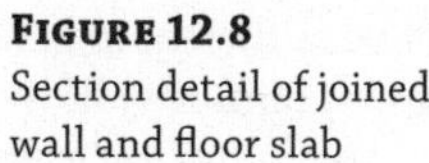

FIGURE 12.8
Section detail of joined wall and floor slab

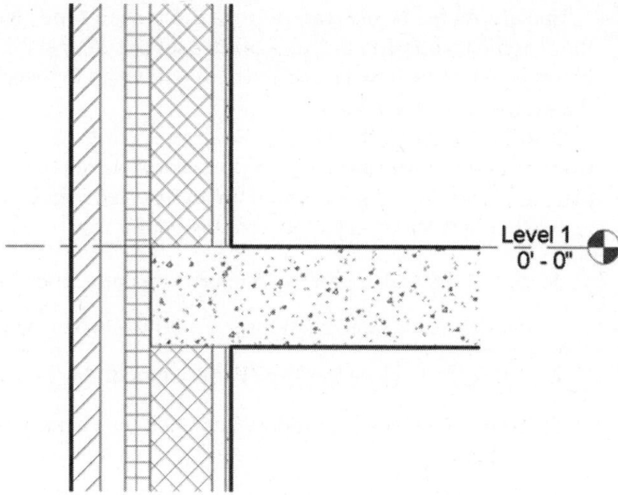

CREATING LAYER WRAPPING

To create a layer-wrapping solution for openings that reflect real-world conditions, you must define two settings. First, select the layer(s) of the wall structure you want to wrap and check the boxes in the Wraps column of the Edit Assembly dialog box. You must then specify the default wrapping behavior for the wall type. These default settings can be set in either the Type Properties dialog box or Edit Assembly, as shown in Figure 12.9.

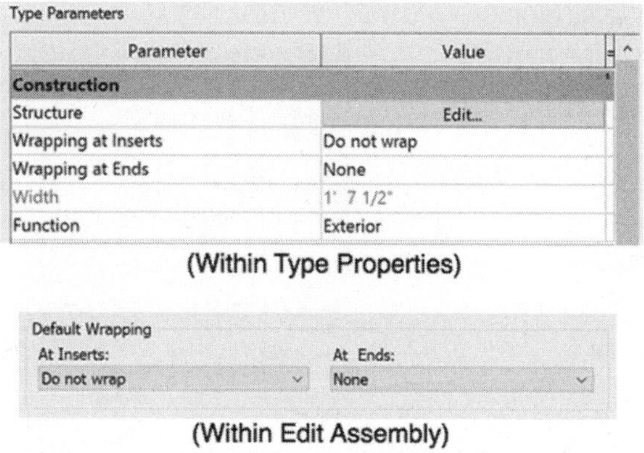

FIGURE 12.9
Default wrapping options can be set in Type Properties or Edit Assembly.

Type Parameters

Parameter	Value
Construction	
Structure	Edit...
Wrapping at Inserts	Do not wrap
Wrapping at Ends	None
Width	1' 7 1/2"
Function	Exterior

(Within Type Properties)

Default Wrapping

At Inserts:	At Ends:
Do not wrap	None

(Within Edit Assembly)

Specifying the layer wrap settings in the wall type alone may not be sufficient to generate the graphic results you desire. Another set of rules established in hosted families allows you to further customize how layers in a wall will wrap to inserted objects. The following exercise will illustrate this functionality.

Begin by opening the file `c12-Wall-Wrapping.rvt` or `c12-Wall-Wrapping-Metric.rvt` from this book's web page, `www.sybex.com/go/masteringrevit2017`. Activate the Level 1 floor plan, and you should see a wall with an inserted window.

Next, follow these steps to create the wall wrap:

1. Select the wall, open the Properties palette, and click Edit Type.

   Notice that Wrapping At Inserts is set to Do Not Wrap, and Wrapping At Ends is set to None.

2. Click OK to close the Type Parameters dialog box.
3. Select the inserted window and click Edit Family on the Modify | Windows tab in the ribbon.
4. When the Window family opens, go to the Project Browser and activate the floor plan named Floor Line.

   You will notice that this window family has been slightly modified from the original Fixed window family in the Revit default library. Two reference planes have been added that allow the depth of the window frame and the wall wrapping to be customized.

5. Select the reference plane that is parallel to the window and just below the window panel. Its name should be displayed at the right end of the plane as Closure. In the Properties palette find the parameter named Wall Closure and make sure the option is checked, as shown in Figure 12.10.

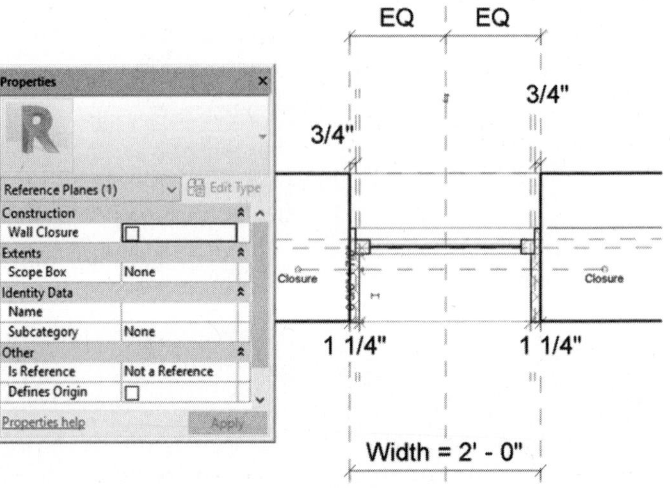

FIGURE 12.10 Assign the Wall Closure parameter to a reference plane.

6. Create a dimension between the exterior face of the sample wall and the Wall Closure reference plane.

   You may need to use the Tab key to ensure that you have selected the wall reference and not the centerline of the wall or any other extraneous reference plane.

7. Press the Esc key or click the Modify button to exit the dimension command, and select the dimension you just created.

8. On the Options bar, find the Label drop-down list and choose <Add Parameter…>.

9. In the Parameter Properties dialog box, type **Exterior Wall Closure** in the Name field and click OK to close the dialog box.

10. Click Load Into Project from the Family Editor panel in the ribbon. You may be prompted to select a project or family if you have more than the two sample files open. When prompted with the Family Already Exists dialog box, select Overwrite The Existing Version.

11. In the Level 1 floor plan of the example project, select the wall and click Edit Type from the Properties palette. From the Structure parameter, click Edit.

12. In the Edit Assembly dialog box, find row 1, which will have a function of Finish 1 [4], and the material Masonry - Brick. Make sure the Wraps option is checked.

13. Set the Wrapping At Inserts option to Exterior, and click OK to close both dialog boxes.

    You should now see the masonry layer wrapping into the opening in the wall created by the inserted window. You can now customize the depth at which the brick will wrap.

14. Select the window and click Edit Type from the Properties palette. Find the Exterior Wall Closure parameter and change the value to **0′-6 5/8″** (**170** mm).

15. Click OK to close the Type Properties dialog box. Notice how the depth of the wrapped masonry layer changes in the plan view.

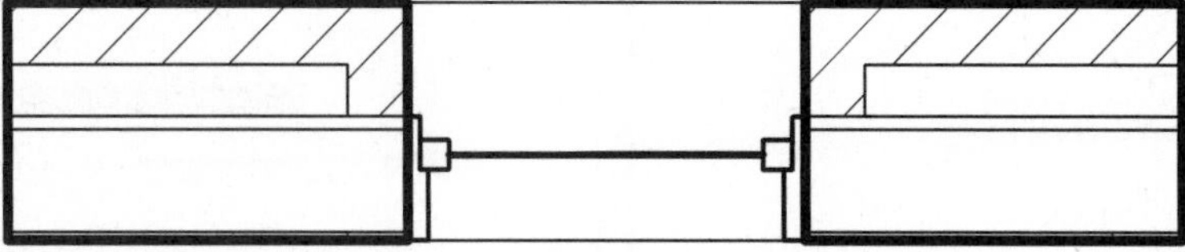

Adding Wall Articulation

If you need to develop more complex and articulated finishes expressed horizontally along the vertical surfaces of certain walls, you can customize wall types in a variety of ways to achieve just about any aesthetic effect. Reveals and sweeps can be added to a wall type, and you can edit the vertical extents of material layers. You can find a good example of this kind of wall in the default project template. The wall type Exterior - Brick and CMU on MTL. Stud (Figure 12.11) contains a variety of sweeps, reveals, and vertical modifications of material layers.

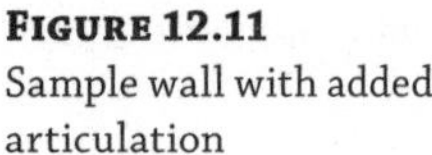

FIGURE 12.11
Sample wall with added articulation

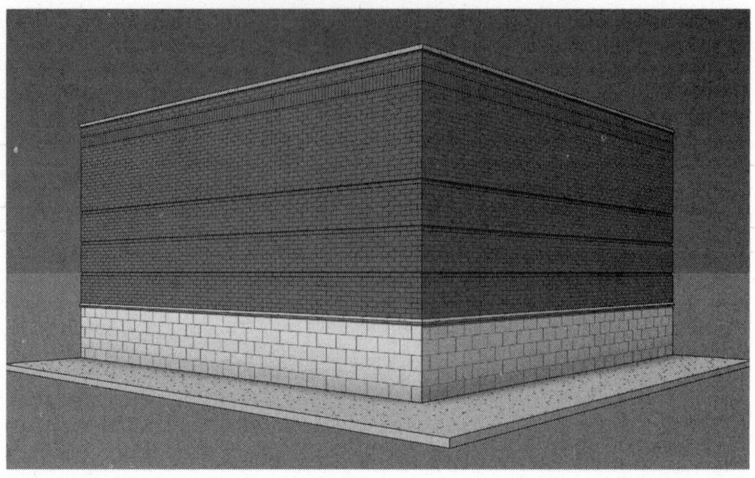

To access these settings, select any wall in your project and click Edit Type in the Properties palette. You can also find the wall type in the Project Browser; double-click it to open the Type Properties dialog box. Once it is open, make sure the preview pane is open and the view in the preview is set to Section. Within the Type Parameters options, click the Edit button in the Structure field to open the Edit Assembly dialog box, and begin modifying the layers and vertical articulation of the wall type, as shown in Figure 12.12.

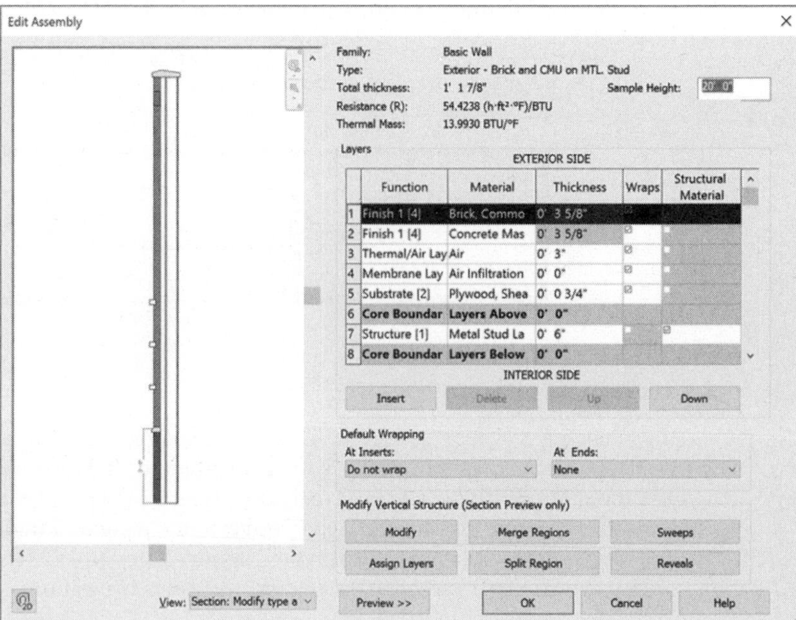

FIGURE 12.12
With the section view active, tools for modifying the vertical structure become active.

In the following sections, we'll examine how to create these types of articulation in your wall type. To begin the exercises, download and open the file `c12-Wall-Articulation.rvt` or `c12-Wall-Articulation-Metric.rvt` from this book's web page. There are two samples of the Exterior - Brick on Mtl. Stud wall type. You will create a new wall type based on this wall throughout the following exercises.

Assigning Two Different Materials on the Finish Face of a Wall

We will begin our series of exercises by creating a new wall type based on an existing layered wall structure. Activate the Level 1 floor plan, select the two wall segments in the exercise file, and then click Edit Type in the Properties palette. In the Type Properties dialog box, click the Duplicate button and create a new wall type named **Mastering - Wall Exercise**. Click OK to accept the settings, click OK to close the Type Properties.

Now let's assume that you need to create a partial region of the finish face where the material is different but is of the same thickness. For example, you might want to use a split-face concrete block at the base of the wall instead of brick:

1. Activate the default 3D view and select one segment of wall in the view. From the Properties palette, click Edit Type, and in the Type Properties dialog box, click the Edit button in the Structure field to open the Edit Assembly dialog box.

   Make sure the Preview pane is open and the view is set to Section.

2. In the upper right of the Edit Assembly dialog box, change the Sample Height value to **6′-0″** (**2000** mm).

   Use either the Steering Wheels button at the lower left of the dialog box (also located in the upper-right corner of the Preview pane) or your mouse wheel to zoom into the shorter segment of wall in the Preview pane.

3. Click the Split Region button under Modify Vertical Structure, and move your mouse pointer along the inside face of the brick layer to a point 4′-0″ (1,200 mm) above the bottom of the sample, as shown in Figure 12.13.

   When you split the layer, the thickness value of the layer indicates it is variable.

4. Select row 2 in the Layers list, and then click the Insert button to add another row immediately below the first exterior layer. Change its function to Finish 1 and its material to Concrete Masonry Units. To open the Material Browser, select the material assignment under the Material column. Using the Graphics tab, set the cut pattern to Masonry – Concrete Block. Then click OK to close the Material Browser dialog box.

5. Click the Assign Layers button, select the new row you created in the previous step, and then click inside the lower portion of the split region in the section preview.

   When the layer is properly assigned to the split region, you will see the fill pattern change to diagonal crosshatch.

6. Click OK to close all open dialog boxes and save your project for additional exercises in this chapter.

After you assign a material row to a split layer, you'll notice that the thickness values of the two layers are linked but you can't change them in the table. To change the thickness of a split wall layer, click the Modify button and select one of the faces in the section preview. Edit the temporary dimensions in the section preview to change the thickness of the layer.

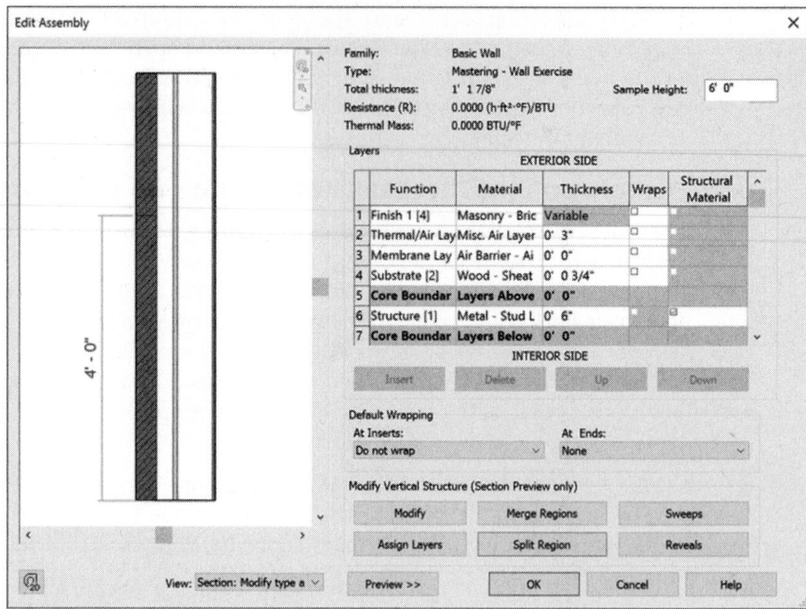

FIGURE 12.13
Splitting the exterior finish into two materials

You may also notice that once a layer is split and an additional layer is assigned to the split portion, the resulting portions can only be the same thickness. In the previous exercise, you split a brick masonry layer to create a region of concrete masonry units (CMU). Although this may achieve the desired graphic result in an elevation view, does it accurately represent the construction of the wall if the CMU is intended to be thicker than the brick masonry? To create a similar result with a vertical layer of varying thickness, you will need to create a stacked wall. We will discuss this later in the section "Creating Stacked Walls."

If you encounter a situation where you need to merge horizontal or vertical layers that already exist in a wall type, use the Merge Regions button and select a line in the section preview between two layers. Once the mouse pointer is over a line between two layers, an arrow indicating which layer will override the other appears, as shown in Figure 12.14.

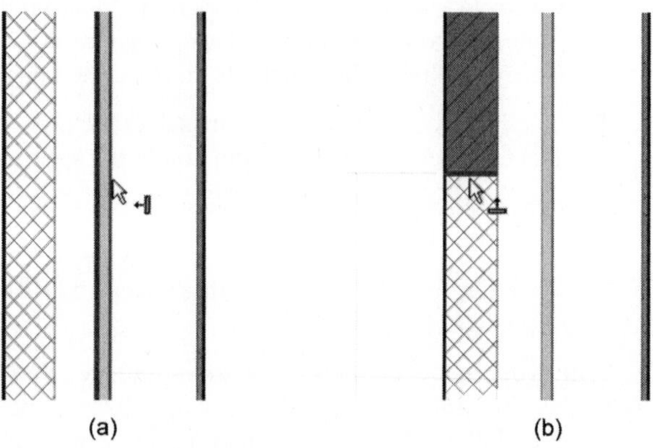

FIGURE 12.14
(a) Merge vertical layers; (b) merge layers that were previously split.

ADDING SWEEPS AND REVEALS

Many walls have horizontal articulations that are either attached to or embedded in the wall assembly. Cornices, soldier courses, and reveals are examples of elements that can be incorporated into wall types. To begin adding these, we will continue our previous exercise of creating a new wall type named Mastering - Wall Exercise. In the following exercise, you will add a bullnose sweep to the wall:

1. Return to the wall's type properties and open the Edit Assembly dialog box.
2. Click the Sweeps button to open the Wall Sweeps dialog box. Click the Load Profile button and open the file `c12-Profile-Bullnose.rfa` or `c12-Profile-Bullnose-Metric.rfa`, which can be downloaded from this book's companion web page.
3. Click the Add button to insert a sweep row. Change the values in the row as follows:
   - Profile: c12-Profile-Bullnose: Type 1
   - Material: Concrete, Precast
   - Distance: 4′-0″ (1,200 mm)
   - From: Base
   - Side: Exterior
   - Cuts Wall: Checked
   - Cuttable: Checked
4. Click Apply and you should see the sweep appear just above the split region, as shown in Figure 12.15.

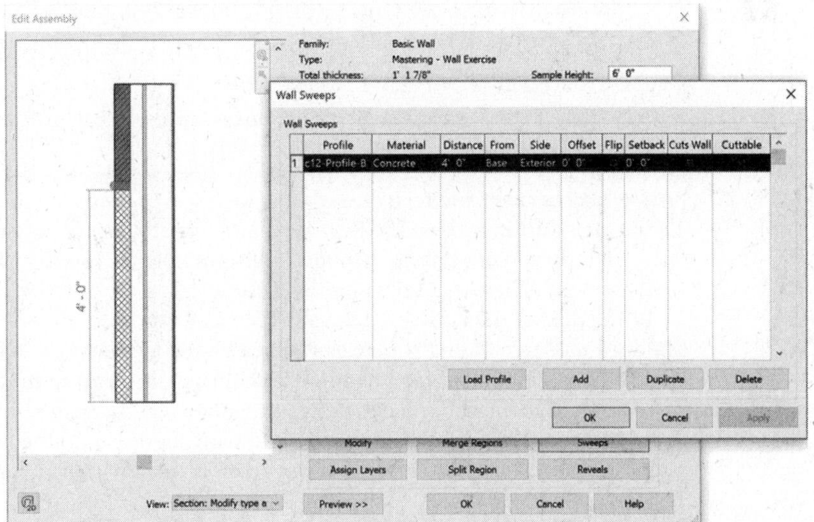

FIGURE 12.15 Bullnose sweep added to wall assembly

Notice that the loaded profile was created for predictable results when placed in a wall assembly. For your own wall, you may need to adjust the offset, flip, and setback values to achieve the desired results. Next, you'll add a different profile to the same assembly.

5. Click OK to close the Wall Sweeps dialog box. In the Edit Assembly dialog box, change the Sample Height value to **12′-0″** (**3650** mm) so that the next sweep addition won't conflict with the one you just added. Adjust the section view as required to see the whole wall.

6. Click Sweeps to reopen the Wall Sweeps dialog box. Click Load Profile again and navigate to the default library. From the Profiles folder select the Walls folder, and select either `Cornice-Precast.rfa` or `M_Cornice-Precast.rfa`.

   If you cannot locate these files in your default library, you can download them from this book's web page.

7. Click Add to create another new row and change the values in the row as follows:

   - Profile: Cornice-Precast or M_Cornice-Precast (Metric)
   - Material: Concrete, Precast
   - Distance: 0′-0″
   - From: Top
   - Side: Exterior
   - Offset: –0′-3 5/8″ (–90 mm)
   - Cuts Wall: Unchecked

8. Notice that the order of the rows is automatically adjusted, based on the vertical relationship of the sweeps added to the wall. Click OK to close the Wall Sweeps dialog box.

   A negative value for Offset was specified to bring the cornice sweep into the exterior finish layer. Vertical adjustments can be made by assigning positive or negative values in the Distance column.

9. Click OK to close all open dialog boxes, and save the project file for additional exercises in this chapter.

The process to create reveals is almost identical to that used to create sweeps. Simply click the Reveals button to open the Reveals dialog box. Experiment with adding your own reveals to the wall type you're creating throughout this chapter's exercises. We've added two reveals to the wall assembly (Figure 12.16) using the default Reveal-Brick Course profile family.

In the default 3D view, switch to the Modify tab in the ribbon, and in the Clipboard panel, choose the Match Type Properties tool. Click the Mastering - Wall Exercise wall segment. The mouse pointer will change to a filled paintbrush, indicating that an existing type is ready to be applied to another object. Select the other wall segment to apply the Mastering - Wall Exercise type. When the types of the two wall segments in the exercise file are matched, you'll see how nicely the sweeps wrap around corners in a 3D or camera view, as shown in Figure 12.17.

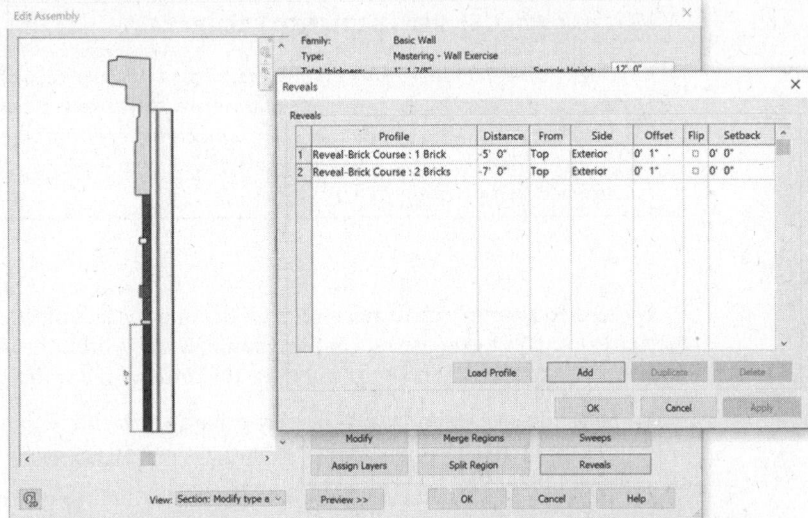

FIGURE 12.16 Reveals have been added to the compound wall assembly.

FIGURE 12.17 Camera view of compound wall with reveals and sweeps

MODIFYING WALL SWEEP RETURNS

In the previous exercises, you learned how to include sweeps and reveals in the assembly of a wall type; however, you can also apply a sweep to a wall if it's needed only in a limited location. For example, you might need to create a chair rail molding in one special room. To accomplish this, go to the Architecture tab in the ribbon and click Wall and then Wall Sweep. You can place a sweep on a wall vertically or horizontally by changing the placement option in the ribbon while the Wall Sweep tool is active. Select a wall sweep type from the Properties palette, and pick the wall faces to which you'd like to apply the sweep. If necessary, the sweep can be adjusted vertically in an elevation or section view.

Moving Wall Sweeps between Projects

Although profile families from RFA files can be used in wall sweep type properties, a wall sweep is a system family that exists only in a Revit project. New sweep types can be created only by using the Transfer Project Standards tool or by duplicating existing types within your active project. And keep in mind that once wall sweeps are added to your project, they can be scheduled like any other project component.

We created a sample chair rail sweep on the interior face of the walls in the `c12-Wall-Articulation.rvt` exercise file. In the default 3D view, orbit the model to view the interior faces. Let's take a look at how to customize the returns of a wall sweep:

1. Select the sweep and it will display grips at each end. Zoom the view closer to the end of the sweep that is aligned with the end of the wall segment.
2. Click the Modify Returns button in the contextual tab of the ribbon.

   There are some additional settings in the Options bar.

   You can change the angle of the return or return it to a straight cut, but for now leave the options as Return and Angle = 90°.
3. You'll notice that the mouse pointer changes to a knife symbol. Click the end of the sweep and then press Esc or use the Modify tool to exit the command.
4. Select the sweep again, and drag the grip at the endpoint you just modified to adjust the length of the sweep return around the corner of the wall.

Figure 12.18 shows how the return can be wrapped around the edge of a wall.

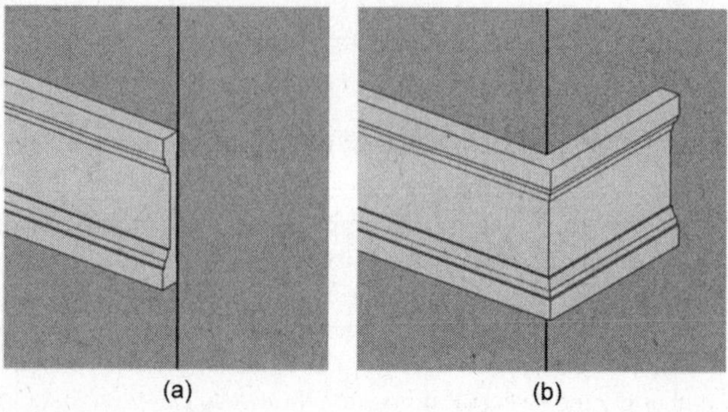

Figure 12.18 Modified wall sweep returns: (a) without the return; (b) with the return checked

Modeling Techniques for Basic Walls

In the previous sections, we explored methods to create a variation within the structure of a basic wall type. When you begin to use these types to assemble your building model, you have still more methods at your disposal to further customize how walls are applied. Let's take a look at techniques you can use for modeling basic walls once they are placed in a project. You can use some of these techniques for stacked walls and curtain walls as well.

Extending Wall Layers

In many types of construction, you'll need layers of materials to extend within or beyond the constraints of the wall. Some common examples include the extension of sheathing and siding on an exterior wall or gypsum wallboard extending only slightly above the ceiling for interior partitions (Figure 12.19).

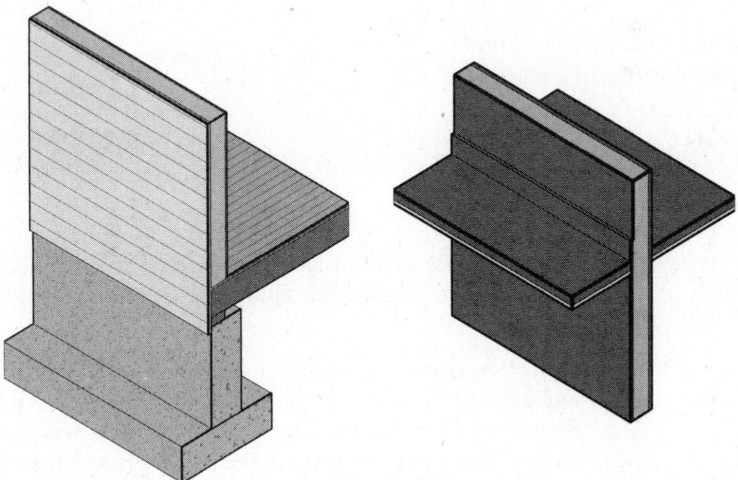

Figure 12.19
Examples of wall layers extending past or within the constraints of the wall

Enabling the extension of layers within a wall assembly requires you to unlock specific edges in the section preview of the Edit Assembly dialog box. Once layers have been unlocked, an instance parameter of the wall becomes active: either Base Extension Distance or Top Extension Distance (depending on which edges you unlocked). You can enter this value directly in the Properties palette or adjust it graphically in a section view by dragging the small blue triangle control at the edge of the unlocked layer. Let's go through an exercise to explore this functionality:

1. From the Architecture tab of the ribbon, click the Wall tool, and from the Type Selector, choose either the Generic - 5″ or Generic - 200 mm type. Click Edit Type to open the Type Properties dialog box.
2. Click the Duplicate button, and name the new type **Exterior Siding**.

3. Click Edit in the Structure field to open the Edit Assembly dialog box.
4. Add a new layer to the exterior of the wall, set its function to Finish 1 (4), use the material Siding, Clapboard, and assign a thickness of **3/4″** (**18** mm).
5. Open the Preview pane and switch to section view. Zoom into the bottom of the wall.
6. Select the Modify button and click the bottom edge of the exterior siding layer. Click the padlock icon to unlock the layer (Figure 12.20).

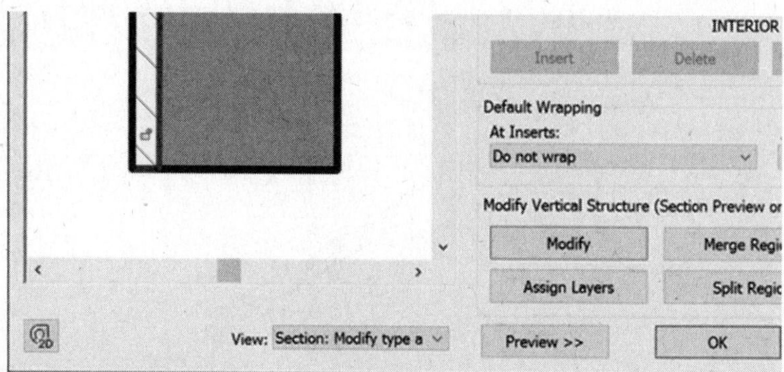

FIGURE 12.20 Using the Modify button, click the padlock icon to unlock layers.

You can unlock as many layers as you like; however, the unlocked layers all need to be adjacent. For example, you cannot unlock wallboard layers on both sides of a framing layer.

7. The siding layer is now unlocked. Click OK to close all open dialog boxes. With the Wall tool still active, create a segment of wall in the project using the Exterior Siding type. Press Esc or click the Modify button, and then select the segment of wall you just created. In the Properties palette, you'll see that the Base Extension Distance parameter is now enabled. Change the value to **–10″** (**–250** mm) for this parameter and observe the wall in the default 3D view.

   You'll see that the siding layer is now extending 10″ (250 mm) below the base of the wall, as shown in Figure 12.21.
8. Create a section view that intersects this wall segment, and then set the Detail Level in the section view to Medium or Fine. Select the wall, and you will see grips at the base of the wall indicating the layers that can be modified (Figure 12.22).

You can drag the controls to the required offset or use the Align tool to set the unlocked edge to another reference object. If you use the Tab key to select just the edge, you can use the Move tool to set a precise distance as well.

There are also controls for layers that are locked. Editing the wall with a control of a locked layer changes the Base Offset or Top Offset value and will automatically adjust any Base Extension or Top Extension distances you previously established.

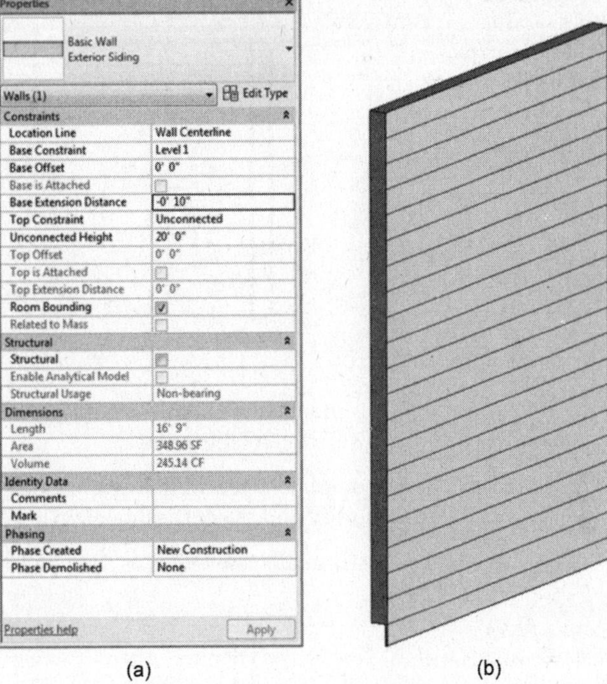

FIGURE 12.21 (a) Modifying the wall layer to have a base extension; (b) the resultant wall with an extended siding condition

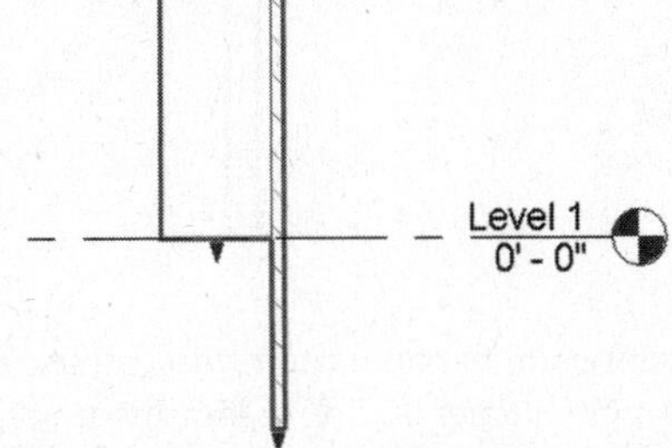

FIGURE 12.22 Unlocked layers can be modified in a section view by dragging or with the Align or Move tool.

EDITING WALL JOINS

In another common design and construction scenario, you may need to specifically control how two or more walls behave when they intersect. There are a number of ways to customize these occurrences. Let's examine two scenarios where wall joins may need to be edited: phasing conditions and acute angled corners.

When you create a model for a renovation of an existing building, you will likely create elements that are existing, demolished, and new. In the example shown in Figure 12.23, a new wall and a wall to be demolished are intersecting an existing wall. Notice that the walls are cleaning up with each other as they normally would if they were all in the same phase.

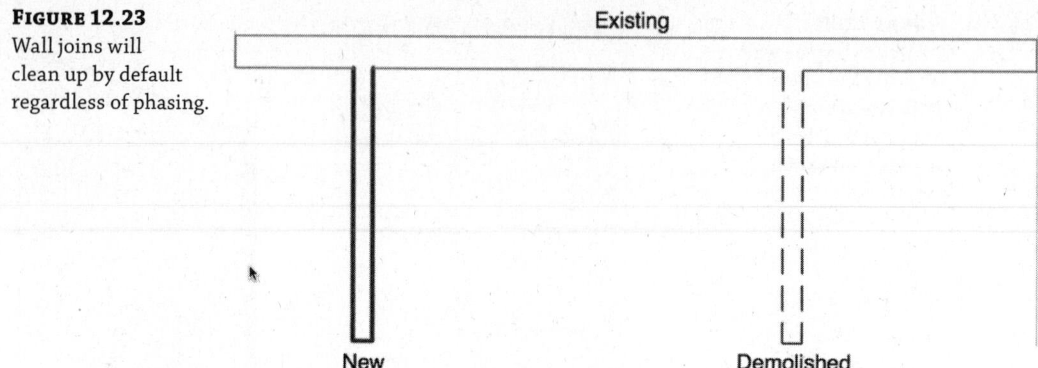

FIGURE 12.23 Wall joins will clean up by default regardless of phasing.

If you would like to change the graphic behavior of the new and demolished walls when they intersect the existing wall, follow these steps:

1. Select the new or demolished wall. Right-click the grip control at the end of the wall you'd like to modify and select Disallow Join.

   This will cause the walls to overlap, as shown in Figure 12.24.

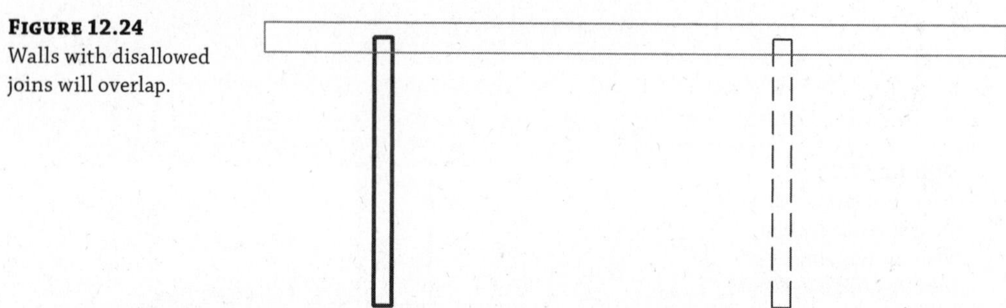

FIGURE 12.24 Walls with disallowed joins will overlap.

2. To complete the operation, you can use the Trim/Extend Single Element or Trim/Extend Multiple Elements tool, or simply drag the endpoints of the walls to create the most appropriate intersecting condition (Figure 12.25).

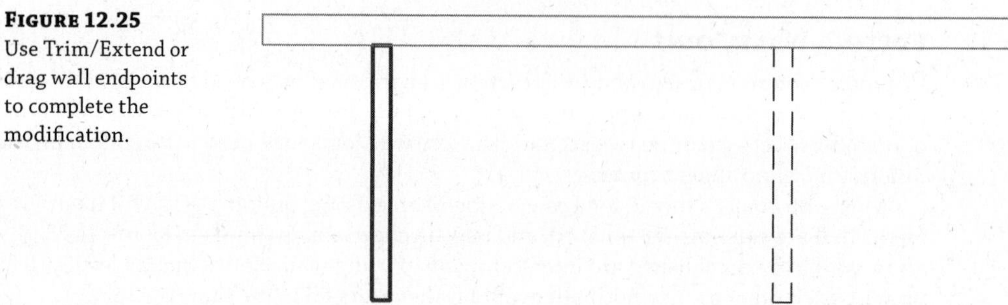

FIGURE 12.25 Use Trim/Extend or drag wall endpoints to complete the modification.

For walls that meet at an acute angle, you can use the Edit Wall Joins tool to control the resolution of the intersection:

1. From the Modify tab in the ribbon, locate the Geometry panel and select the Wall Joins tool.
2. Hover your mouse pointer over an intersection of two walls at an acute angle. You will see a box appear around conditions that can be modified with this tool (Figure 12.26).

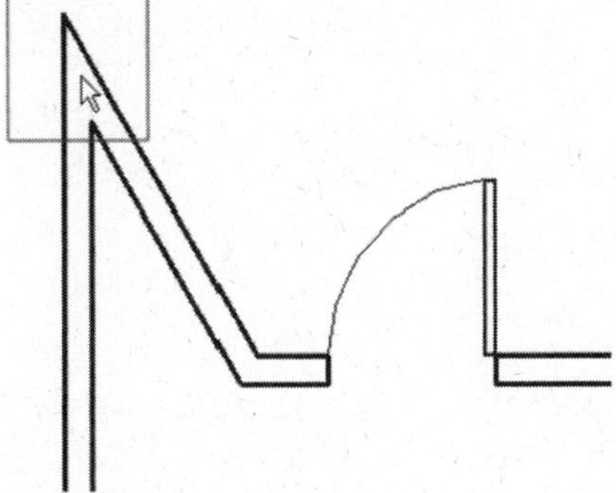

FIGURE 12.26
Use the Wall Joins tool to modify intersecting wall conditions.

3. In the Options bar, you will see a number of choices to help you customize the joining condition between the walls related to the selection.

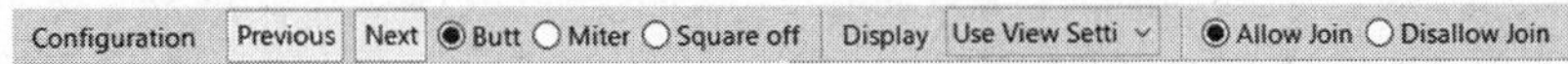

4. To cycle through the available options, choose one of the joining types (Butt, Miter, or Square Off), and then click the Previous or Next button. Some options are shown in Figure 12.27.

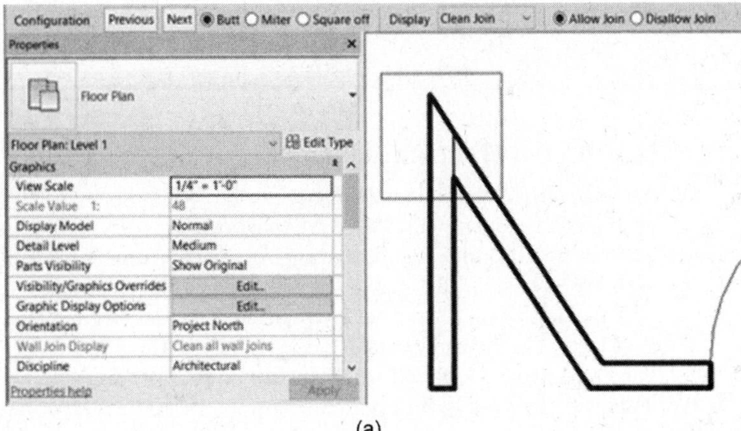

(a)

FIGURE 12.27
You can choose various corner conditions with the Wall Joins tool: (a) Butt, (b) Miter, (c) Square Off.

FIGURE 12.27
(continued)

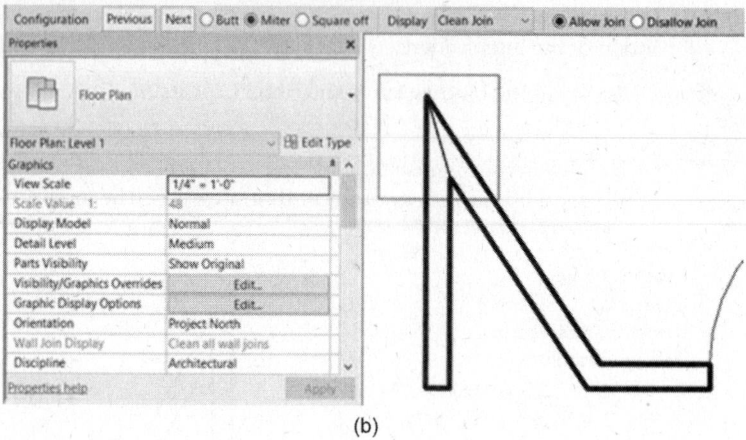

(b)

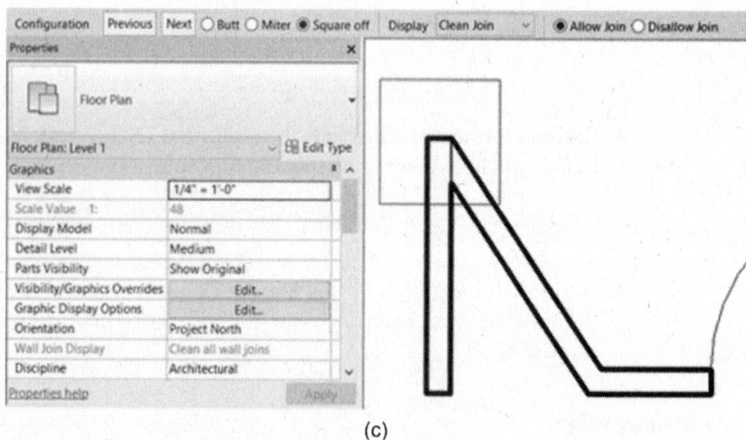

(c)

MODIFYING WALL PROFILES

An important extended modeling technique for walls is the ability to customize the elevation profile of a wall segment. There are two ways you can accomplish this: by attaching the wall's top or base to another element or by editing the sketch profile of the wall. You can apply these methods to basic walls, stacked walls, and curtain walls.

To attach a wall to another element, select a wall segment and you will see the Attach Top/Base button in the contextual Modify tab. Once this command is activated, select either Top or Base, and then pick an object. Walls can be attached to roofs, ceilings, floors, reference planes, and even other walls. Figure 12.28 shows a stacked wall that has been attached to a curvilinear roof by extrusion.

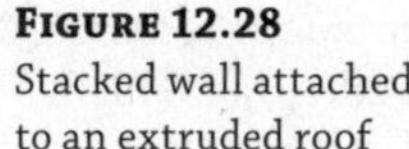

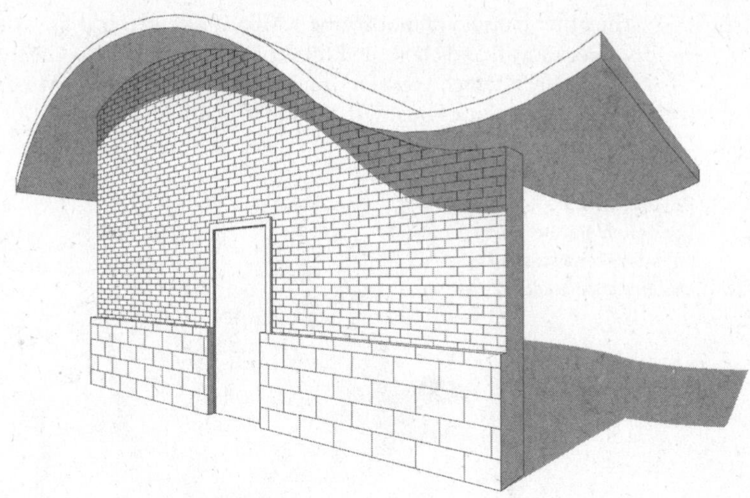

FIGURE 12.28
Stacked wall attached to an extruded roof

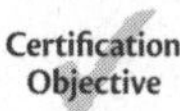

When you use the attach method, be mindful of how the software treats walls that are attached to other objects. After you use this method, the instance parameters Top Is Attached and Base Is Attached will show the status of the selected wall's attachment. These are read-only parameters and are for information only. Be aware that the top constraint and any other offset or height value will not display the actual height of the wall when it is attached to something. For example, if a wall whose base constraint is Level 1 and top constraint is Level 4 is attached to a floor slab on Level 2, the wall's top constraint will still be listed as Level 4 in the Properties palette. This anomaly does not affect other calculations such as wall length, area, and volume.

AUTOMATICALLY ATTACHING WALLS TO FLOORS

When you create a standard floor by sketching a boundary, the floor is hosted on a specific level. After you complete the boundary sketch and finish the editing mode, Revit offers you some help to attach walls to the floor. Any wall whose top constraint is the level on which the floor is hosted can be automatically attached to the bottom of the floor.

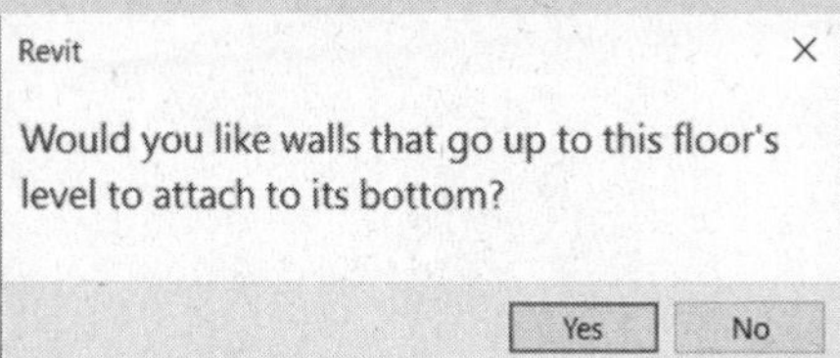

As a bonus, you can access this functionality at any time—not just when you create a floor. If you forgot to attach the walls to the floor when you first modeled the floor, simply select the floor and then click Edit Boundary. Click the Finish Edit Mode button, and you should be prompted to attach walls to the floor.

The other method of modifying wall profiles is to edit the sketch profile of the wall. To do this, select a wall and click the Edit Profile button in the contextual Modify tab. This will open a Sketch mode in which you can draw a new boundary for any edge of the wall shape, as shown in Figure 12.29. Click Finish Edit Mode to complete the operation.

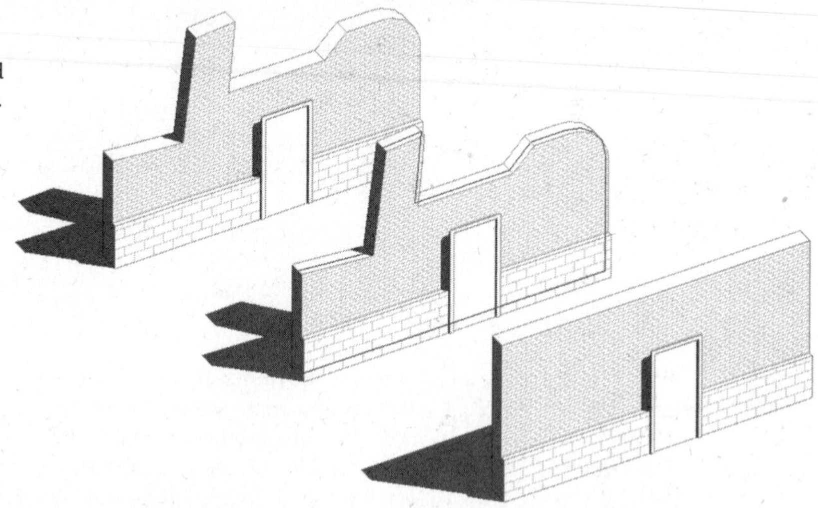

FIGURE 12.29
The sketch elevation boundary for a stacked wall instance is edited.

Creating Custom In-Place Walls

If you are working on traditional architecture, restoration of historic buildings, or free-form design, you may need to create walls that are irregular in shape. The Model In-Place tool, found in the Component drop-down list on the Architecture tab, lets you create any wall style independent of the constraints of the layer structure described in the previous sections of this chapter. Figure 12.30 shows an example of such a wall created with the solid geometry tools also found in the Family Editor.

FIGURE 12.30
Manually constructed wall used to create non-vertical surfaces

You can refer to Chapter 14, "Designing with the Family Editor," to explore the various modeling techniques available in the Model In-Place mode. Remember that the selection of the family category is important to the behavior of the custom geometry. Select the Walls category to allow your custom elements to be scheduled with other walls and to place hosted elements such as doors and windows.

Creating Stacked Walls

Walls in a building—especially exterior walls—are often composed of several wall types made out of different material combinations and with different widths that stack one on top of another over the height of the façade. Because these walls usually sit on top of a foundation wall, you would likely want to establish an intelligent relationship among the different wall assemblies so the entire façade acts as one wall (for example, when the foundation wall moves and you expect walls on top of the foundation to also move). This is where stacked walls can help.

Stacked walls allow you to create a single wall entity composed of different wall types stacked on top of each other. Before you can create a stacked wall, you need to download some basic wall types into your project. So follow these steps to download a variety of stacked walls and then modify one of them:

1. Download and open the file `c12-Stacked-Walls.rvt` or `c12-Stacked-Walls-Metric.rvt` from this book's web page. Activate the Level 1 floor plan view.
2. From the Architecture tab in the ribbon, pick the Wall tool and select Stacked Wall: Exterior – Brick Over Block W Metal Stud (you can find stacked wall types at the bottom of the list in the Type Selector). Draw a segment of wall in the Level 1 floor plan, and then exit the Wall command.
3. Select the wall segment, and in the Properties palette click the Edit Type button. Click the Duplicate button to create a new stacked wall named **Mastering Stacked Wall**.
4. Click the Edit button in the Structure field to open the Edit Assembly dialog box. Open the preview pane and set the view to Section.

   When you're editing the stacked wall type, you'll notice that the Edit Assembly dialog box (Figure 12.31) is slightly different than when you're working with a basic wall. Rather than editing individual layers, in this dialog box you are editing stacked wall types and their relationships to each other.
5. Click the Insert button to add a new wall to the stacked wall assembly. A new row appears in the list and allows you to define a new wall. Select the Generic - 12" (Generic - 300 mm) wall type from the Name list, and enter a Height of **10′-0"** (**3** m) (the Width value is not important in this exercise).
6. At the top of the dialog box, find the Offset drop-down list and change the setting to Finish Face: Interior.

   This will align the interior faces of the stacked walls and allow you to use the Offset field in the Types table to adjust each stacked wall type in a predictable manner.

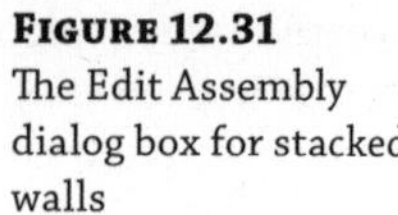

FIGURE 12.31
The Edit Assembly dialog box for stacked walls

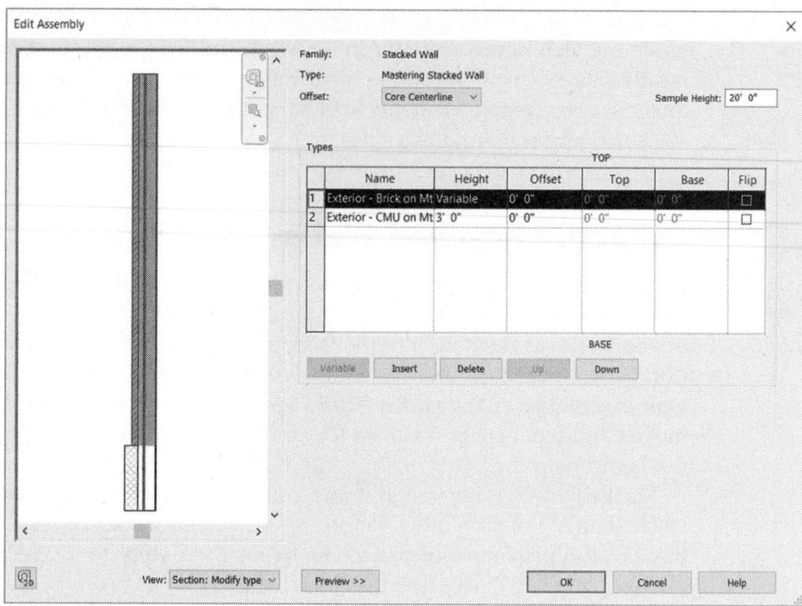

7. Select the row of the generic wall type by clicking the row's number label at the left side of the table. Click the Variable button to allow the wall to vary in height to adjust with varying level heights.

   Note that one row must have a variable height, but only one row in the assembly can be assigned as such. All others must have a specific height value.

8. Go back to the Level 1 floor plan and draw a new wall with the Mastering Stacked Wall type, setting its top constraint to Level 3 in the Options bar or in the Properties palette.

9. Cut a section through the model, and change the heights of Level 1 and Level 3 to see the effect this has on the wall (make sure the level of detail in the section is set to Medium so you can see the layers of the wall).

   You'll see that changing Level 2 does not change the bottom walls because they are of a fixed height; however, changing the height of Level 3 changes the height of the variable wall.

At any time, you can break down a stacked wall into its individual wall types. To do this, select a stacked wall, right-click, and select Break Up. Once a stacked wall is broken up, the walls become independent, and there is no way to reassemble them back to a stacked wall. The base constraint and base offset of each subwall are the same as the stacked wall. For example, if the stacked wall was placed on Level 1, the base constraint for an upper subwall would still be Level 1, with the height difference accounted for in the wall's Base Offset parameter. This can be modified in the Properties palette if necessary.

The following important notes about stacked walls are from the Revit user's guide (from the section "Vertically Stacked Wall Notes"):

- When you create a wall schedule, vertically stacked walls do not schedule, but their subwalls do.

- When you edit the elevation profile of a stacked wall, you edit one main profile. If you break up the stacked wall, each subwall retains its edited profile.
- Subwalls can host sweeps; stacked walls cannot.
- Subwalls cannot be in different phases, worksets, or design options from those of the stacked wall.
- To place inserts such as doors and windows in a stacked wall, you may need to use the Pick Primary Host tool to switch between subwalls composing the stacked wall. For example, the door shown in Figure 12.32 is outside the upper wall because the main host of the door is the bottom subwall.

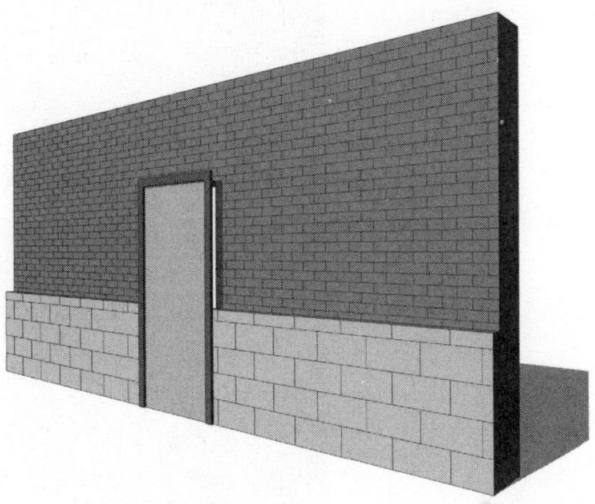

FIGURE 12.32
Inserts may not host correctly in vertically stacked walls.

To place the door properly, select it and then choose Pick Primary Host from the Modify | Doors tab in the Host panel. Place your mouse pointer over the wall and select the upper subwall (you may need to press the Tab key to select the correct component). The door will then be properly hosted in the upper wall, as shown in Figure 12.33.

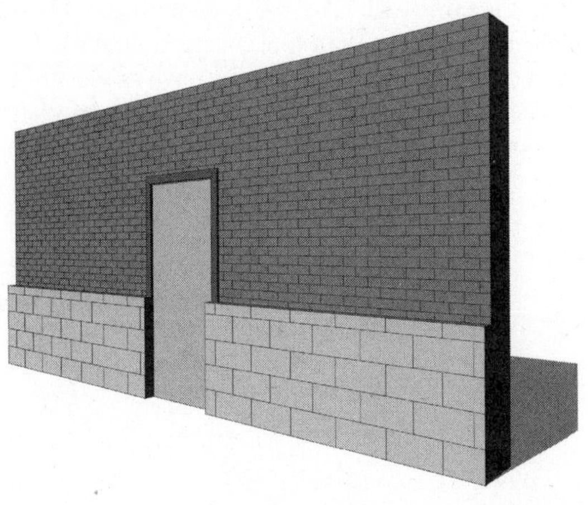

FIGURE 12.33
Use the Pick Primary Host tool to adjust inserts in stacked walls.

Creating Simple Curtain Walls

Curtain walls and curtain systems are unique wall types that allow you to embed divisions, mullions, and panels directly into the wall. They have a distinct set of properties yet still share many characteristics of basic walls. A *curtain system* has the same inherent properties as a curtain wall, but it is used when you need to apply a curtain wall to a face. Curtain systems are usually nonrectangular in shape, such as the glazed dome shown in Figure 12.34.

FIGURE 12.34
Glazed dome created with a curtain system

Before we explore the creation and modification of curtain wall types, you should become familiar with the fundamental components of this object type in Revit. A curtain wall is defined by the following elements and subcomponents:

The Curtain Wall A curtain wall is drawn like a basic wall and is available in the Type Selector when the Wall tool is activated. It has top and bottom constraints, can be attached to roofs or reference planes, can have its elevation profile edited, and is scheduled as a wall type. When a curtain wall is selected in a model, the overall curtain wall definition is displayed as a dashed line with extensions at both ends of the segment.

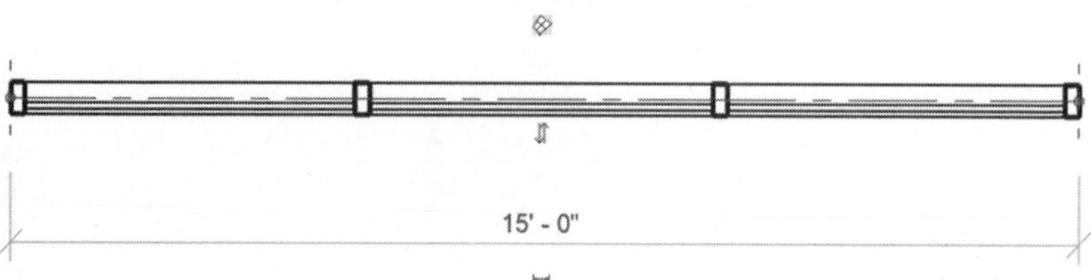

The dashed line of the overall curtain wall definition represents the location line of the wall. This is important if you are placing a curtain system on a face because the placement will be based on the location line. The location line of a curtain wall also determines the measurement of the room area. Even if the Room Area Computation option is set to Wall Finish, a room's area will be measured to a curtain wall's location line.

So how do you adjust the location line of a curtain wall? This is accomplished by modifying the offsets in the mullions and panels you assign to a curtain wall or system. We'll cover this process in the section "Customizing Curtain Wall Types" later in this chapter.

Curtain Grids These are used to lay out a grid, defining the physical divisions of the curtain wall. You can lay out grids freely as a combination of horizontal and vertical segments, or they can be predefined in a curtain wall's type properties in regular spacing intervals. Figure 12.35 shows a freely designed layout of curtain grids and expressive curtain panels in between.

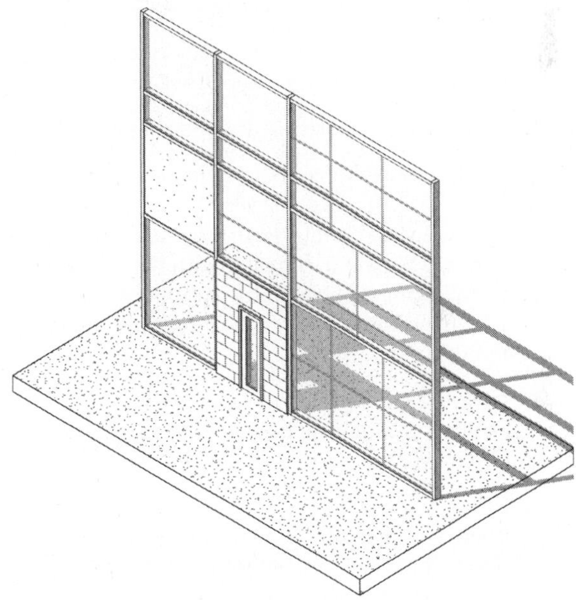

FIGURE 12.35
Curtain wall with regular orthogonal grids and expressive curtain panels

Mullions These represent the structural profiles on a glass façade, and they follow the curtain grid geometry. Mullions can be vertical or horizontal and can be customized to any shape based on a mullion profile family. Offsets specified in a mullion's type properties affect how the mullion is placed relative to the curtain wall's location line.

Curtain Panels These fill in the space between the curtain grids. Offsets in a curtain panel's type properties determine how the panel is placed relative to the curtain wall's location line. Curtain panels are always one of the following:

Empty Panels No panel is placed between the grids.

Glazed Panels These can be made out of different types of glass that can have any color or transparency.

Solid Panels Panels can be created with custom geometry in the Family Editor and can include anything from doors and spandrels to shadow boxes and solar fins.

Wall Types as Infill When you have a panel selected, you can also choose a basic wall type from the Type Selector to fill the space between the curtain grids. All wall types in the project will be available for your selection. An example of this application would be interior office partitions in which the lower portion is a standard wall and glass panels fill the upper portion.

Designing a Curtain Wall

Let's go through a quick exercise to become familiar with the creation of a simple curtain wall. To create a curtain wall, you can either model a standard wall and change its type to Curtain Wall or select a curtain wall type from the Type Selector when the Wall tool is active. To begin the exercise, create a new project and follow the steps:

1. From the Architecture tab in the ribbon, select the Wall tool. From the Type Selector (in the Properties palette) select Curtain Wall 1.
2. In the Level 1 floor plan, draw a single curtain wall. Go to a 3D view to see the result.

   The basic curtain wall definition has no predefined grids or mullions. The wall segment you see is just one big system panel that you will need to divide. If you create a curved segment for a curtain wall, the panels are always straight segments. Thus, if you draw a curved segment in the plan with the Curtain Wall 1 family, there will be only one straight panel segment between the endpoints of the curve until you start to divide it up with curtain grids. Revit doesn't allow for curved glazing outside of a custom family.
3. Divide the wall into panels using the Curtain Grid tool from the Architecture tab. Position your mouse pointer over the edges of the wall to get a preview of where the grid will be placed (select a vertical edge to place a horizontal grid or select a horizontal edge to place a vertical grid).

   There are some snapping options when you are placing curtain grids that will help you divide the panels and subsequent divisions at midpoints and thirds. Watch the status bar for snapping prompts because there are no graphic indicators of the snapped positions other than the mouse pointer pausing. Place grids on the wall segment so that you get something like the wall shown in Figure 12.36.
4. From the Architecture tab, select the Mullion tool.

   Notice that you can select from a variety of mullion types in the Type Selector; however, the default choice is adequate for this exercise. At the right end of the ribbon, you will see the Placement panel with three options for placing mullions: Grid Line, Grid Line Segment, and All Grid Lines. You can place mullions on the curtain wall using any of these methods. Give them a try to see how they work.

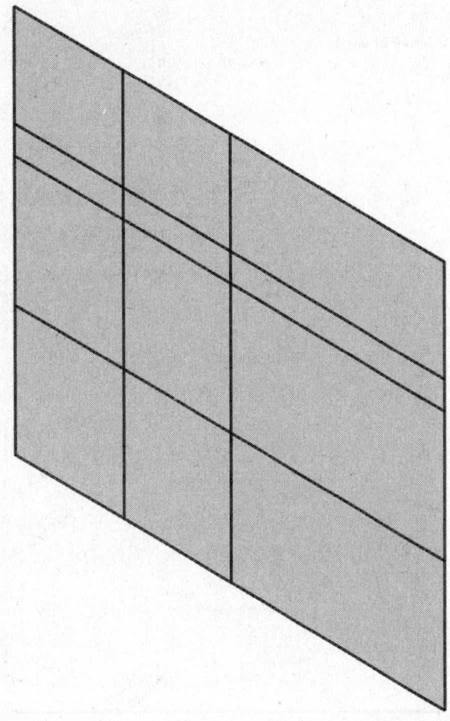

Figure 12.36
Curtain wall with a few manually applied grids

Replacing Panels and Mullions

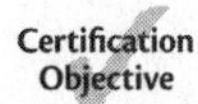

Certification Objective

Next, you'll replace panels in the wall you just created. As we explained earlier, panels are subcomponents of the overall curtain wall, so you may need to press the Tab key to select a panel and view its properties. Special selection tools for curtain walls are available in the context menu when you highlight a mullion or a panel.

In the following exercise, you will replace the narrow band of glazing panels with solid panels:

1. In a 3D view, select one of the glazing panels in the narrow horizontal band (press the Tab key to select it if necessary).
2. Right-click and choose Select Panels ➢ Along Horizontal Grid, as shown in Figure 12.37.
3. With all the glazing panels selected along the horizontal grid, go to the Type Selector and find the type named Solid under the Family System panel (note that the Glazing panel type is in the same family as the Solid panel).

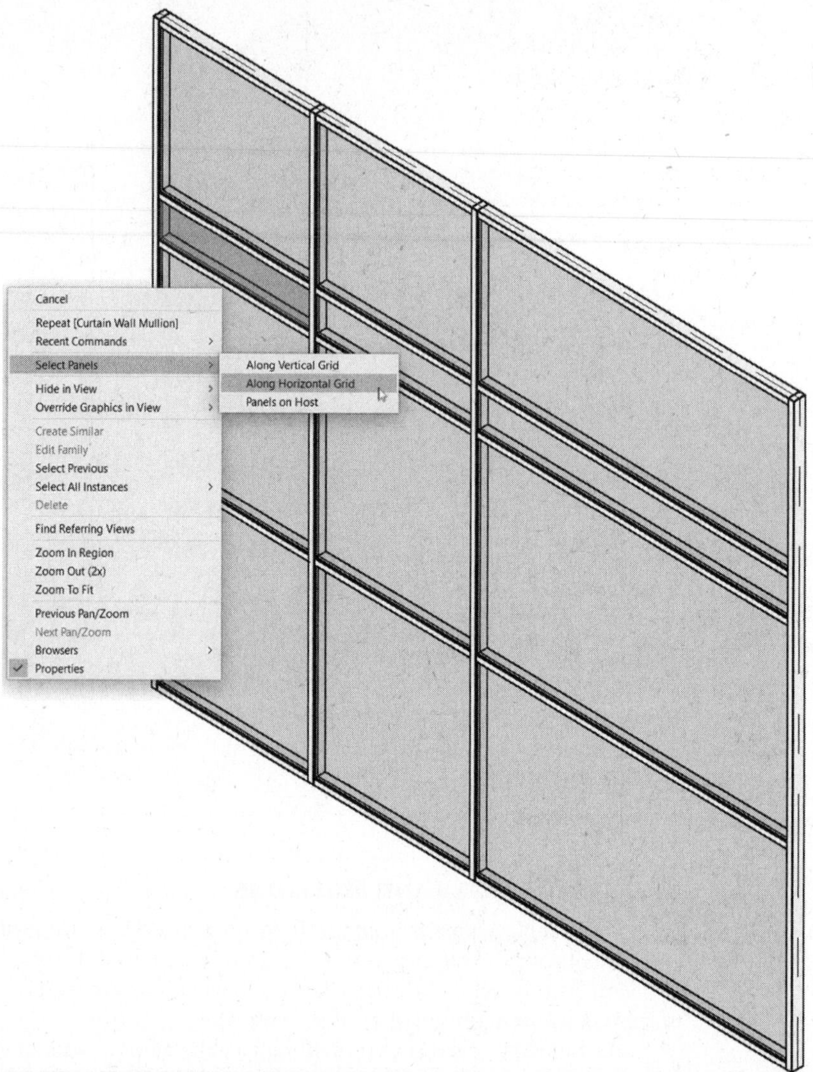

Figure 12.37
Select multiple curtain panels along a grid with commands in the context menu.

Customizing Curtain Grid Segments

In the last part of this exercise, you will practice the techniques for adding or removing segments of curtain grids in order to refine your curtain wall design.

Understanding the Curtain "Grid"

One important fact to remember when working with curtain grids is that they are always implied across the extent of the curtain wall. When we say they are implied, we mean they are not necessarily expressed on all panel segments. In other words, although a curtain grid is always expressed from one end of the wall to the other, you can decide if the grid divides every panel it crosses.

To become more familiar with this technique, you will add a curtain grid to the midpoint of the right-center panel and delete the division between the two panels to the left of the added grid, as shown in Figure 12.38.

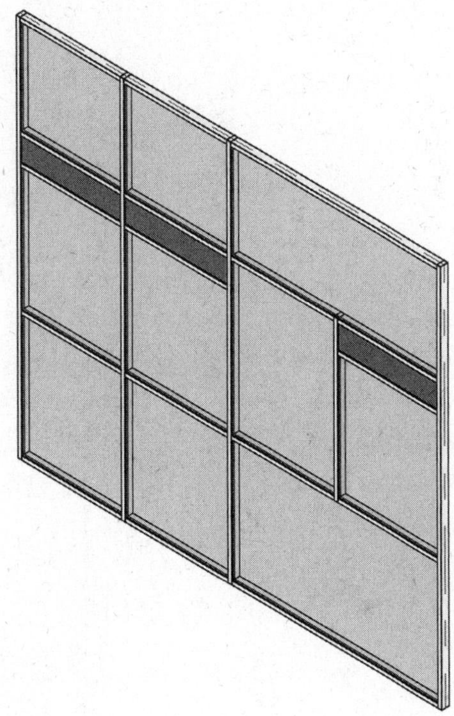

FIGURE 12.38
Individual grid lines are added or deleted to further customize the design.

Follow these steps:

1. Begin by activating the Curtain Grid tool from the Architecture tab. In the Placement panel at the right end of the ribbon, click the One Segment button. Hover your mouse pointer over the bottom edge of the right-center panel and snap to the midpoint of the panel (Figure 12.39).
2. The second step is tricky. You *do not* continue creating another division in the short panel above the center panel. Instead, press the Esc key or click the Modify tool to exit the Curtain Grid command. Select the vertical grid line you created in step 1 (you may need to press the Tab key until you see the dashed line indicating the curtain grid).

   Notice that the grid extends the entire height of the wall (Figure 12.40).

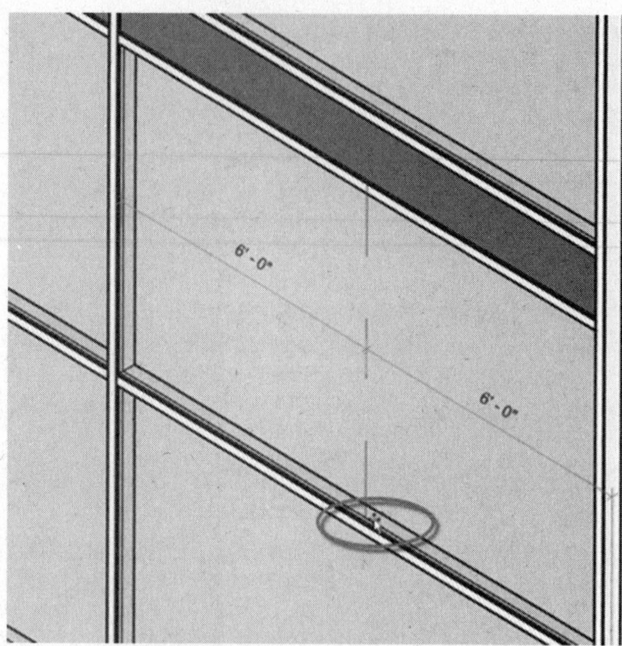

FIGURE 12.39
A single segment is added to the center panel of the curtain wall.

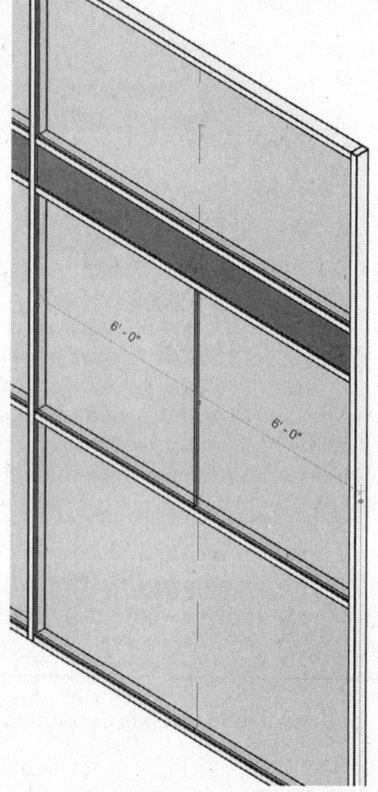

FIGURE 12.40
Select the curtain grid in order to add or remove individual segments along it.

3. With the curtain grid selected, click the Add/Remove Segments button in the Modify | Curtain Grids panel of the Modify tab. Pick the segment of the curtain grid that passes through the short panel. Press the Esc key, and you should see that the short panel is also split in half.

4. Activate the Mullion tool and place mullions on the division between the two center panels, as shown in Figure 12.41.

FIGURE 12.41
Mullions are applied to the segment added in the center panels.

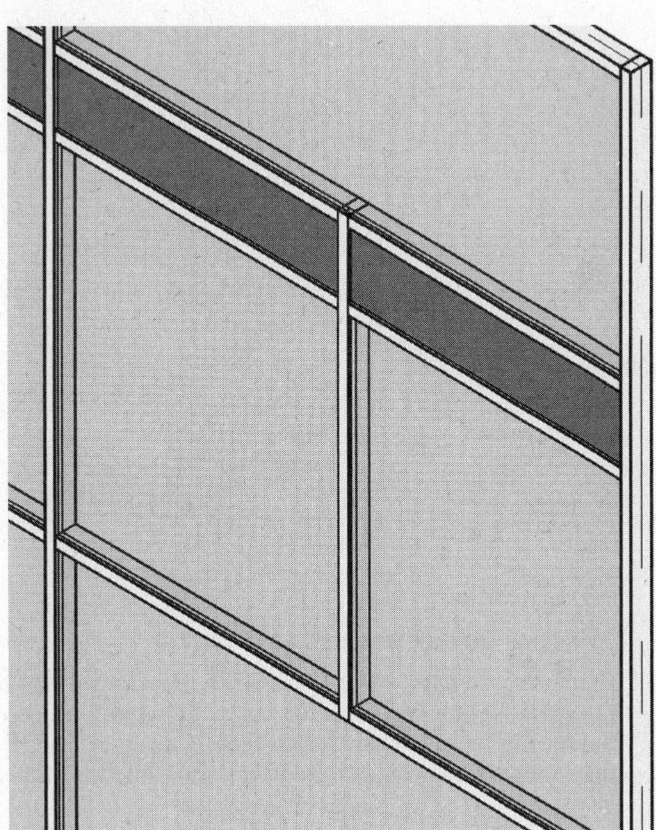

5. Press the Esc key or click Modify. Select and delete the horizontal mullion between the two left panels (this step is optional).

6. Similar to the process of adding grid segments, select the horizontal curtain grid below the narrow band and click the Add/Remove Segments button in the ribbon. Click the segment in the left-center panel.

   If you did not delete the mullion in step 5, a warning will appear prompting you to delete the mullion segment. The result should look like the wall shown in Figure 12.42.

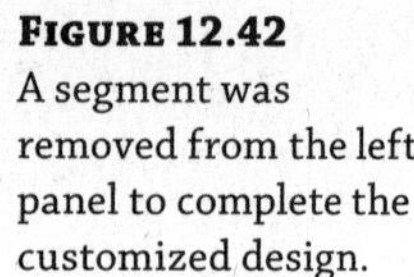

FIGURE 12.42
A segment was removed from the left panel to complete the customized design.

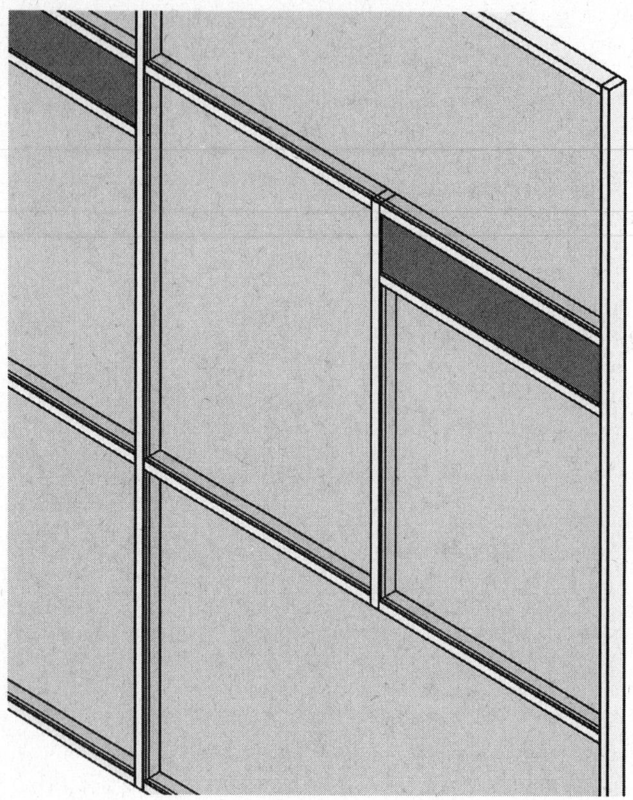

PLACING DOORS IN CURTAIN WALLS

In the next exercise of this topic, you will swap one of the curtain panels for a door panel. Door families for curtain walls can be found in the Doors folder of the Revit default library, but they behave differently than regular doors. The height and width of the curtain wall door are driven by the curtain grids—not the type properties of the door. Follow these steps:

1. From the Insert tab on the ribbon, locate the Load From Library panel and click the Load Family button. Navigate to the Doors folder of the Revit default library and load the `Door-Curtain-Wall-Double-Glass.rfa` or `M_Door-Curtain-Wall-Double-Glass.rfa` family.

   If you can't find these default families, you can download them from this book's web page.

2. Zoom into the bottom-middle panel in your curtain wall. Delete the mullion under this segment, as shown in Figure 12.43. (You don't want to have a tripping hazard at your door!) Remember, you may have to press the Tab key to select the mullion.

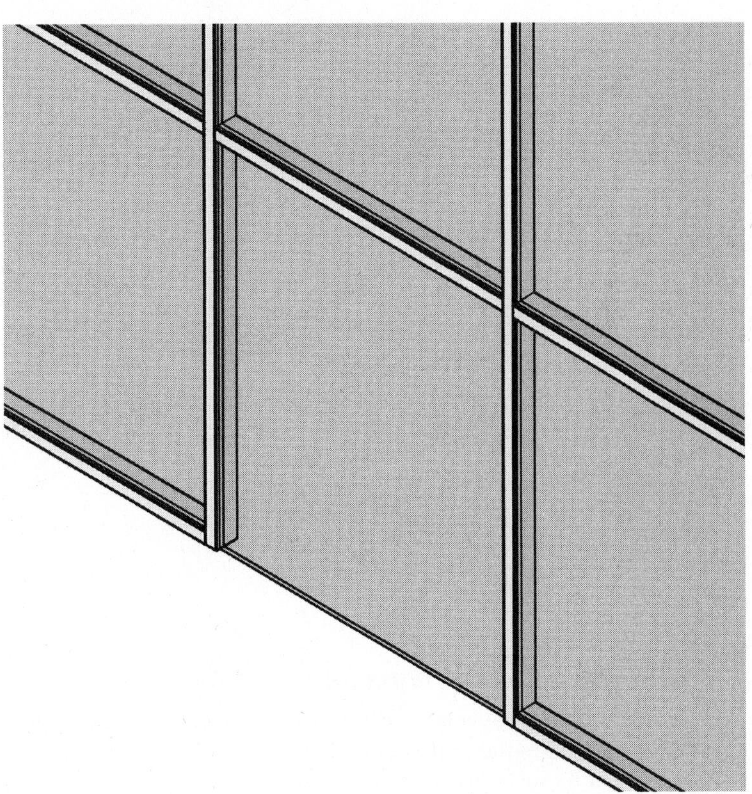

FIGURE 12.43
Delete the mullion below the panel where the door will be placed.

3. Select the bottom-middle panel and go to the Type Selector. Find the door family you just loaded and select it from the list so the results look like the wall in Figure 12.44. (Once hosted, if you only see the glass door panels and do not see the door hardware, change the view's Detail Level to Fine.)

   The door swing can be adjusted in plan as with any other door.

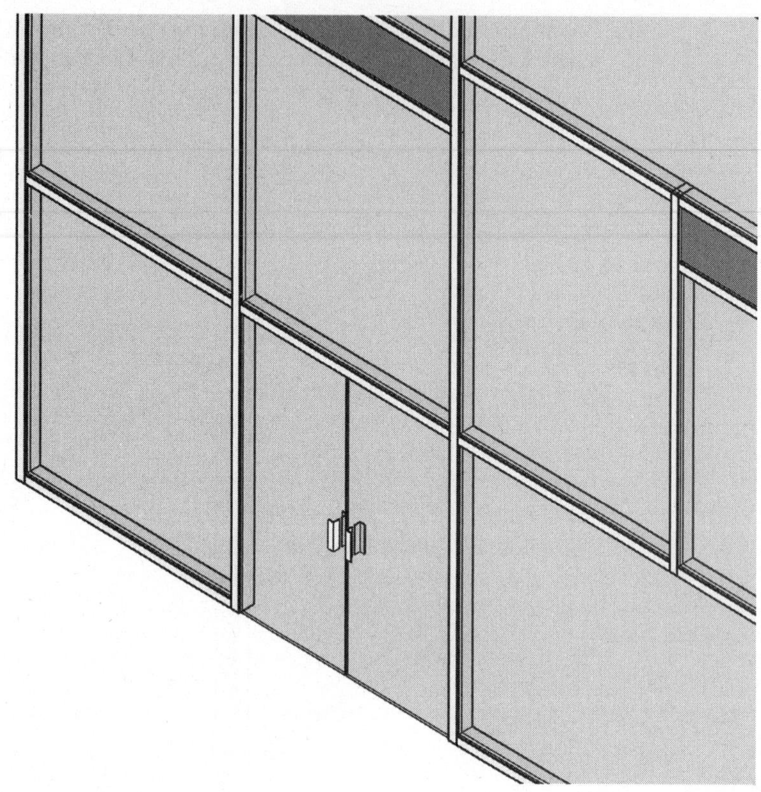

FIGURE 12.44
System glazing panel has been swapped for a double door panel family.

PLACING CORNER MULLIONS

Revit includes special mullions to be used at the corners of two curtain walls. These mullion types are unique in that only one is needed to connect two wall segments. In the default project template, you will find four corner mullion types, as shown in Figure 12.45: (a) V Corner Mullion, (b) Quad Corner Mullion, (c) L Corner Mullion, and (d) Trapezoid Corner Mullion.

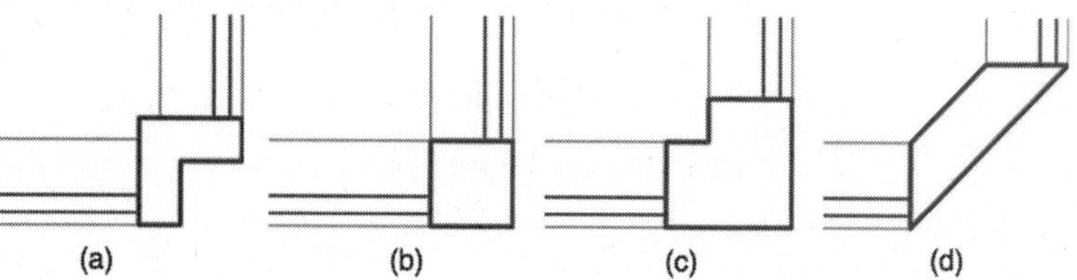

FIGURE 12.45
Available curtain wall corner mullions

Corner mullions cannot be customized beyond the shapes included in the Revit project template; however, you can modify the material assigned to the mullions as well as the offset and depth dimensions in the type properties. When you use corner mullions between two segments of curtain wall, they will automatically adjust to the angle between the segments, as shown in Figure 12.46.

FIGURE 12.46
Corner mullions adapt to angles between curtain wall segments.

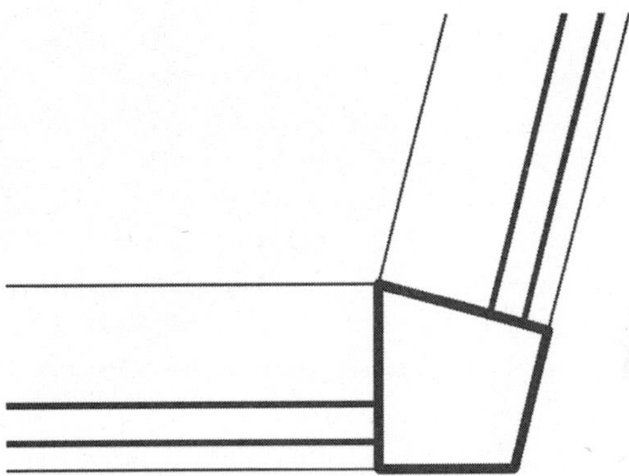

Before you place a corner mullion, make sure the endpoints of the two curtain wall segments are cleanly connected. You can drag the endpoint controls of the walls or use the Trim/Extend To Corner tool. To place a corner mullion, simply use the Mullion tool and select one of the corner edges of either one of the wall segments. If you have already placed a regular mullion at the end of a curtain wall segment, select the mullions along the vertical edge, and then use the Type Selector to choose a corner mullion type. Remember that you can use the context menu (right-click and select Mullions ➢ On Gridline) to make the selection easy.

Customizing Curtain Wall Types

In the previous exercises, you learned the fundamental techniques of building a simple but custom curtain wall design. To reap some additional productivity from the curtain wall tool, you can predefine almost all the properties necessary to generate a complete curtain wall assembly simply by placing the wall in your project. In the following sections, we will examine one of the curtain wall types included with the default project template.

Download and open the file `c12-Simple-Curtain-Wall.rvt` or `c12-Simple-Curtain-Wall-Metric.rvt` from this book's web page. Switch to a 3D view, and you will see that the wall already has vertical and horizontal divisions along with mullions placed on the divisions, as shown in Figure 12.47.

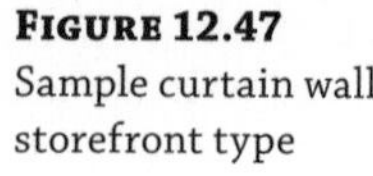

FIGURE 12.47
Sample curtain wall storefront type

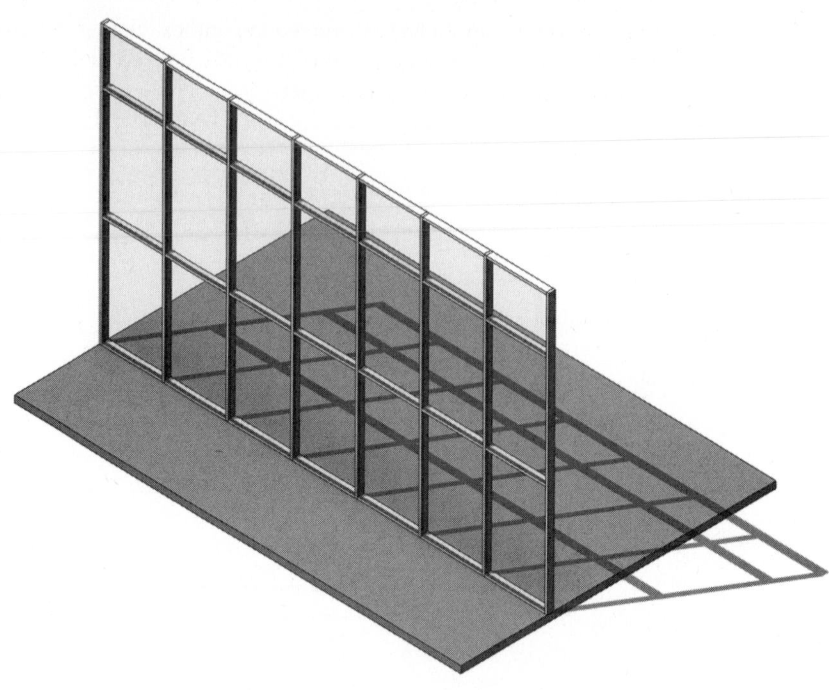

Select the sample of storefront wall in the exercise file and click the Edit Type button in the Properties palette. The settings that drive the generation of this type of wall are relatively easy to understand. Let's review some important options related to these properties:

Automatically Embed When you enable this option, any instance of this curtain wall type will embed itself inside other wall segments. This is useful for modeling extended areas of ribbon or strip glazing (Figure 12.48) instead of using a window family.

FIGURE 12.48
The Automatically Embed option allows curtain walls to be placed inside basic walls.

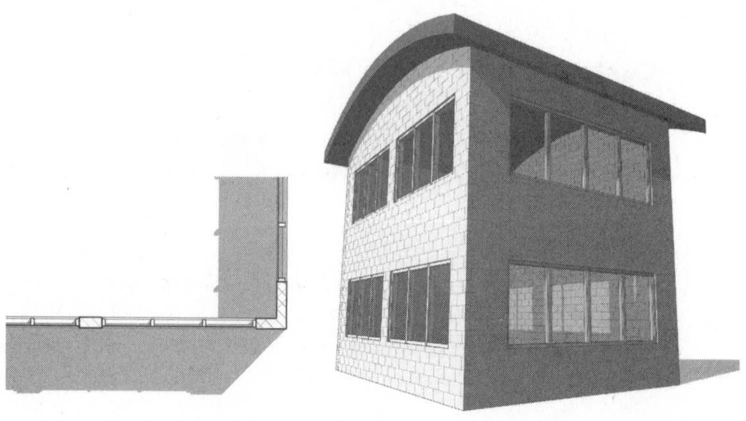

Join Condition This option defines the behavior of the mullion joins. It can be one of the following:

- Not Defined (join conditions can be overridden as necessary)
- Vertical Grid Continuous
- Horizontal Grid Continuous
- Border And Vertical Grid Continuous
- Border And Horizontal Grid Continuous

Display In Hidden Views This option allows you to control the graphic display of individual components over several views. The options for this can be one of the following:

- Edges Hidden By Other Members (the default)
- Edges Hidden By Element Itself
- All Edges
- None

Grid Pattern: Layout There are four options to define how the vertical and horizontal grids will be arranged in your curtain wall:

Fixed Distance The most common setting, which allows you to specify spacing between gridlines. Leftover panel segments must be accounted for in the overall length of the wall.

Fixed Number Divides the wall segment into equally spaced panels. When you select this option, the Spacing parameter becomes disabled. In its place, a new integer parameter named Number will appear in the instance properties.

Maximum Spacing Indicates the maximum spacing distance. Curtain panels will be equally divided over the length of the wall segment, not to exceed the Spacing value.

Minimum Spacing Indicates the minimum spacing distance. Curtain panels will be equally divided over the length of the wall segment, no smaller than the Spacing value.

Mullions This option allows you to specify the mullions that will be automatically applied to the curtain wall. Corner mullions can be applied to either Border 1 or Border 2 for the vertical mullions, but use them carefully—their resolution at corners will depend on how you construct your wall segments. For example, if you define a corner mullion for Border 1 and none for Border 2, you must construct all curtain wall segments of this type in a uniform direction. If you model one wall segment from left to right and another from right to left, you will have overlapping mullions at one corner and none at the other corner.

Modifying Pinned Panels and Mullions

You may have already noticed that when a panel or mullion is selected from a predefined curtain wall type, it appears with a pushpin icon. This indicates that this element is part of a system and cannot be changed without additional action.

To change or delete a predefined panel or mullion in a curtain wall instance, select the element and click the pushpin icon. The icon will change to a pushpin with a red X next to it. At this point, you can change the element using the Type Selector or delete it (only mullions can be deleted).

Pin with Care

Be careful when you attempt to unpin elements from a curtain wall because you cannot re-pin back to the predefined system. Within the active Revit session, you may be able to return to an unpinned curtain wall element and still find the unpinned icon. This allows you to fix any accidental unpinning, but once your project is closed and reopened, you can no longer re-associate the unpinned elements.

Creating Custom Curtain Panels

A curtain panel does not have to be confined to a simple extrusion of glass or solid material. You can create any kind of panel family to satisfy your design requirements. When creating a new panel, be sure to select the Curtain Wall Panel.rft or Metric Curtain Wall Panel.rft family template file. The width and height of the panel are not explicitly specified in the family; instead, the outermost reference planes will adapt to the divisions in the curtain wall into which the panel is embedded. If required, you can adjust the panel geometry to offset within or beyond the reference plane boundaries in the family. This is useful for creating butt-glazed curtain wall assemblies. The following feature contains examples of situations where you might want to consider custom curtain wall panels.

 **Real World Scenario**

Spider Fittings and Sunshades

Generic models can be nested in a curtain panel family. In the example shown here, two instances of the spider component are placed on one edge of the panel. Visibility parameters are assigned to the two spider fittings that enable either the top or bottom spider to be displayed as needed. The spider fittings were downloaded from RevitCity.com, and the sunshade is a Kawneer model 1600 SunShade – Planar, downloaded from Autodesk® Seek (`http://seek.autodesk.com`).

Spandrel and Shadowbox Often in glazing applications, the spacing of horizontal members will consist of a pattern including a narrow band or spandrel to mask the floor and ceiling sandwich. Revit software does not currently have the ability to define two spacing values, but you can create the spandrel or shadowbox in a single panel family. In the example shown here, the spandrel height is a type property of the custom panel family. Standard mullions are applied to the wall.

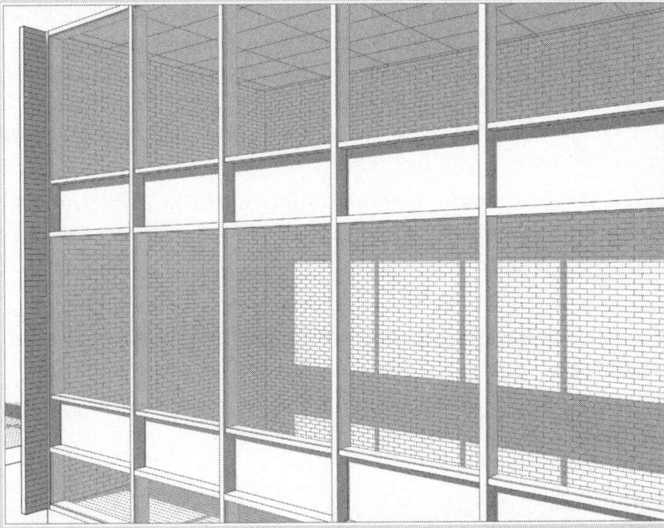

Louvers Our last example shows how metal louvers can be embedded in a curtain panel family. The image shown here is a panel developed with a nested generic model. The louver fins are arranged in a parametric array within the generic model, and then the generic model is placed in the panel. The edges of the louver array are constrained to the reference planes in the panel. This parametric louver curtain panel was downloaded from RevitCity.com.

Creating Complex Curtain Walls

Often at the early stages of design, as an architect or designer you need to be able to model curtain wall systems that indicate more complex design intent. These systems need to be flexible and light enough to allow you to explore design iteration, but they also need to be robust and detailed enough to be useful as your project moves from concept to design development and then on to fabrication.

In Revit you can build complex curtain walls using massing tools. There are two potential workflows. You can model your curtain wall system directly within the project environment from massing forms, or you can build it as a family within a conceptual design environment. Both of these methods are quite similar, but we prefer to use the conceptual design environment because the complexity of modeled elements, such as adaptive components, is better managed in a file that is separate from the project environment.

Project Environment You can build your forms directly within your project environment using the in-place massing tools. When walls are constructed through the In-Place Mass tool, the conceptual design environment does not have 3D reference planes and 3D levels.

Essentially, to create a complex curtain wall within the project environment, you follow these simple steps:

1. Create an in-place mass in the project environment.
2. Divide the surface.
3. Apply a surface pattern.
4. Replace the surface pattern with a pattern-based curtain panel family.

Conceptual Design Environment You create your curtain wall designs in the Revit conceptual design environment (CDE), which is a type of Family Editor. These forms reside outside the project environment. You can then reference these massing families into a project environment, allowing you to explore contextual relationships with the building form.

To create a complex curtain wall within the conceptual design environment, you're going to follow these simple steps:

1. Build a new conceptual mass in the Family Editor.
2. Divide the surface.
3. Apply a surface pattern.
4. Replace the surface pattern with a pattern-based curtain panel family.
5. Load it into your project.

You start by designing a conceptual form that will represent the shape and form of the surface of the curtain wall. You are then able to subdivide the surface of this form using a grid system, referred to as a UV grid. Because surfaces are not always planar (flat), a UVW coordinate system is used to plot location across the surface. This grid system automatically adjusts, following the natural contours of a nonplanar surface or form. The UV grid is then used as a guide for applying a pattern to the surface. You can investigate how you might panelize the surface to make it constructible by applying a geometric pattern to it. This pattern provides a basic graphic representation of how the panel may look. These graphic patterns can then be replaced with parametric components that automatically conform to the divided surface.

Dividing the Surface

Let's take a look at the basic tools that will allow you to divide the surface of a conceptual form:

1. Start by opening `c12-Square-Panel.rfa` from this book's web page.

   This file represents a simple conceptual shape for a curtain wall design (Figure 12.49). The form was constructed by drawing two curves at varying reference levels, and then a surface was generated between them.

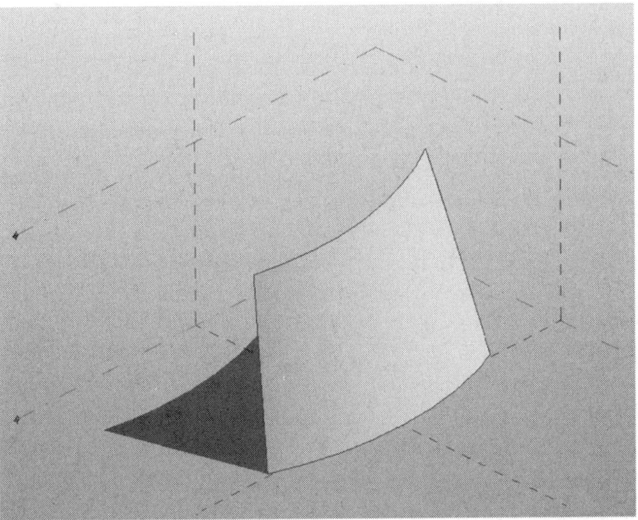

FIGURE 12.49 Conceptual shape to be used as a basis for a complex curtain wall design

2. Select the form and then click Divide Surface on the contextual tab in the ribbon.

   This will divide the surface of the form, and you will see horizontal and vertical grids displayed. This is the *UV grid*.

   You can control the display of the UV grid when it is selected (Figure 12.50). To modify the display, click the U Grid or V Grid button in the UV Grids And Intersects panel on the Modify | Divided Surface tab of the ribbon.

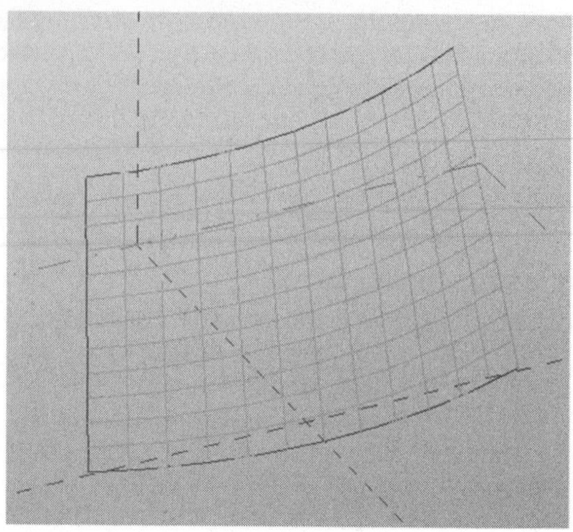

FIGURE 12.50 A surface of the conceptual form has been divided and the UV grid is displayed.

3. With the surface selected, make sure the U Grid and V Grid icons are highlighted in the contextual tab of the ribbon.

   Notice how the Options bar provides a number of settings for you to modify the divided surface. You can control the U grid and V grid by a number or with a specific distance. If you select the Number option, you can enter a number of divisions that will distribute evenly across the surface.

4. Select Distance, which will allow you to enter a specific absolute distance between grids across the divided surface. Under the Distance setting, there is a drop-down menu that also allows you to specify a Maximum Distance or a Minimum Distance value; these are similar to the constraints described earlier in this chapter for basic curtain walls. Make sure the surface is divided by number, with a U grid of 10 and a V grid of 10.

5. With the UV grid selected, you will see a 3D control (x-, y-, and z-axis arrows), and an icon appears in the center of the surface. Click the icon to enable the Configure UV Grid Layout command. The display will change (Figure 12.51), and you can now apply specific settings to control the UV grid even further.

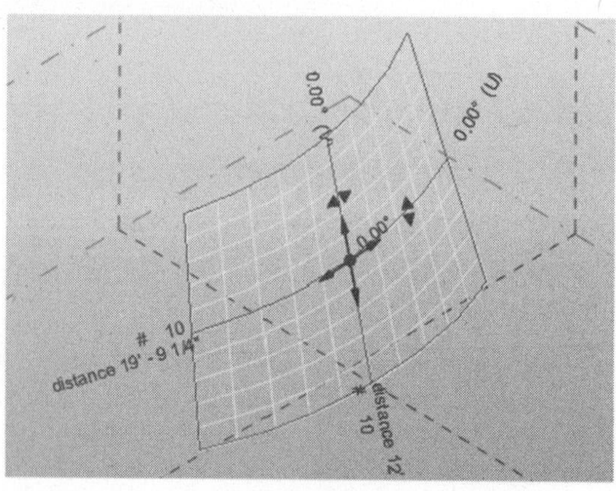

FIGURE 12.51 To configure the UV grid, click the icon at the center of the surface.

You have the ability to alter the rotation of the grid, the UV grid belt, and the justification of the UV grids at the surface borders. These grid configuration parameters can also be found and modified in the Properties palette.

6. In the Properties palette, set the U Grid Rotation value to 45 degrees and the V Grid Rotation value to 45 degrees; then click Apply.

   Notice how the modified values are updated in the 3D view with the Configure UV Grid Layout command activated.

In the Configure UV Grid Layout mode (Figure 12.52), you will see a number of controls—all of which relate to parameters you can also access in the Properties palette. The arrow cross in the middle of the grid is the *grid justification* marker. You can drag it to any side or corner or the center of the grid, which will adjust the value of the Justification property of both U and V grids.

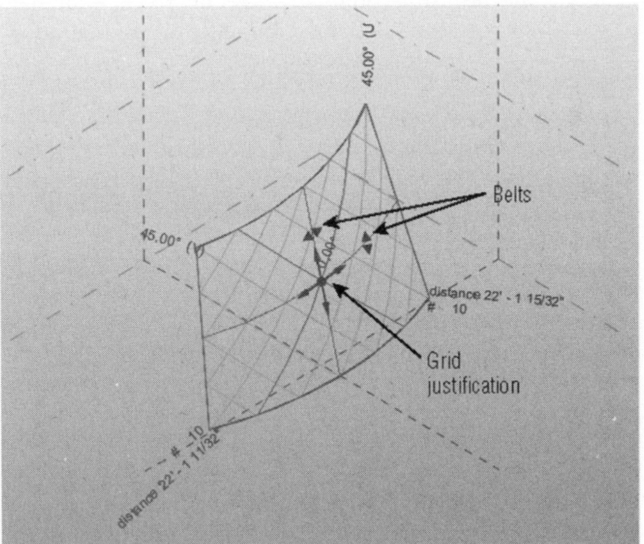

FIGURE 12.52
The UV grid can be modified directly or via the values in the Properties palette.

The *belts* represent the lines along the surface from which the distance between grids is measured. The distance is measured by chords, not curve lengths, and can be seen in the Properties palette as the Belt Measurement parameter for both U and V grids.

Dividing the Surface with Intersects

As you saw in the previous exercise, the Divide Surface tool allows you to divide the surface of a form using the natural UVW grid of the surface. However, if you want to divide the surface with a customized grid pattern, you divide it by intersecting geometry. By using the Intersect feature, you can divide the surface based on the following:

- Intersecting levels, reference planes, and even lines drawn on a reference plane
- A mixture of U or V grids and intersects

Let's take a look at an example based on our previous file, which will demonstrate how you can use a series of defined reference planes to divide a surface:

1. Start by opening the file `c12-Square-Panel-Intersects.rfa` from this book's web page.

   Notice that a series of reference lines are now drawn in the X plane; you will use these reference lines to divide the surface of the form.

2. Select the surface and choose Divide Surface from the ribbon. Click the U Grid tool on the ribbon to disable the display of the U grids.

3. With the surface still selected, click the Intersects button on the ribbon. Select all the reference planes in the X plane, and then click the Finish icon in the Intersects panel on the ribbon.

   This will divide the surface based on where the reference planes intersect the surface of the form. You could also select Intersects ➤ Intersects List to choose named references such as levels or named reference planes instead of picking them in the model view.

4. Go to the Project Browser and open the 3D view named 3D Surface to review the results (Figure 12.53).

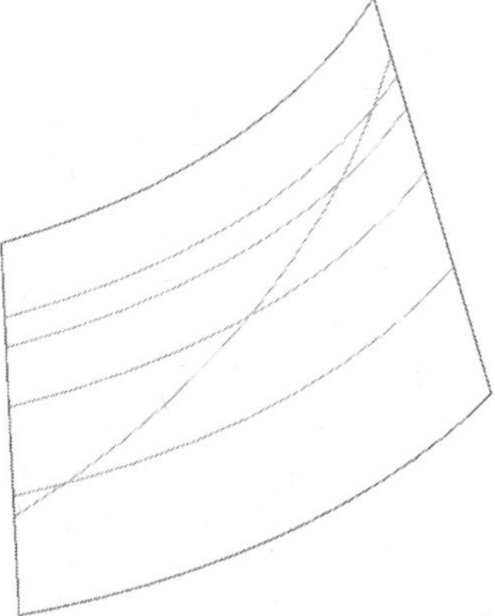

FIGURE 12.53
The surface is divided by intersecting planes and lines.

Applying Patterns

Surface patterns allow you to quickly preview in a graphical manner how a panel will work across the surface of the form. Because you are not working with complex geometry at this stage, the editing and adjustment to the design concept are quick. Revit provides a number of predefined patterns that are available from the Properties palette, and they can be applied to your divided surface. You will now apply a surface pattern to a form:

1. Start by opening `c12-Square-Panel-Pattern.rfa` from this book's web page. Divide the surface following the steps from the previous exercise.

2. With the UV grid on the form selected, you will notice in the Type Selector that the default empty pattern named _No Pattern is applied to the surface. Open the Type

Selector, and you will see that you can apply one of a number of predefined patterns to the surface. Click the Rectangle Checkerboard Pattern type to apply it to your surface (Figure 12.54).

FIGURE 12.54
Surface with Rectangle Checkerboard Pattern applied

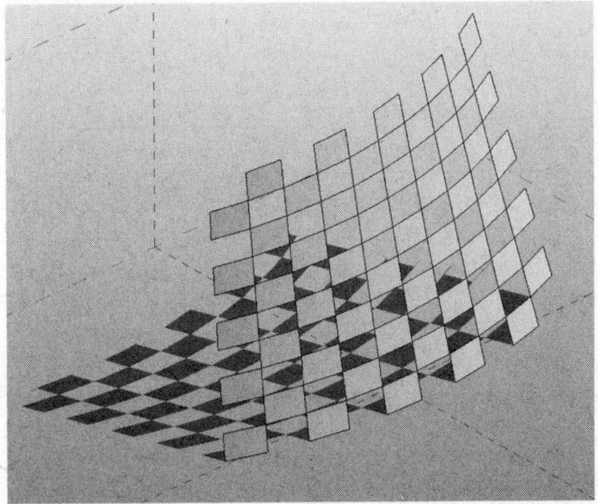

3. Experiment with the various predefined patterns and adjust the UV grid as required to play with the proportions of the patterns.

At any time, you can display both the underlying surface divisions and the pattern surface. With the grid selected, click the Surface button in the Surface Representation panel on the Modify | Divided Surface tab. This display should give you a better understanding of the relationship between the pattern definition and the spacing of the surface divisions.

Editing the Pattern Surface

There will be situations where you will want to edit and control the border conditions for pattern surfaces. Patterned surfaces may have border tiles that intersect the edge of a surface, and they may not end up as complete tiles. You can control the border tile conditions by setting them to Partial, Overhanging, or Empty in the Border Tile instance property of the patterned surface. You will now modify a conceptual curtain wall to examine how the different border conditions affect the surface:

1. Start by opening `c12-Square-Panel-Border.rfa` from this book's web page.
2. Select the surface, and in the Properties palette, locate the Border Tile parameter under Constraints. Set the value to Empty, and click Apply or drag the mouse out of the Properties palette.

   Notice that the tiles at the borders are no longer visible, as shown in Figure 12.55.

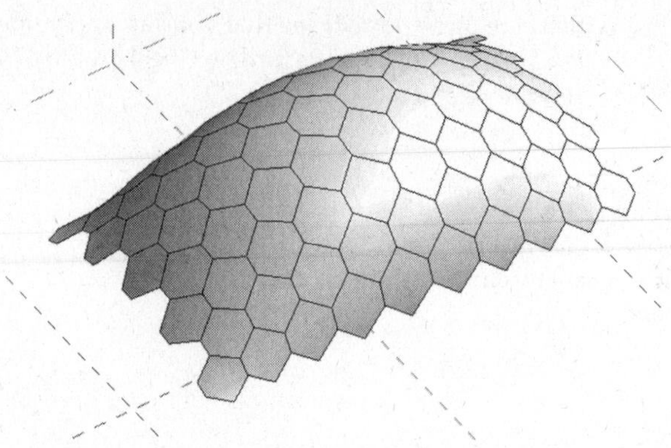

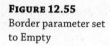

FIGURE 12.55
Border parameter set to Empty

3. Next, change the Border Tile parameter to Overhanging and click Apply.

   The border tiles will now show in their entirety, extending beyond the edge of the surface.

Editing a Surface Representation

When editing a surface in the conceptual design environment, you have the option to choose how surface elements will be displayed. A number of options are available to you, allowing you to customize how you show or hide the various elements that make up a divided surface in a view. If you select either the U or V Grid icon, this will enable or disable the UV grid in the view. The Surface icon allows you to display the original surface, nodes, or grid lines. The Pattern icon allows you to hide or display the pattern lines or pattern fill applied to the surface. The Component icon allows you to hide or display the pattern component applied to the surface. If you decide to make any changes to the display using the Surface Representation tools, these changes will not carry through into the project environment. To globally show or hide surface elements, you will have to alter this from the Visibility/Graphic Overrides dialog box.

In the Surface Representation panel, you will also notice a small arrow in the bottom-right corner. Clicking this arrow will open the Surface Representation dialog box, where you will find additional display options for the surface, patterns, and components. You also have the ability to display nodes and override the surface material of the form. Let's practice controlling the surface representation of your form:

1. Start by opening `c12-Square-Panel-SurfaceRep.rfa` from this book's web page.
2. With the surface selected, go to the Surface Representation panel in the ribbon, and click the arrow in the bottom-right corner to open the Surface Representation dialog box (Figure 12.56).

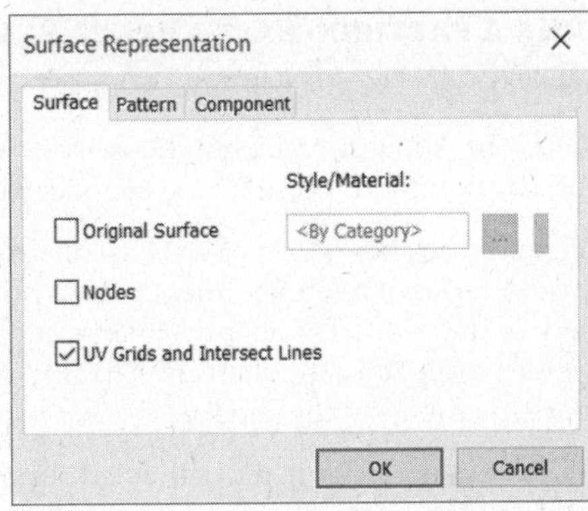

FIGURE 12.56
Use the Surface Representation dialog box to further customize the display of your form.

3. On the Surface tab, enable Nodes if is not already enabled; this will display a node at each intersection of the UV grid, as shown in Figure 12.57.

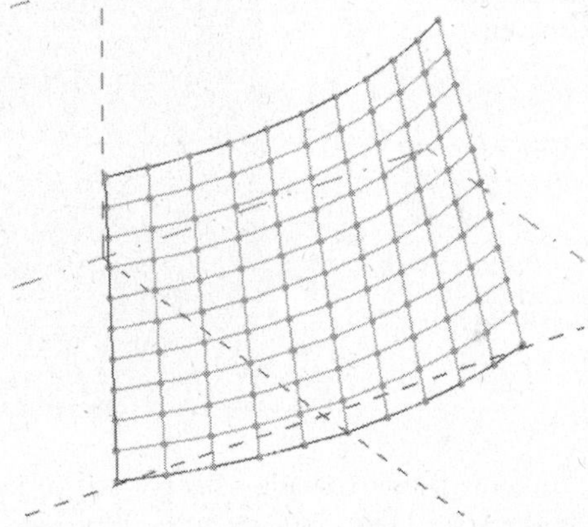

FIGURE 12.57
Nodes are displayed at the intersections of the U grids and V grids.

Adding Definition

So far, you have created a surface, subdivided it, and applied a graphical representation to the form. You can now begin to add actual component geometry similar to mullions and panels. Although the underlying graphic pattern will remain, the component geometry will take precedence. To begin this process, you will create special curtain panel families using the Curtain Panel Pattern Based.rft or Metric Curtain Panel Pattern Based.rft family template. This type of panel family can be applied to the divided surface to populate it with architectural components, adding realistic definition to your conceptual curtain wall surface.

Building a Pattern-Based Panel Family

In the following exercise, you will build a simple rectangular panel and apply it to your divided surface:

1. Click the Application menu, choose New ➤ Family, and select the Curtain Panel Pattern Based.rft or Metric Curtain Panel Pattern Based.rft family template.

   Figure 12.58 shows the pattern-based curtain wall family template, which consists of a grid, a series of reference lines, and adaptive points. The grid is used to lay out the pattern of the panel. The adaptive points and reference lines act as a rig, defining the layout of the panel. You can construct solid and planar geometry within and around the reference lines to form the panel.

   When a panel is applied to a divided surface, the points in the panel adapt to the UV grid and the panel will then flex accordingly. As a general rule, the grid pattern in your curtain panel family should match the pattern on the divided surface to which it is applied. For example, if you have applied a hexagonal pattern to your divided surface, make sure the curtain panel family is also using a hexagonal pattern.

Figure 12.58
The rig in the pattern-based curtain panel family

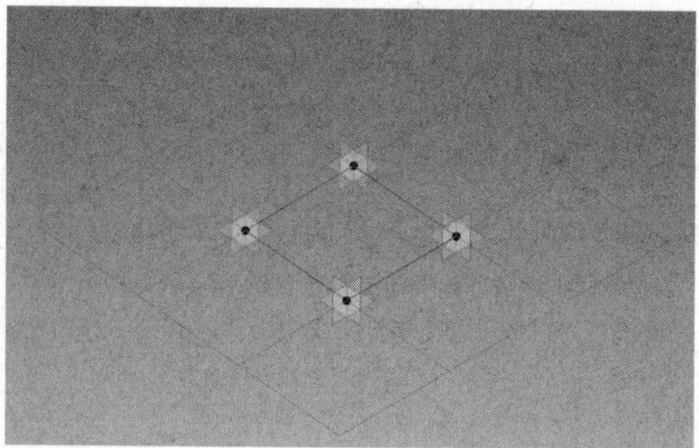

2. You now need to decide what pattern you will use for the component. To change the pattern, select the grid, go to the Type Selector, and change the pattern to Rhomboid. Notice how the adaptive points and reference lines update to reflect the change. Review the various patterns that are available to you. Revert to the Rectangular pattern.

   Modeling a pattern-based curtain panel is similar to how you would sketch and construct a form within the conceptual design environment. You use points, lines, and reference lines to construct geometry.

3. Select one of the adaptive points and drag it. These points move only vertically, not horizontally.

   As you move the point, the reference lines attached to the point will alter the shape. Therefore, as you build geometry on the defined reference lines and an adaptive point is moved or adjusted, the reference lines are altered, and the geometry constructed along the reference lines updates to reflect the change.

4. To reset the adaptive points back to the grid, select the grid and you will notice a Reset Points To Grid button in the Options bar. Click the button to reset the points.

5. Select the four reference lines and click the Create Form ➤ Solid Form button in the ribbon. Two icons now appear in the middle of the model view (Figure 12.59), giving you the option to create an extruded form or a flat planar surface. Select the icon for the planar surface.

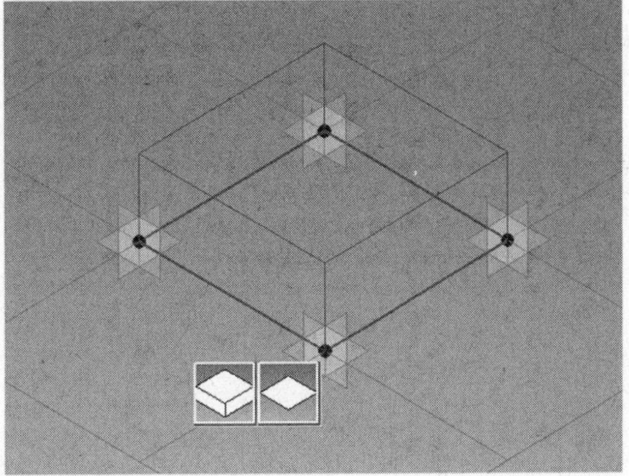

FIGURE 12.59
Geometry options are presented when you are using the Create Form tool.

6. Next, you will flex the geometry to test its consistency. Select one of the adaptive points and move it vertically. Observe how the geometry flexes, as shown in Figure 12.60, and then reset the points to grid.

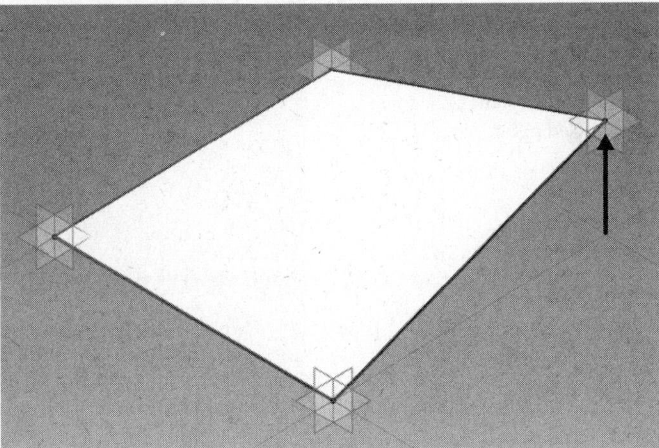

FIGURE 12.60
The panel form will flex when the points are dragged vertically.

7. Switch to the Architecture tab in the ribbon, and from the Draw panel, select the Point Element tool. Place a point on one of the reference planes, as shown in Figure 12.61. This point becomes a hosted point; observe how its symbol is smaller than the symbol for the adaptive points. Select the point, and from the Properties palette change the value of the Show Reference Planes parameter to Always.

This will make it easier to build geometry using the hosted point in later steps.

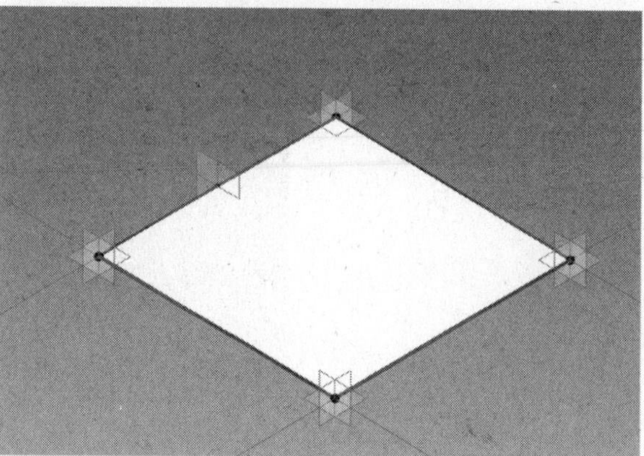

FIGURE 12.61
A reference point is placed on one of the reference lines.

8. From the Architecture tab and the Work Plane panel, click the Set button (Set Work Plane tool) and pick the work plane of the hosted point.

9. Draw a circle with a radius of 6" (150 mm) on the work plane of the hosted point, as shown in Figure 12.62.

   It can be a little tricky drawing the circle onto the active work plane of the hosted point. Therefore, use the Show Work Plane tool to display the active work plane for the point. This will make the process of sketching the circle easier.

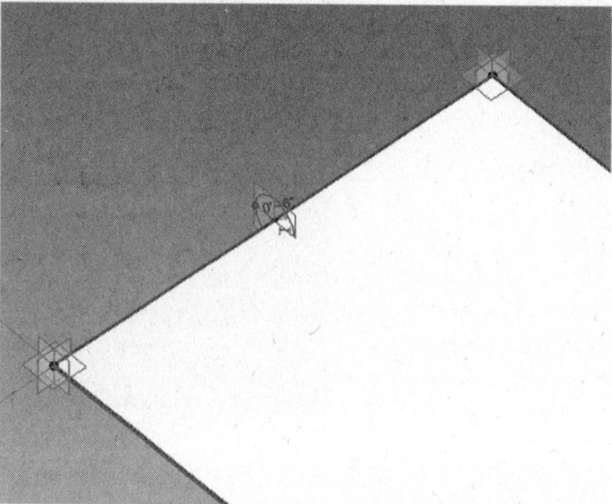

FIGURE 12.62
Draw a circle on the vertical work plane of the hosted point.

10. Select the circle and the four default reference planes, and then choose Create Form ➤ Solid Form.

    This will sweep the circle profile along the four reference planes, as shown in Figure 12.63.

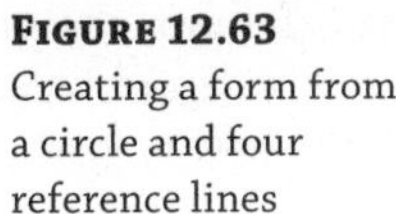

FIGURE 12.63
Creating a form from a circle and four reference lines

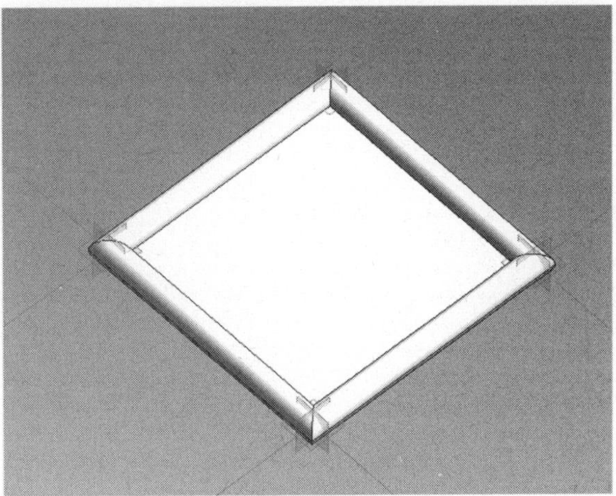

When building your curtain panels, consider how you will assign geometry to appropriate subcategories. This will ensure that you have full control over the elements from a visual and graphical point of view. For details on assigning geometry to subcategories, refer to Chapter 15, "Creating Stairs and Railings."

11. Save the family as `Square-CWPanel.rfa`.

> **CHANGING PATTERNS WITH GEOMETRY**
>
> It is important to understand that if you decide to switch your curtain panel grid pattern after creating solid forms, the geometry will not automatically adapt to the new pattern you choose. The geometry will be left orphaned, and you will need to delete any geometry and remodel, based on the new pattern.

APPLYING COMPONENTS TO A DIVIDED SURFACE

Now that you have created a pattern-based curtain panel family, you'll need to load this family into your conceptual mass family and apply it to the divided surface, replacing the graphical pattern with the actual component.

1. Download and open the file `c12-Square-CWSystem.rfa` from this book's web page.
2. Load the family file `Square-CWPanel.rfa` you created in the previous exercise into this file by clicking Load Family on the Insert tab of the ribbon, or switch to that file and click the Load Into Projects button.
3. In the conceptual mass file, select the pattern and divided surface. In the Properties palette, click the Type Selector, and scroll down the list until you find the name of your pattern-based curtain panel family.

Your new panel family will be listed under the pattern within which it was designed. The component will now be applied to the patterned surface, as shown in Figure 12.64. Note that the more complex the surface and component, the longer it will take to load.

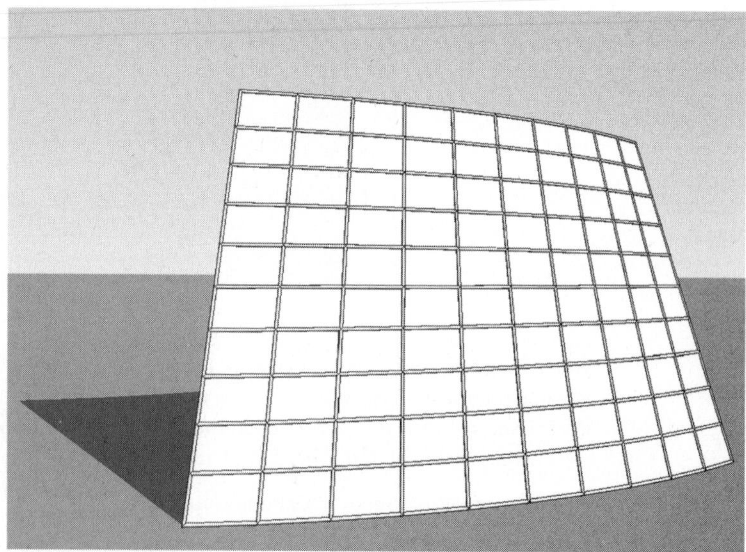

FIGURE 12.64
The pattern-based curtain panel component is applied to a surface in a conceptual mass family.

CREATING A PYRAMID CURTAIN WALL PATTERN-BASED FAMILY

Now that you have mastered the technique of constructing a simple planar curtain panel, let's look at how to create a pyramid type panel. You will add a type parameter to your pyramid curtain panel so that you can vary the apex of the panel:

1. Start a new family using the Curtain Panel Pattern Based.rft or Metric Curtain Panel Pattern Based.rft family template.
2. Place a reference point, ensuring that it snaps to the middle of one of the reference lines included within the template. Place another reference point on the reference line opposite the one you previously placed, as shown in Figure 12.65.
3. From the Architecture tab in the ribbon, click the Reference tool and ensure that 3D Snapping is activated in the Options bar. Draw a reference line between the two newly placed hosted reference points, as shown in Figure 12.66.
4. Place another reference point, so that it becomes hosted, at the midpoint of the previously created reference line (Figure 12.67). Select this reference point, and from the Properties palette, make sure that Show Reference Planes is set to Always.

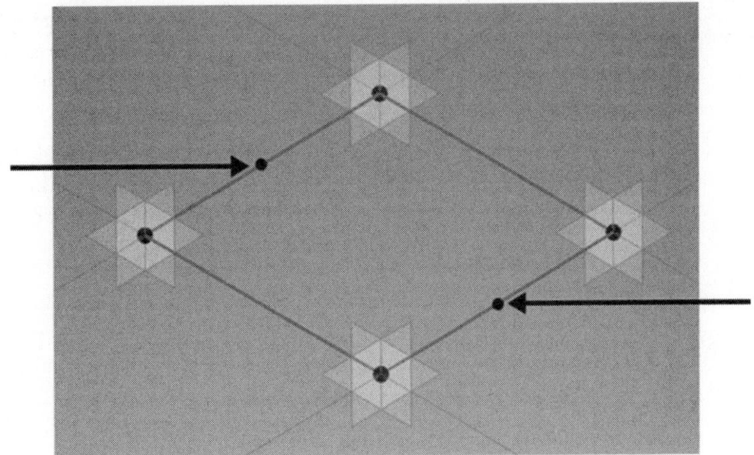

FIGURE 12.65
Hosted points are placed at the midpoint of two reference lines.

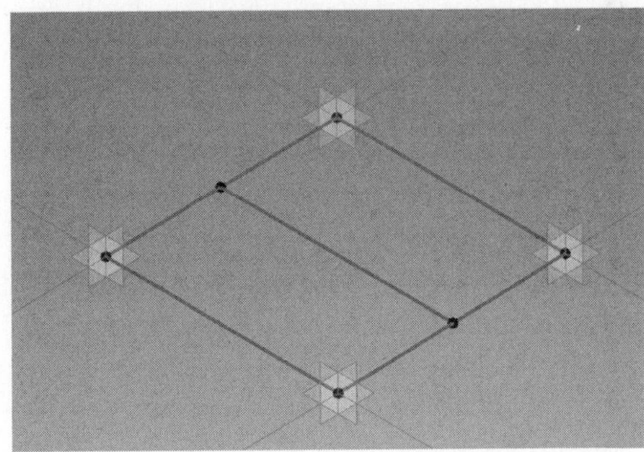

FIGURE 12.66
A reference line is drawn between two hosted points.

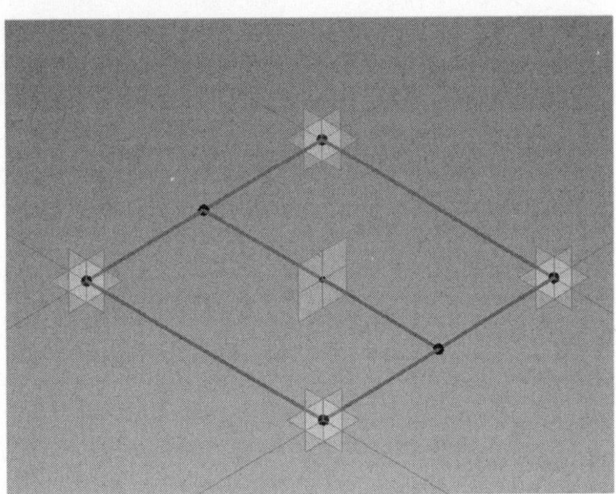

FIGURE 12.67
Place a hosted point at the midpoint of the reference line.

5. From the Architecture tab, choose the Set Work Plane tool and select the work plane of the hosted point at the middle of the previously drawn line. Activate the Reference Line tool and uncheck the 3D Snapping option. Draw a reference line vertically in the Z plane from the hosted point.

   Ensure that the start point of the reference line is locked to the hosted point. You may need to drag the end of the reference line, nearest to the point, in the Z direction before dragging it back to the hosted point. This will ensure that the lock symbol will appear.

6. Select the vertical reference line to display the temporary dimension, and turn this into a permanent dimension by clicking the dimension icon.

7. Select this dimension and then choose <Add New Parameter...> from the Label pull-down in the Options bar. Assigning this dimension to a parameter will allow you to alter the apex of the pyramid panel as needed. In the Parameter Properties dialog box, name the parameter **Apex_Height**. Click OK to close all open dialog boxes.

8. Add a series of reference lines using the 3D Snapping option from the apex to the four points on the base of the pyramid, as shown in Figure 12.68.

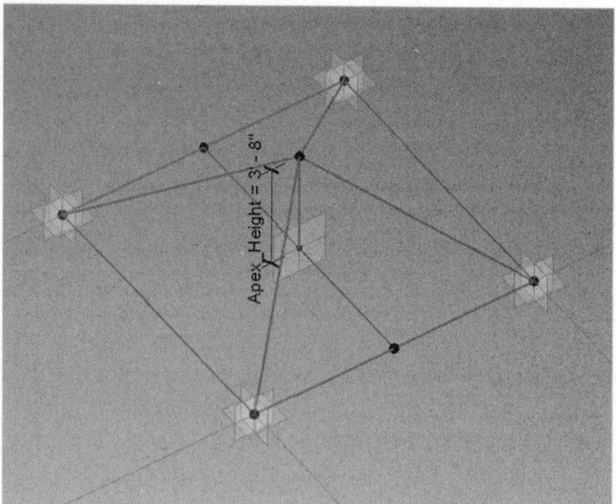

FIGURE 12.68 Reference lines are created from the corners to the apex.

9. You will now create faces on each slope to complete the pyramid shape. To do this, select one reference line from the base and two reference lines on the sloping edges (use the Ctrl key to add lines to your selection), and click the Create Form button. Select the planar triangular face rather than the extrusion (Figure 12.69).

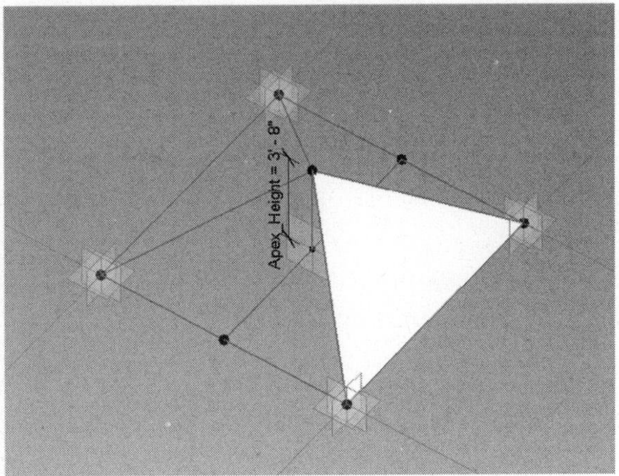

FIGURE 12.69
Select three reference planes, and then use Create Form to generate each face of the pyramid.

10. Repeat step 9 for the three remaining faces until you have a completed pyramid, as shown in Figure 12.70.

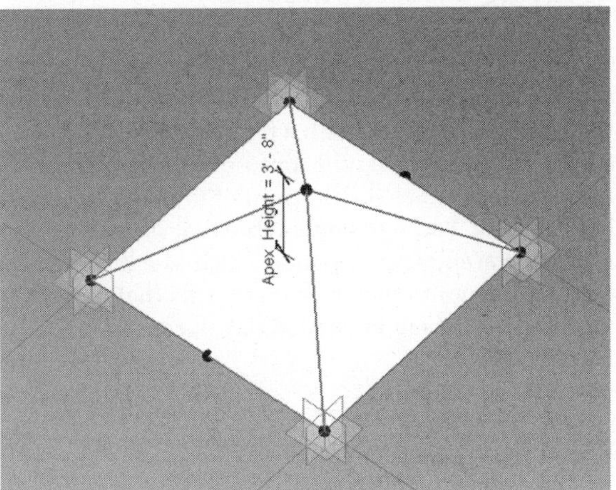

FIGURE 12.70
All four sides of the pyramid have been created.

11. It is important that you flex the pyramid to check that you can control the height of the apex. Open the Type Properties dialog box, and you will see the parameter named Apex_Height. Change the value a few times and click Apply after each change. The pyramid panel should change in height. Save your file as **`Pyramid-Panel.rfa`**.

12. Open the file c12-Pyramid-Project.rfa from this book's web page. Load your `Pyramid-Panel.rfa` family into the `c12-Pyramid-Project.rfa`. Select the surface, go to the Type Selector, and choose Pyramid-Panel.

Your pyramid shape curtain panel will now be populated across the divided surface, as shown in Figure 12.71.

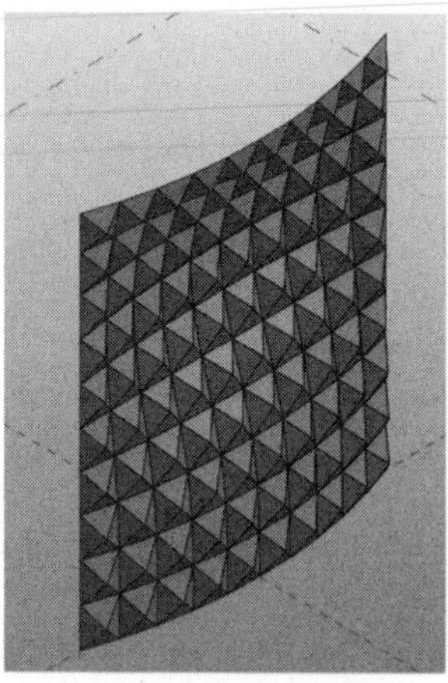

Figure 12.71
The pyramid panel is populated across the entire surface.

Creating Custom Patterns

Although Revit includes a variety of patterns you can use for conceptual curtain walls, at present there is no way to create your own pattern-based curtain panel template. The current patterns shipped with the software are hardwired, so there is no way to modify them either; however, with a bit of creative thinking, you can use the provided templates to construct panels that will conform to a custom pattern concept. When you consider building a custom panel, it is important to take into account how it will repeat vertically and horizontally. You will need to break it down into its smallest module. If you think about a repeating architectural pattern such as a masonry wall, its individual component can be broken down into the brick that forms that pattern, which is in essence is a rectangle. An example of a hexagon-shaped panel, constructed within a rectangular pattern, is shown in Figure 12.72.

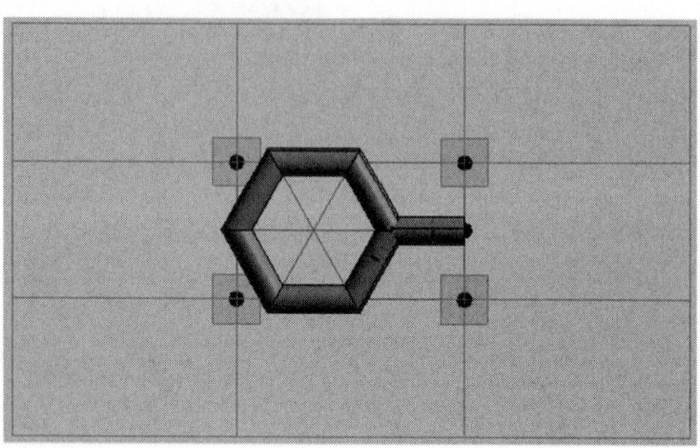

Figure 12.72
A hexagonal panel is constructed within a standard rectangular pattern.

Once you have decided on the design for your panel, look at how the panel could be modularized. To do this, consider laying out the pattern utilizing graph paper. This will certainly help you better understand the layout before attempting to construct the panel using an appropriate template. In Figure 12.73, you can see the hexagonal panel applied across a divided surface.

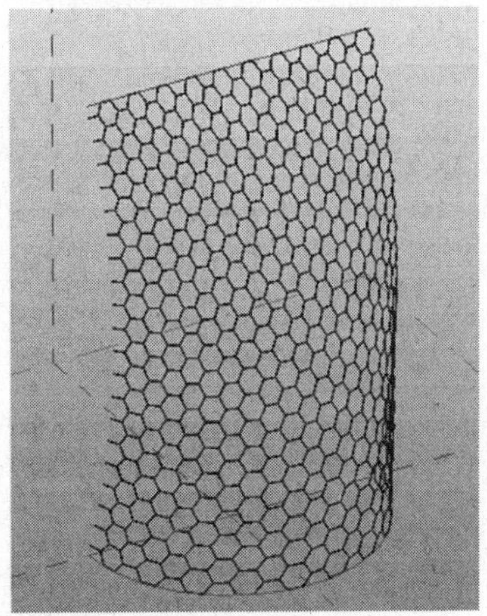

FIGURE 12.73
The hexagonal panel applied across a divided surface

Limiting the Size of Pattern-Based Families

When designing complex curtain wall systems, the goal is to limit the variety of panels. The more variety you have, the higher the cost because you have to create a greater number of unique panels. When you divide a surface, the panel sizes can vary quite dramatically. Although you do not actually have the ability to limit panel sizes, you can start to reduce the size and variety of panels by nesting curtain panels inside other panels. In the following exercise, you will learn how to nest panels to limit size variation:

1. Start by creating a simple pattern-based curtain panel family (use either Curtain Panel Pattern Based.rft or Metric Curtain Panel Pattern Based.rft). Make sure the grid is set to the Rectangular type.
2. Select the four reference lines and use the Create Form tool to generate a planar surface.
3. Similar to the previous exercise, place a hosted point on one of the edges of the surface, and then draw a circle with a 6″ (150 mm) radius on the point's work plane. Use Create Form to generate a swept profile on two edges to represent a mullion, as shown in Figure 12.74. Save this panel as **`Limit-Panel-1.rfa`**.
4. Start another new pattern-based curtain panel family, again using the Rectangular grid pattern. Select the four reference planes, and use Create Form to generate a planar surface rather than an extrusion.

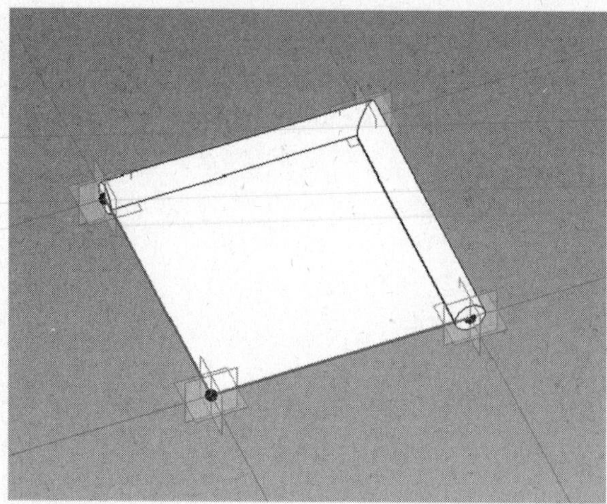

FIGURE 12.74
A panel with a swept profile is created to be nested into another panel family.

5. Select the planar surface and click the Divide Surface tool from the ribbon. You will divide this surface and set the UV grid by number; set U Grid to **2** and V Grid to **2**, as shown in Figure 12.75.

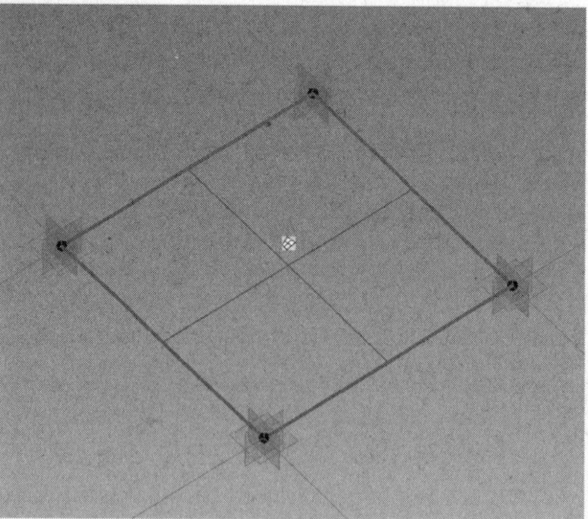

FIGURE 12.75
Create another pattern-based family and divide the surface into a 2×2 grid.

6. Load the Limit-Panel-1 family into the divided surface panel.
7. Select the divided surface and apply your panel to the divided surface by choosing Limit-Panel-1 from the Type Selector. This will nest the panel into the subdivisions of the divided surface (Figure 12.76). Save this panel as **`Limit-Panel-2.rfa`**.

   You can now apply this nested panel into any divided surface. Download and open the file `c12-Limit-Panel-Project.rfa` from this book's web page.

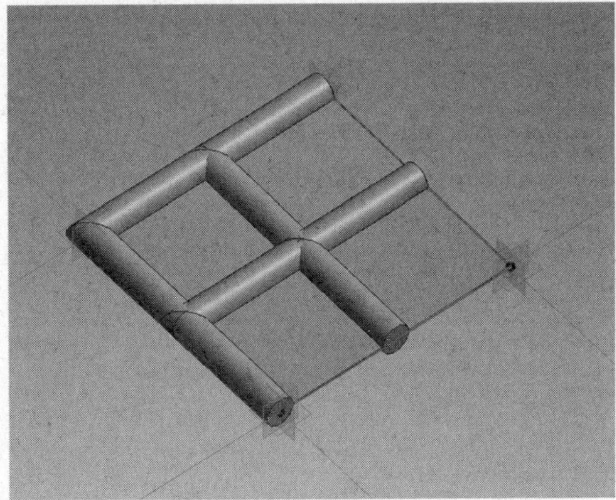

FIGURE 12.76
The simple panel is nested into the divided surface of the host panel.

8. In the `c12-Limit-Panel-Project.rfa` file, select the pattern and divided surface. From the Type Selector, select the name Limit-Panel-2.

   Your new panel family will be listed under the pattern within which it was designed. It will take a few seconds for the software to replace the pattern with the real geometry of the panel. But observe that by nesting the panel inside other panels, you have been able to limit the size and variety of the panels (Figure 12.77).

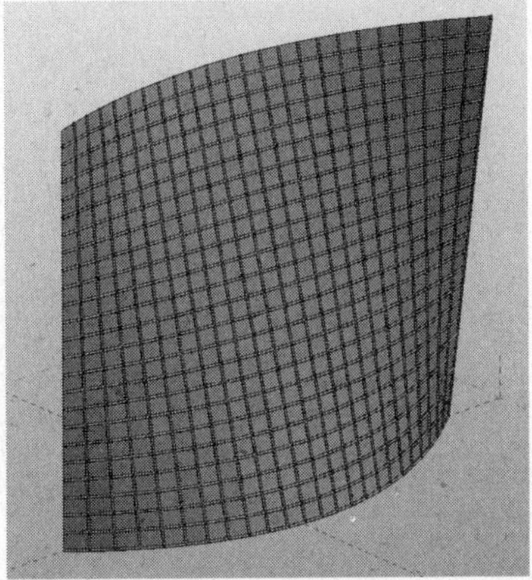

FIGURE 12.77
The host panel containing the nested panel is populated on a divided surface.

Using the Adaptive Component Family

So far, the examples look at using the UV grid to nest in curtain wall pattern–based families; however, there will be situations where you may want to manually place a panel, specifically at border conditions where you may need to construct custom panels. To do this, use the Adaptive

Component functionality that is available to you in the pattern-based curtain panel. This functionality is designed to handle cases where components need the flexibility to adapt to many unique, related conditions. This new functionality also addresses the problems of creating and placing pattern component panels (triangular, pentagonal, hexagonal, and so on) on nonrectangular and irregularly spaced grids. In the following exercise, you will create an adaptive panel and manually place it along the border of a divided surface:

1. Create a simple pattern-based curtain panel family (Curtain Panel Pattern Based.rft or Metric Curtain Panel Pattern Based.rft) and use the rectangular grid pattern. Select each of the four adaptive points and notice that each point has a number from 1 to 4.
2. Select one of the points; from the Properties palette, change the Show Placement Number parameter to Always.
3. Select all the reference planes in the family and choose Create Form; select the Planar Surface option. Save this panel as **`My Adaptive Panel.rfa`**.
4. Download and open the file `c12-StitchSurface-Project.rfa` from this book's web page.
5. Load the `My Adaptive Panel.rfa` family into `c12-StitchSurface-Project.rfa`.

   Notice that in `c12-StitchSurface-Project.rfa` the UV grid has been enabled, as well as the nodes at the intersections of the UV grid (Figure 12.78). You will use these nodes to snap your panel.

FIGURE 12.78
Sample surface with nodes displayed

6. Locate the Families category in your Project Browser and expand the Curtain Panel tree. You will find the My Adaptive Panel type in this list. Drag it into the 3D view window.
7. With the panel attached at your mouse pointer, place the pointer onto one of the nodes on the subdivided surface to place the first point. Place the remaining points onto the corresponding nodes, as shown in Figure 12.79.

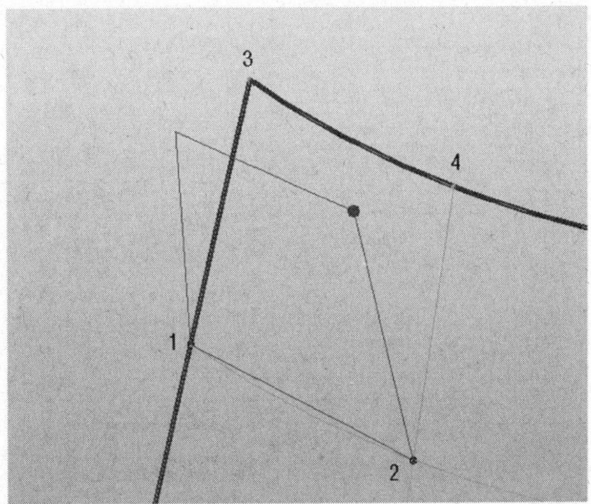

FIGURE 12.79
Placing an adaptive panel into a divided surface

Observe how the panel will adapt based on its placement in the surface division.

Scheduling Pattern-Based Panels

Now that you have completed the design of your pattern-based curtain wall families, you may want to use Revit scheduling capabilities to assess the quantity and area of panels in your conceptual curtain wall system. This can be useful for calculating approximate costs at the early stages of design. You can schedule panels that have been applied to an in-place mass directly in the project environment; however, it is not possible to schedule panels in the conceptual design environment. You will first have to load your concept mass into a project, where you will then be able to schedule the panels. In this example, you will open a sample file, load it into a project, and then create a schedule, which will list all the panels that make up your conceptual curtain wall:

1. Download and open the file `c12-Square-Panel-Schedule.rfa` from this book's web page.
2. Start a new project using either `default.rte` or `MetricDefault.rte`; then load the file `c12-Square-Panel-Schedule.rfa` into your new project.
3. From the Massing & Site tab in the ribbon, click the Place Mass button and select c12-Square-Panel-Schedule from the Type Selector. Make sure that the Place On Workplane icon is selected in the Placement panel, and place the massing component in the Level 1 floor plan.
4. Open the default 3D view to view your model (Figure 12.80).
5. From the View tab in the ribbon, click Schedules and then click Schedules/Quantities. This will open the New Schedule dialog box. Select Curtain Panels from the Category list and click OK.

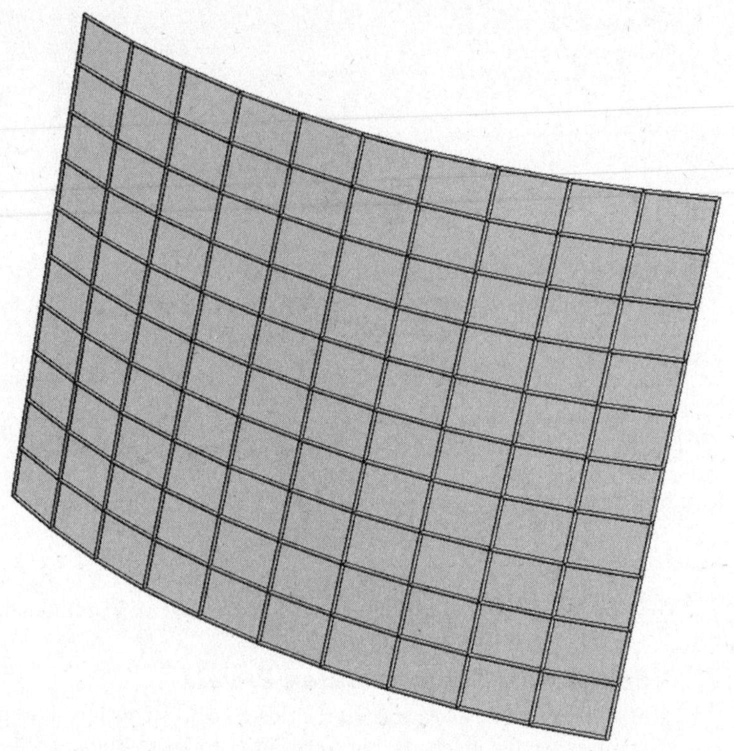

FIGURE 12.80
A conceptual curtain wall is loaded into a project and placed using Place Mass.

6. You will now define the fields that will be included within your panel schedule. Choose Family in the left column and click the Add button to add this field to your schedule. Next, add Area and then Count.
7. Click the Sorting/Grouping tab and check the options for Grand Totals and Itemize Every Instance.
8. Click the Formatting tab and select the Area field. Make sure the Calculate Totals option is selected. Do the same for Count.
9. Click OK, and your schedule will be created. If you scroll down to the bottom of the schedule, the total area and the number of custom panels in your conceptual curtain wall will be listed.

The Bottom Line

Use extended modeling techniques for basic walls. Walls in Revit are made from layers of materials that can represent everything from generic placeholders for design layouts to complete assemblies representative of actual construction.

Master It How can you customize the profile of a wall?

Create stacked walls. Exterior walls are usually composed of several combinations of materials with varying thicknesses. These various wall types can be combined into a single entity called a stacked wall.

Master It How do you create a stacked wall?

Create simple curtain walls. A curtain wall is an assembly of parts including curtain grids, panels, and mullions. They can be created in predefined types with regular horizontal and vertical spacing along with specific panel and mullion types.

Master It How do you add a door to a curtain wall?

Create complex curtain walls. The Revit conceptual massing environment can be used to create complex curtain wall configurations. Pattern-based panel families can be loaded into the massing environment and populated on a divided surface. These populated surfaces can then be loaded and placed in a project model for documentation and scheduling.

Master It How do you create a complex divided surface?

Chapter 13

Modeling Floors, Ceilings, and Roofs

Floors, ceilings, and roofs, which may seem like simple building components, can sometimes prove to be difficult to model and detail in your project designs. In the previous chapter, you learned about creating and customizing walls. Many of the objects in this chapter depend on walls and curtain walls to define their boundaries, but both groups of object types are system families that use a built-up set of layers that are applied to a sketched form. Whereas walls mostly rely on a linear path, floors, ceilings, and roofs rely on a boundary sketch.

In this chapter, you'll learn to:

- Understand floor modeling methods
- Model various floor finishes
- Create ceilings
- Understand roof modeling methods
- Work with advanced shape editing for floors and roofs

Understanding Floor Types

Floors are likely to be one of the first sketch-based elements you will encounter in Autodesk® Revit® software. Some families in the default libraries are floor hosted, so you must first have a floor before you'll be able to place such components. Consequently, floor-hosted components will be deleted if the floor that hosts them is deleted. You can find a more detailed discussion on creating families in Chapter 14, "Designing with the Family Editor," but for now let's review the fundamental types of floors that can exist in a project: a floor, a structural floor, a floor by face, and a pad.

Modeling a Floor

The traditional floor object is a sketch-based element that comprises any number of material layers as defined by the user. The top of the floor object is its reference with respect to the level on which it was created. As such, changes to a floor's structure will affect its depth down and away from the level. You can start modeling floors with generic types, which contain a single layer, and then change the generic floors to more specific assemblies later in the development of your project. You can use floors in a variety of ways to meet the needs of a specific phase of design. In early phases, for example, you can create a floor type to represent the combined floor, structure, plenum, and ceiling assemblies of a building. Commonly referred to as the *sandwich*, a sample is shown in Figure 13.1.

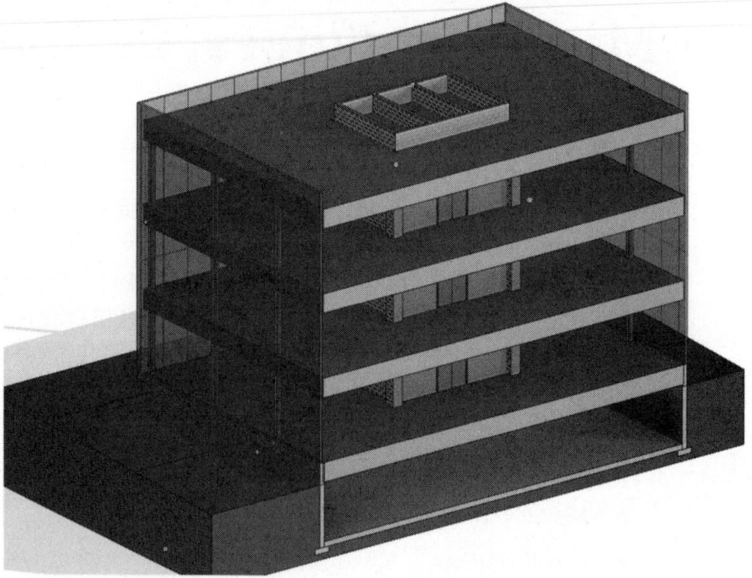

FIGURE 13.1
You can use a single floor type to show the entire floor/ceiling sandwich in early design.

During intermediate phases of design, you can model ceilings so the floor types can include only the floor and a structural layer, as shown in Figure 13.2. Columns may be created, but more precise horizontal structural framing may not be modeled yet. The layer within the floor type represents an assumption of the maximum depth of structural framing.

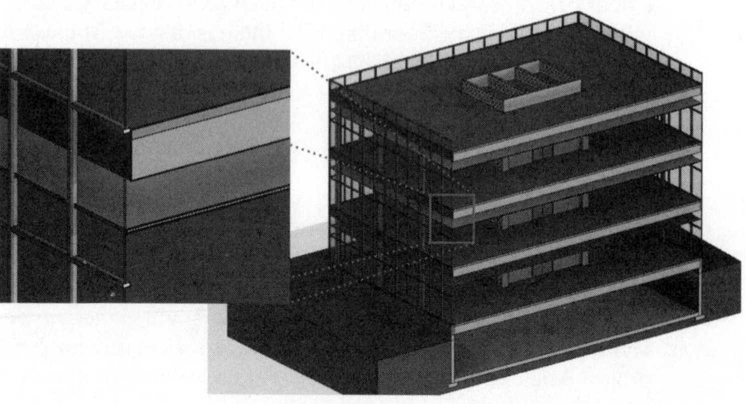

FIGURE 13.2
This floor assembly includes an assumption for the depth of structural framing.

In later phases of documentation approaching and including construction, floors should be modeled as close to actual conditions as possible. You should accommodate detailed finish conditions for floors as well as coordination with a resolved structural system. Accurate modeling of these conditions will help support consistent quantity takeoffs and interference detection. Figure 13.3 illustrates an example of a more accurate floor slab.

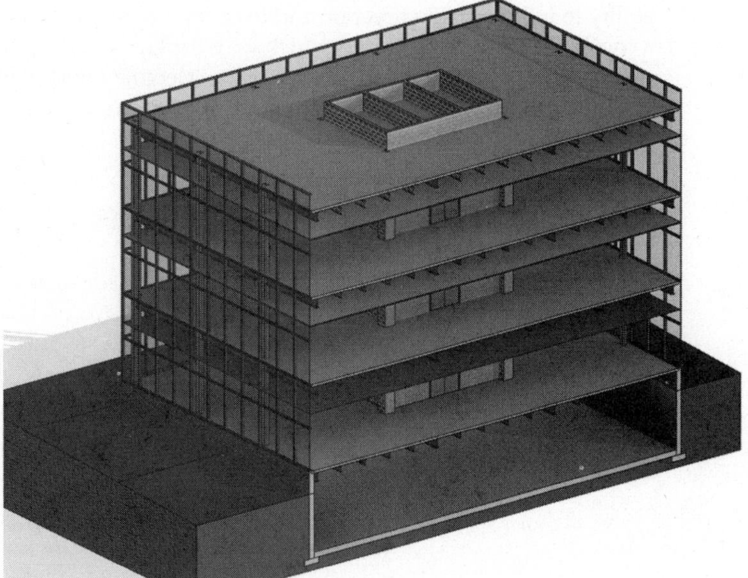

FIGURE 13.3
Floor assemblies for construction should be accurate and separate from structural framing.

These floor assembly types are offered as suggestions for the sake of increased productivity. As such, they should be used with care, especially when performing quantity takeoffs for estimating. For example, the *area* of a floor will be the only accurate value to be extracted from a floor sandwich model in early design, not a volumetric material takeoff. For more information on the use of models by other disciplines, we recommend referring to the AIA document *G202-2013 Project BIM Protocol Form*, which lists authorized uses of a model at various levels of development. You can learn more about AIA contract documents at `www.aia.org`.

COLLABORATION AND THE OWNERSHIP OF FLOORS

Whether or not you are working under an integrated project delivery (IPD) contract, the so-called ownership of floors should be carefully considered for the collaboration process between an architect and a structural engineer. Floors can be one of the most contentious elements of a building design because they can be simultaneously construed as architecture and structure.

The model element author (MEA) for floors should be discussed and clearly defined for each phase in your project BIM execution plan. Remember that element ownership can pass between the architect and the structural engineer when it is appropriate for a given phase. For example, the architect may choose to be the MEA for floors in schematic design but pass ownership to the structural engineer in design development and construction documentation.

With a basic understanding of floors as elements of the building, let's look at some properties of floors that allow expanded uses in the project model. These properties and floor types can help expand your use of floor systems to create better documentation.

Creating a Structural Floor

The structural floor is similar to a traditional floor but has structural functionality, such as the ability to indicate span direction and to contain structural profiles. For example, you can specify a composite metal deck profile, which will display in sections and details generated within your project. You can create a structural floor by selecting the floor element and clicking the instance property called Structural (Figure 13.4). Because Structural is an instance property, any floor type can become a structural floor.

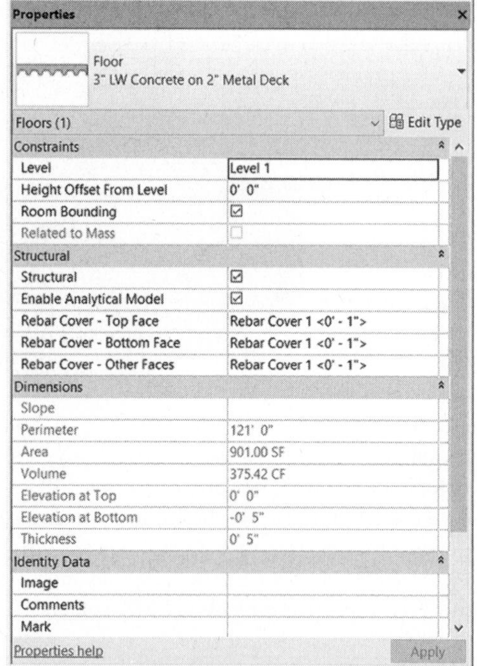

FIGURE 13.4 Structural parameter in a floor's instance properties

After you select the Structural parameter check box for a floor, you can edit its type properties to add a structural decking layer. Let's create a new structural floor so you can explore how this is done:

1. Open the file `c13-Floors-Start.rvt` or `c13-Floors-Start-Metric.rvt` from the book's web page (`www.sybex.com/go/masteringrevit2017`), and activate the Level 3 floor plan.
2. Go to the Architecture tab in the ribbon, and from the Build panel, select Floor ➤ Floor: Structural.
3. In the Draw panel of the contextual tab in the ribbon, make sure your options are set to Boundary Line with the Pick Walls tool, as shown in Figure 13.5.

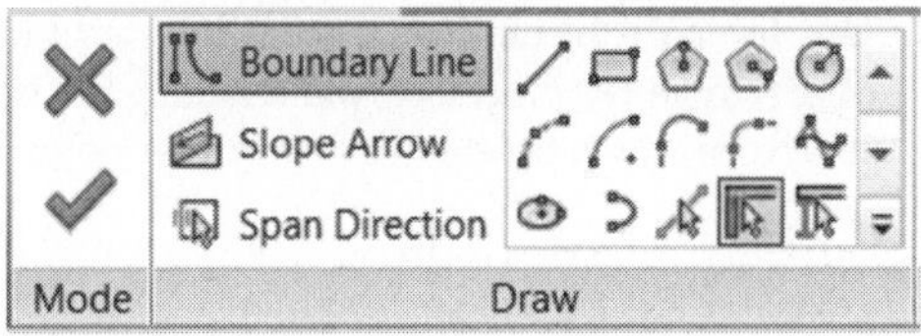

FIGURE 13.5
Use Pick Walls mode to draw boundary lines.

4. In the Options bar, specify an offset of **0′-3″** (**75** mm).

   This setting will place the floor boundary just within the inner face of the curtain wall mullions because the location line of the curtain wall is at the center of the mullions that are 5″ (125 mm) deep.

5. Begin picking the exterior curtain walls by selecting one of the north-south–oriented walls first.

   The first wall that you pick will determine the span direction of the structural floor. You can change this at any time by picking the Span Direction tool from the Draw panel and then selecting one of the boundary lines in the floor sketch.

6. Pick the remaining exterior walls to complete the floor boundary.

   After you finish defining the boundary lines of the floor, you will create a new floor type. If the Properties palette isn't open, press Ctrl+1 on the keyboard, type **PP**, or click the Properties icon in the ribbon.

7. Click Edit Type in the Properties palette. Select Generic - 12″ or Generic - 300 mm as the active type and click Duplicate. Name the new type **Structural Slab**.

8. In the Edit Type dialog box, click the Edit button in the Structure row to open the Edit Assembly dialog box.

9. In the Edit Assembly dialog box, find the layer of the assembly that represents the generic floor you duplicated. This should be row 2. Change the material of this layer to Concrete – Cast-In-Place Concrete and change the thickness to **0′-6″** (**150** mm).

10. Select row 3 and click the Insert button. There should now be four layers. Select the new row 3 and set its function to Structural Deck [1].

    The new Structural Deck properties appear below the layers, as shown in Figure 13.6.

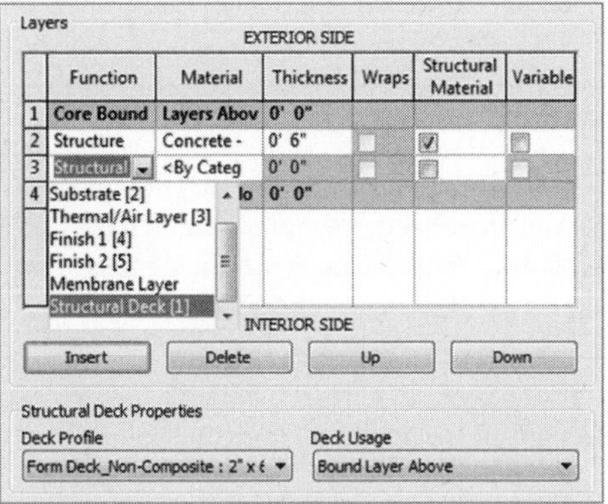

FIGURE 13.6
Setting a layer's function to Structural Deck exposes additional options.

11. The value for Deck Profile should default to Form Deck_Non-Composite: 2′ × 6″ or M_Form Deck_Non-Composite: 50 × 150 mm, but this depends on whether you have a structural deck profile loaded into your project.

    If you don't have a structural deck profile loaded, finish the floor, select the Insert tab of the ribbon, and click Load Family. In your default Autodesk content library, find the `Profiles` folder and open the `Metal Deck` subfolder. Pick an appropriate deck profile and click Open to load it. Select the Structural Slab floor and click Edit Type in the Properties palette to continue the exercise.

12. Activate Wall Section 1 and you should see the completed slab at Level 3.

    Notice that you do not see the details of the structural decking when Detail Level is set to Coarse.

    If you activate the callout at Level 3 (Detail At Level 3), you will see the structural decking because the callout's detail level is set to Medium. This difference is illustrated in Figure 13.7.

FIGURE 13.7
Structural floor as represented in Coarse detail level (left) and Medium detail level (right)

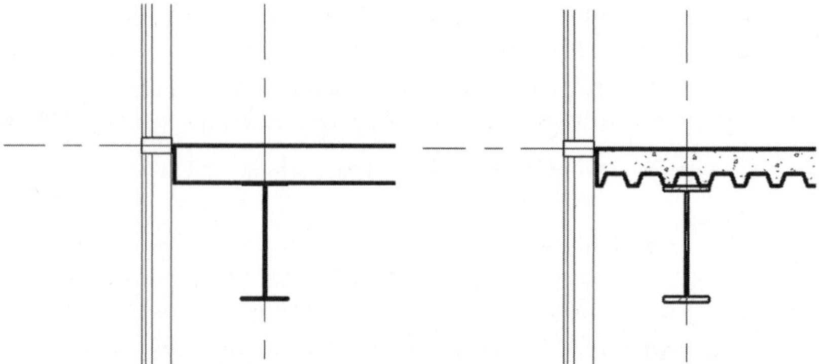

CANTILEVERED METAL DECKING

In Figure 13.7, you can see the metal decking profile shown in a section view; however, when metal deck runs parallel to a support member, the decking cannot cantilever as shown by default when you model a floor. You must customize these slab edges in order to show a more accurate representation of the decking condition.

One easy way to accomplish this is to use the Cantilever options when you are creating or editing the boundary lines of the floor. If you are using a floor type that includes a Structural Deck layer, select any of the boundary lines and you will see Cantilever settings in the Options bar.

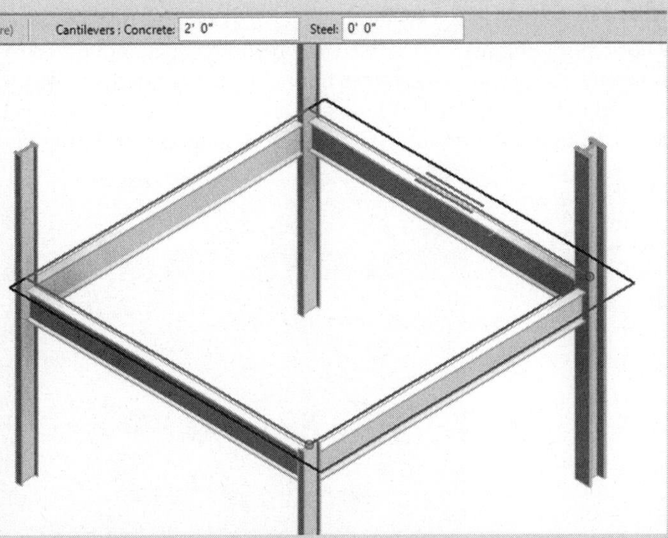

If you define the boundary line at the centerline of the supporting member, define the cantilever value for Steel to be 0′-0″ (0 mm) and Concrete to the value appropriate to your engineered design. Sometimes these values may need to be negative distances to achieve the desired cantilever condition. When you finish the sketch and observe the slab edge in a section view, you will see a more accurate representation of the appropriate construction technique for the floor element.

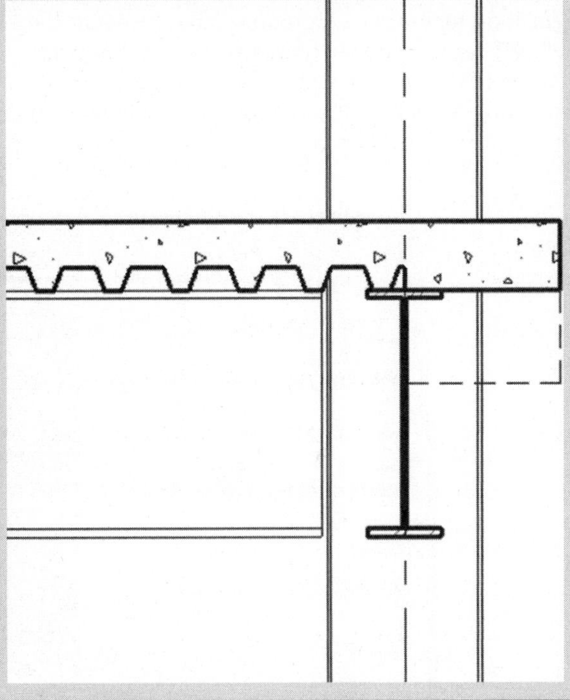

Modeling Floor by Face

This floor modeling method is used when you have generated an in-place mass or loaded a mass family. After you assign mass floors to a mass, you can use the floor-by-face method to assign and manage updates to floors, as shown in Figure 13.8. This type of face-based modeling is discussed in greater detail in Chapter 8, "Advanced Modeling and Massing."

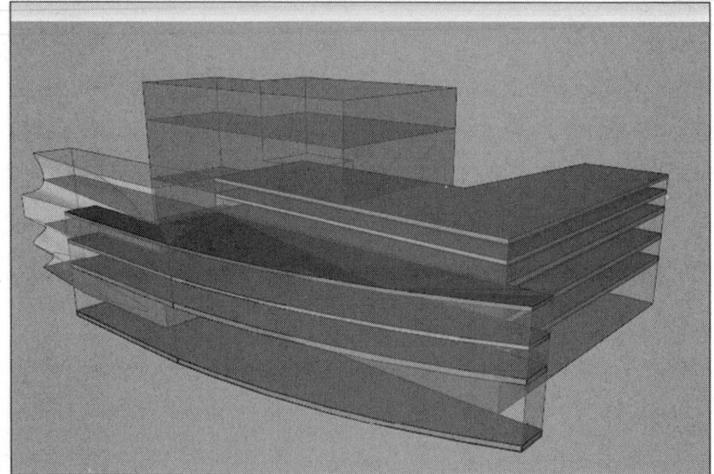

FIGURE 13.8
You can use the Floor By Face tool to manage slabs in more complex building designs.

Defining a Pad

A pad is technically not a floor but has properties similar to a floor. What differentiates a pad is its ability to cut into a toposurface or ground plane and define the lowest limits of a building's basement or cellar. If desired, you can configure the pad to represent a slab on grade, as shown in Figure 13.9. The Pad tool can be found on the Model Site panel of the Massing & Site tab. If you don't see this tab, you can access it by clicking the Application button and choosing Options ➤ User Interface.

For a more detailed exercise on creating building pads, refer to Chapter 3, "The Basics of the Toolbox."

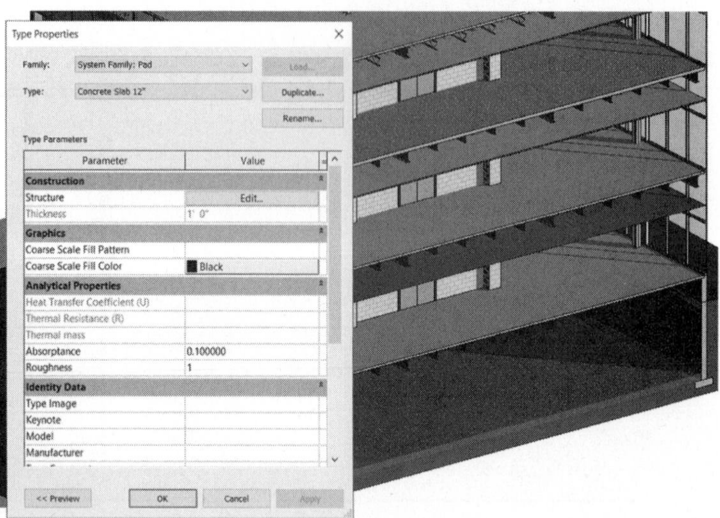

FIGURE 13.9
You can configure a pad as a slab on grade for a basement.

Sketching for Floors, Ceilings, and Roofs

Because floors, ceilings, and roofs are sketch-based objects, the method you use when creating the boundary lines is critical to the behavior of the element to those around it. The recommended method is to use the Pick Walls option, as shown earlier in Figure 13.5.

By selecting the walls to generate the sketch for the roof, you are creating a parametric relationship between the walls and the roof. If the design of your building changes and the wall position is modified, the roof will follow that change and adjust to the new wall position without any intervention from you (Figure 13.10).

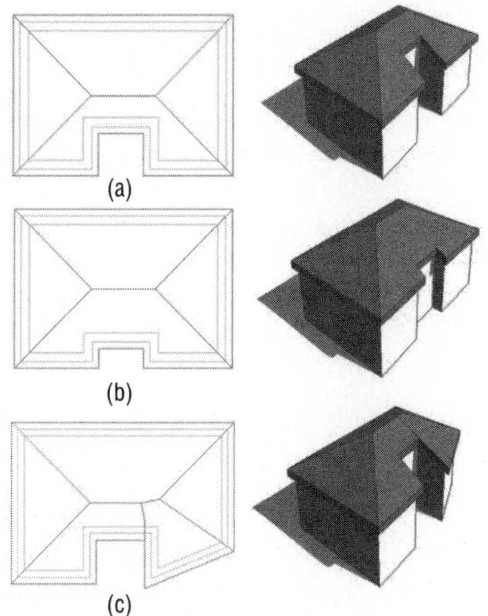

FIGURE 13.10
Using the Pick method: (a) original roof; (b) the entrance wall position has changed, and the roof updates automatically; (c) the angle of the wall to the right of the entrance has changed, and the roof changes to a new shape.

Also notice in Figure 13.10 that the illustrated roof was generated with overhangs beyond the exterior faces of the walls. You can specify an overhang or offset value for a floor, ceiling, or roof in the Options bar *before* picking walls to define the sketch.

If your building design is using curtain walls, be careful with the location lines of these walls. The location line of a curtain wall is defined relative to the offsets specified in the mullion and panel families that make up the curtain wall type. As discussed in Chapter 12, "Creating Walls and Curtain Walls," you have many options when defining the relative location line of your curtain wall types. Refer to the exercise in the section "Creating a Structural Floor" earlier in this chapter for an example of picking curtain walls with an offset based on a centered location line.

Modeling Slab Edges

Slab Edge is a tool that allows you to create thickened portions of slabs typically located at the boundaries of floors. A slab edge type is composed of a profile family and a material assignment. It is important that the material assignment of the slab edge match that of the floor to which you will apply the slab edge in order to ensure proper joining of geometry. Let's explore the application of a slab edge to a floor at grade:

1. Open the file `c13-Design-Floor.rvt` from the book's web page and activate the 3D view named Floors Only.
2. Click the Architecture tab in the ribbon and select Floor ➢ Slab Edge from the Build panel.

   This tool is also available from the Structure tab.
3. If necessary, orbit the 3D view so that you can see the bottom of the lowest floor slab. Pick all four bottom edges of the floor slab at the level named Ground.
4. Activate the view Section 1 and you will see the slab edge applied to and joined with the floor, as shown in Figure 13.11.

   Remember that the material in the slab edge type must match the material in the floor type properties for the geometry to join properly.

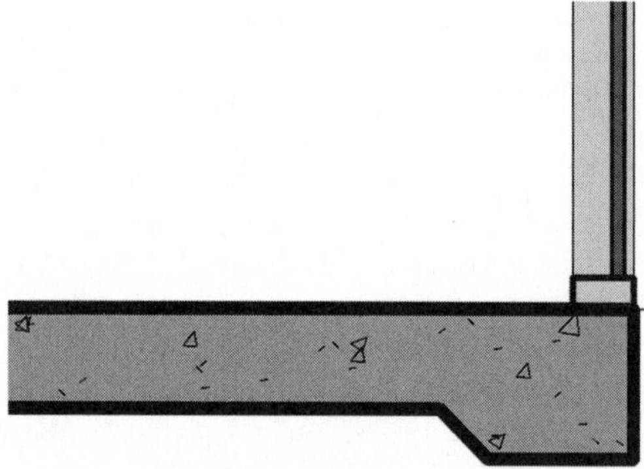

FIGURE 13.11
Thickened slab edge applied to the bottom of a floor

MAKING EARLY DESIGN MODELS

When we first started implementing Revit in early phases of the design, the need to emulate drafting methods was readily apparent. As a design idea for a building was formulated, we would usually make some generic assumptions about more complex systems in order to make the overall design intent as clear as possible. How do you translate this so-called fuzzy design into a building information modeling process?

To bridge the gap between fuzzy design and a highly accurate model, we created a single floor type that contained assumptions not only for the floor but also for the structure and ceiling assembly below. This larger assembly gives a graphic emphasis to building sections without the burden of modeling three different systems before they are close to being resolved. The design floor type also gave us the opportunity to create custom slab edges that are voids instead of solids—voids that approximate a design for ceiling shade pockets or other interface conditions.

Creating a Custom Floor Edge

You can apply a great deal of flexibility to a floor assembly in early design. As we described previously, you can create a floor for early design phases that accommodates the floor, structure, plenum, and ceiling in a single floor type. You can also apply a customized edge to this type of assembly for more creative soffit conditions at exterior walls, as shown in Figure 13.12.

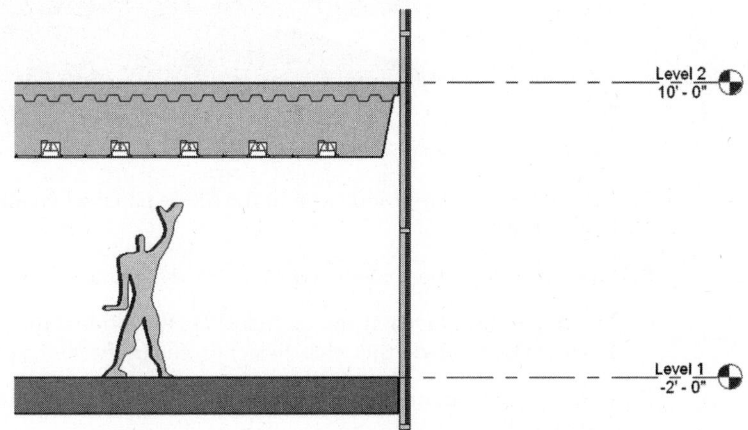

FIGURE 13.12 Customized edge applied to a floor assembly in early design

Let's run through a short exercise so you can practice this skill:

1. Open the file `c13-Design-Floor.rvt` from the book's web page or continue with the file from the previous exercise and activate the view Section 1.
2. Select the floor at Level 1 and open the Properties palette. Change the type to Design Floor Sandwich.
3. Begin a new in-place component by going to the Architecture tab and selecting Component ➢ Model In-Place from the Build panel.
4. Set the Family Category to Floors and specify the name as **Floor Edge-L1**.

   You are now in Family Editing mode, and the ribbon will have different tabs and panels.
5. Click the Create tab and select Void Forms ➢ Void Sweep from the Forms panel.
6. Click the Pick Path tool from the Sweep panel and choose all four top edges at the perimeter of the floor at Level 1.

   You can activate the 3D view Floors Only to complete the picking of all four edges, as shown in Figure 13.13.

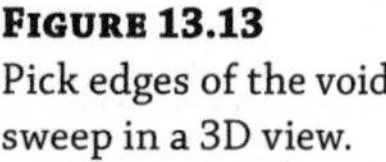

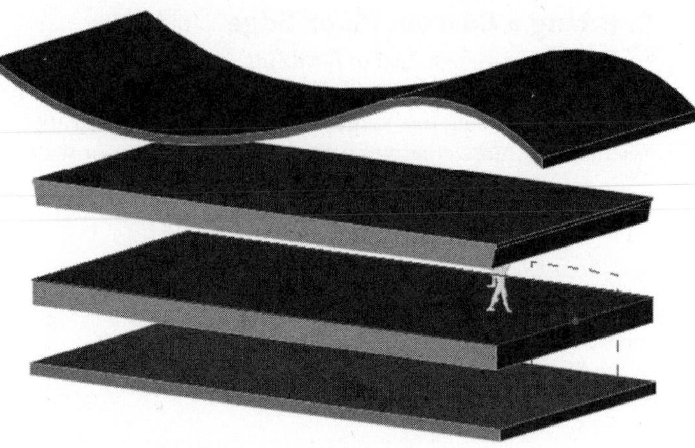

FIGURE 13.13
Pick edges of the void sweep in a 3D view.

7. Click the Finish Edit Mode icon in the Mode panel when all four edges of the floor have been picked.

8. Open the Properties palette if it isn't already visible.

   You might need to reactivate the Select Profile mode if the Properties palette lists only Family: Floors. To do this, click Select Profile in the contextual tab of the ribbon.

9. In the Profile parameter, select SD Sandwich Edge : Type 1 from the drop-down list, as shown in Figure 13.14.

   The SD Sandwich Edge profile has been preloaded for the convenience of this exercise. If you would like to explore how this profile was created, expand the Families tree in the Project Browser and find Profiles ➤ SD Sandwich Edge. Right-click it and choose Edit from the context menu.

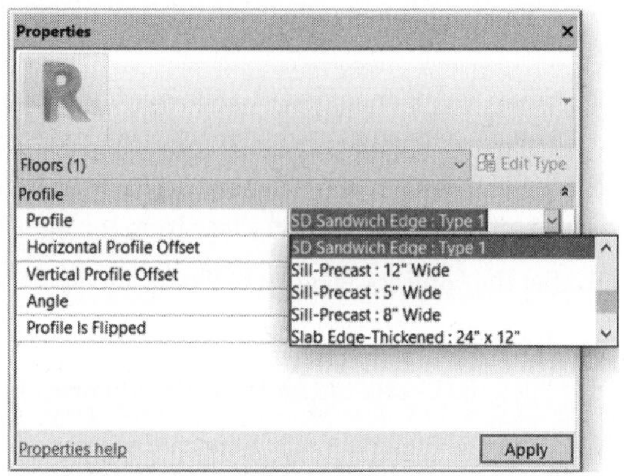

FIGURE 13.14
Select a loaded profile family for the void sweep.

10. You may need to adjust the orientation of the profile so that it faces in toward the floor, as shown in Figure 13.15. To do so, make sure the profile is selected, and click the Flip button in the Options bar or check the Profile Is Flipped option in the Properties palette.

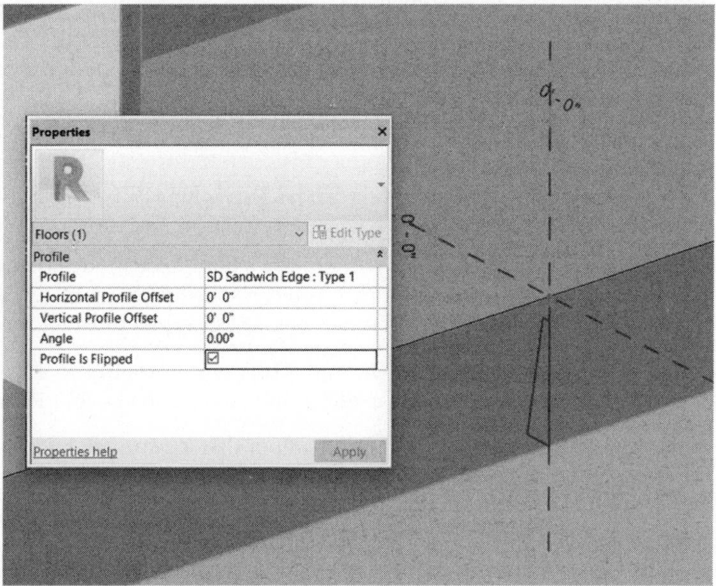

FIGURE 13.15
Make sure the sweep profile is facing toward the floor.

11. Switch to the Modify | Sweep tab in the ribbon and click the Finish Edit Mode icon from the Mode panel.
12. Switch to the Modify | Void Sweep tab in the ribbon and select Cut ➤ Cut Geometry in the Geometry panel. Pick the void sweep and then the floor at Level 1.
13. Click Finish Model in the In-Place Editor panel at the right end of the ribbon.

Activate the Section 1 view, and you should see that the floor sandwich assembly at Level 1 has been customized in a similar way to the floor at Level 2 (Figure 13.16). You can experiment with adding embellishing detail components as shown in the section.

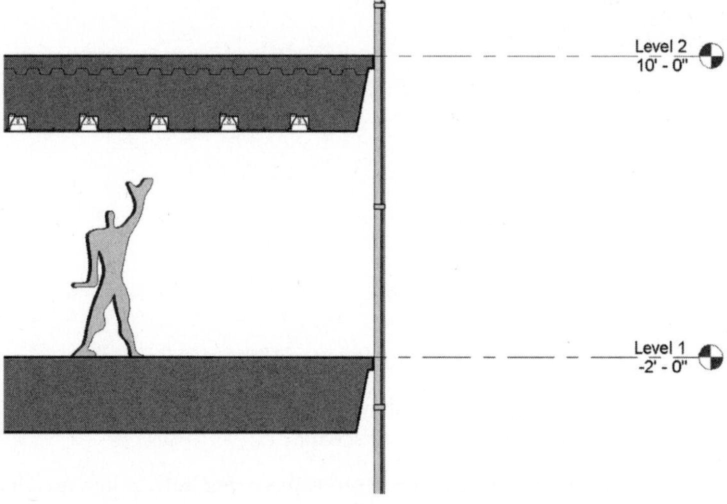

FIGURE 13.16
The edge of the floor sandwich assembly for Level 1 has been customized.

Modeling Floor Finishes

You can apply floor finishes in a variety of ways. Most methods are based on the thickness of the finish material. For example, a thin finish such as carpet might be applied with the Split Face and Paint tools, whereas a thicker finish such as mortar-set stone tile might be a separate floor type.

Using a Split Face for Thin Finishes

One of the easiest ways to divide a floor surface for thin finishes is to use the Split Face and Paint tools. This method will require a floor to be modeled and an appropriate material defined with at least a surface pattern. You can schedule finishes applied with the Paint tool only through Material Takeoff schedules. Let's explore this method with a quick exercise:

1. Open the file `c13-Design-Floor.rvt` from the book's web page or continue with the file from the previous exercise and activate the Level 1 floor plan.

   You will see an area of the floor that is bounded by a wall and two reference planes.

2. Click the Modify tab in the ribbon, activate the Split Face tool from the upper-right corner of the Geometry panel, and pick the floor in the Level 1 floor plan.
3. Draw a rectangle in front of the three interior walls, as shown in Figure 13.17.

   You can constrain—or lock—the sketch lines to the interior walls, reference planes, and floor edge. You may do so in this exercise, but use constraints sparingly in larger projects to avoid slower model performance and updating calculation time.

   Also notice that you generated a complete rectangular sketch instead of only three bounding lines. You do not need to draw the boundary line at the edge of the floor; however, if you don't include that line and the floor shape is modified in the future, the split face may be deleted because it is no longer a closed-loop sketch.

FIGURE 13.17
Sketch a rectangular boundary with the Split Face tool.

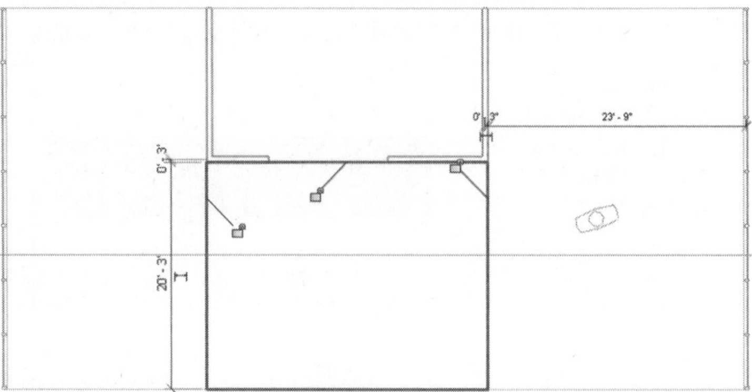

4. Click the Finish Edit Mode icon in the Mode panel.
5. Return to the Modify tab in the ribbon and activate the Paint tool in the Geometry panel, just below the Split Face tool.
6. In the Material Browser, type **carpet** in the filter search at the top.

This will minimize your choices, allowing you to select Carpet Tile from the filtered list (Figure 13.18).

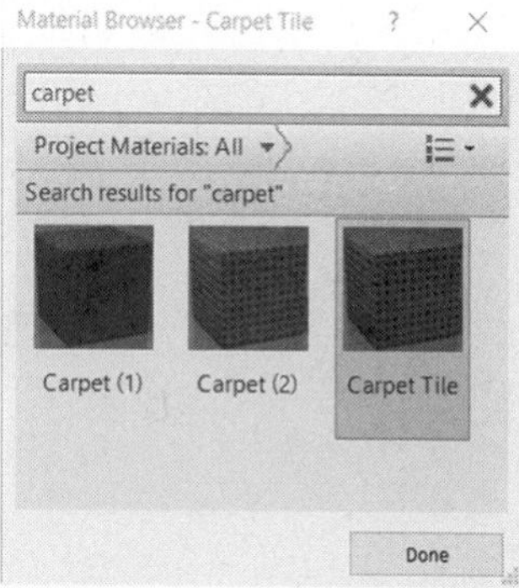

FIGURE 13.18 Choosing the Carpet Tile material

7. In the Level 1 floor plan, click near the edge of the split face you created earlier to assign the material.

   The result should look like Figure 13.19.

8. Click the Done button in the Material Browser to exit the Paint command.

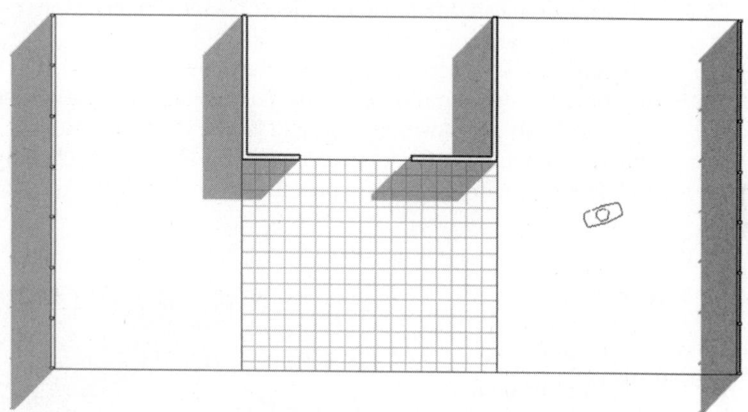

FIGURE 13.19 Completed application of carpet tile material to a split face on a floor

Modeling Thick Finishes

Thicker finish materials such as tile, stone pavers, or terrazzo can be applied as unique floor types and modeled where required. For large areas of finish such as a public atrium or airport terminal, you can assign these materials within the layers of a floor assembly. When you need to add smaller areas of thick floor finishes, you may encounter one of two scenarios: with a depressed floor and without.

In areas such as bathrooms, a thick-set tile floor may require the structural slab to be depressed in order to accommodate the thickness of the finish material. In Figure 13.20, the main floor object has been cut with an opening at the inside face of the walls. Another floor has been modeled with a negative offset value to accommodate the thickness of the tile material, and the tile has been placed as a unique floor element.

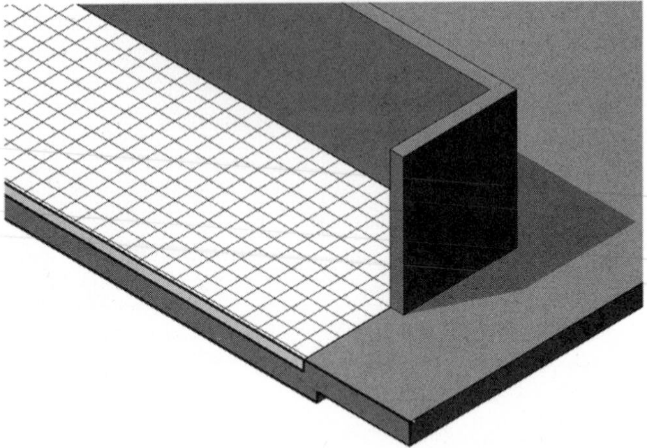

FIGURE 13.20
The thick tile finish and depressed slab are modeled as separate elements.

If you don't need a finish but just a slab depression, you can create it with an in-place void extrusion. Select the Architecture tab in the ribbon and click Component ➤ Model In-Place. Choose the Floors category and create a void extrusion where you need a slab depression. Remember to use the Cut Geometry tool to cut the void from the floor before finishing the family. As an alternative, you can create a floor-based generic family that contains a parametric void extrusion. You can download the file `c13-Slab-Depression.rfa` as an example of this type of family from the book's web page.

Finally, if the structural requirements allow a thick finish to be applied to a floor without dropping the structural slab, a finish floor element can be modeled directly in place within the structural slab. As shown in Figure 13.21, the tile floor has been graphically embedded in the structural floor using the Join Geometry tool. To do this, click the Modify tab in the ribbon and click Join Geometry. Be sure to pick the finish floor *before* the structural floor or you will get an error.

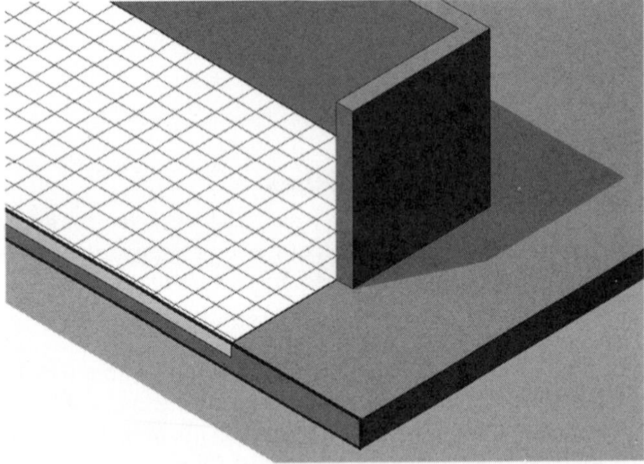

FIGURE 13.21
The thick tile finish floor has been joined with the structural floor.

Creating Ceilings

Ceilings are system families composed of sketch-based elements that also serve as hosts for components such as light fixtures. Like other host elements such as floors and roofs, if a ceiling is deleted, hosted elements on that ceiling are also deleted.

Ceilings are classified as either Basic Ceiling or Compound Ceiling. The Basic Ceiling family does not have a layered assembly and is represented in a section as a single line; however, it does have a material parameter that can display surface patterns in reflected ceiling plans and 3D views. The Compound Ceiling family allows you to define a layered assembly of materials that are visible when displayed in a section view. As with floors, you can change ceiling types by selecting a ceiling in your project and choosing another type from the Type Selector in the Properties palette or with the Match Type Properties tool.

Both the Basic Ceiling and Compound Ceiling types can serve as a host to hosted family components. Ceilings also serve as bounding elements for the volumetric calculation of rooms. This is critical when using environmental analysis programs. For more information about analysis for sustainable design, see Chapter 9, "Conceptual Design and Design Analysis."

You can create a ceiling in one of two ways: automatically or by sketching a boundary. When you select the ceiling tool from the Architecture tab of the ribbon, you can switch between the Automatic Ceiling and Sketch Ceiling modes at the right end of the ribbon.

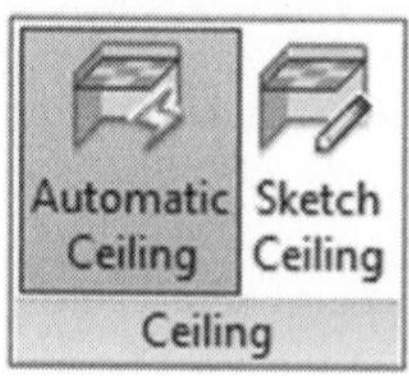

In Automatic Ceiling mode, the software will try to determine the boundaries of a ceiling sketch when you place the cursor inside an enclosed space. If an enclosed space cannot be determined, the cursor will still indicate a circle/slash and you must switch to Sketch Ceiling mode. In this mode, you can use the Pick Walls method as discussed earlier in this chapter to create intelligent relationships with the bounding walls of the ceiling.

CHECK YOUR CEILING HEIGHT

When you are using Automatic Ceiling mode, be aware of the Height Offset From Level property when placing a ceiling within a space. If the Height Offset From Level value is higher than the height of the bounding walls, the ceiling cannot be placed in the space.

Ceilings are best modeled in ceiling plans even though they can be created in a floor plan. When you place a ceiling, its elevation will be based on the level of the current plan with an offset from that level. With the Properties palette open, the Height Offset From Level value can be modified as you create ceilings.

Room Bounding Performance

Floors, ceilings, and roofs all have the ability to be room-bounding elements. This parameter can be found in the instance properties of each object. If you are not using volume calculations for rooms or you don't intend to use the model for environmental analysis, you might consider turning off the Room Bounding parameter in horizontal objects. In larger Revit projects, unnecessary applications of the Room Bounding parameter may lead to reduced model performance.

Understanding Roof Modeling Methods

In today's construction environment, roofs come in a great number of shapes and sizes. They can be as simple as a pitched shed roof or can involve complex double-curved surfaces or intersecting vaults. Once you understand the fundamental concepts, tools, and logic pertaining to roofs, you will be able to design almost any roof shape.

Roofs are similar to floors and ceilings because they are sketch-based elements and can be defined in generic types or with specific material assemblies. You can also change a roof element from one type to another in the same manner as you can a floor or ceiling. A fundamental difference between floors and roofs is that a roof's thickness is generated *above* its referencing level, not below. You can also easily create slopes in roofs by defining slopes in the roof's sketch lines.

In general, roofs can be constructed in four different ways:

- By footprint
- By extrusion
- Modeled in place
- By face

Before we start into how to create the roofs themselves, let's take a look at some of the important instance properties for the roof family. These properties will need to be set properly to get the desired roof type, and they are all found in the Properties palette (Figure 13.22).

Base Level As in other Revit elements, this is the level at which the roof is placed. The roof moves with this level if the level changes height.

Room Bounding When this is checked, the roof geometry has an effect on calculating room area and volume.

Related To Mass This property is active only if a roof has been created with the roof-by-face method (Conceptual Mass tools).

Base Offset From Level This option lowers or elevates the base of the roof relative to the base level.

Cutoff Level Many roof shapes require a combination of several roofs on top of each other—for this you need to cut off the top of a lower roof to accommodate the creation of the next roof in the sequence. Figure 13.23 shows an excellent example of this technique.

FIGURE 13.22
Roof instance properties

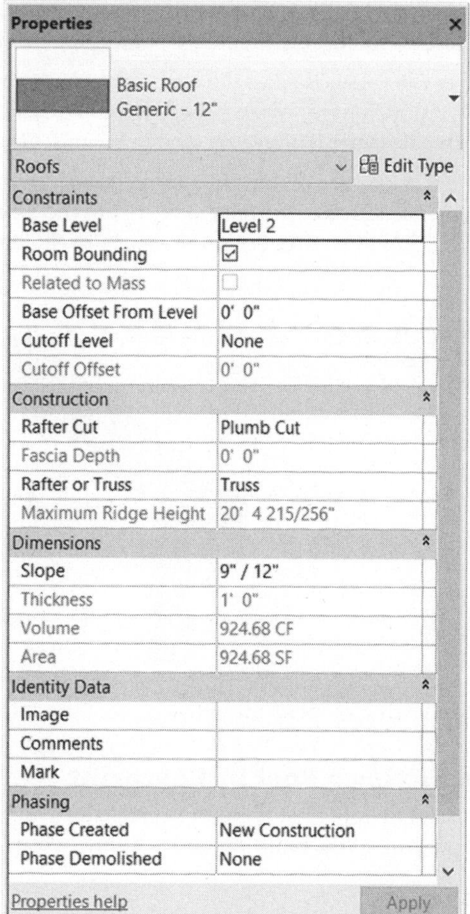

FIGURE 13.23
The cutoff level applied to the main roof, and a secondary roof built on top of the main roof using the cutoff level as a base

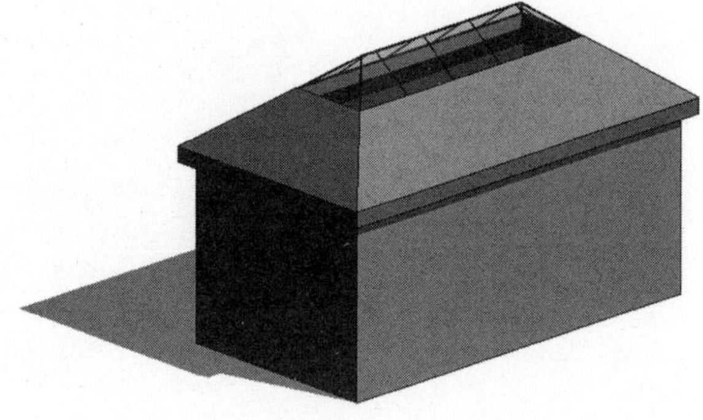

Cutoff Offset When the Cutoff tool is applied, the Cutoff Offset value also becomes active and allows you to set the cutoff distance from the level indicated in the Cutoff Level parameter.

Rafter Cut This defines the eave shape. You can select from Plumb Cut, Two Cut–Plumb, or Two Cut–Square. When either Two Cut–Plumb or Two Cut–Square is selected, the Fascia Depth parameter is activated, and you can set the value for the depth.

Rafter Or Truss With Rafter, the offset of the base is measured from the inside of the wall. If you choose Truss, the plate offset from the base is measured from the outside of the wall. Figure 13.24 illustrates the difference between the Rafter and Truss settings.

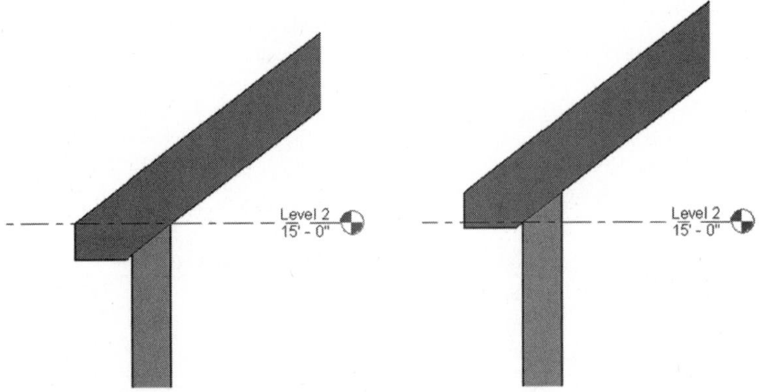

FIGURE 13.24
Rafter setting (left) and Truss setting (right) for roofs

The following sections provide a closer look at the different approaches to modeling roofs.

Constructing a Roof by Footprint

Use the roof-by-footprint method to create any standard roof that more or less follows the shape of the footprint of the building and is a simple combination of roof pitches (Figure 13.25).

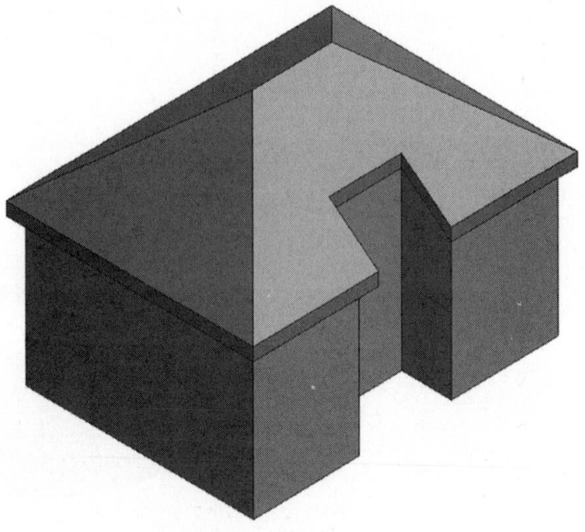

FIGURE 13.25
A simple roof created using the roof-by-footprint method

These roofs are based on a sketched shape that you define in plan view at the soffit level and that can be edited at any time during the development of a project from plan and axon 3D views. The shape can be drawn as a simple loop of lines, using the Line tool, or can be created using the Pick Walls method, which also should result in a closed loop of lines.

To guide you through the creation of a roof by footprint and explain some of the main principles and tools, we offer a brief exercise demonstrating the steps:

1. In a new project using any default template, open a Level 1 plan view and create a building footprint similar to Figure 13.26.

   Make sure the height of the walls is set to Unconnected: 20′-0″ (6000 mm).

Figure 13.26
Sample building outline to be sketched on Level 1

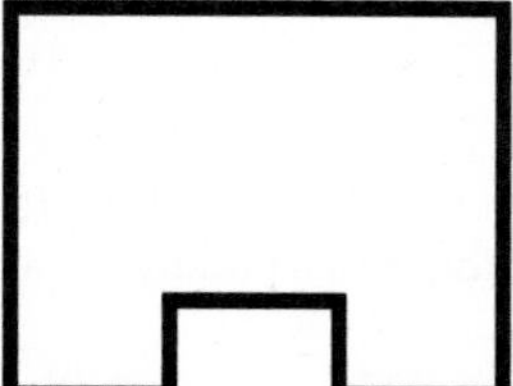

2. Activate the Level 2 plan; then select the Architecture tab in the ribbon and click Roof ➢ Roof By Footprint.
3. From the Draw panel in the Modify | Create Roof Footprint tab, select the Pick Walls tool (this should be the default).
4. When you've chosen to create a roof by footprint, the Options bar displays the following settings (change the Overhang value to **1′-0″** (**300** mm)).

   Overhang: 1' 0" ☑ Defines Slope ☐ Extend into wall (to core)

   To define whether you want a sloped or flat roof, use the Defines Slope check box in the Options bar. The Overhang parameter allows you to define the value of the roof overhang beyond the wall. When the "Extend into wall (to core)" option is checked, the overhang is measured from the wall core. If the option is deselected, the overhang is measured from the exterior face of the wall.
5. After defining these settings, place the cursor over one of the walls (don't click), and using the Tab key, select all connected walls.

   Your display should look like Figure 13.27.

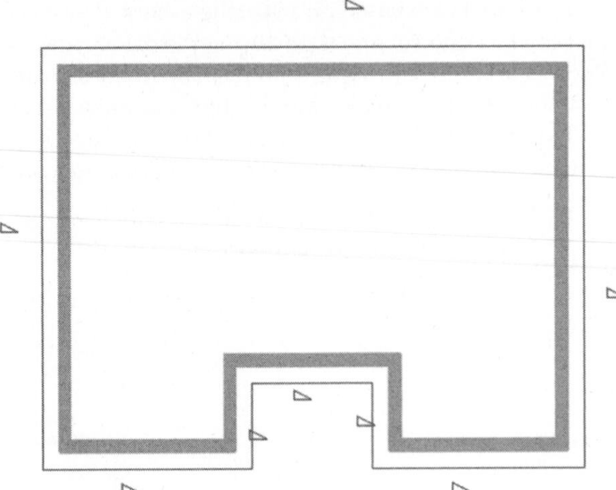

FIGURE 13.27 Roof sketch lines are automatically drawn after Tab+selecting the bounding walls, and they are offset from the walls by the value of the overhang as defined in the Options bar.

6. Select the three walls within the alcove, open the Properties palette, and uncheck the Defines Roof Slope parameter, as shown in Figure 13.28.

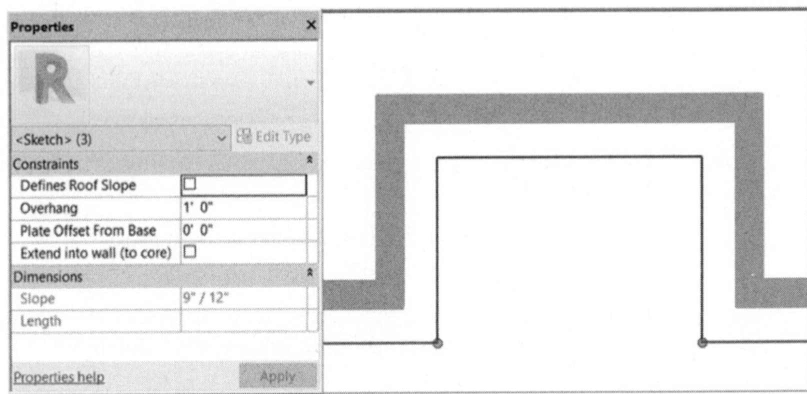

FIGURE 13.28 Uncheck the Defines Roof Slope parameter for two of the roof's boundary lines.

7. Click the Finish Edit Mode icon in the Mode panel of the ribbon. If you are prompted with the question, "Would you like to attach the highlighted walls to the roof?" click the Yes button. Activate a 3D view, and your roof should look like the image in Figure 13.25 shown previously.

If the shape of the roof doesn't correspond to your expectations, you can select the roof and select Edit Footprint from the Mode panel in the Modify | Roofs tab to return to Sketch mode, where you can edit lines, sketch new lines, pick new walls, or modify the slope.

To change the slope definition or angle of individual portions of the roof while editing a roof's footprint, select the sketch line of the roof portion for which you want to change the slope and toggle (check) the Defines Slope button in the Options bar, toggle the Defines Roof Slope parameter in the Properties palette, or right-click and choose Toggle Slope Defining. If you mistakenly made all roof sides with slope but wanted to make a flat roof, you can Tab+select all sketch lines that form the roof shape and clear the Defines Slope box in the Options bar. You can dynamically change the roof slope by selecting the roof and then selecting the blue grips (Figure 13.29) and dragging them either up or down to make the roof pitch steeper or shallower. This is a great way to make quick (although not precise) edits to the roof pitch.

FIGURE 13.29
Select the roof and use the blue grips to dynamically change the roof slope.

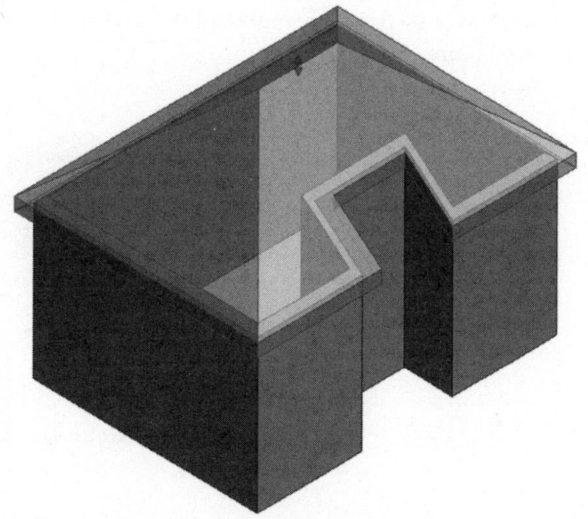

Roof slope can be measured in two different ways: as an angle or as a percentage rise. You can find all slope-measuring options in the Manage tab by selecting Project Units in the Project Settings panel and then selecting Slope to open the Format dialog box (see Figure 13.30). If the current slope value is not in units you want to have (suppose it displays percentage but you want it to display an angle), change the slope units in the Format dialog box—you will not be able to do that while editing the roof slope. Setting it here means specifying the way you measure slopes for the entire project.

FIGURE 13.30
Format dialog box for slopes

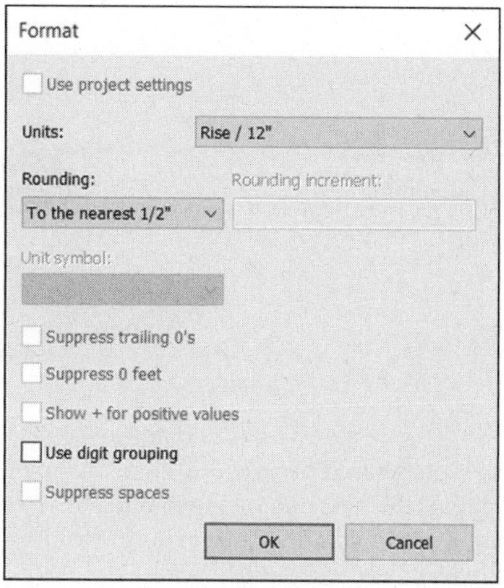

Format
Use project settings
Units: Rise / 12"
Rounding: To the nearest 1/2"
Rounding increment:
Unit symbol:
Suppress trailing 0's
Suppress 0 feet
Show + for positive values
Use digit grouping
Suppress spaces
OK Cancel

Applying a Roof by Extrusion

The roof by extrusion method is best applied for roof shapes that are generated by extrusion of a profile, such as sawtooth roofs, barrel vaults, and waveform roofs. Like the roof-by-footprint method, it is based on a sketch; however, the sketch that defines the shape of the roof is drawn in elevation or section view (not in plan view) and is then extruded along the plan of the building (see Figure 13.31).

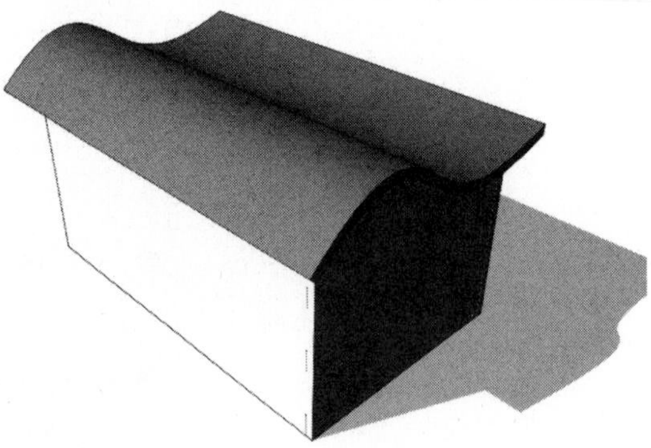

FIGURE 13.31
An extruded spline-shaped roof

Roofs by extrusion do not have an option to follow the building footprint, but that is often needed to accommodate the requirements of the design. To accomplish this, you can use the Vertical Opening tool to trim the edges of an extruded roof relative to the building outline.

Let's briefly review the concept behind the Vertical Opening tool: You create a roof by extrusion by defining a profile in elevation or 3D that is then extruded above the building. The extrusion is usually based on a work plane that is not perpendicular to the building footprint, as shown in Figure 13.32. If the shape of the building is nonrectangular in footprint or the shape of the roof you want to create is not to be rectangular, this tool will let you carve geometry from the roof to match the footprint of the building or get any plan shape you need using a plan sketch.

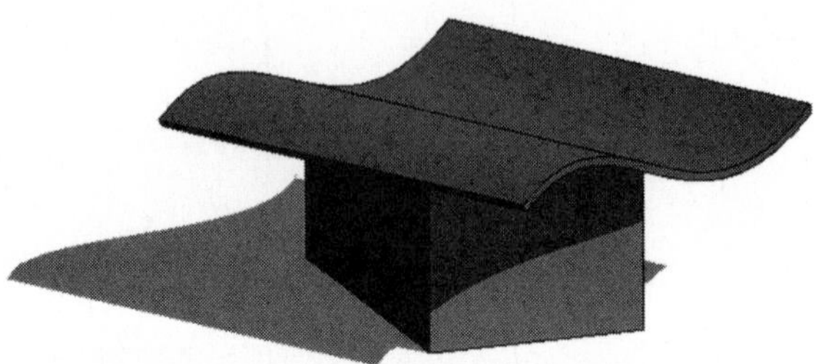

FIGURE 13.32
Extruded roof created at an angle to the building geometry

With sketch-based design, any closed loop of lines creates a positive shape; every loop inside it is negative, the next one inside that negative one will be positive, and so on. In Figure 13.33, a roof by extrusion was drawn at an angle to the underlying walls, but the final roof shape should be limited to a small offset from the walls. To clip the roof to the shape of the building footprint, the Vertical Opening tool was used to draw, in plan view of the roof, a negative shape that will remove the portions of the roof that extend beyond the walls.

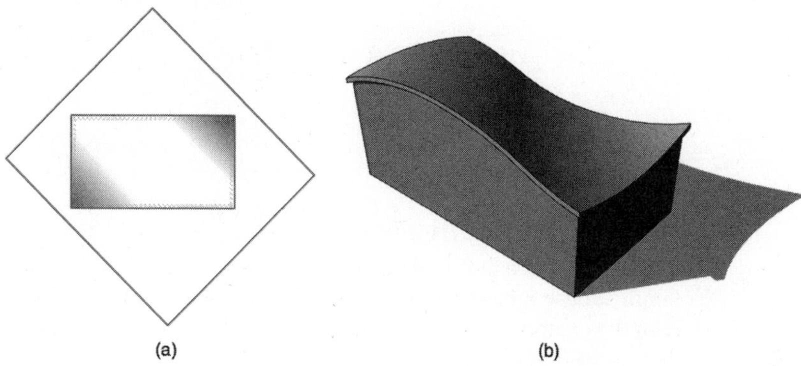

FIGURE 13.33
The Vertical Opening tool with two sketch loops trims the roof to the inner loop.

Roof In-place

The roof in-place technique accommodates roof shapes that cannot be achieved with either of the previously mentioned methods. It is the usual way to model historic roof shapes or challenging roof geometries such as those illustrated in Figure 13.34. The figure shows a barrel roof with a half dome (Extrusion + 1/2 Revolve), a dome roof (Revolve only or Revolve + Extrusion), and a traditional Russian onion dome (Revolve only).

FIGURE 13.34
Examples of modeled in-place roofs

To create an in-place roof, select the Architecture tab in the ribbon and click Component ➤ Model In-Place from the Build panel. Select Roofs from the Family Category list and click OK. While you remain in the In-Place Family editing mode, you can create any roof shape using solids and voids of extrusions, blends, revolves, sweeps, and swept blends (Figure 13.35). More advanced editing techniques are discussed later in this chapter, in the section "Using Advanced Shape Editing with Floors and Roofs."

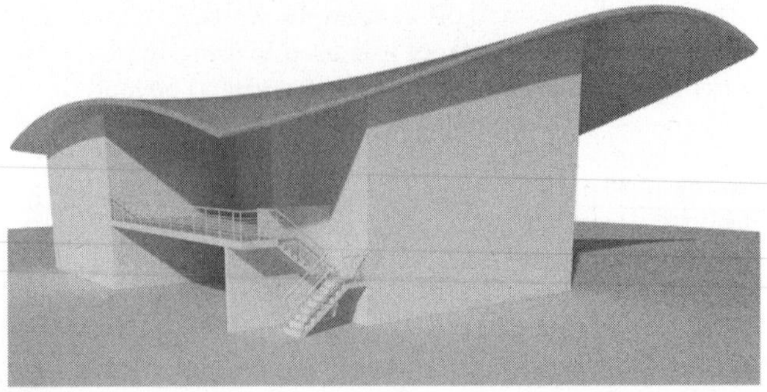

FIGURE 13.35
Organic-shaped roof created using the Swept Blend modeling technique

Creating a Roof by Face

The Roof By Face tool is to be used when you have created an in-place mass or loaded a mass family. These types of roofs are typically more integrated with the overall building geometry than the examples we've shown for in-place roofs. You can find more detailed information about using face-based methods in Chapter 8.

Creating a Sloped Glazing

In Chapter 12, you learned that a curtain wall is just another wall type made out of panels and mullions organized in a grid system. Similarly, sloped glazing is just another type of a roof that has glass as material and mullions for divisions. Using sloped glazing, you can make roof lights and shed lights and use them to design simple framing structures.

To create sloped glazing, make a simple pitched roof, select it, and use the Properties palette to change the type to Sloped Glazing (see Figure 13.36).

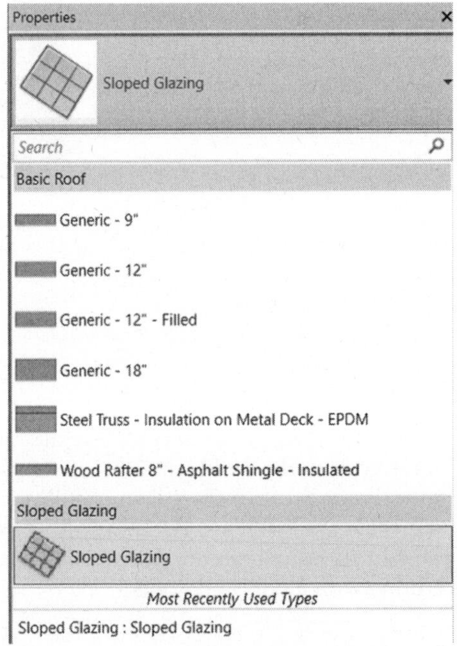

FIGURE 13.36
Sloped Glazing listed in the Properties Window

Once you have done that, activate a 3D view and use the Curtain Grid tool from the Build panel of the Architecture tab in the ribbon to start applying horizontal or vertical grids that define the panel sizes; then you can apply mullions using the Mullion tool in the Build panel. Figure 13.37 illustrates an example of a standard gable roof that has been converted to sloped glazing. Refer to Chapter 12 for more information on using the Curtain Grid and Mullion tools.

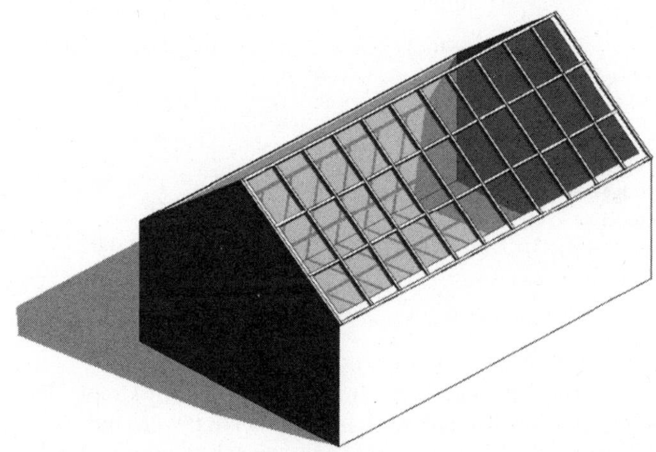

FIGURE 13.37
Sloped glazing is created by switching a standard roof to the Sloped Glazing type and assigning grids and mullions.

Using Slope Arrows

If your design calls for a sloped roof with an unusual footprint that does not easily lend itself to using the Defines Slope property of boundary lines, slope arrows can be added within the sketch of the roof. First, create the sketch lines to define the shape of a roof, but don't check Defines Slope in the Options bar. Instead, choose the Slope Arrow tool from the Draw panel. Draw the slope arrow in the direction you want your roof to pitch. Select the arrow, and in the Properties palette, you can set any of the parameters, as shown in Figure 13.38. The Specify parameter can be set to either Height At Tail or Slope. If you choose Height At Tail, be sure to specify the Height Offset At Head parameter as the end result of the desired slope.

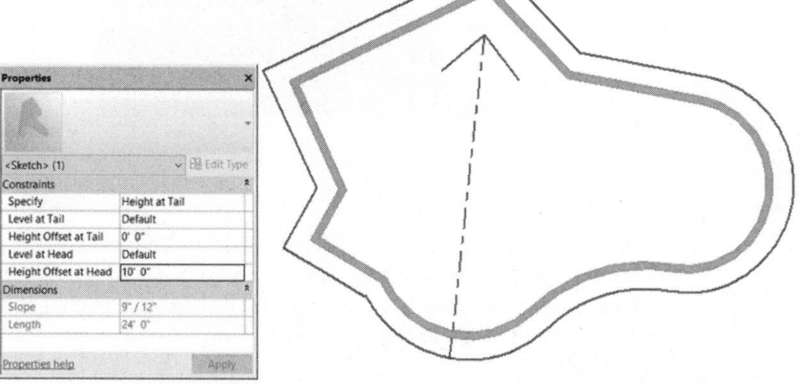

FIGURE 13.38
Defining the properties of a slope arrow added to an irregular footprint roof sketch

Using Additional Roof Tools

The following three roof tools (Figure 13.39) can be found under the Roof flyout:

- Roof : Soffit
- Roof : Fascia
- Roof : Gutter

Each of these tools behaves in a similar fashion—it uses a profile that is swept along the edge of the roof.

FIGURE 13.39
Edge condition roof tools

The difference between these tools is fairly simple. The Soffit tool will sweep a profile to the underside of a roof overhang parallel to the ground. The Fascia tool will sweep a profile along the vertical face of the roof edge, and the Gutter tool will sweep a profile along one of the edges of the roof. Try these tools on the roofs you've created in this chapter to better understand how they react to roof conditions. You can see how the Gutter tool looks using the default profile in Figure 13.40.

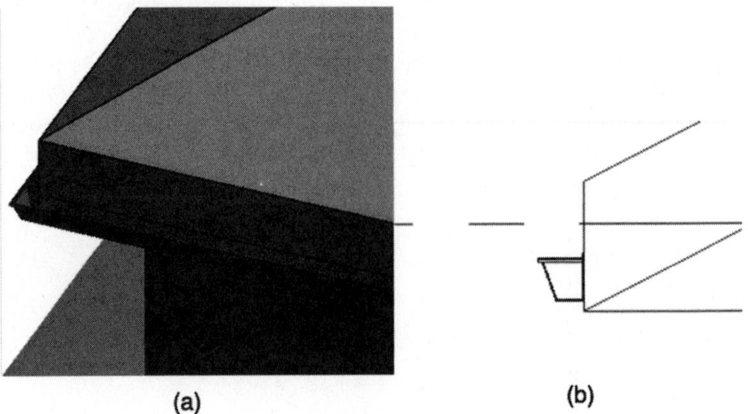

FIGURE 13.40
The Gutter tool

Don't feel you're limited to residential uses with these tools—as an example, the Gutter tool can be used to create a break metal cap for a flat roof parapet. Do be careful when you are picking an edge to apply the Gutter tool. The best approach is to pick in-plan views because the Gutter tool will default to the lower of the two edges so your gutters will be all placed at a consistent level.

Creating a Dormer Step by Step

Roofs with dormers generally cause grief for architects, so we'll guide you through the creation of one:

1. Create the base of a building, set up three levels, and create a roof by footprint with Defines Slope checked for all sides.
2. Approximately in the position indicated in the following illustration, on Level 2 create the four walls of a dormer. Set their height to a value that makes them extend above the roof.

   For easier verification, create a cross section through the dormer to check the height of the dormer walls and, if necessary, modify their height in the Properties palette so that they extend above the roof.

3. Using the Roof By Footprint tool, create a pitched roof on top of the dormer walls.
4. If you switch to a side elevation view, you will notice that the dormer roof probably does not extend to meet the main roof, so you will need to use the Join/Unjoin Roof tool, located in the Modify tab in the Edit Geometry panel, to join the main roof and the dormer. Select the Join/Unjoin Roof tool, select the main roof as the target, and then select the edge of the dormer roof to extend it.

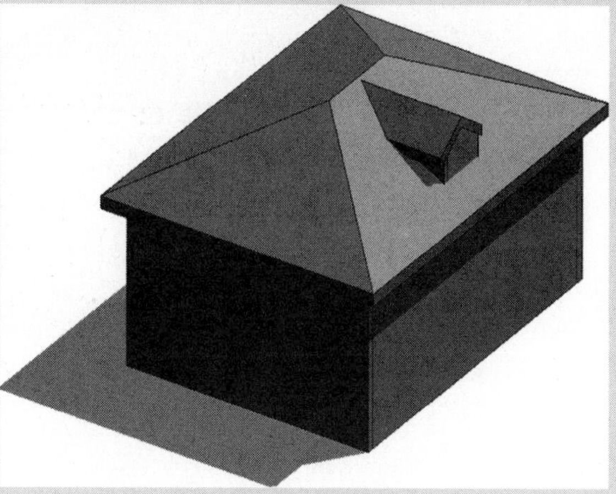

Continues

Continued

5. From the Opening panel on the Architecture tab, select Dormer. Now pick first the main roof and then the dormer roof, and then select the sides of the walls that define the dormer. Select the inside faces of the walls.

   Unlike most sketches, you will not need to provide a closed loop of lines in this case. Finish the dormer opening.

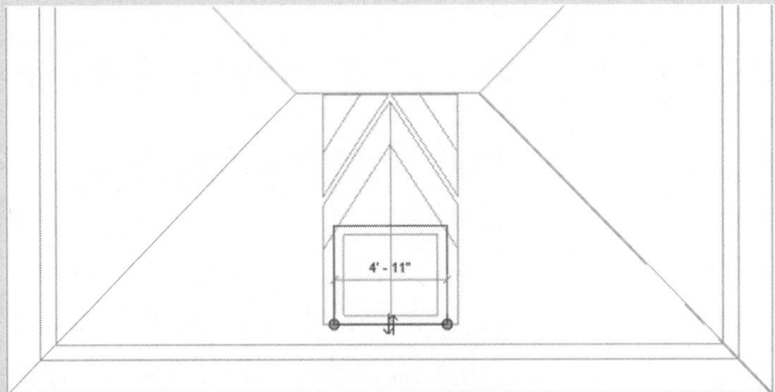

6. Finally, go back to the section view you previously created and edit the elevation profile of the side walls to make sure they don't extend below or above the roofs.

   You should not use the Top/Base Attach tool for tricky modeling scenarios such as the roof dormer, as the attachment may fail. Instead, select the wall and use the Edit Profile tool available in the Mode panel of the Modify | Walls tab to edit its elevation profile and manually resketch the edge lines of the walls to get the triangular elevation profile as shown.

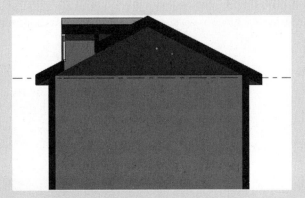

   As a final option, you can convert the front wall of the dormer to a storefront wall type or add a window.

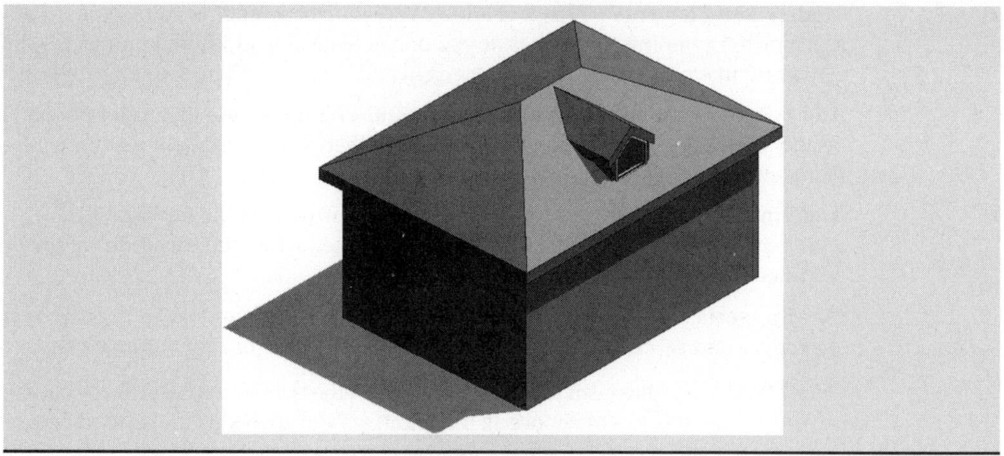

Using Advanced Shape Editing with Floors and Roofs

No flat roof is ever really flat! Fortunately there are tools that allow you to model tapered insulation over a flat roof and similar conditions to give the roof a small pitch. These powerful tools are modifiers that are applicable to roofs and floors and will allow you to model concrete slabs with multiple slopes for sidewalks or roof assemblies with tapered insulation (see Figure 13.41).

FIGURE 13.41
Roof with sloped drainage layer

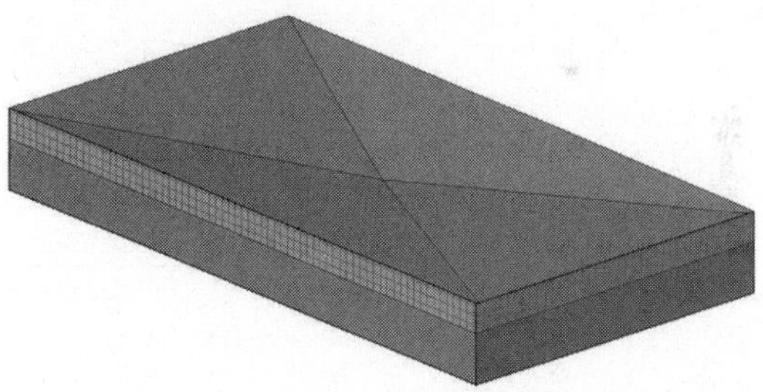

The set of tools available for editing floor and roof shapes appears in the ribbon when you select a flat floor or roof. If the Reset Shape command is inactive, that means the selected element has not been modified with the shape editing tools.

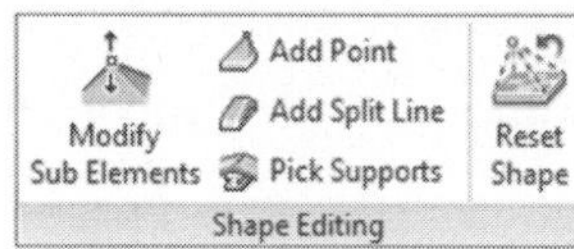

Let's look at what each tool does:

Modify Sub Elements This tool allows you to directly edit element geometry by selecting and modifying points and edges. If you don't create any additional points or split lines before activating this tool, the object's outer edges and corners will be available for editing.

Add Point This tool allows you to add points on the top face of a roof or floor. Points can be added on edges or surfaces and can be modified after placement using the Modify Sub Elements tool.

Add Split Line This tool allows you to sketch directly on the top face of the element, which adds vertices so that hips and valleys can be created when the elevations of the lines are modified using the Modify Sub Elements tool.

Pick Supports This tool allows you to pick linear beams and walls in order to create new split edges and set the slope and/or elevation of the floor or roof automatically.

Once a floor or roof has been modified using any of these tools, the Reset Shape button will become active. You can use this tool to remove all modifications you applied to the selected floor or roof.

Creating a Roof with a Sloped Topping

Let's work through an exercise that shows you how to make a roof with a sloped topping like the one shown in Figure 13.42 (shown in plan view).

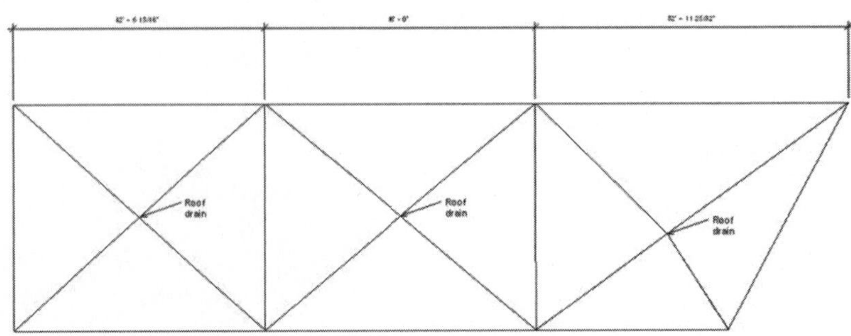

FIGURE 13.42 A roof plan showing a roof divided in segments, with drainage points

Follow these steps:

1. Open `c13-Roof-Edit.rvt` or `c13-Roof-Edit-Metric.rvt` from the book's web page. Activate the Roof floor plan.
2. Select the roof that has already been prepared for you.
3. Activate the Add Split Line tool (the color of the rest of the model grays out while the roof lines are dashed green).
4. Sketch two ridge lines to divide the roof into three areas that will be independently drained.

   The ridge lines will be drawn in blue.
5. Using the same tool, draw diagonal lines within those areas to create the valleys.

Make sure you zoom in closely when drawing the diagonal lines, and be sure that you are snapping in the exact same dividing points. (If you notice that the split lines are not snapped to the correct points, select the Modify Sub Elements tool, pick the incorrect lines, delete them, and try again.)

You have split the roof surface into many regions, but they are still all at the same height and pitch. You should have a roof that looks like Figure 13.43.

Press the Esc key or click the Modify button to stop the editing mode.

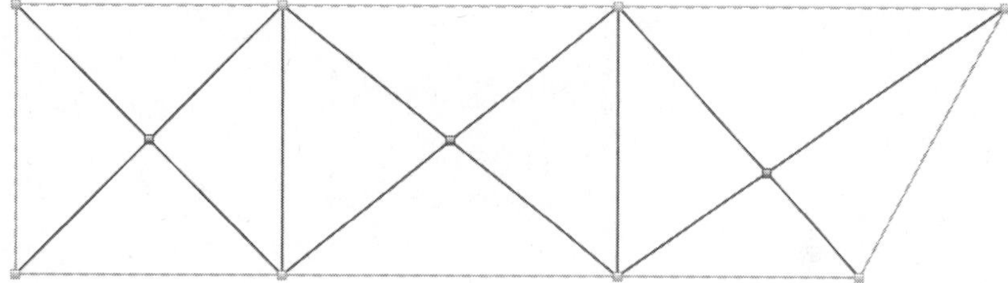

FIGURE 13.43
Using the Add Split Line tool, you can create ridges and valleys.

6. Switch to a 3D view.
7. To add a slope, you need to edit the height of the drainage points or the heights of the edges and ridges created by the split lines. For this exercise, you will raise the elevation of the boundary edges and ridges. Activate the Modify Sub Elements tool and select an edge of the roof (dashed green line). New controls that allow you to edit the text will appear, and you can either move the arrows up and down or type in a value for the height. Type in 1′-0″ (300 mm).
8. Repeat step 7 for all boundary edges and the two north-south split lines forming the ridges between the drainage areas.
9. Make a section through the roof—if possible, somewhere through one of the drainage points. Open the section; change Detail Level to Fine to see all layers.

The entire roof structure is now sloped toward the drainage point.

Applying a Variable Thickness to a Roof Layer

What if you wanted the insulation to be tapered but not the structure? For that, the layers of the roofs can now have variable thickness. Let's see how to apply a variable thickness to a layer of the roof assembly.

1. Continuing with the `c13-Roof-Edit.rvt` or `c13-Roof-Edit-Metric.rvt` file from the previous exercise, select the roof, and in the Properties palette select Edit Type to view the roof's type properties. Click Edit in the Structure row to edit the layers of the roof assembly.

2. Activate the preview. You will notice that in the roof-structure preview, you do not see any slopes. That is correct and will not change. This preview is just a schematic preview of the structure and does not show the exact sloping. Look for the Variable column under Layers, as shown in Figure 13.44. This allows layers of the roof to vary in thickness when slopes are present. Check the Variable option for the insulation material.

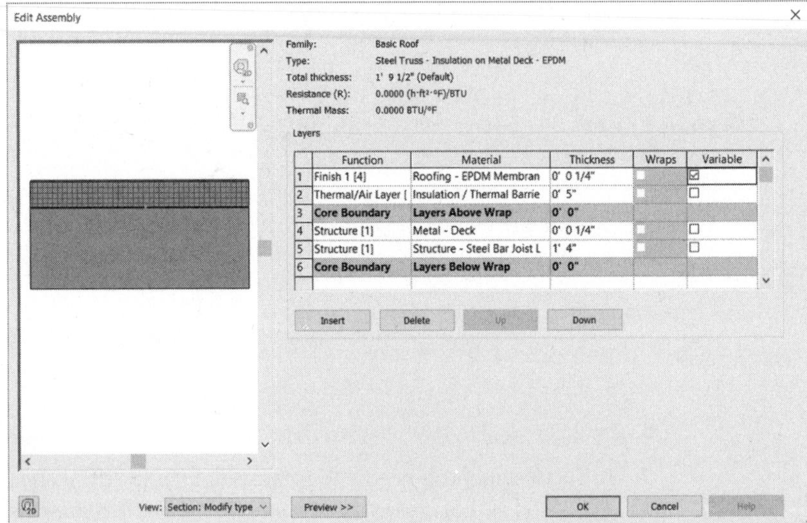

FIGURE 13.44
Specify variable layers of material in the Edit Assembly dialog box.

3. Go back to the section view and observe the changes in the roof assembly.

   As you can see, only the insulation is tapered, while the structure remains flat.

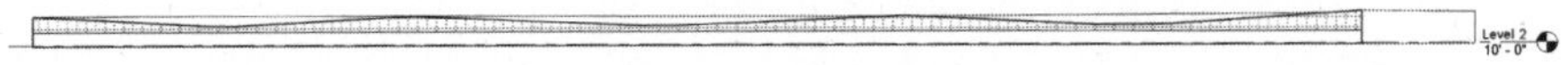

You will only be able to modify an adjustable layer of a floor or roof with a negative value to the next nonadjustable layer of the assembly. In the previous exercise, for example, if you modified the drainage points by more than –0′-5″ (–130 mm), an error would be generated, and the edits to the roof would be removed. You must think about the design requirements of your roof or floor assembly when planning how to model adjustable layers. An alternative approach to the previous exercise might have been to increase the thickness of the insulation layer in the roof assembly to that required at the high pitch points. The drainage points could then be lowered relative to the boundary edges and ridge lines.

The Bottom Line

Understand floor modeling methods. Floors make up one of the most fundamental, sketch-based system families used in a Revit model. You can customize them to accommodate a variety of assumptions at various stages of design.

Master It How can you create a structural floor with integrated metal decking?

Model various floor finishes. Thick and thin floor finishes can be created to support tagging, scheduling, and quantity takeoffs.

Master It How would you represent a thin finish material in your project such as carpet?

Create ceilings. Ceilings are sketch-based system families that can host objects such as light fixtures and HVAC diffusers.

Master It What's the best way to model a ceiling within a space?

Understand roof modeling methods. Roofs can be modeled as simple single-pitch shed roofs or complex extrusions of sinuous curves.

Master It What is the best way to create a single vault roof?

Work with advanced shape editing for floors and roofs. A small but powerful toolset is available for extended editing of floor and roof objects. These tools allow you to create warped floor slabs and tapered layers of roof assemblies.

Master It How do you create a drainage point in a flat roof slab?

Chapter 14

Designing with the Family Editor

In previous chapters, we discussed the modeling techniques for system families such as walls, roofs, floors, and ceilings. Although system families are essentially rule-based assemblies applied to sketch-based forms, component families are more self-contained. Another way to explain the difference is that system families are the objects you usually quantify in terms of linear units, surface area, or volume, whereas component families are most often counted objects. Such families include doors, windows, furniture, light fixtures, plumbing fixtures, specialty equipment, and so on.

In Autodesk® Revit® software, the Family Editor is where you'll create these component families. If you're familiar with other 3D modeling applications, the good news is that it will be easy to get started. But the really great news is that if you've never modeled in 3D, learning to create 3D content for the first time in Revit is a very satisfying process.

So relax, and prepare yourself for getting excited about design. Once you understand how to create parametric content in the Family Editor, you'll probably realize you can do anything in Revit. We'll begin this chapter by discussing some of the general topics that are important to understand about the Family Editor and creating component families. Then you will use some of this knowledge to create your own component family in a detailed exercise.

In this chapter, you'll learn to:

- Get started with a family
- Create the framework for a family component
- Understand family modeling techniques
- Apply extended family management techniques

Getting Started with a Family

Many generic 3D modeling applications allow you to create content that can be used in designing your buildings, and modeling in 3D is certainly a big part of the Family Editor. But the key to the Family Editor is that you're not just modeling but also modeling something specific. The thing that you're trying to design is meant to be a particular thing and behave in a particular way.

So when you're modeling in the Family Editor, you're not just trying to model *how* and *what* something is but also trying to predict how it might change. Anticipating change is essential to creating great, flexible content that is able to quickly and easily reflect your design changes.

For example, take a simple table. If you were to model this table in a program like Rhino, what you'd have when you've finished is exactly what you've modeled. But think about the design process and how often during design you'll need to iterate something like height, length, width, or material. In the real world, each of these parameters is critical. Suppose you have only three options for each of these values—this results in 81 permutations! Who has time to manually create each of these options? But this is what you'd have to do if you were using a generic modeler rather than Revit, where these options are driven by rules. By using parameters to define dimensions, materials, nested elements, and more, you can create additional permutations on the fly.

Understanding In-place Families

In the previous chapter, you learned how to create an in-place void family in order to customize the edge of a floor slab. Although some truly unique content in your project can be modeled using in-place families, it is often a dead-end process that robs you of hours of otherwise productive time for a number of reasons.

First, an in-place family should be used only in cases where the object that you're making is not likely to be moved, rotated, or copied. Any attempt to move, rotate, or copy an in-place family can often have unintended consequences that are difficult to remedy. For example, if you model an in-place family and then create copies in your project, they may all initially look the same, but in fact you're creating new unique families—not just copied instances of the same family. Therefore, if you modify one of the copied instances of an in-place family, the other copy will remain unchanged.

Second, each copied instance will schedule independently from the other instances as separate line items. This is often not desirable because you may want to group like elements together in a schedule.

Finally, there's no way to convert an in-place family into a component family. In some cases, you can copy and paste sketch lines or other 2D elements between the project and family environments. But if you try to copy and paste geometry from the project environment to the Family Editor, you'll get an error stating that you can't copy between family and project. The only way to proceed is to start again in the Family Editor.

Because of these reasons, it is common practice to create in-place families only for conditions that are one-offs, and it is advantageous to model the element in context to the overall design considerations within the project file. An example of this could be a solitary custom reception desk that incorporates its design aesthetics in the surrounding lobby or a unique sculptural element that is part of the environment.

CONTENT GUIDELINES AND STANDARDS

Before you begin to create your own custom content, you should be aware of the vast number of online content providers in the AEC industry. As of this writing, there are over 1000 building product manufacturers providing Revit families. There are also over 20 online content-hosting providers such as Autodesk Seek, RevitCity, National BIM Library, BIMstore, and ARCAT BIM Objects (just to name a few). Because most of these providers offer content for free, how can you be sure that the content you download will be usable or will support extended interoperability and collaboration?

A few of the content-aggregating sites offer content standards or guidelines. One example can be found on the Autodesk® Seek site:

`http://seek.autodesk.com`

In the "For Manufacturers" Area, click on Resources and you will find the Revit Model Content Style Guide. The Style Guide contains very detailed information, including standardized shared parameters, model-object subcategories, and naming conventions. These guidelines are quite thorough, but they only ensure that content is consistent when it is hosted and downloaded from the Autodesk Seek site. There are no international, platform-independent content standards to help you develop content that will offer maximum potential for data interoperability. That said, efforts are under way within the buildingSMART International community (`www.buildingsmart.org`) to help set a standard in the future.

Choosing the Right Family Template and Category

The first thing you'll want to consider in creating a component family is to determine what kind of component you want to build—in other words, you need to select an appropriate category. As we discuss in various chapters throughout this book, there are many predefined categories within a Revit project. You can create a new family from the Application menu by clicking New ➢ Family. This command will open a dialog box where you can choose from a vast selection of family templates (Figure 14.1). Templates for component families use the RFT file format.

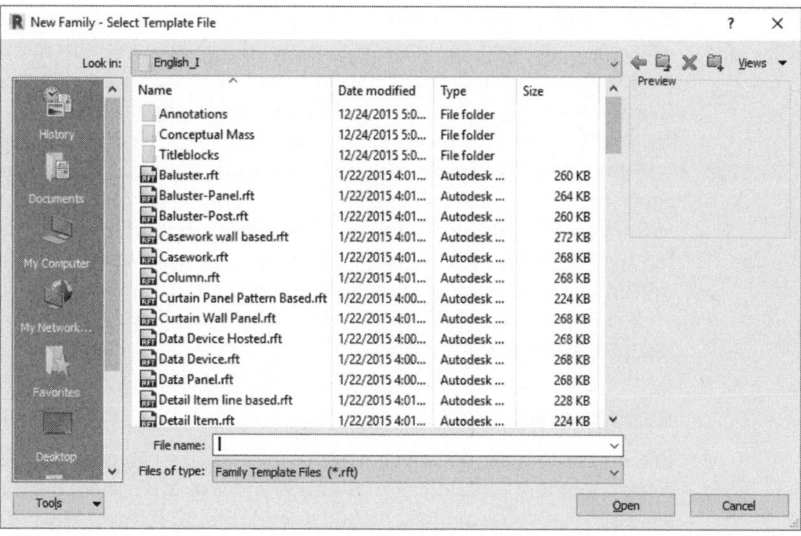

FIGURE 14.1 Select a family template to begin creating a component family.

From the New Family dialog box, select `Generic Model.rft` or `Metric Generic Model.rft` and then click Open. (If you can't find either template file, you can download them from this book's web page at `www.sybex.com/go/masteringrevit2017`.) Selecting the right family template is important because it determines a lot of the family's behavior. For example, a baluster template contains default datum objects that relate to the geometry of a railing (Figure 14.2).

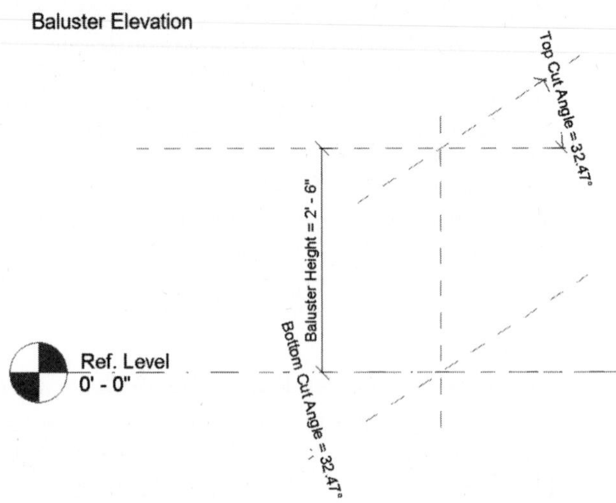

FIGURE 14.2
A baluster family template contains predefined datum objects to manage the geometric behavior.

Aside from some specific cases like balusters, the family template's primary function is to assign a category. In some cases, you can change the category of the family after it has been created. In the family you just started to create, switch to the Properties panel in the Create tab in the ribbon, and then click the Family Category and Parameters button.

In the dialog box shown in Figure 14.3, you will see that this Generic Models family is capable of being assigned to another category. This is helpful if you need to schedule a family in a category different from the one you initially selected. But in many cases, categories cannot be switched, and hosted or face-based components cannot be changed to unhosted (and vice versa). It is also difficult to convert a family that has many modeled elements to another category because you may be forced to reassign all the modeled elements to new subcategories.

Some categories are hardwired for specific behavior, and if you change from one such category to another, you can't go back. For example, if you start a family in one of the baluster templates, you can switch to another category. But after having done so, you cannot switch the family back to being a baluster. Knowing what you want to create before you begin helps you minimize the amount of switching you need to do later in the process.

You should become familiar with the following characteristics that relate to a family's assigned category.

SCHEDULING

Remember that as you start a new component, the category you select controls how the family component will schedule. For example, you wouldn't select the Furniture category to develop a family that you want to schedule as a plumbing fixture. Most of the categories you will use as you develop custom content will be self-explanatory; however, there may be some building elements for which you may need to think about categorization. One example is a vertical circulation component such as an elevator or escalator. You might select the Specialty Equipment category, but that category does not allow the geometry to be cut in a plan or section view. Perhaps you would use the Generic Models category instead, but you would need to use other parameters to schedule these types of families separately from other generic model families in your project.

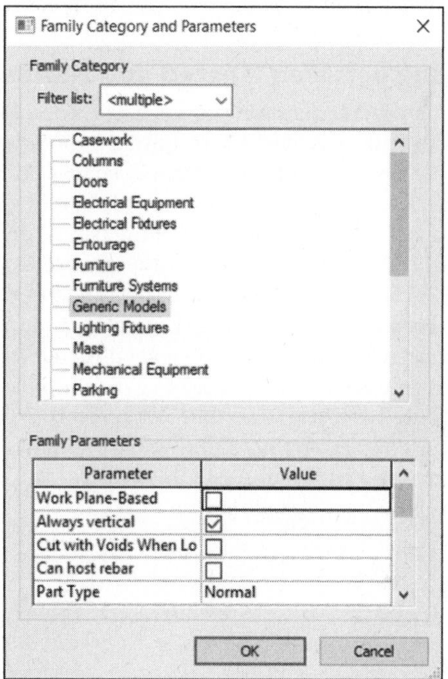

FIGURE 14.3 Switching between family categories

USING PROJECTION AND CUT VALUES

Another important characteristic of the family category is that it will control whether a family will "cut" when intersecting a view plane (plan, section, elevation, and so on). For example, convention dictates that when furniture encounters a cut plane, you should show a projected view rather than a sectional view.

Revit respects this convention by cutting some categories while not cutting others. You can figure out which categories cut or don't cut by going to the Manage tab and clicking Object Styles. As you can see, categories such as Casework, Ceilings, and Columns have line weight values in the Cut column, whereas categories such as Electrical Equipment, Furniture, and Lighting Fixtures do not.

ASSIGNING PARAMETERS

As you start to get into the parameters that can control a family's geometry, material, or other value, keep in mind that it's not always necessary to create components as fully parametric. This is especially true of the first pass. The location and spacing of content are often more important than whether the family can flex geometrically.

Nonparametric families often occur when the component being modeled is specific and highly unique. It may have parameters that control materials or a few other values, but not much more. At this point, little more than selecting the right category and insertion point is necessary. It's often far more efficient to maintain design relationships by modifying the component in the Family Editor and then reloading it into the project—at least until more is known about the design. When more is known, you can open the family and embed more parameters.

Choosing between Hosted and Nonhosted Family Types

The next important question you need to ask yourself as you select your family template is whether the family is meant to be hosted or nonhosted. If you make the wrong decision here, you'll have to start over to switch between these types. To identify the difference between hosted and nonhosted family types, examine the family templates shown previously in Figure 14.1. Some of the filenames are indicated as "ceiling based" or "wall based." These templates are used to create hosted families. Most of the other templates such as `Casework.rft`, `Furniture.rft`, `Metric Casework.rft`, `Metric Furniture.rft`, and `Metric Generic Model.rft` are nonhosted.

First, keep in mind that hosted objects are meant to cut or create an opening or depression in their host. Obviously, a window needs to cut the wall into which it will be placed, or a fire extinguisher case will often need to generate a recess in the host wall. Second, if the component is to be hosted and you're certain that it needs to create an opening in its host, it can cut only one type of host. For example, a lighting fixture that is wall-based may not be hosted by a ceiling.

Want to see a bad example of this? Download and open the `Tub-Rectangular-3D.rfa` family from this book's web page (Figure 14.4).

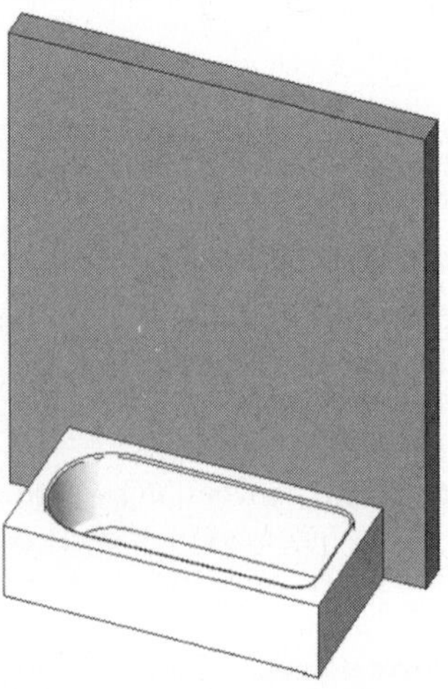

FIGURE 14.4
Wall-hosted plumbing fixtures

What's wrong with this picture? First, this tub is wall hosted and not all tubs need walls, so you'll have to make another family that has no host in order to place the tub where there is no wall. This seems a bit redundant because one tub will do.

Second, if you delete a host, all the hosted elements are deleted as well. This makes some sense when you delete a wall that hosts windows or doors. But it will certainly lead to a lot of frustration if you delete a wall that hosts bathroom fixtures!

We can't stress this enough: As a best practice, avoid creating hosted relationships between objects that do not require hosting (that do not cut or otherwise modify the host). This discussion brings up an interesting point. Rather than use hosted elements, why not make elements face-based? There are some advantages:

- You don't have to decide on a particular host. Any surface will do: Wall, Ceiling, Top of Casework, anything that has a face. This is great if the lighting component you're creating needs to cut into a wall, floor, and ceiling!
- A face-based element can cut the face of geometry in both the project and family editing environment. So the light fixture that cuts a wall in a project can cut the face of a piece of casework in the Family Editor.
- Deleting the host will not delete the component. Is this desirable? Maybe sometimes, but not always. What's important is that you have the option if the component is face-based. You won't have the option if the component is hosted.
- You can place face-based families on host elements from a linked project model. This works great when an architectural model is linked into an engineer's model for placement of electrical or plumbing fixtures.

Creating Other Types of Families in the Family Editor

Now that you understand the importance of selecting between a hosted and a nonhosted family template, you should become familiar with some other types of families you can create in the Family Editor.

Placing Line-Based Components

This is a less common type of family that allows you to place components in the project environment as lines. Line-based families can take advantage of line-based tools such as Trim/Extend and Split and can also support parametric arrays.

Generic model, detail item, and structural stiffener are the only family categories currently available to be used as a line-based component. An example of one is a generic model created by Steve Stafford for his Revit OpEd blog (Figure 14.5). This family is used to lay out egress paths and then calculate the total travel distance in a schedule. You can download this family here:

```
http://revitoped.blogspot.com/2007/01/egress-path.html
```

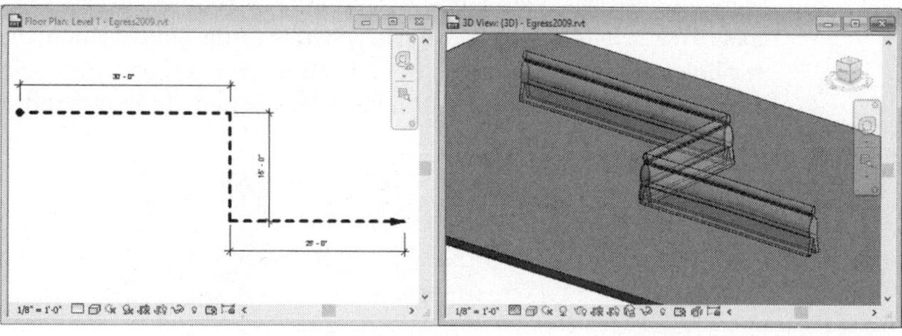

Figure 14.5
An example of a generic line-based family

Using Detail Components

Some types of families consist of only 2D elements—these are called detail components. They are most often used in drafting views; however, detail components can also be placed in plan, elevation, and section views. The benefit of using detail components, as compared to individual lines and filled regions, is that a detail component can be reused many times, thus increasing drafting productivity; quality is increased by allowing control of repetitive detail elements and they support keynote and tagging abilities. We discuss detail components further in Chapter 16, "Detailing Your Design."

Placing Annotation Symbols

Much like detail components, annotation symbols are families that contain only 2D graphics, including lines, text, and fill or masking regions. They are different from detail components because annotation symbols will react to the scale of the view in which they are placed. Aside from the common uses of annotation symbols such as tags, north arrows, or graphic scales, you can nest annotation symbols in other types of model families to customize and better manage your approach to project documentation. Consider some of the families for electrical terminal fixtures in the default library. These families include a 3D representation of a small element, such as a receptacle plate that will be seen in an elevation view, but they also include a generic annotation to represent the object with a scaled symbol in a plan view, as shown in Figure 14.6.

Figure 14.6
A default family illustrating a nested annotation symbol

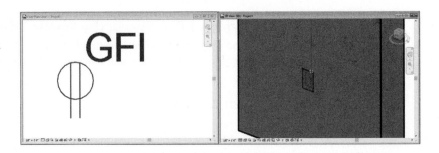

In Chapter 4, "Configuring Templates and Standards," we showed you how to build custom annotation symbols for use in your own projects or templates.

Creating Mass Families

Mass families are special components that are created in a slightly different environment of the Family Editor called the conceptual design environment (CDE). Within this environment, you use tools to sketch lines that are used to generate forms almost automatically. As shown in Figure 14.7, the line tools in the ribbon of the CDE allow you to sketch first, select lines, and then use the Create Form button. After a form has been created, it can be subdivided for additional articulation.

Figure 14.7
Geometry tools in the conceptual design environment

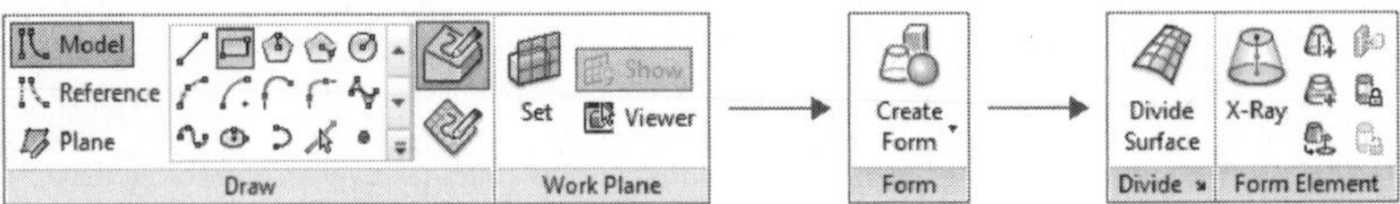

Using Mass Families with an Application

We discuss using mass families with greater detail in Chapter 8, "Advanced Modeling and Massing." If you have an Apple iPad or Android tablet, you might also want to experiment with the free Autodesk® FormIt mobile application. It's also available as a web application here: `http://formit360.autodesk.com`. With this design application, you can quickly generate and study forms—including the ability to analyze gross floor area and shadows (Figure 14.8). When the app synchronizes with your Autodesk® A360 cloud account, it will automatically convert the designs to RVT project files where the modeled geometry is represented as in-place masses.

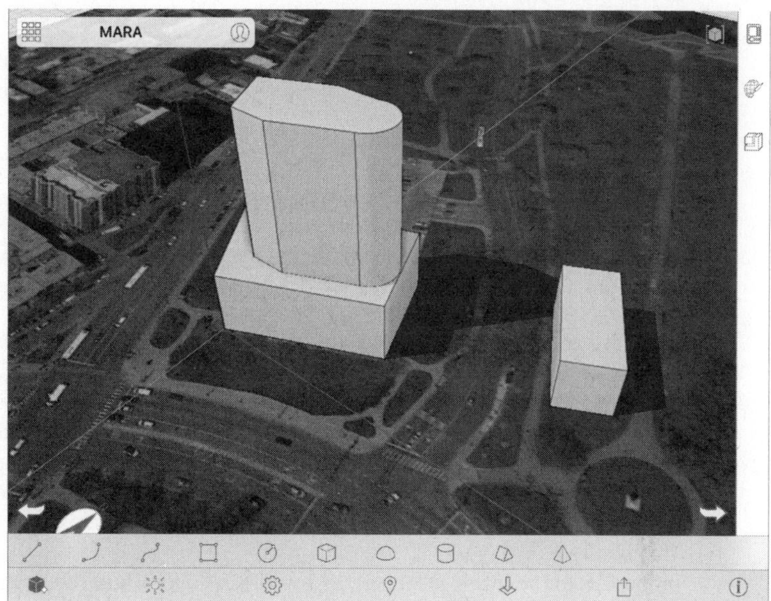

Figure 14.8
The Autodesk FormIt application can be used to generate mass forms.

Using Adaptive Components

Finally, a special type of dynamic family that is used in the CDE is known as an adaptive component. These families are an adaptation of the pattern-based curtain panel concept, but you can use them in geometry other than divided surfaces. You can learn more about creating and using adaptive components in Chapter 12, "Creating Walls and Curtain Walls," and Chapter 9, "Conceptual Design and Design Analysis."

Understanding the Family Editor

The Family Editor isn't a different software application that you need to install. It is simply a unique mode within Revit that has tools and commands specifically designed to create component content. After you launch the command to make a new family and you choose a family template, you will enter the Family Editor. If you happen to have a project file open, you can switch back and forth between a family file and the project just the same way you'd toggle between the open views of a project.

Depending on the type of family you are building, the Create tab in the ribbon will have slightly different tools. In this chapter, you will be using the Furniture family template, and the Create tab will have specific 3D modeling tools, as shown in Figure 14.9.

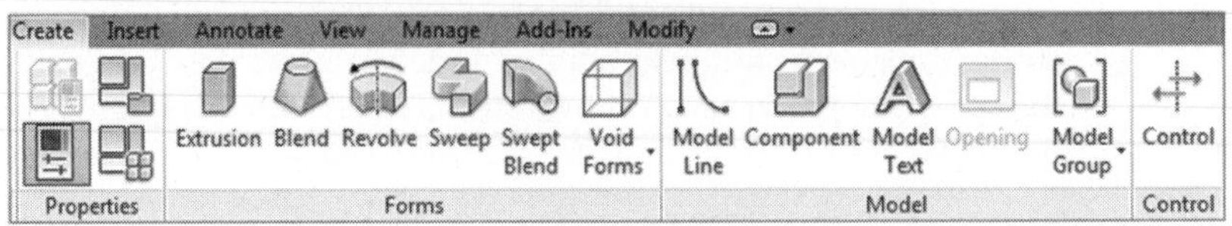

FIGURE 14.9 The Create tab for model families

If you were creating a detail component or annotation family, neither of which can contain 3D geometry, the Create tab displays only 2D tools such as Line, Filled Region, and Label (Figure 14.10).

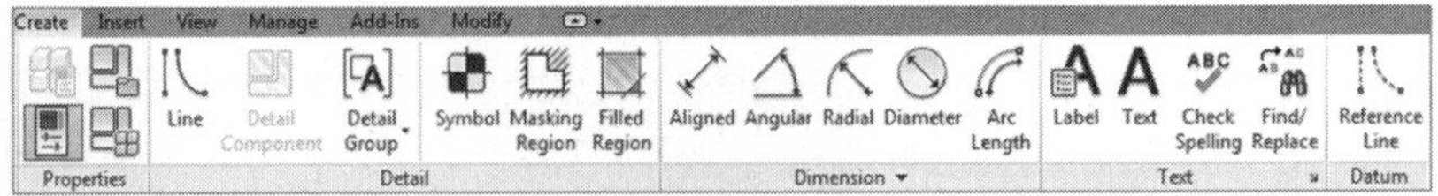

FIGURE 14.10 The Create tab for detail and annotation families

Within the Family Editor, you also have the ability to include imported CAD data. From the Insert tab in the ribbon, you can use the Import CAD tool to utilize 2D or 3D information from another source. You cannot use the Link CAD tool in the Family Editor; therefore, any data imported to a family will not update if the original CAD file is changed.

A feature in Revit is the ability to explode and then manipulate imported 3D solid CAD geometry. You can experiment with this feature by downloading the file `ImportCAD.sat` from this book's web page.

Switch to the Insert tab, click the Import CAD tool, and then browse to the location where you downloaded the sample SAT file. You'll have to change the Files Of Type drop-down list to ACIS SAT Files. Use the default settings and click Open. After the model has loaded, go to the default 3D view and press **ZF** for the Zoom To Fit command. Select the imported geometry, and from the contextual tab in the ribbon choose Explode ➢ Full Explode. Select the solid geometry again, and you'll notice that the imported model is now ready to be manipulated with a series of grip controls (Figure 14.11). Delete the imported geometry before continuing with the exercise in this chapter.

Another tab in the Family Editor that might seem familiar is the Annotate tab. Here you will find tools for dimensions, symbolic lines, and text. In a model component, dimensions and text placed in the Family Editor are not visible when the family is loaded and placed in a project. Although text can be used for reference notes in the Family Editor, dimensions are used to control and drive the geometry. You'll learn much more about parametric dimensions later in this chapter.

The tools in the Detail panel of the Annotate tab in the ribbon allow you to create some 2D geometry within a 3D family. This is especially useful if you have a somewhat complex model that you would like to display as a simplified graphic in a plan view. For example, you may have a detailed 3D model of a bathroom water closet (toilet) fixture. If such a model was composed of complex curved surfaces and solids, displaying many of these components in a project view might ultimately begin to degrade visual performance. Instead, the 3D geometry can be assigned to not display in a plan view, while you include a simple sketch of the fixture in the plan view of the family. Your renderings, sections, and elevations will display the 3D family geometry, while your plan views will remain simple and fast.

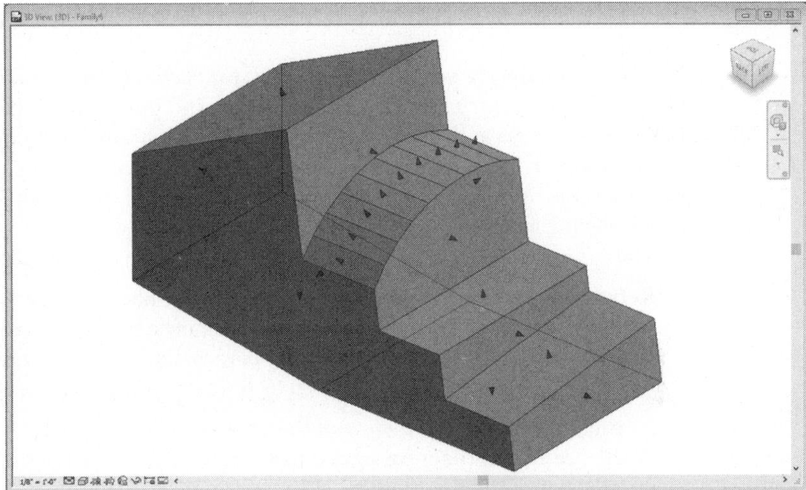

FIGURE 14.11
Imported solid geometry can be exploded and manipulated.

One final aspect to understand about the Family Editor is its ability to use multiple views to visualize your design. Similar to the project environment, it lets you create as many views as you need to help visualize the content in your family. The Ref. Level plan view can be duplicated if you need to examine your family at different elevations. Simply change the View Range properties of each plan view to control the height of the view's cut plane. From the View tab in the ribbon, you can also create camera views and sections within the family.

Developing the Framework for a Family Component

Now that we've discussed some of the basic definitions and rules of the Family Editor, we'll talk about the hierarchy of creating a family component.

In this section you will work through the fundamentals of creating a family in terms of datum objects, constraints, parameters, materials, subcategories, and visibility settings. Later in the chapter, you will learn more advanced modeling and parametric techniques.

Click the Application menu and then select New ➢ Family. Use the `Furniture.rft` or `Metric Furniture.rft` family template, which is available for download with this chapter's exercise files from the book's web page.

Creating the Necessary Reference Planes, Lines, and Points

In the project environment, datum objects are available for you to control and manage the location and behavior of modeled geometry. In previous chapters, we discussed the use of grids, levels, and reference planes, but these data are also extremely important in a component family.

When used in the Family Editor, reference planes, lines, and points will function as the skeleton for the solid and void geometry you build.

To be clear about the usage of datum objects in families, they are not required to construct geometry; however, if you're confident that what you're about to model in the Family Editor will need to flex (have a modifiable length, angle, location, and so on) from within the rules of the family, then it's important that you begin by first creating the rules that will allow the geometry to move.

With few exceptions, you don't want to give parameters to the geometry itself. Instead, you'll want to create the necessary reference planes, lines, and points first. Then associate the parameters to these references and whenever possible test the parameters to make sure the references are flexing properly. Once you're confident the references are flexing, you can build the geometry in context to the references, again testing to make certain that when the references flex, the geometry is flexing as well.

The type of datum object you use is based on how you want the geometry to flex:

Reference Planes These define a single plane that can be set to host sketch lines or geometry. They're best for controlling linear geometric relationships—that is to say, geometry that will flex in a linear fashion. Reference planes don't have endpoints. This is important because you don't want to use reference planes for controlling angular or directional relationships.

As illustrated in the plan view of the `Desk.rfa` family, the linear parameters of Depth and Width are appropriately assigned to reference planes. All of these geometric constraints are parallel to one another (Figure 14.12).

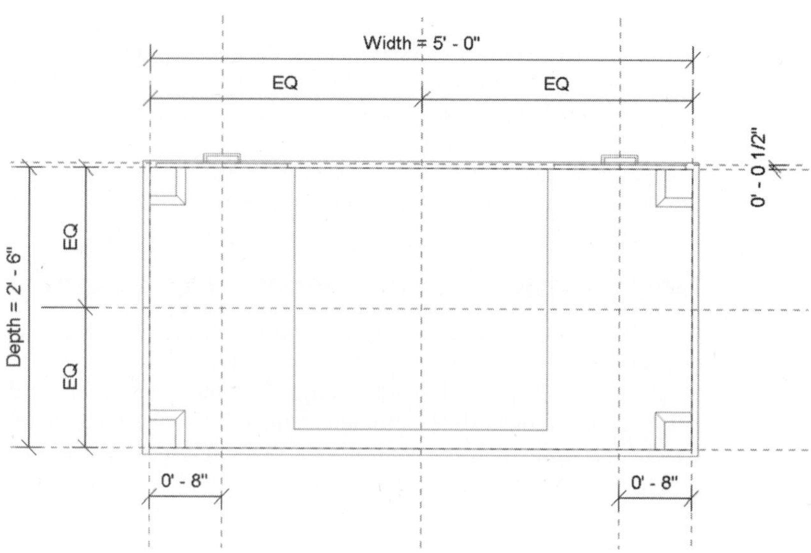

FIGURE 14.12 Reference planes controlling the parameters of the default `Desk.rfa` family

Reference Lines By definition these datum objects have endpoints and are great for controlling angular and directional relationships. They can have four axes of reference, two along the length of the line (which are perpendicular to each other) and one at each end that is perpendicular to the line.

You can also create curved reference lines, but they have only planes that may be used for hosting at each end. There are no references along the curved line, as shown in Figure 14.13.

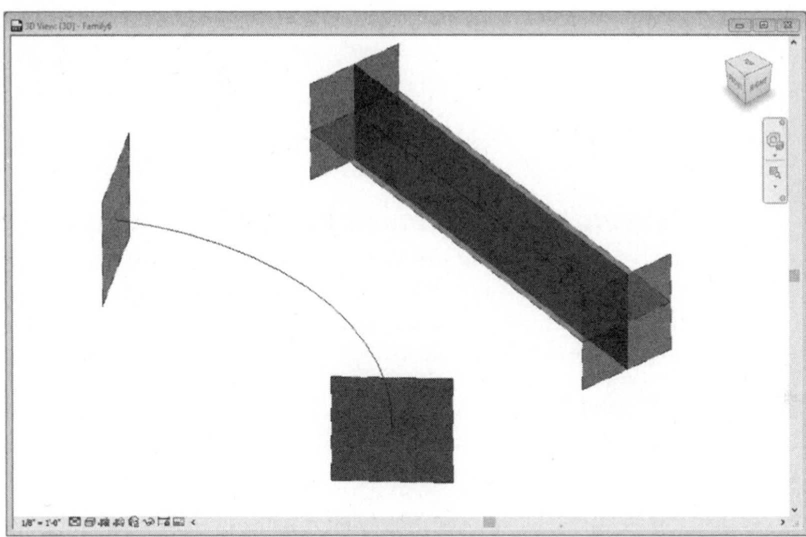

FIGURE 14.13 Straight and curved reference lines

As an example, reference lines can be established in a family with length and angular dimension parameters to control path geometry for sweeps such as the iterations shown in Figure 14.14.

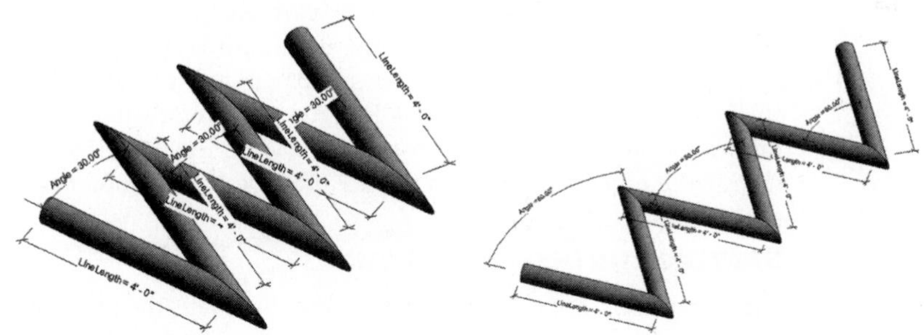

FIGURE 14.14 Sweep geometry using reference lines

Reference Points This type of datum object is available only in certain family templates, including Mass, Generic Model Adaptive, Generic Model-Pattern Based, and Curtain Panel-Pattern Based. Reference points have three planes that can be set to host sketch lines or geometry. You can also use a series of points to control a line or even a spline. Other objects, such as reference lines or other geometric surfaces, can also host reference points. You can select reference points from the Draw panel in the ribbon as shown in Figure 14.15.

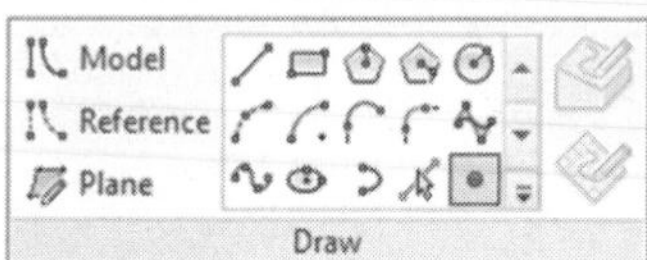

FIGURE 14.15
Reference points in the Draw panel

SETTING THE BEHAVIOR OF REFERENCE PLANES AND LINES

When you place a new reference plane or line or select one already in your family, you will notice a property in the Properties palette called *Is Reference*. This setting is an important factor in how the family will behave when it is placed in a project. It affects how you can dimension or align to the family as follows:

- Not A Reference—The reference will be used only to control geometry in the Family Editor.
- Weak Reference—The reference can be accessed for measurement in the project environment only by pressing the Tab key on the keyboard.
- Strong Reference—The reference has the highest priority for dimensions and alignment. Temporary dimensions are displayed at the strong reference data.

In the Family Editor, reference planes also have other available values for the Is Reference property including Top, Back, Bottom, Left, Right, and Front. These values are all strong references and are provided to help you better organize your family geometry.

You will also notice that symbolic lines have a property called Reference with settings identical to those for the Is Reference property of reference planes and reference lines. We recommend that you treat symbolic lines with the same care as the datum objects.

Use the strong and weak references sparingly throughout your family. The default setting for the Is Reference property is Weak Reference; therefore, there could be a large number of possibilities for measurement within *every component* in your project. For every strong or weak reference, Revit must analyze the reference when you are annotating or designing.

SETTING THE INSERTION POINT

After you've chosen an appropriate family template, the rest is pretty flexible. If you make any mistakes, you'll probably be able to recover most if not all of your work to correct the problem. But some considerations should come before others, which is why we believe that the insertion point is the next most critical criterion on your list for family creation.

First, the insertion point determines the location about which the family will geometrically flex. But second (and often more important), the insertion point is the point of reference when two family components are exchanged. This is critical if the "design" family that you've used as a placeholder is being swapped out for something more specific at a later date. If the insertion points are not established similarly between families, the location of the new family will not agree with the location of the old one.

For example, most of the tables in the default Revit furniture library define the insertion point at the center of the geometry, as shown in Figure 14.16. If you place one table family in your project and then later decide to swap it for a different table family, there should be minimal disruption to the layout of other furniture in your design. The new family will appear in roughly the same spot as the originally placed family. Now what happens if you were to download a table family from a web-based content provider? Will that table also follow the same convention for the location of the insertion point? This concern illustrates the importance of following published guidelines or standards for content creation.

FIGURE 14.16
Insertion point for default table families

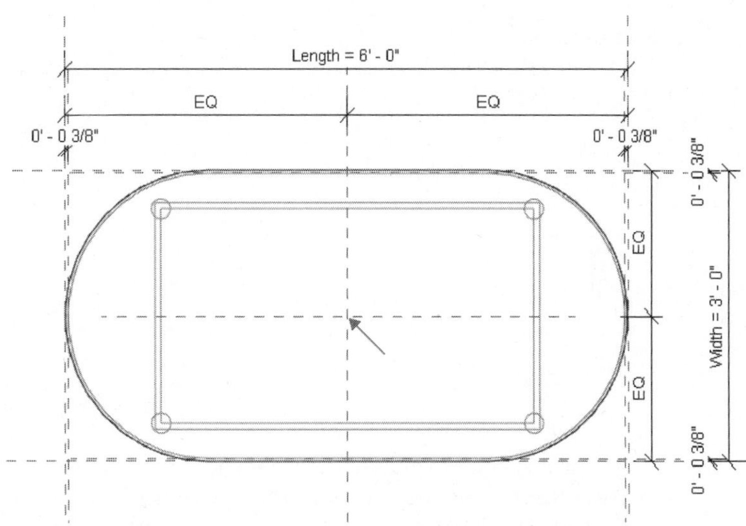

Keep in mind that changing the insertion point is easy. As you might expect, you don't move the geometry to the insertion point. Rather, you simply select two reference planes and then make sure the Defines Origin parameter is selected in the Properties palette. Continuing with this chapter's exercise using the `Furniture.rft` or `Metric Furniture.rft` template, the two reference planes provided already are assigned the Defines Origin property. You will now start to build a geometric framework around these reference planes.

Let's place some reference planes in the new family to officially begin the chapter exercise.

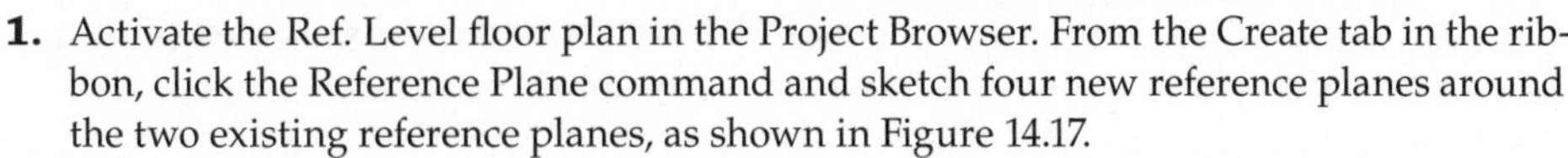

1. Activate the Ref. Level floor plan in the Project Browser. From the Create tab in the ribbon, click the Reference Plane command and sketch four new reference planes around the two existing reference planes, as shown in Figure 14.17.

   The exact placement of the new planes doesn't matter for now.

2. Select the reference plane you added to the left of the center plane, and in the Properties palette set its Name parameter to **Left**. (In Revit 2017, you can select the reference plane, and on both ends you will see the words "Click to name" or the predefined name for the reference plane. Click this area and input the name.)

   Assigning a name to a reference plane will allow you to use it later as a work plane for creating solid forms.

3. Select the reference plane you added to the right and set its Name parameter to **Right**. Select the one near the top of the view and name it **Back**, and then select the one near the bottom of the view and name it **Front**.

4. Activate the Front elevation view and add another reference plane above and parallel to the Ref. Level. Again, the exact placement doesn't matter for now—just make sure it is parallel to the level. In the Properties palette, set the Name parameter for this reference plane to **Top**.

FIGURE 14.17
Adding new reference planes to the exercise family

The Is Reference property for these new reference planes will be set to the default value of Weak Reference. That is acceptable because these will be the major geometrical references of the table family. As an option, you can set the four reference planes in the plan view to Strong Reference and observe later how they behave in the project environment.

Using Dimensions to Control Geometric Parameters

Dimensions are useful for controlling the geometric parameters of your families; however, we recommend they be placed directly on reference planes and lines and not within the sketches of solid or void forms. When you start to construct a component family, you should first lay out any reference planes or lines and then add dimensions to the references—all before you create any solid geometry.

As you complete the exercise steps in this section, you will be creating the framework for solid geometry that you will build in subsequent sections of this chapter.

Aligned

1. With the Front elevation view still active, start the Aligned Dimension command. You can access this command in the Measure panel of the Create tab in the ribbon, in the Annotate tab, or by pressing **DI** to activate the default keyboard shortcut. Place a dimension from the Ref. Level to the reference plane you previously created.

   This process will consist of three mouse clicks: one on the Ref. Level datum object, one on the reference plane above, and a final click in open space to place the dimension string.

2. Press the Esc key or click Modify in the ribbon to exit the Dimension command, and then select the dimension you just placed. To make this dimension parametric, locate the

Label drop-down list in the Options bar and choose <Add Parameter...>. The Parameter Properties dialog box will appear, as shown in Figure 14.18. In the Name field type **Height**, and make sure the Type radio button is selected.

FIGURE 14.18
Assign your first dimension to a new parameter.

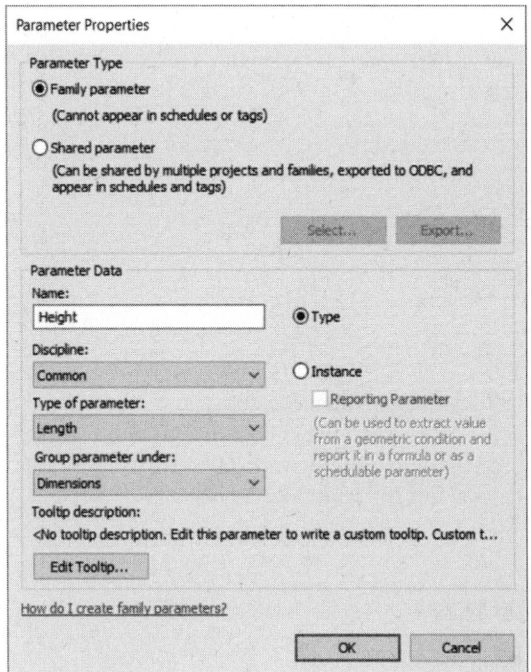

3. Click OK to continue. The dimension will now display with the prefix Height =.

   The exact height doesn't matter because you can control it later on through parameter manipulation.

4. Activate the Ref. Level floor plan. You now need to ensure that the four new reference planes are equally placed around the two planes that define the family origin. After the equality constraints are established, you will place dimensions to control the overall length and width of the shape. The order of this procedure—equality, then overall dimension—should be followed to establish the correct relationship with a center-based origin.

5. Place an aligned dimension between the three vertical reference planes, and then click the EQ symbol near the dimension string. Repeat this process for the horizontal reference planes so that the result looks like Figure 14.19.

6. Next, you will add the dimensions that will actually control the overall size of the shape in plan. Place an aligned dimension between the outer two vertical reference planes, and then place a dimension between the outer two horizontal reference planes.

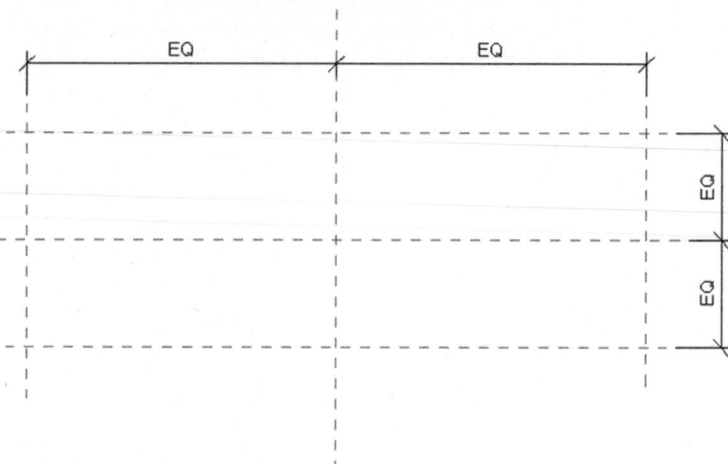

FIGURE 14.19 Set equality constraints on reference planes first.

7. Exit the Dimension command and select the horizontal dimension string. From the Label drop-down list in the Options bar, select <Add Parameter…>. Name the new parameter **Length**, and then click OK. Repeat this process for the vertical dimension string, and name the parameter **Width**.

The result should look similar to Figure 14.20.

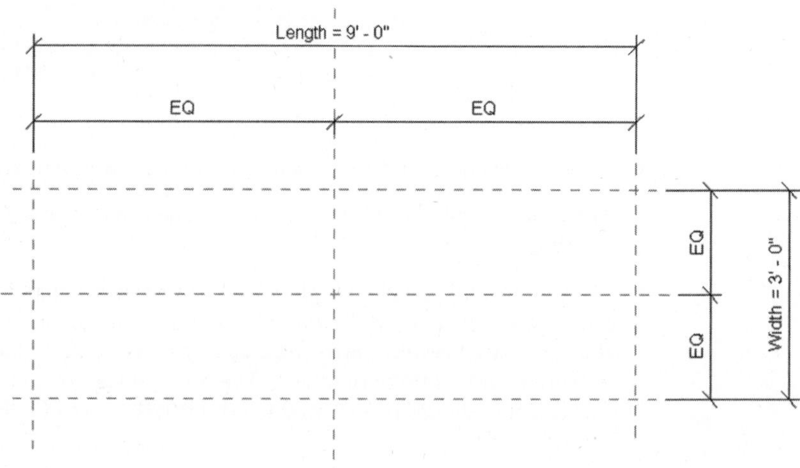

FIGURE 14.20 Establish dimension parameters in the plan.

SHOULD EVERYTHING BE PARAMETRIC?

When you start assigning dimensions to datum objects in your families, take a moment to think about whether you will need to modify those dimensions to create iterations of the component.

Creating too many unnecessary labeled dimensions can make a family more complex, thus potentially degrading performance of your project files. If the dimension is a fixed dimension that will not change between types, then either use an unlabeled dimension or don't dimension it at all. For example, in our table-building exercise, the height might be fixed at 2′-6″ (750 mm); therefore, the Height parameter would not be needed.

Modifying Parametric Dimensions

Now that you have established some dimensions and assigned them to family parameters, it is time to "flex" the geometry—a term that has become popular with Revit users since the early adoption years of the software. You flex your references by applying varying dimension values to confirm that no errors are generated and that the references are behaving the way you intended. Doing this early and often in the family-building process reduces the chance of encountering a problem that you can't solve later on. When you have more forms and more complex parametric relationships, it becomes more difficult to unravel problematic geometry.

There are two ways you can modify the parametric dimensions, thus flexing your family geometry. First, you can simply select a labeled dimension in the drawing area and enter a new value. The second way is different than in the project environment, where you must first select one of the objects a dimension references before editing the value. Although this method seems to be the easiest and most intuitive, you must be careful after you have established defined types within the family because direct manipulation of labeled dimensions will change the value of the active type. For this reason, we recommend that you become accustomed to using the Family Types dialog box to flex your families.

You can create a new reference plane and dimension from the Create panel in the ribbon and then click the Family Types command. Move the dialog box off to the side so you can still see the drawing area and observe the reference planes and dimensions. In the Family Types dialog box, click the New button and create a new type named **Type 1**. Set the dimension parameters as follows, and then click Apply:

Width = 2′-6″ (750 mm)

Length = 6′-0″ (1800 mm)

Height = 2′-6″ (750 mm)

Click the New button again and create a new type named **Type 2**. Set the dimension parameters as follows, and then click Apply:

Width = 3′-0″ (900 mm)

Length = 8′-0″ (2400 mm)

Height = 2′-6″ (750 mm)

If the reference planes and dimensions were created properly, you should not receive any error messages while you are flexing the parameters. In case you do receive any errors, you could delete the dimensions and even the reference planes and start over. If this were to happen later in the process, it would be more difficult to resolve the problem, and many more hours would be lost if you had to start over.

Type Naming

In the previous exercise, you created two types within the family simply named Type 1 and Type 2. You might have also noticed that other families in the default libraries have type names that indicate some sort of size information. For example, the door family Single-Flush has types named according to the respective length and width such as 36″ × 84″. The problem here is that the type name is not automatically linked to any parameters in the family; therefore, if a parameter value is modified and the type is not renamed, the situation can become confusing to users working in your project.

There is no single, correct answer to the type-naming conundrum. You can use specific type names (36″ × 84″) to help the users of your content decide which type to select, or you can choose generic names (Type 1) to avoid conflicts. One possible conflict could arise if you use the type name of a family in a schedule. For example, if you generated a door schedule that used the type name instead of the actual width and height parameters, there might be inconsistency with the actual dimensions versus those in the user-defined name.

A relatively safe methodology is to use more detailed type-naming conventions such as *Material - Nominal Size* to help content users better understand the available choices. An example for a door family might be *Wood - 36 × 84*. And then, as a standard practice, do not use the type name in any schedules for production documentation.

Reviewing the Differences between Type and Instance Parameters

In the previous exercise, you created a few dimension-based parameters that were set to be type parameters. Let's review the difference between a type parameter and an instance parameter—keeping in mind that they can be switched at just about any time.

The key difference between the two is that modifying a type parameter always modifies all instances of the type. Think of a type as a set of identical elements. Change one item in the set, and all the other items of that type in the model change to match. Door sizes are a good example of this. Doors come in standard sizes: 32″, 34″, 36″ (800 mm, 850 mm, 900 mm). On the other hand, an instance parameter modifies only the instances that you have selected. A good use of an instance parameter would be the fire rating on a door. Not every 36″ (900 mm) door will be fire rated, so you'll need to individually identify which ones are. Figure 14.21 shows the parameters of a default curtain wall door family.

In Figure 14.21, the parameters that have the notation (Default) are instance parameters. There are other parameters that can be used to report dynamic values from within the family. These are shown with the (Report) notation. In the example of a standard door, dimensions such as Width, Height, and Thickness would be best established as type parameters because you wouldn't want users to create random or arbitrary values. Also be aware that once a parameter is created, only some aspects of the parameter can be modified. You cannot change the Discipline or Type Of Parameter value after the parameter has been created.

Sorting Parameters

Complex families can have many parameters that control geometry, information, materials, and so on. To make it easier for your team to find parameters efficiently, you can sort them in any way that you deem appropriate for use. When the Family Types dialog box is open in the Family Editor, use the Move Up and Move Down buttons to organize your parameters. When the family is loaded into a project, this sorting order will be seen in the Properties palette and in the Type Properties dialog box.

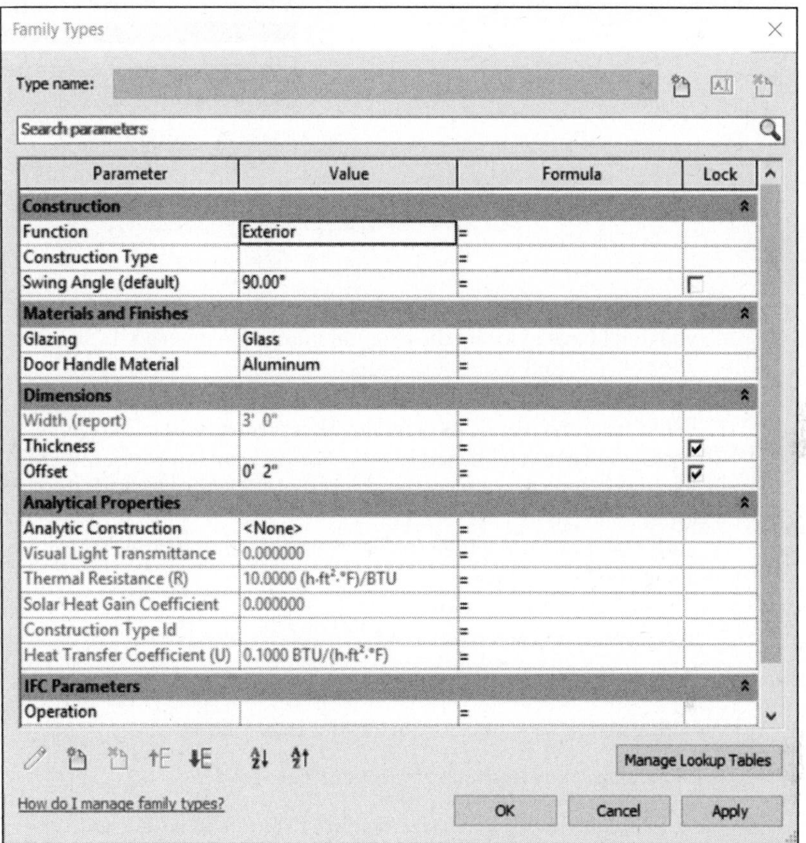

FIGURE 14.21 Parameters of a default curtain wall door family

On the other hand, each new option can create a lot of new types. By default, loading a family into your project will also load all the types. If you want to create the potential for many types but be selective about which types are loaded, you can use a type catalog to load only specific types.

USING TYPE CATALOGS

If you are creating a family that will have many different type iterations, you can consider using a type catalog instead of creating each iteration within the Family Editor. A type catalog is a text file that contains all the iterations of the parameters specified within a family. When you load a family into a project that has an associated type catalog, such as steel framing families, you are presented with a dialog box within which you can select one or more types (Figure 14.22). You can select multiple types by pressing the Ctrl or Shift key.

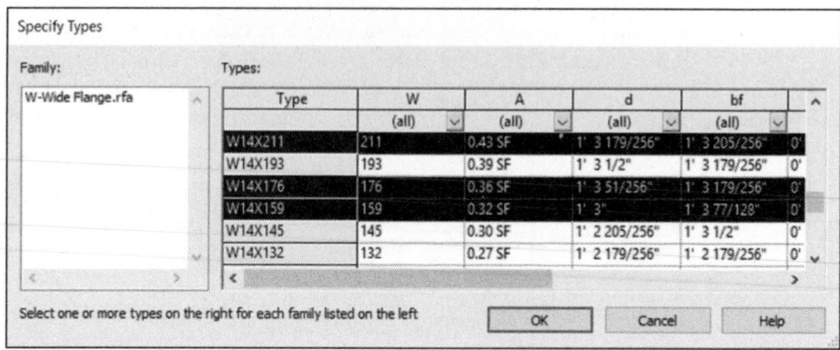

FIGURE 14.22 A type catalog allows you to choose types to load.

If you ever need to load additional types from a family you've already loaded in your project, you don't have to locate the original family file. Instead, locate the family in the Project Browser, right-click it, and then select Reload.

When you generate a type catalog, the easiest method is to first use the Export Types command from the Application menu. This process will export all available parameters and any types you have established in your family to an appropriately formatted syntax. Save the TXT file in the same location as the associated RFA file and with the same filename. For example, the type catalog associated with the `W-Wide Flange.rfa` family file is named `W-Wide Flange.txt`. Using the exact same filename is critical to using a type catalog because that is how Revit will associate the two files.

Open the TXT file with a text editor such as Notepad or Notepad++. Or you can open the file as a comma-delimited table in Microsoft Excel—as long as you save the file back to TXT format when you finish editing.

The first row of the type catalog will be a header that establishes the purpose for each column in the table. The syntax for the header is as follows:

ParameterName##ParameterType##ParameterUnits

Valid entries for *Parameter Type* are listed in Table 14.1 with the proper method for declaring them in the type catalog header. For measurement parameters such as Length and Area, the units can be adapted accordingly. Where the parameter declaration is listed as *ParameterName,* you will substitute a user-defined parameter name. Otherwise, the parameter name is built into the family and cannot be changed.

TABLE 14.1: Types of Parameters Supported in a Type Catalog

TYPE OF PARAMETER	PARAMETER DECLARATION
Angle	*ParameterName*##ANGLE##DEGREES
Area	*ParameterName*##AREA##SQUARE_FEET
Assembly Code	Assembly Code##OTHER##
Cost	Cost##CURRENCY##

TABLE 14.1: Types of Parameters Supported in a Type Catalog *(CONTINUED)*

TYPE OF PARAMETER	PARAMETER DECLARATION
Currency	*ParameterName*##CURRENCY##
Description	Description##OTHER##
Integer	*ParameterName*##OTHER##
Keynote	Keynote##OTHER##
Length	*ParameterName*##LENGTH##FEET
Manufacturer	Manufacturer##OTHER##
Material	*ParameterName*##OTHER##
Model	Model##OTHER##
Number	*ParameterName*##OTHER##
Slope	*ParameterName*##SLOPE##SLOPE_DEGREES
Text	*ParameterName*##OTHER##
URL	URL##OTHER##
Volume	*ParameterName*##VOLUME##CUBIC_FEET
Yes/No	*ParameterName*##OTHER##
<Family Type>	*ParameterName*##OTHER##

For Yes/No parameters in type catalogs, the value is defined as 1 = Yes and 0 = No. For the <Family Type> parameter, enter the complete name of the family with the type designation as *Family Name:Type Name* (without the file extension).

The first column in the table is where you will list the types within the family. In the first row of the table, the first value is blank—that is, the first row will begin with a comma delimiter when it is saved as a TXT file. After the header row is filled with parameter declarations and a list of type names is entered in the first column, you can start populating the values in the rest of the catalog. A sample of a type catalog opened in Excel is shown in Figure 14.23.

FIGURE 14.23 The type catalog for the W-Wide Flange family

	A	B	C	D	E	F
1		W##other##	A##area##inches	d##length##inches	bf##length##inches	tw##length##inches
2	W44X335	335	98.5	44	15.9	1.03
3	W44X290	290	85.4	43.6	15.8	0.865
4	W44X262	262	76.9	43.3	15.8	0.785
5	W44X230	230	67.7	42.9	15.8	0.71
6	W40X593	593	174	43	16.7	1.79
7	W40X503	503	148	42.1	16.4	1.54
8	W40X431	431	127	41.3	16.2	1.34

Organizing Solids and Lines in a Family Editor

When you get beyond the basic geometric controls in families that are dictated by datum objects and dimensions, there are three other ways you can organize the solids and symbolic lines you create in a family:

- Object styles and subcategories
- Visibility settings
- Materials

Each of these three methods of control is directly related to the 3D and 2D content you generate. In other words, you must apply these settings directly to the solids and lines in a family. We will first review each method, and then you will learn about family-modeling techniques in the next section.

Using Object Styles and Subcategories

Let's get back to the exercise file and discuss object styles and subcategories. As mentioned earlier in this chapter, Revit has predefined a number of family categories. These categories define how elements display, schedule, export, and so on. Even though these main object categories can't be modified, you can create subcategories for model, annotation, and imported objects.

Although you can use subcategories to control the visibility of some part of the family, keep in mind that the detail level and visibility settings already manage visibility. The subcategories are most important when you're exporting your project because each category and subcategory is permitted its own CAD layer or IFC classification (Figure 14.24).

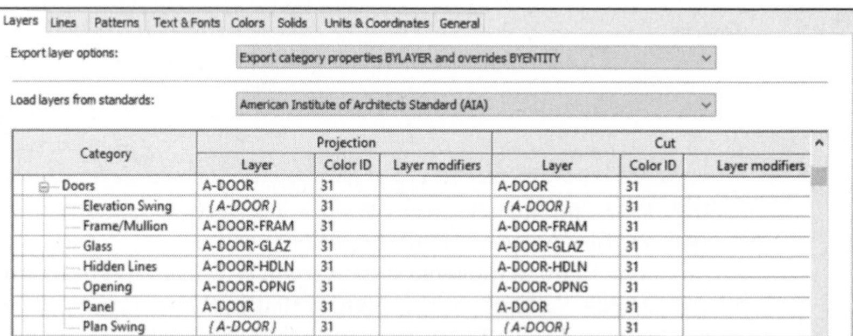

Category	Projection			Cut		
	Layer	Color ID	Layer modifiers	Layer	Color ID	Layer modifiers
Doors	A-DOOR	31		A-DOOR	31	
Elevation Swing	{A-DOOR}	31		{A-DOOR}	31	
Frame/Mullion	A-DOOR-FRAM	31		A-DOOR-FRAM	31	
Glass	A-DOOR-GLAZ	31		A-DOOR-GLAZ	31	
Hidden Lines	A-DOOR-HDLN	31		A-DOOR-HDLN	31	
Opening	A-DOOR-OPNG	31		A-DOOR-OPNG	31	
Panel	A-DOOR	31		A-DOOR	31	
Plan Swing	{A-DOOR}	31		{A-DOOR}	31	

FIGURE 14.24 Export options for categories and subcategories

So if your project is being exported to CAD in such a way that you'll need to associate objects with granular layer settings, creating and assigning subcategories to elements is necessary. Although it's best not to rely on subcategories to manage visibility, we will show you how to create a new subcategory in the exercise file and then assign geometry to it.

In your exercise file, switch to the Manage tab and choose Object Styles. In the Object Styles dialog box, click the New button and create a new subcategory named **Tables**, as shown in Figure 14.25. Click OK to close both dialog boxes.

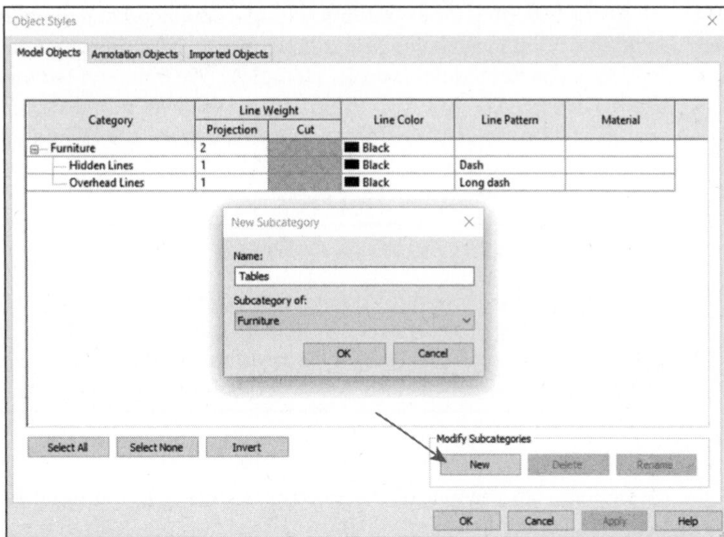

FIGURE 14.25
Create a new family subcategory.

Remember that unless you specifically need to isolate tables from other types of furniture in your project, you shouldn't create too many subcategories because doing so creates an opportunity for inconsistency. What if someone else on your team created a different table family and added a subcategory called Table? When both families are loaded into a project, you will have two subcategories: Tables and Table.

Subcategories must be assigned to solid geometry or symbolic lines in the family in order to be utilized in the project environment. We will discuss this in the "Modeling Techniques in the Family Editor" section later in this chapter.

ASSIGNING VISIBILITY SETTINGS

The time it takes for Revit to generate or regenerate a view depends on how much stuff in the view needs to be displayed. When you're building smaller parts of a larger component (or if the elements are not visible in certain orientations), you should assign those elements to reveal themselves only at a certain level of detail (or in certain views). Doing so prevents the software from managing more information than necessary and helps you keep your views uncluttered.

The Revit Model Content Style Guide published by Autodesk lists guidelines for assigning geometry to the three detail levels available in project views (Table 14.2).

TABLE 14.2: Guidelines for Assigning Detail Level

IF THE GEOMETRY IS:	SET THE DETAIL LEVEL TO:
Smaller than 1′ (300 mm)	Fine
Between 1′ and 3′ (300–900 mm)	Medium
Larger than 3′ (900 mm)	Coarse

Source: Revit Model Content Style Guide by Autodesk

To practice using these visibility settings, download and open the file `c14 Desk Project.rvt` from this book's web page. The sample project contains the default `Desk.rfa` family that is loaded in the Revit default project template. We have created a working sheet in which three 3D views have been placed with different Detail Level properties. Notice that all of the drawer faces and hardware are displayed in every view, despite the Detail Level assignments.

STARTING WITH EXISTING CONTENT

Many of us have downloaded Revit families from a number of widely available online sources to get a first design pass at a piece of content. Autodesk Seek, Revit City, and the AUGI forums are all great places to start. But when you download a family component, take a moment to make sure that the detail level and orientation of detail are appropriate.

Double-click any one of the viewports you see in the sample sheet view to activate a view. Select one of the desks, and then from the contextual tab in the ribbon, click Edit Family. You should be in a 3D view once the `Desk.rfa` family opens. If not, activate the default 3D view. Select the two sets of drawer handles; press the Ctrl key to select multiple items. From the contextual tab in the ribbon, choose Visibility Settings. In the Family Element Visibility Settings dialog box (Figure 14.26), uncheck the boxes for Coarse and Medium. Because these handles are smaller than 1′ (300 mm), they should be seen only when a view's Detail Level is set to Fine. Also uncheck the Left/Right option because viewing the handles from the side might not be that valuable in a section or interior elevation view.

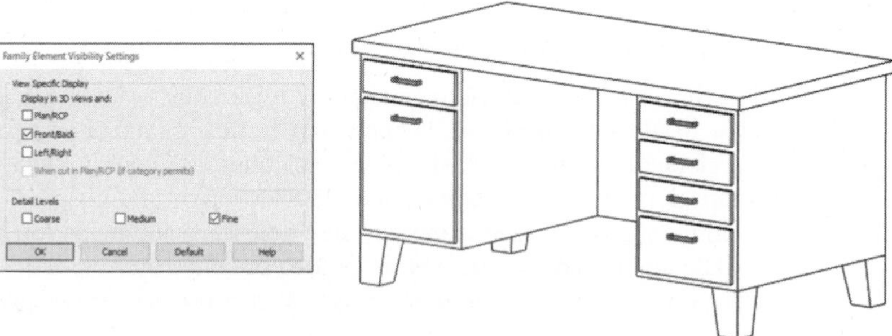

FIGURE 14.26
Family Element Visibility Settings for drawer handles

Notice that the box for the Plan/RCP option is unchecked. This is appropriate for the desk because little more than the surface of the top of the desk needs to show up in the plan. The legs, the hardware, and even the faces of the drawers don't need to show up in the plan. Click OK to close the dialog box.

Next, select the drawer faces and then click the Visibility Settings tool. This geometry range is 1′– 3′ (300–900 mm), so it should display at Medium and Fine detail levels. Also uncheck the Left/Right option (Figure 14.27), and then click OK to close the dialog box.

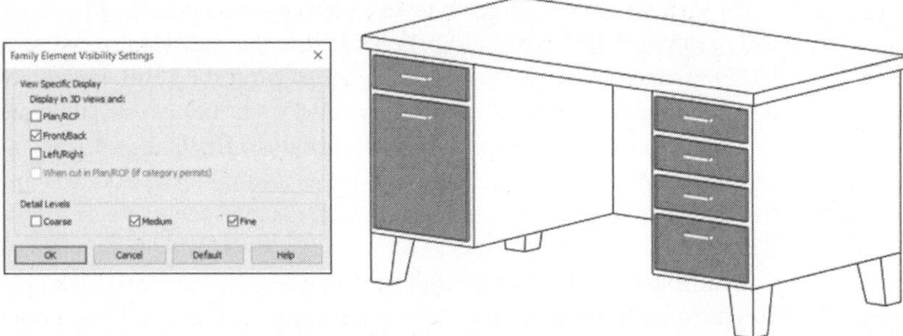

FIGURE 14.27
Visibility settings for drawer fronts

From any tab in the ribbon, choose Load Into Project and then select the `c14 Desk Project.rvt` file if you are prompted. Choose the option to overwrite the existing version, and return to the sample sheet view. You will now see that the appropriate geometry is displaying only at the most appropriate detail levels in each view (Figure 14.28).

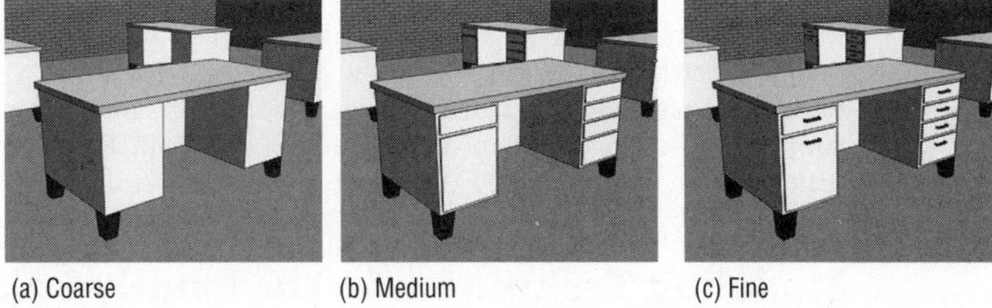

FIGURE 14.28
Views showing a Desk family with appropriate level of detail

USING MATERIALS

Materials are crucial to a family. But what are often more important are the Shading setting and the Transparency value of the material because they communicate much about the intent of your design in the early stages (Figure 14.29).

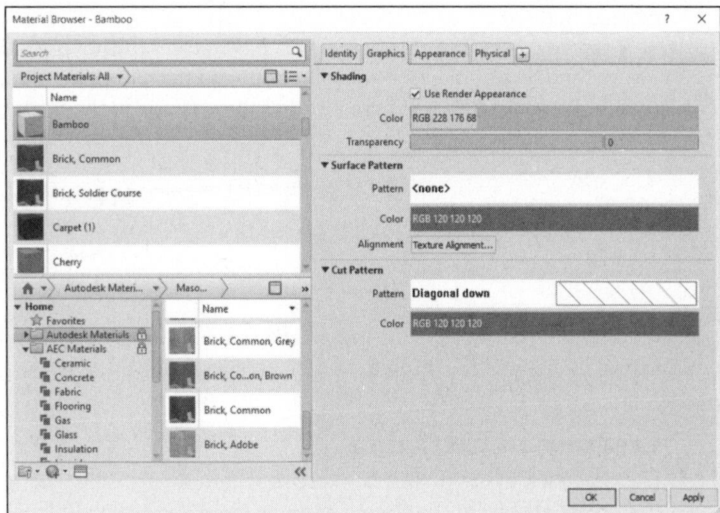

FIGURE 14.29
Shading and Transparency settings in the Material Browser dialog box

In addition, material options are often not easily created in Revit. Yes, a family can have a material parameter. But expressing many different materials for visualization purposes is probably best left to visualization specialists, who understand the subtleties of creating a compelling image, not just a rendering of a working model—and it's unlikely they'll be using Revit for this purpose.

Beyond visualization, however, materials in Revit are used for a host of other things. Graphic representation in construction documents and material takeoffs are two examples. If the materials in your families are something you will need to schedule or view graphically, it's a good idea to define them.

Multiple materials can be assigned to a family. They are assigned based on model solids, so if you have multiple solids (sweeps, extrusions, and the like), each one can be given a unique material.

You have two options to define a material within a family, both being handled in the solid's object properties shown in the Properties palette. By default, the material is set to <By Category>. Select this option and you can change the material to any material shown in the Material Browser dialog box, or you can load a new one from any material library. This is a great use for the family if you know the material is not going to change. If you know that your casework is not going to be anything but blonde maple, for example, go ahead and set the material within the family. Your other option is to use the tiny button [...] to the right of the Material field in the Properties palette to define a new parameter. In this case, you can call the material something like **Casework Material**. If you were to use this same parameter for all your casework families, once it's placed in the model you can change that material via the Material Browser dialog box, and it will update all your casework families at once.

Modeling Techniques in the Family Editor

Creating complex geometry isn't always as easy as opening the Family Editor and starting to model the shape that you think you're trying to create. Sometimes you need to model one form in order to create another form. And sometimes you need to model a complex, parameterized form in order to parameterize the actual shape that you're trying to create. So that you understand these advanced techniques, we'll first cover the available geometry types that can be created in Revit.

There are five discrete geometry types in the Family Editor: Extrusion, Blend, Revolve, Sweep, and Swept Blend. Both solid and void forms can be modeled from these shapes. In this section you'll learn how to create all of these types, along with the Family Editor technique of nesting families.

Which type you select is important, but our advice is to use the simplest form that will express what you're trying to model, keeping in mind how the geometry is likely to change.

Creating an Extrusion

Let's get back to the furniture exercise where we are constructing a table. Activate the Ref. Level floor plan, and from the Create panel in the ribbon click Extrusion. The first action we will take is to specify a work plane to host the extrusion. If you don't specify a work plane, the default plane will be the level associated with the current view.

1. In the Work Plane panel in the contextual tab of the ribbon, click Set. In the Name drop-down list within the Work Plane dialog box, choose Reference Plane : Top, as shown in Figure 14.30.

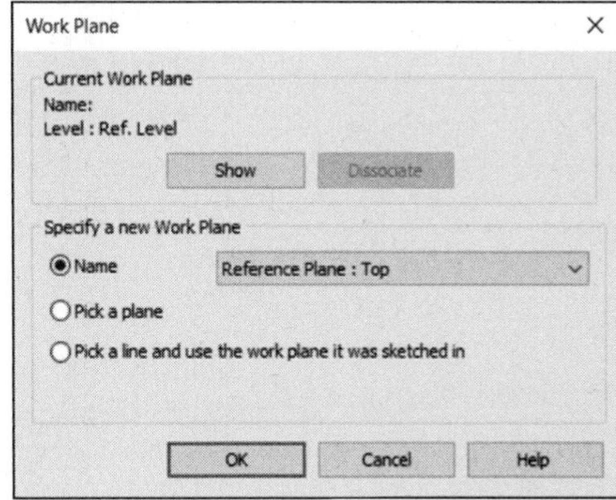

FIGURE 14.30
Set a named reference plane as the work plane.

2. In the Options bar, set the Depth to **–0′-2″** (**–50** mm).

   This will allow the top of the extrusion to be aligned with the Top reference plane, with its thickness extruding downward—away from the work plane.

3. In the Properties palette, set Subcategory to Tables. For the Material parameter, click the small button to the right of the parameter value field.

   This button will allow you to associate a family parameter to the property instead of simply choosing one material to be assigned to the solid.

4. Click the Add Parameter button and create a new parameter named **Tabletop Material**. Click OK to close both open dialog boxes, and then you will see that the Material field is now inactive and the small button now has an equal sign label.

   This means that the property is now being controlled by a family parameter.

5. In the Draw panel, choose the Rectangle tool, and then sketch a rectangle that snaps to the intersections of the outer reference planes (Left, Front, Right, and Back). Immediately after your second click to complete the sketch, you will see padlock icons at each of the four sides of the sketch. Click each one to establish an alignment constraint with the respective reference plane (Figure 14.31). If you click away and the constraint icons disappear, you will either have to delete and redraw the sketched lines or use the Align tool to reestablish the constraint.

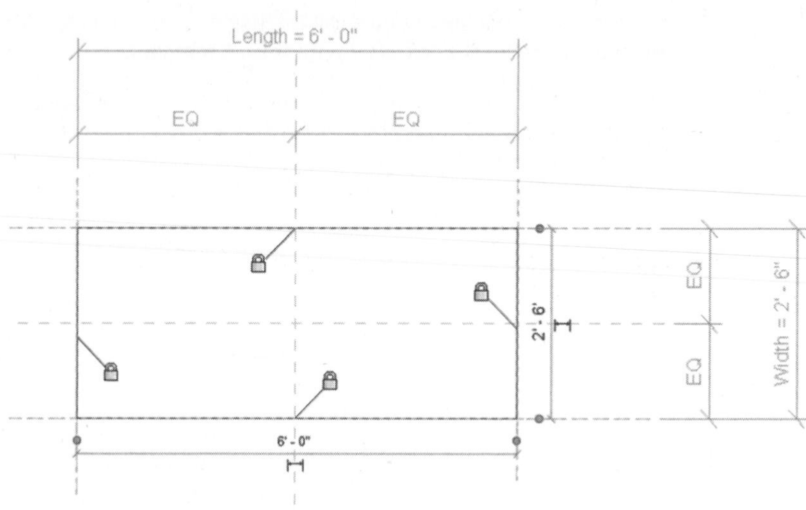

Figure 14.31
Set the constraints of the extrusion sketch to reference planes.

Click Finish Edit Mode from the contextual tab in the ribbon, and you'll see the first solid piece of your exercise family. Activate a 3D view and open the Family Types dialog box. Switch between Type 1 and Type 2, and click Apply to verify that the extrusion flexes like the reference planes did previously in the chapter.

6. Activate the Front elevation view, and add an aligned dimension from the Top reference plane to the bottom of the tabletop extrusion.
7. Select the dimension, and from the Label drop-down list in the Options bar, choose <Add Parameter...>. Name the new parameter **Tabletop Thickness**, and then click OK.
8. Open the Family Types dialog box again, and set the Name drop-down list to Type 2. In the Tabletop Material parameter, click the ellipsis button to launch the Material Browser.
9. From the Material Browser, make sure the library panel is displayed by clicking the icon at the top of the document materials list. Search for "oak" at the top of the dialog box, and then select the material Wood (Oak) from the library panel. Click the up-arrow icon to load the material from the library into the family. In the Graphics tab of the Material Browser, check the box Use Render Appearance (Figure 14.32), and then click OK.
10. Set the Tabletop Thickness value to **4"** (**100** mm) and then click Apply in the Family Types dialog box. Repeat steps 8, 9, and 10 for Type 1, but search for "glass" and load the material named Glass, Green. Set the Tabletop Thickness for Type 1 to **1"** (**25** mm), and then click OK to close the Family Types dialog box.

Creating a Sweep

Let's have a little fun and assign a void sweep to the edge of the tabletop. It will be unique because we only want the sweep to cut the tabletop when Type 2 is selected—it will not cut the top for Type 1.

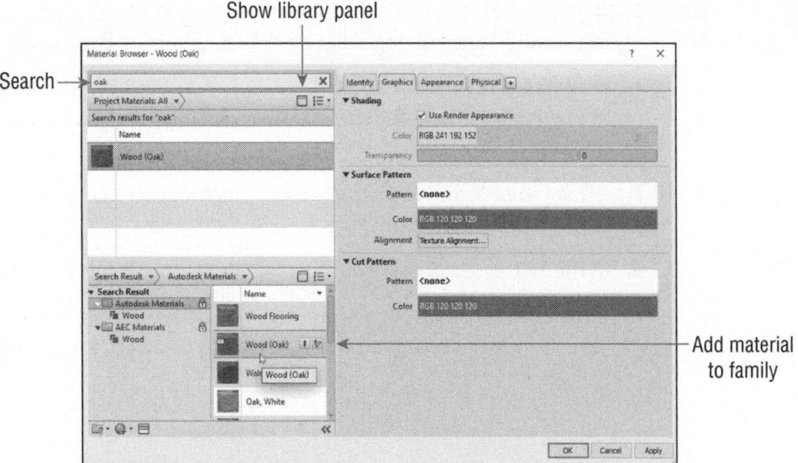

FIGURE 14.32 Adding a material from the library and setting its graphic appearance

A *sweep* is a 2D profile that follows a path. The magic behind sweeps in the Family Editor is that a sweep path can be set to automatically follow other model geometry. A great example is the continuous tubular structure of the chair shown in Figure 14.33. As you can see in the sequence of images, a simpler solid form is generated and then converted to a non-cutting void, a path is generated along the edges of the void geometry, and a tube profile is applied to the path. To explore how this family was made, download the file `c14 Tube Chairs.rvt` from this book's web page.

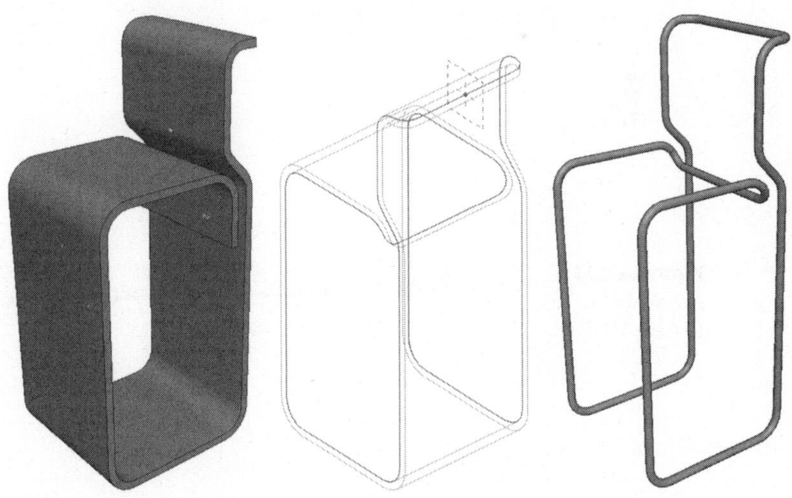

FIGURE 14.33 Solid geometry, converted to a noncutting void used to drive a complex sweep path

In this part of the chapter exercise, you will create a void sweep along the outer edge of the tabletop using the Pick Path tool. You will then assign a parameter to drive the void into or away from the solid extrusion, depending on which type is specified.

1. Activate the default 3D view and set the graphic style in the view control bar to Shaded. Open the Family Types dialog box, select Type 2 in the Name drop-down list, and then click OK.
2. From the Create tab, choose Void Forms ➤ Void Sweep. From the contextual tab in the ribbon, click Pick Path. In the 3D view, pick each of the four upper edges of the tabletop solid (Figure 14.34).
3. Click Finish Edit Mode (the green check mark) in the contextual tab of the ribbon to complete the Pick Path command.
4. In the Sweep panel of the contextual tab, set the Profile drop-down list to c14 Table Void Profile.

   This is a profile family we created and preloaded in the exercise file. You can also download it with the rest of this chapter's exercise files for further exploration.

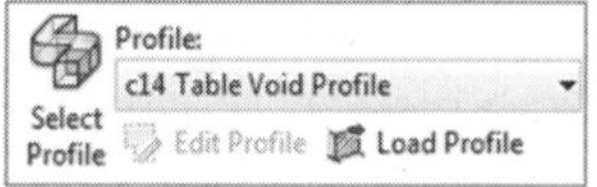

5. Zoom into the area where the profile is applied to the path, and make sure the curved part of the profile is facing toward the tabletop solid (Figure 14.35). If it isn't, click the Flip button in the Options bar.
6. Click Finish Edit Mode in the contextual tab in the ribbon, and the void will automatically cut the tabletop solid.

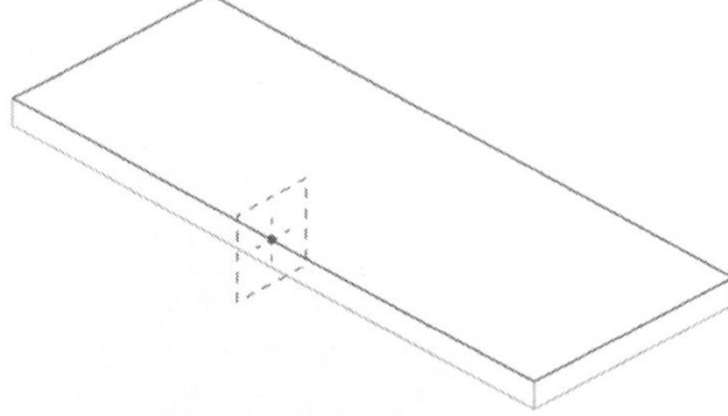

FIGURE 14.34
Use the Pick Path tool to select the edges of the solid tabletop.

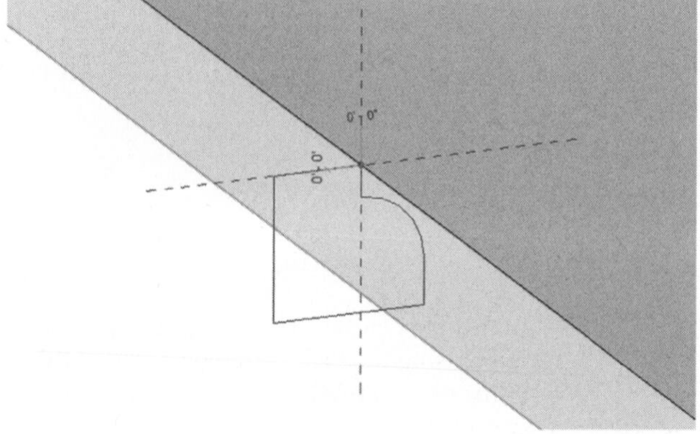

FIGURE 14.35
Adjust the sweep profile to face the solid.

When you create a void in the Family Editor, it will automatically cut any existing solids. If you don't want a void to automatically cut other geometry, you can create the elements as solids first. When you are satisfied with the forms, select the appropriate solids and change them to voids in the Properties palette. Note that once a solid or a void is being cut by another object, you cannot change the solid/void property. You must use the Uncut Geometry tool first.

Because you used the Pick Path method to define the sweep path, the sweep will automatically update as the shape of the tabletop changes. This exercise is a simple example of a powerful tool with a plethora of applications.

Now that you have created a void that cuts the solid geometry of the wood tabletop type, you need to adjust it so that the profile does not cut the solid when the glass tabletop type is specified. Unfortunately, you can't simply turn the void sweep on and off, but you can adjust its horizontal offset so it cuts like a virtual sliding saw.

1. In the 3D view, select the void sweep. In the Properties palette, you will see the parameters that drive the profile within the sweep. Click the Associate Family Parameter button next to the Horizontal Profile Offset value.

2. Click the Add Parameter button. Create a new parameter named **Trigger Cut**, and then click OK to close both dialog boxes.

3. Open the Family Types dialog box, and for Type 2, set the Trigger Cut value to **0′-0″** and then click Apply.

4. Switch to Type 1 and set the Trigger Cut value to **–0′-4″** (**–100** mm), and then click OK to close the dialog box. Figure 14.36 shows the difference between the two types just defined.

FIGURE 14.36
Void sweep cutting Type 2 (wood); not cutting Type 1 (glass)

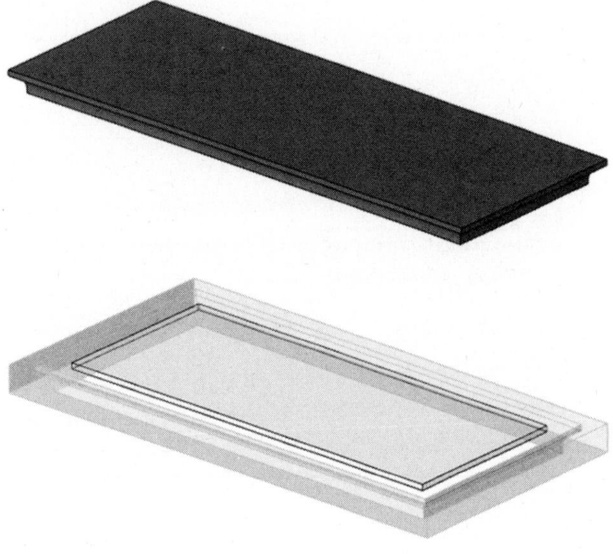

Adding Tooltips

There have probably been times when you have pulled a family out of your library or a previous project to add to your model and you can't remember what the parameters actually control. Parameters like Height or Length are pretty easy, but will you remember what the Trigger Cut does?

In the Family Editor you can add tooltips to your parameters. You can add up to 250 characters to describe your parameter and add some additional notes to how it is intended to be used. In the Parameters Properties dialog box you'll see the Edit Tooltip button.

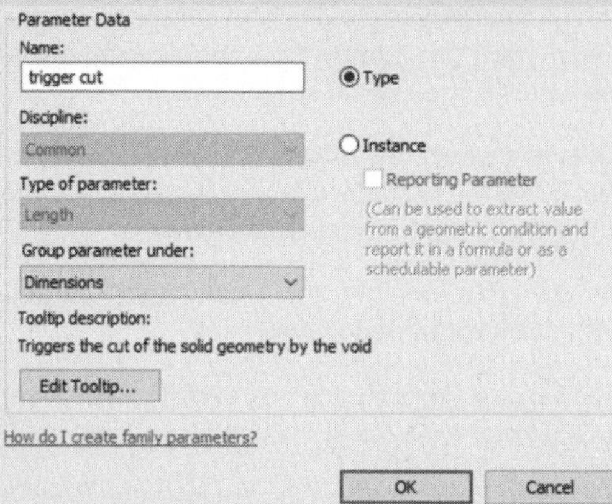

Clicking this button will allow you to add a message or description to your parameter to help explain its functionality.

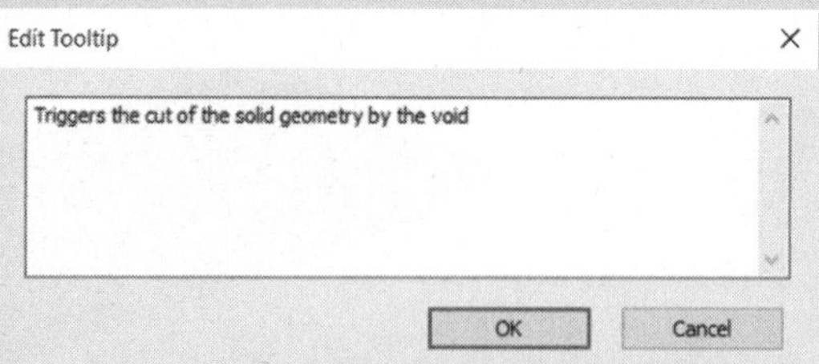

Hovering your mouse over the parameter in the Parameter Properties dialog box will show the tooltip you've created.

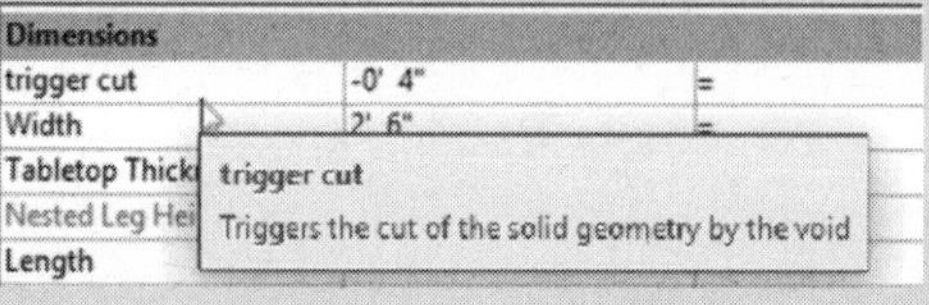

You'll see that adding the negative value to the Horizontal Profile Offset allows you to control whether the void cuts the solid tabletop. We simply assigned the offset value to each family type, but you could explore methods of using formulas with logic such as this:

If Tabletop Thickness < 4″ then Trigger Cut = – 4″ else Trigger Cut = 0″

The actual syntax of this formula to be applied in the Family Types dialog box would be: **if(Tabletop Thickness < 0′ 4″, -0′ 4″, 0′).**

Creating a Revolve

Let's move on to the process of creating the legs for the table. You'll use the Revolve tool to create this shape; however, you will create the shape only once in a separate family that will be loaded into the table family and placed multiple times.

We have created a preloaded family for the purpose of this segment of the exercise. Download and open the file `c14 Table Leg.rfa` from this book's web page. You'll create a revolve form, assign height and material parameters, and then load it into the table family.

1. In the c14 Table Leg file, activate the Front elevation view. You will see that we have sketched a 2D profile consisting of invisible lines.

   These will not display when the leg family is loaded into the table family.

2. From the Create tab in the ribbon, click Revolve. From the Draw panel in the contextual tab, make sure the Pick Lines tool is selected. Hover the mouse pointer over one of the provided profile lines and press the Tab key once, and then click to select all the lines of the profile.

   Don't worry about constraining any of the sketch lines, because this shape won't be dependent on adjacent geometry.

3. Click the Axis Line tool in the contextual tab, select the Pick Lines mode, and then click the vertical reference plane in the drawing area.
4. Click the Finish Edit Mode icon in the contextual tab to complete the Revolve command.
5. Add an aligned dimension between the Ref. Level and the reference plane above the revolve. Select the dimension, and in the Options bar choose <Add Parameter…> from the Label drop-down list. Name the new parameter **Leg Height**, and make sure it is a type parameter.
6. Select the solid revolve, and in the Properties palette click the Associate Family Parameter button for the Material property. Create a new parameter named **Leg Material**, and click OK to close the open dialog boxes.

Before you save the leg family and load it into the table family, you should consider whether the nested family needs to be scheduled—in the case of a table leg, probably not. However, you will load some chairs into the table family later and those will surely need to be scheduled.

Switch to the Create tab, and from the Properties panel click the Family Category And Parameters button. In that dialog box, you will see a list of Family Parameters that contains a parameter called Shared. When this box is checked, the nested family can be scheduled. For example, if you checked the box for the table leg family, loaded it into the table family, loaded the table family into a project, and then placed several instances of the table, you could create a schedule to count the total number of table legs in the project.

Creating a Blend and Swept Blend

When you create a blend, you are essentially combining two different shapes. Say you have a circle and want to transition it to a square. Creating that geometry by using an extrusion and voids would be complicated, but creating it with a blend is simple (see Figure 14.37).

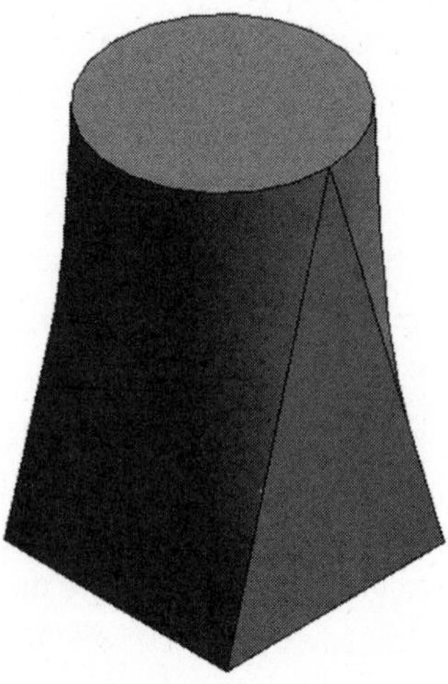

FIGURE 14.37
A simple blend of a square and circle

The only difference between a blend and a swept blend is that a blend is defined along a straight line starting on a work plane. A swept blend is along a user-defined path. Figure 14.38 demonstrates a swept blend between a circle and a square along a user-defined path.

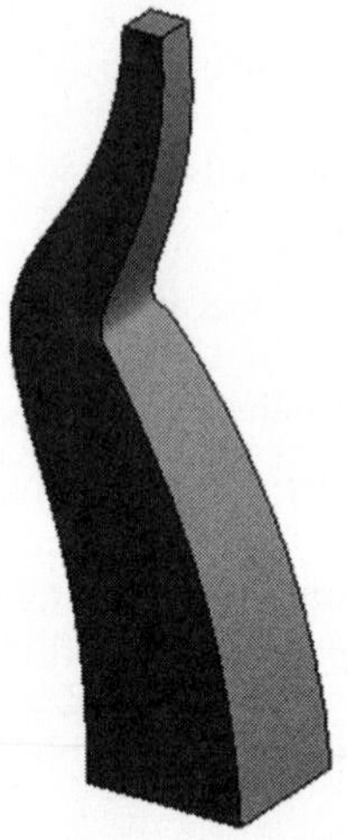

FIGURE 14.38
A swept blend

Both types of blends can incorporate a variety of shapes and profiles. Using the context of furniture that we've established, you'll create a swept blend. You're going to create a wooden stool.

1. To begin, open the default furniture family. You're going to create a three-sided stool, starting with the legs. When you open the default furniture family, you'll be in the Ref. Plane view. In this view, choose the Swept Blend tool from the Create tab.

   The Swept Blend tool has its own contextual menu, shown in Figure 14.39. You will create a path for the sweep and the starting and ending shapes. As you can see, the software first wants you to define a path.

FIGURE 14.39
The Swept Blend contextual menu

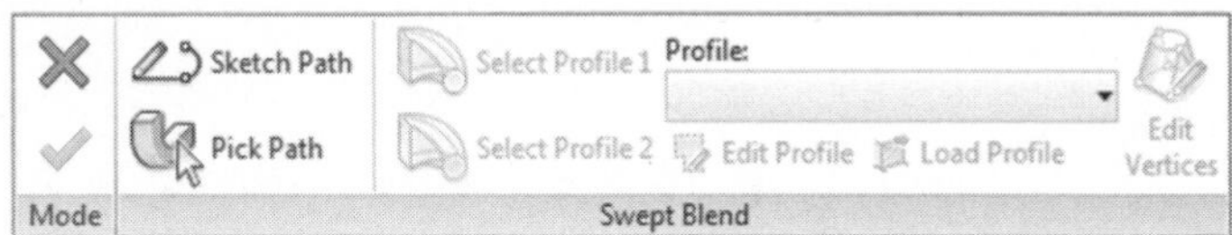

2. Choose the Front elevation view to start the path, and pick the Sketch Path button from the Swept Blend panel. Using the Line tool (which is selected by default), start a line from 10″ (250 mm) to the left of the base and continue until it intersects with the vertical plane at a 73° angle. You'll have a measurement roughly 2′-10″ (865 mm) across the hypotenuse of the triangle (Figure 14.40). Click the green check mark to accept the sweep.

FIGURE 14.40
Creating the leg sweep

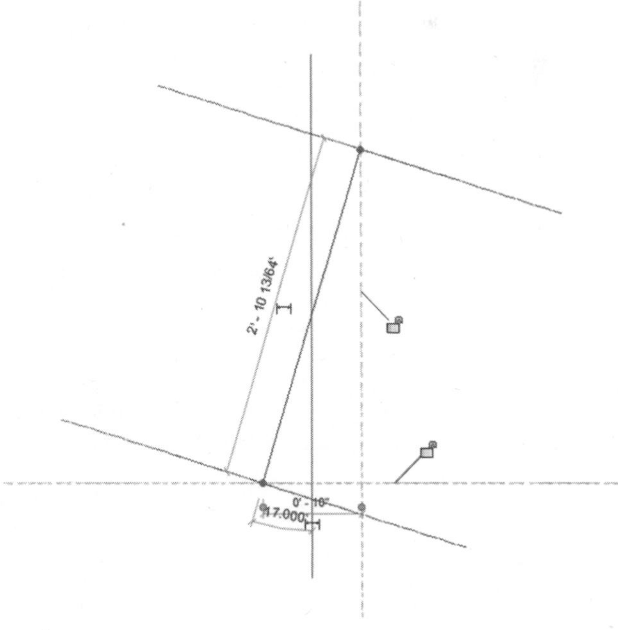

Now you need to make the base of your leg.

3. Open the Ref. View and you'll see two red dots and a line connecting them. The dot on the left is the base of the leg, the dot on the right is the top of the leg, and the line between is the path you just created. Starting with the base, choose the Select Profile 1 button and then the Edit Profile button (Figure 14.41).

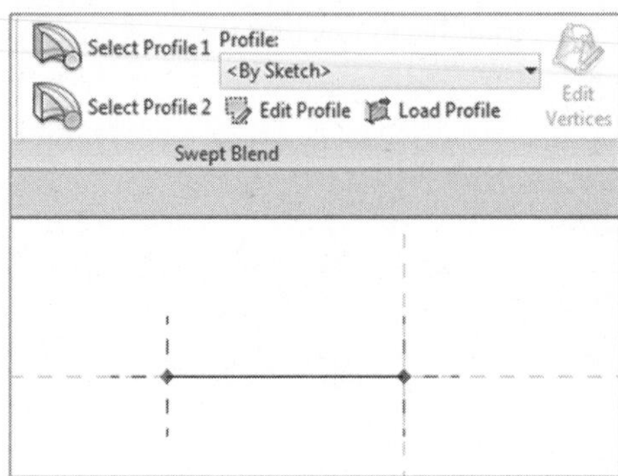

FIGURE 14.41 Modify the two profiles to create the swept blend.

4. Using the left red dot as a center point, create a circle 1″ (25 mm) in diameter. Click the green check mark, then the Finish Edit Mode button, to complete the shape.

   Next, you need to create the top of the leg.

5. Select the Select Profile 2 button and then Edit Profile from the Swept Blend panel. Using the Y-reference plane as the right side of the box, create a rectangle centered on the X-axis 1″ × 3″ (25 mm × 75 mm). Click Finish Edit Mode when you've finished. The two shapes will look like Figure 14.42.

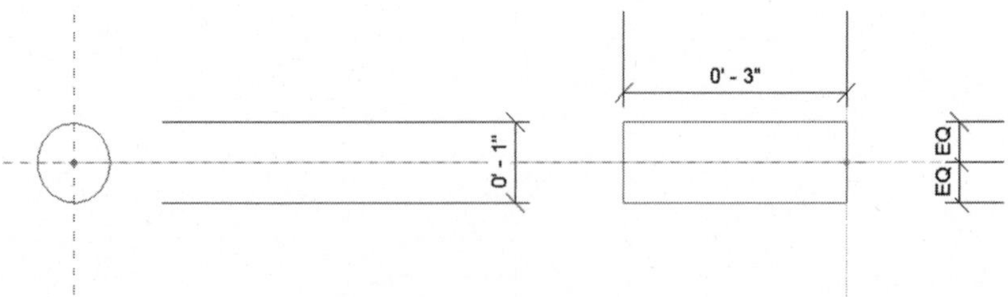

FIGURE 14.42 Finishing the two shapes of the blend

6. With those two profiles and a path complete, click Finish Edit Mode again to complete the sweep. You now have one leg of your stool.

7. To finish the base, select the leg and choose the Array tool. In the Options bar, set these options:
   - Choose a radial array.
   - Leave the Number of arrayed items at 3.
   - Change the Angle to **360**.

- Change the rotation center to the middle of the X-Y reference planes.
- Click OK to finish the array.

You should now have a set of stool legs (Figure 14.43).

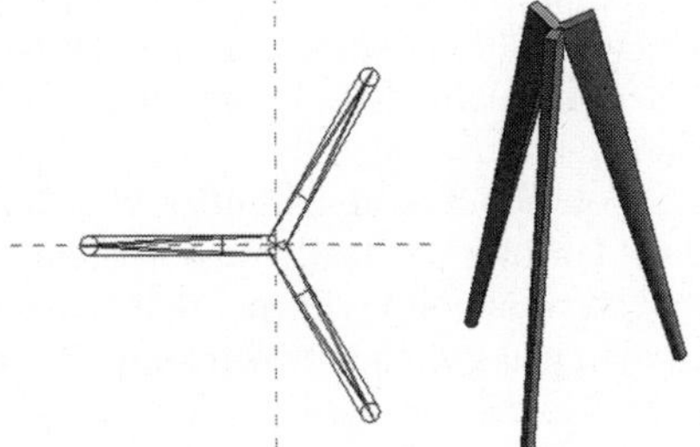

FIGURE 14.43
The completed stool legs

8. From this point, use the techniques explained earlier in the chapter to add a round stool seat and a bar near the base for your feet.

   Our finished stool is shown in Figure 14.44. There are a few ways to create the seat and bar—it can be with a swept blend, an extrusion, or even a revolve.

FIGURE 14.44
The completed stool

The finished family can be found on the book's web page. The file is called `c14-WoodenStool.rfa`. Before we continue with the table-modeling exercise, let's take a moment to discuss the importance of nested families in comparison to modeling repetitive geometry all within one family. Families are used to create individual components. By combining those components, you can use a nested family to add parameters to better define the relationships between those components and best leverage the families within your project.

Nesting Families

Geometry from one family can be loaded into another family. This process is called *nesting*, and it allows you to create a single element that will be used many times in another family. This method is much more efficient than creating an element and then grouping and copying it around the same family. Let's review some benefits of using nested families.

When one family is loaded into another, the nested family behaves as a single, unified component. This means that it will be much easier to change and control the instance placements of a nested family. Even though the nested family may seem like a static component, references and parameters in nested families can be driven by controls in the host family.

A nested family can also be controlled by a Family Type parameter, which will allow you to select from multiple nested families as another parameter in the host family. This feature is incredibly powerful for creating design iteration within families that are in your projects. You will see this functionality later in this chapter when you load two different chair families into the table family and use a Family Type parameter to select between them.

As a final note about nested families, you should always be aware of the insertion point defined in the families you load into other families. As we mentioned previously in this chapter, a consistent insertion point will ensure that a nested family doesn't "flip-flop" in unintended directions when you switch between family types.

Let's get back to the exercise for which you should still be working in the c14 Table Leg family file:

1. Save the leg family and then click the Load Into Project button in the ribbon. The table family should still be open and the leg will be loaded (nested) into it. You will now place multiple instances of the leg family, associate the parameters, and adjust the visibility for control of an optional leg instance.

2. Switch to the c14 Table file, and activate the Ref. Level floor plan. From the Create tab, click the Component tool, and the c14 Table Leg family should be the active component in the Type Selector. Look in the Properties palette at the Host property, and make sure that it is Level: Ref. Level. Place four instances of the leg near the corners of the table and one exactly at the crossing of the center reference planes.

3. Add dimensions for each of the four corner legs, and adjust the legs as necessary so that they are offset exactly 6" (150 mm) from each edge reference plane (Figure 14.45). Lock these dimensions to preserve the offset.

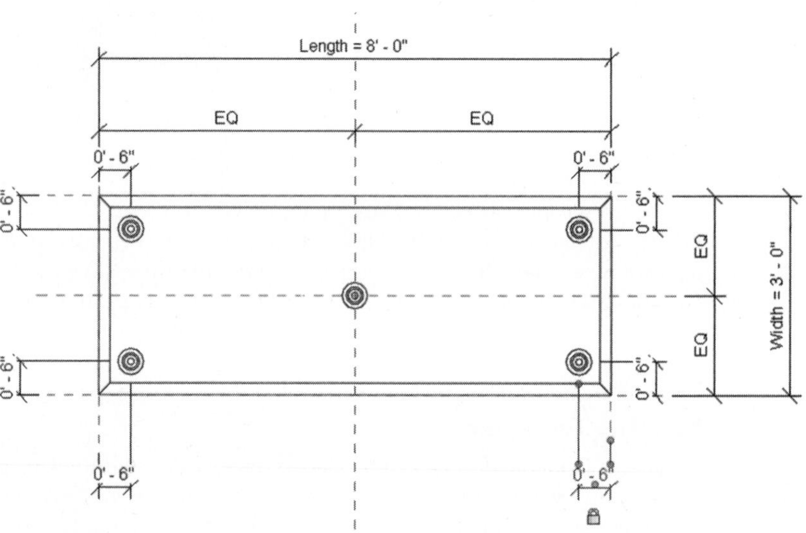

FIGURE 14.45 Leg families are placed and dimensioned in a plan view.

4. Select the middle leg, and in the Properties palette click the Associate Family Parameter button for the Visible property. Click the Add Parameter button, and name the new parameter **Middle Leg**. This will be a Yes/No parameter that can be controlled with a logic formula that will be driven by the length of the table.
5. Open the Family Types dialog box, and in the Formula field for the Middle Leg parameter type the following: **Length > 7′** (for metric, type **Length > 2000 mm**).

   This simple formula will make the middle leg visible when the Length parameter exceeds 7′ (2000 mm) and invisible when it doesn't.
6. Switch to a 3D view, and now you'll need to assign dimensional parameters to drive the leg heights in relation to the table.

   You can do this a few different ways, but when you're dealing with multiple instances of an object, we recommend you feed a value into a nested type parameter rather than align and lock each instance to reference planes within the host family.
7. Select one of the legs, and then click the Edit Type button in the Properties palette. In the Type Properties dialog box, click the Assign Family Parameter (AFP) button for the Leg Height parameter. Add a new parameter named **Nested Leg Height**.
8. Click the AFP button for the Leg Material parameter, and add a new parameter named **Nested Leg Material**. Click OK to close the Type Properties dialog box.

   You must associate the parameters in nested families with parameters in the host family—even if it is simply to allow materials to be assigned to the nested elements.
9. Open the Family Types dialog box. In the Formula field for the Nested Leg Height parameter, type the following: **Height - Tabletop Thickness**.

   Make sure that the parameters are spelled exactly because they are case sensitive. This formula will use the overall height of the table minus the thickness of the tabletop to drive the height of the nested legs.
10. Switch between Type 1 and Type 2 to verify the behavior of the legs. Even though the middle leg is still visible in the Family Editor, it will be invisible when the family is loaded into the project environment.

    Save the table family and load it into the c14 Desk Project file, referenced previously in this chapter. Place some instances of each type and observe the differences in size and number of legs (Figure 14.46).

FIGURE 14.46
The two family types placed in a project

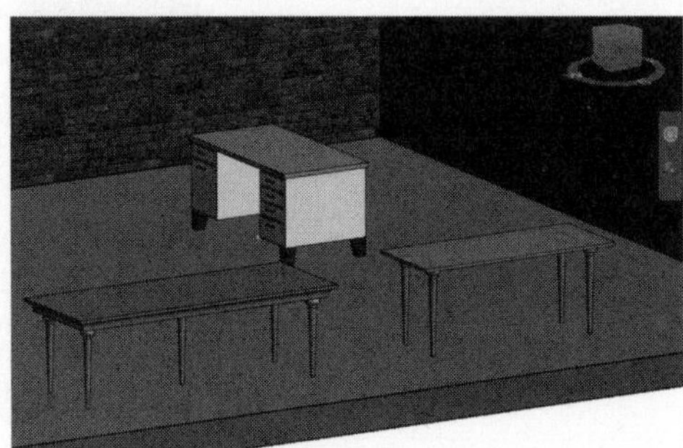

11. Select one of the Type 1 instances of the c14 Table family, and then click Edit Type from the Properties palette. Locate the Nested Leg Material parameter and launch the Material Browser.
12. Search for "white," and load the material named Metal, Paint Finish, White, and Matte from the library into the project. In the Graphics tab, check the box Use Render Appearance, and then click OK in the Material Browser to assign it to the Nested Leg Material. Click OK to close the Type Properties dialog box.
13. Select one of the Type 2 instances and assign the Wood (Oak) material to the Nested Leg Material parameter.

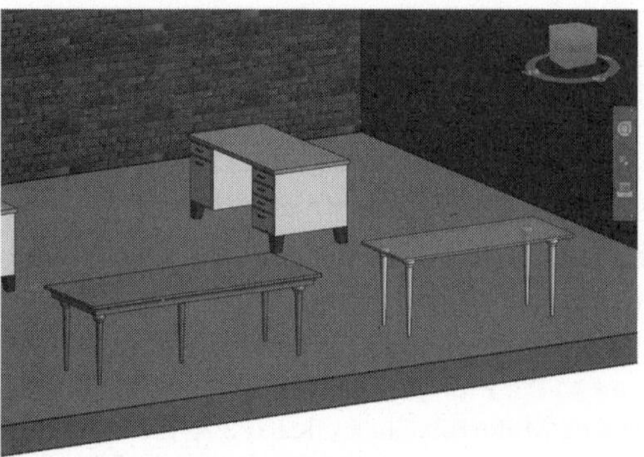

Troubleshooting Techniques

Now that you have created a basic component and explored some of the fundamental modeling techniques, let's look at some additional methods and troubleshooting you might experience working on a real project.

Doing a Visibility Check

In the `c14 Desk Project.rvt` file, open the Visibility/Graphic Overrides dialog box and expand the Furniture category. Uncheck the box for the Tables subcategory, and then click OK to close the dialog box. You'll notice that only the tabletops have been turned off in the drawing area, as shown in Figure 14.47.

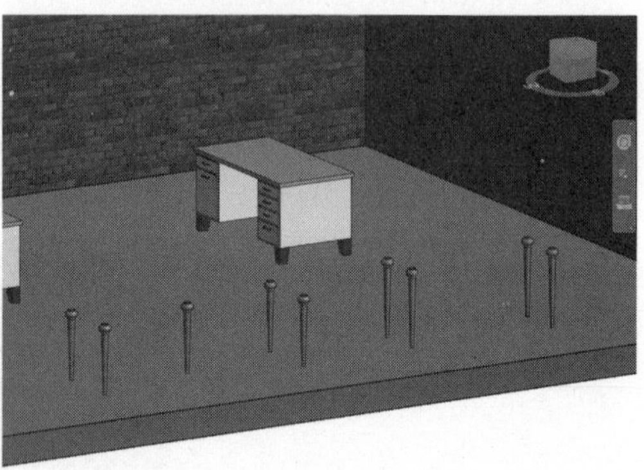

FIGURE 14.47
Visibility settings applied to a subcategory

Open the Visibility/Graphic Overrides dialog box again and uncheck the box for the Furniture category. Click OK, and you will see that the desks and even the table legs have been turned off in the view. Even though the nested table leg family was created with the Generic Model family template, it will behave according to the main category of the host family; however, this does not apply to subcategories. Let's go through the process to fix the problem:

1. Go back to the c14 Table Leg family, and from the Create tab, click the Family Category And Parameters tool. Change the Family Category to Furniture, and then click OK.

   The family category must be changed to Furniture to avoid confusion with object style subcategories. If you create a subcategory under Generic Models named Tables and then reload the nested leg family in the table, there will be two separate subcategories named Tables.

2. Switch to the Manage tab, and then choose Object Styles. In the Object Styles dialog box, click the New button and name the new subcategory **Tables**.

   Remember to use careful planning when naming subcategories within your custom families. As mentioned earlier in this chapter, inconsistency with subcategories can lead to problems with view templates, graphics, exporting, and printing.

3. In the drawing area, select the solid revolve, and in the Properties palette, set the Subcategory parameter to Tables.

4. Save the family, and then click the Load Into Project command in the ribbon. First, reload the leg family into the table family, and then reload the table family into the `c14 Desk Project.rvt` file. When prompted, choose the option to overwrite the existing family.

You will now notice in `c14 Desk Project.rvt` that the table legs are turned off along with the other elements of the tables.

When you are editing a nested family, you could reload the family directly into the project without reloading it into the host family. We recommend working your way back through each family so that the original host family RFA file is maintained in your project content library.

Applying Parametric Arrays and Family Type Parameters

For the final exercise, you will work with additional nested families, but you will now learn how to apply a Family Type parameter and use parametric arrays. The steps in the following exercises must be carefully applied in the correct order or the flexibility in the family may be disrupted. More complex families are prone to errors if you build them quickly and without care, so take your time and review each step along the way.

You will begin by loading two different chair families into the `c14 Table.rfa` family. Download the files `Chair-Dining-1.rfa` and `Chair-Dining-2.rfa` from this book's web page. These modified families were originally downloaded from the `RevitCity.com` website.

1. In the `c14 Table.rfa` file, activate the Ref. Level floor plan. From the Create tab in the ribbon, click the Component tool. If you haven't already loaded the two chair families, click the Load Family command in the ribbon.

2. From the Type Selector, choose the Chair-Dining-1 family and place one chair along the upper edge of the table.

   Remember to press the spacebar to rotate the chair as needed before you place it.

3. Exit the Component command and select the chair you placed in the previous step. In the Options bar, choose <Add Parameter...> from the Label drop-down list. Create a new parameter named **Chair Type**. Note that the parameter type is <Family Type>.

   This kind of parameter will let you apply different families that are nested in the host family.

   Also, it is important that all nested families with which you intend to use a family type parameter must be of the same category. For example, one of the chairs originally downloaded from the `RevitCity.com` website was assigned to the Furniture Systems category, whereas the other was in the Furniture category. Therefore, the two nested families could not be assigned to the same family type parameter.

4. With the chair still selected, click the Edit Type button in the Properties palette. Click the AFP button for the Chair Material parameter. Create a new parameter named **Nested Chair Material**, and then click OK to close the open dialog boxes.
5. From the Modify tab in the ribbon, click the Align tool. As shown in Figure 14.48, click the Back reference plane (1) and then the reference within the chair (2). Finally, click the padlock icon to establish a constraint (3).
6. Add an aligned dimension from the Right reference plane to the center reference of the chair. Set the value to **1′-8″** (**500** mm), and click the padlock to establish the dimension as a constraint.
7. Select the chair, and then from the Modify tab in the ribbon, click the Array tool. In the Options bar, choose the Group And Associate option and the Move To: End radio button.
8. Click once near the chair and then click a second time 2′-8″ (800 mm) to the left. Press the Enter key to accept the number of entities in the array.
9. Use the Align tool to constrain the arrayed chair to the Back reference plane, add an aligned dimension, and then lock the dimension—similar to the previous steps. The plan view should look like the image in Figure 14.49.
10. Select one of the arrayed chairs, and you will again see a line connecting the arrayed objects displaying the number 2. Click this line and then choose <Add Parameter...> from the Label drop-down list in the Options bar. Create a new parameter named **Chair Array**. Click OK to close any open dialog boxes.
11. Open the Family Types dialog box. In the formula field for the Chair Array parameter, type **(Length - 2′) / 2′** (for metric, type **(Length - 600) / 600**).

    This will automatically increase or decrease the number of elements in the array based on the length of the table.

12. Repeat steps 1–10 to place another parametric array along the Front reference plane. When you get to step 3, instead of choosing <Add Parameter...> from the Label drop-down list, you will simply choose the Chair Type parameter, and in step 10 you will choose the Chair Array parameter.

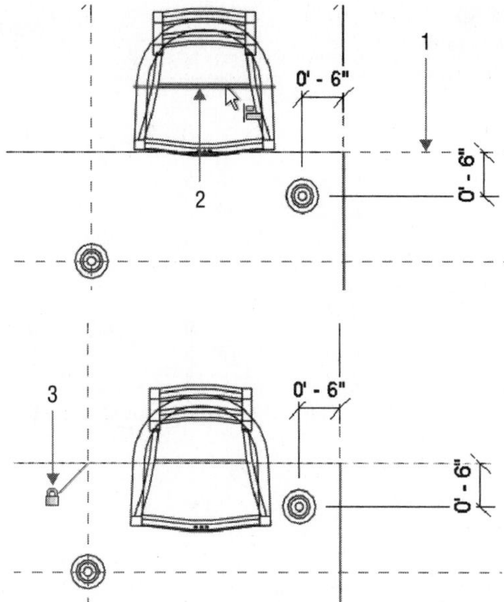

FIGURE 14.48
Using the Align tool

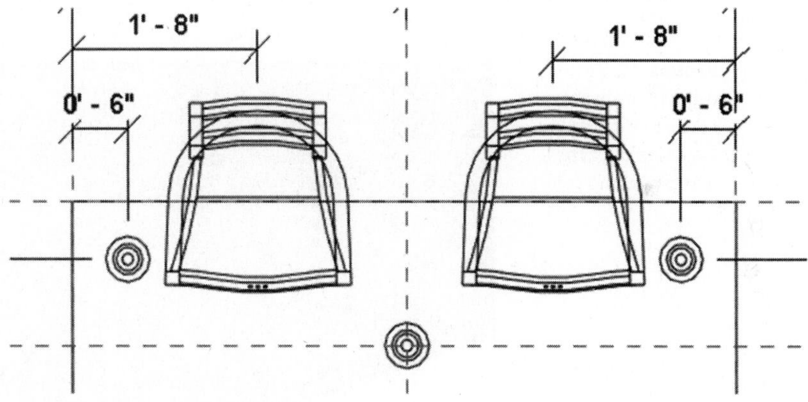

FIGURE 14.49
Two nested chairs are established as a parametric array.

Before you continue with the exercise, take a moment to open the Family Types dialog box and switch between Type 1 and Type 2. Verify that the chairs maintain alignment with the edges of the tabletop. When you select Type 2, there should be six chairs instead of four. Compare your results to the image shown in Figure 14.50.

With Type 2 still active in the Family Type dialog box, set the Chair Type parameter to Chair-Dining-2 and then click the Apply button. You should see all the nested chairs change to the alternate chair family. Save the family and reload it into the `c14-Desk-Project.rvt` file, and choose the option to reload the family and overwrite any parameter values. If the Tables subcategory is still turned off in the view, you may notice that the chairs appear but not the tables. There is likely no realistic need to create another subcategory for chairs, so open the Visibility/Graphic Overrides dialog box and turn on the Tables subcategory.

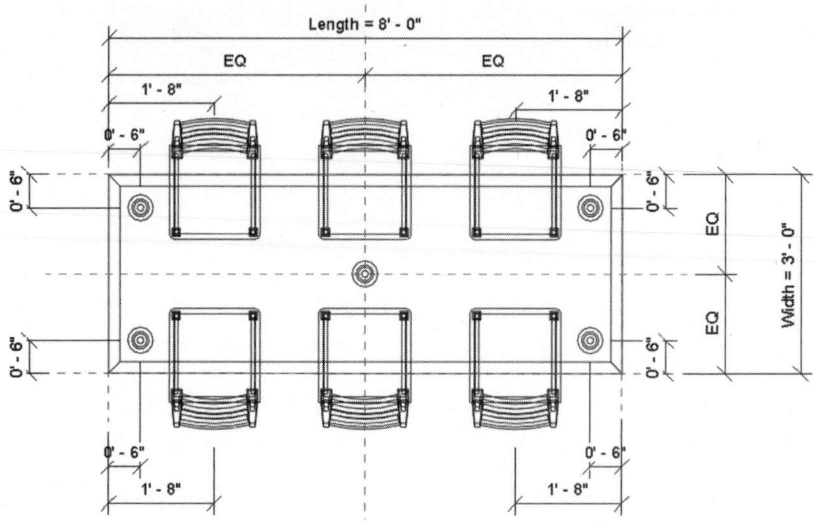

FIGURE 14.50 The complete table family with nested chairs

You can experiment with adjusting the values of the table family, including creating new types with variations in materials (Figure 14.51).

FIGURE 14.51 Adjust family properties to include variations of types, materials, and colors.

The Bottom Line

Get started with a family. Before you start to create your own family components, take a moment to think about how you expect that component to "behave" in your project. The role of the Family Editor isn't just an environment to model geometry; it also determines how the content that you create will behave in the project environment.

Master It Choosing the right template is critical. You can convert from one family template to another, but this is not always the case. Why would you want to choose a door template rather than a Generic Model template?

Create the framework for a family component. Reference planes, points, and lines are the "bones" of your component. Assign parameters to the skeleton, and the geometry will follow along. Be sure to test the parameter and reference relationships before you start to create any solid model geometry.

Master It Why should you build, assign parameters to, and test the references first? Why not just model the geometry?

Understand family modeling techniques. Although the Family Editor contains a wide assortment of modeling and editing tools, you don't always need to build everything in one file. You can use a number of techniques to reduce redundancy and manage complex geometry for a component family.

Master It When would you consider using the technique of nesting families? How could this method improve the efficiency of a component family?

Apply extended family management techniques. Sometimes parametric behavior will depend on the parameters that directly control it, but often these parameters will be expressed as a relationship to something else.

Master It Why are formulas so important? Why not just create the parameters you need and then modify them as needed in the project environment?

Chapter 15

Creating Stairs and Railings

Creating stairs and railings in Autodesk® Revit® Architecture software can be challenging. In addition, stairs and railings are often sculptural as well as functional, and there's a limit to the amount of customization you can design with the provided tools and commands.

An entire book can be written about mastering stairs and railings in Revit, considering the breadth of functionality in these tools and the unlimited number of design configurations they can be used to create. Instead of walking through a few examples of creating stairs and railings, this chapter will give you foundational knowledge about the rules, parts, and key functionality of these tools so that you can use them in the most effective way possible for your own designs. We will also give you some ideas to tackle tougher design challenges by thinking beyond the default tools.

In this chapter, you'll learn to:

- Understand the key components of stairs and railings
- Understand the different stair tools and apply them to custom designs
- Design railings and use the Railing tool for other model elements
- Implement best practices

Designing Stairs and Railings

Designing and iterating complex stairs and railings in any software application can be difficult. You will need to thoroughly understand the rules and constraints of the application—in effect, learn the *language* of the application. To communicate fluently in that language, you need to be able to think fluently. You almost have to be able to think beyond the individual words and begin to arrange whole ideas.

Regardless of how well you know how to use a particular application, you have to incorporate imagination and complex design issues. Sometimes stairs and railings are straightforward and functional (for example, a steel or concrete egress stair), and there's not much room for creative thinking. But in many cases, stairs and railings are conceived as feature elements within a space. They'll be touched and experienced up close. They may be extraordinarily complex and spatial—almost an inhabited sculpture (Figure 15.1).

FIGURE 15.1
Detail of the feature stair in Apple's Fifth Avenue retail store.
Source: Image courtesy of Dougal McKinley

Revit is purpose-built for designing building elements and relating them to the rules of commonly constructed relationships (doors associate with walls, furniture associates with floors, and so on). The software is biased toward relationships specific to designing a building and maintaining those relationships as the design changes. To make things a bit more complicated, there's a specific language for creating stairs and railings in Revit Architecture. For example, Figure 15.2 illustrates the Edit Baluster Placement dialog box for a baluster condition.

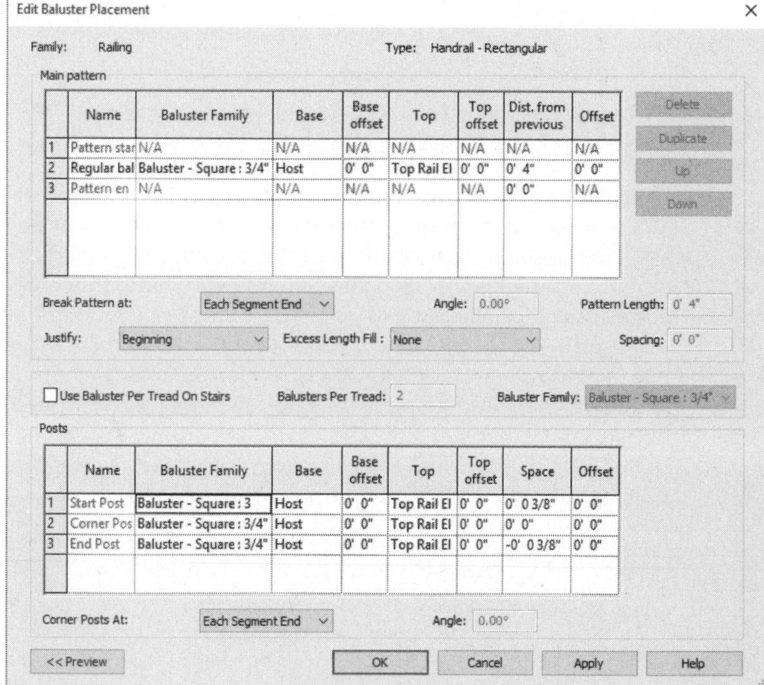

FIGURE 15.2
Edit Baluster Placement dialog box

Before we begin detailed exercises for creating stairs and railings, let's review the main components of each object type and how they are organized within Revit.

Reviewing the Key Components of Stairs and Railings

Stairs and railings are system families, so they exist only within the project environment. As you should already know, these types of families can be shared between projects only by copying and pasting, using the Transfer Project Standards tool, or including them in your project templates. There are several component family templates that serve as subsets of stair and railing system families, such as profiles, posts, and panels.

Reviewing the Basic Rules of Stairs

Before you start to create any stairs in a project, you should become familiar with the basic rules related to these special elements in Revit Architecture. We will discuss the actual geometric components later, but first let's review the parameters that drive the geometry. When you launch the Stair tool, it is assumed that you want a stair to be generated between two levels. If you start the tool from a floor plan view, the base level will be the level associated with the floor plan view and the top will be the next level above. Keep in mind that this may be a level that is not the next major level above; it could be a minor level such as a mezzanine. Always check the instance parameters in the Properties palette when you are creating a new stair (Figure 15.3). You can also assign top- and base-level offsets in the instance parameters the same way you can for walls.

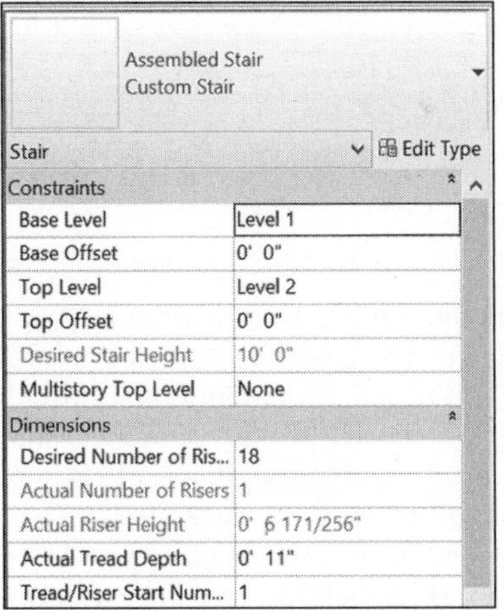

FIGURE 15.3
Instance parameters for a stair

Using the overall height determined by the base and top levels, the stair object will be equally divided into risers. The maximum riser height is defined in the type properties of every stair type. The overall height of the desired stair will be equally divided into risers not exceeding the defined maximum riser height. Tread depth is specified in the stair's type properties as well, but that may be overridden if you manually lay out the treads in Sketch mode.

In addition to the simple rule of overall riser height, some public agencies require a stair calculation to be employed for dimensional compliance. This type of calculation can be enabled from the stair's type properties as well. With either of the stair commands activated, click the

Edit Type button and then the Edit button in the Calculation Rules parameter. This will give you the Stair Calculator dialog box (Figure 15.4), which will allow you to enter the code-based values driving the creation of new stairs.

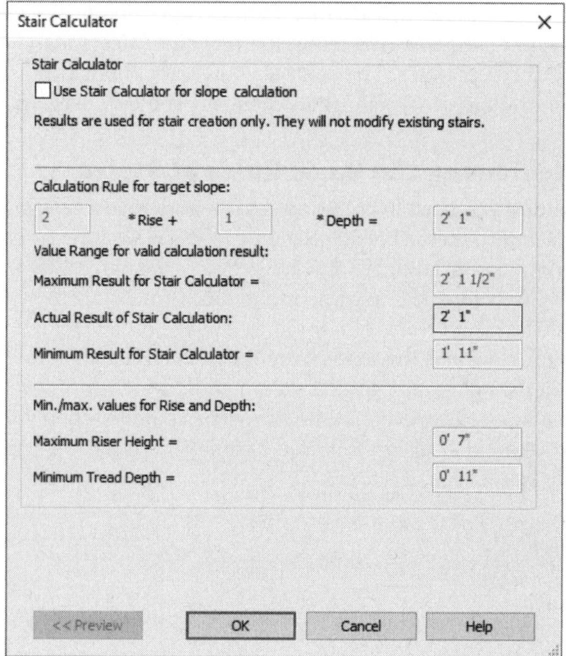

FIGURE 15.4
The Stair Calculator dialog box

Whether you use Stair By Component or Stair By Sketch, the stairs you create will be associated with a base level and top level. You can also assign offset distances to the base and top levels, which allow the stairs to start or end later or sooner depending on the design. Because the stairs remain associated with these datum objects, if the datum objects are adjusted or the offsets are redefined, the stairs will automatically adjust within the calculated rules. This means that if the height reduces, the riser count will remain but each riser will be shorter. In other words, the footprint or plan of the stair will remain unchanged. If the height of a stair run increases and an automatic adjustment would violate the maximum riser height, you will receive a warning that the actual number of risers is different from the desired number of risers. In other words, the footprint of the stair will not change automatically. It is up to you to edit the stair to add more risers where you feel they are appropriate.

Before we discuss the basic component of stairs and railings, download and open the file `c15-00-Stair-Rail.rvt` or `c15-00-Stair-Rail-Metric.rvt` from this book's web page at `www.sybex.com/go/masteringrevit2017`.

Working with Stair Components

With either the Stair By Sketch or Stair By Component tool, the basic elements of a stair are similar. The main part of the stairs—the risers and treads—is called the *run* in Revit. The structural elements that hold the run in place are known as *stringers* in the Stair By Sketch tool, and they are called *supports* in the Stair By Component tool. Finally, *landings* are addressed as unique elements in the Stair By Component tool. In the Stair By Component tool, each of these three basic elements (run, support, landing) is defined with its own unique type properties. When you use Stair By Sketch, they are all defined in the properties of each stair type.

- **Run:** The critical parts of a run are the construction, material definitions, and tread and riser settings. There are two system families for runs in the default project template: Monolithic Run and Non-Monolithic Run. A monolithic run is essentially a single material for the stair, stringer, tread, and riser. Typically, monolithic runs are used for cast-in-place and precast concrete stairs, whereas non-monolithic runs are for stairs made of wood, metal, and various other materials.
- **Support:** The supports for an assembled stair usually take one of two forms. In Revit, these are referred to as *carriage* (open) or *stringer* (closed), as shown in Figure 15.5. Carriage and Stringer are system families you can find in the Project Browser under Families ➤ Stairs. After you select either the Carriage or Stringer option in the stair type properties, you can select one of the respective support types. For example, the Right Support property may be Carriage (open) and the Right Support Type value would be Carriage – 2″ Width. You cannot customize a stringer or carriage profile when you use the Stair By Sketch tool.

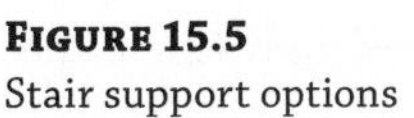
FIGURE 15.5
Stair support options

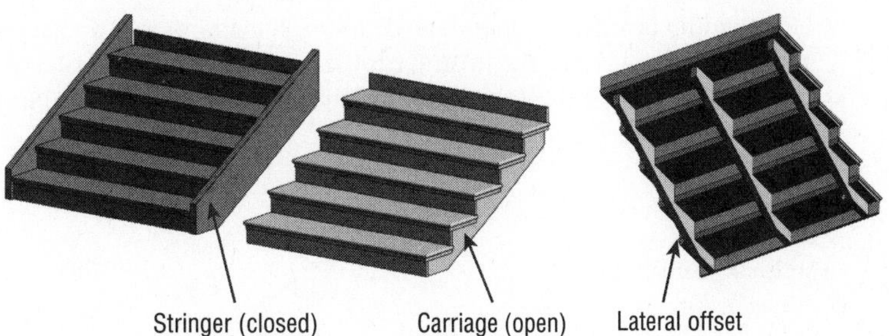

- **Landing:** Landings are the transitional elements between runs. As such, one of the main settings in the type properties for a landing is Same As Run. With this setting enabled, you are left with only the identity data and the material property for monolithic landings. If the Same As Run setting is disabled, you can treat the landing as another tread with the same opportunities to apply a thickness and a nosing profile.

Reviewing the Components of Railings

The major parts of a railing are the profiles, different kinds of balusters, and the nested types within each railing family. Additional functionality is available to help integrate different railing parts into a more cohesive system. In Figure 15.6, a common railing is shown to illustrate the fundamental parts of a railing type.

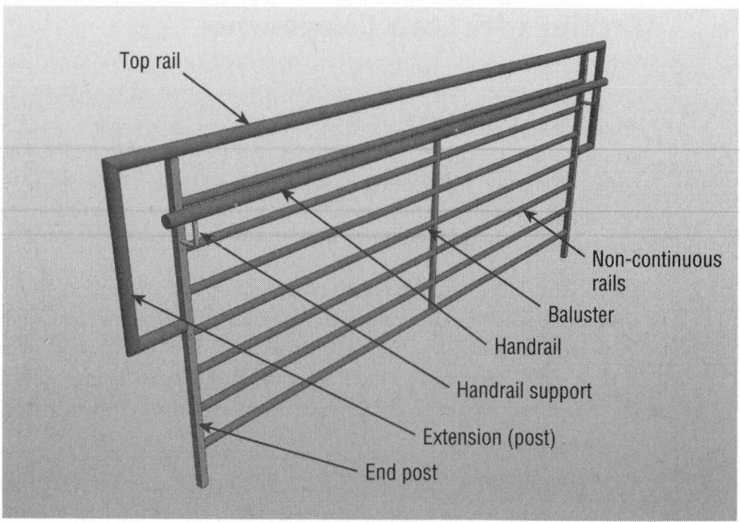

FIGURE 15.6
The integrated parts of a railing type

Let's examine some of these railing components in greater depth:

Profiles The profile is the most basic component used to model a railing. All the rails, posts, and balusters are generated from profile families. You can have as many profiles per railing as you like, but you can't have more than one shape in a profile family (RFA) file. In each profile family, the shape needs to be a closed loop—no gaps or overlapping lines allowed. Furthermore, all the railing profiles will be swept parallel to their host objects. In Figure 15.7, the top rail and all the intermediate rails are simple circular profiles swept along the path of the railing.

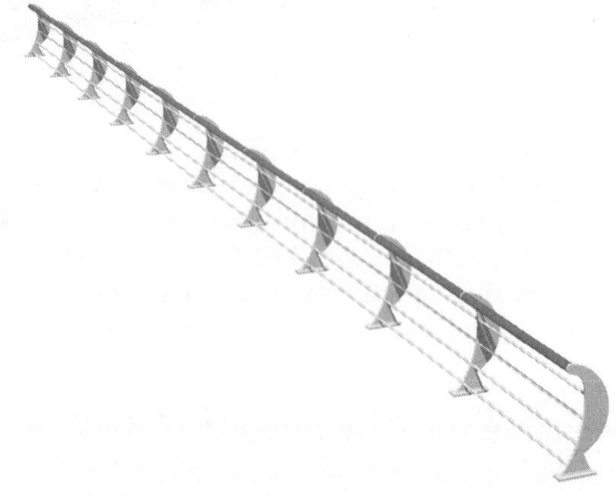

FIGURE 15.7
Multiple profiles per railing

Balusters There are three kinds of baluster family templates you can use to customize a railing type:

- *Baluster posts* have built-in instance parameters to control the height of the baluster so that it can adjust automatically when used within a railing type in a project. The posts are used at the start, end, and transitions of railings.
- *Balusters* are the main, repeated vertical structure of most railing designs. They have instance parameters as well that control the vertical length and the angle of the top and bottom of the baluster (Figure 15.8). When you create your own custom baluster families, you must constrain the geometry to these reference planes so the baluster will adapt to the settings in the railing type.

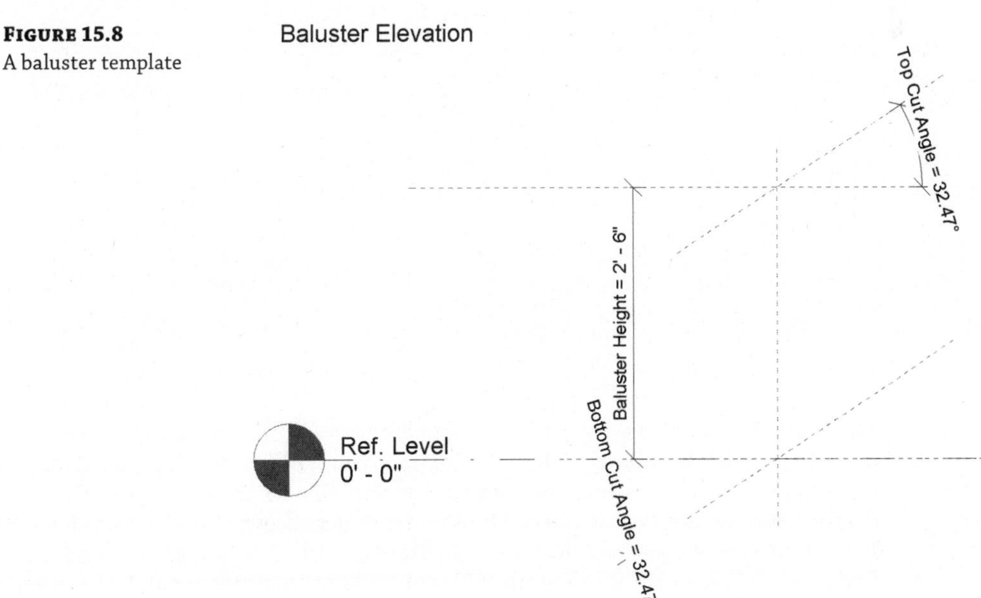

FIGURE 15.8
A baluster template

- *Baluster panels* have controls much like the baluster, but there are additional reference planes to control the overall width of a desired panel (Figure 15.9).

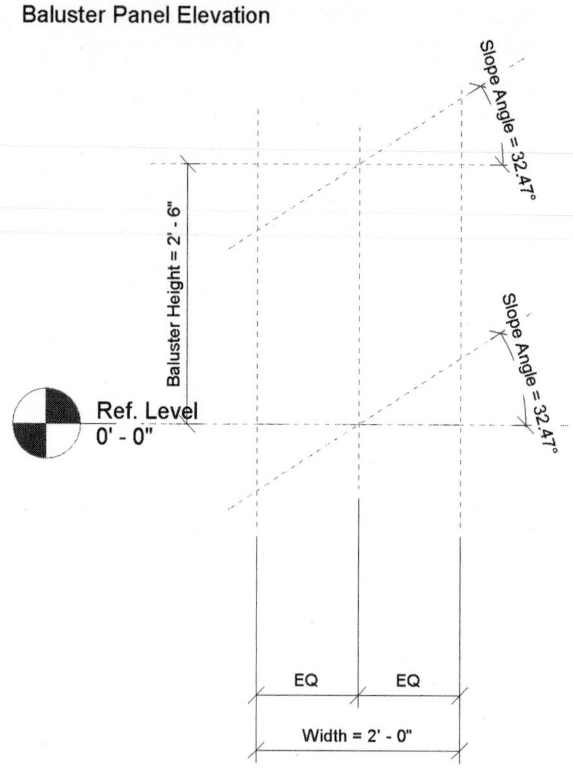

Figure 15.9
A baluster panel template

Top Rail The top rail is a separate component of a railing type. That is to say, it will not appear in the Edit Rails dialog box. Instead, you will find the Top Rail settings in the type properties of the railing and they consist only of a height and a type. The top rail is a nested system family that you can find in the Project Browser under Families ➤ Railings ➤ Top Rail Type. Locate and double-click Circular – 1 1/2″ (Circular – 40 mm). You will find more detailed settings to control this subset of railing functionality (Figure 15.10). Let's take a look at some of the properties of a top rail: Construction, Terminations, and Extensions.

- *Construction* The first category of properties in a top rail defines the basic construction of the rail. Here you will select a profile and specify other behavior such as default join condition, transitions, and hand clearance.
- *Terminations* Another top rail option is defining a termination. This is a family component that can be used at the end of a rail or rail extension. There is only one termination family loaded in the default project template, but you can create your own family using the `Railing Termination.rft` or `Metric Railing Termination.rft` family template. Figure 15.11 shows an example of a termination.

FIGURE 15.10
Top rail type properties

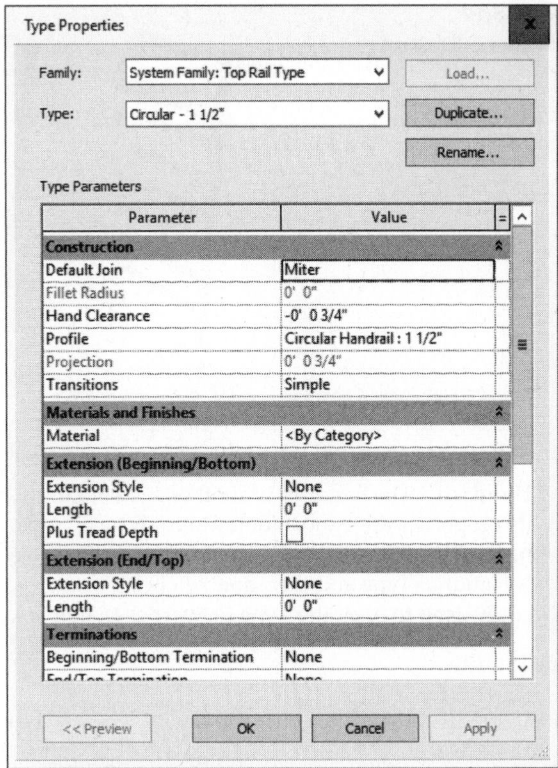

FIGURE 15.11
Rail termination

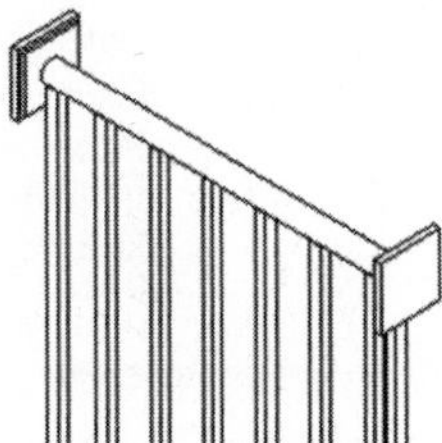

- *Extensions* When you need a rail to extend beyond its main sketch definition of the railing, an extension can be specified as part of the rail type. The extension is an integrated part of the rail, so it's controlled by the same properties like size or materiality. In the settings for Extension (Beginning/Bottom), you can select an option called Plus Tread Depth. This is to accommodate common building codes that require a stair handrail to be extended the length of one tread plus some standard distance. Extension Style is a setting that gives you three predefined designs for the rail extension: Wall, Floor, or Post (Figure 15.12).

FIGURE 15.12
Options for rail extension styles

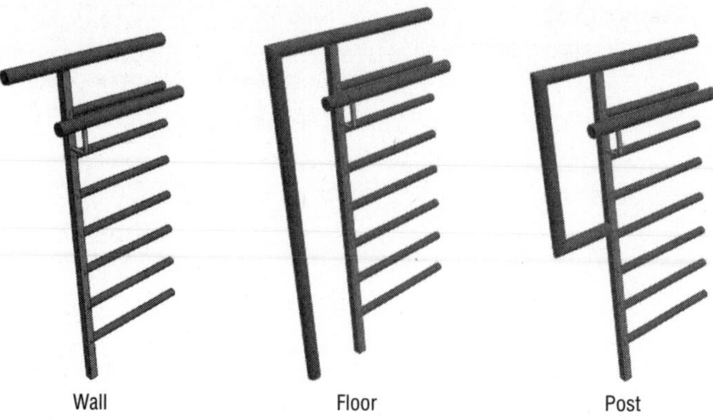

You can customize a rail's extension by pressing the Tab key to select the rail. Then click Edit Rail in the contextual tab in the ribbon, and click Edit Path.

Handrail The handrail is another system family that is nested within a railing family, and its properties are almost identical to those of the top rail family. The one exception is that handrails can use support families. From the Project Browser, navigate to Families ➢ Railings ➢ Handrail Type and then double-click Circular – 1 ½" (or Pipe – Wall Mount in the metric equivalent) to open the Type Properties dialog box for a handrail (Figure 15.13).

FIGURE 15.13
Type properties for handrail supports

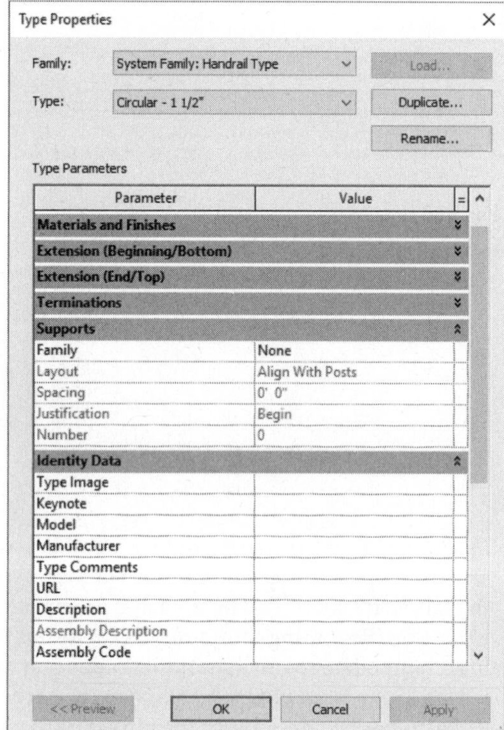

Beyond selecting a support family, you will notice settings for Layout that include Align With Posts, Fixed Number, Fixed Distance, Maximum Spacing, and Minimum Spacing. These are the main controls that will enable or disable the other settings for Supports, including Spacing, Justification, and Number.

Rail Structure (Non-Continuous) Let's return to the type properties of the main railing family. In the Project Browser, navigate to Families ➤ Railings ➤ Railing and double-click Guardrail – Pipe (900 mm Pipe in the metric exercise file). In the Rail Structure (Non-Continuous) parameter, click the Edit button to open the Edit Rails (Non-Continuous) dialog box (Figure 15.14). In this interface, you can insert rails defined by profile families as well as set their relative height, horizontal offset distance, and material. These rails are considered non-continuous because they will be intersected by any balusters you define in the Baluster Placement settings. Click OK to exit this dialog box.

FIGURE 15.14 The Edit Rails (Non-Continuous) dialog box

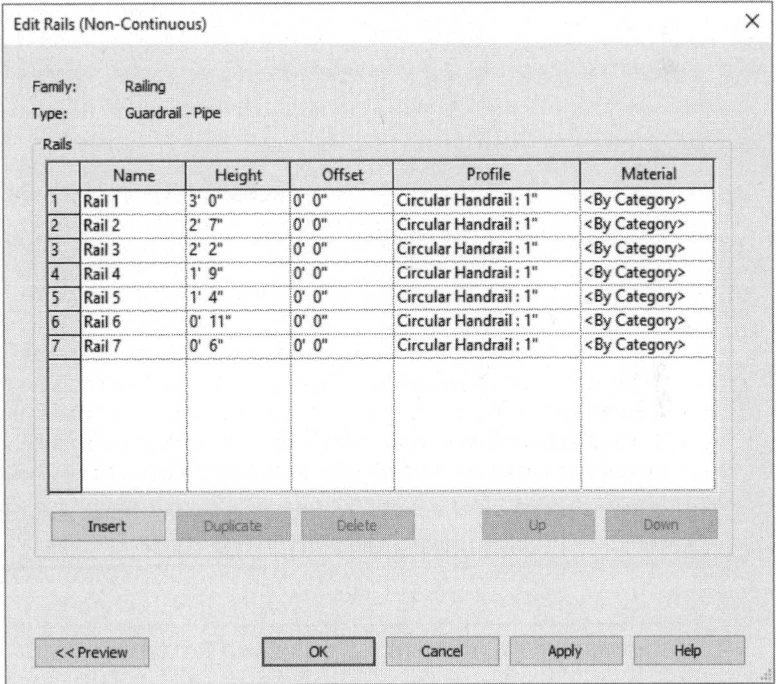

	Name	Height	Offset	Profile	Material
1	Rail 1	3' 0"	0' 0"	Circular Handrail : 1"	<By Category>
2	Rail 2	2' 7"	0' 0"	Circular Handrail : 1"	<By Category>
3	Rail 3	2' 2"	0' 0"	Circular Handrail : 1"	<By Category>
4	Rail 4	1' 9"	0' 0"	Circular Handrail : 1"	<By Category>
5	Rail 5	1' 4"	0' 0"	Circular Handrail : 1"	<By Category>
6	Rail 6	0' 11"	0' 0"	Circular Handrail : 1"	<By Category>
7	Rail 7	0' 6"	0' 0"	Circular Handrail : 1"	<By Category>

Baluster Placement When you return to the type properties of the railing, locate the Baluster Placement parameter and click the Edit button to open the Edit Baluster Placement dialog box (Figure 15.15). As you can see, there are options for the main pattern and the posts and an option for how the balusters will be used on stairs.

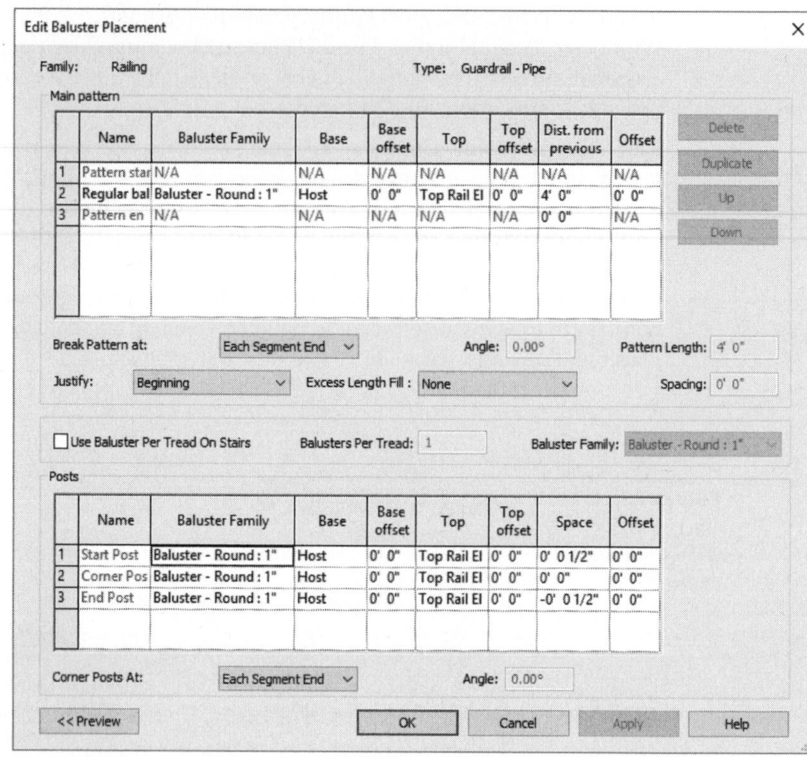

FIGURE 15.15 Edit Baluster Placement dialog box for the Guardrail – Pipe family

The Main Pattern section of the dialog box is where you would assemble all your baluster types and then space and host them accordingly. You can also decide how you want the pattern to repeat (or not repeat) itself at the ends of sketched line segments. The Posts section is used to specify which baluster is used at start, corner, and end conditions (and the frequency of corner posts). Click OK to close both open dialog boxes.

That's a high-level overview of the properties of railings and what they're used for. We've covered the primary features necessary to create great railings.

USING THE TAB KEY WITH STAIRS AND RAILINGS

Railings consist of nested families for top rails and handrails. Stairs are divided into runs, landings, and supports. When you first select a railing or stair, you will be selecting the parent type. You could then click Edit Type in the Properties palette to change the child types; however, there are some unique instance properties and editing capabilities exposed when you use the Tab key to directly select one of the nested elements.

For stairs, one of the important features of a run is whether it begins or ends with a riser. This property is critical in determining how a stair interacts with an adjacent floor slab. Depending on the type of stair you create, these properties are part of either the stair type or the run type. In the newer style of stair, the only way you can access these properties is by hovering your mouse pointer over a stair and then pressing the Tab key once to select the run. The instance properties of the run will then be shown in the Properties palette. You can also access the run width in the same manner.

For railings, you can use the Tab key to access editing functions of top rails and handrails. If you hover the mouse pointer over a top rail and then press the Tab key once to select the rail, you will find an Edit Rail button in the contextual ribbon. Activating this tool allows you to customize the path of the continuous rails to build or customize extensions.

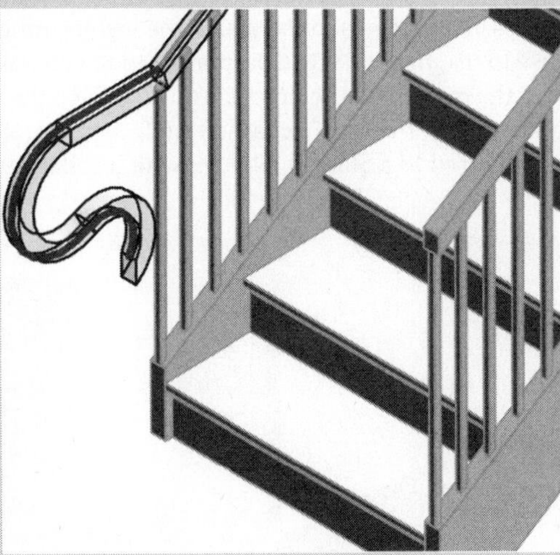

Creating Stairs

Various common configurations of stairs can be created using the tools provided in Revit. Designs that used to require an outside-the-box (workaround) approach are now possible. Examples include three-run stairs (when the stair run turns back onto itself, creating an overlapping condition) and stringers with custom profiles. Despite the improvements to the stair tools, there's still no way to anticipate every unique and sculptural design condition. In these cases, we'll show you techniques that aren't exactly using the stair tools as intended, but the results will geometrically resemble stairs (and their railings).

Understanding the Stair Tools

There are two different tools for creating stairs in a project environment—Stair By Component and Stair By Sketch. Each of these tools uses the core stair parts (runs, supports, landings) in slightly different ways.

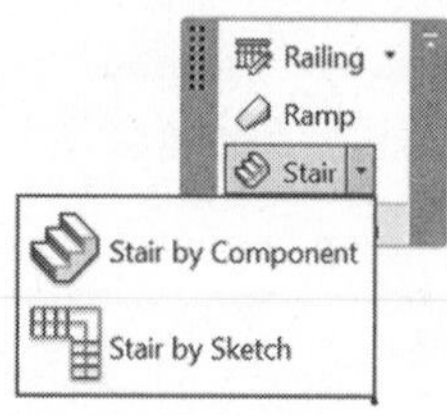

When you choose the Stair By Sketch tool, you are using 2D sketch lines that represent boundaries and risers. Although you have access to a Run function in Sketch mode, it is merely automating the generation of the 2D sketch. You do not have direct access to manipulate the 3D geometry of the stair when you use Stair By Sketch. In addition, the entire stair element is bound to the rules and settings in the stair type—you cannot customize individual parts.

If you choose to use the Stair By Component tool, you have the ability to customize runs and landings within the overall stair element. You also have the unique ability to edit the stair in a 3D view. That is to say, the stair remains visible as a complete model when you edit the stair (Figure 15.16) compared to a Stair By Sketch, which collapses down to the 2D layout lines when edited.

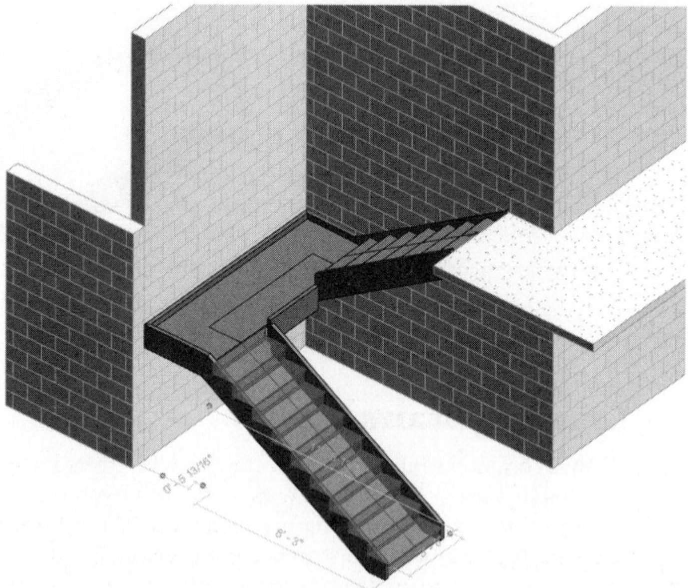

FIGURE 15.16 Editing a Stair By Component in a 3D view

There are additional subcategories of the Stairs object style that allow you to further customize the appearance of stairs and their related elements (Figure 15.17). One of the subcategories is Riser Lines—providing an additional dashed line parallel to the edge of the riser that indicates the nosing length. You can customize the appearance of these elements in Object Styles from the Manage tab in the ribbon. You can also adjust the visibility of the stair elements for any view in the Visibility/Graphic Overrides dialog box and optionally save the settings to view templates.

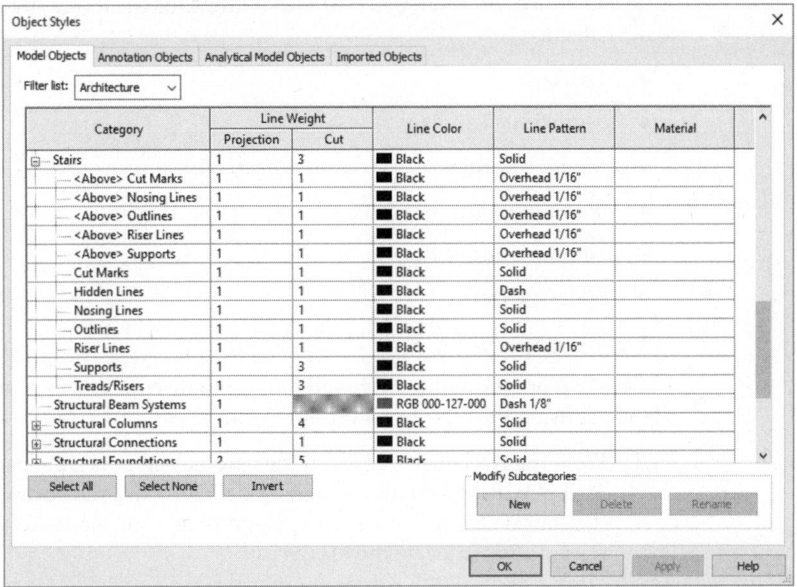

FIGURE 15.17 Additional subcategories are available for stairs.

The fundamental concept behind the Stair By Component tool is that the major components of a stair (run, landing, support) are nested system families that can be independently customized. Although both stair tools are being maintained in the software, understanding the difference between all the families and types can be a challenge.

Let's take a look at the Project Browser under Families ➢ Stairs in the default project template. The family called Stair is the parent system family for the Stair By Sketch tool. If you expand Stair, you will see the stair types that will be available to you if you launch the Stair By Sketch tool.

For the Stair By Component tool, there are three system families that function as the parent families. The following families are the top-level families into which other families are nested:

- Assembled Stair
- Cast-In-Place Stair
- Precast Stair

Under each of these families is where you define a type to be used in your projects. For example, under the Cast-In-Place Stair family, you will find the Monolithic Stair type, which uses nested families for the run, landing, and support. To better understand this nesting, let's look at the family hierarchy of the Monolithic Stair type in a simple list:

- Family: Cast-In-Place Stair
    - Type: Monolithic Stair
        - Run Type: ¾″ Nosing (20 mm)
        - Landing Type: 7″ Thickness (300 mm)
        - Support Type: None

In the Project Browser, you will find listings for the following nested families under the Stairs category:

- Carriage
- Monolithic Landing
- Monolithic Run
- Non-Monolithic Landing
- Non-Monolithic Run
- Stair Cut Mark
- Stringer

Let's explore the ability to directly manipulate component stairs. To begin, create a stair with a landing using the Stair By Component tool:

1. From the Architecture tab, on the Circulation panel, choose Stair ➤ Stair By Component. This will bring you into Sketch mode. Draw the stair from left to right. Base the base of the stair on the left of the screen, and drag your mouse to the right until you place nine risers. Click to locate the ninth riser.
2. Now, move your mouse about 4′ (1.2 m) to the right and click again. This will create a landing and the base for the tenth step.
3. Drag your mouse to the right, placing the other nine risers. Your stair in sketch mode should look like Figure 15.18.

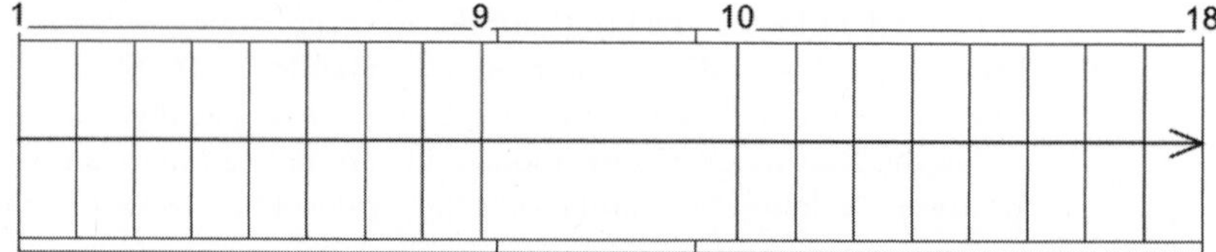

FIGURE 15.18 Creating the component stair with landing

Selecting the runs or the landing will display grips and temporary dimensions that can be used to change the width, direction, and location of the runs or landing.

4. Widen the left run and landing by selecting the portion of the stair and pulling the blue arrow grips down, as shown in Figure 15.19.

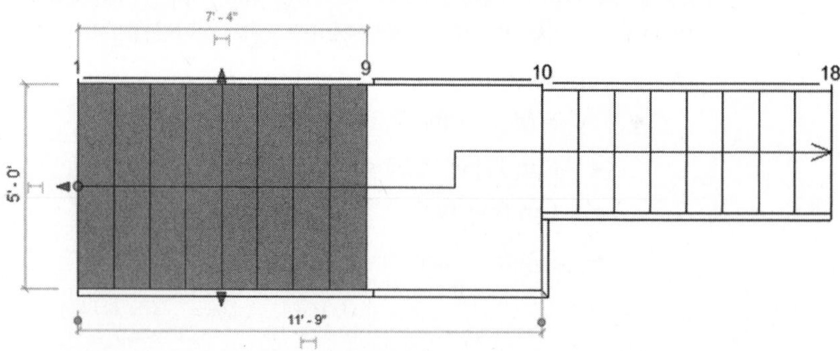

FIGURE 15.19 Widening the left run

5. Now select the landing and move the lower grip to further widen the landing, as shown in Figure 15.20. The landing maintains the connection to the lower run.

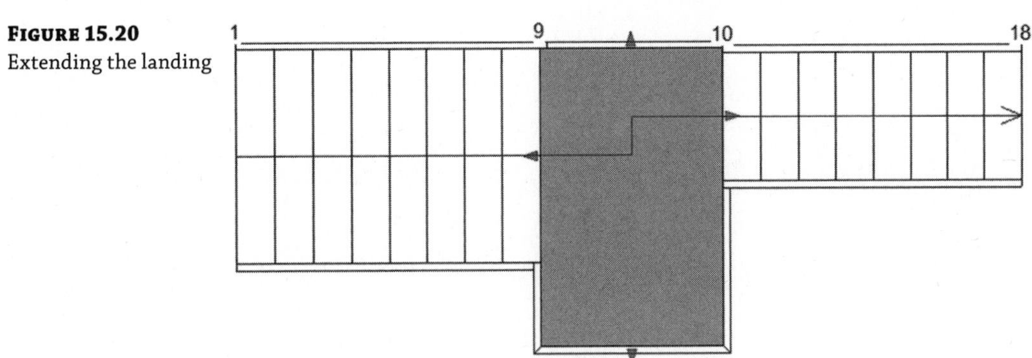

FIGURE 15.20
Extending the landing

6. Changing the shape of the landing is not possible without converting the landing to a sketch-based component. Select the landing and then select Convert from the Tools panel. This will convert the component element to a sketch-based element. Keep in mind that this is irreversible (Figure 15.21).

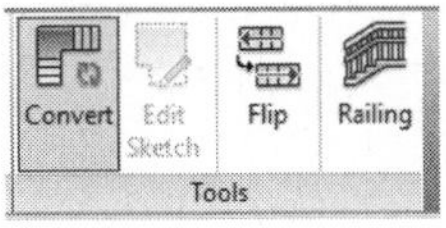

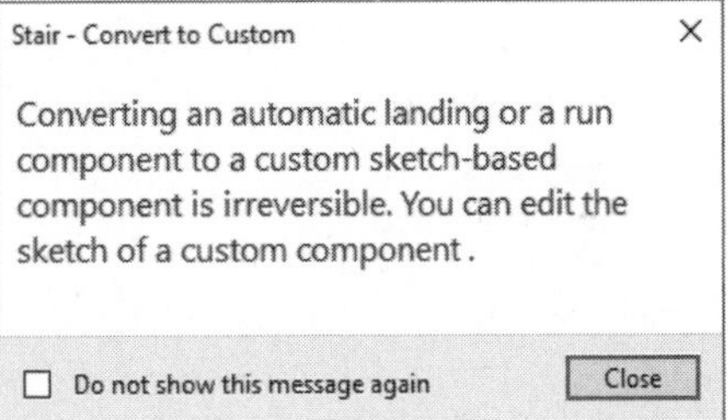

FIGURE 15.21
Converting the landing to a sketch-based component

7. With the landing now sketch based, you can edit its shape and create a form that isn't rectilinear. Select Edit Sketch from the Tools panel. Delete the lower sketch line and then replace it with an arch-shaped boundary, as shown in Figure 15.22. Finish the sketch for the landing, and then click Finish Edit Mode for the component stair.

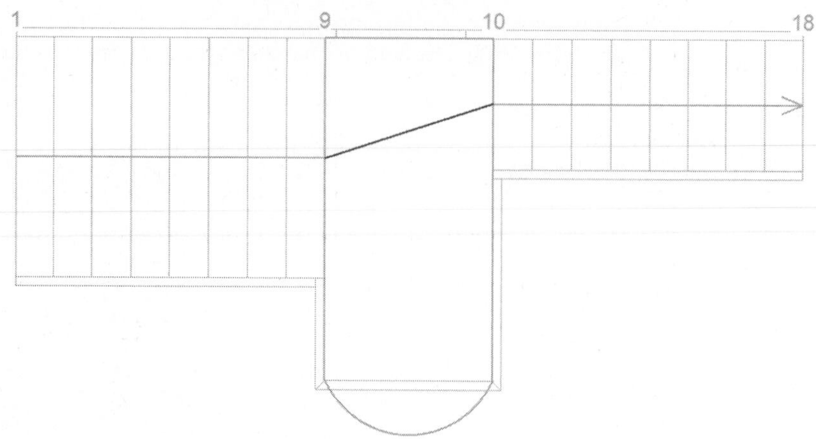

FIGURE 15.22
Sketching the new landing boundary

The resulting stair is shown in Figure 15.23. Don't be afraid to experiment with using both component and sketch-based stair tools in a single stair condition. Just remember that it's often easier to start with the component stair and then modify with sketches when necessary. This is a very powerful, flexible combination and gives you important feedback in 3D rather than going back and forth between sketches and the finished stair. This file can be downloaded from the Chapter 15 folder on the book's web page. Look for the `c15-Stair-Landing.rvt` or `c15-Stair-Landing-Metric.rvt` file.

FIGURE 15.23
Combination component and sketch-based stair

Using the Instance Properties of Stair Components

We have discussed the hierarchy of nested families and types for components in other chapters; stairs follow this same structure. You can Tab+select through the stair to choose either the stair or the rail, but you have other options as well. By hovering over the side of the stair, you can choose just the treads or just the stringer. Both of these selection options come with their own properties, but there are even more parameters available as instance properties of runs, landings, and supports. When you use the Stair By Sketch tool, the Width parameter is available as a simple instance parameter, accessible in the Properties palette when you are sketching the stair or afterward when a stair is selected. When the Stair By Component tool is activated, you can set the width of a run only after it has been created. If you Tab+select the run within a stair assembly, you can access the Actual Run Width property and change it.

The Begin With Riser and End With Riser properties are critical to integrating a stair with adjacent floor slabs. In the Stair By Sketch tool, these parameters are available only in the Type Properties dialog box, which means that you would need to create a new stair type if either of these conditions needed to be customized. For component stairs, these properties can be found in the instance properties of each run. You will need to Tab+select a run within a stair instance to enable or disable these parameters, but it is ultimately more flexible to use throughout your project.

Another important group of instance properties is assigned to the stair supports. If you Tab+select a support for any component stair, you will see parameters, including Lower End Cut and Upper End Cut in the Properties palette. These can be assigned to Vertical Cut, Horizontal Cut, or Perpendicular—options that are not available with the Stair By Sketch tool.

Using Component Stairs in Assemblies

Stairs created with the component method cannot be added to assemblies. Use the Stair By Sketch method if you intend to document a stair with the Assembly functionality. See Chapter 19, "Working in the Construction Phase," for more information about assemblies.

Using the Components for Customizing Stairs

A key concept in making the best use of Revit is to not get hung up on how elements and tools are named or labeled. For example, you can use the Railing tool to create a shading device—which is obviously not a railing. This same concept applies to stairs—don't overlook the nosing profile family as a device for creating interesting shapes that complete the tread because the shape of the nosing is not limited to traditional-nosing profiles. Any shape that needs to extend beyond the face of the tread is fair game to model with the Nosing Profile family. Just remember that you're limited to a single profile per tread and stair run (Figure 15.24). You'll also want to pay particular attention to the insertion point of the nosing profile, because the intersection of the reference planes coincides with the top of the tread and the face of the riser.

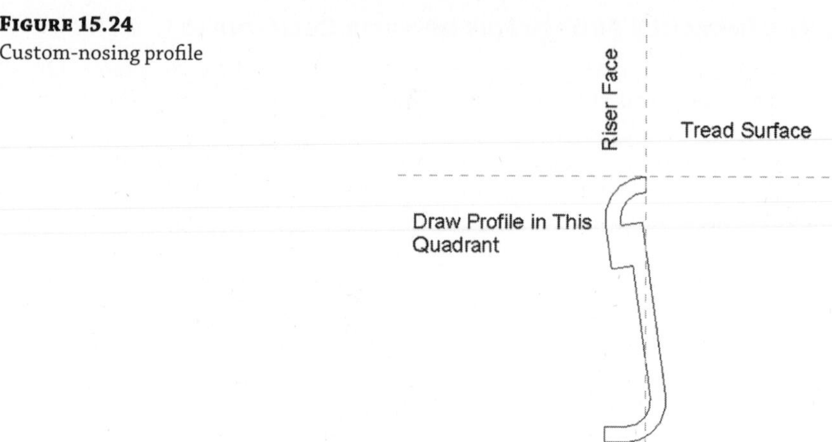

FIGURE 15.24
Custom-nosing profile

Figure 15.25 shows an example from a real stair that was designed to have each tread fabricated from a single plate of steel and then rolled to form the face of the riser above it. Here, each of these treads can be welded behind the lip of the tread above it. It's a fairly elegant idea that can be accomplished by using a custom-nosing profile to create the appearance of a continuous tread. Look closely and you can see where the actual tread ends and where the nosing profile begins. Final linework can be adjusted or hidden (if necessary) when you're creating the details.

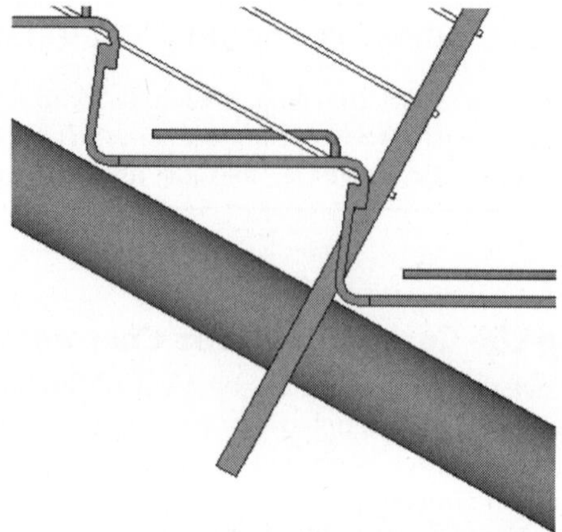

FIGURE 15.25
Continuous tread and nosing profile

Figure 15.26 shows this stair in its final form using our custom profile, but the walls are hidden for clarity. If you'd like to investigate this stair further, it's in the Chapter 15 folder on the book's companion web page and is called `c15-Henrys Stepp.rvt`.

FIGURE 15.26
Example of a customized stair and railing

UNDERSTANDING THE STRINGER

Stringers in Revit are good for creating a number of standard wooden or steel conditions, and the right and left stringers may be customized with profiles. If you need a custom middle profile or a stringer that follows the railing but deviates from the standard left/right stringer location, use the Railing tool (Figure 15.27). The stair will host this railing containing the custom stringer profile (or just the custom profile, with no handrail).

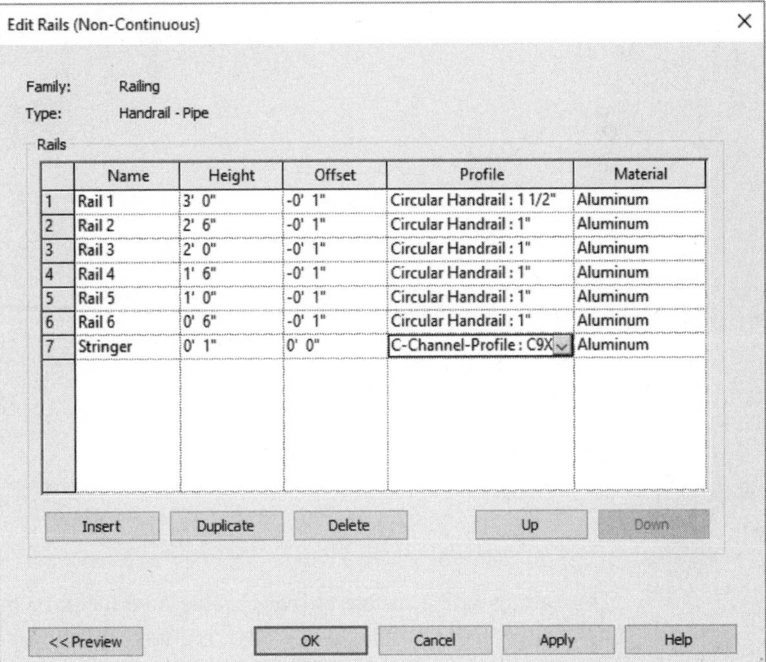

	Name	Height	Offset	Profile	Material
1	Rail 1	3' 0"	-0' 1"	Circular Handrail : 1 1/2"	Aluminum
2	Rail 2	2' 6"	-0' 1"	Circular Handrail : 1"	Aluminum
3	Rail 3	2' 0"	-0' 1"	Circular Handrail : 1"	Aluminum
4	Rail 4	1' 6"	-0' 1"	Circular Handrail : 1"	Aluminum
5	Rail 5	1' 0"	-0' 1"	Circular Handrail : 1"	Aluminum
6	Rail 6	0' 6"	-0' 1"	Circular Handrail : 1"	Aluminum
7	Stringer	0' 1"	0' 0"	C-Channel-Profile : C9X	Aluminum

FIGURE 15.27
Use the Railing tool to create a custom stringer profile.

Notice in Figure 15.27 that the last profile is not part of the traditional portion of the railing. Instead, this profile is used to indicate a custom stringer profile (Figure 15.28). But it has been assigned to the railing to maintain a particular relationship to the stairs.

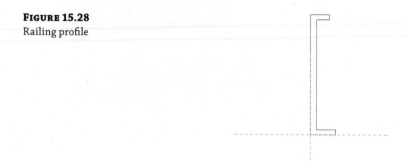

FIGURE 15.28
Railing profile

In Figure 15.29, we've isolated the railing from the stairs to illustrate the finished railing: the handrail, two glazed and continuous panels, and the custom stringer.

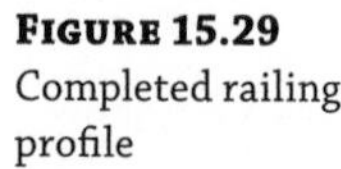

FIGURE 15.29
Completed railing profile

This railing with a custom stringer profile is perfect for a multitude of stair conditions: straight, curved, or even a combination (Figure 15.30). This technique finishes off the stair nicely and exposes the structure in interesting ways.

FIGURE 15.30
Finished stairs

Although the stringer usually occurs to the left or right of the treads, this is certainly not always the case. In some situations you'll want to create a middle stringer using a custom profile. Just remember that this will be a railing that will be hosted by the stair and may not even contain a handrail, just the profile for the stringer (Figure 15.31). In this case, the railing is still being hosted by the stairs; however, there isn't any railing geometry above the tread.

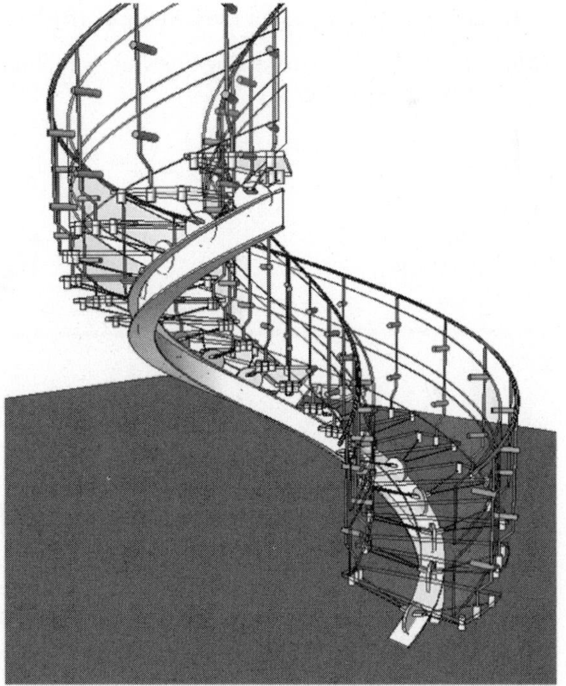

FIGURE 15.31
Custom middle stringer profile

For component stairs, you can also use a custom profile for a stringer, but instead of using a railing family as we previously described, you can assign it to a support type. To accomplish this, you must first create a duplicate support type:

1. Download and open the exercise file `c15-Custom-Stringer.rvt`. In the Project Browser, navigate to Families ➤ Stairs ➤ Stringer, right-click Stringer – Default, and then select Duplicate from the context menu.
2. Double-click the duplicated type to open the Type Properties dialog box. Click the Rename button and set the new name to Stringer – Channel. Click OK.
3. In the Section Profile parameter, select C-Channel-Profile : C9X15 (M_C-Channel-Profile : C250X30 in the Metric file).
4. Check the box for the Flip Section Profile parameter.
5. Finally, change the Structural Depth on Landing to 5″ (125 mm) to set the channel location under the stair. Click OK to close the Type Properties dialog box.
6. Activate the default 3D view and select the stair in the view. In the Properties palette, click Edit Type.
7. Find the Right Support Type parameter and click in the parameter value field. Click again on the small icon in the parameter field to open the Type Properties dialog box for the stringer.
8. In the Type dropdown list, select Stringer - Channel and then click OK.
9. Repeat steps 7 and 8 for the Left Support Type.
10. Click OK to close the dialog box and then observe the change in the stringer support for the stair (Figure 15.32).

FIGURE 15.32
A custom profile can be used as a support type.

This workflow applies to a carriage support as well. Repeat the previous steps, but look for those support types under Families ➤ Stairs ➤ Carriage. As a final note about custom support profiles, you must ensure that the proper usage property is specified in the profile family when you are creating the shape. In the Family Editor, click the Family Category And Parameters button in the ribbon and make sure the Profile Usage parameter is set to Stair Support (Figure 15.33).

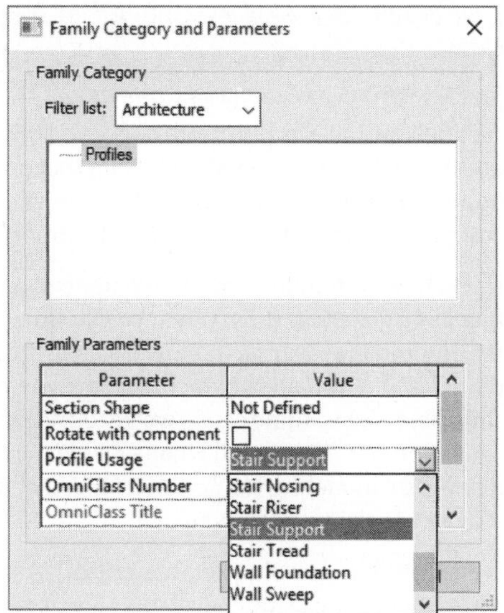

FIGURE 15.33
Setting the Profile Usage parameter for a custom support profile

USING BALUSTERS AS TREAD SUPPORTS

Common tread shapes can be pretty boring, so let's move directly on to custom tread conditions. In situations where you need to be a bit more inventive, you're going to need to know how to create a custom baluster. This technique can either create a custom support element for the default treads or indicate the actual tread.

But instead of the baluster being vertical, it's going to be horizontal. This horizontal baluster will be used in conjunction with the default tread. This baluster may even completely envelop the tread (Figure 15.34).

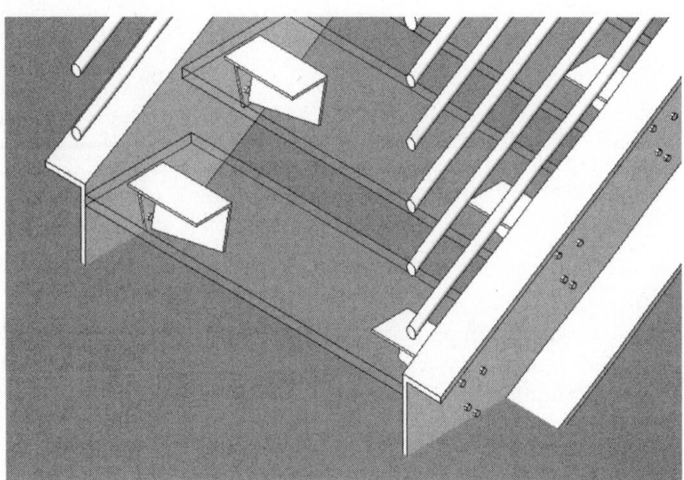

FIGURE 15.34
Baluster as tread support

First, we need to discuss a few rules for creating a customized tread support for the default tread:

- Not every baluster needs a railing. If your baluster support isn't going to be a part of the "actual" railing, simply create a second "railing" that is hosted by the stairs. Sketching another path for your custom railing that only contains the tread support baluster can be accomplished in a few steps. The baluster family template needs to be used for the component that will act as the tread support. Otherwise, it can't be associated to the railing.
- If you have a complex support element, it may be helpful to model the desired support element as a generic family. When you've finished, nest this generic element into the baluster family. You may want to do this because the baluster templates have hardwired reference planes and parameters (which is fine if you're making a baluster that needs to geometrically flex). But in some cases, we've found that these reference planes and parameters may cause your baluster to fail when you load it in the project as a result of these parameters flexing. By modeling the geometry elsewhere and nesting it, you avoid this hassle because it moves as a single component.
- Designating the level of detail is critical. Assigning smaller model elements to only appear when the Detail Level of a view is set to Fine will result in much faster graphics regeneration, view panning, and model rotation. So if you're nesting one component into another family, the detail that you're assigning at the deepest level will be respected through nesting (Figure 15.35).

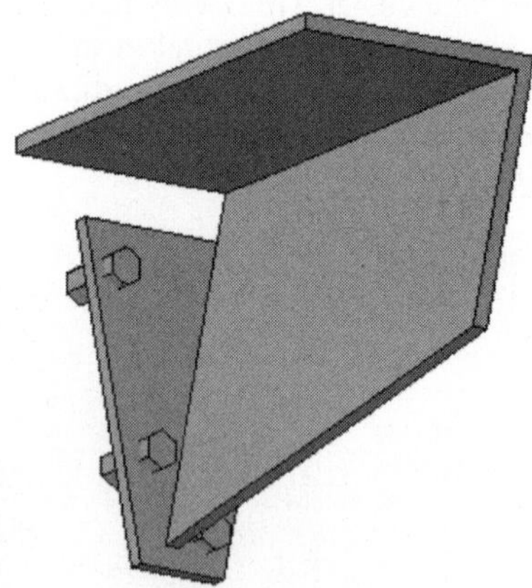

FIGURE 15.35
Single component that will be used as a tread support

Once the component is complete, you can nest it into a baluster template, as shown in Figure 15.36. If necessary, it's also possible to assign parameters to the dimensions in the nested configuration.

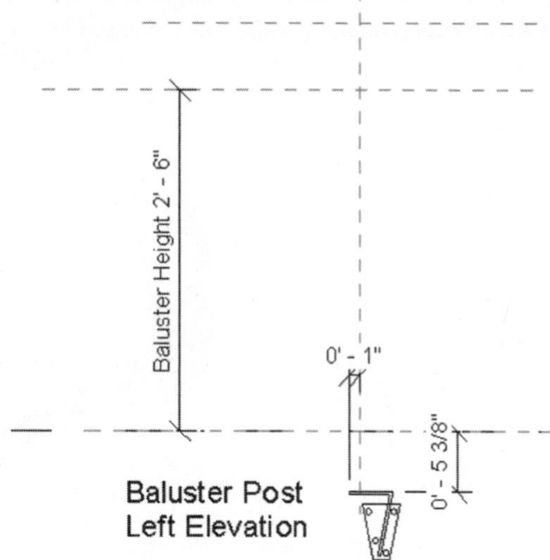

FIGURE 15.36
The generic model nested into a baluster family

The completed stairs are shown in two different configurations in Figure 15.37. Many configurations are possible once you correctly define a single stair type. If you'd like to investigate this stair further, it's in the Chapter 15 folder on the book's web page, and the file is called `c15-Angled-Support-Stair.rvt`.

FIGURE 15.37
Completed stairs with angled tread supports

A custom baluster support might be modeled to contain the real balusters that are intended to support railings. This can simplify and shorten modeling time. In the example shown in Figure 15.38, the baluster support geometry also contains the railing elements on both the right and left sides. If you'd like to investigate this stair further, it's in the Chapter 15 folder on the book's web page; the file is called `c15-Support Tread.rfa`.

Figure 15.38
Complex tread support with balusters

The previous support baluster can be brought together with a custom profile for the center stringer, handrails, and glazed panels to form a complete stair and railing design (Figure 15.39). You can download this example from the Chapter 15 folder on the book's web page; the file is called `c15-Center Baluster Support.rvt`.

Figure 15.39
Completed stair design with custom tread support as a baluster

CONTROLLING THE BALUSTER SUPPORTS

Don't forget to control the number of baluster supports per tread. Revit has an easy way to accomplish this through the railing option Use Baluster Per Tread On Stairs, found in the Edit Baluster Placement dialog box.

Once you've begun to experiment with creating balusters as tread supports for stairs, you'll notice you have options for making more complete and finished conditions.

Start and end posts are useful and can help complete the structure of your custom railing and baluster system, particularly if you want to properly anchor and connect your custom stair and railing. The elements shown in Figure 15.40 are the start and end posts to anchor a custom railing and a baluster that will serve as the tread with integrated support. It builds on the previous example of using a baluster as a support element for a tread.

FIGURE 15.40
Custom post and baluster families

To finish this stair, you need to create start and end posts that anchor the stair. As with the previous handrail-join exercise, you'll want to model the bulk of the custom stair with the custom railing. Then you'll export the stair parts for importing into the baluster template (or the generic model template that will be nested into the baluster template).

Figure 15.41 shows the results after the start and end posts and custom baluster families are applied to a completed stair design.

When it all comes together, the results can be elegant and interesting. All of this is available through the default Stairs tool. You can download this stair from the Chapter 15 folder on the book's web page; it's called `c15-Tube Stair.rvt`.

Now let's go one step further. There's no reason that the baluster support element needs to exactly conform to the shape of the tread. And there's no reason that the support element can't contain the actual baluster that is intended to support the handrail.

Take a look at the support element in Figure 15.42. Not only does it contain the support element, but the support element has been modeled to exceed the shape of the tread that will be modeled by the Stairs tool.

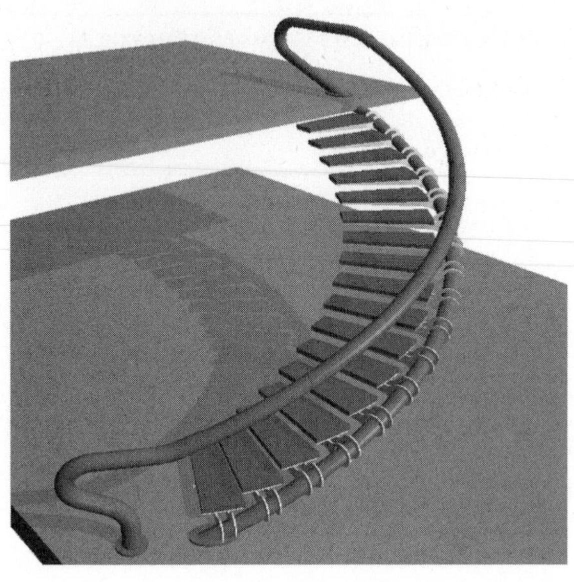

FIGURE 15.41
Finished stair with custom start and end posts

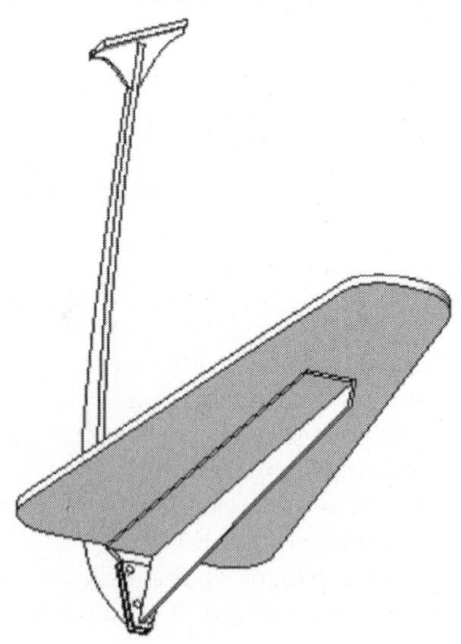

FIGURE 15.42
Support and baluster as a generic model

Keep in mind that we've modeled the support element as a generic model and then nested it into a baluster post template (Figure 15.43). Again, this keeps the baluster unified so it's not affected by the built-in reference planes and parameters.

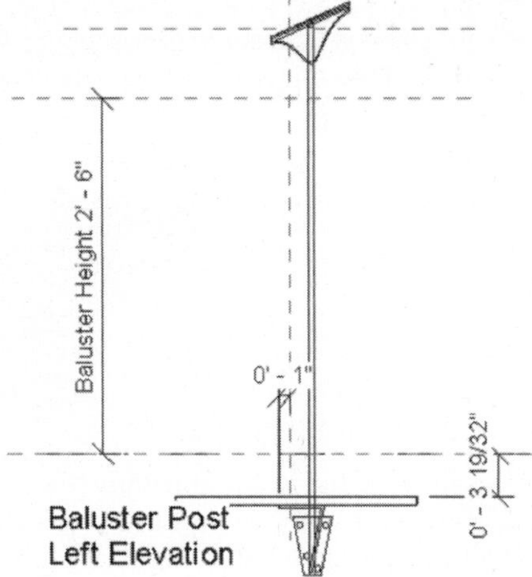

FIGURE 15.43
Baluster and support nested into a baluster post template

Once this custom baluster post is loaded into the project, associate it with the stair and its railings. Remember to select the **One Baluster Per Tread** option. When finished, the default tread is an inlay to the more complete tread support (Figure 15.44). In more complex conditions, it may be desirable to envelop the entire tread with the support geometry. Doing so will allow you to create complex tread shapes that are not dependent on the default tread and use the functionality of the stair and railing objects to properly locate, rotate, and elevate each of your custom treads. If you want to examine this stair further, check out the file `c15-Curved Tread Support.rvt` in the Chapter 15 folder on the book's web page.

FIGURE 15.44
Finished stair with integrated baluster and support

Figure 15.45 shows an example using this technique. The tread support elements have been modeled using blends in order to sweep under the metal plate while changing direction from vertical to angle. This will accommodate the angled pipe rail that will support the stair.

FIGURE 15.45
The top and underside of a tread support

Treads come together in a particularly interesting stair and railing configuration. There is obviously a more conventional outer railing for this stair. But the inner railing doesn't have any elements that occur at hand height. The entire inner railing exists to support the baluster supports (which in turn support the default treads). The end post is being used to anchor the entire structure through the second level. You can find this example, `c15-Highlights.rvt`, in the Chapter 15 folder of the book's web page. Figure 15.46 shows the finished stair. The large structural element is actually a baluster that's been designated as the end post.

FIGURE 15.46
Completed stair with large end post

Creating Stairs with Other Tools

We've discussed a number of different ways the parts of stairs can be manipulated and created. As we approach alternate modeling techniques with the goal of creating elegant stairs, understand that the metadata may not correspond to the geometry. This is usually the only option to complete a design where there are limitations to the default tools while avoiding the need to resort to strictly 2D representation. Because the metadata—the information part of BIM—isn't being coordinated properly, you'll want to take particular care with regard to tagging and scheduling.

A solid spiral wall can be used as a railing, or a support element can easily be created in the Family Editor and then associated with the stair as a start post. Of course, this geometry could also be created as an in-place family, but then you'd lose the advantage of being able to quickly and easily relocate the stair in your project (or create a multistory condition).

In Figure 15.47, you can see part of a spiral stair with default treads and supports modeled as balusters with the Railing tool.

FIGURE 15.47
Baluster used as a support element

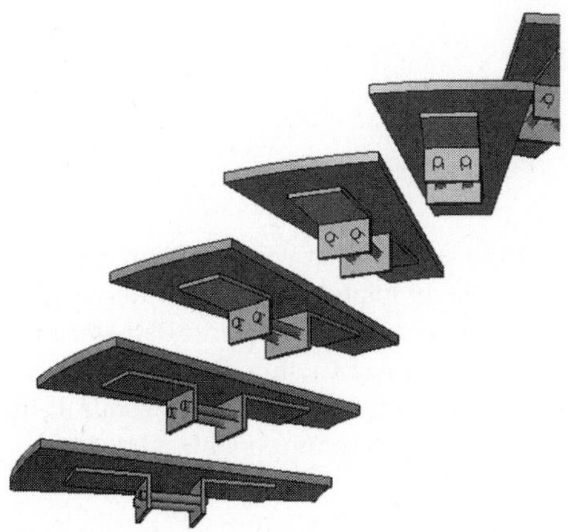

Rather than create the spiral wall (Figure 15.48) as an in-place family under the stair, we modeled the form as a baluster post in order to associate it with the beginning of the railing being used for the support brackets.

FIGURE 15.48
A series of swept blends modeled in a post family.

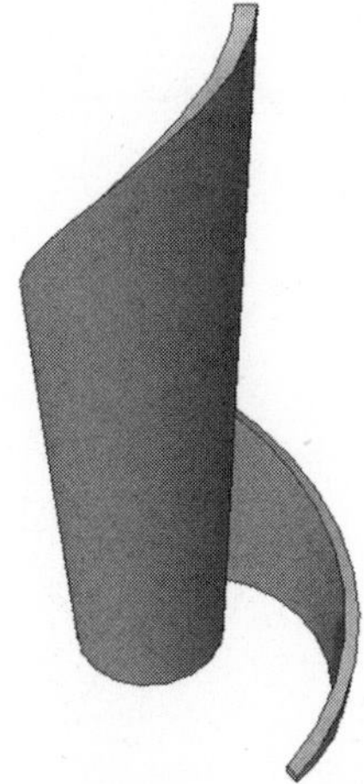

To make sure the path is correct, we copied the run line of the stair into the post family named **Spiral Start Post** (Figure 15.49). Now you can use this path as you create each of the blended sweeps (creating only one swept blend per path). In this case the blends are being modeled so that there's a 3″ (75 mm) gap between the undersides of the default treads.

FIGURE 15.49
Copy the stair run path into the post family.

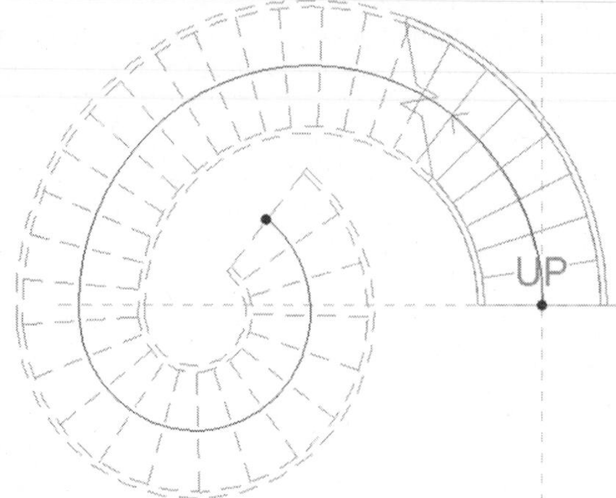

Figure 15.50 shows what you get when it all comes together. The swept blend has been created in a post template. This post is then loaded into the project environment and associated with the railing type named Support Baluster that contains the baluster definition with the support brackets named Custom Baluster. This is also a useful technique if you have to create walls that need to follow either side of a stair. If the condition exists only once, you may opt to create this as an in-place component.

FIGURE 15.50
Finished stair condition

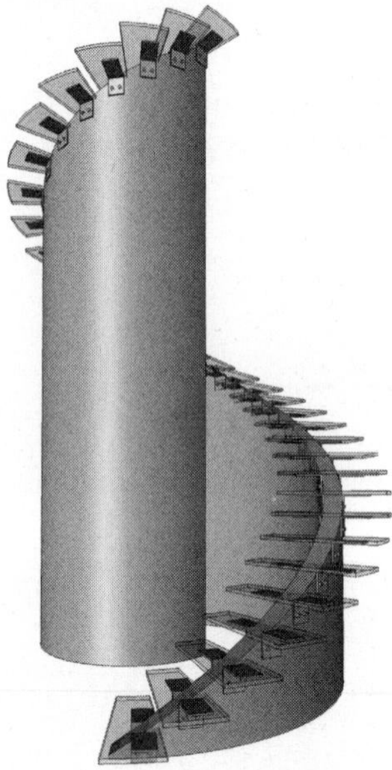

But if it occurs more than once or might be rotated and relocated (as well as occur on many levels), we recommend that you create this as part of the stair and railing definition. Then it will be easier to maintain relationships throughout the project. To investigate this stair, download the `c15-Concentric Stair.rvt` file from the Chapter 15 folder on the book's web page.

Annotating Stairs

Stair treads are annotated using the Tread Number tool, which is located in the Annotate tab of the ribbon. You can use this tool from any plan view. When this tool is activated, place a string of labels on any component stair by simply selecting the stair run. The tread number annotation can be placed at the sides, the middle, or the quarter points along the run width (Figure 15.51).

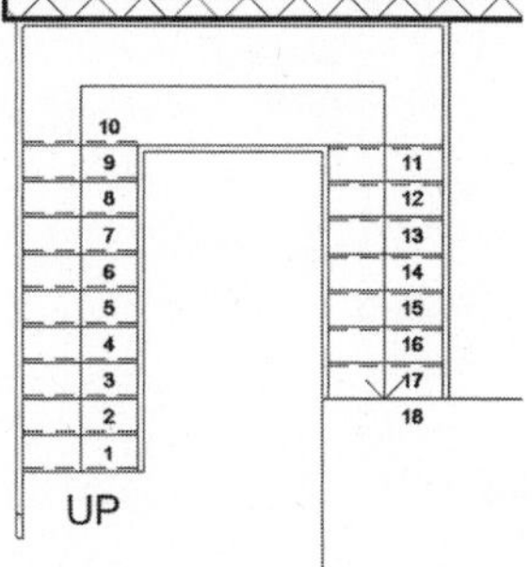

FIGURE 15.51
The tread number annotation counts individual treads or risers.

To customize the tread number annotation, select a tread number instance you have already placed in a view and you will find additional parameters in the Properties palette, such as Number Size, Orientation, and Display Rule (Figure 15.52). You can also change the start number in the Options bar.

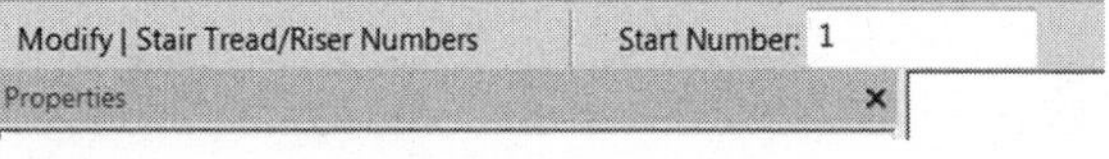

FIGURE 15.52
Customize the tread number in the Properties palette.

The arrow and label for stairs are controlled independently of the stair type for component stairs. If you created a stair with the Stair By Component tool, you will notice that the arrow and label can be selected separately. When they're selected, you can change the type of annotation in the Type Selector, and you have additional parameters in the Properties palette (Figure 15.53).

Because the stair path annotation for component stairs is a separate element, it can simply be deleted when you don't need it in a view. To replace the annotation, go to the Annotate tab in the ribbon, and from the Symbol panel click the Stair Path button and pick a stair to apply the annotation.

Finally, the cut mark that displays with stairs in a plan view can be slightly customized. The settings for cut marks are stored in yet another system family that is nested within the component stair type properties. In the Project Browser, navigate to Families ➢ Stairs ➢ Stair Cut Mark to find the types available in the default project template. Double-click any of these types to observe the properties for customizing the cut mark (Figure 15.54). To assign a Cut Mark Type value, open the Type Properties dialog box for a component stair type and look for the Graphics heading.

FIGURE 15.53
Settings for the stair path annotation

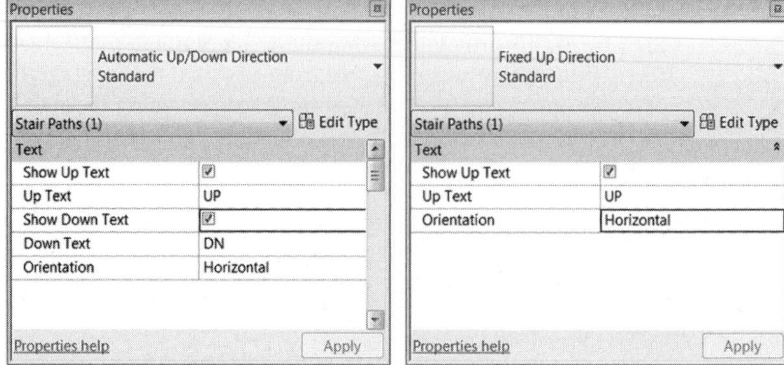

FIGURE 15.54
Parameters for the Stair Cut Mark family

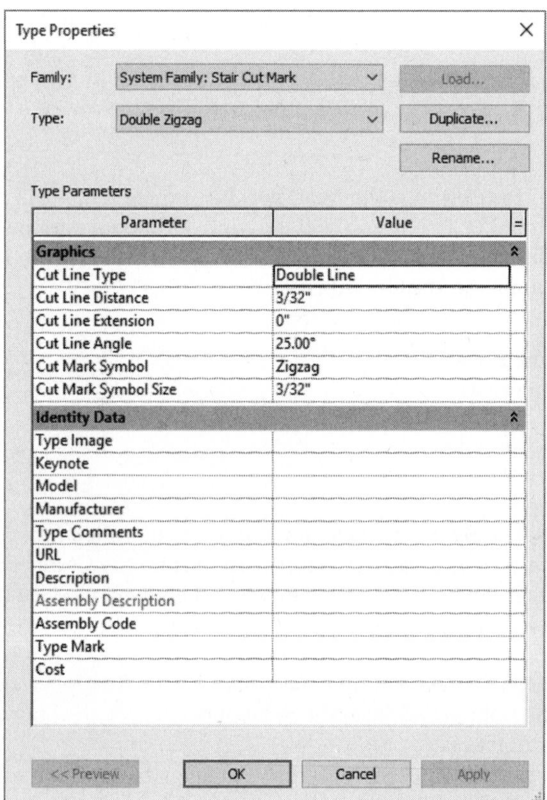

Creating Railings

Railings can be created anywhere in a project. They can be placed on stairs, ramps, floors, and roofs, but they are not hosted elements. The railing does not need to be dependent on a host object to exist. From the Architecture tab in the ribbon, you will find the Railing tool in the Circulation panel. Click the Railing flyout and you will see Sketch Path and Place On Host.

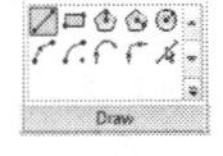

You would use the Sketch Path tool to create a railing on a flat surface such as a slab edge. When the Place On Host tool is activated, you must select a stair or a ramp and the placed railing will follow the slope of the stair or ramp. If you choose this second option, notice in the contextual ribbon that you have the option to specify whether the railing will be oriented above the tread or the stringer (Figure 15.55)—you can always modify this after the railing has been placed.

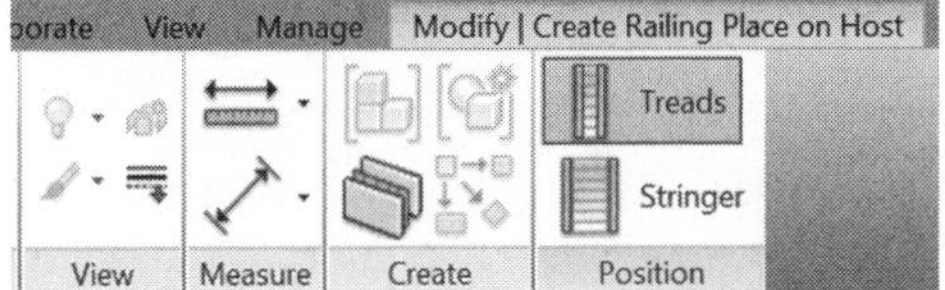

FIGURE 15.55
Set options for tread or stringer placement of railings.

Before we create a railing, we should explain the placement of a railing on a stair a little further. When you use the Place On Host method, the railing path is automatically assigned to the edge of the stair that represents the outside face of the tread and the inside face of the stringer (if one is defined). The railing orientation is simply flipped to either side of this path—toward the tread or toward the stringer. In the Properties palette, you will find a parameter named Tread/Stringer Offset that is set to –0′-1″ (–25 mm) by default. Most rail and baluster families are developed along a center axis; therefore, the Tread/Stringer Offset value pushes the railing to one side or the other of the railing's path. To modify this orientation after a railing has been placed, select a railing and either click the flip arrow that appears in the view window or right-click and select Flip Orientation from the context menu. The Tread/Stringer Offset value will remain the same no matter which way the railing is oriented.

When you use the Place On Host option of the Railing tool, be aware that you will not be able to click stairs that already have railings. You will not be prompted with a warning or an error—you simply can't select the host object. If you do find a stair or ramp on which you would like to place a railing, also be aware that one railing type will be applied to both sides of the host object. If you want a different railing for the outside of a stair element, you can use the Place On Host tool and change one of the rails with the Type Selector either before it is placed or after. If you are using the Stair or Ramp tool, you can choose the option to automatically place railings when the stair or ramp is created.

New to Revit 2017, when you click the Railing button from the Circulation panel on the Architecture ribbon, you will no longer be given a dialog box asking you to pick a railing type. Now, those choices are simply made with the type selector. From the drop-down list in the type selector, you can choose any railing type defined in the project. For stairs only, you can define the placement of the railing to be along the treads or the stringers.

Where would you need to use these sketch segment options for railings? You can use them to customize a railing that has been placed on a host. For example, you may need to continue a railing from a stair run onto a flat landing. Let's try this out in an exercise:

1. Download and open the file `c15-Railing-Tool.rvt` or `c15-Railing-Tool-Metric.rvt` from this book's web page.
2. There is a sample stair from Level 1 up to Level 2, and a railing has already been placed on the stair. Open the Level 2 floor plan. Select the railing along the outer edge of the stair and click Edit Path on the Mode panel in the contextual ribbon.
3. In the Draw panel of the contextual ribbon, select the Line tool and draw a line from the end of the existing railing sketch, as shown in Figure 15.56. Include a short segment extending in the direction of the existing sketch line, and then draw the next segment to the perpendicular edge of the floor landing.

FIGURE 15.56
Draw two new sketch lines to extend the railing path.

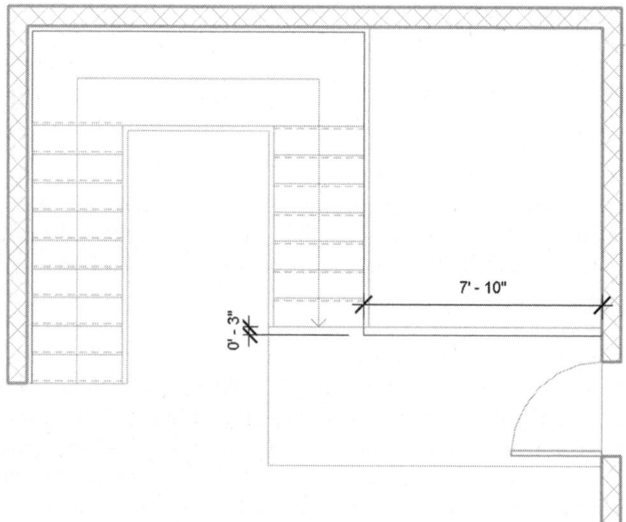

4. Select both new sketch segments you drew in step 3, and from the Options bar, set the Slope option to Flat. Now, this step may not be necessary because the railing sketch should be aware that the floor below is flat, but this is the best way to ensure consistent results with manually sketched railing paths.
5. Click the green check mark in the contextual ribbon to finish the sketch, and activate the Default 3D view to observe your results (Figure 15.57).

FIGURE 15.57
The completed railing has been extended onto the landing.

Creating a Custom Railing

Now that we've reviewed the major components of stairs and railings, let's create a rail. The rail we're going to make is a stainless steel cable railing with flat steel stock posts. Our completed railing will look like Figure 15.58. You can adapt the workflow we're going to complete to create just about any typical railing.

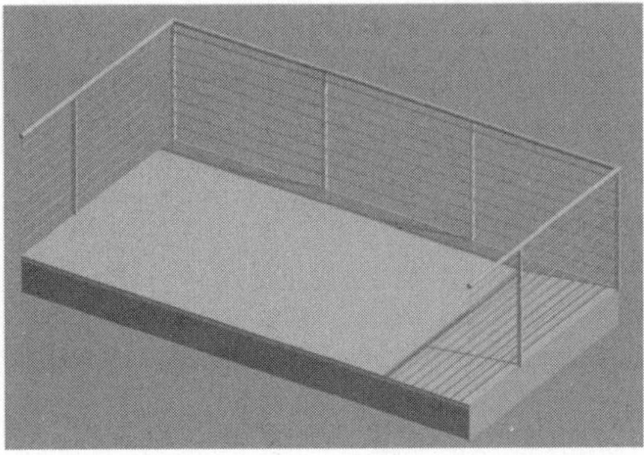

FIGURE 15.58
The finished cable railing

1. To begin, we need to build some of the components of the railing. The rail will have a stainless steel top rail, which is already part of our default project template. However, we will need to create the cables and the posts. Let's start with the cable. Select the Application button and choose New ➢ Family. Select the `Profile-Rail.rft` or `Metric Profile-Rail.rft` family template. You'll see two intersecting reference planes and some text describing the Rail Centerline and the Rail Top.

2. We're going to create the cable, which is a simple, circular extrusion. On the Create tab, select the Line tool from the Detail panel. Use this tool to create a circle that is ½″ (12 mm) in diameter (Figure 15.59). Save this file as **`Cable.rfa`**.

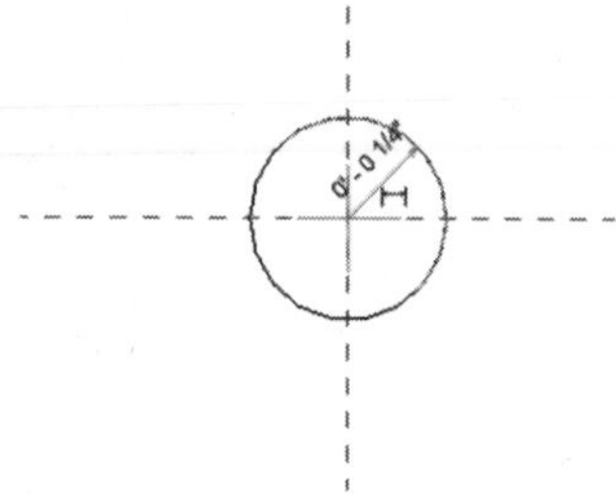

FIGURE 15.59
The cable profile family

3. We need to do a similar thing to create the stainless steel posts. Select the Application button again, choose New ➤ Family, and select `Baluster-Post.rft` or `Metric Baluster-Post.rft` from the list of new families. This will open the Left elevation view of the family. From the Project Browser activate the Ref. Level plan. We're going to make an extrusion that will become our baluster.

4. You'll notice that the tools in this family are different from those in the profile family we just created. The profile family was simple 2D linework that will extrude along a path to create the cable. In this baluster family, we're going to create a 3D element. In the plan view, choose Extrusion from the Forms panel of the Create tab. Using the intersection of the reference planes as the lower-left corner of the form, create a box that measures 1 ½″ × ½″ (40 mm × 12 mm). The shape should look like Figure 15.60. Don't worry about adding the dimensions.

FIGURE 15.60
Using the Extrusion tool to create the post

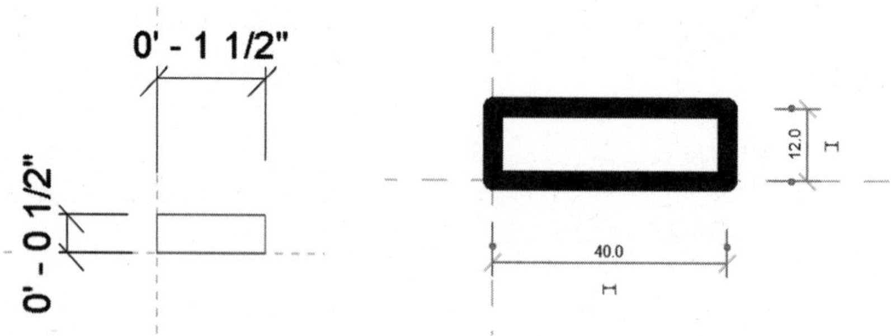

With the shape created, click the green check mark in the contextual tab of the ribbon to make the form. You'll see your box in plan, but for the next step, activate the Front elevation view from the Project Browser. You'll see a short extrusion of the form you just created with the base at the Ref. Level. You'll also see two reference planes above the form—one represents the typical railing height and the other (the higher one) represents the typical guard rail height.

5. Switch to the Modify tab in the ribbon and choose the Align tool, and align the bottom of the extrusion to the Ref. Level and the top of the extrusion to the lower reference plane (Figure 15.61). Make sure to activate the lock after each alignment. When you've finished, save the new family as **SS-Post.rfa**.

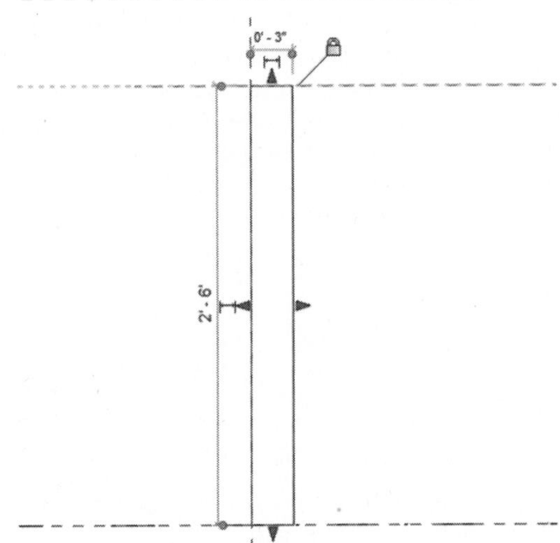

FIGURE 15.61
Align the post to the reference planes.

6. With both of these families created, you can now make the railing. Open a new project file and load both of these families into it. Choose the Railing command and select Sketch Path. Draw a simple line of any length. That will become your railing. Now, while you're in the Railing command, you need to create a new system family type to be your rail. Since this is a system family, like walls or floors, you need to create the rail by duplicating an existing one. Choose Handrail – Pipe and select Edit Type from the Properties palette.

7. In the Type Properties dialog box, choose Duplicate and name the new family **Cable Rail**. Click OK to close the Name dialog box. The family you duplicated shares many of the features of the rail you want. The top rail is a circular pipe, and the rail itself is 3′ (900 mm) tall. You need to modify the Rail Structure (Non-Continuous) and the Baluster Placement options. Begin with the Rail Structure (Non-Continuous). Choose the Edit button to open the Edit Rails (Non-Continuous) dialog box. This dialog box has rails that are spaced 6″ (150 mm) apart using the Circular Handrail profile. You want to change a few things here. First, under the Profile heading, change the profile to Cable : Cable, which is the railing profile you just created. You can do that by selecting Cable : Cable from the drop-down menu. Do this for all of the profiles.

8. Next, you want to change the rail spacing from 6″ (150 mm) to 4″ (100 mm). Modify each of the rails to show a 4″ (100 mm) increment. Your rails from bottom to top will read as follows:

   4″ (100 mm)

   8″ (200 mm)

1′-0″ (300 mm)

1′-4″ (400 mm)

1′-8″ (500 mm)

This won't be sufficient to make it to the bottom of the top rail, so you'll need to add more rails. Click the Insert button to add three more rails: Rail 6, Rail 7, and Rail 8. Make the profile for all of those Cable : Cable and give them a height of **2′-0″** (**600** mm), **2′-4″** (**700** mm), and **2′-8″** (**800** mm), respectively. Here you can also define the materiality of the rail. We've applied Stainless Steel to all of the rails. The completed dialog box will look like Figure 15.62. Once you've finished, click OK.

FIGURE 15.62
The completed Edit Rails (Non-Continuous) dialog box

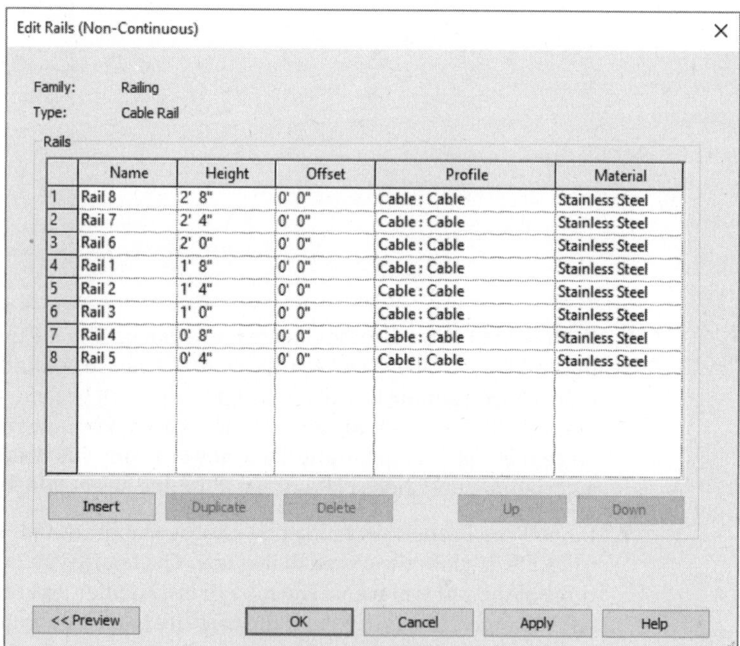

	Name	Height	Offset	Profile	Material
1	Rail 8	2' 8"	0' 0"	Cable : Cable	Stainless Steel
2	Rail 7	2' 4"	0' 0"	Cable : Cable	Stainless Steel
3	Rail 6	2' 0"	0' 0"	Cable : Cable	Stainless Steel
4	Rail 1	1' 8"	0' 0"	Cable : Cable	Stainless Steel
5	Rail 2	1' 4"	0' 0"	Cable : Cable	Stainless Steel
6	Rail 3	1' 0"	0' 0"	Cable : Cable	Stainless Steel
7	Rail 4	0' 8"	0' 0"	Cable : Cable	Stainless Steel
8	Rail 5	0' 4"	0' 0"	Cable : Cable	Stainless Steel

9. Now you need to adjust the baluster. In the Type Properties dialog box, at Baluster Placement, select Edit. This opens the Edit Baluster Placement dialog box.
10. First, like in the rail, you need to modify the family that is used to make the baluster. From the Baluster Family drop-down menu for both the Main Pattern (the upper portion of the dialog box) and the Posts (the lower portion of the dialog box), change the family to **SS Post : SS Post**. Also, you want the post centered under the top rail. Because you built the post family to one side of the reference planes, you need to offset the post to center it. In the Offset column on the far right, enter a value of ¾″ (**19** mm). The finished dialog box will look like Figure 15.63.

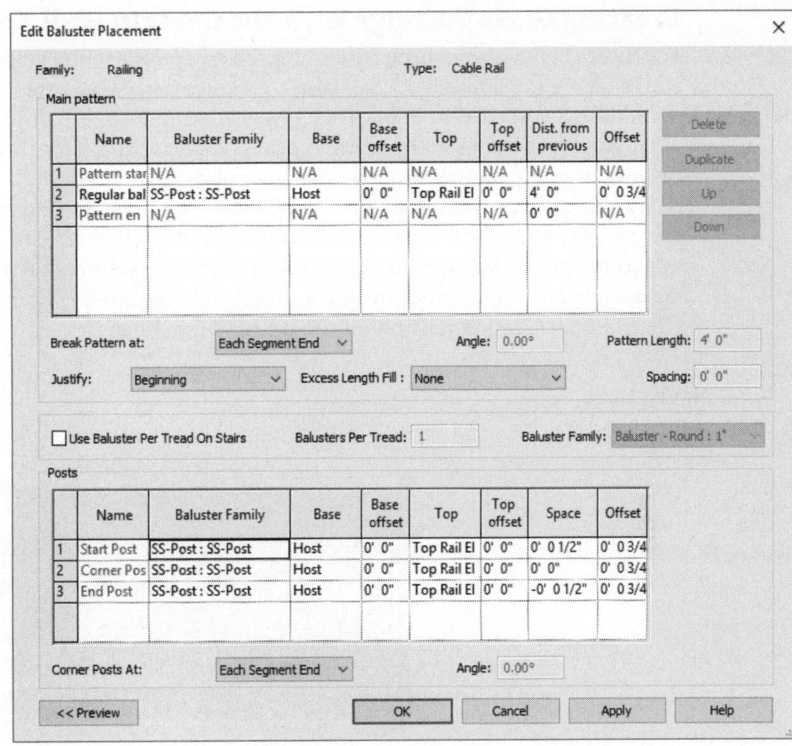

FIGURE 15.63
The completed Edit Baluster Placement dialog box

11. Click OK twice to finish the rail. The completed cable railing will look like Figure 15.64. You can see how quick and easy it is to create some simple railings. You can find the finished railing, `c15-SS Railing.rvt`, on the book's web page.

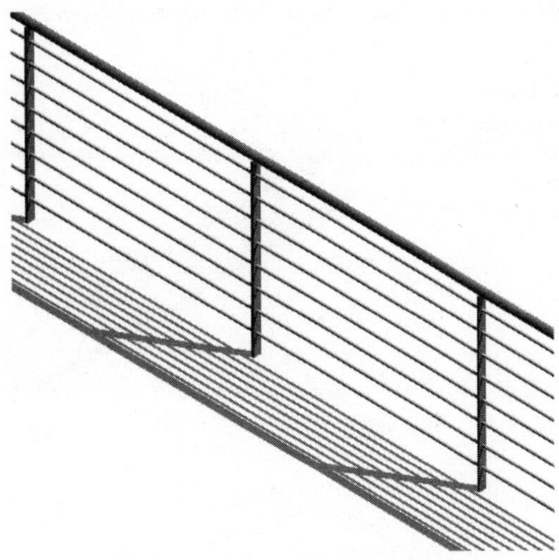

FIGURE 15.64
The completed railing

Creating Glass Railings with the Curtain Wall Tool

The most challenging railings often require exceptions to the rules. This usually means you're trying to manually locate balusters or use panels that are not part of the routine railing definition. If you tried to define each of these exceptions as a different railing type, your project would be overflowing with railing types. The best solution for these types of railings is to diverge from the Railing tool and use the Curtain Wall tool.

By using the Curtain Wall tool, you'll be able to create railings by modeling the balusters and panels inside the Curtain Panel family template (Figure 15.65). Another nice feature about this technique is that the railing is a room-bounding element because it is actually a wall. That makes this perfect for mezzanine conditions that require area calculations—certainly more efficient than creating redundant room-separation lines!

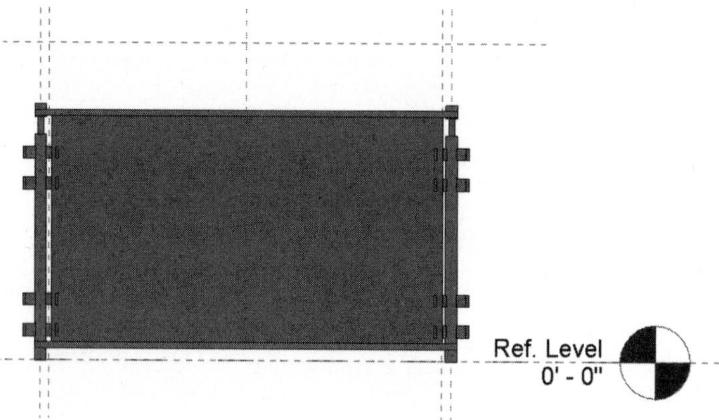

FIGURE 15.65 Curtain panel as a railing

Start by creating a single panel using the Curtain Panel template. The family may contain not only the panel for the railing but also the balusters. Once you load this panel into your project, you can create curtain walls with predefined panel widths (Figure 15.66).

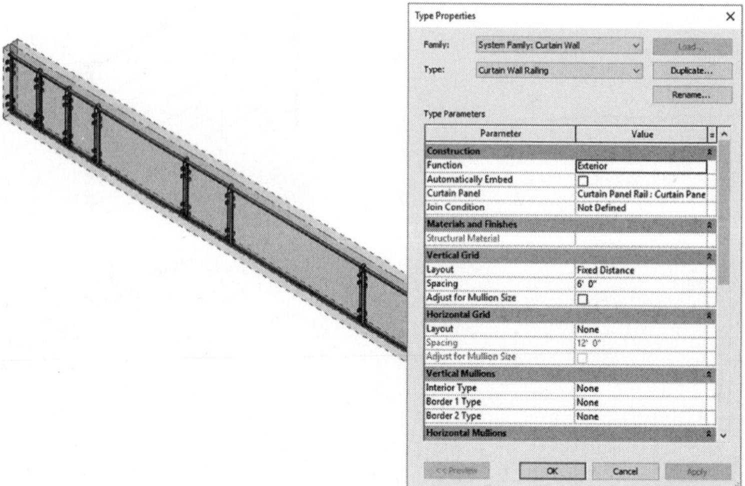

FIGURE 15.66 Curtain panel railing with custom baluster locations

Because curtain panels allow you to unpin predefined grids (as well as create other grid locations), you'll be able to quickly and easily make exceptions to the rules that you previously defined (Figure 15.67) and create several unique baluster locations specific to the installation.

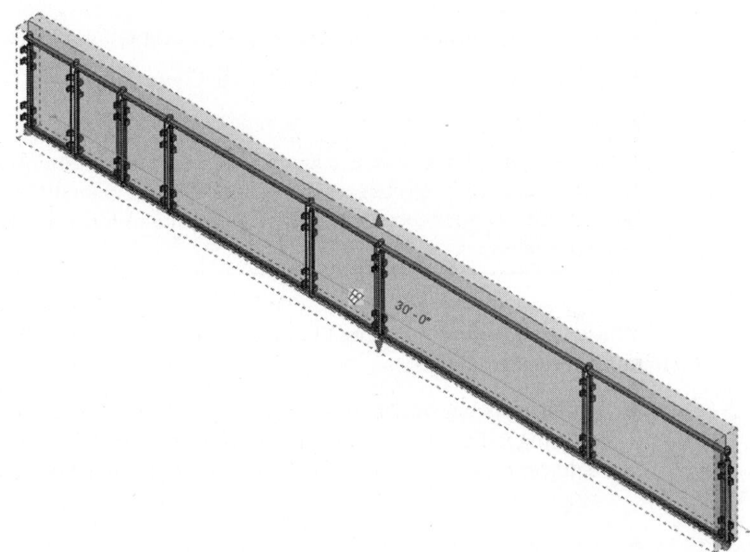

FIGURE 15.67
Adjusted baluster locations

When you're creating railings as curtain walls, be sure to filter your schedules accordingly to prevent these "railings" from being included in your curtain wall schedules. If you want to download this example project, it's in the Chapter 15 folder on the book's web page and is named `c15-CurtainWall-Railing.rvt`.

These outside-the-box techniques should give you some great ideas for making custom railings faster and more interesting than you could ever have imagined.

Using the Railing Tool for Other Objects

Currently, Revit software doesn't have a specific tool to allow components to be quickly and easily distributed along a user-defined path. In some cases you could use line-based families, but these don't work in curved conditions. You could also experiment with adaptive components in the conceptual massing environment, but that could be too complicated for a simple, repeating element. In the meantime, consider using the Railing tool to distribute elements along paths for a variety of uses besides just for railings.

CAREFULLY IDENTIFYING CUSTOMIZED MODEL ELEMENTS

In this chapter we will make a few suggestions to use tools designed to create one type of element to generate other types of model elements. We highly recommend you take care in identifying such elements so that they may be clearly understood by other people who might use your model. If not

Continues

Continued

clearly identified, these elements could cause trouble in BIM applications such as 3D coordination, quantity surveying, and estimating and where specification databases are connected to the design model. Here are some suggestions for identification:

- Use the Assembly Code property to assign an appropriate system description.
- Provide a unique and clearly recognizable Type Name value.
- Provide a clear description in the Type Comments field.

Whatever method you choose to identify these types of customized elements, be sure to indicate the method in your project's execution plan. Whether it is a BIM execution plan, project execution plan, or other similar document, this type of communication and collaboration is essential to the reduction of errors and rework.

When using railing functionality outside of a railing to distribute elements along paths, keep in mind these three rules:

- You'll probably want to nest your family into a baluster family template (rather than creating it directly as a baluster). This is because the existing parameters within the baluster family can cause your geometry to fly apart if it needs to move up and down as a single element.
- Don't expect your nested element to schedule or tag. If you need the elements to schedule or tag individually, you probably want to place them individually (or use another technique, like a line-based family).
- Don't share parameters of nested families in an attempt to schedule. Your element won't schedule properly.

In some cases, you'll want the railing family to have associated profiles, like the shading device in Figure 15.68. The railing profiles are used to create the shading fins, and the balusters are the support elements.

FIGURE 15.68
Railing as shading device

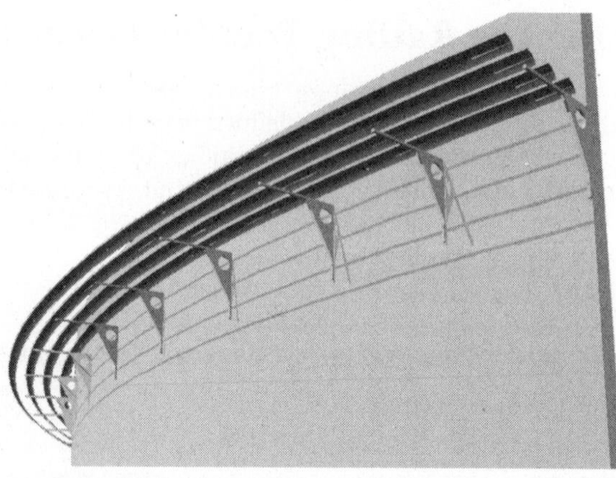

Using railings to quickly and evenly distribute components along a path is great during design and allows for quick iteration. Outdoor elements like lampposts are particularly appropriate for distributed placement (Figure 15.69). In this example, a lamppost has been nested into a baluster family.

FIGURE 15.69
Lamppost nested into a baluster family

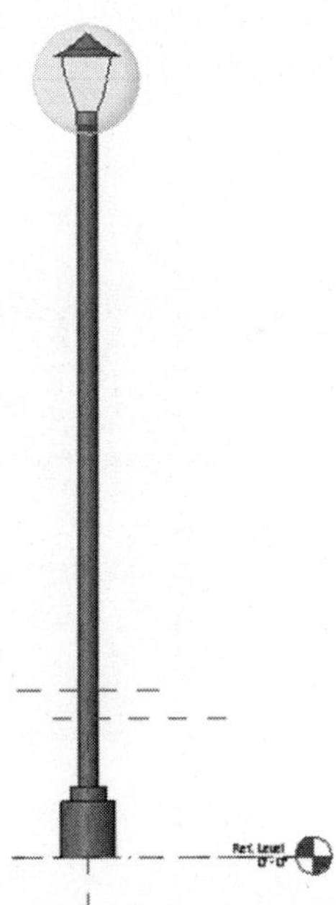

Once this lamppost has been nested in the baluster family, you'll be able to create a custom "railing" with the lamp designated as the "baluster." This will allow you to quickly and easily distribute lampposts along a sketch at specific intervals that can be modified as a parameter. So, for example, if the lamppost was originally distributed on 60′ (18 m) centers, you could very quickly redefine it to occur on 40′ (12 m) intervals (Figure 15.70).

FIGURE 15.70
Lampposts distributed along a path as a baluster family

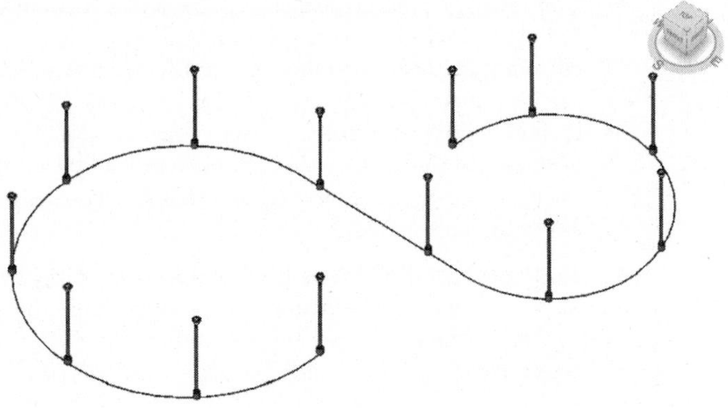

You can use this for any repetitive elements that must be placed on center and evenly distributed along a path. Other uses might include pipe bollards and outdoor planting.

Even a design pass at light rail tracks (including railcars) can be distributed along paths (Figure 15.71). In this case, the rail sleepers are balusters, and profiles are used to create the rails and the rail bed. The monorails are easy too. The vertical supports and railcars are balusters, and the suspended track is the rail profile. This file can be downloaded from the Chapter 15 folder on the book's web page. Look for the `c15-Monorail and Railway Railing.rvt` file.

FIGURE 15.71
Transportation components as railings

Real World Scenario

IMPORTANT BEST PRACTICES

Here are some best practices to consider with regard to creating complex stairs and railings:

- Don't forget to nest your family components whenever possible and appropriate. This will keep the components together when associated with some other template that contains hardwired parameters and reference planes. It will also save you time during design changes and iteration.
- Don't struggle with creating the stairs in this chapter. If you get stuck, you can download the sample stairs from this chapter's files and use them for a starting point when creating your custom stair. Just remember, it's usually easier to build and test a custom stair or railing in a sample project first. Then copy and paste or use Transfer Project Standards to get the custom stair or railing from the test project to your actual project. Download sample files for this document at the book's web page. You'll probably want to copy your custom stairs and railings in an easy-to-access project that contains several finished examples (since they can't be kept as family components).
- The level of detail and visibility is crucial if you care about graphic refresh times and printing. As you model the components of your custom stairs and railings, assign appropriate orientation and level of detail (Coarse, Medium, or Fine). You'll notice a difference when you pan and rotate your model.

- Take care to filter schedules. Using a curtain wall as a railing may have certain advantages, but you also want to make sure your curtain wall schedules are filtered to exclude these types of elements.

Overall, be careful when reaching into your bag of tips and tricks! You need to weigh the cost of implementing a new process against the cost of doing what's familiar. Make sure that you're maintaining a balance between *predictability* and *efficiency*. There are frequently two extremes that you need to avoid:

- *High predictability; low efficiency.* Most people will grasp the solution that you intend to implement; they'll fully understand the technology and technique. But they'll also quickly realize that managing design changes and iteration will be highly manual and time-consuming. And the rest of the team will doubt your leadership and understanding of the technology and processes.
- *High efficiency; low predictability.* The solution will be very efficient to manage the design, but only you or a few team members will understand what you've created. Everyone else on the team will resist making any changes to your creation out of fear that they'll break it.

So, what's important with creating interesting and innovative stairs and railings is that you manage to strike a balance between these two extremes. Just remember these four simple characteristics:

- **Beneficial:** Not just to you but to the project team
- **Efficient:** Implementation and changes that are fast and predictable
- **Elegant:** Understood by the team and by any new team members
- **Repeatable:** Can be used on many projects

If you can't remember these guidelines, the handy acronym of **BEER** should help. When you are not sure which solution is the best one to follow, your team will tend to gravitate to whatever allows them to have a beer at the end of the day.

In other words, whatever allows them to decompress, reenergize, and come back to work the next day refreshed, focused, and enthusiastic will ultimately win out. And keep in mind that this principle isn't just important to stairs and railings or Revit or BIM but also important to having an interesting life.

The Bottom Line

Understand the key components of stairs and railings. Having a complete understanding of the components of stairs is important. You don't want to set about breaking the rules until you understand how best (and when) those rules can be broken.

Master It What are the essential parts of stairs?

Understand the different stair tools and apply them to custom designs. Designing in a spreadsheet is hard. Step back and consider what you're trying to accomplish. If you'll look at the components that make up stairs, you'll see some interesting opportunities.

Master It How would you create a continuous tread that wasn't monolithic? What would you do if you wanted to create a custom stringer? Are balusters always vertical and used to support handrails? What if your particular stair just can't be modeled in the Stairs tool?

Design railings and use the Railing tool for other model elements. From model patterns to geometric intricacy, there's a lot that can be created with the Railing tool. When this doesn't work, look to the Curtain Wall tool for "railings" that can contain space and allow "balusters" to be conveniently unlocked.

Master It Why would you not use a railing to manage repetitive relationships? What if you need to accurately distribute geometry along a path?

Implement best practices. There are specific best practices when creating custom stairs and railings. Pay attention to nesting geometry, maintaining the right level of detail, and filtering schedules so the metadata ends up in the right place.

Master It Is it possible to create solutions that are too efficient? What's the big deal with detail levels? And finally, what's the most important thing to remember before creating an elegant workaround?

Part 5

Documentation

Up to now, we've discussed how to create an Autodesk® Revit® Architecture model and use BIM to derive interesting forms, create parametric content, and perform analysis on your design. Part 5 focuses on how to document those designs in the construction document phase and ultimately present those drawings to project stakeholders.

We will walk through the process of creating detail views and 2D content (detailing); generating different types of plan views and sheets (documenting); and finally, how to add text, notes, and dimensions (annotating).

Chapter 16

Detailing Your Design

As you've seen so far, you can show information in Autodesk® Revit® Architecture software in a variety of ways, including 3D views, plans, sections, and elevations. In each of these cases, the geometry is typically modeled based on design intent, meaning that your goal isn't to model everything but to model enough to capture the overall scope of the proposed building. To this end, it becomes necessary to embellish the model in specific views with more detailed information. These take the shape of 2D detail elements that you will use to augment views and add extra information.

In this chapter, you'll learn to:

- Create details
- Add detail components to families
- Learn efficient detailing
- Reuse details from other files

Creating Details

If you are accustomed to using 2D CAD software applications to create drawings, you should first be aware of how the detailing process in Revit differs from CAD drafting. In Autodesk® AutoCAD® software, for example, you would create a new DWG file and then add lines, arcs, circles, hatch patterns, text, and dimensions to develop a detail. You might use blocks to combine repeatable elements to increase efficiency and maintain consistency. In Revit, you will create additional views within the project file, to which you might add 2D embellishment along with annotation and dimensions. Details can incorporate parts of the 3D model or can be empty views exclusive to 2D elements.

View Types for Detailing

Before we discuss the process of detailing, let's review the fundamental views in which you can create details: detail views and drafting views.

Detail Views Detail views are essentially subsets of the views we've discussed previously in this book such as plans, elevations, and sections. When you create a new section or callout, you have the option to select Detail View from the Type Selector. The model is still displayed in a detail view, although you can set the Display Model view property to Do Not Display if necessary.

Because you can use detailing tools in any view, we will refer to any view that displays the model as a detail view throughout the remainder of this chapter.

Refer to Chapter 2, "Applying the Principles of the User Interface and Project Organization," for more information about the difference between callouts and detail views.

Drafting Views Drafting views do not display model content. Instead, they are simply a blank canvas within which you can create details using only 2D elements such as lines, arcs, circles, or 2D families. Drafting views can be associated with sections or callouts, but those view references will display a reference label such as SIM (similar) or TYP (typical). You can customize the Reference Label value in the type properties of each view.

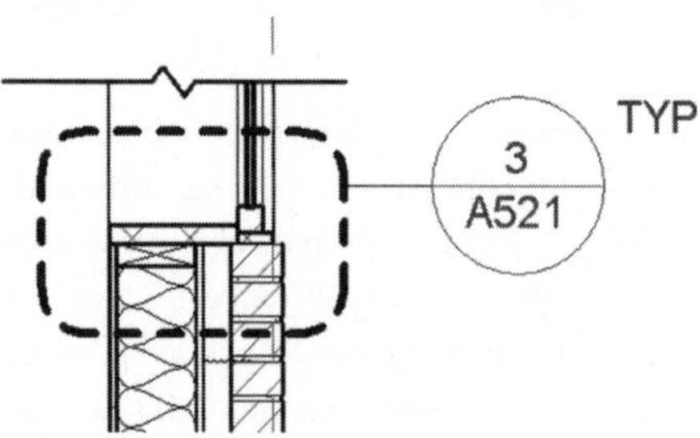

Download and open the file `c16-Sample-Building.rvt` or `c16-Sample-Metric.rvt` from this book's web page (`www.sybex.com/go/masteringrevit2017`).

From the Project Browser, activate the view Section 2, and you will see an overall section of the building. We will create a more detailed section callout of the exterior wall at the right side of the view. Let's walk through the steps to generate this view:

1. Switch to the View tab in the ribbon, locate the Create panel, and then click Callout ➤ Rectangle.
2. In the Type Selector, change the view type to Wall Section.
3. Sketch a rectangular region around the exterior wall at the right side of the building.
4. When you finish sketching the new callout, it should look like the section view shown in Figure 16.1. Double-click the callout head to activate the new view.

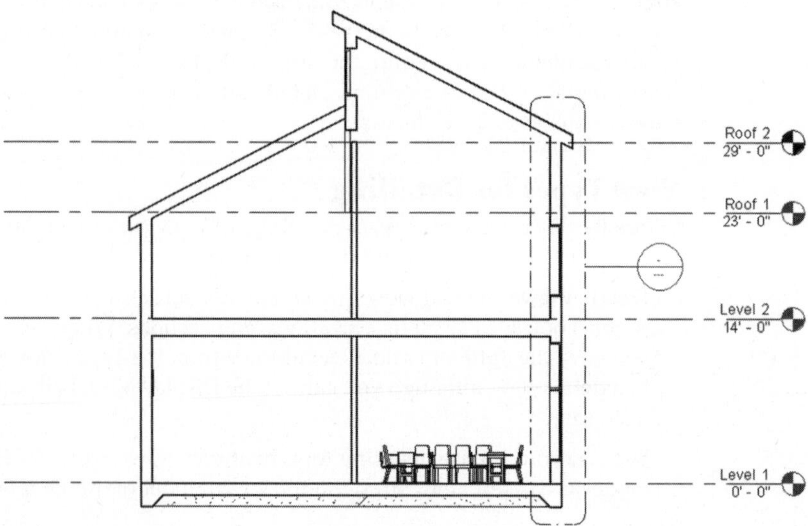

FIGURE 16.1
Wall section callout added to building section view

5. In the Properties palette, change the View Name to **Wall Section North**, set the Detail Level to Medium, and change the Scale to 1/2″=1′-0″ (1:25).

   You have taken the first step toward creating the path from the overall down to the specific. From the plan and an overall section, you have created a wall section. Before we drill down even further, let's break the view down in order to isolate only the transition conditions at floors and roof.

6. Select the crop region in the wall section view and you will see a number of view break icons. Click one of the Horizontal View Break icons along either vertical edge of the crop region.
7. You now have two crop subregions, but you will need to create one more. Select the crop region again, and then click and drag the grip at the bottom of the upper subregion to stretch it downward. Do not drag it too close to the lower subregion because it will rejoin the subregions back into the original crop boundary.
8. Use the grips at the top edge and bottom edge of the three subregions to show the intersection conditions with the Level 1, Level 2, and Roof.
9. Select the crop region once again, and you will see vertical double arrows at the middle of each subregion. Use these arrows to move the subregions closer together.

The final result of this exercise should look like the image in Figure 16.2.

FIGURE 16.2
Wall section view broken into subregions

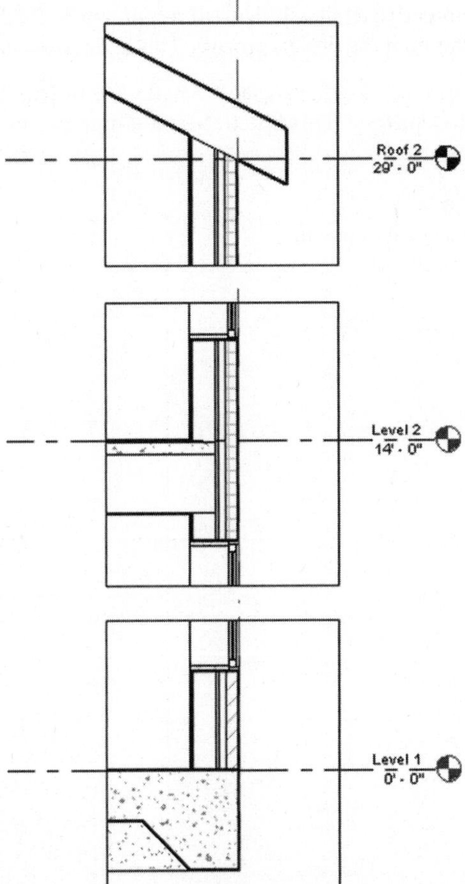

Working with the Detailing Process

Now that you have completed the setup of a detail view, we will discuss three different methodologies with which you can approach the detailing process: stand-alone detailing, hybrid detailing, and model detailing. These are terms we invented to help you understand and plan your detailing efforts as your skills improve in the Revit environment.

Stand-alone Detailing (Beginner) If you are relatively new to the Revit environment, you might choose to develop your details without any part of the 3D model serving the detail. In this scenario, you can use either detail views or drafting views; however, you may tend to use more of the latter. If you use detail views, the Display Model view property (in the Property Palette with the view selected) will most often be set to Do Not Display. This setting allows you to see the model components in a regular line weight, half tone, or not at all in a detail view.

With a stand-alone detailing approach, you forfeit some ability to ensure your details accurately reflect the modeled condition. In a detail view, you may temporarily return the Display Model view property to Normal or Halftone, but you may be able to draft more comfortably using the blank canvas of an empty view.

Hybrid Detailing (Intermediate) As you become more experienced with detailing in Revit, you may start to use a more balanced number of detail views and drafting views. With a hybrid approach you will maintain the model in any detail views and you will add detail components to embellish the 3D model. This approach tends to yield a more accurate representation of the intended design, but it will require more time and care to maintain as the model evolves throughout the design process. This is the workflow used by most teams detailing in Revit.

In Figure 16.3, you can see a detail view in which the Display Model view property has been set to Halftone. This illustrates the difference between what is modeled and what is a detail component.

FIGURE 16.3
Example of a detail view with embellished drafting

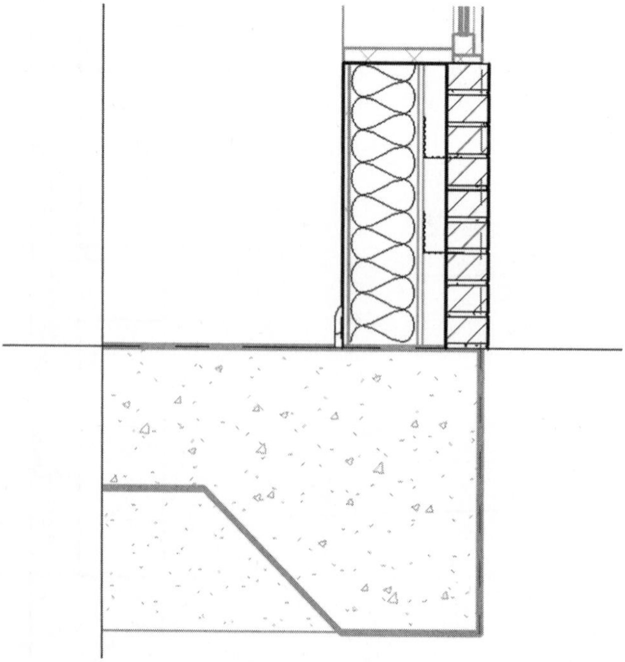

Model Detailing (Advanced) The most complex approach to detailing can also be the most efficient—once you become familiar with creating families and customizing your project templates. The approach we refer to as model detailing still involves the use of some detail components; however, they are embedded into model elements where applicable. For example, in a wood-framed structure, detail elements such as sill plates, studs, joists, or anchors can be embedded in wall type definitions. The details will display automatically when the walls are displayed in a section detail view.

With any of these three methods we've described, there is a range in which you can use the model to help generate your details. You should plan your approach before you begin detailing in your project. As always, the more time you spend preparing your template content in the beginning, the less time you will need to develop your details later in the project.

Detailing Tools

Even when you're creating details, Revit has a variety of parametric tools to allow you to leverage working in a BIM environment. You can use these tools to create strictly 2D geometry or to augment details you are trying to create from 3D plans, sections, or callouts. To become truly efficient at using Revit to create the drawings necessary to both design and document your project, it's important to become acquainted with these tools—you will find yourself using them over and over again throughout your process. All of these tools are located on the Detail panel of the Annotate tab.

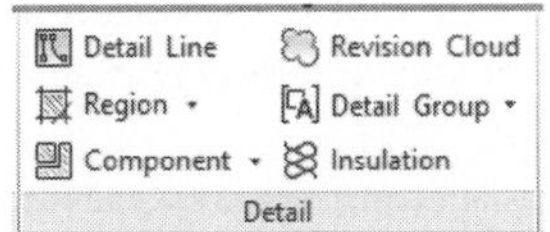

This small but very potent toolbox is what you will need to familiarize yourself with in order to create a majority of the 2D linework and components that will become the details in your project. To better demonstrate how these tools are used, let's step through them to explain each one's purpose. Note that some of the tools may not be available depending on the active view. For best results, make sure you have a plan or detail view active before continuing.

Using the Detail Line Tool

The Detail Line tool is the first tool located on the Detail panel of the Annotate tab. This tool is the closest thing you'll find to CAD drafting because it allows you to create view-specific linework using different line styles and it provides tools for drawing and manipulating different line shapes.

Detail lines are view specific—they appear only in the view in which they're drawn. They also have an arrangement to their placement, meaning that you can layer them underneath or on top of other objects. This is especially important when you begin using a combination of regions, detail lines, and model content to create your details.

Using the Detail Line tool is fairly easy. Selecting the tool will change your ribbon tab to look like Figure 16.4. This new tab will have several panels that allow you to add and manipulate linework.

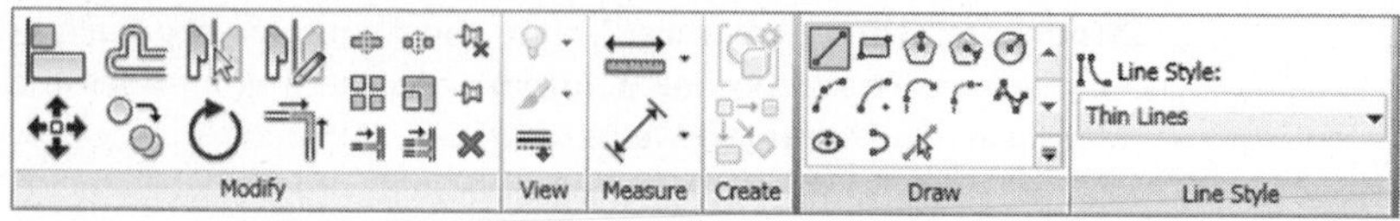

Figure 16.4
The Detail Line toolset on the Place Detail Lines context ribbon

There are three major panels on this new tab: Line Style, Draw, and Modify. Because of their use sequence (selecting the line type, creating the shape, and modifying the line), we'll talk about them in order from right to left.

Line Style This panel includes a drop-down menu that allows you to choose a line style in which to produce the linework in this view. The drop-down menu has all the default Revit line styles as well as any custom ones you might have made for your project or to accommodate office or client standards. The active line will be the one displayed in the drop-down window before it's expanded.

New line styles can be added at any time in the project, and many offices find it necessary to add custom line styles beyond the thin, medium, and wide ones available in Revit out of the box. To add more styles or to just see the complete list, choose Additional Settings from the Manage tab and select Line Styles. For more information about creating your own custom line styles, refer to Chapter 4, "Configuring Templates and Standards."

Draw The Draw panel contains a number of geometry tools to draw within the active view. The tools allow you to create lines, boxes, circles, splines, ellipses, and arcs. The last tool in the bottom row is the Pick tool. This tool allows you to select a line previously drawn or portion of a model element (say an edge) and add linework on top of the existing shape.

Modify The Modify panel has several tools that you can use to modify any of the linework already placed within the view. The larger tools, from left to right, are Align, Offset, Mirror (axis), Mirror (line), Move, Copy, Rotate, and Trim.

Using the Linework Tool

Although not part of the Annotate tab, the Linework tool helps you make your detail composition more legible. Default settings for object styles and line weights will manage most of a view's composition automatically, but you sometimes need to adjust a line or two to clarify a detail. The Linework tool allows you to modify the edges of model elements in a view-specific context. Note that this tool is not available in a drafting view because it works only on model elements.

To use the Linework tool, switch to the Modify tab in the ribbon, locate the View panel, and click Linework. This will add the familiar Line Style selector panel at the end of the ribbon. Simply choose the line style you want to assign, and then select an edge of a model element.

The edges you pick can be almost anything: cut lines of walls, families, edges of floor slabs, and so on. Selecting the edge of an element will change the default line style to the style you have chosen. To return an edge to its original line style, use the Linework tool again, but select <By Category> from the Line Style drop-down list.

You can also choose to remove lines using this tool. By selecting the <Invisible Lines> line type, you can make some edges disappear. Use this method instead of covering unwanted lines with masking regions.

Another great use of the Linework tool is to indicate the edges of overhead ceilings or floors in a floor plan view. To accomplish this task, set the Underlay property of the active view to the level where the ceiling, floor, or roof is associated. If necessary, set the Underlay Orientation to Reflected Ceiling Plan. Start the Linework tool, select an overhead line style, and then pick any edges you'd like to see in the floor plan view. When you're finished, set the Underlay property back to None, and not only will the lines you created with the Linework tool remain, but they will update if the overhead model object is modified.

Let's use the Linework tool to continue our exercise with the wall section detail by following these steps:

1. Switch to the Modify tab in the ribbon, locate the View panel, and then click the Linework tool.
2. From the Line Style drop-down menu in the contextual tab of the ribbon, choose Medium Lines.
3. As indicated in Figure 16.5, click the inside face and the outside face of the exterior wall. Also click the edge of the wall below the window sill.

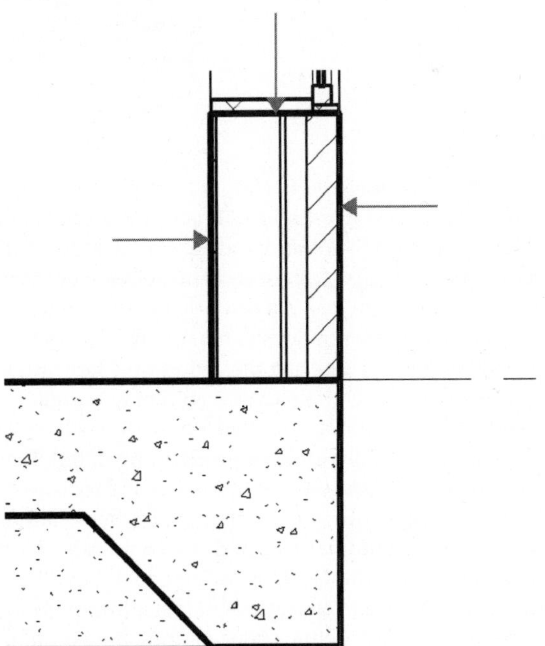

FIGURE 16.5
Use the Linework tool to modify the cut lines of the wall element in a detail.

DOORS AND SYMBOLIC LINES

In the architecture industry, doors are typically modeled in a closed position but shown as open and with a door swing direction in plan view. To get this dual representation, in the Family Editor turn off the visibility of the door panel (extruded solid form) in the plan view and draw the 90-degree open door panel and its swing using symbolic lines. Control this visibility in the family environment using the Visibility settings explained in the next section of this chapter.

Symbolic lines can be controlled using the same Visibility settings available for detail components and the solid model elements in the family. You can use the same logic and draw the dashed lines that represent the door-opening direction in elevations.

Using Filled Regions and Masking Regions

The next tool on the Detail panel of the Annotate tab is the Region tool, which contains two individual commands: Filled Region and Masking Region. *Regions* are two-dimensional areas of any shape or size that you can fill with a pattern. This pattern (much like a hatch in AutoCAD software) will dynamically adjust based on changes to the region boundary. You can manipulate the draw order of regions in the same manner as detail lines. Regions also have a type property (Background) that can be set to Opaque (hiding the objects they are placed over) or Transparent (letting the elements below show through).

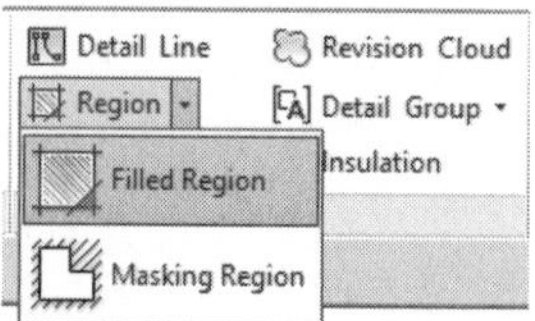

Filled regions allow you to choose from a variety of hatch patterns to fill the region. These are commonly used in details to illustrate materials like rigid insulation, concrete, or plywood. *Masking regions*, on the other hand, do not include a fill pattern. Masking regions are typically used to "hide" or *mask* certain content from a view that you don't want shown or printed. As an example, there might be a particularly detailed way in which two walls join and their materials overlap. In some cases, it doesn't make sense to model that condition, and it makes more sense to use detail lines to describe the condition. Here you would need to mask a portion of the view so you can essentially draw over it with new content.

When selecting the Region tool, you will be taken directly into Sketch mode, and you'll have a series of tools similar to those for drawing detail lines. The Draw panel allows you to create any number of shapes with all the associated tools to move, copy, or offset the linework.

When creating either kind of region, it's important to note that you cannot complete Sketch mode unless the boundaries you draw are in closed loops. You can create as many closed-loop boundaries as you want as long as they do not overlap and are all formed with closed loops (Figure 16.6). Notice in the figure that, in addition to the use of multiple closed loops, you can use any combination of line styles to draw the boundary of a region.

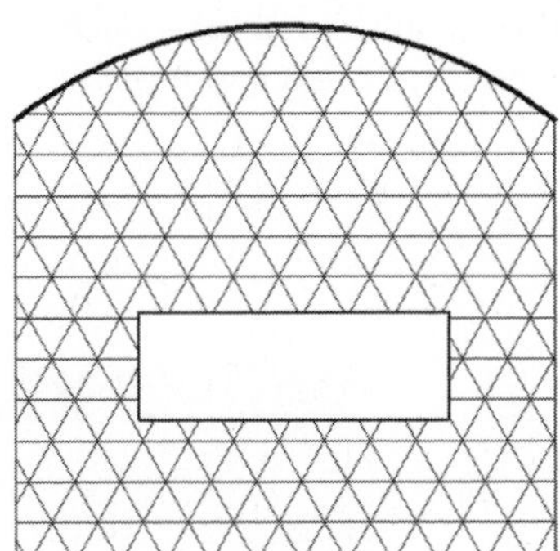
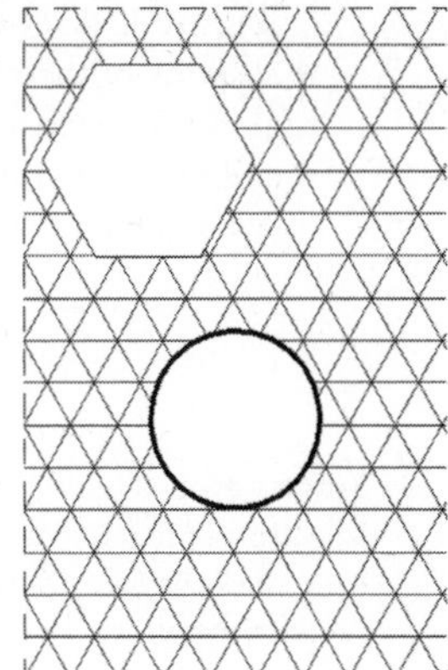

FIGURE 16.6
Multiple shapes within a single filled region

Another consideration for using regions is the linework that borders a region. When starting the Region tool, you'll be able to choose the line style you want to use for the border of the region from the Line Style drop-down (similar to working with detail lines). You can change line styles for any of the segments of the region and even make them all different if needed.

One especially useful segment line style is <Invisible Lines>. When drawn in Sketch mode, these appear as gray lines, but once the sketch is completed, they become invisible lines. When used with a masking region, this line style can create a completely invisible box that allows you to hide elements that are unwanted in a particular view. Figure 16.7 shows the same masking region in two instances, one selected and the other not selected. You can see how the masking region seems to disappear, covering the filled region. Use caution if you decide to use masking regions with invisible boundary lines because you will not be aware of their existence unless you hover the mouse pointer over them. In the example shown in Figure 16.7, the end result can also be achieved by modifying the filled region and drawing two additional invisible lines.

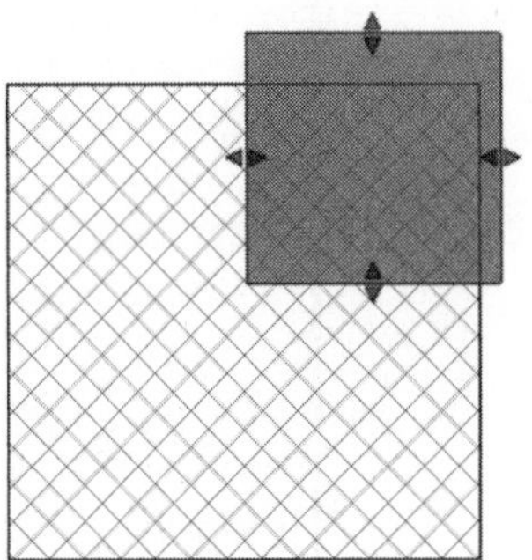

FIGURE 16.7
A masking region selected and not selected

Filled regions have slightly more options because, unlike masking regions, they let you control the parameters of the fill pattern. Filled region types are another type of Revit system family. A region type created in one view can be used in any other view, and modifying the type properties of a region in one view changes it in all the other views.

Figure 16.8 shows the list of filled region types from one of our office templates. You'll notice that many of the region names are indicative of various materials. Instead of naming the filled region types according to their graphic properties, such as Diagonal-Up, it's a good idea to use the identity parameters such as Type Mark and Assembly Code to help extend the effectiveness of even 2D detail elements.

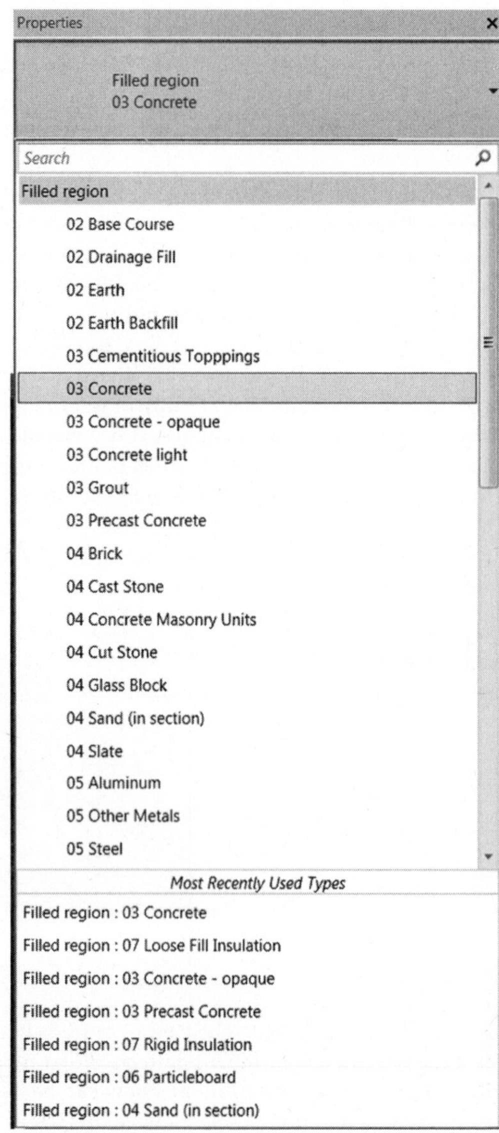

FIGURE 16.8
Selecting a filled region type from the Type Selector within the Properties palette

STANDARDIZING TYPE NAMES FOR FILLED REGIONS

Having some sort of naming convention applied to your filled region types can help you organize the Type Selector in a way that is easy for the project team to understand. You'll notice in Figure 16.8 that we've organized the region names around a two-number MasterSpec division prefix. Because MasterSpec is tied to the keynoting system as well, project teams tend to be familiar with the naming convention. This approach also keeps similar material types together rather than all of the materials being sorted alphabetically. Take Concrete and Precast Concrete as an example. You can see in Figure 16.8 that those material types are very close together in the drop-down list based on their prefix.

The filled regions also have additional properties. By highlighting any placed region, you can open its type properties from the Properties palette by clicking Edit Type (Figure 16.9). These properties allow you to control the fill pattern, background opacity, line weight, and color of the region. Remember that these properties are by type, so if you want a region that is opaque and then decide you also want one that is transparent, you'll need to create another type.

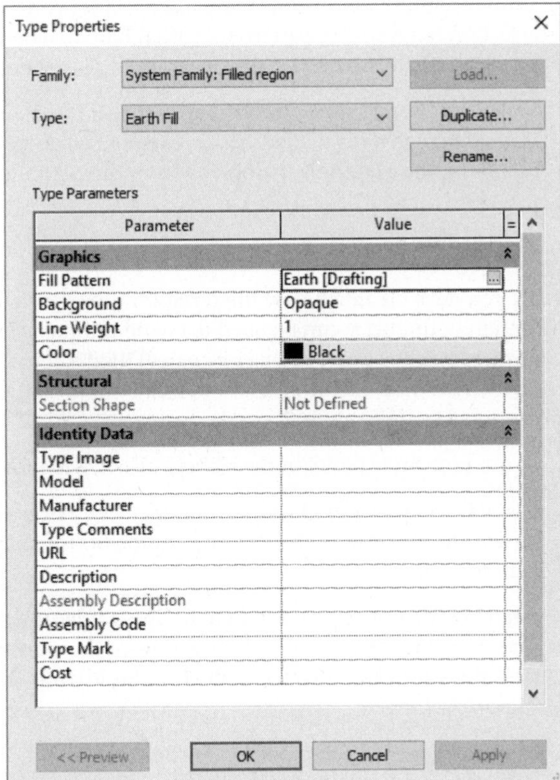

FIGURE 16.9
Type properties for a filled region

As we discussed in Chapter 4, filled regions can use either a drafting pattern or a model pattern. Refer to Chapter 4 for instructions on how to create a custom fill pattern. For now, let's review the process of creating a new filled region type.

Creating a New Filled Region Type

To create a new filled region type, begin by duplicating an existing region and then modify its properties. Follow these steps to get started:

1. Switch to the Annotate tab in the ribbon, and on the Detail panel click Region ➤ Filled Region. Click the Edit Type button in the Properties palette.
2. Click Duplicate in the Type Properties dialog box.
3. Name your new region **Earth Fill**, and then click the button in the Fill Pattern field to open the Fill Pattern dialog box.
4. Make sure you have Drafting selected at the bottom of the Fill Patterns dialog box. Select the pattern named Earth.

   Note that you can create filled region types with model patterns; however, you must make sure the region types are named clearly so you can recognize the difference between similar regions. For example, the filled region you would use to indicate brick masonry in a section is a drafting pattern (diagonal hatch), whereas a brick surface pattern is a model pattern and can be used in an elevation or plan view.
5. When you finish, click OK until you exit all the dialog boxes. The same region patterns that you created for a filled region can also be associated with material surfaces or cuts by accessing the Materials dialog box from the Manage tab in the ribbon.

Placing a Filled Region

Now that you have created a new filled region type, let's add a region to the detail and explore how different boundaries can be used to create unique graphics without separate linework. If you continue from the previous exercise, the Filled Region command will still be active. If not, switch to the Annotate tab of the ribbon, locate the Detail panel, and then click Region ➤ Filled Region and follow these steps:

1. In the Line Style panel in the ribbon, select Wide Lines from the drop-down menu.
2. In the Draw panel of the contextual tab in the ribbon, select the Line tool and then sketch an area to the right of the slab edge at the bottom of the detail view. Use the image in Figure 16.10 as a guide.
3. After you complete a closed loop of lines, hold down the Ctrl key while selecting the lines to the right and below the top line of the sketch, as shown in Figure 16.10. With multiple lines selected, go back to the Line Style drop-down menu in the ribbon and choose <Invisible Lines>.
4. Click the green check mark in the ribbon (Finish Edit Mode). The resulting filled region will look similar to the image shown in Figure 16.11.

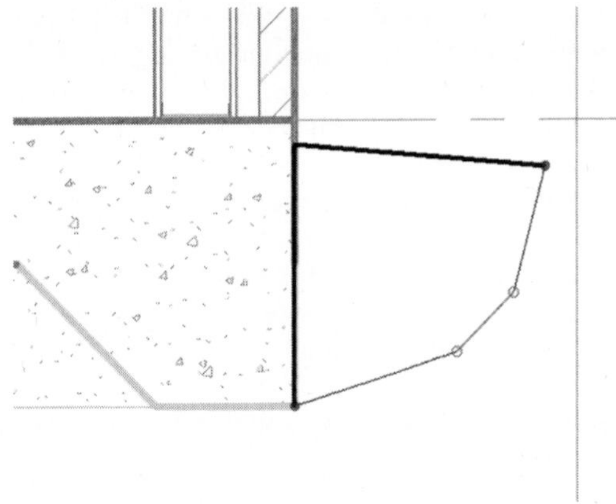

FIGURE 16.10
Set some sketch boundary lines to be invisible.

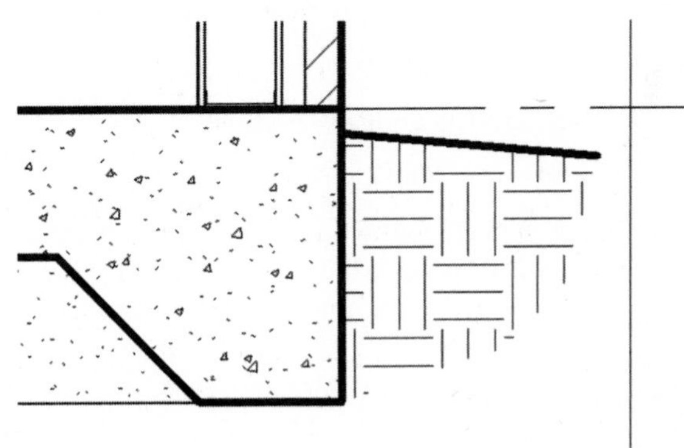

FIGURE 16.11
The completed filled region added to the detail

The sketch line in the filled region boundary that is coincident with the edge of the slab should be of the same line weight as the setting for the slab. In this sample file, both Floors and Wide Lines are set to a line weight of 5.

Adding Detail Components

Another important tool for detailing is the detail component—a family that consists of exclusively 2D geometry. You can schedule detail components, tag them, and assign keynotes. Because they are families, they can also be stored in your office library and shared easily across projects.

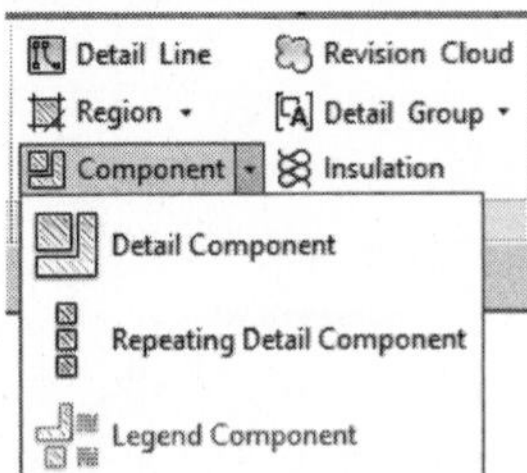

To add a detail component to a view, select Detail Component from the Component drop-down list located on the Annotate tab, and use the Type Selector to choose from components that are already loaded into the model. If you don't see a detail component you want to insert in the Type Selector, click the Load Families button in the contextual tab of the ribbon, and load one from the default library or your office library.

Remember, in the Autodesk default family library, detail components are stored in the Detail Items folder, under which the folders are organized according to MasterFormat or a similar standard coding system. Many building objects are represented in the default library with detail components. For example, if you are looking for a detail component representing a steel beam, don't look in the library under Structural Framing—instead look in the Detail Items folder.

Adding Detail Components and Embellishing the View

We have preloaded some detail component families into the sample building project you downloaded earlier in this chapter. Use the following components to further embellish the bottom, middle, and top portions of the wall section (the metric equivalents may have an *M_* prefix):

- Base Molding - Section
- Nominal Cut Lumber - Section
- Corrugated Wall Tie - Section

These detail components are all specifically designed to be used in a section detail. There are other similar detail components in the default library that can be used in a plan detail or when the object is to be shown from the side. An example of some detail embellishment is provided in Figure 16.12.

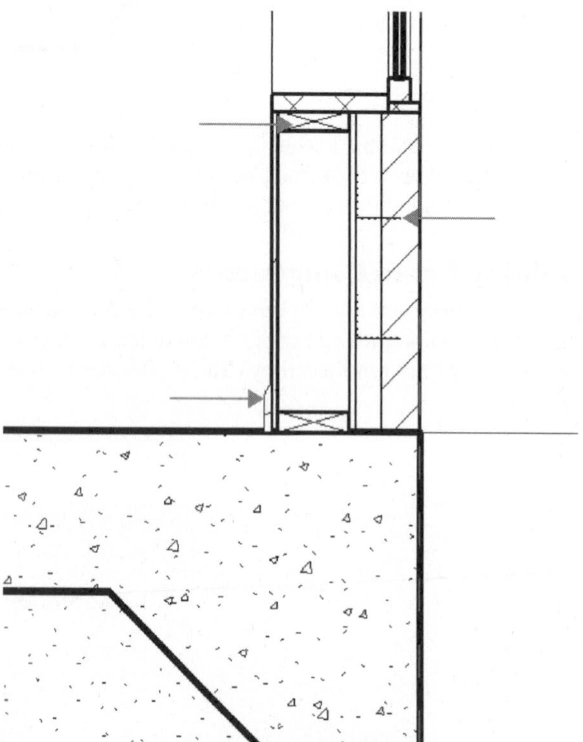

Figure 16.12
Detail components have been added to the detail view of the model.

You might notice that there are only three types loaded for the detail component family named Nominal Cut Lumber - Section. What if you need to load more types from that same family? This scenario occurs sometimes when you use families that have a type catalog. Refer to Chapter 14, "Designing with the Family Editor," for more information about families and type catalogs.

To reload a family for access to additional types within the family, one option is to start the Detail Component tool again, click Load Family, and find that family in the library. A simpler solution is to locate the family in the Project Browser (the Families branch is toward the bottom), right-click the family name, and then choose Reload from the context menu. If the family's source file (the RFA file) is available and the family has an associated type catalog, the Type Catalog dialog box will appear and allow you to select additional types to be loaded into the project.

Follow these steps:

1. In the Project Browser, expand the Families branch of the tree, locate and expand the Detail Items branch, and then locate Nominal Cut Lumber-Section or M_Nominal Cut Lumber-Section.
2. Right-click the family name and select Reload from the context menu.

   Note that you may be prompted to select a family file if the original RFA file cannot be located. In that case, we have provided the RFA and the accompanying type catalog in TXT format along with this chapter's exercise downloads.
3. Select the types 2 × 10 and 2 × 14 (50 × 200 mm and 50 × 300 mm) from the Specify Types dialog box, as shown in Figure 16.13, and then click OK.
4. Use the additional types to continue adding detail components to the view within the floor element at the middle of the detail view.

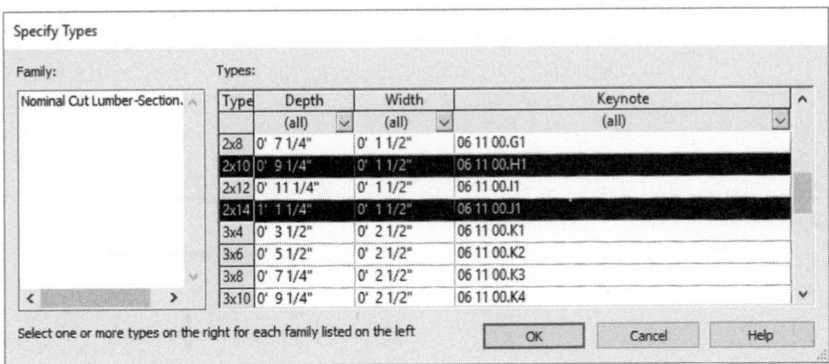

FIGURE 16.13 Select types to be loaded from a family type catalog.

ARRANGING ELEMENTS IN THE VIEW

So far you have created all of the content in order and have not had to change the arrangement of any of the elements. However, knowing how to change the arrangement is an important part of detailing, so you don't have to draw it all in exact sequence. Arrangement allows you to change the position of an element, such as a line or a detail component, relative to another element. Much like layers in Adobe Photoshop or arrangement of objects in Microsoft PowerPoint,

Revit allows you to place 2D elements in front of or behind others. You'll see the Arrange panel on the far right once an element or group of elements is selected and the Modify menu appears (Figure 16.14).

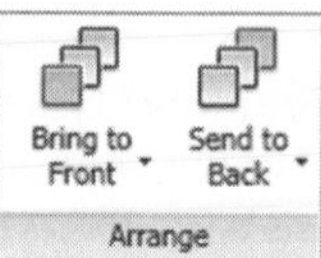

FIGURE 16.14
The Arrange panel

From here, you can choose among four options of arrangement:

Bring To Front This brings the selected objects all the way to the front of the stack. In Figure 16.15, there are two detail lines on top of a masking region, which is also on top of a filled region. By selecting the detail lines and choosing Bring To Front, we moved the lines on top of all the other elements.

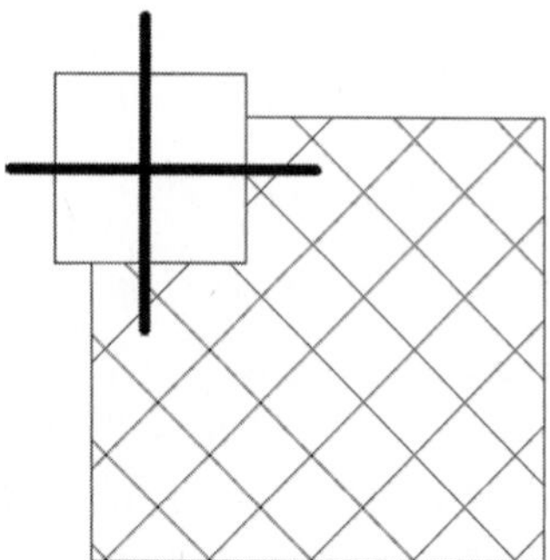

FIGURE 16.15
Bring To Front

Bring Forward This option brings the selected elements one step closer to the front in a given sequence. In Figure 16.16, we've selected the masking region and chosen Bring Forward, and now it appears on top of one of the detail lines. Note that each of the detail lines is its own layer within this stack.

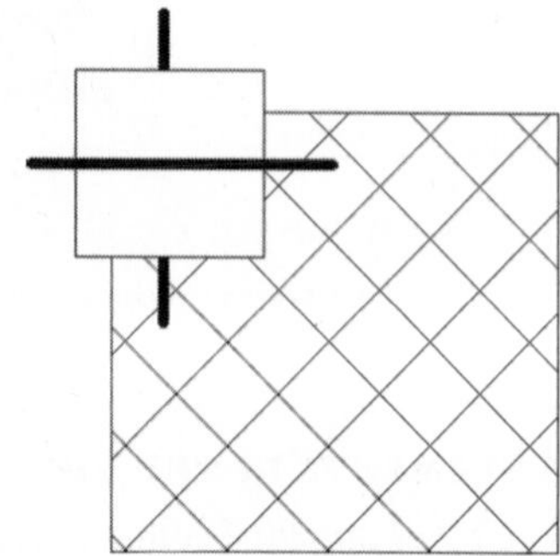

FIGURE 16.16
Bring Forward

Send To Back This option does the exact opposite of the Bring To Front tool and will send an object all the way to the back of the stack. In Figure 16.17, we've chosen the masking region again and sent it to the back.

FIGURE 16.17
Send To Back

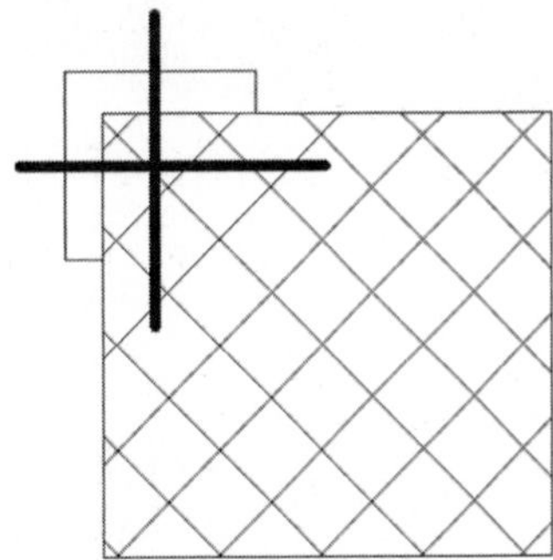

Send Backwards The fourth option, Send Backwards, will step the selected elements one step backward in the stack. In Figure 16.18, we've chosen the horizontal detail line and sent it backward; it now appears behind the filled region.

FIGURE 16.18
Send Backwards

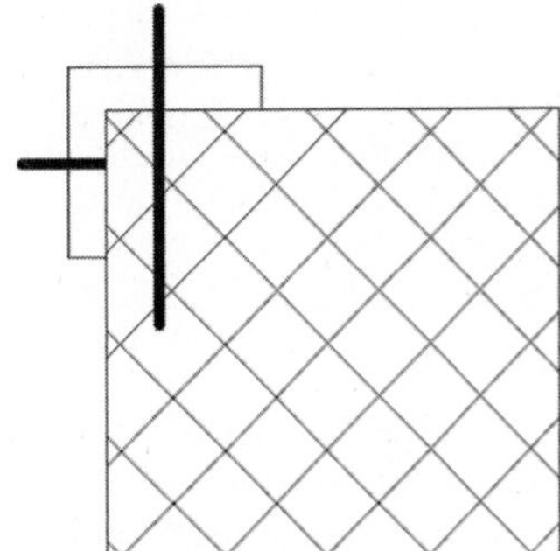

Repeating Detail Component

Repeating elements are common in architectural projects. Masonry, metal decking, and wall studs are some common elements that repeat at regular intervals. The tool to help create and manage these types of elements is called the Repeating Detail Component, and it's located in the Component flyout on the Annotate tab (Figure 16.19).

FIGURE 16.19
Choosing Repeating Detail Component

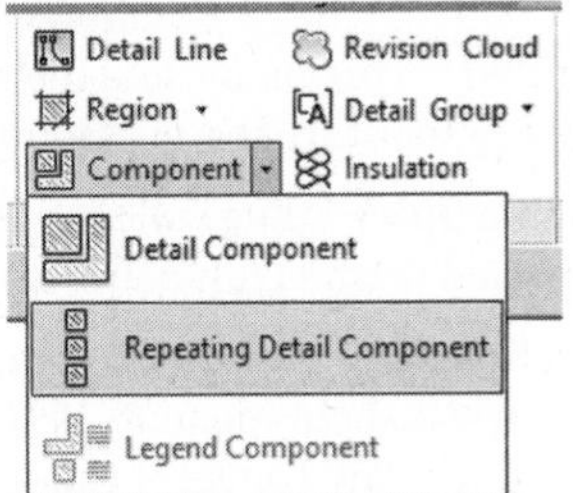

This tool lets you place a detail component in a linear configuration where the detail component repeats at a set interval. This allows you to draw a "line" that then becomes your repeating component. The default repeating detail is common brick depicted in section, repeating in regular courses (Figure 16.20). Creating elements like this not only lets you later tag and keynote the materials but also gives you some easy flexibility over arraying these elements manually.

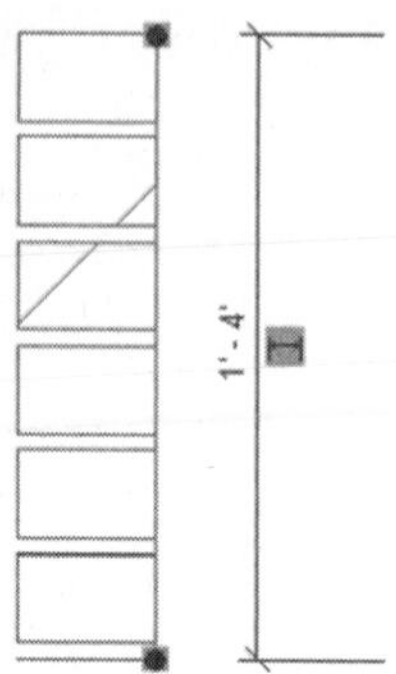

FIGURE 16.20
A brick repeating detail

> **BEWARE THE LIMITATIONS OF REPEATING DETAIL COMPONENTS**
>
> Before you decide to use the Repeating Detail Component tool in any of your details, you should be aware of its limitations. Although repeating detail components can be scheduled, they cannot be tagged or assigned a keynote as you would for a simple detail component. If your annotation methodology relies on tags and/or keynotes, we recommend you avoid the use of repeating detail components. Instead of the repeating detail component, you can use a single detail component and then use the Array command.

Before you create a repeating detail component, we'll cover the properties behind one so you can get a better idea of how they work. Start the Repeating Detail Component command and draw a sample line using the Brick type. Exit the command by pressing Esc or clicking the Modify button, and then select the Brick repeating detail. In the Properties palette, click Edit Type to open the Type Properties dialog box.

Let's review what each of these settings does:

Detail This setting allows you to select the detail component to be repeated.

Layout This option offers four different modes:

- **Fixed Distance** This is the absolute spacing between components, for example, a strictly defined center-to-center measurement.
- **Fixed Number** This mode sets the number of times a component repeats itself in the space between the start and endpoint (the length of the sketched path).
- **Fill Available Space** Regardless of the value you choose for Spacing, the detail component is repeated on the path using its actual width as the Spacing value.
- **Maximum Spacing** The detail component is repeated using the set spacing, and the number of repeated components is set so that only complete components are drawn. Revit creates as many copies of the component as will fit on the path.

Inside This option adjusts the placement of the last detail component in the repeating detail. If Inside is selected, the last component will be drawn inside the endpoint of the repeating detail line. If Inside is not selected, the last component will be drawn outside or overlapping the endpoint of the line.

Spacing This option is active only when Fixed Distance or Maximum Spacing is selected as the method of repetition. It represents the distance at which you want the repeating detail component to repeat. It doesn't have to be the actual width of the detail component.

USING FORMULAS TO PERFORM MATH

In the example of the imperial brick, you have a distance of 2-2/3″ or 2 171/256" vertically between bricks stacked in a wall. Because there are three brick courses in every 8″ (225 mm is standard in the UK), you don't need to know the exact distance between each brick—you can use Revit to calculate that value. Revit is formula driven, so you can enter = 8″/3 in the Spacing field and it will calculate the distance for you, similar to using a formula in Microsoft Excel.

Detail Rotation This option allows you to rotate the detail component in the repeating detail.

In the `c16-Sample-Project.rvt` file, we have already created a repeating detail to illustrate brick and mortar coursing. At the base of the exterior wall, you will see that a portion of the modeled wall assembly already contains a layer assigned with a brick material; however, individual brick courses are not shown. Let's embellish the view with a repeating detail component to better communicate the design intent.

1. Zoom closer to the bottom portion of the detail view, at the base of the exterior wall. From the Annotate tab in the ribbon, locate the Detail panel, and click Component ➢ Repeating Detail Component.
2. From the Type Selector, choose the Brick repeating detail type. Starting at the bottom of the inside face of the brick layer, draw a line up to the bottom of the window sill, as shown in Figure 16.21.

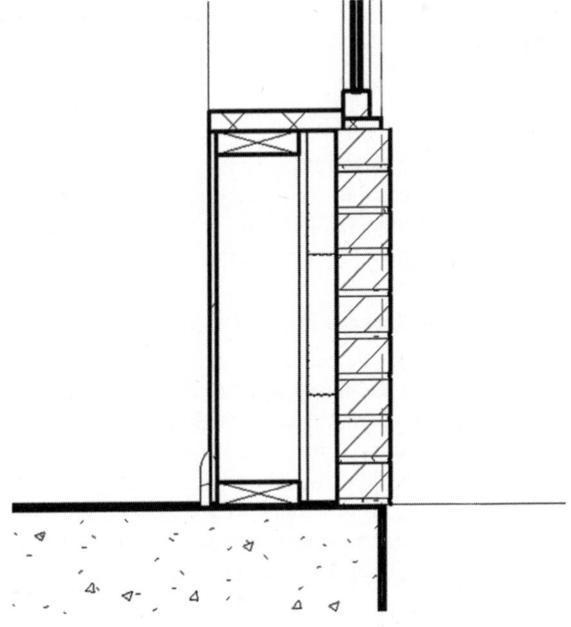

FIGURE 16.21
The brick repeating detail component applied to the view

If the last brick detail does not appear at the top of the sketched line, you can either drag the line farther up or edit the type properties of the repeating detail family and toggle the Inside parameter.

3. Press the Esc key or click the Modify button to exit the Repeating Detail Component command. Select the corrugated metal wall tie components you placed in the Detail Components exercise. Hold down the Ctrl key while clicking each component.
4. From the Arrange panel in the contextual tab of the ribbon, click Bring To Front. If necessary, you can use the arrow keys on the keyboard to nudge the wall tie components so that they display in proper relation to the mortar lines of the repeating brick detail (Figure 16.22).

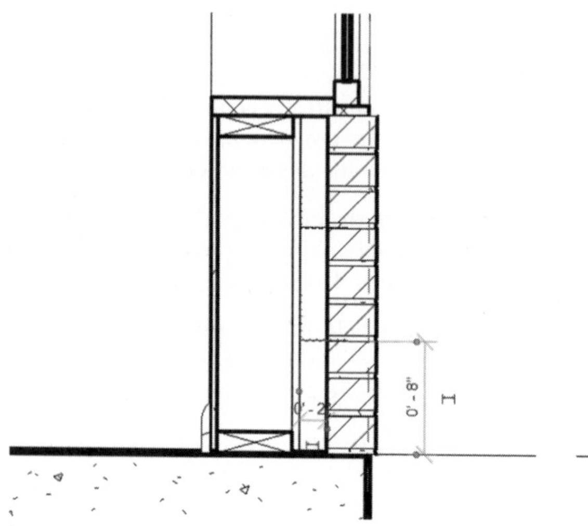

FIGURE 16.22 Adjust the draw order and position of previously placed detail components.

Although this detail still needs annotations before you can think about placing it onto a sheet, you can begin to see how you have used the 3D geometry of the model and were able to quickly add some embellishment to it to create a working project detail. For now, save this detail. You'll return to it later in the chapter.

Using Line-Based Detail Components

Although there isn't a command dedicated to line-based detail components, this category of 2D elements can be quite powerful. As their name suggests, line-based detail components are 2D elements that behave like lines. Some examples of building elements you can illustrate with these components include waterproofing, gypsum board, plywood, and even repeating elements such as brick. Why would you use a line-based detail component for brick instead of a repeating detail component as we previously discussed? Because you can tag and schedule a line-based detail component. You can use any modifying commands on line-based detail components such as Trim, Extend, and Align.

In the default content library you will find components in the Detail Items folder such as Gypsum Wallboard, Rigid Insulation, and Drainage Board. Start the Detail Component command, click Load From Library, and load a few of these families. In a detail view, practice drawing these elements to embellish the modeled design further.

Drafting Insulation

The best way to think of the Insulation tool is as a premade repeating detail. You'll find this tool on the Detail panel of the Annotate tab.

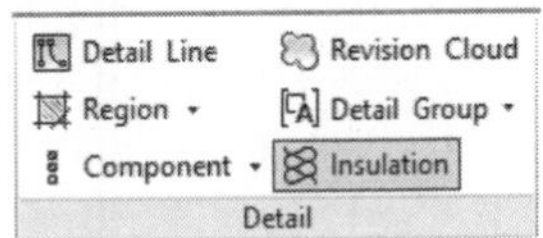

Selecting this tool allows you to draw a line of batt insulation, much like a repeating detail. Figure 16.23 shows a typical line of insulation.

FIGURE 16.23 The insulation detail component drafted in a view

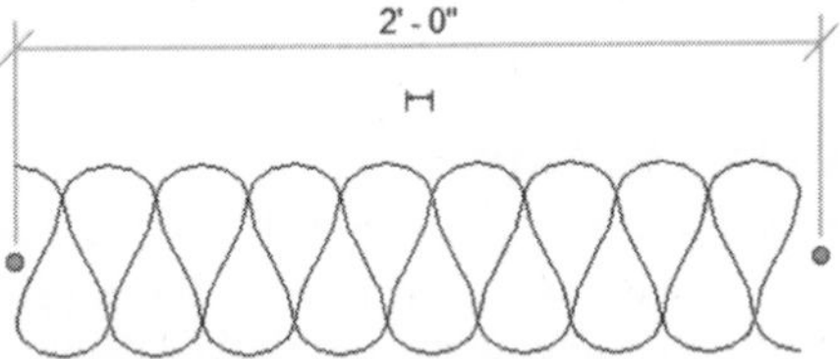

When selecting the Insulation tool, you can modify the width of the inserted insulation from the Options bar or the Properties palette. In the Properties palette, you can also control the Insulation Bulge To Width ratio, which adjusts the amount of curve in the insulation. The default value is 2.0. By default, insulation is inserted using the centerline of the line of batt, but you can control the offset in the Options bar once the tool is activated. You can also modify the width either before or after inserting insulation into your view.

Let's continue to embellish the wall section view in the c16-Sample-Project file. Follow these steps to begin adding insulation detail components:

1. From the Annotate tab in the ribbon, click the Insulation tool. In the Options bar, set the Width value to **5″** (**150** mm) and the Offset to 0″ To Center.

   You can customize the Offset value depending on how you would like to sketch the insulation by drawing the line representing the center of the insulation or either edge.

2. Within the wall assembly, hover the mouse pointer at the midpoint of one of the nominal wood framing detail components you placed previously in this chapter. Use the midpoint snaps of the framing components to set the start point and endpoint of the insulation component.

3. Continue to add insulation components in the remaining wall, floor, and roof structure layers in the detail view.

   A sample of the result is shown in Figure 16.24.

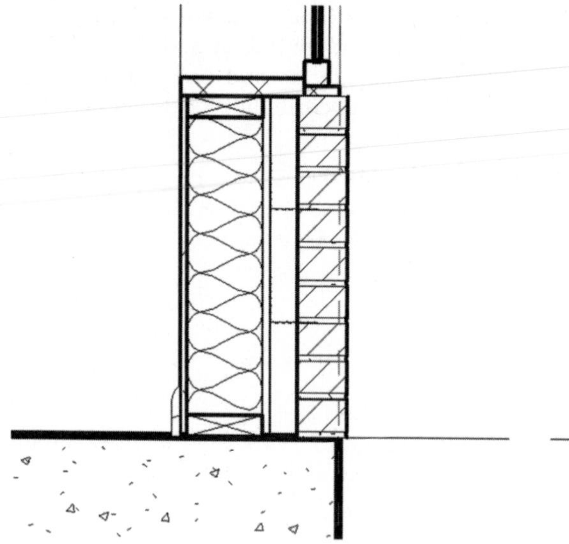

FIGURE 16.24
Insulation detail components added to the wall section

Creating Detail Groups

Detail groups are similar to blocks in AutoCAD and are a quick alternative to creating detail component families. They are collections of 2D graphics and can contain detail lines, detail components, or any other 2D elements. You will probably want to use a detail component to create something like wood blocking; however, if you plan to have the same configurations of wood blocking in multiple locations, you can then group those configurations and quickly replicate them in other details. As with blocks in AutoCAD, manipulating one of the detail groups will change all of them consistently.

There are two ways to make a detail group. The more common one is to create the detail elements you'd like to group, select all of them, and then click the Create Group button in the Create tab of the contextual tab of the ribbon. When you're prompted for a group name, use a naming convention that will help you organize and recognize the contents of each group rather than accept the default name (Group 1, Group 2, and so on).

The other way to create a detail group is by clicking the Create Group button in the Detail Group flyout on the Annotate tab (Figure 16.25). You will then be prompted for the type of group (Model or Detail) and a group name before you can select any elements for the group. If you are working in a drafting view, you can only create a detail group; the Model option is inactive in this case.

FIGURE 16.25
Click the Create Group button on the Annotate tab and then select the elements.

After defining a group name, you'll be taken into Edit Group mode. Your view will have a yellow transparency overlaid on top of it, and elements within the view will appear gray. To add elements to the group, click the Add button in the Edit Group panel (Figure 16.26). Here you can also remove unwanted elements from your group. When you finish, simply click the Finish green check mark.

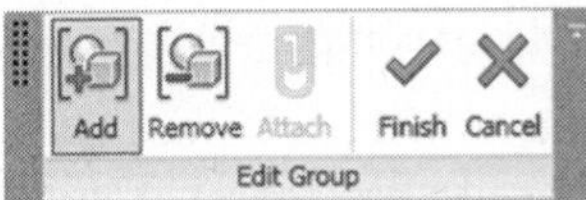

FIGURE 16.26
The Edit Group panel

You can place any group you've already made using the Place Detail Group button from the Detail panel of the Annotate tab (Figure 16.27) and selecting the group from the Type Selector. You can also drag and drop any group from the Project Browser into the active view.

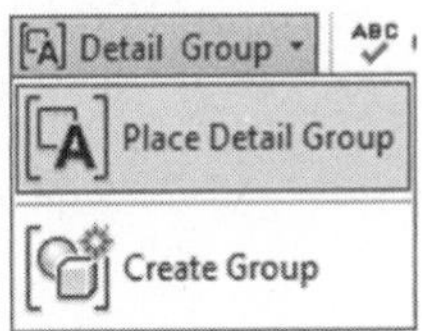

FIGURE 16.27
Placing a detail group

> **DETAIL COMPONENTS AND PROJECT TEMPLATES**
>
> If you find you are inserting the same detail components over and over again, load them into your project templates and make them readily available when you begin any new project.

Adding Detail Components to Families

In this chapter, you have read about the number of ways you can embellish a 3D model with 2D detailing. We have discussed how to add detail elements as needed in the project environment, but you can also include 2D elements inside families. The possibilities for this method are almost limitless. You can add any kind of symbolic line to 3D families, but in this section we will focus on nesting a detail component in a profile family, which will then become the basis for the curtain wall mullions in the sample project.

A more detailed review of curtain wall modeling is provided in Chapter 12, "Creating Walls and Curtain Walls." For now, we will simply edit the mullions already provided in the sample building project to add some 2D detailing. Let's get started by following these steps:

1. Continue working with the `c16-Sample-Building.rvt` or `c16-Sample-Metric.rvt` file you downloaded from this book's web page. In the Project Browser, locate and activate the section view named Section At Curtain Wall. It is located under the Sections (Wall Section) branch of the Project Browser.
2. In the Project Browser, expand the Families branch, locate and expand the Profiles branch, and then right-click Pr-Mullion-Horizontal or M_Pr-Mullion-Horizontal. Choose Edit from the context menu, and the mullion profile family will open.

   The basic reference planes and profile lines have already been created.

   You should already have downloaded the RFA files included with this chapter's exercise files. Among them are a series of detail components that represent the internal extrusion details of the mullions in the sample project's curtain wall system.
3. From the Create tab in the ribbon, click the Detail Component command. Browse to the location where you downloaded this chapter's exercise files and load the file named `Kawneer-1600-Sys1-Horizontal.rfa` or `M_Kawneer-1600-Sys1-Horizontal.rfa`.

4. Place the detail component to fit exactly within the profile boundary.

   You may need to rotate the component before placing it by pressing the spacebar. The result should look like the image in Figure 16.28.

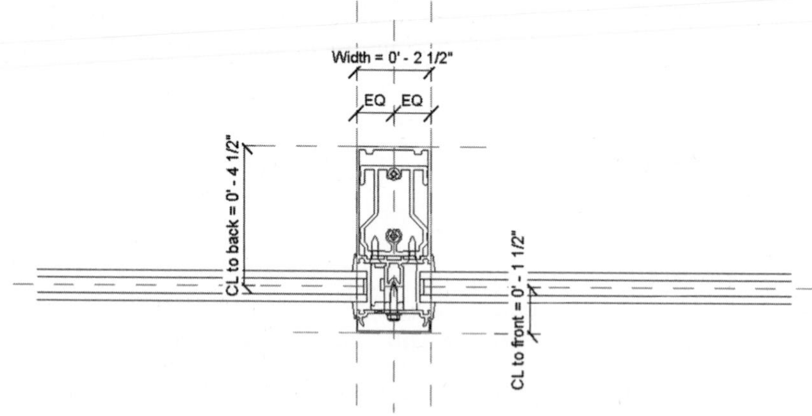

FIGURE 16.28 Detail component added to the profile family

5. Click the Modify button and then select the detail component you just placed in the view. From the contextual tab in the ribbon, click Visibility Settings. In the Family Element Visibility Settings dialog box, uncheck the Coarse and Medium settings. The only setting that should be checked is Fine. Click OK to close the dialog box.
6. Click the Load Into Project button from the ribbon and load the revised profile family into the sample building project file. When prompted, select the option to override the existing version.
7. From the View tab in the ribbon, locate the Create panel and click Callout ➢ Rectangle. In the middle portion of the wall section, sketch a rectangle around the mullion near the top of the floor associated with Level 2, as shown in Figure 16.29.

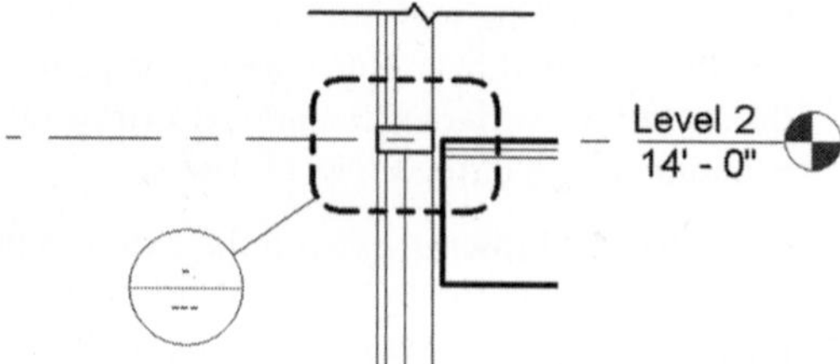

FIGURE 16.29 Create a callout of the wall section.

8. Double-click the callout head to activate the callout view. In the Properties palette or the view control bar, change the View Scale to **3″=1′-0″ (1:5)** and set Detail Level to Fine.

   After you have made these changes, you will see the nested detail component appear in the curtain wall mullion, as shown in Figure 16.30.

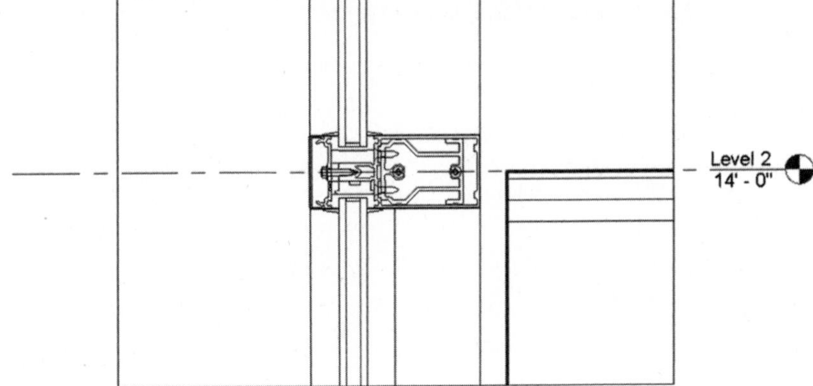

FIGURE 16.30
The nested detail component will appear when Detail Level is set to Fine.

9. Repeat the steps in this exercise for the head and sill mullion families. Edit the profile families listed here (starts with Pr-Mullion) with the associated detail components (RFA files) or their metric equivalents:

   Pr-Mullion-Head > `Kawneer-1600-Sys1-Head.rfa`

   Pr-Mullion-Sill > `Kawneer-1600-Sys1-Sill.rfa`

The detail components we used for this sample exercise were excerpted from real manufacturer's content that is available for free from the Kawneer website (`www.kawneer.com`). Complete curtain wall system components for Revit are also available from the website.

You might have noticed that the curtain wall modeled in this chapter's sample building is somewhat simplified. For example, the portion of the glass panels inside the mullions is not modeled; however, this condition appears in the detail component once you get down to a fine level of detail. This exercise illustrates a hybrid approach to the balance between modeling and detailing. If you download one of the Revit models from the Kawneer website (one sample, ASCMDDH3a .dwg, is provided with this chapter's downloaded content), you will see that the glass panels are more accurately modeled to include the mullion bite (Figure 16.31). In that scenario, you would not need to include masking regions to simulate the glass panel in the mullion detail component.

FIGURE 16.31
More detailed modeling will require less detailing.

LEARNING EFFICIENT DETAILING

As you get more practice creating details in Revit, you'll find certain workflows support more flexibility and speed. Here are some tips to keep in mind when creating your details:

- If your modeling is reasonably detailed to begin with, the detailing will go much faster because you will need to add fewer components. However, you must strike a balance and not make an overly detailed model because that would negatively impact performance. When wondering what to model or what to make into a detail component, ask yourself the following questions:
    - Will I see or use this in other views in the project?
    - Will it affect other aspects of the project (like material takeoffs)?
    - How large is it? (Our office tends to use 2D detailing for details 1 1/2″ (40 mm) and smaller.)
- There is no limit to how much information you can place in a detail component. If you will be seeing similar conditions throughout the model, put in as much as you can.
- You can use detail components at every scale within the model, so it is a great way to draw the information only once.

If the lines describing small components seem to merge when printed, there's little point in showing that geometry at that scale. You might consider making the model simpler.

Reusing Details from Other Files

As you develop details of common building features, you will likely find the need to reuse this content in future projects. You might even have an existing library of details that were created in a CAD application. In either situation, there are tools and commands available in Revit software that allow you to maximize the usage of the material you produce over time.

Using CAD Details

It is quite common to have details that were originally created in a CAD program. Sometimes these are details taken from a manufacturer's website, and sometimes they can be details drawn in other projects or from an office library, and you simply want to reuse them in your project rather than re-create them. Regardless of where they originated, you have the ability to work with 2D detail elements and import or link them into the model for use in your project.

In Chapter 7, "Interoperability: Working Multiplatform," we provide detailed guidance on using linked DWG files for the basis of project details.

Real World Scenario

TIPS ON IMPORTING CAD DETAILS

At times in the project, your workflow will necessitate using 2D information from a past project, a manufacturer's library, or another resource in your current Revit project. To optimize the performance of your imported CAD files within your model, we recommend that you take some steps to prepare the CAD file before import. Here are some general tips to help your import process:

- If the file you'd like to import contains hatches or annotations, delete them before importing and use filled regions and the Revit Text or Keynote tool for annotations. This will help keep your graphics consistent (in the case of hatch) and allow you to edit the verbiage and location of any notes.
- Import only one detail at a time so you can take better advantage of the software's ability to manage sheet referencing. If you have a series of details organized in a single CAD file that you want to use in documenting your project, isolate each detail, save it as a separate file, and then import it.
- Make sure you import the CAD details using the proper line weights, colors, and styles. Check your CAD file before importing into your Revit project to make sure it is consistent with your office's standards.
- If the imported geometry is something you really want or need to edit, it's better for your model and overall file size to import the CAD file into a detail component (if it's 2D) and explode it and edit it in the Family Editor. This way, when you import it into your project file, it is still a single object rather than thousands.
- Revit software doesn't allow line segments shorter than 1/32″ (0.8 mm). Although this is seemingly a very small line, many manufacturer details have small segment lines in them. When CAD details are exploded, those short lines will be deleted and can leave your linework looking incomplete.

For additional tips on leveraging CAD data, refer to Appendix B, "Tips, Tricks, and Troubleshooting."

Using Details from Other Revit Projects

As we begin to discuss the reuse of detailing content, we must return to the three methodologies introduced at the beginning of this chapter—stand-alone detailing, hybrid detailing, and model detailing. As you approach a project with more detailed modeling, you will reduce the amount of drafting needed in the project environment; however, you will be less able to reuse content as standard details or detail templates. This is because the best way to reuse 2D content is with drafting views.

There's an App for That

If you have many details in DWG format that you would like to quickly import to a project file, a few add-ins are available to automate the process. One example is the Detail Link tool that is part of the Revit Express Tools suite that Cad Technology Center developed. This tool allows you to select multiple DWG files and import each one to its own drafting view in Revit. You can learn more about the Detail Link tool from the website `www.cadtechnologycenter.com` and the Autodesk Apps Exchange (`http://apps.exchange.autodesk.com`).

Saving a Single Detail

If you are working in a detail view of the model or a drafting view, you can save all of the 2D elements to an external file for reuse in other Revit projects. In the case of a single 2D detail, it can be quick work to get the file from one project to the next:

1. Open the file with the detail you'd like to collect, and activate the view in which this detail appears. Select all the 2D geometry and annotation within the drafting view, and create a group using the Create Group button on the contextual tab of the ribbon.

   Note that if you are in a callout or detail view in which model elements are displayed, two groups will be created—a model group and a detail group.

2. Give the group a name, making sure the name is unique enough not to overlap with any view names in your current project or the project you're going to import into.
3. With the detail grouped and named, expand the Groups node in the Project Browser. Now, expand the Detail Group node and find the group you just created. Right-click the group and choose Save Group from the context menu.
4. As part of the Save As process, you'll get the Save Group dialog box (Figure 16.32). This will allow you to create a separate RVT file for your group—basically a stand-alone project file. Save the group in a location where you'll be able to find it again and close your project file. There's no need to name the group because the new file will reflect the group name.

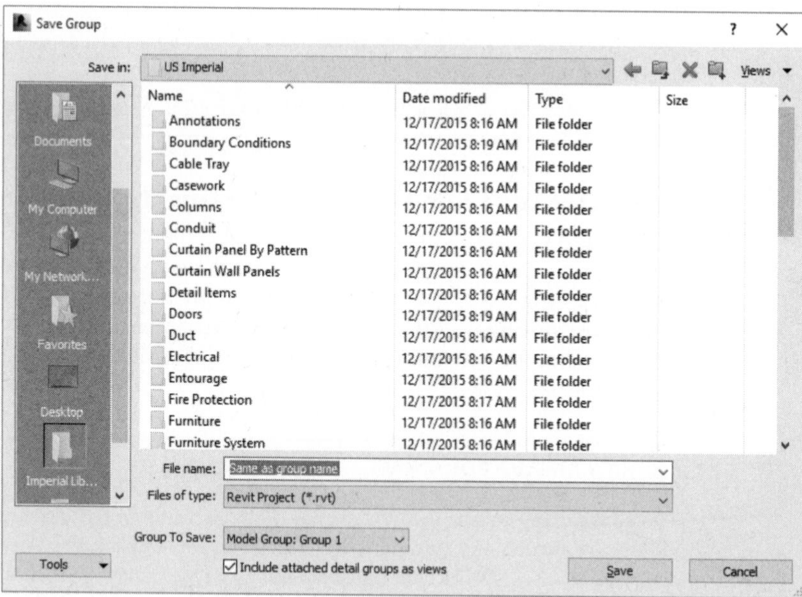

FIGURE 16.32 The Save Group dialog box

   We have created a sample file using this method for use in the remainder of this exercise. Make sure you download the file `c16_JambDetail.rvt` from the book's companion web page.

5. Continue with the sample building project file saved from the previous exercises in this chapter.
6. From the View tab, click Drafting View to create a new view, and name it **JAMB DTL**.

The scale does not matter because it will inherit the scale of the imported detail.

7. From the Insert tab of the ribbon, choose Insert From File and then Insert 2D Elements From File.
8. In the Open dialog box, navigate to and select the `c16_JambDetail.rvt` file. You will then see the Insert 2D Elements dialog box, which is shown in Figure 16.33. Highlight Drafting View: JAMB DTL from the list box, and select the Transfer View Scale check box. Click OK to close the dialog box and begin the import.
9. Click anywhere in the drafting view to place the imported elements, and then click the Finish button in the ribbon to complete the command.

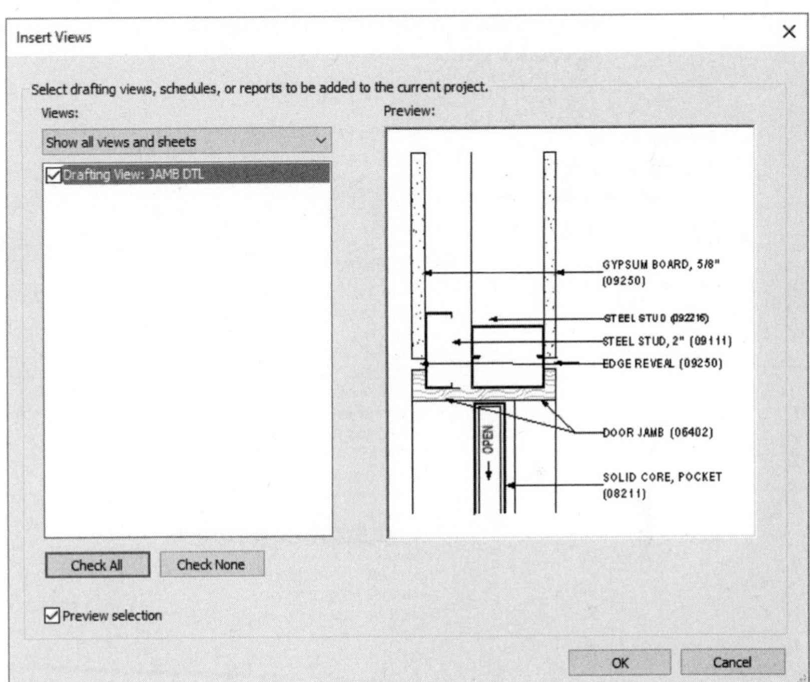

FIGURE 16.33 Choose the detail group from the Insert 2D Elements dialog box.

SAVING MULTIPLE DETAILS

As you create more details in Revit projects, you will inevitably want to save some of them to an office library or some sort of localized resource so you can quickly locate the good ones again. Revit allows you to selectively save multiple views from a single project into a separate, standalone file. This workflow will work for both 2D and 3D content.

A quick way to get any view with 2D elements isolated to an external file is to right-click the view in the Project Browser and choose Save To New File from the context menu. Note that this option is not available for any view that does not contain 2D detail elements. It might take the software a few moments to compile the view content, but you will be presented with a dialog box asking you to locate the new file. Once the view is exported, it functions like any other RVT file. You can open these new views directly and edit or manipulate any of the content or elements within the file. You'll also see a streamlined version of the Project Browser having only the nodes that relate to the content you've exported.

Another way to export multiple views is to click the Application menu and choose Save As ➤ Library ➤ View. This command allows you to save multiple views into a single RVT file that acts as a library for those views. Here are the steps:

1. Start by opening the file with the views you want to save. Click the Application menu and select Save As ➤ Library ➤ View.
2. This will give you the Save Views dialog box (Figure 16.34). It will show a list of view names on the left and a preview window on the right. Click the check box for each of the views you want to save into a separate file. Once you have all your view names established, click OK.

FIGURE 16.34 Exporting multiple views to a separate file

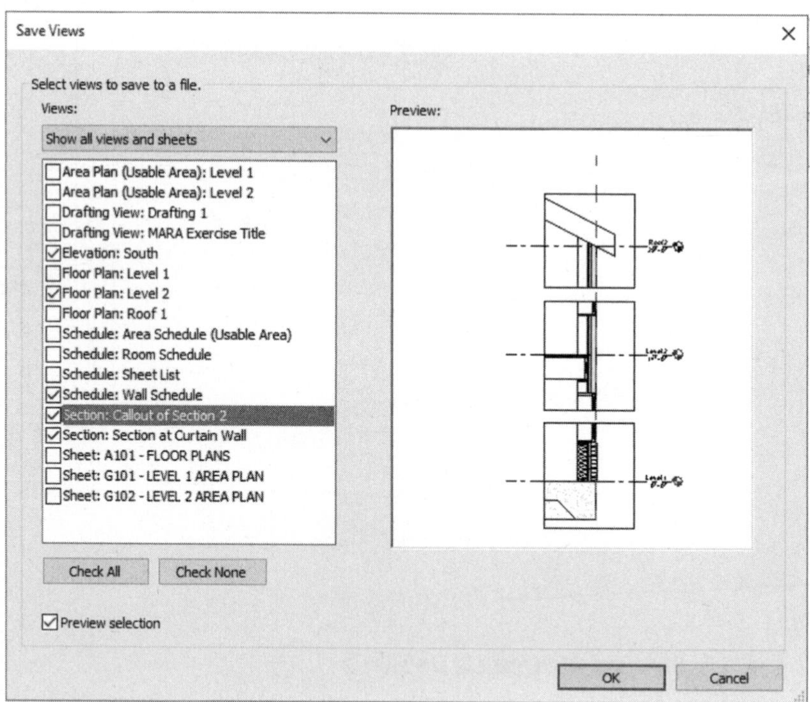

The software might take a few moments to export the views, depending on how many you've chosen and how large the overall file size is. Once the process is complete, you'll have a separate file to import those views back into Revit projects. This import process is just as simple as exporting. Here's how to import the views:

1. Open the project where you want to put the imported views. From the Insert tab on the ribbon, choose Insert From File and then Insert Views From File.

2. The new dialog box will look similar to the Save Views dialog box. You will have a list of the views you can import from the column on the left and a preview of those views on the right. Check the box for the views you want to import and click OK (Figure 16.35).

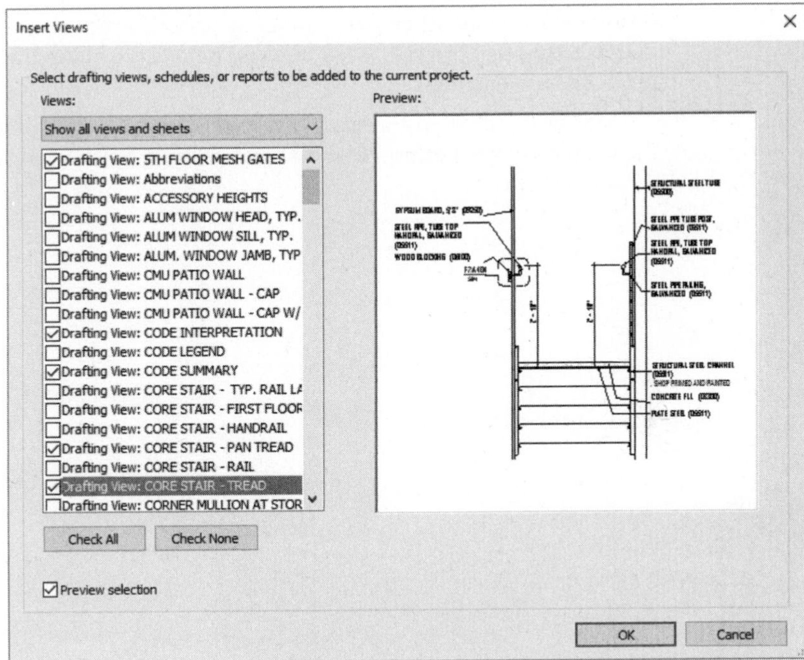

FIGURE 16.35
Importing multiple views into a project

You can also import entire sheets of details using this method. If sheets exist in the file you have selected with the Insert Views From File command, they are listed as options to insert. When sheets are inserted, the details placed on each sheet are automatically imported into the project as well.

The Bottom Line

Create details. Details in Revit are a combination of 2D elements layered on top of 3D model elements or sometimes just stacked on top of each other. Creating good, easy-to-read details typically requires some embellishment of the 3D model.

Master It What are the three primary categories of detail elements and how are they used?

Add detail components to families. You can make creating details in Revit easier by adding some of the detail elements directly to the family. In this way, when you cut sections, make callouts, or enlarge plan conditions, your "smart" details can begin to construct themselves.

Master It Because you don't always want elements to appear in every scale of a view, how can you both add detail elements to your families and still limit the amount of information that is shown in any given view?

Learn efficient detailing. As you master detailing in Revit, you'll begin to learn tips and tricks to make your process of creating details more efficient.

Master It To help you assess how much effort you should be putting into your details, what are three questions you should be asking yourself before starting any detail?

Reuse details from other files. In many project workflows, you will need to incorporate details from other projects. Reusing these details can aid in the speed and efficiency of project documentation.

Master It There are several ways to reuse details from other projects. Name one and list the steps to perform the tasks necessary to quickly move a detail from one project to another.

Chapter 17

Documenting Your Design

While the industry continues to move toward a 3D building information model as a construction deliverable, today we still need to produce 2D documents for a construction document set or design reviews. Using the integrated documentation tools in Autodesk® Revit® Architecture software, you can create these sets with more accuracy and reliability than in the past. In this chapter, you will take the elements you have previously modeled and detailed and begin to create the documentation for your design.

In this chapter, you'll learn to:

- Document plans
- Create schedules and legends
- Lay out sheets

Documenting Plans

In this chapter, we'll introduce a scenario that will mimic what might happen on a real project in a preliminary design phase. We are going to assume that you'll be using the `c17-Sample-Building-Start.rvt` or `c17-Sample-Metric-Start.rvt` model from the book's web page: `www.sybex.com/go/masteringrevit2017`.

Here's the story: You have recently completed some preliminary design work in advance of your upcoming client meeting. You'll need to lay out the plans, elevations, and perspectives on some presentation sheets for the meeting, but you'll also have to include some building metrics, such as area plans and schedules of overall spaces.

In the following sections, you'll set up those views and sheets, starting with the area plans. For the purposes of program verification, you have decided you need to establish the spatial areas for the building so the client can get some preliminary pricing from the contractor. Before you create your area plans, we'll discuss some of the various ways you can calculate areas in Revit.

Calculating Space Using Room Objects

The simplest way to calculate the space in a building design is to use room objects. Room tags can be used to report room name, department, area, and any of the other properties of a room. These properties can also be scheduled to report the total area of all rooms within a design. With rooms, however, the areas that they report are limited to how those spaces are defined. With the `c17-Sample-Building-Start.rvt` or `c17-Sample-Metric-Start.rvt` model open, choose the Architecture tab, and then access the expanded panel under the Room & Area panel. Click Area And Volume Computations, which opens the Area And Volume

Computations dialog box. You will see the options for room area computation in the project. The choices are as follows:

- At Wall Finish
- At Wall Center
- At Wall Core Layer
- At Wall Core Center

Because each of these settings affects the entire project, a level of consistency is ensured for room calculations; however, the global nature of the settings makes it difficult to use the room objects for gross area calculations. Room calculations can give you an accurate net area—or *carpet area*—that refers to the area between the finished wall surfaces considered as occupied space. This value can also be reported in the room tag or in a schedule by selecting the first choice under the Room Area Computation settings, At Wall Finish, in the Area And Volume Computations dialog box (Figure 17.1). Select this option and click OK.

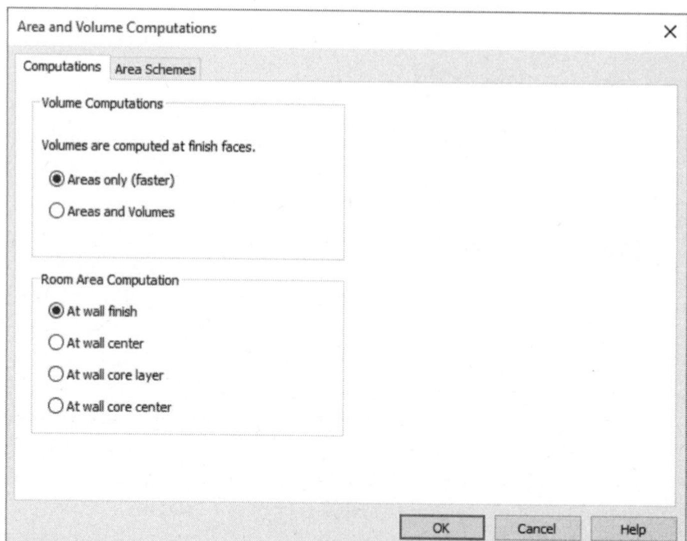

FIGURE 17.1
The Area And Volume Computations dialog box

Let's see how this looks in the floor plans. Activate the Level 2 floor plan. In this view, we have already established the rooms and added room tags; however, the tags do not show the room areas. To modify this setting, follow these steps:

1. Select any of the room tags, and from the Properties palette, choose Edit Type.
2. In the Type Properties dialog box, choose the Show Area check box. Click OK to exit the dialog box.

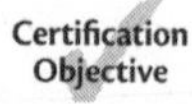

Now you should see the areas reflected in the room tags, as shown in Figure 17.2. This is because the Show Area setting was created as a Yes/No type parameter assigned to the visibility property of the area label within the room tag family. If you want to explore this functionality further, you can open the tag family. Select the room tag and click Edit Family in the contextual tab of the ribbon.

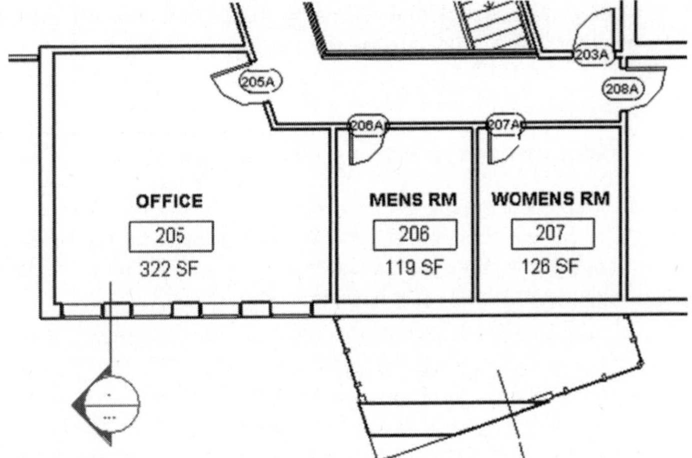

FIGURE 17.2
Room area reflected in the room tag

If you select any one of the room tags, you can also see the area that it is calculating displayed with a red outline (Figure 17.3). When adding rooms, you are not limited to only rooms that are bound on all sides with walls. If you note the lounge and lobby spaces on Level 1, shown in Figure 17.3, there isn't a wall dividing the two rooms, yet they are shown as being independent of each other. This separation is achieved by using room separation lines, which can be placed with the Room Separator tool located on the Room & Area panel of the Architecture tab. Note that these lines will print and export with other model and annotation elements, but you can adjust their visibility in the Visibility/Graphic Overrides dialog box. If you decide to change the visibility of the room separator lines and turn them off within a view, they will continue to divide the room objects. You will find these elements in the Visibility/Graphic dialog box on the Model Elements tab, under Lines, <Room Separation>.

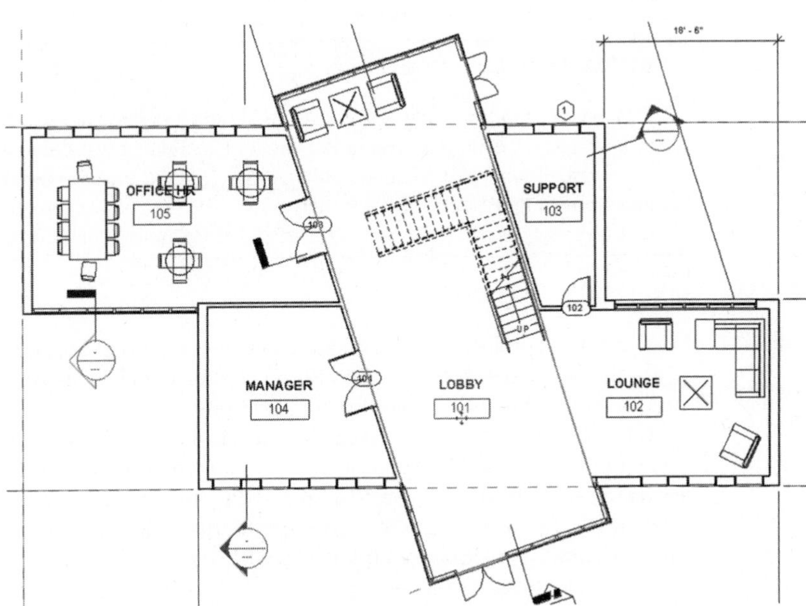

FIGURE 17.3
The room object shows what area is being calculated.

Because area calculations using rooms don't usually include wall thicknesses, let's look at another way to calculate areas—using area plans.

Working with Rooms and Areas

Rooms and areas are the two object types you will use to annotate and report the occupied space within your building designs. You can use room tags and area tags to visualize data such as a room name or number, but the tags merely report the data that exists in the object itself. So, how do you work with objects that have no solid geometry?

Both rooms and areas have a reference that can be seen if you hover the mouse pointer within a space. Sometimes these references can be difficult to find, but there is something you can do to improve your efficiency when working with these objects. In the Visibility/Graphic Overrides dialog box, locate Areas or Rooms in the Model Categories tab. Expand the category for either object and you will see Interior Fill and Reference. These subcategories are turned off by default, but you can turn them on if you will be frequently editing these objects.

Creating Area Plans

Area plans are views of the model used to calculate defined, two-dimensional spaces within the model according to prescribed calculation standards but with the added ability to customize the area boundaries. The software allows you to create as many area calculation schemes as you need to depict the design. Area boundaries can exist only in area plans and can be either manually placed or automatically associated with walls. If they are automatically placed, the areas within them will be calculated based on the BOMA standard.

BOMA Area Calculations

BOMA stands for the Building Owners and Managers Association. Widely used in the United States by architects, developers, and facility managers alike, it was created to help standardize building development and spatial needs. BOMA uses its own set of standards for calculating areas that have some nuances relating to exactly where the area boundaries between spaces fall, depending on the Area Type property. You can find more information on BOMA standards at `www.boma.org`.

The default project template includes some predefined areas. To add to the list of available area schemes, access the expanded Room & Area panel in the Architecture tab of the ribbon, and then click Area And Volume Computations.

When the Area And Volume Computations dialog box opens, choose the Area Schemes tab, shown in Figure 17.4. Here you can add as many new area schemes as your design requires. For each area scheme, you can create associated plans, schedules, and area boundary layouts; however, be careful not to add too many superfluous area schemes on larger projects because doing so can degrade performance and increase file size.

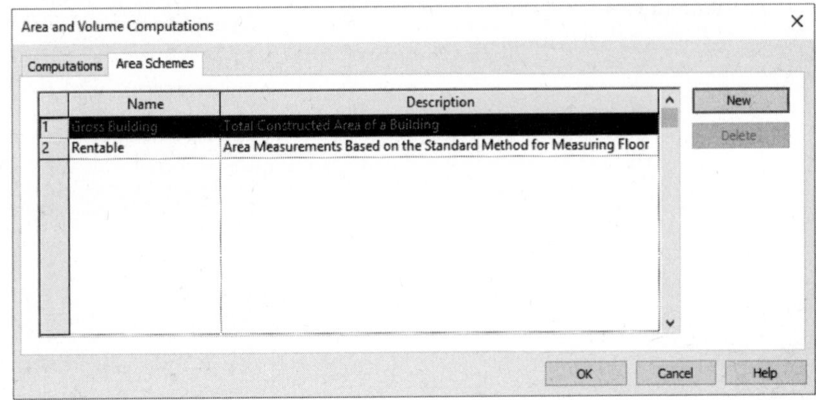

FIGURE 17.4 The Area Schemes tab in the Area And Volume Computations dialog box

Create a new area scheme by clicking the New button. By default this will be a rentable type plan based on BOMA calculation rules. You will see a new area scheme in the list. Click in the Name field of the new row and rename the scheme **Usable Area** (Figure 17.5). Click OK to close the Area And Volume Computations dialog box.

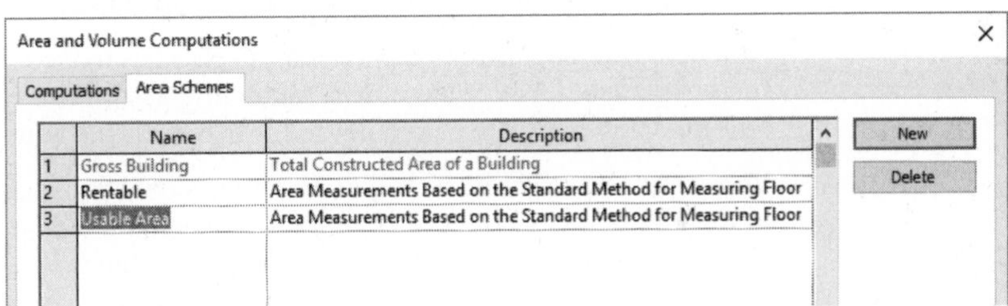

FIGURE 17.5 Create a new area scheme.

To continue the exercise, you will need to create area plans for your presentation. You can create an area plan from either of two locations: One is located on the Room & Area panel of the Architecture tab; the other is located on the Create panel of the View tab. Follow these steps:

1. From the Architecture tab in the ribbon, find the Room & Area panel, click Area, and then click Area Plan. You are prompted with the New Area Plan dialog box, shown in Figure 17.6.
2. From the Type drop-down menu, choose Usable Area. While pressing the Ctrl key, select both Level 1 and Level 2.
3. Click OK. You are prompted with the option to automatically generate area boundaries for exterior walls. Because you selected more than one level, you will receive a prompt for each level for which a plan is being generated. Go ahead and click OK to generate the plans automatically.

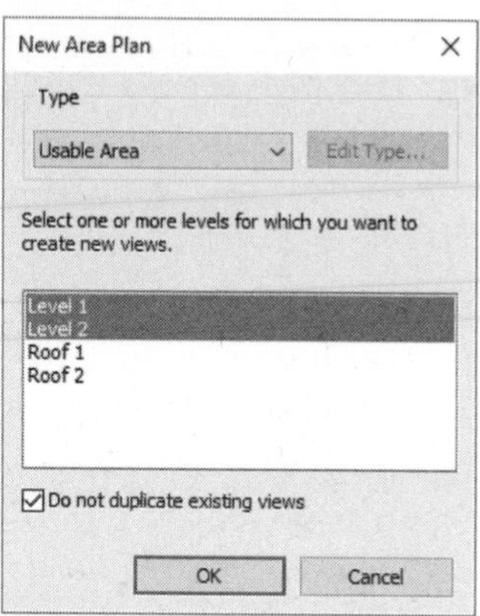

FIGURE 17.6
Creating new area plans

This creates new area plans under a new node in the Project Browser: Area Plans (Usable Area). The name in the parentheses will always be associated to the area calculation type you used.

4. In the Project Browser, select both Level 1 and Level 2 under Area Plans (Usable Area). Right-click and select Apply View Template from the context menu.
5. In the Apply View Template dialog box, choose Area Plan from the list of view templates, click OK to apply the template, and close the dialog box.

   Note: This method applies the template properties to the views, but it does not associate the template with the views. To permanently assign the view template to the views, edit the View Template parameter in the Properties palette.

   View references, furniture, and floor patterns are turned off based on the settings defined in the view template (Figure 17.7). For more detailed information on using view templates, refer to Chapter 4, "Configuring Templates and Standards."

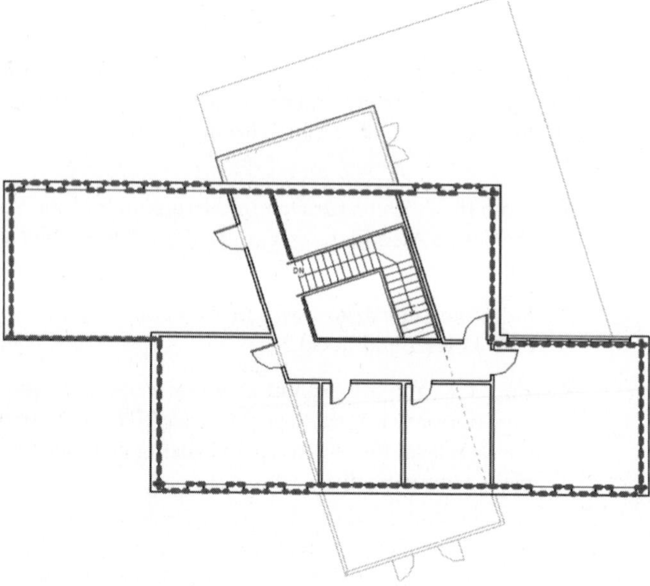

FIGURE 17.7
Area boundaries have been automatically assigned to the exterior walls.

When looking at the area plan on your screen, you'll notice a thick, purple line running around the inside face of the exterior wall. This is the Area Boundary line. *Note that we have changed the default properties of the Area Boundary line type in the figures within this project for clarity.* The software has attempted to calculate your plan area based on some predefined rules. For the most part, it does a reasonable job of figuring out where the boundaries are, but from time to time those lines need some adjusting. You will learn over time whether this automation works based on the complexity of the perimeter walls in your designs. If they are complex and not clearly closed, the results of the automated boundary placement may be undesirable.

In the Project Browser, find the node Area Plans (Gross Building) and open either of the plans. Notice the difference in the application of the area boundaries to the exterior walls. The area boundaries are applied to the outside faces of the exterior walls. In the Usable Area plans (Figure 17.7), the boundaries are assigned to the inside faces of the exterior walls—also adapting to window elements.

To complete this part of the exercise, you will place additional area boundaries to subdivide the interior space into different spaces.

6. Activate the Level 1 area plan for Usable Area. From the Architecture tab, select the Room & Area panel; click Area Boundary.

   The default drawing method is set to Pick, and in the Options bar, the Apply Area Rules setting is checked. Remember that this setting determines whether the location of the boundary will be affected by the Area Type property of the areas placed on either side of the boundary.

7. Pick the interior walls indicated in Figure 17.8.

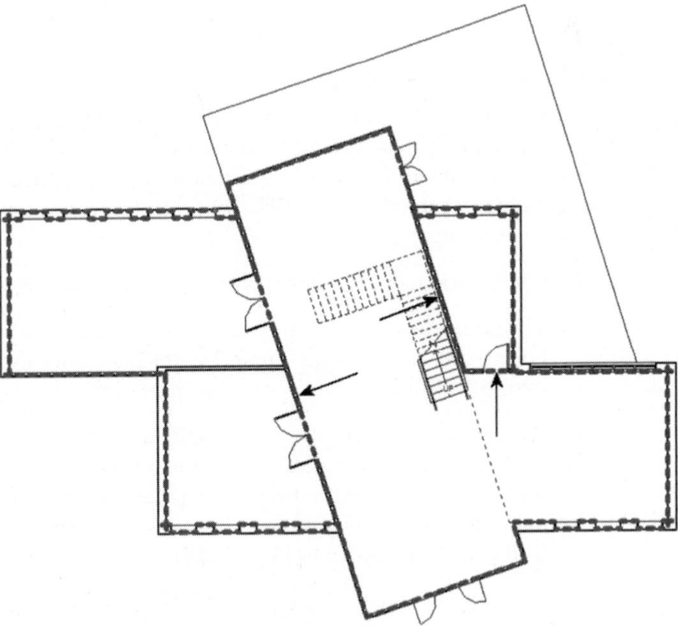

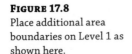

FIGURE 17.8
Place additional area boundaries on Level 1 as shown here.

8. Activate the Level 2 area plan for Usable Area, and using the same method as in Level 1, add area boundaries to the interior walls indicated in Figure 17.9. You will need to use the Trim tool to adjust the line for the wall at the end of the corridor.

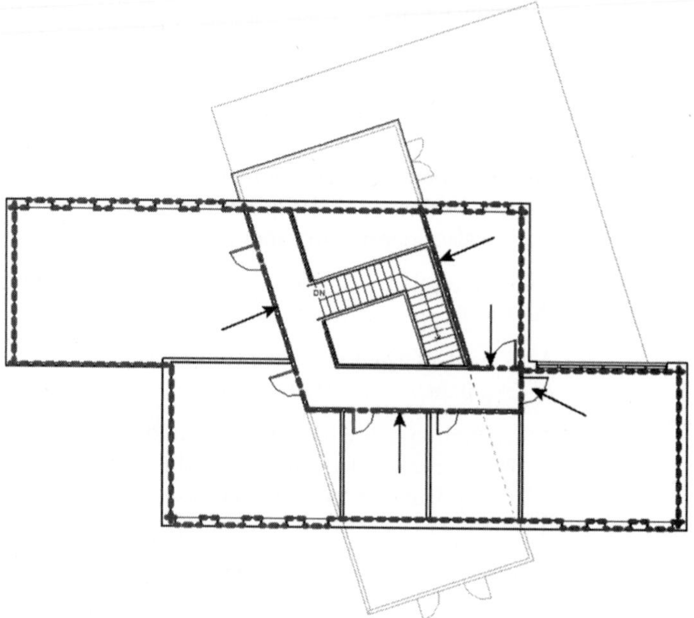

FIGURE 17.9
Place additional area boundaries on Level 2 as shown here.

Adding Area Objects

Like room objects, areas need a closed boundary in order to be placed, and they have properties to which you can add attributes that are "taggable." You can have any number of areas visible in an area plan, but unlike rooms, areas can be seen and tagged only in area plans. In this section's exercise, you will place area objects within the boundaries you created in the previous exercise:

1. On the Room & Area panel on the Architecture tab, choose the Area tool.

   The Area tool places an area in a manner similar to placing a room, and it gives you a bound area with a large X in it (Figure 17.10). The area of the space bound by the purple boundary lines will be reported as part of the area tag.

2. Place areas in each of the zones defined by the boundary lines in the Level 1 floor plan for Usable Area. To modify the names of the areas, you can select the area object and then modify the name in the Properties palette, or you can select the area tag, click the name, and then type the new value. Change the names of the areas to **OFFICES**, **LOBBY**, and **SERVICES**, as shown in Figure 17.11.

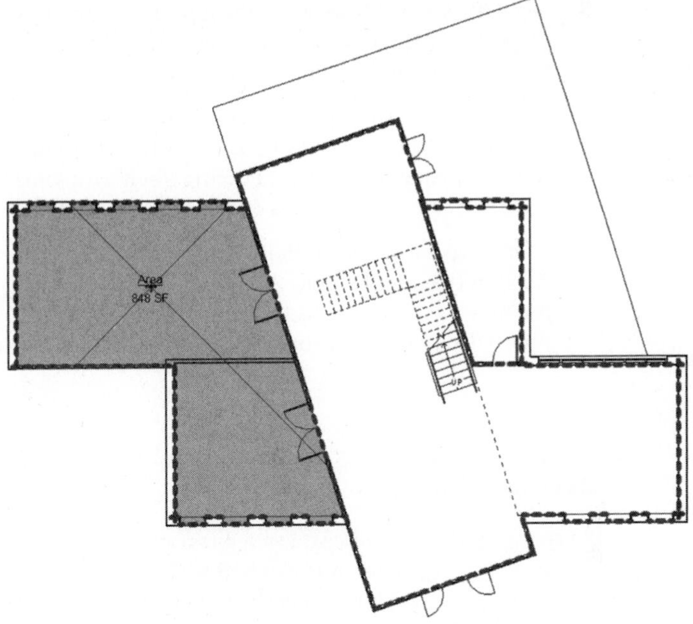

FIGURE 17.10
The placed area element with area tag

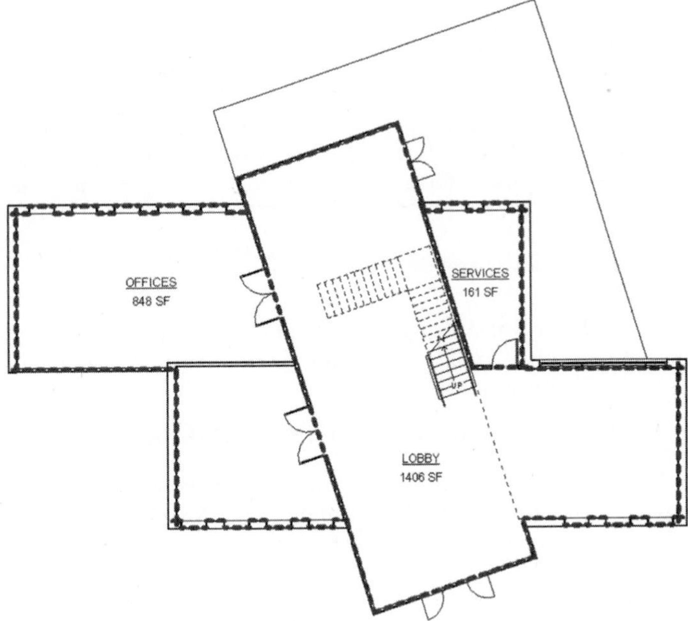

FIGURE 17.11
Rename the areas placed on Level 1.

3. Select the OFFICES area (not the tag), and in the Properties palette, change the Area Type property to **Office Area**. Select the SERVICES area and change its Area Type property to **Building Common Area**.

   Notice that some of the area boundaries change to different wall faces as the Area Type property is modified. This behavior is based on the BOMA area measurement standards and is dependent on either allowing Revit to automatically assign area boundaries or using the Apply Area Rules option when you are placing the boundaries yourself.

   Rooms are not visible in the area plans, based on the settings in the view templates provided in the sample project. If you do not turn off the visibility of rooms in area plans, you may mistakenly select a room object instead of an area. Always be sure to check the Type Selector to verify that you have selected an area or a room.

Deleting Areas

As you complete this exercise, you may accidentally place an area outside the boundaries of the design, or you may place two areas within the same space. First, realize that you must delete the area, not just the area tag, to remove the area element; however, the area actually remains in your project. You are prompted with a warning as shown here:

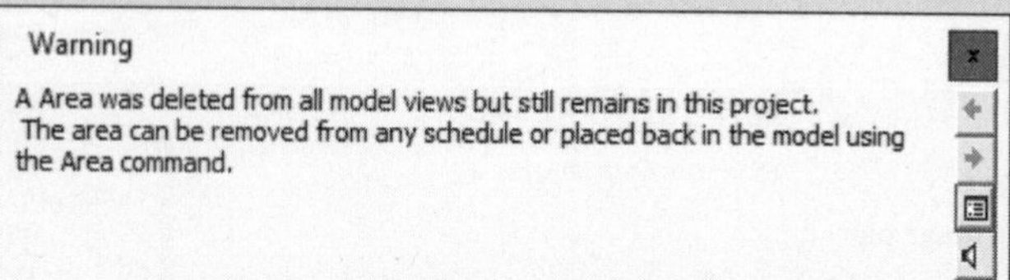

To completely remove an area from your project, you must remove it from an area schedule. The Area and Level properties of deleted areas are shown in a schedule as Not Placed. You can pick these rows in a schedule and choose Delete from the Rows panel of the ribbon.

4. The next step in our area plan is to follow steps similar to those for Level 1. Activate the Level 2 area plan for Usable Area and place areas in the zones defined by the area boundaries.
5. Rename the areas **OFFICES**, **CIRCULATION**, and **SERVICES**, as shown in Figure 17.12.
6. Select the OFFICES area and change the Area Type property to **Office Area**. Select the CIRCULATION area and change Area Type to Major Vertical Penetration. Select the SERVICES area and change the Area Type to Building Common Area.

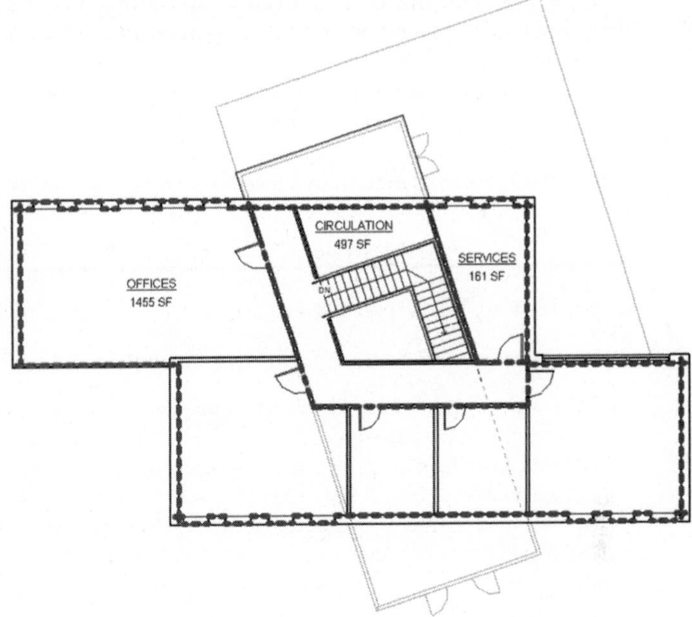

FIGURE 17.12
Rename the areas placed on Level 2.

7. Select the area tag for SERVICES, and from the Options bar, activate the Leader setting. This will allow you to move the tag away from the area object without generating a warning. With the SERVICES area tag still selected, move it outside the area boundary lines and adjust the leader line as necessary.

Modifying Area Plans

Like rooms, areas can be modified at any time during the design process. They will be adjusted automatically if the boundary lines are locked to a wall or other element that has been moved as part of the design, or they can be modified manually.

If you delete an area line, you'll get the warning message shown in Figure 17.13. This message tells you that you have removed one or more of the boundary lines for an area and the software can no longer calculate the area.

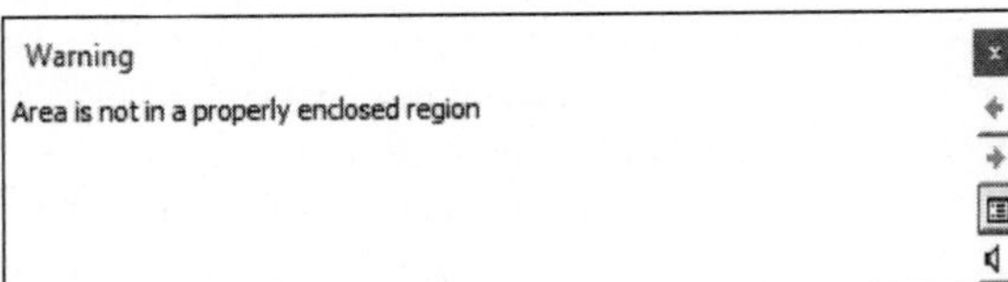

FIGURE 17.13
Modifying an area boundary generates a warning.

If you are in the midst of modifying a space, finish your modifications and replace any area lines that you've deleted or removed as part of the design change. Once the area is completely bound, it will recalculate the space.

In this section, you've created an area plan that will give you a graphic representation of the space you've defined with boundary lines. But what if you want to show this same information in a spreadsheet format? All you need to do is set up a view type in the model that allows you to look at the same information in a tabular format. For this, you can use a schedule.

Real World Scenario

WORKING WITH AREA PLANS ON LARGE PROJECTS

On a large project where our client was a government agency, our team was required to create many different area schemes to comply with the documentation deliverables. These area schemes included gross floor area, rentable area, and individual department areas. Because the project was so large in overall area and number of spaces, performance of our Revit project file was suffering because the software was simultaneously analyzing the parametric relationships between all the physical building elements while maintaining all the calculations in our area plans for each of the area schemes.

To alleviate some of the degraded performance, we decided to create a separate project file into which we linked our architectural model. In this file, we re-created the required area schemes, area objects, and area plans. Even the sheets dedicated to the area calculations were created in this project file.

Although this approach improved the performance of the main architectural model, there were some limitations. The main limitation was that we could not use the Pick Walls method to assign the area boundaries to the walls in the linked model. Thus, the Apply Area Rules option did not function, which required us to manage the area boundaries manually in relation to their associated walls.

If you decide to pursue this method of working with area plans on large projects, consider the work involved against the benefits gained in performance before you decide to implement it.

Creating Schedules and Legends

Schedules are lists of elements and element properties within the model. They itemize building objects such as walls, doors, and windows as well as calculate quantities, areas, and volumes. They can also list document elements such as sheets, keynotes, and views. Schedules are yet another live way to view a Revit model. Once created, they are constantly kept up to date with any changes that occur to the model itself.

Legends are views in which you can display building components or annotations used in your model without affecting quantity schedules of the actual project model. Legends can be created for displaying information such as door types, wall types, key plans, or general notes. Legends and schedules are unique in their behavior as a view because they are the only views that can be placed on multiple sheets.

Creating Schedules

In a project workflow, creating schedules of objects, areas, or quantities is usually one of the most laborious tasks for architects. When this process is performed manually, it can take a very long time and typically results in errors that require validation of the design data.

In Revit, all building elements have information about their properties defined within the model. You also have the option to include additional information with any element. For example, doors have properties such as size, material, fire rating, cost, and so on. All of this information can be scheduled and quantified. Because the schedule is a live tabular view of the element within the model, modifying values in a schedule changes the element in the model, and vice versa.

There are several types of schedules, all of which you can access from the Create panel of the View tab. You can also create schedules by right-clicking the Schedules/Quantities node in the Project Browser. You can create six primary types of schedules:

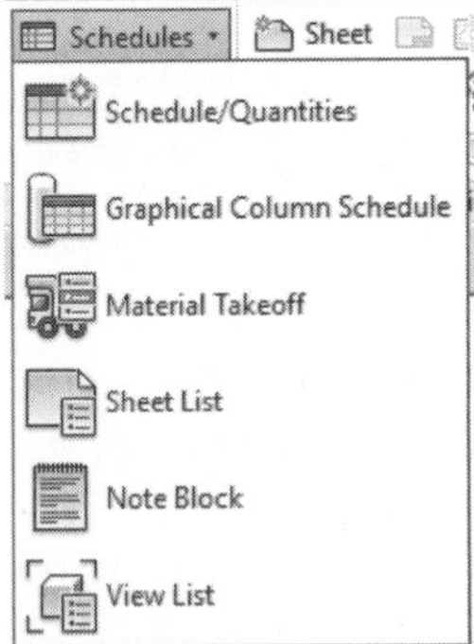

Schedule/Quantities As the most commonly used schedule type, this schedule allows you to list and quantify all element category types. You would use this type to create tabular views for doors, walls, windows, areas, rooms, and so on.

Graphical Column Schedule This type of schedule can graphically show the structural columns in the project and their attributes.

Material Takeoff This type of schedule can calculate the area or volume of materials across any family category. For example, you might want to know the volume of concrete within the model. Regardless of whether the concrete is in a wall, floor, or column, you can configure the schedule to report the total amount of that material in the project.

Sheet List This schedule allows you to create a list of all the sheets in the project. In addition to the number and name of the sheet, you can include the current revision number, date, and revision description.

Note Block This type of schedule lists the parameters of generic annotation families that are used in your project. These are different from element tags because the values reported in the Note Block schedule come from the annotation families—not the model objects. You can also use a note block to list the annotation symbols (centerlines, north arrows) used in a project.

View List This schedule generates a list of all the views in the Project Browser and their properties. A view list is useful for managing your project because the schedule is a bidirectional view, which allows you to edit many view properties such as name, scale, and phase.

Each of these schedule types gives you the ability to select related element properties that you can mix and match to track elements within the model. When you create a new schedule, you must first select a category of objects to itemize (Figure 17.14). You can also filter the schedule based on the various disciplines by selecting the Filter List drop-down menu at the upper left.

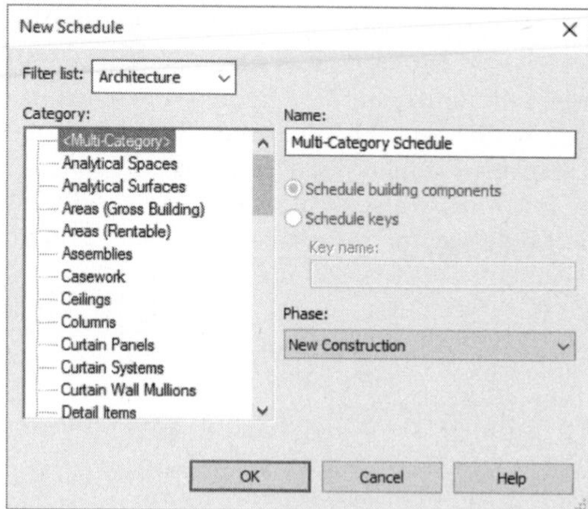

FIGURE 17.14
Creating a new schedule

Although the most common schedules are based on a single object category, you can also create schedules that span categories. The first option in the dialog box in Figure 17.14 is the <Multi-Category> schedule. You might want to schedule all the casework, furniture, and furniture systems in a project simultaneously, or all the windows and doors if they are being ordered from the same manufacturer. Although this type of schedule allows you to span multiple categories, many specific parameters cannot be included. First, it is difficult to isolate just two categories (such as windows and doors) in a multi-category schedule. Second, you cannot include critical parameters in the schedule such as length, width, and height. Another limit of this schedule type is that you cannot schedule host elements (walls, floors, ceilings, and so on), only their materials and family components.

SCHEDULE KEYS

There is a special kind of schedule that gives you the ability to populate a list of values before placing any actual objects in your model as well as manage these values from one location. Known as a schedule key, it can be selected when you first create a schedule. A common example of the use of a schedule key is to manage room finishes. In this use case, you create a schedule key named Room Finish Type. You add the parameters Floor Finish, Base Finish, Wall Finish, and Ceiling Finish to the schedule. In the schedule, use the New Row button to create room finish types. For example, you could create types for Executive Office, Standard Office, Service Corridor, and Rest Room.

The parameter Room Finish Type will then appear in the element properties of every room object. The parameters that are assigned to a schedule key can be edited only in the key schedule—not in the room properties. This might seem inconvenient; however, you can manage large numbers of objects with common parameters. For example, if the floor finish for all the rooms in your project that were assigned as an Executive Office type needed to change from carpet to ceramic tile, you would simply change the schedule key and all instances of that room type would update.

Creating a Room Schedule

Certification Objective

To become familiar with the general functionality of creating a schedule, you will create a room schedule. You're going to continue working in the model, `c17-Sample-Building-Start.rvt` file or `c17-Sample-Metric-Start.rvt` you opened earlier in this chapter. Later in this chapter, you will apply your skills to create an area schedule based on the previous exercises.

From the View tab in the ribbon, click Schedules ➤ Schedule/Quantities. In the New Schedule dialog box, select Rooms from the list of categories, and click OK to continue. You are then presented with the Schedule Properties dialog box. This is the main interface by which you set, and later modify, any of the organizational or appearance characteristics of your schedules. The dialog box consists of five tabs: Fields, Filter, Sorting/Grouping, Formatting, and Appearance. Let's step through each of these tabs and examine how they affect the form and function of the schedule:

Fields The Fields tab (Figure 17.15) lets you select the data that will appear in your schedule. The list of available fields on the left will vary based on the category you choose to schedule. If you've assigned any custom parameters to those categories, they will be available here as well. Also notice the option Include Elements In Linked at the lower-left corner. Enabling this option will allow you to schedule across multiple files, and it can be a great tool for larger projects. The order of the fields you add to the Scheduled Fields list at the right side (top to bottom) determines the order of columns in your schedule from left to right.

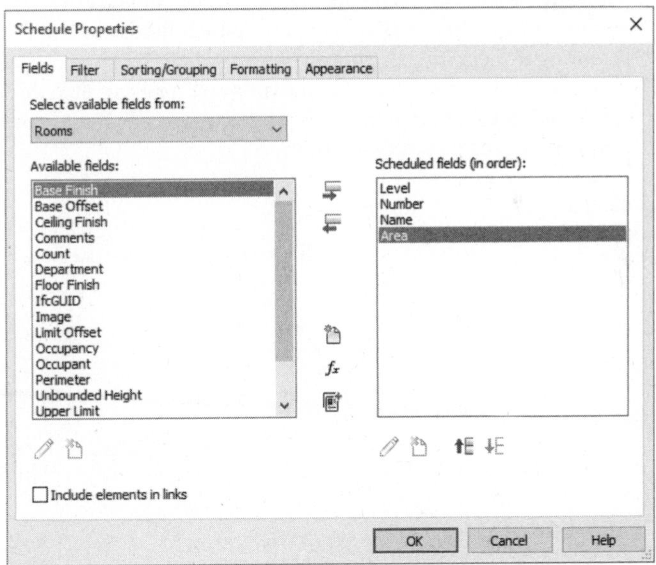

Figure 17.15 The Fields tab

From the list of available fields on the left, add Level, Number, Name, and Area to the list of scheduled fields on the right.

Filter On the Filter tab (Figure 17.16), you can filter out the data you don't want to show in your schedule. Filters work like common database functions. For example, you can filter out all the sheets in a set whose names don't begin with the letter A. Or you can filter a material list so that it shows only items containing Concrete. Filters operate only on certain schedule fields. For instance, you can't apply a filter to the Family And Type field.

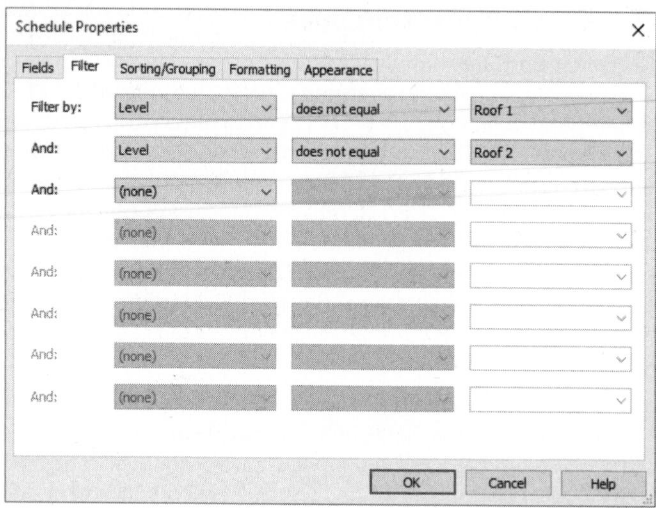

FIGURE 17.16 The Filter tab

Set the first group of filter drop-downs to Filter By: Level: Does Not Equal: Roof 1. Set the second group of filter drop-downs to Filter By: Level: Does Not Equal: Roof 2.

Sorting/Grouping The Sorting/Grouping tab (Figure 17.17) lets you control the order in which information is displayed and which fields control that order. For instance, if you are creating a sheet index, you can choose to sort by sheet number or sheet name, depending on how you'd like the information displayed. You can also decide whether you want to show every instance of an item or only a summary of object types by using the Itemize Every Instance check box at the bottom.

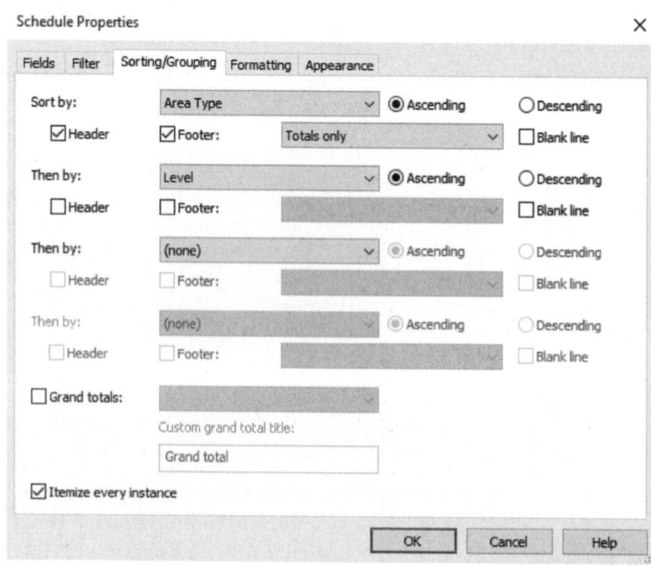

FIGURE 17.17 The Sorting/Grouping tab

In the first Sort By options, set the drop-down to Level, select the Header and Footer options, and set the Footer drop-down to Count And Totals.

In the Sorting/Grouping tab, you have the ability to summarize the reported information in group footers or as a grand total at the bottom of the schedule; however, you must designate one or more fields to calculate totals in the Formatting tab to display these results.

Formatting The Formatting tab (Figure 17.18) controls the display for each field and whether the field is visible on the schedule. It also controls other elements of the field, such as justification, display name, and orientation of the header. This tab also allows you to use the Calculate Totals check box for use with the footer or Grand Totals options in the Sorting/Grouping tab. Note that you may also need to use the Calculate Totals option for certain numerical fields if you intend to deselect the Itemize Every Instance option in the Sorting/Grouping tab. For example, if you include the Area property of walls and choose not to itemize every instance, the area appears as a blank field in the schedule unless you check the Calculate Totals option.

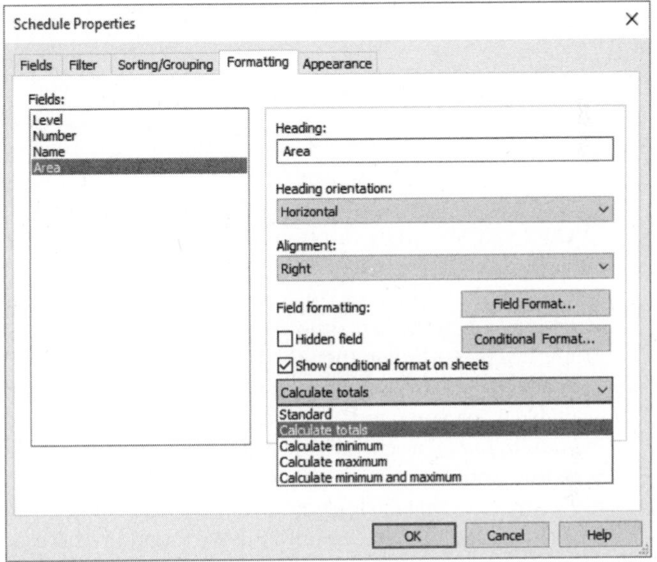

FIGURE 17.18
The Formatting tab allows you to change unit formats and specify fields in which you need to calculate totals.

The Hidden Field option is also an important feature to help you customize your schedules. You can use this option when you need to include a field just for filtering or sorting but you don't want to see it in the schedule, such as a custom sorting parameter for drawing sheets. You can also select it when you want to use a field as the header of a group of elements in a schedule. For example, you may include the Family and Type fields, but you want only the family listed as a grouping header because you don't need to show the family name repeatedly in every row of your schedule.

For this exercise, select the Level field and then activate the Hidden Field option. Select the Area field, set the Alignment to Right, and then activate the Calculate Totals option.

Appearance The Appearance tab (Figure 17.19) controls the graphical aspects of the schedule, such as font size and style of text for each of the columns and headers in the schedule. It also allows you to turn the schedule grid lines on and off and modify the line thickness for the grid and boundary lines. For revision schedules, you can also specify whether the schedule reads from top to bottom or from bottom to top.

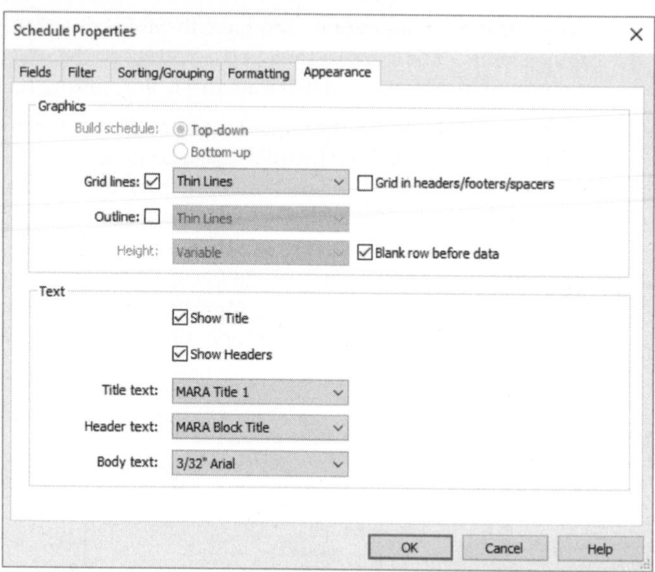

FIGURE 17.19
The Appearance tab

Select the Outline check box and set the Outline drop-down to Wide Lines.

Once you've worked through each of the tabs in the Schedule Properties dialog box, click OK and you will see the working layout of the schedule. The schedule settings can be modified at any time, but this gives you a basis from which to begin. To modify the schedule, you can access any tab of the Schedule Properties dialog box from the five corresponding buttons in the Properties palette when the schedule view is active.

A special tab on the ribbon is active when you are editing a schedule. This ribbon is not available when you select a schedule that has been placed on a sheet but available only in the editing mode. To edit a schedule on a sheet, you must right-click the schedule and then select Edit Schedule from the context menu. The Modify Schedule/Quantities tab shown in Figure 17.20 has many tools that enable you to modify field selection, hide columns, merge cells, and perform other functions that are similar to those found in Microsoft Excel.

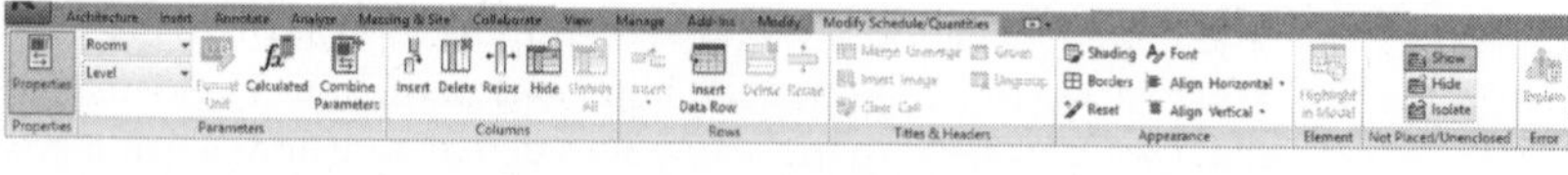

FIGURE 17.20
The contextual tab in the ribbon for schedules

In some schedules, such as room schedules, area schedules, and sheet lists, the Insert Data Row button is active. This command allows you to add rows to the schedule in order to prepopulate the project with values before you actually create an element. In the example of rooms, if you first create a room schedule and then generate a list of rooms using the Insert Data Row command, you can place rooms in your model using the predefined data in the Room drop-down from the Options bar.

In addition to the various formatting tools in the contextual tab for schedules, you will find a panel named Parameters. The drop-downs in this panel allow you to select some cells in the schedule and point them to other parameters within the project. As an example, we inserted a row beneath the title row and set the left cell to Project Information: Project Number. The two remaining cells in that row were merged and the cell's parameter was set to Schedule: Phase using the two drop-downs in the Parameters panel. As you can see in Figure 17.21, you can even change the phase of the schedule directly in the cell of the schedule.

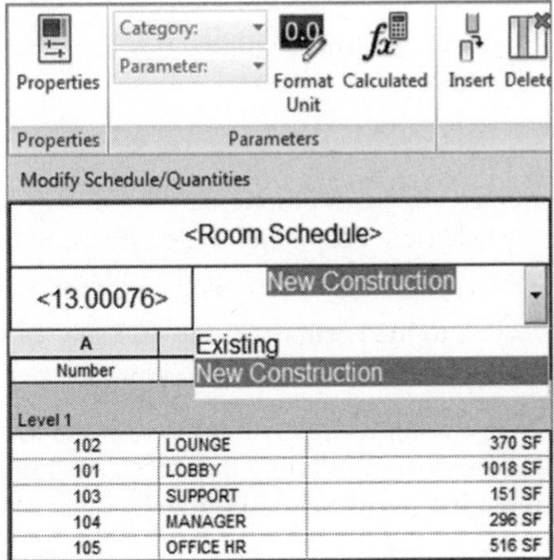

FIGURE 17.21
Additional information can be added to a schedule with tools from the Parameters panel.

Another key feature of the contextual tab for schedules is the Highlight In Model button. This button allows you to select any element in the schedule and locate that element within the model. Let's say you want to locate a particular door from your door schedule. Select the respective row in the schedule and click the Highlight In Model button; Revit will pull up a different view with that door highlighted. This technique can be a useful way to locate elements in the model, especially for larger models.

Now that you have an idea of the elements that compose a schedule, let's explore the workflow with the following two exercises. You will first create a simple wall schedule and then create a Usable Area schedule based on the areas you defined earlier in this chapter.

Making a Wall Schedule

In this exercise, you will create a schedule of building elements that is filtered to report only certain types of walls and is simplified to show only a summary of each unique wall type within the project. Make sure you have the `c17-Sample-Building-Start.rvt` or `c17-Sample-Metric-Start.rvt` file open, and then follow these steps:

1. From the View tab in the ribbon, locate the Create panel, click Schedules, and then click Schedules/Quantities.

   The New Schedule dialog box opens.

2. Choose Walls from the Category list and click OK.

3. In the Fields tab, choose the following wall properties from the Available Fields list and add them to the Scheduled Fields list (in order):

   - Function
   - Family

- ◆ Type
- ◆ Area

4. Switch to the Sorting/Grouping tab, set the first Sort By field to Family, and check the Header and Blank Line options. Leave the Itemize Every Instance option checked for now.
5. Click OK to close the dialog box and observe the amount of data that is available for this schedule.

   Let's refine the schedule even further.

6. In the Properties palette, scroll down to find the Edit buttons related to the five tabs in the Schedule Properties dialog box. Click the button next to Filter. Set the first filter drop-down list to Function: Equals: Exterior.
7. Switch to the Formatting tab and select the Function field from the list. Check the Hidden Field option and click OK to view the result in your schedule.

   Note that now only the exterior walls are being listed. Walls with any other function property are not being itemized. Although the Function field is not shown, it must be included in the Scheduled Fields list to be used as a filter.

8. From the Properties palette, click the Edit button related to the Sorting/Grouping tab. Uncheck the Itemize Every Instance option and check the Grand Totals option. From the Grand Totals drop-down list, choose Totals Only.

<Wall Schedule>

A	B	C
Family	Type	Area
Basic Wall		
Basic Wall	Exterior - EIFS-Brick on Wd Stud	491 SF
Basic Wall	Exterior - EIFS-Brick on Wd Stud	540 SF
Basic Wall	Exterior - EIFS-Brick on Wd Stud	252 SF
Basic Wall	Exterior - EIFS-Brick on Wd Stud	325 SF
Basic Wall	Exterior - EIFS-Brick on Wd Stud	478 SF
Basic Wall	Exterior - EIFS-Brick on Wd Stud	149 SF
Basic Wall	Exterior - EIFS-Brick on Wd Stud	641 SF
Basic Wall	Exterior - EIFS-Brick on Wd Stud	150 SF
Basic Wall	Exterior - EIFS on Mtl. Stud	491 SF
Basic Wall	Exterior - EIFS-Brick on Wd Stud	317 SF
Basic Wall	Exterior - EIFS on Mtl. Stud	360 SF
Basic Wall	Exterior - EIFS on Mtl. Stud	219 SF
Basic Wall	Exterior - EIFS on Mtl. Stud	364 SF
Curtain Wall		
Curtain Wall	Exterior Glazing	44 SF
Curtain Wall	Exterior Glazing	132 SF
Curtain Wall	Exterior Glazing	39 SF
Curtain Wall	Exterior Glazing	271 SF
Curtain Wall	Exterior Glazing	108 SF
Curtain Wall	Exterior Glazing	648 SF
Curtain Wall	Exterior Glazing	164 SF
Curtain Wall	Exterior Glazing	152 SF
Curtain Wall	Exterior Glazing	106 SF
Curtain Wall	Exterior Glazing	271 SF

9. Switch to the Formatting tab and select the Family field from the list. Check the Hidden Field option. Next, select the Area field, check the Calculate Totals option, and set the Alignment to Right.

10. Click OK to close the dialog box and observe the final modifications to your wall schedule (Figure 17.22).

FIGURE 17.22
The finished wall schedule displays a summary of elements.

<Wall Schedule>		
A	B	C
Family	Type	Area
Basic Wall		
Basic Wall	Exterior - EIFS on Mtl. Stud	4773 SF
Curtain Wall		
Curtain Wall	Exterior Glazing	1936 SF
		6709 SF

In this simple wall schedule exercise, you saw that a large amount of model data can be succinctly itemized and displayed using a combination of parameters within the elements. Only the exterior wall types were itemized, and the total area for each type was reported, including a grand total of all types.

MAKING AN AREA SCHEDULE

In our next exercise, you will create an area schedule specifically for the Usable Area scheme you established earlier in this chapter. The process is similar to that of creating a wall schedule.

If you are working through all the exercises in this chapter, continue with the `c17-Sample-Building-Start.rvt` or `c17-Sample-Metric-Start.rvt` file from this book's web page. To create the schedule, follow these steps:

1. From the View tab in the ribbon, select Schedules and then Schedule/Quantities. From the Categories list, select the Area (Usable Area) schedule type and click OK.

2. On the Fields tab, notice that the available fields in an area table are much more limited than they were in the Walls table in the previous exercise. For this schedule, you need only four fields:

   - Area Type
   - Level
   - Name
   - Area

   Choose those from the Fields list on the left, and using the Add button, move them to the right or double-click the names to move them from one side to the other.

   Remember that the order of the fields in this list will determine the order of the columns in your final schedule. Use the Move Up and Move Down buttons as needed to order the list correctly.

3. Next, choose the Sorting/Grouping tab. From the first pull-down menu, choose to sort by Area Type and check the Header and Footer boxes with the Totals Only option. In the second pull-down, choose to sort by Level. Check the Itemize Every Instance option at the bottom.

4. In this schedule, you want to make the areas read as they would in a spreadsheet—right-justified and totaled. Choose the Formatting tab and select Area from the list on the left. Change the Alignment to Right and check the Calculate Totals box. Select the Area Type field and check the Hidden Field box.

5. Click OK to close the dialog box and observe your results (Figure 17.23). The areas placed on each level should be listed under a header and the total area should be calculated at the bottom of each grouped level. Finally, the sum of all areas is displayed as a grand total at the bottom of the schedule.

FIGURE 17.23
The final schedule is an organized list of areas according to their level.

<Area Schedule (Usable Area)>

A	B	C
Level	Name	Area
Building Common Area		
Level 1	LOBBY	1406 SF
Level 1	SERVICES	848 SF
Level 2	SERVICES	156 SF
		2411 SF
Major Vertical Penetration		
Level 2	CIRCULATION	513 SF
		513 SF
Office Area		
Level 1	OFFICES	162 SF
Level 2	OFFICES	1444 SF
		1606 SF

ADDING SCHEDULES TO YOUR TEMPLATES

As you continue to document your designs, you will likely use the same schedules on many projects. Spend the time to make them consistent with your office's graphic standards, and add them to your office template. That way, you won't have to create them from scratch each and every time. As you add content to your model, the schedules will automatically populate, in effect filling themselves out.

If you have a schedule in another project and you want to add it to your current project, there's no need to re-create it. Open both projects in the same instance of Revit. Go to the sheet on which the schedule you want to copy appears. If it's not on a sheet, you'll need to place it on one. Then simply select it and copy it to the Clipboard (press Ctrl+C). In your destination project, go to any sheet and press Ctrl+V to paste it. Once the paste is finished, the schedule should be there with all the formatting from the previous project but with all the information from your current model.

Another way to save a schedule separate from a project file is to save the view. Choose the Application button and click Save As ➤ Library ➤ Save Views. From here you can select several schedules to export as a small, separate RVT file. This file can then be inserted into other project files to add the schedules. If you want to export only one schedule, you can right-click on the schedule in the Project Browser and select Save To New File from the context menu.

CREATING A SHEET LIST

Using a sheet list schedule, you can create a tabular view of sheets in your project—even including drawings provided by consultants. This type of schedule allows you to create placeholders for sheets that are not yet created or that will not be a part of your discipline's drawing set.

In the sample workflow, you have created area plans for the Usable Area scheme. Eventually, you may want to create another area scheme based on departmental spaces. You haven't created them yet, but you want to create your sheet list, including the area plans that you will create later. To do so, follow these steps:

1. From the View tab in the ribbon, click Schedules ➤ Sheet List.
2. In the Fields tab of the Sheet List Properties dialog box, add the fields named Sheet Number and Sheet Name to the list of scheduled fields.
3. On the Sorting/Grouping tab, choose to sort by Sheet Number and make sure the Itemize Every Instance check box is checked. Click OK to close the dialog box.
4. To begin adding sheets to the sheet list, go to the Rows panel in the ribbon and then click Insert ➤ Data Rows. This will give you a row with the next sequential number based on the last number you entered. Change the sheet number in the new row to **G101** and click the Data Rows button again. The next new row should be G102. Change the names of G101 and G102 to **LEVEL 1 AREA PLAN** and **LEVEL 2 AREA PLAN**, respectively.

<Sheet List>

A	B
Sheet Number	Sheet Name
A101	FLOOR PLANS
G101	LEVEL 1 AREA PLAN
G102	LEVEL 2 AREA PLAN

   You can continue populating the schedule in this way, adding any sheet names you need or plan to have in the presentation package. Next, you will begin to create a sheet directly from a row in the sheet list.

5. Start by selecting the New Sheet button from the Modify Schedules/Quantities tab on the ribbon. This will give you a dialog box similar to Figure 17.24.
6. Select the type of sheet border you'd like to use from the list at the top. Choose the C size sheet border for this exercise.
7. Select G101 - LEVEL 1 AREA PLAN from the list of placeholder sheets and click OK.

This will create a sheet from the line item in the schedule using the same name and sheet number. The new sheet will appear under the Sheet node in the Project Browser with the correct number and name. You will begin to add views to this sheet later in this chapter.

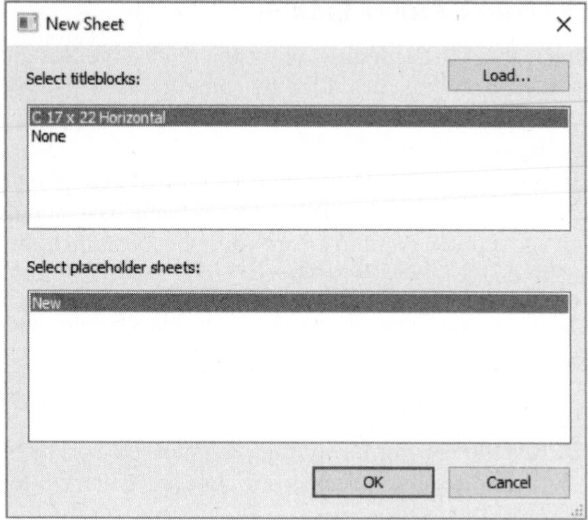

FIGURE 17.24
Converting a placeholder into a sheet

Using Legends

Legends can become great tools for general notes, key plans, or any other view type that you will want to have consistent across several sheets. It's also important to note that anything you place inside a legend view—doors, walls, windows, and so on—will not appear or be counted in any schedules. Legend elements live outside of any quantities present in the model.

The Legend tool is located on the Create panel in the View tab. You can create two types of legends from this menu: a *legend*, which is a graphic display, or a *keynote legend*, which is a text-based schedule. Both legend types can be placed on multiple sheets, but for this exercise, you'll focus on the graphic legend. The keynote legend will be handled in more detail in Chapter 18, "Annotating Your Design."

As part of the sample workflow, you may want to present some of the wall types from your presentation package to demonstrate the Sound Transmission Class (STC) of the walls and the overall wall assembly. Because these wall types will be appearing on all the sheets where you are using them in plan, you'll make them using a legend.

To make a legend, choose the Legend button from the View tab under the Legends flyout. Creating a new legend is much like creating a new drafting view. You'll be presented with a New Legend View dialog box (Figure 17.25), where you can name the legend and set the scale. For this legend, name it **WALL LEGEND** and choose 1 1/2″ = 1″–0″ (1:10) for the scale.

FIGURE 17.25
Creating a legend

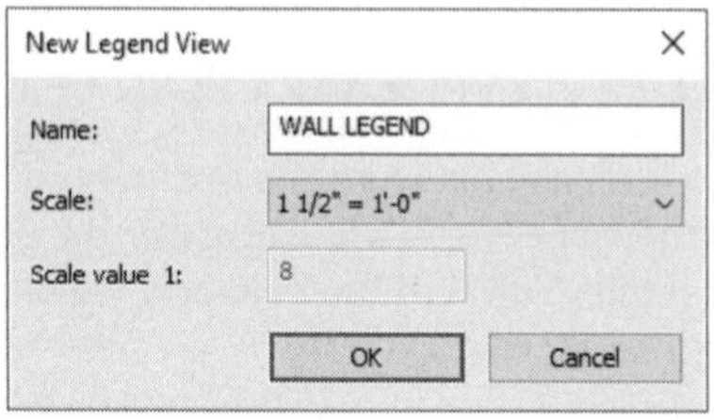

New Legend View
Name: WALL LEGEND
Scale: 1 1/2" = 1'-0"
Scale value 1: 8
OK
Cancel

The legend you've created will look like a blank view. At this point, it's up to you to add content. The simplest type of legend would be adding notes such as plan or demolition notes that would appear in each of your floor plans. You could do this simply by using the Text tool and adding text within this legend view; however, in this example you want to add more than just text.

To add wall types or any other family to the legend view, expand the Families tree in the Project Browser and navigate to the Wall family. Expand this node and then expand the Basic Wall node. Select the Interior – 4 7/8″ (138 mm) Partition (1-Hr) wall type, drag it into the view, and insert it anywhere.

With the family inserted into the view, it will appear as a 3′ (1000 mm)-long plan wall. Change your view's detail level from Coarse to Medium or Fine so you can see the detail within the wall. With that done, select the inserted wall and look at the settings in the Options bar. These options will be consistent for any of the family types you insert. The Options bar for legend elements consists of three sections:

Family This drop-down menu allows you to select different family types and operates just like the Type Selector does for other elements within the model.

View The View option lets you change the type of view from Floor Plan to Section.

Host Length This option changes the overall length (or in the case of sections, height) of the element selected.

Let's make some minor adjustments to the wall sample in the legend. Let's change View to Section and change Host Length to **1′-6″** (**500** mm).

The wall now looks like a sectional element. By adding some simple text, you can embellish the wall type to better explain the elements you're viewing (Figure 17.26).

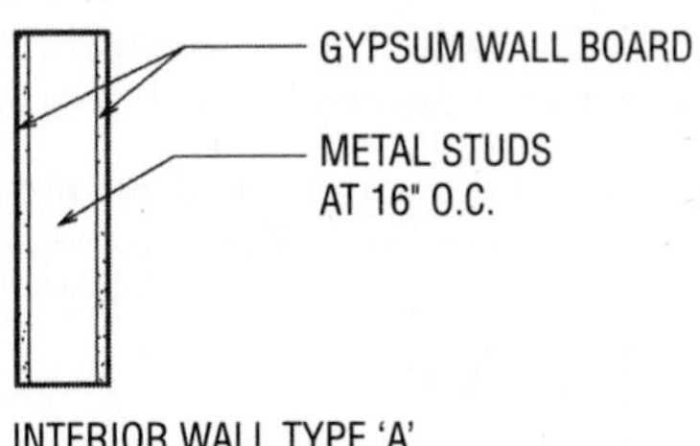

FIGURE 17.26
Add other annotation to embellish the wall type section.

Continue the exercise by adding the Exterior – EIFS On Metal Stud wall type to the legend along with some additional text notes to Figure 17.26.

Laying Out Sheets

Throughout this chapter, you have created different kinds of views, including area plans, schedules, and legends. Eventually you will need to lay those out onto sheets so they can be printed or exported as PDF or DWF files and sent to others for review.

Creating sheets is easy. As you've already seen, you can create sheets through a sheet list schedule. You can also create sheets by right-clicking the Sheet node in the Project Browser and selecting New Sheet from the context menu. Regardless of which method you use to create them, in the following sections we'll walk you through laying out these views on sheets and show you how to manipulate each view further once it's placed on a sheet.

Adding the Area Plan

In the following exercise, you will continue to use the `c17-Sample-Building-Start.rvt` or `c17-Sample-Metric-Start.rvt` file saved from previous exercises in this chapter:

1. Open the G101 – LEVEL 1 AREA PLAN sheet in the view window by double-clicking it in the Project Browser. Now, let's add your first view—the Usable Area plan for Level 1. To do this, simply drag and drop it from the Project Browser onto the sheet. The view will show at the proper scale and with a view title already established. You can then drag the view across the sheet to place it where you'd like to have it, which in this case is centered at the top of the sheet.

   When views are placed on sheets, they are referred to as viewports. Select the view you just placed on the sheet and look at the Properties palette. The instance properties of the viewport are actually the view properties of that view. These properties can be modified at any time in the Properties palette for a viewport that has been placed on a sheet. A viewport also has type properties that determine the view title family, the visibility of the view title, and the formatting of the optional title extension line. We discuss viewport management with greater detail in Chapter 20, "Presenting Your Design."

   After placing the view on the sheet, you'll notice that the purple area boundary lines are still visible. If you print the sheet at this point, the software will print those lines as thick, black lines that border your floor plate. This may be undesirable, so you need to do some view management to turn those lines off. One way you can do this is by activating the area plan from the Project Browser and working within the view itself. Since you have the view already established on a sheet, there's no reason to go back to the original view when you can work on it directly through the sheet.

2. Right-click the view on the sheet and choose Activate View from the context menu. You can also double-click a view placed on a sheet to activate it.

Activating a View

Activating a view is like working in model space through a paper space viewport in Autodesk® AutoCAD® software. You're working on the actual view but you're doing so while it is placed on the sheet. This gives you the benefit of seeing how changes to the view will affect the layout of the view on the sheet. For example, it could be undesirable to enlarge the crop window for the view to show more information on the sheet. Doing so will take up valuable sheet real estate and should be balanced by the amount of space the other views on this sheet need. You'll also notice that once the view is activated, all the surrounding materials (the sheet and any other views) turn gray. This is to alert you to the fact that you're working in the view and are not active on the sheet.

In this view, however, you want to make some modifications to the visibility and turn off the area boundaries so they are not visible when you print. To do this, open the Visibility/Graphic

Overrides dialog box by pressing VG on your keyboard or navigating to the command via the context menu.

In the Visibility/Graphic Overrides dialog box, pan down in the Model tab (activated by default) and choose the Lines node. Uncheck the box for <Area Boundaries> and click OK. The boundary lines should disappear from the view.

Now you're ready to get out of the activation mode and add some additional views to the sheet. To do this, right-click anywhere within the view and choose Deactivate View from the context menu. You can also double-click outside the viewport to deactivate the view.

Deactivate Active Views

Keep the following in mind: Once you activate a view and complete your edits, you must deactivate it. As you can see on the sheet, activated views gray out the surrounding sheet context. If you were to print at this point, the sheet would print as gray with only the activated view showing in black.

To deactivate a view, you can do one of three things. You can click Deactivate View from the context ribbon, right-click the mouse and choose Deactivate View from the context menu, or simply double-click outside of the view area.

With the view on the sheet, you will want to make some other adjustments to help clean up the sheet layout a bit. One thing you will want to do is modify the view title's location and length. To do this, select the viewport, and the view title will activate. With the view title active, you'll notice the blue grip at the end of the title line. By grabbing and dragging the grip, you can shorten the view title. Press the Esc key or click the Modify button in the ribbon to deselect the viewport.

Now select the view title itself—not the viewport—and then click and drag the title closer to the view itself (Figure 17.27).

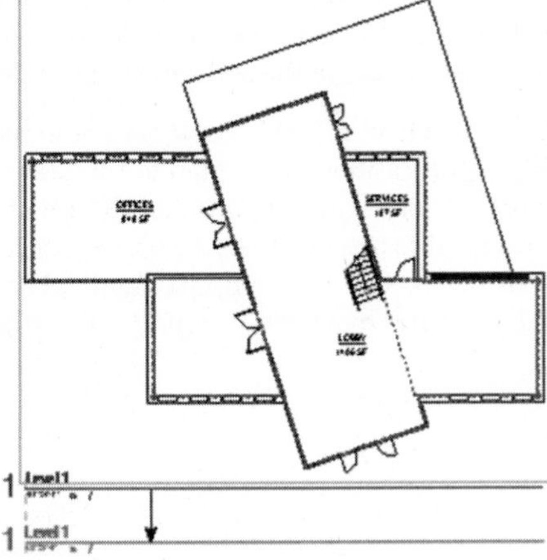

Figure 17.27
Move the view title by selecting it directly, not by selecting the viewport.

Using Guide Grids

If you have multiple plans, elevations, or sections that need to be placed at the same location on a series of sheets, the Guide Grid command can help you manage this. Guide grids are nonprinting grids that can be associated with sheets. The grids allow you to snap or align elements such as reference planes, other grids, or crop regions to specific locations relative to the sheet border.

You can create as many unique guide grids as required in a Revit project. First, activate the G101 sheet to establish your first guide grid. Complete the following exercise before placing the next area plan on a new sheet:

1. From the View tab in the ribbon, select Guide Grid from the Sheet Composition panel. Name the new **grid C-Sheet Area Plans**.
2. When you see the grid appear on the sheet, select it and look at the Properties palette. Change the spacing to **3″** (**75** mm).
3. Select the outer boundary of the guide grid and activate the Move command (press **MV** on the keyboard). Snap to one of the grid intersections within the guide, and then move it to the upper-left intersection of the inner sheet border.

   Where you place the guide grid and the spacing of the grid itself will depend on exactly how you plan to use it. In our example, we need to identify only a single common point to which we will align our area plans. The location of the boundary of the grid is not important; the boundary cannot be snapped to.
4. Access the view properties of the sheet and scroll down to find the Guide Grid property. Make sure it is set to C-Sheet Area Plans.
5. Select the area plan already placed on sheet G101 and activate the Move command. Snap to the intersection of the two reference planes visible in the plan and then to a nearby intersection on the guide grid.

   Note that some traditional modifying methods do not work with guide grids. For example, you cannot use the Align command.
6. If you haven't already done so, create a new sheet using the G102 - LEVEL 2 AREA PLAN placeholder. In the Properties palette, make sure the guide grid is specified and note that it is now in exactly the same location as on the previous sheet.
7. Drag the Level 2 Usable Area plan onto the sheet, and then use the Move command to adjust the location of the plan to the same location as on the previous sheet (Figure 17.28). Note that only crop regions and datum objects will snap to the guide grids; therefore, you may need to activate the area plans and enter Reveal Hidden Elements mode in the view control bar. This will temporarily display reference planes in the exercise file. Deactivate the view and move the viewports into alignment with the guide grid.

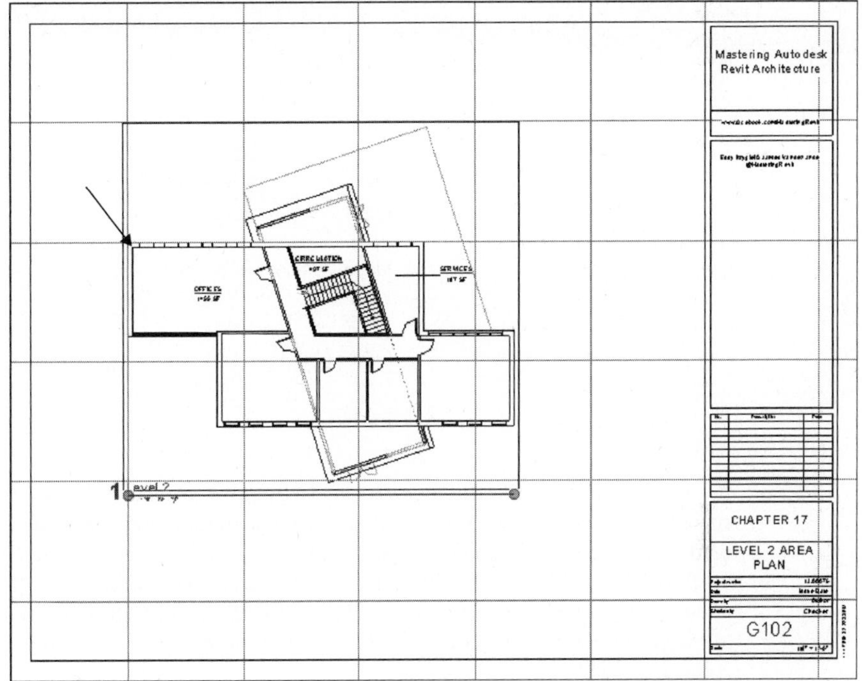

FIGURE 17.28 Use Guide Grids to help align views among a series of sheets.

If you haven't noticed already, model views of the same scale will always snap to each other without any special grids. What you might not realize is that this also works between views of different types as long as they are of the same scale. For example, you can drag an elevation from the Project Browser onto sheet G102 and see how it snaps in relation to the plan. Sections can also be aligned with elevations and with plans. Even 3D views can be aligned with each other.

Adding the Schedule

With the largest view, the area plan, on the sheet, you can use the bottom portion of the sheet to lay out your other views. For the second view, let's add the area schedule you created. To do this, drag and drop it from the Project Browser in much the same way you added the area plan. The inserted view will look like Figure 17.29. You'll notice some differences in how this view looks from the way a schedule looks when it's not on a sheet. Specifically, you can now see the header text and the fonts you chose in the schedule properties. You'll also be able to see the grid lines and their associated line weights from the Appearance tab of the schedule properties.

FIGURE 17.29
A schedule placed on a sheet

Area Schedule (Usable Area)		
Level	Name	Area
Building Common Area		
Level 1	LOBBY	1406 SF
Level 1	SERVICES	848 SF
Level 2	SERVICES	156 SF
		2411 SF
Major Vertical Penetration		
Level 2	CIRCULATION	513 SF
		513 SF
Office Area		
Level 1	OFFICES	162 SF
Level 2	OFFICES	1444 SF
		1606 SF

With the schedule on the sheet, it looks a bit tight. You have the ability to redefine the column spacing so you can make any visual adjustments to the schedule while it is on the sheet to help it read better. These adjustments do not change the actual schedule—just its appearance on the sheet.

To do this, highlight the schedule by selecting it. The schedule will turn blue, and you'll have a few new grips to help you make adjustments (Figure 17.30). The blue inverted triangles will allow you to modify the column widths. Grab them and drag them left or right to change the column sizing.

FIGURE 17.30
A schedule's appearance can be manipulated when it is placed on a sheet.

Area Schedule (Usable Area)		
Level	Name	Area
Building Common Area		
Level 1	LOBBY	1406 SF
Level 1	SERVICES	848 SF
Level 2	SERVICES	156 SF
		2411 SF
Major Vertical Penetration		
Level 2	CIRCULATION	513 SF
		513 SF
Office Area		
Level 1	OFFICES	162 SF
Level 2	OFFICES	1444 SF
		1606 SF

You'll also notice a blue cut symbol on the schedule. This cut symbol lets you break the schedule into multiple vertical columns on the same sheet. This tool can be especially handy if you have a long schedule like a room schedule or door schedule and it has too many rows to fit vertically on your sheet. Selecting this tool will break the schedule in half (and you can break it into half again and again) so that you can take advantage of the horizontal real estate. If you choose to separate your schedule in this fashion, it will still retain all the necessary information and all the portions will continue to automatically fill themselves out dynamically as a single schedule would. You also have the opportunity to change the overall height of the schedule once it is broken up by grabbing the grips at the bottom of the schedule and dragging up and down (Figure 17.31). Doing so will draw or push rows from the adjacent schedule portion so that all of your information is continuous.

FIGURE 17.31
Changing the schedule height

Area Schedule (Usable Area)		
Level	Name	Area
Building Common Area		
Level 1	LOBBY	1406 SF
Level 1	SERVICES	848 SF
Level 2	SERVICES	156 SF
		2411 SF
Major Vertical Penetration		

Area Schedule (Usable Area)		
Level	Name	Area
Level 2	CIRCULATION	513 SF
		513 SF
Office Area		
Level 1	OFFICES	162 SF
Level 2	OFFICES	1444 SF
		1606 SF

To rebuild a split schedule—essentially returning it to a single list—select the schedule on the sheet so it highlights and the grips are displayed. Click one of the move icons and drag the split portion on top of the other schedule segment. The split schedule will then become whole again.

Finishing the Sheet

Now that you have those two views on the sheet, it is a simple matter to add the remaining views. To add the wall legend you created, you will drag and drop it from the Project Browser in much the same way you did with the other two views.

In this case, the wall legend came onto the sheet needing little modification. Following this same workflow, you can also add a drafting view from the imported detail to the sheet, completing Sheet **G102** (Figure 17.32).

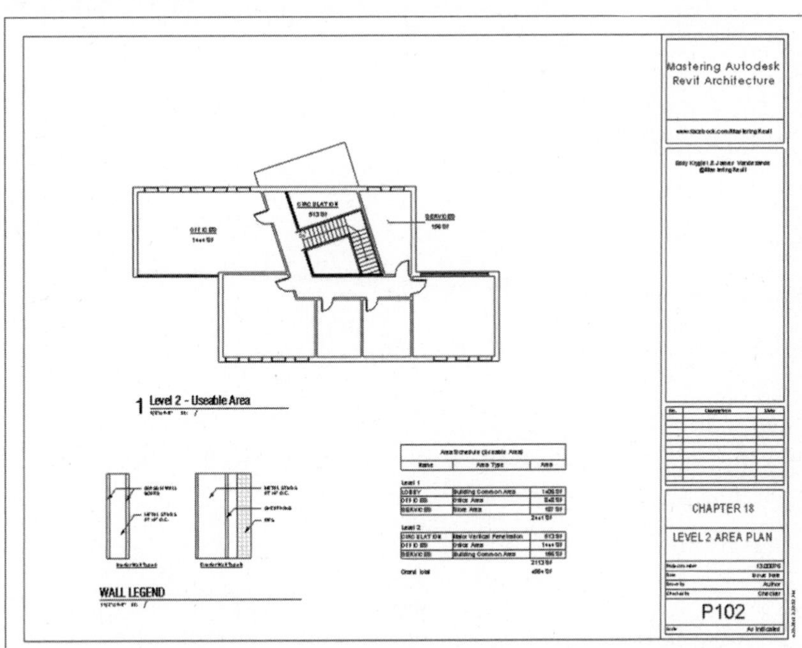

FIGURE 17.32
The finished sheet

The Bottom Line

Document plans. With floor plans you can create visual graphics that help define how a space is laid out. However, Revit provides other tools such as area plans to help you describe space.

Master It List the four types of area plans that you can create and note the two that Revit creates automatically.

Create schedules and legends. Schedules are another view type; they allow you to show information about the model in a nongraphic format. Schedules can also be used to dynamically report quantities of elements inside the model.

Master It Understand how to create schedules and report additional information about the elements in the model. How would you create a simple casework schedule showing quantities of types?

Lay out sheets. Eventually in a project it will become necessary to create sheets that will become the documentation set. Knowing how to create a good sheet set provides you with another venue to communicate with contractors, clients, and other team members.

Master It To properly create a sheet set, you need to understand the dynamics of adding views to a sheet. In the Revit environment, there is only one way to add views to a sheet. What is it?

Chapter 18

Annotating Your Design

No set of documents is complete without the annotations to describe the drawings. Even when you are using a digital, parametric model, you still need to provide annotated documents. It is necessary to add dimensions, tags, text, and notes to the drawings to properly communicate with owners, contractors, and the rest of the design team.

In this chapter, you'll learn to:

- Annotate with text and keynotes
- Use tags
- Add dimensions
- Set project and shared parameters

Annotating with Text and Keynotes

Notes are a critical part of communicating design and construction intent to owners and builders. No drawing set is complete without descriptions of materials and the work like the ones you can see in Figure 18.1.

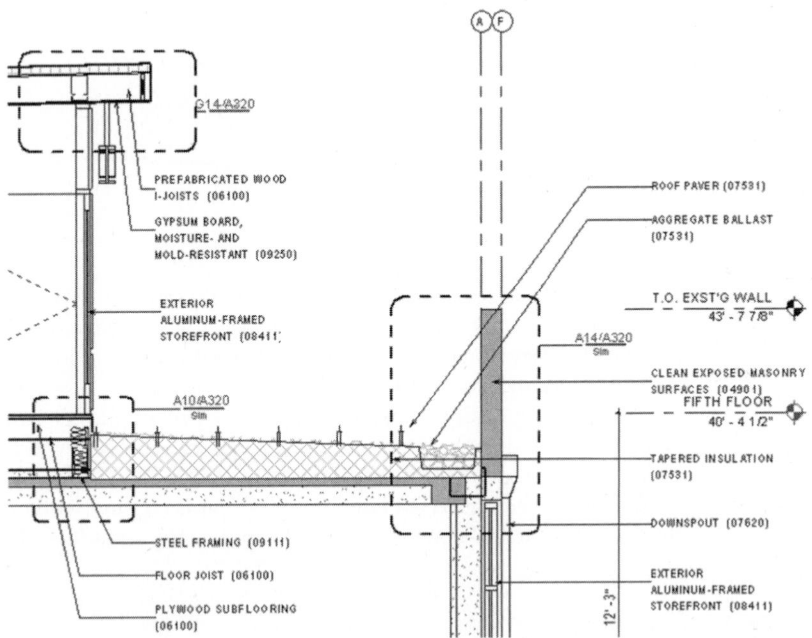

FIGURE 18.1
An annotated detail

There are two ways to add notes to your drawings in Autodesk® Revit® Architecture software. Both are located on the Annotate tab and highlighted in Figure 18.2. One of these methods is the Text command (shown on the left), and the other is the Keynote command (shown on the right).

FIGURE 18.2 The Text and Keynote commands

The text object consists of a resizable field into which you can enter text with optional features, including leaders, bullets, or numbers. Text can be used for annotations, sheet notes (such as general notes), or legends; it can be used generally anywhere you need to add a description or a note.

Keynotes are predefined text fields that are linked to elements and materials through a data file. Keynotes can be scheduled and standardized across the project but can't be directly edited within the application. Both keynotes and text have specific uses. Let's look at how both of these can be used in a project.

Using Text

Text is quick and easy to add to any view (including 3D views), and like other drafting elements it is view-specific. Text added to one view will not appear in any other location within the model, nor will the information that you insert into the text box hold any sort of parametric values.

You can access the Text tool from the Text panel on the Annotate tab (shown previously in Figure 18.2). To begin adding text, select the Text tool and first observe the settings in the contextual ribbon (Figure 18.3). You can specify an option for a leader, the position of the leader, and the justification of the text. It is easier to set these options before you place a text object, but they can always be adjusted later.

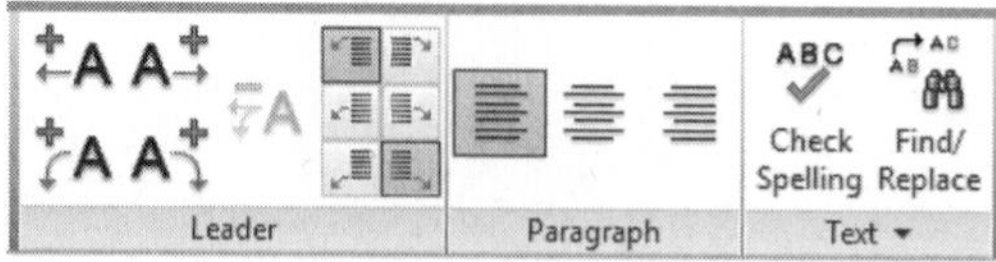

FIGURE 18.3 The contextual ribbon for the text tool

After you have selected the most appropriate settings for your annotation, go to a place in a view where you'd like to place the text object. You will have the opportunity to use one of two methods to create the text object. If you click once, the location you clicked will be the origin of the text object and the text will not have a defined width. Using this method, you may need to use the Enter key to fit the text to your needs—pressing Enter will create a line break in the text box. This method may cause some difficulty in the future if you need to resize the text box or if you change the scale of the view.

The other option is to hold down the left mouse button while you click to place the origin of the text. Then drag the mouse pointer to specify the boundary of the text object, creating a box.

Don't worry about the vertical extents of the boundary; you just need to set the width of the text box. Using this option gives you greater flexibility if you need to resize the text box or if the scale of your view changes, because the word-wrapping will be handled automatically. With the Text command active, you'll be presented with the standard mouse pointer crosshair, but it will have a small *A* in the lower-right corner to let you know you are adding text and not other elements. In either case, if you need to adjust the width of your text box, you can do so at any time using the grips.

If you select one of the leader options in the ribbon before placing the text object, your first one or two clicks (depending on the leader option selected) will be to place the leader. For example, if you choose the two-segment line leader option, your first click will be the arrowhead of the leader. Your second click will be the elbow of the leader, and then the third click will be the beginning of the text box. At this third click, you can still drag the mouse pointer to predefine the width of the text box. Try this a few times until you become familiar with the implicit placement and snapping alignment of text objects and leaders.

Once you place a text object in a view, you can write much as you do in applications such as Microsoft Word. Once you finish typing, click outside the text box. Your finished text box will look like Figure 18.4.

FIGURE 18.4
A highlighted text box

REMOVE EXISTING WOOD
WINDOWS. STORE ON SITE.
CLEAN EXISTING MASONRY
OPENING. SAND PATCH
MORTAR AS NEEDED USING
TYPE-N MORTAR AND COLOR
APPROVED BY ARCHITECT.
REPLACE EXISTING WOOD
SILLS WITH CAST STONE.
PROFILE TO MATCH.

New to Revit 2017 are some additional text formatting tools. With the text inside the text box activated or as you're typing, you'll notice some new text formatting features. For anyone familiar with any other text editor, these tools should be fairly self-explanatory, and for anyone familiar with Revit over the past few years, these come as some long-sought-after text-editing improvements. The new tools, shown in Figure 18.5, will allow you to do the following:

- Format the font to bold, italic, or underlined text
- Add subscripts or superscripts
- Change font size visually
- Add bullets, numbers, or alphabetical lists
- Indent text
- Change the position of text in a list by adding or removing incremental tabulation

FIGURE 18.5
New text formatting tools

You'll also notice that once you finish with your initial text or you select an existing text object, a few tools are available with which you can modify the text:

Grips The round grips on either side of the text box allow you to resize the width of the box.

Move There is a move icon that appears in the upper-left corner of the text box. In addition, hovering your mouse anywhere within the highlighted text will also display a move cursor. You can click and drag from within the box or click the move icon on the upper-left corner to relocate it. When you're moving text with the move icon (or the Move command), the text *and* leader will relocate together. When you're moving text by dragging, the leader end will remain pinned while you relocate the text box. These methods let you move either the text or the text and the leader, depending on your need.

Rotate The upper-right corner shows a rotate icon. Clicking this icon allows you to rotate the text box as you would any object in a project. Remember that text will always position itself to be read left to right if it is horizontal or bottom to top if it is vertical in a view.

A text family behaves like other families because it maintains a parametric relationship throughout the project. Making type property changes to a text object in one location (changing font, font size, color, and so on) changes all the instances of that type throughout the model. To modify text type properties, select a block of text or choose the Text tool and then observe the Properties palette, as shown in Figure 18.6.

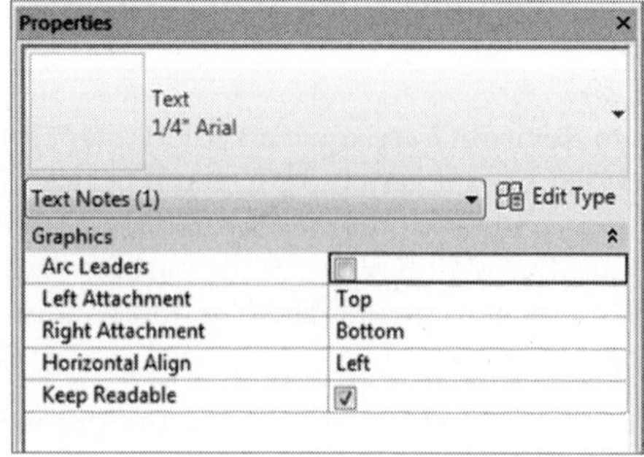

FIGURE 18.6
Type Selector for text

The instance properties for text objects are rather limited and deal primarily with controls such as alignment, location, and so on, which you can also set on the ribbon. The Type Selector also allows you to select a different text type or edit the properties of the currently selected type. Click the Edit Type button to open the text family's type properties. Figure 18.7 shows the properties for the default 1/4" Arial text type.

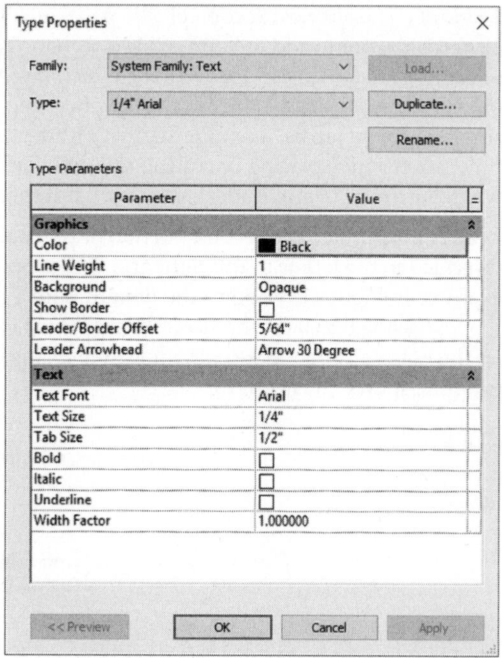

FIGURE 18.7
Type Properties dialog box

In the Type Properties dialog box, you have more control over the style of the text from a type perspective. While you can now edit specific text in a text box, there are still many reasons that you want to control text with the Type tool. In the Type Selector, you can modify text type properties, such as font, size, and width factor. You can also add formatting to the text, such as bold, italic, and underline. Other important settings to consider include Show Border, Background, and Leader Arrowhead. The Show Border property simply allows all text object instances to be enclosed with a line boundary. The Background property can be set to either Opaque or Transparent, which will control whether the text will obscure objects beneath it. Finally, the style of leader arrowhead is defined in the text type properties to help you maintain consistency throughout your design documents.

CONTEXTUAL TEXT FORMATTING

When any text *object* is selected in a view (not the text itself), additional formatting tools become available on the ribbon. The Format panel is divided into four sections that allow you to modify the instance of the text you've placed. Figure 18.8 shows the Format panel when the overall text object is selected and when you activate the text within the object. Let's look at this panel in more detail to better understand the toolset:

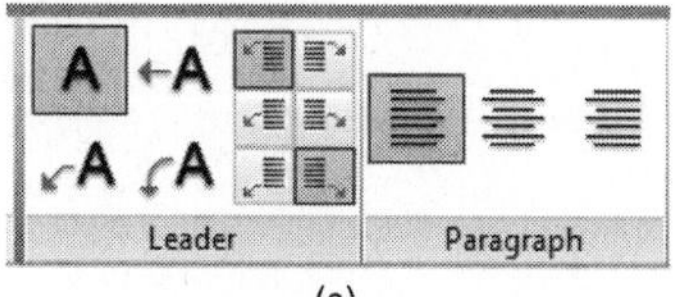

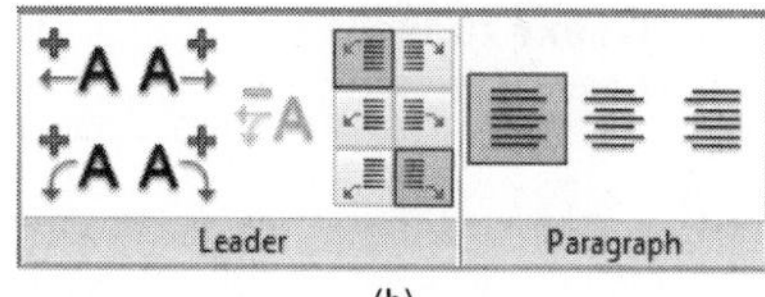

FIGURE 18.8
The Format panel in the contextual tab of the ribbon when placing text (a) and selecting a text object (b)

Leaders The leftmost section of this panel (a) allows you to designate the type and style of leader you want to add to your text box. When you activate the Text tool, the upper-left A is selected by default (as in Figure 18.8), which designates that no leader is currently added. The other choices all add a leader to the text. Reading from left to right, the options are no leader, a single-segment leader, a double-segment leader, and an arc leader. Leaders can be added at any time when you're placing or editing text and can also be removed at any time. Remember that when you're removing leaders, they will disappear in the order in which they were added.

Leader Location The second portion of this panel (b) dictates leader location. Leaders can be added to the left or to the right and at the top, middle, or bottom of the text box. The top example in Figure 18.9 shows the default with a left leader springing from the upper left of the text; leaders that spring from the right side typically come from the end of the text box (at the bottom). A double-segment leader springing from the left and right will look like the example shown in Figure 18.9.

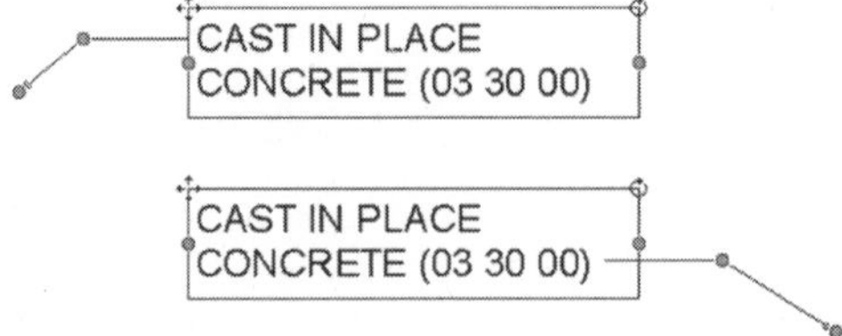

FIGURE 18.9 Text with leaders attached to different sides

Using Keynotes

Keynotes are annotations that use a parameter to connect specific elements or materials in the model to descriptive information stored in an external TXT file. You can control the formatting of the keynote's font style, size, and justification in the same manner as you can format standard text, but keynotes are essentially a tag family. Formatting changes must be made in the keynote's family (RFA) file and reloaded into the project.

Inserting a keynote allows you to choose a value from the TXT file and apply it to a material or element. Because keynotes act as families, they can also be scheduled where standard text cannot. Before we discuss how to add different keynote types, we'll explore the various ways a keynote can be displayed.

Without official corroboration from Autodesk, it appears that the keynoting functionality was designed to support the American Institute of Architects (AIA) proposal of the ConDoc system, in which a short numeric reference (usually based on MasterFormat by the Construction Specifications Institute) followed by a two-letter suffix is used to label elements in a drawing. The keynote then references a list or legend that is located on the same sheet as the note and has a longer definition of the note. For example, a keynote on a detail might read 033000.A1, with a leader pointing to an element in the drawing. The associated list on the side of the sheet would read CAST IN PLACE CONCRETE. Figure 18.10 shows an example of a keynote legend.

FIGURE 18.10 A keynote legend

KEYNOTE LEGEND	
03300.AO	CIP CONC FLOOR SLAB (03300)
04810.BF	STONE CLADDING (04810)
05120.AC	STEEL BEAM (05120)
05310.AH	COMPOSITE FLOOR DECK (05310)
05500.BB	STEEL COLUMN (05500)
05500.BU	STEEL ANGLE (05500)
06105.AB	WOOD FURRING (06105)
06105.AC	PLYWOOD (06105)
06105.AD	1X IPE WOOD SUNSCREEN (06105)
07210.AB	RIGID INSULATION (07210)

Despite the intended use of a keynote, you are not restricted to using only the numeric code. You can also display the full, written description directly within the detail or view without the numeric reference key. Figure 18.11 shows an example of keynotes that display the full description instead of the key.

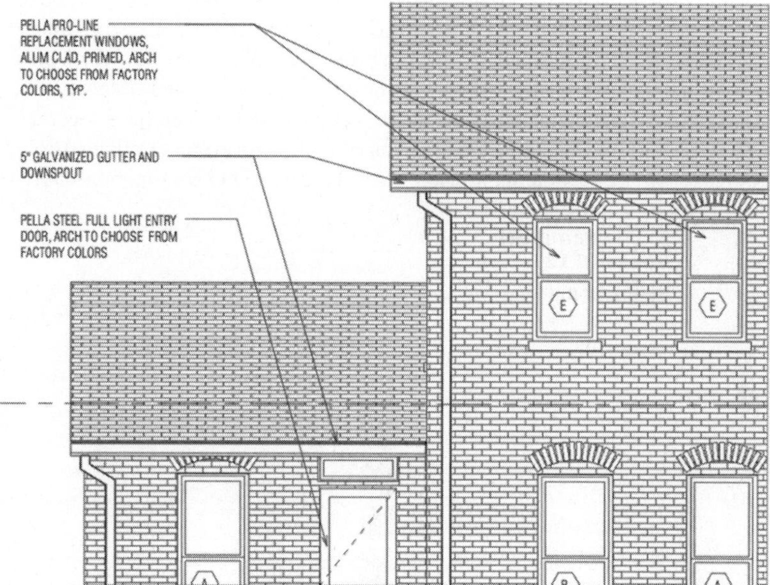

FIGURE 18.11
Keynotes displaying full text descriptions

There is no wrong way to use keynotes, and Revit supports several methods of using them for annotation. Regardless of the method you use, keynotes will adhere to the same process for use. Once an element is tagged with a keynote, it will retain that keynote in all other views in the model. If an element has been tagged with a keynote in one view and is then annotated in another view, it will automatically display the same keynote value. This can become a powerful tool you can use to add consistency throughout the project for annotated elements.

New to Revit 2017 is the ability to pin keynotes. Pinned keynotes will retain their location even if the element they have tagged has been moved.

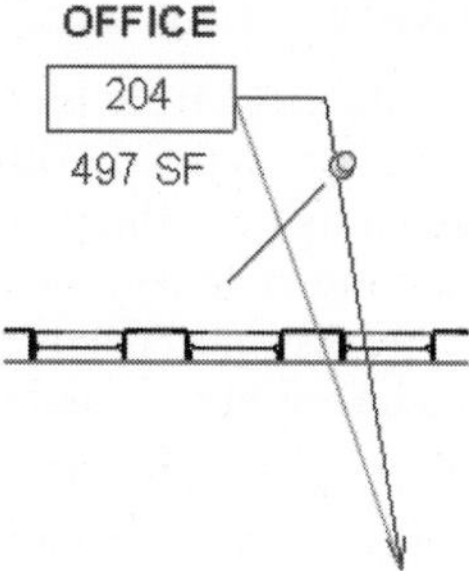

The Keynote command is located on the Annotate tab in the ribbon. When you select the Keynote tool, you have three options:

Element Use Element keynotes to annotate elements and assemblies within the model, such as walls, doors, floors, or other family instances. This type of note is typically used if you want to annotate an entire assembly (such as a wall, roof, or door). Moving the Element keynote leader arrow off the object will change the value of the note based on the element to which it points. The keynote value for a family type can be preset within the family. We'll go into that later in this chapter.

Material Using the Material keynote type will allow you to annotate specific materials within any elements. You can add notes for materials like concrete, gypsum board, rigid insulation, metal studs, and so on. Moving the Material keynote leader arrow from one material to another will change the value of the note based on the material to which it points even if it's within the same element. So, a wall with multiple materials can have several Material keynotes. Material keynotes can also be predefined as part of your project template through the Materials tool on the Manage tab. Material keynotes can also be used in conjunction with Element keynotes (Figure 18.12).

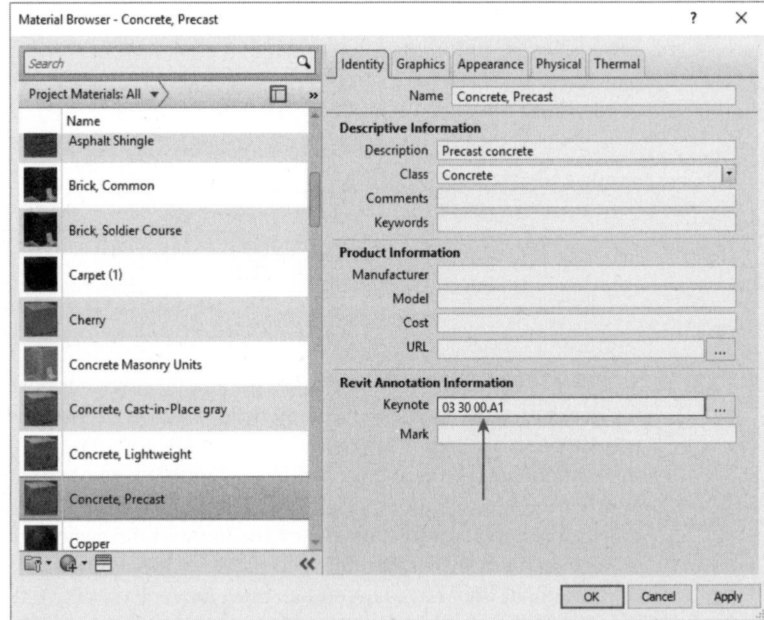

FIGURE 18.12 Adding a Keynote value to the identity data for a material

User User keynotes are different from Element and Material keynotes because they are view-specific and cannot be predefined. Although they are still tied to the same TXT file and will update in the same manner as other keynotes, they are not associated with any model objects. User keynotes are meant to be used for all the instances when you don't have a modeled element or material but you still need to define a note. Some examples of things you wouldn't necessarily model might be sealant, backer rod, or flashing.

User keynotes are used primarily in drafting views. To use any keynote, a given view must have at least one model element or component visible within it. In the case of a drafting view, you will need to insert a 2D component (such as wood blocking or a steel stud) because keynotes cannot be used to note linework. Because User keynotes are not locked to specific model geometry, once they are inserted they can easily be copied or moved around within the view and pointed toward any element. In this way, if you have sealant or flashing shown as linework, you can add a User keynote to the view and then adjust the note leader and the note value to call out the sealant properly. You can change the value of a User keynote at any time simply by double-clicking the note value; this modification will not affect any other notes within the project.

You can use all of these note types in conjunction with one another. Using an Element note to add a keynote to a wall doesn't mean you cannot also use a Material note to call out the individual materials in the wall assembly.

Assigning Keynotes and Editing

A core concept of the Keynote tool is how the notes react within the model. Assigning a keynote to an object lets you associate a text or numeric value with a family's keynote type parameter. This value is consistent for every instance of that element within the model or project. For example, all walls have a type parameter called Keynote that lets you set the keynote value. If you keynote a wall anywhere within the model, the keynote value in the type parameter will reflect that note. Consequently, any other wall of that type will be prepopulated with that keynote value. Changes to this keynote value will dynamically update the type parameter value and update any keynotes placed within the model tagged to this wall.

All keynotes within a project are tied to an external TXT file. This TXT file is the only location where the value of the keynotes can be edited. You can modify this file at any point to add or remove notes, and you can make the edits while the project is actively open. Figure 18.13 shows a sample of the file.

Figure 18.13
The keynote TXT file

RevitKeynotes_Imperial_2004a.txt - Notepad

File Edit Format View Help

```
12 48 00.B2	Tire Tread Mat	12 48 00

Division 13	Special Construction
13 49 00	Radiation Protection	Division 13
13 49 00.A1	1/2" Lead Lined Gypsum Wallboard	13 49 00
13 49 00.A2	5/8" Lead Lined Gypsum Wallboard	13 49 00
13 49 00.B1	Sheet Lead Shielding	13 49 00
13 49 00.B2	2" Lead Corner Strip	13 49 00
13 49 00.B3	2" Lead Joint Strip	13 49 00

Division 14	Conveying Equipment
14 12 00	Electric Dumbwaiters	Division 14
14 12 00.A1	Dumbwaiter	14 12 00
14 24 00	Hydraulic Elevators	Division 14
14 24 00.A1	Hydraulic Elevator	14 24 00
14 28 00	Elevator Equipment and Controls	Division 14
14 28 00.A1	1 1/2" Elevator Door Saddle Extension	14 28 00
14 28 00.A2	2" Elevator Door Saddle Extension	14 28 00
14 28 00.A3	3" Elevator Door Saddle Extension	14 28 00
14 28 00.A4	4" Elevator Door Saddle Extension	14 28 00
14 28 00.B1	3 3/8" Elevator Door Saddle	14 28 00
14 28 00.B2	4" Elevator Door Saddle	14 28 00
14 28 00.B3	4 7/8" Elevator Door Saddle	14 28 00
14 28 00.B4	5 1/2" Elevator Door Saddle	14 28 00
14 92 00	Pneumatic Tube Systems	Division 14
14 92 00.A1	Pneumatic Tube System	14 92 00
```

This external file is designed to keep the annotations consistent by storing them in one repository. Every time you add or change a note value and reload the TXT file back into the Revit model, all the keynotes dynamically update.

You can edit this TXT file or add one to the project at any time. You can have multiple keynote files for various projects, but you can have only one TXT file associated with a project at a time. You cannot assign multiple keynote files to one project model.

Managing Keynotes

A great way to ensure consistent use of notes throughout multiple projects is to create a master keynote file for each of your various project types. This master note list can be linked to elements and materials within your project template so that you can immediately begin inserting common notes into any project. Because this master list will likely be quite long, project teams can make a copy of the list and place it in their project directory. They can then safely delete the notes they won't be using over the course of the project, giving them fewer options to hunt through when they need to add a keynote.

A single keynote file also gives project management a level of control over the consistency of the notes that you won't be able to get if you use regular text. Spelling accidents or mislabeling can happen in a project when you use regular text objects. For example, it's easy to overlook a note that reads CIP CONCRETE on one detail and CAST-IN-PLACE CONCRETE in another. By placing all the notes into one file, the project manager or project architect has better control over how the note reads, thus ensuring consistency throughout all the sheets and details.

Because the keynote list is a separate TXT file, if you are transferring files to other offices or clients, you may need to include the TXT file along with the RVT file. If you don't send the TXT file, others will be able to see all your keynotes but they won't be able to change or edit any of them.

Using the Keynote File

Three default keynote text files are available at the library locations. In Windows 7, Windows 8, or Windows 10, they are found at `C:\ProgramData\Autodesk\RVT 2017\Libraries\US` (there is also a default keynote file in the Metric folder). Another way to find these files is to start a new project using the default template and go to the Annotate tab. Click the Keynote drop-down arrow on the Tag panel and select Keynoting Settings. In the Keynoting Settings dialog box, click the Browse button and you will be taken to the default library location.

These four keynote files are

`RevitKeynotes_Imperial.txt`

`RevitKeynotes_Imperial_2004.txt`

`RevitKeynotes_Imperial_2010.txt`

`RevitKeynotes_Metric.txt`

You can edit any of these files in Notepad or Excel and follow the format already established within the file. Let's look at the format of this file so you can understand how to customize the keynotes.

The first few rows of the file (Figure 18.14) designate the grouping of the notes. In this example, they consist of a label (Division 03) followed by a tab and then a description (Concrete).

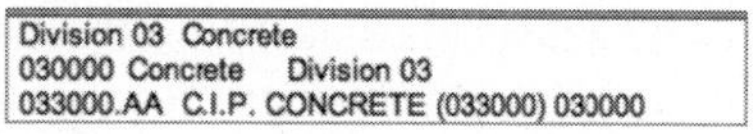

FIGURE 18.14
The keynote TXT file header

```
Division 03 Concrete
030000 Concrete    Division 03
033000.AA C.I.P. CONCRETE (033000) 030000
```

Directly below this header is a secondary, or minor, grouping. This secondary grouping follows the same format as the primary group and provides better control over how the keynotes are displayed within Revit. This line follows the same format as the first: Label (030000), then a tab, then a description (Concrete), then another tab, and then a reference to the parent code (Division 03). This last entry must match the label in the line above. This designates the second line as a subset to the first line. You can add as many or as few subgroups as you'd like. In our case, we have subcategories for each division, but that's not necessary.

Below the grouping are the contents of that group. These lines are articulated in the following format:

Label [tab] Description (note body) [tab] Grouping

In the example shown in Figure 18.14, this reads as follows (where the [tab] is an actual tab, not the text):

033000.A1 [tab] C.I.P. CONCRETE (033000) [tab] 030000

To get an idea of how this will all look once loaded into Revit, see Figure 18.15, which shows you the Keynotes dialog box with Division 03 expanded.

FIGURE 18.15
The Keynotes dialog box

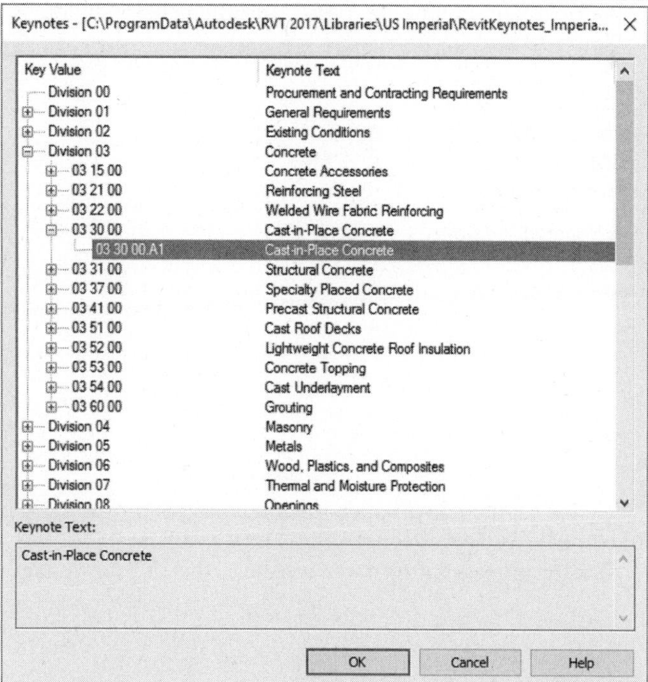

Using the keynote file approach lets you add, remove, or edit notes and groups of notes. It might seem frustrating to have to open and load a separate TXT file every time you want to add or remove notes from the keynote list. However, remember that this also maintains consistency and a level of control over the master list that isn't available with simple text objects. Although it might be slow at stages to get all the project notes into the TXT file, it also means that the time you'll spend checking and verifying the notes is dramatically reduced.

If you find that editing keynotes in an external TXT file that is segregated from the project environment does not suit your needs, tools are available online to help you manage keynotes using a graphical interface. Revolution Design has created a tool called Keynote Manager (`www.revolutiondesign.biz`) that will manage your keynote list, create headings and subheadings, and format the TXT file in a way that Revit can read it. Tools like this are great for speeding up the editing process for keynotes and maintaining proper formatting of the TXT file.

Accessing Keynote Settings and Loading the TXT File

Now that the keynote TXT file is established and you've begun populating it with annotations, you need to link it to your project. Loading this file into the project is simple and needs to happen only once. Additionally, loading this keynote file is a project setting, not a user setting. Once the file is linked, all team members will have access to the keynotes. As a side note, if you are working in a team environment, make sure to place the keynote file in a location everyone has access to, like a network resource. Placing it on your C: drive will allow you access to it but will not allow others on your team to see the notes.

To access the keynote settings and load the keynote text file, go to the Annotate tab in the ribbon, locate the Tag panel, and then click Keynote ➤ Keynoting Settings, as shown in Figure 18.16.

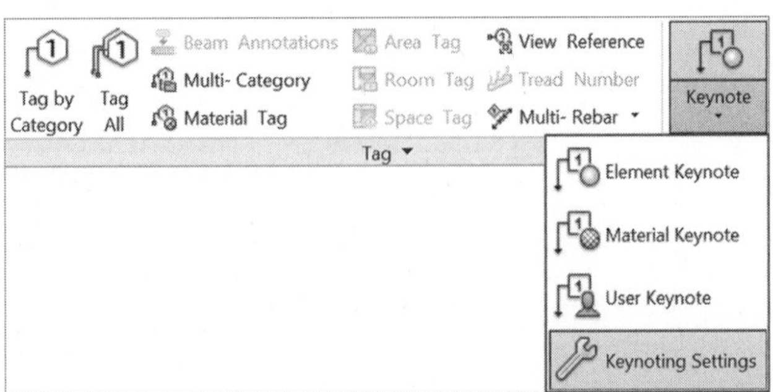

Figure 18.16 Accessing the Keynoting Settings

This command will open the Keynoting Settings dialog box (Figure 18.17). Here, you can define the project's keynote file as well as adjust some other settings. To load the keynote file, click the Browse button and navigate to the TXT file you created.

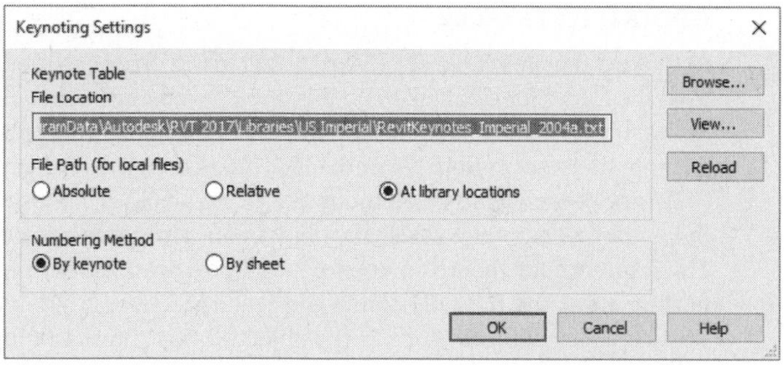

FIGURE 18.17
The Keynoting Settings dialog box

Here are some other variables that you can set in the Keynoting Settings dialog box:

File Path File Path defines how Revit Architecture looks for your text file using one of three methods:

Absolute The Absolute option follows the UNC naming conventions and navigates across your network or workstation for a specified location.

Relative This option locates the text file relative to your RVT project file. If you move the RVT file and the text file and maintain the same folder structure, the keynote file will be found and automatically loaded.

At Library Locations This option lets you put the text file in the default library location defined in the File Locations tab of the Options dialog box (Application ➤ Options).

Numbering Method Numbering Method defines how the keynotes are numbered:

By Keynote This option allows you to number keynotes as they come from the associated text file.

By Sheet With this option enabled, the keynotes are numbered sequentially on a per-sheet basis.

LOADING OR RELOADING KEYNOTES

Once the keynote TXT file is loaded into Revit, it is available for the team to use. As we've mentioned, changes can be made to this file on the fly while the project is open and active. Although this is true, if changes are made to the keynote file while the project is open, the keynote file will need to be reloaded into the project for the changes to be visible to other team members. There are two ways to do this:

- Open the Keynoting Settings dialog box and click the Reload button. Once this is done, you'll need to use Synchronize With Central (if the project is workshared), and your team members will also need to use SWC to gain access to the changes.
- Close and reopen your project file.

Adding Keynotes

Download the project file `c18-Sample-Building-Start.rvt` and the keynote file `MARA_Keynotes.txt` from the folder for Chapter 18 on this book's web page at `www.sybex.com/go/masteringrevit2017`. Make sure you place them in the same folder on your computer because the path setting for the keynote file is set to Relative in the RVT file. Open the RVT project file to begin the exercise.

To add keynotes to an element in a project model, choose one of the three keynote types from the Annotate tab; then select the object you want to annotate in your view and insert a keynote. The sequence for inserting keynotes is arrowhead, leader segment, and then keynote. Similar to placing a tag, the Keynote command (even the User keynote) requires an object to be selected to start the insertion sequence. If the object doesn't have a note already defined, you'll be prompted to pick a note from the Keynotes dialog box. Figure 18.18 shows a sample of this list.

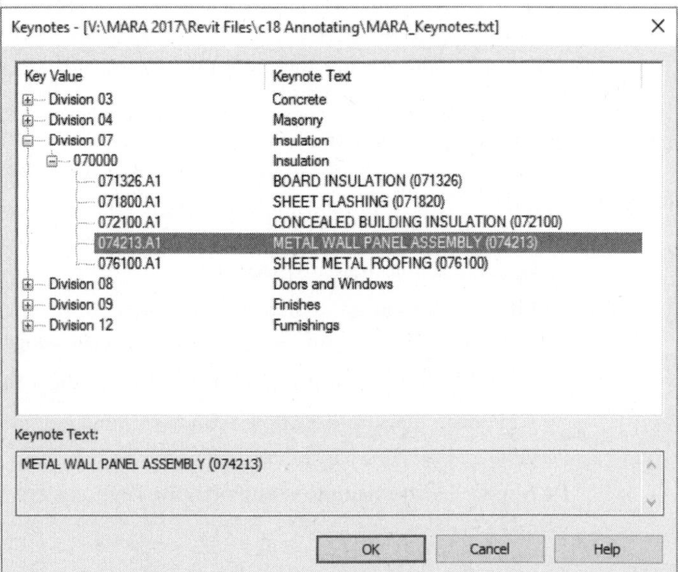

Figure 18.18 Choosing a keynote to insert

Let's explore this functionality with a quick exercise in which you will annotate a detail with keynotes. Follow these steps:

1. From the Project Browser, expand the Sections (Wall Section) heading and activate the view named Window Sill Detail.
2. Go to the Annotate tab in the ribbon and select Keynote ➢ Element Keynote on the Tag panel.
3. Select the window in the view and then place the leader and keynote.

   You will see that the keynote code has already been populated because the keynote has already been defined in the type properties for the window family.
4. With the Element Keynote command still active, click the wood sill detail component and place another keynote. This time, the Keynotes dialog box will appear because no keynote was defined in the wall's type properties. Select the keynote labeled 061100.A1 and then close the dialog box.

5. Go back to the Annotate tab in the ribbon and select Keynote ➤ Material Keynote.
6. Select the cross-hatched material at the right side of the wall below the window. Again, the Keynotes dialog box will appear because a keynote value was not defined in that material's identity data. Select the keynote labeled 071300.A1 and then close the dialog box.

The results will look like the image in Figure 18.19.

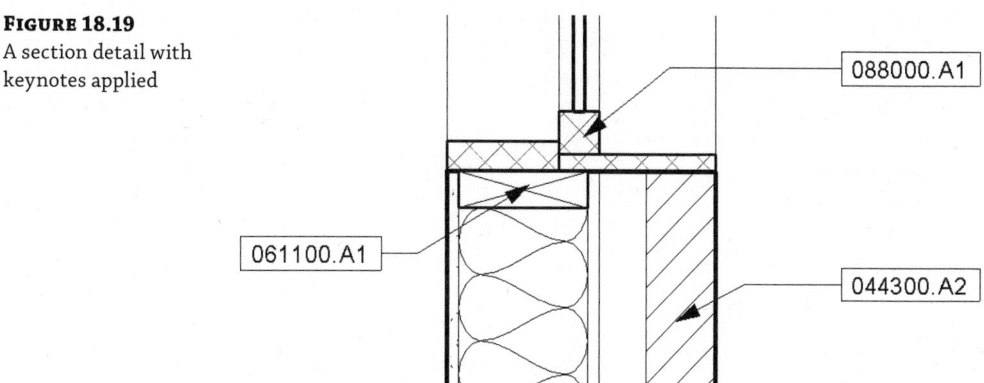

FIGURE 18.19 A section detail with keynotes applied

CREATING KEYNOTE LEGENDS

Depending on your choice of keynote and your workflow, you might want to create a legend on each sheet for your notes. You might want only the keynotes that are shown on a given sheet to dynamically appear in the legend. Or you might want to have one legend that will show all keynotes used throughout the project.

These legends usually reside on the side of a sheet near the title block information and can take one of two forms. The first type is all-inclusive and shows every note within the project. This style has the benefit of consistency between sheets in the set. The same note will always be in the same location in the list; however, this type of list can become quite long for larger projects. The other type of keynote list includes only the notes that show up on a particular sheet. This has the advantage of supplying a list of notes customized for each sheet without extraneous information. Creating either list manually has traditionally been challenging. One of the benefits of Revit Architecture is the ability to completely automate either list type, thus removing much of the chance for error in the process. Let's review how to create both types of lists.

Creating a keynote legend is simple: Choose the Legends button on the View tab and select Keynote Legend from the drop-down list (Figure 18.20). Once you launch the command, name the keynote legend, and then click OK.

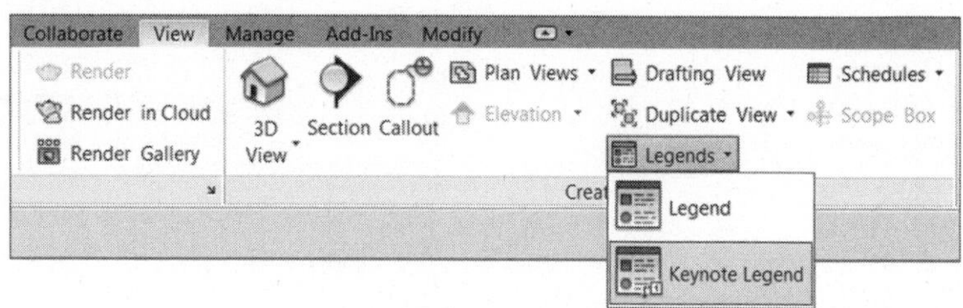

FIGURE 18.20 The Keynote Legend button

You'll be presented with what looks like a typical schedule dialog box, called Keynote Legend Properties. There are only two fields available in a keynote legend, and by default, they are both loaded into the Scheduled Fields side of the Fields tab (Figure 18.21). Those fields are as follows:

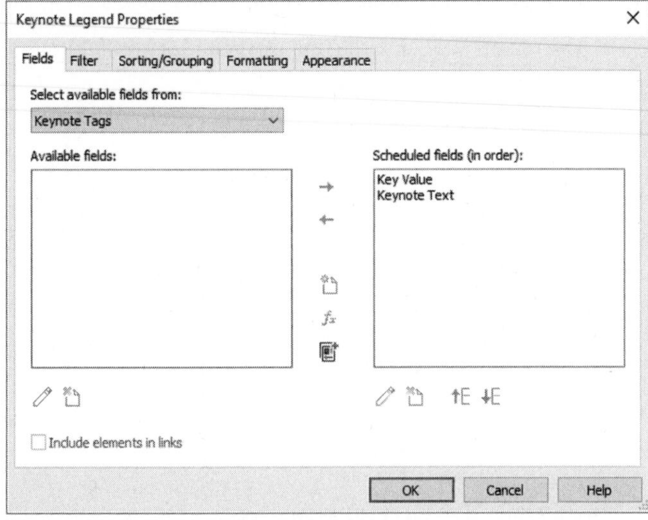

FIGURE 18.21
The Fields tab of the Keynote Legend Properties dialog box

Key Value This field contains the numeric value of the keynote.

Keynote Text This field contains the text description for the keynote.

A keynote legend works like any other schedule as far as formatting and appearance go. By default, the sorting and grouping are already established because the key value is used to sort. The one special item of note is located on the Filter tab. At the bottom of this tab is a feature unique to this type of schedule: a Filter By Sheet check box (Figure 18.22). Selecting this box gives you the ability to filter the list specifically for each sheet set; leaving the box deselected will supply a full list of the keynotes over the entire project.

FIGURE 18.22
The Filter By Sheet option on the Filter tab in the Keynote Legend Properties dialog box

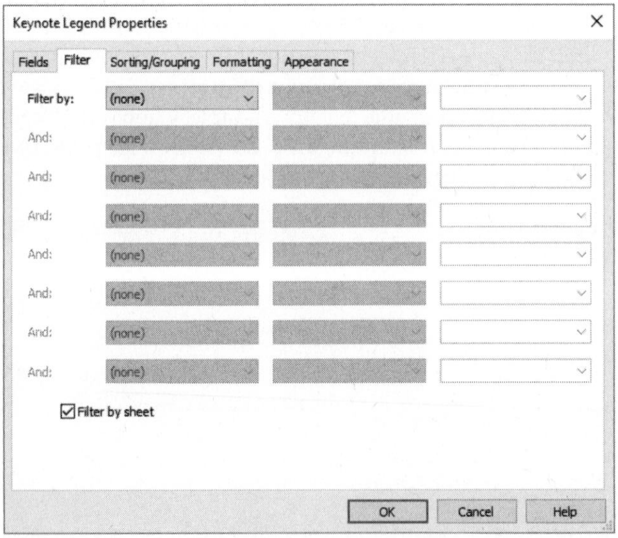

Like any other type of legend, a keynote legend can be placed on sheets again and again within the project. You're not limited to only one instance of the legend on a sheet as you are with other view types. Additionally, if you choose the keynote legend that filters by sheet, it will dynamically modify the note list based on individual sheet contents. As views are added or removed from a sheet or notes are added to the project, the keynote legend updates accordingly.

Keynote legends are considered to be another type of legend view and will appear under the Legends node of the Project Browser.

A Schedule for Keynotes

Creating a schedule for keynotes is a great way to find single-use notes and typos in a project. If you are working on a project team, there's always a chance that someone could be inserting an incorrect keynote into the project. Scheduling the notes is an efficient approach to managing the annotation process and gives you the tools to verify consistency. Scheduling keynotes allows you to do three things:

- List all the notes within a project and verify their spelling and accuracy.
- Find odd or one-off instances. Sometimes this can mean the note was accidentally placed in lieu of another note.
- Make sure all the keynotes in the project are represented in the specifications.

Using the Keynote Family

Revit Architecture comes with a default keynote family that allows you to produce both keynotes and text notes using the default keynote TXT file. The family name is `Keynote Tag.rfa`. This family has four types that let you change note styles within the project, as Figure 18.23 shows.

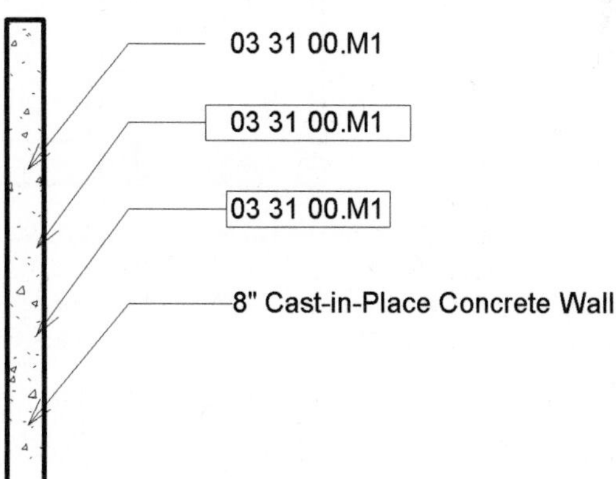

Figure 18.23 Keynote styles available in the default tag

Here are the four default styles:

- Keynote Number
- Keynote Number – Boxed – Large
- Keynote Number – Boxed – Small
- Keynote Text

Each of these tag types pulls information from the text file we discussed previously in this chapter and reports it at the end of the leader. To change your keynotes between any of these options, select the keynote and choose a different type in the Type Selector.

Annotating with Tags

Tags are text labels for elements such as doors, walls, windows, rooms, and several other objects that architects typically need to reference in a set of drawings. In Revit Architecture, tags are intelligent, bidirectional graphics that report information stored in an object's properties. Once you've tagged an element and entered a value in the tag, the tagged model element will retain that value until you remove it. The value lives with the model elements in a project; it is not a property of the tag. That means you can delete or remove tags without fear of losing the data entered into the tag. It also means that once an element is tagged with information in one view, if the tag is configured to report a type property, the same or similar elements will report the same information in any other view in which they are tagged without the necessity of entering the information twice. To understand this a bit better, take the example of a wall tag.

You've placed a wall tag in a view. The tag initially had "**?**" as a value, meaning that the Type Mark property for that wall was blank. In the wall tag, you've entered a wall type value of **A1**. In another view, you can now tag the same wall type and it will automatically display a value of A1. You can also delete any, or even all, of the tags for that wall, and new tags you place will still report the type number of A1.

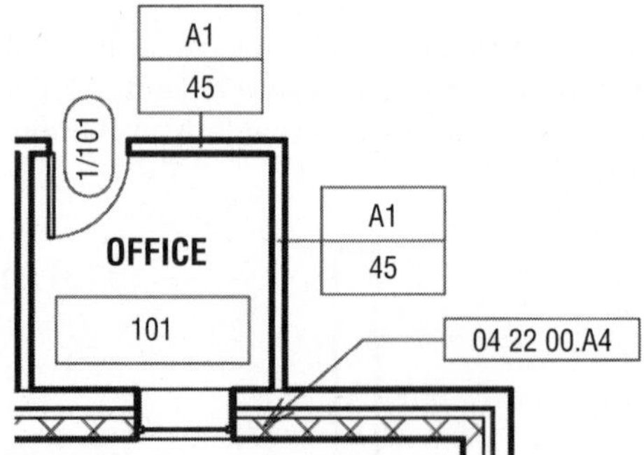

Keep in mind that you can also tag elements that are in linked models. Although you cannot edit the properties of these elements (for example, you cannot change the wall type or door number), you can add tags to any of the linked elements as if the same elements were part of your project file.

Tags are versatile elements for annotating your designs. A tag can display a door number, but it can just as easily display any other properties of the door, such as fire rating, cost, or material type.

Inserting Tags

Tags can be automatically inserted when a model element, such as a door or room, is placed within the project (by checking the Tag On Placement option in the contextual tab of the ribbon), or they can be inserted later. The options to place a tag are all located on the Tag panel of the Annotate tab (Figure 18.24).

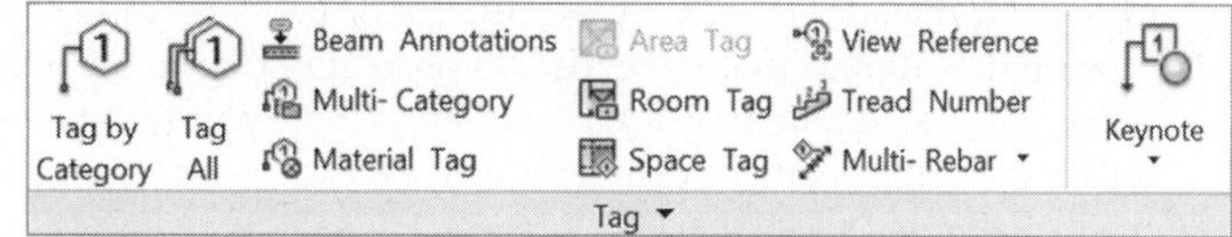

FIGURE 18.24
Tag tools in the Annotate tab

When you're adding tags, it's not necessary to find or choose the right tag—they will be assigned automatically. Tag families are specific to the elements to which they are being tagged. For example, you use a door tag to tag a door, but you can't use a door tag to tag a wall or other element within the project. Figure 18.25 shows you some of the tags that are available; there is a tag for each type of object. You can customize each of the tag family types so you can graphically differentiate your door tags from wall tags, room tags, area tags, and so on.

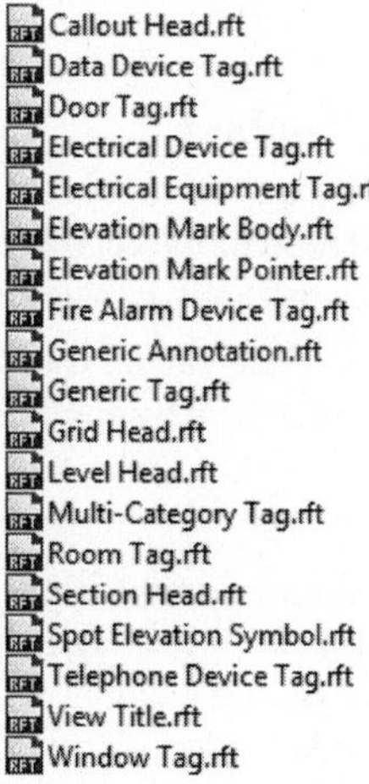

FIGURE 18.25
Listing of various tag families

When inserting a tag, you'll have several placement options available in the Options bar, as shown in Figure 18.26.

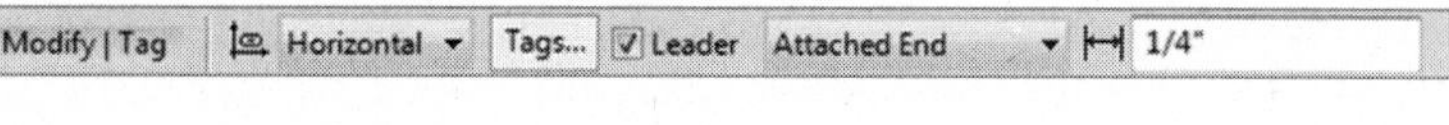

FIGURE 18.26
The Options bar when placing a tag

Orientation The first option allows you to orient the tag horizontally or vertically. Tags, like text, will always read from either the bottom or the right side of the sheet or view.

The Tags Button Clicking this button opens the Loaded Tags and Symbols dialog box, where you can load various tags.

Leader The final three options relate to the tag leader. You can select the Leader check box (or turn it off) to have a leader show (or not show). Although attached leaders are the default for tags, the Leader drop-down can be changed from Attached End to Free End if you don't want to associate the end of the leader with the element you've selected. Using the Free End option allows the leader to float free of the object. The final option of this set for leaders is the default leader length. By default, the value is set to 1/2" (12 mm). When you're placing tags like wall tags that have leaders perpendicular to the wall they are tagging, it is a good idea to set a default length with which you are comfortable. You can adjust the tag location after inserting them, but sometimes it's easier to set a good default value in leader length.

New to Revit 2017 is the ability to pin tags. Like Keynotes, a pinned tag will retain its location even if the element it has tagged has been relocated. This can be beneficial to keep small changes to elements from impacting several views prior to a deadline, but it can be equally problematic by allowing elements that have been dramatically changed to look incorrectly tagged.

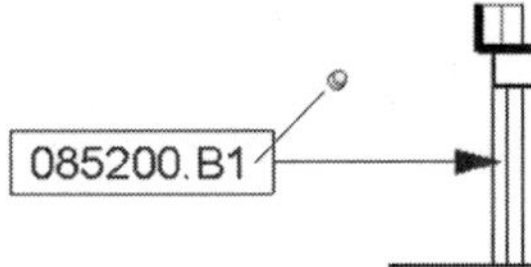

Using the Tag Toolset

On the Annotate tab, you'll find several tools that you can use to insert tags. Look back at Figure 18.24 to see these tools. Each has a different purpose and can be used in conjunction with other tools or separately to help document your project. Let's take a look at each one:

Tag By Category The Tag By Category button is possibly one of the most frequently used Tag commands. As we mentioned before, several tags are available, allowing you to tag a host of elements in the model. Click the Tag By Category button when you want to tag one element at a time, regardless of its category.

Using this tag command will allow you to select a door, a window, a wall—whatever single element you want to apply a tag to in the model. As you hover over elements, the tag type that corresponds to that element will be shown. Should the element you are trying to tag not have the associated tag loaded in the project, you will be prompted to load it (Figure 18.27).

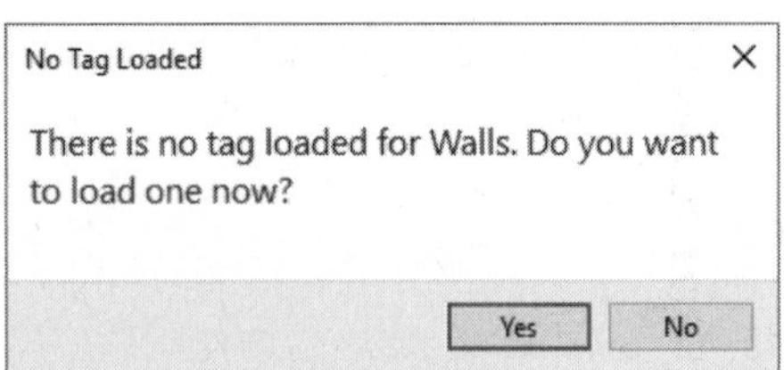

FIGURE 18.27
Loading a tag for a specific element type

Tag All The Tag All button, which activates the Tag All Not Tagged command, will do exactly that: tag all the untagged elements of a selected category within a given view. For example, you can tag all the doors. Or you can tag all doors, walls, and rooms—or any combination of any list of elements. When you select the Tag All command, the Tag All Not Tagged dialog box will appear (Figure 18.28). This dialog box displays a list of the elements in the view for which you have already loaded tags. Here, you can specify which elements can get tagged, what tag will be used, and if that tag will have a leader assigned to it. Use the Ctrl key on your keyboard to select more than one element from the list. When you've selected the categories you would like tagged, click OK.

FIGURE 18.28
Tag All Not Tagged dialog box

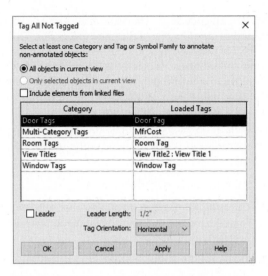

Tag All Not Tagged

Select at least one Category and Tag or Symbol Family to annotate non-annotated objects:

(•) All objects in current view
( ) Only selected objects in current view
[ ] Include elements from linked files

Category	Loaded Tags
Door Tags	Door Tag
Multi-Category Tags	MfrCost
Room Tags	Room Tag
View Titles	View Title2 : View Title 1
Window Tags	Window Tag

[ ] Leader Leader Length: 1/2"
Tag Orientation: Horizontal

OK Cancel Apply Help

Tagging all the elements within a view can be a wonderful time-saver—but only if you're okay with the software choosing the location for each of the tags. For example, the tags will be placed in the middle of the rooms. For most spaces, that will work just fine. For other tag types, such as walls or doors, you might have to adjust tag locations to make sure everything reads properly.

Room Tag and Area Tag These two tag types work in much the same way. They will tag the room elements or area elements, depending on the type of view in which you happen to be. In other words, Room tags will work only in plans and elevations, whereas Area tags can be placed only in area plans. To tag rooms or areas, simply select the tag type you want and select the room or area object. When you place rooms or areas initially, the tag option is selected by default.

Material Tag The Material tag is used to annotate specific materials within a model element, similar to the Material keynote. The main difference from the keynote is that the tag does not use an external TXT file to read additional information about the tagged element. The default Material tag will display the Material Description value (Figure 18.29, left) as opposed to the Keynote value. You can always customize the Material tag to display other values such as the Mark, as shown in Figure 18.29 (right).

FIGURE 18.29
Two options for tagging materials

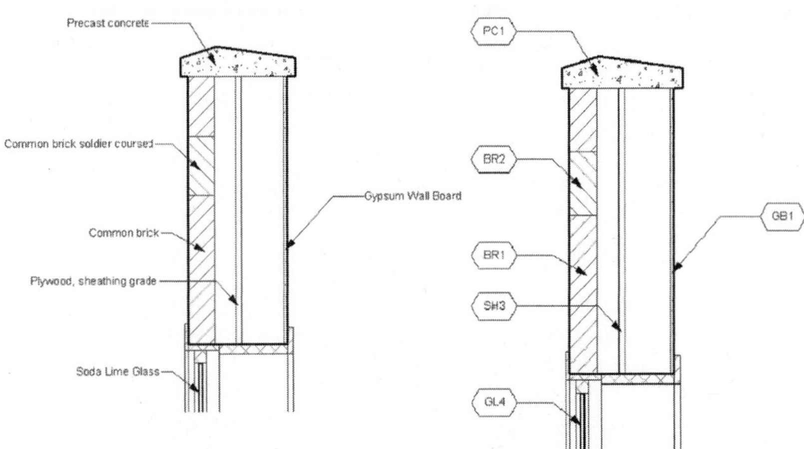

Multi-Category Tag The Multi-Category tag allows you to use the same tag style in a project to tag elements of different categories. This tag type can be useful in a number of ways. Let's say you want to tag several elements in a floor plan and call out their manufacturer and unit cost. Typically, you would have to create a few different tag families to tag furniture, casework, lighting, and so on. Now a single tag type can do this for you by tagging the same field (like manufacturer or unit cost) across different element types. Let's step through making a Multi-Category tag.

From the book's web page, download the `c18-Sample-Building-Start.rvt` or `c18-Sample-Metric-Start.rvt` file or continue with the exercise file from the previous section. Then follow these steps:

1. Activate the Level 1 floor plan.
2. Click the Application menu and choose New ➤ Family. This will take you to the default family templates. Open the Annotations folder and choose Multi-Category `Tag.rft` or Metric Multi-Category `Tag.rft`.
3. In the Family Editor, go to the Create tab and select the Label tool. Click near the intersection of the reference planes in the view to place a label.
4. Once the label is placed in the view, the Edit Label dialog box opens (Figure 18.30). Here you'll see a list of the parameters that are common across multiple family types—Assembly Code, Cost, Family Name, and Model, among others. Select Manufacturer and Cost from the list and click the icon with the green arrow to add them to the Label Parameters list. Make sure the Manufacturer parameter is above the Cost parameter (you can do this by selecting Manufacturer and then the Move Parameter Up button). Select the Break option in the Cost row. Click OK to close the dialog box.

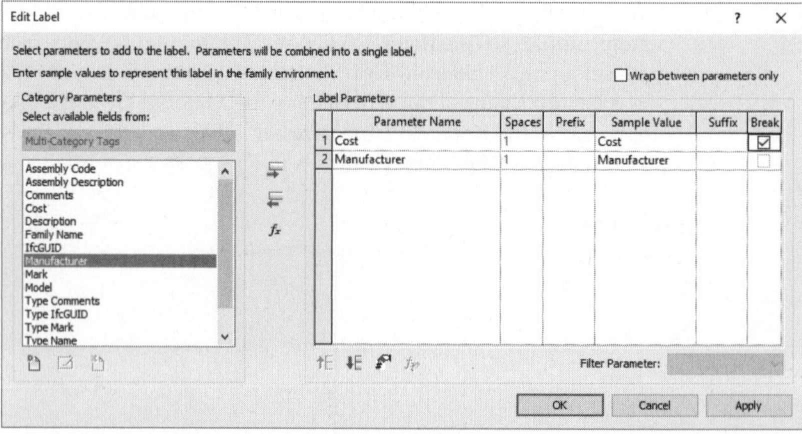

FIGURE 18.30
Adding parameters to a label

5. Save the family as **`MfrCost.rfa`** and then click the Load Into Project button in the ribbon. If you have multiple project files open, select the `c18-Sample-Building-Start.rvt` project file when prompted.

6. Back in the project file, switch to the Annotate tab in the ribbon, locate the Tag panel, and then click the Multi-Category button. Click one of the chairs in the space named LOUNGE. When the tag is placed, you will see a question mark, indicating that this element has no predefined value for either Manufacturer or Cost. Press the Esc key twice or click Modify to exit the Tag command, select the tag you just placed, and then click the question mark.

7. The Change Parameter Values dialog box (Figure 18.31) opens. This dialog box is used only when a tag has multiple parameters assigned to a single label. Otherwise, you would usually be able to type a value directly into a tag. Enter values for both Manufacturer and Cost, and then click OK. You'll get a dialog box stating that you're changing a type parameter that could affect many other elements. Click Yes and then OK to accept that change.

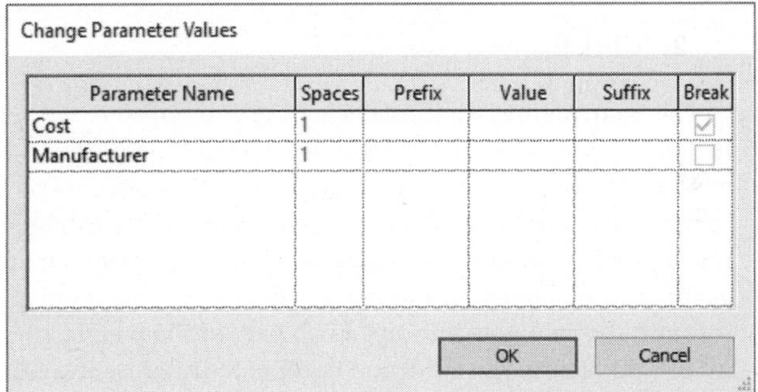

FIGURE 18.31 Changing the parameter values

8. As you hover your mouse over other elements in this view, you'll notice the same behavior as with other tags. Elements that have predefined values will show the tag filled in while elements without values will have question marks. Add a few more tags, and you can begin to see some of the versatility of the Multi-Category tag.

Adding Dimensions

Dimensions are used to convey the distance or angle between elements or parts of elements. In Revit, a dimension is a bidirectional annotation, which means that you can edit the distance directly within the dimension string to move elements a specific distance apart and the dimension updates automatically as the distance between elements changes. Dimensions are annotations, making them view-specific elements that appear only in the view in which they're drawn. The Dimension tools are located on the Annotate tab.

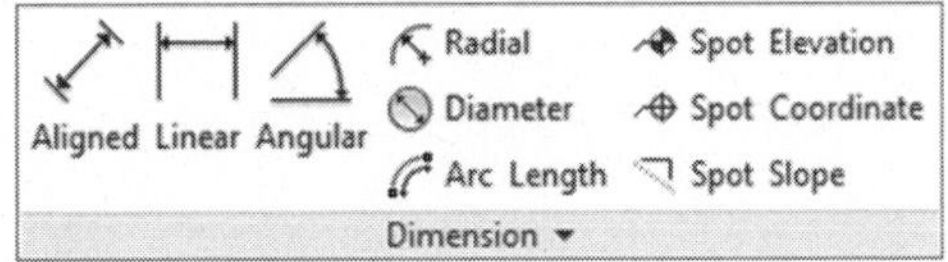

Like all annotations in Revit, dimensions will automatically adjust to the scale of the view. If you change the view scale, the dimensions automatically resize. By default, a Linear string of dimensions only dimensions parallel entities. Nonparallel elements by their very nature have a dynamic dimensional relationship. Dimensions in Revit Architecture always read from the bottom or from the right, following standard architectural sheet layout conventions.

To place a dimension, choose any Dimension tool and begin selecting multiple entities. You can keep selecting multiple entities in any sequence, creating a dimension string across your view. Click anywhere in an open area of the view to finish selecting entities and place the dimension string.

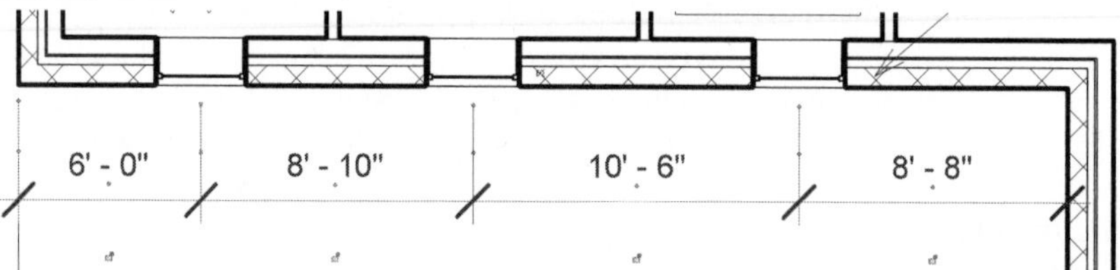

When any Dimension tool is active, you will see two settings available in the Options bar that are specifically related to walls. The first drop-down list allows you to specify the default method for dimensioning wall geometry. You can choose from wall centerlines, wall faces, center of core, or faces of core. This setting merely establishes the defaults—what will be selected when you first click a wall with the Dimension tool. If you need to select a different part of a wall, hover the mouse cursor over a wall segment and then press the Tab key to cycle through the available options. Each part of the wall segment geometry will highlight at the mouse pointer as you continue to repeatedly press the Tab key.

The second option allows you to pick either individual references (default) or entire walls. When the Entire Walls option is selected, click the Options button to modify the Auto Dimension settings, shown in Figure 18.32. In this example, we have chosen to dimension opening widths as well as intersecting walls. The dimension string shown was placed with a single click on the exterior wall!

FIGURE 18.32
Changing the Auto Dimension option

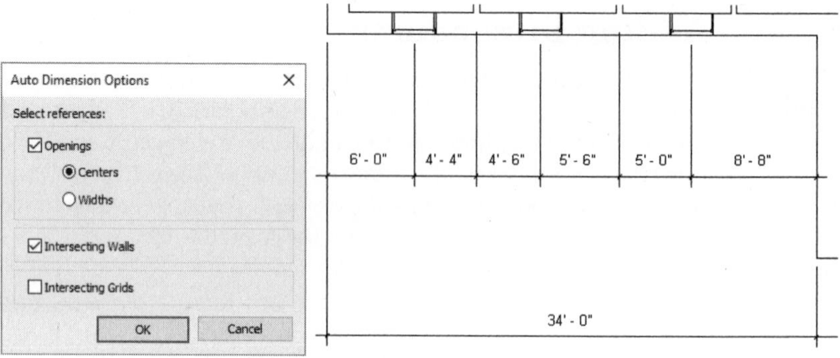

Once a dimension string is placed, you have several options to customize the string, the dimension values, and the witness lines (the linework that makes up the dimension). In Figure 18.33, you can see a typical aligned dimension string that has been selected after placement. Let's take a look at each of the available controls:

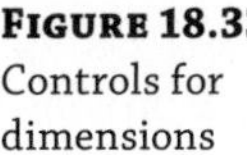

FIGURE 18.33
Controls for dimensions

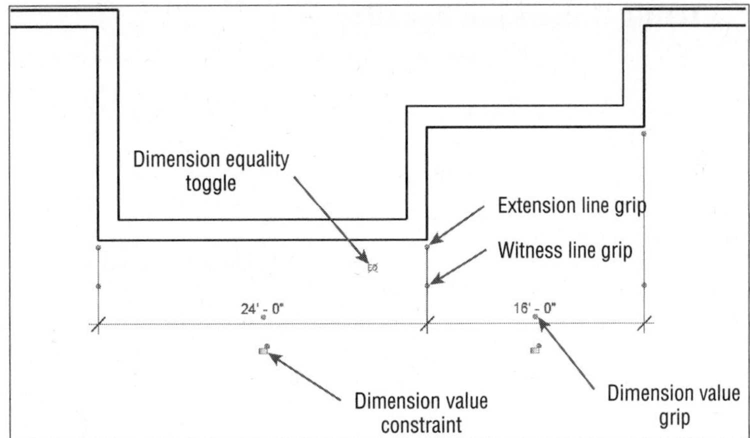

Dimension Value Grip To adjust the position of any of the dimension values, especially for shorter dimension strings where the value might overlap the witness lines, click and drag the dimension value grip to relocate the text. The leader settings associated with dimension values are found in the dimension type properties. If you need to reset the position of the dimension value, right-click the dimension string and select Reset Dimension Text Position from the context menu.

Extension Line Grip The predefined distance that separates the dimensioned object from the beginning of the extension line is specified in the dimension type properties as Witness Line Gap To Element; however, you may need to manually adjust the extension line in some circumstances. Click and drag the extension line grip, and you will also notice that the grip will snap into place near the predefined distance if you need to return the extension line to its original gap distance.

Witness Line Grip The grip on each extension line that is closer to the dimension string is the witness line grip. This control allows you to move the witness line to a different entity. Click and drag this control to another object in the project and the dimension string will automatically update.

Dimension Value Constraint The *lock* symbol allows you to preserve a dimension value so that it cannot be changed unless the constraint is removed. This functionality can be used to preserve dimension values for minimum widths of corridors, floor-to-floor heights, and other special features of your designs. As powerful as this feature is, you should use it only when absolutely necessary, because an overly constrained model can create problems you may have difficulty unraveling. Remember, with great power comes great responsibility.

Dimension Equality Toggle Another powerful control included with dimensions is the ability to set all the values of a selected dimension string to be equal. And because the dimension is a bidirectional annotation, the model elements associated with the dimensions will be spaced equally as well.

Using Dimension Equality

When you choose to use the dimension equality toggle, there are a few unique options to customize how the values are displayed. In the type properties of a dimension style, you can specify the default text displayed as well as a formula and how the witness lines are displayed (Figure 18.34).

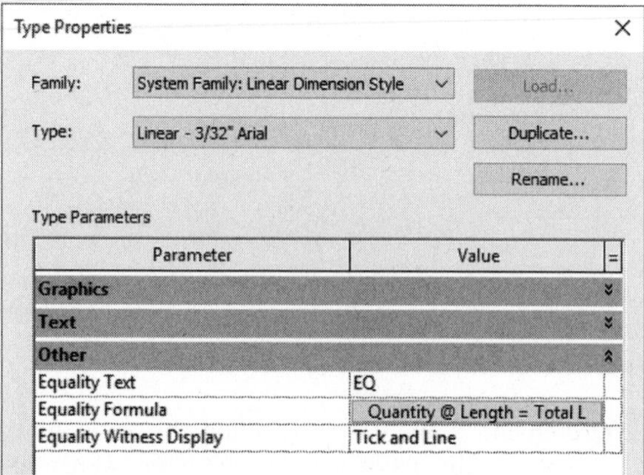

FIGURE 18.34 Equality settings in the dimension style type properties

When you click the Equality Formula button, you can specify a customized string of values to best express the intention of the equality and, new to Revit 2017, how those values will be shown on the dimension string. In the example shown in Figure 18.35, the parameters Number Of Segments, Length Of Segment, and Total Length are selected with suffix symbols to display the complete result in the dimension string, as shown at the bottom of the figure.

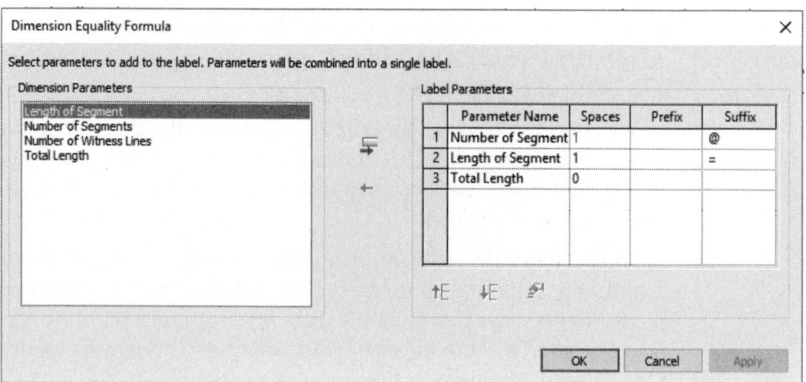

FIGURE 18.35 Using a customized equality formula

Customizing Dimension Text

One of the main benefits of dimensions in Revit Architecture is that they cannot be overridden to display a different length or angle other than what is actually being measured. This may come as a shock if you have used Autodesk® AutoCAD® software in your past experience, but this restriction is necessary to maintain the integrity of the building information model.

Even though you cannot override the value of the dimension, you have the ability to either append some text to a dimension value or override the length or angle with a text string. To access these settings, double-click any dimension string to open the Dimension Text dialog box. In the example shown in Figure 18.36, the text HOLD has been added to appear below the dimension string, indicating that the dimension is to be maintained during construction.

FIGURE 18.36
Custom text appended to a dimension value

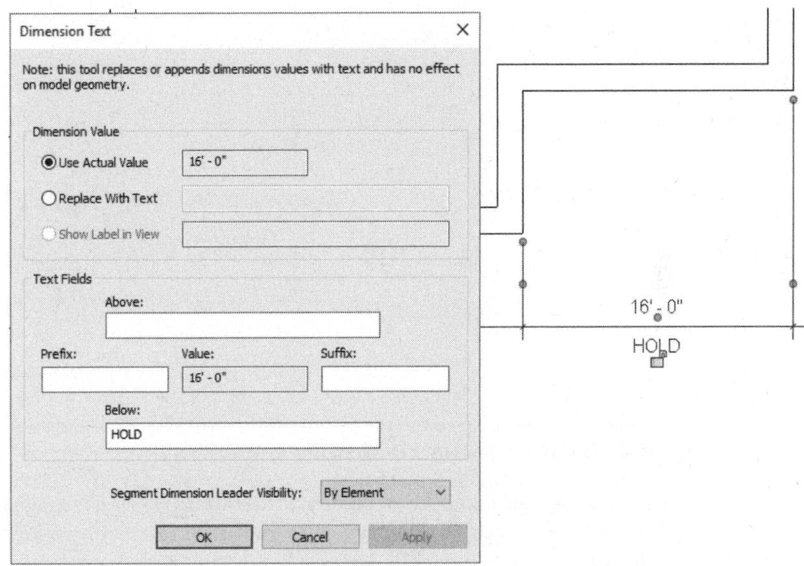

You'll notice the option Replace With Text at the top of the Dimension Text dialog box. You might think you can override the dimension value with a string representing another length or angle value, but a warning will prevent you from entering any numeric values.

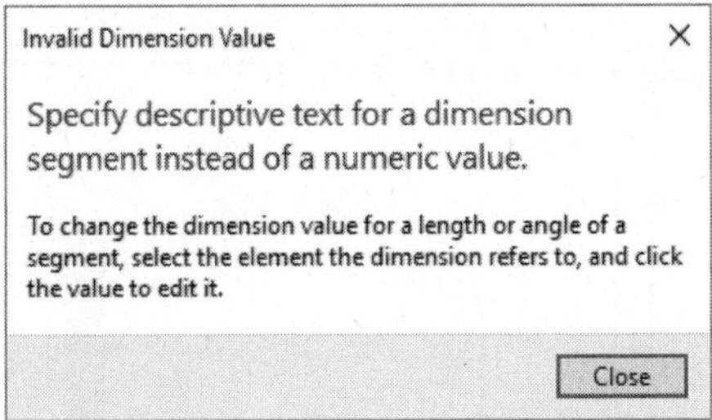

The Replace With Text option can be used to indicate various conditions for the purpose of construction tolerances. For example, you may have a series of similar conditions where new construction abuts existing conditions and you simply want the dimension to display VARIES, as shown in Figure 18.37.

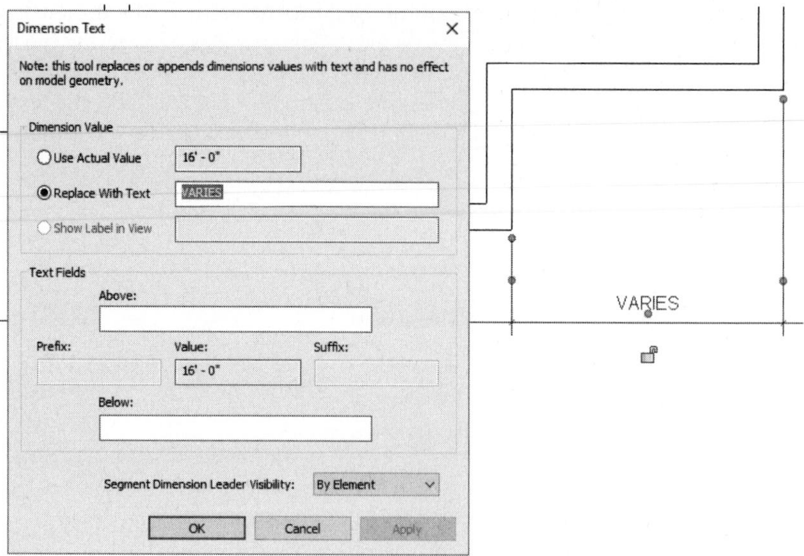

FIGURE 18.37 Custom text replacing a dimension value

USING DIMENSIONS TO MODIFY GEOMETRY

We have trained hundreds of new Revit Architecture users through the years, and one of the most misunderstood concepts is how to use dimensions to modify model geometry. We just discussed the method for customizing dimension text, but users often will use this same method to make a change to model elements. This results in frustration when all you get is the Dimension Text dialog box.

To develop a clearer understanding of this concept, remember that a simple dimension string is a measurement between two objects. If you select the dimension, the software does not know which object you are intending to move. Instead, pick the model element first and then select an associated dimension to change its value, and the element will be moved.

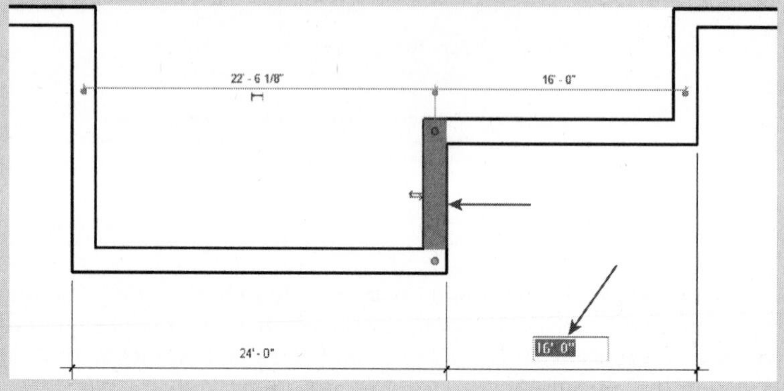

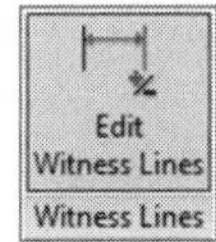

Editing Dimension Strings

As you continue to annotate your project with dimensions, you will likely need to edit dimension strings to combine, split, or add new witness lines. Most of these editing functions can be done with the Edit Witness Lines command. You will find this command in the contextual ribbon when you select a dimension string in a view.

Let's walk through each of these dimension-editing scenarios with some exercises. Download and open the file `c18-Dimensions-Start.rvt` or `c18-Dimensions-Metric-Start.rvt` from this book's web page, and then follow these steps:

1. Activate the Level 1 floor plan and zoom in to the lower-left portion of the layout. You will see that some dimensions have already been placed and you will need to edit them (Figure 18.38).

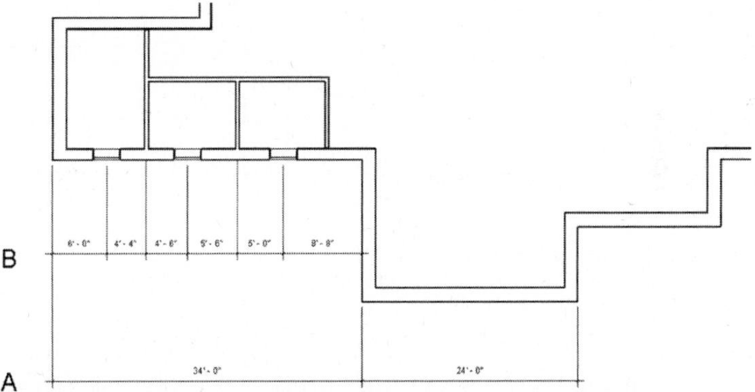

FIGURE 18.38 Sample project with dimension strings

2. Select the lower dimension string (indicated as A in the view) and then click the Edit Witness Lines command in the contextual ribbon.
3. Click the next vertical wall segment to the right of the layout and then the corner point. You might need to press the Tab key to place the dimension on the outer face of the wall and to snap to the angled corner.
4. To complete this editing command, click an open area of the view. Do not press the Esc key or you will lose the edits you just made.

   The results should look like Figure 18.39.

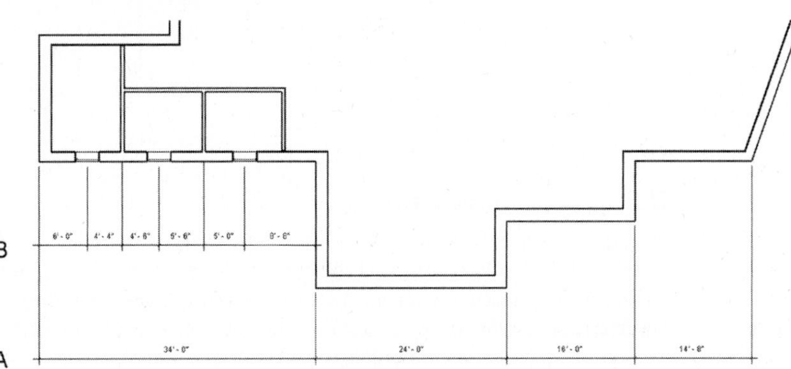

FIGURE 18.39 Adding witness lines to a dimension string

5. Now select the upper dimension string labeled as B in the view and once again activate the Edit Witness Lines command.
6. Click each of the intersecting interior partitions to remove them from the dimension string. Click an open area of the view to complete the command, and the results should look like Figure 18.40.

FIGURE 18.40
Removing witness lines from a dimension string

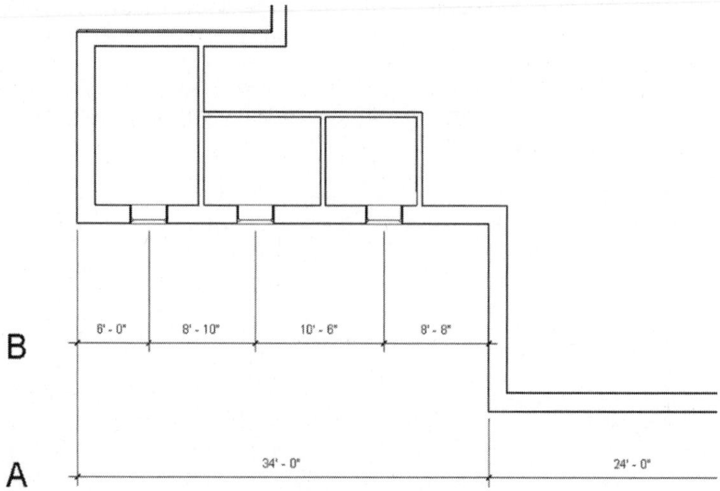

You can also delete any inner segment of a dimension string if you hover your mouse pointer over one segment in a dimension string and press the Tab key once. An individual segment will highlight; select this segment and then press the Delete key. Try this with the outer dimension segment from the previous exercise (Figure 18.41).

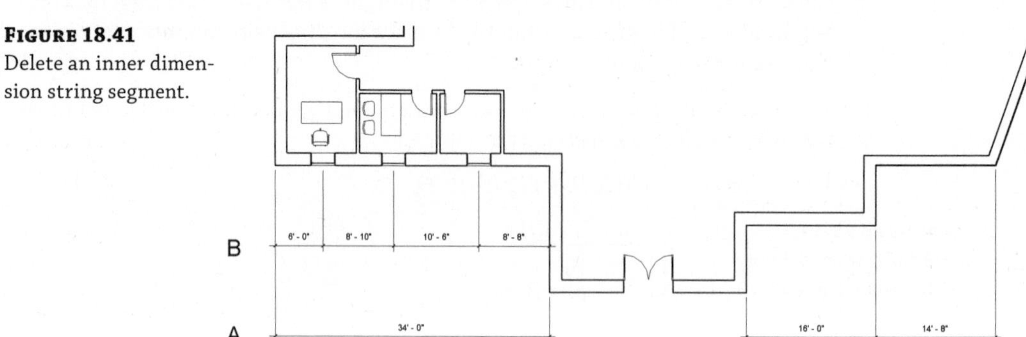

FIGURE 18.41
Delete an inner dimension string segment.

Using Alternate Units

Alternate Units allow you to show mixed Imperial and metric units within a single annotation. You can do this either to the right of the base dimension or below it. Just select one of the dimension strings and open its type properties. The Alternate Units settings are highlighted in Figure 18.42. Set Alternate Units to Below to show the alternate units below the dimension string.

FIGURE 18.42
Alternate Units settings

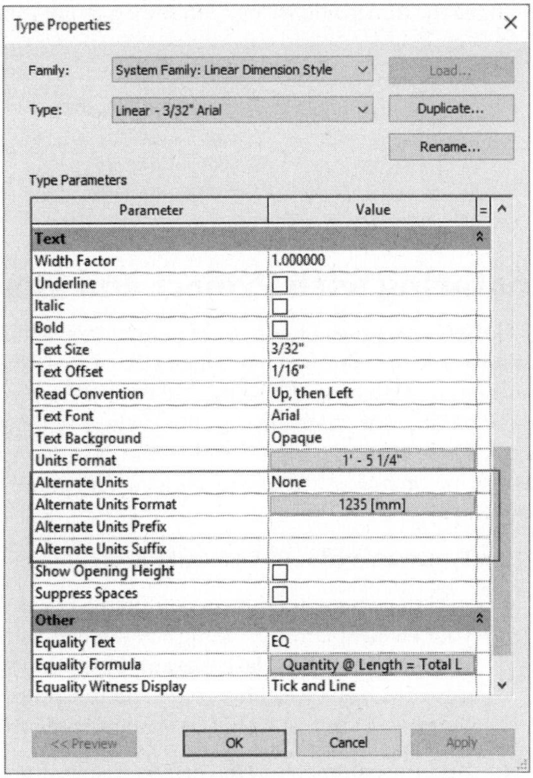

Type Properties

Family: System Family: Linear Dimension Style — Load...

Type: Linear - 3/32" Arial — Duplicate...

Rename...

Type Parameters

Parameter	Value
Text	
Width Factor	1.000000
Underline	☐
Italic	☐
Bold	☐
Text Size	3/32"
Text Offset	1/16"
Read Convention	Up, then Left
Text Font	Arial
Text Background	Opaque
Units Format	1' - 5 1/4"
Alternate Units	None
Alternate Units Format	1235 [mm]
Alternate Units Prefix	
Alternate Units Suffix	
Show Opening Height	☐
Suppress Spaces	☐
Other	
Equality Text	EQ
Equality Formula	Quantity @ Length = Total L
Equality Witness Display	Tick and Line

<< Preview | OK | Cancel | Apply

Let's explore how to use this tool:

1. Continuing from the previous exercise, select the dimension string B and click the Edit Type button in the Properties palette. You don't want all the dimensions to show both sets of units, so click the Duplicate button and name the new dimension string **Linear – 3/32″ Arial I/M** (**Linear - 2.5mm M/I** for the metric file).
2. In the same Type Properties dialog box, change Alternate Units to Below. Set the Alternate Units Format to Millimeters in the Imperial file (Feet And Fractional Inches in the metric file). So that you know the other number is a measurement in an alternate unit, in Alternate Units Suffix add **mm** in the Imperial file. The settings will look like Figure 18.43.
3. Click OK to close the dialog box.

FIGURE 18.43
Alternate Units Format settings

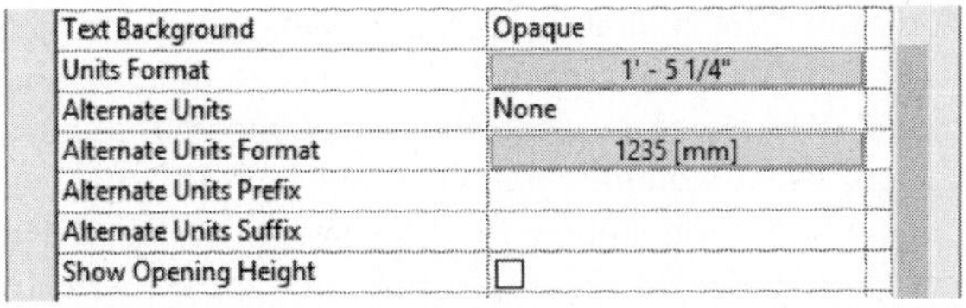

Parameter	Value
Text Background	Opaque
Units Format	1' - 5 1/4"
Alternate Units	None
Alternate Units Format	1235 [mm]
Alternate Units Prefix	
Alternate Units Suffix	
Show Opening Height	☐

You'll see the dimension string with Imperial units above and metric units below (Figure 18.44).

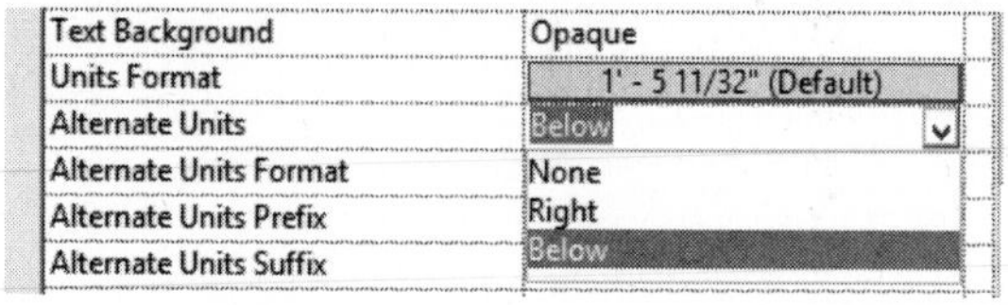

FIGURE 18.44
Alternate units in the model

Text Background	Opaque
Units Format	1' - 5 11/32" (Default)
Alternate Units	Below
Alternate Units Format	None
Alternate Units Prefix	Right
Alternate Units Suffix	Below

Annotating with Project and Shared Parameters

Every element in a project has a list of parameters. Some of these parameters, such as Assembly Code and Mark, are common parameters that are assigned to almost all object types. Others, such as Length, Height, and Volume, are unique to specific element types. Despite the plethora of default parameters, there are situations where you may need to add custom parameters to elements. These custom parameters, like the default ones, can be tagged and scheduled.

Depending on how you'd like to use a custom parameter, you can add them to your elements in a few ways:

- If all you want to do is schedule the new parameter, you have a couple of options:
  - Add the parameter directly within the schedule itself. This will add a new parameter to your element family. Adding a parameter using this method adds it only to the element family in the schedule. For example, say you want to schedule the sound transmission class (STC) of a wall. You could add this property directly within the wall schedule and the new parameter would be available only to objects in the Walls category.
  - Add the parameter to the project. Using this method, you can still schedule the new parameter, but you will have the option to add it to multiple categories. So, if you want to add a parameter for Unit Cost, you can add that to both your door and window categories at the same time.
- If you want to be able to both schedule *and* tag your parameter, you will need to create a *shared parameter*. This parameter is created as part of a separate file that is shared among the tag family, the element family, and the project. An example of this kind of tag might be for door security hardware. You can create a parameter that is assigned to a door family as well as a door tag that will allow you to designate whether or not a door has a card reader to gain entrance to a room.

In the following sections, we will discuss how to create both of these parameter types as well as the pros and cons of each.

Creating Project Parameters

You can create custom project parameters at any time in the project cycle. Depending on how you create the parameters, you can assign them to one or more element categories within the model. You can also assign them to elements that have already been created or to element categories for elements that you have yet to create.

The following steps will allow you to make a custom parameter that can be scheduled but not tagged. For this example, pretend you are working on an existing building and reworking a space. Much of what is onsite will need to be demolished, but you would like to reuse all the elements that are salvageable. As you are documenting the existing conditions, you want to schedule the elements you want to keep. To do this, you'll make a parameter called Reuse. Continue with the project file from the previous exercise (`c18-Dimensions-Start.rvt` or `c18-Dimensions-Metric-Start.rvt`).

To add a new project parameter, follow these steps:

1. Go to the Manage tab in the ribbon and click the Project Parameters button.

   This will display the Project Parameters dialog box (Figure 18.45).

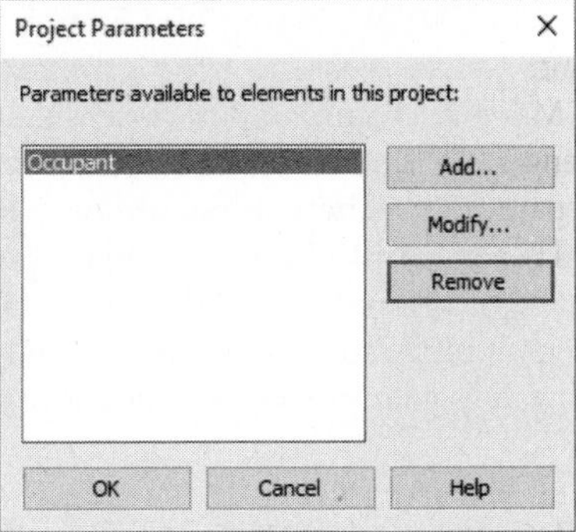

Figure 18.45
The Project Parameters dialog box

2. Click the Add button to open the Parameter Properties dialog box. Here you will be asked to define a list of properties for the new parameter.

   Let's step through what these selections will be (Figure 18.46 shows a view of the completed dialog box).

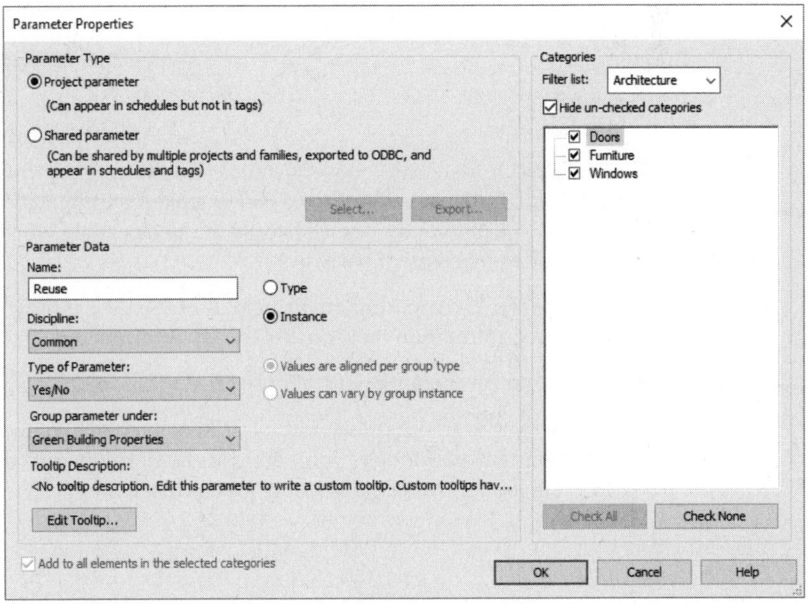

Figure 18.46
Setting the parameter properties (shown with Hide Un-checked Categories selected)

3. Set Parameter Type to Project Parameter.

   Choosing between project and shared parameter is the first choice you'll need to make. We'll get to shared parameters later, so for now, leave it at the default of Project Parameter.

4. For Name, type **Reuse**. The name is used for describing the parameter as well as referencing it in schedules and the Properties palette.

5. Leave the Discipline setting at Common.

   The Discipline drop-down menu will give you a few choices: Common, Structural, Electrical, HVAC, Piping, and Energy.

6. Set Type Of Parameter to Yes/No.

   This setting dictates the format or behavior of the parameter. As you can see in Figure 18.47, a variety of parameter types are available. It's important to understand some of these options and, more specifically, their differences. If you start creating formulas with your parameters, you'll quickly understand how important it is to use the proper type. For instance, you cannot multiply Angle × Volume. Text cannot be added to a formula. Integers do not have decimal values. Many of these values are easy to understand if you apply a bit of logic.

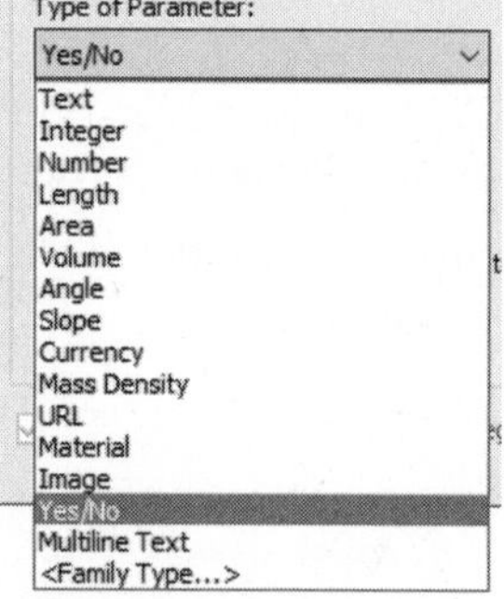

FIGURE 18.47 Listing of available parameter types

7. For Type Or Instance, choose Instance. This setting controls the uniqueness of the parameter itself. Both parameter types can be mixed within a given family. In this example, use an instance parameter because you want to designate whether something is reusable on an element-by-element basis.

   See Chapter 2, "Applying the Principles of the User Interface and Project Organization," for more information on type and instance parameters.

8. For Group Parameter Under, choose Green Building Properties.

   This setting is an organization tool. When you open your element properties, depending on how many parameters you add, you can develop quite a long list. This tool allows you to group new parameters into any given category.

9. In the list of categories, check the boxes for Doors, Furniture, and Windows.

   Categories is the list of element types in which this new property will appear. This is where you define all the category types you'll associate with the new parameter. Category selections are flexible. If you decide you need to change categories after you create your parameter, you can easily come back to the Project Parameters tool and modify your selection.

10. When you finish, click OK. This will take you back to the Project Parameters dialog box, where you can choose to add another parameter or, in our case, just click OK to exit completely.

Back in the model, you can now select a door (because it is one of the categories you chose) and see that you have added a Reuse parameter in the form of a check box to the bottom of the Properties list (Figure 18.48).

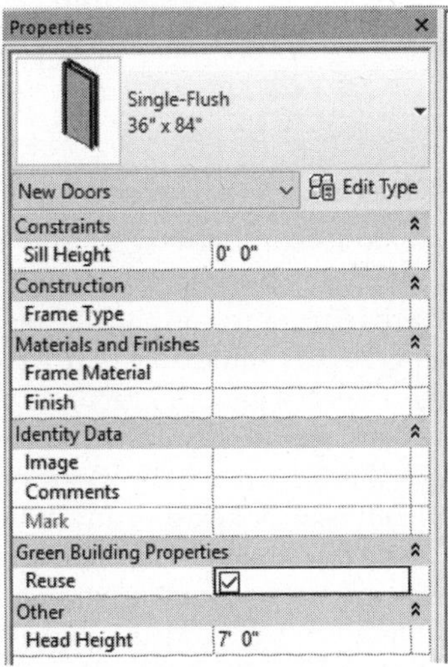

FIGURE 18.48
The Reuse parameter in the family

Now that you've created a custom parameter in the project, it's even easier to create one while in a schedule. You can create a custom parameter while creating a schedule or after the fact by modifying one. To create a parameter in a schedule, click the New Parameter button in the Schedule Properties dialog box (Figure 18.49). Doing so opens the same dialog box that you see when you click the Project Parameter button, with the exception that the Categories selections will be grayed out because you can create parameters in schedules only for the element being scheduled.

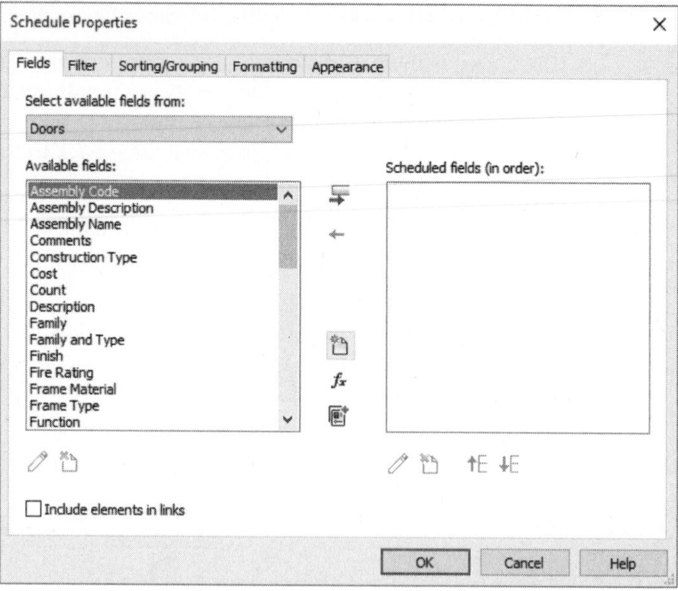

FIGURE 18.49 Adding a parameter while in a schedule

Creating Shared Parameters

When you want to schedule *and* tag a custom parameter, you will need to use shared parameters. Previously in this chapter, you learned that customized project parameters are useful for scheduling the STC rating on a wall. You can also use them to schedule which doors have security systems as part of the door hardware set, for example, or to specify which equipment in a lab will require special gases (oxygen, argon, and so forth). None of these parameters exist by default in any families, but they are all values that you might want to tag or schedule, depending on the type of project you are working on.

These parameters do not exist in any of the tags either, so in order to tag these parameters, you need to create them in both the tag and the element families.

Don't worry—it's not as complicated as it all sounds, but you will need to follow some steps fairly closely. Once you have added a shared parameter to your project, you cannot modify it. If you want to change it, you'll need to delete it and add the parameter again. So it behooves you to make your choices thoughtfully.

Let's look at the workflow behind creating a shared parameter. You'll do this by creating a custom wall parameter called STC so you can tag the sound transmission class of the wall types. To get started, continue using the `c18-Dimensions-Start.rvt` or `c18-Dimensions-Metric-Start.rvt` example from the previous exercise.

Creating the Shared Parameter

The first thing you do is create a new, shared parameter file. This file translates the values of the shared parameter between the tag, family, and project. Follow these steps:

1. To create a shared parameter, go to the Manage tab in the ribbon and click the Shared Parameters tool.

Doing so opens the Edit Shared Parameters dialog box (Figure 18.50).

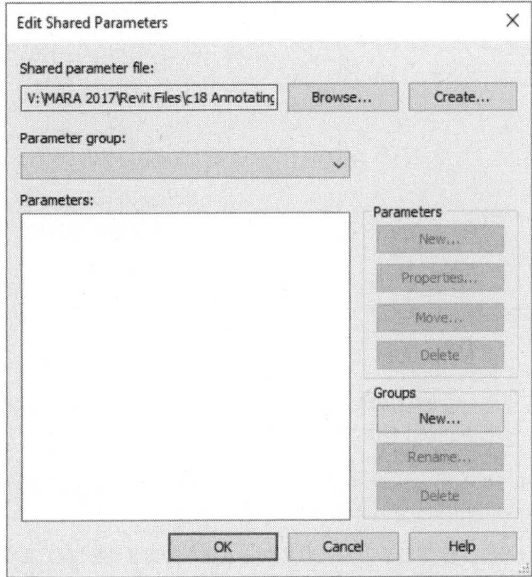

FIGURE 18.50
Creating the shared parameter

2. Click the Create button to open the Create Shared Parameter File dialog box. Name your shared parameter file. For our example, we've named it STC; however, if you plan to make more than one shared parameter, you might want to name it something more universal. All of the shared parameters for a given project will ultimately live in the same file. Give the file a name and location that will make sense to the project team. Then click Save.
3. Now that you've saved the TXT file, you'll return to the Edit Shared Parameters window, where you'll assign this parameter to a group by selecting New under the Groups option (this keeps like elements grouped together). This group is a hierarchical collection. So, for the wall's STC, you will want to create a group called **Wall Properties** (Figure 18.51). This grouping allows you to easily sort different parameters within project categories. Once you name the group, click OK.

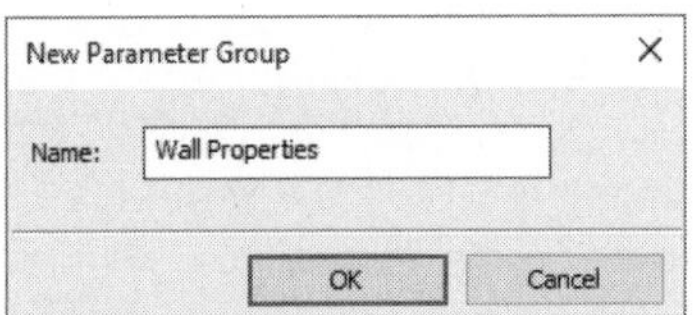

FIGURE 18.51
Creating a shared parameter group

4. Once you have a group, you'll see that the Parameters buttons are now active. Click the New button and name the parameter **STC**. Leave the Discipline setting at Common. For Type Of Parameter, choose Integer. Because STC ratings are whole numbers, you can use the Integer type and eliminate any decimal places you'd have if you used Number as the type (Figure 18.52). Once you've entered the settings, click OK.

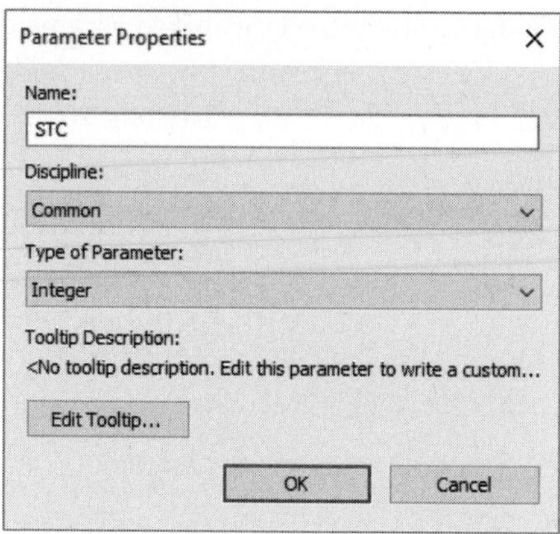

FIGURE 18.52 Naming the parameter and setting the type

5. You should see the new STC parameter in the Edit Shared Parameters dialog box. Click OK to exit this dialog box.

You've now created a shared parameter. The next step is to assign it to a category.

Assigning the Shared Parameter to a Category

The shared parameter is now defined, but you don't have it associated with any categories yet. To do so, follow these steps:

1. From the Manage tab in the ribbon, click the Project Parameters button to open the Project Parameters dialog box. You want to add a new parameter, so click Add.
2. The Parameter Properties dialog box opens. This time, select the Shared Parameter radio button, and then click Select. In the Shared Parameters dialog box, select the **STC** parameter you just created, and then click OK. You'll see that many of the fields are now grayed out in the Parameter Properties dialog box. This is because you have already specified this information in the shared parameter. In the Categories list, select Walls (Figure 18.53). Click OK to exit the dialog box.

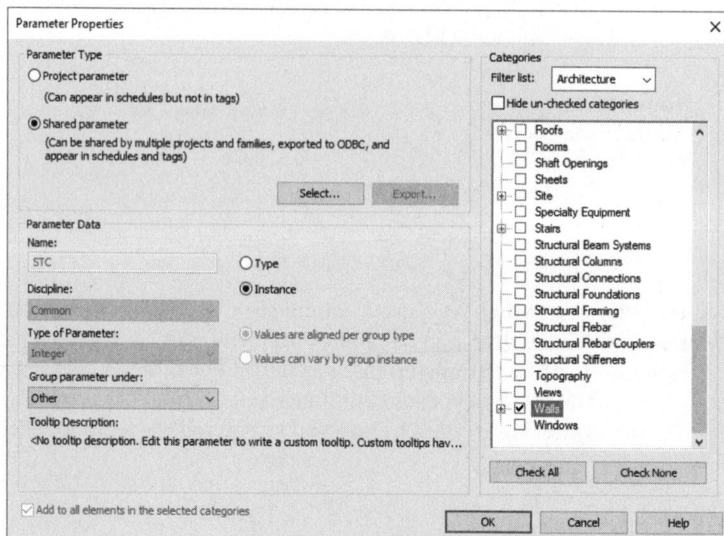

FIGURE 18.53 Assigning the shared parameter to a category

3. You'll see the new shared parameter (STC) below your previous project parameter (Reuse) in the Project Parameters dialog box (Figure 18.54). Click OK to close the dialog box.

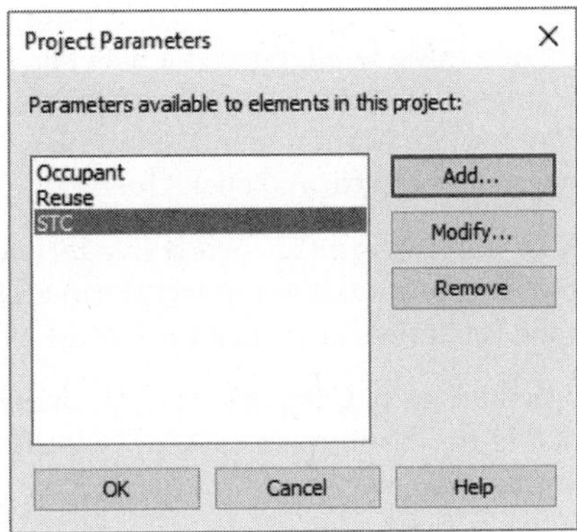

FIGURE 18.54
The shared parameter is now part of the project.

4. Now that the **STC** parameter is part of the project, you can begin assigning values to it. Open the Level 1 floor plan and select one of the interior walls on the left side of the plan. By scrolling down in the Properties palette, you'll notice that the STC parameter is now at the bottom (Figure 18.55). Enter a value of **45** and click Apply, or simply move your mouse out of the palette to set the value.

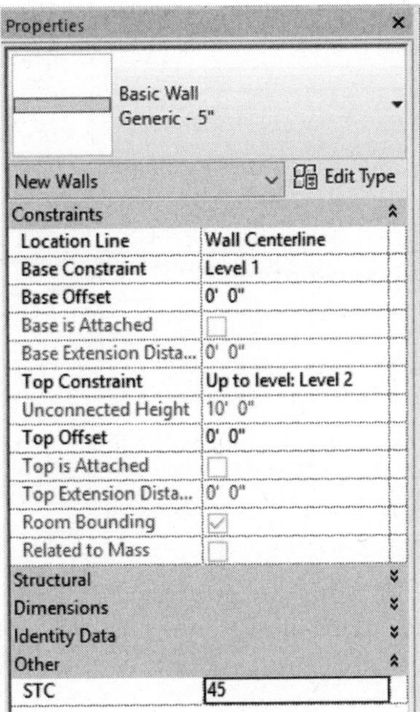

FIGURE 18.55
Giving the new parameter a value in the project

TAGGING THE SHARED PARAMETER

So far, you've created a shared parameter and added it to the Walls category in a project. These are all features you could have leveraged with a project parameter. The benefit of using a shared parameter is being able to tag it. The final step in this process is creating a tag to display the STC parameter in the wall:

1. The first thing you'll need is a new tag. Because you're tagging a wall, and there isn't a default wall tag type, you'll need to make a generic tag and apply it to a wall condition. From the Application menu, select New ➢ Family. Open the Annotations folder, select `Generic Tag.rfa`, and click Open.
2. Next, you'll assign the correct category to the tag. By default, a generic tag is just that: generic. You want it to report information from the Walls category, so on the Create tab, in the Properties area click the Family Category And Parameters button.
3. With the Family Category And Parameters dialog box open, choose Wall Tags from the list (Figure 18.56), and click OK. Delete the red text note in the tag family template before continuing.

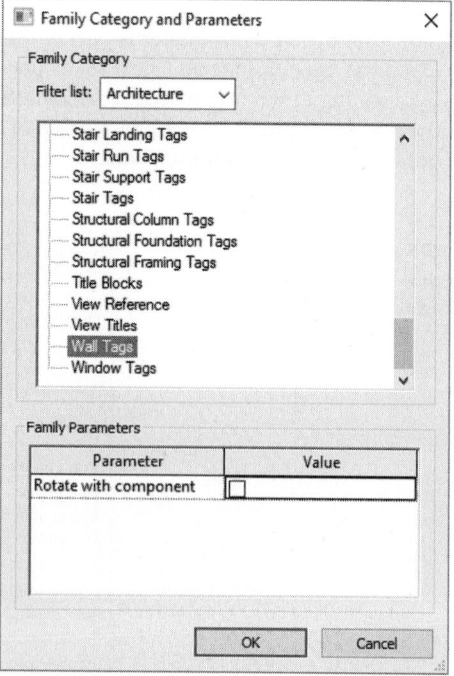

FIGURE 18.56 Selecting the Wall Tags category

4. With the proper category selected, you need to add a label for your tag. From the Create tab in the ribbon, select the Label tool on the Text panel, and then click just above the intersection of the two reference planes in the view.

5. In the Edit Label dialog box, select Type Mark from the list of category parameters and add it to the Label Parameters list to the right (Figure 18.57). This will call out the wall type and help you associate the proper wall with the STC rating. Click OK to close the dialog box and zoom in closer to the label you just placed.

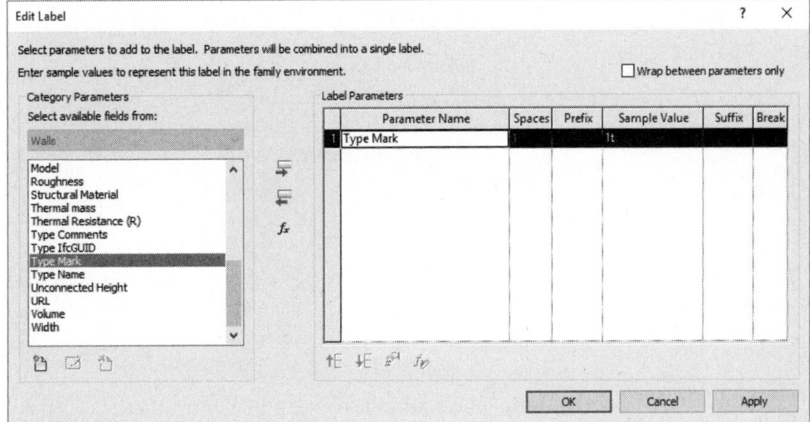

FIGURE 18.57 Adding the Type Mark parameter

6. With the Type Mark parameter placed, let's add the STC parameter. Activate the Label tool again, and then click just below the intersection of reference planes in the view. In the Edit Label dialog box, click the Add Parameter button at the bottom of the Category Parameters list. This opens the Parameter Properties dialog box (Figure 18.58). Click Select to open the Shared Parameters dialog box. Select STC and click OK, and then click OK again.

Parameter Properties

Parameter Type

Shared parameter

(Can be shared by multiple projects and families, exported to ODBC, and appear in schedules and tags)

Select... Export...

Parameter Data

Name:

<No parameter selected>

Discipline:

Type of Parameter:

OK Cancel Help

FIGURE 18.58 Choosing the shared parameter

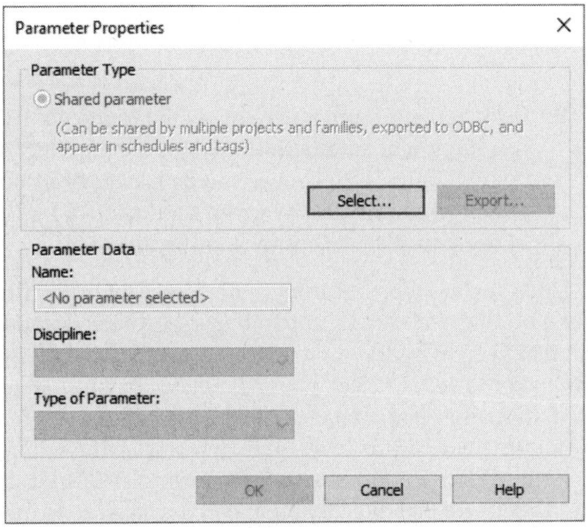

7. You'll now see the STC parameter in the Category Parameters list. Select it and add it to the right side of the dialog box (Figure 18.59). Click OK to close the dialog box.

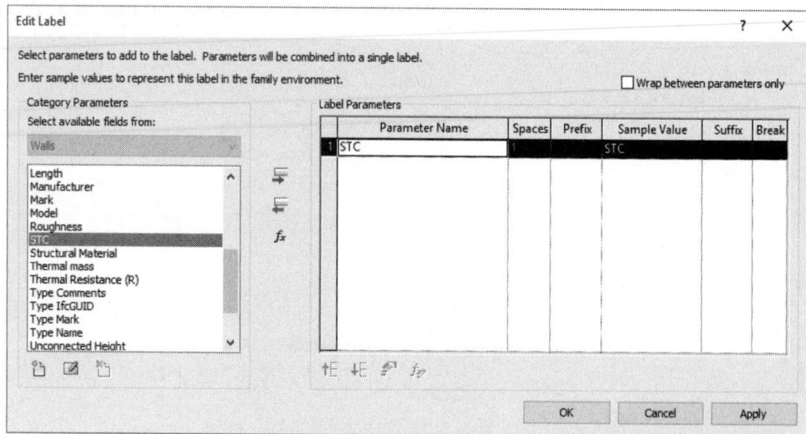

FIGURE 18.59 Adding the STC parameter to the label

8. With all the labels added, you can brush up the tag with a bit of linework to help differentiate the tag from the rest of the drawing. On the Create tab, choose the Line tool from the Detail panel. Using the default options, draw a box around the two labels and a line between them (Figure 18.60). Once this is done, save the family as **`Wall-STC.rfa`** and then load it into the project by clicking the Load Into Project button.

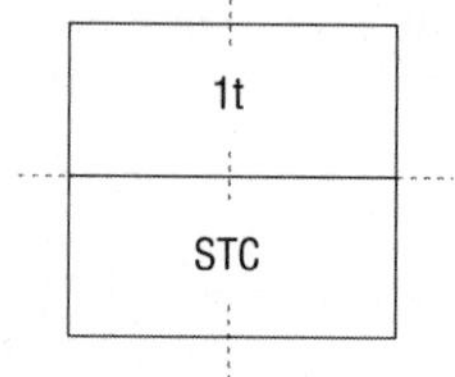

FIGURE 18.60 The customized wall tag

9. Back in the project, you're ready to tag the wall. Once you insert the tag into the project file, Revit will automatically begin the tagging command. However, the other way to begin tagging is to choose Tag By Category from the Annotate tab. Select the wall to which you have already given a value of 45 for the STC. You'll see the wall type and STC rating populate within the tag (Figure 18.61).

Once you've stepped through this workflow a few times, it will quickly become familiar and you'll be able to add custom parameters to projects and tag them without a second thought. One thing to keep in mind while you're doing all this, however, is that once you have added a shared parameter to your project, you will not be able to change any of the properties of the parameter itself. If you set the parameter type to Integer but you really wanted Number, you'll need to delete the parameter and start over. Also, when working with a team, remember that shared parameters work much like keynotes with their external TXT files. If you are sharing the project file with the idea that it will be edited by another team, be sure to include the shared parameter file.

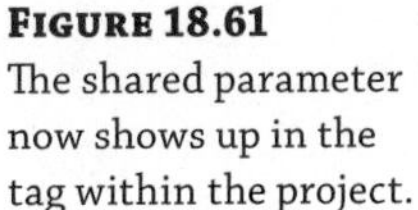

FIGURE 18.61
The shared parameter now shows up in the tag within the project.

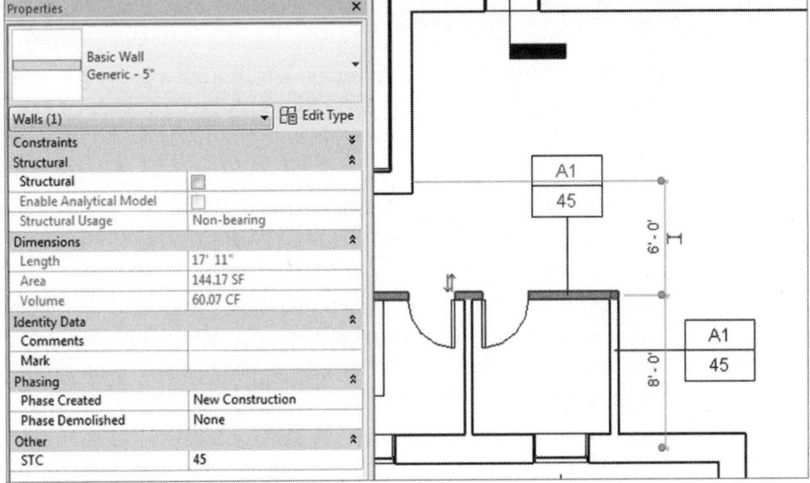

SHARED PARAMETERS BEYOND TAGGING

We have just finished a section on how to create your own shared parameters and use them to create tags that are not a part of the default Revit categories. But, as with all parameters, your use of shared parameters is not limited to only tagging. In one project, for example, we were designing a manufacturing facility. This facility had a large amount of process equipment, and the various pieces of equipment had special design needs like argon and nitrogen gases, compressed air, or special electrical power. We wanted to tag the equipment in our drawings, but we also wanted an easy way to visualize which pieces of equipment needed what kinds of services.

To do this, we combined the shared parameter file we created for the tags and used color filters (discussed in Chapter 10, "Working with Phasing, Groups, and Design Options") to color the equipment in plan and help the design teams make sure we were supplying the right services to the right elements.

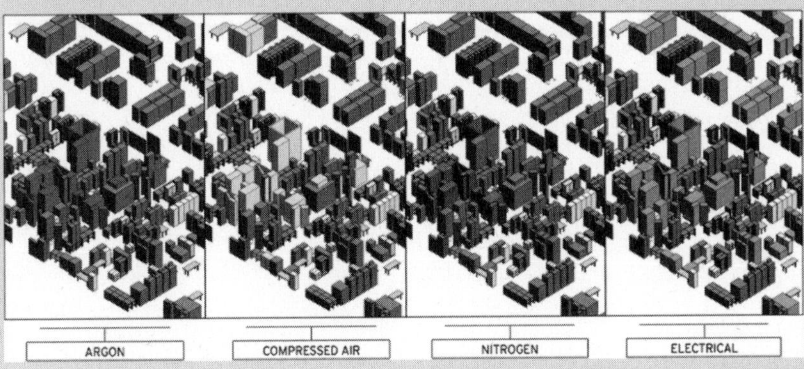

The Bottom Line

Annotate with text and keynotes. Although a picture is worth a thousand words, you will still need notes to make drawings understandable and be able to call out key elements in each view. Know how to create and modify text and keynotes for a complete set of documents.

Master It To properly use the keynoting feature, you'll need to understand what each of the three keynote types do and how they're used. List each and explain how they can be used in a project.

Use tags. Tags are text labels for elements such as doors, walls, windows, rooms, and several other objects that architects typically need to reference in a set of drawings. These tags typically refer back to other schedules or information in other portions of the drawing set and are unique to the view in which they are inserted.

Master It Inserting tags quickly can be a good way to make documentation time more efficient. How can you quickly tag a number of elements in the model at the same time?

Add dimensions. Dimensioning is a critical part of the project documentation, allowing you to communicate the distance elements are from one another.

Master It Adding dimensions is a necessary part in any project. However, in a project workflow you will typically want to change the location of a dimension's witness line without having to re-create the entire dimension. How do you move a witness line without remaking the entire dimension?

Set project and shared parameters. Revit Architecture lets users add as many custom parameters to an element as are needed to document the project. These parameters can be both tagged and scheduled, depending on how they are made.

Master It You need to add a custom parameter for your project to track the percentage of recycled content in materials. What's the best way to go about doing this?

Part 6

Construction and Beyond

In the previous chapters, we focused on the architect's role in design and construction using Autodesk® Revit® Architecture software. As the software continues to expand beyond being a tool for design documentation, we want to touch on several other uses outside the traditional scope of the designer. In the chapters in Part 6, we discuss how Revit can be used to augment design and documentation after construction documents are complete.

Chapter 19

Working in the Construction Phase

In this chapter, we will explore the use of Autodesk® Revit® Architecture software in the construction phase by design teams and builders. For design teams, the use of Revit Architecture usually entails markups, sketches, and revision management; however, a builder may approach building information modeling (BIM) tools in unique ways. Many different BIM programs are available for builders to use in preconstruction and construction phase tasks, so we will not assume that Revit is the primary tool used by the majority of them.

In this chapter, you'll learn to:

- Add revisions to your project
- Use digital markups
- Model for construction

Using Revisions in Your Project

Revisions allow designers and builders to track changes made to a set of construction documents during the construction phase of a project. Because the construction documents usually consist of numerous sheets, this methodology allows everyone on the team to track and identify which changes were made and when they were made during construction. The purpose is not only to ensure correct construction but also to create *as-built* documentation recording how the building was actually created to be delivered to building owners upon occupancy.

In a typical drawing set, revisions will look like Figure 19.1 when they are created and issued as part of the drawing set. Revision clouds themselves are created within views that are placed on the sheets. The revision tag is also placed within the view, but once the view is then placed on a sheet, the revision will dynamically appear in the sheet properties and on any revision schedule on the sheet itself.

Creating a Revision Cloud

To create a revision cloud in your project, switch to the Annotate tab in the ribbon, locate the Detail panel, and then choose Revision Cloud. This places you in a revision cloud drawing mode, similar to Sketch mode, and allows you to bubble the revised detail or drawing. When you finish, click the green check mark to complete the sketch and your annotation is done. We'll step through this in more detail later in this chapter.

FIGURE 19.1
Typical revisions

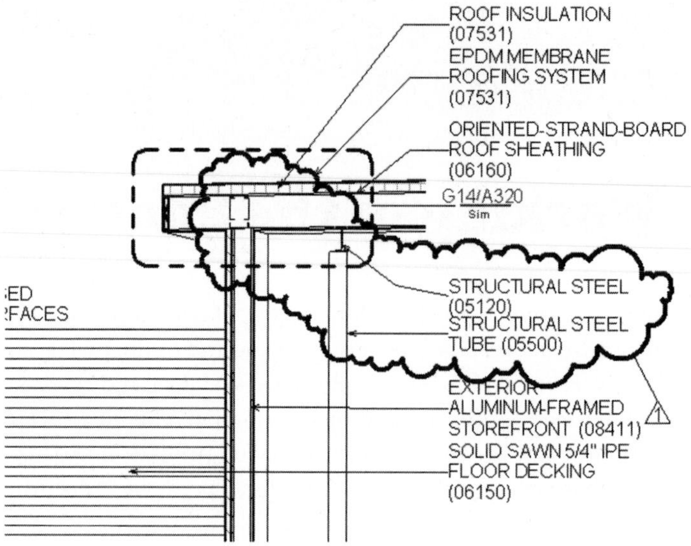

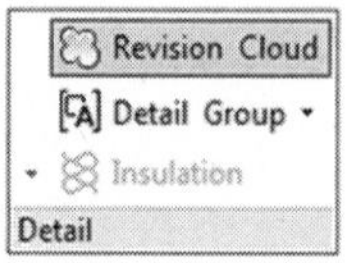

You will usually have several rounds of revisions to a document set. Revit provides a way to manage the revision list and gives you the ability to name and date the various revisions in your project to better track them. The Sheet Issues/Revisions tool is located in two places within the application. You can find it on either the View tab in the Sheet Composition panel or the Manage tab under Additional Settings.

Either one of these buttons will open the Sheet Issues/Revisions dialog box (Figure 19.2). Here you can add, merge, issue, and define the visibility of revisions.

Before you begin creating revisions in your sheet set, it's good to start with this dialog box to give those revisions some order. Let's review the major components of the Sheet Issues/Revisions dialog box, beginning with the table of revisions:

Table of Revisions The Sheet Issues/Revisions dialog box starts with one default revision already in place, even though you may not have made a revision yet. This is only to give you a place to start—no revision will appear in your title blocks until you add revision clouds to your views. Each revision has a fixed number of parameters that you can enter. As you can see in Figure 19.2, the parameters include Numbering, Date, Description, and an Issued check box in addition to Issued To and Issued By columns and options for showing clouds and tags.

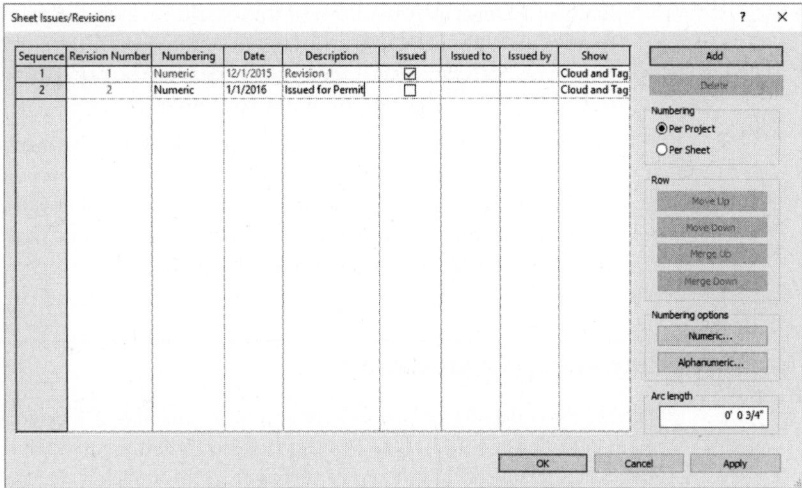

FIGURE 19.2
The Sheet Issues/Revisions dialog box

Numbering (Table Column) The Numbering option allows you to number each revision numerically, alphabetically, or not at all. If you choose an alphabetic sequence, the sequence is defined in the Customize Numbering Options. In the Numbering Options box in the lower right, choose either Numeric or Alphanumeric to set your sequence and remove letters you don't want to use. For instance, some firms don't use the letters *I* and *O* because they are often confused with the numbers *1* and *0*, respectively. Figure 19.3 shows a sample of the dialog box. By default, an entire alphabet appears here. The None option allows you to add project milestones—unnumbered entries that appear in revision tables—to sheets without having to add revision clouds.

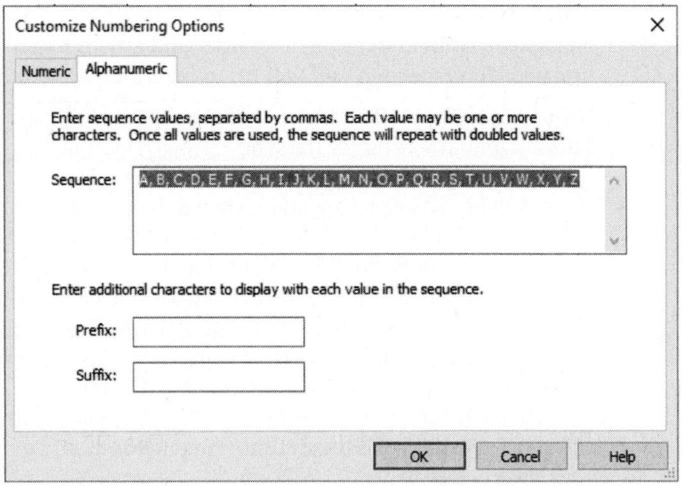

Customize Numbering Options

Numeric | Alphanumeric

Enter sequence values, separated by commas. Each value may be one or more characters. Once all values are used, the sequence will repeat with doubled values.

Sequence: A, B, C, D, E, F, G, H, I, J, K, L, M, N, O, P, Q, R, S, T, U, V, W, X, Y, Z

Enter additional characters to display with each value in the sequence.

Prefix:

Suffix:

OK | Cancel | Help

FIGURE 19.3
Customize Numbering Options allows you to use any order of letters or numbers.

Date and Description Both of these fields are user-driven only. The date is not tied to any functionality within Revit, nor is the description—both are simple text fields. However, both fields will schedule as part of your revision table on your sheets and are useful in organizing and tracking your revisions.

Issued To issue a revision, click the check box in the Issued column. Doing so locks the revision clouds and tags placed on sheets or in views associated with that revision, preventing them from being moved, deleted, or otherwise edited. The parameter values in the dialog box become inactive. This is to guarantee that the clouds and data do not change downstream once you issue a set of drawings.

REVISIONS IN A LIVE MODEL

During the construction process, the project model may still be changing. When you issue a revision, keep this in mind: Although the clouds can become fixed in the project, the model will not be static. As you continue to make revisions to the model, it will always be up to date. This means that you might have multiple revisions in the same location on your sheet set. So if you need to maintain an archive of all project phases or each revision, be sure to export the sheets as either DWF or PDF files as a snapshot of the sheets at time of issue.

Issued To/Issued By You may enter notes to the project team in these fields for whom the revisions are to be issued and who issued them.

Show This table column controls the visibility of revision clouds and revision tags that have been issued. As issues occur, you may want to hide just the clouds or just the tags from previous revisions. For example, if you've issued one revision and then add revisions to a later issue and want to clean up your drawing, you can choose to show the issued revision as the tag only—typically a small triangle with the revision number inside it—or not show anything at all by using the None option.

Add Button This function is used to create a new revision. The new revision will automatically be placed in sequential order and only the sequence number will be automatically updated. You'll need to add your own description and date.

Numbering (Radio Buttons) You can choose to number revisions by sheet or by project. This is a global setting for the whole project, but one can be swapped for the other at any point. Which method you choose mainly depends on how your firm chooses to track revisions. The Per Sheet setting allows you to have as many revisions as you want within the drawing set, but on each sheet, the list of revisions will remain sequential. For example, an issue named "Issued for Design Development" may be revision number 4 on one sheet and number 7 on another. Using the Per Project setting will order your revision clouds based on the sequence established in the Sheet Issues/Revisions dialog box. In other words, all revisions with the same issue date would have the same revision number regardless of how many revisions appear on any given sheet. This approach might give you a greater degree of consistency throughout your document set but may limit the number of overall revisions you can use in the project. Either numbering method can be configured in advance and added to your project template.

Placing Revision Clouds

If you want to place a revision, open a view in which changes to the project have occurred and use the Revision Cloud tool found in the Detail panel on the Annotate tab. Use the familiar sketching tools from the Draw panel in the contextual tab of the ribbon to generate a cloud around the area you are calling out as a revision. The tool automatically starts with the Box command, allowing you to draw a box around your revision. If you'd like something more fluid, you can switch to the Line tool on the Draw panel. Lines are automatically created that make a *cloud* (or series of arcs), as shown in Figure 19.4. The size of the arcs will be determined by the Arc Length setting found in the Sheet Issues/Revisions dialog box we described in the previous section. When you finish creating the cloud, click the Finish Sketch button (the green check mark) in the contextual tab of the ribbon. Note that the Revision cloud tool doesn't require you to form a closed loop—you can finish the sketch at any point.

FIGURE 19.4
Adding a revision cloud to a view

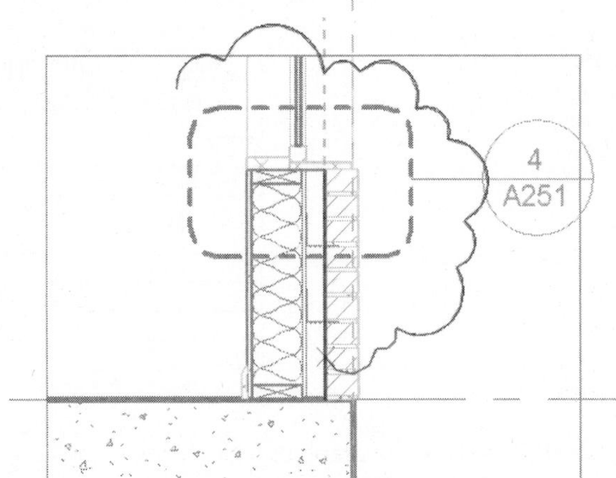

By default, each new revision cloud will be assigned to the last revision in the Sheet Issues/Revisions dialog box. If you need to change the revision to which a cloud is assigned, select the cloud and use the Properties palette to modify its revision number (Figure 19.5).

FIGURE 19.5
The revision cloud's issue assignment can be changed in the Properties palette.

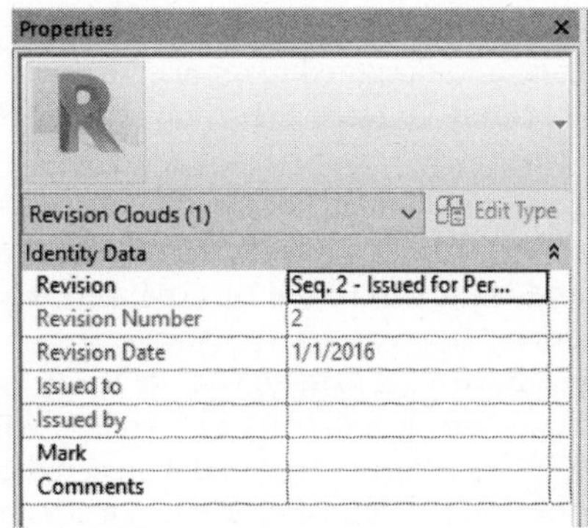

Revision Clouds in a Live Model

During the construction process, the project model may still be changing. As you create revisions, you might need to create more than one within the same view or sheet. Where you place the revision cloud can be as important as the revision itself. For instance, do you place it within the view or on the sheet? As a best practice, we suggest you place the revision in the location where the content is changing. So, if you're modifying a flashing detail, place the revision bubble in the view. If you're changing the name of the detail on the sheet, place it on the sheet itself. This will help you downstream, when you make another change to that same view or element.

As soon as you have placed a revision cloud on a sheet, any revision schedules placed in your title block will update to include the revision number, description, and the date you assigned in the Sheet Issues/Revisions dialog box earlier (Figure 19.6).

Figure 19.6
The updated title block with the revision information

No.	Description	Date
2	Issued for Permit	1/1/2016

Like other objects, the graphics for revision clouds are controlled from the Object Styles dialog box, found in the Settings panel on the Manage tab. Settings for revisions are located on the Annotation Objects tab. The default setting for the line thickness is 1. We recommend that you increase the default thickness for revisions in your project template to more clearly illustrate and communicate your design modifications.

Tagging a Revision Cloud

Revision clouds can be tagged like many other elements. Similar to other tags, revision tags are intelligent and designed to report the revision number or letter that has been assigned to the revision cloud. To place a revision tag, use the Tag By Category tool in the Tag panel on the Annotate tab.

If a tag for revisions is not in your template, you will be warned that no such tag exists in your project. To continue, simply load a revision tag. The default tag is named `Revision Tag.rfa` and is located in the Annotations folder of the family library within a standard installation.

Once you have a tag loaded, you are ready to tag revision clouds. Hover the cursor over a revision cloud and click to place the tag. You will see a preview of the tag prior to placing it (Figure 19.7). Once the tag is placed, you can drag it around the cloud to reposition it and turn the leader on and off. With or without a leader, the revision tag will stay associated with the cloud.

FIGURE 19.7
Tagging a revision cloud

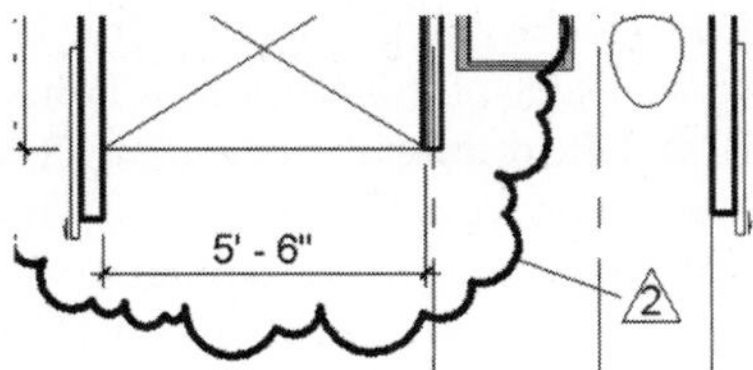

Disabling the Leader

You can choose to use a leader line between the tag and the cloud, depending on your preference or your office standards. In many cases, the tag just needs to be near the cloud and a leader is not necessary. Disable the leader by selecting the tag and clearing the Leader option in the Options bar. It's good to note here that if your firm's standards are to hide the cloud and you have the leader activated, you'll see the revision tag plus the leader but no cloud since the leader and tag are connected.

BIM AND SUPPLEMENTAL DRAWINGS

The process of making supplemental drawings (SDs)—also known as supplemental sketches (SKs)—entails making a change to an existing drawing and then issuing that change as a separate document during the construction process. Sometimes this can be a single 8 1/2″ × 11″ [A4] or 11″ × 17″ [A3] sheet where the new detail is then pasted over the old one in the document set. From a workflow perspective, this can be a little disruptive for two reasons:

- Placing a view into a smaller sheet to issue the individual view can lead to other problems. Because there is only one instance of the view, it requires you to take the view off your Construction Document sheet to place the view in a new sheet. The problem is that the new sheet/detail is meant to replace a portion of your original document set, so your set is now out of sequence. You will need to remove the view from the sheet it was issued on temporarily (and remember to put it back) or duplicate the view and hope that you do not need to make last-minute additional changes.
- A supplemental drawing, once issued, is like a snapshot in time. It becomes a numbered change made to the drawing set at a given date. Because the model and all the views in the model always reflect the most current state of the project, making separate SD sheets and views within Revit will show any additional changes made to that view.
- As an alternative, you can reissue the full sheet. This is easiest for a Revit workflow, but it depends on your firm's standards for supplemental drawings.

Using Digital Markups

Both Autodesk® A360 (`www.autodesk360.com`) and Autodesk® Design Review offer an efficient way to view and mark up 2D digital documents and 3D models. This workflow is different from revisions and is geared more toward informal design review rather than the management of sheet issues. For example, if your drawings must be reviewed for quality control and overall comments by a senior designer who might not be familiar with Revit software, this tool can streamline the process. The senior designer, consultant, or any other third party can make comments and review changes directly in the digital file and return them to the Revit Architecture user who needs to modify the original model.

In this section, we're going to focus on the use of Design Review for DWF markups. Both applications are capable of this workflow. Think of the A360 tool as an online version of the DWF markup tool. It additionally has many powerful collaboration tools to help the overall project process—markups are only a portion of what the tool does. Feel free to explore A360 to see the full effect it can have on team collaboration.

Using Design Review, you can view files in DWFx or DWF format. If you export sheets to DWFx and the markups are linked back into Revit, the markups will be automatically placed on the corresponding sheet. So there is no need on your part for any sort of alignment or placement of the revisions.

Design Review is a free tool that you can download from the Autodesk website: `http://usa.autodesk.com/design-review`. Once it's installed, you can open and mark up any DWFx or DWF file produced by any Autodesk or other CAD/BIM software package.

Publishing to Design Review

There are two ways to share your model using Design Review: as 2D drawings or as a 3D model. If you publish to 3D, you create a single 3D representation of your model that can be orbited, control visibility of element categories, and be queried for the properties of any of the elements. Publishing to 2D can create either a single view or a whole collection of interconnected views and sheets packaged as one file. You can even combine 2D views and a 3D model in one DWFx file.

Exporting DWFx Files

You can export to DWFx from any view, except a schedule. To export your views or sheets, select the Application menu and choose Export ➤ DWF/DWFx. The DWF Export Settings dialog box (Figure 19.8) will open. Here you can choose views/sheets to export in addition to specifying how the results will be published.

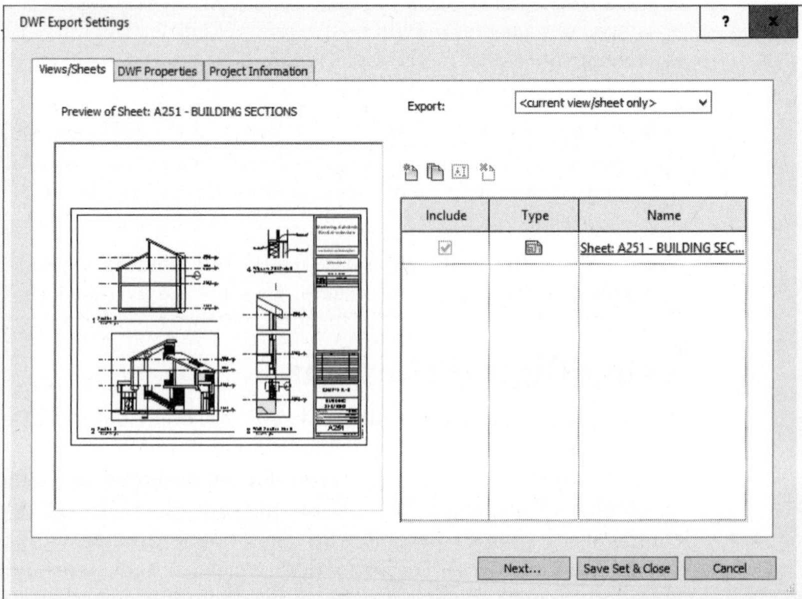

Figure 19.8 The DWF Export Settings dialog box

In the following exercise, you will open a Revit file and create a DWFx file for review:

1. Open the `c19-Sample-Building-Start.rvt` model, which can be downloaded from this book's web page, `www.sybex.com/go/masteringrevit2017`.
2. Open Sheet A101 from the sheet list in the Project Browser. Click the Application menu and select Export ➢ DWF/DWFx to open the dialog box shown in Figure 19.8.
3. Click the New Set icon at the top of the list of views and name the set **MASTERING SHEETS**.

   Once you create the set, you will see a new drop-down list appear in the dialog box; you can use it to control which views are displayed in the view list (Figure 19.9).

FIGURE 19.9
The Show In List drop-down is available only with a view set.

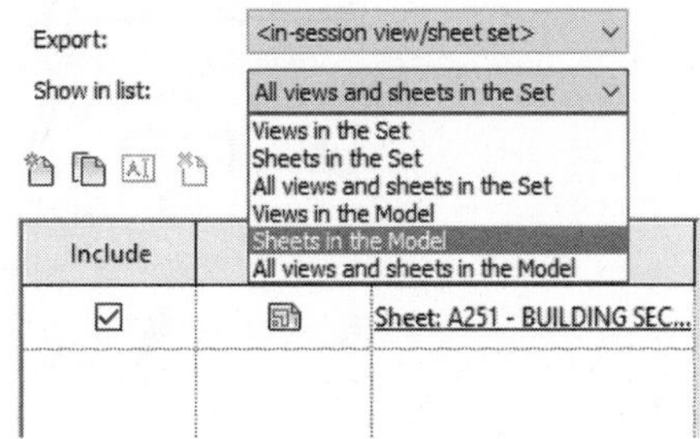

4. From the Show In List drop-down, select Sheets In The Model, and then select sheets A101 and A102.

   These sheets will be added to the set to be published.

   You can sort the list of views by any of the columns by clicking a column header. Try this by clicking the Name header.
5. To check the export size, select the DWF Properties tab and click the Print Setup button. In the resulting dialog box, you can set explicit sizes for your export. Click the option Use Sheet Size to automatically detect sheet sizes based on the title blocks you are using in the project.

   This dialog box mirrors the one used for printing.
6. Click Next and specify the name of the file and a location in which to save it. Make sure you check the box to combine all sheets into a single DWFx file (see Figure 19.10).

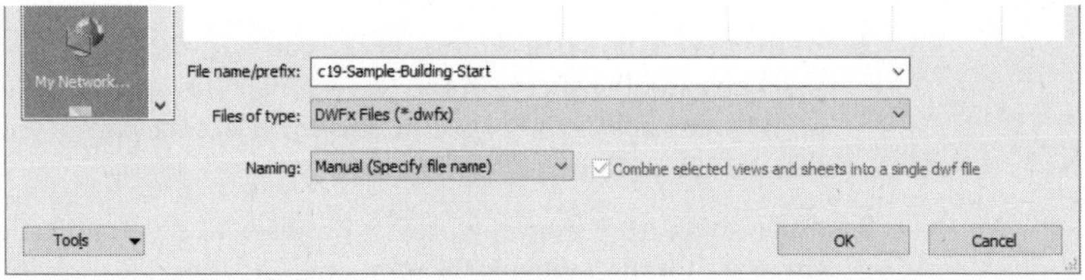

FIGURE 19.10
Manual file naming is available when you combine views for publishing.

7. Open the published DWFx file in Autodesk Design Review. Choose the Markup & Measure tab, and then add a few comments and markups on the A101 sheet.

   Using the Shapes and Draw tools on this tab, you can add clouds, arrows, and text to insert your comments or changes into the drawings. This can be done in a variety of colors and line weights to give them extra visibility on the page. Once all your changes are created, save the file and it will retain all your changes. Figure 19.11 shows an example of a markup.

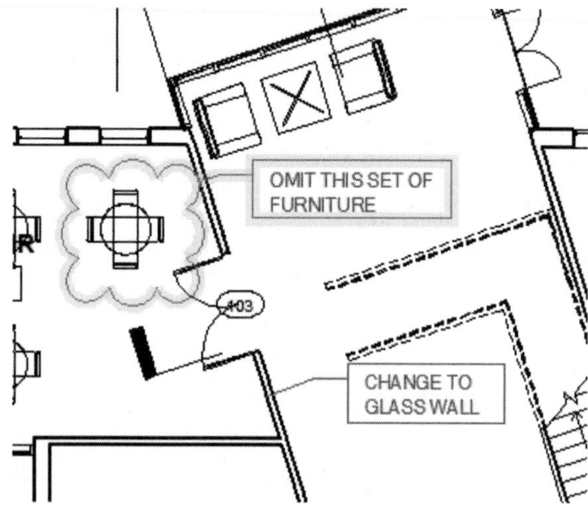

FIGURE 19.11
A marked-up DWFx file

IMPORTING A DESIGN REVIEW MARKUP

Once you've added markups to the DWFx file, save the file and close Design Review. You can then link the marked-up DWFx file back into the RVT project file. Continue to use the sample file from the previous exercise. You can also download the file `c19-Sample-MarkedUp.dwfx` from this book's web page. This file already contains some markups to use in the following exercise. Perform these steps to import the marked-up file into the project file:

1. On the Insert tab, choose DWF Markup from the Link panel and then select the DWFx file you saved in the previous exercise.

   This is a simple import dialog box. There are no settings in the window.

   When you select a DWFx file, only the markups will be shown—not the entire DWFx file. If there are no markups in the file, nothing will be visible in Revit.

2. In the next dialog box (Figure 19.12), you will see the views in the DWFx file that contain markups and the sheets in the Revit project to which they will coordinate. You can insert all the markups or only specific sheets. Select the sheets you'd like to import; be sure to select A101, and then click OK.

3. Open sheet A101 from the Project Browser, and you will see the markup as an overlay in the same location where it was created in Design Review (Figure 19.13).

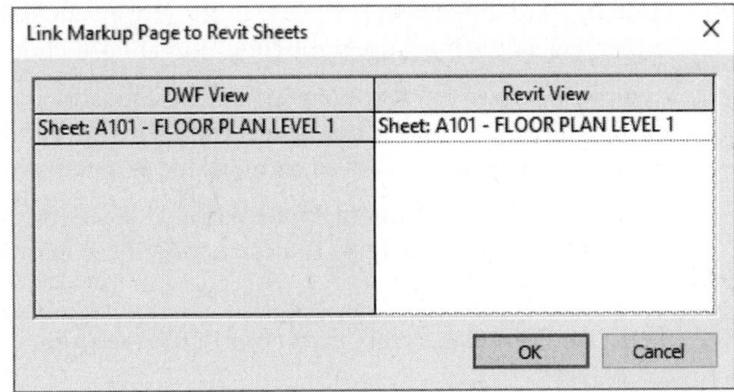

FIGURE 19.12 Sheets with associated markups are shown.

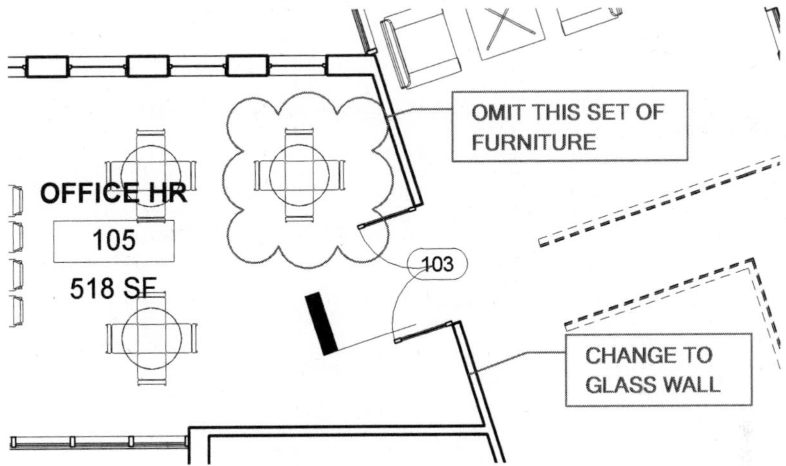

FIGURE 19.13 The marked-up sheet linked into Revit

Markups can be linked only to sheets. If you export a view and mark it up, you will not be able to link that view back into the model. Also, none of the other linework from the DWF will link into the model—any of the building geometry, backgrounds, sheet content, and so on. The only thing that will be visible in Revit is content created with the DWF Markup tool.

You cannot move or delete linked DWF markups—they appear with a pin if selected; however, you can do a number of things to graphically indicate that you've reviewed a markup:

Change its graphic appearance. Let's say you have 20 redline markups on your sheet. You need to keep track of which ones you've picked up. One way to do this is to graphically override each markup as you make the requested modifications. Select the markup, right-click, choose View ➤ By Element, and click Override Graphics. Choose a color to indicate "done." Yellow works well because it suggests a highlight marker.

Hide it. This approach is similar to the graphic override, but you hide the markup altogether. Select the markup, right-click, and choose Hide In View ➤ Element.

Remove it. You can remove markups by choosing Manage Links from the Manage tab. In the Manage Links dialog box, select the DWF Markups tab, select the markup, and click the Remove button. This removes all markups associated with the link.

Another way you can interact with a linked DWF file is by modifying the status or appending comments to each markup. You can access these features in the Properties palette when you select a markup, as follows:

1. In the A101 sheet view, select one of the markups you created and go to the Properties palette.
2. Change the Status drop-down list to Done and then click the Edit button in the Notes field. In the Edit Text dialog box, enter some text related to the completion of the design modification requested in the markup (Figure 19.14).

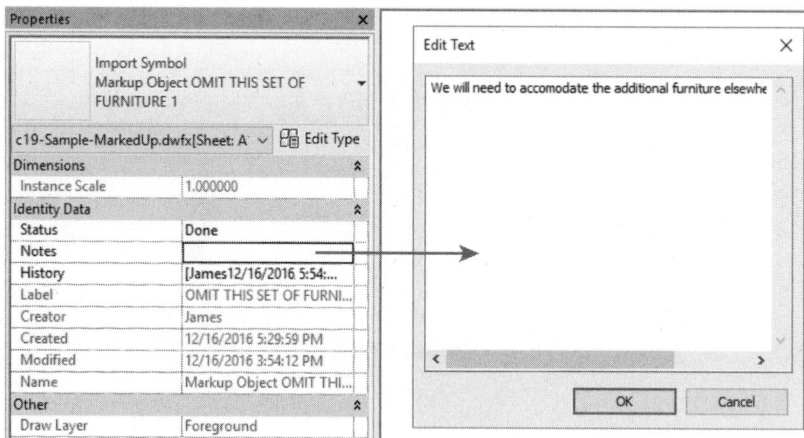

FIGURE 19.14 Modifying the properties of the markup

3. Click the Apply button at the bottom of the Properties palette or move the mouse pointer out of the Properties palette.
4. Switch to the Insert tab in the ribbon, and from the Link panel choose Manage Links. Select the DWF Markups tab.
5. Select the row containing the DWFx file you linked in the previous steps, and then click the Save Markups button at the bottom left of the dialog box.

   There is no alert or notification that the save process has completed, so just wait a few seconds.
6. Click OK to close the Manage Links dialog box.

7. Open the DWFx file again in Design Review, and you will see that the status of the markups has been updated.

The comments you added can be seen in the Markup Properties palette (Figure 19.15).

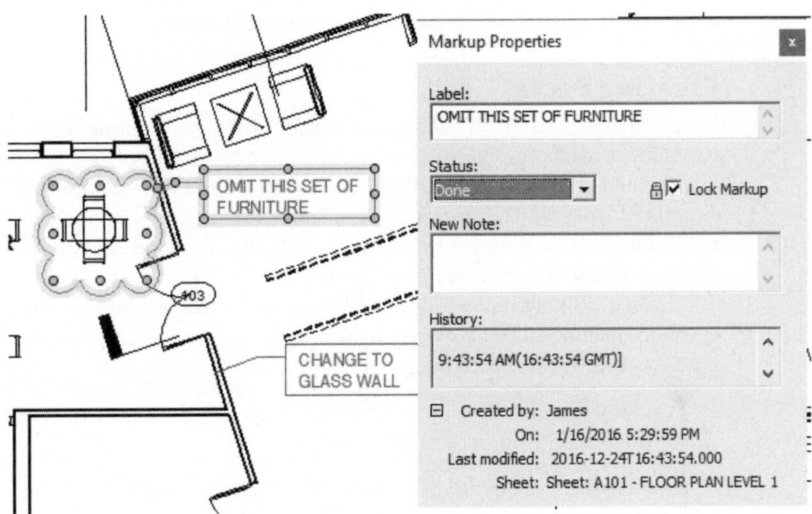

FIGURE 19.15 Modifying the properties of the markup

Using the DWFx file format along with the integrated tools within Revit, you have closed a communication and coordination loop that has traditionally been an area of difficulty. This workflow also benefits larger project teams because you don't have to manage a central pile of drawing markups that need to be shared or distributed among several teammates. All the staff working on a project will have access to the same linked DWF markups.

Modeling for Construction

Now that we have reviewed some basic functionality a design team might use during the construction phase, let's take a look at how a builder (contractor, subcontractor, or construction manager) might use Revit in the industry today.

Revit is often referred to as a design application; however, contractors are using the software more frequently as both a model-authoring and project-analysis tool. Although builders use BIM tools to obtain different results than design professionals do, many of the processes and functions are the same; they are merely applied in particular ways according to the needs of the various users.

Functionality introduced back in Revit Architecture 2012 supports a more interactive and flexible approach to construction modeling. The first addition was the ability to create parts, which are individual subsets of more complex layered elements such as walls and floors. The other addition allowed you to generate assemblies, which are segregated subsets of the project model with their own associated views, annotations, and sheets. These tools are used to take large elements and break them down into smaller components as they'd be used on the job site. As an example, in an architectural model, a cast-in-place concrete floor would be a single element for the entire floor plate. In practice, the contractor would never pour the floor that way. The concrete would be poured in a series of pads, and the contractor would have to divide the slab into those series of pours for his or her schedule. The potential to minimize data loss between the design and construction stakeholders of a project can start to change how we approach collaboration and delivery of our buildings.

Creating Parts

Parts are designed to aid the user in subdividing larger model elements into smaller components for construction planning. Each part maintains a persistent relationship with the elements from which it was derived, and it can be subdivided into smaller parts if necessary. Parts can be generated from walls, floors, ceilings, and roofs, as long as they are of consistent thickness. They also have their own properties, such as volume, area, and height; as such, they can be scheduled independently of their original elements.

While it is likely that designers will use parts to customize architectural elements, we are going to discuss only the workflow intended for the builder. To get started with the basic workflow for creating and dividing parts, follow these steps:

1. Open the file `c19-Parts-Start.rvt` or `c19-Parts-Metric-Start.rvt`, which you can download from this book's web page.
2. Activate the Default 3D view if it isn't already open.

   Notice that each of the wall, floor, ceiling, and roof elements in this sample model is composed of one object. A section box has been activated in this view that is exposing the layers within each element (Figure 19.16).

FIGURE 19.16
The beginning Parts model

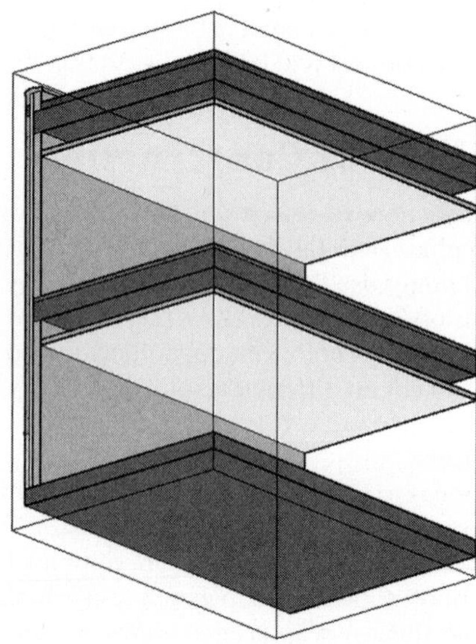

3. Select the floor at Level 2. On the Create panel in the contextual tab of the ribbon, click the Create Parts button.

   Notice that the original object has been visually replaced in the current view by the parts representing each layer of the floor assembly. It is still in the project model—it has not been deleted.

   There is a new view property in the Properties palette named Parts Visibility whose default value is Show Parts. This means that if parts have been created for any object, they will be displayed instead of the original. This property can also be set to Show Original or Show Both.

4. In the Project Browser, right-click the Default 3D view and choose Duplicate View and then Duplicate. Rename the copy of the view **Original Model**.
5. Activate the view named Original Model. From the Properties palette, find the Parts Visibility parameter and change it to Show Original.
6. In the Project Browser, rename the {3D} view to **Parts Model**.
7. Activate the Parts Model view, and repeat the process of creating parts for the wall, the ceilings, and the roof in the sample model. Simply select each of these elements and choose the Parts tool from the context menu as before.

In the previous exercise, you created an alternative way to view your model that begins to explore constructability. Without additional modification, you can start to interact with these individual components by examining their properties or even hiding them or overriding their graphic display.

Modifying Parts

In addition to creating parts from original model elements, you can divide these parts into smaller ones. You can even change the phasing properties at the part level and use grips to modify the extents of the parts. Let's begin with an exercise to divide some parts using planes and sketched lines:

1. Go back to the Parts Model view and select the top part of the roof at the Roof level.

   This will be the layer representing insulation.

2. From the Part panel in the contextual ribbon, click Divide Parts.

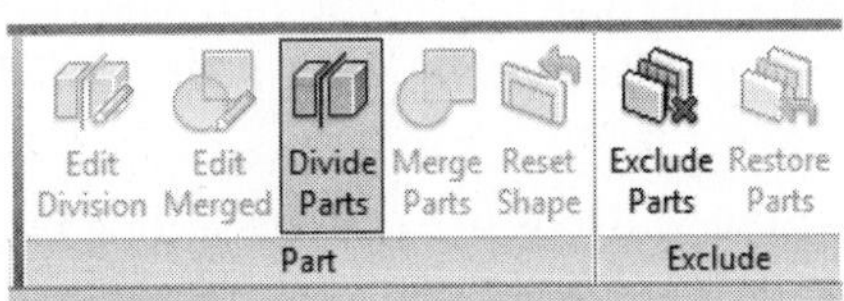

You will enter Sketch mode, where you can either select intersecting datum or draw your own dividing lines.

3. Click the Intersecting References button in the contextual ribbon. You are presented with the Intersecting Named References dialog box (Figure 19.17). From the Filter drop-down list, select All and notice that you can choose from levels, grids, and named reference planes.

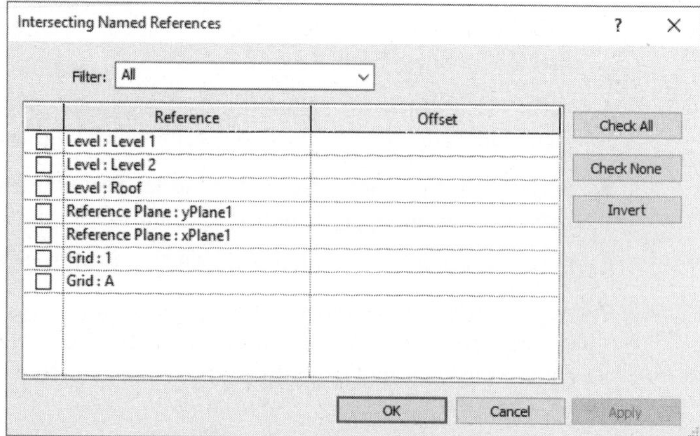

FIGURE 19.17 You can use a datum as one way to divide parts.

Note that if a reference plane has not been named, it will not appear in this list.

4. Check the boxes for the two reference planes named xPlane1 and yPlane1. Click OK to close the dialog box. You'll see two green datum objects highlight in the model.
5. Click the green check mark in the contextual ribbon to finish Edit mode.

   After you complete the process for dividing the part, notice that the part has now become four separate pieces. To experiment with how the parts maintain their relationship to the original object as well as the intersecting reference planes, go to the Level 1 floor plan and move the reference planes around, but try to keep them within the boundary of the sample floor. When you return to the 3D view, you will see that the divisions stay synchronized with the reference planes.
6. Activate the ceiling plan for Level 1. In the Properties palette for the view, change Parts Visibility to Show Parts. Select the Gypsum Wall Board part on the bottom of the ceiling below the Level 2 floor.

   Graphically, this will look like you're selecting the entire ceiling because it will all highlight blue.

   You can make sure you have the correct part selected by examining the Properties palette. The category filter at the top should display Parts (1) and the Material parameter should indicate Gypsum Wall Board – Ceiling (Figure 19.18).

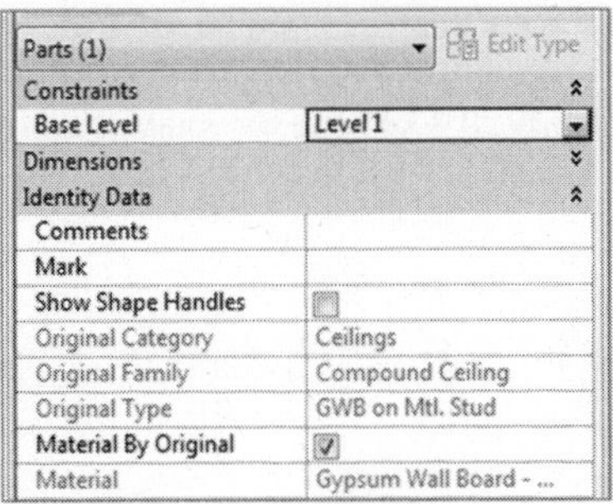

FIGURE 19.18
Verify your selection of the gypsum ceiling by making sure you have (1) part selected and the material is Gypsum Wall Board.

7. Click the Divide Parts button in the contextual ribbon, and then click the Edit Sketch button to activate Sketch mode. Draw a diagonal line across the part from left to right, as shown in Figure 19.19.

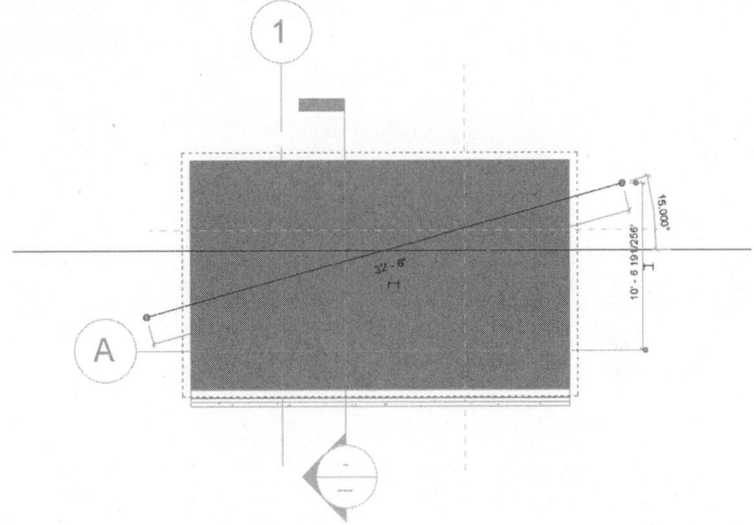

FIGURE 19.19
Sketch a line to divide a part.

If you need to sketch lines to divide parts, the lines do not have to be in closed loops, but they must intersect the boundaries of the part. Keep in mind that if the original element is edited so that its boundaries extend beyond any sketched part divisions, the part divisions will be deleted.

8. Click the green check mark in the contextual ribbon to finish the sketch, and then click it again to finish the part-dividing mode.

9. Activate the Parts Model view, and orbit the model so you can select the inside face of the wall. Select the part of the wall that would represent the gypsum wall board at the interior face of Level 2.

10. From the Properties palette, find the Show Shape Handles parameter and check the box. You will see triangular shape handles on all four sides of the part, as shown in Figure 19.20. Drag the top shape handle down to indicate that the gypsum wall board is not to be installed to the full height of the wall assembly.

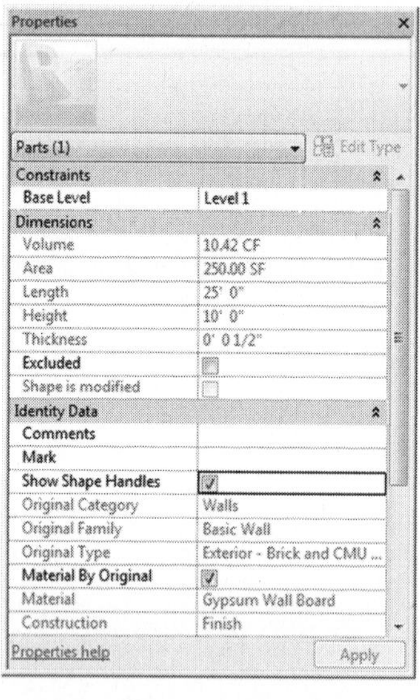

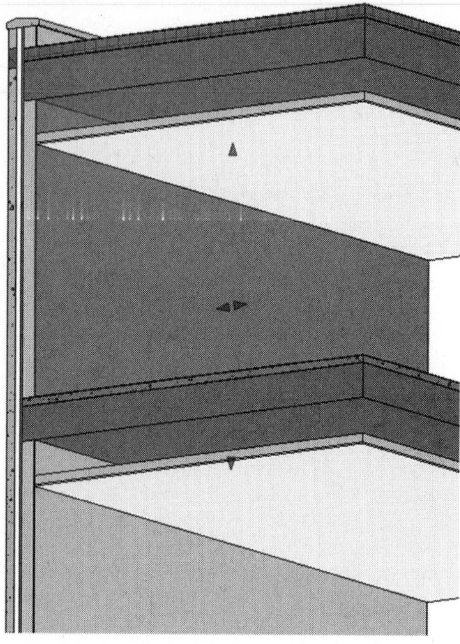

FIGURE 19.20
Use the Properties palette to enable shape handles for parts.

There are several other ways you can interact with parts in your project model. Select any of the parts and observe the Properties palette. You will see that you can override each part's material, phase created, and phase demolished (Figure 19.21).

FIGURE 19.21
Some part properties can be overridden.

Original Category	Walls
Original Family	Basic Wall
Original Type	Exterior - Brick and CMU on MTL....
Material By Original	☑
Material	Gypsum Wall Board
Construction	Finish
Phasing	
Phase Created	New Construction
Phase Demolished	None
Phase Created By Original	☑
Phase Demolished By Original	☑

USING PARTS

So far in this chapter, you've seen how you can use parts to subdivide building elements such as walls and floors. While the workflow outlined can take away from quickly laying out walls and floors, the Parts tool is very useful if leveraged correctly. As an example, one use for the Parts tool would be to define precast panels. In many instances, the precast paneling follows architectural grid lines. Controlling those with hosted voids or sweeps can be cumbersome and lead to a lot of manual coordination. Hosted sweeps can also be problematic around windows or other openings in the panels. This workflow would allow you to dynamically update the design and have it resonate through the documents quickly and clean up more easily than sweeps.

Knowing when to make use of a tool in Revit is almost as important as knowing how to use the tool. Tools like parts that allow a granular manipulation of building geometry are typically better left until later in the design process.

Dividing Parts with a Gap

In the previous exercise, you learned how to divide parts using datum objects and simple sketches. You also have the ability to divide parts with a defined gap as well as with a custom profile. Let's explore these options with another exercise:

1. Continue to work with the sample file `c19-Parts-Start.rvt` or `c19-Parts-Metric-Start.rvt` from the previous exercise. Activate the Parts Model 3D view and orbit the model to view the exterior face of the wall.
2. Select the main part of the exterior wall face that has the material assignment Concrete, Precast. Click the Divide Parts tool in the contextual ribbon.
3. In the Properties palette, set the Divider Gap parameter to **1"** (**25** mm).
4. Click the Intersecting References tool in the ribbon, set the filter to All, and then select Level 2, Reference Plane: yPlane1, and Grid: 1. Click OK to close the dialog box.
5. Click the green check mark in the ribbon to finish Divide Parts mode, and the panel will be divided with a continuous gap, as shown in Figure 19.22.

Figure 19.22
Parts divided with a continuous gap

In addition to simple gaps, parts can be divided with a custom profile. A family template called `Division Profile.rft` (`Metric Division Profile.rft`) is available in the default family template library. This profile family is similar to other profiles except that the completed sketch in the family does not need to be a closed loop. That said, the sketch must extend completely between the two reference planes associated with the Width parameter in the template.

A number of division profiles are loaded in the default architectural project template. You can find these in the Project Browser under Families ➤ Division Profiles. To examine how any of these are created, right-click Tapered Notch and select Edit from the context menu.

Let's explore how you can edit an existing division and apply a custom profile to the gap. Follow these steps:

1. Continue to work with the project file `c19-Parts-Start.rvt` or `c19-Parts-Metric-Start.rvt` from the previous exercise. Activate the Parts Model 3D view, and orbit the model to view the exterior face of the wall.
2. Select any one of the divided parts of the main precast concrete portion of the wall. Once a part has been divided, you won't need to select all the parts to edit the division—select just one. From the contextual ribbon, click Edit Division.

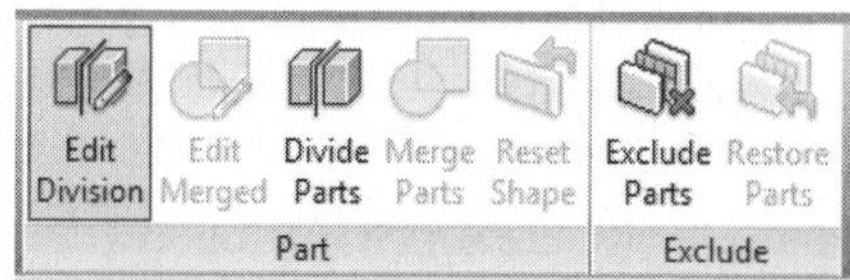

3. In the Properties palette, change the Division Profile parameter to Angled Step: Angled Step. Once you select a profile type, additional parameters are available in the Properties palette. Set the Edge Match parameter to Complementary (Figure 19.23).

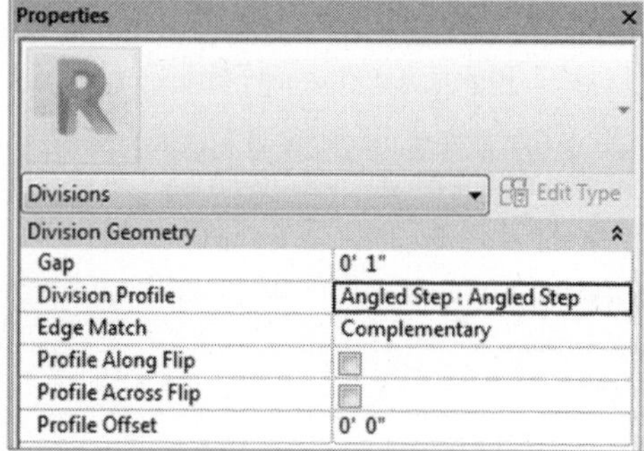

FIGURE 19.23
Assigning a division profile to a part

4. Click the green check mark in the ribbon to finish the division edits, and you will see that the updated profiles are applied to all edges of the divided parts (Figure 19.24).

FIGURE 19.24
Parts divided with a division profile

5. To explore different functionality with division profiles, repeat steps 2 through 4, but select the profile Notch and set the Edge Match parameter to Mirrored. Observe the change in behavior using a different matching property.

   When you apply a custom profile to a division of parts, the profile is applied to all divisions. If you need to assign different profiles to different divisions, you must apply each of those unique divisions separately. Let's try this approach by continuing the exercise.

6. In the Parts Model view, select any of the precast concrete parts you generated earlier in this exercise. Click Edit Division in the contextual ribbon.
7. Click the Intersecting References button in the ribbon, and in the Intersecting Named References dialog box, set the Filter drop-down to All, and then deselect Reference Plane: yPlane1.
8. Click OK to close the dialog box, and then click the green check mark in the ribbon to finish editing the division.
9. While pressing the Ctrl key, select the two larger precast concrete panels to the right side of the wall. Click the Divide Parts button in the ribbon.
10. Click the Intersecting References button in the ribbon, set the Filter drop-down to All, and then select Reference Plane: yPlane1. Click OK to close the dialog box.
11. In the Properties palette, set the Divider Gap parameter to **0″–1″** (**25** mm). Click the green check mark in the ribbon to finish editing the division.

You will now see that the custom profile was maintained for the other part divisions, but the rightmost vertical division has only a simple gap.

Merging Parts

Parts can be merged to form larger, more contiguous geometry; however, the parts to be merged must have the same material and the same creation and demolition phases, and the merged geometry must consist of a single connected component. Parts with gaps assigned to the divisions will not be merged.

To merge parts, press the Ctrl key while selecting multiple parts. In the contextual ribbon, click Merge Parts. Once parts have been merged, you can always edit them in the future. To edit merged parts, select the part and then select Edit Merged from the contextual ribbon.

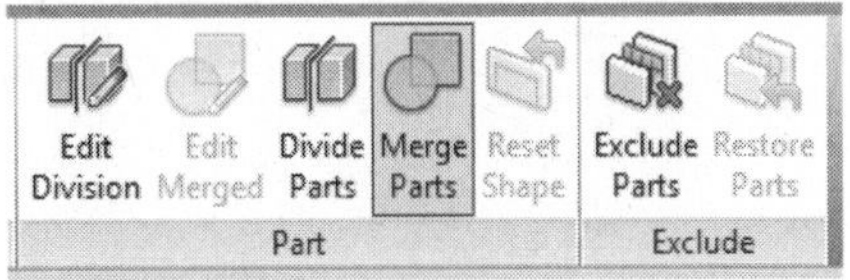

Excluding Parts

Parts can also be excluded from a model to support more detailed construction conditions. To exclude a part, select the part and click Exclude Parts from the Exclude panel of the contextual ribbon. Excluded parts will not appear in any schedules; however, they are easily restored. To restore an excluded part, hover over the area with your mouse pointer where the part was excluded. You will be able to select the excluded part, but it will be indicated with a special icon. Click the icon on the excluded part or click Restore Parts in the contextual ribbon.

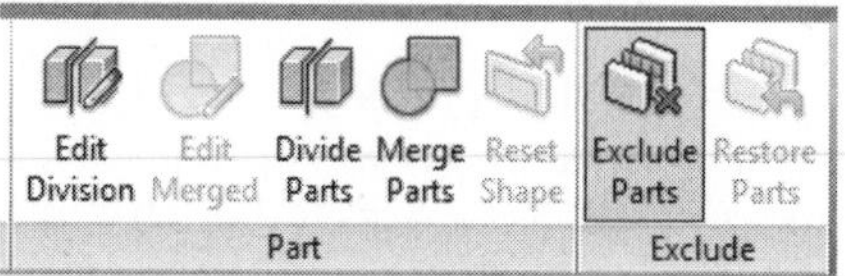

Be Aware of the Parts Category

Because parts are considered a separate category of elements, you should pay careful attention to how they might affect your views and view templates. Take a look at the visibility and graphic overrides for any view, and you'll see that Parts is listed as an object category. This means that once you create parts for a model element—whether the original object was a floor, ceiling, wall, or roof—the parts are all treated as a singular type of object. For example, if you have surface patterns for floors hidden in a view and you create parts for a floor, the surface pattern will appear again unless you have hidden surface patterns for the Parts category as well.

Scheduling Parts

Another valuable aspect of using parts is the ability to schedule them—essentially a cleaner way to generate material takeoffs. You can create a parts schedule in the same manner as you would for other object categories. On the View tab, click Schedules ➤ Schedule/Quantities, and choose the Parts category.

Select the Fields tab of the Schedule Properties dialog box, and you will see the available fields (Figure 19.25). With a part schedule, you can report the original category of the object along with the part material and the usual geometric information.

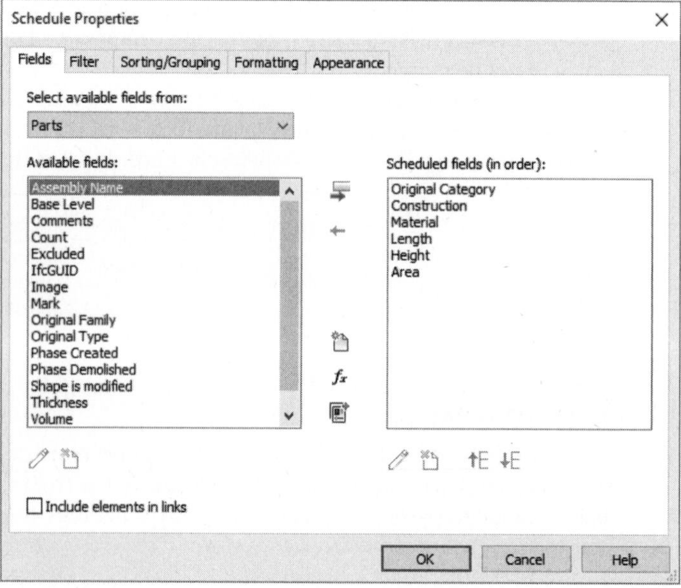

Figure 19.25
A part schedule has access to some unique fields for reporting.

There is also a field named Construction that indicates whether the part was derived from a Core layer or a Finish layer. This field can then be used as a filter and/or sorting criterion in your schedule. An example illustrating the results of a part schedule is shown in Figure 19.26.

FIGURE 19.26
An example of a completed part schedule

<Part Schedule>					
A	B	C	D	E	F
Original Category	Construction	Material	Length	Height	Area
Ceilings					
Ceilings	Core	Metal - Stud Layer			361 SF
Ceilings	Core	Metal - Stud Layer			361 SF
Ceilings	Finish	Gypsum Wall Board - Ceiling			361 SF
Ceilings	Finish	Gypsum Wall Board - Ceiling			153 SF
Ceilings	Finish	Gypsum Wall Board - Ceiling			208 SF
Floors					
Floors	Finish	Vinyl Composition Tile			375 SF
Floors	Core	Concrete, Lightweight			375 SF
Floors	Core	Metal - Deck			375 SF
Floors	Core	Structure - Steel Bar Joist Layer			375 SF
Roofs					
Roofs	Finish	Roofing - EPDM Membrane			375 SF
Roofs	Core	Metal - Deck			375 SF
Roofs	Core	Structure - Steel Bar Joist Layer			375 SF
Roofs	Finish	Rigid insulation			79 SF
Roofs	Finish	Rigid insulation			109 SF
Roofs	Finish	Rigid insulation			108 SF
Roofs	Finish	Rigid insulation			78 SF
Walls					
Walls	Trim	Concrete, Precast	25' - 0"		
Walls	Trim	Brick, Soldier Course	25' - 0"		
Walls	Trim	Concrete, Precast	25' - 0"		
Walls	Finish	Concrete Masonry Units	25' - 0"	3' - 4"	83 SF
Walls	Finish	Gypsum Wall Board	25' - 0"	10' - 0"	250 SF
Walls	Finish	Gypsum Wall Board	25' - 0"	0' - 8 1/2"	18 SF
Walls	Finish	Gypsum Wall Board	25' - 0"	10' - 0 5/8"	251 SF
Walls	Finish	Concrete, Precast	25' - 0"	0' - 8"	17 SF
Walls	Finish	Air	25' - 0"	24' - 0"	600 SF
Walls	Finish	Plywood, Sheathing	25' - 0"	24' - 0"	600 SF
Walls	Core	Metal - Stud Layer	25' - 0"	10' - 0"	250 SF

Creating Assemblies

An assembly organizes related elements within your project. The feature is designed to help users track and schedule a collection of elements as a single entity. In the case of precast concrete, for example, a column made of multiple families, including reinforcing bars, mounting hardware, and corbels, can be collected into a single assembly.

As you identify objects to be included in an assembly, you can also choose from a variety of views in which to document the element in isolation from the rest of the project model. A collection of assembly views can be thought of as shop drawings. Let's take a look at the workflow for creating an assembly.

In the following exercise, you can use any sample model to illustrate the process of creating assemblies:

1. In any view of your project, select a few model elements. Try to pick a few that are relatively close to each other.

2. From the contextual tab in the ribbon, click Create Assembly. You will be prompted to name the new assembly (Figure 19.27).

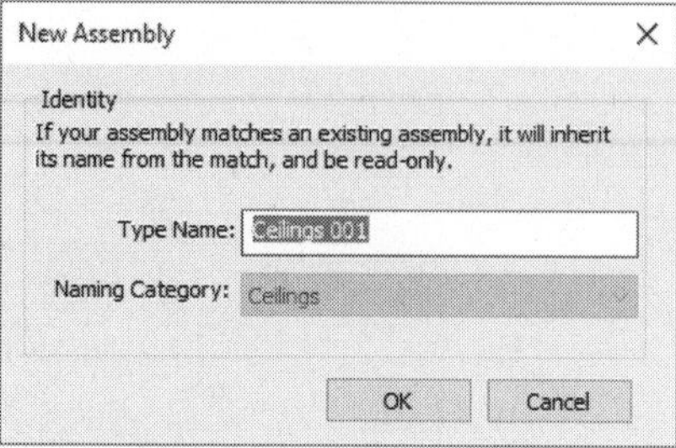

FIGURE 19.27
Enter a name for the new assembly.

If you selected objects of different categories such as a wall and a ceiling, you have the opportunity to select which category the assembly will inherit. Choosing one category or the other does not seem to have an effect on the functionality beyond the organization that is exposed to the user.

USING IDENTICAL ASSEMBLIES

When you create a new assembly, the software automatically determines whether another identical assembly exists in your model. If one exists, the new assembly inherits the name of the identical assembly. In a somewhat similar situation, if you were to create copies of an assembly throughout your project, the matching assemblies would function in a similar way to how groups function. The fundamental difference between assemblies and groups is in the propagation of changes. If you have identical assemblies in a project and you change one of them, the name of the modified assembly is changed and it is treated as a unique assembly.

Creating Assembly Views

After you have created an assembly, you can create a series of views that are dedicated to that assembly. In other words, you will see only the elements included in the assembly within these views. In addition to plans, sections, and 3D views, you can generate parts lists and quantity takeoffs for an assembly.

To generate assembly views, select an assembly in any view and select Create Views from the Assembly panel in the contextual tab of the ribbon. You are prompted with a dialog box in which you choose the views assigned to the assembly (Figure 19.28).

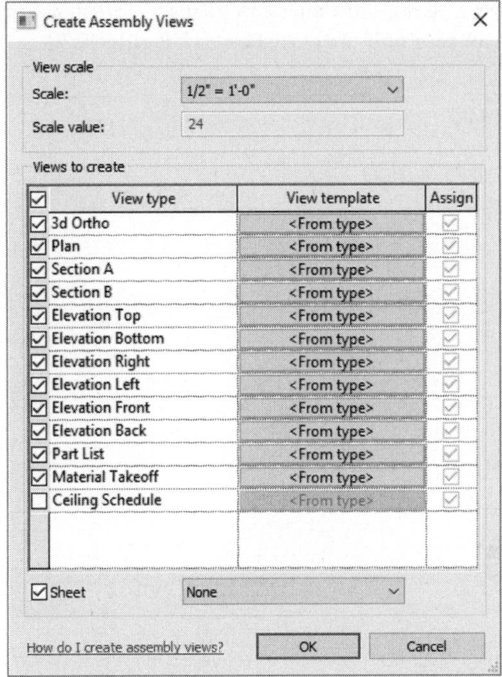

FIGURE 19.28
Select views to be created with the assembly.

After you click OK, you will find the assembly views at the bottom of the Project Browser. Under the Assemblies grouping, you will find each assembly listed with all the associated views (Figure 19.29).

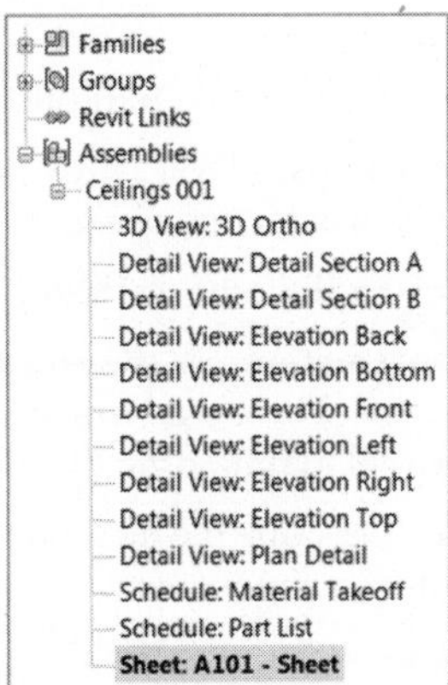

FIGURE 19.29
Assembly views are found at the bottom of the Project Browser.

Although sections are automatically placed for the included elements, the individual views are not placed on the assembly sheet. To do this, activate the sheet within an assembly and then drag and drop the views onto the sheet. Note that assembly views can be used on non-assembly sheets and regular views can be placed on an assembly sheet. An example of views compiled into an assembly sheet is shown in Figure 19.30.

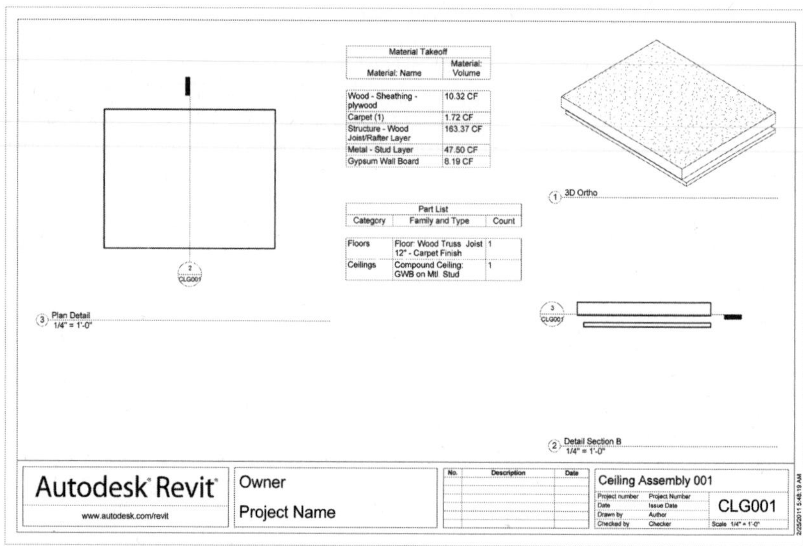

FIGURE 19.30
An example of a simple assembly sheet

The Bottom Line

Add revisions to your project. You need the ability to track changes in your design after sheets have been issued. Adding revisions to a drawing is an inevitable part of your workflow.

Master It How do you indicate revisions on a drawing sheet?

Use digital markups. DWFs provide a lightweight means to digitally transfer and mark up multiple sheets in a document set.

Master It Explain the workflow using DWF markups.

Model for construction. Parts and assemblies allow a model element to be broken down into smaller parts. These subelements can be used in more detailed ways for the construction process while still maintaining their association with the original element.

Master It Describe the method for breaking down a design-based model assembly into its individual components.

Chapter 20

Presenting Your Design

Although Autodesk® Revit® Architecture software is most often used to create parametric content for documentation, it is often necessary to show designs to clients and other project stakeholders to make critical decisions. Revit has tools that you can use to embellish views or create new graphics to help present the design.

In this chapter, you'll learn to:

- Understand color fill legends
- Use 3D model views in your presentation
- Work with viewport types
- Create "exploded" axonometric views

Understanding Color Fill Legends

There are many times in the design process when you will need to go beyond documentation for construction and portray spaces in a building in a different way. For example, you may need to communicate design intent, departmental adjacencies and allocations, or room finishes. Because Revit software has these functions, you can use its parametric capabilities to do more than just generate annotation—you can graphically show all kinds of model parameters.

The tool for creating this kind of view is called the Color Fill Legend. You can use this tool to color areas and rooms in plans, sections, and elevations. It allows you to assign different colors to just about any of the room or area properties within a view. Here are just a few examples of the types of views you can create:

- Floor plans showing departments.
- Floor plans showing spaces based on area value. An example might be rooms smaller than 500 square feet (50 sq m) as one color, rooms that are between 500 and 1000 square feet (50 sq m to 100 sq m) as another color, and rooms bigger than 1000 square feet (100 sq m) as a third color.
- Building sections showing different departments in different colors as in a stacking diagram.
- Plans, sections, or elevations portraying room finish types.

There is an almost endless list of the types of color fills you can create to help communicate a wide variety of project-specific details. The Color Fill Legend tool is located on the Color Fill panel of the Annotate tab (Figure 20.1).

FIGURE 20.1
The Color Fill Legend tool

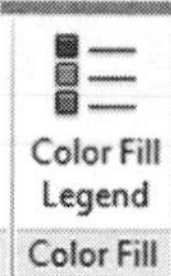

To better demonstrate some of the uses of the Color Fill Legend tool, let's make a simple color fill plan showing room types.

Making a Color Fill Legend for Rooms

In many projects, it becomes necessary to display plans with some additional information about the spaces. Typically during the design phases, clients need to see how different departments are located adjacent to one another. Even in a simple residential design, it can be helpful to see how public spaces such as kitchens and living areas are located relative to the more private spaces of bedrooms and bathrooms.

In the sample building project used in Chapter 17, "Documenting Your Design," you may want to visually show the various space types in the floor plans. You want to graphically demonstrate which spaces have been assigned to various departments defined in the building's program of requirements. To get started, download and open the `c20-Sample-Building-Start.rvt` or `c20-Sample-Metric.rvt` model from the book's web page, `www.sybex.com/go/masteringrevit2017`. You will begin by creating a new type of floor plan that will help organize the Project Browser and automatically assign an appropriate view template.

To get started, follow these steps:

1. Switch to the View tab in the ribbon, locate the Create panel, and then choose Plan Views ➤ Floor Plans. In the New Floor Plan dialog box, click the Edit Type button to open the Type Properties dialog box for the Floor Plan type.
2. Click the Duplicate button and then name the new view type **Color Fill**.
3. Click the button in the parameter field named View Template Applied To New Views. In the Apply View Template dialog box, select Color Fill Plans and then click OK to close the Type Properties dialog box.
4. Using the Ctrl key, select both Level 1 and Level 2 in the New Floor Plan dialog box, and then click OK.
5. Return to the Project Browser and you will see a new heading called Floor Plans (Color Fill). Change the names of the new floor plans to **Level 1 - Dept - Color** and **Level 2 - Dept - Color**.

6. Activate each of the new color fill plans and use the Tag All Not Tagged tool to add room tags to each plan.

   For more information on tagging, see Chapter 18, "Annotating Your Design."

7. Open the Level 1 - Dept - Color floor plan and click the Color Fill Legend button in the Color Fill panel of the Annotate tab. This will activate the Color Fill Legend tool and ask you to place a legend somewhere in the active view. Anywhere for now is fine—just place it to one side of the plan or the other.

   Once the legend is placed, you can then define and customize its characteristics.

8. After the legend is placed, you'll be presented with a dialog box similar to the one in Figure 20.2. This dialog box will prompt you to choose from a list of space types available in the current view and color schemes that have already been established within the model. From the Space Type drop-down list, select Rooms, and from the Color Scheme drop-down list, choose Name and click OK.

FIGURE 20.2
Choose Space Type and Color Scheme after you place the legend in a view.

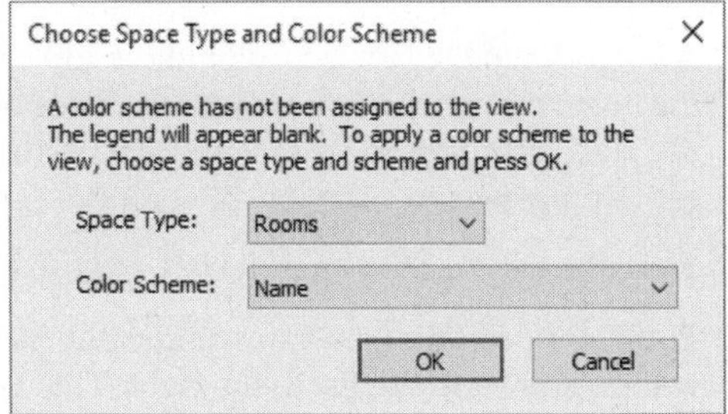

The color scheme will automatically generate a legend based on your room names and color the rooms on the plan.

If you already created a color scheme that you wanted to use in this view, it would be a simple matter of selecting it from this list and clicking OK, and the legend and view would be complete. The default project template contains a few simple color schemes from which you can choose when you place your first legend. You started with a basic one that automatically assigns a color for each unique room name in the project; however, this type of presentation is not usually that useful.

In the subsequent steps of the exercise, you will create different color schemes to further explore more complex methods of presentation.

Certification Objective

9. After the legend is placed, you can then alter its properties or choose a different color scheme. To modify a legend, select the legend, and in the Modify | Color Fill Legends context menu, click the Edit Scheme button.

   This opens the aptly named Edit Color Scheme dialog box (Figure 20.3). This dialog box allows you add, rename, or delete color schemes on the left side and define the graphic properties and attributes of these schemes on the right.

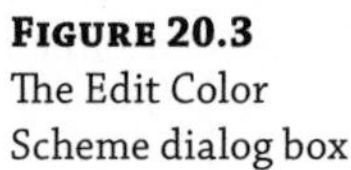

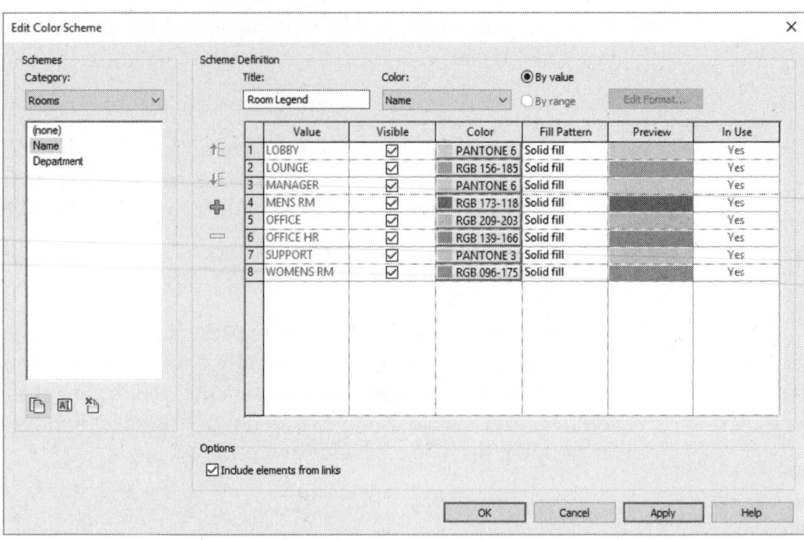

FIGURE 20.3 The Edit Color Scheme dialog box

A drop-down list labeled Color at the top of the Scheme Definition area appears. This is the property by which the color scheme is being defined. It is currently assigned to color the plan according to room name. Each unique room name in the project is automatically generating its own color for the legend.

10. From the list of schemes at the left, choose Department.

The Color drop-down list now indicates the Department parameter, but there are no values defined in the list to the right. This is because text has not been added to the Department parameter for any of the room elements in the project.

Any parameter available to be used in a color fill legend needs to have values in its properties. You can enter the value in the Properties palette either by selecting the item and finding that property or by predefining values in the color scheme. In the following steps, you will predefine values for the departments and then assign them to the rooms later.

11. Now let's predefine some values. At the left side of the table under Scheme Definition, click the green plus sign to add values to the color scheme for Department. Create four new values as follows:

- MANAGEMENT
- OPERATIONS
- PRODUCTION
- SALES

For now, you can use the automatic color and pattern assignments.

12. Click OK to close the dialog box.

You will notice in the floor plan that the legend now shows the title Department Legend and it displays No Colors Defined (Figure 20.4). Even though you defined some Department values, they will not show on the legend until you assign values to the rooms placed in the project.

FIGURE 20.4
Department legend with no defined color scheme

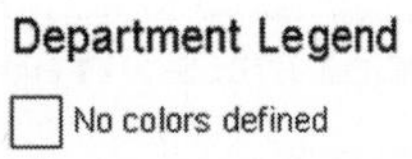

Department Legend

No colors defined

13. Back in the floor plan, select the Manager room on the lower left of the plan and look in the Properties palette. Find the Department property and click in the value field to access a drop-down list (Figure 20.5).

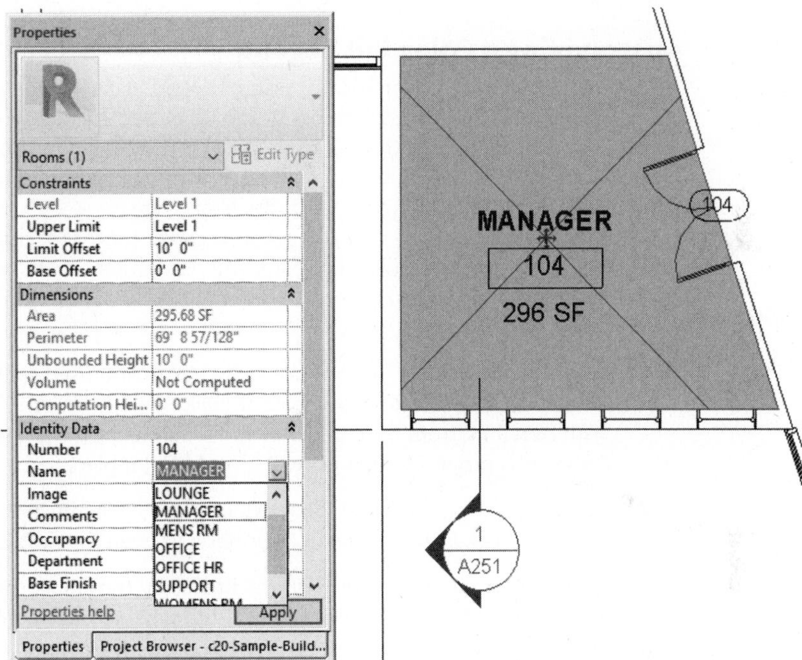

FIGURE 20.5
Assign values to room properties based on data assigned to a color scheme.

The values available in the list are the values you added to the color scheme in step 5.

14. Assign the two rooms at the left side of the plan to the MANAGEMENT department, assign the LOUNGE space to the SALES department, and assign the SUPPORT space to the OPERATIONS department.

    As you make these assignments, the color fill legend will update and the space will fill with the matching color.

15. Activate the **Level 2 - Dept - Color** floor plan and repeat steps 7 through 14 to assign some department values.

Because you already created a color scheme defined by department value, you don't need to repeat steps 9 and 10.

Assigning Color Fills without a Legend

In the previous exercise, you generated color fills on a plan by adding a legend and then customizing the color scheme through the legend. You don't have to place a legend in order to color a plan with a color scheme. In the Properties palette for a view, you can find the Color Scheme property. Click the button in the value row to open the Edit Color Scheme dialog box and choose a color scheme to be assigned to the view. The plan will display the respective colors even without a legend shown on the view. You can always add a legend later by using the Legend tool in the Color Fill panel of the Annotate tab in the ribbon.

Customizing a Color Fill Legend

Although the software automatically assigns colors to each value in a color scheme definition, you'll likely want to change the colors or the fill patterns to suit your presentation needs. In this section you will customize the color scheme and the legend created in the previous exercises. Because many firms typically have standards for presentation color schemes, it's a good idea to add your customized schemes to your office template.

In the following exercise you will create a copy of the department-based color scheme to use black line patterns instead of color fills. Download and open the file `c20-Sample-Building2-Start.rvt` or `c20-Sample-Metric2-Start.rvt` from the book's web page. Then follow these steps:

1. Return to the Level 1 - Dept - Color floor plan you used for the exercise in the previous section. In the Project Browser, right-click Level 1 - Dept - Color and choose Duplicate With Detailing from the context menu. Rename the duplicated view **Level 1 - Dept - Black**. Repeat this process for the Level 2 - Dept - Color plan.

2. Activate the Level 1 - Dept - Black floor plan, select the legend located to the right of the plan, and click Edit Scheme in the ribbon to open the Edit Color Scheme dialog box.

3. Select Department from the list of schemes on the left side and click the Duplicate icon at the bottom of the list. Name the duplicate scheme **Department (Black)**.

4. You can change any of the assigned colors by selecting any of the buttons in the Color column. Doing so opens the Color dialog box (Figure 20.6) and allows you to select colors based on RGB values or PANTONE colors. Change the colors for each of the departments to black (R:**0**, G:**0**, B:**0**) and then click OK.

   After you have defined the colors, take note of a couple of other features in the Edit Color Scheme dialog box, shown previously in Figure 20.3. The first is the Options area at the bottom of the dialog box, which contains a single check box that allows you to pull values from linked projects. If you are working on a large building that is split into multiple files, this is a good way to tie all that information together into a single graphic presentation.

5. The other option you have is the ability to exclude various scheme definition values for a color scheme. Notice the Visible column next to the Value column in the scheme definition, as shown in Figure 20.7.

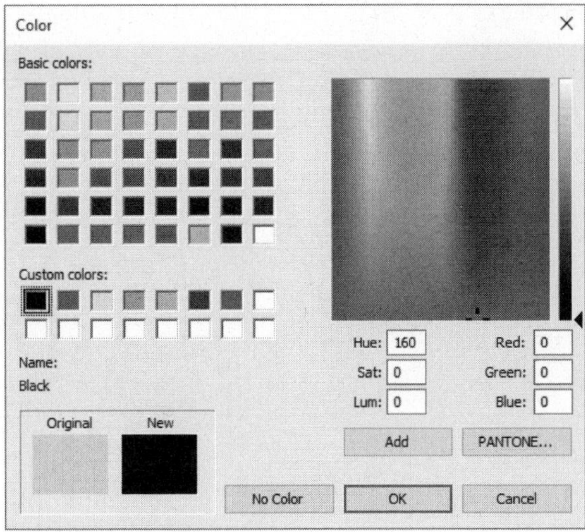

FIGURE 20.6
Click the button in the Color column to select a different color.

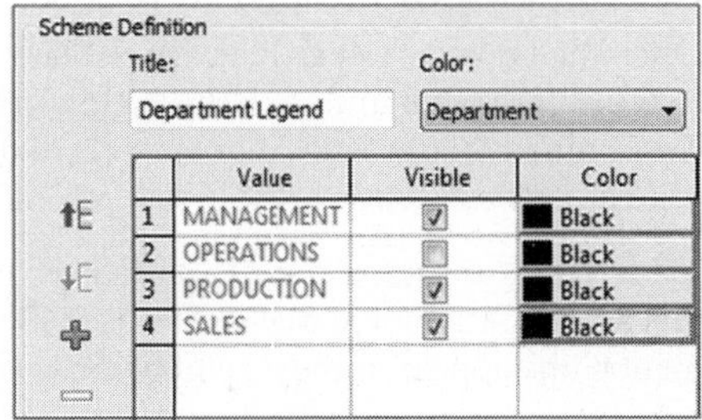
Scheme Definition

Title: Department Legend

Color: Department

	Value	Visible	Color
1	MANAGEMENT	☑	Black
2	OPERATIONS	☐	Black
3	PRODUCTION	☑	Black
4	SALES	☑	Black

FIGURE 20.7
Use the Visible option to exclude values from the legend.

Uncheck the box in the Visible column next to the value for OPERATIONS.

This setting will exclude the selected value wherever this color scheme is applied to a view. In this example, we might assume that the client does not need to see spaces that belong to the OPERATIONS department in color—just the remaining departmental spaces.

6. Click each of the fields under the Fill Pattern column to change the fill pattern to a variety of line-based patterns, as shown in Figure 20.8.

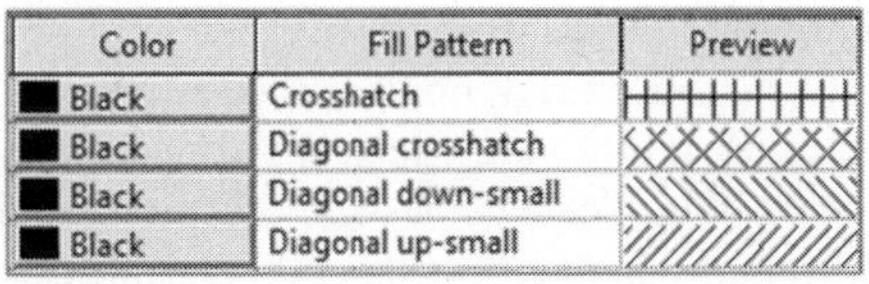

Color	Fill Pattern	Preview
Black	Crosshatch	
Black	Diagonal crosshatch	
Black	Diagonal down-small	
Black	Diagonal up-small	

FIGURE 20.8
The pattern for each value can be customized.

7. Click OK and you'll notice that the color fills have dynamically changed to reflect the modifications you made in your color scheme properties, as shown in Figure 20.9.

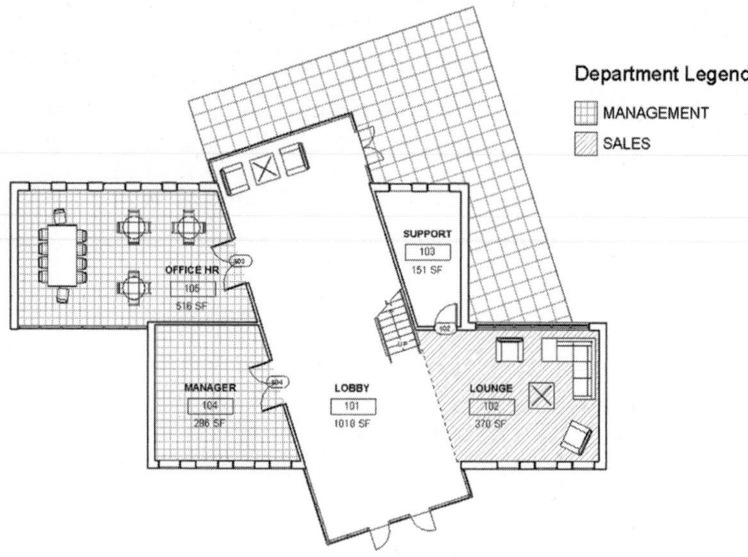

FIGURE 20.9
The floor plan after scheme colors and patterns are altered

8. Open the Level 2 - Dept - Black floor plan. In the Properties palette, locate the Color Scheme parameter and click the button in the value field that is currently assigned to Department. In the Edit Color Scheme dialog box, choose the Department (Black) color scheme and click OK.

The pattern fills are automatically placed according to the department assignments. Also notice that spaces assigned to the OPERATIONS department are not colored, nor does the department name appear in the legend because the Visible setting was turned off in step 5.

Modifying Other Settings

By now, you've created a color fill legend and placed it within a view, and you've seen a number of the settings and properties of the legend. Those settings reflect how the color fill legend will look and react to the plan or view in which it's placed, but there are other settings you can modify as well. The legend key itself has several properties that control fonts and swatch sizes. Select the legend and click the Edit Type button in the Properties palette to explore some of the other properties you can modify.

Figure 20.10 shows the type properties for a color fill legend. In this dialog box, you can change the font size and type as well as the size of the color swatches that appear in the legend.

An important type property for color fill legends is Values Displayed. The two options for this property are By View and All, and the default setting for color fill legends is By View. You might have noticed that none of the spaces on Level 1 are assigned to the PRODUCTION department, and so that value does not appear in the legend placed on Level 1.

Try creating a duplicate color legend type named All Values and change the Values Displayed property to All. This legend type shows all department names, regardless of the department assignments on each level. This setting does not override the Visible options you specify in the color scheme settings; therefore, the OPERATIONS department will still not display when you use the Department (Black) color scheme.

In summary, you can combine any color scheme with any color legend type—the two are not dependent on each other.

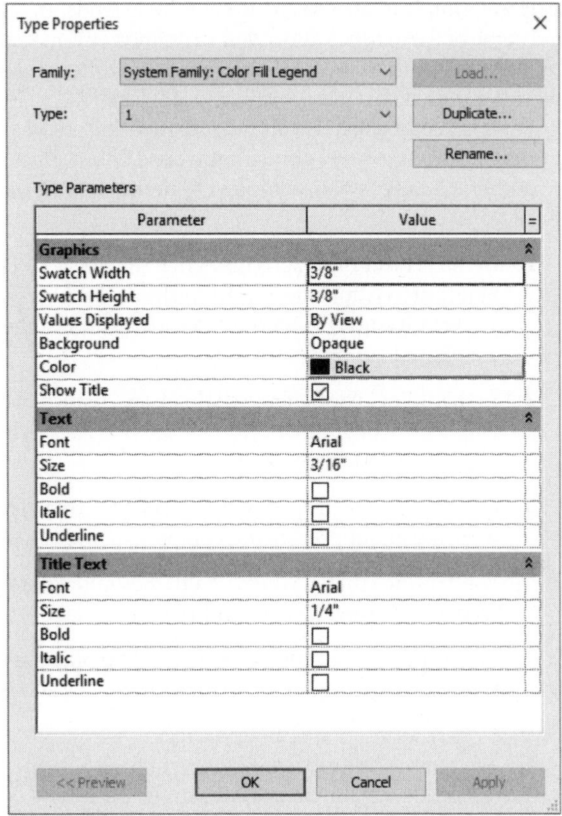

FIGURE 20.10 Edit the visual and functional characteristics of a color fill legend in the Type Properties dialog box.

> **DON'T FORGET YOUR STANDARDS**
>
> It can take several tries between creating color fill plans and printing them to get the colors just right. You'll find yourself making multiple adjustments along the way. When you have one that works for you, take the time for a couple of extra steps so you don't have to re-create this work in the future.
>
> First, if it is a type of project that you'll be doing again and again, add the legend to your project template. This is as easy as placing the legend on a view and the view on a sheet (similar to a schedule) and copying it to the Clipboard. Open your project template (in the same instance of Revit) and paste it onto a sheet, and your settings, colors, and naming conventions will be quickly transferred and saved for future use.

Using Numerical Ranges for Color Schemes

In the previous exercises, you explored how to use color schemes to create presentation material based on specific object properties. You can also create color schemes that display ranges of numerical values. In the following exercise, you will continue with the `c20-Sample-Building 2-Start.rvt` or `c20-Sample-Metric2-Start.rvt` file. With the Room color fill legend defined, you have seen an example of how to create color fill legends. A variety of other legend types are available, and some of these types allow you to define your own parameters when creating the legend itself. Let's step through this process again using a different legend type so you can see how you can define your own parameters in a color fill legend.

The next color scheme you will create is based on areas. Whereas the Department color scheme was defined by rooms that were already placed on plans, the area scheme is defined by numerical ranges you will need to define within the color scheme properties. Follow these steps:

1. In the Project Browser, right-click the Level 1 - Dept - Black floor plan and choose Duplicate With Detailing from the context menu. Rename the duplicated plan **Level 1 - Area Range**. Select the color fill legend in the view, and click Edit Scheme in the contextual tab of the ribbon.
2. In the Edit Color Scheme dialog box, create a copy of the Name color scheme, using the Duplicate icon at the bottom of the list. Name the new scheme **Area Range**. Also change the Title field to Area Range.
3. From the Color drop-down list, choose Area. Click OK if you are presented with a warning about preserving colors.

   You'll notice that all the room names and colors will disappear; they are replaced with values representing each unique room area.

   This type of schedule—like a schedule of room names—is probably not that useful as a presentation method. Instead, let's create a series of colored area ranges to easily identify which spaces are within specific ranges.
4. Next to the Color drop-down list in the Scheme Definition field, select the By Range option. The static area values in the list below are now split into two columns labeled At Least and Less Than (Figure 20.11).

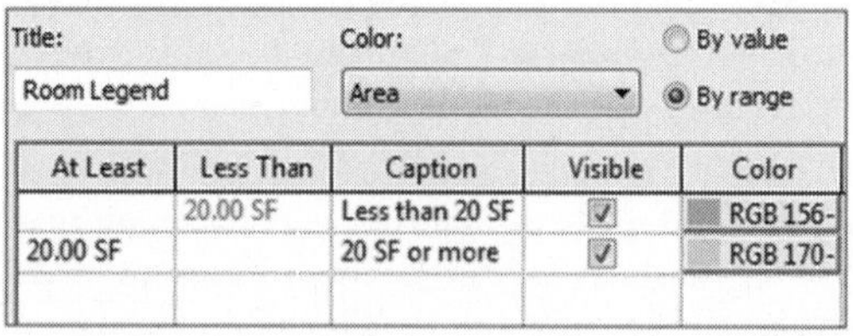

FIGURE 20.11 Select By Range to change the scheme definition.

Title: Room Legend — Color: Area — By value / By range

At Least	Less Than	Caption	Visible	Color
	20.00 SF	Less than 20 SF	☑	RGB 156-
20.00 SF		20 SF or more	☑	RGB 170-

5. Select one of the rows so the green plus button is active. Click that button two times so that you have four rows in the list of value ranges.
6. Starting from the bottom row, change the values to **800**, **500**, and **200**, as shown in Figure 20.12.

FIGURE 20.12
Modifying the values in the Scheme Definition field

At Least	Less Than	Caption	Visible
	200.00 SF	Less than 200 S	☑
200.00 SF	500.00 SF	200 SF - 500 SF	☑
500.00 SF	800.00 SF	500 SF - 800 SF	☑
800.00 SF		800 SF or more	☑

You can also try changing some of the colors assigned to each of the value ranges to make the presentation more meaningful or simply easier to read.

7. Click OK to update the color fill scheme and view the results in the plan (Figure 20.13).

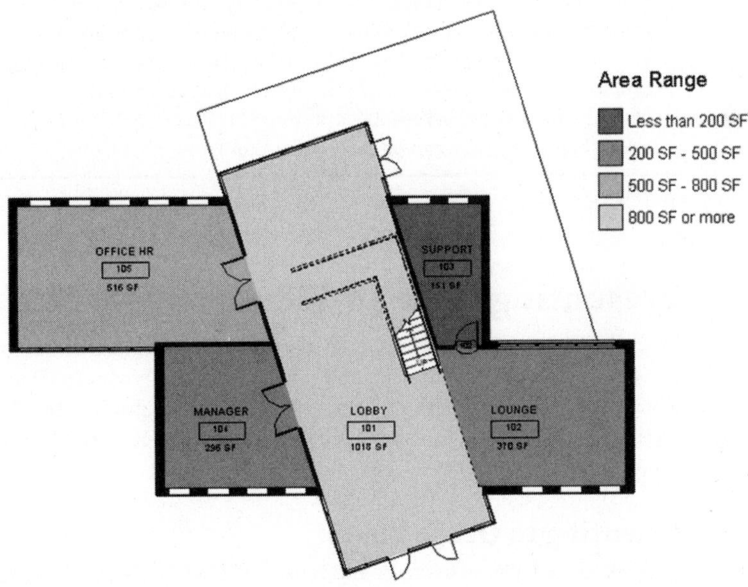

FIGURE 20.13
The finished floor plan with color fills by area range

The rooms now have colors based on their sizes rather than their names.

8. In the Project Browser, right-click Level 2 - Dept - Black and choose Duplicate With Detailing from the context menu. Rename the duplicated view **Level 2 - Area Range**.

9. In the Level 2 - Area Range floor plan, select the existing color fill legend and click Edit Scheme from the contextual tab in the ribbon. In the Edit Color Scheme dialog box, select Area Range and then click OK.

The rooms on Level 2 are now also represented with the same color range as we assigned for Level 1.

PROGRAM VERIFICATION WITH COLOR FILLS

Another more advanced presentation technique can be achieved with color fills by using value ranges for verification of your project's program of requirements. We showed you how to create a color fill scheme to illustrate ranges of spatial area; however, the results can be made even more useful for effective decision making.

The Area property of rooms will always display the actual value of the enclosed space. To compare the actual or designed area with the required area, you must create and populate a user-defined parameter. There are other applications that can accomplish this integration with Revit, including Trelligence Affinity (`www.trelligence.com`) and dRofus (`www.drofus.com`); however, the ability of an external application to feed the required program areas into the Revit model is irrelevant. The key is to compare the required area with the designed area and feed the difference into another user-defined room parameter. This can be accomplished using the Revit application programming interface.

Once the difference in area is captured in a room parameter, a color scheme can be established to color the ranges in the difference. For example, if the designed area is divided by the required area, you will get a percentage that can be included in a color scheme range. Color the higher percentages (positive and negative) with a noticeably visible color and the lower percentages with a more subtle color. If the range of acceptable differences is between 95 percent and 105 percent of the required area, then that range can be assigned no color and no pattern.

Presenting with 3D Views

In addition to using 2D views such as plans, sections, and elevations to convey your design intent, you can present the 3D model in a variety of ways. In Chapter 11, "Visualization," we discussed the methods for creating analytic and photorealistic visualizations; the following sections will help you to establish a new repertoire of presentation techniques for design and construction documents.

Orienting to Other Views

A quick and easy way to create more useful 3D views is by utilizing the Orient To View command. This command, which is somewhat hidden within the ViewCube®, allows you to create a 3D view that mimics the settings of a 2D view.

In the following exercise, you will continue to use the `c20-Sample-Building2-Start.rvt` or `c20-Sample-Metric-Start.rvt` file. You will first adjust the view range settings for the floor plans and then create a 3D view for each level. Finally, you will assemble the views on a sheet to complete the presentation.

1. Select Level 1 from the Project Browser and go to the Properties Palette to examine the view properties. Click the Edit button in the View Range property.
2. In the View Range dialog box (Figure 20.14), change the Top value under Primary Range to Level Above and set the corresponding offset value to **–1′-8″** (**–0.5** m). Repeat this step for Level 2.

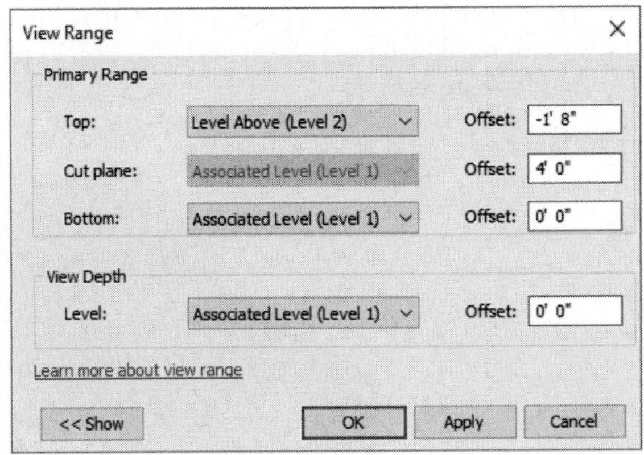

FIGURE 20.14 Adjust the Top values for the plan's view range.

Although you are changing the top of the view range of the floor plans, you will not see any difference in their graphic display.

3. Right-click the Default 3D view {3D} in the Project Browser and create two duplicates. Rename the duplicate views **Box-Level 1** and **Box-Level 2**.
4. Activate the view Box-Level 1 and right-click the ViewCube. Select Orient To View ➤ Floor Plans ➤ Floor Plan: Level 1, as shown in Figure 20.15.

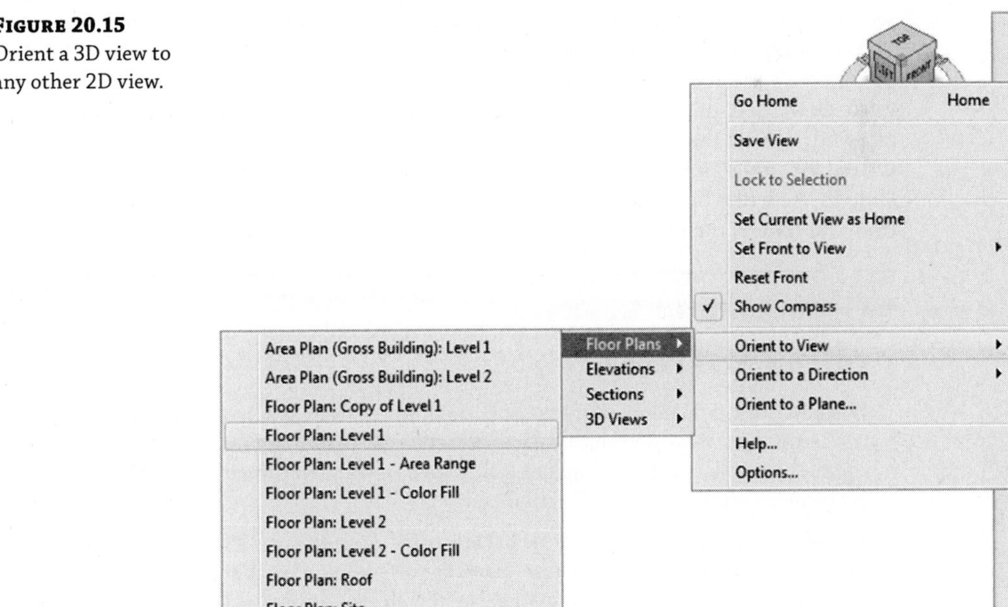

FIGURE 20.15 Orient a 3D view to any other 2D view.

The view will be set to a plan orientation, but more important, a section box has been enabled that matches the extents of the Level 1 plan view. Try orbiting the view to see the results (Figure 20.16).

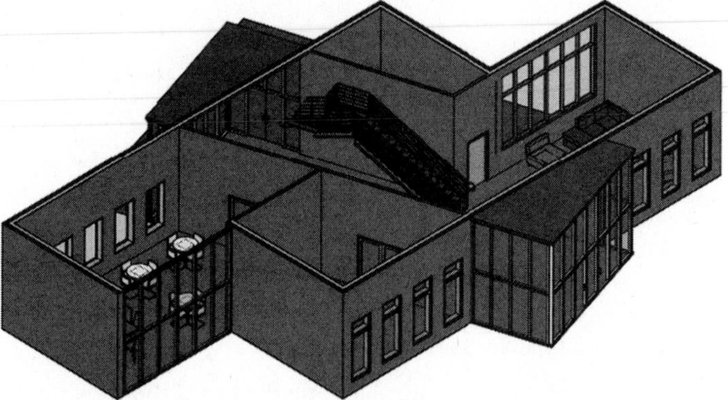

Figure 20.16
A 3D view after being oriented to a plan view

5. Right-click the ViewCube and select Orient To A Direction ➤ Southwest Isometric.
6. Repeat steps 4 and 5 for the Box-Level 2 view.
7. Create a new sheet using the title block in the project file, and drag the **Box-Level 1** and **Box-Level 2** views onto the sheet.

Place the Box-Level 2 view directly above the Box-Level 1 view and you'll notice that the views will align vertically. You can align model views of various types on sheets as long as they are the same scale. This does not work for drafting views or perspective views.

You can continue to experiment with the view settings of these 3D views on the sheet. Even though the section boxes won't print by default, you may want to hide them anyway. You can't uncheck the Section Box property because the view would no longer be three-dimensionally cropped. To hide the section box, select the viewport and then click Activate View in the contextual tab in the ribbon. Select the section box, and from the contextual tab in the ribbon, click Hide In View (the light bulb icon) ➤ Hide Elements. Right-click and choose Deactivate View from the context menu, and then repeat this process for the other 3D view.

 **Real World Scenario**

Cutting to the Core

We have worked on many building projects in which there was a central core of vertical circulation: stairs, elevators, and shafts. After years of legacy experience using 2D views to explore these complex yet isolated three-dimensional spaces, we found it difficult to imagine an easier way to perform this design and coordination task.

The ability to quickly generate a 3D view that is based on an enlarged stair plan or elevator shaft section has proven to be immensely valuable. Teaching this technique to the senior architects and engineers on your team will bring you plenty of praise! There's even an app for that—the COINS Auto-Section Box add-in is a free download that can be found in the Autodesk Exchange app store (`http://apps.exchange.autodesk.com`). The Auto-Section Box tool has become one of our most used add-ins.

Annotating 3D Views

Once you add a 3D view to your sheets, you're likely want to annotate it. To add annotations to your 3D view, you first need to lock it before adding text and tags as you would in a 2D view. This functionality is quite simple to implement.

In any orthographic 3D view, you will find the Lock/Unlock View button in the view shortcut bar, as shown in Figure 20.17. Once you lock the view, you can begin to add tags, text, and dimensions, but you cannot change the orientation of the view unless it is unlocked.

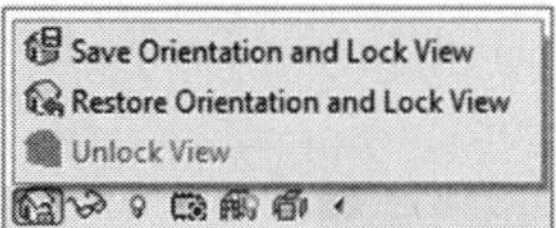

FIGURE 20.17 The 3D view can be locked from the view control bar.

In the example shown in Figure 20.18, a section box was first applied to a 3D view and then annotated.

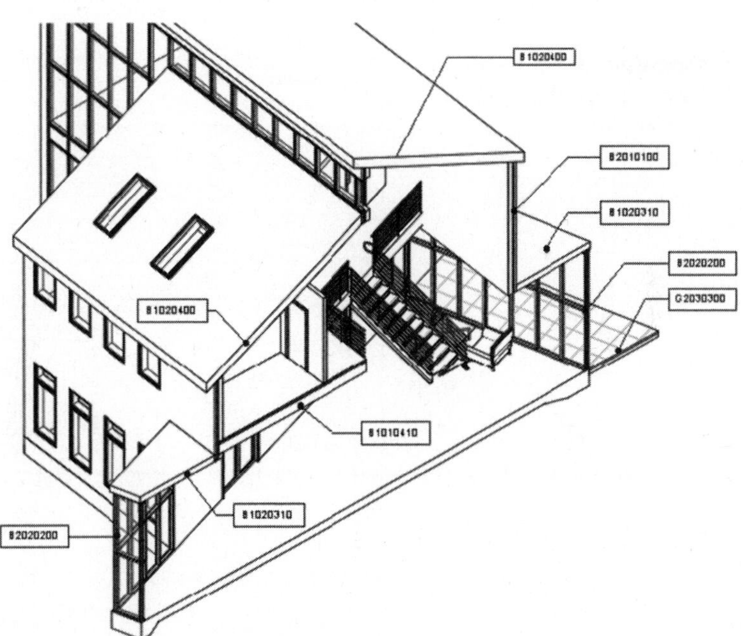

FIGURE 20.18 Annotation can be applied to a 3D view with locked orientation.

Once you have added annotation to a view, you may need to rotate the view. Return to the locked view tool and click Unlock View. You are now free to orbit the 3D view; notice how your annotations orbit with your model. The annotations will appear a bit skewed as a result of this rotation. If you want to return the view to the originally saved orientation, click Restore Orientation And Lock View. The annotations will reappear in their original locations.

Editing Viewport Types

In the previous exercises, you might have noticed that the 3D views placed on the sheet displayed the default view title; however, we don't need the titles every time we place a view on a sheet. Options and properties related to the display of views on sheets are stored as *viewport* types. Although the name conjures up memories of model space and paper space in Autodesk® AutoCAD® software, it is actually quite different in Revit. The viewport does not determine the scale or anything else about the view itself but simply sets the parameters for how a view sits on a sheet.

Let's examine how to customize viewport types by completing an exercise that continues from the previous example of placing 3D views on a sheet:

1. Using the sheet with the two stacked 3D plan views, select one of the views and click Edit Type in the Properties palette.

   The Type Properties dialog box appears (Figure 20.19).

   There are only a few properties in a viewport type, most of which are related to the extension line in the title. You can change the View Title family selection in the Family drop-down list. However, in this exercise you will not need a view title. We're going to create a new viewport type that does not use a title.

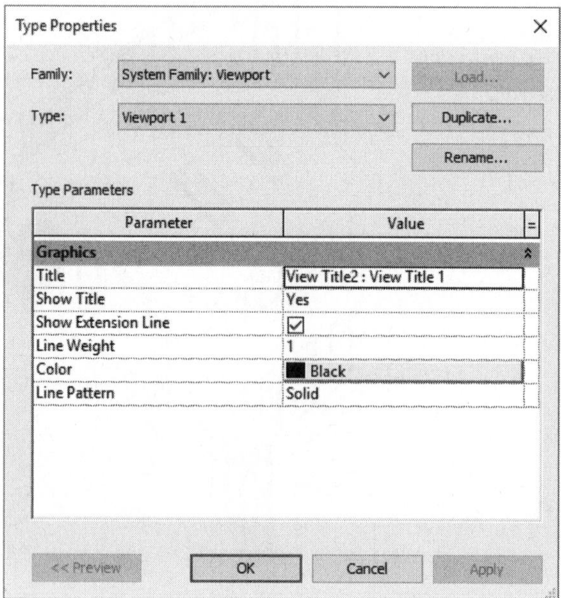

FIGURE 20.19 The type properties of a viewport

2. Click the Duplicate button to create a new viewport type named No Title.
3. Click the Show Title drop-down list and select No.
4. Next, for the Show Extension Line setting, uncheck the box.

Before you click OK to make the new type, let's verify an important property in this dialog box. The Show Title property is set to When Multiple Viewports, which will display the titles only when multiple views are placed on a sheet. The view title is not displayed if only one view is placed on a sheet, as in an overall floor plan.

5. Click OK to close the Type Properties dialog box, and you'll see that the viewport you had selected is already changed to the new type. Select the other viewport and switch it to No Title in the Type Selector.

When you have completed the exercise, you can also add some detail lines to the sheet to further embellish the descriptive presentation, as shown in Figure 20.20. Although you cannot snap to the geometry within the viewports, you can use the arrow keys to nudge the lines into alignment as required.

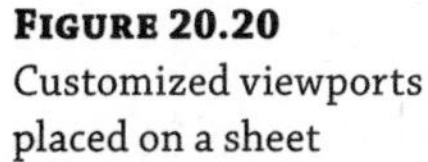

FIGURE 20.20
Customized viewports placed on a sheet

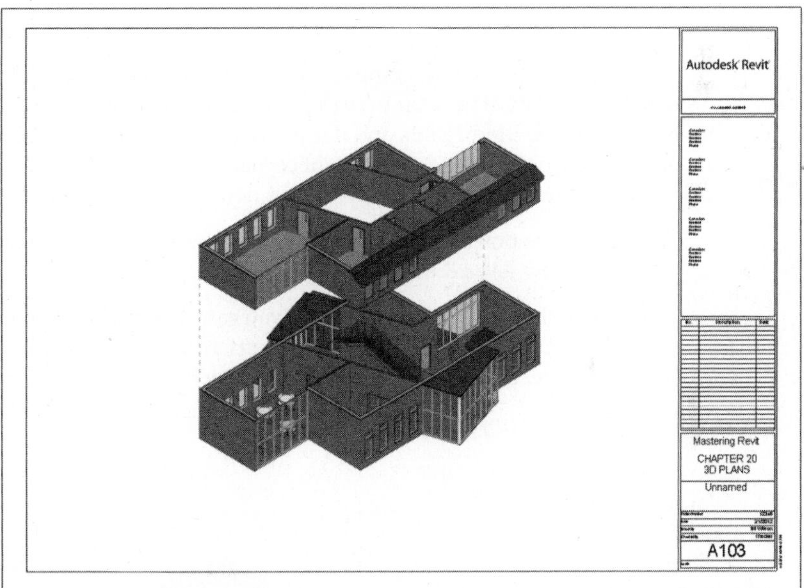

Creating "Exploded" Axonometric Views

A very useful tool to help you present your designs in a unique way is the Displace Elements tool. This tool allows you to create an "exploded" axon—essentially allowing you to take the geometry of a 3D view and move it without impacting the model. In Figure 20.21, you can see the use of the Displace Elements tool on the left and the original model on the right. The displacement is view-specific, so in all other views the model integrity remains.

FIGURE 20.21
Using the Displace Elements tool

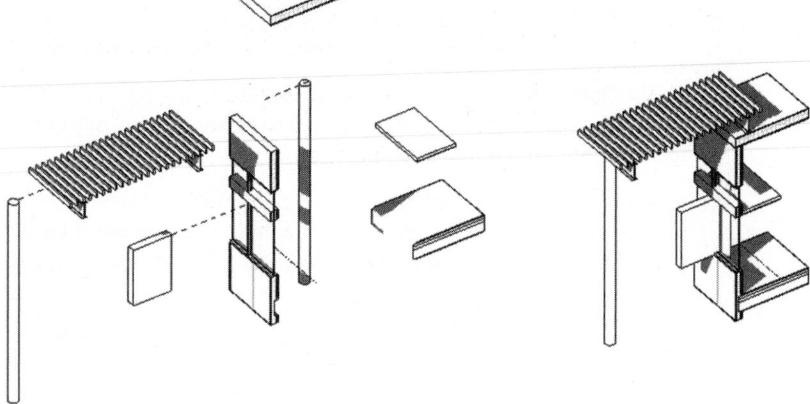

In this exercise, you're going to continue using the `c20-Sample-Building2-Start.rvt` or `c20-Sample-Metric2-Start.rvt` file to create a displaced element. The Displace Elements tool is found on the Modify tab, and it is active when you select an object in a 3D view. It is located on the View panel in the upper-right corner.

You'll start this exercise by creating a new view:

1. Take the Box-Level 1 view you created in the previous exercise and duplicate it. Rename the view **Axon-Level 1**.
2. With the new view established, you can change the orientation. Right-click the ViewCube, select Orient To A Direction, and select Southeast Isometric. Alternatively, you can select the corner of the ViewCube where the Front, Right, and Top sides connect.

   Your starting view will look like Figure 20.22.

FIGURE 20.22
Baseline view for the displaced elements

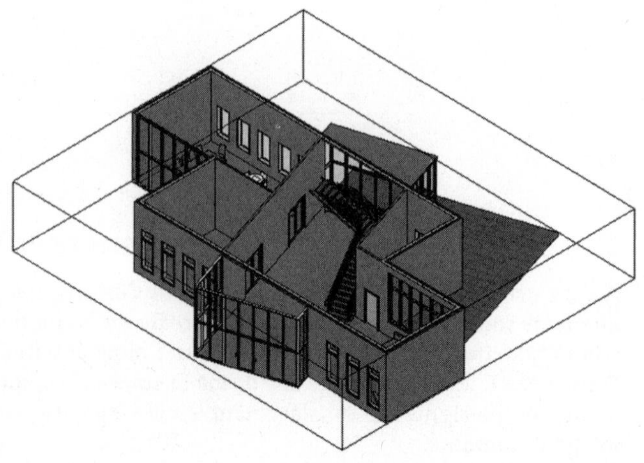

3. One thing that you'll notice about this view is the section box. In other situations, the scope box would create a limit for what you could change, because anything outside the scope box would effectively disappear within the view. Because the changes you are making using the Displace Elements tool are only view-specific and not actually manipulating model content, you can leave the scope box where it is.

   So that it doesn't interfere with the view, however, you can turn it off. Right-click the scope box and choose Hide In View ➢ Element from the context menu.

4. Now, you can begin displacing elements. When using this tool, elements will be grouped based on selection. So, if you were to pick multiple elements and then displace them, they would all move together, keeping a relative distance to one another.

   To demonstrate this, select both of the walls on the right of the view (Figure 20.23).

FIGURE 20.23
The first selection for displacement

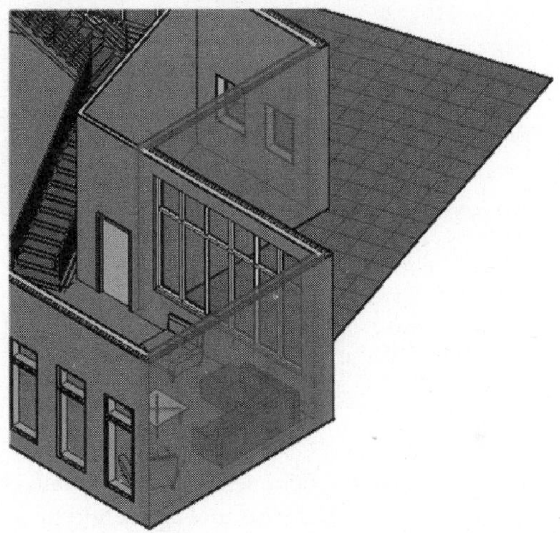

5. Select the Displace Elements tool from the View panel of the Modify tab. Both walls will remain highlighted now, but you'll see a 3D control tool appear (Figure 20.24).

FIGURE 20.24
Using the 3D control to move the displaced elements

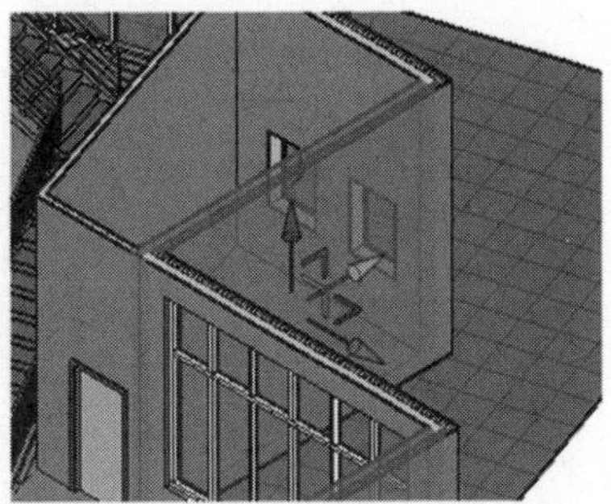

6. Grab the red control (the one that points to the lower right) and pull it away from the building. The walls should move in a plane parallel to their original position.

   You'll see the walls you selected visually unjoin from the building (Figure 20.25). If you were to move these walls without the use of this tool, you would receive error messages about rooms being unbound or elements being unjoined. None of that is happening because the changes you're making are just view-specific and not impacting the actual model.

FIGURE 20.25
The displaced walls

7. For the next displacement, select the three walls on the backside of the building (Figure 20.26). Select the Displace Elements tool again, and drag these using the green arrow (the one pointing to the upper right).

FIGURE 20.26
The second displacement

Notice how the door moved without selecting it (instead the wall was selected) but the storefront system did not move. As you create these types of views, you'll need to make sure you're selecting all of the elements you want to relocate. If you don't get it exactly right, however, don't worry. With these displaced walls highlighted, some new tools are active in the Modify | Displaced Elements tab: Edit, Reset, and Path. The Reset tool will undo the displacement you have created and reset the walls to their original locations.

8. To complete this step, you need to use the Edit button. Select Edit and notice how the view has changed. The elements within the displacement group are highlighted orange, and a new Edit Displacement Set panel has popped up that is similar to the Edit Groups panel.

9. In this view, choose Add from the Edit Displacement Set panel. Choose the storefront system that you didn't select in step 7 (Figure 20.27).

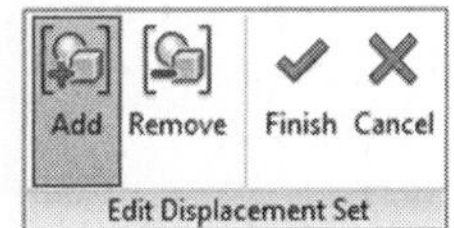

FIGURE 20.27
Add the storefront wall to the displacement set.

It will immediately move to its proper location within the wall and turn orange like the rest of the set (Figure 20.28). Click Finish from the panel to exit this view.

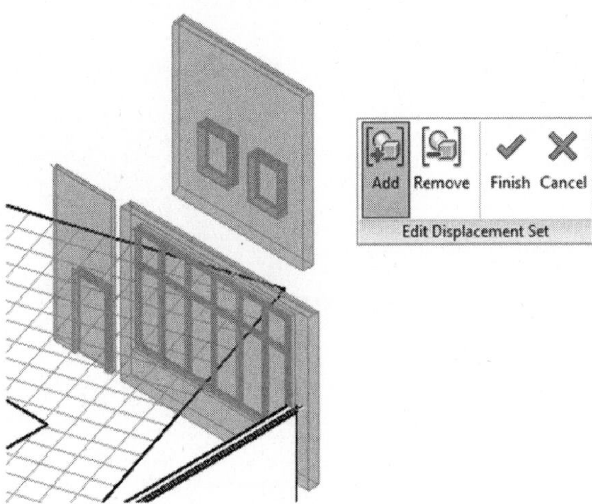

FIGURE 20.28
Displace the wall next to the stairs.

10. You're going to make one more displacement: the wall to the right of the stairs. Select it, choose the Displace Elements tool, and move the wall away from the stairs just a bit (Figure 20.29).

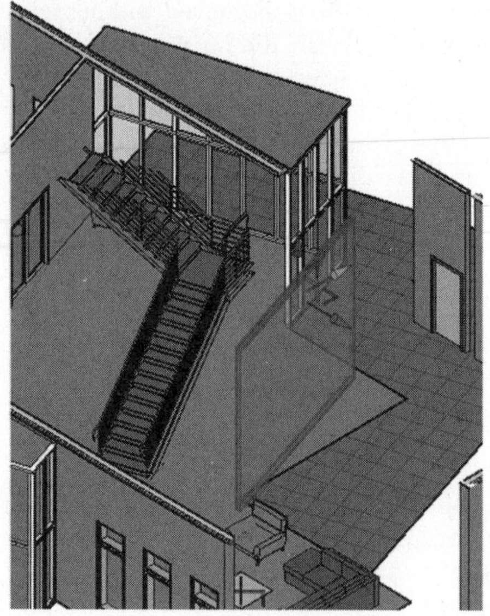

FIGURE 20.29
Using the Path tool to trace the displaced elements to their origin points

11. With all the elements displaced for this view, we're going to touch on one more tool. Highlight the first set of walls you displaced and select the Path tool from the Displacement Set panel. With this tool selected, click the lower portions of the walls you moved. It creates a dashed line or a "path" that the walls are pulled out upon. This will help to add visual clues to the view so you can see the origin point of specific elements. Do this for the other elements you've displaced (Figure 20.30).

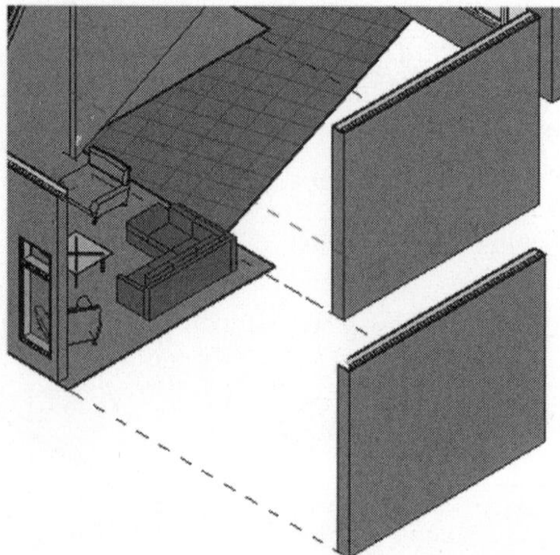

FIGURE 20.30
Completing the displacement of elements

In addition to moving building elements along their logical displacement plane, you can move them in any other direction if it increases the clarity of your 3D presentation. The path will be jogged for elements that are displaced out of plane.

12. The final view with the paths and displaced elements will look like Figure 20.31.

FIGURE 20.31
The finished view

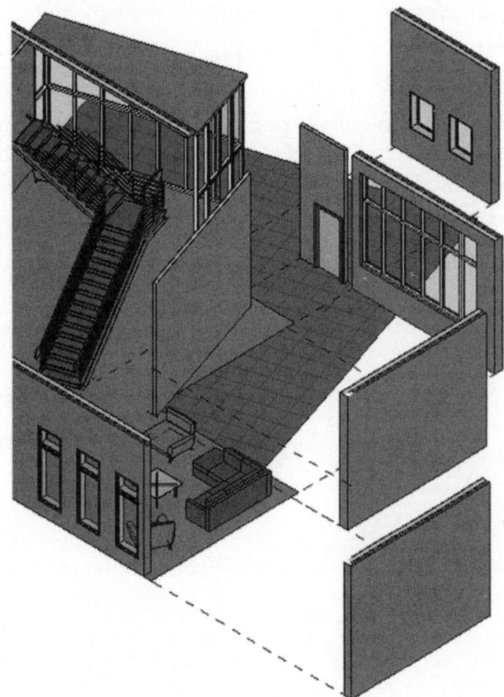

As with any other view in Revit, this view is parametric as well. Changes you make to elements within the model will update elements within this view and to the paths too.

If you now open the **Default 3D** view, you'll see that the integrity of the model has not changed—all the building's elements are exactly where you would expect them. You can even begin to experiment with making modifications to the walls you have displaced—add a door or a window and you can see that updated within the displaced view. You can quickly begin to see how useful this type of visualization can be!

The Bottom Line

Understand color fill legends. Color fills are a great way to illustrate data that otherwise might appear only in a schedule, such as department assignment, designed areas, and room finishes.

Master It There are a variety of ways to graphically display information using color fills. It can initially take a bit of time to get things organized, but once you create the legends, they can easily be transferred between views and projects. Describe how to add a color fill legend, once created, to your project template.

Use 3D model views in your presentation. Revit provides a variety of ways to help you visualize your designs—both while designing and during presentation. Understanding where these features are located and how and when to use them can help expedite the presentation process, depending on the look and feel you want to create with your images.

Master It Describe the process for creating an exploded 3D view of each level within your project.

Work with viewport types. Viewport types are simple to manage, but they are powerful when applied to the views you place on sheets. You can customize the view titles for any use case, from design presentations to construction documents.

Master It Describe the process for adding a new viewport type to your project.

Create "exploded" axonometric views. The Displace Elements command is used to create exploded axonometric views that used to be drafted by hand or created manually in a separate model. Understand the best ways to use this tool to help visualize and communicate design ideas.

Master It Describe the process for creating a displaced view.

Chapter 21

Computational Design with Dynamo

For a typical Revit user, the term *computational design* can evoke visions of obscure tools used for advanced form-making. This preconceived notion has proven difficult to curtail, even as parametric modeling and design computation become more commonplace. New tools providing parametric design environments enable users to not only create unique geometry but also develop automated processes and sophisticated data manipulation techniques.

The application of computer programming in design and construction has given rise to architects and engineers extending the capabilities of "out-of-the-box" Revit software by developing custom tools with the Revit application programming interface (API). The results provide more flexibility and expediency to the design process. Learning to code can be a difficult task, necessitating the rise in use of visual programming as a vehicle for computational design. With this process, users can create algorithms and manipulate data graphically, rather than textually.

Visual programming is diagrammatic and easier to understand than code, with *nodes* representing entities and *wires* mapping out how nodes relate to each other. This is known as a *data flow,* and in most visual programming languages the flow of data occurs from left to right.

In this chapter, you'll learn to:

- Get started with Autodesk Dynamo®
- Understand the Dynamo UI
- Connect nodes to make data flow
- Use additional Dynamo tools

Getting Started with Dynamo

Dynamo is a visual programming interface plugin for Revit. It is also available as a stand-alone application known as Dynamo Studio. With Dynamo for Revit, users can create custom design and automation methods with node-based diagrams that instantly affect both project and family files. Geometry and data generated with Dynamo become flexible; minor tweaks to a Dynamo definition file can deliver major results. Figure 21.1 shows an example of this.

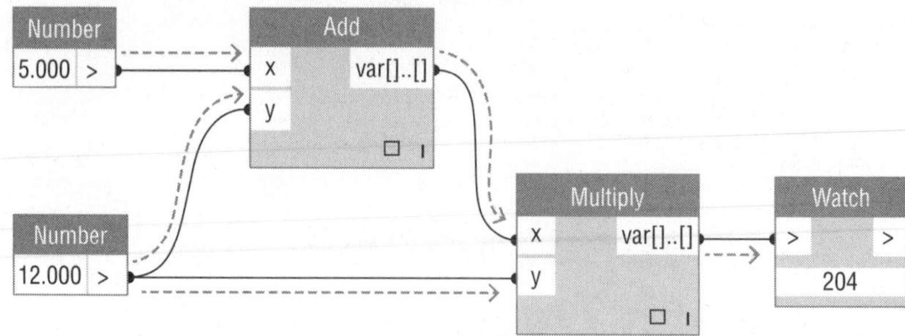

Figure 21.1 Using nodes and wires to create the equation [(5+12)×12]

Downloading Dynamo

Dynamo is an open source application. You can download the official released version of Dynamo from `http://www.dynamobim.com`. On the home page, browse to the dedicated download page and choose the latest version. Figure 21.2 shows the Dynamo BIM homepage.

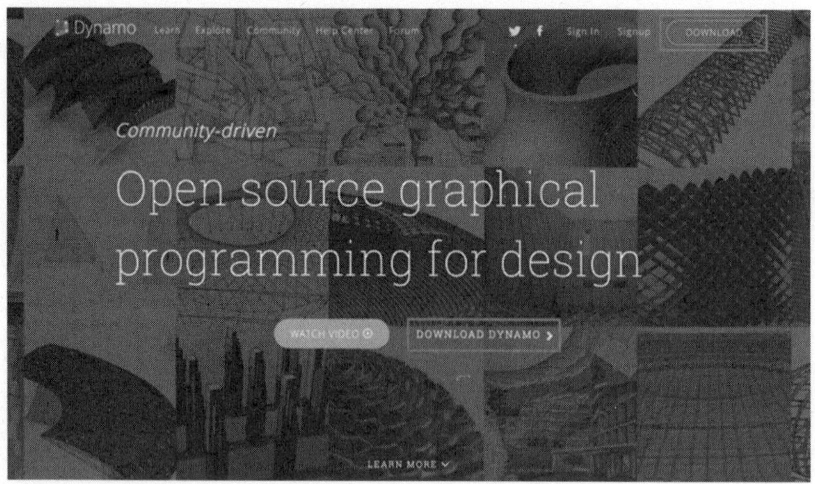

Figure 21.2 The Dynamo BIM homepage

Installation

Once Dynamo is downloaded, run the executable file to complete the installation if you're planning to use the stand-alone version (Figure 21.3). Make sure Revit and any other applications are closed. During the installation you can customize the installed components, including what versions of Revit you want to add Dynamo to (if you want to install this for earlier versions of Revit). (In Revit 2017, Dynamo is installed automatically with Revit.) Make sure Dynamo Training Files is selected, as these are an invaluable learning resource.

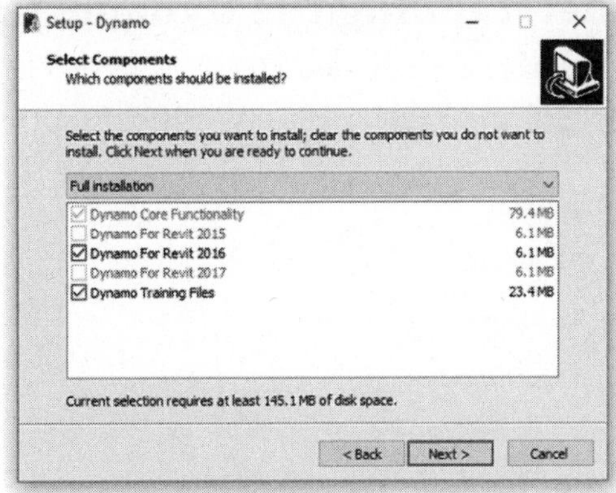

FIGURE 21.3
Dynamo installation. Make sure to install all available options.

Opening Dynamo

Once Dynamo is installed, open Revit to use the application. Dynamo will be available in the Manage tab of the ribbon. You might notice that Dynamo is grayed out initially. To open Dynamo, you must have a Revit project file or family file (typically a Conceptual Mass) open to connect to Dynamo. Dynamo will run only in the file in which it was opened. If you have multiple files open within Revit, make sure that the file you want to connect to Dynamo is the active window before clicking the Dynamo button.

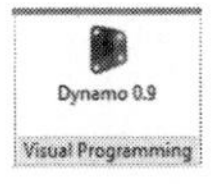

Click the Dynamo button to start the application. It will open in a new window (Figure 21.4). To create a new Dynamo file, with the extension *.dyn, click the New icon on the Start Page. A Dynamo file is referred to as a *definition* and can be thought of as a dynamic diagram that performs a function or process.

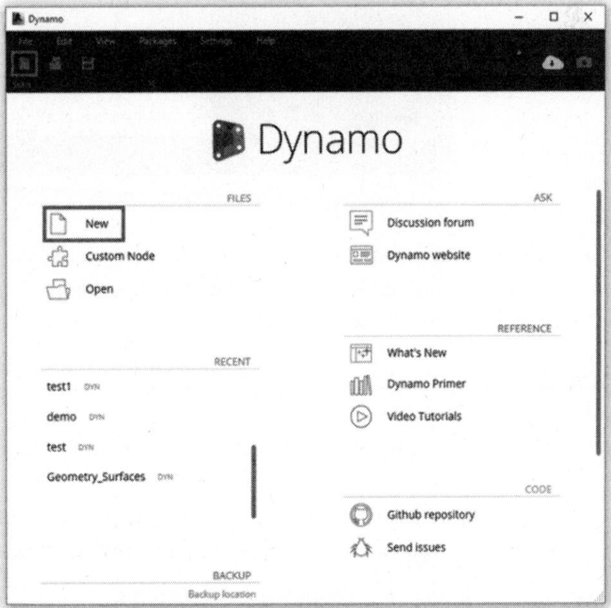

FIGURE 21.4
Dynamo Start Page

Understanding the Dynamo UI

Although connected to a Revit file, Dynamo has its own user interface and window separate from the Revit window. Dynamo's user interface is divided into four areas, as shown in Figure 21.5.

A. Toolbar

B. Node Library

C. Workspace

D. Execution Bar

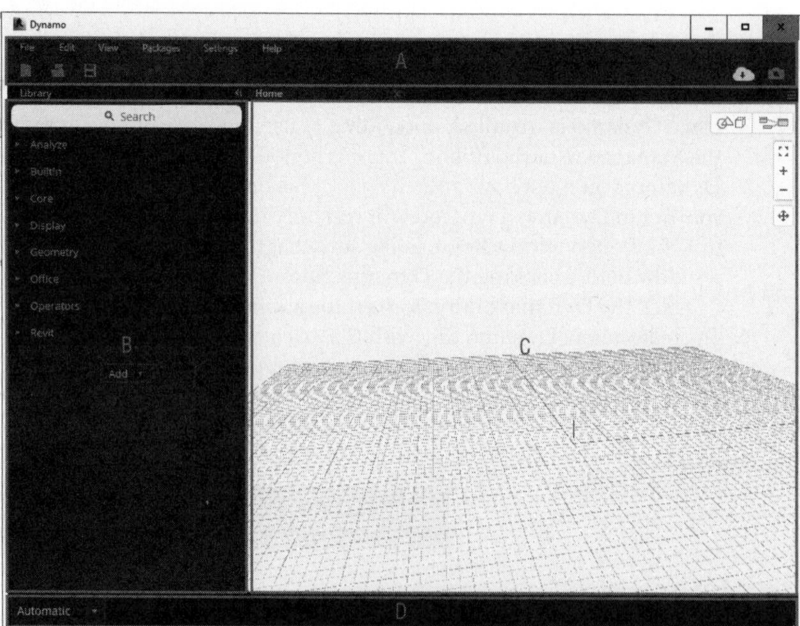

FIGURE 21.5 The Dynamo UI

Toolbar Like most Windows-style software, the toolbar contains the basic application functionality for managing files, selections, and settings. It includes drop-down menus as well as icons for quick access. Hovering over an icon will display its functionality and hotkey in a contextual box.

Node Library The Node Library is a categorized repository for all available nodes. *Nodes* are objects within Dynamo that connect to form a routine or program and are connected with elements called *wires*. Wires are what visually demonstrate the flow of data between nodes. We'll go into the parts of a node a bit later in this chapter.

The nodes are organized hierarchically within nested libraries based on how nodes relate to one another. You can browse the Node Library by clicking the menus and submenus until you reveal a set of nodes and their descriptions. As an example, point-related nodes can be found in the Geometry menu and then the Point submenu (throughout this chapter we will use the convention Geometry ➤ Point to describe where to locate a specific node). Within the submenu, nodes are further categorized by color: green is Create, red is Action, and blue is Query. Hovering over a particular node will reveal a contextual box with the node description including necessary inputs for the node and what it will output when used properly. The search bar at the top of the Node Library palette can be used in lieu of browsing the library's hierarchy to search for a specific node by name. Finally, clicking a node will place the node into the Graph View of the workspace.

Workspace The workspace is where you interact with nodes and relationships while developing your Dynamo definition. The workspace is an area where two views are overlaid: the Graph View and a 3D Preview. The Graph View is the display of your Dynamo definition showing the mapping of the nodes and formulas; the 3D Preview is the display beyond the Graph View (in the background) and shows any geometry being created by your Dynamo definition. Both are rendered simultaneously.

As you create a Dynamo definition that includes geometry nodes, you will see a preview of the results, or an *instantiation*, not only within the workspace but also within the project or family environment. The preview geometry cannot be selected and should be thought of as a by-product of what you are creating in your definition. It is shown as a visual reference only.

It is important to note that your mouse will behave differently depending on whether the Graph View or 3D Preview is activated. Refer to Table 21.1 for mouse controls in each of these view types.

TABLE 21.1: Dynamo Mouse Controls

MOUSE CONTROL	GRAPH VIEW	3D PREVIEW
Left-click	Select Node	
Middle click	Hold to Pan	Hold to Pan
Middle scroll	Zoom	Zoom
Right-click	Contextual menu: Node Search	Contextual menu: Hold to Orbit

Toggling between the two views to control the extent and orientation of each view is possible by selecting the Toggle Preview icons at the top-right corner of the workspace, as shown in Figure 21.6 (A). Any geometry that is displayed in the 3D Preview is visible only within the workspace. Unless you have created a definition that converts Dynamo geometry into model geometry using particular Revit element nodes, you will be unable to see any geometry visible in the Revit project or family file you have connected to this Dynamo session. We suggest playing with the two different view types and the mouse controls. While it might not sound intuitive when reading the workflow, it functions fairly simply when you are in the Dynamo environment.

Also shown in Figure 21.6 are additional navigation tools. Dynamo definitions can become rather large, and at times you will want to zoom in or zoom out to work in greater detail or to see the overall workflow. From top to bottom in area B, these tools will allow you to zoom to fit, zoom in, zoom out, and pan within the view.

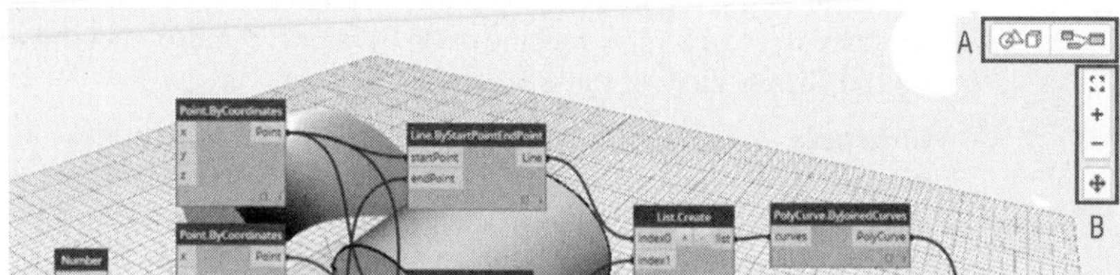

FIGURE 21.6
The workspace navigation tools

Execution Bar The Execution Bar is where you run the Dynamo definition or perform the process that you have laid out in the view. A new definition defaults to Automatic as a run style. This means that the definition is running automatically and updates immediately when it is modified. Automatic execution is appropriate for smaller and leaner Dynamo definitions. However, it can create performance issues when you are modifying larger definitions where small changes can take considerable time to update. If you notice a lag in performance or are working with large definitions, switch to Manual where the definition is processed only when the user chooses.

Connecting Nodes Makes Data Flow

Now that we have looked at the user interface, let's take an in-depth look at a node's structure and state and how you can create a visual program when connecting nodes with wires.

Node Structure

Dynamo nodes are the building blocks of a visual program. The flow of data within a node (and ultimately through the entire Dynamo definition) enters through the left and exits out the right side via ports. Nodes can store, analyze, and process both data as well as geometry; they can even report and access information that exists outside of the Dynamo environment. A node is broken down into five key parts, as shown in Figure 21.7.

A node consists of the following:

A. Node name: This is the common name of the node. The system of naming is *Category. NodeName.* For example, you can define a point in space with `Point.ByCoordinates`. Throughout the chapter this convention will be used to define nodes.

B. Input ports: These are receiving locations for data from another node. You can hover over a port to see a contextual pop-up containing the type of data required. Some nodes do not have input ports, meaning that their primary function is either to act as an input for other nodes (for example, the Integer node) or to access and report information from the Revit file you have tethered to the Dynamo file (for example, the Wall Type node).

C. Output ports: These are transmitting locations to send data from the current node to the input port of another. Whatever the function of the node might be (whether you are creating a point or calculating the volume of a solid mass), you can supply the results further along the Dynamo definition. Some nodes do not have output ports, meaning that their primary function is to either display information from a preceding connected node (`Watch`) or perform a transaction (`Excel.WriteToFile`).

D. Node preview: This tool allows you to preview the resultant data from the node. You can hover over the icon to see a contextual pop-up of the data or click the icon to open and close a preview pane.

E. Lacing option: This tool illustrates the lacing option applied to the resultant data (more on lacing options later) and is relevant only when your node contains a list of data, which it often does.

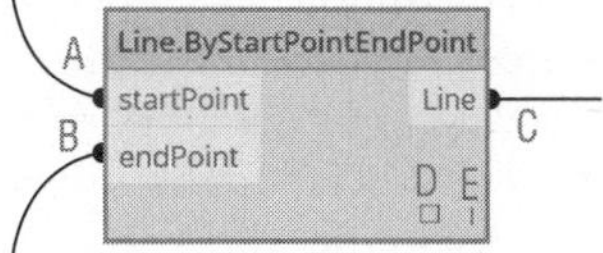

FIGURE 21.7
The anatomy of a Dynamo node

Using Nodes

You can place a node into the workspace by browsing through the Node Library categories and clicking one of the node options available. The node will appear in the center of your workspace when selected. A node can be moved by simply selecting and dragging it to a new location.

SEARCH BAR

Once you get a handle on the naming conventions of the Node Library, another method for node selection and workspace placement is to use the search bar available at the top of the Node Library palette. When nothing is selected in the Dynamo environment, the search bar is automatically active; simply typing at any point will begin a dynamic search. As you type, the Node Library will limit the available nodes based on what is being typed. Dynamo will try to predict the node you are searching for and highlight a node as you continue typing. If the highlighted node is the desired node, pressing Enter on your keyboard allows you to place it, as shown in Figure 21.8. Pressing Escape will clear the text in the search bar and restore all available nodes. If you are having trouble with the search bar being automatically active, press Escape prior to typing a search query.

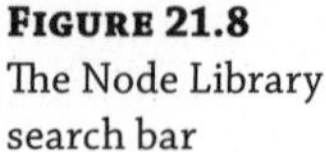

FIGURE 21.8
The Node Library search bar

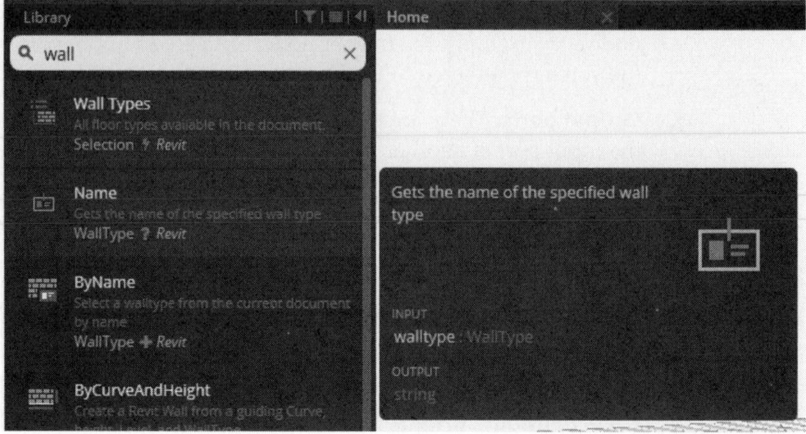

CONNECTING NODES WITH WIRES

Nodes are linked together using wires, a graphical representation denoting the flow of data within the Dynamo definition. To connect two nodes, left-click the output of one node (the right side of the node), then move the mouse to the inputs of another node (on the left side) until the intended input port highlights, and left-click again to complete the connection. A connected node will look like Figure 21.9. To disconnect, left-click the output port of your node and then again in an empty area in the workspace.

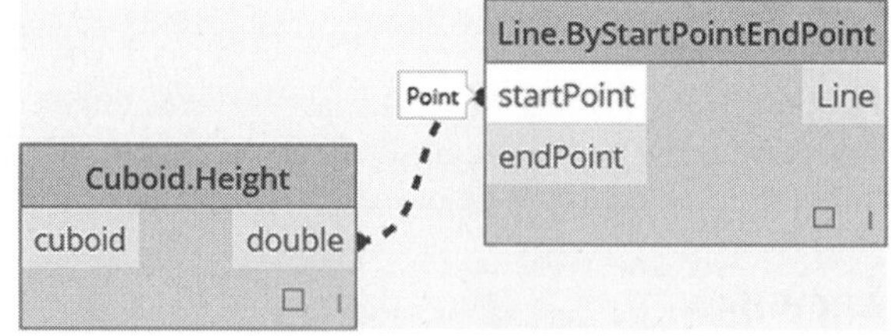

FIGURE 21.9
Connecting nodes

NODE STATES

As shown in Figure 21.10, a node can have various visual states depending on how it is connected to other nodes, whether the user is interacting with it, and whether the definition is valid. Here are some examples of node coloration:

A. Active: The node's header is dark gray with all inputs connected and (when running automatically) the type of data is correct.

B. Idle: The node's header is gray and disconnected from other nodes.

C. Warning: The node is yellow; it is in an error state because of the type of data being fed to it or the structure of the data it is attempting to interpret.

D. Selected: The node has a blue stroke around the perimeter. Any connected wires will also highlight as blue.

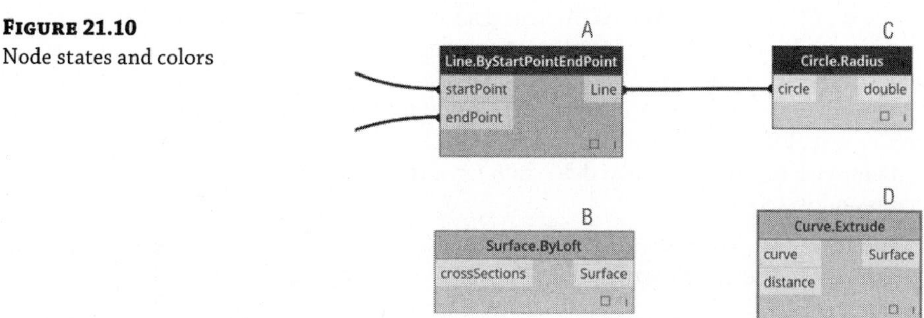

FIGURE 21.10
Node states and colors

Organizing a Definition

As you develop a Dynamo definition, it can start to look a lot like spaghetti if you are not careful. Organization and legibility are important, regardless of whether you are a beginner or an advanced user. There are many reasons why you would want to stay organized.

- You are possibly sharing your definition with your colleagues.
- Your definition is large and/or complex.
- You are working on your definition intermittently and might not remember your line of thinking between opportunities to work on it.
- You have realized you have made an error and need to go back through your definition and troubleshoot.

Fortunately, Dynamo includes some tools to help you with organizing your definition.

Notes Notes are editable text fields you can add to your Dynamo definition, allowing you to add descriptions and characterize areas of your definition in plain language. To add a note to the workspace, select Edit in the toolbar and choose Create Note (or use Ctrl+W). You can move the note around with your mouse similar to how you do with a node. Double-clicking the note opens an Edit Text window.

Selection Alignment Making your definition look neat and tidy by manually moving nodes with your mouse can be difficult, if not impossible. To align a set of nodes, drag-select them and right-click. In the context menu, choose Align Selection. There are a variety of alignments available including average and distribution options.

Grouping Grouping is an effective way to organize your definition, allowing you to highlight selections of nodes with color and annotate with text. To group a set of nodes, drag-select them and right-click. In the context menu, select Create Group. A green rectangle will appear around your selected nodes. You can drag the group with your mouse similar to how you move a node and edit the group annotation by double-clicking the group. To change the group color or ungroup the selection, right-click the group and select the appropriate option.

Using Visual Programming

With that background, let's start programming! Once you have an understanding of the user interface and node structure, it is time to delve into visual programming by creating small snippets of Dynamo definitions. As you read through the exercises, use Dynamo to re-create the images shown in this section. Each aspect covered includes relevant material, advice, and where/how to find depicted nodes. You can also use the automatic search function within Dynamo to quickly find a node if you are familiar with the node name (in other words, the header text at the top of each node).

Before we begin, we have to delve into the two types of nodes we are going to use: input nodes and watch nodes.

Input Nodes Input nodes are how a user can define values or parameters within a definition. There are a variety of different types of inputs.

- **Number and Integer:** These nodes allow you to manually input a numeric value.
- **String:** A string is another word for a series of characters or text. An example of a string could be "Room Name" or "Fire Rating."
- **Number Slider and Integer Slider:** These nodes are similar to `Number` and `Integer` but give you dynamic control of the output with a slider. By clicking the down arrow at the left of the node, you can reveal the default values controlling the slider granularity.
- **File and Directory Path:** These nodes allow users to access and utilize files or directories available on the workstation.

Watch Nodes Watch nodes are preview nodes. They serve a similar function to clicking the Node Preview button, but they create a continuous reveal that is useful for troubleshooting and data management. There are two types of watch nodes:

- **Watch:** This node creates the standard data list preview.
- **Watch3D:** This node creates geometric results, acting like a small workspace view. It might seem redundant at first glance, but if you are creating a definition with multiple geometric solutions, the overlap within the workspace can be illegible and cumbersome. You can hide a geometry's preview in the workspace by right-clicking the node and selecting Preview.

In Figure 21.11, watch nodes surface solutions from data that has been both created and derived from manual inputs.

With an understanding of the node types, you're ready to begin creating a Dynamo definition. This definition is going to start with a simple shape. Shapes can be points, curves, and surfaces. Let's explore each type.

Points Point nodes can be found by browsing Geometry ➤ Point in the Node Library. In Figure 21.12, two points are created using the `Point.ByCoordinates(x,y,z)` node. The coordinates for the first point are defined by `Number` nodes, while the second point is defined by an `Integer Slider` node. Both points require user input for their coordinate values. Note the point in the lower right of Figure 21.12.

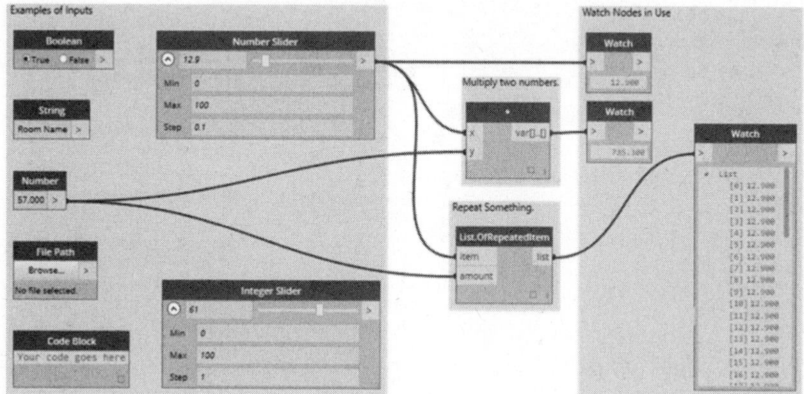

FIGURE 21.11 Input nodes and watch nodes

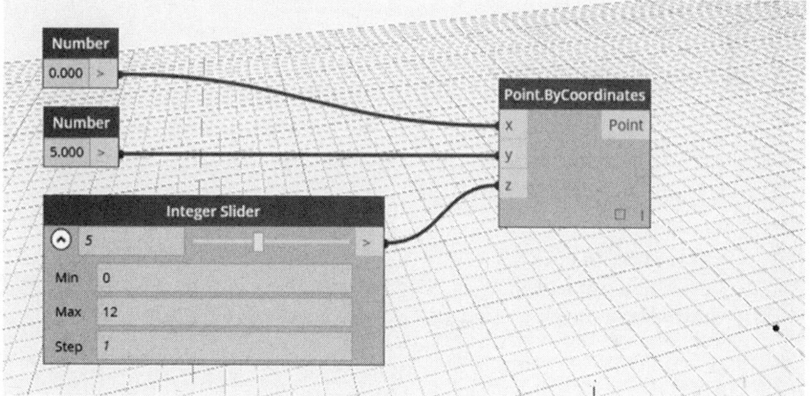

FIGURE 21.12 Using input nodes to create a point

To create a point, simply drop in the following nodes:

- `Number` (you'll need two instances of this)
- `Integer Slider`
- `Point.byCoordinates` node

Once the nodes are placed, connect them, mimicking Figure 21.12. With the Execution Bar set to Automatic, modify the `Number` node values, and slide the arrow on the `Integer Slider`. You should see the location of the points update in the 3D Preview beneath the Graph View.

Curves By browsing for Geometry in the Node Library, you can find a number of categories corresponding to types of curves such as Line, Curve, and NURBS Curve. In Figure 21.13, a `Line.ByStartPointEndPoint` node is used to create a curve with two point nodes as inputs. We can use this to create a curve attached to our point.

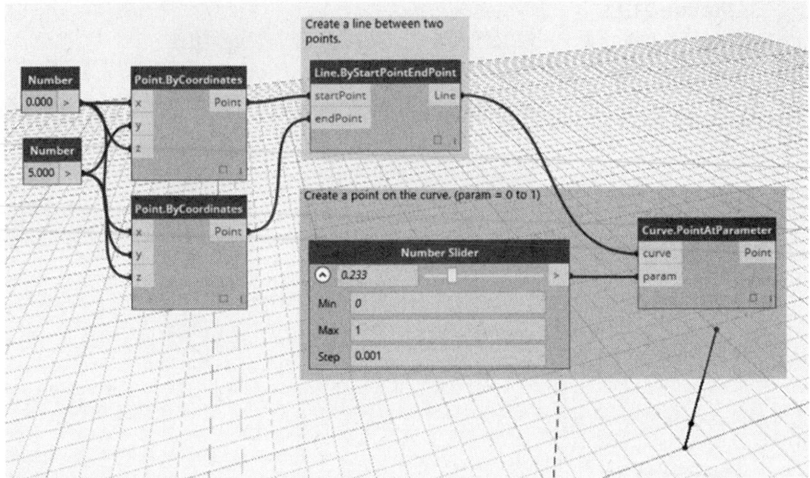

FIGURE 21.13 Creating a curve by start point and end point

1. Start by detaching the `Integer Slider` node. You are going to use a similar tool, the `Number Slider` (shown in Figure 21.14), in the following steps. This slider allows you a higher level of granularity but works effectively the same way as the `Integer Slider`. After you detach the `Integer Slider`, connect the `NumberSlider` following the same layout (Figure 21.14).

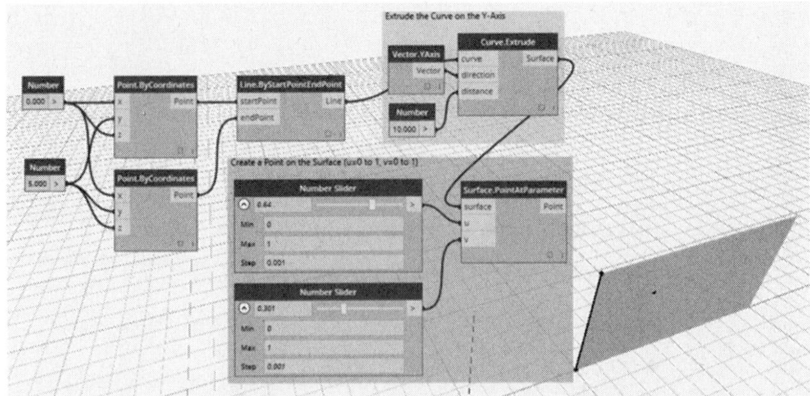

FIGURE 21.14 Creating a surface by extruding a curve

2. Add another `Point.ByCoordinates` node and connect them as shown in Figure 21.13. Set your first `Number` node to zero and connect it to the X and Z connections on the first `Point.ByCoordinates` node and to the Y on the second `Point.ByCoordinates` node. Set the second `Number` node to 5 and connect it to the remaining Y and X and Z connections.
3. Add a `Line.ByStartPointEndPoint` node. Connect the Point connections from the `Point.ByCoordinates` nodes to the startPoint and endPoint connections of the new node.
4. Add a new `NumberSlider` node and a `Curve.PointAtParameter` node.

5. Connect the Line connection from the `Line.ByStartPointEndPoint` node to the Curve connection in the `Curve.PointAtParameter` node. Finally, connect the `NumberSlider` output to the Param connection of the `Curve.PointAtParameter` node.

Now, by changing the values of the `Number` node or the slider, you can change the location of the point on the line or the line's start and end points.

Real World Scenario

THE VALUE OF COMPUTATIONAL PROGRAMMING

Seems like a lot of work for a line, right? Remember, one of the benefits of visual programming is the ability to rapidly change the output based on a string of values. As you become more practiced with Dynamo, you can use definitions like this to feed geometry within families and rapidly change a building's façade design or other aspects of the form.

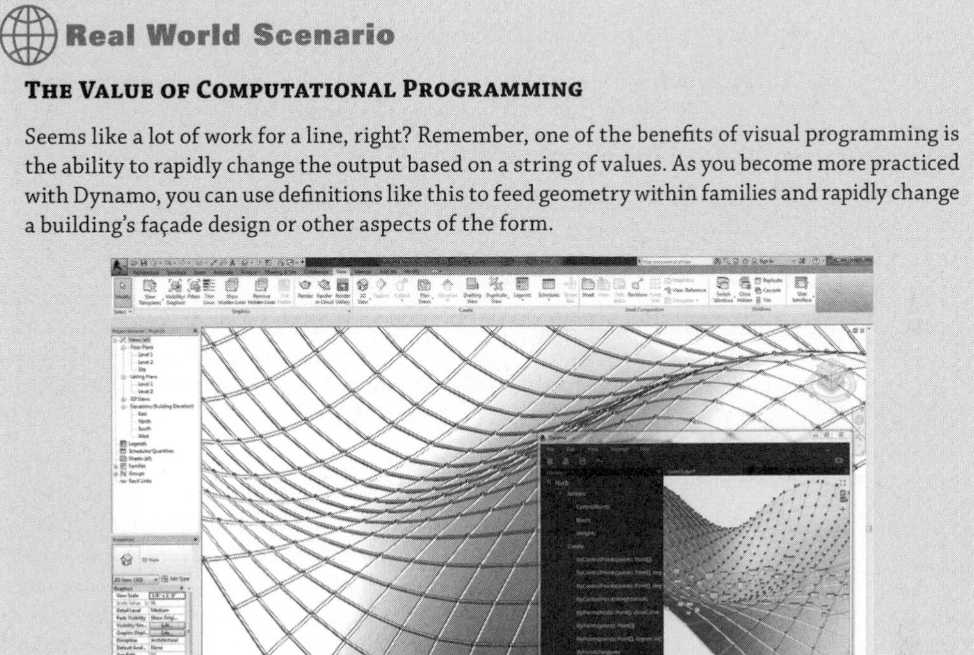

Source: Colin McCrone

Surfaces Now that you have created a point and a curve, you can use what you have to create a surface. There are a number of surface categories to browse under the Geometry heading of the Node Library such as Surface, Sphere, and Polysurface. There are also surface nodes that are "hidden" within other categories. To continue this exercise, you are going to use the `Line.ByStartPointEndPoint` from the previous example (Figure 21.13). You will create an extruded surface using a `Curve.Extrude` node, which can be found under Geometry ➤ Curve. Notice how the extrusion of the curve is controlled with the `NumberSlider` nodes in this example.

1. This example will get a bit more complex. Start by removing the `NumberSlider` and `Curve.PointAtParameter` nodes. You are going to connect a few additional nodes between your original content and the sliders.

2. Add `Vector.YAxis`, `Number`, and `Curve.Extrude` nodes (shown in the green box in Figure 21.14). With those nodes added, do the following:
   - Connect the output of `Line.ByStartPointEndPoint` to the Curve input of `CurveExtrude`.
   - Connect the Vector output of `Vector.YAxis` to the Direction input of `CurveExtrude`.
   - Connect the output of the `Number` node to the Distance input of `CurveExtrude`.
   - Give the `Number` node a value of 10.
3. Add two `NumberSlider` nodes and a `Surface.PointAtParameter` node, as shown in the blue area of Figure 21.14. With those nodes added, connect the following:
   - The output of first `NumberSlider` to the U input of `Surface.PointAtParameter`
   - The output of the second `NumberSlider` to the V input of `Surface.PointAtParameter`
   - The output of the `CurveExtrude` node to the Surface input of `Surface.PointAtParameter`

Now, by changing the sliders, you can update the curve and the surface! As we've demonstrated in this basic example, once your definition is created, it can be a simple matter to use the definition to manipulate forms. Next, you'll look at some advanced elements in Dynamo.

Additional Dynamo Tools

Now that you have stepped through some basic examples of using Dynamo to create points, lines, and surfaces, you can learn how those tools can be leveraged for more complex shapes. In this section, you'll explore some additional tools and see how they can be leveraged to create more robust Dynamo definitions. Because providing exercises to fully explain all the aspects of Dynamo could easily fill an entire book, the following content will simply explain the concepts and refrain from more step-by-step examples.

Code Blocks

Code Blocks are nodes that you can use to define a snippet of DesignScript, a simple programming language developed by Autodesk. DesignScript is a programming language available in many Autodesk tools such as AutoCAD that allows for more robust control of parametric content. You can create a Code Block by searching for it in the Node Library or just double-clicking an empty area in the workspace. The basic structure of DesignScript works by creating a line of code followed by a semicolon, as shown in Figure 21.15. Code Blocks can come in handy in a variety of ways. The following are two commonly used Code Block functions:

- **Creating inputs:** A Code Block can be used in lieu of inputs. Simply typing a numeric value followed by a semicolon will create an output. Multiple outputs can be created using the same node.
- **Creating expressions:** Adding an expression with variables will reveal inputs. This minimizes the need for additional nodes for mathematical equations that can make a definition bulky and difficult to follow.

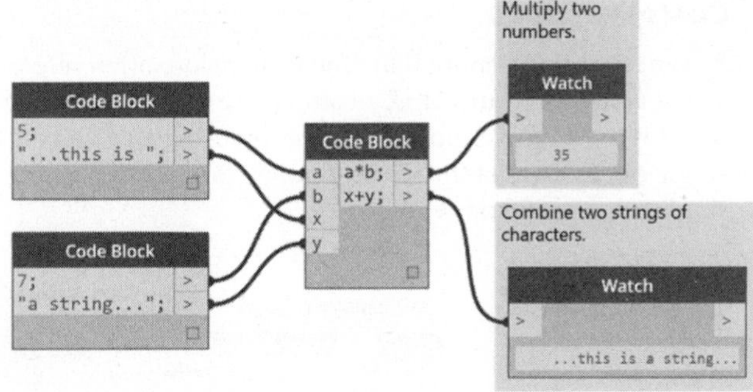

FIGURE 21.15
Code Blocks for creating inputs and expressions

You can find resources for learning more about Code Blocks and DesignScript at `www.dynamobim.com`.

Managing Data

Situations will arise using Dynamo where you will create data flows that are collections of items, and in some cases, they are associated with other collections. Any data flow containing multiple items is known as a *list* (sometimes described as an *array*). List nodes can be found under Core ➤ List. Understanding the principles of data management in Dynamo is critical for successfully developing useful definitions. Take some time to peruse and experiment with all the various list nodes available. Each of the images accompanying the following topics can be used to practice the concept and replicate the Dynamo definition.

SIMPLE LISTS

A simple list is a line of items, as shown in Figure 21.16. A `List.Sequence` node has been used to create the list 1, 2, 3…. Let's examine Figure 21.16 more closely. In the first `Watch` node, you will notice that each item in the list has an index value in brackets signifying its location in the list. Index values are integers and begin with the value [0]. To select an item from a list, you have to use its index value. In the second half of the definition, items [0] and [3] have been singled out using `List.GetItemAtIndex`.

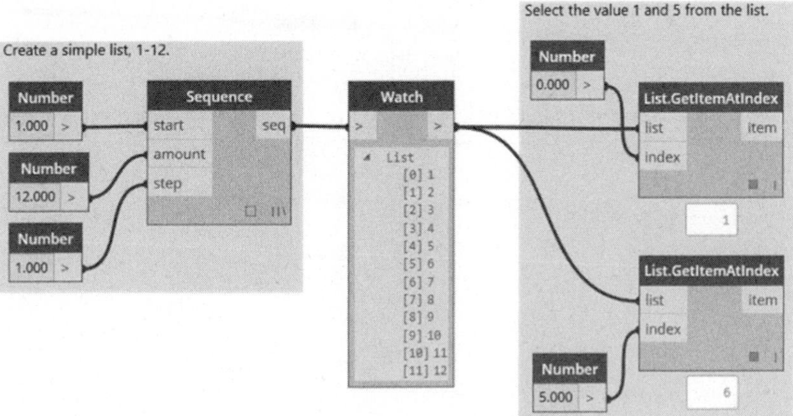

FIGURE 21.16
Creating a simple list and retrieving items

Complex Lists

A complex list has more than one dimension, often referred to as a list of lists or a multidimensional array. In Figure 21.17, a complex list is generated from a simple list using `List.Chop`. The result is a list of five sublists, each containing two values. Using `List.GetItemAtIndex` will single out an item of the highest order, as shown in the `Watch` node. It can then be used again to single out a particular value.

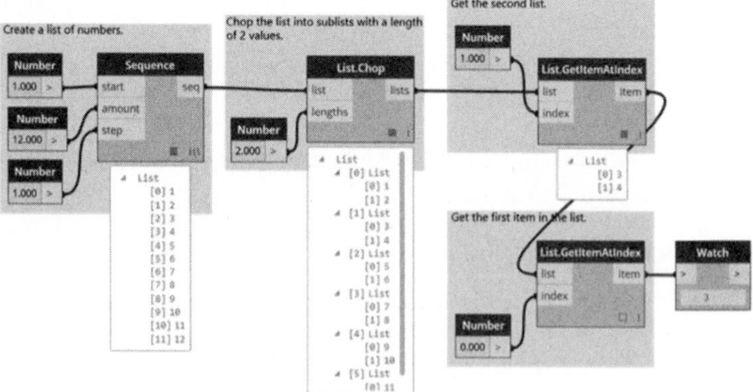

Figure 21.17
Creating a complex list and retrieving items

Structuring Lists

Certain nodes require list inputs. For example, the `Curve.ByPoints` node has one input port, "curves." A simple list of points will produce a single curve. To create multiple curves, you must break up the list supplied into sublists. By organizing data correctly, a single node can have a robust output. In Figure 21.18, we use the `List.Create` and `List.Transpose` nodes to reorganize point data. Code Block nodes, in the blue field, are used to reduce the size of the definition for clarity. You can also use Code Blocks to create lists. As you can see, `0..6..1;` creates a list from 0 to 6 with a step of 1.

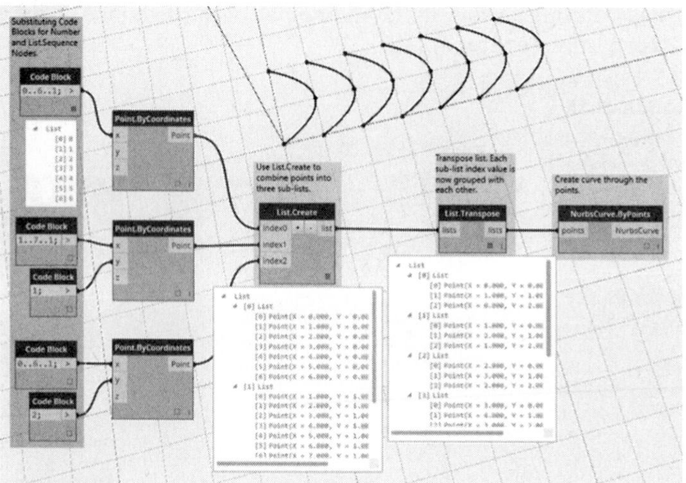

Figure 21.18
Creating and restructuring complex lists

LACING

Lacing is another word for data matching, or the method in which a Dynamo node interprets and associates differently sized inputs. There are three methods available, each one producing different results. To modify the lacing method of a node, right-click the lacing icon on the lower-right corner of the node. In the cascading menu, hover over lacing and make a selection. The following lacing methods are illustrated using points and lines to establish their behavior:

Shortest List The default lacing option for Dynamo is Shortest List, as shown in Figure 21.19. For each list, associate each corresponding list item until there are no more items in one list.

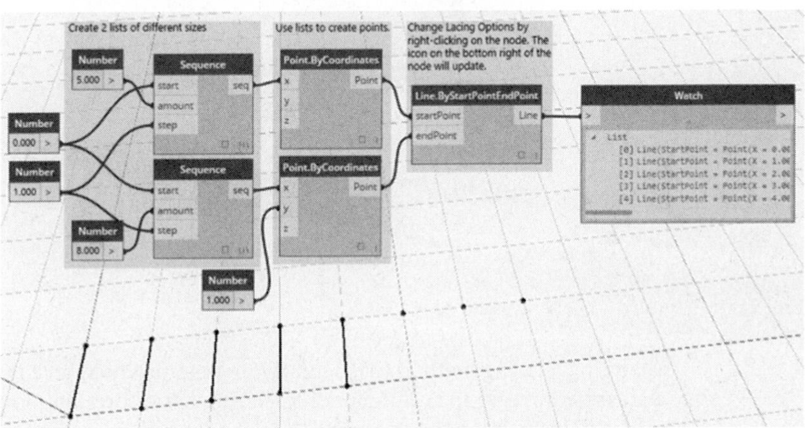

FIGURE 21.19 Using the Shortest List algorithm

Longest List Figure 21.20 shows the longest list lacing option. For each list, associate each corresponding list item, duplicating the last item in the shorter list until there are no more items in either list.

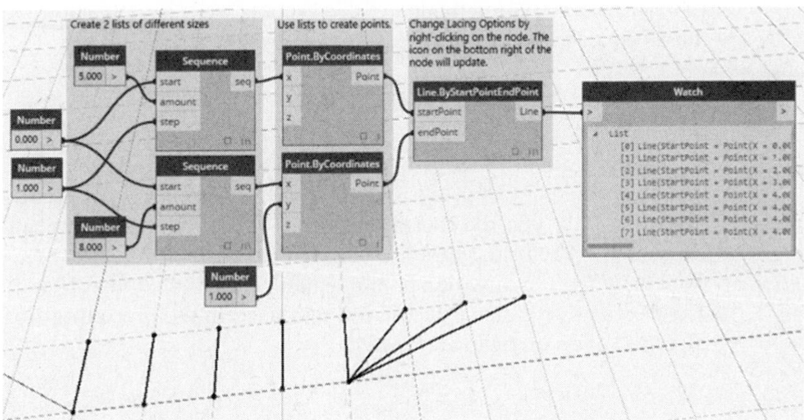

FIGURE 21.20 Using the Longest List algorithm

Cross Product As shown in Figure 21.21, the cross product lacing option makes all possible connections. For each list, associate each list item with every other item in the corresponding list.

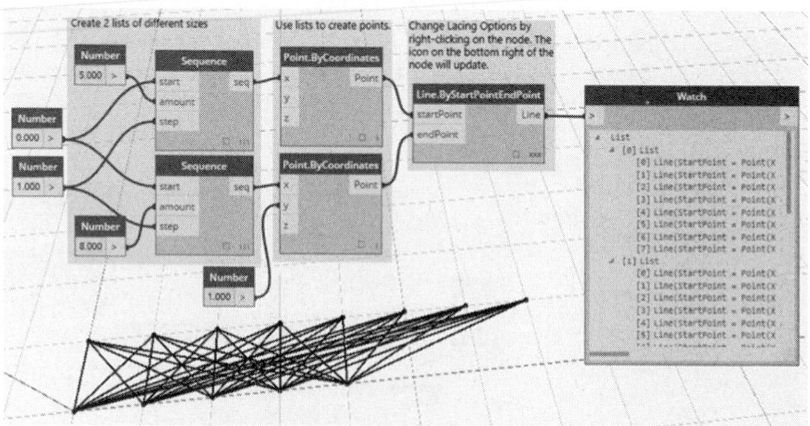

FIGURE 21.21 Using the Cross Product algorithm

Changing a lacing method (particularly to cross product) on a large definition can generate a massive increase in node solutions, leading to performance issues and the possibility of Dynamo freezing and not responding. It is good practice to save your file first, disconnect any subsequent nodes before switching lacing methods, and then use a `Watch` node to best ensure the intended outcome.

Geometric Manipulation and Analysis

Beyond the creation of geometry, nodes can also manipulate existing geometry or perform analysis against an existing model. In this section, we'll explore some of the node types that allow those functions.

VECTORS

A vector is a quantity that has a direction and magnitude. The input of a vector is similar to that of a point (x,y,z), but the node calculates the relative difference between the origin, in this case (0,0,0), and the coordinate input. Vector-related nodes can be found by browsing Geometry ➢ Vector in the Node Library. In Figure 21.22, a `Points.ByCoordinates` node is used to define the direction of a line using the `Line.ByStartPointDirectionLength` node. The `YAxis` node is also a vector and was used in the preceding surface example to define the direction of an extrusion.

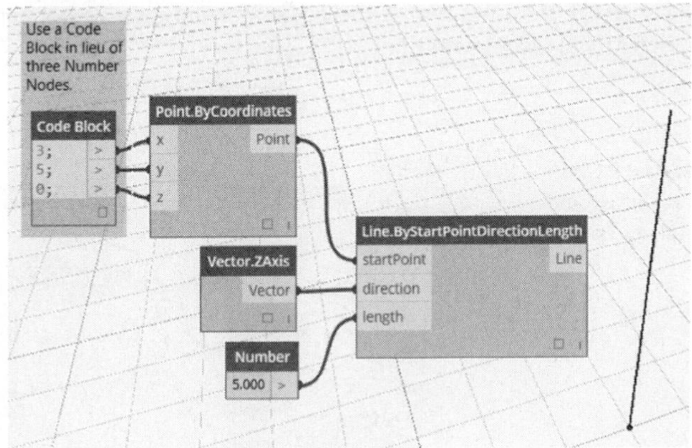

FIGURE 21.22 Using a vector to signify a curve's direction

COORDINATE SYSTEMS

Coordinate systems are two-dimensional abstract planes, similar to construction planes in CAD software, and are used to create local coordinates for evaluating existing geometric conditions and creating new ones. Coordinate system nodes can be found by browsing Geometry ➢ Vector or Geometry ➢ Plane in the Node Library. In Figure 21.23, a `Surface.CoordinateSystemAtParameter` node was used to locate a coordinate system on a surface at (U:0.5, V:0.5).

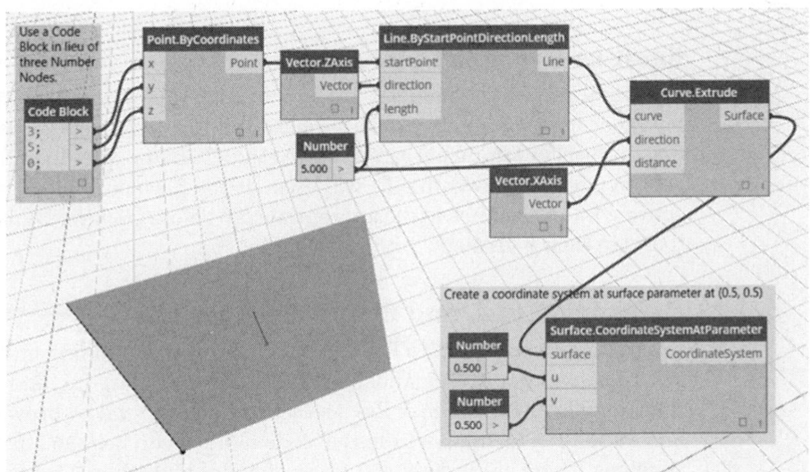

FIGURE 21.23 Placing a coordinate system onto a surface

GEOMETRIC TRANSFORMATIONS

A transformation is a general term for methods used to manipulate the orientation, size, and location of a shape. Common transformations are translate (move), scale, rotate, and reflect.

Figure 21.24 shows two of these transformations. Vectors and coordinate systems are critical for defining a transformation.

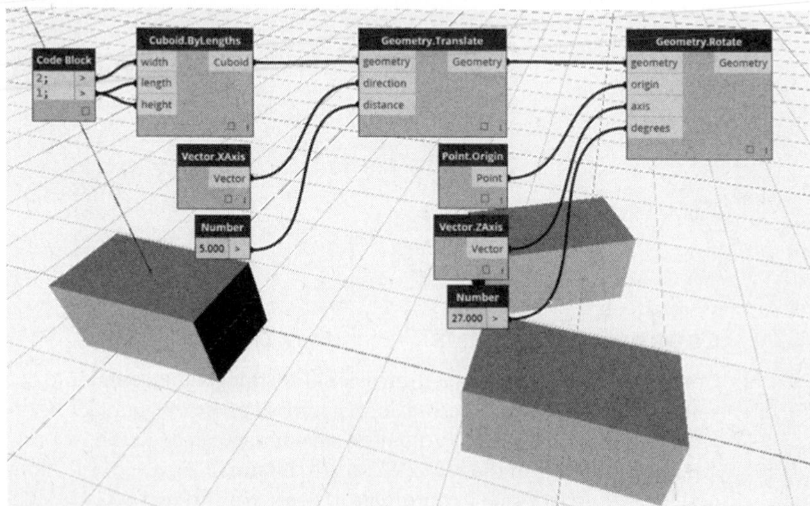

FIGURE 21.24 Translating and rotating a cuboid

Revit to Dynamo to Revit

The real utility of Dynamo lies in its connection to Revit, enhancing the design process by combining design computation with a robust building information database. Information from a Revit project or family file can be ported into Dynamo, provided that you opened the Dynamo session when your existing file was open. If you have multiple files open, make sure that the active window belongs to the appropriate file before clicking Dynamo. Revit-related nodes are found in their own menu within the Node Library.

Category, Type, and Element Selections

Controlling the quality of a Revit project file through auditing and *en masse* model changes are two prospects ripe with manual technical solutions, plug-ins, and workarounds developed over the years. Dynamo's suite of Revit selection nodes, found by browsing for Revit ➢ Selection and for Revit ➢ Element within the Node Library, can help you develop your own dynamic solutions. There are two general types of nodes that when used together can query and select elements in a Revit file: menu selection nodes and All Elements nodes.

- **Menu selection nodes** are more difficult to find because they do not have a standard naming convention, but they all share two common features: no input ports and an embedded drop-down menu. These nodes can give you access to Revit categories and types. There is also the `Element Types` node, a node where the term *element* is used broadly to describe nearly *anything* in Revit, from sun settings to voltage types to phase filters.
- **All Elements nodes** select all the elements in a project based on a particular qualification, usually one of the tiers within the Revit hierarchy (Category ➢ Family ➢ Type ➢ Instance).

Auditing a Revit Project

Figure 21.25 shows two project file audits being performed. Using the `Categories` and `Element Types` nodes connected to `All Elements` nodes, you can identify all walls that have been placed in the model as well as all wall types that are available to place. An extra node, `Element.Parameters`, shows the wall type properties as a series of sublists corresponding to the order of the list of wall types.

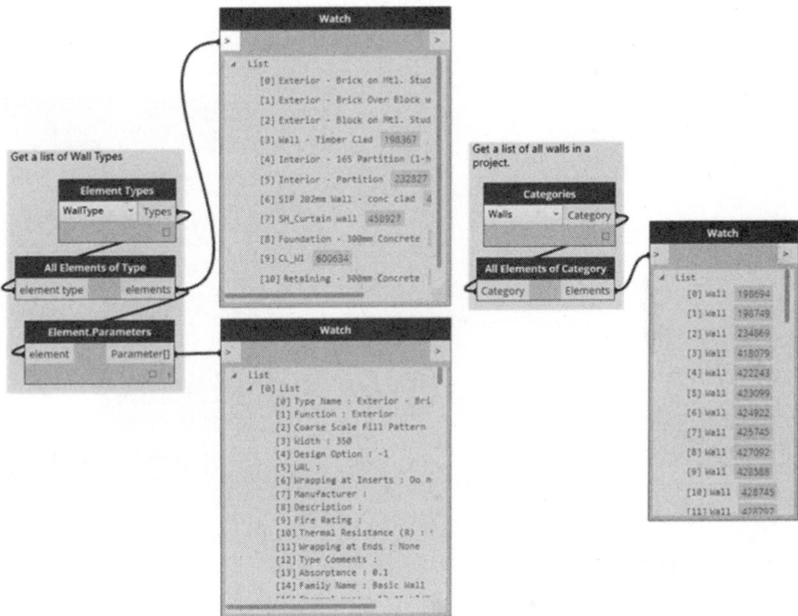

FIGURE 21.25 Auditing wall types and walls placed

Placing Revit Families

In addition to auditing, you can use menu selection and `All Elements` nodes to help place Revit families. In Figure 21.26, a Dynamo definition creates a series of floors. All elements of category Levels are retrieved from the model. The level elevations are used to define a series of points. These points define planes where a rectangle is placed. A `Floor.ByOutlineTypeandLevel` node uses a "longest list" lacing option to combine the outlines, floor type, and levels to create a series of floor elements in the project.

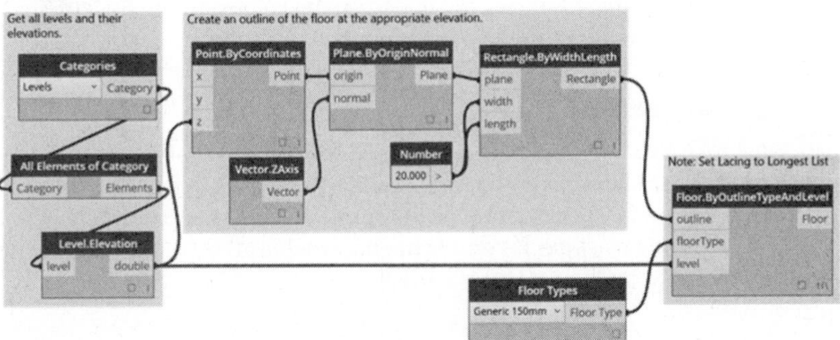

FIGURE 21.26 Using Dynamo to build a series of floors

Manual Selections

There are a variety of manual selection nodes available in Revit ➤ Selection (or you can type **select** in the search bar). These are point-click nodes that allow you to select model elements as well as parts of model elements. These nodes tend to be more useful in Conceptual Mass families than project files. Once selected, the element is visible in the workspace 3D Preview. The node is now dynamically linked to the object, recognizing any modifications that might occur in the Revit file and displaying the element ID below the select button, as shown in Figure 21.27.

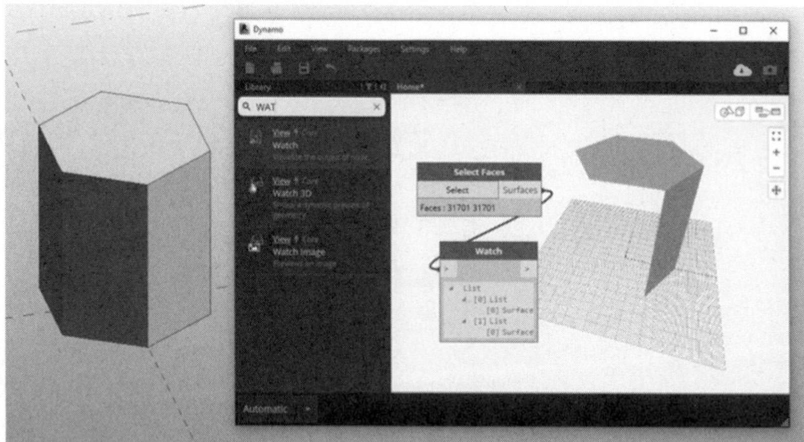

Figure 21.27
Selecting faces of a conceptual mass

Interoperability

There is an entire ecosystem of software being used by architects and engineers during the design process. Each particular platform in that ecosystem has its own file formats and protocols. Moving from one file format to the next can result in both data loss and geometric "impurity." Interoperability, a term heard often when discussing BIM processes and workflows, is a property of one piece of software that enables it to work with another. More generally, the term has come to mean the ability to send and receive data seamlessly.

Using database formats like spreadsheets is a pragmatic (and democratic) solution to the problem of interoperability. If you can convert design data into a tabular form, Dynamo proves quite useful. Dynamo has the ability to read and write in both Microsoft Excel and CSV formats. The Excel nodes, `Excel.ReadFromFile` and `Excel.WriteToFile`, can be found in their own menu named Office. CSV nodes can be located in the BuiltIn and Core menus. Using either format will require File Path inputs.

Excel to Revit

An Excel spreadsheet can be used to create a set of points. `File.Path` and `File.FromPath` are used to convert the browsed path to an input for `Excel.ReadFromFile`, as shown in Figure 21.28. A `String` input is used to locate the correct sheet in Excel. Keep in mind, strings are *case sensitive*. If you are having trouble accessing the data from a spreadsheet, check to make sure your sheet name is correct.

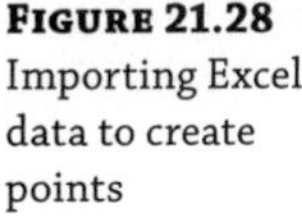

FIGURE 21.28 Importing Excel data to create points

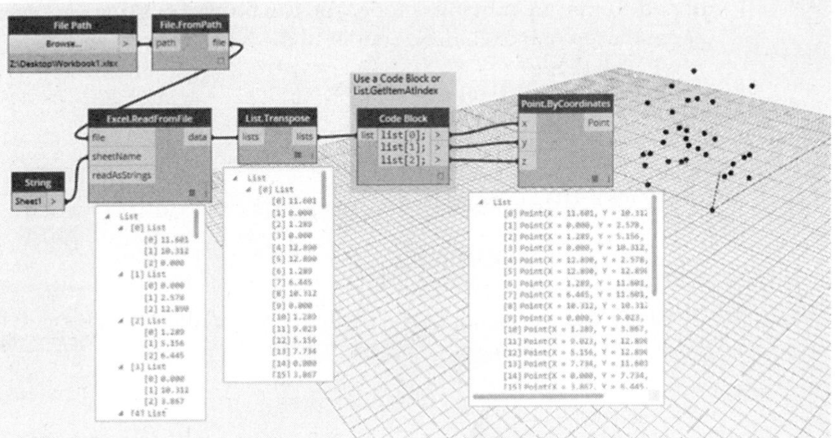

The original data is three columns corresponding to x, y, and z values. As you can see in the output of the `Excel.ReadFromFile` node, Dynamo understands the data in a way that might seem unconventional at first. The highest-order list defines a row, and the three items in that list define the three columns. Each list could be considered a point, in effect, but `Point.ByCoordinates` requires three inputs. The `List.Transpose` node is used to transpose the data, similar to transposing a spreadsheet (swapping columns and rows). Once transposed, there are three lists each with all values x, y, or z. A Code Block is used in lieu of `List.GetItems` to quickly create three outputs that can be used to create the point geometry.

REVIT TO EXCEL

Data can just as easily be sent to Excel from Revit (via Dynamo). In Figure 21.29, room data is retrieved from a project file and exported to a newly created Excel file. The resultant spreadsheets were added to emphasize the connections in Figure 21.29. Using selection nodes, all elements of category Room are retrieved, and room parameters are obtained using `Element.GetParameterValueByName`. The room names and areas are then combined into a `List.Create` node. If the data was placed into `Excel.WriteToFile` at this point, the result would be 14 columns of data including one row of room names and one row of room areas. By transposing the data before writing to Excel, you can create a more conventional spreadsheet.

Package Manager

The Dynamo Node Library is extensive and built for a variety of applications across a range of industries, but there is always missing functionality or modifications to existing nodes that might pique a user's interest. Dynamo is open source and welcomes community involvement. The package manager is a portal for Dynamo users to develop and publish additions to the Node Library to extend Dynamo's core functionality.

Packages are available to download in the Online Package Search by choosing Search for a Package in the toolbar. The list might take a few moments to load. Packages can include a suite of nodes or be an individual node. You can browse existing packages or search using the search bar at the top of the window. Similar to the Node Library, searching will limit the results related to what you type.

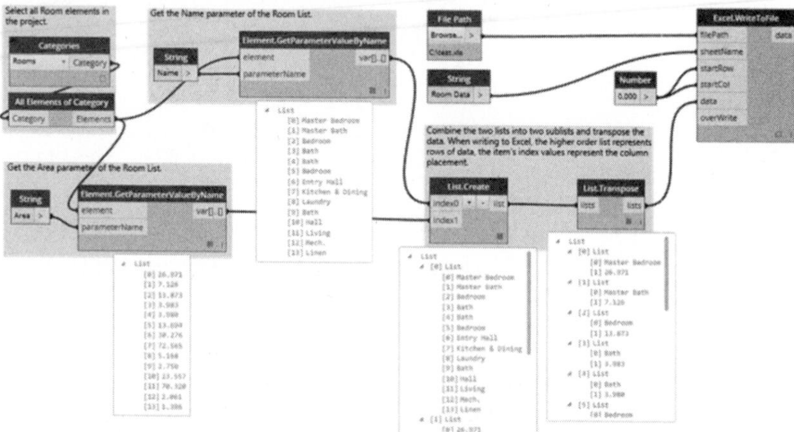

FIGURE 21.29
Exporting room data to Excel

To install a package, select the download icon and *voilà*! At the bottom of the Online Package Search window, the downloaded package is highlighted in cyan. The location of the new node(s) depends on how the developer has structured the package. In some cases, installing a new package might create an additional menu in your Node Library; in others, it might be blended to fit within the library. Use the search bar if you are unsure where an installed package has been located.

Additional Resources

Sample definitions are included during installation; you can access them in the Dynamo toolbar under Help ➤ Samples. Learning Dynamo can be both rewarding and arduous, but you are not alone! The community of Dynamo users is continuously growing. At DynamoBIM (`www.dynamobim.org`) you can find additional tutorials, forums, user galleries, and a blog. A simple online search query for help with a Dynamo issue can yield many results, but it is important to realize that Dynamo is (currently) a perpetual beta software that has undergone many changes since 2011. Online search results that are more than a year old can yield obsolete solutions.

The Bottom Line

Get started with Autodesk Dynamo. Dynamo is a visual programming interface that runs parallel with Revit and allows you the ability to code forms and shapes within your Revit environment. Dynamo creates definitions by connecting *nodes* with *wires* to convey data.

Master It There are five parts to a node. What are they, and what do they do?

Understand the Dynamo UI. Dynamo has a simple, straightforward UI. Becoming comfortable with the parts of the user interface can allow you more flexibility and lower frustration when learning the application, either as a novice or on your road to an expert.

Master It What are the four primary sections of the user interface?

Connect nodes to make data flow. Connecting nodes is the true power behind Dynamo. The connections visually and programmatically show data flow and the path of information from beginning to end to create the form, run the analysis, or provide whatever is the desired output. Understanding the basics of connecting nodes is the first step to creating your own Dynamo definition.

Master It Describe the workflow to create a series of nodes and connect them properly.

Use additional Dynamo tools. While Dynamo is a robust programming application, there are additional tools you can use to further leverage its capabilities.

Master It Describe some of the tools external to Dynamo and how they can be used to push the capabilities of the application even further.

Part 7

Appendixes

In this section you will find:

- **Appendix A: The Bottom Line**
- **Appendix B: Tips, Tricks, and Troubleshooting**
- **Appendix C: Autodesk Revit Architecture Certification**

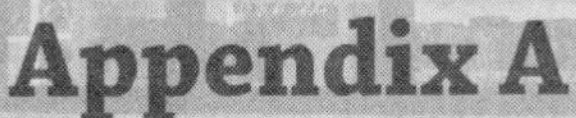

Appendix A

The Bottom Line

Chapter 1: Introduction: The Principles of BIM

Focus your investment in BIM. Since using Revit software is a change in workflow, it is also important to understand the change in staffing and who is needed to perform what roles on a project.

Master It What are the three primary roles in a Revit project, and what are the responsibilities of those roles?

Solution Every successful Revit project will need three roles accounted for. These roles do not need to be individual people; one person can assume all three roles at any point in the project. The roles are architect, modeler, and drafter. These roles are responsible for understanding and articulating the design, creating model content, and laying out and annotating the documentation, respectively.

Understand a BIM workflow. Understand how projects are completed in BIM and how the use of Revit software on a project can change how information within a project is created.

Master It Explain one of the primary differences between a more traditional 2D CAD-based workflow and producing documents using Revit.

Solution In a 2D CAD-based workflow, documents are created by team members by creating plans, sections, elevations, and details, all as separate drawings, and then manually coordinating that content for the project set. In a BIM or Revit workflow, the plans, sections, elevations, and perspectives are a by-product of creating the virtual building model and are coordinated through updates made to the model itself.

Leverage BIM processes. Understanding the level of risk your firm is willing to take in new technologies will help you establish goals for your future use of BIM.

Master It Using the three areas of firm integration (visualization, analysis, and strategy), define how those areas overlap for your firm or project.

Solution Remember, there is no wrong answer in mapping a path forward for your firm or project. The important thing is to identify which areas are critical to the workflow of your firm to help you focus your future efforts.

Chapter 2: Applying the Principles of the User Interface and Project Organization

Understand the user interface. In addition to understanding how your project is organized, to use the Revit software well you must understand how the UI is organized. Once you grasp both of these concepts, you will be ready to move ahead.

Master It The "big" areas of the UI are the ribbon, the Properties palette, the Project Browser, and the drawing area. How do these areas work together, and what tabs correspond to an iterative design process?

Solution The Architecture tab is where you'll turn in your early design process because it contains datum objects, system families, component families, and spaces. As the design develops, you'll establish your views from the View tab. When you start to get into documentation, you'll work from the Annotate tab. Having panels from the Modify tab pulled off and close at hand will keep you from having to go between one contextual tab and another.

Understand project organization. The compelling advantage of being able to design, document, and manage your project across multiple disciplines—the architectural, structural, and mechanical disciplines—is something that you can do only in Revit, and understanding project workflow is key to getting off on the right foot.

Master It Thinking back to the Revit organizational chart shown in Figure 2.21, what are the main components of a Revit project, and how can you apply them to your design process? How do these categories directly affect your design workflow?

Solution The top-level categories of a Revit project are datum, content, views, and management. They correspond to the design process of maintaining relationships, repetition, representations, and restrictions. Keep these corollaries in mind as you move sequentially from schematic design, design development, construction documentation, and construction management.

Chapter 3: The Basics of the Toolbox

Select, modify, and replace elements. Many fundamental interactions are supported by Revit software to select just what you need and to modify elements efficiently.

Master It How can you quickly select only the door tags in a plan view and switch them to another type?

Solution First, window-select the entire plan. Then, using the Filter tool in the Modify tab of the ribbon, select only the Door Tags category, close the Filter dialog box, and change the type in the Properties palette.

Edit elements interactively. The editing tools in Revit are similar to those found in other CAD and BIM software programs. Tools such as Move, Copy, and Trim are available on the Modify tab of the ribbon.

Master It How do you create a parametric repetition of an element?

Solution Select an element and activate the Array tool from the Modify tab of the ribbon. Specify a linear array with the Group And Associate option, and choose either Move To 2nd for specific element spacing or Move To Last for consistent overall length with varied element spacing.

Use other editing tools. Beyond the basic editing tools are more advanced commands to help you consistently and intelligently populate a building model with content.

Master It How do you copy model elements in the same location for a multistory building?

Solution Select the required elements and copy them to the Clipboard (Ctrl+C). From the Clipboard panel in the Modify tab, select Paste Aligned To Selected Levels, and then choose the levels to which you'd like to paste the copied content.

Create site context for your project. The site tools allow you to create context for your building models, including topographic surfaces, graded regions, and property lines.

Master It Describe the different methods used to create a topographic surface.

Solution A topographic surface can be created by placing points at specific elevations relative to internal project coordinates, by using an imported 3D CAD file from a civil engineering software program, or by using a text file that contains the x-, y-, and z-coordinates of a field of points.

Chapter 4: Configuring Templates and Standards

Define settings for graphic quality and consistency. The fundamental building blocks for any template are the customized settings for object styles, line styles, fill patterns, materials, and more.

Master It How can a complex custom-fill pattern be imported?

Solution Use a text-editing application to create a custom pattern or copy a pattern from another application. Be sure to add lines to the pattern definition that describe the units and pattern type. In the New Pattern dialog box, choose Custom and click the Import button to select your custom pattern file. Adjust the pattern as necessary for the desired result.

Organize views for maximum efficiency. The project template can be used to capture a framework supporting your visual and organizational standards.

Master It How can you customize the Project Browser to support your business needs?

Solution Filtering folders based on view types and documentation helps team members quickly find what they're looking for in a project. Your project template can also exclude views that are not needed based on a specific task. For example, if you're in design development, you can exclude previous views and sheets that were part of a previous schematic design stage.

Create custom annotation families. Developing a graphic style to match your standards will usually require you to edit some annotation families or create them from scratch.

Master It Can a single label display more than one parameter? How are custom view tags loaded into a project?

Solution A single label can show more than one parameter—and even custom parameters. Just remember to place the label with the Label tool. Assign the label to report the desired parameters.

Start a project with a custom template. Making your custom template available for new projects ensures that all future projects will maintain the same level of graphic quality and efficiency you expect.

Master It How do you set your own custom project template to be the default for new projects?

Solution Click the Application button, select the Options button, and navigate to the File Locations tab. Click the Browse button for the Default Template File field, and navigate to the location of your custom project template. From now on, click the Application button, select New Project, and select New in the Recent Files window—or press Ctrl+N—to use your new template as the basis for the new project.

Develop a template management strategy. Organizing your standards, content, and settings while using Revit tools to transfer content will make your effort more efficient.

Master It How do you insert your standard details from one Revit project to another? How do you transfer settings such as materials?

Solution 2D content such as standard details can be stored in separate Revit project files and loaded when needed. One way to do this is with the Insert Views From File tool in the Insert tab. Select an RVT project file, and then choose eligible views such as drafting views, sheets, or schedules. They are transferred into your active project with all associated parameters. To transfer settings and styles such as materials, select the Manage tab and click Transfer Project Standards. Remember to open another project from which you'd like to transfer settings before running this tool.

Chapter 5: Working in a Team

Understand key worksharing concepts. Once the team has created local files, it is necessary to understand how to keep both the local files and the central file up to date as changes occur on the project. Doing so ensures that everyone is working from an updated and recent copy of the model at all times.

Master It Once you have begun working in your local file, how do you publish your changes to the central file? How do you download changes from the central file to your local file?

Solution The easiest way to do this is by using the Synchronize With Central command, which is accessible from the Collaborate tab and also from the Quick Access toolbar. To download changes from others without uploading your latest work, use the Reload Latest (RL) command.

Enable worksharing on your project. Knowing how to activate and use worksharing is indispensable to working in a team environment using Revit.

Master It How do you transition a single-user Revit file to a multiuser environment using worksharing?

Solution To activate worksharing, click the Worksets button on the Collaborate tab. This will initiate the worksharing feature and divide your model into the two default worksets. To allow others to access the model, you will need to choose File Save As and save the file to a network location. After this, close the file. Each team member then makes a local copy of this network file and works exclusively within his or her local copy.

Organize worksets in your model. There is no single rule for organizing worksets in your project models; however, they can be used to your team's advantage. You can use worksets to better organize larger projects and for additional visibility control.

Master It How do you assign objects to worksets? How do you change an object's workset assignment?

Solution As model elements are added to a project, they are assigned to the active workset selected by the user. The active workset is visible either in the Collaborate tab in the ribbon or in the status bar. An object's workset assignment can be changed in the Properties palette at any time.

Manage workflow with worksharing. Once the central file has been created, you will need to organize and structure the model into logical worksets to maintain workflow with Revit.

Master It How do worksets differ from layers in 2D CAD? What are some logical ways to create worksets within a model?

Solution 2D CAD layers were logically divided around individual elements in isolated files. In Revit, because everything is in one file and you are working with 3D objects, not just model lines, you need to use worksets to divide the building in different ways. Some logical workset divisions would be Shell And Core, Interiors, FF&E, and Site.

Understand element ownership in worksets. Editing elements in a central file means you have sole ownership over further changes to those elements. Understanding the permissions is critical to working in a team.

Master It How do you edit an element in the model if someone has already taken ownership of it in a worksharing environment?

Solution Trying to edit the element initiates a request for permissions in Revit. When you alert the other team member of your desire to have ownership of this element, that person can grant your permission request using the Editing Requests button on the Collaborate tab.

Collaborate in the cloud. Not all of your team members will be Revit-savvy and know how to use the tools. In addition, not everyone on the team will have a copy of Revit, but you might still need their input and comments on the design. Learning to leverage complementary tools to Revit is critical to keeping a project moving smoothly.

Master It How do you use the cloud to get feedback from non-Revit users on a project team?

Solution Create a series of views in your project, making sure to name them in a way that is easy for other team members to understand. These views can be plans, sections, elevations, or 3D views. Share the Revit model with team members using `http://360.autodesk.com`. The site will allow them to browse the views and add comments.

Chapter 6: Working with Consultants

Prepare for interdisciplinary collaboration. Proper planning and communication are the foundation of effective collaboration. Although only some client organizations may require a BIM planning document, it is a recommended strategy for all design teams.

Master It What are the key elements of a BIM execution plan?

Solution An effective BIM execution plan will first list the goals and uses of building information modeling as well as the scope of the data to be developed. It will also list the software platforms to be used, information exchange process, delivery strategy, and technology infrastructure.

Collaborate using linked Revit models. The most basic tool for collaboration is the ability to view consultants' data directly within the context of your own model. Project files from other disciplines can be linked and displayed with predictable visual fidelity without complex conversion processes.

Master It How can worksharing complement the use of linked Revit models?

Solution Placing each linked model on a unique workset allows team members to choose when to load or unload the linked models without affecting their teammates. Worksets within linked models can also help you manage graphic quality using the ability to load or unload worksets globally.

Use Copy/Monitor between linked models. The Coordination Monitor tools establish intelligent bonds between elements in a host file and correlating elements in a linked model. They also support a workflow that respects the needs of discrete teams developing their own data, perhaps on a different schedule than that of other team members.

Master It How can grids in two different Revit projects be related?

Solution The Copy/Monitor tool allows you to copy elements such as grids from a linked file into a host file and monitor the linked element for changes.

Run interference checks. Interference checking—also known as *clash detection*—is one of the most important components of building information modeling. It is the essence of virtual construction and has the greatest potential for cost savings during the physical construction process.

Master It How do you find interfering objects between two linked Revit models?

Solution On the Collaborate tab, locate the Coordinate panel and choose Interference Check Run Interference Check. If you are using linked models, select the desired linked project in the Categories From drop-down list while keeping the other column set to Current Project. Select the desired object categories in the left and right columns (for example, choose Structural Framing from a structural model and Ducts from an MEP model). Click OK to run the check. The results can be exported to a report for coordination with others.

Chapter 7: Interoperability: Working Multiplatform

Use imported 2D CAD data. CAD data can be integrated into your Revit project in a number of ways: as plans of existing conditions, as fixture layouts from consultants, or as standard details from your company's library.

Master It How can CAD details be used in a Revit project?

Solution Create a new drafting view for a single detail. From the Insert tab, choose Link CAD and select a DWG detail file. During linking, set the colors to Black And White.

Make sure the scale of the drafting view matches the notation scale of the CAD detail. Use the Query tool to turn off unwanted layers within the linked file.

Export 2D CAD data. The ability to deliver quality 2D information to other constituents involved in your project is as important as importing it into the Revit environment. Appropriately formatted views, standardized layer templates, and proper coordinate settings will result in happy team members and a smooth coordination process.

Master It Does Revit software comply with the National CAD Standard?

Solution Yes, you have the ability to map Revit model categories to standardized layers in the Export Layers dialog box. Access this tool by clicking the Application menu and selecting Export Options Export Layers DWG/DXF. Load industry-standard layer conventions using the Standard button.

Use imported 3D model data. Model data generated outside of the Revit environment can be integrated into your projects as whole-building systems, massing studies, or unique components.

Master It How can a building's structural model created with the Bentley Structure be integrated into a Revit project?

Solution Create a structural framing family into which the DGN model will be inserted. When the family is finished, the DGN geometry will be displayed as any other Revit structural-framing component.

Export 3D model data. Your modeled elements don't have to remain in the Revit environment forever. Data can be exported to 3ds Max, SketchUp, AutoCAD MEP, and more.

Master It How can you coordinate your architectural Revit model with an engineer using AutoCAD MEP?

Solution The engineer will likely require one DWG model per level for efficient coordination. Create duplicate floor plans for exporting and adjust the View Range settings for Top to Level Above, Offset: 0 and Bottom to Associated Level, Offset: 0. Create duplicate 3D views for each level, right-click the ViewCube®, choose Orient To View Floor Plans, and find the corresponding floor plans. These 3D views can be batch-exported to DWG format and referenced by the MEP engineer in the designs.

Work with IFC imports and exports. Industry Foundation Classes (IFC) is a vendor-neutral model format designed to support interoperability in the AEC industry. It is widely used by some major BIM platforms available around the world.

Master It How is an IFC model integrated into a Revit project for coordination?

Solution You can open an IFC file by clicking the Application menu and selecting Open IFC. Once the file is open, the data can be saved as an RVT Revit project file and linked into another Revit file for continued coordination.

Chapter 8: Advanced Modeling and Massing

Create and schedule massing studies. Starting the design process with actual building elements can lead to a lot of unexpected frustration. Walls lead to rooms, which get room tags and eventually scheduled. But if you've failed to fulfill the client's program, you'll wonder where to start over!

Master It You're faced with creating some design studies of a large hospital complex. How would you go about creating a Revit project that would allow you to create a massing study and schedule it against the design client's program?

Solution Massing studies allow you to create schedules of the surface, floor areas, and volumes of a mass. This is incredibly helpful for resolving the design intent and client's program before committing to walls, floors, and other building geometry.

Know when to use solid and surface masses. Solid masses and surface masses can both be used to maintain relationships to host geometry like walls and roofs, but surface masses can't be volumetrically scheduled or contain floor area faces.

Master It You've been asked to create a complex canopy system for the entry to a hotel project. The system will consist of a complex wave of triangular panels. What kind of mass would you create?

Solution You're probably going to be better off not creating a solid mass because you don't need a solid—you need only a surface. It's best to use solids when you have to calculate the client's overall design program: floor areas, surface, and volume. For limited, surface-based relationships, just use surface massing. Surface masses will help you resolve the overall design idea first. Then you can move on to patterns and eventually component-level geometry.

Use mathematical formulas for massing. Not all massing is going to involve intuitive, in-the-moment decision making. By discovering the underlying rules that express a form, you can create the formulas that can iterate and manipulate your massing study. So rather than manually manipulating the mass, you manipulate the formulas related to your mass.

Master It What's the best way to discover and create these formulas?

Solution Never stop sketching! Staring at a blank spreadsheet is a one-way road to frustration. Sketch the idea and try to discern the rules that make the form change and morph into your design idea. Once you think you've discovered the rules that contain the idea, start testing the rules. Once you find that the idea or principle is valid, it's simply a matter of scale.

Chapter 9: Conceptual Design and Design Analysis

Embrace energy analysis concepts. Understanding the concepts behind sustainable design is an important part of being able to perform analysis within the Revit model and a critical factor in today's design environment.

Master It What are four key methods for a holistic sustainable design?

Solution Four key methods for a sustainable solution are (1) understanding a building's climate, (2) reducing building loads, (3) using free energy when possible to power those loads, and (4) using efficient systems.

Create a conceptual mass. Understand ways to generate building forms quickly and easily to explore a variety of shapes and orientations.

Master It Describe how you can use families to quickly generate form.

Solution By using adaptive components and masses, you can quickly create geometry that can be dynamically modified by pushing or pulling reference lines or by formulas.

Analyze your model for energy performance. Being able to predict a building's energy performance is a necessary part of designing sustainably. Although Revit doesn't have an energy-modeling application built into it, it does have interoperability with many applications that have that functionality.

Master It Explain the steps you need to take to get a Revit model ready for energy analysis.

Solution The steps are as follows:

1. Make sure the building has walls, floors, and roofs. Those all need to meet and join so there are no unrealistic gaps in the model.
2. Make sure each of the regions in the model has a room element inserted into it and that the room element's height is set to the bottom of the floor above.
3. Under Area And Volume Calculations, select Room Volumes.
4. Export the model to gbXML and import that into an energy-analysis application.

Chapter 10: Working with Phasing, Groups, and Design Options

Use the Phasing tools to create, demolish, and propose a new design. Time is such an important element to the design process and nearly impossible to capture with traditional CAD tools. Don't use phasing for construction sequencing (there's a better way). Embrace phasing for *communication*, not just *illustration*.

Master It How can you use phasing to communicate your design across a series of key stages? What kind of project is best suited to phasing?

Solution From the Manage tab, you can access the settings for phases. You can create phases for the major stages of work in your project as well as define filters and graphic overrides to illustrate the overall design approach. Use the Phase and Phase Filter view properties to customize project views, including schedules. Set the Phase Created and Phase Demolished properties of model elements to adapt to the project phases. Any kind of project can use phasing, but tenant improvement projects benefit the most from the ability to document existing conditions and demolition.

Understand and utilize groups. Groups are great for creating collections of both host and family component geometry. Just remember to apply best practices, and you'll avoid a lot of common roadblocks. Individual model elements within groups will always appear properly in schedules, as you'd expect. And creating exceptions in groups allows you to make subtle changes without creating a new group.

Master It Why shouldn't you mirror groups?

Solution Although mirroring works conceptually, it breaks down in implementation. Just because you can mirror something in Revit Architecture doesn't mean that it can actually be manufactured that way. And even more confusion can result if the mirrored object has to be powered, accessed, maintained, and so on in an impossible condition. Mirroring groups has been known to create so much hassle that you are better off avoiding it.

Create and use design options. Like groups, design options work great when you follow the rules. Design options are intended for design iteration that is bounded and well-defined—not for putting multiple buildings in one project file. Remember that links, groups, and phasing can exist within design options. Always keep hosted elements with their host when using design options.

Master It Suppose you have a multistory tower. How could you show multiple design options for the entire vertical exterior enclosure?

Solution Put each enclosure option in a different project file. You can link these files into one master project file. Then associate each of the links with a different design option. Eventually you set and accept the primary option. Then bind the link, and the chosen enclosure model will become a group within your project. The group can be ungrouped to continue editing the final design.

Chapter 11: Visualization

Create real-time and rendered analytic visualizations. Analytic visualization is the concept of communicating information about your project in a nonliteral way, and it's very important! It's not about showing real materials in the project but about using filters to visualize important metadata.

Master It During the renovation of a space, you want to reuse the doors rather than throw them away. How would you illustrate this?

Solution Assign an instance parameter to the doors called Recycled. Then apply this value to all the doors fulfilling these criteria in your project. Now you can use this parameter to create a view filter to illustrate where these reused doors are being used.

Render emotive photorealistic visualizations. Photorealistic visualization is about communicating design ideas but in emotive ways that are much closer to how the space will be experienced, including real lighting, materials, and entourage. Just remember that the time it takes to calculate and render your views will change dramatically based on the quality and resolution of your views.

Master It Would the rendering for a PowerPoint presentation differ from a rendering being printed for a marketing brochure?

Solution The rendering for the PowerPoint presentation needs to be only about 150 dpi, whereas the rendering for the printing needs to be 300 dpi. A 300 dpi image will take much longer to render than a 150 dpi image, even though they'll look the same on the screen.

Understand the importance of sequencing your visualization workflow. The sequence of design—building, content, materials, and cameras—is not the same as the sequence for visualization (geometry/cameras, lighting, materials). Lighting is far more important than materials of actual objects. Get the lighting right and the materials will look great, but not the other way around.

Master It How do you create a rendering environment that replaces the actual materials with matte materials in order to study the effects of lighting on your design?

Solution Use Phase Filter to create a material override, and assign this analytic filter to the view that you're rendering.

Chapter 12: Creating Walls and Curtain Walls

Use extended modeling techniques for basic walls. Walls in Revit are made from layers of materials that can represent everything from generic placeholders for design layouts to complete assemblies representative of actual construction.

Master It How can you customize the profile of a wall?

Solution A wall can be attached to another object such as a roof, floor, or reference plane. Select a wall, activate the Attach Top/Base tool, and pick the object to which the wall should be attached. You can also edit the profile of a wall in elevation by selecting a wall, activating the Edit Profile tool, and modifying the sketch of the wall.

Create stacked walls. Exterior walls are usually composed of several combinations of materials with varying thicknesses. These various wall types can be combined into a single entity called a stacked wall.

Master It How do you create a stacked wall?

Solution You must duplicate an existing stacked wall type within a project. In Type Properties, open the Edit Assembly dialog box and add any combination of basic walls into the stacked wall structure.

Create simple curtain walls. A curtain wall is an assembly of parts including curtain grids, panels, and mullions. They can be created in predefined types with regular horizontal and vertical spacing along with specific panel and mullion types.

Master It How do you add a door to a curtain wall?

Solution Use the Tab key to select a single panel in a curtain wall segment. If the panel is part of a predefined system, you must unpin the panel first. From the Type Selector, choose a curtain panel door family.

Create complex curtain walls. The Revit conceptual massing environment can be used to create complex curtain wall configurations. Pattern-based panel families can be loaded into the massing environment and populated on a divided surface. These populated surfaces can then be loaded and placed in a project model for documentation and scheduling.

Master It How do you create a complex divided surface?

Solution From the Recent Files window, select New Conceptual Mass. Add a second level to the family and draw a curved line on each level. Select the two lines and click Create Form; choose the Planar Surface option. Select the new form and click the Divide Surface button on the ribbon.

Chapter 13: Modeling Floors, Ceilings, and Roofs

Understand floor modeling methods. Floors make up one of the most fundamental, sketch-based system families used in a Revit model. You can customize them to accommodate a variety of assumptions at various stages of design.

Master It How can you create a structural floor with integrated metal decking?

Solution You can create a structural floor by going to the Architecture tab of the ribbon and clicking Floor Structural Floor. This tool activates the Structural parameter in a floor's instance properties. Once this is activated, edit the floor's type properties to add a Structural Deck layer and assign a deck profile.

Model various floor finishes. Thick and thin floor finishes can be created to support tagging, scheduling, and quantity takeoffs.

Master It How would you represent a thin finish material in your project such as carpet?

Solution Activate the Split Face tool from the Modify tab of the ribbon, select a floor, and define the boundaries of the area to be assigned as the thin material. Activate the Paint tool, select the appropriate material, and click the split face you created within the floor.

Create ceilings. Ceilings are sketch-based system families that can host objects such as light fixtures and HVAC diffusers.

Master It What's the best way to model a ceiling within a space?

Solution Ceilings are best created in a ceiling plan. Activate the Ceiling tool from the Build panel in the Architecture tab of the ribbon. Specify a value for the Height Offset From Level setting of the ceiling in the Properties palette, and use Automatic Ceiling to fill a bounded space with a ceiling object.

Understand roof modeling methods. Roofs can be modeled as simple single-pitch shed roofs or complex extrusions of sinuous curves.

Master It What is the best way to create a single vault roof?

Solution That roof is best created with the Roof By Extrusion method. Go to the Architecture tab of the ribbon and click Roof ➢ Roof By Extrusion. Specify a wall or reference plane as the work plane and switch to an elevation, section, or 3D view. Draw the profile of a vaulted roof and click Finish Edit Mode. Adjust the extents of the extrusion as desired.

Work with advanced shape editing for floors and roofs. A small but powerful toolset is available for extended editing of floor and roof objects. These tools allow you to create warped floor slabs and tapered layers of roof assemblies.

Master It How do you create a drainage point in a flat roof slab?

Solution Select a roof object and activate the Add Split Line tool from the Shape Editing panel in the ribbon. Draw two crossing lines from the four corners of the roof boundaries. Activate the Modify Sub Elements tool and select the point where the split lines cross. Change the value that appears to create a low drainage depression in the slab.

Chapter 14: Designing with the Family Editor

Get started with a family. Before you start to create your own family components, take a moment to think about how you expect that component to "behave" in your project. The role of the Family Editor isn't just an environment to model geometry; it also determines how the content that you create will behave in the project environment.

Master It Choosing the right template is critical. You can convert from one family template to another, but this is not always the case. Why would you want to choose a door template rather than a Generic Model template?

Solution Balusters, curtain panels, detail components, and hosted elements all have specific, predefined behavior. Plan ahead when you're creating these categories. Objects that need to "cut" their host, like doors and windows, must be created in templates that are hardwired to contain a portion of the host that will be cut. This allows you to create the door or window and also cut the host in the way that it needs to cut in the project.

Create the framework for a family component. Reference planes, points, and lines are the "bones" of your component. Assign parameters to the skeleton, and the geometry will follow along. Be sure to test the parameter and reference relationships before you start to create any solid model geometry.

Master It Why should you build, assign parameters to, and test the references first? Why not just model the geometry?

Solution Testing the references and parameters before you add geometry keeps things simple and helps you troubleshoot parametric behavior before building the geometry. Remember to keep parametric dimensions outside of Sketch mode so you and others can easily find them later. After you've tested the parameters and references successfully, you can be confident that your geometry will behave predictably.

Understand family modeling techniques. Although the Family Editor contains a wide assortment of modeling and editing tools, you don't always need to build everything in one file. You can use a number of techniques to reduce redundancy and manage complex geometry for a component family.

Master It When would you consider using the technique of nesting families? How could this method improve the efficiency of a component family?

Solution Anytime you need to create a repetitive element within a family, you should consider using a nested family. This method allows you to build the repetitive element only once, and you will maintain better control of the placement of the nested component within its host. You can also use multiple nested families as a way to explore various design solutions for a component or to efficiently manage subcomponents, such as different hardware types for a door.

Apply extended family management techniques. Sometimes parametric behavior will depend on the parameters that directly control it, but often these parameters will be expressed as a relationship to something else.

Master It Why are formulas so important? Why not just create the parameters you need and then modify them as needed in the project environment?

Solution Formulaic relationships help maintain rules within a family so that changing one rule can have an effect on many others. Using formulas, therefore, allows you to drive one parameter based on the value of another, and the result can drive a length, material, or other rules-based value. When you have many parametric-type permutations, it's better not to weigh your project down with a lot of options that you'll probably never use. Whenever this happens, don't load all the possible types in your project—just turn to a type catalog in order to select only the family types that you need. Since you don't want to have to remember all of these relationships manually, allow Revit to maintain them for you.

Chapter 15: Creating Stairs and Railings

Understand the key components of stairs and railings. Having a complete understanding of the components of stairs is important. You don't want to set about breaking the rules until you understand how best (and when) those rules can be broken.

Master It What are the essential parts of stairs?

Solution Baluster posts, balusters, and baluster panels along with handrail profiles are the essential parts of any railing. Nosings, stringers, and treads are the essential parts of stairs. Having a firm understanding of how these components react to changes in their respective dialog boxes is critical.

Understand the different stair tools and apply them to custom designs. Designing in a spreadsheet is hard. Step back and consider what you're trying to accomplish. If you'll look at the components that make up stairs, you'll see some interesting opportunities.

Master It How would you create a continuous tread that wasn't monolithic? What would you do if you wanted to create a custom stringer? Are balusters always vertical and used to support handrails? What if your particular stair just can't be modeled in the Stairs tool?

Solution Try using the nosing profile to complement the shape of your tread. And don't forget that a handrail profile can be used to create a custom stringer profile with little trouble. Although balusters often support handrails, this is not always the case. Balusters may also consist of the support element that will support the tread. A complex baluster family associated with the railing as the start post can create the most complex railing conditions quickly and easily. But if all else fails, remember that there's still the Family Editor. Just model it the way you want it, and then put it in the project. It's probably more sculpture than stair at this point. Modeling it in the Family Editor means that you'll be able to move, elevate, rotate, and copy the results throughout the project. If you have to make changes (and you will), you'll simply open the component in the Family Editor.

Design railings and use the Railing tool for other model elements. From model patterns to geometric intricacy, there's a lot that can be created with the Railing tool. When this doesn't work, look to the Curtain Wall tool for "railings" that can contain space and allow "balusters" to be conveniently unlocked.

Master It Why would you not use a railing to manage repetitive relationships? What if you need to accurately distribute geometry along a path?

Solution Modeling these railings as components in the Family Editor is often faster than creating groups and then copying them throughout the project. Railings are also helpful for creating geometry that needs to be distributed along paths, even if the results aren't actually railings. Finally, don't use geometry when a model pattern will do. This will keep your project light.

Implement best practices. There are specific best practices when creating custom stairs and railings. Pay attention to nesting geometry, maintaining the right level of detail, and filtering schedules so the metadata ends up in the right place.

Master It Is it possible to create solutions that are too efficient? What's the big deal with detail levels? And finally, what's the most important thing to remember before creating an elegant workaround?

Solution You're not the only person working on the project! Design is a team sport, and any out-of-the-box exceptions to the rules need to be understood by the entire team. "Over modeling" is often misunderstood to mean "too much geometry," but geometry is critically important to understanding how your design is going to be assembled. So if you'll take the time to assign levels of detail to components, it'll help refresh views and printing. Finally, remember that the best solution is the one that is implementable. If your team doesn't understand your "custom hack," you're not playing a team sport and the project will ultimately suffer.

Chapter 16: Detailing Your Design

Create details. Details in Revit are a combination of 2D elements layered on top of 3D model elements or sometimes just stacked on top of each other. Creating good, easy-to-read details typically requires some embellishment of the 3D model.

Master It What are the three primary categories of detail elements and how are they used?

Solution Detail lines are used to create two-dimensional linework of various weights and styles. They are used for drafting, much as you would draft in a CAD application. Filled regions and masking regions are the two region types that are used to apply patterns (even if that pattern is a solid-white field) against your details. These can help to show context such as materiality. Components like detail components and detail groups are used to create 2D families that can be used and reused in a variety of details within the model. They are historically used to create elements like blocking, metal studs, metal deck, and so on.

Add detail components to families. You can make creating details in Revit easier by adding some of the detail elements directly to the family. In this way, when you cut sections, make callouts, or enlarge plan conditions, your "smart" details can begin to construct themselves.

Master It Because you don't always want elements to appear in every scale of a view, how can you both add detail elements to your families and still limit the amount of information that is shown in any given view?

Solution Using the detail levels (Coarse, Medium, and Fine), you can control the visibility of any element within a family to show, or not show, at those settings. By controlling the detail level, you can keep the family simple in a Coarse view and add more detail as the drawing gets increasingly complex.

Learn efficient detailing. As you master detailing in Revit, you'll begin to learn tips and tricks to make your process of creating details more efficient.

Master It To help you assess how much effort you should be putting into your details, what are three questions you should be asking yourself before starting any detail?

Solution Before starting any detail, ask yourself:

- Will I see or use this in other views in the project?
- Will it affect other aspects of the project (like material takeoffs)?
- How large is it?

Reuse details from other files. In many project workflows, you will need to incorporate details from other projects. Reusing these details can aid in the speed and efficiency of project documentation.

Master It There are several ways to reuse details from other projects. Name one and list the steps to perform the tasks necessary to quickly move a detail from one project to another.

Solution Here are the steps to save views from one project for use in another project:

1. Start by opening the file with the views you want to save. Click the Application menu and select Save As Library Views.
2. The Save Views dialog box shows a list of view names on the left and a preview window on the right. Click the check box for each of the views you want to save into a separate file; click OK.
3. To import the views, open the project you'd like to import the views into, and choose Insert From File from the Insert tab. Choose Insert Views From File.
4. In the resulting dialog box, you will have a list of the views you can import from the column on the left and a preview of those views on the right. Check the box for the views you want to import and click OK.

Chapter 17: Documenting Your Design

Document plans. With floor plans you can create visual graphics that help define how a space is laid out. However, Revit provides other tools such as area plans to help you describe space.

Master It List the four types of area plans that you can create and note the two that Revit creates automatically.

Solution The four types of area plans are rentable area, gross area, usable area, and BOMA area. The software provides automatic calculations to show rentable and gross areas.

Create schedules and legends. Schedules are another view type; they allow you to show information about the model in a nongraphic format. Schedules can also be used to dynamically report quantities of elements inside the model.

Master It Understand how to create schedules and report additional information about the elements in the model. How would you create a simple casework schedule showing quantities of types?

Solution Here are the steps to create a schedule within Revit:

1. On the View tab, choose Schedule/Quantities from the Schedule button.
2. Choose Casework as a schedule category.
3. On the Fields tab, choose Family And Type followed by Quantity.
4. On the Sorting tab, choose to sort by Family And Type; make sure Itemize Every Instance is checked. When that's done, click OK.

Lay out sheets. Eventually in a project it will become necessary to create sheets that will become the documentation set. Knowing how to create a good sheet set provides you with another venue to communicate with contractors, clients, and other team members.

Master It To properly create a sheet set, you need to understand the dynamics of adding views to a sheet. In the Revit environment, there is only one way to add views to a sheet. What is it?

Solution Views can be added to a sheet by dragging them from the Project Browser and dropping them onto the sheet. From that point, they can be edited or manipulated to properly place them relative to other views that appear on that sheet.

Chapter 18: Annotating Your Design

Annotate with text and keynotes. Although a picture is worth a thousand words, you will still need notes to make drawings understandable and be able to call out key elements in each view. Know how to create and modify text and keynotes for a complete set of documents.

Master It To properly use the keynoting feature, you'll need to understand what each of the three keynote types do and how they're used. List each and explain how they can be used in a project.

Solution Element keynotes annotate assemblies such as walls, floors, and roofs. Material keynotes designate materials within Revit, such as concrete, gypsum board, or rigid insulation. User keynotes are not tied to an element or a material and can be used to note other aspects of the view or detail.

Use tags. Tags are text labels for elements such as doors, walls, windows, rooms, and several other objects that architects typically need to reference in a set of drawings. These tags typically refer back to other schedules or information in other portions of the drawing set and are unique to the view in which they are inserted.

Master It Inserting tags quickly can be a good way to make documentation time more efficient. How can you quickly tag a number of elements in the model at the same time?

Solution Use the Tag All tool. This tool allows you to load several tags for different elements at the same time and populate a view with all those tag types at once. You will probably need to manipulate the location of some of the tags, but most should be placed cleanly and accurately, saving you time for other portions of the project.

Add dimensions. Dimensioning is a critical part of the project documentation, allowing you to communicate the distance elements are from one another.

Master It Adding dimensions is a necessary part in any project. However, in a project workflow you will typically want to change the location of a dimension's witness line without having to re-create the entire dimension. How do you move a witness line without remaking the entire dimension?

Solution Highlight the dimension string and grab the blue grip that is below the text string. By clicking and holding this element, you can now select a new host for the witness line.

Set project and shared parameters. Revit Architecture lets users add as many custom parameters to an element as are needed to document the project. These parameters can be both tagged and scheduled, depending on how they are made.

Master It You need to add a custom parameter for your project to track the percentage of recycled content in materials. What's the best way to go about doing this?

Solution Since the items you want to track need to be scheduled but not tagged, it's easiest do to this with a project parameter. Add one to the project for a percentage of recycled content, and then track that in a Multi-Category schedule showing all the material types you want to track.

Chapter 19: Working in the Construction Phase

Add revisions to your project. You need the ability to track changes in your design after sheets have been issued. Adding revisions to a drawing is an inevitable part of your workflow.

Master It How do you indicate revisions on a drawing sheet?

Solution First, a revision must be created in the Sheet Issues/Revisions dialog box. Then, a revision cloud is drafted in either an active view or a sheet. The revision cloud is assigned to one of the project revisions in the Properties palette. Finally, the revision cloud is tagged. The revisions are automatically tracked in revision schedules that are part of the title block.

Use digital markups. DWFs provide a lightweight means to digitally transfer and mark up multiple sheets in a document set.

Master It Explain the workflow using DWF markups.

Solution Once your views are drawn and placed on sheets, export the sheets to a DWFx format. They can be shared with other members of your team for markup. Others will open the DWFx in Design Review and create the comments, and then send the marked-up set back to the design team. This set is then linked back into the drawing set, and the markups will be visible on the drawing sheets.

Model for construction. Parts and assemblies allow a model element to be broken down into smaller parts. These subelements can be used in more detailed ways for the construction process while still maintaining their association with the original element.

Master It Describe the method for breaking down a design-based model assembly into its individual components.

Solution Select a wall, floor, roof, or ceiling and use the Create Parts tool. The view may need to be set to Show Parts. Once parts are created, they can be divided, merged, or excluded.

Chapter 20: Presenting Your Design

Understand color fill legends. Color fills are a great way to illustrate data that otherwise might appear only in a schedule, such as department assignment, designed areas, and room finishes.

Master It There are a variety of ways to graphically display information using color fills. It can initially take a bit of time to get things organized, but once you create the legends, they can easily be transferred between views and projects. Describe how to add a color fill legend, once created, to your project template.

Solution To add a color fill legend from a project to your project template, add it to a view and add the view to a sheet. Legends can be transferred like schedules: Once they are added to a sheet, they can be copied to the Clipboard and then pasted to the sheet in the project template. This will transfer all the colors, fonts, and other settings from the project to the template.

Use 3D model views in your presentation. Revit provides a variety of ways to help you visualize your designs—both while designing and during presentation. Understanding where these features are located and how and when to use them can help expedite the presentation process, depending on the look and feel you want to create with your images.

Master It Describe the process for creating an exploded 3D view of each level within your project.

Solution After adjusting the view range of your plan views to accommodate the actual bottom of the level up to the top, open a 3D view and right-click the ViewCube. Select Orient To View and choose the floor plan for each level.

Work with viewport types. Viewport types are simple to manage, but they are powerful when applied to the views you place on sheets. You can customize the view titles for any use case, from design presentations to construction documents.

Master It Describe the process for adding a new viewport type to your project.

Solution After placing a view on a sheet, select the view and click Edit Type in the Properties palette. Click Duplicate and create a uniquely named type. Once you have modified the settings, apply the new type to other views by selecting a viewport and picking the new type from the Type Selector.

Create "exploded" axonometric views. The Displace Elements command is used to create exploded axonometric views that used to be drafted by hand or created manually in a separate model. Understand the best ways to use this tool to help visualize and communicate design ideas.

Master It Describe the process for creating a displaced view.

Solution Starting in a 3D view, select elements to visually displace. The selections will be based on how you would like to see the elements grouped as you move them around within the view. By selecting elements and then selecting the Displace Elements tool, you can begin staging your axonometric view.

Chapter 21: Computational Design with Dynamo

Get started with Autodesk Dynamo. Dynamo is a visual programming interface that runs parallel with Revit and allows you the ability to code forms and shapes within your Revit environment. Dynamo creates definitions by connecting *nodes* with *wires* to convey data.

Master It There are five parts to a node. What are they, and what do they do?

Solution The five parts are Node Name, Input Ports, Output Ports, Node Preview, and Lacing options. These parts control the input and output of a node.

Understand the Dynamo UI. Dynamo has a simple, straightforward UI. Becoming comfortable with the parts of the user interface can allow you more flexibility and lower frustration when learning the application, either as a novice or on your road to an expert.

Master It What are the four primary sections of the user interface?

Solution The following are the four primary sections of the Dynamo UI:

- The Toolbar
- Node Library
- Workspace
- Execution Bar

Connect nodes to make data flow. Connecting nodes is the true power behind Dynamo. The connections visually and programmatically show data flow and the path of information from beginning to end to create the form, run the analysis, or provide whatever is the desired output. Understanding the basics of connecting nodes is the first step to creating your own Dynamo definition.

Master It Describe the workflow to create a series of nodes and connect them properly.

Solution Nodes are added by searching for them in the Node Library and adding them to the workspace. This can be done via dynamic search or by browsing through the library and clicking a node. Once added to the workspace, nodes output on the right and input on the left. Connecting nodes is done by dragging the right (output) of one node to the left (input) of another node, creating a sequence for the data to flow. The sequence or *definition* is the visual program.

Use additional Dynamo tools. While Dynamo is a robust programming application, there are additional tools you can use to further leverage its capabilities.

Master It Describe some of the tools external to Dynamo and how they can be used to push the capabilities of the application even further.

Solution There are several applications that can interface with Dynamo. The first and most obvious one is Revit. Revit can be used as a workspace of sorts to create geometry or as a data set to pull information from if you want to perform any type of analysis on your project file. Excel is another application that can help feed long lists of data (numbers, strings, and so on) into Dynamo to cut down on manual entry or as a pass-through application. In this last example, you might pull room areas from a Excel-based building program and push them into Dynamo to test designed room sizes. Finally, there is the Dynamo package manager that allows more advanced users a way to give back to the Dynamo community and create their own nodes and other content.

Appendix B

Tips, Tricks, and Troubleshooting

This appendix provides some tips, tricks, and troubleshooting to help keep your project files running smoothly. Listed here are some pointers to keep you from getting into trouble as well as a peppering of time-savers and other great ideas.

In this appendix, you'll learn to:

- Optimize performance
- Use best practices
- Maintain quality control
- Apply tips and shortcuts

Optimizing Performance

It should make sense that a smaller Revit file on a fast computer with a good network will run the quickest. There is no real "typical" project file size for Autodesk® Revit® Architecture projects, and a file can range anywhere from 10 MB to well over 800 MB. We've found that a project with less square footage and with a lot of geometry and detail (like a medical office building) can be larger in file size than a warehouse project—which has a lot of empty square footage. Because documentation is often an indication of project complexity, we've found as a good rule of thumb that for each documented sheet, your file should be about 1 MB. So a completed project of 100 full-size sheets should be about 100 MB.

Much of the variation depends on the level of detail in the model itself, the presence of imported geometry (2D CAD files, SketchUp, and so on), the number of views you have, and the overall complexity. Obviously, your hardware configuration will also be a factor in determining the speed and operation of your models.

You can optimize your hardware in a number of ways to get the most out of the configuration you have. You should first look at the install specifications and recommended hardware specs for a computer running Revit software. Autodesk has published those requirements on its website, and they are updated with each new version of the software. You can find the current specs at `www.autodesk.com/Revit`; then choose System Requirements from the right side of the menu at the top of the page.

Beyond the default specifications, you can do things to help keep your files nimble. Here are some other recommendations:

Use a 64-bit OS. Revit Architecture likes RAM, and the more physical RAM it can use, the more model you can cache into active memory. Windows offers several versions of a 64-bit

OS, but since Revit 2014, Windows 7 has been a minimum requirement. You can use this in a 32-bit or 64-bit version, but a 64-bit OS allows you to use as much RAM as you can pack into your machine. Note that Windows 8.1 and Windows 10 are also supported.

Get a faster hard drive. Chances are you're working on Revit on a local hard drive. If you're working on a large project with a central file, your local file will be on your computer's hard drive. If you're working on a small project without worksharing enabled, there's a chance you might be working on your local drive if you're taking the file home or if you don't have a network. Regardless, one of the things that will affect performance is your drive speed. This is how fast your computer can read/write to the local drive (input/output or I/O speed). With the large files Revit can create, a faster drive will equal less read/write time; so if it's within your budget, try to get the 7200 rpm drive as a minimum or even an SSD (solid state drive). We've found the SSD, especially in a laptop, is a huge performance boost. You'll appreciate the difference.

Get a good graphics card. Revit is also very graphics-intensive and will push the limits of any video card you have in your computer. Although many graphics cards are available at a variety of performance and price levels, a good starting point is looking for ones that have been tested and approved by Autodesk for use with Revit. You can find recommended system hardware as well as graphics hardware and driver specifications at `www.autodesk.com/graphics-hardware-detail`.

Figure out how much RAM your project will need. Before you email your IT department requesting 64 GB of RAM, figure out how much you're actually going to use on your project. Your OS and other applications like Outlook will use some of your RAM, but you can calculate how much RAM Revit will need to work effectively. The formula is as follows:

```
Model size in Explorer × 20 + Linked file size(s) × 20 = Active RAM needed (in megabytes)
```

Let's look at a couple of examples to demonstrate how it works. You have a Revit file with no linked files, and your file size on your server is 150 MB. So you'll need 150 MB × 20 = 3000 MB, or 3 GB, of RAM just for Revit to operate effectively. In another example, you have a 120 MB file, a 50 MB structural model linked in, and four CAD files at 1 MB each. The calculation is as follows:

```
(120 MB × 20) + (50 MB × 20) + (4 MB × 20) = 3480 MB or 3.5 GB of RAM
```

Once you've put as much RAM into your workstation as is practical, your next recourse for improving model performance is to reduce your file size so you're not using as much RAM. Here are some tips to do that and thereby improve your file speed:

Manage your views. There are two things you can do using views to help improve performance. First, the more views you have open at once, the more information you will load into active RAM. It's easy to have many views open at once, even if you're concentrating on only a few views. Close windows you're not using to help minimize the drain on your resources. You can always close all the windows except your active one using the Close Hidden Windows tool. Choose the View tab and click the Close Hidden button (Figure B.1). You can map a keyboard shortcut to this command such as "XX," or you can find it in the Quick Access toolbar. The Close Hidden Windows command will close the hidden windows in your active project as well as all other open projects and families in your current session of Revit.

FIGURE B.1
Closing hidden windows

The other way to manage your views is to get rid of the ones you don't need. Revit allows you to make different views within your model quickly and easily. This can sometimes lead to having a lot of views (sometimes hundreds) that you aren't using in your document set and don't plan to use. Adding too many views can raise your overall file size even if you haven't added any geometry or annotations within those views. Get rid of those unused views—typically views that are not on sheets—to help keep your file running smoothly. We discuss how to create a schedule to help identify the unused views later in this chapter.

Delete or unload unused CAD files. There are many times in a project process when you'll want to load content from another source as a background. This could be a client's CAD as-built drawings or a consultant's MEP design. You might link these files into your drawing and, during the busy course of the project, forget about them. As you've seen from the earlier tips on RAM use, all these small files add up. Getting rid of them can speed up your Revit project file and is just good housekeeping. If the CAD file is linked, you can remove it using the Manage Links button on the Insert tab. If the CAD files have been inserted instead of linked, right-click an instance of the CAD file in a view and choose Select All Instances from the context menu. Then click Delete to remove all the instances in the entire model as opposed to only the CAD file in the active view.

LINK, DON'T IMPORT

As a general rule of thumb, we highly recommend linking CAD files instead of inserting them. You will notice a significant difference in model performance as you get more and more CAD files into your model.

Don't explode imported CAD files. A CAD file, when imported into Revit Architecture, is a collection of objects that is managed as a single entity. If you explode a CAD file, the single object immediately becomes many objects—and these all take up space in the file, requiring more resources to track and coordinate.

If you're importing DWG files, leave them unexploded as much as possible. If you need to hide lines, use the Visibility/Graphic Overrides dialog box to turn layers on and off. Explode only when you need to change the imported geometry, and start with a partial explode to minimize the number of new entities. Figure B.2 shows the tools available on the ribbon when you select an imported or linked DWG file. Also note that lines smaller than 1/32" (~1 mm) are not retained when CAD files are exploded. This can result in unusable imports.

FIGURE B.2
Explode options

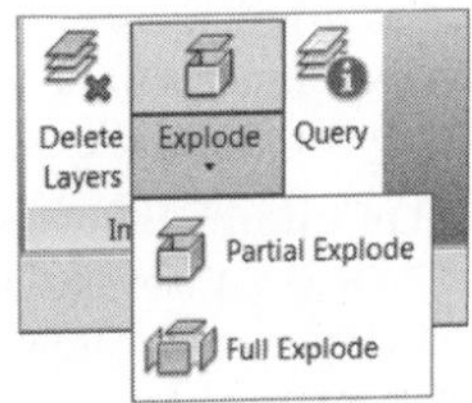

A better workflow than importing your CAD files directly into the project is to import them into a Detail Component family and then load that family into the project. This approach will also aid in keeping accidents from happening, like a novice user exploding the imported CAD. An example of this workflow is to import a SketchUp model into a mass family and then load the mass family into a project file. This workflow is covered in more detail in Chapter 7, "Interoperability: Working Multiplatform."

Turn on volume computation only as needed. Calculating the volumes on a large file can slow down your model speed immensely. This setting is typically turned on when exporting to gbXML, but sometimes teams forget to turn it back off again. Volumes will recalculate each time you edit a room, move a wall, or change any of the building geometry. Turn these off using the Area And Volume Computations dialog box found at the bottom of the Room & Area panel on the Home tab (Figure B.3).

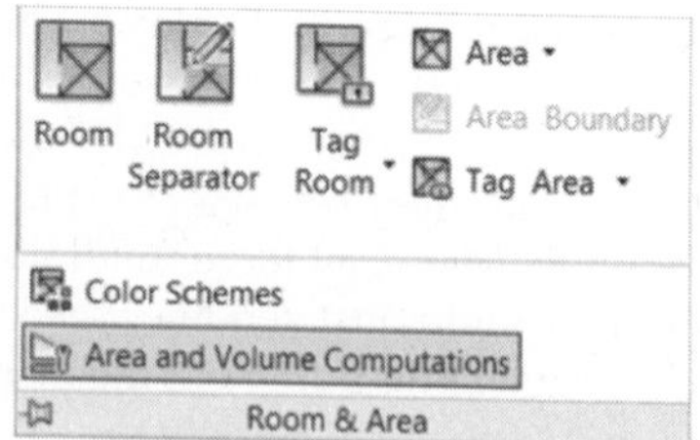

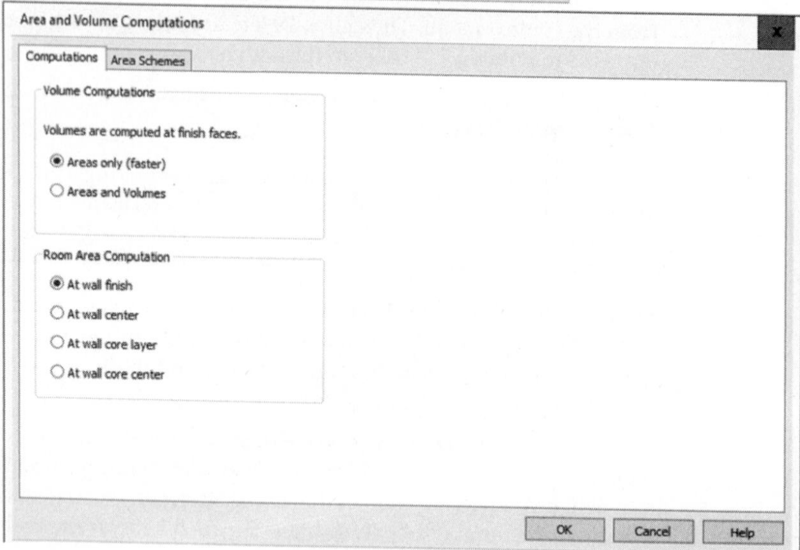

FIGURE B.3 Choose the area calculations to minimize unneeded computations.

Use Best Practices

Good file maintenance is critical to keeping your files running smoothly and your file sizes low. The following are some best practices and workflows that were identified in other areas of the book but are consolidated here as a quick reference:

Manage the amount of information shown in views. Learn to manage the amount of information needed in a given view. Minimize the view depth and the level of detail so you don't show more than you need to show in a view. Here are some simple tips to keep your individual views working smoothly:

Minimize the level of detail. Set your detail level, found in the view control bar, relative to your drawing scale. For example, if you're working on a 1/32″ = 1′-0″ (1:500) plan, you probably don't need Detail Level set to Fine. This will cause the view to have a higher level of detail than the printed sheet can show, and you'll end up with not only black blobs on your sheets but also views that are slow to open and print.

Minimize view detail. Along with the amount of detail you turn on in the view using the Detail Level tool, make sure you're not showing more than you need to. For instance, if you have wall studs shown in a 1/16″ = 1′-0″ (1:200) scale plan or the extruded aluminum window section shown in a building section, chances are it will not represent properly when printed. Turning off those elements in your view will keep things moving smoother as well as printing cleaner.

Minimize view depth. View depth and crop regions are great tools to enhance performance. As an example, a typical building section is shown in Figure B.4. The default behavior causes Revit to regenerate all of the model geometry to the full depth of that view every time you open the view. To reduce the amount of geometry that needs to be redrawn, drag the section's far clip plane (the blue dashed line when you highlight the section) in close to the cutting plane.

FIGURE B.4
Minimizing the view depth

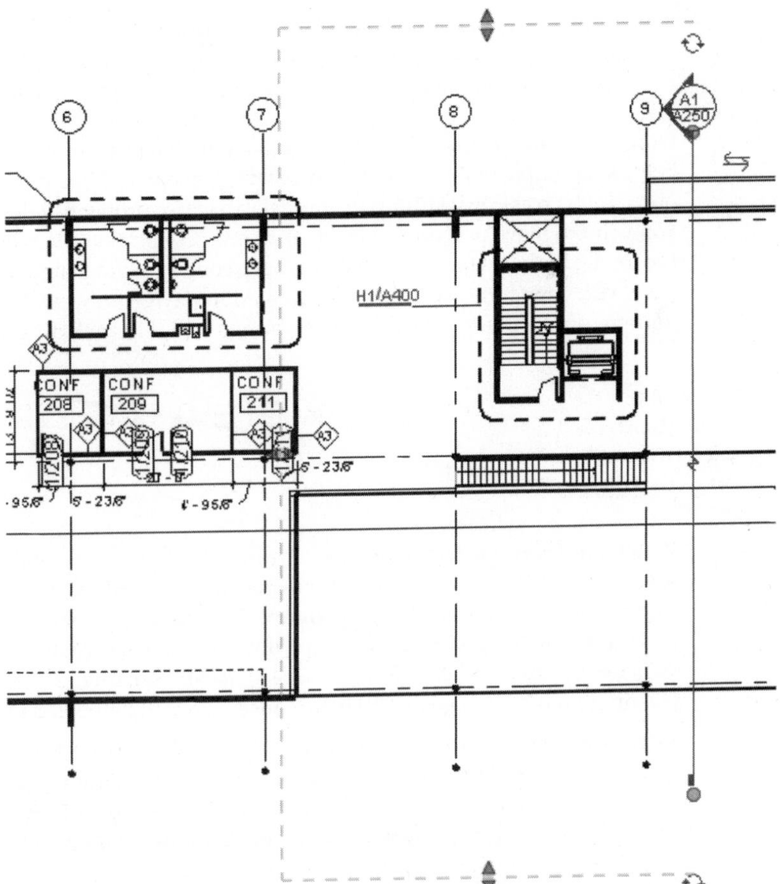

Model only what you need. Although it is possible to model to a very small level of detail, don't fall into the trap of over-modeling. Be smart about what you choose to model and how much detail you plan to show. If it's not conveying information about the project, maybe it's not really needed. The amount of information you do or do not model should be based on your project size and complexity, your timeframe, what you need to document, and your comfort level with the software.

How much to model: Use these three rules of thumb. When you are trying to decide how much detail to put into a model or even a family, there are three good rules of thumb to help you make the right decision for the particular element you're looking to create:

- **Scale:** What scale will this detail be seen in? If it's a very small scale (such as 3" = 1'-0"), it might be simpler to just draw it in 2D in a drafting view.
- **Repetition:** How many times will this detail appear in the drawing set? If it will appear in only one location or only one time, it might be easier to just draft it in 2D rather than try to model the element. If it will appear in several locations, modeling is the better solution. The more exposure an element has in the model (the more views it shows in), the more reasons you have to model it. For example, doors are good to model. They show in elevations and plans all over the sheet set.
- **Quality:** Be honest—how good at modeling families are you? Don't bite off more than you can chew. If you're new to the software, keep it simple and use 2D components. The more projects you complete, the better you'll understand the transition to a BIM workflow.

Don't over-constrain. Embedding user-defined constraints into families and the model helps keep important information constant. However, if you don't need to lock a relationship, don't do it. Over-constraining the model can cause problems later in the project process when you want to move or modify locked elements. Constrain only when necessary. Otherwise, let the model be free. However, if you do over-constrain your model, Revit has a new feature to show you where the constraints are located in any given view. In the View Control bar at the bottom of the screen is the Show Constraints tool (Figure B.5).

FIGURE B.5
Finding constrained objects with the Show Constraints tool

1/8" = 1'-0"

Watch out for imported geometry. Although you have the ability to use geometry from several other file sources, use caution when doing so. Remember that everything you link into a project or a family takes up around 20 times the file size in your system's RAM. So linking a 60 MB NURBS-based ceiling design will equal 2 GB of RAM and more than likely slow down your model. Deleting unused CAD files, using linking rather than importing, and cleaning up the CAD geometry before insertion will help keep problems to a minimum.

Purge unused files and family types. You will find that you won't use every family, group, or material you create in your model. Revit Architecture has a tool that will allow you to get rid of those unused elements to help keep your file sizes down to a reasonable level. This tool, Purge Unused, can be found on the Manage tab in the Settings panel. If your file is very large, it can take several minutes to run, but eventually you'll be presented with a list (Figure B.6) of all the unused elements within your file.

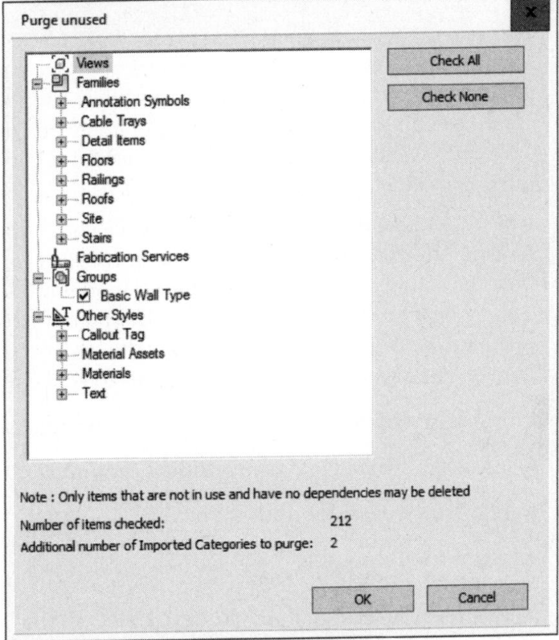

FIGURE B.6 Use the Purge Unused dialog box to reduce file size.

We'll discuss the Purge Unused command in greater detail later in this appendix.

Model correctly from the beginning. As you refine your design, it's critical to model correctly right from the beginning, not taking shortcuts, so you don't have to fix things later. If you can begin by thinking about how your project will be assembled, it will save you a lot of time later in the process. It's good practice to plan ahead, but remember that the software will allow you to make major changes at any stage in the process and still maintain coordination. If you are still in an early phase of design and do not know the exact wall type, use generic walls to capture your design intent; changing them later will be simple.

Manage workshared files. When employing worksharing on a project, you'll want to follow additional tools and tips. Check out Chapter 5, "Working in a Team," for more details.

Make a new local copy at least once a week. In a workshared environment, your local copy can begin to perform poorly or grow in file size while the central file remains small and nimble. If this is the case, it might be time to throw out the old local copy for a new one. Keep in mind that Revit allows you to make a new local copy upon opening the central file. When you choose a central model from a network location, Revit will automatically make a new local copy and place it in your Documents folder. If you choose not to follow that workflow, keep in mind that if you're accessing a project on a daily basis, it's a good idea to make a new local copy at least once a week.

Divide your model. For larger projects or campus-style projects, you can break up your model into smaller submodels that are linked together. You can also do this on a single, large building, although it is a bit more complex. Dividing a model helps limit the amount of information you are loading into a project at one time.

This is a particularly good idea if your project is going to be delivered in separate phases or bid packages. As the project progresses and you complete each delivery, you'll start the next phase by creating a new project file and then linking in the previous project file as context. Doing so will greatly simplify your document set (because you'll be able to start over after each phase) and avoid inadvertently modifying the previous phase (since the geometry and documentation are in a linked file).

If you decide to divide your project, make your cuts along lines that make sense from a holistic-building standpoint. Don't think of the cuts as you would in CAD, but think about how the actual assemblies will interact in the building. For example, don't cut between floors 2 and 3 on a multistory building unless you have a significant change in the building form or program. A good place to cut might be between the building and the adjacent parking garage. Here's a list of some good places to split a model:

- At a significant change in building form or massing
- At a significant change in building program
- Between separate buildings on the site
- At the building site

Don't want to divide your model? Use Collaboration for Revit. Collaboration for Revit is a service that synchronizes your model with other model users in your office or other locations. It is a paid service that allows you similar functionality to something like Revit Server, but without the need to manage the installation process across your network. In lieu of your files being saved on your Revit Server installation, the central file resides on the Autodesk® A360 website. For more information about the service, visit `www.autodesk.com/products/collaboration-for-revit/overview`.

Collaboration for Revit, or C4R, is included in the default Revit installation starting with Revit 2017. The service is designed for teams working in different locations to work within the same model at the same time without having to manage a Revit Server installation.

To use C4R, open Revit and choose the Collaborate tab. On the Manage Collaboration panel, you can activate C4R by choosing the Collaborate button (Figure B.7).

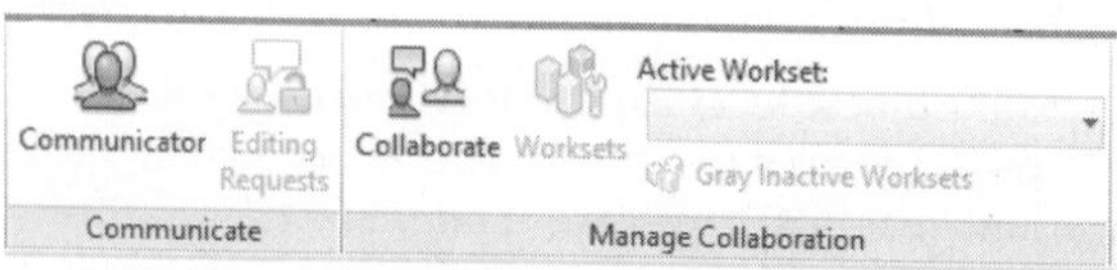

FIGURE B.7
Activating Collaboration for Revit

Revit will ask you to save your model and then ask whether you want to collaborate across your network or collaborate using A360 (Figure B.8). Collaborating within the network will limit you to working only with people who have access to your LAN. If you're working with other firms on the same model, you would want to use the A360 option. When you save your model, it will either save to a central location on the LAN or save to the A360 site, allowing you to coordinate with anyone else, anywhere.

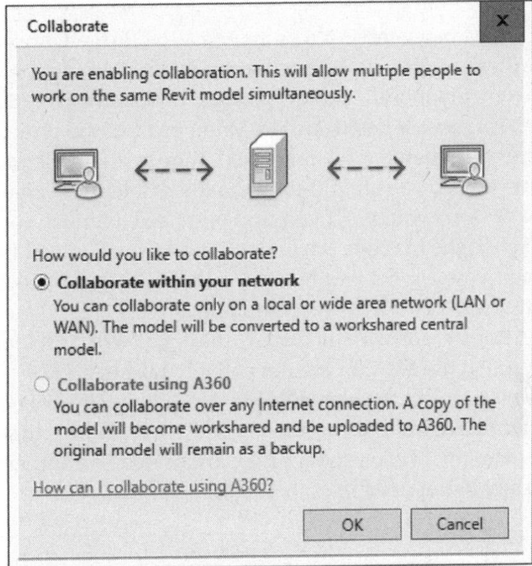

Collaborate
You are enabling collaboration. This will allow multiple people to work on the same Revit model simultaneously.
How would you like to collaborate?
Collaborate within your network
You can collaborate only on a local or wide area network (LAN or WAN). The model will be converted to a workshared central model.
Collaborate using A360
You can collaborate over any Internet connection. A copy of the model will become workshared and be uploaded to A360. The original model will remain as a backup.
How can I collaborate using A360?
OK
Cancel

FIGURE B.8
Collaborating across the LAN or with A360

Quality Control

In any project process, you should always maintain a level of quality control to ensure a solid workflow. When working in a BIM environment, good model maintenance is an imperative part of the process. A well-maintained model will open quickly and be responsive when you're changing views or manipulating content. A model that is not well maintained can have a very large file size, take a long time to open or save, or even become corrupted. Letting the quality of your model suffer can negatively impact the team's overall production and lead to frustration because members cannot be as efficient as they'd like to be. The model size will grow, it will take a long time to save locally or SWC (Synchronize With Central), and the file can suffer corruption or crashes.

Maintaining a good, healthy model is not difficult. It takes about as much effort as regularly changing the oil in your car. The important thing, as with your car, is actually doing the regular maintenance so you don't have to fix a bigger problem that could have been avoided. In the following sections, we'll cover some simple things you can do using the tools already built into Revit software.

Keeping an Eye on File Size

The size of your file is a good metric for general file stability. A typical Revit file size for a project in construction will be between 100 MB and 500 MB. Note that 500 MB is really on the high side of file sizes; beyond that, the model will be slow to open and hard to rotate in 3D views. Other views, such as building elevations and overall plans, will also be slow to open.

Should your file become large or unwieldy, you have several ways to trim your file and get your model lean and responsive again. We've discussed some ways to make your computer faster to accommodate larger files sizes. Now, let's discuss ways to optimize the file itself.

Purging Unused Families and Groups

On the Manage tab is a command called Purge Unused. This command removes all the unused families and groups from your model by deleting them. There are many times in a design process when you will change window types or wall types or swap one set of families for another. Even if those elements are not being used in the project, they are being stored within the file, and therefore, when the file is opened, they are being loaded into memory. Depending on the stage of your project, you should periodically delete these elements from the model to keep your file size down. Don't worry—if you find you need a family you've removed, you can always reload it.

Select the Manage tab and choose Purge Unused from the Settings panel. Depending on the size of your model and how many families you have loaded, it might take the software a few minutes to complete this command.

After the software is done thinking, it will provide you with a list of all the families and groups in the file that are not actively within a view (Figure B.9). At this point, you have the option to select the elements you want to delete or keep, and remove the rest. You can select either entire families or just unused types. Notice that some of the families cannot be selected for deletion, because either they are nested in another family or other types of that family are already being used in your project.

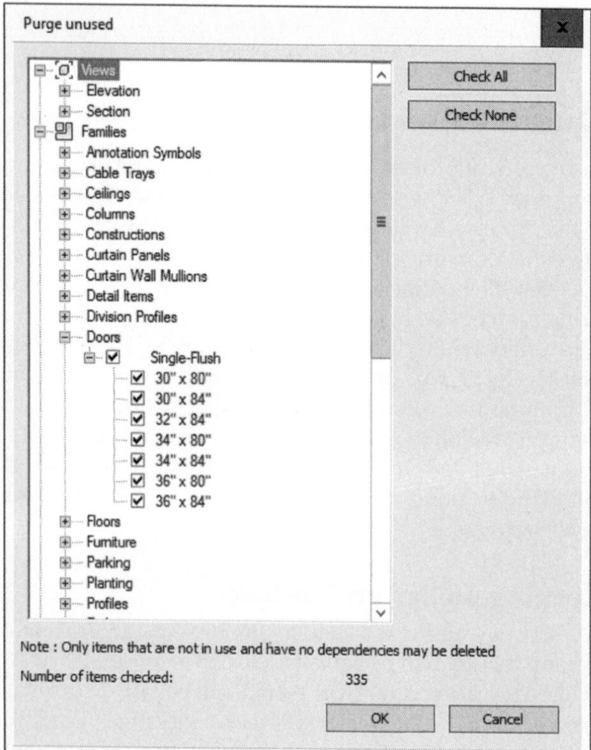

Figure B.9
The Purge Unused dialog box

In addition to families, unused materials and property sets can be removed using the Purge Unused command. Imported categories can be purged as well; however, you don't have the option to choose which ones to delete.

We don't recommend that you use this command in the early stages of design, because your file size won't be that large early on, and purging would eliminate any preloaded families that you might have included in your template. During schematic design and design development, you are typically going through design iteration and will likely be adding and removing content regularly. It can become a hassle to have to constantly load or reload families into the model. If your model is not suffering from performance issues or the file size isn't unruly, it's not necessary to perform a Purge Unused.

You might also consider using the Save Families tool before purging all unused families. From the Application menu, click Save As Library Family and you can export all of the families in your project to a folder. After you purge unused families, you can always return to the folder in which you saved the families and reload them as necessary.

Cutting Down on the Number of Views

The ability to quickly create views within a model is one of the benefits of using Revit; however, this ability can be a detriment if it is not managed. Beyond the simple hassle of sorting through many views to find the one you need, too many views can also negatively affect your performance and file size.

Obviously, a number of views are needed within the model to show design intent and create the construction documentation. Beyond those views, you will find yourself creating views to study the design, deal with model creation, or simply view the building or project from a new angle. These types of working views will never make it to the sheet set, and some will be used for only brief periods.

Before you go through the effort of counting all your unused views, remember that a Revit model is a database. You can use this feature to let the software perform the counting for you, using schedules. To create a schedule that will track unused views, open the `AppB-Foundation.rvt` file found on the book's web page at `www.sybex.com/go/masteringrevit2017`. Next, select the Schedules flyout from the View tab and choose View List.

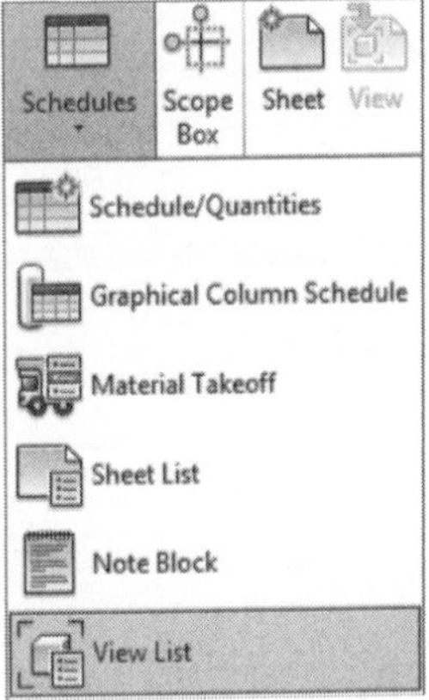

How Many Working Views Are Too Many?

How many working views are too many to have in your model? The obvious answer is that when performance begins to suffer, you need to start looking at ways to make the model leaner and speed up response times. We had a project team new to Revit software, and they were complaining about the file being slow to open and manipulate. When reviewing their model, we saw their file size was over 900 MB! We were surprised they were able to do any work at all.

One of the first things we did to get the file size down to something more reasonable was look at all the views that were not on sheets. We found they had more than 1200 views not being used. Deleting those views and running a File Save (with the Compress box checked) brought the file size down to 500 MB. Although the size was still high, this example demonstrates the impact that too many views can have on your file size.

The View List Properties dialog box allows you to select the fields you want to have in your schedule. For your View List schedule, select the following fields (in order):

- Sheet Number
- View Name
- Title On Sheet

Use the Add button to move those fields from the left column to the right one and sort them in the order listed (Figure B.10).

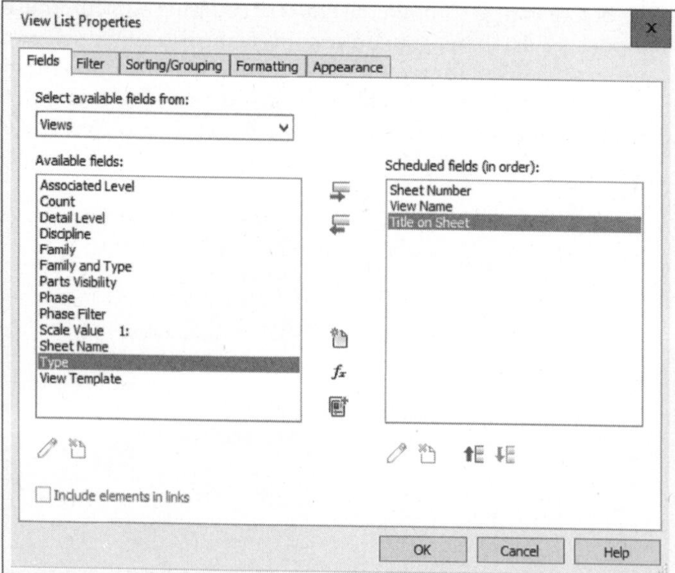

Figure B.10
Selecting fields for your View List

If you were to click OK right now, you'd create a schedule of all the views you have within the model. Since you want to see only the views that are not on sheets, you have a bit more formatting to do. By selecting the Filter tab, you can choose to see only the views not placed on sheets. In the sample model, there are two sheet types: those that begin with an *A* and ones that begin with a *K*.

1. On the Filter tab, choose to filter the sheets by sheet number.
2. From the drop-down menu, choose Does Not Begin With as a filter type.
3. Finally, in the text field, enter a capital **A** (Figure B.11).

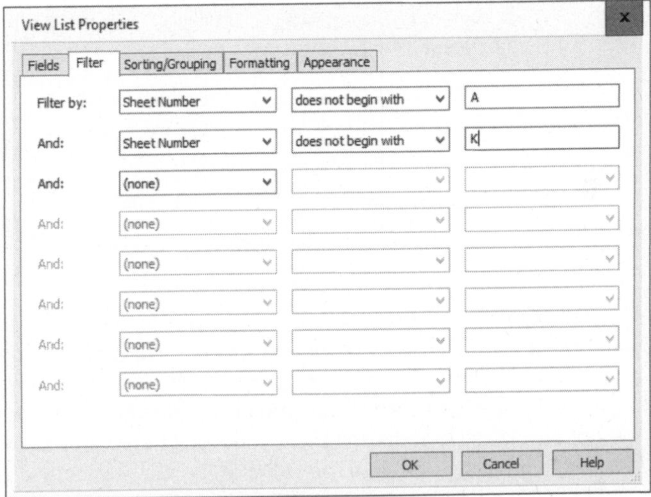

FIGURE B.11
Filtering out views on sheets

Remember that because these are database functions, they are also case sensitive. Before moving on to the next tab, choose to add another filter selection. Copy the one you just created to filter A sheets, but now filter out all the K sheets.

FILTERING IS AND, NOT OR

Remember that filtering is not an OR command (this OR that)—it's an AND command. So, if you have more than one filter, what you see in the schedule needs to meet both requirements, not just one.

As a last bit of formatting, select the Sorting/Grouping tab. On this tab, from the drop-down menu select Sheet Number. Should you have missed a sheet number type (for instance, if you have G sheets in your list), it would appear at the top. Be sure to have the Grand Totals and the Itemize Every Instance check boxes selected (Figure B.12). Click OK when you've finished.

FIGURE B.12
Sorting the schedule by sheet name

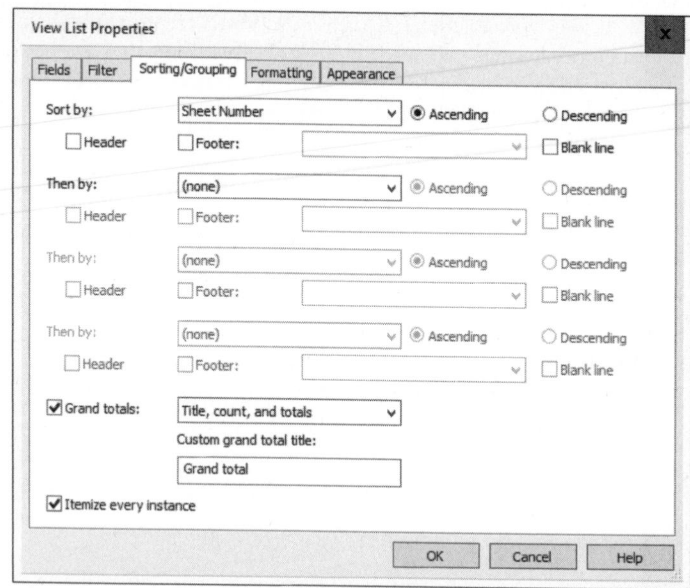

The result of this exercise will be a schedule that looks similar to Figure B.13; it shows a list and the total of all the views not on sheets in your model. You can see that in our model we have 19 views not currently on sheets. No matter how many views you have in this schedule, you'll want to be selective about what you eliminate and what you choose to keep. Just because a view is not on a sheet, that doesn't mean it doesn't have value to your project. Ideally, someone familiar with the project will assess the value of the views in this schedule to determine what to keep and what to remove.

FIGURE B.13
The finished schedule

<View List>

A	B	C
Sheet Number	View Name	Title on Sheet
	3D section	
	Level 3	
	3D View 1	
	3D View 2	
	3D View 3	
	Roof Plan	
	3D View 7	
	arcade	
	entry - northeast	
	Level 2	
	Level 3	
	3rd floor terrace	
	Perspective	
	telefund	
	northwest	
	!Opening View	
	Sunshade Detail	
	{3D}	
Grand total: 18		

It is also a good idea to add this schedule to your office template where it will keep a running list of views not on sheets that you can refer to at any time in the project process.

Using Schedules

As you saw in the previous example, using schedules is a great way to use tools already in the software to perform quality control on your projects. Don't think that all schedules need to be placed on sheets. There are several uses for schedules as a quality assurance measure. In the previous example using views, you used schedules to help troubleshoot poor model performance; however, you can use schedules to help you control quality for all kinds of things. The following sections highlight two more examples.

Multicategory Schedules

An excellent way to monitor the contents of your building model is through the use of multicategory schedules. For the purpose of quality control, you might not be too concerned with extensive quantity takeoffs. Thus, you will need to create a schedule with a limited number of fields, organized in a way that doesn't list each and every object instance in the project. We'll show you how to do this in the following exercise:

1. Continuing with the `AppB-Foundation.rvt` file, go to the View tab in the ribbon, click the Schedules flyout, and select Schedule/Quantities.
2. Choose <Multi-Category> at the top of the Category list and change the name to **Multi-Category QA Schedule**.
3. In the Fields tab of the Schedule Properties dialog box, add the following fields (in order) to the Scheduled Fields list:
   - Category
   - Assembly Code
   - Assembly Description
   - Family And Type
   - Count
4. Switch to the Sorting/Grouping tab, set the first sorting parameter to Category, and select the Header option. For the second sorting parameter, choose Assembly Code, and set the third sorting parameter to Family And Type. Finally, uncheck the Itemize Every Instance option at the bottom of the dialog box (Figure B.14).
5. Switch to the Formatting tab and select the Category field. Check the box to make it a hidden field and then click OK to view the results (Figure B.15).

With this type of schedule, you can manage the entire scope of contents actively placed in your model. Objects that don't have the proper assembly codes can be corrected in this schedule. For other issues such as family- or type-naming conventions, you will need to make those adjustments in the Project Browser. In addition to verifying that the correct content has been used throughout your project, you can check the Count field for rows where a small number of elements have been placed—perhaps indicating that a family has been placed in error.

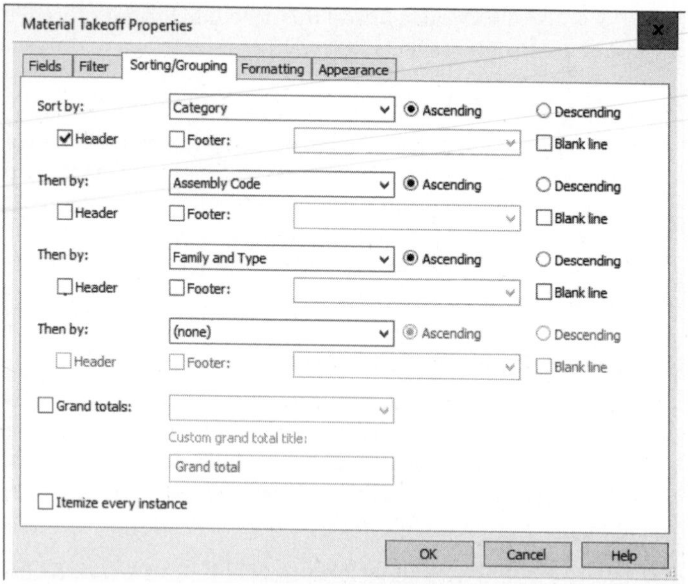

FIGURE B.14
Specify the sorting and grouping options for the multicategory schedule.

Material Takeoff Properties

Fields | Filter | Sorting/Grouping | Formatting | Appearance

Sort by: Category — Ascending / Descending
Header — Footer: — Blank line

Then by: Assembly Code — Ascending / Descending
Header — Footer: — Blank line

Then by: Family and Type — Ascending / Descending
Header — Footer: — Blank line

Then by: (none) — Ascending / Descending
Header — Footer: — Blank line

Grand totals:
Custom grand total title:
Grand total

Itemize every instance

OK | Cancel | Help

FIGURE B.15
The multicategory schedule shows all elements in the project.

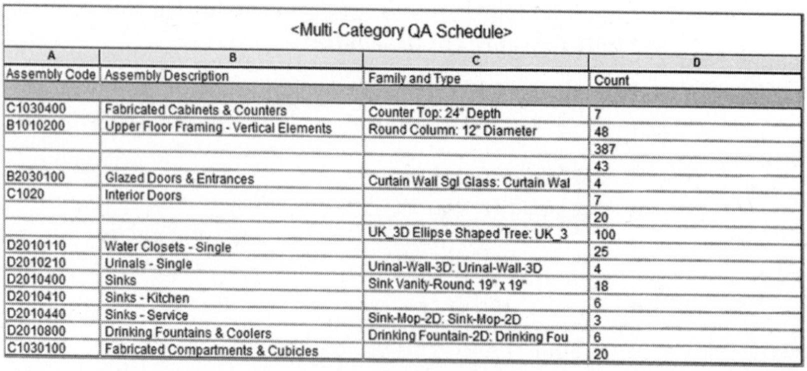

<Multi-Category QA Schedule>

A	B	C	D
Assembly Code	Assembly Description	Family and Type	Count
C1030400	Fabricated Cabinets & Counters	Counter Top: 24" Depth	7
B1010200	Upper Floor Framing - Vertical Elements	Round Column: 12" Diameter	48
			387
			43
B2030100	Glazed Doors & Entrances	Curtain Wall Sgl Glass: Curtain Wal	4
C1020	Interior Doors		7
			20
		UK_3D Ellipse Shaped Tree: UK_3	100
D2010110	Water Closets - Single		25
D2010210	Urinals - Single	Urinal-Wall-3D: Urinal-Wall-3D	4
D2010400	Sinks	Sink Vanity-Round: 19" x 19"	18
D2010410	Sinks - Kitchen		6
D2010440	Sinks - Service	Sink-Mop-2D: Sink-Mop-2D	3
D2010800	Drinking Fountains & Coolers	Drinking Fountain-2D: Drinking Fou	6
C1030100	Fabricated Compartments & Cubicles		20

DISCOVER A BUNDLE OF SCHEDULES

Did you know that there are some valuable elements hidden in project templates provided by Autodesk? If you create a new project file using the Construction-Default template, you will find many schedules related to quality assurance (QA) or quantity surveying (QS). There is also a sheet named 000 - Temporary Schedule Sheet, from which you can copy any number of schedules and then paste them into your own project.

NOTE Another way to save your schedules is to simply right-click them in the Project Browser and choose Save to New File. This will export the schedule to an RVT file and is a good way to save any view type.

Keynotes

As a final example illustrating the use of schedules to manage the consistency of a project, we'll discuss how to use keynotes in the construction document process. Regardless of whether you use numerical keys or text-based keys, you will invariably need to use one of them to add annotations to your project. Although the software can easily produce both types of annotation, for the sake of ease and consistency we will refer to them as *keynotes* for the remainder of this section because that is the name of the Revit command.

If you are keynoting a project, you are adding annotations that call out specific materials or conditions within your details. Those notes not only need to be consistent across multiple details but will also link directly back to the project specifications—a separate set of documents published outside of the Revit environment. Historically on a project, to maintain any sort of consistency between notes in different views, you needed to manually coordinate all the notes and manually check them. When you are talking about hundreds of sheets in a drawing set and thousands of notes, there is plenty of room for error. In a manual process, you can have notes on one sheet that read "Cast-in-Place Concrete," whereas on another sheet they read "CIP Concrete," and on a third sheet "Cst in Place Conncrete" (note the typos).

The Keynote tool has some built-in checks and balances to ensure a level of consistency when it is being used, and we explore the tool further in Chapter 18, "Annotating Your Design." However, it should be pointed out that a keynote legend is another good way for the project manager to maintain a level of oversight throughout the project. A keynote legend will give you a running list of what notes are being used in a project—even though it is intended to be placed on sheets to complement your documentation. This overall list can also be cross-checked against the specifications so you can ensure that everything you've added to the model has a corresponding section.

To create a keynote legend, follow these steps:

1. On the View ribbon, select the Legends drop-down, and choose Keynote Legend.

   The fields for a keynote legend are limited to **Key Value** and **Keynote Text**.

2. Switch to the Filter tab and you will notice an option unique to this type of legend. Check the box labeled Filter By Sheet if you want the legend to display only the keynotes shown within the same sheet on which the legend is placed. Remember, you can place a legend on as many sheets as necessary.

3. In the Sorting/Grouping tab, you have one additional option to help you review the keynotes used in your project. If you select the Footer option and choose the Title, Count, And Totals option (Figure B.16), you can view how many times each keynote is used throughout your project. Remember that this option will also affect the instances of the keynote legend already placed on sheets. Use this option sparingly and disable it after your quality control tasks.

Figure B.16
Use the Footer option to show a count of each keynote.

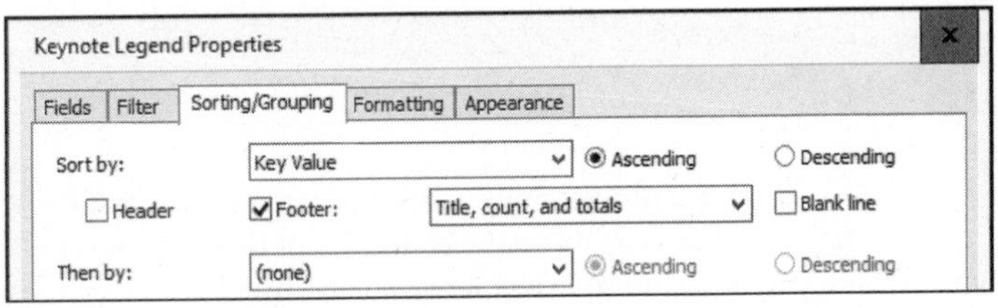

The finished schedule will look like Figure B.17. If you look at the elements displayed in the schedule, you'll notice that it is organized by Construction Specification Institute (CSI) division, and every note will be listed so you can verify the spelling and accuracy of each item.

FIGURE B.17
The Keynote Legend view

<Keynote Legend>

A	B
Key Value	Keynote Text
033000.AG	LIGHTWEIGHT CONCERETE FILL (033000)
042300.AB	HOLLOW GLASS BLOCK (042300)
053100.AH	GALV. METAL DECK (053100)
084413.AV	INSULATED SPANDREL PANEL (084413)
092216.BA	STEEL STUD (092216)
092900.AA	GYPSUM BOARD (092900)
096813.AA	CARPET TILE, CT(XX) (096813)

Reviewing Warnings

A seemingly obvious place to troubleshoot your model is the Review Warnings tool. Although this technique will do very little to affect your overall file size, the Warnings dialog box will alert you to problems within the model that should regularly be addressed to ensure file stability. To locate this dialog box, go to the Manage tab in the ribbon, find the Inquiry panel, and click the Warnings button.

Selecting this tool will give you the dialog box shown in Figure B.18, which lists all the warnings still active in your project file.

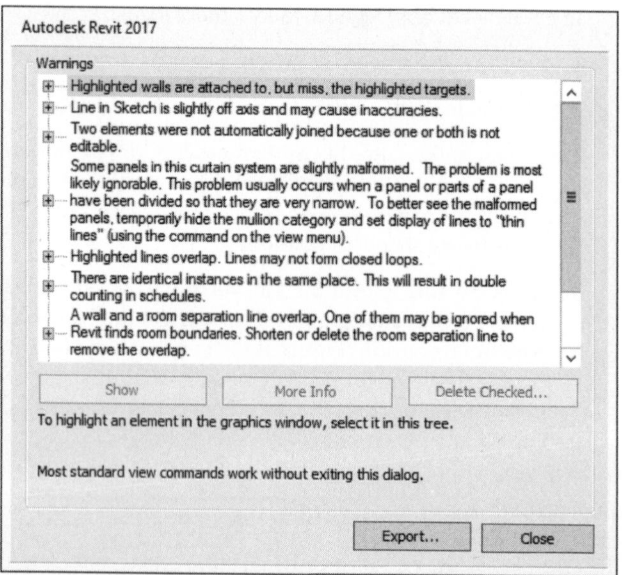

FIGURE B.18
The Warnings dialog box

Warnings are notifications of all types of issues the software has resolving geometry, conflicts, or formulas that do not equate. Examples of things that will appear in this dialog box are instances where you have multiple elements sitting directly on top of each other, thereby creating inaccurate schedule counts; wall joins that do not properly clean themselves up; wall and room separation lines overlapping; stairs that have the wrong number of risers between floors; and so on. This dialog box shows you all the times the yellow warning box appeared at the bottom-right corner of the screen and you did not take action to solve the problem. Warnings that go unchecked not only can compound to create other errors but can also lead to inaccurate reporting in schedules or even file corruption. You'll want to check the Warnings dialog box regularly as part of your periodic file maintenance and try to keep the number of warnings to a minimum. You might also notice that the dialog box has an Export feature. This feature exports your warning list to an HTML file, allowing you to read it at your leisure outside the model environment (Figure B.19). Pulling this list into a Microsoft Word or Excel document allows you to distribute the warnings across the team for them to be resolved.

FIGURE B.19 Exporting the warnings

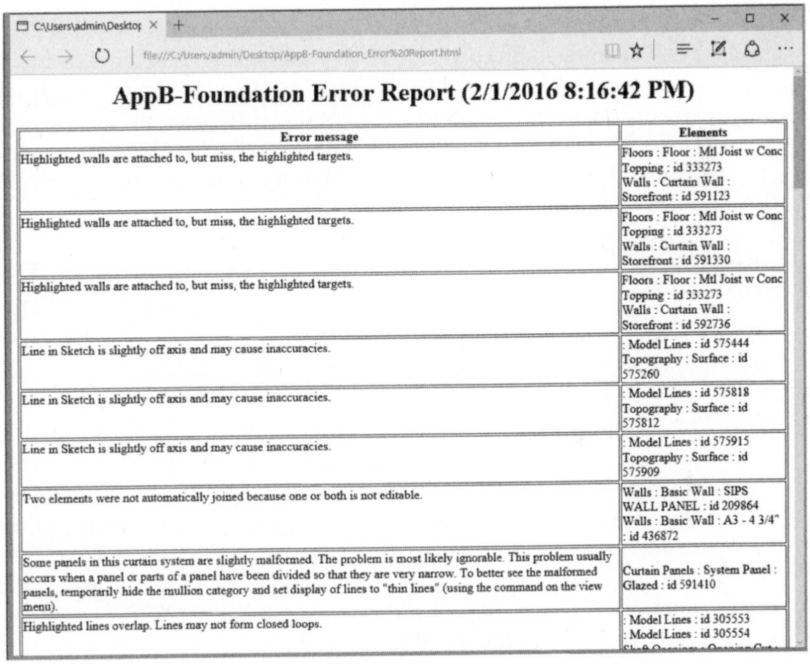

AppB-Foundation Error Report (2/1/2016 8:16:42 PM)

Error message	Elements
Highlighted walls are attached to, but miss, the highlighted targets.	Floors : Floor : Mtl Joist w Conc Topping : id 333273 Walls : Curtain Wall : Storefront : id 591123
Highlighted walls are attached to, but miss, the highlighted targets.	Floors : Floor : Mtl Joist w Conc Topping : id 333273 Walls : Curtain Wall : Storefront : id 591330
Highlighted walls are attached to, but miss, the highlighted targets.	Floors : Floor : Mtl Joist w Conc Topping : id 333273 Walls : Curtain Wall : Storefront : id 592736
Line in Sketch is slightly off axis and may cause inaccuracies.	: Model Lines : id 575444 Topography : Surface : id 575260
Line in Sketch is slightly off axis and may cause inaccuracies.	: Model Lines : id 575818 Topography : Surface : id 575812
Line in Sketch is slightly off axis and may cause inaccuracies.	: Model Lines : id 575915 Topography : Surface : id 575909
Two elements were not automatically joined because one or both is not editable.	Walls : Basic Wall : SIPS WALL PANEL : id 209864 Walls : Basic Wall : A3 - 4 3/4" : id 436872
Some panels in this curtain system are slightly malformed. The problem is most likely ignorable. This problem usually occurs when a panel or parts of a panel have been divided so that they are very narrow. To better see the malformed panels, temporarily hide the mullion category and set display of lines to "thin lines" (using the command on the view menu).	Curtain Panels : System Panel : Glazed : id 591410
Highlighted lines overlap. Lines may not form closed loops.	: Model Lines : id 305553 : Model Lines : id 305554

In the example shown in Figure B.19, we have 47 warnings in the file. How many warnings in a file are too many? That depends on your model, computer capabilities, what the warning types are, and your deliverable. For instance, if you are delivering a model to your client or to the contractor, you might have a zero-warning requirement. In that case, all warnings must be resolved prior to delivering the model. If you are still actively in the design phase of the project, however, you will always have some warnings—it is an inescapable part of the process of iteration. As you refine the drawings, problems will be resolved, and as you add new content to the model that is in need of resolution, new ones will be created. If you are not worried about a model deliverable, you can get away with having fewer than 1000 warnings in the project without too much trouble. That said, the cleaner the model, the smoother it will run.

Another option for finding and resolving warnings is available in the contextual tab of the ribbon. When you select one or more objects that have warnings associated with them, you will see the Show Related Warnings button at the end of the ribbon. Click this tool to display the warning dialog box, and only the warnings related to the selected elements will be displayed. This is a good way to resolve model issues as you and your team develop a project. Being proactive about model quality will save you time in the long run. As Benjamin Franklin once said, "An ounce of prevention is worth a pound of cure."

Other Tips and Shortcuts

Beyond all the things you can do to hone your skills, you will begin to learn a number of tips and shortcuts as your experience grows using Revit Architecture. Here is a compilation of some of those tips and tricks:

Let the software do the math. Revit Architecture is like a big calculator, and it's very good at doing math correctly. Don't want to spend the time trying to figure out what your room size is after you subtract a 3 5/8″ stud and 5/8″ piece of gypsum board from an 11′-2″ room? Don't. If you need to modify a dimension, simply add an equal sign and a formula (Figure B.20), and Revit will calculate the value for you. You can do a lot of math within the Properties palette. Revit will support everything from simple calculations to the more complex Boolean equations.

FIGURE B.20
Use an equal sign to perform calculations.

Dimensions	
Thickness	= 4'5" - 2 13/16"
Panel Width	2' 11 5/8"
Rough Width	3' 2 1/4"
Rough Height	7' 1 1/8"

Make elevators visible in your plans. You want to create a shaft that will penetrate all the floors of your building and put an elevator in it that will show in all your plans. You could do that with an elevator family and cut a series of holes in the floors by editing floor profiles, but sometimes those holes lose their alignment. Fortunately, you can do both things at once using the Shaft tool found on the Opening panel of the Architecture tab. Here, not only can you cut a vertical hole through multiple floors as a single object, but you can also insert 2D linework to represent your elevator in plan (Figure B.21). Every time the shaft is cut in a plan view, you will see the elevator linework.

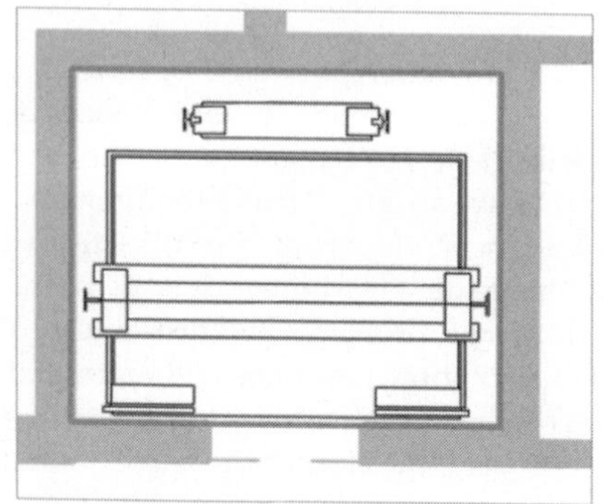

FIGURE B.21
Adding an elevator to a shaft

Orient to view. Creating perspective views of isolated design elements can be quick and easy in a plan or section, but let's say you want to see that same element in 3D to be able to work out the details. Here's how:

1. Create a plan region or section cut isolating the area in question. If you're using a section, be sure to set your view depth to something practical.
2. Open the Default 3D view or any axon of the project.
3. Right-click the ViewCube®, select Orient To View, and select your view from the context menu.

Now, your 3D view will look identical to your section or plan region, but by rotating the view, you'll be able to see that portion in 3D.

Tune your shortcuts. You can edit your keyboard shortcuts without the hassle of rooting through your hard drive looking for a TXT file. To edit your shortcuts, click the Application menu and select Options. Choose the User Interface tab and then click the Customize button. The Keyboard Shortcuts dialog box (Figure B.22) will allow you to edit those shortcuts. Consider making common shortcuts the same letter. So instead of pressing VG to get to your Visibility/Graphic Overrides dialog box, make the shortcut VV for quicker access.

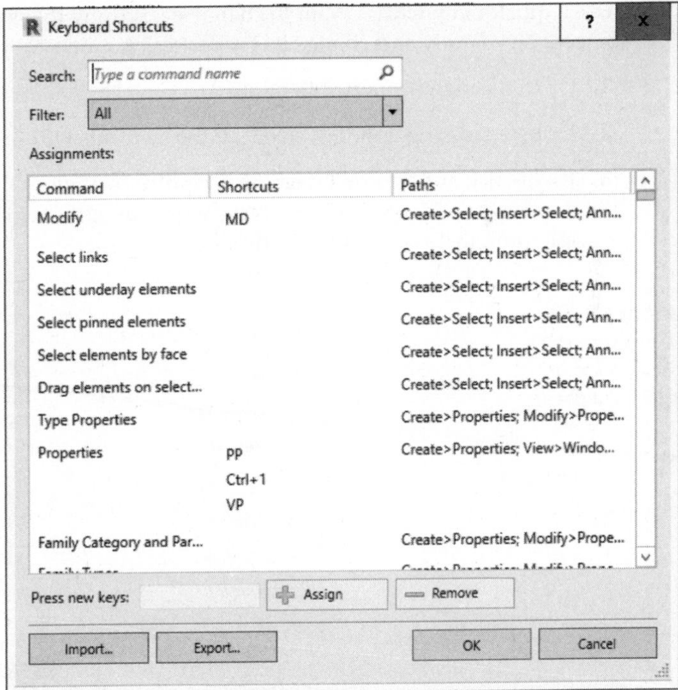

FIGURE B.22 Editing your keyboard shortcuts

Drag and drop families. You need to load a family into a project, you have the Explorer window open, and you know where the family is, but you don't want to go through the laborious effort of navigating across your office's server environment to get there. No problem. You can drag and drop families from Explorer directly into the project file.

Double-click families to edit. You no longer need to highlight a family and then mouse all the way to the ribbon to choose Edit Family. If you want to edit the family, simply double-click it and the family will launch in the Family Editor. You can customize other double-click settings in the Options dialog box, accessed on the Application menu.

Double-click the mouse wheel to activate the Zoom To Fit command for even faster view navigation!

Copy a 3D view. You made the perfect 3D view in your last project, and you can't figure out how to get it into your current project. Fortunately, there's a way to copy views from one project to another. Open both files in the same running instance of the software and then follow these steps:

1. In your perfect view, right-click the 3D view in the Project Browser and choose Show Camera from the context menu.
2. Press Ctrl+C to copy the selected camera.
3. In your new model, use Ctrl+V to paste the camera, and your view and all its settings are now there.

Use a quick-cut poché. Want to change everything that's cut in a view without having to select every family and change its properties? A quick-cut poché is, well, quick:

1. Open the view you want to modify.
2. Using a crossing window, select all the elements within the view.
3. Right-click and choose **Override Graphics In View ➢ By Element** from the context menu. As shown in Figure B.23, you can choose any filled region in the project and assign it to anything that is cut within your model.

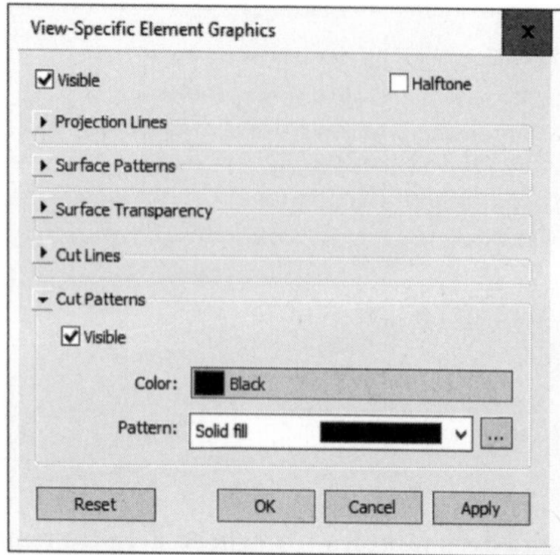

FIGURE B.23 Using Override Graphics for a quick-cut poché

Move your ribbon. Did you know that you can reorganize the tabs on the ribbon and place them in any order you'd like? Hold down the Ctrl key and select a tab (like Insert). You can drag it left or right to change the order in which they appear.

Additional Resources

A number of resources are available to help you along the way to improve your Revit Architecture skills, solve problems, or create new content. In our digital age, there is a wealth of information online to help you learn or communicate with users far and wide. So before you spend hours trying to solve a particularly challenging problem on your own, you might check some of these tools:

Help Clicking the question mark icon in the upper-right corner of the application will take you to the Autodesk Help site at `http://help.autodesk.com/view/RVT/2017/ENU`. This site will give you a basic synopsis of all the tools, buttons, and commands available in the application. If you don't wish to use the online help resource, you can switch to the traditional local help file by searching your computer for the version of the `Revit.ini` file specific to your version of Revit software. For the individual user, the `Revit.ini` is located here:

`C:\Users\username\AppData\Roaming\Autodesk\Revit\Autodesk Revit 2017`

Edit the file in a text-editing application. Find the section heading named Documentation, and edit the values as follows:

```
[Documentation]
UseHelpServer=0
HelpFileLocation="C:\Program Files\Autodesk\Revit 2017\Program\Help\
en-US\WBH\index.html"
HelpBrowser=0
```

The value for HelpFileLocation in the example above may vary, depending on the localized version of the software or modifications to the default installation path. You can also change the HelpFileLocation variable to any location on your company's server.

UseHelpServer can be set to **0** for offline help or to **1** for online help. HelpBrowser is an integer that controls the Internet browser used when calling the help content. Set this variable to **0** to use the default browser or to **1** to always use Internet Explorer. The variable OnlineHelpLocale can be used to direct links to online help into a specific language. Use a locale designation such as **enu** for English-United States or **fra** for French.

Subscription Support If you have purchased Revit Architecture on subscription, Autodesk offers web-based support. Autodesk's responses are speedy, the advice is top-notch, and chances are your problem has been seen before. Subscription Support can be accessed online at `http://subscription.autodesk.com`.

AUGI Autodesk User Group International (AUGI) is a source for tips and tricks as well as excellent user forums. The forums are free to participate in, and they're a great place to ask questions, find answers, or discuss project workflows. AUGI is located online at `www.augi.com`. Once you're there, head to the AEC forums.

YouTube Here's a great reason to tell your IT department you need access to YouTube: Autodesk has its own channel that has some great content, is free, and has hundreds of short videos showing you how to perform specific tasks in Revit. See `www.youtube.com/user/autodeskbuilding`.

AECbytes AECbytes is a website dedicated to following the trends in the AEC industry, with a strong focus on BIM, technology, and the direction of the industry, put together by Lachmi Khemlani. See `www.aecbytes.com`.

RevitForum RevitForum is a user-based forum for all the Revit questions you could ever ask. It has international membership and language translation. It's a great resource where you can ask questions and receive feedback; see `www.revitforum.org`.

Appendix C

Autodesk Revit Architecture Certification

Autodesk® certifications are industry-recognized credentials that can help you succeed in your career, providing benefits to both you and your employer. Getting certified is a reliable validation of skills and knowledge, and it can lead to accelerated professional development, improved productivity, and enhanced credibility.

This Autodesk Official Press guide can be an effective component of your exam preparation and was current at the time of this book's press. Autodesk highly recommends (and we agree!) that you schedule regular time to prepare, review the most current exam preparation road map available at `www.autodesk.com/certification`, use Autodesk Official Press guides, take a class at an Authorized Training Center (find ATCs near you here: `www.autodesk.com/atc`), and use a variety of resources to prepare for your certification—including plenty of actual hands-on experience.

Certification Objective

To help you focus your studies on the Autodesk® Revit® Architecture skills you'll need for these exams, the following table shows objectives that could potentially appear on an exam and in what chapter you can find information on that topic—and when you go to that chapter, you'll find certification icons like the one in the margin here.

Table C.1 is for the Autodesk Revit Architecture 2017 Certified Exam Sections and Objectives and lists the topics, exam objectives, and chapter where the information for each objective is found.

These Autodesk exam objectives were accurate at publication time. Please refer to `www.autodesk.com/certification` for the most current exam road map and objectives.

Good luck preparing for your certification!

TABLE C.1: Autodesk Revit Architecture 2017 Certified User Exam Sections and Objectives

TOPIC	OBJECTIVE	CHAPTER
Collaboration	Copy and monitor elements in a linked file	Chapters 5, 6
	Use worksharing	Chapter 5
	Import DWG files into Revit	Chapter 7
	Use Worksharing Visualization	Chapter 5
	Assess or review warnings in Revit	Appendix B

TABLE C.1: Autodesk Revit Architecture 2017 Certified User Exam Sections and Objectives *(CONTINUED)*

TOPIC	OBJECTIVE	CHAPTER
Documentation	Create and modify filled regions	Chapter 17
	Place detail components and repeating details	Chapter 17
	Tag elements (doors, windows, and so on) by category	Chapter 18
	Use dimension strings	Chapter 18
	Set the colors used in a color-scheme legend	Chapter 20
	Work with phases	Chapter 10
Elements	Change elements within a curtain wall: grids, panels, mullions	Chapter 12
	Create compound walls	Chapter 12
	Create a stacked wall	Chapter 12
	Differentiate system and component families	Chapters 12, 13, 14
	Work with family parameters	Chapter 14
	Create a new family type	Chapter 14
	Use family creation procedures	Chapter 14
Modeling	Create a building pad	Chapter 3
	Define floors for a mass	Chapter 8
	Create a stair with a landing	Chapter 15
	Create elements such as floors, ceilings, or roofs	Chapter 13
	Generate a toposurface	Chapter 3
	Model railings	Chapter 15
	Edit a model element's material: door, window, furniture	Chapter 11
	Change a generic floor/ceiling/roof to a specific type	Chapter 12, 13
	Attach walls to a roof or ceiling	Chapter 12, 13
	Edit room-aware families	Chapter 3

TABLE C.1: Autodesk Revit Architecture 2017 Certified User Exam Sections and Objectives *(CONTINUED)*

TOPIC	OBJECTIVE	CHAPTER
Views	Define element properties in a schedule	Chapter 17
	Control visibility	Chapters 3, 11, 16, 17
	Use levels	Chapters 2, 12, 13, 15
	Create a duplicate view for a plan, section, elevation, drafting view, etc.	Chapter 17
	Create and manage legends	Chapter 17
	Manage the view position on sheets	Chapter 19
	Organize and sort items in a schedule	Chapter 17

Index

B

C

D

E

G

H

I

J

K

M

P

Q

R

S

T

W

X

Y